D1619004

The Encyclopedia of Contemporary American Fiction 1980–2020

The Encyclopedia of Contemporary American Fiction 1980–2020

Volume II
L–Z

Edited by
Patrick O'Donnell, Stephen J. Burn,
and Lesley Larkin

WILEY Blackwell

This edition first published 2022
© 2022 John Wiley & Sons Ltd

All rights reserved. No part of this publication may be reproduced, stored in a retrieval system, or transmitted, in any form or by any means, electronic, mechanical, photocopying, recording or otherwise, except as permitted by law. Advice on how to obtain permission to reuse material from this title is available at http://www.wiley.com/go/permissions.

The right of Patrick O'Donnell, Stephen J. Burn, and Lesley Larkin to be identified as the authors of the editorial material in this work has been asserted in accordance with law.

Registered Offices
John Wiley & Sons, Inc., 111 River Street, Hoboken, NJ 07030, USA
John Wiley & Sons Ltd, The Atrium, Southern Gate, Chichester, West Sussex, PO19 8SQ, UK

Editorial Office
The Atrium, Southern Gate, Chichester, West Sussex, PO19 8SQ, UK

For details of our global editorial offices, customer services, and more information about Wiley products visit us at www.wiley.com.

Wiley also publishes its books in a variety of electronic formats and by print-on-demand. Some content that appears in standard print versions of this book may not be available in other formats.

Limit of Liability/Disclaimer of Warranty
While the publisher and authors have used their best efforts in preparing this work, they make no representations or warranties with respect to the accuracy or completeness of the contents of this work and specifically disclaim all warranties, including without limitation any implied warranties of merchantability or fitness for a particular purpose. No warranty may be created or extended by sales representatives, written sales materials or promotional statements for this work. The fact that an organization, website, or product is referred to in this work as a citation and/or potential source of further information does not mean that the publisher and authors endorse the information or services the organization, website, or product may provide or recommendations it may make. This work is sold with the understanding that the publisher is not engaged in rendering professional services. The advice and strategies contained herein may not be suitable for your situation. You should consult with a specialist where appropriate. Further, readers should be aware that websites listed in this work may have changed or disappeared between when this work was written and when it is read. Neither the publisher nor authors shall be liable for any loss of profit or any other commercial damages, including but not limited to special, incidental, consequential, or other damages.

Library of Congress Cataloging-in-Publication Data

Names: O'Donnell, Patrick, 1948– editor. | Burn, Stephen, editor. | Larkin, Lesley, editor.
Title: The encyclopedia of contemporary American fiction 1980-2020 / edited by Patrick O'Donnell, Stephen J. Burn, and Lesley Larkin.
Description: First edition. | Hoboken, NJ : Wiley-Blackwell, 2022. | Includes bibliographical references and index.
Identifiers: LCCN 2021054298 | ISBN 9781119431718 (cloth)
Subjects: LCSH: American fiction–20th century–Encyclopedias. | American fiction–21st century–Encyclopedias.
Classification: LCC PS379 .E53 2022 | DDC 813/.540903–dc23/eng/20220207
LC record available at https://lccn.loc.gov/2021054298

Cover Design: Wiley
Cover Image: © AerialPerspective Works/Getty Images sebastian-julian/Getty Images

Set in 10/12.5pt MinionPro by Straive, Pondicherry, India
Printed and bound by CPI Group (UK) Ltd, Croydon, CR0 4YY

Contents

Volume I

Alphabetical List of Entries   vii
About the Editors   xi
Contributors   xiii
Introduction   liii

Contemporary American Fiction 1980–2020 A–K   1

Volume II

Contemporary American Fiction 1980–2020 L–Z   787

Index   1479

Lahiri, Jhumpa

MARSHALL BOSWELL
Rhodes College, USA

Jhumpa Lahiri's lyrical, finely wrought fiction explores the complications experienced by Indian immigrants as they confront the challenges of assimilating to their adopted United States while also maintaining allegiance to their Indian heritage. She experienced success right from the start as her debut story collection, *Interpreter of Maladies* (1999), won the 2000 Pulitzer Prize for Literature. The wide readership she earned from that first book helped make her debut novel, *The Namesake* (2003), both a bestseller and the basis of a well-received motion picture starring Kal Penn. She is also the author of *Unaccustomed Earth* (2008), a second story collection, and the novel *The Lowland* (2013). Eschewing the freewheeling magical realism of Salman Rushdie, her work is rigorously realistic, grounded in the conventions of literary fiction and focused on her characters' psychological development. As her immigrant characters struggle with both their newfound country and the India they left behind, Lahiri defamiliarizes US culture, uncovering its strangeness and contingency even as she illuminates the concrete particulars of her parents' native Bengal. In her complex and layered rendering of the immigrant experience, Lahiri discloses the universal existential longings that lie at the heart of her characters' search for a stable identity and a sense of belonging.

Lahiri's childhood in the United States, as the daughter of Bengali immigrants, fueled her sense of divided loyalties, a doubleness that sits at the heart of her fiction. As she explained in 2006, "When I was growing up in Rhode Island in the 1970s I felt neither Indian nor American... My perception as a young girl was that I fell short at both ends, shuttling between two dimensions that had nothing to do with one another" (Lahiri 2006). Born in London in 1967 to Indian parents, she was christened Nilanjana Sudeshna Lahiri. At the age of two she moved with her family to South Kingstown, Rhodes Island, where her father, Amar K. Lahiri, worked at the University of Rhodes Island and her mother, Tapati Lahri, worked as a schoolteacher. Along with her younger sister, Jhelum Lahiri, she spent her Americanized childhood in the environs of a sprawling college campus, a situation she has bestowed upon many of her fictional characters, including *The Namesake*'s Gogol Ganguli and Bela Mitra of *The Lowland*. Her kindergarten teacher, acknowledging that her actual name was too difficult for her to pronounce, called Lahiri by her family "pet name," Jhumpa, an event she playfully fictionalizes in

The Namesake. In 2007 she told British journalist Benjamin Anastasis, "I remember going to school and watching my teachers as they called out the names on the roster. When they came to mine, you could tell they felt like they had to split the atom . . . Watching them, I used to think, 'God, I wish I could just be Beth Jones'" (Anastas 2007). From kindergarten on, she has answered to Jhumpa, using it also as her official pen name.

In 1985 she began her undergraduate studies at Barnard College of Columbia University in New York, from which she was graduated in 1989. After a few years working as a research assistant in Cambridge, she began graduate work at Boston University, from which she earned an MFA in creative writing as well as a PhD in Renaissance studies, focusing specifically on Italian traces in Jacobean drama, thus planting a fascination with Italian culture that would bloom in later years. During this same period, she honed her craft, with her first major publication, the story "The Real Durwan," appearing in *The Harvard Review* in 1993. This piece, along with eight other stories, she later included in *Interpreter of Maladies*. In 1998, the title story appeared in *Agni Review*, published out of Boston University, while the collection's opening piece, "A Temporary Matter," inaugurated her career-long relationship with *The New Yorker*, which established a "first-right of refusal" arrangement with her. Two additional pieces from the collection – "Sexy" and "The Third and Final Continent" – also appeared in *The New Yorker* in 1999, the same year her first collection was published.

In the justly celebrated title story, an Indian tour guide named Mr. Kapasi takes a Westernized Indian American family on a sightseeing tour of Odisha, India. A failed scholar who once dreamed of an academic career, Mr. Kapasi now works as a tour guide and a Gujarati translator for a local physician. Mrs. Das, the mother of the American family, is the only person on the tour to engage directly with Mr. Kapasi, and this special attention, coupled with her aura of sexual confidence, he misreads as a special bond. Similarly mistaking his role as an "interpreter of maladies" for that of a psychologist, Mrs. Das confesses to him that her male child is illegitimate, shocking and disillusioning Mr. Kapasi. The double misunderstanding at the story's heart discloses the cultural chasm that separates Mr. Kapasi, an Indian longing for acceptance by a glamorous American, from Mrs. Das, an Americanized Indian who mistakenly interprets Indian culture.

"Sexy," Lahiri's entry in the ninth edition of *The Norton Anthology of American Literature*, flips the script by viewing the Indian/American divide from the perspective of a white American. The story's point of view character is a single woman in her twenties named Miranda, who becomes the mistress of an older Indian American man named Dev. Whereas Dev is drawn to Miranda's youth, she is fascinated by his Indian heritage, which renders him both exotic and remote. At the Boston Mapparium, she stands at one of the maps and listens as Dev, standing at the other end, whispers, "You're sexy" (Lahiri 1999, p. 91). Their physical distance, overlaid against the global map, captures the underlying dynamic of their affair, which a child clarifies when he later defines "sexy" as "loving someone you don't know" (p. 107).

Several stories focus on the romantic struggles of young couples who, in addition to dealing with the standard problems of intimacy and separateness, must also contend with competing approaches to assimilation. In "This Blessed House," a staid, steady husband named Sanjeev finds himself bewildered by his exuberant, irreverent wife, Twinkle, who, upon discovering a storehouse of tacky Christian paraphernalia left over by their house's previous tenants, insists on displaying them as kitsch. Her approach to the artefacts matches her playful, improvisational approach to her own mixed identity, contrasting with Sanjeev's dogged effort to assimilate to the West, as typified by his dutiful attention to the liner notes to his classical CDs. Similarly, Shoba, in "A Temporary Matter," is too blind and self-absorbed to realize that his more outgoing wife, Shukamar, has outgrown him. A series of planned blackouts in their neighborhood, the "temporary matter" of the title, provides the couple with an occasion to air their secrets, which become increasingly more urgent and culminate in a final, devastating betrayal, revealed at the exact moment the lights return.

The two stories with the deepest autobiographical undercurrents are "When Mr. Pirzada Came to Dine" and "The Third and Final Continent." The former describes a young Indian American girl's reaction to the Indo-Pakistan war, news reports of which she watches with her family, Bengali Hindus, and the Mr. Pirzada of the title, a Pakistani Muslim. The narrator struggles to understand not only the animosity driving the war but also the indifference of her American friends to this calamity. "The Third and Final Continent," which concludes the collection, dramatizes in fictional form Lahiri's father's arrival to the United States, which Lahiri deftly connects to the 1969 Apollo moon landing.

The title story won an O. Henry Award and was included in *Best American Short Stories*, as was "The Third and Final Continent." In addition to the Pulitzer Prize, the collection also earned a PEN/Hemingway Award for Best Fiction Debut of the Year and *The New Yorker*'s award "Best Debut of the Year." In 2001 Lahiri married *Time* magazine writer Alberto Vourvoulias Bush in a traditional Bengali ceremony that took place in Calcutta, home of Lahiri's extended family and a regular destination for her throughout her years growing up. Not long after the marriage, the couple welcomed their first child, a son. Finally, a 2002 Guggenheim Fellowship helped her finish her much anticipated first novel, *The Namesake*, which appeared in 2003 to generous acclaim.

The novel is several things at once – a *Bildungsroman* couched in an immigrant narrative that is also a multigenerational family saga. Although Lahiri has insisted the novel is not autobiographical, she has admitted that much of it "sticks pretty closely to the general way I was raised" (Mudge 2003). Gogol Ganguli, the "namesake" of the title, focuses his confusion about his identity as an Indian American on his curious name. As Lahiri explained in a promotional interview for the book, "All the Bengalis I know personally . . . have two names, one public, one private" (Lahiri 2007). In Bengali practice, the "private" name is their "pet name," used by family members, while their "public" name is the one they put on the dotted line. In Gogol's case, his parents are forced against their practice to put his pet name on his birth certificate as they await a letter from his Bengali grandmother that will supply them with his proper name. Unfortunately, the letter never arrives. What's more, his schoolteachers reject the provisional "proper" name his parents later assign him, thereby elevating his pet name to his proper name.

Gogol's father names his son after his favorite writer, Nikolai Gogol, whose stories he was reading when he barely survived a devastating train wreck. Although Gogol considers the odd name an embarrassment, and one more impediment to his desire to assimilate and melt into the American mainstream, Lahiri's use of the name perhaps signals her vision of art and literature as a way to transcend barriers. Similarly, food and cooking function in the novel as both markers of ethnic and national identity and an invitation to hybridity, as in the novel's richly suggestive opening scene, in which Gogol's mother, on the eve of giving birth to the novel's protagonist, improvises a snack combining Rice Krispies, Planters peanuts, red onions, and green chili peppers, thus producing a "humble approximation of the snack sold for pennies on Calcutta sidewalks" (Lahiri 2003, p. 3).

For much of the novel Gogol resists his parents' effort to connect him with his Bengali heritage, choosing instead to embrace his American life, even to the point of moving into the home of a free-spirited New York WASP who curiously still lives with her sophisticated, wealthy parents. The death of his father sends Gogol back into the fold of his Bengali heritage, where he experiences an even deeper betrayal. The novel ends with Gogol finally reading the volume of Gogol stories his father gave him on the eve of his departure for college, suggesting that, in the end, literature is a place where the contradictions of the immigrant experience can remain in fruitful tension.

Following the triumphant release of *The Namesake*, Lahiri returned in 2004 to the short form with "Hell-Heaven," her first *New Yorker* short story publication since "Nobody's Business" in 2001. Additional stories appeared in 2006 and 2007, the whole of which she gathered together to comprise her 2008 collection, *Unaccustomed Earth*. More ambitious than its celebrated predecessor, the volume features five stand-alone stories and a three-part story cycle featuring two star-crossed lovers named Hema and Kaushik. The book's epigraph, which also provides the book's title, is drawn from "The Custom-House," Natheniel Hawthorne's famous preface to *The Scarlet Letter* (1850): "Human nature will not flourish, any more than a potato, if it be planted and replanted, for too long a series of generations, in the same worn-out soil. My children have had other birthplaces, and, so far as their fortunes may be within my control, shall strike their roots into unaccustomed earth." Accordingly, Lahiri's characters flourish amid the confusions of cross-Atlantic travel and multicultural misunderstandings. Whereas *Interpreter of Maladies* explored the ambiguities of newlyweds and children, *Unaccustomed Earth* expands its scope to address generational conflicts between children and parents as both navigate the Indian American experience.

The collection's near novella-length title story reprises the dual misunderstanding of "The Interpreter of Maladies" but applies the trope to that of an Americanized daughter and her widower father. Ruma, a new mother, feels obligated, according to Bengali custom, to invite her newly single father to live with her and her husband in Seattle. Yet she also feels deep guilt about her reluctance to go through with her invitation. Her father, meanwhile, hides from his daughter a burgeoning love affair he has lately begun with an Indian widow with whom he has been traveling. Similarly, "Hell-Heaven" resembles "When Mr. Prizada Came to Visit," only in this case the visitor is a dashing Bengali immigrant named Pranab, with whom the narrator's mother falls in love. As in the earlier story, the female protagonist revisits this episode in her parents' life from the vantage point of her own adulthood, yet whereas "Mr. Prizada" stays confined to the 1971 period of the Indo-Pakistani War, "Hell-Heaven" follows its narrator well into college and beyond, where she learns that, upon learning of Pradu's marriage to an American girl named Deborah, whom the narrator idolizes, her mother attempted suicide. The shocking ending marks a dark shift in Lahiri's work that she will develop more fully in her next novel.

The three stories that make up the "Hema and Kaushik" cycle represent three different approaches to point of view. "Once in a Lifetime" is a dramatic monologue in which Hema, addressing Kaushik directly, describes the girlish crush she had on him when he and his family moved into Hema's home during the late 1970s. Only later does Hema learn that Kaushik's mother is dying of breast cancer, the cause of their surprise return to the

United States. Kaushik takes over as narrator of the second piece, "Year's End," which details the resentment he feels when his widower father remarries a Bengali woman vastly plainer and more banal than his glamorous mother. In the final piece, "Going Ashore," Hema and Kaushik reencounter each other on the eve of Hema's marriage to a dull but suitable young man. Their affair rounds out the flirtation begun in the first story while also invoking the collection's other failed love affairs.

The collection was not only a bestseller but another award winner, this time snagging the Asian American Literary Award and the Frank O'Connor International Short Story Award. Living now in Brooklyn with her husband and two children – a girl arrived in 2005 – Lahiri turned her attention once again to the long from. The resulting work, the 336-page novel *The Lowland*, revisits many of her by now characteristic themes and tropes, including another detailed depiction of an Indian American childhood spent in a college milieu. Yet as with *Unaccustomed Earth*, Lahiri has deepened her art and widened her canvas, producing a work that functions as a dark counterpart to *The Namesake*'s hopeful vision of the American assimilation.

The novel opens in Calcutta in the 1960s, during the period of the Naxalite insurgency. The Naxalites, a group of communists determined to eradicate poverty and inequality, capture the imagination of Udyan Mitra, a poor Calcutta college student. His near-twin brother, Subhash, resists the pull of politics and devotes himself to his scientific studies. After Subhash leaves for America to complete his education, Udyan falls in love with a fellow Naxalite sympathizer named Gauri, who gets embroiled with Udyan in a political intrigue that ends with Udyan's violent murder. Subhash, confused but determined to honor his brother, marries Gauri, who moves with him to America. Their marriage, forced upon them by political upheaval, mirrors the arranged marriages of Bengali custom.

Yet rather than depict another couple gradually growing fond of each other – "out of habit if nothing else" as the narrator of "Hell-Heaven" says of her own parents – Lahiri this time traces the deepening chasm that grows between Subhash and Gauri following the birth of their only child, Bella (2008, p. 81). Unsatisfied by motherhood, Gauri finds fulfillment in philosophy, which she pursues all the way to the graduate level, often leaving Bella alone in the house so that she can attend lectures and work on her dissertation. When she is offered a fulltime teaching position on the West Coast, she abandons the family entirely. The novel's final movement recounts Gauri's emotional attempt to reconnect with Bela following the news of Subhash's death. The novel ends on an unsettling note in contrast to the neat, tidy conclusions of Lahiri's earlier fiction.

By the time *The Lowlands* appeared in 2013, Lahiri had relocated her family to Rome, Italy, thereby fulfilling a lifelong fascination with Italian culture. While there, she dedicated herself to mastering Italian, and began writing in that language in an attempt, as she would explain in her Italian-language short story "The Exchange," to become "another person." In 2015 she described her experience with her new language in an essay published in *The New Yorker* titled "How To Teach Yourself Italian," which was translated into English. Her most recent book, *In Altere Parole* (2015), is a collection of Italian-language stories and essays that was translated and published in the United States as *In Another Language*. The work explores her love of Italy, the challenges of writing in another language, and how her life in Italy, and her immersion in the Italian tongue, has given her the sense of belonging that had eluded her for most of her life. Most recently she has returned to the United States as Director of the Creative Writing Program at Princeton University, where she has been on the faculty since 2015, and where Toni Morrison famously served as the Robert F. Goheen Professor in the Humanities.

A rare phenomenon in literary studies, Jhumpa Lahiri is a critically lauded writer of artful literary fiction who has also managed to achieve widespread popularity. Even Barack Obama is a fan. Her four major works of fiction seem all of a piece, and possibly mark the end of a major phase in her career, as exemplified by her recent shift to Italian. Although it is unclear what direction her work will take going forward, her achievement thus far remains singular in US fiction, and her stature shows no sign of diminishing.

SEE ALSO: Debut Novels; Globalization; Multiculturalism; Realism after Poststructuralism

REFERENCES

Anastas, Benjamin. (2007). Inspiring adaptation. *Men's Vogue* (March 2007). https://web.archive.org/web/20080622163028/http://www.mensvogue.com/arts/books/articles/2007/02/jhumpa_lahiri (accessed July 7, 2021).

Lahiri, Jhumpa. (1999). *Interpreter of Maladies*. Boston: Houghton Mifflin.

Lahiri, Jhumpa. (2003). *The Namesake*. Boston: Houghton Mifflin.

Lahiri, Jhumpa. (2006). My two lives. *Newsweek* (March 5, 2006). https://www.newsweek.com/my-two-lives-106355 (accessed July 7, 2021).

Lahiri, Jhumpa. (2007). "I inherited a sense of exile from my parents": A conversation with Jhumpa Lahiri. *The Economic Times* (April 10, 2007). https://economictimes.indiatimes.com/i-inherited-a-sense-of-exile-from-my-parents/articleshow/1880249.cms (accessed July 7, 2021).

Lahiri, Jhumpa. (2008). *Unaccustomed Earth*. New York: Knopf.

Mudge, Alden. (2003). Family values. Bookpage.com. https://bookpage.com/interviews/8215-jhumpa-lahiri-fiction#.YTeKIZ1KjIU (accessed September 7, 2021).

FURTHER READING

Freidman, Natalie. (2008). From hybrids to tourists: children of immigrants in Jhumpa Lahiri's *The Namesake*. *Critique: Studies in Contemporary Fiction* 50 (1): 111–126.

Pauydal, Binod. (2015). Breaking the boundary: reading Lahiri's *The Lowland* as neo-cosmopolitan fiction. *South Asian Review* 36 (3): 15–31.

Reddy, Vanita. (2013). Jhumpa Lahiri's feminist cosmopolitics and the transnational beauty assemblage. *Meridians: feminism, race transnationalism* 2 (2): 29–59.

Wilhite, Keith. (2016). Blank spaces: outdated maps and unsettled subjects in Jhumpa Lahiri's *Interpreter of Maladies*. *MELUS* 41 (2): 76–96.

Wutz, Michael. (2015). The archaeology of the colonial – un-earthing Jhumpa Lahiri's *Unaccustomed Earth*. *Studies in American Fiction* 42 (2): 243–268.

LaValle, Victor

LEAH MILNE
University of Indianapolis, USA

Though the work of essayist and novelist Victor LaValle primarily veers towards the genres of horror and fantasy, critics are quick to append the qualifier "literary" to the beginning of their generic descriptions, a sign of how LaValle's work actually refuses to stay within the boundaries of any one category. Even his most fantastical texts have elements of literary realism. In an interview with Terry Gross (Gross 2012), LaValle noted that fiction differs from journalism because "journalism's job is to tell you what happened, and fiction to some degree is to make you understand how it felt to go through a certain experience." He thus populates his stories with monsters, trolls, and other fantastical creatures because these feel like the best way to get readers to empathize with the experiences of his characters. For instance, just as Godzilla became a metaphor for the war-related ravaging of Japan, the protagonist of LaValle's third novel,

The Devil in Silver (2012), encounters a bison-headed monster roaming the halls at night, giving readers a sense of how a sane man might feel if he were trapped in a mental hospital.

Many of LaValle's earlier works are more realistic, and often partly autobiographical. Born in 1972 and raised by his single mother and grandmother, both of whom are Ugandan immigrants, LaValle grew up in the densely populated and diverse neighborhoods of Flushing and Rosedale in Queens, New York. He often includes elements of this formative upbringing in his texts. For example, his first collection of interconnected short stories, *Slapboxing with Jesus* (1999), portrays a group of primarily Black and Latino men attempting to survive city life in the 1970s and 1980s. Equal parts gritty, funny, and vulnerable, the stories examine friendship and family, mental illness, gang violence, and sex. Garnering critical attention, the collection earned LaValle a PEN Open Book Award as well as the key to Jamaica, a neighborhood in southeast Queens.

One of the characters featured most prominently in the second half of *Slapboxing with Jesus* is Anthony James, a 15-year-old morbidly obese Puerto Rican rebel who returns as the protagonist of LaValle's first novel, *The Ecstatic* (2002). The novel was a finalist for the PEN/Faulkner Award and the Hurston-Wright Legacy Award, and also earned LaValle favorable comparisons to authors such as Haruki Murakami, John Kennedy Toole, and Edgar Allan Poe. In *The Ecstatic*, Anthony – now age 23, a college dropout suffering from bipolar disorder and also possibly schizophrenic – finds himself back in the basement of his family home in Queens cleaning houses and having run-ins with prisoners and loan sharks before joining his family on a road trip to the US South.

Though LaValle did his best to obscure many of the book's autobiographical influences – especially those related to mental illness – he reveals in numerous interviews how certain aspects of the novel hurt his mother and sister (and would have offended his grandmother, too, if she had still been alive). Anthony's experiences are at least partly inspired by LaValle's own, as he flunked out of Cornell as an undergraduate after suffering through academic issues and struggles with physical and mental health. After working hard and seeking professional help, LaValle graduated and began to place more confidence in his abilities.

Undoubtedly, music also played a role in this recovery, as it has at other times in his life. He speaks often of how his childhood friends in Flushing – representing a rainbow of diverse cultures – particularly enjoyed heavy metal, including the music of Metallica, Slayer, and Iron Maiden, and later discovered hip-hop. In an interview with Tara Anderson (2017), he describes the two genres of hip-hop and metal as "the two great working-class male music forms that America has created." LaValle makes numerous allusions to musicians and songs in all of his works, so it is especially fitting that *The Ecstatic*'s title inspired rapper Mos Def's album of the same name, released in 2009.

Mos Def would blurb LaValle's next novel, *Big Machine* (2009), as "the first great book of the next America." (Music – in this case, the rapper KRS-One and the band Megadeth – also plays a role in the novel.) Though his previous books had certainly garnered critical attention, *Big Machine* is in many ways LaValle's breakout novel. Invited by the Amsterdam-based film institute, Binger Filmlab, to adapt *Big Machine* to film, LaValle would go on to win numerous honors for his novel, including the Shirley Jackson Award for Best Novel in 2009 and the American Book Award and the Ernest J. Gaines Award for Literary Excellence in 2010.

Part of the reason for *Big Machine*'s success, LaValle mentions in an interview with Jack Boulter, is his relationship with fellow fiction writer and essayist Emily Raboteau, whom he married in 2010. They have since gone on to have two children, a son and a daughter. He and Raboteau are also both professors: Raboteau is a professor of English at the City College of New York, where she also directs the creative writing MFA program; LaValle is an associate professor in the Columbia University School of the Arts writing program, from which he himself graduated with a master of fine arts in 1998. He was an assistant professor in the program at the time when he was writing *Big Machine*, which is pointedly less autobiographical than his other novels, maybe partly due to his family's disenchantment with his use of personal details in his previous works.

Big Machine also marks LaValle's more definitive pivot towards fantasy, horror, noir, the supernatural, and an overall stubborn defiance of generic categorization. The main character, Ricky Rice, is a recovering addict and a survivor of a suicide cult who is working at his cleaning job when he is mysteriously recruited to join a secret society of fellow Black ex-junkies and criminals known as the "Unlikely Scholars." Provided food, shelter, clothing, and a modest stipend for their services, the Unlikely Scholars conduct odd and disorienting research assignments as paranormal investigators in a place in Vermont called the Washburn Library.

Like many of LaValle's works, *Big Machine* deals with faith, free will, and resilience. "Doubt is the big machine. It grinds up the delusions of women and men," states one of the book's characters (2009, p. 205). In numerous flashbacks, Rice grapples with his disturbing past as part of his family's cult, as well as with his country's own disturbing treatment of African Americans, both of which hold questions of morality and belonging at their center. However unsettling his cult had been, his aunts established it both as a form of self-creation and as a way to rectify American claims to Christian tenets with its decidedly un-Christian practice of slavery. Given the big questions of *Big Machine* in regard to history, terrorism, racism, and religious fundamentalism, it is no wonder that LaValle has alluded in a number of interviews to the possibility of a sequel.

Though the aforementioned *The Devil in Silver* is not a sequel per se, LaValle discusses the subsequent 2012 novel as existing in the same mostly realistic but somewhat off-kilter world as *Big Machine*. There are also elements of his first novel, *The Ecstatic*, in *The Devil in Silver*'s final pages, making his books appear as though they were part of a broad universe of overlapping (though never quite intersecting) lives and experiences. Though the novel – written in an opinionated and parenthetical-riddled third person – is a departure from his previous first-person works, LaValle's preoccupations with faith, class, and mental health – not to mention stories that are set in Queens – return in this novel.

The Devil in Silver tells the story of Pepper, an awkward and temperamental 42-year-old who has a run-in with police. The police, too tired from a long shift to worry about processing Pepper at an actual police station, instead admit him, without his consent, to the labyrinthine psychiatric unit of New Hyde Hospital, where the law and the hospital's understaffed inattention kick in to keep him medicated rather than to assess his sanity and offer hope of an authorized release. That first night, he is nearly killed by an old man with the head of a bison, and he decides to join forces with a few fellow patients to protect them from the monster. A companion novella, *Lucretia and the Kroons* (2012), expands on the story of one of *The Devil in Silver*'s youngest secondary characters.

Though marketed solely as a horror or thriller, the novel's dark humor, social satire, and its care in presenting its cast of characters suggest LaValle's signature blending of genres. In many ways, the bison-headed old man notwithstanding, the book is Kafkaesque in its depiction of a nightmarish and convoluted world. For instance, when Pepper insists that the system that imprisons him does not work for people like him, his doctor notes, "A wise man once said that every system is designed to give you the results you actually get ... The system is working *exactly* right for those it was *intended* for" (2012, p. 306). New Hyde becomes a microcosm for the world that Pepper now seems barred from reentering. Meanwhile, the characters themselves are Dickensian – whether they are the forgotten poor who haunt the halls of the hospital alongside the giant Minotaur-like monster or the overworked, disillusioned, and occasionally abusive staff and doctors who feel beleaguered or apathetic to improve their workplace's treatment of its patients. In his author's note, LaValle credits his sympathetic portrayal of these characters to the "offices" where he wrote the book: the two donut shops in Washington Heights near the New York apartment he shares with his wife and kids.

Aside from Dickens and Kafka, LaValle's work is replete with more pointed allusions to other authors, artists, and works that have inspired him. These references notably span genres and time periods and include authors such as Shirley Jackson, Harlan Ellison, James Joyce, and Ramsey Campbell, a British horror writer. The long-suffering doctor in *The Devil in Silver* leads a hospital book group in its debut selection, Peter Benchley's *Jaws* (1974), through which Pepper learns to sympathize with the monster who haunts him. (Pepper is also obsessed with Vincent Van Gogh.) Meanwhile, *Big Machine* alludes to Homer, Octavia Butler, Richard Wright, and – most notably – Ralph Waldo Ellison's *Invisible Man* (1952).

Rather than being an allusion, LaValle's 2016 second novella, *The Ballad of Black Tom*, can be interpreted as an all-out retelling or repurposing of H.P. Lovecraft's 1925 short story "The Horror at Red Hook." LaValle grew up reading the works of Lovecraft, along with other horror authors like Richard Matheson, Shirley Jackson, and Stephen King. LaValle likes to remark that the relatively mundane book covers of the horror books on the spinner shelves of grocery stores contributed to this preference, as his mother was more likely to buy those innocuous-looking tomes rather than the romances with their more salacious covers. Though Lovecraft was a favorite of his, he identifies King's *IT* (1986) as the first book he ever loved, and Jackson's *The Haunting of Hill House* (1959) as the book he has probably reread the most. Lovecraft's racist fears actually inform much of the earlier author's works, and "The Horror at Red Hook" is arguably Lovecraft at his most xenophobic. For instance, Lovecraft's narrator refers to Red Hook's immigrant community as "a maze of hybrid squalor." LaValle's *The Ballad of Black Tom* is both criticism and tribute to Lovecraft, whose racism he only recognized much later when rereading his works.

The novella takes place in Harlem in 1924 and centers on a hustler named Charles Thomas Tester. Tommy is a trickster figure of sorts, able to don a suit and convince white people that he is a blues musician despite only knowing a few songs on the guitar taught to him by his father, Otis. One of those people Tommy manages to fool is the source of mystery at the center of Lovecraft's story: Roger Suydam, an eccentric millionaire and occultist who promises a paycheck that will help him care for himself and Otis. Two racist detectives hound Tommy for information on the reclusive Suydam, one of whom is the extremely violent Mr. Howard, whose last name is the "H" of H.P. Lovecraft. The other is the Irish-born policeman Detective Malone, Lovecraft's protagonist from "The Horror at Red Hook" and the subject of the second half of *The Ballad of Black Tom*.

Despite the oppressiveness and devastation caused him by the New York police, Tester and the people he meets stand as a defense of the diverse and crowded New York that Lovecraft openly abhorred in his works. LaValle pointedly avoids mimicking Lovecraft's stylistic flourishes, instead telling Tommy's story in an unaffected and matter-of-fact tone and even fleshing out the flattened character of Malone. LaValle's literary rebuttal and homage to Lovecraft's story would win numerous honors, including the Shirley Jackson Award for Best Novella, the 2016 Nebula Award for Best Novella, the 2017 Hugo Award for Best Novella, and the 2017 World Fantasy Award.

In one of the most emotional scenes in the novella, Tommy reacts with rage at a violent act committed by the cops by quoting a line from Mary Shelley's *Frankenstein* (1818), when her monster declares war against humanity. The line foreshadows LaValle's next work, the *Destroyer* comic series (2017), a continuation of *Frankenstein*. The story follows the titular family's last living descendants, Dr. Jo Baker and her 12-year-old son Akai, the latter of whom is a victim of police violence. Published on the eve of the bicentennial anniversary of Shelley's novel, *Destroyer* also contends with other problems that humanity has wrought, including war, environmental disaster, sexism, and greed.

In addition to horror novels, LaValle grew up reading comic books and remembers being surprised that popular genres could also discuss political topics. He tells interviewer Tara Anderson how much he enjoyed the mutants and captivating characters in *X-Men* and then realizing, "Oh my God, this is about prejudice and institutional power being used to crush minorities" (2017). LaValle's aforementioned tenure at the Binger Filmlab would also help him contend with how to transform his written text to the visual language of comics, though he credits most of the work's sweeping landscapes, resonant imagery, and clever visual allusions to illustrator Dietrich Smith, colorist Joana LaFuente, and cover artist Micaela Dawn. The series would win the Bram Stoker Award for Superior Achievement in a Graphic Novel and would be listed as a finalist for the Dwayne McDuffie Award for Diversity in Comics.

The same year that *Destroyer* came out, LaValle would experience even more success with *The Changeling* (2017), which would win the World Fantasy Award and the American Book Award, among others. *The Changeling* tells the story of Apollo Kagwa, an antique book dealer born of a single immigrant mother and an absentee father, who falls in love with librarian Emma Valentine, with whom he has a child named Brian. Apollo is part of a generation that the novel refers to as "New Dads," a group who are so deeply involved in child-raising that they also post multiple pictures of their children on social media. *The Changeling* deals with loss, parenthood, privacy, and class while riffing on Maurice Sendak's chilling children's story, *Outside Over There* (1981), in which goblins steal a baby.

Billed as a fairy tale horror novel, *The Changeling* takes place in the congested apartment complexes and suburban boroughs of Queens, but also in a more mythical version of New York populated by secret islands and haunting forests. In the midst of telling a fairy tale, the second half of the novel also contends with the very nature of what fairy tales are historically meant to do in terms of providing insights into morality and adulthood. The novel further deals with issues outside of the realms of fairy tales. For instance, Apollo confronts his mother, Lillian, about his childhood and his father, and he worries about his best friend and fellow book dealer, Patrice, an Army veteran dealing with post-traumatic stress disorder (PTSD). *The Ballad of Black Tom* and *The Changeling* are also in development as television series by SYFY AMC and FX, respectively.

LaValle's admiration for the work that genre fiction can do is evident in how he writes all of his works. For instance, in *The Devil in Silver*, while the titled devil makes his appearance in all of his buffalo-like glory, the real fear comes from the bureaucratic quagmire and ineptitude of the underfunded American healthcare system and the ease with which a sane person can become entrapped by it. In *The Changeling*, terror arrives not only when encountering the novel's monster, but also when Apollo and Patrice, two Black men, find themselves in a white suburban neighborhood at night – a danger particularly keen if any of the residents decide to be as "proactive" as does the ostensibly white person who calls the cops on Akai when she mistakes his Little League baseball bat for a rifle in *Destroyer*. In an interview with friend and fellow author Marlon James, LaValle notes how the category of literary realism is itself a fallacy, built on what a "very specific subset of American or European life" have agreed upon as the general experience of real life (Shapiro 2019). In his genre-defying work, LaValle proffers another version of reality that makes room for other stories and experiences.

SEE ALSO: Butler, Octavia; Cole, Teju; Gomez, Jewelle; Illness and Disability Narratives; James, Marlon; Jones, Stephen Graham; King, Stephen; Mixed-Genre Fiction; Mosley, Walter; Whitehead, Colson

REFERENCES

Anderson, Tara. (2017). Five things: writer Victor LaValle on comic books, Metallica, and Malcolm X. Interview with Victor LaValle. *WFPL*. https://wfpl.org/five-things-writer-victor-lavalle-on-comic-books-metallica-and-malcolm-x/ (accessed July 8, 2021).
Gross, Terry. (2012). Author interviews: Victor LaValle on mental illness, monsters, survival. *NPR*. https://www.npr.org/2012/08/29/160246687/why-monsters-stalk-mentally-ill-in-devil-in-silver (accessed July 8, 2021).
LaValle, Victor. (2009). *Big Machine*. New York: Spiegel & Grau.
LaValle, Victor. (2012). *The Devil in Silver*. New York: Spiegel & Grau.
Shapiro, Lila. (2019). A conversation with Marlon James and Victor LaValle. *Vulture* (February 5, 2019). https://www.vulture.com/2019/02/marlon-james-and-victor-lavalle-have-a-conversation.html (accessed August 26, 2021).

FURTHER READING

Ali, Abdul. (2013). A conversation with Victor LaValle. *Wasafiri* 28 (4): 23–27.
Francis, Vievee. (2010). Beauty and fiends: an interview with Victor LaValle. *Callaloo* 33 (4): 949–967.
Sloan, Aisha Sabatini. (2010). A forecast for Blackness: the work of Victor LaValle. *Callaloo* 33 (4): 979–981.

Leavitt, David

FIORENZO IULIANO
University of Cagliari, Italy

David Leavitt's production covers a time span of more than thirty years; his wide-ranging output includes novels, short stories, novellas, travel books, essays, and the editing of classics and anthologies. Since 2000 he has taught Creative Writing at the University of Florida. Leavitt's extensive production resists any possible attempt at classification. A "gay writer" according to the critics that have reviewed his books over the years, he has repeatedly voiced his suspicion about the existence of anything like gay literature (Leavitt 2003, pp. xxii–xiii and xxxviii). His substantial lack of interest in the academic debates about gender and identity politics, moreover, has earned him the criticism, when not the open hostility, of scholars in gay studies, who have attacked his characters' longing for normativity, maintaining that Leavitt "suburbanized the queers" (Woodhouse 1998, p. 140). Although his 1985 essay "The New Lost Generation" was acclaimed – and can still be read – as the manifesto of the yuppie generation, his writing shares little or nothing with the works of the so-called literary Brat Pack of the 1980s, nor does it have much more to do with minimalism, another label that has frequently been attached to his works and that he has rejected or distanced himself from. Finally, his Jewish American legacy, despite being evoked through many of his characters, never takes center stage either. Leavitt has often remarked on his annoyance with the labels that the US literary market seems obsessed with, and has actually referred to George Eliot's *Middlemarch* (1871; naming many of his characters after its protagonists) and E.M. Forster's *A Room with a View* (1908) as two of his major sources of inspiration. To such authors Leavitt owes the plain and limpid style in which his narrative is written, and also the motifs that most frequently recur in his work, more reminiscent of themes addressed by late Victorian and early modernist authors than comparable with the blank fiction of the 1980s, when his literary career began.

Central to many of Leavitt's stories is his characters' need to find a place that they can, at least provisionally, call home, and that can hopefully function as an idealized site of emotional balance and social stability. The possibility to adjust one's own desires, emotions, and aspirations to often unfamiliar or even hostile contexts, which marks the experience of numerous protagonists of his novels and stories, is epitomized by the "crane-child" that gives *The Lost Language of Cranes* (1986) its title. A baby raised without maternal care, the crane-child spends his first months basically alone, in a poor apartment close to a construction site. Having, for this reason, mastered no language, it only replicates with his body and arms the moves of the cranes he can spot from his window. The need to find something to identify with and to love, together with the necessity to regain a pristine site of affect and belonging, are among the central motifs of Leavitt's narrative, acquiring every time different patterns and accents. The home and the family, rather than places that his protagonists can claim as part of their own identity and location in society, are frequently designed as either ultimate horizons of desire and expectation or repositories of memories and loose recollections from the past, by now lost.

"The New Lost Generation" can prove precious to appreciate the role of these themes in Leavitt's narrative. Here he argues that his generation is "born too late and too early" (Leavitt 1985, p. 88): he and his peers are younger than their elder siblings, who went through the politically saturated 1960s, but were at the time too old to absorb the (supposedly) apolitical individualism of the 1980s. The lost generation of young people born in the 1960s, thus, struggles to carve out its own identity and position in the present US society, feeling perpetually out of place, uprooted, and deprived of any site of cultural and symbolic identification. His characters' quest for a place of origins to head back to is, thus, understandably central to Leavitt's narrative, yet it is destined to be perpetually frustrated given the impossibility to ever find a site of full belonging even when they are portrayed as presumably enjoying their lives, their jobs, their relationships, and their leisure time. Their inability to find a niche they can fully recognize as their own is counterbalanced by their attempts to both constantly appropriate the places they happen to visit and attune to the people they run into, trying to detect a remote trace of intimacy even in the most distant and foreign experiences.

Both the endeavor to familiarize with the unfamiliar, and a powerful sense of estrangement from what should be close or even intimate, characterize Leavitt's narrative from his very debut book. Especially his early works insist on the household as, at the same time, the most proximate and the most distant of the contexts young people (as were his characters and himself, too) could experience and relate to. His first two novels, *The Lost Language of Cranes* and *Equal Affections* (1989), are centered on two families facing unexpected troubles: in the former Philip Benjamin, a young man from New York, comes out to his family, only to later discover, to his mother's and his own utmost surprise, that his father Owen is gay too. The story is intertwined with the Benjamins' domestic worries due to the gentrification of Midtown Manhattan, which urges them to move out to other areas of the city and thus reconfigure their whole existence. Though narratively essential in *Equal Affections* as well, homosexuality gradually loses its thematic centrality, as this second novel features illness as the thematic kernel around which the story of the Coopers, a Jewish family from California, revolves. Louise, the strong and passionate mother and wife, discovers that she has cancer, the event triggering a process of self-analysis through which she tries to come to terms with her own past and with her present condition as a woman disillusioned with her marriage and her own identity and religious legacy. Whereas in *The Lost Language* the protagonists' coming out only serves to emphasize the gap between two generations of gay men, in *Equal Affections* the homosexuality of Danny and April, the Cooper siblings, is almost peripheral to the whole unfolding of the story.

In *Martin Bauman* (2000), the autobiographical novel in which Leavitt also describes the literary scene of the 1980s New York, the protagonist, a young writer and the author's alter-ego, reports that especially gay scholars and critics were attacking his characters' desire for normality, which was actually at odds with the rebellious demands expressed by previous generations of gay writers. The stories authored by Martin are criticized because of their lukewarm interest in the impact that AIDS was having at the time on gay communities and for their penchant for family matters and mothers dying of cancer. If it is actually true that AIDS seldom takes center stage in Leavitt's narrative, with few, though outstanding, exceptions, illness recurs in a number of stories, such as "Counting Months," "Radiations" (*Family Dancing*, 1984), and "Gravity" (*A Place I've Never Been*, 1990), in which, besides being explored with regard to its emotional and social impact on the characters' lives, it also gives Leavitt an opportunity to reflect on the human body as a simultaneously phenomenological and political datum. Corporeality is in fact addressed as a barrier that, being perceived as porous and vulnerable, reveals how fragile and precarious the human condition is, and how difficult it is to disentangle one's own individuality from its sometimes hardly detectable connections with the outer world and with other people. This is the case, for instance, of "Saturn Street" (*Arkansas*, 1997), in which Leavitt juxtaposes discourses about AIDS with science fiction in order to suggest a new possible epistemology of the body. Here science fiction provides an interesting foray into American society and culture, highlighting some of its desires or fixations, such as the need to overcome fears and anxieties by envisaging an idealized time and place in which everything is perfectly functioning. It also makes the story's protagonists figure an originally immaterial idea of corporeality, in which the external barriers of the body's surface have broken up, allowing for a more intimate connection among human beings. Whether this final collapse is due to illness, which actually lacerates the bodily surface exposing scars, sores or cuts, or to some futuristic image of incorporeal bodies, does not seem to make much difference. Cognate to the focus on science fiction in stories like "Saturn Street" or "Aliens" (*Family Dancing*) is the increasing intimacy between humans and machines, widely celebrated by the 1980s cyborg cultures, whose downsides are explored in the story of the addiction of Walter, one of the protagonists of *Equal Affections*, to digital pornography and internet-based communication – a theme also addressed in "The List" (*The Marble Quilt*, 2001).

If that of the multiple ways through which human relationships can be shaped, undone, and infinitely reconfigured is one of the leitmotifs of Leavitt's narrative, at least two more themes are to be mentioned as peculiar to his production: geography and spatiality first, and then his characters' troublesome relationship with history and with the past. The former, in particular, probably represents one of the most immediately recognizable traits of Leavitt's narrative, most of which explores space not as a simple material datum, but as a complex category according to which his characters arrange and shape their emotional worlds and their relationships with other people. Not only do the actual spaces he represents resonate with his characters' feelings, impressions, and reflections; spaces are made all the more significant insofar as they encapsulate the polarizations, the juxtapositions, and the overlappings that make up Leavitt's stories. As for geography, the author himself has declared his fondness for maps, as witness, for instance, *While England Sleeps* (1993), in which the realistic topography of London is constantly compared with its abstract representation, provided by the map of the subway. The same novel also features a complex interplay of geographical oppositions (the city and its map, the center, and the periphery of London, England and Spain), in which each place acquires a specific and identifiable role in the narrative economy of the story. Something similar happens in *The Two Hotel Francforts* (2013), in which Lisbon, the most western outpost of Europe, is explored and narrated as a city of doubles, where two almost homonymous hotels, located in distant areas, stand for the opposite choices that the novel's four protagonists make with regard to their lives and their conditions as exiles.

The role played by cities and spaces in Leavitt's narrative also reflects the meaning that they have in the life and in the imagination of his characters, and what is true for the American cities in which most stories are set is also evident when his American characters visit or move to Europe. Often chosen to symbolically counterbalance the widths of American spaces, Europe becomes the idealized "other" upon which most of Leavitt's characters project their dreams. This is partially noticeable in the already mentioned *The Two Hotel Francforts*, in which Lisbon is recounted through the perspective of two American couples, but is especially evident in the numerous stories Leavitt sets in Italy. The backdrop of a number of long narratives, among which "The Wooden Anniversary" (*Arkansas*) and *The Page Turner* (1998) (a novel partially set in Rome and featuring an aspiring pianist who gradually acknowledges his lack of talent), Italy is also the setting of many short stories, such as "A Road to Rome" (*A Place I've Never Been*), "Crossing St. Gotthard," or "The Marble Quilt" (*The Marble Quilt*), besides being the central motif of *Italian Pleasures* (1996), *In Maremma: Life and a House in Southern Tuscany* (2001), *Florence, A Delicate Case* (2002). Leavitt locates himself in a long-standing tradition of English (and gay) writing about Italy, as witness his direct references to E.M. Forster's *A Room with a View* and Henry James's *Daisy Miller* (1878) in the autobiographic "The Term Paper Artist," also included in *Arkansas*. Here the protagonist compares the two writers with regard to their ability to understand Italy, and his predilection for Forster is explained in words that can be referred to Leavitt's writing about Italy as well. James, he maintains, "never gets under Italy's skin, which is odd, because Forster does, and he spent so much less time there" (Leavitt 1998, p. 23). Yet, getting under Italy's skin means for Leavitt catching and portraying that universe of senses – smells, tastes, ephemeral visual impressions – that presumably make up both urban and rural Italian landscapes. Sometimes Leavitt's Italy, thus, sounds more idealized than real, especially when, as in "The Wooden Anniversary," it becomes the land in which it seems that any form of pleasure can be fully satisfied, food, sex, art and the landscape all coalescing in a unique, diversified, sensuously enjoyable (albeit sometimes bothersome) experience, or when, as in *Shelter in Place* (2020) (published in Italian as *Il decoro*, a few months before the English original) it is envisaged as the best place to move to after the 2016 United States presidential election.

The role of memory, finally, is essential to understand Leavitt's work, which includes stories set in the past and dealing with his protagonists' need to retrieve and reconcile to personal or collective memories. In "The Infection Scene" (*The Marble Quilt*), which combines the life of Lord Alfred Douglas with that of a young man living in present-day US, or in *The Indian Clerk* (2007), which goes through the life of the famous Indian mathematician Ramanujan, fiction and biographical data are mixed up, as in the biography of Alan Turing, *The Man Who Knew Too Much* (2006), which Leavitt authored for the series "Great Discoveries" released by Norton. *While England Sleeps* and *The Two Hotel Francforts*, on the other hand, are choral novels in which tragic love affairs are set against the backdrop of the Spanish Civil War and World War II respectively. Especially in *While England Sleeps*, the war represents a fracture in any linear understanding of temporality that questions the very idea of progress as intrinsic to history. The crisscrossing between private and public spheres is one of the novel's most interesting and best accomplished features. His almost philological reconstruction of the past, moreover, cost Leavitt a legal complaint from British poet Stephen Spender, whose autobiography *World Within World* (1951) he was accused of having plagiarized. The book was withdrawn from the market and reissued only in 1995, after being revised by the author, this episode marking, according to Drew Patrick Shannon, the beginning of a gradual loss of interest in Leavitt's works from critics and readers (Shannon 2001, pp. 315–316).

Memory is paramount not only in Leavitt's works set in the past, but more broadly in his numerous stories that address his protagonists' relationship with their individual pasts. This often means that the Jewish-American legacy turns out to be central to many of his stories, though reference to Leavitt's production is curiously absent from most essays and collections about Jewish-American literature. In *Equal Affections*, it is experienced as a contested site of identification for Louise, whose personal past and final (and frustrated) decision to convert to Catholicism occupy a significant part of the overall narrative. In *Martin Bauman*, the protagonist and his boyfriend's controversial relationship with the religious beliefs and practices of their own families marks some of the most compelling episodes of the novel. Finally, "Family Dancing," the story that gives Leavitt's first book its title, provides one of his most insightful and impressive accounts of the rituals of a Jewish-American family. The distress experienced by Seth, one of the protagonists, derives both from his being a closeted gay young man, whose sexuality his parents do not even suspect, and from his double bind as, at the same time, a standard American teenager and the son of a traditional Jewish-American family. Being Seth for his friends and Sethela for his (especially older) relatives bespeaks his simultaneous belonging to two, at least in his eyes, contrasting worlds. The motif, typical of much Jewish-American literature, of the young protagonist's troubled relationship with the Jewish legacy is here adapted to the generation coming of age in the 1980s. Intimately dovetailing with the broader concern with identity as, at the same time, a reassuring promise and a menacing trap, this is one of the most intriguing and thought-provoking oppositions that frequently emerge in Leavitt's writing.

SEE ALSO: After Postmodernism; Fiction and Affect; Illness and Disability Narratives; Minimalism and Maximalism; Queer and LGBT Fiction; Urban Fiction

REFERENCES

Leavitt, David. (1985). The new lost generation. *Esquire* (May): 85–95.
Leavitt, David. (1998). *Arkansas: Three Novellas.* London: Abacus; 1st ed. 1997.
Leavitt, David. (2003). Introduction. In: *The New Penguin Book of Gay Short Stories* (ed. David Leavitt and Mark Mitchell), xiii–xxix. New York: Penguin.
Shannon, Drew Patrick. (2001). Courage in the telling: the critical rise and fall of David Leavitt. *International Journal of Sexuality and Gender Studies* 6 (4): 305–318.
Woodhouse, Reed. (1998). *Unlimited Embrace: A Canon of Gay Fiction, 1945–1995.* Amherst: University of Massachusetts Press.

FURTHER READING

Annesley, James. (2006). *Fictions of Globalization: Consumption, the Market and the Contemporary American Novel.* London: Continuum.
Bleeth, Kenneth and Rivkin, Julie. (2001). The "limitation David": plagiarism, collaboration, and the making of a gay literary tradition in David Leavitt's "The term paper artist." *PMLA*, 116 (5): 1349–1363.
Guscio, Lelia. (1995). *"We Trust Ourselves and Money. Period": Relationships, Death and Homosexuality in David Leavitt's Fiction.* Bern: Peter Lang.
Iuliano, Fiorenzo. (2017). Il futuro è un groviglio che gira in tondo. Guerra, storia e identità in *Mentre l'Inghilterra dorme* di David Leavitt. In *Raccontare la guerra. I conflitti bellici e la modernità* (ed. Nicola Turi), 309–327. Florence: Florence University Press.
Lo, Mun-Hou. (1995). David Leavitt and the etiological maternal body. *Modern Fiction Studies* 41 (3/4): 439–465.

Lee, Chang-rae

JI-YOUNG UM
Seattle Pacific University, USA

Chang-rae Lee is an American author of five novels to date, perhaps best known for his portrayals of Korean American and Korean diasporic experience. But to describe Lee's writing as simply "Korean American" would be reductive. His writing is, as Lee himself has put it, often concerned with the inner conflicts of the individual in response to the demands of the larger context around them, whether that context is a Long Island suburb or the legacy of America's wars in Asia. That he has chosen to explore these tensions through the immigrant's perspective and/or experience is not a proof of limited imagination or range. Rather, Lee's works show that the so-called immigrant literatures or narratives are not limited to the scope of a particular group's history and experience but are vital to the ways in which we read, understand, and make sense of literary texts and their relationship to the broader social world.

Lee came to prominence with the publication of *Native Speaker* in 1995, which went on to win the American Book Award and the PEN/Hemingway Award among others. It is also the novel that perhaps remains most closely identified with Lee himself. The protagonist and narrator, Henry Park, like the author, is a young Korean American man from the suburbs of New York. The novel's intense focus on Henry and his inner life, his family dynamics, and its most prominent setting, Queens, all would appear to support the idea that Lee drew heavily from his own life. Lee is not by any means the first

Korean American published writer. Younghill Kang's 1931 autobiography *The Grass Roof* is widely recognized as the first publication by a Korean American writer. Lee is, however, arguably the first Korean American writer to receive such wide, popular recognition from both literary circles (readers and critics) and scholarly communities. Lee has taught creative writing at various higher education institutions and is currently on faculty at Stanford University.

The publication and recognition of Lee's work also emerged in the wake of significant sociohistorical and cultural shifts. The rise and mainstreaming of multiculturalism in the 1970s and 1980s shifted the dominant national paradigm on race, from a nation-state that enacted racist policies (Jim Crow laws and race-based immigration restrictions, among others) to one that aimed to promote a diversity of identities and cultures. By the 1990s, visual and print media would see some of the era's most important landmark cultural productions from writers of color, including Toni Morrison's *Beloved* (1987), Sandra Cisneros's *The House on Mango Street* (1984), and Amy Tan's *Joy Luck Club* (1989), to name a few. The publication of *Native Speaker* in 1995 was part of a similar wave of significant, award-winning works by Asian American writers, including Jessica Hagedorn (*Dogeaters*, 1990), Susan Choi (*The Foreign Student*, 1998), and Jhumpa Lahiri (*Interpreter of Maladies*, 1999).

This is not to suggest that only felicitous social conditions allowed Asian American and other writers of color to gain prominence or recognition – as, perhaps, some detractors of multiculturalism may claim. But dismissing the significant sociopolitical changes in the period leading up to Lee's (and others') publications would imply that Asian Americans publishing before the 1990s were just not very skilled writers, a conclusion that is simply inaccurate. Moreover, although representation of and works by racial minorities were made visible more broadly, and often heralded as signs of racial progress, it is important to note that material conditions for these groups were not similarly transformed. Therefore, we might consider Asian American writing in this period as an arbiter of both significant change and ongoing struggle, and not as an end point or as a sign of the realization of the "American Dream."

Lee's subsequent novels feature, in varying but nonetheless prominent ways, Korean American/Korean diasporic characters (with the notable exception of *On Such a Full Sea* (2014), Lee's most recent novel to date). *A Gesture Life* published in 1999 centers on "Doc" Hata, whose seemingly quiet and peaceful life in the suburbs masks a troubled inner life. Hata is, of course, a Japanese surname, hiding both his origins as an ethnic Korean who was adopted by a Japanese family and his traumatic past in the Japanese imperial army during World War II, during which he was tasked with looking after Korean women who had been forced into sexual service to the soldiers. But Lee's second novel also complicates the more readily recognizable Korean American immigrant experience as portrayed through Henry Park in *Native Speaker*. Hata's background and his past, in contrast, highlight the violence and lasting legacy of Korea's subjugation under Japanese colonial rule. The history and legacy of the Korean War (1950–1953) and US involvement would be further explored in Lee's fourth novel, *The Surrendered* (2008). Both of these novels and the historical context they invoke demonstrate the significance of histories of imperialism (Japanese as well as US) for Koreans in the United States. As Asian American literary scholar Lisa Lowe has noted in *Immigrant Acts*, the large number of Asian immigrants (from countries that have been directly affected by US militarism and/or colonialism) to the United States after the 1965 Immigration Reform Act represents the "return" of "material legacy of the repressed history of US imperialism in Asia" (Lowe 1996, p. 16).

This "repressed history" is fully borne out in the three central characters of *The Surrendered*: June, a Korean war orphan who eventually immigrates to the United States, Hector, a white American soldier who crosses paths with June both in the Korean orphanage and again in the United States, and Sylvie, who runs the orphanage along with her missionary husband and helps to facilitate adoption of Korean orphans by American families. The Korean War and the Vietnam War, and America's involvement in both, are often characterized as "proxies" for the Cold War between the two post-World War II superpowers, the United States and the Soviet Union. The binary logic of the Cold War subsumed long, complex histories and politics of newly independent and/or decolonizing countries such as Korea and instead reduced them to proxy client nations for either the United States or the Soviet Union. Thus, American intervention in the civil war between North and South Korea would be narrativized as defense of democracy and freedom, "saving" South Korea from communism. The three characters, their relationship to one another and to the war, work to complicate the binary logic of war (victory vs. defeat, good vs. evil, male vs. female, etc.). While the three characters may simply appear to reproduce common tropes in war stories – the war orphan, the GI, the nurturing/sacrificing mother – in Lee's novel, all three represent and embody the damages of war and imperialism.

It is not only Lee's Korean American characters who must grapple with the violent histories and legacies of US militarism and imperialism, as *The Surrendered* shows. It is a past that all Americans must reckon with, in one form or another, even as liberal multiculturalism became the defining national ethos and identity. While the term "multiculturalism" may have lost the aspirational cachet and power it once wielded, the idea – that the United States is a nation made up of many races, cultures, languages, and that this uniquely defines and strengthens our national community – remains powerful. In this context, two of Lee's earlier novels, *Native Speaker* and *Aloft* (2004), disrupt (immigrant) narratives of assimilation and expose the promises and contradictions of multiculturalism.

If the Korean American narrator/protagonist of *Native Speaker* was read as the author's stand-in, the white, multigenerational Italian American narrator/protagonist of *Aloft* would seem to signal the opposite. Although some critics interpreted this choice as a gesture of resistance or backlash against being pigeonholed as an "ethnic" writer on Lee's part, *Aloft* also explores and complicates stories of and about immigrants in a multiracial society, as with his previous novels. *Aloft*'s protagonist, Jerry Battle, and his mixed-race, multiracial family may seem to embody the promise and dream of multicultural America, yet as the strands of family drama unravel throughout the novel, Jerry – and we, the readers – can see that racial difference and racial trauma do not merely disappear as a result of familial and other intimate bonds. The histories of military and imperial violence in Asia haunt the characters here as well, largely through Jerry's Korean ex-wife Daisy, whose troubled mental health and suicide hint at unresolved trauma from this past.

Native Speaker perhaps offers the most direct and clearest critique of multiculturalism, in its portrayal of the tensions and contradictions of multiculturalism with no easy resolution. The interracial and intercultural dynamics in the novel reflect the aftermath of the Los Angeles riots of 1992. The uprising – or the riot, as most news and media outlets called it – was in response to the acquittal of police officers accused of brutally beating Rodney King, an African American man. Much of the violence was contained in the Koreatown area of Los Angeles, and the conflicts were largely represented as either misplaced anger against white supremacy or the eruption of long-simmering tensions between the African American community and Korean American entrepreneurs. Both analyses offer incomplete and oversimplified explanations; yet it was through these mainstream news media outlets' portrayals that Korean Americans were propelled into national consciousness in the wake of the 1992 riots/uprising.

Lee's novel references these events mainly through one of its central characters, John Kwang, a Korean American New York city councilman. *Native Speaker* deploys John Kwang as the primary arbiter for both highlighting and potentially resolving interracial conflicts. In one scene, Kwang is shown defusing a potential conflict between a Korean American business owner and an African American customer, while in another, Kwang addresses a group of African American religious leaders, calling for unity on the basis of shared histories of exclusion and oppression: "Know that what we have in common, the sadness and pain and injustice, will always be stronger than our differences" (1995, p. 153).

Yet the novel – and Lee – seems to recognize that Kwang's vision and Kwang himself represent a fantasy. Kwang's eventual fall from grace in many ways echoes the limits and failures of multicultural ideologies. But this resolution in the novel, or its lack of resolution, should not be read as failure of imagination or an expression of cynicism. Instead, we should, as literary scholar Daniel Kim suggests, value "not the politics that it as a novel could never give us anyway but the politics that it might make us want" (2003, p. 250). Kim's point also serves as a useful reminder that works of art, particularly those that might be categorized as "realist," do not merely serve as mirrors to our world but as sites for imagining other possibilities, outcomes, and futures. Even at their most real – that is to say, closest to or most resembling our material world and experiences – Lee's characters, their stories, backgrounds, and struggles, engage with or grapple with a fantasy: if that "fantasy" which is both imagined and destroyed in *Native Speaker* is that of the promise of multicultural America, we can see how Lee's subsequent novels also grapple with other such fantasies at their heart.

Likewise, even a dystopic fantasy novel may be deeply rooted in and reflect "real" worlds, lives, and conditions. Lee's most recent novel, *On Such A Full Sea*, perhaps represents the biggest departure from his previous works, at least at an initial glance. The novel unfolds as a dystopian fantasy in an unspecified future America that has been transformed by devastating climate change. It may not, sadly, require a great leap of imagination on the part of contemporary readers to imagine a society besieged by environmental catastrophe that is also deeply and sharply stratified along class lines. The future "America" of Lee's novel is divided into three groups: the "Charters" – the elite, managerial class – who live in towns with all the recognizable privileges of their status; those who live in "facilities," the class of workers who provide the Charters with goods and services; and the "counties," the vast rural in-between places, populated by poor people abandoned and left to fend for themselves.

The novel's central character, Fan, is a worker at one of the facilities ("B-Mor") and serves as the reader's guide through this world. B-Mor, and presumably other such facilities, are largely populated by descendants of Chinese immigrants, a choice that signals at once the long history of America's relationship to racialized migrants and their labor, from the transatlantic slave trade to Japanese and Filipino workers in the sugar plantations of Hawaii to the braceros program and more, as well as recent and ongoing economic tensions between the United States and China. America's history of immigration and immigration legislation have always been contingent upon the need and demand for labor. That this population of B-Mor is described as descendants of Chinese immigrants (who fled when climate change rendered large areas of China uninhabitable) further emphasizes the history of Asian migration to the United States and the exploitation of racialized bodies for labor. Fan's departure from B-Mor is precipitated by the mysterious disappearance of her boyfriend, but it also mirrors a migrant's journey into a strange and unfamiliar world with unknown rules (if any) and strangers who may be, in turn, hostile or friendly.

It is no wonder that Lee himself has stated that "all immigrant novels are dystopian novels. They're just not dystopias for most of the readers ... Where people don't see you as fully human, where you don't speak the language, and where all the conduct and practices are a mystery and maybe sometimes dangerous" (Kachka 2014). Lee's comments here invite the reader to reverse the lens through which immigrant and other minority writings often get read: instead of approaching them as stories about people who are marginalized, othered, and/or otherwise differentiated from dominant culture, we should center and see the world through these perspectives. The peculiarities of the content and form of *On Such a Full Sea* perhaps illustrate this idea in the most direct way. But if we can take this quote at its face value and approach Lee's earlier works as dystopian novels, we might better see not only the dystopic nature of our current world through re-centering of immigrant positionalities and experiences, but also more just and substantive possibilities for powerful change beyond mere fantasies.

SEE ALSO: Contemporary Fictions of War; Hagedorn, Jessica; Lahiri, Jhumpa; Mixed-Genre Fiction; Morrison, Toni; Multiculturalism; Nguyen, Viet Thanh; Tan, Amy

REFERENCES

Kachka, Boris. (2014). Pigging out with writers Gary Shteyngart and Chang-rae Lee. *Vulture* (January 7, 2014). https://www.vulture.com/2014/01/gary-shteyngart-chang-rae-lee-feast-interview.html (accessed July 8, 2021).

Kim, Daniel Y. (2003). Do I, too, sing America?: vernacular representations and Chang-rae Lee's native speaker. *Journal of Asian American Studies* 6 (3): 231–260.

Lee, Chang-rae. (1995). *Native Speaker*. New York: Riverhead Books.

Lowe, Lisa. (1996). *Immigrant Acts: On Asian American Cultural Politics*. Durham, NC: Duke University Press.

FURTHER READING

Cho, David. (2017). *Lost in Transnation: Alternative Narrative, National, and Historical Visions of the Korean-American Subject in Select 20th-Century Korean American Novels*. New York City: Peter Lang.

Naimon, David. (2014). A conversation with Chang-rae Lee. *The Missouri Review* 37 (1): 120–134.

Nguyen, Viet Thanh. (2015). The emergence of Asian American literature as an academic field. In: *The Cambridge History of Asian American Literature* (ed. Rajini Srikanth and Min Hyoung Song), 289–305. Cambridge: Cambridge University Press.

Page, Amanda M. (2017). *Understanding Chang-rae Lee*. Columbia: University of South Carolina Press.

Park, Josephine. (2016). *Cold War Friendships: Korea, Vietnam, and Asian American Literature*. New York: Oxford University Press.

Lee, Don

KYUNG-SOOK BOO
Sogang University, South Korea

Don Lee (b. 1959) is an American writer of Korean descent, whose fiction has won numerous awards and honors. Lee's father, a second generation Korean American, was a career State Department officer, so Lee grew up in a transnational context, spending much of his childhood in Seoul and Tokyo, attending American schools abroad before coming back to the United States to attend UCLA and earn an MFA from Emerson College. Lee's fiction reflects both his transnational understanding of local American life and his interrogation of how minoritized Americans negotiate the gap between legal and cultural citizenship as they construct identities that refuse to be bound by the binary of the hyphen in which ethnic identity and American national identity are set up falsely as competing identities. Lee's works can be read on two different levels simultaneously: one, where the characters' dilemmas and conflicts are universally American and very much rooted in localities; and another, where those very same universal dilemmas and conflicts have been shaped transnationally and complicated due to specific ethnic histories and the racialization of ethnic bodies. Rather than being interested in the dual personality question that was central to much of twentieth-century Asian American literature, Lee's twenty-first-century works explore the relationship between the private and public spheres as individuals navigate and negotiate institutional America in their personal lives through characters who embody both a rejection of the false binary of the hyphen and the consequences of American society's attempts to mark and bind those bodies by that binary.

Don Lee has published one short story collection and four novels; a second story collection, *The Partition*, will be published in 2022. His first book, *Yellow* (2001), which won the Sue Kaufman Prize for First Fiction from the American Academy of Arts and Letters as well as the Members Choice Award from the Asian American Writers' Workshop, is a collection of eight stories of various people whose paths cross in the fictional Californian small town of Rosarita Bay.

It contains short stories published previously for which he also won awards, such as a Pushcart Prize for the first story in *Yellow*, "The Price of Eggs in China," or an O. Henry Award for the sixth story in the collection, "The Possible Husband." Lee's second book and first novel, *Country of Origin* (2004), explores the complex relationship between ethnicity, race, gender, and nationality in constructions of American identity by placing two US citizens, one of Japanese and African American parentage and the other of Korean and European American parentage, in the space of Japan, outside of the United States, yet where the United States is still present in many ways. Lee was awarded an American Book Award, the Edgar Award for Best First Novel, and a Mixed Media Watch Image Award for Outstanding Fiction for *Country of Origin*.

In his second novel, *Wrack & Ruin* (2008), which was a finalist for the Thurber Prize, Don Lee returns to the space of Rosarita Bay, carefully set up previously through the interlinked eight stories in *Yellow*. Here he explores questions about gentrification, the possibility of space for artists in a neoliberal and late capitalistic America, and the process of racialization for certain American bodies according to the different spaces they inhabit through two American brothers who happen to be of Korean and Chinese descent. Lee's third novel, *The Collective* (2012), continues to explore the figure of the artist in America by intertwining an examination of the positionality of both the racialized Asian American body and the contemporary artist through the lives of three Asian American artists who form the 3AC, or the Asian American Artists Collective. Lee was awarded the Asian/Pacific American Award for Literature from the Asian Pacific American Librarians Association for *The Collective*.

Don Lee's most recent novel, *Lonesome Lies Before Us* (2017), weaves together many of the questions explored in his earlier works to interrogate the influence of racialization, institutional America, and capitalism on the identity formation and lives of individual US citizens, but focuses on the musician as the figure of the artist in contemporary America rather than that of the writer or visual artist. In addition to these five books, Lee's stories, essays, and book reviews have been published widely in a range of forums including literary magazines, anthologies, and popular media (such as *American Short Fiction, The Boston Globe, Charlie Chan Is Dead 2* [1993], *Electric Literature, GQ, The Gettysburg Review, Glimmer Train, Harvard Review, The Kenyon Review, Manoa, Narrative, The North American Review, Screaming Monkeys* [2003], *The Southern Review, The Stranger, The Village Voice, The Virginia Quarterly Review*, etc.). Lee has also served as editor of the literary journal *Ploughshares,* founded the online literary journal *TINGE* Magazine, and has been teaching in the MFA program at Temple University since 2009.

A close examination of the world of Rosarita Bay is central to understanding how Don Lee's fiction probes the gap between legal and cultural citizenship for racialized American bodies while simultaneously refusing to even entertain questioning of the Americanness of such bodies. In *Yellow*, Lee introduces Rosarita Bay (a fictionalized version of Half Moon Bay, California) as a typical small town in America:

> On the surface Rosarita Bay looked like a nice seaside town, a rural sanctuary between San Francisco and Santa Cruz. It billed itself as the pumpkin capital of the world, and it had a Main Street lined with gas street lamps and old-time, clapboarded, saltbox shops and restaurants. Secluded and quiet, it felt like genuine small-town America, and most of the eight thousand residents preferred it that way, voting down every development plan that came down the pike.
>
> (2001, pp. 22–23)

The eight stories Lee anchors in this generic "rural sanctuary" can be read as stories of any typical resident of "genuine small-town America," the narratives being about love, companionship, family, coming of age, loss, chance, and careers, issues that are so universal that they have the ability to render Lee's characters practically anonymous as representations of the average, "genuine" American. Lee's protagonists struggle with various issues simply as ordinary Americans, who by the way happen to be of Asian descent just as they happen to be from or live in Rosarita Bay; their main conflicts are not necessarily generated by or confined to their racial or ethnic backgrounds and are shared with other Americans across regional, racial, gender, generational, and class lines.

The people populating Rosarita Bay are not immediately or predominantly identified through their race or ethnicity, nor are their stories determined mostly by a specific ethnic context. This is one of the two projects of *Yellow*: to show that Americans of Asian descent are simply Americans. *Yellow* establishes this matter-of-factly through its portrayal of the generically "genuine" and mundane lives of its characters as they participate in American society; in other words, *Yellow* establishes the Americanness of its characters firmly and clearly, without hesitation, qualification, or explanation, by confirming the cultural citizenship of its Asian American characters. This quiet refusal to even open up the possibility of questioning their belonging in American society in turn disinvites any questioning of their legal citizenship by refusing to open up any space between perceived and confirmed membership in the nation, and as a result, establishes their full American citizenship.

Yellow also shows, however, that the ordinary and typical American lives of these single, married, or widowed artists, surfers, restaurant owners, lawyers, charterboat operators, database programmers, math teachers, businessmen, students, and so on, *are* complicated by being racialized. This is the second project of *Yellow*: to expose and question how American citizens' lives are constructed, changed, constricted, complicated, and challenged by racism, just because of the happenstance that they are of Asian descent rather than Western European. Lee's main strategy for showing us how race and racism affect his Asian American characters' lives is similar to the one he uses to establish his characters as "genuine" Americans first and foremost: he begins by showing us the ordinariness and universality of a character's life, focusing the narrative on an issue that is not necessarily ethnicity or race specific, then he colors that narrative with particular details that refer to the history of Asian Americans or incorporates flashbacks that give us insight into how racialization lies at the root of what seems like a personal quirk or problem.

It is important to note that while the Americans of Asian descent in *Yellow* seem to represent all walks of life, the closer they are to institutionalized America, the more race becomes an issue, and the security of their individual status becomes shaken. In the America symbolized by Rosarita Bay, institutional America is still largely represented as being white: Gene Becklund, a sergeant from the sheriff's office, Julie Fulcher, a social worker from the San Vincente County Department of Family and Children's Services, and Ariel Belieu, Rosarita Bay's reference librarian, are all white. A close examination of the positions Asian Americans occupy in *Yellow* reveals that their individuality is preserved best when they remain in the private realm, and that the further they enter into public space, the more they have to contend with generalization based on perceived racial identity.

For example, in "Casual Water," Patrick and Brian Fenny go from the private realm to the public world of social institutions when their father abandons them to pursue a golfing career eight years "after their mother had repatriated to the Philippines" (2001, pp. 125–126): they go from being 17-year-old high school senior Patrick and 11-year-old sixth-grader Brian to being identified primarily as "Amerasians" (p. 133) or "Filipinos" (p. 144) when Sergeant Becklund brings social worker Julie Fulcher to take Brian into state custody and place him in foster care. The narrative reveals that Brian learns the term *Amerasian* for the first time from Fulcher, representative of the state:

> He [Brian] stopped suddenly and asked, "Are we Amerasian?"
> Patrick looked at his brother. "Who told you that?"
> "The woman [Julie Fulcher]. She asked if kids ever tease me because I'm Amerasian."
> "We're not Amerasian," Patrick said. "That's what they call people whose mothers are Vietnamese."
> "Was Mom a bargirl before she met Dad?"
> "What are you talking about?"
> "Billy Kim saw it in a movie. That's what they call hookers in the Philippines."
>
> (2001, p. 133)

It is Fulcher's naming of Brian as Amerasian and her assumption that Brian's schoolmates would also see him primarily as a body with that racialized identity inscribed on it that robs Brian of his individual identity and places him suddenly in a generalized group. Patrick's response reveals that he has been taught by the American media coverage of the Vietnam War to associate the term *Amerasian* with a particular ethnic group, and that he does not realize that the racialized framework of the term that prompts Fulcher to automatically include him in the group designated by the term, regardless of any ethnic distinctions to which he may adhere or deem integral to his understanding of himself. It is the designation of *Amerasian* that exposes Brian to the thought that his mother may be included in the American media's stereotypical hypersexualized portrayal of Filipina women as prostitutes. This racializing of Brian is reinforced when Fulcher tries to make a "race-specific" foster family placement with a Filipino couple who barely speak English (2001, p. 144). Brian is initiated into the world of racialized identifications when he enters the world of social and state institutions and is taught that he is primarily seen as a racial category and not as an individual by being interpolated as an "Amerasian." Interpolating Brian as "Amerasian" is a public act that wrenches open a gap between Brian's cultural and legal citizenship and contests his Americanness, which is restored only when he is taken back into the private sphere through Evelyn Yung's guardianship, which occurs outside of the formal public foster family system.

It is not just the courts that operate as regulatory forces policing American identity racially; the world of art also belongs to the public sphere that participates in the racialized policing of American identity. In the opening story of the collection, "The Price of Eggs in China," Caroline Yip (who happens to be Chinese American) and Marcella Ahn (who happens to be Korean American) are referred to by name and recognized as individuals as long as the narrative is about their personal interactions as private citizens, whether as someone's girlfriend, or a client buying a custom-made chair, or the alleged victim or suspect in a stalking case, in the "genuine" America of Rosarita Bay, but the moment they emerge as poets, in other words, as artists who engage in the public sphere, they are rendered nameless, faceless, and indistinguishable as "Oriental Hair Poet No. 1" (2001, p. 17) and "Oriental Hair Poet No. 2" (p. 13).

It is not the private act of writing poetry that transforms them from individual to racialized stereotype, but the public act of being published and critically reviewed that suddenly erases all personal distinctions, including name, ethnicity, personality, class, and poetic style, and leaves them simply as orientalized body parts. When *Speak to Desire*, Marcella's highly erudite poetry, and *Chicks of Chinese Descent*, Caroline's slangy, contemporary poetry, happen to be published as first books at the same time, the critics focus on the two women's racial identity and physicality instead of their poetry, "reviewing them together, mocking the pair," "as 'The Oriental Hair Poets,' 'The Braids of the East,' and 'The New Asian Poe-tresses'" (2001, p. 20). The two very different women lose their status as individuals and citizens and become reduced to messes of hair as punishment for entering the public sphere as speaking voices.

Yellow reinstates Caroline and Marcella's individuality and citizenship by allowing them to speak again, in the public sphere of art that has created Rosarita Bay: the narrative gives them a space in which to regain their voices to speak and act as unique individuals while the narrative also simultaneously speaks about the systemic and institutionalized racism that seeks to silence them, to prevent them from stepping into the tradition of Whitman in which one can sing a song of one's self and have it be the American song too. *Yellow* provides a space for Caroline and Marcella to carry on Langston Hughes's (1925) project of claiming America, singing America as an American "*I, too.*" By voicing the way their lives as Americans are complicated by racism while leaving them free from any burden or obligation to play the role of spokesperson, Don Lee shows how the racialization of Asian Americans generates complex negotiations of identity for Americans of Asian descent without permitting questioning of their belonging to occur. In addition, he also shows how literature as an engagement of the private and the public spheres can provide an effective space for negotiations of citizenship to occur without the loss of individuality or the elision of historical contexts.

Don Lee extends his exploration of literature as a powerful space for negotiations of citizenship for racialized Americans beyond US borders, reminding us of the transnational context of domestic US identity negotiations. Multiple references to America's military and political presence in Asia are scattered throughout the stories centered in Rosarita Bay in *Yellow*: Joe Konki, in "The Lone Night Cantina," is said to have "enlisted in the Navy, making ports of call in the Philippines, where he had the dragon tattoo drawn on his arm, in Japan, and even in Korea" (2001, p. 112); Davis Fenny, who abandons his sons in "Casual Water," is said to have done "two tours at Subic Bay, returned to Tempe with a Filipina wife, Lita Bautista" (p. 136); Janet McElroy Kim is said to have been "an Army brat on Yongsan" (p. 170) in "Domo Arigato"; Duncan Roh, in "The Possible Husband," remembers seeing "an air show, the Blue Angels in their Phantom F-4s flying acrobatic stunts" and buzzing the Han River, dropping "napalm onto the sandbars, terrific billows of flames rising into the air" when his father was stationed at Yongsan, not understanding until later that it had been "the arrogance of the demonstration, dropping live bombs during peacetime into the river of a foreign capital, merely to entertain the troops" that had disturbed him amidst the thrill he felt (p. 165); and in the last story of the collection, also entitled "Yellow," Danny Kim reflects on how the Vietnam War, which to him was "a blatantly racist war, as were the last two American wars" against the "yellow peril," rendering the Japanese, the Korean, and the Vietnamese as all "inhuman and atavistic" (p. 220), had marred his "otherwise genial years" of college "and heightened his desire to repudiate his Asian-ness" (pp. 220–221). Danny's public anti-Vietnam War stance is complicated by his private consideration of enlisting, because for him, "for any Asian, there were deeper questions of patriotism which could not easily be ignored – a legacy of the days of internment" (p. 220). Danny connects the history of America's involvement overseas in Asia with that of interning its own citizens of Japanese descent on US soil, actions that together constitute a transnational context for understanding Rosarita Bay and the constant and continuing racialization of its Asian American inhabitants.

Rosarita Bay, then, goes from being a relatively isolated and typical small town affirming mainstream American notions of the nation to a space located within transnational negotiations of Americanness. Rosarita Bay's inhabitants are Americans whose everyday tribulations are contextualized by both the specifics of "genuine small-town America" (2001, p. 23) and transnational understandings of the nation-state of America. Each of the eight stories in *Yellow* stand alone as a portrait of a particular current or former resident of Rosarita Bay, but one has to read through the entire collection to piece together a more comprehensive picture of each character, as the histories of each are scattered throughout the collection, connecting the stories as a cohesive whole while constructing a metanarrative about ethnicity and race in America. The structure of *Yellow* reflects the thematic project of each story in its refusal to allow readers to neglect the significance of interconnectivity or historical and sociopolitical contexts that inform personal and cultural particulars, and in its insistence that readers look beyond the surface appearance of things to identify and address entrenched systemic and institutionalized problems. Don Lee continues this exploration and interrogation in all of his works, sometimes returning to Rosarita Bay or surrounding areas in California, and other times going to New York, Cambridge, or even outside of the US nation-state.

SEE ALSO: Jen, Gish; Kingston, Maxine Hong; Multiculturalism; Nguyen, Viet Thanh; Ozeki, Ruth; Story Cycles; Literary Magazines; Yu, Charles

REFERENCES

Hughes, Langston. (1925). "I, too." *The Survey Graphic* 53 (11): 61.
Lee, Don. (2001). *Yellow*. New York: Norton.

FURTHER READING

Boo, Kyung-Sook. (2014). Korean American literature. In: *Asian American Society: An Encyclopedia* (ed. Mary Yu Danico), vol. 1, 591–596. New York: SAGE.
Ho, Jennifer. (2013). Acting Asian American, eating Asian American: the politics of race and food in Don Lee's *Wrack and Ruin*. *Eating Asian America: A Food Studies Reader* (ed. Robert Ji-Song Ku, Martin F. Manalansan IV, and Anita Mannur), 303–322. New York: New York University Press.
Lee, Don. (2020). The partition. *The Virginia Quarterly Review* 96 (2): 40–55.
Lee, Kun Jong. (2015). The making of an Asian American short-story cycle: Don Lee's *Yellow: Stories*. *Journal of American Studies* 49 (3): 593–613.
Wills, Jenny Heijun. (2017). Formulating kinship: Asian adoption narratives and crime literature. *Adoption & Culture* 5: 64–88.

Le Guin, Ursula K.

SARAH FARRELL
University of Texas at Arlington, USA

Urusula K. Le Guin was born on October 21, 1929, in Berkeley, California, and was the youngest child of three older brothers. Her parents were both scholars in their respective fields: Alfred L. Kroeber was an anthropologist and Theodora K. Kroeber was a writer. During her youth, the family would go to their summer home in Napa Valley, called Kishamish, surrounded by forty acres. Bucknall concludes, "much of Le Guin's delight in describing journeys on foot stems from these early explorations of what must have seemed unlimited territory" (Bucknall 1981, p. 2). Many academics, graduate students, writers, and scholars, as well as Indians and relatives, frequented this residence and helped to create a rich foundation for culture and the respect for "different ways of life that human beings can adopt" (p. 2). Along with these personal associations, reading was a frequent activity in the Kroeber household. Growing up, she was influenced not only by science fiction stories, but also by the Romantics, like Tolstoy and Dickens. Her scholarly ambitions were fueled from infancy, as she was continually encouraged to have "impassioned, intellectual conversations" with her family and was treated as an equal among her male siblings (Freedman 2008, p. 29). This acceptance motivated her love of writing from a very young age, as she completed her first short story at the age of 11. She attended both Radcliffe College, earning a BA in 1952, and Columbia University, earning an MA with a focus on French and Italian literature. Le Guin has published works in numerous genres, including novels, short stories, essay collections, children's works, and translations. In addition to these genres, she has received various types of accolades: among her awards are a National Book Award, nine Hugo Awards and six Nebula awards.

Ursula K. Le Guin's life experiences, especially her relationship with her father and the familial interest in anthropology, were major influences on the subjects tackled in her writings. Her works revolve around the notion of world building and the creation of lands based on customs, languages, and specific characteristics of a people. Le Guin is able to develop these ideas through the genres she is most known for: science fiction and critical utopias. As she states in an interview from 1982, science fiction provides her with avenues to "help people get out of their cultural skins . . . in science fiction you are often expected to get into the skin of another person from another culture" (Freedman 2008, p. 27). In this way, her works attempt to show human connection through fictional lands, helping her readers to see the complex relations of those who may be different from themselves and how such societies are formed. Consequently, the major themes in her writings often deal with political and social concerns, as world building helps readers to questions their own views of reality as it relates to gender, religion, and sexual preference. Another major influence on her writings is the concept of Taoism: a philosophy that fosters the idea of discovery versus invention and creates a writing that goes against control, promoting a lack of interference.

The reason why a reader finds these concerns to be so interesting and complex is related to the great care this author takes in connection to the realism of the character – her characters are built from very accurate representations of their psychological platforms. These psychological platforms are often Jungian in nature, as "the worlds and countries through which her people travel are places of the mind" and mainly highlight common archetypes found in myth: universal characters that humans have been able to associate with for centuries (Bucknall 1981, p. 151). These ideas flourish through the Jungian terms as certain archetypes often take center stage in her works, including this idea of shared experiences: "humans all share such universal experiences as leaving home, challenging the status quo, and developing a mature identity through rebirth" (Reid 1997, p. 4). In Le Guin's works, she often reflects on the notion of Jungian good and evil as well, often situating these terms in complete conflict – a Western viewpoint. Blending her Taoist philosophy on life, Le Guin shows an ambiguity to these views. As such, the majority of Le Guin's heroes "observe before acting . . . and succeed when they learn this [type of] wisdom, appreciating the interdependence of action and inaction, light and dark, and even of order and chaos" (p. 4). While she does show the interconnectivity of what many may see as opposites in terms of Western ideas, her views on genre are a bit more structured. Le Guin has a strong claim to the terms of science fiction. For Le Guin, in order to write a good science fiction, there must be an "[inclusion of] us in the universe" as these details bring up fundamental truths about "the relationships human beings have in the world" (Freedman 2008, p. 53). This view can be found in some of her most famous texts, including *Earthsea Cycle* (1968–2001), *The Dispossessed* (1974), and *The Left Hand of Darkness* (1969).

The relationship of the human in the world, especially within the *Earthsea Cycle*, is one of pure fantasy. For Le Guin, this distinction is clear: "Both realism and science fiction deal with stories that might be true. Fantasy, on the hand, tells a story that couldn't possibly be true" (Freedman 2008, p. 92). Truth, however, is complex – as her characters do present lessons to be learned and applied to reality. In this work, the author provides coming-of-age stories for older young adults and generates a unique type of magic through this context. It is a magic that is governed by the laws of the psyche – very Jungian in nature. She also creates a very interesting view on death, as there is a powerful association between acceptance and the reassurance of death. This work also provides a faithful account of her views about geography, highlighting the importance of the accuracy of geography in a work as it relates to the movement of the characters. In fact, the first item Le Guin invented was a map for this trilogy, proving that the building blocks for fiction should be situated within some type of systematized landscape. This type of accuracy is very Tolkien-esque in nature and helps to provide reality to the places within these fantastical worlds.

Within the book *The Dispossessed*, world building is enhanced through both a political context and a linguistic one. She builds on the idea of anarchism, a frequent political model in her works, and shows the importance of the stranger (the individual) in her writing: "The person who comes into a world or a society that isn't their own, and has to try to understand and be understood, [making a language] that becomes almost a metaphor for comprehension and communication" (Freedman 2008, p. 145). As such, language in this text becomes a part of a class system, and her anarchism also becomes "closely linked to her Taoism in its taste for an organic order rather than an imposed one" (Bucknall 1981, p. 10). It is through this genre, the critical utopia that had its infancy in the 1970s, that she shows the difficult situations that must be overcome by society. As such, her world produces a location to enquire about the correct roles of humanity, especially within communal and capitalist environments. These dualities are enhanced by the competing principles of the two planets in her work. In this context, Le Guin does not create easy solutions in the work, showing that even societies built on utopian values can easily crumble. This type of critical evaluation of the human in society is also found in one of her other more famous works, *The Left Hand of Darkness*.

In this work, a pure science fiction by most accounts, the author creates characters who revolve around a proto-feminist agenda as she creates a world of androgynous characters – a new theme for the year in which it was published, 1969. This emphasis on androgyny is one of the most critically evaluated aspects of this work, as these characters were meant to show a stance connected to second-wave feminism and to the New Wave of science fiction. New Wave science fiction "promoted political upheaval" (Bernardo and Murphy 2006, p. 16), while second-wave feminism "moved beyond simply seeking equality among women and men to directly challenging gender roles themselves, calling into question the social role of women and, more broadly, the very definition of what it means to be a woman" (p. 31). In this case, Le Guin attempts to use her Taoist models of holism to show there is not a real difference between the genders in *The Dispossessed*. Unfortunately, the critics, including powerful voices like Joanna Russ, found her characters to be too masculine. This analysis is in direct correlation with the fact that Le Guin uses masculine pronouns throughout her work. She also created relationships based purely in heterosexual terms – a viewpoint found in terms like kemmering – the ability to produce children but only through heterosexual norms. Le Guin's response was straightforward, as she stated the following: "I dissatisfy a lot of my gay friends and I dissatisfy a lot of my feminist friends, because I don't go as far as they would like" (Freedman 2008, p. 40). She tries to mitigate these issues by stating that the overall goal of this work was to promote the "hatred of oppression and love of freedom [as] they affect the individual" (Bucknall 1981, p. 152). Therefore, the theme of the novel was connected more to individualism and the idea of betrayal. However, she does later admit that her novel is perhaps not as convincing as is needs to be in depicting androgyny, as it may leave out too much: "One does not see Estraven as a mother, with his children, in any role which we automatically perceive as 'female': and therefore, we tend to see him as a man. That is the real flaw of the book" (Bernardo and Murphy 2006, p. 33). In response to this criticism, Le Guin generated a very astute and honest article titled: "Is Gender Necessary? Redux." In this essay, she shows her growth as a writer in this time and genre, accepting that she is starting to perceive these views in a clearer light and beginning to notice how the terms of androgyny need to be further complicated. Despite these challenges, she learned from her battles and found peace with her writer's voice in this arena.

Le Guin's more famous works have been previously discussed, but there are several genres on which she has also been given a lot of accolades. First, there is her ability for translations. Some of her more famous translations are the following: *The Twins, The Dream/Las Gemelas, El Sueño* with Diana Bellese in 1997, *Selected Poems of Gabriela Mistral* published in 2003, *Kalpa Imperial* published in 2003, and *Tao Te Ching: A Book About the Way and the Power of the Way* published in 1997 and again in 2009. Le Guin has stated on numerous occasions that this type of work, translating, is a thankless job and one a writer does because of the pure joy one can gleam from it on a personal level. As a younger writer she started to explore this genre, but it wasn't until later in life, her seventies especially, that she took more of an interest in translating. However, her renditions are often considered to be more like second originals than pure translations. Ria Cheyne writes the following about Le Guin's version of *Tao Te Ching*: ". . . these texts, as Le Guin's translations, are not necessarily translations in the traditional sense of the word. She refers to her version of the *Tao Te Ching*, for example, as a 'rendition, not a translation'" (Cheyne 2006, p. 457). Le Guin stated the following in terms of her view of translations:

> Translation is entirely mysterious. Increasingly I have felt that the art of writing is itself translating, or more like translating than it is like anything else. What is the other text, the original? I have no answer. I suppose it is the source, the deep sea where ideas swim, and one catches them in nets of words and swings them shining into the boat . . . where in this metaphor they die and get canned and eaten in sandwiches.
>
> (Kroulek 2018)

This viewpoint also helps to foster a translation that often relates to some of her fictional works. For example, in *Kalpa Imperial* she reworks fairy tales in connection to political commentary where "beggars become emperors, democracies become dictatorships, and history becomes legends and stories" (Le Guin n.d.a). Her views on individuality and the fluidity of governments that help to situate people and places take center stage just as they do in her own creations, such as *The Dispossessed*. These same ideas relate to the fact that many of Le Guin's heroes are translators and many of her worlds are multilingual (Cheyne 2006, p. 457). Language, therefore, is a pivotal point in any genre that she creates. Her perhaps most famous translation, *Tao Te Ching: A Book About the Way and the Power of the Way*, also perpetuates the themes found in her original works. While Le Guin has been educated on the *Tao Te Ching* for over forty years, she "consulted the literal translation and worked with Chinese scholars" in order to create a more modern version that can speak to the current era (Le Guin n.d.b). As such, translations do not exist merely in terms of bringing a work back into view, but they are used as ways to bridge the gap in cultural understanding and to bring a new awareness about everyone and how we all create a distinct and valuable place in the world.

Her other nonfiction works, in particular her essays, adhere to a similar dictum – as they ask us to think deeply about the world in which a text is created and how the author will go about creating their works. Some of these works include the following: *Dancing at the Edge of the World* (1989), *The Language of the Night* (1992), *Cheek by Jowl* (2009), *The Wave in the Mind* (2004), *No Time to Spare* written in 2017, *Words are My Matter* in 2017, and *Conversations on Writing* in 2018. Many of these essays deal with complicated topics about the female writer and their relationship to the creation of a text. Lisa Rashley wrote the following in terms of Le Guin's essays and biography: "In fact, though, Le Guin's essays represent fictions of a sort in themselves: autobiographical narratives that interrogate the relationship between the woman artist's body and her experience of gender, especially in terms of how she might choose to narrate that female body" (Rashley 2007, p. 29). As such, when one reads her essays one cannot help to see her views on the world seep through these complex connections where the "relationship between bodies and language, and particularly the power language has to convey an individual's truth through storied narrative, is a complex and vexed one" (p. 29). To reflect on her essays is to reflect on the same reflections being narrated in her fictional settings.

The last genre to discuss, as Le Guin could accomplish every genre with complexity and power, is that of her children's books. Her *Catwings* books, written between the years of 1988 and 1999, have captivated young and old for their inventiveness and fresh perspective. Part of this perspective relies on her ability to discuss adult-themed ideas, as one critic states: "Although [this work] has been criticized for being too frightening, she does not sugarcoat trauma. In fact, these winged creatures have wings because it is the hope that they can fly away from their neighborhood" (Lindow 1997, p. 33). In this way, the cats are a symbolic representation of getting past one's circumstances through some type of intrinsic gift. Many also believe these works foster her Jungian idea about the self and other. For example, Mike Cadden states that these creatures are more than "a 'normal' cat with human thoughts and consciousness, because it allows us to move from the self toward the other without the false impression that we have actually gotten all the way there" (Cadden 2008, p. 13). The cats in this context may take on human attributes, but they are still very much playing with the notion of understanding the other. This is most definitely addressed in the idea that while the cats are anthropomorphized, "the winged siblings in *Catwings* may argue like human brothers and sisters, but the way their mother sends them out into the world is the behavior of a real feral cat . . . the mask of humanity is thin and semi-transparent – the strongest impression is of a glimpse into an alien way of seeing and living. That glimpse of the alien Other . . ." (Attebery 2006, p. 199). The alien other also pervades into the issue of power struggles and the questioning of authority. As stated by Len Hatfield, in *Catwings* there is an:

> ambivalence [that] arises from the ways that narrative texts in general claim authority for themselves, and these tactics for claiming textual authority recur in Le Guin's other children's books. Le Guin frequently provides her readers with mimetic situations that expose problems with adult authority. In *Catwings*, for example, when Susan and Hank find the winged kittens playing in an empty field, the children keep the secret because they are convinced that people (the adults) will fail to understand and preserve these wonders.
>
> (Hatfield 1993, p. 45)

The view of power and power relations was a huge part of her reality, as well, as she used this platform in connection to political agendas.

Continuing her efforts to show the complexity of the individual and the acceptance of various views, she campaigned through numerous political activisms. Her work with the National Organization for Women, Abortion Rights Action League, and Women's International League for Peace and Freedom enhanced her connection to nonviolence and ecological awareness. As such, her life mimicked the beliefs often found throughout her fictitious worlds. In essence, Le Guin saw writing as a continuation of her world, as she stated numerous times in various interviews: "Writing is simply a major part of the way I live … like having kids or being a member of the family or cooking meals. It's one of the things I do, one of the important things I do" (Freedman 2008, p. 47). This importance constitutes a lasting legacy, as her death in 2018 left a lasting praise to those works that ask us to challenge misconception and to foster the appreciation of varied views in this world.

SEE ALSO: Ecocriticism and Environmental Fiction; Multiculturalism; Queer and LGBT Fiction

REFERENCES

Attebery, Brian. (2006). Ursula K. Le Guin beyond genre: fiction for children and adults. *Children's Literature association Quarterly* 31 (2): 199–202.

Bernardo, Susan M. and Murphy, Graham J. (2006). *Ursula K. Le Guin: A Critical Companion*. Westport: CT: Greenwood Press.

Bucknall, Barbara J. (1981). *Ursula K. Le Guin*. New York: Ungar.

Cadden, Mike. (2008). *Ursula K. Le Guin: Beyond Genre*. London: Taylor & Francis.

Cheyne, Ria. (2006). Ursula K. Le Guin and translation. *Extrapolation* 47 (3): 457–470.

Freedman, Carl H. (ed.) (2008). *Conversations with Ursula K. Le Guin*. Jackson: University of Mississippi Press.

Hatfield, Len. (1993). From master to brother: shifting the balance of authority in Ursula K. Le Guin's *Farthest Shore* and *Tehanu*. *Children's Literature* 21: 43–65.

Kroulek, Alison. (2018). 10 Ursula K Le Guin quotes about languages and translation. The Language Blog. https://k-international.com/blog/ursula-k-le-guin-quotes-about-languages/ (accessed July 16, 2021).

Le Guin, Ursula K. (n.d.a.). *Kalpa Imperial: The Greatest Empire That Never Was*. https://www.ursulakleguin.com/kalpa-imperial (accessed July 16, 2021).

Le Guin, Ursula K. (n.d.b.). Non-fiction translations. *Lao Tzu: Tao Te Ching: A Book About the Way and the Power of the Way*. https://www.ursulakleguin.com/translations-non-fiction (accessed July 16, 2021).

Lindow, Sandra J. (1997). Trauma and recovery in Ursula K. Le Guin's "Wonderful Alexander": animal as guide through the inner space of the unconscious. *Foundation* (Summer): 32–38.

Rashley, Lisa. (2007). Revisioning gender: inventing women in Ursula K. Le Guin's nonfiction. *Life Writing and Science Fiction* 30 (1): 22–47.

Reid, Suzanne E. (1997). *Presenting Ursula K. Le Guin*. New York: Twayne.

FURTHER READING

Burns, Tony. (2010). *Political Theory, Science Fiction, and Utopian Literature: Ursula K. Le Guin and* The Dispossessed. Lanham: Lexington Books.

Cummins, Elizabeth. (1993). *Understanding Ursula K. Le Guin*. Charleston: University of South Carolina Press.

Davis, Laurence and Stillman, Peter G. (2005). *The New Utopian Politics of Ursula K. Le Guin's* The Dispossessed. Lanham, MD: Lexington Books.

Gorodischer, Angélica. (2003). *Kalpa Imperial: The Greatest Empire That Never Was* (trans. Ursula K. Le Guin). Easthampton, MA: Small Beer Press; originally published in two vols as *La Casa del Poder* and *El Império mas Vasto*, 1983.

Lao Tzu. (1997). *Tao Te Ching: A Book About the Way and the Power of the Way* (trans. Ursula K. Le Guin). Boston: Shambhala.

White, Donna R. (1999). *Dancing with Dragons: Ursula K. Le Guin and the Critics*. Columbia, SC: Camden House.

Lerner, Ben

ALISON GIBBONS
Sheffield Hallam University, UK

"I decided to replace the book I'd proposed with the book you're reading now, a work that, like a poem, is neither fiction nor nonfiction, but a flickering between them" (Lerner 2014, p. 194); so reflects the narrator of Ben Lerner's acclaimed second novel, *10:04* (2014). This highly metatextual, self-referential statement is indicative of the recurring tropes and preoccupations that resonate across Lerner's oeuvre to date. Ben Lerner (b. 1979) began his literary career as a poet (so the comparison to poetry is fitting). He has published three collections – *The Lichtenberg Figures* (2004), *Angle of Yaw* (2006), and *Mean Free Path* (2010) – which have subsequently been collated, alongside additional writings, in *No Art* (2016). He is also the author of three novels: *Leaving the Atocha Station* (2011), *10:04*, and *The Topeka School* (2019). All three novels involve a "flickering" between fictional and nonfictional forms of writing, the latter primarily including autobiography, poetry, and literary and art criticism. It is this flickering, this tension, that has come to characterize Ben Lerner's contemporary American fiction.

Contemporary literary works that "flicker" between fiction and autobiography are widely referred to as examples of autofiction, a genre descriptor coined by French writer Serge Doubrovsky in 1977. Marjorie Perloff explains that "American autofiction combines the clearly fictional with the seemingly accurate biographical history of its authors" (2018, p. 12). All three of Lerner's novels fall under the umbrella of autofiction, with Lerner described in *The New York Times Magazine* as "one of its most gifted exponents" (Harvey 2019). Moreover, speaking of his work as autofiction in a podcast-interview for British newspaper *The Guardian*, Lerner describes his three novels to date as "a trilogy" which "feels like a closed circle" (Lea, Irvine, and Armistead 2019). Alex Preston similarly argues for conceptualizing the three books as an autofictional "trilogy, in that the basic facts of life being presented are clearly those of Lerner himself – growing up in Topeka, Kansas, moving to Brooklyn via an interlude in Spain, writing poetry and then novels, and becoming the father of two girls" (2019). Herein, I explore Lerner's novels through the lens of autofiction and consider the thematic and biographical interconnections that allow them to be read together as a trilogy.

10:04 is Lerner's most overt autofiction: the narrating character "Ben" is "a published author" (2014, p. 11) whose "previous novel, despite an alarming level of critical acclaim, had only sold around ten thousand copies" (p. 154) and was "unconventional but really well received" (p. 155). *10:04* fictionalizes the author's life over a period of approximately fourteen months – datable because of the way in which the novel is bookended by Hurricane Irene (which occurred in August 2011) in its opening and Hurricane Sandy (in late October 2012) at its close – during which "Ben," like the real Lerner, lives in Brooklyn, New York, where he struggles to write his second novel. In contrast, the autofictional dimensions of *Leaving the Atocha Station* and *The Topeka School* are more covert because the fictionalized avatar of the author – Adam Gordon – is differentiated from Lerner by name. In *Leaving the Atocha Station*, Adam is a young aspiring poet who, during 2004 (as with *10:04*, a historical event – this time, the Atocha Station bombings of March 11, 2004 – grounds the novel in time), moves to Madrid as the recipient of "a prestigious fellowship" (2011, p. 53). Lerner's author bio for the book emphasizes his accomplishments as an award-winning poet who previously undertook a Fulbright scholarship in Spain and was awarded a Howard Foundation Fellowship. Such biographical details consequently encourage a reading of character Adam in relation to author Ben Lerner and of the novel as, at least partly, autobiographical. Indeed, the fictionalized author of *10:04* even laments that – because of the autofictionality of his first novel – on romantic dates, "he'd likely be asked which parts of his book were autobiographical" (2014, p. 67) whilst in moments of anxiety, he feels as though he has "become the unreliable narrator of [his] first novel" (p. 148).

Although Adam Gordon also features in *The Topeka School*, Lerner's third and most recent novel is more polyvocal with its fifteen chapters alternating between the points of view of four characters: Jonathan and Jane Gordon (two chapters each), their son Adam (four chapters), and Darren – a troubled teenager on the fringes of Adam's social circle (seven chapters). Three of the four Adam chapters detail his adolescence when he trains for, and competes in, the National Debating Championships in which – not incidentally – the real Ben Lerner won the award for International Extemporaneous Speaking in 1997. The biographical parallels do not stop there: Jonathan and Jane Gordon are psychologists who work at "the Foundation – which was in fact a world-famous psychiatric institute and hospital" (Lerner 2019, p. 50), just like Lerner's real parents who practiced at the Topeka Menninger Foundation; in the mid-1980s, Harriet Lerner – the author's real mother – began publishing popular feminist psychology books on women's mental health and relationships and was even invited to talk about her first work, *The Dance of Anger* (1985), on *The Oprah Winfrey Show*, while in *The Topeka School*, the strikingly similar success and influence of Jane Gordon's first book on family life is the subject of both Jane's and Jonathan's reflections (Lerner 2019, pp. 89–94, 179). Correspondingly, in *Leaving the Atocha Station*, Adam tells his Spanish friends that his parents are "both psychologists" and that his mother "is a well-known feminist" (2011, p. 60).

Although, unlike *The Topeka School*, *10:04* is set in New York and *Leaving the Atocha Station* in Madrid, Topeka – where the real Ben Lerner grew up – nevertheless exerts its influence on the narrators' memories. In *Leaving the Atocha Station*, at a party, Adam accidentally pours himself a drink of tequila, the smell and taste of which remind him vividly of a formative adolescent experience:

> At seventeen I had made myself violently ill drinking tequila and had never had it again, except to taste it every couple of years to see if it still disgusted me, which it always did. I thought back to that night in Topeka, vomiting for an hour near a bonfire then sleeping in the bed of a pickup in the middle of the winter. I could smell the campfire and felt cold and a little dizzy.
>
> (2011, p. 140)

Likewise, in *10:04*, the narrator speaks of his "entire childhood in Topeka" (2014, p. 14), recounts a story that his father told him on a journey back to Topeka (pp. 138–139), and, walking through an empty school in New York, finds himself transported into his own childhood memory: "do you know what I mean if I say that when I reached the second floor and disposed of the wax paper, I was in Randolph Elementary School and seven. . .?" (pp. 14–15). Notably in *The Topeka School*, Randolph Elementary is mentioned repeatedly as an institute of Adam's education (e.g. 2019, p. 83). In these examples from *Leaving the Atocha Station* and *10:04*, the memory becomes so vivid as to make it seem phenomenologically real: Adam experiences the sensation of being drunk by the campfire whilst Ben seems to walk into his past or, at least, the school that the fictional Adam Gordon and the real Ben Lerner attended.

In *10:04*, the narrator problematizes the reliability of personal recollections by considering the perceptual dynamics of memories. Discussing his walks around the city of New York, Ben reflects: "Whenever I walked across Manhattan Bridge, I remembered myself as having crossed the Brooklyn Bridge" (2014, p. 134). This act of misremembrance is refined, in relation to his most recent Bridge crossing, as Ben admits, "I was starting to misremember crossing in the third person, as if I somehow watched myself walking beneath the Brooklyn Bridge's Aeolian Cables" (pp. 134–135). The idea of third-person memory is taken up in *The Topeka School*, particularly in moments of traumatic personal experience. Jonathan, for instance, recollects a visit to New York's Metropolitan Museum of Art on a bad acid trip: "I remember the next several hours of the Episode in both the first and third person, probably because I've depended heavily on Jane's account" (2019, p. 49). The same language is also present in Jane's personal revelation of historical abuse: "Now I remember that night in third person, like I'm looking into the living room from Sima's vantage on the porch swing – I misremember that moment as the moment I started to recall more fully what had happened, but it wasn't" (pp. 82–83). Lerner's use of the phrase "third person" thus exploits a distanced narrative perspective – in contrast to the immediacy of first-person point of view – as a means of representing the ways in which memories alter and are misremembered, falsified, even fictionalized. In their interrogation of the intensity and reliability of memory, Lerner's works are characteristic of autofiction in which, according to Dyx, "lived experience is itself subject to the distortions of the imagination and the act of fictionalizing affects the content of the memories" (2018, p. 6).

As the quotations from *The Topeka School* above show, the chapters focalized by Jonathan and Jane Gordon are realized in the first person, bestowing their words with a sense of conversational immediacy. This is particularly the case with the Jane chapters in which she addresses a second-person "you" who appears to be her son. For instance, just as she is about to recount a memory of Adam that could be potentially quite embarrassing for him, she taunts her addressee, "I bet you won't put this in your novel" (2019, p. 94). At other times, the addressee interrupts or responds to her:

> I could go on. This is the backdrop against which Sima and Dad's own relationship got out of hand, but you'll have to ask him –
> – If I want details.
> If you want details. I'm interested in how you remember the trip to New York. Looking back, it was a horrible idea. I was doing an event at the Ninety-Second Street Y, a kind of public conversation about my work. . .
>
> (2019, p. 103)

The first-person chapters of Jane and Jonathan consequently feel colloquial. This is particularly true of Jane's narrative, which seems styled to resemble an interview transcript through: the addressee's conversational interruptions signaled by the dash; Jane's self-conscious references to her own speech ("I could go on") and to memory ("Looking back"); metatextual intimations about the writing process of *The Topeka School* ("I bet you won't put this in your novel"). Along with the biographical connections between the Gordons and Ben Lerner's own family, these stylistic traits generate a nonfiction effect, as though *The Topeka School* is, in some ways, a collection of remembered testimonies.

Whilst in *The Topeka School* Jane's aside to a "you" addressee seems aimed at Adam as an avatar of author Ben Lerner, the character Ben's first-person narrative in *10:04* makes striking use of second-person "you" to incite an extratextual addressee. In the aftermath of Hurricane Sandy, for example, Ben walks with his friend Alex through Manhattan, an act he narrates by articulating: "reader, we walked on" (2014, p. 234). In Union

Square, they stop briefly and Ben claims: "A reporter was filming a segment nearby and I walked within range of the camera and tungsten lights and waved; maybe you saw me" (p. 235). Lerner's explicit prior reference to the "reader" leaves no doubt that this "you" should be interpreted as addressing the reader. This effect is intensified by Lerner's cheeky hypothetical "maybe you saw me," which emphasizes the possibility that real readers could have seen narrator Ben in the background of a real-world news report about the aftereffects of Hurricane Sandy. Such extratextual asides from Lerner's avatar "Ben" therefore imply that real readers share the same ontological plane as the narrator, a semantic proposition only possible if "Ben" is Lerner and the events of the novel really took place; that is to say, if *10:04* is, in some way, autobiographical and thus nonfictional.

Whilst the author-characters of *Leaving the Atocha Station* and *10:04* function as the novels' sole first-person narrators, in *The Topeka School* the three Adam chapters focusing on his youth are written in the third person. It is only the last of the four Adam chapters, itself the final chapter of the book, which is written in the first person. This is a significant shift in narrative voice. There is also a spatiotemporal shift to present-day New York, where a grown-up Adam now lives with his Spanish-speaking wife Natalia and their two daughters, Luna and Amaya; though of the latter, he worries, "why does it feel dangerous to fictionalize my daughters' names?" (2019, p. 265). The question is placed in parenthesis, an act which marks it out as distinct from narration, and thus outside of the frame of the story. Additionally, the self-conscious reference to the act of fictionalizing suggests that the aside represents the real Ben Lerner's own authorial anxieties. Reflecting on a plotline from *Leaving the Atocha Station* (2011, p. 29), the character Ben cites similar concerns in *10:04*:

> In my novel the protagonist tells people his mother is dead, when she's alive and well. Halfway through writing the book, my mom was diagnosed with breast cancer and I felt, however insanely, that the novel was in part responsible, that having even a fictionalized version of myself producing bad karma around parental health was in some unspecifiable way to blame for the diagnosis.
>
> (2014, p. 138)

Lerner claims that the metatextuality of his writing is designed to provoke consideration of the uses of fiction within our external reality. In his words, "the self-referentiality of my novel [*10:04*] is a way of exploring how fiction functions in our real lives – for good and for ill – not a way of mocking fiction's inability to make contact with anything outside of itself" (Lin 2014). Lerner thus argues that fiction is not an insular, isolated ontology but, rather, essential to reality and thus our stories have the potential to impact reality. In this view, fiction is never distinct from nonfiction and the flickering between the virtual and the actual can have personal and social consequences.

Adam's life in this final chapter of *The Topeka School* is notably reminiscent of narrator Ben's in *10:04*: not only do Adam and Natalia live in New York, the chapter opens with them walking the city's streets, not dissimilarly to the many descriptions of Ben and Alex walking in *10:04* (in *Leaving the Atocha Station*, Adam is also frequently depicted walking around Madrid); at the end of *The Topeka School*, readers discover that Adam is "monitored closely by doctors for signs of a genetic syndrome I prayed nightly I had not bequeathed to my girls, tracking the dilation where the aorta meets the heart" (2019, pp. 269–270), while in *10:04* Ben learns that he has Marfan syndrome, a "genetic condition" affecting the heart's connective tissue which can lead to "fatal tearing of the aorta" (2014, p. 5);

during a visit back to Topeka, the stopped clock of the Foundation's tower reminds Adam of the film *Back to the Future*, itself a notable intertext of *10:04* and narrator Ben's "favorite movie" (p. 111). In the final chapter of *The Topeka School*, Adam and his family participate in an #OccupyICE demonstration at the Jacob Javits Building in Manhattan. Identifiable from the political chant – "FAMILIES AND CHILDREN, we yelled, then the others: DESERVE TO BE SAFE" (2019, p. 279) – the real-world protest, in June 2018, was against the "zero tolerance" immigration policy of the Trump administration, which initially led to children being separated from their parents (Kalmbacher 2018). Including this in the final chapter explicitly frames the prior events of *The Topeka School* in retrospective. The perceptual and temporal shift (from Adam's third-person perspective in the 1980s to first-person "I" in Trump-era America), along with the autofictional resonances between Lerner's three novels (moving from 1980s Topeka through 2004 Madrid and 2011–2012 New York to the near present), indeed casts *The Topeka School* as, in Lerner's words, "the prehistory of the other two books, the unconscious of the other two books in a certain way" (Lea, Irvine, and Armistead 2019).

This entry has focused on the autofictional dimension of Lerner's novels. His work can also be considered, amongst other things, as part of his poetic praxis, in relation to his critical writing, as well as for the way in which the narratives are grounded in time by historical events. However, it seems undeniable that *Leaving the Atocha Station*, *10:04*, and *The Topeka School* each fictionalize aspects of Ben Lerner's life. Not only are there recurring biographical details which thread through the novels, but stylistic refrains and techniques echo between them as they contemplate the value, reliability, and intensity of memory in personal experience. If – as Lerner claims and as this entry has demonstrated – the three novels are so inextricably intertwined as to be read as a self-contained autofictional trilogy, what future track Lerner's fiction takes, and how that might diverge from autofiction, is yet to be seen. It is nevertheless possible that – as avid readers of Ben Lerner's contemporary American fiction and to quote from *The Topeka School* – you may have already "been told most of what happens next, must remember it in the third person" (2019, p. 97).

SEE ALSO: After Postmodernism; Fiction and Affect; Realism after Poststructuralism

REFERENCES

Dyx, Hywel. (2018). Introduction: autofiction in English: the story so far. In: *Autofiction in English* (ed. Hywel Dyx), 1–23. Cham, Switzerland: Palgrave Macmillan.

Harvey, Giles. (2019). To decode white male rage, first he had to write in his mother's voice: how Ben Lerner reinvented the social novel for a hyper-self-obsessed age. *The New York Times Magazine* (October 8, 2019). https://www.nytimes.com/interactive/2019/10/08/magazine/ben-lerner-topeka-school.html (accessed July 5, 2021).

Kalmbacher, Colin. (2018). Parents with babies occupy ICE offices to demand reunification of children separated from families. *Law & Crime* (June 21, 2018). https://lawandcrime.com/immigration/parents-with-babies-occupy-ice-offices-to-demand-reunification-of-children-separated-from-families/ (accessed July 5, 2021).

Lea, Richard, Irvine, Lindesay, and Armistead, Claire. (2019). Ben Lerner and Meena Kandasamy on autofiction: books podcast. *The Guardian* (December 17, 2019). https://www.theguardian.com/books/audio/2019/dec/17/ben-lerner-and-meena-kandasamy-on-autofiction-books-podcast (accessed July 5, 2021).

Lerner, Ben. (2011). *Leaving the Atocha Station*. London: Granta Books.

Lerner, Ben. (2014). *10:04*. London: Granta Books.

Lerner, Ben. (2019). *The Topeka School*. New York: Farrar, Straus and Giroux.

Lin, Tao. (2014). Interview with Ben Lerner. *The Believer* (September 1, 2014). https://believermag.com/an-interview-with-ben-lerner/ (accessed July 5, 2021).

Perloff, Marjorie. (2018). *The Story of "Me": Contemporary American Autofiction*. Lincoln: University of Nebraska Press.

Preston, Alex. (2019). *The Topeka School* by Ben Lerner review: a work of extraordinary intelligence. *The Guardian* (November 5, 2019). https://www.theguardian.com/books/2019/nov/05/the-topeka-school-ben-lerner-review#maincontent (accessed July 5, 2021).

FURTHER READING

Bilmes, Leonid. (2018). "an actual present alive with multiple future": narrative, memory and time in Ben Lerner's *10:04*. *Textual Practice* 34 (7): 1081–1102. https://doi.org/10.1080/0950236X.2018.1515789

Gibbons, Alison. (2018). Autonarration, "I," and odd address in Ben Lerner's autofictional novel *10:04*. In: *Pronouns in Literature: Positions and Perspectives in Language* (ed. Alison Gibbons and Andrea Macrae), 75–96. London: Palgrave Macmillan.

Katz, Daniel. (2017). "I did not walk here all the way from prose": Ben Lerner's virtual poetics. *Textual Practice* 31 (2): 315–337.

Manshel, Alexander. (2017). The rise of the recent historical novel. *Post45* (September 29, 2017). https://post45.org/2017/09/the-rise-of-the-recent-historical-novel/

O'Dell, Jacqueline. (2019). One more time with feeling: repetition, contingency, and sincerity in Ben Lerner's *10:04*. *Critique: Studies in Contemporary Fiction* 60 (4): 447–461.

Lethem, Jonathan

JOSEPH BROOKER
Birkbeck, University of London, UK

The novelist Jonathan Lethem (b. 1964) was born and raised in Brooklyn, New York. The borough has been central to some of his most important work and has figured large in his reputation. While Lethem has been a vivid chronicler of Brooklyn in particular, and of New York in general, his literary imagination has in fact stretched further – notably to California, a prominent setting in six of his novels, and a state in which he has lived for two extended spells. Beyond that, Lethem's fiction has also envisaged alternative worlds, virtual spaces, and even an alien planet. His work has at some moments been deeply rooted in recognizable realities – street names, shops, shards of cultural history – while at others lifting off to great imaginative freedom. Lethem has been both highly realistic and a practitioner of the literature of the fantastic, and one of his major strategies has been to unite these contrasting approaches, or to bring them into collision.

Lethem was the precocious child of bohemian radicals. His father is a painter; his mother, a political activist, died of cancer in 1978, an event which would leave a strong mark on much of Lethem's fiction. Another of her legacies was a typewriter, on which Lethem commenced writing fiction in his teens. A voracious reader, he absorbed large quantities of science fiction (SF), and its powerful influence shows across his early work. Lethem did not start from notions of the realist tradition or the great American novel: his impulse was toward the fabulation of alternative, often dystopian worlds. His single greatest inspiration in this was the California-based novelist Philip K. Dick (1928–1982), whose paranoid imagination Lethem consumed enthusiastically and reworked into his own fiction.

Lethem's first short stories appeared in magazines like *Interzone* and *Isaac Asimov's Science Fiction Magazine*. Several were collected in *The Wall of the Sky, the Wall of the Eye* (1996). More than many other celebrated writers of his generation, he emerged within a realm of genre, with what critics have called a "megatext" of motifs and narrative options – from robots to time travel. Lethem would deploy many motifs and plot elements that squarely belong to SF: from the infinite traffic jam and consumerist technology in his story "Access Fantasy," to the virtual reality entertainment of "How We Got In Town And Out Again"; from the robotic exoskeletons that allow basketball players to use the skills of former greats of the sport in "Vanilla Dunk," to the mysterious alien beings who roam New York in "Light and the Sufferer." The same is true of his early novels. *As She Climbed Across The Table* (1997), the third to be published, centers on a hole in the universe that scientists name Lack, and explores the possibilities of alternate dimensions beyond it. This novel is at least set in a satirical version of contemporary California. Others more openly depart the naturalistic plane. Lethem's debut *Gun, With Occasional Music* (1994) is set in twenty-first-century San Francisco and features a police state, a drug-pacified population, and animals that have been given human intelligence by genetic modification. *Amnesia Moon* (1995) limns a postapocalyptic environment in which various American communities have retreated into their own delusions and distortions – what one character calls "Finite Subjective Realities." Both novels also concretize the notion of social status: in the first, citizens' karma points are recorded on an electronic card and can be reduced by the police; in the second, the town of Vacaville assigns every citizen a quotient of "luck," which then determines their life chances. Lethem's fourth novel, *Girl in Landscape* (1998), goes further still: from a future Earth suffering disastrous climate breakdown, a family travels to make a new life on a distant planet inhabited by a mysterious alien race called the Archbuilders.

One could, therefore, say that until his mid-thirties Lethem was an SF writer. Yet he occupied this role in a complex way. Unlike "hard," science-oriented SF, his fiction tends to eschew great detail about the logic of its alternate worlds: the science of genetics in *Gun* or climate alteration in *Girl in Landscape* are unapologetically sketchy, primarily occasions for allegory or political reflection. Moreover, several of his narratives do not even make a pretense of such an empirical basis, and instead simply unfold unexplained scenarios which might be labeled as fantasy or Gothic: "Five Fucks," "The Insipid Profession or Jonathan Hornebom," and the novella *This Shape We're In* (2001) are examples.

Moreover, if the early Lethem had a signature mode it was the deployment not just of a genre, but of more than one at once. "Light and the Sufferer," for instance, introduces its mysterious "space aliens" from "another dimension" into an otherwise mundane, though brutal, world of New York crime. *Gun, with Occasional Music*, most strikingly, explores its future dystopia through a hard-boiled detective whose attire, adventures, and wise-cracking narrative voice are all modeled on Raymond Chandler's Philip Marlowe. As Lethem openly explained, the novel "is a piece of carpentry. I wanted to locate the exact midpoint between Dick and Chandler" (Clarke 2011, p. 51). The collision of SF and hard-boiled genres creates a frisson, while casting both genres in a fresh light. The detective proves an ideal figure to explore and explain an estranged world, while this dystopia takes Chandler's "mean streets" to another level. One of Lethem's great themes, memory – and more especially its counterpart, forgetting or amnesia – is crucially in play, as free drugs encourage the population to forget their experiences and memory is eventually outsourced altogether to compliant machines. Memory and the reconstruction of history are central to the work of a detective, but are more compromised than ever in a state condemned to forget.

Girl in Landscape also combines genres. It is evidently SF, but much of its mood, language, and imagery is taken from the genre of the Western. The planet, with its vast broken arches abandoned by a previous generation of aliens, resembles the Monument Valley in which John Ford directed numerous classic Westerns: above all, *The Searchers* (1956), in which John Wayne's Ethan Edwards plans to find and kill his niece Debbie who has been abducted by a Comanche tribe. In Lethem's novel, Efram Nugent, the earliest human settler on the planet, takes on Wayne's physical presence, diction, and values, expressing contempt for the remaining Archbuilders, who are a kind of Indigenous people. Lethem's heroine Pella Marsh is a pubescent girl who comes to harmonize with the planet, even mentally occupying the bodies of its tiny fauna which spy on human settlers. Lethem has described the novel as *The Searchers* retold from Debbie's point of view: "What might it be like to see John Wayne through her eyes?" (Clarke 2011, p. 55). The shifted setting gives Lethem scope to make a kind of revisionist Western. At the same time, Pella's is also a coming-of-age story, one centered on mourning her mother who has died of illness at the start of the book: another generic strand, this time closely entwined with Lethem's own history.

Lethem's fifth novel, *Motherless Brooklyn* (1999), was a break from the pattern, in being set in present-day New York with no SF elements; at the same time, it marked a return to the hard-boiled crime mode of his debut and it demonstrated again his immersion in the possibilities of genre. Lionel Essrog is an orphan who has grown up in Brooklyn under the wing of the shady local businessman Frank Minna. When Minna is murdered, Lionel investigates. Minna's business has already been euphemistically labelled a "detective agency," but in seeking the killers, Lionel truly becomes a detective for the first time. As in *Gun*, the motifs of the genre are on show: the criminal kingpin in his lair, the ominous heavy, the femme fatale, and an intricate plot of illegal deals and betrayal. Again, though, the operation of a genre comes with deliberate interference. For one thing, as with *Girl in Landscape*, the genre is blended with another kind of narrative, showing Lionel's development as he progresses through the case: in Lethem's words, "it's really a Bildungsroman, a family romance, a coming-of-age story, whatever" (Clarke 2011, pp. 35–36). But most crucially, Lionel's defining characteristic is Tourette's syndrome, which makes him spectacularly ill-suited to work in this genre. Where the private detective should be cool, sardonic, in control, Lionel lacks control of his own speech and gestures. Lionel's syndrome gives *Motherless Brooklyn* membership of another, tentative subgenre: what Marco Roth has called the "neuro-novel," in which formal experiment is founded in a contemporary fascination with the chemistry of the brain. Lionel's extraordinary outbursts typically take an existing phrase and twist it into new mutations: thus, his own name, "the original verbal taffy," becomes "Liable Guesscog," "Final Escrow," "Ironic pissclam," (Lethem 1999, p. 7) "Viable Guessfrog" (p. 92), "Criminal Fishrug" (p. 97), "Lyrical Eggdog! Logical Assnog!" (p. 104), "Lullaby Gueststar," "AlibyebyeEssmob" (p. 109), and "Unreliable Chessgrub" (p. 229). This verbal distortion, sprinkled liberally across the novel, gives Lethem an outlet for sheer wordplay in the lineage of James Joyce's *Finnegans Wake* (1939). Yet for all this, *Motherless Brooklyn* is also a compelling detective story. So much was confirmed when it won the 2000 Gold Dagger award for crime fiction, in a field composed and judged entirely by specialist crime writers.

The Fortress of Solitude (2003) completed Lethem's homecoming. Its first part recounts the youth of Dylan Ebdus, a near surrogate for Lethem, in 1970s Brooklyn. After a hinge section ingeniously framed as a CD liner note, the long final part follows Dylan in the late 1990s as he reconnects with his past, returning to Brooklyn to find upscale bistros appearing on the once rough streets. A story of gentrification, *Fortress* is also one of race: the white Dylan befriends his mixed-race contemporary Mingus Rude, and the two share an obsession with comic books. The young Lethem's fascination with superheroes thus at last finds full fictional expression, in a narrative vastly more distended and detailed than his previous novels: his Brooklyn is described immersively in terms of the cracked slates of the sidewalk and the cries of children playing street games. Lethem thus reveals a new aspect as a writer, dedicated to the painstaking recreation of the recent historical past, while the novel's final stretch is a sometimes satirical scan of contemporary America. Yet *Fortress* holds a wild card: a magic ring that grants the power of flight. Discovering this item, Dylan and Mingus concoct the hero Aeroman, bringing superheroes from comic-book pages into the real Brooklyn. In the midst of Lethem's *Bildungsroman*, the ring is an estrangement effect, daubing a streak of fantasy across his great mimetic achievement. In this the novel exemplifies Lethem's impulse "to push together realistic character, and emotion, and naturalistic or mimetic textures, with the stuff of dream, fantasy, symbol" (Clarke 2011, pp. 122–123).

Lethem has borrowed the critic Manny Farber's duality of "white elephant" and "termite" art (Lethem 2011, pp. xxi–xxii). The white elephant novelist would produce earnest epics about the great questions of his time, while the termite artist – Lethem's preferred option – would make nimbler, more unpredictable and subversive cultural interventions. Occupying genre fiction was a way to be a termite. The scale and seriousness of *The Fortress of Solitude* at last risked, as Lethem acknowledged, putting him into an elephant suit. Having started in *Interzone*, he could now be found writing tales of the Upper East Side in *The New Yorker*. He has thus periodically attempted stratagems to escape this comfortable role and regain the element of surprise. The follow-up to *Fortress* was a deliberately breezy romantic comedy set in 1990s Los Angeles, *You Don't Love Me Yet* (2007); another was a comic book written at the invitation of Marvel Comics, a 2008 revival of the 1970s title *Omega the Unknown*, which reprised Lethem's love of superheroes in a fresh medium. Lethem also authored two short books about popular culture: a 2010 study of John Carpenter's film *They Live* (1989), crystallizing his interest in pulp and paranoia, and a 2012 analysis of the Talking Heads LP *Fear of Music* (1979). In short fiction, too, Lethem has tried surprising moves. In the 2015 collection *Lucky Alan*, while some stories occupy essentially mimetic worlds, one, "Their Back Pages," is told as a fragmented description of comic book panels, and another, "The Dreaming Jaw, The Salivating Ear," is a surreal materialization of an online "blog" into real space, narrated backwards.

Yet Lethem did not shun the challenge of large, imposing novels. *Chronic City* (2009) turned his attention to Manhattan, in a reality-shifted metropolis where the *New York Times* produces a war-free edition, a gray cloud mysteriously covers Manhattan's financial district (the closest Lethem's novels have come to an allegory of the effects of 9/11), and a giant tiger is rumored to be tearing up buildings on the Upper East Side. Ingenuous actor Chase Insteadman befriends the obsessive cultural critic Perkus Tooth, whose paranoid theories of the politics of Norman Mailer, Marlon Brando, and the Rolling Stones offer an exaggerated outlet for one aspect of Lethem's imagination. Chase's world ultimately comes to appear dominated by simulation; even his romance with a doomed astronaut stranded in space turns out to be a fiction played out in the press to distract the public. Chase himself can scarcely remember the truth of the story: once more Lethem posits collective amnesia as a strategy of the cynical state.

Dissident Gardens (2013) is still more ambitious, a family saga that reaches back to the 1930s and forward to the moment of Occupy, as Lethem sketches a history of the American political Left. *Dissident Gardens* reimagines a version of Lethem's mother in the form of Miriam Zimmer, a rebellious young Jewish leftist who traverses the coffee-house scene of the 1960s folk revival. The novel stands out in Lethem's oeuvre thus far in having scant truck with the fantastic or with popular genre forms – unless the historical novel and family saga themselves are counted as such. Much closer to Philip Roth than Philip K. Dick, *Dissident Gardens* might have suggested that the later Lethem would be following a more conventionally respectable literary path than his younger self. Yet his two novels since then have not altogether confirmed this. *A Gambler's Anatomy* (2016), published in the UK as *The Blot*, is Lethem's least classifiable novel, depicting a backgammon player's escapades in Berlin and Berkeley. A tumor inside the protagonist's face appears to give him psychic powers, making the novel, in its way, as fantastic as Lethem's earlier work. Thomas Pynchon is a presiding literary spirit over this digressive story of Californian counterculture's ambiguous complicity with commerce and power. The same can be said of *The Feral Detective* (2018), in which Phoebe Siegler, a young woman from New York, travels to inland California in search of a missing friend. Enlisting the help of shaggy detective Charles Heist, she returns Lethem to the territory of a familiar genre, albeit in an eccentric fashion. Rather as Lionel Essrog's Tourette's interferes with his detective narrative, Phoebe's is mediated through her wise-cracking millennial's monologue. Her journey from East to West coast, meanwhile, follows Lethem's own: in 2010 he had relocated to Claremont, California, to take a full-time chair in creative writing.

Lethem's most definitive statement is the 2007 essay "The Ecstasy of Influence." Playing on and against Harold Bloom's notion of the "anxiety of influence," Lethem proposes that art is made from other art, and it can cheerfully acknowledge this rather than neurotically repress it. The essay also carries legal and political implications, drawing on theories of intellectual property and the excessive scope of copyright and arguing for a "Commons" of cultural life. Remarkably, Lethem's essay is largely constructed from quotations from other sources, invisibly patched together without quotation marks. A key at the essay's end names the dozens of sources, from Thomas Jefferson to David Foster Wallace. The essay's form thus enacts its assertions, in a bravura exercise in imitative form. It is the closest Lethem has come to issuing a credo, as its underlying sense of the intertextuality of all art can be viewed as a thread through his entire career: from *Gun*'s blatant borrowing from Chandler, to *Girl in Landscape*'s from Ford, to the collection *Kafka Americana* (1999), co-written with Carter Scholz, which openly rewrites Kafka's work. As his career develops, Lethem can even be seen recycling his own materials: a talking kangaroo in *Gun* is recalled by a more naturalistic one in *You Don't Love Me Yet*; the incongruous presence of a Buddhist Zendo in *Motherless Brooklyn* is matched by one at the other end of the country in *The Feral Detective*; and numerous character names playfully recur across novels written decades apart.

Lethem has been publishing novels for over a quarter of a century. Remarkably extensive – eleven novels, multiple collections of stories and essays – his oeuvre has also been diverse and unpredictable. From the strategies he has already essayed – SF, crime, superheroes, contemporary realism – one can hardly guess what he will do next. The safest presumption is that it will unabashedly – even ecstatically – draw on the extant library of literature and art, forging novel combinations from the archive of the cultural past.

SEE ALSO: Chabon, Michael; DeLillo, Don; Egan, Jennifer; Eggers, Dave; Erickson, Steve; Millhauser, Steven; Mixed-Genre Fiction; Pynchon, Thomas; Tartt, Donna; Wallace, David Foster

REFERENCES

Clarke, Jaime. (ed.) (2011). *Conversations with Jonathan Lethem*. Jackson: University Press of Mississippi.
Lethem, Jonathan. (1999). *Motherless Brooklyn*. New York: Doubleday.
Lethem, Jonathan. (2011). *The Ecstasy of Influence*. New York: Doubleday.

FURTHER READING

Brooker, Joseph. (2020). *Jonathan Lethem and the Galaxy of Writing*. London: Bloomsbury.
Coughlan, David. (2011). Jonathan Lethem's *The Fortress of Solitude* and *Omega: The Unknown*, a comic book series. *College Literature* 38 (3): 194–218.
Galchen, Rivka. (2009). In between the dream and the doorknob: on Jonathan Lethem's fictions. *Ecotone* 5 (1): 162–180. https://ecotonemagazine.org/nonfiction/in-between-the-dream-and-the-doorknob-on-jonathan-lethems-fictions/
Luter, Matthew. (2015). *Understanding Jonathan Lethem*. Columbia: University of South Carolina Press.
Peacock, James. (2012). *Jonathan Lethem*. Manchester: Manchester University Press.

Literary Magazines

DONAL HARRIS
University of Memphis, USA

While the first literary magazines date back to the seventeenth century, the modern version emerged in the late nineteenth and early twentieth centuries, first in Europe and the United States, and later in Russia, the West Indies, Argentina, Japan, India, and Ghana. "The history of contemporary letters has, to a very manifest extent, been written in such magazines," claimed Ezra Pound (1930, p. 702), because they incubated the as yet unsung authors and literary forms that commercial publishers ignore. These magazines often were, and continue to be, simultaneously dismayed with the current state of commercial publishing and inspired by the ideal of a world republic of letters, where local literatures might contact and communicate outside the bounds of national borders. Literary magazines are by nature difficult to shoehorn into a single, comprehensive narrative, but their numerousness, geographic range, eclecticism, and openness to unpopular and experimental artistic styles make them an essential component of the twenty-first-century literary field.

DEFINED BY DIVERSITY

The field of literary magazines is best imagined as an archipelago of variously sized islands rather than a solid body of land that a writer or researcher can navigate. According to the most recent survey by the Community of Literary Magazines and Presses (CLMP), which was founded in 1967 to help direct federal, state, and private arts funding to small presses and magazines, there are over 1,100 literary magazines or small presses operating in the United States, with circulations ranging from several dozen to tens of thousands (CLMP 2021). Because CLMP only counts magazines after they print three issues, a fairly high bar for a self-financed periodical, the actual number is certainly much higher.

While that aggregate number has been relatively stable since the mimeograph revolution of the 1960s, the fate of individual magazines is less so. When Michael Anania surveyed the field in 1978, he found that almost 70% of publications had opened shop after 1970, and only 9% existed before 1960. According to a 2011 analysis of the magazines catalogued in *Library Journal* (Nester and Black 2011), less than half of the literary magazines between 1980 and 1995 lasted ten years. There are outliers, of course – Harriet Monroe's *Poetry* has continuously published since 1912 – but the norm is for an individual title to burn brightly and then flare out.

Literary magazines also tend to resist easy classification because of what John O'Brien of Dalkey Archive Press refers to as the "vision of change" that motivates them (O'Brien 2016, p. 128). That is, magazines are born out of the feeling that a particular style of writing, authorial identity, regional affiliation, or literary topic have been excluded from other outlets. This iconoclasm defines some of the most influential journals of the last forty years. For example, in 1976 Charles Henry Rowell founded *Callaloo* to showcase the writing and arts of the Black South by individuals such as Ernest Gaines, Alice Walker, and Yusef Komunyak, whom he felt were intentionally left out of primarily white Southern literary journals. That same year, equally inspired by the punk poetry of Patti Smith and anarchic UK underground music zines, Dennis Cooper co-founded *Little Caesar* in Los Angeles to bring the energy of New York's music scene to the poetry world. In 1979, Bill Buford resuscitated Oxford University's *Granta* to document the rise of what he called "dirty realism" by Raymond Carver, Bobbie Ann Mason, and Frederick Barthelme; champion "postcolonial" writers such as Salman Rushdie; and support the long-form, meticulously researched personal essays that would later coalesce into the genre of creative nonfiction. In 1980, Nicolas Kanellos moved *The Americas Review* (formerly *La Revista Chicano-Riqueña*) to Houston, Texas, where it offered a platform for Latinx and Chicanx writers who were ignored by mainstream US publications. Each of these examples began with the same idea – to create an outlet for a new style of writing and new type of writer – but the content of that idea looks quite different in each instance.

As the histories of *Callaloo*, *Granta*, and *The Americas Review* make clear, the location and structure of individual titles can change over time, too. *Callaloo* and *The Americas Review* have moved between several universities, and *Granta* has seen several editors, as well as owners, who each had their own idea for the magazine's direction. All three speak to a general trend, beginning in the 1980s, of the professionalization of formerly small-scale and independent magazines. Some moved in-house to university English departments as one wing of growing creative writing programs, while others joined publishing collectives or sought partnerships with book publishers to supplement their finances. *Granta*, for example, struck an early partnership with Penguin US that gave them access to an uncommon level of distribution and marketing. Finally, since the late 1990s, the development of "born digital" magazines and online-only content for print titles has become the field's biggest area of growth, making the definition of "literary magazine," as well as the concept of publishing, even murkier.

This diversity of size, scope, and duration is endemic to literary magazines, and it relates to a feature that distinguishes the magazine, as a periodical, from other forms of publication: that is, seriality. Unlike a bound novel or book of poetry, magazines publish individual issues at relatively regular intervals that are both stand-alone objects and representatives of a larger, longer publishing project. The seriality of literary magazines affords a number of opportunities to editors and writers alike: special issues on specific topics, long articles or fiction that is published over the course of multiple issues, and the ability to incorporate reader feedback in the form of letters to the editor or editorial responses to reviews of past issues. Thus, there are obvious differences *between* literary magazines, but there is also variety *within* each title, a variety that in theory is endlessly renewable, reborn with each new installment. In short, it is especially hard in the twenty-first century to count, let alone to conceptualize, the full warp and weft of contemporary literary magazines in all of their academic and amateur, commercial and coterie, paper-based and "post-print" variety.

THE "LITERARY" AND THE "LITTLE"

The English word "magazine" is related etymologically to the French *magasin* and, even earlier, the sixteenth-century Arabic term *makazin* (plural of *makzan*), both of which designate a storehouse. And, on the surface, a "literary magazine" is just that: any periodical that houses fiction, poetry, and criticism that will be picked up and used by some adventurous reader. Thus, in the broadest definition, legacy titles such as *The New Yorker* or *Harper's*, with regular circulations in the hundreds of thousands, are just as much literary magazines as *Little Caesar* or *Callaloo*, which have much shorter lifespans and more specialized subscriber lists, respectively. Researchers in the fields of communications, journalism, and media studies, such as the contributors to *The Routledge Handbook of Magazine Research* (Abrahamson and Prior-Miller 2015), tend to favor the descriptor "literary" because it emphasizes the genre's position in relation to other types of magazines, particularly commercial or general interest magazines. Thus, a literary magazine occupies an analogous space in the periodical market to that of a news magazine like *Time*, fashion magazine like *Vogue*, regional magazine like *Southern Living*, or conservative magazine like *The National Review* (Dietz 2014). Trade organizations and publishing collectives like CLMP also tend to favor the term "literary," at least partially because doing so reflects the National Endowment for the Arts' and National Endowment for the Humanities' inclusion of literature as a target funding area, and hence opens up federal and state grant money to their member magazines.

However, the dominant term in literary studies for these serialized storehouses is "little magazine," which serves several purposes. First, building on Pierre Bourdieu's (1996) idea of restricted production, it draws a circle around those journals aimed at an audience of other writers and scholars rather than those for a general readership. Thus, one hallmark of contemporary little magazines is the practice of publishing "forums," "conversations," or "roundtables" on a topic related to the craft or business of literature. For example, Jena Osman's and Juliana Spahr's *Chain*, which ran from 1994 to 2005, often opened issues with an editorial forum on that volume's general topic, and *BOMB* magazine, which began in 1981, solely publishes author interviews. *BOMB* consists of "artists talking to artists about art," and because of this it "*belonged* to its community of artists and writers," as longtime editor Betty Sussler put it, rather than to some "general" reader outside of the arts or literary world (2015, p. 22). Thus, little magazines are aimed at the insiders of literary culture, even if they also often position themselves on the outside of mainstream publishing.

"Little" rather than "literary" also subtly allows for the full range of verbal and nonverbal arts. It links contemporary magazines to early-twentieth-century forebears such as Gilbert Seldes's *Seven Lively Arts*, Alfred Stieglitz's *Camera Work*, Margaret Anderson's *The Little Review*, and Maria MacDonald and

Eugene Jolas's *transition*. In different ways, these publications situated literary modernism's "revolution of the word" alongside experimental works in sculpture, photography, radio, film, painting, and other media. This historical connection can be seen in Ian Morris's and Joanne Diaz's *The Little Magazine in Contemporary America* (2015), which argues that "new little magazines are surprisingly similar to their modernist antecedents from the 1920s" in their commitment to "avant-garde aesthetics, their global engagement, and their eagerness to influence poets, critics, and scholars who might then influence a wider readership" (p. x). "Little" magazines are literary, then, but they also exemplify how "the literary" rubs against other contemporary art forms.

Finally, the scalar descriptor "little" signals anticommercialism and anti-institutionalism. In his postmortem on the "small magazines," Ezra Pound argued, "When [a journal's] motivation is merely a desire for money or publicity, or when this motivation is in great part such a desire for money directly or publicity as a means indirectly of getting money," then it cannot speak to the literary currents of its time (1930, p. 689). Likewise, the field-shaping *The Little Magazine: A History and a Bibliography* (Hoffman, Allen, and Ulrich 1946) defined its subject against the commercial expediency of the mainstream magazines. Elliot Anderson's and Mary Kinzie's *The Little Magazine in America* – which itself started as a special issue of the *Tri-Quarterly Review*, a literary magazine based out of Chicago – flatly announced, "as a rule they do not, and cannot, expect to make money" (1979, p. 3).

Contemporary magazines tend to align themselves with one side of this divide between "literary" and "little" in their editorial voice and formal design. For example, the editors of *n+1* modeled the magazine's house style on the contrarian voice of titles like *The Baffler* and *The Partisan Review*. The editors early on published fiction by Helen DeWitt, Sam Lipsyte, and Benjamin Kunkel, but its first issue, published in the summer of 2004, was explicitly styled as an antidote to the typical literary magazine. It contained a number of "state of the field" articles on periodical culture: a think piece on the postmodern neoconservatism of *The Weekly Standard*, a critique of *The New Republic*'s staid literary taste and regressive politics, and two articles on the author David Eggers and his San Francisco-based magazines *McSweeney's* and *The Believer*. Through and through, *n+1* bore the history of the little magazine's insistence on iconoclasm.

McSweeney's, for its part, also sided with the little magazines. Founded in 1998, the magazine initially focused on publishing work that had been rejected by other venues, and included contributions by Joyce Carol Oates, David Foster Wallace, David Shields, and Jonathan Lethem. But it also brought smallness to the level of typography. In fact, format was just as important as the author list for establishing the *McSweeney's* style: early issues often included manifestos and position statements in exceptionally small print on the spine, copyright page, and other disregarded portions of the bound volume. In addition, the magazine rarely looked like a magazine. It published issues in a range of formats, from a Victorian-era triple decker with a magnetized spine, to a cigar box made to resemble the personal kit of a World War I soldier, to a paperback made to look like a 1930s pulp story collection. For Jeffrey Lependorf, these design techniques mirror the editorial focus on rejected material, in that both elevate "the 'inessential' and overlooked to the level of literature," in a sense doubling down on the "littleness" of the magazine's scope (2015, p. 2).

Granta, on the other hand, uses its publication method to align itself with the commercial press, even if it is just as dedicated to elevating marginalized writers. Because of an early partnership with Penguin, *Granta* was published in codex form, like a book, rather than as a magazine, and it gained access to wider distribution and promotion than a typical literary journal. By affiliating with the commercial press both in administration and design, then, *Granta* asserted itself as a mainstream literary magazine in a way that the self-consciously little magazines do not.

THE CAMPUS AND THE CITY

One of the most significant developments in literary magazines in the last fifty years has to do with a different kind of institutional affiliation. Whereas the majority of early-twentieth-century literary and little magazines were independent – bigger literary magazines funded through advertising revenue, or "little magazines" funded by the editor or a wealthy patron – the balance has tipped to university-based publications, rather than literary movement or scene-based production.

This type of literary magazine is often housed in an English department and run by creative writing faculty and graduate students. In April 2020, *Poets & Writers* compiled a list of over 160 MFA-based literary magazines currently publishing in the United States, with some programs sponsoring multiple journals: for example *The Columbia Poetry Review*, *Hair Trigger*, *Hotel Amerika*, and *Punctuate* are all listed as affiliates of Columbia College in Chicago, and Louisiana State has at least three creative writing magazines or reviews attached to it (Staff 2020). Certainly, there is a long history of universities promoting literary magazines: *Virginia Quarterly Review* began in 1925, University of Nebraska-Lincoln's *The Prairie Schooner* was founded in 1926, and *The Kenyon Review* dates to 1939. However, the sheer number of such magazines, along with the fact that they are primarily operated by graduate students, marks a sea change in the field.

This transition echoes a larger change in contemporary American literary culture that Mark McGurl (2009) refers to as "the program era." That is, a defining feature of postwar literary production and readership as a whole has been the indelible mark of creative writing programs, especially graduate-level programs. They brought novelists and poets (but rarely playwrights) into the fold of previously "academic" literature departments and, in the process, made creative writing an accreditable domain of higher education, subject to all of the institutional pressures (budgets, annual evaluation, tenure) faced by other faculty members and students in the English department. It is telling that the Association of Writers and Writings Programs and the Community of Literary Magazines and Publishers were both founded in 1967, as both organizations mark a self-conscious professionalization of authorship and the literary magazines that publish those authors' work.

This isn't to say that MFA programs have a monopoly on contemporary literary magazines, especially at the highest and lowest ends of magazine publishing. Underground literary and arts "zines" such as *Cometbus*, *Genda*, and *Biracial Bandit* survive outside of "the program," and commercial magazines like *Harper's* and *The New Yorker* continue to turn profits and expose readers to new fiction and poetry. Rather than present an antagonistic relationship between university and commercial magazines – "MFA vs. NYC," as Chad Harbach (2014) puts it – it is probably more accurate to see the program's rise as a separate but related path to professionalization as the apprenticeship model of cultural hubs like New York and London. Instead of "MFA vs. NYC," then, both campuses and literary cities offer potential safe havens and financial support to editors and writers attempting to make a mark.

TECHNOLOGICAL CHANGE: PRINT, "DIGITTLE," AND THE FUTURE OF LITERARY MAGAZINES

The history of literary magazines is indelibly tied to transformations in print technology, especially since the mimeograph revolution of the 1960s. Mimeograph machines and later Xerox copiers lowered the bar of entry for self-publishing and the hand-made, rough-hewn aesthetic can be seen in titles such as *Floating Bear*, edited by Amiri Baraka and Diane DiPrima (perhaps most famous for publishing a William S. Burroughs piece, "Roosevelt After the Inauguration," which led to Baraka's and DiPrima's arrest on obscenity charges); *Fuck You/a magazine of the arts*, edited by Ed Sanders; and *Umbra*, published by the long-running and still active Black arts collective Society of Umbra. These small-run journals took inspiration from the artistic experimentalism of modernist little magazines, as well as their outsider status: part of the allure of mimeograph and copier machines was the promise of artistic and editorial control over the magazine itself, and their cheap, fast mode of publication reflected the editorial mission of capturing an arts scene in real time. These titles were some of the first to publish future literary stars such as Frank O'Hara, Charles Bukowski, Ishmael Reed, and Nikki Giovanni, among countless others, but the method of production, for many, was an aesthetic of its own.

In a similar way, the widespread availability of desktop publishing programs in the 1990s allowed fledgling editors to make professional-quality magazines on their own, without the specialized skills of typesetters or computer programmers. Programs like Aldus's PageMaker (launched in 1985), Quark (launched in 1987), and Adobe's InDesign (launched in 1999) offered WYSIWYG ("what you see is what you get") layout capabilities, so that designing a magazine became nearly as user-friendly as typing into a word processor and cropping images. *McSweeney's*, in San Francisco, and *Fence*, in New York City, both founded in 1998, are emblematic of the newly available refinement in design that desktop publishing made available.

The Internet, and digital technology in general, has also fundamentally changed how literary magazines circulate. Like mimeographs, Xerox copiers, and desktop publishing before, the abundance of cheap domain space has provided a new generation of writers and editors low-cost entry points into the literary field. Sometimes this takes the form of online supplements to legacy titles, such as the *Harriet* blog associated with *Poetry* magazine. It is also common for print journals to reorganize as digital publications, such as with Andrei Codrescu's *Exquisite Corpse*, which operated in print between 1983 and 1995, then migrated into an online-only format. And still others, like *The Rumpus*, *Drunken Boat*, and *Scalawag*, conceived of their publication projects as web-based from the beginning. According to CLMP, which began cataloguing web-based titles in 2000, online literary magazines continue to be the fastest-growing segment of the field (Lependorf 2015).

Many of these web-based literary magazines intentionally follow in the wake of their print-based forebears, while taking advantage of the particular affordances of digital publication. In fact, the cross-referencing capabilities of hyperlinks and hashtags, along with the ability to easily add new content, fit quite well with the inherent seriality of print-based literary magazines. From a certain vantage, the serial publication and collaborative production of print magazines looks like an earlier version of the Internet's promise of endlessly renewable, endlessly diverse content. But Internet-based literary and little magazines also make more direct use of their digital presence. For example, *Scalawag* focuses on the writings and multimedia art of marginalized communities in the global South, much like *Callaloo* before it. But unlike *Callaloo*, whose offices followed Charles Henry Rowell as his academic career traversed different universities, *Scalawag*'s address is its "url" rather than a physical location, so it stays in place despite the fact that its three editors live in three different states.

Literary magazines have been shaped by digital technology in other ways, too, especially under the guise of remediation. For most of the twentieth century, archives and indexes of small-press literary magazines were, at best, difficult to access because they were cordoned off in the Special Collections departments of research libraries. This began to change in the late 1950s, when university librarians experimented with transferring their periodical holdings onto microfilm and microfiche rolls, which could then be copied and shared with other libraries. It was a move toward greater accessibility and, ideally, greater preservation. However, the process also irreparably damaged many magazines: to make the microfilm, librarians pulled off the covers, tore out the bindings, and often discarded the "nonliterary" content, such as advertising pages.

More recently, the print-based little magazines of the twentieth century have found new life as digitized images, which are held in a range of public and private databases. Online archives such as the Modernist Journals Project (a joint effort by Brown University and the University of Tulsa), *Jacket2*'s Reissues platform, Kenneth Goldsmith's Ubuweb, and Jed Birmingham and Kyle Schlesinger's *Mimeo Mimeo* collection make a whole array of short-run and hard-to-find titles available for anyone with wi-fi connection. At the same time, sites like *Monoskop* and *From a Secret Location* use the capabilities of web publication to build ever larger compendiums of defunct literary and arts magazines from both the United States and abroad, making available magazines published far from the literary hubs, from Cleveland, Ohio to Cairo, Egypt. Eric Bulson refers to these digital reproductions of print-based literary magazines as "digittle magazines" (2017, p. 268). Unlike their paper-based originals, these are scanned images housed on servers, ostensibly unbound by the limits of print runs or physical proximity. They are accessible and available on thousands of computer screens around the world all at once, without ever moving. This transformation of media format brings with it a range of questions concerning the materiality of publication and the phenomenology of reading, as well as basic questions about the politics of access to these materials.

This new availability arises at the same time that the field of literary studies has adopted methodologies from book history, print culture studies, the digital humanities, literary sociology, and media studies that lend themselves to the large-scale study of periodicals. Though organizations like *VIDA: Women in Literary Arts* have undertaken this type of comprehensive analysis for over a decade – the *VIDA* Count annually tracks gender disparity in publishing – newer projects, such as the NEH-sponsored *Circulating American Magazines* database, make longitudinal and comparative analysis of enormous numbers of magazines possible like never before.

Since the beginning of the twentieth century, both producers and scholars of literary magazines have defined them by their amplification of underrepresented artistic communities, dedication to peripheral literary practices, and incubation of new narrative, poetic, and intermedial modes of expression. In fact, one might argue that the measure of a healthy literary culture is an overabundant magazine culture, especially one that pushes at the borders of what constitutes "the literary." If this is the case, then the twenty-first-century Anglophone literary field is truly humming.

SEE ALSO: Big Data; Burroughs, William; Carver, Raymond; Cooper, Dennis; Eggers, Dave; Gaines, Ernest; Intermedial Fiction; Lethem, Jonathan; Mason, Bobbie Ann; Oates, Joyce Carol; Program Culture; Reed, Ishmael; Walker, Alice; Wallace, David Foster

REFERENCES

Abrahamson, David and Prior-Miller, Marcia. (eds.) (2015). *The Routledge Handbook of Magazine Research: The Future of the Magazine Form*. New York: Routledge.

Anania, Michael. (1978). Of living belfry and rampart: on American literary magazines since 1950. *Tri-Quarterly* 4: 6–23.

Anderson, Elliot and Kinzie, Mary. (1979). *The Little Magazine in America: A Modern Documentary History*. New York: Pushcart Press.

Bourdieu, Pierre. (1996). *The Rules of Art: Genesis and Structure of the Literary Field* (trans. Susan Imanuel). Palo Alto, CA: Stanford University Press.

Bulson, Eric. (2017). *Little Magazine, World Form*. New York: Columbia University Press.

Community of Literary Magazines and Presses. (2021). Directory of publishers. https://www.clmp.org/readers/directory-of-publishers/ (accessed July 15, 2021).

Dietz, Laura. (2014). Online versus print: the reputation of literary fiction magazines. *Short Fiction in Theory and Practice* 4 (1): 6–20.

Harbarch, Chad. (ed.) (2014). *MFA vs. NYC: The Two Cultures of American Fiction*. New York: Farrar, Straus and Giroux.

Hoffman, Frederick John, Allen, Charles, and Ulrich, Carolyn Farquhar. (1946). *The Little Magazine: A History and Bibliography*. Princeton: Princeton University Press.

Lependorf, Jeffrey. (2015). A decade or so of little magazines: one reader's perspective. In: *The Little Magazine in America* (ed. Ian Morris and Joanne Diaz), 1–18. Chicago: University of Chicago Press.

McGurl, Mark. (2009). *The Program Era: Postwar Fiction and the Rise of Creative Writing*. Cambridge, MA: Harvard University Press.

Morris, Ian and Diaz, Joanne. (eds.) (2015). *The Little Magazine in Contemporary America*. Chicago: University of Chicago Press.

Nester, Daniel and Black, Steve. (2011). Here today, gone tomorrow: on the lifespan of the literary magazine. *Bookslut* (February 2011).

O'Brien, John. (2016). 19 things: more thoughts on the future of fiction. In: *Literary Publishing in the Twenty-First Century* (ed. Travis Kurowski, Wayne Miller, and Kevin Prufer), 120–130. Minneapolis: Milkweed.

Pound, Ezra. (1930). Small magazines. *English Journal* 19 (9): 689–704.

Staff. (2020). Literary journals associated with MFA programs. *Poets & Writers* (April 24, 2020). https://www.pw.org/content/literary_journals_us_mfa_programs (accessed July 15, 2021).

Sussler, Betty. (2015). The history of BOMB. In: *The Little Magazine in Contemporary America* (ed. Ian Morris and Joanne Diaz), 19–27. Chicago: University of Chicago Press.

FURTHER READING

Henderson, Bill. (ed.) (1980). *The Art of Literary Publishing: Editors on Their Craft*. New York: Pushcart Press.

Kurowski, Travis, Miller, Wayne, and Prufer, Kevin. (eds.) (2016). *Literary Publishing in the Twenty-First Century*. Minneapolis: Milkweed.

Phillips, Rodney and Clay, Steve. (1998). *A Secret Location on the Lower East Side: Adventures in Writing, 1960–1980*. New York: Granary Books.

Sklar, Morty and Mulac, Jim. (1978). *Editor's Choice: Literature and Graphics from the U.S. Small Press, 1965–1977*. New York: Pushcart Press.

Weddle, Jeff. (ed.) (2018). Alternative publishing: little magazines, zines, and such. Special issue of *Serials Review* 44.

Literature of the Americas

ANTONIO BARRENECHEA
University of Mary Washington, USA

An academic discipline, "Literature of the Americas" has been challenging the traditional study of American Literature for decades. Definitions remains unclear, however, and separate terms describe a number of academic approaches today. Some of these – including "Inter-American Studies" and "Hemispheric Studies" – are (by definition) less committed to the particularities of language and literature, and adopt instead a cultural "studies" approach attuned to politics and ideology. Closer to the original meaning is "inter-American," which suggests a meeting of international participants on both sides of a punctuation dash. "Hemispheric," on the other hand, has opened a grammatically modified path for American Studies based upon US "hemispheric" relations with neighbors from Spanish America, Brazil, Canada, and the Caribbean. My choice of "Literature of the Americas" in this entry is consistent with the international origins of the discipline before it veered toward US national literature. This narrowing has led to its place in this volume on "American Fiction," suggesting continuity between "America" and "Americas."

Developing out of South America in the 1930s, Literature of the Americas began as the study of the Western Hemisphere, in other words, the literary output of nations comprising the "Americas." The nomenclature does not indicate a new US literary studies formation, but a consortium of nations of which the United States is one member. To study the hemisphere means to dive into languages and literary traditions that go back more than a century before British arrival in North America. Luis Alberto Sánchez's *Nueva historia de la literatura americana* (1944) is the first published history of the literature of the Americas. While its author had already penned an authoritative literary history of his native Peru, this book expanded the domain of American letters to US and Brazilian authors. Written in exile while Sánchez taught in Chile, Argentina, and the United States, the *Nueva historia* was, indeed, a "new" development in "American" historiography. For the first time ever, a scholar juxtaposed hemispheric literary currents toward a Greater American vision. This book would lead into Sánchez's *Historia comparada de las literaturas americanas* (1973–1976), the most ambitious history of literature of the Americas ever written. Across its four volumes and 1,600+ pages, Sánchez examines the United States, Brazil, the French Caribbean, and Spanish America in comparative literary relation. Sánchez responds to Herbert E. Bolton's call for a hemispheric treatment of literature (among other subjects) at the end of his presidential address to the American Historical Association from 1932. In "The Epic of Greater America," the historian established conceptual parameters for studying the Western Hemisphere "to supplement the purely nationalistic presentation to which we are accustomed" (1933, p. 448). Literature of the Americas dates to this "Good Neighbor" era of cooperation. By 1976, Sánchez would answer the call as a comparatist with strong footing in each of the literatures under analysis.

His *Historia comparada* begins with the pre-Columbian era, treating Quechua drama and other genres alongside North American transcriptions of oral traditions. Sánchez then turns to "discovery" chronicles from Christopher Columbus, John Smith, and other writer-explorers. This leads into the emergence of "New World" colonial literatures in New England and the Spanish viceroyalties in Mexico City and Lima. The author discusses the seminal writings of El Inca Garcilaso de la Vega and Baroque Hispanic luminaries next to those by the Puritans, Cotton Mather and Anne Bradstreet. After addressing the Enlightenment and the rise of independent literatures in the Americas, Sánchez covers hemisphere-wide movements ranging from romanticism to naturalism. Vanguard literature, such as modernismo and the writings of the US "lost generation," lead into the 1970s rise of the Latin American Boom. Indeed, to read Sánchez today is to recuperate a veritable "lost" archive for Literature of the Americas. These texts from centuries past have gone missing in recent approaches that stress US "hemispheric" gain over the hemisphere. Sánchez places national literatures under the Western Hemisphere. He developed the comparative model despite being a critic of US imperialism, and a persecuted intellectual from Peru's leftist party, APRA (American Popular Revolutionary Alliance). In short, Sánchez is the unacknowledged (and untranslated) founder of Literature of the Americas.

Following Sánchez's example is Joaquim de Montezuma de Carvalho's *Panorama das literaturas das Américas* (4 volumes, 1958–1965). Coordinated by a Portuguese scholar working in colonial Angola, it is the first and only collaborative history of literature of the Americas. As master editor, Carvalho tackles the enterprise nation by nation, and in the four major European languages of the Western Hemisphere. He commissioned top scholars (such as Luis Leal, from Mexico and Max Enríquez Ureña, from the Dominican Republic) to contribute surveys of the literatures of their home countries, and in their national languages. Although Carvalho mostly limited the task to literature after 1900, this still makes for twenty-four mini-panoramas totaling 2100 pages (Canada has one in English and one in French). The project took seven years to complete from South Africa. Incredibly, Carvalho had not set foot in America at the time of its publication, having cultivated his interest through reading and scholarly networks. He privileges nonetheless deep local knowledge – the particularities of literary expression from Ecuador and Haiti, for example – within a hemispheric map of parallel and intersecting cultures. The work features a preface from José Mora, secretary general of the Organization of American States; an address from Gabriela Mistral; a prologue by the Brazilian poet Manuel Bandeira; original artwork by the Uruguayan painter Carlos Paéz Vilaró; and a lead poem by Juana de Ibarbourou, also from Uruguay. The volumes challenge the Anglophone reader (only US and Canadian entries appear in English). Carvalho's familiarity with languages and hemispheric cultural agents makes one thing clear: Literature of the Americas is a lifelong journey, one pursued ideally from the larger standpoint of Spanish and Lusophone-based Latin American Studies.

Within the United States, one notable essay coincides with Sánchez's *Nueva historia*. Written by a Canadian-born comparatist and published in the US-based journal *Hispania*, George W. Umphrey's 13-page article "Spanish American Literature Compared with That of the United States" offers a crash course in literature of the Americas from colonial to contemporary times based upon "a notable similarity in the main trends of the literatures of the New World" (1943, p. 21). Given the emerging field's home within Latin American Studies, it is fitting that *Hispania* was the flagship journal of the American Association of Teachers of Spanish and Portuguese, and that its author was a professor of Spanish in the United States. Four years later, readers would gain unprecedented access to US and Latin American literature in one volume.

Guy A. Cardwell's *Readings from the Americas: An Introduction to Democratic Thought* (1947) is the first Literature of the Americas anthology, one designed for college students. The book takes a novel (and user-friendly) approach to sharing primary texts across borders – translation. Cardwell, an English professor at the University of Maryland, continues Sánchez's comparatist periodization from colonial times to the present. As the book's subtitle indicates, however, he shares the primary concern of American Studies as the discipline took shape after World War II: US democracy. As was the case with F.O.

Matthiessen and other academic flagbearers, a national ethos guides the book and its selections. Still, reprinted translations placed side-by-side provide Anglophone readers with a mini canon of Latin American authors and historical figures, such as Andrés Bello and César Vallejo, vis-à-vis writings by Thomas Jefferson and Emily Dickinson. Cardwell wants this archive to "constitute material easily adaptable for classes in American civilization where the emphasis is upon our literary, social, and political heritage" (1947, p. iii). The comparative "inclusion of Latin-American selections" intends to highlight unseen democratic ties, but also to "combat tendencies toward nativism, racism, or unqualified nationalism" (p. iv). While Cardwell is an inter-Americanist pioneer, *Readings from the Americas* also marks the beginning of the Americanization of Literature of the Americas.

Indeed, a new model of hemispheric inquiry was emerging at the dawn of American Studies, and with the aim of disrupting Cold War nationalism and challenging US imperialism. The biggest contribution is by Yale Sterling Professor Stanley T. Williams, who co-taught the first course in American Studies on record, "American Thought and Civilization." Williams's *The Spanish Background of American Literature* (2 volumes, 1955) is Hemispheric Studies avant la lettre. It is a revolutionary study of Hispanic contexts and sources for nineteenth-century US letters. The first volume is a history of public and private archives available to the nation's authors, all of which created, to quote from one chapter heading, a "widening consciousness of Spanish culture" (1955, vol. 1, p. 21). Travel writing, periodicals, paintings, translations, and scholarly books make up most of this repository. In the second volume, Wiliams includes biographical sketches of eight giants of national literature "eager to plunder for the young Republic the cultural riches of Spain" (vol. 1., p. xx). The select few were dedicated Hispanists despite the persistence of a "Black Legend" that had turned Spain and its colonies into a Latin foil (Catholic, inquisitorial, etc.) to Anglo-Protestant prosperity. In Williams's progressive narrative, Washington Irving, William Cullen Bryant, Henry Wadsworth Longfellow, and others comprise a literary canon with a US multicultural bent. *The Spanish Background of American Literature* thus forms a Hispanist alternative to Matthiessen's *American Renaissance: Art and Expression in the Age of Emerson and Whitman* (1941). Williams's emphasis on the contributions of Hispanic peoples to the cultural development of the United States challenged longstanding stereotypical views of Spain and its former colonies. At the same time, these efforts steered Literature of the Americas back toward one national literature looking in on itself. Instead of an archive of texts in multiple languages and representing several traditions (and inside which Spain's value is plain to see) Literature of the Americas would lend a "hemispheric" political inflection to American Studies.

These hemispheric enterprises were decades ahead of their time; they now constitute a prehistory of Literature of the Americas. Nonetheless, Sánchez and Williams are the two pillars of the discipline as it has evolved. Scholars today generally split their allegiance between the trails they blazed. Those trained in Comparative Literature and Latin American Studies tend to follow Sánchez's member-nations approach to literature; English and American Studies partisans are more likely to heed Williams's contextual decoding of US culture. The modern discipline begins in 1982, when US-based scholars found collective expression at the tenth congress of the International Comparative Literature Association (ICLA). Held at New York University, the ICLA conference headlined a colloquium on "Inter-American Literary Relations." It featured a keynote address by the Mexican author Carlos Fuentes. The papers in the published conference proceedings – many of them written by inter-Americanists who came to prominence in the 1980s and 1990s – highlight New World traditions placed in two- and three-way literary dialogue. All of the contributors approached "America" as a multilingual and international object of study. American Literature was, during this era, a comparative literature of the Western Hemisphere.

This ethos would guide publications that bolstered the movement. Appearing in 1982 and 1986, respectively, were A. Owen Aldridge's *Early American Literature: A Comparatist Approach* (the first such monograph), and Bell Gale Chevigny and Gari Laguardia's *Reinventing the Americas: Comparative Studies of Literature of the United States and Spanish America* (the first such edited collection). As can be seen by their titles alone, during this first wave, US Literature existed within a framework pertaining to Bolton's "Greater America." Another comparatist pursuit was the two- and three-author study connecting the Americas, such as José Ballón's *Autonomía cultural americana: Emerson y Martí* (1986) and Vera M. Kutzinski's *Against the American Grain: Myth and History in William Carlos Williams, Jay Wright, and Nicolás Guillén* (1987). Lois Parkinson Zamora's first book, *Writing the Apocalypse: Historical Revision in Contemporary U.S. and Latin American Fiction* (1989) closed out the 1980s by tracing the eschatological drive of six canonical New World authors, including Gabriel García Márquez, John Barth, and Thomas Pynchon. For comparatist and Latin Americanist scholars entering the field at this time, the juxtaposition of national literatures was essential. Close readings in original languages was a gateway to accessing differences in political histories, but also religion, culture, and other intangible facets of life across time and place in the Americas.

Several publications carried inter-Americanism into the 1990s. Gustavo Pérez Firmat's *Do the Americas Have a Common Literature?* (1990) served as a methodological guidebook for the first wave. An edited collection of essays, it placed the problematic of the field at the titular forefront. Pérez Firmat addressed his own query by advancing different ways to read literature of the Americas, including intertextuality, parallel development, and pan-American topicality. Earl E. Fitz's *Rediscovering the New World: Inter-American Literature in a Comparative Context* (1991) applies such theories to identify themes specific to New World consciousness. José David Saldívar's *The Dialectics of Our America: Genealogy, Cultural Critique, and Literary History* (1991), Zamora's *The Usable Past: The Imagination of History in Recent Fiction of the Americas* (1997), and Santiago Juan-Navarro's *Archival Reflections: Postmodern Fiction of the Americas (Self-Reflexivity, Historical Revisionism, Utopia)* (2000) considered the impact of historical thinking in literary production. I trace the end of this first wave of Literature of the Americas to three books concerned with race: Doris Sommer's *Proceed with Caution, When Engaged by Minority Writing in the Americas* (1999), Deborah Cohn's *History and Memory in the Two Souths: Recent Southern and Spanish American Fiction* (1999), and George Handley's *Postslavery Literature in the Americas: Family Portraits in Black and White* (2000). While providing a fitting end to an era keen on gathering voices from outside the United States, the international gains would yield to the scope and influence of English and American Studies departments, whose scholars were just then undertaking a "hemispheric turn" of their own.

The second wave of Literature of the Americas (as "Hemispheric Studies") begins with Janice Radway's 1998 presidential address to the American Studies Association

(ASA). Here, the sitting ASA president considered renaming the organization the "Inter-American Studies Association" so that "America" no longer defaults to the United States. Still, the conference, which took place in Seattle under the heading "American Studies and the Question of Empire: Histories, Cultures and Practices," was a nation-based affair. As indicated by the title, "Empire" (not the Western Hemisphere) and "Cultures" (not literatures) were of paramount importance to Americanists at the turn of the century. This politicized and self-critical orientation attests to the influence of Amy Kaplan and Donald E. Pease's *Cultures of United States Imperialism* (1991), particularly its focus on race, gender, and ethnicity. Through essays by major scholars, the anthology consolidated the concern with culture and power from 1980s postcolonial studies, identity politics, and debates about the Western canon. The point for Americanists was to fight US nationalism through a multiculturalist agenda, and to recognize that American economic exploitation around the world was a factor in the formations and evaluation of national literature.

As advocated by Pease and John Carlos Rowe, respectively, "New American Studies" and "Post-National American Studies" would find their hemispheric correlative in Caroline F. Levander and Robert S. Levine's *Hemispheric American Studies* (2008). The collection is the upshot of research that first appeared in a 2006 special issue of the journal *American Literary History*, in which the editors attempted "a reconsideration of US literary and cultural histories in the larger territorial (and discursive) frame of the 'American' hemisphere" (2006, p. 397). *Hemispheric American Studies* offers fresh insight into how the United States, Latin America, and even Canada conjoin through neocolonial relations. This work formed part of a new reorientation of American Studies from a Eurocentric transatlantic perspective to a North-South trajectory across US national borders. While the roots are in Williams's *The Spanish Background of American Literature*, the political emphasis on US-Hispanic borderlands brought together Latino, ethnic, Indigenous, race, gender, and other subfields of American Studies in operation since the 1970s. As such, Hemispheric Studies forms a multi-front demystification of literature and its covert support for the imperialist status quo. A favored approach is the tracing of US hemispheric imaginaries and their geopolitical bases, as is the identification (and implicit celebration of) authorial interventions from the nation's margins. The colonial Americas, however, is one area in which *Hemispheric American Studies* pursues comparatist work closer to the first wave (as evidenced by Ralph Bauer and Anna Brickhouse). Rather than a literature-centered survey, *Hemispheric American Studies* proposes a new cultural studies-based orientation to the reading of documents (fiction, history, comics, maps, etc.) as informed by what Rita Felski calls "the hermeneutics of suspicion." Over the past twenty years, the most recognizable form of Literature of the Americas has been this one. Panoramas recede before targeted examinations of minority cultures and, most especially, US investment in the Americas. A babel of languages and literatures finds a lingua franca in scholarship meant to disturb US privilege from within.

With Literature of the Americas intersecting so many scholarly fields, the discipline exists in a state of continual crisis and autocritique. Already in the 1980s and 1990s, books blasted US imperialism in the academy, as American Studies departments encroached upon the turf (and limited university resources) of Latin American Studies. More recently, Comparative Literature has ceded ground to English and American Studies. The latter access international literatures in translation, particularly in the classroom.

In conjunction, they deploy theoretical frameworks that were once the domain of Comparative Literature as it sought a common ground for discussing numerous European literatures. Departments of English and American Studies have also fared better when it comes to adapting discourses of identity politics and "diversity, equity, and inclusion" that have become staples of the neoliberal university. French Canadian and Caribbean Studies programs are also imperiled, as the academic lingua franca is now English. Given the consumer model of university operations, nation-based studies of historically marginalized peoples tend to substitute for (rather than coexist with) courses on non-US languages and literatures, including from Latin America. As the latter transforms into an undefined variant of the former, the non-Anglo majority of the Western Hemisphere becomes a "minority" or "marginal" part of the one nation in charge. This is troubling, particularly given the place of Latin America in the historical span of the Americas, and the Hispanic origins of the discipline that US "hemisphericists" would now claim to profess. In an essay titled "Inter-American Studies or Imperial American Studies?" (2005), Sophia A. McClennen lambasts Radway's ASA address, and traces its implications for Hemispheric Studies from her vantage point as a Latin Americanist and Comparative Literature scholar. She claims the speech advances lines of thinking that "represent themselves as post-national, but which ultimately have no cultural referents beyond the borders of the United States, and consequently are not post-national in any meaningful way" (2005, p. 402).

There is also a less controversial dimension to Literature of the Americas: classroom pedagogy. Bolton, the founder of hemispheric American history, taught the popular course "History 8" at UC Berkeley. In his textbook *History of the Americas: A Syllabus with Maps*, he calls the offering "a general survey of the history of the Western Hemisphere from the discovery to the present time" (1928, p. iv). Forays into Literature of the Americas during the 1980s and 1990s likewise tackled teaching, acknowledging that testing inside the classroom guaranteed the field's validity and impact. In sum, how does one get students to rethink American Literature in line with some version of Literature of the Americas? Earl E. Fitz, a professor of Portuguese, Spanish, and Comparative Literature at Vanderbilt University, has asked this question with the most vigor and steadfastness. Since designing the nation's inaugural courses in Literature of the Americas at Penn State University in 1979, Fitz has been a program builder and custodian of the discipline. Because answers to pedagogical questions carry political weight, the consideration of teaching falls heavily upon such scholars of the Americas. Classroom instruction helps establish allocation of university resources, defines new professorships, and guides the future of the conversation. The commitment to pedagogical reflection is evident in, most recently, *Teaching and Studying the Americas: Cultural Influences from Colonialism to the Present* (2010), a volume edited by Anthony B. Pinn, Caroline F. Levander, and Michael O. Emerson. A care for pedagogy to keep the field intact and politically relevant continues to mark the discipline. The research on teaching sometimes follows an intellectual history approach by considering the provenance of library collections and other official and unofficial networks of inter-American scholarly exchange. It can also turn to class methodologies and/or program building, including the fine points of taking graduate and/or undergraduate students through a semester's syllabus.

With its myriad outlooks, and a history featuring as many bridges as walls, how might Literature of the Americas transform the study of "contemporary American fiction"? While my answer is to combine the two approaches, the existing tensions require careful parsing. Both Literature of the Americas and Hemispheric Studies can be umbrellas for multiple subfields. Hemispheric Studies serves as a landing spot for Latino Studies and its historical pursuit of social justice, with Chicano Studies being a strong subwing. This Latino/Literature of the Americas fusion brings race, gender, class, and ethnicity to American fiction within post-1980 contexts of trans-hemispheric migrations, and accommodation to US labor and other dominant patterns of life. It also addresses history that has come to define US-Hispanic relations and Latino borderlands, such as the Monroe Doctrine (1823), the Treaty of Guadalupe Hidalgo (1848), the Platt Amendment (1903), the Panama Canal (1903–1914), and the Good Neighbor Policy (1933). This type of scholarship recalls Williams's *The Spanish Background of American Literature*, but it places marginalized voices at the center of cultural history. The point here is to show how underrepresented Latinos have helped define the nation. Contemporary Chicana authors Sandra Cisneros and Gloria Anzaldúa, and Dominican-American writer Junot Díaz, fit this mold. Their personal narratives possess a hemispheric outlook within contemporary US globalization. Their injection of Spanish idioms into Anglophone US literature helps preserve Hispanic voices inside a monolingual canon. One way to amplify this approach beyond the nation, however, is by considering history's effects elsewhere. For example, the War of the Pacific (1879–1884) remapped South American borders, and carried cultural implications for Peru and Chile. In addition, reading Spanish-language authors, such as the Mexican Yuri Herrera, adds inter-American vistas. His celebrated book *Señales que precederán al fin del mundo* (2009) [*Signs Preceding the End of the World*, translated in 2015] liberates the US–Mexico border from its positioning in academia. Border Studies need not default to one side.

Any discussion of inclusiveness will inevitably lead us to consider the missing pieces. From a historical standpoint, the most important contact zones in the Americas were places where European agents (Spanish, French, Portuguese, Dutch, and English) battled for material wealth and prestige. Here, too, Indigenous nations served as resistance fighters, functioned as translators, and fell victim to violence. As native peoples succumbed to smallpox during the sixteenth century, the colonial system brought African slaves to the New World via transatlantic trade networks. All forms of hemispheric study tends to emphasize these three groups, as their interactions create the early Americas, and subsequent formations of racial and cultural mixture (from mestizo colonial architecture to Afro-Cuban jazz). This orientation distinguishes the bulk of Hemispheric Studies from multicultural American Literature. Whether in the US variant, or as Literature of the Americas, the hemisphere is still the lynchpin. This is not to decree that one cannot undertake an ethnic studies approach to the literature of the Americas by studying, for example, the Asian diaspora in the New World (not just in San Francisco, but also in São Paulo).

Literature of the Americas can also pursue Black consciousness across nations with a deep African presence. Juxtapositions of classic slave narratives by Frederick Douglass or Harriet Tubman with those of the Cuban Juan Manzano or the Bermuda-born Mary Prince uncovers an inter-American picture that shaped national literatures. Later, the United States and the Caribbean share a line of cultural transmission in the Harlem Renaissance and Martinique's *négritude* movement. Placed in interconnection, such pan-Africanist vanguards respond to the hemispheric experience of Black Americans, beyond language and national affiliation. In the context of contemporary American fiction, one may read Toni Morrison's *Beloved* (1987) in light of slavery in Latin America. Morrison, who consulted Brazilian slave records while writing her masterpiece, fuses North and South American experiences that tend to detangle in African American Studies readings. Furthermore, slavery has been at the core of South America since its national literary beginnings. Thus, we might turn to Manuel Zapata Olivella's novel *Changó, el gran putas* (1983) [*Chango, the Biggest Bad Ass*, translated in 2010], which traces historical Blackness beyond North America. Written by an Afro Colombian, this encyclopedic narrative traverses Brazil, the Caribbean, and New England while reflecting histories of African ancestry, the Black diaspora, and centuries of rebellion. It is a gateway novel for the hemispheric study of African-based literatures of the Americas. It challenges European impositions of language and nations in the Americas, yet also reflects the distinctions that exist within specific communities.

Leslie Marmon Silko's *Almanac of the Dead* (1991) is another gateway text, this time challenging American Literature via Hemispheric Indigenous Studies. Written in contestation to the Columbian quincentenary, *Almanac of the Dead* returns to pan-Indigenous text and visual traditions (including the Maya codices) in a weave of intersecting stories that denounce past injustices and prophesy a hemispheric revolution. The oral, pictographic, and literary range of the Laguna Pueblo author is the culmination of cosmopolitan and Indigenous ways of knowing inside American Literature. Silko is a key member of Kenneth Lincoln's "Native American Renaissance," but she is likewise a hemispheric cultural agent who blends the epistemologies of Native American, Latino, Latin American, and Border Studies. Her novel's recruitment of Latinos into a united front (with the US Southwest as a hemispheric nucleus, a collective *Aztlán*) celebrates the legacy of indigeneity beyond settler nations, and from the Arctic Pole to the Tierra del Fuego. For Silko, Latin American literature is an Indigenous archive by another name, even when comprised of mestizo authors from Spanish-speaking countries. Furthermore, one can read Silko alongside contemporary Latin American writers, among them Carlos Fuentes, whose mega-novel *Terra Nostra* (1975) is a Neo-baroque fusion of European and Indigenous life to restage the birth of Latin America. Given their panoramic display, historical consciousness, and hybridity, *Terra Nostra* and *Almanac of the Dead* are hemispheric novels, par excellence.

One final approach to Literature of the Americas traces the hemispheric imaginaries of established writers within uneven geopolitical contexts. While the authors may or may not have traveled beyond their respective nations, they still help to construct the hemispheric "other" for readers at home. Such an analysis, based largely upon biography and ideology, also stems from Williams's *The Spanish Background of American Literature*. A reading list includes William H. Prescott's histories of the Spanish "Conquista" in Latin America, short fiction and translations of Mexican literature by Katherine Anne Porter, and even "Great American Novels" of hemispheric cultural provenance, such as Herman Melville's *Moby-Dick* (1851) and Jack Kerouac's *On the Road* (1957). In short, how do canonical US authors expand in meaning given their own imaginative investment beyond an Anglophone tradition? Jacques Poulin's *Volkswagen Blues* (1984) provides a contemporary example from outside the United States. A Quebecois novel about the history of North America and the long span of Indigenous and French Canadian relations, the work reflects the evolution of Quebec under globalization. At the same time, *Volkswagen Blues* is concerned with deeper roots for such migrations, across hemispheric borders and via archives that its characters peruse on a trip to San Francisco. It is another gateway novel, intersecting various times and nations. It creates an ideal multi-layered terrain for encountering, reflecting upon, and studying cultural and historical differences in the world. Most importantly, "master" fictions like those above place literature within an inter-American continuum that calls for more close reading. They provide access to an intertextual chain of texts of the Western Hemisphere.

From the beginning, Literature of the Americas has advanced a maximalist and survey-based approach to learning across traditions. What Literature of the Americas has lost in scope and comparatist vision over the past twenty years, it has gained in precision, and in a political enthusiasm fueled by US scholars. As Literature of the Americas evolves at a time of global nationalist resurgence, this evolution calls for a thoughtful navigation between its outward and inward trajectories. They are both important. Still, less navel-gazing and more inter-American knowledge production may help correct the near-sightedness that threatens the discipline in the 2020s. I contend that Literature of the Americas must encompass the anti-nationalist critiques of US-based Hemispheric Studies. For full pedagogical impact, however, it must avoid a status quo distancing from literature that, today, preserves US academic privilege. Instead, Literature of the Americas must remain worldly, forever in pursuit of linguistic expression in the face of political expediencies, including those of cultural studies-based ideological critiques. Through ignorance and divisive rhetoric, the contemporary era has resurrected old stereotypes. It has minimized the Western Hemisphere. Fortunately, for Literature of the Americas, bigger is always better.

SEE ALSO: Black Atlantic; Border Fictions; The Culture Wars; Globalization; Indigenous Narratives; Periodization; Silko, Leslie Marmon

REFERENCES

Bolton, Herbert Eugene. (1928). *History of the Americas: A Syllabus with Maps*. Boston: Ginn.

Bolton, Herbert Eugene. (1933). The epic of Greater America. *The American Historical Review* 38 (3): 448–474.

Cardwell, Guy A. (1947). *Readings from the Americas: An Introduction to Democratic Thought*. New York: The Ronald Press Company.

Levander, Caroline F. and Levine, Robert S. (2006). Introduction: hemispheric American literary history. *American Literary History* 18 (3): 397–405.

McClennen, Sophia. (2005). Inter-American studies or imperial American studies? *Comparative American Studies: An International Journal* 3 (4): 393–413.

Umphrey, George W. (1943). Spanish American literature compared with that of the United States. *Hispania* 26 (1): 21–34.

Williams, Stanley T. (1955). *The Spanish Background of American Literature*. 2 vols. New Haven, CT: Yale University Press.

FURTHER READING

Bauer, Ralph. (2009). Hemispheric studies. *PMLA* 124 (1): 234–250.

Fox, Claire F. (ed.) (2005). Critical perspectives and emerging models of inter-American studies. Special issue of *Comparative American Studies* 3 (4).

Kutzinski, Vera M. (2012). Afterword: America/*América*/Americas. In: *The Worlds of Langston Hughes: Modernism and Translation in the Americas*, 221–240. Ithaca, NY: Cornell University Press.

Rausert, Wilfried. (ed.) (2017). *The Routledge Companion to Inter-American Studies*. New York: Routledge.

Zamora, Lois Parkinson and Spitta, Silvia. (eds.) (2009). The Americas, otherwise. Special issue of *Comparative Literature* 61 (3).

M

Mailer, Norman

JAMES EMMETT RYAN
Auburn University, USA

Norman Mailer's fiction after 1980 followed decades of a writing career positioned at conceptual boundaries between history, fiction, journalism, and autobiography. By 1980, his experimentation with "fiction" as a literary genre was uniquely complicated by Mailer's political activities, public celebrity, and personal appearance within a number of his notable earlier books of journalism, especially those that negotiated boundaries between fiction and nonfiction, such as *Miami and the Siege of Chicago* (1968), *The Armies of the Night: History as a Novel/The Novel as History* (1968), and *Of a Fire on the Moon* (1970). Mailer's public statements about fiction during the decades before 1980 likewise illustrate his ambivalence about his aims and aspirations for literary fiction as such. For example, in a preface to his novel *Why Are We in Vietnam?* (1967), Mailer reflected that "Sometimes, I think the novelist fashions a totem as much as an aesthetic, and his real aim, not even known necessarily to himself, is to create a diversion in the fields of dread, a sanctuary in some of the arenas of magic. The flaws of his work can even be a part of his magical strength, as if his real intent in writing is to alter the determinations of that invisible finger which has written and moved on. By such logic, the book before you is a totem, not empty of amulets for the author against curses, static, and the pervasive malignity of our electronic air" (2018, p. 872). *Why Are We in Vietnam?* marked the beginning of a hiatus in Mailer's work as a novelist, even as his fame grew throughout the 1970s as an essayist, journalist, and political figure.

Mailer's later 1970s return to the novel brought him widespread acclaim and a Pulitzer Prize for Fiction with the publication of *The Executioner's Song* (1979), a lengthy, factual "true life novel" (as the book was marketed) closely based on the life of convicted murder Gary Gilmore. Interviews by Mailer with Gilmore, his family members, and acquaintances were crucial in developing a fictionalized but thoroughly researched and journalistic treatment of Gilmore's life. And while *The Executioner's Song* was specifically advertised as a "novel" and received literary awards as fiction, its content was almost entirely a work of investigative journalism focusing on Gilmore, the first man to be executed after the 1976 American reintroduction of the death penalty for capital crimes.

Between 1968 and 1983, Mailer ascended the heights of cultural celebrity while publishing

---

The Encyclopedia of Contemporary American Fiction 1980–2020, First Edition. Edited by Patrick O'Donnell, Stephen J. Burn, and Lesley Larkin.
© 2022 John Wiley & Sons Ltd. Published 2022 by John Wiley & Sons Ltd.

twenty books, but none of them novels, with only a partial exception in *The Executioner's Song* (his "true life novel") and *Of Women and Their Elegance* (1980), a book sometimes described as a fictional autobiography of its central figure, Marilyn Monroe. *Of Women* presents photography featuring primarily women subjects – specifically the work of notable New York fashion photographer Milton Greene (1922–1985), a close friend and business partner of Marilyn Monroe. Greene's photographs of Marilyn Monroe (1926–1962) are prominent in the book, which was lavishly produced as a quarto-sized art volume on fine paper with excellent photo reproduction in a range of sizes from postage-stamp images to full-page renderings. *Of Women* also includes photographs previously published in notable mass-market periodicals such as *Esquire, Glamour, Harper's Bazaar, Life, The Saturday Evening Post,* and *Town & Country*. These images go beyond the stated subject of "women" to include male celebrities and artists such as Laurence Olivier, Marlon Brando, Omar Sharif, Richard Avedon, Jimmy Durante, Dizzy Gillespie, and others. In addition to Marilyn, whose imagined interior voice sets out the theme of women's "elegance," the book also features images of iconic female celebrities including as Judy Garland, Candice Bergen, Jane Fonda, Sophia Loren, Diahann Carroll, Ava Gardner, and Marlene Dietrich. More than a typical photography book, *Of Women* includes a lengthy essay that avoids discussion of specific photographs of Marilyn Monroe and the other celebrities featured in Milton Greene fashion images. Instead, Mailer delves imaginatively into the mental, moral, and sexual world of the mid-twentieth century's most glamorous woman, following a line of fictional thought that imagines Monroe's views about marriage, celebrity, and femininity. More darkly, Mailer suggests that the varieties of Monroe's exploitation at the hands of various men, never fully to be known by the public, hinted at "some unquenchable horror, some incubus that lay over all later success" (1980, p. 285).

Mailer stipulates in an introductory note to *Of Women* that "The book, while based on episodes in Marilyn Monroe's life, and on the reminiscences of Amy and Milton Greene, does not pretend to offer factual representations and in no way wishes to suggest that these are the actual thoughts of Miss Monroe or of anyone else who appears in these pages" (1980, n.p.). Mailer does open *Of Women* with a brief excerpt from a Marilyn Monroe interview with *Life* magazine, published only a day before her death and touching memorably on her experience of celebrity and glamor. Otherwise, the text included in *Of Women* draws on Mailer's imagined interior dialogue: a sort of fictional diary of the iconic and surpassingly photogenic star.

Mailer's attitude toward literary fiction during these years is partially captured in a 1979 interview comment that "I'm not sure the Great American Novel can be done anymore. Everything's gotten so complicated, and you have to know so much by now. I think John Dos Passos came as close as anyone with *U.S.A.*" (quoted in Lennon 2006, p. 94). Still, as *The Executioner's Song* was being published to great acclaim as a highly realistic work. Mailer attested in another interview that he wanted that book "to read like a novel, to feel like a novel, to smell like a novel" (quoted in Lennon 2006, p. 96). Writing in the author's note that concluded *Of Women*, Mailer inconclusively addressed the question of fictionality: "My last book, *The Executioner's Song* [1979] which to many seemed a work of nonfiction, was called fiction by me. . . . Now, I face the problem of what to call this book with its splendid photographs. I am frankly at a loss. . . . Perhaps we may call this an imaginary memoir, an as-told-to-book, a set of interviews that never took place between Marilyn Monroe and Norman Mailer" (1980, pp. 284–285).

The long-awaited *Ancient Evenings* (1983) is a bloated, poorly organized magical-historical novel focused on four reincarnated lives narrated by a voluble twelfth-century CE protagonist named Menenhetet. Written over a ten-year period (1972–1982), *Ancient Evenings* defies easy summary but basically is a frame narrative that unfolds from the perspective of a boy called Meni, a descendant of Menenhetet who serves as audience for his great grandfather's nightly recounting of sexual and military adventures among the Egyptian elite and pharaohs. Menenhetet, uninhibited and frank about the experiences of his remembered four lives, becomes the central voice of the novel, although he is less memorable for his personality or the clear direction of those ancient lives than for the recurrent themes that he emphasizes.

As with Mailer's *The Naked and the Dead* (1948), *Ancient Evenings* conveys epic battles and the brutality of warfare in memorable terms. The mythical dimensions of the novel are enhanced by Mailer's occasional use of characters who are gifted with clairvoyant and telepathic mental powers, which have the effect of blurring boundaries between individuals and coherent human identities or memories. However, *Ancient Evenings* frustrates because of its diffuse narrative lines, scores of characters, and undisciplined plot. In spite of these shortcomings, though, Mailer manages to render a work of complex imagination notable for its crudely sexual vignettes and flat characterization, but wed to a picaresque quality reminiscent of Petronius's *Satyricon* and occasionally redeemed by the kind of narrative power familiar from epic works such as *Gilgamesh* or the *Iliad*. The freewheeling behavior of gods and goddesses is in turn emulated by Menenhetet's social world, in which earthily violent and freewheeling sexuality, luxurious court amenities, and a backdrop of tribal warfare are relayed from overlapping family memories.

Ancient Evenings is notable for its representation of ancient sexuality in extravagant terms. Sexual aggression and sexual fluidity, recalled over several generations, mark *Ancient Evenings* in a powerful and sometimes pornographic way. Mailer provides a view in *Ancient Evenings* of coercive sexual power – especially homosexual and incestuous sexual modes – that emulates but also goes well beyond frankly sexual literary precursors such as *Satyricon* or the *Iliad*. Egyptian court and family life according to *Ancient Evenings* was profoundly queer, relentlessly bisexual, frequently incestuous, and occasionally reverts to bestiality or cannibalism. The Egyptian youth Meni listens as Menenhetet details his many lives of sexual adventure, noting that his story began in humble peasant circumstances and yet led to a privileged and decadent life in the Egyptian court. Out of the murky and unrecorded history of ancient Egyptian lives, Menenhetet in his final life – at age 60 the same age as Norman Mailer – becomes a profound and unapologetic voice of recollection and storytelling, or as he remarks very late in the novel: "The memory of my first three lives hovered in my mind like three ghosts standing before my door" (1983, p. 680). Like *Ancient Evenings* taken as a whole, the novel's voluble storyteller is a voice spoken across generations and shaped profoundly by overlapping frames of sexual identity and sexual power. Interviewed years after the novel's publication, Mailer admitted that *Ancient Evenings*, which he deemed his most ambitious book, was perhaps only partly successful.

Tough Guys Don't Dance (1984) appeared soon after the critical and commercial disaster of *Ancient Evenings*, notable for its ancient historical perspective and avoidance of contemporary political and social culture. A shorter novel of more typical scale and conventional (crime novel) genre status, *Tough Guys* returns Mailer to social commentary and fictional examination of criminality, the upper class drug trade, and popular culture, with the interesting twist that Mailer's summer home community of Provincetown, Massachusetts, is used for its setting. Mailer has asserted in various interviews that he wrote *Tough Guys* strictly for financial reasons and pressures from his publisher, but in fact its taut construction, focused presentation, and sensitivity to late-twentieth century American life make it one of the most successful and popular of his later novels. That popularity is reflected in the commercial funding provided for Mailer to write and direct a 1987 comedy-drama film adaptation of *Tough Guys Don't Dance* that featured leading Hollywood actors Ryan O'Neil and Isabella Rossellini in the starring roles.

Mailer returned to the epic scale of *Ancient Evenings* with his gargantuan *Harlot's Ghost* (1991), a novel based on the American security state, exemplified by the CIA's birth in the years after the World War II. *Harlot's Ghost*, Mailer's most important post-1980 novel, blends fictional characters with real historical figures, a method probably influenced by best-selling novels by E.L. Doctorow, such as *The Book of Daniel* (1971) and *Ragtime* (1975), both of which drew on techniques of docudrama to illuminate aspects of twentieth-century American history. Political leaders such as John Kennedy, Fidel Castro, Allen Dulles, and J. Edgar Hoover, among many others, make cameo appearances in *Harlot's Ghost*, while Mailer's invented characters recount and inhabit an imaginative history of the CIA's formation, including its ideological and social quirks.

Born as a secretive agency in the years just after World War II, the CIA was at first staffed mainly by socially elite men recruited from the Ivy League, and so *Harlot's Ghost* unfolds to reflect the CIA's early demographics and sensibilities. The social and intellectual firepower of its main characters make the narrative compelling as a culturally apt portrait of the agency's early leaders, especially in the case of CIA agent Harry Hubbard, who has taken more than a year to write a memoir of the CIA that is presented in the novel as a frame narrative, but one preserved on microfilm and recounted at great length in *Harlot's Ghost* while Hubbard is on assignment at a Moscow hotel. The product of Mailer's considerable research into the agency's founders, *Harlot's Ghost* represents the CIA's earliest leaders as having a substantial education in contemporary literature, art, and philosophy. Like his protagonists, Ivy League-educated and comfortable at intellectual exchange at rarified levels, Mailer puts his spy characters into conversation about high culture (especially male producers of high culture) at numerous junctures in the novel. The book is filled with references to famous literary figures such as William Faulker, Dashiell Hammett, Henry Miller, Ernest Hemingway, Herman Melville, Henry James, Marcel Proust, and James Joyce, among many others. *Harlot's Ghost* unfolds not only in the blue-blood enclaves of New England, New York, and the far reaches of espionage secrecy in Washington DC, but also in South America and Berlin, Germany, where its key spy characters navigate the murky world of ex-Nazi spies and conduct secretive regime-change projects on behalf of the CIA. In keeping with Mailer's view of history as powerfully shaped by sexual mores, Berlin figures not only as the epicenter of Cold War espionage, but – as in *Ancient Evenings* – also as a theater for unfolding scenes rife with an atmosphere of sexual adventurism and S/M homosexual subcultures undergirding twentieth-century politics and culture.

Mailer's self-consciousness about Jewish identity is essential in many of his works, but perhaps never more ironically so than in *The*

Gospel According to the Son (1997) in which he recreates the fictional world of the biblical Jesus. This attempt at rehearsing the four books of the New Testament – all from the point of view of Christ himself – again features the later Mailer working to inhabit the consciousness of an important historical figure, in novels that have alternately featuring celebrities of transcendently great or profoundly criminal accomplishment. Whereas in other works of fiction or journalism he attempted to do so with Muhammad Ali (*The Fight* [1995]), Marilyn Monroe (*Marilyn* [1973]) Lee Harvey Oswald (*Oswald's Tale* [1995]), and Gary Gilmore (*The Executioner's Song*), in *The Gospel According to the Son* he takes on perhaps his greatest test of sympathetic religious imagination in one of his shorter post-1980 novels.

The last published novel by Mailer, *The Castle in the Forest* (2007) revisits the World War II subject matter of his best-selling first novel, *The Naked and the Dead*. Unlike the earlier wartime novel by Mailer, *The Castle in the Forest* confronts instead an important example of a historically momentous individual – Adolf Hitler – tragically divided between humanity and sheer, demonic evil. Rather than following the life of soldiers in an ordinary combat platoon as in his pathbreaking earlier novel, however, Mailer focuses instead on an imagined history of the Nazi dictator's childhood. Structuring the story is a narrative centered around the recollections of a fictional character named Dieter, a demonic German man who outlines the influences (including possible incest) that shape Hitler into a grotesquely evil human being. Sharing experimental narrative techniques developed in *Ancient Evenings*, which explored the overlapping memories, intersecting consciousness, moral compass, and sexual legacy of reincarnated family members in ancient Egypt, *The Castle in the Forest* confronts similar themes in a twentieth-century historical context. But it does so as a way of highlighting Adolf Hitler as a prototypically immoral Nazi committed to totalitarian racial supremacy and murderous ethnic cleansing. The narrator Dieter takes the form of a German SS officer who reports to Heinrich Himmler, who in turn helped lead the Nazi party and served as architect of the Holocaust, but who in this novel assigns Dieter the task of investigating Hitler's background for any signs of Jewish heritage. Only a Satanic colleague like Dieter, Mailer seems to suggest, could serve adequately to understand the autobiographical textures of the twentieth century's most notorious villain. Readers appeared to agree, as *The Castle in the Forest*, Mailer's final work of fiction and published in the last year of his life, became his eighth novel to be listed as a *New York Times* bestseller. As with most of his novels since 1980, this concluding work in his career as a creative writer is notable for its diminishing preoccupation with Mailer's own personal celebrity and its lessened reliance on the daringly experimental blend of New Journalism and "true life" techniques that characterized his books before 1980.

SEE ALSO: Contemporary Fictions of War; Doctorow, E.L.

REFERENCES

Lennon, J. Michael. (2006). Norman Mailer: novelist, journalist, or historian? *Journal of Modern Literature* 30 (1): 91–103.

Mailer, Norman. (1980). *Of Women and Their Elegance*. New York: Simon & Schuster.

Mailer, Norman. (1983). *Ancient Evenings*. New York: Little, Brown.

Mailer, Norman. (2018). Preface to *Why Are We in Vietnam? Four Books of the 1960s: An American Dream, Why Are We in Vietnam?, The Armies of *the Night, Miami and the Siege of Chicago.* New York: Library of America; 1st ed. 1967.

FURTHER READING

Lennon, J. Michael. (2013). *Norman Mailer: A Double Life*. New York: Simon & Schuster.
Mailer, Norman. (1979). *The Executioner's Song*. New York: Little, Brown.
Mailer, Norman. (2003). *The Spooky Art: Some Thoughts on Writing*. New York: Random House.
Mailer, Norman. (2015). *Selected Letters of Norman Mailer* (ed. J. Michael Lennon). New York: Random House.
Whalen-Bridge, John. (ed.) (2010). *Norman Mailer's Later Fictions: Ancient Evenings through Castle in the Forest*. New York: Springer.

Major, Clarence

KEITH BYERMAN
Indiana State University, USA

Clarence Major, African American novelist, short story writer, painter, poet, and essayist, is one of the country's most prolific artists. He has published eight novels, two books of short fiction, fourteen collections of poetry, four works of nonfiction, and a volume of his paintings.

He was born in Atlanta on December 31, 1936, and spent his early years in the nearby small town of Lexington, a cotton-farming community. Several members of his immediate and extended family were mixed race, including his mother. This reality has affected his writing as well as his personal life. His Black male protagonists are frequently in mixed-race relationships, and he tends to move between Black and white worlds.

Because of domestic conflict, his mother relocated to Chicago, where, because of her light skin color, she was able to get work in businesses usually restricted to white women. Eventually, she brought Clarence and his younger sister Serena to live with her on the city's south side. The neighborhood in which they lived was something of a Black artists' community, with Lil Armstrong, the former wife of Louis Armstrong, living nearby and Lionel Hampton staying in the boarding house where they lived when he was in town. He attended high school with Herbie Hancock, later a renowned jazz keyboardist.

This environment encouraged Major's own artistic efforts, though in different directions. From early school days he did drawings that earned him the attention of his teachers. In high school, he received a scholarship to attend drawing classes at the Art Institute of Chicago. He also took up poetry; at a young age, he got an uncle to print up fifty copies of his first poems. He also started reading serious literature while in school, including a number of French poets and novelists. This self-education prepared him to undertake more experimental and erotic material.

After graduating from high school, he did a tour of duty in the air force as a clerk. He spent much of the time reading philosophy, history, biography, and literature. He also began sending stories and poems to little magazines, an experience that served him well when he returned to Chicago and started his own magazine. In the mid-1960s, he moved to New York and lived in Greenwich Village. It was here that he wrote his first novel, *All-Night Visitors* (1969). It brought together three previous attempts, concerning Vietnam, Chicago, and New York. The unifying factor was the protagonist, a young Black man obsessed with his own sexuality. Major was unsuccessful in finding a mainstream publisher and turned in desperation to Olympia Press, which mainly focused on pornography. Conflicts over the sexual content of the story led the author to randomize the chapters, thus creating for him a reputation as an experimental novelist.

In his second novel, *NO* (1973), published by an African American company that specialized in social science texts, he developed the theme of incarceration. Unlike the work of some of his contemporaries, such as John Wideman and Ernest Gaines, Major uses the concept metaphorically rather than literally. The narrator, Moses Westby, is named after his father, who has a reputation for toughness and indifference to the suffering of others. The son feels trapped by racial hostilities, sexual demands and failures, toxic masculinity, and impositions by others on what his identity should be. He achieves his liberation, not through escape, but through constructing the narrative of his imprisonment. A number of elements form the context for this novel. Growing up in his neighborhood in Chicago, Major was expected to focus on making money and creating a middle-class life. His first marriage reinforced this sense of turning away from his ambitions as an artist to becoming a breadwinner. Even the publication of his first novel, with the demands of the publisher, was not truly liberation. By telling the story of the ways a young Black man can be restricted by society, Major opens the gates of his prison.

A key to his new possibilities was the affiliations he made in New York. One was Umbra, a group of young Black artists based on the Lower East Side whose goal was to bring together social activism with a commitment to aesthetics. The group included Ishmael Reed, Tom Dent, Calvin Hernton, and David Henderson; they held workshops and produced the literary magazine *Umbra*. More important for his career, he joined the Fiction Collective, a group of experimental writers who had become frustrated with what they considered to be the narrow-minded perspective of the mainstream publishing houses. They set up their own process of selecting, editing, printing, and advertising their own work. They were based primarily in New York, but some, including Major, took creative writing positions at the University of Colorado when that university decided to expand its program by emphasizing more radical approaches to fiction. While most of the writers remained little known, some, such as Russell Banks and Charles Johnson, went on to have successful careers, winning literary prizes and producing bestsellers.

For Major, the group became the community that he had never had. He published his next three novels through them. *Reflex and Bone Structure* (1975) deconstructs the detective narrative. The central female character is killed, not once, but multiple times, as the narrator, who also claims to be the author, keeps changing the circumstances of her death. As a character in the story, he also is a suspect in the murder. This mystery is also a metaphor for the creation of fiction. At various points, the text states that these characters are, after all, only words on a page. When the "author" puts down those words, these figures come to life; when he finishes writing, they cease to live. At best, they exist within the prison of narrative he has generated. In effect, then, every novel is a mystery, with the reader seeking to understand the motives, ambitions, and desires for this literary creation.

In *Emergency Exit* (1979), Major seeks to break free of the traps that fiction writing leads him into. He undertakes to make the novel into a life experience that the reader must try to make sense of, rather than a clearly artificial construct with clearly established conventions. At the same time, he knows that what he presents is done with words and not living things. To handle this conundrum, Major repeatedly draws attention to the verbal play that is fiction. Characters talk back to the narrator, who in this work is not part of the action. The Ingram family is said to be Black, but struggle to maintain a racial identity. They visit Africa, but do so in part so that Jim can carry on his work as a spy for the CIA. The text also incorporates a series of images, mostly paintings by Major, which may or may not have anything to do with the storyline. In one instance, there is a photograph of Major standing in a field of cows. These serve as nonverbal experiences for the reader, thereby subverting the expectations of engaging words.

The third Fiction Collective publication, *My Amputations* (1986), uses the device of stolen identity to explore the complexities and absurdities of race in America. Mason Ellis, who has the letters ME tattooed on his chest, reads the work of the author Clarence McKay while in Attica Prison and comes to believe that he is the real McKay. Once free, he searches for and kidnaps that author and takes over his life. He gives readings and lectures at various universities and goes on European tours. He both believes that he is McKay and fears that his identity theft will be exposed. But the play with identity goes beyond this theft. McKay's initials are, of course, those of Major himself; in addition, they are also those of the Harlem Renaissance poet Claude McKay. We are also told that Ellis was born in Georgia, moved with his mother to Chicago, tries to become a writer, and serves in the military. After his service, he returns to Chicago and has several children whom he abandons. This material is the same as Major's own early life. In addition, Ellis reads only at the universities and international locations where Major lectured. By matching details in this way, but then assigning them to a character who may be insane, he is free to satirize or criticize people who had been his colleagues without being seen as overtly attacking them.

After this final work for the Fiction Collective, Major largely turns away from the experimental mode that had defined his reputation. In part, this shift probably had to do with the fact that he made very little money from the early works. In fact, the authors of the Collective were expected to pay a substantial part of the costs of publication.

This change in narrative approach can be seen in a brief analysis of the openings of the two novels. *My Amputations* begins:

> Again, as in a recurring dream, Mason opened the closet door and stepped hesitantly into its huge darkness, its nonlineal shape: he pulled the door shut then crouched there on the floor – which seemed to be moving – with the breathing of The Imposter. This dimness was not illuminated by the glowing Mason felt. He could smell the man: his sweat, his urine, his oil. The skin of Mason's eyes was alive with floaters. Faintly in the background – perhaps coming through the wall from the next apartment – Sleepy John Estes was singing "Married Woman Blues." Mason pushed hard for *the* beginning, some echo or view. Anglosaxon monosyllables clustered there. He couldn't remember how it all started nor even his muse's birth. He called her Celt CuRoi.
>
> (Major 1986, p. 1)

The text continues in this manner for two and a half pages of fragmentary, surreal narrative. It is useful to keep in mind that Mason is in fact the imposter of the story; thus Major establishes from the beginning the problem of identity that dominates his early fiction. We also see the blending of cultural materials, as when he juxtaposes a blues reference and one from Celtic mythology.

This passage is in sharp contrast to the opening of *Such Was the Season* (1987):

> Last week was a killer-diller! I don't know if Juneboy brought good or bad luck. First news he was coming down here came from Esther. She called me one night from Chicago, where she lives, oh bout a week fore he was to get in. She said, "Annie, my son Adam is coming down there to speak at Spelman bout his research at Howard University Hospital."
>
> I said, "What kinda research, Esther?"
>
> She said, "Annie Eliza, I done told you bout Adam's research so many times, I swear you don't never listen to nothing I say."
>
> Then I said to my baby sister, "You tell that boy he better stay with me when he gets here, I won't stand him staying in some hotel or with nobody else."
>
> (Major 1987, p. 1)

What he creates in this new work is the narrative voice of an older Black woman, who tells the story of her prosperous family in Atlanta. Its down-home style is profoundly different from the postmodernist voice of *My Amputations*. *Such Was the Season* is published at the peak of the popularity of Black women's fiction. Alice Walker's *The Color Purple* comes out in 1982, with Toni Morrison's *Beloved* following in 1987 and Gloria Naylor's *Mama Day* in 1988. All three women tended to use sophisticated but otherwise traditional narrative methods. They were also regularly appearing on the *New York Times* bestseller list. While Major claims in interviews that the work was in fact experimental, what he meant by that was the choice of narrator. In addition, having published a dictionary of African American slang in 1970 and having spent his childhood in rural Georgia, Major was familiar with the speech patterns of a character like his Annie Eliza. Her folksy manner serves as a counterpoint to the book's critique of Black preachers and also, though more subtly than other Black male writers of the time, of the feminism of young Black women.

A book published a year later, though begun much earlier, goes in a different direction entirely. While living in Colorado, Major became interested in Native American cultures. He spent three years researching Zuni traditions. The result was a pair of books: the poetry collection *Some Observations of a Stranger at Zuni in the Latter Part of the Century* (1989) and the novel *Painted Turtle: Woman with Guitar* (1988). The subtitle of the fiction suggests connections with Major's other art form, painting, since it is associated with modernist art. However, the novel itself is conventional. The narrator, a Navajo-Hopi man, is asked to get the title character to adopt a more modern musical style. They become lovers, in part because both are alienated from their traditional cultures: Painted Turtle because she was raped and attempted to drown the twins that were the result of that assault, and the narrator because he is not pure Hopi. By the end of the story, they are joined by their mutual acceptance of being outsiders.

Dirty Bird Blues (1996) marks Major's return to the world of Black music he knew while growing up in Chicago. He sets the novel in the post-World War II North, an environment used by Richard Wright and a number of his associates. But Major is not particularly interested in social realism; rather, he focuses on the creation of art in the midst of an often hostile environment. Manfred Banks, the central character, has three obsessions: blues music, his wife Cleo, and Old Crow bourbon (the "Dirty Bird" of the title). The three cannot coexist, and the narrative is Man's struggle to negotiate among them. The one constant in his life is that he can always create music; in fact, his speech patterns are as much blues lyrics as they are ordinary English. Ultimately, he gives up drinking, and Cleo returns to him. In essence, Major's claim is that art is the resolution to one's problems.

Major's last (to date) novel, *One Flesh* (2003), also focuses on art, in this case painting. With this work, he undertook to enter the mainstream, arranging for it to be published by Dafina, an imprint that focuses on African American genre writing. The story is a traditional romance, using ethnic differences as the source of conflict. John Canoe, the protagonist, has a white mother and Black father, whose relationship has failed. His love interest, Susie, is a Chinese American who is alienated from her family because they want her to marry a Chinese man. Though John, like Manfred Banks, has a strong belief in his artistry, we virtually never see him producing art. Similarly, Susie, who is a poet, is never shown writing. In a work intended as a romance, what is curious is the main character's lack of passion. John lacks intensity about family, relationships, and even his art. It is as though he has become so secure in his aesthetic vision that he no longer needs to struggle.

Briefly, his short fiction demonstrates the same range of strategies as his novels. *Fun and Games* (1990) includes "Maggy: A Woman of the King," which appears to be a brief episode not used in his first novel. Other pieces, such as "The Vase and the Rose" and "Number Four," make use of changing narrative voices that create a disorienting effect. The concluding section, "Mobile Axis: A Triptych," consists of three pieces about the making of art, especially painting. Scenes are depicted and then shifted as if the narrator is imaging compositional possibilities. There are no significant narratives involved, though the narrator asserts the presence of various emotions.

The second collection, *Chicago Heat* (2016), is Major's most recent literary publication. About half of the stories were previously published, including two that appeared in *Fun and Games*. In it, his interest is primarily in using a range of narrative voices. Among them are a composer in New York, a boy whose mother develops a relationship with a white man, a young woman reuniting her parents in Chicago, a summer social worker in Harlem, a painter, and a biographer doing research in Venice. Those in the third person generally are told with a focal character. Several take the point of view of women. The selection gives some credence to Major's claim that *Such Was the Season* was in fact experimental, not in the sense of postmodernism, but rather in taking on the challenge of a variety of voices across time, space, gender, race, and register.

Art is the central concern for Clarence Major. Whether it is finding experimental modes for literary expression, or finding a variety of voices to express his concerns, or exploring the identity of the artist, he has sought to find meaning through narrative forms of expression.

SEE ALSO: Banks, Russell; Burroughs, William; Erdrich, Louise; Everett, Percival; Federman, Raymond; Gaines, Ernest; Jones, Gayl; McKnight, Reginald; McMillan, Terry; Momaday, N. Scott

REFERENCES

Major, Clarence. (1986). *My Amputations*. New York: Fiction Collective.
Major, Clarence. (1987). *Such Was the Season*. San Francisco: Mercury House.

FURTHER READING

Bell, Bernard. (ed.) (2001). *Clarence Major and His Art: Portraits of an African American Postmodernist*. Chapel Hill: Univerity of North Carolina Press.
Bunge, Nancy. (ed.) (2002). *Conversations with Clarence Major*. Jackson: University Press of Mississippi.
Byerman, Keith E. (2012). *The Art and Life of Clarence Major*. Athens: University of Georgia Press.

Marcus, Ben

PATRICK O'DONNELL
Michigan State University, USA

One of the premiere experimental writers of his generation, Ben Marcus is the author of two novels, three collections of short stories, an illustrated novella, and numerous essays; he is the editor of two key collections of contemporary American fiction, *The Anchor Book of New American Short Stories* (2004), and the Vintage Contemporaries edition of *New American Stories* (2015). Marcus has a significant online presence via his website, benmarcus.com, where he publishes essays, reflections, and work in progress, and under the "Smallwork" tab, work by other writers. By no means a diminutive, the invented word "smallwork" occupies an important place in Marcus's fiction, where (as in *The Flame*

Alphabet [2012]) it signifies intricate details that can be discerned in linguistic processes as well as material objects, often jolted out of context to generate the contrast, mechanics, logic and (contradictory) illogic of naming, description, and things. One of Marcus's concerns throughout his work is the relationship between language and communication: how does language – gendered, localized, dialectical – operate as an unwieldy, "glitched" vehicle for human understanding and the mis/communications that haunt our lives? What is the relationship between language and politics, sexuality, maturation, and socialization? Marcus writes compelling allegories in which the linguistic act, by inversion, is the subject of a story limited to the capacities of the language in which it is being written as an object to be scrutinized, as if linguistic signs were literal signs drawing our attention or distracting us from our goals. Thus regarded, Marcus's fictions primarily might be viewed as language experiments – but experiments manifesting a social order that, in its repressive codes and systems, reveals its fragility.

Marcus was born in 1967 and grew up primarily in Austin, Texas, the state capital known for the University of Texas, Austin City Limits, eccentric customs and characters, and liberal politics. He is the son academic parents; his mother was the well-known feminist scholar, Jane Marcus, who, in numerous works such as *Virginia Woolf and the Languages of Patriarchy* (1987) helped to establish the foundations of second and third-wave feminist thought in the United States: she is also a "character" in Marcus's first novel, *Notable American Women* (2002). Marcus earned a BA at New York University, and an MFA in Creative Writing at Brown University; currently, he is Professor at the Columbia University School of the Arts. He has been the recipient of a Guggenheim Fellowship, the Berlin Prize Fellowship, and the Morton Dauwen Zabel Award from the American Academy of Arts and Letters.

While often labeled a collection of short stories, Marcus's first book, *The Age of Wire and String* (1995), is an assemblage of short takes on contemporary life, work, society, and structure, or as the book's "Argument" states, "a catalog of the life project as prosecuted in *The Age of Wire and String* and beyond, into the arrangements of states, sites, and cities and, further, within the small houses that have been granted erection or temporary placement on the perimeters of districts and river colonies" (1995, loc. 102). Complete with a bevy of charts, graphs, and cartoons by Catrin Morgan, the book contains forty-one stories divided between eight sections entitled "Sleep," "God," "Food," "The House," "Animal," "Weather," "Persons," and "Society"; each section concludes with a list of "Terms" that, by contingency, refer to the foregoing stories; each section contains five stories, save for the last, which contains six. This, then, appears to be a highly structured collection of stories, with an emphasis on fabrication and mathematical precision, and indeed this is confirmed by one of the epigraphs to *The Age of Wire and String*, "Mathematics is the supreme nostalgia of our time," by Michael Marcus, an eponym for Ben Marcus's father who is a retired mathematician and university professor. The stories – both mathematically precise and exotically abstract – often combine detailed structures, geographies, climates, and objects with surrealistic conditions and circumstances, such as in "Food Storms of the Original Brother," which describes a decaying cosmos comprised of "atmospheric" food particles that "can be utilized in assembling the fall of man" including "[b]its of rain containing beef seeds (rains of the Americas derive from the cattle colonies of the South, often stealing beef from the livestock to thicken the water coverage of storms)" (1995, loc. 379).

The influence of Donald Barthelme, Donald Antrim, George Saunders and, further back, Jorge Luis Borges can be detected in these brief narratives that cover "topics" ranging from the relationship between snoring and speech to an apocalypse in which the weather is somehow destroyed, "food costumes," and the meticulous construction of an automobile composed of various mechanical and organic parts. The terms that follow each section in which the stories appear, giving *Age* the feel of a guide or textbook, are expansive rather than explanatory: thus, in the section entitled "Food," terms such as "Choke Powder," "Food Posse," and "Storm Lung" appear, the latter defined as an "[o]bject which can be swallowed to forestall the effects of weather upon a body" (1995, loc. 477). Like his influences, Marcus views fiction in *The Age of Wire and String* as a series of linguistic trials engaged with the formation of a new language to describe intersections between objects in the world and human emotion. The title of the work suggests that it is at once a set of inventions, an arrangement of abstract trajectories, and a form of paleontology focused on a past era that also could possibly be an apocalyptic, posthuman future. As a first and founding fiction, *The Age and Wire of String* thus predicates much of what is to come in Marcus's *oeuvre*.

Marcus first novel, *Notable American Women*, appeared in 2002, and like *Age*, it is a remarkable narrative experiment. Many first novels are autobiographical, and it would seem this might be the case with *Notable American Women* as it contains voices or characters bearing the names of Michael Marcus, Jane Marcus, and Ben Marcus. But these entities are as so clearly differentiated from whatever the real Ben Marcus might conceive his real life or childhood to be that they become parodies of the paternal type, the maternal principle, the subjugated child. Instead of autobiographical scenes, the novel consists of a series of monologues, mini-histories, constructed recollections, and apparent chapters from an instruction manual on parenting and communication that vie with each other in a satire on the affective states of family life, domestic culture and communication, and contemporary identity. Language itself is one of the primary subjects of *Notable American Women*, especially as seen on occasions when its power to repress is evident, or, conversely, when its failure to convey meanings beyond the iconic are apparent. As the title of the novel suggests, the exploration of language as gendered is paramount, especially when one regards the activities of the charismatic "Jane Dark" who comes to inhabit the Marcus household as Ben's tutor, and who is the leader of the "Silentist" movement which advocates a form of materialized women's speech having the power to generate a silence and paralysis that will overcome the noise of the language of patriarchy and all bodily movement associated with the production of that language.

In the end, however, the novel is not to be understood simply in terms of a binary contestation between patriarchal language and some form of matriarchal language (or silence) that could replace it if the novel's notable American women, led by Jane Dark, could succeed. The paradox that Marcus explores here and throughout his work lies in the capacity of language to "harden" into forms of categorial thinking that underlie a repressive social order running opposite to its innate mutability, its sheer expressivity and its roots in the unconscious, pitched against an all-encompassing silence that reveals how much cannot be expressed. This paradox reveals itself most tellingly, and often hilariously, in mixed-up metaphors of Marcus fiction concentrated on wind, weather, breathing, eating, and bodily secretion. From *Notable American Women*: "Mother sprayed a fine mist of behavior water at me that night" (2002, p. 112); the "contract against motion does not imply a legal agreement against nutrient input or other body-sustenance strategies ... Gesture-free nutrition intake is permissible and advisable, whether through intravenous methods or a food-entry system that can be accomplished without the technique of chewing, handling, or in any way moving in relation to the nutrient stuffs" (p. 172); "Possibly this was a form of unison breathing. Crowds of women breathing in sequence, a political breathing, precisely timed, producing their audible wind, then entering a hard inhale all together, clearing the room of oxygen, stifling anyone not following their calibration" (p. 153). The surrealistic phraseology of these representations are indicative of Marcus's complex view of language as both a force to contend with and a human limitation.

Marcus's notable engagement with a fellow author over the capacities of language and fiction offers a further elaboration on his views about both. In 2002, Jonathan Franzen, having achieved considerable recognition for the 2001 publication of *The Corrections*, wrote a sweeping opinion piece in the *New Yorker* about the state of contemporary American fiction. The essay, entitled "Mr. Difficult," while expressing admiration for William Gaddis's *The Recognitions* (1955), critiqued Gaddis's later novels as well as a host of experimental fiction by contemporary American writers as violating what Franzen referred to as "the Contract" that should exist between readers and writers: that authors "do the work" in order for the client/reader to experience sufficient understanding and pleasure worthy of their time. Those authors who do not pursue this contract – especially those whose work is apparently overly-difficult, opaque, or abstruse in Franzen's view, including those works that are highly self-referential in linguistic terms – are "Status" writers who apparently ask the reader to do an unreasonable amount of work in order to "read" (i.e. get through, comprehend, take pleasure in) their fiction.

To go into the details of this argument requires more than the available space, but suffice it to say that to this reductionist characterization of experimental, avant garde writing (the kind that falls into the category of "Status" fiction) Ben Marcus responded with a counter-argument in the ironically titled "Why Experimental Fiction Threatens to Destroy Publishing, Jonathan Franzen, and Life as We Know It: A Correction," in a 2005 issue of *Harper's*. Marcus's response is both obvious and complex: for him, fiction from the beginning has always been about pushing the boundaries of its own form, it has been consistently a language experiment, from Cervantes to Pynchon, and the job of literature in general deserving of the name is to expand minds and explore new ways of thinking about language, world, identity: this is the proper "work" of both reader and writer, in Marcus's view. But beyond engaging Franzen in what is, in effect, a rather old debate about the purposes of literature and the role of the avant garde, Marcus goes on in his response to explore and critique the assumptions about realism, language, reading comprehension and difficulty, and audience that underlie Franzen's screed, with tongue-in-cheek references to "scientific" readability tests that show Franzen to be a far more "difficult" writer (in the terms of these tests) than Gaddis. Marcus's point in all of this is not primarily to defend Gaddis's writing or his own, but to attack the premise that one kind of writing should be privileged above another, or seen as more worthy of the reader's attention, because it situates itself within confines that are more comfortable (according to some specious standards of "comfort"). One can see in this response the lineaments of Marcus's innate fictional concerns: to show the possibility and limitations of language and linguistic systems when explored when operating within a social order in disarray, blown-up, and exposed for its pretensions. For Marcus, that order, insufficiently exposed, is what Franzen might find "comfortable."

Linguistic systems exposed, undermined, and reinvented can serve as a characterization of Marcus's most important work to date, *The Flame Alphabet*, published in 2012. Perhaps the debate with Franzen lent fuel to the fires that light this extraordinary novel, a *tour de force* that explores how families, clans, cults, and nations form around linguistic conventions and systems of communication built upon sand. At the center of *The Flame Alphabet* is the story of a parent's search for a lost child and a, seemingly, impossible attempt to preserve the nuclear family in the face of a collapse of the social order and the reorganization of society into iconoclastic, oppositional groups (children vs. adults; men vs. women; cults of fascistic order vs. cults of anarchy), each speaking (or not speaking) its own incomprehensible language. In the world of *The Flame Alphabet*, the speech of children at certain stages of maturity has become toxic to adults such that they must be quarantined until they grow out of the stage of poisonous talk. Indeed, communication between all parties has become so fraught with danger that the invention of Rube Goldberg devices distancing speech from bodies and filtering out the "weather" accompanying speech is necessary in order for information to be imparted. *The Flame Alphabet*, in effect, stages a language apocalypse in which the reality that human language describes and shapes has become infected with a virus spread through the "disease" of language itself, its capacity for sublimination disabled. The novel might be seen as a survival narrative where the protagonist must learn a new language made of the fabric of silence to endure in a landscape where human language has outlived both its power and its use.

Since the appearance of *The Flame Alphabet*, Marcus has published two collections of short stories, *Leaving the Sea* (2014) and *Notes from the Fog* (2018). Both collections are made up of stories Marcus has published individually in such venues as *Granta*, *Harper's*, *Electric Literature*, *The New Yorker*, and *Tin House*. *Leaving the Sea*, which also includes two stories, "The Moors" and "The Father Costume" published separately as chapbooks, appears to have a scattering of stories on (for Marcus) unremarkable subjects – a family reunion, a sea cruise with a protagonist who is a teaching a creative writing workshop, a son (or daughter) at their mother's deathbed – but these are punctuated with narratives that construct situations revealing the complexities of family, identity, impersonation, and language that fascinate him. Alongside stories about the difficulties of caring for a child with serious medical issues or a dying mother there is "First Love" which begins "I could not sleep until I had labored through a regular lust application performed with motion, gesture, and languageflower" (2014, p. 197), or "Origins of the Family," which begins with a descriptive sentence turned strange: "A man and woman sometimes gather in the evening to discuss their future projects together, a conversation that takes place in a hushed, bone-free room" (p. 209). Part Two of the collection is comprised of two questionnaires, the first beginning with the question "How long have you been a child?" and the response "Seventy-one years" (p. 113), the second with the question "People are pursuing different strategies during the hardship ... [how long have you advocated the cave?]," and the response "Advocate is a strong word. If I occupy a life raft out on the ocean, and people are drowning, I don't 'advocate' the raft to them. I enjoy the raft and my relative security" (p. 119). In both cases, Marcus uses the genre of the questionnaire to conduct examinations of childhood and adulthood, survival, and the relationship between language and behavior that are evident throughout the assemblage. "The Father Costume" serves as a key story in that it focuses on the relationship between a father and his sons – a familiar fictional theme – but Marcus's "father" in the narrative is both archetypal and alien, "I wish I could say my father's name. I do not know the grammatical tense that could properly remark on my father. There is a portion of time that my own language cannot reach. . . . In this portion of time is where my father is hidden. If I learn a new language, my father might come true. If I reach deep into my mouth and scoop out a larger cave. If I make do with less of myself, so that he might be more" (p. 183). Here the strangeness of the father and the familiar are revealed, once more, by both the inherent uncanniness and limitations of language and speech.

In *Notes from the Fog*, the weather is misty in narrated worlds where indeterminacy is the order of the day. For example, in "Blueprints for St. Louis," a story about a couple tasked with designing a memorial for the city of St. Louis where a terrorist's bomb has gone off in a crowded office building killing thousands, the husband-wife team has "made their mark by designing large public graves where people would gather and where maybe really cool food trucks would also park" (2018, p. 56). They experience the disintegration of their relationship while attempting to design a monument to fear and disorder – a project that involves, among other "smallwork," "bids from the pharmaceuticals . . . vying to be the providers of the chemical component that every memorial these days was more or less expected to have: a gentle mist to assist the emotional response of visitors and drug them into a torpor of sympathy. . . . A mood was delivered via fog" (p. 271). As in much of his fiction, Marcus suggests here that public affect is commodified, an artificial construct produced out of the need to provide a "proper" response to the confusion and social alienation produced by mass violence – a condition all too familiar in the United States in the wake of 9/11 and nearly weekly mass shootings. Other stories of the collection consider the plight of a child who declares that he no longer loves his parents ("Cold Little Bird"); the gradual decline of a man who works for a voracious business that develops "cutting edge" products such as an app that can pair people with similar moods, a "jug" containing all the bionutrients one needs, delivered daily to your home or office, and a way of delivering nutrients via light ("The Grow-Light Blues"); and the downward trajectory of an eccentric man who is fired from his job as a teacher for not "fitting in," whose wife dies, and who continues on in a life of low-paying jobs and single parenting ("Notes from the Fog"). The mordant summary of this last story does little to explain its final lines that seemingly offer respite in a world of noise and muddle: "Sometimes when the kids get antsy and want to go inside, I hold them close and ask them to wait. Just a little longer, I say, outside in the shade. Just wait with me under the tree here a little bit longer. Something amazing is coming" (p. 266). Marcus's most recent collection to date, replete with stories of impersonation, distancing, family, and mind/body estrangement in its piercing dissection of contemporary life, thus allows a few rare moments of solace, though it must be understood that the "amazing" thing coming might be as terrifying as it might be beautiful.

SEE ALSO: After Postmodernism; Antrim, Donald; Franzen, Jonathan; Gaddis, William; The New Experimentalism/The Contemporary Avant-Garde; Saunders, George

REFERENCES

Franzen, Jonathan. (2002). Mr. Difficult. *The New Yorker* (September 30, 2002): 100–111.
Marcus, Ben. (1995). *The Age of Wire and String*. New York: Knopf. Kindle ed.
Marcus, Ben. (2002). *Notable American Women*. New York: Vintage.

Marcus, Ben. (2005). Why experimental fiction threatens to destroy publishing, Jonathan Franzen, and life as we know it. *Harper's Magazine* (October, 2005): 39–52. https://harpers.org/archive/2005/10/why-experimental-fiction-threatens-to-destroy-publishing-jonathan-franzen-and-life-as-we-know-it/ (accessed September 10, 2021).

Marcus, Ben. (2014). *Leaving the Sea*. New York: Viking.

Marcus, Ben. (2018). *Notes from the Fog*. New York: Knopf.

Marcus, Ben. (n.d.). benmarcus.com (accessed September 10, 2021).

FURTHER READING

Berry, R.M. (2006). The question of writing now: FC2 responds to Ben Marcus. *Symplokē* 14 (1–2): 316–318.

Huehls, Mitchum. (2013). The post-theory novel. *Contemporary Literature* 56 (2): 280–310.

Schneiderman, Davis. (2006). Notes from the middleground: on Ben Marcus, Jonathan Franzen, and the Contemporary Fiction Combine. *ebr: The Electronic Book Review* (September 2006). https://electronicbookreview.com/essay/notes-from-the-middleground-on-ben-marcus-jonathan-franzen-and-the-contemporary-fiction-combine/

Soldat-Jaffe, Tatiana. (2014). Zombie linguistics. In: *The Year's Work at the Zombie Research Center* (ed. Edward P. Commentale and Aaron Jaffe), 361–388. Bloomington: Indiana University Press.

Vanderhaeghe, Stéphanie. (2013). Ben Marcus & the question of language (some notes & a parenthesis). *Revue Française d'Études Américaines* 135: 66–79.

Marshall, Paule

PAULINE AMY DE LA BRETEQUE
Sorbonne Nouvelle University, France

Paule Marshall is one of the most prominent Black American women writers in the United States. Her fiction offers an incredible insight on a great variety of topics such as West Indian migration, the African diaspora, racism, Black feminism, and neocolonialism. Militant as a Black feminist, Marshall depicts in her novels and short stories the point of view of strong women fighting for emancipation. At the crossroads of North America and the Caribbean, her work tackles the quest for identity from the perspective of female characters. Her writings are an attempt at finding reconciliation between the multiple aspects of her identity and within the African diaspora.

Marshall was born on April 9, 1929, in Brooklyn under the name Valenza Pauline Burke and died on August 12, 2019. Her parents, Adriana Viola Clement Burke and Sam Burke, both came from Barbados and settled in the 1910s in the West Indian community of the Bedford-Stuyvesant neighborhood in Brooklyn. Marshall was the middle child in a family of two girls and one boy. When she was 13, her father had become more and more involved with a spiritual and cult leader, Father Divine, and was barely part of the family household anymore. Marshall's mother had to raise her children alone and worked hard to prevent the family from falling into poverty.

Growing up far from her parents' native country, Paule Marshall was nevertheless deeply influenced by the Caribbean community around her. When she was nine years old, she traveled for the first time to Barbados and met her family there. Her experience in Barbados as an American child is retraced in her partly autobiographical short story "To Da-Duh, in Memoriam" (1967) and in her memoir.

Marshall is most often considered as an American author and is indeed part of a line of African American writers, such as Langston Hughes, who contributed to the launching of her literary career. She was close to civil rights activists like June Jordan or Pauli Murray, for instance. Yet, her writings are really at the intersection of the West Indies, the United

States, and Africa, and they create a link between various spaces of the African diaspora, from Barbados to Brooklyn, Brazil, or Africa. Her work constantly reminds us of the diasporic dimension of her culture, as she testifies in her last publication, *Triangular Road: A Memoir* (2009). She actually considers West Indians and African Americans as one people and equally claims both her American and her West Indian heritage, thus refusing strict classification. The writer and her work represent the bridge that links the different parts of the African diaspora.

Marshall was able to reconnect further with her Caribbean origins during the numerous trips she made to the Caribbean and South America when she worked as a journalist for *Our World* (1953–1956), a magazine mainly addressed to an African American readership. Before that, she worked as a librarian while she attended graduate school in English literature at Hunter College in New York City, after graduating from Brooklyn College. Her college education and her professional career show how passionate she was about literature. When Marshall was a child, her mother reproached her for being too absorbed in books.

Writing had almost a therapeutic function for Marshall, and her work can be regarded as an attempt to answer the questions she had been asking herself about her identity. In an interview with Joyce Pettis, she mentions her difficulties in reconciling her Caribbean and her American identities (Pettis 1991). She also used writing to try to elucidate the question of the meaning of life, and of how one can make the most of one's life.

Marshall was deeply engaged in unveiling historical truth about Black people in the Americas and in producing a counter-discourse to the denigrating colonial and racist image that was dominating when she grew up in the United States. She therefore gives another image of Black people, highlighting their struggle for survival, their culture, and their creativity. Her interest in history was paired with strong political views about resistance and achievement of independence.

Women are an essential part of her writing, as she focuses mainly on female characters. In an interview with Joyce Pettis, she explains that women were more part of her world and experience than men (Pettis 1991). She grew up among women from the Barbadian community, and these had a most important influence on her works. Marshall was well aware that women were not central characters of canonical literature, and had in mind to center her fiction on powerful and creative women. Some of them are writers (such as the main character of *Daughters*, who has a project to write a PhD dissertation on maroonage). In an interview with Daryl Cumber Dance, Marshall expresses her determination to create a literature with which Black women will be able to identify (Dance 1992). She also explains that she started writing at a time when Black women were not taken seriously in the United States and she found herself in a hostile environment for Black women to write in. She was denigrated by publishers, and had difficulties accessing other Black women's literature. Marshall was a great reader, but she was mostly exposed to the European and American literary canon when she read books from the Brooklyn Public Library. She therefore based her first writings on the works of classical white male writers such as Thomas Mann. When she started writing her first novel, *Brown Girl, Brownstones*, in the 1950s, she was barely aware of the works of Black writers. She discovered Black women's literary works quite late in her life, but she was then deeply influenced by Gwendolyn Brooks and Zora Neale Hurston.

Marshall thus reveals Black women characters' perspectives on migration and transculturalism, and on identity building in relation to the African diaspora. She tackles the questions of sexual and racial discrimination and of power relations inherited from colonialism and slavery in the Caribbean and in the United States. She addresses in her works the issues of cultural hybridity, the constant evolution of identities, as well as memorial recovery – in *Praisesong for the Widow* (1983) or in *The Chosen Place, the Timeless People* (1969), for instance.

Marshall is the author of five novels, three short story collections, and a memoir. She was awarded the Guggenheim Fellowship for her work in 1960, the American Book Award in 1984, the Langston Hughes Medal in 1986, and the John D. and Catherine T. MacArthur Fellowship in 1992. She was also a teacher of creative writing at Yale, Columbia, Virginia Commonwealth University, and New York University.

Brown Girl, Brownstones was first published in 1959 and is greatly inspired from the writer's own life. The plot takes place in the 1930s in Brooklyn and relates the story of Selina, a young girl born in the United States to Barbadian parents. The novel starts when Selina's father, Deighton, inherits a piece of land in Barbados and dreams of going back to his home island, while Selina's mother, Silla, wants him to sell the land so they can buy a house, a brownstone, in Brooklyn – a symbol of social achievement and integration. The coming-of-age novel relates Selina's development as a young woman conscious of the double cultural influence shaping her identity. As the story unfolds, Selina is increasingly aware of the racial and gender bias that prevails in the United States. She finds strength and freedom in dancing and in artistic expression. As the author's alter ego, she aims at becoming a poet at the end of the book.

It took a long time for Marshall to complete her second novel, *The Chosen Place, the Timeless People*, which was published ten years later, in 1969. Writing it was quite a long process, as Marshall did extensive research on maroonage, sugar cane, as well as peasant life in the Caribbean. She admitted that it was not easy to transform her research into fiction.

The Chosen Place, the Timeless People is set on an imaginary Caribbean island called Bourne Island, modeled on Barbados and other anglophone Caribbean islands. The novel starts when a group of American anthropologists, Allen, Saul, and his wife Harriet, settle in Bournehills, an underdeveloped region of Bourne Island, to lead a field survey for an American aid organization. Bournehills is depicted as a backward place, and somewhat stuck in the past. No humanitarian mission had ever succeeded in the region, due to the inhabitants' resistance to any change imposed from outside.

The novel explores the characters' quest for identity in their own past and highlights the role of history in identity building. Merle, one of the main characters, who is descended from both slaves and planters, encapsulates this quest for identity because of her profound in-betweenness and her resistance to categorization. She is fond of history, and more particularly the local history of Bournehills, and teaches the story of maroonage to her pupils at school.

Marshall's fiction takes a stronger political turn with this second novel, which opens a complex reflection on the limits of the independence of former colonies. Indeed, Marshall underlines the continuity between the colonial past and the contemporary Caribbean, where hierarchies remain the same, and where the so-called independent governments are still directed by foreign powers. She thus denounces foreign interventionism and the perpetuation of colonization through projects to bring civilization and development to poorer countries.

The whole novel highlights how different parts of the Americas interconnect through economical domination and racial power relations inherited from colonialism and slavery. One of the characters, Harriet, epitomizes the involvement not only of the South of the United States in the system of slavery, but also of the North, which is often considered as disconnected from slavery. Marshall stresses the interests that some Northern traders had always had in slavery in the United States, and thus shows how widespread the roots of slavery were.

Marshall's third novel, *Praisesong for the Widow*, further examines the theme of the African diaspora and highlights the role of cultural remembrance in the emergence of a feeling of diasporic belonging. The novel explores Avey Johnson's – an upper-middle-class African American living in New York – acceptance of her origins. At the beginning of the novel, she is on a cruise in the Caribbean with two of her friends. On a sudden impulse she decides to leave the cruise, after a dream she has had about her old Aunt Cuney from Tatem Island in South Carolina with whom she used to spend summer holidays when she was a child. Aunt Cuney and she would take a ritual walk to the sea and, more particularly, to a place called the Ibo Landing, where, during the times of slavery, slaves from Nigeria rebelled and drowned in the sea. In the dream she refuses to follow her aunt to the Landing, thus signifying her rejection of her African origins. Indeed, Avey and her late husband had forgotten and denied their African American cultural legacies to feel better integrated in a prevailingly white American culture. While willing to go back to New York, Avey encounters in Grenada an old man, Lebert Joseph, who convinces her to go with him on the yearly ritual excursion to the small island of Carriacou. There, Avey develops an awareness of her African origins and a responsibility as a carrier of memory. Slowly, vague memories from the past resurface from the contact with some cultural rituals in Carriacou, and Avey forges for herself a new diasporic identity connected with Caribbean cultures.

Daughters, Marshall's fourth novel, published in 1991, was born from a quote that the author read one evening on the leaflet of a dance program in New York: "Little girl of all the daughters,/You ain't no more slave,/You's a woman now." It made the author imagine a group of women in the shadows, behind the stage, who would come forward and become the main characters of her story. The novel is set between New York and another fictional Caribbean island called Triunion. Ursa Mackenzie lives in New York but was born in Triunion from a Triunionian father and an American mother. Ursa's life in New York is torn between failure to lead an academic career, an unsatisfying long-lasting relationship with a man, and the systemic racism that threatens Black populations in the United States. Ursa's father is the Prime Minister of Triunion, and was formerly full of ambitions and ideals for his newly independent country. Going back home for the elections in Triunion, Ursa is disillusioned by the political achievements of her father. She discovers an island poorer than before, and corrupted by foreign real estate developers. The relationship between Ursa Mackenzie and her father mirrors the relationship between the Caribbean and the USA – it is anchored into seduction, dependency, but also domination. The novel depicts both relationships through a fight for autonomy and independence, at the level of individuals, but also at the level of countries and regions.

Marshall's fifth and last novel, *The Fisher King*, published in 2001, relates the story of Sonny-Rett Payne, the child of a West Indian domestic in Brooklyn, who becomes a renowned jazz pianist in Paris after having fled racism and family pressure in the United States. He breaks off all ties with his home country, and dies in France. Many decades later, Sonny-Rett's brother Edgar organizes a concert commemorating his brother, and decides to reconnect with Sonny-Rett's family in Paris. Once again, Marshall tackles racism and discrimination issues, as well as migration, transnationalism, and remembrance. The story is set between the Caribbean, the United States, and Europe, with jazz music as a backdrop and acting as a cultural binder of the African diaspora.

Marshall is also the author of three short story collections. She wrote *Soul Clap Hands and Sing* (1961) when she was in Barbados, revising her first novel. She already had *The Chosen Place, the Timeless People* in mind, but writing *Brown Girl, Brownstones* had taken so much of her energy that she was not sure she would be able to write another novel, and so she turned to short fiction. The title of the collection is a quote from W.B. Yeats's poem "Sailing to Byzantium" (1928). It mirrors the common concern of the four short stories in the collection, which ask the question of how to live a life fully. Marshall also wanted to know if she would be able to write convincingly about men, as she had rather favored female characters in her novels. Each novella is thus about a middle-aged man who has failed to live his life fully and becomes suddenly conscious of the fact during a moment of epiphany that occurs at the end of the story. The collection also embraces various parts of the Americas, from Brooklyn to Barbados, Brazil and British Guiana. Some of the short stories contained in *Soul Clap Hands and Sing* were republished by The Feminist Press at the City University of New York in the collection *Reena and Other Stories* (1983), which also includes Marshall's very first short story, "The Valley Between" (1954), and the novella "Merle," based on *The Chosen Place, the Timeless People*. In this collection, all the stories are preceded by autobiographical comments by Marshall. In 1985, *Reena and Other Stories* was republished by Virago Press under the title *Merle: A Novella and Other Stories*.

Committing herself fully to writing and to becoming a writer was not an easy decision for Marshall. She doubted her ability to devote herself entirely to writing. In two major essays, she recounts her birth as a writer. The first, "Shaping the World of My Art," was published in 1981 in *Women's Studies Quarterly*. The second, "The Making of a Writer: From the Poets in the Kitchen," was first published in the *New York Times Book Review*'s series entitled "The Making of a Writer" in 1983, and appears as the introduction to her last two short story collections. Marshall was a great reader, but she was also strongly exposed to orality and to storytelling in the environment where she grew up, in the Barbadian community of Brooklyn. She was deeply influenced by her mother's language and by the conversations she had with other women from the Barbadian community in the kitchen of the family's brownstone in Brooklyn. Marshall calls the women who inspired her "the poets in the kitchen." Their language and their culture were passed on to the writer, who discovered how language and speech could help overcome the hardships of life. Marshall was imbued with their rhetoric, with the rhythm of their speech, and with their mastering of the art of storytelling.

Marshall's last published piece of work is her memoir entitled *Triangular Road: A Memoir* (2009). Much interest is to be found in this autobiographical writing about the author's childhood, her career as a writer and as a teacher, but also about her literary and historical approach and her political engagement. Her memoir is an adaptation of a series of lectures delivered at Harvard University in 2005 on the theme "Bodies of Water" and their impact on Black history and culture throughout the Americas. The book is thus divided into three main parts, covering three bodies of water, all intimately linked to the history of slavery and of the African diaspora: the James River, the Caribbean Sea, and the Atlantic Ocean. In her last work, Marshall highlights more than ever the links between the different parts of the African diaspora, and how they have shaped her as a writer and as a political activist.

SEE ALSO: Black Atlantic; Globalization; Literature of the Americas

REFERENCES

Dance, Daryl C. (1992). An interview with Paule Marshall. *The Southern Review* 28 (1): 1–20.

Pettis, Joyce. (1991). Interview: Paule Marshall. *MELUS* 17 (4): 117–129.

FURTHER READING

Brathwaite, Edward K. (1970). Review: West Indian history and society in the art of Paule Marshall's novel. *Journal of Black Studies* 1 (2): 225–238.

DeLamotte, Eugenia C. (2016). *Places of Silence, Journeys of Freedom: The Fiction of Paule Marshall*. Philadelphia: University of Pennsylvania Press.

Francis, Donette A. (2000). Paule Marshall: new accents on immigrant America. *The Black Scholar* 30 (2): 21–25.

Olmsted, Jane. (1997). The pull to memory and the language of place in Paule Marshall's *The Chosen Place, the Timeless People* and *Praisesong for the Widow*. *African American Review* 31 (2): 249–267.

Pettis, Joyce. (1995). *Toward Wholeness in Paule Marshall's Fiction*. Charlottesville: University of Virginia Press.

Maso, Carole

ROBIN SILBERGLEID
Michigan State University, USA

Beginning with the publication of *Ghost Dance* in 1986, Carole Maso has been widely recognized as a feminist experimental writer. The author of ten books – spanning fiction, nonfiction, and genre-bending works – as well as numerous pieces of short fiction and criticism, Maso is a writer for whom language itself provides major subject matter. As evidenced in both content and form, including a shift toward nonfiction and hybrid works, Maso's writing relentlessly interrogates traditional narrative structures and strives toward what feminist theorist Hélène Cixous describes as "a language that heals as much as it separates" (quoted in Maso 1993, p. 163). Her works' radical challenge to summary – its desire for "open" form – in many ways makes traditional criticism, including this sort of overview, not only difficult but counterintuitive. Such disconnect might account for the relative lack of sustained literary criticism on Maso's oeuvre to date and makes an argument for alternate, reader-centered practices, such as affective, performative, or "reparative" modes of criticism as means of approaching her work.

Born March 9, 1956, in Paterson, New Jersey, Maso graduated from Vassar College and, as she has noted, held a series of odd jobs (among them: waitress, artist's model) while working on her craft (what she terms her "apprenticeship") before publishing *Ghost Dance*. With life partner Helen Lang, she has an adult daughter, Rose, whose birth is the subject of the journal *The Room Lit by Roses* (2000). Although she has notoriously stated that she never attended a graduate program in creative writing, Maso has taught at Illinois State University, George Washington University, Columbia University, and Brown University, where she has been on faculty since 1995 and has served as director of the Program in Literary Arts; her teaching method, she claims, is almost exclusively to ask questions of her students (2000b, p. 36). Among her accolades, Maso is the recipient of a Lannan Literary Award, a National Endowment for the Arts Literature Fellowship for fiction, and the 2018 Berlin Prize.

Much of Maso's work is metafictional, incorporating self-reflexive discussion of the efficacy and ethics of writing about loss and desire and questioning the usefulness and value of traditional narrative forms, including the limitations of language itself. Maso's novels are highly intertextual, whether through subtle allusion or blatant parody, and the majority of her characters are artists, writers, or professors whose lives echo the author's in substantial ways. Language is arguably her central subject and interest. Aptly characterizing herself as a "lyric artist," each of Maso's novels adopts a distinct strategy in its exploration of lyricism and anti-narrative methods; her book *Break Every Rule* (2000) collects a number of shorter essays that serve partly as manifesto, as well as autobiographical, aesthetic, and critical contexts. Attempting to characterize the lyrical novel, she asks in "Notes of a Lyric Artist Working in Prose," "How to incorporate the joys and pleasures, tenderness, delicacies, the generosities and seductions of the novel and its narrative capacities with the extraordinary, awesome capabilities of poetry?" (2000a, p. 53). Published mainly by small innovative presses such as Dalkey Archive, Maso is not shy in her condemnation of the mainstream publishing industry (she once notoriously described Knopf as a "whorehouse").

Building on Maso's own arguments about her work, as suggested in extant criticism on her writing, anti-narrative and lyrical modes in Maso's books are connected thematically to loss and melancholia (e.g. Stirling 1998), on the one hand, and female sexuality and desire on the other (e.g. Chevaillier 2017; Quinn 2001); the relationship between these drives is compelling but largely underexplored. Although she is not a writer of strict historiographic metafiction, her books are nonetheless historically grounded; the personal tragedies of her protagonists are tied to the major catastrophes of the twentieth century, including the AIDS epidemic, World War II, and the Gulf Wars. *Ghost Dance*, a book in five parts, is organized around central image patterns, as protagonist Vanessa comes to terms with the unexpected death of her mother in the explosion of a Ford Pinto; it takes its title from Native American mourning rituals. At its center is Vanessa's mother, the acclaimed poet Christine Wing, whose psychological instability serves as both the well-spring of her creativity and the major obstacle in terms of maintaining a real grasp on the world (she notoriously has difficulty dressing appropriately for the weather) and parenting her children; this character is the first in a series of artist-protagonists who struggle with mental illness. Beyond its immediate focus on the Turin family, *Ghost Dance* is in some ways very much ahead of its time in its keen awareness of climate change and the related disaster of capitalism, facts which become more prescient upon twenty-first-century rereadings. This early book sets up formally some of the experimentalism of Maso's later work, including its fragmented structure and its reliance on image patterns and refrain.

Maso's second novel, *The Art Lover* (1990), builds on this reliance on fragmentation and imagery; staged as a multileveled narrative of loss, the book centers on the novelist Caroline, whose work-in-progress forms part of the fiction, and who searches for a way to work through her friend's AIDS diagnosis; the recent death of her father, Max, an art historian; and the early childhood loss of her mother, Veronica, to suicide. In each of its three levels, the book asks the extent to which the production of art might provide solace; Caroline's attempts at mourning are paralleled in the novel-within-a-novel she is writing, a narrative of a family that has recently broken apart as a result of divorce. Set in New York in the mid-1980s, the novel is a brilliant exploration of the AIDS crisis as well as a triumph of Maso's formal innovation, incorporating three narrative levels and a collage of visual images. While some of Maso's more recent works seem more invested in the imaginative realm than documentation, *The Art Lover* is grounded both temporally and spatially in its narrative present with explicitly dated sections, including numerous sections that reference the Challenger explosion that took place on January 28, 1986. Most tellingly, given Maso's later turn toward nonfiction, the novel radically breaks from the fictional narrative about Caroline to incorporate elements of autobiography, as Maso devotes the penultimate section "More Winter" to the AIDS-related death of her friend, artist Gary Falk, whose life is mirrored in the novel through the tale of Caroline's friend Steven, also dying of AIDS. The book is visually innovative through its incorporation of photography, reproductions of Falk's paintings, newspaper clippings, and other graphic means. With its explicit focus on "art lovers" and metafiction, the book offers a serious interrogation of the efficacy of art to confront both personal and cultural loss. As Maso writes through the persona of Caroline, "I am sick of myself trying to give shape to all this sorrow, all this rage, all this loss – and failing" (1990, p. 148). If the production of the novel suggests Maso's success, it is telling that the book ends not with fiction and written text but with the actual photograph of Carole and Gary.

Such work on the loss of faith in narrative sets up *The American Woman in the Chinese Hat* (1994) – the third of Maso's books, although it was published fourth – which features Catherine, a writer visiting France and grieving the breakup of a long-term romantic relationship. Set in Vence, the novel arguably presents a version of the assignment Ava Klein offers her students to "rewrite *Death in Venice* as a feminist text" (Maso 1993, p. 31). After all, as Jeffrey DeShell aptly states, the difference between "Vence" and "Venice" is an "I" (1997, p. 198). In addition to Mann's *Death in Venice* (1912), the novel builds on the thematic focus on mental health and American women's literary tradition evidenced by Kate Chopin's *The Awakening* (1899) and Sylvia Plath's *The Bell Jar* (1963), among others. *American Woman* is Maso's barest narrative, mirroring Catherine's breakdown and loss of faith in words, as the novel whittles to a minimalist lexicon as Catherine struggles to learn French and communicate basic needs and desires. *American Woman* is also Maso's truest instance of "autofiction" – through its thinly veiled autobiographical fiction – as the plot of the novel closely mirrors what Maso has revealed of her own experience going to France after winning the Lannan prize. Splitting Catherine into subject and object, as marked in the shift between first and third person, the end of this novel features the death of the protagonist – at least one version of the protagonist – who has lost a sense of herself as subject. According to Marjorie Worthington, "By grappling with the seemingly inexorable pull of traditional narrative forms, this novel illuminates the heterosexism and violence toward the feminine inherent in those forms and represents a successful attempt to provide space for an agenic female subject" (2000, p. 243).

If *American Woman* is in some way the lowest point of Maso's narrative, the following narrative *AVA* (1993) is her celebratory triumph. On a formal level, *AVA* is the most radical of Maso's novels, virtually devoid of plot; instead, like Virginia Woolf's *The Waves* (1931), it presents a multivoiced series of short fragments of Ava Klein's memory on the last day of her 39 years, organized into three movements of "Morning," "Afternoon," and "Night"; the book presents itself as Ava's consciousness, incorporating snippets of books she recalls from her "passionate, promiscuous reading of the literature of this world" (1993, p. 114), memories of her three husbands and numerous lovers, a miscarried pregnancy, alongside occasional references to the hospital where, in the novel's present, she is in treatment for a rare blood disease. The book resists linear narrative and quite literally creates space, in the form of interlinear blanks; in this way, the book is deliberately a reader-centered text in which, as Maso says, "a reader can write the story right along with me" (Chevaillier 2017, p. 118). Haunted by the deaths of Ava's family members in Treblinka, the book offers an example of post-Holocaust narrative and situates itself consciously against the works of Claude Lanzmann and Paul Celan (Silbergleid 2010). As Maso's most explicitly intertextual book, *AVA* features a substantial "sources" section, inviting her readers to gather the books Ava has read as professor of comparative literature. According to Maso, the characters from *AVA* reappear in a longer work-in-progress called *The Bay of Angels*, of which only a handful of excerpts have been published to date. Alongside its thematic focus on the Holocaust, *AVA* is also a formal illustration of Maso's investment in what she has characterized as feminine writing; within *AVA*, direct quotations from Woolf, Cixous, and Nathalie Sarraute scaffold this critical conversation. The book is highly influenced by the work of Hélène Cixous and takes her call for a "language that heals" as a critical refrain. Maso's book *Aureole* (1996), which she has characterized as a series of "erotic etudes," is arguably exemplary of this sort of experimentation with feminine form and content. Attempting to build a new language of desire, "with Whitmanesque exuberance," Steven Moore says, "Maso sings of the joys of lesbian sex, channeling Sappho as her narrative persona" (1997, p. 211).

In direct opposition to the open, reader-centered form of *AVA* and the celebratory tone of *Aureole*, *Defiance* (1998) – Maso's only "commercial" novel, published by Dutton – offers a brash parody of narrative convention; taking on the incest narrative which became a common trope of mainstream fiction in the 1990s, its heroine, Bernadette O'Brien, whose childhood is marred by a family history of abuse, is a professor of physics on death row for murdering two of her male students whom she characterizes as her "sweet phallocentrics." The production of this "lurid" tale counters her years spent as an elective mute. Forced to write from her cell, she likewise describes plot-driven narrative as a "vise" or "prison." She is another one of Maso's feminist characters for whom there is no real way out. In this way, her situation serves as a metaphor of the publishing industry as a whole. Perhaps not surprisingly, then, after the publication of *Defiance*, Maso did not publish any fiction again until *Mother and Child* (2012), which, in both subject and form, one might speculate is the result of Maso herself becoming mother. Counter to the aggressive perspective offered in *Defiance*, *Mother and Child* is a third-person imaginative narrative that might be understood as one of the fairy tales that the mother-writer Christine might have told her children in *Ghost Dance*; in its highly metaphorical prose, puberty becomes "the transformation," a dwelling in the country is "a house of leaves," and a tree "a great pillar." Such elevated language both offers a delightful rereading of daily life with children and also risks complete inaccessibility; speaking of bats in the house that require the mother and child receive rabies shots, for example, "the mother realized they had been exposed to something that could not be reversed" (2012, p. 13). In its exploration of childrearing and domestic life, *Mother and Child* brings together and collapses the ordinary and the surreal; it is also worth noting that the book was written in the shadow of 9/11, with a central image of a tower on fire. At its best, as Flore Chevaillier says, the book "redefines fiction writing both in its content involving realistic and fairy tale traditions and in its fragmentary elusive form" (2017, pp. 115–116).

Not surprisingly, given her characters' continued interrogation of the possibilities of narrative fiction, the majority of Maso's books published since 2000 have been pieces of nonfiction or hybrid works that bridge creative and critical writing. As such, she explores the space between imagination and veracity; "truth," if not "fact," is critical to Maso's project. In the first of these, *Break Every Rule* (2000), Maso collects pieces that explain her development as a writer and major literary influences, as well as reflect on the state of twentieth-century literary production and her relationship to the mainstream publishing industry. These essays include a lengthy meditation on Gertrude Stein which borrows her title "A Novel of Thank You" and the titular "Break Every Rule," which asks "Might the novel, one day, like the old ways of thinking about gender and race and sexuality, simply appear silly, outdated, quaint?" (2000a, p. 159). Writing a new story of queer family, *The Room Lit by Roses* thus tells the story of Maso's pregnancy and the birth of her daughter in 1998. Published in 2000, alongside the emergence of the "momoir" as literary genre, the book considers questions of narrative form and the fragmented quality of diaries themselves, exploring reproduction as metaphor for narrative, and narrative as metaphor for reproduction, in lieu of a more straightforward journalistic account. Her book on Mexican painter Frida Kahlo, *Beauty is Convulsive* (2002), brings together poetry, diary, and criticism as an homage to Kahlo and consideration of feminist/female artistic production. Although the book jacket describes the work as "prose poems," they are more aptly shaped as highly fragmented and lyrical meditations or "votives" (as many of the sections are titled) that are as much about the author as they are about her subject, in some ways building on the collapse of fiction and nonfiction in *The Art Lover* as well as the pregnancy journal; as the "I" and the "you" of the project become virtually indistinguishable, Frida becomes a vehicle through which Maso might address her own issues, including the tradition of female artistic production. Although none of these three books are in a strict sense memoir, they provide background on the production of Maso's novels, discussion of her influences, and do critical work on framing and setting the context in which one might read the novels. Given the paucity of substantial scholarship on Maso's oeuvre – at present no monograph exists – this is particularly notable; concerns about the intentional fallacy aside, Maso is a capable reader of her own work, and, with characteristic fragmentation and collage, her nonfiction is as formally innovative as her novels.

Taken as a whole, Maso's books to date (1986–2012) reveal a sustained interrogation of narrative form, genre, and the limits of language, under the pressures of heteropatriarchy, capitalism, world war, and pandemic. As the field of literary studies works toward more expansive and engaged models of criticism, Maso's work offers critical points of entry for feminist and narrative intervention, opening themselves to readers who accept the invitation to enter.

SEE ALSO: After Postmodernism; Mixed-Genre Fiction; Post-9/11 Narratives; Queer and LGBT Fiction; The New Experimentalism/The Contemporary Avant-Garde; Third-Wave Feminism

REFERENCES

Chevaillier, Flore. (2017). *Divergent Trajectories: Interviews with Innovative Fiction Writers*. Columbus: Ohio State University Press.

DeShell, Jeffrey. (1997). Between the winding sheets: The American Woman in the Chinese Hat. *The Review of Contemporary Fiction* 17 (3): 194–120.

Maso, Carole. (1990). *The Art Lover*. San Francisco: North Point.

Maso, Carole. (1993). *AVA*. Normal, IL: Dalkey Archive.

Maso, Carole. (2000a). *Break Every Rule: Essays on Language, Longing and Moments of Desire*. Washington, DC: Counterpoint.

Maso, Carole. (2000b). *The Room Lit by Roses: A Journal of Pregnancy and Birth*. Washington, DC: Counterpoint.

Maso, Carole. (2012). *Mother and Child*. Berkeley, CA: Counterpoint.

Moore, Steven. (1997). A new language for desire: Aureole. *The Review of Contemporary Fiction* 17 (3): 206–214.

Quinn, Roseanne Giannini. (2001). "We were working on an erotic song cycle": reading Carole Maso's AVA as the poetics of female Italian-American cultural and sexual identity. *MELUS* 26 (1): 91–113.

Silbergleid, Robin. (2010). Speaking (in) the silences: gender and anti-narrative in Carole Maso's *Defiance*. *Tulsa Studies in Women's Literature* 29 (2): 331–349.

Stirling, Grant. (1998). Mourning and metafiction: Carole Maso's *The Art Lover*. *Contemporary Literature* 39 (4): 586–613.

Worthington, Marjorie. (2000). Posthumous posturing: the subversive power of death in contemporary women's fiction. *Studies in the Novel* 32 (2): 243–263.

FURTHER READING

Chevaillier, Flore. (2013). *The Body of Writing: An Erotics of Contemporary American Fiction*. Columbus: Ohio State University Press.

Cooley, Nicole. (1995). Carole Maso: An interview. *American Poetry Review* 24 (2): 32–35.

Harris, Victoria Frenkel. (ed.) (1997). Special issue on Carole Maso. *The Review of Contemporary Fiction* 17 (3): 104–215.

Silbergleid, Robin. (2007). "Treblinka, a rather beautiful word": Carole Maso's post-Holocaust narrative. *Modern Fiction Studies* 53 (1): 1–26.

Stirling, Grant. (1998). Exhausting heteronarrative: *The American Woman in the Chinese Hat*. *MFS Modern Fiction Studies* 44 (4): 935–958.

Mason, Bobbie Ann

ALEX JONES
Vanderbilt University, USA

Hailing from Western Kentucky, Bobbie Ann Mason (b. 1940) is a writer who bears a vexed relationship to contemporaneity. With the appearance of her short story "Still Life with Watermelon" in a 1983 issue of *Granta Magazine*, Mason was quickly grouped with an emerging group of writers known as the "dirty realists." A loose collection of authors including Raymond Carver and Jayne Ann Philips, the dirty realists focused on the gritty, mundane experiences of working-class characters in heartland America. Mason's mastery of the short story form – particularly in her first collection *Shiloh and Other Stories* (1982) – was of a piece with the minimalist understatement perfected by the dirty realists. Mason's fiction features working-class characters guzzling Coca-Cola, and devotedly tuning in to late night reruns of $M*A*S*H$, hardly typical content in late twentieth-century literature. Yet her focus on the enclosure of the rural landscape of Kentucky and the daily rhythms that accompany it is a peculiar characteristic for a writer bearing the moniker of "contemporary" in the 1980s. In Mason's fiction, the rural–urban dialectic is one in which the former is still holding out, though barely. Mason is fixated by the rootlessness of modernity and the troubled search for a rural home in a world of urban transients, a fait accompli in the work of her fellow dirty realists and of postmodern writers. To read Bobbie Ann Mason is to grapple with a writer deftly balancing a certain belatedness and a particular contemporaneity.

In her Pulitzer Prize-nominated memoir *Clear Springs* (1999), Mason dwells on "[t]he allure of rootlessness" that severs her from the soil, speech patterns, and shifting landscape of Western Kentucky (1999, p. 6). Mason delivers a set of rhetorical questions in her memoir's opening chapter, "The Family Farm, 1994": "What happened to me and my generation? What made us leave home and abandon the old ways? Why did we lose our knowledge of nature? Why wasn't it satisfying? Why would only rock-and-roll music do? What did we want?" (p. 11). "The Family Farm" reads as a rewrite of Leo Marx's *The Machine in the Garden: Technology and the Pastoral Ideal in America* (1964), but here personally reconfigured by the prodigal daughter. As Marx used the sight and sound of a train disrupting Thoreau's idyllic paradise, so Mason views Seaboard Farms' chicken-processing plant that looms above the family farm as a threat to an entire "way of life" (1999, p. 14). Turning her gaze towards the highway that bisects the farm, Mason's nostalgia is bitterly tempered by "the wires and poles, the asphalt, the Detroit metal, the discarded junk-food wrappers and beer cans thrown from cars that have 'twentieth century' written all over them" (p. 8). Mason marshals both nostalgia and critique, but her assessments of the family farm are seldom unequivocal. Seaboard Farms employs many people in Clear Springs. Mason's mother "approves of progress, even though she finds much of it scary and empty." The highway, littered and disruptive as it is, "called" Mason and her siblings to careers in writing, Hollywood, and the corporate world (p. 11). And most importantly, Mason's parents are glad that their children are spared a life of agonizing toil ploughing the soil.

Mason has narrated this tension most sustainedly in the character of Nancy Culpepper, a close stand-in for the author. First featured in the titular short story "Nancy Culpepper" and then "Lying Doggo" (both collected in *Shiloh*), Culpepper then reappeared in the novella *Spence + Lila* (1988) and *Zigzagging Down a Wild Trail: Stories* (2001), before her accumulated appearances were collected and rounded out in the life-spanning *Nancy Culpepper* (2006). Like Mason, Culpepper left her native Western Kentucky to attend graduate school in the Northeast. And, like Mason, Culpepper wrestles with her allegiances to her parents, her grandmother (known as "Granny" throughout), and to her former rural existence that she has consciously, anxiously spurned. Culpepper, Mason's most conflicted character, is a quintessential transient and dabbler. She is variously a stay-at-home mother, a bohemian traveler, a vice principal at her son's primary school, and an amateur historian, realizing towards the end of her life that she has never had a career to anchor her. Upward mobility often comes at the price of a general nomadism in Mason's fiction and dramatizes the pitfalls of tying one's identity to a profession rather than a specific place. This eternal wandering is literalized in *The Girl in the Blue Beret* (2011), where the protagonist is an airline pilot. In Nancy's last appearance in "The Prelude" (2006), Culpepper, well into her sixties, reunites with her estranged husband Jack in the English Lake District. With her sister, Nancy has sold the Culpepper farm in Kentucky (see "The Heirs"); Nancy and Jack have likewise sold their home in Boston, leaving the pair peripatetic by the time readers leave Nancy. "Where *can* we live?" Nancy asks Jack in the story's final line (2006, p. 224; original italics).

Yet Mason's return to Nancy across the span of her career suggests a fictional world of solidity, integrity, and ongoingness. (The Culpepper family is mentioned a few times in Mason's early twentieth-century historical novel *Feather Crowns* [1993].) Nancy floats into and out of Mason's short story collections and novels – her fleeting permanence rather oxymoronic. Her habitual reappearances give Mason's fictional world a sense of organic wholeness, but this wholeness is only achieved through Nancy's capacity to remain largely offscreen, waiting in the wings. In *Nancy Culpepper* our access to Nancy is temporally compartmentalized: we drop into Nancy's life in different settings in 1980–1982, 1985, 1994, 2002, and then 2005. Each event that happens in these selected years is necessarily metonymic for that time. A rootless life is one where small events must stand in for a fragmentary whole.

It is important to understand that Mason's use of Nancy to explore "the allure of rootlessness" is not simply a matter of geography but an interpersonal affect (2006, p. 6).

Rootlessness takes place in Nancy's strained relationship with Jack when he accuses his wife of overemphasizing her Southern heritage and then resists her sporadic urges to visit Kentucky. Jack is frustrated that Hopewell – the setting for *Feather Crowns*, *In Country* (1985), and for the bulk of Mason's short stories – remains the stable referent for "home" in his relationship, no matter how much Hopewell itself changes, and no matter how far Nancy drifts from Western Kentucky. Hopewell is thus a tenacious setting, a holdout against the forces of modern economic necessity. It is also a richly peopled dossier for Mason, who deploys Hopewell multiple times as a rooted counterpoint to a world succumbing to mass rootlessness.

Rootlessness is generative for Mason, posing the interlocking problems of inheritance, continuity, and futurity. It is often the perils of the chemical world that give these problems narrative form in Mason's fiction. In the novel *An Atomic Romance* (2005), Reed Futrell is a hedonistic engineer at a uranium enrichment plant. His budding romance with Julia, a student of molecular biology, is thrown off course when Julia learns of reports of radioactive spillage in the local Fort Wolf Wildlife Refuge where the two have recently gone camping. Reed must scrutinize his own complicity in papering over the human and environment threats posed by his employer, which led him to knowingly take Julia to the refuge. *An Atomic Romance* is an exploration of the cascading nature of compromise. It is about the politics of romance, and how compromise at work in turn compromises romantic relationships. At the end of the novel, when Julia tells Reed that she is pregnant, the couple rejoice. Yet for the reader, the threat of birth defects caused by Reed's multiple exposures to neptunium clouds the happy scene. The novel is schizophrenically balanced between hopes for the future generation and its precarious chemical inheritance.

In Country, Mason's most well-known and enduring novel, probes a young woman's "inheritance" of the Vietnam War that is also chemically suffused (1985, p. 89). Eighteen-year-old Sam Hughes longs to understand the experiences of her father, a young man killed in action in Vietnam in the late 1960s. Set in the middle of the Reagan years, Sam's limited access to her father's experience is mediated by a motley collection of taciturn veterans in the small Kentucky town of Hopewell. Sam's two main points of contact among the vets are her uncle Emmett, whom she lives with, and her crush, Tom, a local mechanic. The epistemological gap that Sam confronts is overlaid by a gender divide. As one vet admonishes Sam, "You don't know how it was, and you never will. There is no way you can ever understand. So just forget it" (p. 136). War is men's business. Yet the war has feminized Emmett, who, like Klinger in *M*A*S*H*, wears women's dresses and – like many of the vets in Hopewell – has difficulties making a commitment to women. Sam fears that Emmett's pimply skin is actually chloracne, a symptom of Agent Orange. She suspects that Emmett has been chemically castrated by Agent Orange, much like Tom, who cannot gain an erection when trying to seduce Sam. Sam's particular inheritance of the Vietnam War is thus also a meditation on the problem of reproductive futurity, because Agent Orange ripples out from Hopewell into the stretches of deep time. To be "in country" is to reside in a chronotope of extended wartime, encompassing what is brought home from Vietnam to the rural country of Western Kentucky. War hovers, chemically, in the perpetual present.

For Mason, reflections on reproduction, history, and deep time are especially suited to longer forms like the novel. Mason is adept at planting counter-histories into the minds of her characters that would alter the course of the present. In *An Atomic Romance*, Reed wonders "If his father hadn't died in a chemical accident, would he now be suffering from leukemia or liver cancer?" (2005, p. 109). In *Spence + Lila*, Spence shudders at the thought of Lila having had a stroke in the "lonely trails" of Florida while on a family holiday rather than at home in Kentucky (1988, p. 35). Mason skillfully exploits the anxious grooves of the subjunctive. Character development in Mason is a byproduct of such apprehensive inner questioning. The thought of whether things could have been different shapes and distorts the present.

Scrambling contexts is accordingly another favored Mason technique. Mason's characters long to be transported to other worlds. After a few drinks at a veterans' dance in *In Country*, Sam tipsily desires to experience Vietnam: "A pool of orange light from a mercury lamp was the color of napalm. A napalm bomb frozen in time, she thought. Palm trees under the light. Nay-palm. No palms" (1985, p. 124). Alternatively, other characters resist such bewildering transportation. In an enormous Wal-Mart parking lot in *Spence + Lila*, Spence forgets where he is, perceiving that "The vertical lines of street lamps tower in the landscape like defoliated trees," a horrific reminder of the use of pesticides on his family farm (1988, p. 58). The ultimate lesson – positive and brutal simultaneously – simply involves persevering through this historical thicket and "replacing your own life with new ones," as Lila muses while confronting the possibility of cobalt treatments for breast cancer in *Spence + Lila* (p. 29).

Given their brevity, Mason's short stories tend to eschew considerations of ultimate lessons, making her work particularly suitable to *The New Yorker*, which published four short stories from *Shiloh*. Like other dirty realists, Mason's stories are, in the words of Bill Buford, "unadorned, unfurnished, low-rent tragedies about people who watch day-time television, read cheap romances or listen to country and western music" (Buford 1983).

There was a taste among readers, Buford further noted, for tales about "the belly-side of contemporary life" in Reagan's neoliberal America. As Maggie Doherty (2015) has shown, the dirty realists' sparse sentences led to a flurry of awards and prizes. *Shiloh* won the prestigious PEN/Hemingway Award for first fiction in 1983 and led to a Guggenheim Fellowship for Mason. Yet her early career success left Mason with the particular curse of the precocious: her work would forever be judged by how it measured up to *Shiloh* and *In Country*.

Yet literary culture in the 1980s was split on the question of whether dirty realism represented a revolution from below in the subject matter and style of literary fiction, or if the slew of MFA graduates publishing clipped prose heralded what John Aldridge dismissively labeled "the new assembly-line fiction," strenuous editing a poor substitute for genuine innovation (Aldridge 1992). Yet Mason was not an MFA graduate like fellow dirty realists Tobias Wolff and Richard Ford. (Indeed, she published her PhD dissertation in 1974 on Vladimir Nabokov's postmodern epic *Ada, or Ardor* [1969]). Mason's MFA-less status makes it likewise difficult to graft Mason into the cast of characters forming what Mark McGurl has termed "the program era" (McGurl 2009). Mason has rejected the minimalist and "K-Mart realist" labels, asserting that the pared back style of her prose is inspired by the clipped rhythms of Kentucky speech (see the interviews collected in *Patchwork* [2018]).

Reading Mason's short story collections, an overarching subject emerges: a couple negotiate the pressures of long-term commitment against the backdrop of a modernizing Western Kentucky dotted with subdivisions, malls, and big-box stores. Often what tests the couple is exactly this notion of home – suburbanized, modern – so different from the generation or two before. Strained romantic relationships amidst a generalized rootlessness is the blueprint for Mason's short stories. This broad template is found in "The Retreat," "Graveyard Day," "Shiloh," "The Rookers," "Third Monday," "Residents and Transients," and "Still Life with Watermelon" in *Shiloh*; "Sorghum," "Midnight Magic," "Memphis," "Big Bertha Stories," "Piano Fingers," and "Coyotes" in *Love Life: Stories* (1989); and "Tunica," "The Funeral Side," "Window Lights," and "Charger" in *Zigzagging*. Slightly more than her novels, Mason's short story collections are united by their thematic similarity, which has changed remarkably little in the two decades separating the publications of *Shiloh* and *Zigzagging*.

In "Still Life with Watermelon," Louise Milsap's husband Tom has left her to work on a ranch in Texas. "[D]etermined to get along without Tom," Louise, who has lost her job at the local Kroger, starts painting watermelons, hoping to sell her work to a wealthy collector from Paducah (1982, p. 61). When Tom finally returns, Louise realizes that her desire to paint does not stem from artistic pleasure but arises "out of spite" for her drifting husband. Louise's gaze is frustratingly anchored to Tom's wandering star. Her self-righteous notion of domestic responsibility actually conceals her admiration for her drifting husband. Louise ultimately realizes that "perhaps the meaning of home grows out of the fear of open spaces" (p. 73).

"Charger," the concluding story of *Zigzagging*, follows a 19-year-old who frets that he is prematurely entering into a dull middle age. His girlfriend, Tiffany, still in high school, wants to get married, and Charger intuits that he is unlikely to rise above his minimum wage job at a local fertilizer company. When the couple go on a trip to Nashville, Charger abruptly veers west toward Texas, hoping to miraculously run into his roaming father, who recently abandoned his family to head for the Lone Star state. Spurred by the disappearance of his father, Charger feels as if he "had been catapulted forward," stuck in a predetermined future (2001, p. 202). The story ends in a Memphis hotel room, with Charger hoping that "If he got an early start on what his father had gone to see, maybe he would not mind what was to come later. It would be a way to fool destiny" (p. 209). Going on the road paradoxically allows and then disallows Charger the agency to alter his bleak future.

Mason's interests in anticipation and belatedness have received a different inflection in her intermittent turn to historical fiction. Set in 1980, *The Girl in the Blue Beret* is based on the experiences of Mason's real-life father-in-law. The novel chronicles mandatorily retired pilot Marshall Stone in his search to find and thank the members of the French Resistance who helped him escape the Nazis in World War II. Marshall was a cocky fighter pilot shot down on the French–Belgium border on his way back from his tenth bombing mission in 1944. Set adrift from the logbooks, maps, and strict flight schedules that locked him firmly in the present, 60-year-old Marshall feels unanchored, his murky past "in front of him" (2011, p. 23). The novel's method is to exploit repressions, carefully hidden remembrances, and faulty memories. Marshall is shocked to recall that a fellow crew member did not die when the aircraft crashed but was actually with Marshall when he crossed the Pyrenees into Spain, only to then tragically disappear amidst scattered gunfire from the Nazis at this pivotal moment. But the novel never pursues these caesuras beyond pointing to Marshall's tireless rigidity and attachment to routine that heretofore prohibited the backward glance. *Blue Beret* is ultimately overdependent on a simple view of the malleability of the past, which seems a lackluster use of the affordances of historical fiction.

Feather Crowns, Mason's more assured contribution to the genre of historical fiction, transforms uncertainty about the past into the vexed quality of singular historical events. In 1900, Christianna Wheeler, the wife of James, gives birth to quintuplets in Hopewell, Kentucky. The event, unrivalled across the continent, elicits an immense amount of excitement in the locality and interstate. Amidst this hubbub, however, all five babies tragically die. A local funeral owner chemically preserves the quintuplets in an "eternal bed," another variation of a chemical afterlife (1993, p. 318). An untrustworthy promoter, Greenberry McCain, offers the Wheelers the chance to tour the babies across the South, the closest Mason ever comes to Southern gothic. *Feather Crowns* raises a series of questions that register as strained silences between Christianna and James. Was the decision to charge admission to see the quintuplets justified given the family's debt, or was the handling of babies by strangers what ultimately resulted in their deaths? Is the experience of touring the quintuplets cathartic for Christianna, or does her hatred for the gawking crowds overpower her journey through the grieving process? Mason leaves all such questions unanswered. The novel subtly explores the erosion of the private sphere and casts Mason in the role of historical diagnostician, identifying the early twentieth-century fascination with spectacle and the profit-seeking forces impinging upon home. While *Feather Crowns* reaches deeper into the past than any of her other fictions, the Wheelers' problematic decision to leave home for the perils of the outside world is vintage Mason, recasting rootlessness into a time period when it does not feel anachronistic. For the rest of her oeuvre, however, Mason would wrestle with the dual strains of belatedness and contemporaneity in a world of fiction otherwise resistant to the lures of rural life.

SEE ALSO: Carver, Raymond; Contemporary Regionalisms; Ford, Richard; Illness and Disability Narratives; Minimalism and Maximalism; Phillips, Jayne Anne

REFERENCES

Aldridge, John W. (1992). *Talents and Technicians: Literary Chic and the New Assembly-Line Fiction*. New York: Scribner's.

Buford, Bill. (1983). Editorial. *Granta* 8 (June 1, 1983). https://granta.com/dirtyrealism/ (accessed July 9, 2021).

Doherty, Maggie. (2015). State-funded fiction: minimalism, national memory, and the return to realism in the post-postmodern age. *American Literary History* 27 (1): 79–101.

Mason, Bobbie Ann. (1982). *Shiloh and Other Stories*. New York: Harper & Row.

Mason, Bobbie Ann. (1985). *In Country*. New York: Harper & Row.

Mason, Bobbie Ann. (1988). *Spence + Lila*. New York: Harper & Row.

Mason, Bobbie Ann. (1993). *Feather Crowns*. New York: HarperCollins.

Mason, Bobbie Ann. (1999). *Clear Springs: A Memoir*. New York: Random House.

Mason, Bobbie Ann. (2001). *Zigzagging Down a Wild Trail: Stories*. New York: Random House.

Mason, Bobbie Ann. (2005). *An Atomic Romance*. New York: Random House.

Mason, Bobbie Ann. (2006). *Nancy Culpepper: Stories*. New York: Random House.

Mason, Bobbie Ann. (2011). *The Girl in the Blue Beret*. New York: Random House.

Mason, Bobbie Ann. (2018). *Patchwork*. Lexington: University Press of Kentucky.

McGurl, Mark. (2009). *The Program Era: Postwar Fiction and the Rise of Creative Writing*. Cambridge: Harvard University Press.

FURTHER READING

Armstrong, Rhonda Jenkins. (2012). Transformational spectacle in Bobbie Ann Mason's *Feather Crowns*. *The Southern Literary Journal* 45 (1): 39–55.

Docarmo, Stephen N. (2003). Bombs from Coke cans: appropriating mass culture in Bobbie Ann Mason's *In Country*. *Journal of Popular Culture* 36 (3): 589–599.

Hinrichsen, Lisa. (2008). I can't believe it was really real: violence, Vietnam, and bringing war home in Bobbie Ann Mason's *In Country*. *The Southern Literary Journal* 40 (2): 232–248.
Price, Joanna. (2000). *Understanding Bobbie Ann Mason*. Columbia: University of South Carolina Press.
Wilhelm, Albert. (1998). *Bobbie Ann Mason: A Study of the Short Fiction*. New York and London: Twayne.

Maupin, Armistead

TED ATKINSON
Mississippi State University, USA

Armistead Maupin emerged as an author of note in the mid-1970s, earning a reputation for dismantling binary oppositions constructed within the framework of restrictive cultural norms: straight/queer, conservative/liberal, and puritanical/permissive, to name a few. Drawing praise from critics while landing on bestseller lists, Maupin became a literary celebrity whose ties to the likes of British expat author Christopher Isherwood and Hollywood movie idol Rock Hudson confirmed that he had arrived in the American cultural firmament. From the outset, Maupin's literary production has defied conventions of style and genre used by taste makers to define "popular literature" for the masses in contrast to "literary fiction" regarded as more aesthetically refined to the preferences of sophisticated readers. Maupin's notoriety rests largely on the *Tales of the City* series comprising nine novels published between 1978 and 2014. Add to that television adaptations as adept as the original source material at pleasing critics and popular audiences alike, and Maupin can be viewed as the creator of a cultural franchise. At the center is the storied 28 Barbary Lane in San Francisco, where an apartment complex converted from a Victorian-style house becomes home to a group of characters whose lives and experiences evince historical and cultural touchstones over roughly three decades. The proprietor, Anna Madrigal, functions as the surrogate mother in what Maupin brands a "logical family" constituted not by blood but by bonds of mutual consent and a shared sense of countercultural identification. Maupin has also published two novels that stand apart even as they are revealed to exist within the *Tales* expanded universe: *Maybe the Moon* (1992) and *The Night Listener* (2000). In 2017, he published *Logical Family: A Memoir*, which became the basis of a Netflix documentary film, *The Untold Tales of Armistead Maupin* (2017). Maupin's life story reads as a study in personal and professional contradictions and transformations, unfolding much like the serialized path of twists and turns he charts for his most indelible characters. From youth and young adulthood spent as a closeted son of the conservative South to a stint in the military, from a tour of duty in Vietnam to coming out and coming into his own as a gay man in San Francisco, Maupin positioned himself to become a skilled chronicler of the ongoing conflict between cultural and countercultural forces in American society. He has done so by adapting and queering traditional literary genres and forms to produce a body of work regarded for its finely observed depictions of the features and bugs that give shape and meaning to the human experience.

The origin story of Maupin's signature series begins in 1976, the United States Bicentennial, when the *San Francisco Chronicle* published the first installment of a regular column under the banner, "Tales of the City." In short order, the column attracted a devoted group of readers who became engrossed in the serialized sketches, taking in the view of San Francisco presented through the eyes of the protagonist, Mary Ann Singleton, a recent transplant to the West Coast from the Midwest. Mary Ann's struggle to find her way in a strange land populated by a large cast of eccentrics bears resemblance to Dorothy's adventures in Oz except with "friends of Dorothy" and adult subject matter and themes instead of the beloved children's fare. Maupin compiled and revised the initial run of sketches, shaping them into *Tales of the City*, a novel published in 1978. The same process of revising and reshaping serialized stories yielded three more novels published in steady succession: *More Tales of the City* (1980); *Further Tales of the City* (1982); and *Babycakes* (1984). The fifth book in the series, *Significant Others* (1987), came from material in the *San Francisco Examiner*, where the column moved for the remainder of its runtime as a newspaper serial. At the time, it appeared that *Significant Others* might mean the end of *Tales* once and for all. But Maupin delighted his followers by publishing *Michael Tolliver Lives* in 2007; it was the first in the series composed as a novel from start to finish. The book is also notable for the dramatic shift in perspective from the distant third-person narration that serves as an effective mechanism for Maupin's keen powers of social observation and ear for dialogue on display in the first six installments to a first-person perspective affording an intimate view of the titular character, Michael "Mouse" Tolliver, a founding member of the Barbary Lane logical family. The mood of reflection and contemplation in *Michael Tolliver Lives* permeates the remaining two books published in the series as it stands now: *Mary Ann in Autumn* (2010) and *The Days of Anna Madrigal* (2014).

The title of the column and first novel made plain one of the most indelible influences on Maupin's work: Charles Dickens. The name alone confirms that *Tales of the City* pays titular homage to *A Tale of Two Cities* (1859). Indeed, the famous opening passage of the Dickens classic ("It was the best of times, it was the worst of times...") has an epigraphic resonance when applied to Maupin's debut novel, despite the fact that Maupin borrowed a line from Oscar Wilde, not Dickens, for the actual epigraph. The element of duality – the inherent tension between opposing forces defining a given era – that Dickens evokes is key for Maupin in subverting dominant narratives and restrictive social constructions of gender, race, class, and sexuality by subjecting them to the destabilizing pressure of nonconformity. It stands to reason that the small but astute body of scholarship on Maupin to this point pays heed to his Dickensian predilection (Kellerman 2016; Warhol 1999; Bram 2012). The publication history of *Tales* is a common point of comparison, given that the serialized novel was Dickens's literary modus operandi in the Victorian era. Working in that mode, as Maupin has observed on numerous occasions, meant that the gap between composition and publication was never wide and often too close for comfort. It is all the more remarkable, then, that the author managed to keep track of the multiple characters' paths intersecting and storylines unfolding (another Dickensian parallel) while writing to deadline. Although the tight schedule generated pressure, it imbued the fiction with an air of contemporary relevance strengthened by Maupin's knack for tapping into the zeitgeist for creative inspiration. That talent was still evident after he had abandoned the column and then decided to reboot the series after a hiatus of nearly two decades. The documentary component of Maupin's literary production, like that of Dickens, means that over time the works transform from serial novels rooted in their time to social novels of their time without seeming outdated. Maupin's literary canvas evinces a technique that resists painting the grand strokes of history in the making as a backdrop in favor of rendering it at the granular level of San Francisco through the lives of characters playing out in intricately woven plots reminiscent of those fashioned by Dickens.

The suspension of the series for an extended time makes it possible to categorize the early phase of the *Tales* series published thus far as a sextet, the remainder as a trilogy. While the groupings are chronological, they also reflect an unmistakable shift in tone, mood, and method heavily influenced by the social, cultural, and political changes that took place in American society in the interim. The first six novels coincide with a timespan encompassing the ongoing sexual revolution in the 1970s to the onset and outbreak of the AIDS epidemic in the first half of the 1980s. Part of what makes Mary Ann Singleton's acclimation to San Francisco at the front end of this period so difficult is that she flinches at the open expressions of sexual liberation she observes in the city, as represented by the main cast of neighbors and friends she meets at Barbary Lane: Michael Tolliver, a gay man who plays the field as he holds out hope for long-term commitment; Brian Hawkins, a heterosexual waiter/Lothario; and Mona Ramsey, a woman whose artistic aspirations are thwarted by working in advertising and whose bisexuality splits the difference. Methodically, Maupin tantalizes readers with the prospect of a deep, dark secret kept by the enigmatic Anna Madrigal before revealing it to be that she is transgender, having undergone sexual reassignment surgery in Denmark when the procedure was in its infancy. With the straight and putatively strait-laced Mary Ann rounding out the core group, Maupin renders 28 Barbary Lane a gender and sexuality spectrum that grows more colorful as the narrative scope widens to encompass the whole cityscape and sometimes points beyond. In addition to the representative characters, Maupin incorporates into the serialized narrative historical references that serve as temporal markers in the overall narrative progression. Typically, it is possible to trace historical timelines through characters' storylines as they unfold over the course of several installments. Michael Tolliver's arc in the first six novels, for example, is a microcosm of the burgeoning AIDS crisis. Accordingly, he moves from indulging in the hedonism of dance clubs and bathhouses in the Castro District to losing a former lover to AIDS to testing positive himself for HIV before the development of AZT and various other drug cocktails prolong his life so that he is able to become a small business owner and to experience a long-term, serodiscordant relationship complete with joint home ownership. Along the way, actual historical figures enter the picture, often in appearances that suggest Maupin is testing the limits of readers' credulity. In bizarre storylines fueled by happenstance, fictional characters encounter such notables as a seemingly resurrected Jim Jones, the infamous cult leader responsible for the Jonestown massacre, and Queen Elizabeth II and Prince Philip during their official visit to California in 1983. These and other cases in point enhance the playful surrealism that is a hallmark of Maupin's storytelling.

In the span between *Sure of You* (1989), the presumptive final installment of *Tales*, and the reboot that occurred with the publication in 2007 of *Michael Tolliver Lives*, the American cultural landscape experienced dramatic change, particularly with regard to the matter of gay rights and queer representation. The Michael who narrates the series reboot offers ruminations on the past depicted in the first six novels that are tinged with nostalgia for the relatively carefree days before AIDS struck and laced with melancholy owing to the decimation of his community the plague caused, but he is also aware that culture at large has grown generally more accommodating to gay men and lesbians. The two subsequent novels share the recognition of a new social reality for gays and lesbians, depicting characters' lives and relationships playing out in a post-marriage equality landscape shaped by a reversal in public opinion and significant gains in civil rights after decades of social and political activism in the face of rampant homophobia and oppressive heteronormative standards. In many respects, the milieu of the later novels seems far removed from *More Tales of the City*, in which Michael comes out to his family in the form of a letter written at a moment of pique after learning of his mother's support for Anita Bryant's homophobic Save Our Children campaign. Incidentally, when the missive first appeared in Maupin's newspaper column, it was the author's means of coming out to his parents without a direct confrontation. Michael's poignant expression of overcoming shame to take pride in his identity served the same purpose for many gay men who used Michael as a proxy for coming out to family and friends, giving "Letter to Mama" a life of its own outside the novel. In *Michael Tolliver Lives*, though, his mother, now in a Florida nursing home, is more tolerant, if not always accepting, of Michael's "lifestyle," as are his conservative brother and his evangelical Christian wife. Now in a long-term, serodiscordant relationship with Ben, a much younger man he met online, Michael and his partner take a cross-country trip to Orlando, the place he once called home. This visit lays the groundwork for a melodramatic, soap operatic climax when Michael eventually chooses to remain in San Francisco with the suddenly hospitalized Anna Madrigal and his logical family rather than return to Florida for a second time when he learns that his biological mother has taken a turn for the worse and is near death. Over the course of this novel and the remainder of the trilogy, the logical family at Barbary Lane is reunited (upon Mary Ann's return to San Francisco) and reconstituted to extend the sexuality and gender spectrum even further. In the sextet, transgender representation is largely confined to Anna Madrigal (whose name is revealed as an anagram for "a man and a girl"), but by the trilogy that scope broadens considerably to reflect how transgender issues have moved to the vanguard of the struggle for equality (especially in the wake of marriage equality) along with a proliferating set of identities expressed by the symbol at the end of the now commonly applied acronym LGBTQ+. The use of flashbacks in *The Days of Anna Madrigal* makes clear that the doyenne of Barbary Lane is the overarching figure whose lifetime encompasses the decades of struggle, resilience, tragedy, and triumph that define the contours of queer history.

Like Anna Madrigal and the other central characters in *Tales*, Maupin made his way to San Francisco in search of a place where he could feel at home instead of restricted by home as had become increasingly the case in the South of his youth. For Maupin, as for Michael Tolliver, this journey meant following the standard script for queer people in American cultural production. It dictates that escaping hidebound midsize cities and rural towns to find freedom in a proverbial gay mecca (San Francisco or New York) is essential for queer people not only to survive but also to thrive on the strength of authenticity. The notion that Maupin abandoned the South, however, diminishes the importance of regional influences that have remained with him in his life and, in turn, have informed his writing. As noted, critics have identified Dickens as Maupin's most direct literary forebear, but another prospect emerges when considering his work in the context of southern literature: Thomas Wolfe. Maupin showed admiration for his fellow North Carolinian when he spearheaded a successful effort in 1966 for his graduating class at the University of North Carolina, Chapel Hill, to bequeath a campus memorial dedicated to Wolfe. The influence on Maupin is apparent when turning to Wolfe's debut, *Look Homeward, Angel* (1929). Among the settings in this sprawling novel with autobiographical elements is a boarding house run by a woman based on Wolfe's mother and populated by a cast of eccentric tenants. For readers steeped in *Tales*, it is sure to call to mind Anna Madrigal and her apartment complex at 28 Barbary

Lane. Another signature work by Wolfe, the posthumously published *You Can't Go Home Again* (1940), suggests further connections by registering seismic historical events in the making from the perspective of a character feeling their impact in his immediate surroundings and in the course of his own life. In this regard, Wolfe's George Webber, a southerner in exile witnessing the rise of Hitler and fascism in Germany among other historical milestones, has much in common with Maupin's Michael Tolliver as he observes and experiences firsthand the devastating effects of the AIDS crisis as a denizen of San Francisco. Moreover, the title of this signature Wolfe novel serves as an apt thematic expression of the unsettling and alienating effects of returning to a place that once was but no longer can be home that Maupin depicts in the Orlando section of *Michael Tolliver Lives*.

While Wolfean notes of autobiographical fiction with southern inflections are detectable in *Tales*, they register as pronounced echoes in *The Night Listener*, a roman à clef praised by critics as a complex work of literary fiction written in an elevated style relative to the more famous *Tales*. The Maupin analogue is the narrator, Gabriel Noone, a gay man who fled his native South for San Francisco before becoming a renowned author. Noone's fame is enhanced by *Noone at Night*, a popular program on National Public Radio featuring the author reading from a series of serialized sketches he pens. The particular audience member referenced in the title is Peter Lomax, a 13-year-old boy and the reputed author of a forthcoming memoir based on his traumatic childhood experience of enduring sexual assault and exploitation for years at the hands of his parents and contracting full-blown AIDS as a result. Over time, Noone and Lomax form a long-distance friendship that provides emotional sustenance to Noone as his long-term relationship is coming to an end. The foundation of the burgeoning friendship cracks, however, once people close to Noone and eventually the author himself come to believe that Lomax is a persona crafted by an impostor rather than a real person. The novel is based on an actual experience Maupin (along with other celebrities) had with someone claiming to be a teenage boy, sexual assault survivor, and AIDS patient named Godby Johnson. Among many parallels between Noone the narrator and Maupin the author are tours of duty in the Navy, coming-out letters to family embedded in fiction, and emotionally distant fathers who regard virulent racism as part of being a gentleman of the old school. On one level, *The Night Listener* is a variation on *Michael Tolliver Lives*, in this instance the veil between author and narrator existing literally in name only. As such, it contributes to a probing exploration of the uncanny aspects of postmodern identity formation and a metafictional reckoning with the effects of celebrity status on an author's life and work. For Maupin, it has meant garnering a measure of fame and fandom while queering traditional genres and forms in producing a body of work widely regarded for exhibiting the rare combination of literary merit and mainstream appeal.

SEE ALSO: Contemporary Regionalisms; The Culture Wars; Queer and LGBT Fiction; Urban Fiction

REFERENCES

Bram, Christopher. (2012). *Eminent Outlaws: The Gay Writers Who Changed America*. New York: Twelve.

Kellerman, Robert. (2016). Goodbye, Barbary Lane: the passage of time in the recent novels of Armistead Maupin. *The Journal of American Culture* 39 (1): 41–54.

Warhol, Robyn R. (1999). Making "gay" and "lesbian" into household words: how serial form works in Armistead Maupin's *Tales of the City*. *Contemporary Literature* 40 (3): 378–402.

FURTHER READING

Browning, Jimmy D. (1993). Something to remember me by: Maupin's *Tales of the City* novels as artifacts in contemporary gay folk culture. *New York Folklore* 19 (1–2): 71–87.

Einstadter, Werner J. and Sinclair, Karen P. (2012). Lives on the boundary: Armistead Maupin's complete *Tales of the City*. *Journal of the History of Sexuality* 1 (6): 682–689.

Friend, Tad. (2001). Virtual love. *The New Yorker* (November 26, 2001): 88–94, 96–99. https://www.newyorker.com/magazine/2001/11/26/virtual-love-2

McBride, James

GERALD DAVID NAUGHTON
Qatar University, Qatar

One of the most interesting writers on race to emerge in the last decade of the twentieth century, James McBride (b. 1957) is an African American novelist, memoirist, and jazz musician. His memoir, *The Color of Water: A Black Man's Tribute to His White Mother* (1995), which spent two consecutive years on the *New York Times* Best Seller list, established him as a major figure in contemporary American literature. His novel *The Good Lord Bird* won the 2013 National Book Award for fiction. Both books revel in McBride's ability to find a new lexicon of race that embraces models of hybridity, heterogeneity, and racial complexity. Other significant works include *Miracle at St. Anna* (2001), *Song Yet Sung* (2008), and *Kill 'Em and Leave* (2016). He has written screenplays and teleplays in collaboration with both Spike Lee (*Miracle at St. Anna* [2008], *Red Hook Summer* [2012]) and David Simon (*Parting the Waters* [2000]). In 2015, McBride was presented with the National Humanities Medal by President Obama, who praised his work "for humanizing the complexities of discussing race in America" (Dwyer 2016).

All of McBride's major work is alive to the possibilities of racial redefinitions and dismissive of strict racial binaries. As such, it reflects a particular mode of writing and thinking about race that was ascendant at the turn of the twenty-first century; McBride's centering of hybridity in his writing has led some critics to position him within notions of "post-race" (Elam 2011, p. 46) – a frequently derided term, and one which McBride himself has always viewed with suspicion. America's "post-racial moment," which was being loudly heralded around the time of Barack Obama's rise to prominence in 2007, is a specific cultural period in which tropes of transracialism and post-racialism become the loci of important national debate (Turner and Nilsen 2014). As Sika Dagbovie-Mullins argues, the whole debate is fueled by "a national fantasy of transcending race, or at least, with escaping the divisive and bad feelings that dwelling on racial injustice seems to cause" (2013, p. 6). Today, as Ta-Nehisi Coates has written, "the term *post-racial* is almost never used in earnest" (2015).

Despite this, much of McBride's writing – particularly his 1995 memoir *The Color of Water* – has often been discussed as an exemplar of America's "post-racial moment" (Naughton 2018). Though not quite "post-racial" in outlook, McBride's writing is shaped by his own mixed-race background, and particularly by the influence of his mother, Ruth McBride Jordan, a white, Jewish woman who chose to marry a Black man in the 1940s, and raised her large family in the Projects of Red Hook in Brooklyn. Ruth McBride lived in Black communities her whole life without asserting any specific racial identity. Her racial ambiguity was the cause of much consternation for her mixed-race son growing up. Her best answer to his persistent questions simply "God is the color of water. Water doesn't have a color" (McBride 1996, p. 210). Obviously, taking this statement as the basis of his book,

McBride is also attracted to the notion of "not having a color," or rather of not conforming to America's racial taxonomy. Though he dislikes the term post-racial (Dagbovie-Mullins 2013, p. 86), he is equally (or more) suspicious over claims of racial essentialism. In *The Color of Water*, he tells the story of coming of age in Brooklyn and encountering versions of Blackness that were at odds with his hybrid reality. He describes the prevalence of Black essentialism in the urban North and finds, as William Ramsey has noted, that such essentialism "threaten[s] his sense of self as a mixed race person, a contradiction containing both the white oppressor and the black Other" (Ramsey 2005, p. 134).

Similarly, modes of racial contradiction occur in McBride's best-known novel, *The Good Lord Bird*, which plays on tropes of racial and gendered misidentification. Telling the story of John Brown's raid on Harpers Ferry, the novel is a farcical treatment of historical fiction that plays on many of the nineteenth century's most loaded racial symbols. Most notably, The *Good Lord Bird* satirizes nineteenth-century archetypes of mixed-race protagonists and passing narratives. Beginning in the middle of John Brown's ride through Kansas in the mid-1850s, the novel moves from a confused shoot-out in which the narrator, Henry Shakelford (later renamed Onion), is taken up as a good luck charm by Brown, who mistakes Onion for a girl. Onion spends seventeen years as a free Black woman and becomes the only Black survivor of Brown's ill-fated raid on Harpers Ferry in 1859. He is present both at Brown's infamous Pottawatomie massacre and at the chaotic battles at Black Jack and Osawatomie; he comes with Brown on a fundraising tour to Boston; he meets Frederick Douglass in Rochester, New York, and meets Harriet Tubman in Canada, and stays by Brown's side as he plans and attempts to execute the raid on Harpers Ferry. Onion's story is therefore rooted in historical record, but it is also an absolutely outlandish and barely believable yarn. As a preface, the novel follows the practice, established in nineteenth-century slave narratives, of including "authenticating material" to attest to the veracity of Onion's narrative. This document, however, seems clearly bogus, thus undercutting any such notion of authenticity, legitimacy, or purity in the text which follows.

One of the most telling ways in which *The Good Lord Bird* mocks authenticity is through McBride's ironic engagement with the well-worn antebellum tradition of the tragic mulatta narrative. As a Black male who "passes" into femininity, Onion is metatextually aware that his story presents an inversion of the typical nineteenth-century passing narrative – which typically occurs when racially mixed or hybrid female characters make the transgressive choice of passing into the white world. The protagonist of *The Good Lord Bird* instead "passes" as a mixed race female – thus passing from a stable identity category into a model of unstable racial and gender indeterminacy. At one point in the novel, as Onion is in danger of having his "true" identity uncovered, he claims for himself the ideological protection of the near-white, mixed-race tragic mulatta. He replies to the question of who he "really" is with the words, "the best part of me nearly as white as you, sir. I just don't know where I belongs, being a tragic mulatto and all." "Then," Onion tells us, "I busted into tears" (McBride 2013, p. 28). What this vignette reveals to us is McBride's ability to deconstruct categories of race as a mark of "belonging" (p. 28). Onion's claims of not knowing where he belongs are genuine – this is a novel of adolescence that has already been compared frequently to *The Adventures of Huckleberry Finn* (1884) (Hesse 2013) – but his attribution of this uncertainty to racial categorization is, in a sense, "false." His incongruous decision to pass is presented in the novel as a form of racial performance that shows up all of America's long-held identity categories as, in a sense, performative too.

McBride's other major work, *Miracle at St. Anna*, *Song Yet Sung*, and *Kill 'Em and Leave*, reveals his fascination with retelling Black history, and exploring the connection between performance, narrative, and historiography. Like *Good Lord Bird*, *Miracle at St. Anna* is a fictional treatment of Black history. In it, McBride retells the story of the African American 92nd Division's deployment to Italy during World War II. The novel was inspired by McBride's step-uncle, a veteran, who once commented to him as a child, "Boy ... back in the war, the Italians, they loved us! And the French ... oh, la, la! We was kings over there!" (McBride 2002, p. 259). Thus, the novel provides a transnational framework in which to reconfigure notions of racial and national belonging. McBride's second novel, *Song Yet Sung*, is set in a small Chesapeake Bay town just before the outbreak of the Civil War – a place where the reality of slavery was more ambiguous than in other parts of the country. Into this liminal space, McBride weaves a narrative of history and fantasy, as his protagonist, Liz Spocott, a young runaway slave, awakes from a coma with the ability to dream accurately of the future – from the near future to the twentieth-century Civil Rights movement, and beyond. Liz's visions help her and her fellow slaves to escape to freedom, but her knowledge of what that freedom will entail (the "song yet sung" of the novel's title) ironically undercuts that narrative progression. In *Kill 'Em and Leave*, McBride mixes memoir with biography, telling the story of the legendary soul musician James Brown. The book brings together many of McBride's constant literary obsessions: the role of music and performance is foregrounded, but the construction of Black identity through complex family structures is perhaps one of the book's most interesting aspects. McBride provides a detailed explanation of the singer's very complex family tree and explores how it informs and shapes the production of Brown's music and of his identity.

What McBride has contributed, then, to the shape of contemporary American literature is a hybridization of form, theme, and identity that runs through his diverse treatments of race and history in America. A jazz musician by trade, he has continued to experiment and improvise on the forms of fiction, historical fiction, and nonfiction. Significantly, this expansion of form has gone hand-in-hand with McBride's ongoing efforts to expand the very categories of identity with which McBride's characters continuously wrestle. In opening up new discussions of race, authenticity, and hybridity, McBride represents – particularly in his two best known books, *The Good Lord Bird* and *The Color of Water* – a writer who continues to shape our understanding of race in America.

SEE ALSO: Multiculturalism; Post-Soul and/or Post-Black Fiction; Whitehead, Colson

REFERENCES

Coates, Ta-Nehisi. (2015). There is no post-racial America. *The Atlantic* (August 2015). https://www.theatlantic.com/magazine/archive/2015/07/post-racial-society-distant-dream/395255/ (accessed October 11, 2021).

Dagbovie-Mullins, Sika. (2013). *Crossing Black: Mixed-Race Identity in Modern American Fiction and Culture*. Knoxville: University of Tennessee Press.

Dwyer, Colin. (2016). At White House, a golden moment for America's great artists and patrons. *NPR* (September 22, 2016). https://www.npr.org/sections/thetwo-way/2016/09/22/495011305/at-white-house-a-golden-moment-for-americas-great-artists-and-patrons (accessed October 11, 2021).

Elam, Michele. (2011). *The Souls of Mixed Folk: Race, Politics, and Aesthetics in the New Millennium*. Stanford: Stanford University Press.

Hesse, Monica. (2013). Novelist James McBride on bringing John Brown to life. *Washington Post* (December 3, 2013). https://www.washingtonpost.com/lifestyle/style/novelist-james-mcbride-on-bringing-john-brown-to-life/2013/12/03/61d48ca2-5c22-11e3-be07-006c776266ed_story.html (accessed October 11, 2021).

McBride, James. (1996). *The Color of Water: A Black Man's Tribute to His White Mother*. New York: Riverhead.

McBride, James. (2013). *The Good Lord Bird*. New York: Riverhead.
McBride, James. (2002). *Miracle at St. Anna*. New York: Riverhead.
Naughton, Gerald David. (2018). Posthistorical fiction and postracial passing in James McBride's *The Good Lord Bird*. Critique 59 (3): 346–354.
Ramsey, William M. (2005). Knowing their place: three Black writers and the postmodern South. *The Southern Literary Journal* 37 (2): 119–139.
Turner, Sarah E. and Nilsen, Sarah. (2014). *The Colorblind Screen: Television in Post-Racial America*. New York: NYU Press.

FURTHER READING

Dubey, Madhu. (2010). Speculative fictions of slavery. *American Literature* 82 (4): 779–805.
Gubar, Susan. (1997). *Racechanges: White Skin, Black Face in American Culture*. New York: Oxford University Press on Demand.
Hobbs, Allyson Vanessa. (2014). *A Chosen Exile: A History of Racial Passing in American Life*. Cambridge, MA: Harvard University Press.
Mickle, Mildred. (2018). *Critical Insights: James McBride*. Hackensack, NJ: Salem.
Newman Judie. (2020). African American history and the short story: James Mcbride's "The Under Graham Railroads Box Car Set." *Studies in the American Short Story* 1 (2): 180–186.
Newman, Judie. (2020). Folklore, fakelore, and the history of the dream: James McBride's *Song Yet Sung*. In: *21st Century US Historical Fiction* (ed. Ruth Maxey), 17–32. London: Palgrave Macmillan.
Rockquemore, Kerry Ann and Brunsma, David L. (2007). *Beyond Black: Biracial Identity in America*. Lanham, MD: Rowman & Littlefield.

McCarthy, Cormac

DAVID COWART
University of South Carolina, USA

The Cormac McCarthy canon may be likened to a great house, an imposing example of eclectic postmodern architecture – half Southwestern hacienda, half gothic pile inherited from Faulkner's Emily Grierson (central figure in the widely anthologized story "A Rose for Emily" [1930]). The extensive grounds of this literary edifice, along with the vast estate to its south (property of a neighbor decidedly ambivalent towards trespassers), lend themselves to nomadic wanderings, whether those of some cowboy Odysseus like John Grady Cole of *All the Pretty Horses* (1992), or those of the meanest picaro, like "the kid" in *Blood Meridian* (1985), or simply those of the desperate father and son of *The Road* (2006). This landscape, the geography of McCarthy's imagination, provides the setting for Casa Cormac itself, its rooms the author's varied subject matter and themes. Through this door, for example, readers enter the American past; through that one, the future. Another leads to a library devoted to literary history, where one tries, perhaps, to situate the McCarthy genius within a tradition that subsumes Hawthorne and Melville and Faulkner to the exclusion of figures – Emerson, Whitman – unwilling to contemplate the depths of human depravity. These and other rooms flank a great gallery, the house's most striking feature, whose very scale makes it a metaphor for the distinctive style of one who so capably navigates the dictionary's vast river of words.

No one reads much McCarthy without marveling at the style. In the extraordinary richness of the vocabulary and in the author's stately, near-biblical cadences, language itself seems the counterweight to the prodigies of human anguish catalogued from volume to volume. One wonders, perhaps, whether the mannered sentences and the out-of-the-way yet precise words might simply disguise or compensate for a calculated thematic askesis. What, after all, does a tree of dead babies *mean*? Vereen Bell (1988, p. 128) sees *Blood Meridian* (where that tree is rooted) as "haunted by the mystery that its own language challenges the very nihilistic logic that it gives representation to." In more positive terms, one discerns in the McCarthy style what James Joyce would call an "apostolic succession." Joyce himself influences that style, as do Faulkner, Dostoyevsky, and Melville, not to mention the King James Bible (Woodward 1992, pp. 28–31).

The intellectual growth of a great writer can offer a microcosm of literary history. Thus, Joyce's career seems contained in the idea his character Stephen Dedalus articulates that literary expression progresses by stages from subjective to objective, from lyric to epic to dramatic forms. Like Joyce, McCarthy starts with the personal or subjective, evoking the region, southeastern Tennessee, where the author himself grew up and received, like the great Irish writer, a Catholic education. The early novels *The Orchard Keeper* (1965), *Outer Dark* (1968), and *Child of God* (1973) seem to move centripetally, converging inwards from the Blue Ridge and Great Smoky Mountains to a Knoxville depicted, in *Suttree* (1979), as virtually all underbelly (but that city, and the river that runs through it, is as exhaustively documented as Joyce's Dublin and its fluvial artery, the Liffey). McCarthy's *Portrait of the Artist as a Young Man*, *Suttree* features a protagonist who, like Joyce's (1916) hero, struggles to free himself from family, religion, and the other nets designed to impede the soul's free career.

Moving to the Southwest, self-exiled like Joyce, McCarthy writes in an epic vein, his always elevated style well suited to the genre. In John Grady Cole and Billy Parham, protagonists of the Border Trilogy (1992–1998), the reader encounters heroes in the ancient mold: resourceful, considerate towards those weaker than themselves, courageous, persevering. Like his predecessors in Homer and Virgil, the McCarthy hero undergoes trials of courage and endurance, including incarceration in a Mexican prison (the archetypal descent to the underworld, as it were), to emerge as an embodiment of the national character. But repeatedly, contemplating the fate of distinction such as theirs in a post-heroic age (neither John Grady nor Billy participates in the great climacteric of World War II), McCarthy denies his heroes anything more than temporary triumphs, Pyrrhic victories.

Epic's sibling is that most exalted form of drama, tragedy, the audience for which traditionally experiences pity and fear on behalf of a splendid, flawed, and doomed protagonist. Often thought uncongenial to the modern temper, tragedy may seem to subsist only as its journalistic simulacrum, yet we still measure the stature of flawed protagonists – notably those of McCarthy – by the magnitude of the forces before which they do not bow. The author's credentials as tragedian, half-glimpsed in his various plays and screenplays, figure most prominently in the novels, in fiction that, in the cold eye it casts on heroic agency, approximates Joyce's idea of the disinterested perspective, the objectivity, of drama. One admits, however, that the fate of a McCarthy protagonist may sort oddly with the tragic criteria articulated by Aristotle and later theorists. Characters see little in the way of *anagnorisis*, the "recognition" whereby, to paraphrase Wordsworth, tragic suffering enables one to see into the very life of things. Nor, pity and fear having become existential givens, does the reader experience much more than a painful postmodern parody of catharsis.

More than epic and tragedy are hybridized as this author crosses multiple boundaries of genre and artistic fashion, thereby participating, in his own distinctive way, in the engagement, increasingly common at the end of the twentieth century and beginning of the twenty-first, with borderlands, liminality, liminal spaces, and cultural hybridity. How interesting that the author's 1985 novel *Blood Meridian*, with its movements back and forth across the Mexican border, precedes by two years one of the seminal theoretical meditations on this subject, Gloria Anzaldúa's *Borderlands/La Frontera* (1987). Both McCarthy and Anzaldúa enact discursive hybridity by mixing Spanish and English, forcing readers to experience otherness as the very price of understanding. McCarthy, to be sure, foregrounds the otherness of gender much less than Anzaldúa, yet the women in his next borderlands novel, *All the Pretty Horses*, define a kind of distaff continuum: the mother who divorces the father, goes on the stage, and declines to let the son take over the grandpaternal ranch; the lover – Alejandra – who gives John Grady up to save him; and the aunt – Alfonsa – who articulates what may be gender's Mexican reality principle when she interdicts her niece's love. "Males makes the rules and laws," Anzaldúa observes, but "women transmit them" (1987, p. 16).

In a more positive light, Alfonsa speaks for historical perspective. Lecturing John Grady on Mexico's tragic past, she amplifies the heteroclite historicism introduced in *Blood Meridian*, develops its negative, so to speak, from a later temporal vantage and from a differently gendered point of view. For whatever reason, she cannot and will not countenance the notion of a mésalliance – the crossing of a class border – between Alejandra and her cowboy paramour. The author himself is not altogether without bias: he imagines border crossing into dangerous experience as reserved to those with the Y chromosome. Engaged in an archetypal yet inchoate quest, in adventures at once picaresque, romantic, epic, and tragic, the McCarthy protagonist bears no small resemblance to the universal hero of Lord Raglan or Joseph Campbell. As tradition dictates, he crosses a threshold – the Mexican border – to begin a dangerous journey, a series of trials that ought to eventuate in triumphant return. As in the shadowy quest that structures Eliot's *The Waste Land* (1922), however, no grail materializes, nor does McCarthy's Southwestern knight marry the princess and become king. He limps home sans prize or boon.

Collectively known as the Border Trilogy, *All the Pretty Horses*, *The Crossing* (1994), and *Cities of the Plain* (1998) chronicle the twilight phase of America's westward expansion. These fictions distil the romance mythoi of the frontier only to expose them to the icy winds of postmodern skepticism. Telescoped in the three related texts, these mythoi give way, at the end, to recognitions that complement or reframe the terrible insights marshaled in *Blood Meridian*. The closing pages of the trilogy, set in the mid-century present, function as a kind of palinode, a retraction of such mythographic shapeliness as has figured in previous pages and volumes.

McCarthy's protagonists, John Grady Cole in the first volume, Billy Parham in the second (they appear together in the third), exhibit all the virtues of mythic frontier masculinity: bravery, resourcefulness, respect for women, a fierce loathing of injustice in all its forms. Each of these splendid ephebes comes of age amid violent and horrific experiences. Eventually, chastened by loss, each returns, intact against the odds. The author presents as no small feat their self-deliverance and their bringing home of the little that remains to them. John Grady returns with his horse and the mounts of two comrades (one murdered in Mexico); Billy Parham, who survives three journeys south of the border, returns at last with the mummified remains of his lost brother. In a memorable scene at the end of the first volume, John Grady displays the thigh wound he has sustained in his heroic journey. This injury, which recurs in the literary and religious imagination of the West, conflates Odysseus's scar, the damaged body of the Fisher King, and the stigmata of Christ. Like the Greek hero, John Grady has survived an incredible odyssey; like Jesus he looms in our memory as an heroic innocent who has suffered terribly for the universal corruption. Like the Fisher King, finally, he will prove unable to reverse the laying waste of a homeland already taken over by oil wells, pickup trucks, post-frontier commerce.

This world provides the setting for *Cities of the Plain*, the trilogy's last volume, which brings John Grady Cole and Billy Parham together, only to reveal them as a pair of living anachronisms. In his first two volumes, McCarthy has crossed his own artistic border – into romance. Now, like his characters, he crosses back, refusing to imagine that a once-vital ethic of self-reliance – not to mention heroism such as his young protagonists have shown – might survive its historical moment. All along, in fact, McCarthy observes that moment at its farthest extreme, long after the high tide of frontier élan. By mid-century (*Cities of the Plain* begins in 1952), the West has passed fully into a meretricious modernity, hopelessly uncongenial to heroic action. John Grady finds himself enamored of a woman forcibly prostituted by a vicious Mexican brothel keeper. Unable to deliver either his Dulcinea or himself from degradation, the hero of *All the Pretty Horses* perishes in a sordid knife fight.

Billy Parham suffers a similarly anticlimactic fate – only more prolonged. In his youth, recounted in *The Crossing*, he has, like John Grady, survived his own violent coming of age. Early on, he frees and rescues a trapped wolf, which becomes at once the helpful animal companion of folktales and the metonym for his own innocence, his own wild and perfect integrity. But when, like John Grady, he descends into dangerous Mexico, the splendid animal – more than ever a part of himself – is subjected to the most appalling torments (it is captured and made to fight other animals). Forced to witness this degradation, Billy at last delivers the wolf from its suffering. A few years later, in *Cities of the Plain*, he can only watch as John Grady gets himself killed, a Beowulf who takes down the dragon (i.e. Eduardo, the Mexican pimp) at the cost of his own life. In the end, half a century later, Billy dwells under a bridge, a derelict given to reminiscing about the old days. Such, McCarthy suggests, is the fate of our Western vision, our Western myth – a history that, neither romantic nor tragic, can only end with the shabby pathos of some appalling abjection before the loosening sphincter of death.

An abjection preferable, perhaps, to what characters in *No Country for Old Men* (2005) and *The Road* will experience. As McCarthy continues to dwell in and write about the Southwest, he presents additional constructions of the liminal. A conceptual border is crossed when the archetypal trappings of a mythic West (cowboys, horseflesh, resolute frontier lawmen) make way for the era depicted in *No Country*, with green hair, heroin addiction, human trafficking, and villainy on such an appalling scale that the aging sheriff, a good man, backs away, concedes his inadequacy, quits. An elemental breach in the very fabric of romance has opened up while the watchmen (or murengers) took a break or simply nodded off. The title *No Country for Old Men*, after all, comes from William Butler Yeats's "Sailing to Byzantium," and the paradigm shift chronicled and lamented in the novel reframes the new and brutal dispensation heralded in another Yeats poem, "The Second Coming," which famously concludes with the imminent birth of a rough beast that will inaugurate a new dispensation of unprecedented violence. Small wonder, perhaps, that *No Country* should be followed by *The Road*, in which McCarthy imagines regression to the Hobbesian state of nature and lives "solitary, poor, nasty, brutish, and short."

McCarthy the historical novelist, then. Never an admirer of Henry James, who despised the historical novel, McCarthy is its unapologetic practitioner. Like a number of his contemporaries (one thinks of Barth, Doctorow, Ishmael Reed, Pynchon, Morrison, Colson Whitehead), McCarthy embraces the aesthetics of postmodern historiography in fictions that take the measure of a past riddled with gaps, omissions, and silences. The most interesting of contemporary historical novels are not so much about this past as about how ideology dictates its representation. The reader of this body of fiction discovers, among other things, that the routine iconoclasm of the modernists (their desire to "shock the middle class") has become something more epistemologically radical. Thus, like Thomas Pynchon or Don DeLillo, McCarthy deconstructs the modernist predilection for mythopoesis and mythography and metanarrative. Where the moderns saw myth as universal, instinctive truth, the postmoderns expose it as factitious construct. Myth regresses, as it were, to *mythos* in its original Greek sense of "plot" or "story" – story with neither the obloquy of untruth nor the pretense of cultural universality and plot as what manifests itself in paranoid dread of political manipulation or historiographical *méconnaissance*.

This subversion of the "mythic method," as T.S. Eliot called it in his review of *Ulysses* (1923, p. 482), complements and even abets the new historiography that calls into question the shapely (and tendentious) narratives of traditional history. In other words, history as traditionally written proves inevitably and even systematically fictive. Paradoxically, the necessary corrective is not to eradicate the fictive element but to bring it fully to consciousness and, in the process, to give a voice to those silenced or passed over in the historical narratives of empire. Since the historian cannot make up or imagine the past, it falls to the storyteller to do so and thereby to do justice to its victims. Realizing that unproblematic representation of the past is a chimera, postmodern novelists candidly emphasize the *story* in history. At its best, their fiction captures this past, closes with its truth, achieves something denied to the historian.

History at once gratifies and confounds the desire for meaningful retrospect. Thus, the historically inflected vision of McCarthy's Western novels involves little in the way of *telos*. The author dismantles the narrative of Manifest Destiny – the narrative so central to America's historical perception of itself. Thus, to seek the center of McCarthy's literary oeuvre – its "meridian" – is to come again to the transitional fiction that so fascinates and troubles every reader who manages to get through it. In *Blood Meridian*, which presents a version of the frontier experience profoundly subversive of the American national myth, McCarthy avoids romanticizing history's victims. Rather than depicting the greed and brutality of white men and the innocence of Indigenous populations, that is, he represents a carnivalesque rapacity, a universal blood lust untrammeled by ethical restraint. On virtually every page he presents a new, more horrific atrocity: beatings give way to murders, knifings to beheadings, scalping to pedophile rape, massacre to that never-to-be-forgotten tree of dead babies. McCarthy bases his story on the real-life exploits of a band of ragtag mercenaries called the Glanton Gang, among them a couple of central figures, Judge Holden and a youth called only "the kid." The first gives the lie to ideas of westward expansion as a civilizing process; the second, a Huck Finn caricature, mocks the very idea of youthful innocence and its benign influence. The judge presides over this fiction, a figure of enormous energy, cunning, and Machiavellian *virtù* – but all in the service of the dark energies he embodies. He reminds us that the great literary archetypes of evil, from Lucifer to Kurtz to Hannibal Lecter, are to be understood as fallen versions of angelic natures.

Denying foundational metanarratives of morality and history, Judge Holden occupies a vantage that looks like postmodernism *avant la lettre*. "What's he a judge of?" the kid asks at one point (McCarthy 1985, p. 135). One answer lies in etymology: the word "judge" derives from the Latin *judex, judicis*, which combines *jus* (law) with *dicere* (to say). A judge "speaks the law." But the law spoken by this character is that of perfectly amoral nature. One sees in the judge – and hears from him – certain unsparing universal principles come to conscious form. When not gratifying appetites even more unspeakable than those of Conrad's Kurtz, the judge articulates precepts that mock precisely what one might think him professionally responsible for upholding:

> Moral law is an invention of mankind for the disenfranchisement of the powerful in favor of the weak. Historical law subverts it at every turn. A moral view can never be proven right or wrong by any ultimate test . . . Man's vanity may well approach the infinite in capacity but his knowledge remains imperfect and howevermuch he comes to value his judgements ultimately he must submit them before a higher court. Here there can be no special pleading. Here are considerations of equity and rectitude and moral right rendered void and without warrant and here are the views of litigants despised. Decisions of life and death, of what shall be and what shall not, beggar all questions of right. In elections of these magnitudes are all lesser ones subsumed, moral, spiritual, natural.
>
> (1985, p. 250)

Faulkner-like in its rhythm and gravid tonality, the language in this passage serves a vision wholly bereft of the Faulknerian humanity. It brims with legal and judicial terms: law, court, pleading, void and without warrant, litigants, decisions. Ironically, however, this is the vocabulary, the lexicon, of human law, predicated on morality at once subjunctive and deeply provisional. The idea that heroic purpose might be superior to the meaningless and relentlessly bloody flux of existence is dismissed as little more than wishful thinking, window dressing for the gratification of appetites "judgeable" only by those who think that the "moral law" has some universal standing vis-à-vis the "historical law" that shrugs at humanity's need to contain or make shapely stories out of the world's violence.

The unsparing darkness of its vision, along with the disturbing stylistic energy with which it is conveyed, places McCarthy's fiction in rare literary company. The novels of Thomas Hardy or Nathanael West or Bret Easton Ellis seem relatively cheerful; nothing since *King Lear* has been so horrifically bleak, so powerful, so true. Yet, however grim the message, the experience of reading McCarthy remains exhilarating. His art shares with all great literature the ability to transmute life's basest metal into a strange, sometimes terrible beauty.

SEE ALSO: Barth, John; Border Fictions; Contemporary Regionalisms; Coover, Robert; DeLillo, Don; Doctorow, E.L.; Everett, Percival; Pynchon, Thomas; Reed, Ishmael; Whitehead, Colson

REFERENCES

Anzaldúa, Gloria E. (1987). *Borderlands/La Frontera: The New Mestiza*. San Francisco: Aunt Lute.
Bell, Vereen. (1988). *The Achievement of Cormac McCarthy*. Baton Rouge: Louisiana State University Press.
Eliot, T.S. (1923). Ulysses, order, and myth (review of *Ulysses* by James Joyce). *The Dial* 75 (5): 480–483.
McCarthy, Cormac. (1985). *Blood Meridian*. New York: Penguin Random House.
Woodward, Richard B. (1992). Cormac McCarthy's venomous fiction. *New York Times Magazine* (April 19, 1992): 28–31.

FURTHER READING

Chamberlain, Samuel. (1996). *My Confession: Recollections of a Rogue* (ed. William H. Goetzmann). Austin: University of Texas Press.
Guillemin, Georg. (2004). *The Pastoral Vision of Cormac McCarthy*. College Station: Texas A&M University Press.

Jillett, Louise. (ed.) (2016). *Cormac McCarthy's Borders and Landscapes*. New York: Bloomsbury Academic.

O'Gorman, Farrell. (2005). Joyce and contesting priesthoods in *Suttree* and *Blood Meridian*. *Cormac McCarthy Journal* 4 (1): 100–117.

Sepich, John. (2008). *Notes on Blood Meridian Revised and Expanded Edition*. Austin: University of Texas Press.

McElroy, Joseph

BRIAN McHALE

The Ohio State University, USA

Joseph McElroy (b. 1930) is notorious for having written one of the most "unreadable" major novels of the postmodern era, *Women and Men* (1987). "Unreadability," of course, is in the eye of the *marketplace*: an "unreadable" novel is one that lacks commercial potential. So uncommercial is *Women and Men* that it is frankly astonishing that it was ever published in the first place. It is ambitious, demanding, strange, uncompromisingly difficult, and intimidatingly long (1192 pages, or 850,000 words, by one estimate; Karl 1990, p. 181). Nevertheless, if in some places it can seem almost impenetrable, in others it is deeply engaging, and it keeps readers interested in the very same ways that the most calculatedly commercial bestseller does, by arousing curiosity, suspense, and surprise. It is undoubtedly McElroy's magnum opus, routinely ranked alongside Gaddis's *The Recognitions* (1955) and *J R* (1975), Pynchon's *Gravity's Rainbow* (1973), DeLillo's *Underworld* (1997), Gass's *The Tunnel* (1995), Wallace's *Infinite Jest* (1996), and other outsized masterpieces of postmodern American fiction, and it inevitably overshadows the rest of McElroy's long and productive career. By 1987, McElroy had already published five novels, four of them large-scale "mega-novels" (Karl 1990) – *A Smuggler's Bible* (1966), *Hind's Kidnap* (1969), *Ancient History* (1971), and *Lookout Cartridge* (1974) – while the fifth, *Plus* (1977), makes up in density what it lacks in length – an imploded mega-novel. Hard on the heels of *Women and Men*, McElroy published an atypical short novel, the affecting coming-of-age story *The Letter Left to Me* (1988), then lapsed into near-silence, apart from some short stories and occasional writings, for fifteen years. In the interval, the publishing industry shifted out from under him, undergoing waves of acquisitions and consolidation (DiLeo 2018), and it was left to small presses to bring his earlier novels back into print. When new work from McElroy began to appear in the twenty-first century, it was with small presses: two novels, *Actress in the House* (2003) and *Cannonball* (2013), and a collection of twelve stories dating from the 1980s through the 2010s, *Night Soul and Other Stories* (2010). While none of these works rival *Women and Men* in accomplishment – or in length – they do share many stylistic, narratological, and thematic features with it.

Women and Men might read in the twenty-first century like historical fiction, but it is, in fact, a topical novel, a fiction of the present day – or rather, of the day before yesterday. Published in the 1980s, it is set in 1976/7 – the Bicentennial moment – and immersed in the concerns, anxieties, and material culture of the 1970s: technoculture, second-wave feminism, environmentalism, and the toxic politics of Pinochet-era Chile, test bed of what would come to be called neoliberalism (Harvey 2005, pp. 7–9). But if *Women and Men* is a topical novel, it is also a genre fiction – or rather, a fiction of multiple genres. McElroy already had a track record of flirting with popular genres: three of his previous novels displayed kinship with thrillers, while *Plus* was an experiment in science fiction, deeply colored by the space program of the 1960s and 1970s and by contemporary brain science. *Women and Men*, too, displays genre markers of the thriller, in particular, in its subplots focused on the activities of the Chilean agent

De Talco. (We are surely meant to associate him with the 1976 car bomb assassination of the Chilean refugee Orlando Letelier by agents of the Pinochet regime in Washington, DC.) *Women and Men* also experiments with science fiction, especially in Jim Mayn's daydreams (if that's what they are) of teleportation to and from an orbiting space station. The adventures of Mayn's grandmother Margaret, an intrepid female reporter who travels to the Southwest in the 1890s and attracts the romantic attentions of a Navajo "prince," read like a Wild West dime novel. Finally, the novel's main plot (insofar as it has one) derives from romantic comedy: Jim Mayn and Grace Kimball, who live in the same Manhattan apartment building and have many acquaintances in common, are in some sense made for each other, fated to meet – yet perversely, the entire narrative conspires to prevent that from happening, both eliciting and frustrating our pop-genre expectations.

Generically composite, *Women and Men* is also composite in another sense. It comprises about twenty-four or twenty-five (depending on how one is counting) relatively self-contained episodes, short story- or novella-length, about various New Yorkers who are connected with each other, sometimes directly, sometimes at one or two degrees of separation (Mathews 1990, pp. 214–215). Over a dozen of these episodes had already appeared as free-standing short stories in literary magazines, two of them in *The New Yorker*, and one as a separate chapbook (*Ship Rock*, 1980), before being folded into the fabric of *Women and Men*. (Two other episodes, *Preparations for Search* and "The Unknown Kid," originally earmarked for *Women and Men*, were withheld and published elsewhere). This description makes *Women and Men* sound like a story cycle in the modernist mode of *Dubliners* (1914), *Winesburg, Ohio* (1919) or *Go Down, Moses* (1942), but that is misleading, because the self-contained stories are actually anything *but* self-contained.

They are, in fact, surrounded, framed, and all but overwhelmed by a series of interchapters, five in all, that McElroy perversely calls "breathers" – which would normally imply moments of relief between episodes of exertion, but not in this case. *These* "breathers," rather, are supplementary narratives that connect and complicate the shorter ones around them and are conducted in a first-person-plural voice – *we* – perplexingly identified as the voices of *angels* (Mathews 1990). Plural angel voices seem to enjoy unrestricted freedom of access to all kinds of knowledge unavailable to mere characters – insight into the past and distant places, interior views of characters' minds. In effect, they embody and make literal the narratological abstraction of the *omniscient narrator*.

Women and Men has been called a *systems novel* (LeClair 1989) and a *field novel* (Wilson 1996), both terms indicating an *allover* structure that subsumes individuals and their doings into complex, elusive forms of organization much bigger than themselves, and perhaps invisible to them. Its characters are complexly connected with one another in ways that they are often ignorant of, or that they only become aware of as the novel unfolds. Everyone seems to have "friends in common" (McElroy 1987, p. 947) or at least "acquaintances in common" (p. 883) with everyone else, or they "share a messenger" (p. 1153) with others, or otherwise stay in touch through intermediaries. These networks of connection are also circuits of exchange. Objects pass from hand to hand around the circuit: a white Cadillac, a used bicycle, an opera score of *Hamlet*, a Colt pistol, and, grotesquely, a tapeworm retrieved by a Native American fisherman from a Great Lakes pike and shipped to a fashionable East Coast physician, who administers it to an opera diva as a desperate weight-loss measure. More typically, however, it is not objects but information that circulates, often in the form of stories – for instance the strange tales told to Mayn at bedtime by his grandmother Margaret about her adventures among the Navajo, which Mayn in turn retells years later to his daughter Flick, who transmits them to her friend the journalist Linc (link?), who repeats some of them at the feminist consciousness-raising workshop led by Grace Kimball, who ends up absorbing them into her own dreams.

A network-fiction like *Women and Men* runs the risk of stiffening into what modernist critics taught us to call a *spatial form* (Frank 1945), a pattern of motifs, verbal echoes, and internal cross-references, as in *Ulysses* (1920) or *The Waste Land* (1922). To compensate for the potential inertness of spatial form, McElroy mobilizes the resources of *epistemological desire* – the irresistible readerly hunger to *know,* which dynamizes his narrative and keeps it in motion. If *Women and Men* is characterized by excess of information, it is also characterized by the strategic deployment of informational *gaps* that energize the narrative. Withholding information, supplying it belatedly and obliquely, teasing us with tantalizing glimpses of possibility, surprising us with new information that we literally could not have seen coming, the narrative keeps us leaning forward. In other words, *Women and Men* deploys the classic narrative resources of *curiosity, surprise* and *suspense* (Sternberg 1990, 1992) to counter the potential inertness of pattern making and systems modeling.

Curiosity is the form of narrative interest intrinsic to murder mysteries – *whodunit?* – and *Women and Men* is a plentiful generator of mysteries: Why did Mayn's mother, Sarah, kill herself – or did she? Who is buried in her grave? Was the Chilean journalist Mayga Rodriguez murdered, and if so, by whom? What became of Amy, assistant to a refugee economist? What is the secret agent De Talco up to, and what becomes of him at the novel's end? *Surprises,* in the form of unanticipated revelations, especially of family secrets and relationships, come thick and fast as the novel's end approaches: the sleazy information-broker Spence turns out to be Jim Mayn's brother (maybe); the amorous Navajo "prince," who in 1894 pursued Mayn's grandmother Margaret from the Southwest all the way to Maplewood, New Jersey, was shot dead by her husband-to-be, Alexander. Finally, *Women and Men* is surprisingly *suspenseful,* especially with respect to its romantic comedy subplot: will Mayne and Grace Kimball ever get together, and if so, how? They are neighbors; they hear about each other from mutual acquaintances; they are even both seated in the same audience at an interrupted dress rehearsal of the *Hamlet* opera. But with perverse irony, McElroy prevents their meeting: Mayne rings Grace's doorbell, but leaves before she can answer the door!

Short fictions bridge the gap in McElroy's career between *Women and Men* and his twenty-first-century novels. They include the 150-page novel *The Letter Left to Me*; the 70-page novella *Preparations for Search* (1984, 2010, 2012), an outtake from *Women and Men* itself; and the dozen stories in *Night Soul,* two of which pre-date *Women and Men,* while two others date from the early 1990s and the rest from the twenty-first century. (Another short work, *Taken from Me,* appeared in 2014 in a Kindle-only edition.)

McElroy's attachment to genre fiction formulas persists in the short fictions. *Preparations for Search* is an inconclusive detective story hinging on a missing persons search for an absconded father. Muted thriller motifs figure in the post-9/11 stories "No Man's Land" and "Mister X." "The Last Disarmament but One" resonates with *Women and Men*'s science fiction experiments, and even casts a sly sidelong glance at motifs dating back to *Plus*. McElroy also experiments with the coming-of-age genre in *The Letter Left to Me* and the story "Character," and even with political satire in "The Campaign Trail," a droll riff on the Democratic primary election season of 2008 (Clinton vs. Obama), which anticipates the more pronounced satirical dimension of *Cannonball*.

Like *Women and Men*, though on a miniature scale, many of the shorter fictions model systems through networks of connection and circulation. *The Letter Left to Me*, so dissimilar to *Women and Men* in other ways, tracks the "dissemination" through various social circuits of a letter whose platitudinous content is much less important than the very fact of its circulation. "No Man's Land," "Mister X," "Canoe Repair," "Silk," and "Particle of Difference" all map networks of connection and circulation among disparate characters in complex urban (or, in the case of "Canoe Repair," small-town) milieus.

Many of the same strategies of informational gapping and gap-filling that imparted narrative dynamism to *Women and Men* recur in the short fictions. Sometimes delayed disclosure of information seems relatively inconsequential: Iraqi refugee Ali's teacher turns out to be the underemployed poet Mo's wife in "No Man's Land"; the "California-looking fellow" who might have vandalized Zanes's laundromat in "Canoe Repair" turns out to have been the builder of the birch bark canoe that Zanes is repairing; and in "Mister X" a whole series of more or less trivial coincidences connect Val the acupuncturist to the stranger who fixed Mister X's flat bicycle tire. It's a small world, but so what? Elsewhere, however, apparently trivial informational gaps prove to be highly consequential indeed: in "Particle of Difference," the minor mystery of a family photo album's disappearance is resolved when the protagonist realizes his estranged wife has taken it, and infers that she will ask him for a divorce.

The slight uncanniness with which the husband attains this insight is typical of these stories, and not only reminds us of similarly uncanny moments in *Women and Men*, but also anticipates the undercurrent of uncanniness in the late novels. In *Preparations for Search*, for example, other characters somehow know what the narrator, Bet, is thinking without his having uttered it aloud, and Bet recognizes Korn the detective without ever having seen him before. In "No Man's Land," the narrator Mo somehow channels private conversations among Ali's family, though Mo is never physically present and has no realistic means of knowing what has been said. "Mister X" is narrated by one of "us" in X's circle of friends, but the narrator's access to others' minds and private moments is inexplicable in realistic terms. Uncanniest of all is the story "Silk, or the Woman with the Bike," where the unnamed protagonist encounters an enigmatic woman who brings a bike onto the subway, then abandons it there. He tells his story to a co-worker, who in a flash of something like clairvoyance or telepathy intuits that the woman wanted to give him her bike, and later, in another moment of insight, intuits that the woman is dying. The co-worker is inexplicably right on both counts.

Several of the stories from the *Night Soul* collection, "Mister X" in particular, read like outtakes from McElroy's twenty-first-century novels, *Actress in the House* and *Cannonball*. *Actress* confirms yet again McElroy's affinity for genre fiction. It opens like a hardboiled detective story with a shocking act of violence – an actress gets her nose bloodied onstage by a mimed slap that turns out to be real – and a phone call out of the blue to the lawyer (not private eye) Daley at his office from this same actress, who begins entangling him in her complicated life. Is she the femme fatale of film noir, or a victim in need of protection, or both? *Cannonball*, though it displays elements of both coming-of-age story and thriller, is something of a departure for McElroy: it is mainly a deadpan satire of post-9/11 American life, somewhat in the vein of "The Campaign Trail," hinging on the purported discovery in Iraq during the US occupation of a scroll containing an interview with Jesus in which He endorses capitalist competition and the free market. The scroll is fraudulent, needless to say.

Both of the late novels exploit McElroy's signature strategies of withheld information, delayed disclosure, and the opening and closing of narrative gaps. *Cannonball* is partly a missing person investigation – what has become of Umo, the Chinese illegal immigrant and talented diver? – and partly an exposé of a government conspiracy. Its gappiness is heightened by radical displacements of chronological order, where "before" and "after" are often exchanged and effects are narrated before causes, including an entire sequence told moment-by-moment in reverse order, as in Christopher Nolan's celebrated film *Memento* (2000). *Actress*, too, has its mysteries: was Becca the actress sexually abused in her childhood by her father and much older half-brother? What role has the elusive businessman Ruley Duymens played in Daley's life, and more pointedly, in that of Daley's late wife? But the most startling, delayed disclosure in *Actress* is not the solution of a mystery but a surprising revelation that readers could not have anticipated: Daley, we learn very belatedly, was complicit in a Vietnam-era war crime, when he was at the controls of a helicopter from which five Vietcong suspects – including an adolescent girl and a female translator – were thrown to their deaths.

This is an especially shocking revelation because we have been on such intimate terms with Daley throughout. He is focalizer of the entire storyworld, and it is through him that all our knowledge of other people and events is filtered – everything but this one crucial piece of information about Daley himself, which has been repressed. Indeed, Daley knows much more than he should, according to the norms of realistic fiction. He "always [knows] things" about other people (McElroy 2003, p. 104); he somehow intuits strangers' backstories on first meeting them; he has, we are reminded again and again, a "gift" (a keyword in this novel). Daley, in short, is an uncanny mind reader and clairvoyant like the ones we encounter throughout McElroy's short fiction. Uncanny, inexplicable insight also characterizes Zach, the first-person narrator of *Cannonball*. Zach has an uncanny capacity to grasp situations and connections intuitively, and in common with his equally gifted sister, Em, he appears to have the power of prophesy. "It came to me" is a recurrent refrain, signaling moments of superhuman insight. Most powerful of all these moments of insight is the novel's final scene, which flashes back to an earlier point in time when Umo (not yet gone missing) exchanges gifts with Zach's eccentric polymath friend, called the Inventor. This is a private moment, where only Umo and the Inventor are present; Zach was not there, and could not have heard about it from either of them, yet he *knows*, and movingly narrates, what transpired between them.

One way of describing the uncanny insightfulness of characters in McElroy's fiction is to say that they literalize the kind of routine mind reading that goes by the name of "Theory of Mind" (Zunshine 2006): the capacity of people in everyday interactions, and also of characters in realistic fictions, to make hypotheses about what other people are thinking on the basis of their speech, facial expressions, body language, and so on. In this sense, the insightfulness and apparent clairvoyance of McElroy's "gifted" characters only dramatize and make explicit what realistic characters routinely do anyway. Alternatively, we could say that McElroy's clairvoyants and telepaths intuit things (like Umo's private meeting with the Inventor) that no one could realistically know who did not share their own author's privileged perspective on their world. In this sense, the uncanny insightfulness of some of McElroy's characters converges with the uncanny, omniscient angelic voices of *Women and Men*, the we that, transcending the epistemological limitations of merely human characters, seem capable of seeing everywhere and connecting everything.

SEE ALSO: Contemporary Fictions of War; DeLillo, Don; Gaddis, William; Gass, William H.; Hypertext Fiction and Network Narratives; Minimalism and Maximalism; Mixed-Genre Fiction; Post-9/11 Narratives; Pynchon, Thomas; Story Cycles; Wallace, David Foster

REFERENCES

DiLeo, Jeffrey R. (2018). Independent presses. In: *American Literature in Transition, 1990–2000* (ed. Stephen J. Burn), 362–377. Cambridge: Cambridge University Press.

Frank, Joseph. (1945). Spatial form in modern literature. *The Sewanee Review* 53 (2): 221–240.

Harvey, David. (2005). *A Brief History of Neoliberalism*. New York: Oxford University Press.

Karl, Frederick. R. (1990). *Women and Men*: more than a novel. *Review of Contemporary Fiction* 10 (1): 181–198.

LeClair, Tom. (1989). *The Art of Excess: Mastery in Contemporary American Fiction*. Urbana: University of Illinois Press.

Mathews, Harry. (1990). We for one: an introduction to Joseph McElroy's *Women and Men*. *Review of Contemporary Fiction* 10 (1): 199–226.

McElroy, Joseph. (1987). *Women and Men*. New York: Knopf.

McElroy, Joseph. (2003). *Actress in the House*. Woodstock, NY: Overlook.

Sternberg, Meir. (1990). Telling in time (I): chronology and narrative theory. *Poetics Today* 11 (4): 901–948.

Sternberg, Meir. (1992). Telling in time (II): chronology, teleology, narrativity. *Poetics Today* 13 (2): 463–541.

Wilson, William Smith. (1996). Joseph McElroy: fathoming the field. Toward a definition of a postmodern genre: the field-novel. *Electronic Book Review*. http://electronicbookreview.com/essay/joseph-mcelroy-fathoming-the-field/ (accessed July 9, 2021).

Zunshine, Lisa. (2006). *Why We Read Fiction: Theory of Mind and the Novel*. Columbus: Ohio State University Press.

FURTHER READING

Joseph McElroy Issue. (2011). Special issue of *Golden Handcuffs Review* 1 (14).

Walser, Andrew. (ed.) (2004). *A Joseph McElroy Festschrift*. http://electronicbookreview.com/essay/a-joseph-mcelroy-festschrift/ (accessed July 9, 2021).

McKnight, Reginald

MILO W. OBOURN
SUNY Brockport, USA

Reginald McKnight, in a 2001 *African American Review* interview with Dr. Bertram Ashe, repeatedly returns to the phrase "The map is not the territory," a phrase which provides a useful lens through which to think about his work as a body (2001, p. 429). McKnight is referring here to the difference between studying African literature and allowing life in Africa to hold a mirror up to his experiences as a deracinated Black man – the difference between intellectual knowledge of self and place, and somatic processing of identity and space. McKnight's major works explore racism on an embodied level – the trauma and joy of embodied Blackness for Black people in the United States, as well as the harm that anti-Black racism does to non-Black people's capacities for critical thinking, expansive feeling, interpersonal connection, and personal and political action. McKnight's work – which includes two novels, *I Get on the Bus* (1990) and *He Sleeps* (2001); three collections of short fiction, *Moustapha's Eclipse* (1988), *The Kind of Light That Shines on Texas* (1992), and *White*

Boys (1998); and two edited texts, *African American Wisdom* (1994) and *Wisdom of the African World* (1996) – offers literature that is of the body. His texts attempt to be not a map but, to the extent that language can be so, the territory.

McKnight was born on February 26, 1956, in Fürstenfeldbrook, Germany. He grew up with a parent serving in the air force, which led his family to live in a number of locations, including New York, Texas, Louisiana, California, and Colorado. He served in the marine corps, from which he was honorably discharged in 1976, before attending college. McKnight then received his AA from Pike's Peak Community College (1978), his BA from Colorado College (1981), and his MA from the University of Denver (1987). McKnight has won numerous awards and fellowships. These include the Thomas J. Watson Fellowship, which permitted him to spend a year living and writing in Africa (1985); the Bernice M. Slote Award for Fiction from the University of Nebraska for "Uncle Moustapha's Eclipse" (1985); and the Drue Heinz Literature Prize from the University of Pittsburgh Press for stories collected in *Moustapha's Eclipse*. McKnight is a Bread Loaf Fellow (1988). He won an Ernest Hemingway Foundation Award from PEN American Center (1989) and both the Kenyon Review New Fiction Prize and the O. Henry Award for "The Kind of Light that Shines on Texas" (1989). He received a National Endowment for the Arts Grant for Literature (1991), a Whiting award (1995), and a Pushcart Prize (2016). McKnight has had two extended stays in Dakar, Senegal – one to teach English (1981/2) and another as part of his Thomas J. Watson fellowship (1985).

McKnight talks about visiting Africa as what both allowed him to self-identify as a writer and also what gifted him the writing practice that allowed him to start to express in language the thoughts and experiences his body had been holding. He also says in his interview with Ashe that "part of being black is the search for blackness" (Ashe 2001, p. 435). McKnight's work pushes readers to search not only for Blackness, but for the ways Blackness functions in and on Black and white bodies to reveal broad human interrelations. His novels, short fiction, and collections all gesture toward a sense of infinite canonization of the idea of Blackness. It's not that it doesn't exist or isn't a material reality, but more that it is always relational, always contextual, always just beyond full articulation, and always deeply embodied.

Reginald McKnight's novels *I Get on the Bus* and *He Sleeps* both follow African American characters through a series of surreal experiences in Senegal. Both novels deal with the search for Blackness, in that they have main characters who have come to Africa to find a community or identity that could inform their feelings of being both unavoidably Black and not Black enough in the United States. Both novels are structured as detective stories, thereby centering the literal narrative of a search and also placing the reader in a position of not knowing. The ways in which the characters somatically experience dislocation, both physically and psychically, is replicated in the reader's destabilization in relation to reality and dependence on a disrupted, sick, cursed, surreal, and/or magical interpretive framework.

In *I Get on the Bus*, Evan Norris, a young Black man from Denver, goes to Senegal with the Peace Corps and finds himself feeling ill, unclear about what he is actually doing versus what he is imagining, and most bizarrely, constantly appearing without reason on a public bus in Dakar. In a malarial stupor brought on by refusing to take his quinine, he is taken in by Aminata, a Georgetown University student, and her father, the village *marabou* (healer). Evan starts to believe that Aminata's father has put a *jinn* (curse) on him and that a *demm* (soul eater) is after him. Finally, he is told by a friend that to be rid of the jinn he must kill another African American living in Senegal named Africa Ford Mambada.

Despite the fact that the intrigue of the novel is based largely on the reader's desire to figure out what all these enigmatic Senegalese happenings mean, what is most engaging about the book is the central trope of the novel – Evan's consistent reemergence on the bus. It is clear that Evan is neither dreaming nor hallucinating, as he never finds himself back where he started. He simply will suddenly be on the bus instead of where he was and have to get off and start over from there. The bus is a matter of, as Evan puts it, "believ[ing]/disbeliev[ing]" (1990, p. 72), a space of in-betweens, of halves. As Evan says, "I am half-lost, half-bemused, half-terrified, half-aghast – half-clearheaded, half-placid, half-confident" (p. 23). This in-between psychic space echoes and amplifies what McKnight has referred to as a state of being a "cultural mulatto" – a deracinated Black person informed by a Eurocentric culture, who in this case is not navigating African culture, language, and society. His search, as well as his movement through his environment (both the psychical impact of it and the actual mode of public transportation), here becomes an embodied experience, not a mapping. Evan is living the embodied experience not of mapping a place, but of being mapped by the place, his body itself coming to hold the territory.

He Sleeps was published approximately ten years after *I Get on the Bus* and is in many ways a rewriting and refining of the earlier novel. Bertrand, our Evan-like main character, is a young anthropologist from Colorado who has come to Senegal to write his dissertation and finds himself having surreal experiences that he is unable to explain. Like Evan, Bertrand stands in a relation of wanting to know and map Africa, and wanting to mine it for some kind of truth, having come to Africa to "help all black people by recovering our forgotten things" (2001, p. 112).

In *He Sleeps*, the surreal embodiment of the territory manifests itself in Bertrand's sleeping and dreaming, often for days at a time. Since Bertrand had never dreamt before coming to Senegal, he had always "suspected" that when people spoke of dreams they "were talking about something they'd invented, imagined." He writes in his journal, "I always believed dreams took one's will. But this thing *happened* to me" (2001, p. 22). *He Sleeps* illuminates the ways in which one's confrontation with global difference can undermine one's sense of rootedness, while at the same time the ideological boundaries that come with that rootedness greatly affect one's experience of global difference. What begins for Bertrand as a disconcerting interaction with a foreign culture that was also supposed to be his home culture, quickly turns into cataplexy, severe insomnia, narcolepsy, bodily violence, and near insanity and death. McKnight takes very seriously the aspects of national identity and ideology that defy conscious choices to belong or feel comfortable in a space that is both foreign and progenitor, while at the same time, in this later novel, allowing his main character to survive the experience of losing the stability of being the one who maps.

Intersections between race/racism and sexuality/heteronormativity/sexism are also a central theme of *He Sleeps*. Bertrand is constantly fantasizing about another man's wife, and he often reports dreaming about sex. The fact that he is married to a white American woman and is attracted to a Black African woman is also a recurrent issue for Bertrand. He believes his dreams to be closely connected, if not fully derived from, a letter from his wife that said only, "Go ahead. Find your black girls. Fuck them all" (2001, p. 21). Over the course of the book, larger themes of castration, slavery, and racial identity are revealed to be related much more directly to US history than to any fantasy about Africa as a site of difference. These themes take on alternate forms because, like much of what appears in Bertrand's dreams, they don't "fit in with what he would call the main narrative" (p. 34). Histories of racial violence are a form of trauma in the body that cannot fit national "main narratives." In the context of the novel, the embodiment of these traumas appears in dream segments, side stories about travel outside the village, and unfinished notes for Bertrand's dissertation.

The end of the novel is composed of a letter from Bertrand to his wife in which he tells her stories of his past, using them as figurative devices that might allow feelings and experiences that do not fit the main narrative to emerge within it. Through his rereading of these stories from his past and remapping of his own territory, Bertrand is able to tell his wife that he had been afraid to live with her because, he says, "I was afraid they'd track us down, chuck rocks at our windows, burn crosses on our yards" and "there were other times when I was also ashamed. You can't be aware of a thing without in some small, subtle, deeply subconscious way believing it" (2001, p. 210). The novel ends in the territory of the United States even as it is lived and embodied through Bertrand's experience in Senegal. The writing is a remapping and re-embodying of a territory that was too violent for Bertrand to live with full consciousness in the territory itself.

Much of McKnight's short fiction reads like focused explorations of the themes in his novels. Many stories are about Black American men who find themselves disoriented, dreaming, or ungrounded in West Africa. Many are stories about interracial love affairs. Possibly the most striking, however, and the ones that diverge a bit more from the main themes of his novels are those stories that focus on family relationships and inherited trauma. In many of his stories, as in his novels, the experience of embodied race and the impacts of living in a racist society are narrated so as to make the territory of white supremacist America and the global dynamics in which that territory is situated accessible via the somatic experiences of his characters. Intergenerational and racialized traumas are played out on an interpersonal level, which gives the reader a way of understanding the through line between systemic oppression and somatic embodiment.

In *Moustapha's Eclipse*, McKnight's first published collection of stories, there is a common theme of parsing relations between race, masculinity, and sexuality. One of the shorter of the stories, located in the center of the collection, "Getting to be Like the Studs," is a study of the ways in which white cisnormative masculinity, anti-Black racism, anti-woman sexism, and compulsive heterosexuality are interdependent and internalized through US social systems, particularly school systems. This story is narrated and focalized through a nameless white teenage boy who does not fit in and who befriends Lenny, the only Black boy in his school. Our narrator feels compelled to be "more like the studs" (1988, p. 61). And while he can't do this via sexual conquest of women – "with those guys [the studs] around the girls didn't have much use for a guy like me" (p. 54) – he can do it via violence to a Black body and, as a result, violence to himself. There are suggestions that both Lenny and our narrator are queer in some way, whether because they do not fit dominant forms of masculinity (our narrator because he has big ears and girls don't like him; Lenny because he would be beaten up for dating a white girl and there are only white girls in his class) or because they are actually attracted to one another. Lenny says he doesn't like girls, our narrator is referred to as "sweetheart" by one of the studs, and at one point the narrator calls

Lenny a faggot and Lenny responds, "You are if I am" (pp. 54–55). Our narrator, though he enjoys his friendship with Lenny, feels the need to get away from him, as though Lenny's Blackness is what is keeping the narrator from achieving access to dominant white masculinity. He develops an internalized disgust at being associated with Lenny, which manifests in him calling Lenny "a damn, stupid dog" in front of the class (p. 60). This act of violence and self-harm (in that it destroys his only friendship and keeps him from the one person who actually supports him) comes after he remembers the studs yelling anti-Semitic slurs at a Jewish boy who was talking to a white girl they liked. He mimics this racism in an attempt to achieve white male privilege, justifies it to himself by saying at least he did not physically assault or call Lenny the n-word. In the end what he achieves is one of the studs saying "yo to me every now and then," though, he admits, "I really ain't made no real friends yet" (p. 61).

The Kind of Light That Shines on Texas, published six years after *Moustapha's Eclipse*, moves deeply into what I am calling McKnight's embodied writing – less map and more territory. It begins with a story that is about the consumption of one's writing. "The Homunculus: A Novel in One Chapter" is written as a kind of parable about writing, in which a brilliant writer closes himself off in a frenzy of creation only to find he has manifested a miniature version of himself who then proceeds to eat his masterpiece, grow to be a mirror image of the author, vomit the manuscript back out, and disappear. Here McKnight establishes consumption and growth from ingestion of your desires and words as a theme. One becomes the territory in part by ingesting the map of one's territory. This collection ends with a story entitled "Soul Food," set in an unnamed dystopia that is not so different from modern capitalism in which a man, who must steal to eat, witnesses a man's finger being cut off so that another thief can get to his ring. Our main character goes through the man's wallet, finds a picture of the man's family, thinks of crying but cannot. Instead, fantasies of eating the body arise. He heaves up saliva. And finally, he cries.

This "sandwiching," if you will, of the middle stories by allegories/fantasies of ingestion and expulsion draws the reader's attention to the embodiment of larger racial, sexual, and gendered systems in individual characters in the stories, again often accessed via interpersonal relationships that play out the effects of these systems on (primarily) Black bodies. "Roscoe in Hell" and "Quitting Smoking" both use love stories – the former between mother and son and the latter between romantic partners – to provide the reader access to a mapping of how the territories of the body take in racism and sexism and hold or expel them. In "Roscoe in Hell" a young man dies and goes to a hell where he is expected to party all the time. In life he was a drug user, not because he wanted to party but because he learned the coping mechanisms of stories and substance abuse from his mother, who would drink and read to him. "Quitting Smoking" is an epistolary story about a Black man who is told by the white woman he is dating about a sexual assault she experienced prior to knowing him. He recalls a time that he and a few friends witnessed the abduction of a woman and did not intervene. Their relationship becomes distanced, and tense, and he believes that it is due to the fact that he can't face his complicity in the assault of another woman. The story ends with the girlfriend telling him that her assailant was Black and that he should be shocked she does not hate all Black men. Our narrator writes, "I felt sick and dead and I couldn't breathe right. It was like my veins'd been tapped and were leaking all over the floor" (1992, p. 172). This embodied experience of racism as it manifests via gender and sexual relations is felt by the reader as an unexpected climax to the story. The ways in which US society uses gender and sexuality to internally assault Black bodies becomes tangible for the reader, while not erasing the trauma of sexual assault that the narrative had focused on until this point.

McKnight's third collection of stories, *White Boys*, brings together the themes and strategies of the two previous collections. The title story follows two military families in Louisiana – one white, one Black. Derrick, our main character, is the middle child in the Black family who has just moved from Texas. He comes with stories from his friends about how Black people are lynched in the South. Derrick's family moves in next door to a white family with a father who might be the grown version of our main character from "Getting to be Like the Studs." The father is deeply upset by the arrival of a Black family in his neighborhood and aims to use his youngest son's (Garret's) friendship with Derrick to terrorize the family by planning a camping trip with the boys where they will "pretend" to lynch Derrick. Garret believes that his father is actually going to lynch his friend, and to protect Derrick, Garret calls Derrick the n-word repeatedly, saying things to him like "you're a n***** and I'm not. I'm better than you" (1998, p. 213). Though we end with Derrick and his constant need for vigilance in a racist world, the story physically and emotionally leaves us with the resonating sickness of Garret as he falls to the ground and "heaved as though he were passing all his innards, but he gave up only a trickle of saliva" (p. 214). The ways in which white supremacy and anti-Blackness are incubated and fostered in the body of a white child are attended to even as we see how violent this child has now become.

In all of McKnight's work there is a deep attentiveness to the ways racism not only has somatic effects but is itself an embodied practice and embodied violence, replicated not only in the structures in which we live but through the ways we come into physical, emotional, and spiritual relation to one another.

SEE ALSO: Black Atlantic; Illness and Disability Narratives; Post-Soul and/or Post-Black Fiction; Trauma and Fiction

REFERENCES

Ashe, Bertram D. (2001). "Under the umbrella of Black civilization": a conversation with Reginald McKnight. *African American Review* 35 (3): 427–437.
McKnight, Reginald. (1988). *Moustapha's Eclipse*. Pittsburgh: University of Pittsburgh Press.
McKnight, Reginald. (1990). *I Get on the Bus*. New York: Little, Brown.
McKnight, Reginald. (1992). *The Kind of Light That Shines on Texas*. New York: Little, Brown.
McKnight, Reginald. (1998). *White Boys*. New York: Henry Holt.
McKnight, Reginald. (2001). *He Sleeps*. New York: Henry Holt.

FURTHER READING

Govan, Sandra Y. (2009). A stranger on the bus: Reginald McKnight's *I Get on the Bus* as complex journey. In: *Contemporary African American Fiction: New Critical Essays* (ed. Dana A. Williams), 136–159. Columbus: Ohio State University Press.
Murray, Rolland. (2005). Diaspora by bus: Reginald McKnight, postmodernism, and transatlantic subjectivity. *Contemporary Literature* 46 (1): 46–77.
Nicholas, Xavier. (2006). A conversation with Reginald McKnight. *Callaloo* 29 (2): 304–321.
Walsh, William. (1994). We are, in fact, a civilization: an interview with Reginald McKnight. *The Kenyon Review* 16 (2): 27–42.

McMillan, Terry

RITA B. DANDRIDGE
Virginia State University, USA

A *New York Times* bestseller, Terry McMillan's *Mama* (1987) captures the historic practice of Black mothers fending for themselves and their children when they are either without a legal mate or with one unable to support adequately his offspring. Set in the 1960s, nearly 100 years after slavery, *Mama* depicts Mildred Peacock, mother of five, married to a low-wage sanitation worker named Crook. Her precarious situation connects to the historic issues of race, gender, and class. As a Black woman, she is marginalized economically, faced with spousal abuse, and trapped on the lowest rung of America's class ladder. After Crook's death, Mildred becomes head of her household and, at first, appears to become a statistic of what Daniel P. Moynihan, advisor to President Richard Nixon, derogatorily referred to in the 1960s as a matrifocal "family structure" that has led to the deterioration of Black families (Moynihan 1965, p. 8). Moynihan's stereotype was purposed to reveal a historic dissimilarity in family structures of Blacks and whites and to cast blame on Black mothers for the disintegration of the female-centered Black family. McMillan repurposes the stereotype to depict a strong Black mother meeting the challenges of poverty, providing for her children, and guiding them to purposeful societal responsibility. Mildred is representative of many Black mothers fiercely resisting the obstacles that weaken the Black family structure.

As a Black popular culture text, *Mama* is a counternarrative. It debunks the Eurocentric narrative of motherhood anchored in Judeo-Christian belief that assumes a "mother should bear her children in tranquility, passivity and delight" in a patriarchal family structure (Dandridge 1998, p. 406). Mildred Peacock is an unmarried teenager when she has her first child, Freda. After her marriage to Crook, she has four more children in rapid succession. In her pretense to be the ideal mother, Mildred dons a platinum wig, metaphorically suggesting "the halo encircling the head of Christ's mother" (p. 408). In reality, the wig camouflages her devalued life as a Black mother, as Crook snatches the wig from her head and physically abuses her. Mildred's despair as a mother is evident when she muses, "I'm twenty-seven years old, and I'm sick and tired of this shit" (McMillan 1987, p. 14). Her profanity captures the aesthetics of the counternarrative which reveals that deference to the beauty myth fails to improve Black women's lives.

Mama expands the canon of African American literature by contemporizing the urban Black mother's plight while fictionalizing details about McMillan's family. It updates motherhood stories found in African American novels such as Nella Larsen's *Quicksand* (1928), Ann Petry's *The Street* (1946), Toni Morrison's *The Bluest Eye* (1970), and Arthenia Bates's *The Deity Nodded* (1973). Setting her novel in the North during the 1960s Civil Rights movement, McMillan magnifies the continuous struggles and the sacrifices that Black mothers make to protect and provide for their children.

Mama's expansion of the canon connects with its revelatory telling of McMillan's family story. Born in South Park in Port Huron, Michigan, the setting of *Mama*, Terry McMillan is the oldest of five children and the daughter of Madeline Washington Tillman McMillan, a day worker, and Edward Lewis McMillan, a sanitation worker, nicknamed "Crook." Her mother's child-bearing cycle is echoed in *Mama*. Madeline had a baby every ten or eleven months (Patrick 1999, p. 33). Similar to Mildred in *Mama*, Madeline confronted the rage of her alcoholic husband. After his death when Terry was 16 years of age, Madeline provided for her family by working odd jobs. To help her mother, Terry worked at the local library where she discovered Louisa May Alcott and James Baldwin (pp. 45–47). Terry and her sisters were taught to have "high standards" and to "depend on no man for everything" (p. 34). Madeline inspired Terry to further her education, just as Mildred inspired Freda. McMillan received her BS in journalism (1979) from the University of California at Berkeley and then enrolled in a master's program in film writing at Columbia University in New York.

McMillan's second best-selling novel, *Disappearing Acts* (1989), updates the historic role that education has played in Black male–female relationships. It portrays the difficulty the twentieth-century educated Black woman has in finding an eligible and educated Black male partner. In the nineteenth century, "252 [Black] women" compared to "2272 [Black] men" not only had finished normal school but also had received baccalaureate degrees (Du Bois 1900, p. 55). The number of Black women graduates was smaller because they often saw no need to continue their education when they could marry an educated Black man with a job paying enough for him to support a family. In 1985, the approximate setting for *Disappearing Acts*, the high school graduation rate nationwide was 58.4% for Black males and 60.8% for Black females (*Statistical Abstract of the United States* 2002, table 209, p. 139). These 1980s statistics present a precipitous decline in the Black male's education and his breadwinner capability compared to that of his nineteenth-century counterpart. The data also suggest that Black females with more education will have a smaller pool of educated-eligible Black men to choose from and will encounter more competition from other females in their search for educated Black men. Moreover, a Black woman may lessen the importance of a Black male's insufficient education but emphasize another asset to complete his "romantic market value" in a relationship (Davis 1993, p. 25). *Disappearing Acts* presents the consequence of this 1980s phenomenon in the relationship between Zora Banks, a high school teacher, and Franklin Swift, a high school dropout and self-employed carpenter.

To manifest tension between Zora and Franklin, *Disappearing Acts* employs the Black aesthetics' strategy of call-and-response, a two-part motif in which the second tune comments on or responds to the first. Call-and-response is apparent in their live-in relationship when Franklin telephones Zora on her 30th birthday and says he has "to work overtime and wasn't able to cash his check"; Zora responds by offering "to lend him fifty dollars" (McMillan 1989, p. 119). Franklin accepts her offer, but Zora's uneasiness surfaces as she muses, "I felt stupid because here it is my birthday and I was lending him money to take me out" (p. 119). Her anxiety increases when she learns the next day from a friend that Franklin has been laid off for a week.

Disappearing Acts expands the African American literary canon by enlarging the domestic abuse theme used to include the educated Black woman. It reveals that the heroine must admit to the truth about her reason for staying in an injurious relationship. Only then will she be motivated to transform trauma into meaningful survival.

The domestic abuse theme allows Terry McMillan to retell her story about her turbulent live-in relationship with Leonard Welch, a 30-year-old carpenter working as a floor installer in the brownstone where she lived at 42 Fort Greene Place in Brooklyn. Similar to Franklin, Welch was married, the father of two children, but separated from his wife. In 1984, he became the father of McMillan's son, Solomon Welch, but McMillan dissolved the abusive relationship. When Welch read *Disappearing Acts*, he "filed a $4.5 million dollar lawsuit against [McMillan] and her publisher claiming defamation of character" (Richards 1999, p. 7). In 1991, the court decided in McMillan's favor.

McMillan's best-selling third novel, *Waiting to Exhale* (1992), revisits African American women's history of women-centered bonding for communal and personal wellbeing. The idea for the novel materialized after McMillan conversed via telephone with a female friend about the dismal dating scene for professional Black women. The novel limns the bonding experiences of four Black women: Savannah Jackson, Bernadine Harris, Gloria

Matthews, and Robin Stokes, a member of Black Women on the Move, a professional Black women's community association. The women's connectedness reveals the inanity of Black women's altering their appearances through expensive cosmetics, wigs, and clothes in an attempt to attract male interest.

As popular literature, *Waiting to Exhale* articulates a Black aesthetics theory that litcrati Larry Neal and Molefi Asante argue for. Neal proposes "a separate symbolism, mythology, critique, and iconology" for Blacks (1968, p. 29), while Asanti advocates deposing a Eurocentric worldview for an African one (1987, p. 3). The Black aesthetics discourse in *Waiting to Exhale* defies the Eurocentric beauty myth as a means to identify Black women's gender success. It exposes the deception inherent in a cosmetics-based beauty myth and lauds the genuineness of a Black aesthetic sensibility.

Waiting to Exhale expands the African American literary canon, especially its 1960s and post-1960s discourses on Black aesthetics. It unfolds the need for Black women to embrace their natural beauty and reminds readers of the protagonist's senselessness in Toni Morrison's *The Bluest Eye* in which the impoverished Pecola Breedlove wishes for blue eyes to make herself beautiful. Few African American novels have had such instant success as *Waiting to Exhale*. It sold more than two million copies, reached the *New York Times* bestseller list, garnered top-rated reviews, and was made a movie in 1995.

McMillan's next novel, *How Stella Got Her Groove Back* (1996), updates the historical tradition of African American women's travel adventures. It puts into perspective that Black women's travel narratives function as subversive literature and date back to Nancy Prince's *Narrative of the Life and Travels of Mrs. Nancy Prince* (1850). A free Black woman, Prince overturned the sexist idea that women should be homebound creatures. Whereas Prince traveled as a missionary to Russia and Jamaica with her husband, Stella Payne, the protagonist in McMillan's novel, travels to Jamaica, where she finds romance.

How Stella Got Her Groove Back articulates an African American aesthetic through a romance counternarrative. It defies the Eurocentric myth of romance wherein man and woman meet, fall in love, marry, and live happily ever after. Stella meets, falls into lust with the Jamaican Winston Shakespeare, and even pays for his trip to California. Before his three weeks' visit ends, Stella muses, "I'll be glad when he's gone" (McMillan 1996, p. 358). The short duration of Stella's relationship defies the longevity that the Eurocentric myth proposes.

How Stella Got Her Groove Back expands the canon of African American travel literature. It reveals a single Black woman traveling alone to a foreign place, experiencing romance and cultural diversity, returning home, and sending for the man of her affections to come to America. The novel's expansion of the canon links to the novel's genesis. McMillan wrote the first draft of her novel in twenty-three days after her 1995 summer vacation to Jamaica, where she had a whirlwind romance with Jonathan Plummer, the fictional Winston Shakespeare. McMillan and Plummer married and then divorced when he announced his homosexuality. By fictionalizing her personal experiences, McMillan confirms the novel's relevance to the African American literary canon in which much of its fiction is built upon reactions to real-life race and gender issues.

In "Author's Note," McMillan informs readers that *A Day Late and A Dollar Short* (2002) "was inspired by [her] emotions and personal responses to issues that have arisen for many families, and . . . perhaps even in [her] own." With its emphasis on a middle-aged protagonist, the novel depicts Viola Price, a chronic asthmatic facing declining health along with her children's and grandchildren's problems of incarceration, divorce, spousal abuse, and child molestation.

A Day Late and A Dollar Short applies Black cultural aesthetics found in Black mourning narratives. It manifests "the spirit's persistence" even in death (Holloway 1997, p. 33). In a performative post-mortem ritual, Viola Price's spirit persists. At her request, her family gathers at Thanksgiving to read letters she has written prior to her death. To her husband and four children, her instructive missives of love and advice enhance the members' identity and immortalize her maternity. For its exceptional writing, this novel received the NAACP Image Award and became a television movie.

As a mourning narrative, *A Day Late and A Dollar Short* expands the canon of African American literature. It enlarges the presentation and development of protagonists found in mourning narratives. Unlike Ossie Davis's *Purlie Victorious* (1971), Ernest Gaines's *A Lesson Before Dying* (1993), and Toni Morrison's *Sula* (1973), that delineate dying Black men and a young Black woman, respectively, McMillan's novel depicts a middle-aged Black matriarch whose demise strengthens the living rather than weakening survivors.

The Interruption of Everything (2005) gives an updated version of the gender-based work that has historically hindered Black women from having substantial opportunity for self-time. It probes the midlife of protagonist Marilyn Grimes, pregnant mother of three and wife of a suspected errant husband. Her gender-based tasks extend to caring for her live-in mother-in-law with Alzheimer's, her senile mother, and her addicted foster sister and small children.

In *The Interruption of Everything*, the "Africanity" family structure acknowledges Black cultural aesthetics. It depicts patterns of African "consanguineal kin groupings" that include multiple generations, their rules and rituals (Hudgins and Holmes 1990, p. 2). The beauty of the "Africanity" model in McMillan's novel is its divergence from the Western nuclear family structure and its embrace of the African paragon with its interlacing descent, filiation, and marriage.

With the woman at the center of the family, *The Interruption of Everything* again expands the canon of African American literature. It deconstructs the myth of the Black woman as "the mule of the world." When popularized in Zora Neale Hurston's *Their Eyes Were Watching God* (1937), the myth lauded the Black woman's strength while decrying her abuse. In *The Interruption of Everything*, the protagonist's weariness undermines the superwoman stereotype. Protagonist Marilyn Grimes tells her husband, "[I am] tired of being the mule of the world that carries the burden for everything and everybody in this house" (McMillan 2005, p. 89). Voicing weariness, Marilyn subverts the exploitation associated with the myth and offers an enlarged view of the Black woman character in African American literature.

The sequel to *Waiting to Exhale*, *Getting to Happy* (2010), delves into the historical anxieties that middle-aged Black women experience. It revisits the female foursome found in *Waiting to Exhale* and illuminates how those women have aged in fifteen years. Savanah, now 51 years old, is married to Isaac Hathaway, a passionate churchgoer and cybersex enthusiast. Robin, still unmarried, has a 15-year-old daughter Sparrow, whose father is incarcerated. Bernadine has divorced John and married Jesse Hampton, alias James Wheeler, a bigamist. Gloria loses her husband in a drive-by shooting. All the women, except Gloria, have matured in loveless relationships.

Getting to Happy is a Black aesthetic text limning the struggles and celebrations of Black women. It makes effective use of naming, call-and-response, and blues idioms. Irony is used to strengthen McMillan's integration of Black cultural material into the Western idiom: Bernadine is "our black Julia

Child"; Robin names her dogs "Romeo" and "Juliet"; and Jesse Hampton, Bernadine's husband, is nicknamed "Jesse James" because he steals from women to enrich himself.

Getting to Happy expands the canon of African American literature by signifying on other ethnic women's novels. It has "the four-woman novel form" popularized in Louisa May Alcott's *Little Women* (1868) and appropriated in Amy Tan's *The Joy Luck Club* (1989) and in Julia Alvarez's *How the Garcia Girls Lost Their Accents* (2010) (Richards 1999, p. 122). McMillan's novel enlarges the technique of four blood sisters or relatives in the aforementioned novels by including four unrelated Black women maintaining a friendly sister-type relationship. Their stories of unrequited love, addiction, and child-rearing speak specifically to a tradition of anxieties that African American women experience. In sharing their trauma, the women reach a plane of happiness,

Who Asked You? (2013) records a litany of twenty-first-century issues that Black women have historically confronted. Caring for a bed-ridden husband with Alzheimer's, drug-dependent adult children, and abandoned grandchildren top the list for protagonist Betty Jean Butler. Everyone freely gives advice, but she does not ask for it.

Who Asked You? blends Black cultural aesthetics with white icons. Characters are named after well-known personages such as R&B-soul-pop-disco singer Luther Vandross (Betty Jean's grandson) and the white country and western singer Tammy Wynette (Betty Jean's white neighbor). Different cultural hairstyles are observed, also. Diverse racial aesthetics increase whites' knowledge of Blacks but also reveal Blacks' faultfinding. The dreadlock coiffeur is glorified when worn with "a sense of pride" but condemned when not shampooed. Tammy thinks about her non-greeting "black racist" neighbors and admits, "I am not intimidated by black people anymore, and I refuse to apologize for being white" (McMillan 2015, p. 35).

The significance of *Who Asked You?* to the African American canon is its acknowledged similarities in the lives of American Blacks and whites. Both races experience births, deaths, family disagreements, divorces, out-of-wedlock pregnancies, abandonment of children, male incarceration, elder children's neglect of parents, and race prejudice. *Who Asked You?* motivates readers to see beyond racial divisiveness.

McMillan's next novel, *I Almost Forgot about You* (2016), links to African American women's history as a text of remembrance. Recalling the past has traditionally enabled a critique of Black women's struggles and survival. The protagonist, Dr. Georgia Young, an oversexed middle-aged ophthalmologist, sets out to locate her bygone male friends as a means to find out why their relationships did not work. Her journey exposes how the way one lives her life often determines how one finds herself in middle and old age.

The novel's Black aesthetic component is a jazz-like riff. The riff begins with Dr. Young having pizza delivered to her home by an economically disenfranchised young Black boy with dreams of going to college. The passage functions as one of many thematic variations on the hopeful, yet unfulfilled, Black male and the sexually frustrated Black woman. The melody is played and replayed as Dr. Young, the soloist–protagonist, orchestrates the tune about all the men she has dated, married, or had sex with.

The use of the riff in *I Almost Forgot about You* expands the canon of African American literature. Not since the improvisational structure of Toni Morrison's *Jazz* (1992) has the riff been revisited, composed, and performed with such thematic intensity as it is in McMillan's *I Almost Forgot about You*. The strength of the novel's thematic riff lies in its double entendre: some Black women's release of their sexual inhibitions satisfies profound loneliness, and Black men do have ambitions other than sex.

A masterful literary artist, Terry McMillan interweaves African American history, culture, and expansion of the African American literary canon into each of her novels. She expands the African American literary canon in her novels by widening Black women's historic and advancing struggles for identity, autonomy, and gendered empowerment. Her novels not only enlarge Black women's communal position found in canonical African American novels, but they also update matters related to Black women's health, caretaking, careers, spousal abuse, incarceration, and death. In addition, McMillan's works broaden the functionality of cultural strategies found in the African American literary canon and add contemporary gender-based counternarratives to displace outmoded Western myths. While some critics argue that McMillan's works and those of other "popular" writers are distinct from and lesser than those in the African American literary canon, her use of history and culture manifests a timely and meaningful expansion of the African American literary canon in which she should be included.

SEE ALSO: Alvarez, Julia; Illness and Disability; Morrison, Toni; Tan, Amy; Trauma and Fiction; Urban Fiction

REFERENCES

Asanti, Molefi Kete. (1987). *The Afrocentric Idea*. Philadelphia: Temple University Press.

Dandridge, Rita B. (1998). Debunking the motherhood myth in Terry McMillan's *Mama*. *CLA Journal* 41 (4): 405–416.

Davis, Larry E. (1993). *Black and Single: Meeting and Choosing a Partner Who's Right for You*. Chicago: The Noble Press.

Du Bois, W.E.B. (1900). *The College-Bred Negro*. Atlanta: Atlanta University Press.

Holloway, Karla. (1997). Cultural narratives passed on: African American mourning stories. *College English* 59 (1): 32–40.

Hudgins, John L. and Holmes, Bernadette J. (1990). *The Impact of Family Structure Variations among Black Families on the Gender Enumeration of Black Males*. Center for Survey Methods, Washington, DC: Research Bureau of the Census.

McMillan, Terry. (1987). *Mama*. New York: Houghton.

McMillan, Terry. (1989). *Disappearing Acts*. New York: Viking.

McMillan, Terry. (1996). *How Stella Got Her Groove Back*. New York: Viking.

McMillan, Terry. (2002). *A Day Late and a Dollar Short*. New York: Signet.

McMillan, Terry. (2005). *The Interruption of Everything*. New York: Viking.

McMillan, Terry. (2015). *Who Asked You?* New York: Signet; 1st ed. 2013.

Moynihan, Daniel P. (1965). *The Negro Family: The Case for National Action*. Office of Policy Planning and Research. Washington, DC: United States Department of Labor.

Neal, Larry. (1968). The Black Arts Movement. *The Drama Review* 12 (4): 28–39.

Patrick, Diane. (1999). *Terry McMillan: The Unauthorized Biography*. New York: Thomas Dunne.

Richards, Paulette. (1999). *Terry McMillan: A Critical Companion*. Westport, CT: Greenwood Press.

Statistical Abstract of the United States: The National Data Book. (2002). U.S. Department of Commerce Economics and Statistics Administration. Table 209, p. 122. Washington, DC: Government Printing Office.

FURTHER READING

Bell, Bernard W. (2004). *The Contemporary African American Novel: Its Folk Roots and Modern Literary Branches*. Amherst: University of Massachusetts Press.

Dandridge, Rita B. (1997). Debunking the beauty myth with Black pop culture in Terry McMillan's *Waiting to Exhale*. In: *Black Popular Cultures into the Twentieth-First Century: Language, Rhythm, and Sound* (ed. Joseph K. Adjaye and Adrianne R. Andrews), 121–133. Pittsburgh: University of Pittsburgh Press.

Dandridge, Rita B. (1999). Terry McMillan. In: *Contemporary African American Novelists* (ed. Emmanuel S. Nelson), 319–326. Westport, CT: Greenwood Press.

Ellerby, Janet M. (1997). Deposing the man of the house: Terry McMillan rewrites the family. *MELUS* 22 (2): 105–117.

McMillan, Terry. (2020). *It's Not All Downhill from Here*. New York: Ballantine Books.

Mengestu, Dinaw

CORINNE DUBOIN
Université de La Réunion, France

Ethiopian-born writer Dinaw Mengestu is a twenty-first-century novelist and freelance journalist. The son of refugees, he grew up in the Midwest and, since his first visit to Africa in his twenties, he has been publishing essays and magazine articles on Ethiopia and present-day conflicts in Africa. Since 2006, he has produced three award-winning novels in which he portrays a diverse set of characters, African exiles and refugees or their descendants, and tackles the themes of migration, dislocation and loss, diaspora, and the forging of new identities in multicultural America. As a member of the new African diaspora in the United States, he has become a major voice in contemporary multiethnic American literature.

Dinaw Mengestu was born in Addis Ababa in 1978 during the Ethiopian Red Terror. After the communist revolution and the overthrow of Emperor Selassie I in 1974, a Marxist–Leninist military junta headed by Mengistu Haile Mariam seized power and led a ruthless campaign of repression from 1976 to 1978. Political opponents and dozens of thousands of people were arbitrarily arrested, tortured, incarcerated, or executed. The Red Terror remains a persistent historical trauma for Ethiopia and its worldwide diaspora. Dinaw Mengestu's own family was directly affected. While some of his relatives turned into influential figures, others became victims of the new regime: his father's older brother, a lawyer, died under suspicious circumstances after being taken into custody; one of his mother's brothers was also arrested and another one escaped to Sudan.

Facing such a serious situation, Mengestu's father, who worked for Ethiopian Airlines, requested asylum in 1978 while on a trip to Italy, shortly before his son's birth. In 1980, his wife, daughter, and two-year-old son Dinaw joined him in Peoria, Illinois. Hired as a worker at Caterpillar, a major construction equipment company, Mengestu's father climbed up the corporate ladder as an executive before he was laid off. He and his family consequently moved to Forest Park, a suburb of Chicago, and eventually settled in the Washington, DC, area where they had relatives. During his college years, Dinaw Mengestu began his studies at Georgetown University and earned his bachelor's degree in English in 2000. He then pursued graduate studies in New York and received a master of fine arts in fiction from Columbia University in 2005.

As Mengestu himself has pointed out in many interviews, he lived a "prototypical American childhood" (Scrivani 2015) and had to face the challenges of growing up Black in America. A son of immigrants, he also had to come to terms with his dual identity and bridge the gap between two cultures. As a child, he had no memories of his native land and little information about his parents' past lives, and he inherited their sense of loss and alienation. Thus, during his teen years, he showed a growing interest in Ethiopia, and in his early twenties he pressed his father to tell him about his uncle who was killed during the Red Terror and interviewed close relatives, tape-recording his painful family story.

Mengestu made his first trip to Ethiopia in 2005. Since 2006, he has reported for *Rolling Stone*, *Harper's*, *The New Yorker*, *The Wall Street Journal*, and the like, and has published both personal essays and articles on African politics and conflicts in Darfur, Uganda, and the Congo. He lived for a few years in Paris with his wife. They moved to New York in 2012 with their two sons. Since 2016, Mengestu has been Professor of Written Arts and Director of the Written Arts Program at Bard College in New York State.

Mengestu's family history, his own experience in multiethnic America, and his trips to Africa as a journalist have been ongoing sources of inspiration for his fictional writings. He has rapidly emerged as a talented young American novelist and has been the recipient of many literary awards and distinctions. In 2007, after the publication of his debut novel, *The Beautiful Things that Heaven Bears* – also released in the United Kingdom under the title *Children of the Revolution* (2007) – he was selected as one of the National Book Foundation's "5 under 35" honorees. He also won the French *Prix du premier roman étranger* that same year and the *Guardian* First Book Award in 2008. In 2010, Mengestu published his second novel, *How to Read the Air*, and *The New Yorker* listed him as one of the most promising "20 Under 40" American writers. In 2012 he received the Ernest Gaines Award for Literary Excellence. His third and most recent novel, *All our Names* (2014), also earned immediate critical acclaim, and *Granta*'s "Best of Young American Novelists of 2017" confirmed him as a major literary figure of his generation. In addition, he was awarded a Lannan Fiction Fellowship in 2007, was a 2012 McArthur Foundation Fellow, and was the Lannan Foundation Chair in Poetics at Georgetown University from 2012 to 2015.

Mengestu's works of fiction have contributed to the renewal and growing diversification of contemporary American literature in the past decades, resulting from the increasing presence of African, Indian, and Asian immigrants in the United States, and from the emergence of new diasporas in the era of globalization. With other recent African diaspora authors, such as Nigerian American Chris Abani, Chimamanda Ngozi Adichie, and Teju Cole, or Ghanaian Taiye Selasi, Zimbabwean NoViolet Bulawayo, and Cameroonian Imbolo Mbue, Mengestu unsettles traditional assumptions on the definition of Black identity in America. In parallel with African American authors, this new generation of fiction writers has also contributed to reshaping the contours of Black American writing. However, unlike the above-mentioned authors, who lived in Africa (and some in Europe) before coming to America as students or expatriates, Mengestu is a second-generation immigrant who grew up in the United States and who has built an American identity that incorporates his Ethiopian heritage. As an American writer of Ethiopian descent who claims to be the heir to a Western literary tradition in all its diversity and richness, he calls for a new approach to immigrant literature as an integral American genre that does not categorize, if not marginalize, writers along ethnic lines.

In his debut novel, *The Beautiful Things that Heaven Bears*, Mengestu portrays a lonely Ethiopian immigrant, Sepha Stephanos, who has lived in Washington, DC, for seventeen years. He escaped the Red Terror after his father's arrest and puzzling death and now owns a failing grocery store in Logan Circle, a redeveloped Black neighborhood. This first-person narrative, written from the perspective of an African exile, alternates between the account of Sepha's frustrating life in America and his memories of home and family in Addis Ababa. In moments of nostalgia mixed with sarcasm, he and his émigré friends, "Joe from the Congo" and "Ken the Kenyan," look back upon political coups in Africa. Also, Sepha briefly dates his white American neighbor Judith, a divorced mother and professor of American history.

Mengestu's novel moves away from the conventional immigrant story. The author revises the perception of the United States as a unique land of opportunity and contests the traditional representation of the newcomer who successfully integrates into American society. Feeling helpless and lonely, caught in a state of melancholia, his central character ends up trapped in-between two unattainable worlds: the lost homeland he had to flee and will never return to, and a prosperous America that seemed promising but brings only disappointments. Sepha's economic failure and his final eviction as a store owner, as well as his romantic setbacks, are emblematic of his failed attempt at assimilation. His narrative expresses the aspirations, anxieties, and disillusions of African immigrants who build fragile diasporic identities in an ever-changing, complex social environment. The impermanence and precariousness of their world in movement, from Addis Ababa to Washington, DC, and the fragmentation of society are symbolized by the gradual transformation of Logan Circle, a predominantly African American neighborhood that undergoes gentrification. Sepha, who left his homeland and its capital city torn apart by the revolution, is witness to ethnic tensions that divide African Americans, African newcomers, and new white homeowners. Thus, Mengestu exposes the lure of the American dream together with America's illusory democratic principles.

Sepha often spends time in his store reading books aloud to Judith's daughter, Naomi. These moments of intimacy remind him of the times when his father would tell him stories which he had invented. Literature and storytelling are recurring themes in Mengestu's fiction. His main characters, all first-person narrators, are readers (in *The Beautiful Things that Heaven Bears* – the title is actually a line from Dante's "Inferno"), storytellers (in *How to Read the Air*), and would-be writers (in *All our Names*). The author thus highlights the soothing power of shared words. For his characters living in the diaspora, writing, reading, or storytelling help them (re)connect with people, the past, and their memories of home, and help them engage in the definition of their own migrant selves.

In his second novel, *How to Read the Air*, Mengestu further explores the central theme of migration by exposing the transgenerational impact of forced mobility. The narrative superimposes two road trips. American-born Jonas – an English teacher and former public letter-writer, and the son of Ethiopian refugees – leaves New York and drives down South, retracing the route his parents, Yosef and Mariam, took thirty years before, in 1977, from Peoria, Illinois, to Nashville, Tennessee. They had just reunited and settled in the United States as a young couple, after three years of separation in the context of the Ethiopian revolution.

In this multilayered narrative that weaves together the broken trajectories of first- and second-generation immigrants in the United States, Mengestu uses the classic American road trip as a metaphor for the emergence of new ties, the building of a new sense of self, the will to give meaning and direction to one's life, and the appropriation of diasporic territories, whether real or imagined. The novelist shows how Jonas's wanderings, his personal quest for answers, and his need to reconnect with his parents' elusive past so as to come to terms with it, all lead him to a journey into creative imagination. Jonas fabricates stories and memories so as to fill in the missing pieces and record the untold painful history of invisible migrants, such as that of his father's perilous odyssey to America, through Sudan and Europe.

Jonas's retrospective narrative sheds light on Yosef's inability to build strong, intimate bonds with his wife and son. His sudden fits of violence were the expression of a silent pain deeply rooted in his repressed, traumatic memories of exile – his escape from Ethiopia involved crossing the seas to reach America, hidden in a box in the hold of a ship. As an immigrant, he had developed a feeling of insecurity and had thus learned "how to read the air" and watch out for signs of trouble. Mengestu's novel demonstrates how the failure of immigrant parents to clearly articulate the truth about their lived experience of displacement and their resulting psychological distress affects their children. In common with the Chinese American daughters in Amy Tan's *The Joy Luck Club* (1989) or the Bengali American Gogol/Nikhil Ganguli in Jhumpa Lahiri's *The Namesake* (2003), Jonas lacks a firm sense of his own self; he also questions his commitments. Mengestu thus shows the complicated routes, the back roads and short cuts taken by the children of immigrants to gain a clearer sense of belonging and put down roots. More broadly, he interrogates American identity.

Jonas is haunted by Yosef's shadowy past. After his father's death, he feels the urgent need to tell his students about Yosef's improbable journey. Playing fast and loose with the truth, Jonas gets carried away, embellishes his fascinating tale, captures the attention of his young audience, and triggers empathy. In a similar way, when he worked at a refugee resettlement center, Jonas would edit the migrants' written testimonies and make deliberate untruthful statements that reported dire experiences and grossly distorted facts. In both situations, Jonas invents memories, turns history into stories and legends to pass on: remembering implies re-vision and the fictionalization of history. With his imaginative account of his father's epic passage, Jonas associates Yosef with America's migrant past; through the reclamation of a legacy, of a lost memory, he also negotiates his own diasporic identity, his Ethiopian filiation.

Mengestu highlights the healing, redemptive power of storytelling and self-writing for Jonas. Ironically enough, the narrator weaves a web of lies in his search for the truth. He becomes a subversive master of words, a deceiver and a *bricoleur* who stands at intersections between past and present, Africa and America, facts and fiction, hoping to patch up his own life. Through his unreliable narrator, the novelist reminds his readers about the evocative power of imagination and about the relation of literature to history: narrative fiction does not aim to achieve veracity (that is what historiography does), but it involves rewriting lived history and exploring the emotional truth of personal and collective past experiences that inform the present.

Looking back on the pivotal early seventies, Mengestu's third novel, *All our Names*, confirms the writer's preoccupation with the impact of a history of displacement on the formation of unstable, fluid identities. He addresses the themes of self-consciousness, interracial relations, and social and cultural diversity through a cross-national perspective, beyond boundaries of difference. The novel combines two stories told in alternating chapters by two first-person narrators: Isaac, an African student who fled from Uganda to the United States after being involved in a merciless revolution; and Helen, a white American social worker stuck in her Midwestern hometown and designated to assist Isaac as a newly arrived refugee. She belatedly discovers that the young man has concealed his true identity as he used his friend's name (Isaac) and passport to come to America. Through the two protagonists' intersecting lives and short-lived romance, the author revisits a period of political unrest and social transformation in both post-independence Africa and post-Civil Rights America.

Through Isaac's narrative, Mengestu reconsiders Pan-Africanism and its democratic ideals as the movement rapidly turned into a utopian dream and gave way to brutal dictatorial regimes based on the logic of power. By depicting a naïve young man and his close friend, who plan a student rebellion, get involved in a revolution, and participate in mass killing, the writer shows how everyone can be caught up in collective madness and easily fall into the trap of violence, abjection, and inhumanity. The novelist portrays morally ambiguous, multifaceted characters and exposes the complexity of their emotions, the intricacies of human nature. He thus avoids the distortions of a one-sided representation of Africa and responds to facile, patronizing Eurocentric depictions. Mengestu also reimagines the past in the light of more recent examples of barbaric acts and tragic events he has covered as a journalist: deadly conflicts from Rwanda to Darfur, genocides, the enrollment of child soldiers. He merges together past and present events so as to make an oblique assessment of the legacies of history in contemporary Africa.

Once Isaac reaches America, the narration shifts perspective. Helen's personal account, which intersects with the story of Isaac, depicts their disturbing encounter, which destabilizes her certainties about America and Africa, about her own path in life and her sense of self, about her construction of race and gender. Helen's narrative mainly focuses on her interaction with Isaac, her response to foreignness and Otherness, and her complicated interracial love affair with Isaac, which exposes her to racism in America.

Mengestu creates a parallel between Isaac's and Helen's wavering worlds. The author's dual narrative builds a bridge between the hopes and disillusions of newly independent Africans, and those of Americans in a racialized society. His remapping of the Black Atlantic as a transnational space in the twentieth century, with a focus on Africa and its new diasporas, highlights persisting transcontinental connections and renewed circulations, with the forced displacement of refugees.

While Mengestu's previous novels concentrate on the plight of immigrants and the difficulties they face in finding their place, *All our Names* takes another direction as it does not dwell upon Isaac's American experience as a newcomer, but on his traumatic memory of past actions that led him to flee, on his difficulty in revealing the truth to Helen, and on the possibility of envisioning healing, thanks to Helen's unconditional support and love. In that sense, the novel recalls Haitian American Edwidge Danticat's *The Dew Breaker* (2004), which intertwines the individual stories of a former *tonton macoute* (Haitian paramilitary soldier) in exile who lies to his family and hides his feelings of guilt and shame, while his victims, who have also resettled in the United States, struggle to build themselves up and overcome the trauma of a haunting past. Both multivocal fictions raise difficult ethical questions about postcolonial societies and the possibility of redemption through the reconstruction of identity away from home.

The title of the novel *All our Names*, as well as the main character's renaming, evoke the multiple identities, and the fluctuating sense of being and belonging, that are determined by encounters, displacements, and relocations, in a constant process of renewal. Yet, Mengestu's novels are not simply immigration stories. They embrace a broad range of key themes that bring to light the complexities of human relationships, thus transforming unique individual immigrant experiences into fluid collective destinies that transcend differences. Therefore, Mengestu's fictional exploration of personal trajectories, across borders, leads his readers to rethink American literary and cultural diversity.

SEE ALSO: Adichie, Chimamanda Ngozi; Black Atlantic; Cole, Teju; Danticat, Edwidge; Lahiri, Jhumpa; Multiculturalism; Tan, Amy; Trauma and Fiction

REFERENCE

Scrivani, Maria. (2015). Babel: novelist and journalist Dinaw Mengestu. *The Public* (November 11, 2015). http://www.dailypublic.com/articles/11112015/babel-novelist-and-journalist-dinaw-mengestu (accessed July 22, 2021).

FURTHER READING

Duboin, Corinne. (2017). African and American selves: "contact zones" in *All Our Names* by Dinaw Mengestu. *Etudes Littéraires Africaines* 44: 95–111.

Ledent, Bénédicte. (2015). Reconfiguring the African diaspora in Dinaw Mengestu's *The Beautiful Things That Heaven Bears*. *Research in African Literatures* 46 (4): 107–118.

Masterson, John. (2018). "DestroyedMichygen": rerouting the postnational in contemporary diaspirant fiction. *Research in African Literatures* 49 (1): 1–21.

Varvogli, Aliki. (2017). Urban mobility and race: Dinaw Mengestu's *The Beautiful Things That Heaven Bears* and Teju Cole's *Open City*. *Studies in American Fiction* 44 (2): 235–257.

Millennial Fiction

SCOTT MCCLINTOCK
Independent scholar, Big Bear, USA

As used here, the term "millennial" encompasses the adjective "millennial" as applied to fiction written on either side of the "millennium" of the year 2000, by authors of any generation (literary periodization); "Millennial" as an adjective delineating authors born in the decades from around the 1980s to the 1990s (that is, a concept of literary generations); and "millennialism" or "millenarian," to characterize a rhetoric of the "end of days" present in American literature from the beginnings, a preeminent way the American community has been imagined and reimagined over the course of its history and literature, and how narratives of both the origin and end of the American nation have been imagined apocalyptically. How Millennial fiction merges with the apocalyptic strain across the history of American literature, yet reflects the new information order, social media landscape, and globalized economy corresponding to the growing ethnic diversity of twenty-first-century fiction, will be discussed below. Evidently, the text selection for this entry does not distinguish genre fiction and literature, instead preferring to emphasize thematic groupings of cultural texts.

THE MILLENNIAL THEME IN MILLENNIAL FICTION

The millennial theme of the "end of days" is not unique to writing by Millennials as a generation; indeed, it has typified American literature from the beginning, but seems, perhaps unsurprisingly, to particularly define writing by Millennials in the generational sense. Michael Wigglesworth, the Puritan minister, doctor, and poet whose poem "The Day of Doom" (1662) was a bestseller in early New England, illustrates the influence of millennialist or millenarian rhetoric on an emerging American literature and its sense of national identity in the colonial period (the American as the "new man" after the end of history, God's Elect in New England as what the poem styles the "chosen Generation"). The rhetoric of apocalypse, millennialism, and end-of-time discourse both founded the national idea of America as the new Republic redeeming the failure of European nationhood, and casts doubt on this foundational rhetoric in narratives of the collapse of the nation and social institutions in American life in various apocalyptic scenarios that will be discussed in more detail below.

Stephen J. Burn's edited collection of essays, *American Literature in Transition, 1990–2000* (2018), locates American fiction written around the final decade of the American Century ("millennial" as a term of literary periodization) within the longer arc of millennialism as a theme in American literature, citing such authors as John Updike (*Toward the End of Time* [1997], set in the year 2020); John Barth's story, "The End: An Introduction" (in *On With the Story* [1996]), a story that is partly a parody of the "end of everything" discourse that Barth says proliferated in the 1990s, what the story refers to as "endism"; Richard Powers's *Gain* (1998); and David Foster Wallace's *Infinite Jest* (1996); to which could be added T.C. Boyle's *World's End* (1990), and the mordantly comic post-apocalyptic short fiction of George Saunders in *CivilWarLand in Bad Decline* (1996), among many others.

Another culturally significant strain of the apocalyptic in millennial fiction is the popularity of young adult (YA) fiction that is post-apocalyptic, for example Susan Collins's Hunger Games (*The Hunger Games* [2008]; *Catching Fire* [2009]; and *Mockingjay* [2010]), and Veronica Roth's Divergent series, novels that are about surviving after apocalyptic events that have foundered the nation. If the nation is seen to be a broken community, both of these novel cycles portray communities of solidarity (what Thomas Beebe refers to as "apocalyptic communities") that resist totalitarian control in a postapocalyptic setting. As in much postapocalyptic fiction, nation-states are survived by city-states, and the postapocalyptic landscape is also a postnational one. Other Millennial fiction in the generational sense focusing on postapocalyptic plots set in cities and representative of the increasing ethnic diversity of this genre includes Susan Ee's *Angelfall* (2012), Julie Kagawa's *The Immortal Rules* (2013), Tochi Onyebuchi's *War Girls* (2019), Victoria Lee's *The Fever King* (2019), N.K. Jemisin's *The City We Became* (2020), and Lilliam Rivera's *Dealing in Dreams* (2020).

In Roth's Divergent series, the individual and the body politic correspond: the personality traits identified by the names for the various factions in the postapocalyptic city-scape of Chicago are both individual (discovered through a kind of psychometric testing) and social or collective. The psychologist Joy Paul Guilford, whose concept of "divergent thinking" as nonlinear cognition was influential in theories of intelligence, applied psychometric measurement to creativity similar to how the "divergent" personality of Roth's books may not be exclusively identified with any one of the factions, mirroring within the fictional world of Roth's books the tendency of Generations X, Y, and Z to reject exclusive, singular identifications such as nationality, race, gender, or sexuality, but rather to embrace the overdetermination of multiple, intersectional identities (Crenshaw 1991) in belonging to different social groups simultaneously, much as Brett Easton Ellis rejects his identity as a gay man defining his writing, or Ocean Vuong, for whom his gay sexuality seems more significant than his Vietnamese ethnicity.

In the more recent fiction discussed below, Ling Ma's *Severance* (2018) represents Millennial novels concerned with the theme of apocalypse. Space does not allow for consideration of Cherokee author Daniel H. Wilson's *Robopocalypse* (2011), or its successor, *Robogenesis* (2014), but they could easily be prime examples of science fiction genre conventions involving artificial intelligence as what Thomas Beebe (2009) dubs "eschatechnology" and "reflective dissonance," as it relates to Native American reimaginings of "Western" genres. One of the recent trends among Gen X and Millennial Native American authors is the turn to genre fiction, especially apocalyptic science fiction, by Ohkay Pueblo author Rebecca Roanhorse, Blackfeet author Stephen Graham Jones, and others. In Native American fiction, apocalyptic scenarios represent an imaginative vision of a history in which the apocalypse has already occurred to Native people with the European conquest. To examples like these could be added realist fiction such as Yuri Herrera's *Signs Preceding the End of the World* [*Señales que precederán al fin del mundo*] (2015), a novel reflecting what anthropologist Ruth Behar (1993) termed "translated" identities addressing the transnational experiences of border crossers from Mexico and Latin America, which, although not an example of apocalyptic science fiction like the others, does open with a striking scene centering on the portentous sign of the end of the world for a man, a dog, and a cat, who are swallowed up when a sinkhole rips a breach in the road, a dreamlike, apocalyptic episode recalling Chicano author Tomás Rivera's novel, ...and the Earth Did Not Devour Him [... y no se lo tragó la tierra] (1971).

THE NEW WORK ORDER IN MILLENNIAL FICTION

Ling Ma, author of *Severance*, was born in China and emigrated to the United States, where she received an MFA in writing from Cornell. Her debut novel, *Severance*, is a crossover, genre-straddling novel blending elements of Millennial workplace fiction, immigration stories, and apocalyptic survivor fiction like the genre classic *Earth Abides* by George R. Stewart (1949). In *Severance*, a SARS or Wuhan coronavirus-type global pandemic originating in the Shenzhen region of China causes its victims to withdraw into an autistic-like solipsistic condition in which they continue to carry out repetitive, habitual tasks while becoming increasingly absorbed in their interior personal memories, like quasi-zombies, before succumbing physically. The disease, it is suspected, spreads through the transnational global exchanges of people and things characterizing the distributed global networks of the new capitalist economy, such as the specialized publishing production firm, Spectra, where the novel's narrator, Candace Chen, is employed producing boutique Bibles. With its corporate headquarters in New York City and its supply chain in China, the firm epitomizes the replacement of the traditional workplace, of industrial mass-market capitalism in which corporations were located primarily within the boundaries of nation-states by the geographically distributed, science-and-technology-driven "fast" capitalism, in which the application of information technology to production makes possible "mass customization," just-in-time production for specialized niche markets for which competition is extremely fierce and which must be able to rapidly and flexibly adapt, as opposed to traditional, "Fordist" mass production before the end of World War II (Gee, Hull, and Lankshear 1996).

In Ma's novel, the apocalyptic event of the nation's collapse is referred to unoriginally (deliberately so) as The End, and the chapters of the novel alternate between the narrator's struggle to survive in the postapocalyptic scenario with a small group of fellow survivors and chapters flashing back to events leading up to The End, or more distant memories of Candace Chen's childhood or early adulthood, including her moving from Salt Lake City, Utah to New York City as a young adult after the death of her parents. Early chapters detail Candace's relocation to New York City, where she begins a photoblog titled "New York City Ghost" featuring cell phone camera snapshots of the urban landscape of the city, explaining at one point that the "ghost" of her blog's title is herself. The motif of the "ghost" in *Severance*, echoed in the fictive corporation Spectra, possibly reverberates with "ghosting," a term used in social media and dating for the social distancing of someone totally withdrawing from all communication without explanation (like the "zombies" of the novel). Regardless, when Candace describes herself as a "ghost," she portrays herself as "walking around aimlessly, without anywhere to go, anything to do," just a "specter haunting the scene" (Ma 2018, p. 41).

The kind of management literature surveyed by Gee, Hull, and Lankshear (1996) is parodied in Ma's novel by the economist and author Steven Reitman, the title of whose fictional book, *You're Not the Boss of Me: Labor*

Values and Work Ethic Among America's Millennial Youth, reflects the generational gap between older, Boomer-era managers and their Generation X and Y employees, and the complaints about the alleged "slacker" work ethic among Millennials in the workforce. This new work order constructs employees as no longer "workers" but "associates" or "partners," socialized into the "vision" and values of the company to which everyone owes a total commitment, employees who are "empowered" to take on more of the routine administrative tasks over their own productivity that used to be performed by middle-level managers, must be "eager to stay" but "ready to leave" when the needs for flexibility and adaptivity of the corporation demand (Gee, Hull, and Lankshear 1996, p. 19). And indeed Candace herself displays exactly these characteristics of the ideal employee in the new capitalist work order. At one point she writes, "They kept me on because my output was prolific and they could task me with more and more production assignments. When I focused, a trait I exhibited at the beginning of my time there, I could be detail-oriented to the point of obsession" (pp. 16–17), illustrating the "over-the-top" dedication of workers in the new capitalist economy. Her boyfriend, Jonathan, too, we learn, once worked as an assistant editor at an independent cultural magazine in Chicago, which he leaves when it is acquired by a larger media company. His description of the corporate culture that induced him to leave lampoons the "flexible" structure and conditions of work in fast capitalism:

> By the end of his first year, the corporate owners made changes to the vacation benefits policy: Instead of allowing for unlimited rollover vacation days, they would only rollover a maximum of ten from that year to the next. In response, some of the older employees, many of whom had been there since the eighties, took early retirement in order to capitalize on the months' worth of vacation days they'd amassed before the policy could go into effect. It was essentially a forced retirement of senior employees with higher salaries.
>
> (2018, p. 136)

The passage continues with one of the few references to "severance" in the novel:

> By the end of his second year, corporate announced that policy regarding severance packages would be changed. Severance would no longer be scaled according to the number of years that employees had worked, but the company would provide a flat fee for all employees who'd worked there for fewer than ten years. Within the following year, almost all of the senior staff had been laid off, given their diminished severance payouts. The editor who'd hired him was also let go.
>
> (2018, pp. 136–137)

The theme of "severance" in Ma's novel, then, corresponds to an economic order in which the cutting of contractual bonds between employees and their employers foregrounds how ties between individuals and various communities or systems become unstable, and how individuals withdraw within themselves with the breakdown of community.

Candace and Jonathan in Ling Ma's novel are thus prototypical Millennial workers in the new, knowledge-based economy organized by the application of information technology to production, and the globally distributed networks of supply and production characteristic of late capitalism, a new work order in which the boundaries between national markets have been erased, and in which "motivated" workers acting independently as "partners" within the organization cannot be "bossed" around by supervisors as in traditional command, hierarchical workplaces, but must be "developed" and "coached" to internalize the vision and purpose of the corporation and, independently or in teams, carry out provisional work assignments, and in which the traditional lifelong career has been superseded by a "personal portfolio" one carries from temporary work assignment to temporary work assignment. The result of this new work order is the frequently underemployed or unemployed status of many Millennial workers, who find themselves engaged in aimless activity when employed at all, wandering around directionlessly like the "fevered" near-zombies of *Severance*.

Ling Ma's novel, then, despite the superficial genre conventions associating it with "survival fiction" and postapocalyptic fiction, is really nothing so much as a "workplace novel" along the lines of David Foster Wallace's *The Pale King* (2011). In this, it could be joined with Helen DeWitt's *Lightning Rods* (2011), Catherine Lacey's *The Answers* (2017), Halle Butler's novel, *The New Me* (2019), and Hilary Leichter's *Temporary* (2020), among others.

The globalization of capital flows and workplaces enabled by the application of information technology to production under the "new work order" (Gee, Hull, and Lankshear 1996) represents a postnational phase of capitalism, in contrast to the nationally based corporations under the Fordist, mass production economic order of the period from the early twentieth century to the early 1970s, a transformed workplace about which millennial fiction seemingly confirms the adage that "it is easier to imagine the end of the world than the end of capitalism" (Fisher 2009, p. 2).

ETHNIC, CULTURAL, AND GENDER DIVERSITY OF MILLENNIAL FICTION

Werner Sollors's concept of ethnic modernism, as the incorporation of ethnic difference within the perpetual renewal and regeneration of American literature (*Beyond Ethnicity: Consent and Descent in American Culture*, 1986), as well as the "translated" experience earlier associated with Yuri Herrera's *Signs Preceding the End of the World* (2015), could also describe novels illustrating the increasingly globalized, transnational character of Millennial American fiction, such as the Balkan magical realism of Téa Obreht's *The Tiger's Wife: A Novel* (2011); the debut novel of Yaa Gyasi, born in Ghana, raised in Alabama, and a graduate of the Iowa Writers' Workshop, *Homegoing* (2016); and Ocean Vuong's *On Earth We're Briefly Gorgeous* (2019), all novels of memory about other homelands by foreign-born, American-based younger authors, and examples of the increasingly ethnically diverse character of Millennial fiction resulting from the high representation of immigrant authors in it.

Thomas Beebe, in *Millennial Literatures of the Americas, 1492-2002* (2009), describes literature as an "eschatechnology" (pp. 6-7 and passim) and identifies how a dominant discourse of millennialism in the Protestant tradition is answered by what he calls the "reflective dissonance" by which this rhetoric becomes hybridized in the Americas as it is contested by racial or ethnic "others," an observation carrying over into the increasing diversity of American fiction in this survey. However, while American fiction has become increasingly ethnically diverse during the decades since the 1980s, a tendency has simultaneously emerged in Millennial authors in the generational sense toward a post-ethnic sensibility in a way to be discussed further, below.

Standing out among authors in her concerns with reenvisioning national history from the kind of hybridized perspective Thomas Beebe refers to as "reflective dissonance" is Boomer-generation, Laguna Pueblo Native American author Leslie Marmon Silko, whose most ambitious novels bracket the decade of the 1990s and, like other authors previously mentioned, frequently illustrate the traits of both what Linda Hutcheon (1988) called "historiographic metafiction" and a concern with millennialist, apocalyptic themes, most obviously in her novel *Almanac of the Dead* (1991), but also *Garden in the Dunes* (1999). Silko's fiction employs a sweeping, ironic, critical perspective of American history that shares this quality with other writers of "historiographic metafiction" previously mentioned, but inscribing the dissenting perspective of Native Americans and others culturally marginalized that is more centered on ethnicity and cultural difference than other more culturally mainstream authors. Native American authors like Daniel H. Wilson and Leslie Marmon Silko undertake to counter "terminal narratives," as anthropologist Michael V. Wilcox has called them, of Native American cultural extinction, by emphasizing the survival and cultural persistence of Native Americans, or what Gerald Vizenor dubbed "post-Indian" identity.

POST-ETHNICITY AND THE END OF HISTORY IN MILLENNIAL AMERICAN FICTION

Ottessa Moshfegh's *My Year of Rest and Relaxation: A Novel* (2018) has been described as "slacker fiction," but it could be better characterized as a novel of fatigue, ennui, and idleness related to underemployment of Millennials, rather than "slacking," exactly.

A deracinated narrative sensibility is conveyed in a novel by a Persian American author whose narrator is a blond WASP woman (because why not write about a character from the most culturally validated, desirable elite), whose own body image ideal is Whoopi Goldberg, reflecting a trend in Millennial fiction in the generational sense toward a post-ethnic sensibility. The narrator describes her boss at an art gallery where she gets one of her first jobs in New York City as "the kind of mysteriously ethnic woman who would blend in easily in almost any country. She could have been from Istanbul or Paris or Morocco or Moscow or New York or San Juan or even Phnom Penh in a certain light, depending on how she wore her hair" (Moshfegh 2018, p. 36). Culture, ethnicity, and nationality are indeterminate in a way that is characteristic of much Millennial fiction.

The novel's narrator works not because she needs to (her inheritance from her deceased parents provides her financial independence), but because if she "did normal things – held down a job, for example," she could "starve off the part of me that hated everything" (2018, p. 33). About her job at the art gallery she says, "for the most part, the little effort I put into the job was enough" (p. 36). At the art gallery job, the narrator starts taking hour-long naps during lunch break, sneaking them in the supply closet at the gallery, which starts the narrator's need for even more sleep, what she calls going into "hibernation," self-sedating with Ativan, Ambien, and Nembutals and other pill combinations, and little else all day, thinking that if she could just sleep all day, she could "become a whole new person" (p. 26), like the character Millie in Halle Butler's *The New Me*, or Mary Parsons and the Identity Distance Therapy in Catherine Lacey's *The Answers*, and could forget the feeling of being dead and hating everybody (p. 19). The urge to sleep, what the narrator dubs "somnia" or "somnophilia," reflects the deep desire and narrative structure in American literature and culture for self-regeneration or renewal. Sleeping all day "felt productive. Something was getting sorted out. I knew . . . that when I'd slept enough, I'd be okay. I'd be renewed, reborn. I would be a whole new person, every one of my cells regenerated enough times that the old cells were just distant, foggy memories. My past life would be but a dream, and I could start over without regrets, bolstered by the bliss and serenity that I would have accumulated in my year of rest and relaxation" (p. 51). Upon being fired from her job at the art gallery, the narrator describes her reaction to her last day on the job: "There was no sadness or nostalgia, only disgust that I'd wasted so much time on unnecessary labor when I could have been sleeping and feeling nothing" (p. 49). The theme of "wasted" time recurs in writing by Millennials, the sense of life spent roiling around in futile activities, allying its sensibility with nothing so much as Marcel Proust's epic a century earlier of wasted time, *temps perdu*, which has been translated variously as "lost time" or "things past," but contextually, within the framework of Proust's novel, conveys strong connotations of wasted time, time spent in vain, frivolous or useless activities. "Time, I guess, passes," says Millie, in Butler's *The New Me* (2019, p. 67), dilating the sentence with the diffidence of how time is passed.

Besides being a workplace novel, *My Year of Rest and Relaxation* is a 9/11 novel, the narrator of which has been seeking oblivion for the year leading up to September 11, only to wake to the horrible reality of that day at the end of the book. Passages describing the narrator's perfunctory forays into the New York City dating scene resembling Candace Bushnell's *Sex and the City* (1997) provide the background necessary to understand her choice of a first pick-up boyfriend, Trevor, who works for an investment bank in the World Trade Center, whom she prefers to the art school hipster guys who "focused on 'abstract ideas' and developed drinking problems to blot out the self-loathing they preferred to call 'existential ennui'" (Moshfegh 2018, p. 33), even though he is just manipulating the narrator as a rebound girlfriend between affairs with older women. As the narrator undertakes her "relaxation project," she experiments with different drug combinations to induce her desired state of semi-aware borderline unconsciousness, spending her days on the sofa eating animal crackers and watching second-hand video tapes on what was already, in the year 2000, becoming obsolete technology, to be replaced by DVDs and, later, streaming media. As the novel progresses, the narrator discovers that while she was asleep, she has been sleepwalking, a plausible side effect of the drugs she has been taking. She wakes to find the furniture in her apartment rearranged, cartons of uneaten takeout food stacked here and there, or containers of melted ice cream, new clothes she does not remember buying, subscriptions to magazines she does not recall ordering, new credit cards she cannot remember applying for; she finds that she has been online chatting with strangers without remembering it, uncannily realizing that while she has been asleep, she has not been doing nothing, but rather leading a double life hidden from herself, in which she does things uncharacteristic of herself she cannot recall doing. Her friend Reva periodically interrupts the narrator's pill-induced haze seeking consolation which the narrator is unable to give her for her mother's death and break-up with her supervisor with whom she's been having an affair. To get rid of her, the supervisor has had Reva promoted to a new position working for a counterterrorism firm located in the Twin Towers (p. 203). It is January 2011. The climactic image of the novel is one of the terrible, iconic 9/11 images, which the narrator accidentally sees on the television news coverage because her VHS player has broken down and she can no longer doze off with videos, the female counterpart of the "Falling Man" of Don DeLillo's novel of that title, of a woman tumbling into space from the 78th floor of the south tower, one of the "jumpers" whose unidentifiable figures outline both the individuality and anonymity of the victims, who reminds the narrator of Moshfegh's novel of her friend, Reva, whom she knows she will never see again, but who is just a "human being, diving into the unknown ... wide awake" (p. 289).

The relaxation project of the narrator of Moshfegh's novel and the Shen Fever zombies of Ling Ma's *Severance* similarly point to the way in which many Millennials in more recent fiction feel self-alienated from their own lives, highly intelligent narrators trapped in repetitive, routine jobs and actions they feel disconnected from, yearning for a better life commensurate with the better version of themselves they hazily wish to become. Although Moshfegh's novel is set in the portentous fall of the year 2000 counting down to September 11, 2001, it is a 9/11 novel only by apophasis, studiedly avoiding mentioning what the reader already knows, and refusing any sentimental identification with the apocalyptic event of 9/11, rejecting being "defined" by it, individually or generationally, but recognizing the beauty and fragility of individual lives in the novel's final passage. It shares this avoidance of making 9/11 the central reference point with Catherine Lacey's *The Answers*, which glancingly mentions it in connection with a narcissistic character, illustrating the tendency of more recent American fiction to eschew generational labels defined by relation to epochal events or national narratives, but instead value individuality and personal stories.

Indeed, a distinguishing feature of Millennial American fiction in the generational sense, as delineated by authors born between the early 1980s and about 1995, are discussions around the lack of a defining Millennial novel as there was for previous generations, even in the 1980s: Generation X had Bret Easton Ellis and generationally epitomizing novels like *Less than Zero* (1985) and *American Psycho* (1991). Earlier generations – such as the Lost Generation of the 1920s, or Beats of the 1950s – wrote fiction defined by world wars in a way that 9/11 has failed to individuate the Millennial generation or Gen Z.

The 9/11 novels of the first two decades of the 2000s are in fact by Boomers, or even "Silent Generation" authors such as Thomas Pynchon, whose novel *Bleeding Edge* (2013) weaves together the Y2K apocalypse and 9/11, and Don DeLillo, whose *Underworld* (1997) is historical fiction concerned with "last things" among other themes, and whose *Falling Man* (2007) is usually on the list of 9/11 fiction, who share with other writers of their generation like Philip Roth (*The Plot Against America* [2004]; *The Human Stain* [2000], about identity politics in 1990s America) an interest in explorations of American nationality and history in larger contexts of globalization. Indeed, rather than Thomas Pynchon's more overtly thematic 9/11 novel, *Bleeding Edge*, it may be the more oblique treatment of 9/11 utilizing genre conventions of pulp Weird Fiction in his earlier novel, *Against the Day* (2006), from which a line can be traced to the more contemporary writing by Millennial authors and its use of pulp genres. While writing by earlier generations such as the Silent Generation that lived through World War II or the Boomer generation that followed it was concerned with the attempt to define national culture and was historiographic in its effort to identify the uniquely defining characteristics of particular periods of American history, writing by Millennial authors seems rather to move beyond generational or ethnic categories, almost as if, with Gen Z, a limit has indeed been reached exhausting the usefulness of generationally or ethnically identifying labels, along with letters of the alphabet.

SEE ALSO: Border Fictions; Fictions of Work and Labor; Globalization; Indigenous Narratives; Periodization; Post-9/11 Narratives; Young Adult Boom

REFERENCES

Beebe, Thomas. (2009). *Millennial Literatures of the Americas, 1492–2002*. Oxford: Oxford University Press.

Behar, Ruth. (1993). *Translated Woman: Crossing the Border with Esperanza's Story*. Boston: Beacon Press.

Burn, Stephen J. (ed.) (2018). *American Literature in Transition, 1990–2000*. Cambridge: Cambridge University Press.

Butler, Halle. (2019). *The New Me*. New York: Penguin Books.

Crenshaw, Kimberle. (1991). Mapping the margins: intersectionality, identity politics, and violence against women of color. *Stanford Law Review* 43 (6). https://doi.org/10.2307/1229039

Fisher, Mark. (2009). *Capitalist Realism: Is There No Alternative?* Ropley, UK: O Books.

Gee, James, Hull, Glynda, and Lankshear, Colin. (1996). *The New Work Order: Behind the Language of the New Capitalism*. Boulder, CO: Westview Press.

Hutcheon, Linda. (1988). *A Poetics of Postmodernism*. New York: Routledge.

Ma, Ling. (2018). *Severance*. New York: Farrar, Straus and Giroux.

Moshfegh, Ottessa. (2018). *My Year of Rest and Relaxation: A Novel*. London: Jonathan Cape.

Sollors, Werner. (1986). *Beyond Ethnicity: Consent and Descent in American Culture*. Oxford: Oxford University Press.

FURTHER READING

Konstantinou, Lee. (2009). The brand as cognitive map in William Gibson's *Pattern Recognition*. *boundary 2* 36 (2): 67–97.

Rowe, John Carlos. (ed.) (2000). *Post-Nationalist American Studies*. Berkeley and Los Angeles: University of California Press.

Spicer, Andre. (2020). Sci-fi author William Gibson: how "future fatigue" is putting people off the 22nd century. *The Conversation* (January 23, 2020). https://theconversation.com/sci-fi-author-william-gibson-how-future-fatigue-is-putting-people-off-the-22nd-century-130335

Tulathimutte, Tony. (2016). Why there's no "millennial" novel. *The New York Times* (December 7, 2016). https://www.nytimes.com/2016/12/07/books/review/why-theres-no-millennial-novel.html

Wood, James. (2000). Human, all too inhuman. *The New Republic* (July 24, 2000). https://newrepublic.com/article/61361/human-inhuman

Millhauser, Steven

JAMES P. ZAPPEN
Rensselaer Polytechnic Institute, USA

Steven Millhauser is the author of four novels, including Pulitzer Prize-winning *Martin Dressler: The Tale of an American Dreamer* (1996), and numerous novellas and short stories. Following two early and ostensibly realist novels, Millhauser turned in the mid-1980s to mixes of reality and fantasy and created imaginative worlds grounded in historical contexts and extensively, often elaborately, detailed descriptions. These works explore the creative imagination in the arts and architecture; consumer culture; and isolation, boredom, and loneliness. Sometimes read as magical realist or modernist for their mix of reality and fantasy, their exploration of the worlds of art and architecture, and their multiple perspectives and lack of closure, these works may also be read as postmodernist insofar as they create imaginative worlds that shift from reality to fantasy and from the possible to the impossible and thereby defy traditional notions of rationality and causality.

Millhauser's mix of reality and fantasy suggests a kinship with magical realism (Alexander 2006, pp. 62–64), and his interest in art, multiple perspectives, and open endings allies him with the early modernists (Ingersoll 2010). These modernist worlds are Millhauser's worlds – from "August Eschenburg" and "In the Penny Arcade" (*In the Penny Arcade*, 1986) to "The Barnum Museum" and "Eisenheim the Illusionist" (*The Barnum Museum*, 1990) to *Martin Dressler*. But some of Millhauser's best work transcends the modernist world view that is bound to traditional notions of causality by creating imaginative worlds wherein causal explanations do not apply (McHale 1987, pp. 3–11, 73–83; Plotnitsky 2017, pp. 68–74). Brian McHale explains that whereas modernist fiction poses epistemological questions about how to interpret the world, postmodernist fiction raises ontological questions about worlds of different kinds (1987, pp. 6–11), and Arkady Plotnitsky claims that from modernist to postmodernist fiction we are passing from the presumptive causality of relativity theory – wherein God "does not play dice" – to the multiplicity, incompleteness, and randomness of quantum mechanics – wherein causal forces are indeterminate (2017, p. 73). These postmodernist worlds, too, are Millhauser's worlds – from some of the tales in *From the Realm of Morpheus* (1986) to "Cathay" (*In the Penny Arcade*) and "The Invention of Robert Herendeen" (*The Barnum Museum*) to the "Impossible Architectures" stories (*Dangerous Laughter*, 2008) to "We Others" (*We Others*, 2011) and "Miracle Polish" (*Voices in the Night*, 2015). But the modernist stories often stretch the limits of plausibility, and the postmodernist stories can often be explained as flights of the imagination, so Millhauser's work eludes overly simple categorization.

The two early novels are dark tales of adolescent isolation and boredom, suicide games, and murder, their detailed descriptions suggesting literary realism but sometimes drifting between reality and fantasy. *Edwin Mullhouse: The Life and Death of an American Writer 1943–1954 by Jeffrey Cartwright* (1972) is an apparent parody of a literary biography, a parody because the biographer, Jeffrey Cartwright, portrays the writer, Edwin Mullhouse, as the gifted author of *Cartoons*, who dies eleven years after he was born, at precisely the same day and time, the victim of an apparent suicide but actually killed by his biographer to ensure the closure and finality of the biography. But the novel also provides a foreshadowing of Millhauser's later work in its portrait of childhood isolation and loneliness; its exploration of childhood's creative imagination, which "sooner or later . . . is beaten out of us" (Millhauser 1996, p. 75); and its merging of reality and fantasy, especially in *Cartoons*, which, Jeffrey insists, is more real than the unreality it presents to us. *Portrait of a Romantic* (1977) is a fictional memoir, a grim tale of adolescent boredom and deadly games, in which an adult Arthur Grumm recounts his complicity in the suicide of his friend William Mainwaring. Arthur seeks relief from his boredom in innocent board games; an unfulfilled suicide pact with his friend Philip Schoolcraft; visits with classmate Eleanor Schumann; and, finally, a suicide pact with William, with real bullets, ending in William's death at his own hand. With Eleanor, Arthur enters the make-believe worlds of her dolls and toys, her Childhood Museum, and their staged marriage and deaths, these encounters perhaps foreshadowing Millhauser's later fantasy worlds but pulled back into reality by the spiders in Eleanor's dollhouse and the cramped blackness of her closet.

From the Realm of Morpheus marks Millhauser's transition into the world of fantasy, best represented by his exploration of the creative imagination in "The Tale of Ignotus," which describes the narrator Carl Hausman's encounter with the *Portrait of a Young Man*, Thomas Eden, third Baron Hall – a painting so realistic that Lord Hall, aka Ignotus, is able to emerge from the canvas as a real, live man. Ignotus falls in love with a young girl, Julia von Harnack, and plans to marry her until his hopes are shattered by a magician, Stromboili, who learns Ignotus's secret of moving in and out of the canvas and coerces him into displaying his *magic* in public performances, under threat of exposing his secret. His marriage plans delayed and eventually ended by Julia's entry into a convent, Ignotus attempts to end his own life and destroy the painting, unsuccessfully however, and so is doomed to live forever – for the realism of the painting, he acknowledges, was the work not of genius but of mediocrity: "For it's never your Raphaels – your Titians – what have you – that step out of the frame – but only we accursèd ones – spawn of fiery dullness and enraptured mediocrity" (Millhauser 1986, p. 119).

Millhauser's modernist works frequently merge reality into fantasy within possible if not always plausible worlds. These works revisit the theme of the creative imagination, conceived as a childlike innocence, transcending the limits of realistic imitation, but threatened by consumer culture, and often accompanied by isolation and loneliness. In "In the Penny Arcade," a 12-year-old boy revisits a penny arcade, hoping to re-experience the enchantment that he felt as a child, but feeling disappointment as he sees the arcade figures of a fortune teller, a cowboy, and a circus woman, now aging and decaying. But the boy recaptures his childlike innocence as he steps into a dark alcove and imagines the figures seemingly alive, enchanting, captivating, as he had seen them as a child. Reflecting on his experience, he resolves to remain vigilant, lest he become ordinary, "part of the conspiracy of dullness" (Millhauser 1998a, p. 145). In "August Eschenburg," August works with his father, a watchmaker, in a small German city but is inspired by a magician's clockwork automaton to create little figures of his own and is soon engaged by a Berlin department store owner, Herr Preisendanz, to create automatons to lure customers to his store. August initially enjoys some success, but his creativity is threatened when a rival automaton maker at a competing store creates sexually suggestive automatons that compete for customers more successfully than his own, and August, refusing to compromise his art, is terminated and returns to work with his father. August's rival, Hausenstein, lures him back to Berlin to create automatons for his Magic Theater, but Hausenstein is still driven by a culture of mediocrity that he calls the Untermensch (underman), his counter to Friedrich Nietzsche's Übermensch (overman). He therefore creates a rival theater with even more crudely sexual automatons, and August leaves Berlin, questioning his art and his life, but carrying his automatons with him, defeated but not compromised, his future uncertain, the story open-ended and seemingly unfinished.

"The New Automaton Theater" (*The Knife Thrower and Other Stories*, 1998), however, offers promise that an automaton maker might escape the culture of mediocrity. The narrator in an unnamed German city observes the city's pride in its automaton theater and explains the automaton maker's art as mimetic or illusionistic but not realistic – thus a mimesis that surpasses the realistic portraiture that gave life to Ignotus or Hausenstein's crude attempts to imitate human sexuality. The narrator then recounts the life of a master automaton maker, Heinrich Graum, who by age 24 had mastered the art of "scrupulous imitation" and by age 36 had brought the art to its richest expression but who then fell silent for twelve years (Millhauser 1999, p. 101). Upon his return, Heinrich reveals automatons of a new kind, no longer mere imitations of humans but "new beings, inserted into the universe by the mind of Graum the creator" (p. 109). His audience, initially shocked, is eventually drawn into the new automatons' joys and sufferings, is filled with rapture in their presence, and the new automaton theater is born.

But the artist's creative imagination is often accompanied by isolation and loneliness. In "The Little Kingdom of J. Franklin Payne" (*Little Kingdoms*, 1993), Franklin is inspired by his father's photographic imaging, develops an interest in drawing, and creates a comic strip for a local newspaper. Franklin enters into an uneasy marriage with Cora Vaughn, with her has a daughter, Stella, and soon, against Cora's wishes, moves to a new job, where he meets his version of Hausenstein, Max Horn, his rival both in art and in love. Outside of work, Franklin develops animated cartoons, is consumed by his drawings, and

Cora and Max are drawn together, leaving Franklin isolated and alone. Increasingly lured into the illusory world of the cartoon, Franklin creates his longest animation; conducts a screening for Stella; and, in a flight of the imagination, sees others entering the screening room, first Cora and Max, then his boss, then his mother and father, all, at the end, applauding his accomplishment – and Franklin, his future uncertain, is nonetheless satisfied, for "he had done what he set out to do" (Millhauser 1998b, p. 115).

In "August Eschenburg" and "Franklin Payne," the creative imagination is threatened by consumer culture when the artist overreaches the culture of mediocrity of ordinary people. The creative imagination is also threatened when it succumbs to mediocrity. In "The Barnum Museum," visitors enter a maze of multiple halls filled with mermaids; a turbaned man on a flying carpet; wandering jugglers, clowns, and peanut vendors; a children's museum; and much more, descending through three subterranean levels. The museum may be a fantasy of the creative imagination, but, as the circus name *Barnum* suggests, it may also be a spoof of "the Barnum-esque strain in American culture" (Ingersoll 2014, p. 60). Other stories more directly spoof that culture. In "A Change in Fashion" (*Dangerous Laughter*), the Age of Revelation in women's fashion is followed by an Age of Concealment during which women's clothes increasingly cover their bodies until the clothes completely separate from them, standing alone, the women elsewhere, at which point, not surprisingly, fashion reverts to earlier styles. In "The Next Thing" (*We Others*), a new structure, again with multiple subterranean levels, develops next to a mall, initially encompassing office spaces and shopping areas, then a food park, automated shopping services, a housing development, and utilities and eventually becoming a small town, with rumors of more towns to follow and without any suggestion of a return to simpler times.

Martin Dressler draws together the themes of the creative imagination, isolation and loneliness, and consumer culture in its portrait of the American dream. Like August Eschenburg and Franklin Payne, Martin is a visionary but on a larger scale, a dreamer and architect of New York City restaurants and hotels at the turn of the twentieth century, driven not to acquire wealth but to create new worlds, which overreach the mediocrity of the ordinary and merge reality into fantasy, captured in Millhauser's richly detailed descriptions. Martin learns early in life that he has a gift for consumer culture (and in this respect he is perhaps his own Hausenstein), initially creating a window display for his father's cigar store; then working his way through the ranks at the nearby Vanderlyn Hotel; simultaneously developing a series of restaurants; and eventually purchasing the Vanderlyn, his first hotel and the beginning of his life's adventure of creating new worlds: the Dressler, then the New Dressler, and finally the Grand Cosmo. Meanwhile, Martin also learns early that he must separate his sex life from his business life. He has a sexual encounter with a Vanderlyn hotel guest; visits prostitutes; marries another Vanderlyn guest, Caroline Vernon, who speaks little and only occasionally tolerates sex; initiates a sexual affair with a hotel chambermaid, Marie Haskova; and engages Caroline's sister, Emmeline, to assist with his restaurant and hotel management.

But as Martin revels in the success of his restaurants, the renovated Vanderlyn, and the Dressler, his imagination sours into new worlds that overreach popular consumer culture, his marriage falls apart, and his dream shatters. The New Dressler has multiple levels, above and below ground, including a hotel, a landscaped park, a department store, vacation retreats, and a labyrinth. In a foreshadowing of Martin's ultimate collapse, Caroline moves into Emmeline's apartment, and Marie simply disappears, a casualty of the City's regular cycle of renovations. The ultimate collapse is the Grand Cosmo: "a new concept in living, ... a world in itself, a city within the city," encompassing a variety of living spaces (Millhauser 1997a, p. 264); parks, theaters, and exhibits; a new kind of department store, with "meandering aisles" and "festive plazas" filled with exotic displays (p. 269); and rumors of "darker and more disturbing entertainments" on the lower levels (p. 271). But critics are either mystified or provoked, the public is confused, occupancy plummets, and Martin is forced to close the Grand Cosmo and face an uncertain future. Like Franklin Payne, however, Martin is satisfied, "for he had done as he liked, he had gone his own way, built his castle in the air" (p. 288).

Millhauser's postmodernist works further shift the balance from realism to fantasy and venture into impossible worlds that elude causal explanations. "Eisenheim the Illusionist" provides a bridge to these impossible worlds. Eduard Abramowitz, known as Eisenheim, is inspired by a traveling magician to create stage performances that become increasingly mysterious: traditional magic tricks, a reflection in a mirror that takes on a life of its own, the unexplained disappearance of a rival magician, a brilliant performance by a rival magician who is revealed to be Eisenheim himself, materializations of physical objects, and then manifestations of real people. But the manifestations appear to cross the boundaries between life and art, reality and illusion, and Eisenheim is pursued by the law and compelled to give his final and most impressive performance – his own disappearance – leaving behind only speculations about lenses and mirrors versus dark magic versus Eisenheim himself as mere illusion, the multiple perspectives and open endings of modernism offering a brief glimpse of the impossible worlds of postmodernism.

Other stories portray what are indeed impossible worlds. In "Cathay," the Emperor's Court Magician is selected in a contest in which two finalists compete for the Emperor's favor. The first turns a jade statue into a live woman, and the second turns a similar jade statue into a live statue – an echo of the theme that true creativity surpasses realistic imitation. In "The Invention of Robert Herendeen," the adolescent Robert, solitary and bored, uses his imagination to create a person, Olivia, who is neither a human being nor a work of art "but rather a being who existed in a realm parallel to the other two – a third realm" (Millhauser 1997b, p. 189). But his imagination then creates another person, Orville, who intrudes upon his relationship with Olivia, then creates a house full of revelers, which collapses, as Robert is forced to wonder what will happen next. In "Impossible Architectures," readers experience the replication of an entire kingdom in miniature, minutely detailed but invisible to the naked eye; an "other town" that precisely replicates the original (Millhauser 2009, p. 133); a Dome that covers the continental United States, with plans to cover the globe and perhaps all of space; and a Tower that reaches to the floor of heaven before it finally collapses. In "Miracle Polish," a man purchases a mirror polish that reflects his own and his friend Monica's real but enhanced selves, of which she disapproves because she wants him to appreciate her as she really is – another comment on the vagaries and perils of realistic imitation.

Other postmodernist stories are haunting tales of isolation and loneliness. "A Game of Clue" (*The Barnum Museum*) tracks two stories in the parallel worlds of the real-life players and the fantasy characters in the game. The players gather for a family birthday party and the game but are troubled and distant from each other, and the characters are troubled and separated by their insecurity and sexual tension, the separation between the players and the characters reflecting the isolation and loneliness within both the family and the game. "We Others" explores the parallel worlds of a lonely man and a lonely woman, the man leaving his home on a dark night, finding refuge in the woman's attic, and finding the woman equally alone. The man is one of the *we others*, lost figures who roam about, sometimes seen, sometimes not seen by others, and who occasionally meet to explore who they are. The man roams about the woman's house, the woman sees him and accepts his presence, but she becomes unsettled when her niece visits her and encounters the man in her bedroom. The man disappears and continues to wander about in the night.

SEE ALSO: Periodization

REFERENCES

Alexander, Danielle, Ponce, Pedro, and Rodríguez, Alicita. (2006). Steven Millhauser. *Review of Contemporary Fiction* 26 (1): 7–76.
Ingersoll, Earl G. (2010). Steven Millhauser, a very late modernist. *Journal of the Short Story in English/Les Cahiers de la nouvelle* 54: 1–16.
Ingersoll, Earl G. (2014). *Understanding Steven Millhauser*. Columbia: University of South Carolina Press.
McHale, Brian. (1987). *Postmodern Fiction*. London: Routledge.
Millhauser, Steven. (1986). *From the Realm of Morpheus*. New York: William Morrow.
Millhauser, Steven. (1996). *Edwin Mullhouse: The Life and Death of an American Writer 1943–1954 by Jeffrey Cartwright*. New York: Random House; 1st ed. 1972.
Millhauser, Steven. (1997a). *Martin Dressler: The Tale of an American Dreamer*. New York: Random House; 1st ed. 1996.
Millhauser, Steven. (1997b). *The Barnum Museum*. Normal, IL: Dalkey Archive Press; 1st ed. 1990.
Millhauser, Steven. (1998a). *In the Penny Arcade*. Normal, IL: Dalkey Archive Press; 1st ed. 1986.
Millhauser, Steven. (1998b). *Little Kingdoms*. New York: Random House; 1st ed. 1993.
Millhauser, Steven. (1999). *The Knife Thrower and Other Stories*. New York: Random House; 1st ed. 1998.
Millhauser, Steven. (2009). *Dangerous Laughter*. New York: Random House; 1st ed. 2008.
Plotnitsky, Arkady. (2017). Philosophical skepticism and narrative incredulity: postmodern theory and postmodern American fiction. In: *The Cambridge Companion to Postmodern American Fiction* (ed. Paula Geyh), 63–80. Cambridge: Cambridge University Press.

FURTHER READING

Chénetier, Marc. (2003). An interview with Steven Millhauser. *Transatlantica: Revue d'études américaines/American Studies Journal* (1). https://journals.openedition.org/transatlantica/562
Max, D.T. (2008). The illusionist. *The New York Times* (February 24, 2008). https://www.nytimes.com/2008/02/24/books/review/Max-t.html?register=google
McGrath, Patrick. (1998). Artists and automatons. *The New York Times* (May 10, 1998). https://www.nytimes.com/1998/05/10/books/artists-and-automatons.html
Millhauser, Steven. (1995). Replicas. *Yale Review* 83 (3): 50–61.
Rodríguez, Alicita. (2006). Architecture and structure in Steven Millhauser's *Martin Dressler: The Tale of an American Dreamer*. *Review of Contemporary Fiction* 26 (1): 110–126.

Minimalism and Maximalism

STUART J. TAYLOR
University of Glasgow, Scotland

Minimalism and maximalism are key tendencies in late-twentieth- and early-twenty-first-century American fiction, and can include such major writers as Raymond Carver, Frederick Barthelme, Amy Hempel (minimalism) and William Gaddis, John Barth, Joyce Carol Oates, Thomas Pynchon, and David Foster Wallace (maximalism).

According to Edward Strickland, minimalism is "a movement, primarily in postwar America, towards an art – visual, musical, literary, or otherwise – that makes its statement with limited, if not the fewest possible, resources, an art that eschews abundance of compositional detail, opulence of texture, and complexity of structure" (2000, p. 7). Narration in minimalist fiction favors short words, compact and simply structured sentences and paragraphs, imitative of easy-to-understand colloquial dialogue. Descriptions of characters, their backgrounds, and settings are restricted in minimalist fiction, while brand names are frequently used as a shorthand for such description. This descriptive trope tends to heighten the perceived superficiality of literary minimalism's objects, suggested by the derogatory title of "Kmart realism" (Kenney 1986, p. 16). Minimalist stories usually contain very little action, and their tendency to be written in the present tense emphasizes a lack of dramatic arc and thus a nihilistic suspension of resolution. Maximalism, by contrast, is not so much a movement as a repudiation of many minimalist principles. Maximalist fiction is expansive, featuring linguistic digression, redundancy, and verbosity that distinguish such fiction from literary minimalism's concision. The nihilistic or poignant stasis of minimalism contrasts with maximalism's exuberance, and complex vocabulary, sentence structure, and lengthy paragraphs often result in very long works with high page counts. Such enthusiastic extensiveness led to maximalist fiction being granted its own derogatory labels such as "hysterical realism" (Wood 2000).

Both literary minimalism and maximalism can be considered responses to shifting cultural media hierarchies – such as the continued ascendancy of television and the innovations of Internet connectivity – as well as geopolitical transformations, with Stephen Sestanovich arguing that the strategies by which the United States sought to assert global exceptionalism have oscillated between the maximalism (confrontational, extensive commitments to change) of Truman and Reagan, and the minimalism (accommodating retrenchment) of Nixon and Carter. Indeed, there is a general consensus among critics that the literary postmodernism, which sought to respond to the apocalyptic conditions of impending nuclear Armageddon, was challenged by the stark "tell it like it is" minimalist short stories of Raymond Carver (and his profoundly influential editor, Gordon Lish), a challenge that picked up considerable momentum with its propagation through creative writing MFA programs. By the 1990s, this challenge was, in turn, countered by the door-stop, maximal novels by older writers associated with postmodernism, such as Thomas Pynchon and Don DeLillo, as well as younger literary figures, notably David Foster Wallace, William T. Vollmann, Richard Powers, and others. While in many ways accurate and useful, this framework risks overlooking the fundamental – and, recently, increasingly emphasized – connection between each of these two "-isms," where the shortest story can have maximal scope. Thus, miniaturism is also considered here as a mode that connects minimalist and maximalist fiction.

Between Raymond Carver and his editor Gordon Lish, a signature American minimalist style was forged in the 1960s and 1970s. Bearing traces of Hemingway's paratactic sentences and late Beckett's structural brevity, Carver's stories – as severely edited by Lish – frequently culminate in stasis in which the narrator is trapped, even as they will (or, perhaps, resist) transformation. This style was very influential on 1980s minimalism. In *What We Talk About When We Talk About Love* (1981), the hallmarks of Lish's significant linguistic surgery are even more apparent. In "A Serious Talk," Burt and Vera are characterized by the products they consume:

He drank the cup of cranapple juice and vodka. He lit a cigarette and tossed the match into the big ashtray that always sat on the kitchen table. He studied the butts in it. Some of them were Vera's brand, and some of them weren't.

(Carver 2009, p. 294)

In "The Bath," characters are denied names – "the mother" and "the baker" – while "the child's" name "SCOTTY would be iced on" a spaceship-styled birthday cake "in green as if it were the name of the spaceship." Terse and static, the baker is a quintessential minimalist character, speaking only the "barest information, nothing that was not necessary" (2009, p. 251). While the baker's expression renders him a figure of some levity, such linguistic austerity becomes crucial to minimalist representations of trauma.

Through its reticent prose, minimalist fiction evokes trauma's unutterable pain, an aspect of which is the need to express in order to heal and the existential guilt of being unable to do so. As Mark McGurl suggests, it is through this "affective dialectic of shame and pride" that minimalist fiction energizes its radical linguistic economy against maximalism's effluence (2009, p. 286). In Amy Hempel's "In the Cemetery where Al Jolson Is Buried" (1983), which she wrote in Gordon Lish's writing class, the narrator struggles to connect with her terminally ill friend, a gulf symbolized in the disconnected prose and objectifying descriptions. When the narrator is invited by a male doctor to leave her hospitalized friend and "spend an hour on the beach":

"Bring me something back," she says. "Anything from the beach. Or the gift shop. Taste is no object."
He draws the curtain around her bed.
"Wait!" she cries.
I look in at her.
"Anything," she says, "except a magazine subscription."
The doctor turns away.
I watch her mouth laugh.

(Hempel 2007, p. 33)

The equivocation between a commercial and natural gift flattens the setting, while the exclamation against "a magazine subscription" nihilistically undercuts the publication of Hempel's short story itself. The disembodying description "I watch her mouth laugh" contrasts with the agency of the doctor who "turns away," suggesting both patient and narrator in a state of passive disintegration. The story concludes with the narrator imagining her own unspeakable grief – following the burial of her friend – through that of a chimpanzee fluent in basic sign language. To its young, the chimpanzee had signed:

Baby, drink milk.
Baby, play ball.
And when the baby died, the mother stood over the body, her wrinkled hands moving with animal grace, forming again and again the words: Baby, come hug, Baby, come hug, fluent now in the language of grief.

(Hempel 2007, p. 40)

The reduction of grief to these sparse phrases, further reduced into nonlinguistic actions, is notable for the distance evoked between narrator and her friend, and yet these concise communicative acts articulate an aching immediacy of the loss of articulation in the presence of pain.

This minimalist reduction as a means to inscribe particularly female trauma – rather than assert, in the case of Carver and Frederick Barthelme, a clipped masculine reticence – is also seen in longer works of fiction, notably Hempel's novella *Tumble Home* (1997) and Jayne Anne Phillips's *Machine Dreams* (1984). Still, the style continues to reinforce the individualistic repression of middle-class America, often with stifling irony, through domestic settings, such as the Phillips family in Andrea Lee's *Sara Phillips* (1984) and the Vincents in Susan Minot's *Monkeys* (1984). Sandra Cisneros, another Iowa Writers' Workshop alumnus, displays the style throughout *The House on Mango Street* (1984), a short story cycle that recounts the development of Esperanza Cordera in the Hispanic quarter of Chicago. The opening vignette, "The House on Mango Street," functions as a frame-tale for the rest of the narrative, and features a nun asking Esperanza where she lives.

> There, I said pointing up to the third floor. You live *there*?
> *There*. I had to look to where she pointed – the third floor, the paint peeling, wooden bars Papa had nailed on the windows so we wouldn't fall out. You live *there*? The way she said it made me feel like nothing. *There*. I lived *there*. I nodded.
>
> (Cisneros 2004, p. 5)

The repetition of, and accumulation of meaning in, "*there*," demonstrates a minimalist reduction of elements while reinforcing the shameful, repressive stasis of the narrative. Esperanza reflects on the experience: "I knew then I had to have a house. A real house. One I could point to. But this isn't it" (2004, p. 5). Yet, despite being reassured her plight is "Temporary," Esperanza finds, at the end of the cycle, little progress. In the penultimate vignette, "A House of My Own," her dream of escape is largely defined in the negative – "Not a flat. Not an apartment in back. Not a man's house" – indicating both imaginative and economic limitations (p. 108). The promise of escape is still ambiguous in the closing story, where Esperanza acknowledges the liberating potential of writing:

> I put it down on paper and then the ghost does not ache so much. I write it down and Mango says goodbye sometimes. She does not hold me with both arms. She sets me free.

> One day I will pack my bags of books and paper. One day I will say goodbye to Mango. I am too strong for her to keep me here forever. One day I will go away.
>
> (2004, p. 110)

But not today. Despite the future verb structures, the vignette is locked in present tense, amplifying the sense of ache and longing. The friction between the individual and their surroundings is continually framed as one of loss in minimalist US fiction: an abdication of agency to fate. Cormac McCarthy's border trilogy – *All the Pretty Horses* (1992), *The Crossing* (1994), and *Cities of the Plain* (1998) – recasts the West as an agent of contraction rather than a landscape of expansion. *All the Pretty Horses* opens in the house of John Grady Cole's dead grandfather, the last of his name. As in Cisneros, the dwelling symbolizes limitation and scarcity, despite its apparent physical capacity:

> The House was built in eighteen seventy-two. [. . .] The original ranch was twenty-three hundred acres out of the old Meusebach survey of the Fisher-Miller grant, the original house a oneroom hovel of sticks and wattle. That was in eighteen sixty-six. [. . .] [Cole's great-grandfather] built the house and by then the ranch was already eighteen thousand acres. In eighteen eighty-three they ran the first barbed wire. By eighty-six the buffalo were gone. That same winter a bad die-up. In eighty-nine Fort Concho was disbanded.
>
> (McCarthy 2012, pp. 6–7)

This is in dramatic contrast to the ranch of Don Hector Rocha y Villareal that Cole finds across the US–Mexican border, which:

> occupied part of the broad barrial or basin floor of the bolson and was well watered with natural springs and clear streams and dotted with marshes and shallow lakes or lagunas. In the lakes and in the streams were species of fish not known elsewhere on earth and birds and lizards and other forms of life as well all long relict here for the desert stretched away on every side.
>
> (2012, p. 100)

In this fecund land, however, Cole seeks to dominate, to tame or restrict nature under his control, aspiring to be the "comandante" of all horses (p. 132). Yet, Cole's trajectory is toward prison, a place that parallels his grandfather's ranch as a site of stunted progress, where the prisoners are "Like passengers in a halted train" (p. 184).

Despite being a *Bildungsroman*, *All the Pretty Horses* concludes with ambivalent promise, as Cole rides and "The bloodred dust blew down out of the sun." The final line of the novel states that Cole "Passed and paled into the darkening land, the world to come," with the comma in that sentence caught between past and future tenses, emphasizing a present beyond Cole's agency or control (2012, pp. 309–310). *Cities of the Plain* consolidates this tension, denying meaningful choices in the present, while acknowledging alternatives that exist just beyond the reach of increasingly isolated individuals. Here, "Choice is lost in the maze of generations" and, emphasizing the present, characters are trapped in a world that "takes its form *hourly* by a weighing of things at hand" (1998, p. 195).

While the trauma in McCarthy's trilogy exemplifies the plight of the reticent stoic male, Alicia Erian's debut novel *Towelhead* (2005) redeploys minimalist restriction to probe both the trauma of sexual abuse and the repression of various misogynistic moral systems. The novel features an epigraph from Raymond Carver's "On an Old Photograph of My Son" – "We all do better in the future" – which yields a kind of irony as, despite narrating in the past tense, *Towelhead*'s Jasira seems trapped in an adolescent voice, evoking minimalism's stasis rather than redemptive reflection. The novel opens with short, declarative sentences: "My mother's boyfriend got a crush on me, so she sent me to live with Daddy. I didn't want to live with Daddy. He has a weird accent and came from Lebanon." Jasira's feelings about her father are articulated only in the simplest words: she "got depressed about" visiting him, but "when it was time to go home again, I got happy." The depressing tension is encapsulated in a clear image: "Once I spilled some juice on one of his foreign rugs, and he told me that I would never find a husband" (Erian 2005, p. 1). The connection between objects ("juice" and "foreign rugs") and moral judgments aligns with minimalism's reductive, superficial descriptions. In *Towelhead*, this effectively characterizes the repressive attitudes of many of the often well-meaning adult characters and the formative influence they have on Jasira.

In particular, descriptions of domestic settings are used to assert socioeconomic conditions and to signal emotional distance. While her mother "was a middle-school teacher, so she couldn't afford very much," Jasira's father "was making a good salary at NASA" (2005, p. 3), and their new suburban home foregrounds objects as a substitute for a relationship:

> Daddy and I each had our own bathroom. [...] It was my responsibility to keep my bathroom clean, and Daddy bought me a can of Comet for under the sink.
>
> (2005, p. 5)

The domestic setting and its objects combine to curtail the possibility of hope and a liberated future for Jasira:

> That night, on the vinyl bed, I thought about my future. I imagined it as day after day of misery. I decided nothing good would ever happen to me, and I began to fantasize about [my mother's boyfriend,] Barry. [. . .] We would live in a house on the other side of town, and I could wear whatever I wanted to the breakfast table.
>
> (2005, p. 4)

More recently, minimalist style has been used to effectively evoke the scarcity of post-apocalyptic environments that, with the escalation of the climate crisis, are an increasingly dominant feature of cultural discourse.

McCarthy's *The Road* (2006) evokes the bleakness of the world through a tightly constricted narrative voice:

> He [...] looked out over the wasted country. The road was empty. Below in the little valley the still gray serpentine of a river. Motionless and precise. Along the shore a burden of dead reeds. Are you okay? he said. The boy nodded. Then they set out along the blacktop in the gunmetal light, shuffling through the ash, each the other's world entire.
>
> (2006, p. 4)

Even while written in the past tense, the frequent absence of *to be* verbs – "Along the shore [was/is] a burden of dead reeds" – suggests being trapped in the present. Such omission continues to characterize the relationship between the man and the boy:

> They sat that evening by the fire and the boy drank hot soup and the man turned his steaming clothes on the sticks and sat watching him until the boy became embarrassed. Stop watching me, Papa, he said.
> Okay.
> But he didn't.
>
> (2006, p. 270)

A complex of possible emotions – fear that the boy is terminally ill, grief over the hopelessness of his future, parental love – is implied but never stated. By contrast, Peter Heller's *The Dog Stars* (2012) commits to the present tense throughout, using short sentences to maintain energy and evoke the quick, practical thinking – specifically of its combat pilot narrator, Hig – necessary to survive in a desperate postpandemic landscape. The novel opens:

> I keep the Beast running, I keep the 100 low lead on tap, I foresee attacks. I am young enough, I am old enough. I used to love to fish for trout more than almost anything.
> My name is Hig, one name. Big Hig if you need another.

While *The Dog Stars* propels its story with a clipped narrative voice, the inherent excitement of airplanes in a risky postapocalyptic world is divergent from the minimalism of the 1980s short story. Minimalist narratives of postapocalyptic peripheries are, in some ways, more faithful to the impressionistic heights of the style. Honed in the depictions of unnamed characters in *Dept. of Speculation* (2014), Jenny Offill's minimalism, for example, is deftly applied to climate catastrophe in *Weather* (2020). In *Weather*, Lizzie is trapped in an administrative position – as the assistant to a celebrity climate academic, Sylvia – that increases her awareness to the slow-moving Armageddon of "climate departure" (2020, p. 67), while emphasizing her peripheral position to both the cataclysm and attempts to forestall it. Here, the end of the world is static and domestic, with the final lines of the novel emotionally flat, detached, and yet aching with grief:

> The dentist gave me something so I won't grind my teeth in my sleep. I consider putting it in, decide against it. My husband is under the covers reading a long book about an ancient war. He turns out the light, arranges the blankets so we'll stay warm. The dog twitches her paws softly against the bed. Dreams of running, of other animals. I wake to the sound of gunshots. Walnuts on the roof, Ben says. The core delusion is that I am here and you are there.
>
> (2020, p. 201)

The minimal style of *Weather* also contributes to a moral stance against excess. Reflecting on the social media ecosystems of the early twenty-first century, Lizzie notes that "There is advice everywhere, some grand, some practical. The practical advice spreads quickly and creates consequences" (2020, p. 115). Here, her limited narrative voice reads as both an acceptance of individual inefficacy and a moral stance against particularly privileged discourse: "First conference with Sylvia.

One thing I'll say about it: lots of people who are not Native Americans talking about Native Americans" (p. 37). Thus, *Weather* emphasizes the inescapable moral imperative dividing minimalist and maximalist fiction, which McGurl argues is "[g]rounded in an affective dialectic of shame and pride" (2009, p. 286).

While "leaver-outers" of minimalism write in both short stories as well as longer forms, the "putter-inners" favor the novel – especially "big books, mega-novels, total novels" – as the preeminent form of literary maximalism (Kuehl 1989, pp. 104, 108). With signature traits of digression, redundancy, and verbosity, the maximalist novel demonstrates its author's will "to see and record the world in great detail, as well as manage the resultant text, which might be tumescent in size, troublingly dense in complexity, or tedious in its obsession with particulars" (Levey 2016, p. 9). This tendency to excess was often indistinguishable from the superabundance of disconnected images that characterized literary postmodernism in the mid-twentieth century. William Gaddis's *The Recognitions* (1955) is often seen as a clear example of a type of postmodern maximalism, sometimes called literary encyclopedism, that seeks to bring a vast amount of information under control, although is often doomed to collapse under its own weight.

The glut of gluttonous works that followed *The Recognitions* in the 1960s and 1970s – by John Barth, Nabokov, Marguerite Young, Gaddis, Pynchon, and DeLillo – is regularly cited as the catalyst for igniting literary minimalism's reactive rise in the 1980s. Yet, the maximalist novel continued to develop in this decade – including notable publications of Alexander Theroux's *Darconville's Cat* (1981); the beginning of Joyce Carol Oates's Gothic saga (*Bellefleur* in 1980, *A Bloodsmoor Romance* in 1982, and *Mysteries of Winterthurn* in 1984); Richard Powers's first two novels, *Three Farmers on Their Way to a Dance* (1985) and *Prisoner's Dilemma* (1988); and, within twelve months, Joseph McElroy's *Women and Men* (1987), Toni Morrison's *Beloved* (1987), and David Foster Wallace's debut, *The Broom of the System* (1987).

Such works demonstrated literary maximalism to be a fitting response to the increasing digital connectivity and the deluge of data in the late twentieth to early twenty-first centuries. *Darconville's Cat*, for example, exemplifies the maximalist characteristic of generative redundancy, particularly in a late chapter, entitled "Why don't you –?," which consists of five pages of archaic imperative statements with which Dr. Crucifer impels the eponymous Darconville to commit atrocities upon his love interest, Isabel:

> Stab her with a bung-starter! Mail her a poison suit! Employ the scaphism! Hurl her down the Gemonian steps with tincans tied to her ears! [. . .] Screw a spout into her mouth and porcelainize her for a men's room in Kabool!
>
> (Theroux 1981, pp. 662–667)

Rather than such complex redundancy, Oates's maximalism tends toward torrential verbosity and a plethora of elements. This is clearly illustrated in *Bellefleur*'s opening paragraph, a single sentence of 214 words, which begins "It was many years ago in that dark, chaotic, unfathomable pool of time before Germaine's birth (nearly twelve months before her birth)" and ends "it was on this tumultuous rainlashed night that Mahalaleel came to Bellefleur Manor on the western shore of the great Lake Noir, where he was to stay for nearly five years." The intervening clauses represent Germaine's orgiastic conception, demonstrating the characters' lust as "too ravenous to be contained" through an effluence of "groping, careless, anguished words" (Oates 1981, p. 3). In this way, Oates overloads the narrative present with the weight of a past whose description, potentially, could be infinitely swollen.

While Oates's narrative present is suffocated by an excessively inflated description of the past and its inexhaustible variations, Richard Powers's writing tends to expand the past through discrete historical artifacts placed in manifold informational networks. His debut novel, *Three Farmers on Their Way to a Dance*, takes a single element – a real-life 1914 photograph by August Sander entitled "Young Farmers" – and uses it to fuel a complex intertwining of contemporary and historical narratives, with a fluctuating voice that variously identifies as a Mr. P-, who both is and is not Powers himself. This centrifugal overflow of boundaries from a single object exemplifies the systemic excess Powers would deploy across his other works – such as *Galatea 2.2.* (1995), which also features a character called Mr. Powers – often with contradictory aims to archive a vast wealth of information yet undermine, through narrative instability and reflexivity, the durability of any such archive.

The literary maximalism of Toni Morrison, on the other hand, takes African American experience as a "discourse of difference" in what McGurl calls "high cultural pluralism" (2009, p. 62). In *The Bluest Eye* (1970), Morrison dismantled the superficial identity of "Dick and Jane" stories in order to explode room for violently marginalized voices. In *Beloved*, the excesses of intergenerational trauma are reconstructed in a haunted house that inverts the (white) minimalist's tranquilizing domesticity. Dedicated to the "Sixty Million and more" Africans estimated to have died in captivity during the Middle Passage of the transatlantic slave routes, *Beloved* is a complexly structured novel that creates space for repeated suffering, atonement, and catharsis. While apparently minimalist in their simplicity, the first sentences of each of the novel's three sections – respectively, "124 was spiteful" (2005, p. 3), "124 was loud" (p. 199), and "124 was quiet" (p. 281) – actually indicate the vast transformative cycles within the work, in which the atrocities and traumas of slavery are repeatedly evoked, heightened until they spill over and are disrupted through the supernatural presence (and occasionally voice) of "Beloved," and finally resettle in a new form.

Morrison's work is fundamentally opposed to minimalist stasis, framing dynamic inclusion as an effective means to force confrontation – of both reader and writer – with America's original sin. Indeed, space is created to be filled in Morrison's maximalism, and it is filled by voices from the margins. Other maximalist excesses in literature are more overtly structural, such as David Foster Wallace's *Infinite Jest* (1996). Perhaps the defining novel (and publishing event) of the 1990s, *Infinite Jest* is thoroughly a printed information system. Across 1079 pages, *Infinite Jest* tells the near-future stories of tennis prodigy Hal Incandenza's mental decline, substance abuser and burglar Don Gately's recovery, and a larger political plot in which Quebecois separatists seeking to bring an end to the Organization of North American Nations (ONAN) by distributing an experimental video entitled "Infinite Jest" which causes those who view it to fatally lose the ability to do anything else. The way these narratives and their related details are dispersed across the novel's main text and its 388 endnotes are a crucial part in the reading experience, and the effort required – on behalf of the reader to decide which details are important, and on behalf of the author to balance between difficult and engaging sections – is a signature aspect of Wallace's maximalism that seeks to unite reader and author in meaningful conversation and connection. While indebted to the maximalist fictions of Pynchon (*Gravity's Rainbow* [1973]) and DeLillo (*Ratner's Star* [1976]; *End Zone* [1972]), Wallace's novel pushes alienating difficulty to collapse, uncovering a means to move past irony into some kind of realism that exists within the vast networks of the information age – a turn regularly described as "new sincerity" (Kelly 2010).

In the year following *Infinite Jest*, Pynchon and DeLillo published their own late-millennial maximalist fictions, *Mason & Dixon* (1997) and *Underworld* (1997), which both returned to key dates in US history (colonial cartography and the Cold War nuclear arms race) as a dumping ground for contemporary angst. Following the September 11 attacks, however, both writers took divergent approaches in their subsequent works. While Pynchon analogously incorporated the attacks into the Tunguska event of 1908, in the 1062-page *Against the Day* (2009), DeLillo turned away from writing massive novels. The original cover art of *Underworld* – depicting the approach of an ominously silhouetted aerial object to the Twin Towers of the World Trade Center – became prophetic, yet DeLillo's subsequent novels, including those directly about the attacks such as *Falling Man* (2007), were considerably pared down works, all under 300 pages of sparse prose. Meanwhile, Roberto Bolaño's labyrinthine *2666* (2004) catalogues a uniquely dangerous post-9/11 occident, while Jonathan Safran Foer's *Extremely Loud & Incredibly Close* (2005) sought to walk the line between sincerity and sentimentalism. Foer's novel retains the exuberance of maximalist fiction, manipulating (like Powers's *Farmers*) actual photographs to probe textuality and transformation. Similarly, Donna Tartt's *The Goldfinch* (2013) dramatizes image forgery as excessive, transformative proliferation, albeit through relatively orthodox prose. More recently, Lucy Ellmann's *Ducks, Newburyport* (2019) emphasizes formal experimentation on a large scale. At 1030 pages, comprising mainly a single-sentence stream-of-consciousness-style narration by an Ohio housewife, the novel exuberantly incorporates representations of social media, music, film, and a national history from pre-colonial America to the Trump presidency in free-association internal dialogue. The 19,354 repetitions of the phrase "the fact that" that punctuate the main narrative can be, at times, hypnotic and irritating, yet force the consideration of the issue of space – and who gets to make and occupy it – at the heart of literary maximalism.

Ducks, Newburyport is a quintessential maximalist novel that demonstrates many of the features and failings of generative redundancy. As Nick Levey argues, maximalist fictions emphasize the "importance of specificity and detailed 'noticing' in the literary arts and wider culture" (2016, p. 10). Levey clarifies that "what might otherwise be seen as excess or redundancy [...] becomes necessity if these texts are to be experienced as enjoyable" (p. 9). And yet, such works can prove just as tiresome and numbing as the flattest, most narcotic minimalist texts. Indeed, while the two are often considered as opposite poles, Mark McGurl effectively unites them in terms of a dialectic (2009, p. 377). Inspired by Bharati Mukherjee's literary use of ancient Indian miniature painting techniques – clearly demonstrated in *The Holder of the World* (1993), which spans 300 years in under 300 pages – McGurl argues that, by masterfully balancing inclusion and exclusion (as well as other taxonomic binaries), this dialectic produces literary miniaturism, or "maximalism in a minimalist package" (2009, p. 375). Key examples range from Jorge Luis Borges's "The Aleph" (1945), through Thomas Pynchon's *The Crying of Lot 49* (1965) and Donald Barthelme's "The Balloon" (1981), to more recent examples from Lydia Davis and George Saunders. Saunders's *Lincoln in the Bardo* (2017) demonstrates how literary miniaturism continues to be deployed in the novel form to balance contemporary historiographic concerns within a single historical scene. However, Carmen Maria Machado's experimental memoir *In The Dream House* (2019) is perhaps the strongest contender for a work that encapsulates the compactness of minimalism, the systems of maximalism, and the equilibrium of miniaturism. With self-contained chapters that each use a unique genre, trope, or form (from high-modernist techniques in "*Dream House as* Epiphany" to pop-culture appropriations in the devastating "*Dream House as* Choose Your Own Adventure®"), Machado's text is in constant dialogue, through footnotes, with Stith Thompson's *Motif-Index of Folk-Literature* (1955–1958) to elaborate an intense investigation of queer domestic abuse and race. Machado's memoir signals the continuing relevance of the minimalist–maximalist–miniaturist dialectic in contemporary American fiction, foregrounding literary fiction as a cultural anchor in an increasingly turbulent century.

SEE ALSO: After Postmodernism; Barth, John; Border Fictions; Carver, Raymond; DeLillo, Don; Foer, Jonathan Safran; Gaddis, William; Hempel, Amy; McCarthy, Cormac; Morrison, Toni; Oates, Joyce Carol; Powers, Richard; Pynchon, Thomas; Trauma and Fiction; Wallace, David Foster

REFERENCES

Carver, Raymond. (2009). *Collected Stories* (ed. William L. Stull and Maureen P. Carroll). New York: Library of America.

Cisneros, Sandra. (2004). *The House on Mango Street*. London: Bloomsbury.

Erian, Alicia. (2005). *Towelhead*. London: Headline Review.

Heller, Peter. (2012). *The Dog Stars*. New York: Knopf Doubleday.

Hempel, Amy. (2007). *The Collected Stories of Amy Hempel*. New York: Simon & Schuster.

Kelly, Adam M. (2010). David Foster Wallace and the new sincerity in American fiction. In: *Consider David Foster Wallace: Critical Essays* (ed. David Hering), 131–146. Austin, TX: Sideshow.

Kenney, Edwin J. (1986). Take April as she is (book review). *The New York Times* (November 2, 1986): 16. https://www.nytimes.com/1986/11/02/books/take-april-as-she-is.html (accessed August 4, 2021).

Kuehl, John. (1989). *Alternate Worlds: A Study of Postmodernism*. New York: NYU Press.

Levey, Nick. (2016). *Maximalism in Contemporary American Literature: The Uses of Detail*. New York: Routledge.

McCarthy, Cormac. (1998). *Cities of the Plain*. New York: Knopf.

McCarthy, Cormac. (2006). *The Road*. New York: Knopf.

McCarthy, Cormac. (2012). *All the Pretty Horses*. London: Picador; 1st ed. 1992.

McGurl, Mark. (2009). *The Program Era: Postwar Fiction and the Rise of Creative Writing*. Cambridge, MA: Harvard University Press.

Morrison, Toni. (2005). *Beloved*. London: Vintage Books; 1st ed. 1987.

Oates, Joyce Carol. (1981). *Bellefleur*. New York: Warner.

Offill, Jenny. (2020). *Weather*. London: Granta Books.

Rebein, Robert. (2009). *Hicks, Tribes, and Dirty Realists*. Lexington: University Press of Kentucky.

Sestanovich, Stephen. (2014). *Maximalist: America in the World from Truman to Obama*. New York: Knopf.

Strickland, Edward. (2000). *Minimalism: Origins*. Bloomington: Indiana University Press.

Theroux, Alexander. (1981). *Darconville's Cat*. New York: Doubleday.

Wood, James. (2000). Human, all too inhuman. *The New Republic* (July 24, 2000). https://newrepublic.com/article/61361/human-inhuman (accessed July 16, 2021).

FURTHER READING

Clark, Robert C. (2015). *American Literary Minimalism*. Tuscaloosa: University of Alabama Press.

LeClair, Tom. (1989). *The Art of Excess: Mastery in Contemporary American Fiction*. Urbana: University of Illinois Press.

Mixed-Genre Fiction

MICHAEL BASSELER
Justus Liebig University Giessen, Germany

Where do genres come from? Quite simply from other genres. A new genre is always the transformation of an earlier one, or of several: by inversion, by displacement, by combination.

(Todorov 1990, p. 15)

> [A]ny narrative longer than a headline or a joke almost inevitably uses multiple generic conventions and strategies.
>
> (Rieder 2010, p. 197)

It is practically impossible to conceive of the bulk of contemporary US fiction as anything but mixed-genre fiction. As a matter of fact, many of the most acclaimed novels of the past 40 years or so owe a great deal of their success and literary historical significance to the ways in which they combine and transform existing genres, blur and push generic boundaries, and create new hybrid genres. Paul Auster's *The New York Trilogy* (1985–1986), for instance, has become famous for its pastiche of detective fiction, mystery fiction, and postmodern philosophy; Louise Erdrich's *Love Medicine* (1984) interweaves canonical European literary genres such as the family saga and fairy tale with Native American forms and traditions of storytelling; Toni Morrison's *Beloved* (1987) fuses the African American slave narrative with the ghost story, Southern gothic, and magical realism; Michael Chabon's *The Amazing Adventures of Kavalier & Clay* (2000) merges historical fiction, romance, and adventure with comic-book superhero stories; Dave Eggers's *A Heartbreaking Work of Staggering Genius* (2000) deliberately blurs the boundaries between fiction and nonfiction (especially memoir and fantasy); Jonathan Safran Foer's 9/11 novel *Extremely Loud & Incredibly Close* (2003) draws on the repertoires of such diverse genres as the *Bildungsroman*, historical novel, and postmodern metafiction and combines these with multimodal, visual forms of storytelling to process the trauma of the attacks; Junot Díaz's *The Brief Wondrous Life of Oscar Wao* (2007) has been hailed for its "odd amalgam of historical novel, bildungsroman, postmagical realism, sci-fi, fantasy, and super-hero comic romance" (Saldívar 2011, p. 585); and Jennifer Egan's *A Visit From the Goon Squad* (2010) oscillates between short story collection and novel, incorporating extra-literary genres such as PowerPoint slides. The list could go on and on, yet what these examples already show is that genre-mixing can be regarded as the rule, rather than an exception, in contemporary US fiction. We need to remind ourselves, however, that this is not an entirely new phenomenon. Not only has hybridity been considered a hallmark of postmodernism as the period under which most of these works are usually subsumed (cf. Hassan 1987, p. 170), it can be found throughout virtually all literary periods, reaching back as far as antiquity (see Fowler 1982, p. 181). We may also think of Virginia Woolf's famous dictum of the novel as a cannibalistic genre, "which has devoured so many forms of art" (1958, p. 18). Or, in the words of David Shields: "The novel has always been a mixed form; that's why it was called *novel* in the first place" (2010, p. 14).

When talking about the very meaning of the term "genre" in mixed-genre fiction, a few clarifications are indicated. First, when used by literary scholars and especially by genre theorists, genre typically denotes a particular class or kind of literature (see Fowler 1982), manifesting in certain textual repertoires, conventions, as well as reading practices or, in more recent terms, cognitive schemata (see Sinding 2005). Apart from the traditional classification of literary texts into the broad forms of lyric, drama, and narrative, these forms are divided into genres, such as "tragedy" or "novel," which again are then further segmented into a plurality of subgenres such as "*Bildungsroman*," "novel of manners," or "historical novel." This distinction is usually based on particular thematic and/or formal characteristics. In a second, quite distinct usage of the term, genre is often used by critics as a marker to separate high-brow forms of literature from popular, middle- and low-brow forms. Particularly in combination with "fiction," genre tends to indicate differences in valency, suggesting a stable and clear-cut dichotomy between serious, that is, "literary," fiction and popular genre fiction (e.g. crime fiction, mystery fiction, and science fiction): "Genres are separated from one another in categories titled 'mystery,' 'romance,' 'fantasy,' and the like, and all separated from the miscellaneous titles classified as 'literature' or 'literary fiction' or just 'fiction'" (MacKay 2010, p. 135).

While we have good reasons to doubt that this dichotomy ever held water – after all, what we now consider to be the canon of "literary fiction" is populated by plenty of ghosts, vampires, mad scientists, and other characters typically confined to "genre fiction" – it seems outright preposterous when applied to the contemporary novel, as the above list shows. As "authors with recognized high-cultural cachet now increasingly make forays into popular genres" (Hoberek 2007, p. 238), the very distinction becomes poriferous. Mark McGurl has described this turn to genre as a significant shift in what he calls "the program era" (2009) of US literature, where it increasingly replaced notions of individual originality by turning creativity into "a question of social practice" (Dorson 2017, p. 6) reflected in genre. And scholars like Ramón Saldívar have pointed out the "generative power of generic hybridity" (2013, p. 6), especially within the field of "ethnic minority fiction." Although genre still smacks of aesthetic inferiority and guilty pleasure, and as a result "often ceases to be when it encounters the academy" (Lanzendörfer 2016, p. 2), the tendency of an increasing amalgamation of literary and genre fiction toward something like "literary genre fiction" (Dorson 2017) is undeniable – even if, as Jeremy Rosen claims, "literary writers take pains to mark themselves as distinct from the realm of genre fiction, not 'contributors' to it" (2018, fn. 3).

This entry sketches out the poetics and cultural dynamics of mixed-genre fiction in US literature of the past few decades, with a focus on works produced in the twenty-first century. While the combination and displacement of genres was already popular among the writers associated with the heyday of postmodern fiction, several critics have pointed out that the recent turn to amalgamated or hybrid genres is one signal of an important shift toward a new cultural paradigm (see, e.g. Hoberek 2007; Lanzendörfer 2016). Accordingly, the entry will outline what this shift entails, how it manifests in the literature produced over the past few decades, and what broader cultural contexts it involves. Given the ubiquity of genre-mixing in recent fiction, the examples introduced are, at least to an extent, contingent; many others could have been chosen and are conspicuous by their absence here. Taken together, however, the texts discussed below may serve to show the spectrum of mixed-genre fiction that oscillates between the poles of pop-cultural entertainment and literary art; a distinction that, as a result, has become increasingly difficult to uphold.

MASHUP FICTION AS A CATALYST FOR GENERIC HYBRIDITY

Originally taken from ethnomusicology, where it describes the creative merging of elements from two or more existing songs by using computer technology, the term "mashup" has been introduced in literary studies to refer to works that combine a literary classic with popular genres, thus creating a generic hybrid. A well-known example would be Seth Grahame-Smith's *Pride and Prejudice and Zombies* (2009), which parodically displaces the material of Jane Austen's classic romance/novel of manners, combining it with generic elements and conventions from horror stories, ninja, and especially zombie fiction. While leaving about 80% of the original text intact, Grahame-Smith transforms it – "one bloody page at a time"

(2009, p. 10) – into a story about a zombie uprising. As a result, as Heta Pyrhönen (2013) has convincingly argued, *Pride and Prejudice and Zombies* not only applies what she calls the "Austenian dominant construction principle" in its generic setup (as does, e.g., Ben H. Winters's *Sense and Sensibility and Sea Monsters*, 2009); it also ironizes and debunks idealized notions of the transformative aspects of love inherent in Austen's original and the romance genre at large by casting it against a modern, strictly physical notion of love played out in the protagonists' bodies, their violence and sexual attractiveness. If genre "is central to the social organisation of knowledge" (Frow 2010, p. 4), Grahame-Smith's mashup exploits this to foreground the changing cultural and historical notions of love built into its colliding generic structures.

In his subsequent *Abraham Lincoln: Vampire Hunter* (2010), Grahame-Smith employs a similar strategy, even though the book has no single original pretext. Instead, it makes use of the convention of the frame story: the fictional author Grahame-Smith relates how he came into the possession of Abraham Lincoln's secret, ten-volume journal in which the Great Emancipator recorded "the central struggle of his life," that is, being "one of the greatest vampire hunters of his age" (2010, pp. 14–15). In what follows, the narrator weaves together a story that contains numerous quotations from (real and invented) historical letters, speeches, and newspaper clippings, as well as paintings and photographs, all of which contribute to reveal the hidden truth behind "the towering myth of Honest Abe, the one ingrained in our earliest grade school memories" (p. 15). In generic terms, *Abraham Lincoln: Vampire Hunter* might best be described as a biographical novel, in which numerous historical references to Lincoln's early life and political ascent are blended with the fictional elements of the vampire story. The book's underlying idea, reflected in its generically hybrid form, is that slavery and vampirism formed an unholy alliance in the Old South, a parodic illustration of the monstrosity of the peculiar institution as well as a comment on the practice of "doing" history (see Salvati 2016). Other examples of popular mashup fictions include Nick Mamatas's Beatnik horror novel *Move Under Ground* (2004) and Ben H. Winters's *Android Karenina* (2010), obviously a sci-fi rewriting of Tolstoy's realist masterpiece. Though perhaps already waning as a cultural phenomenon, in the early 2000s mashup fiction has arguably served as a catalyst for the generic hybridization that characterizes much of contemporary literary writing, and to which we will now turn.

THE POLITICS OF GENRE-MIXING IN THE CONTEMPORARY US NOVEL

While the mass popularity of mashups reached its peak around 2010 (both *Pride* and *Lincoln* have been made into genre-mixing films), the turn to genre fiction is by no means restricted to popular writers. Or, to put it differently, as critically acclaimed writers such as Cormac McCarthy, Michael Chabon, or Colson Whitehead frequently draw on genre fiction, the lines between genre and literary fiction seem to blur or even vanish completely. What we can see in contemporary US literature, perhaps, could be described as an increasing tendency to amalgamate allegedly "literary" genres such as the *Bildungsroman* with (i) "popular" genres such as science fiction, crime fiction or vampire fiction, as well as with (ii) genres traditionally subsumed under the label "non-fiction," for example, autobiography and memoir (thus creating a generic hybrid called "autofiction"). This section will deal with the former, while the next will turn to the latter. Although quite dissimilar in their aesthetics and politics of genre amalgamation, the turn toward both "literary genre fiction" and "autofiction" attests to the novel's ability to absorb all kinds of genres into its form, an ability that has been exploited by a variety of US authors over the past decades.

A novel that has frequently been discussed as a prime example of the recent trend toward "literary genre fiction" is *Zone One* (2011), African American author Colson Whitehead's tongue-in-cheek contribution to the post-millennial zombie fad. Whitehead, who has emerged as one of the most prolific and critically acclaimed writers of the past ten years or so, has become famous for his "exhilarating culture-, genre- and media-crossing art," or simply "New Eclecticism" (Whitehead and Selzer 2008, p. 393). Whereas *Pride and Prejudice and Zombies* can hardly be distinguished from the now popular genre of fan fiction in its almost mechanical rewriting of an original text, *Zone One* exploits the popularity of the zombie genre to create a complex and generically hybrid text that enables new forms of expression and social criticism. Set in Lower Manhattan in the aftermath of a zombie apocalypse, the novel follows the protagonist, Mark Spitz, and his Team Omega as they rummage through the small refuge of humanity that is Zone One – surrounded by the living dead – in a doomed effort to reconstruct human society. The reconstruction is driven by capitalism and corporatism (here the book echoes themes from Whitehead's earlier novels, particularly *Apex Hides the Hurt* [2006]), which thus emerges as the form of life that has even survived what the novel refers to as "the Last Night." In the end, however, this reconstruction turns out to be an illusion when the wall that keeps out the "skels" (as the zombies are called in the novel) collapses, leaving Spitz no other choice than to dive into the "sea of the dead" (Whitehead 2011, p. 259).

Several scholars and literary critics have recognized that *Zone One*, through its mixing of literary and popular genres, presents a utopian/dystopian vision of contemporary US social structures and politics. Ramón Saldívar, for instance, has read the novel as an example of "postrace fiction" (2011). While the near extinction of humanity in the zombie apocalypse levels racial differences among the surviving (that the novel's protagonist is Black is only revealed very late in the novel), "Whitehead proposes that it may well be necessary first to imagine the end of the world before we may imagine the historical end of racialization and racism" (Saldívar 2013, p. 13). In this context, genre-mixing, and especially the amalgamated form of "speculative realism," is part and parcel of Saldívar's conception of postrace aesthetics in contemporary American literature. Just as the invention of the generic hybrid of the "historical romance" by writers like Walter Scott was a reaction against neo-classicism in the early nineteenth century, Saldívar avers that the "contradictory and oxymoronic blending of history and the speculative genres" is central to postrace writers (on genre-mixing and border-crossing in multiethnic fiction, also see Totten 2016; Behling 2003). This results in a "hybrid crossing of the fictional modes of the speculative genres, naturalism, social realism, surrealism, magical realism, 'dirty' realism, and metaphysical realism" (Saldívar 2013, p. 5) that also characterizes *Zone One*. As "the representation of social justice requires a formal medium incorporating states of fantasy that occupy and override previous attempts to represent the real" (Saldívar 2011, p. 594), these "amalgamations of novelistic form and generic styles ... by virtue of their surface complexities inaugurate a new stage in the history of the novel" (p. 594) and, through their very form, account for democratic deficits and the shortcomings of liberalism itself, especially with regard to matters of race and ethnicity.

While race is the focus of Saldívar's reading of the novel's genre-mixing politics, the zombie plot has also been read as a commentary on, and extension of, the utopian imagination with regards to alternatives to capitalism. Although the novel doesn't offer any closure by sketching out what a utopian vision of a post-capitalist society could look like, the novel's zombie apocalypse presents a brief "moment of imaginable systemic change" (Lanzendörfer 2014, p. 44). Drawing on Fredric Jameson's notion of fantasy as a genre that distracts and emancipates us from our own defense mechanisms against reality, Lanzendörfer concludes that "[t]he use of genre by writers of literary fiction speaks to the need to find new ways of imagining modes of political expression beyond the constraints of social realism, which, while it can depict the existing, cannot imagine the future" (p. 45). Blending the different reading frames of literary fiction with genre fiction, Whitehead's novel thus expands the expressive possibilities of literary fiction, in this case using zombie fiction to "produce new reading frames" (p. 50) in order to diagnose social relations in the "real" world.

Other examples of such genre-mixing between the poles of realism and fantasy include Octavia Butler's *Fledgling* (2005) and Tananarive Due's *My Soul to Take* (2011), two novels that explore racial relations and questions of social justice through vampire plots. Butler, who has been at the vanguard of speculative realism at least since the publication of her masterpiece *Kindred* (1979), tells the story of Shori, a mysterious Black girl who at the beginning of the novel "awoke to darkness" (2007, p. 1) with near-fatal injuries and no memory, only to find out that she is the last surviving member of a family of vampires (or Ina, as they're called in the novel) erased in a raid instigated by another Ina family. There is one thing that separates Shori from her kin, however; she is Black, the result of her family's genetic experiments with human DNA to make the Ina less susceptible to sunlight and thus fitter for survival in a world densely populated and dominated by humans. Hybridity is the novel's main theme, reflected in its plot and form: a generic hodgepodge of female coming-of-age story, crime fiction, courtroom drama, science fiction, vampire fiction, and even neo-slave narrative, *Fledgling* exploits genre to reflect on meanings of race, identity, sexuality, and belonging, all of which are culturally constructed and prefigured through these very genres. Race and gender are also central in Due's *My Soul To Take*, a novel that draws heavily on Butler's Afrofuturist approach to generic hybridity and her reinvention of the Black vampire genre. Like in *Fledgling*, the future of the community depends on interspecies transgression, and so the novel "depicts mortal/immortal hybridity as a positive, transformative power for the formation of a global, multiracial community" (Hoydis 2015, p. 79).

Although embraced by ethnic writers as a means of "exerting their force against the realist imagination" (Saldívar 2011, p. 581) that has produced social injustice and discrimination, "speculative realism" is by no means restricted to "minority" or "ethnic" writers. One might even argue that the merging of realist and fantastic genre conventions in fact constitutes a major lifeline for the contemporary US novel at large, providing it with new narrative possibilities. A case in point would be George Saunders's Booker Prize-winning *Lincoln in the Bardo* (2015), a wildly inventive mix of historical novel, (fictional) biography, ghost story, and Buddhist philosophy, infused with a good portion of satire. The novel revolves around the death of Abraham Lincoln's son Willie, a historical fact that the novel depicts in the form of short citations from real and invented sources. While there is no superordinate narrative voice, these citations form one section of a large chorus of voices; the other section is comprised of dozens of ghost-like figures who linger in a state between death and rebirth – the bardo of Tibetan Buddhism – at Oak Hill cemetery, Georgetown, where Lincoln buried and mourned his son. Blending the genres of historiography, biography, and ghost story, the novel creates a highly idiosyncratic, even disturbing and disorienting storyworld in which the reader is forced to reconcile the allegedly "realist" story conveyed in the citations with a supernatural world in which spirits communicate with each other and possess the ability to move in and out of – and thus blend with – living humans as well as with each other. Not unlike *Abraham Lincoln Vampire Hunter*, Saunders draws on the national myth of Lincoln to infuse it with fantastic elements; whereas in Grahame-Smith's mashup this blending results in a straightforward, action-driven vampire plot meant for entertainment (thinly veiled by allusions to slavery), however, *Lincoln in the Bardo* is closer to Saldívar's notion of speculative realism in that it invites for deeper reflections on questions of social justice, ethics, and empathy and their significance for a US society that is perhaps as polarized as it was during the Civil War.

BLURRING THE BOUNDARIES
BETWEEN FICTION
AND NONFICTION: AUTOFICTION
AS A MIXED GENRE

The methodical mixing of genres is also a central strategy in a number of works that "push toward the boundary between fiction and the 'real' by way of the collision between fictional storylines and nonfictional events" (Manshel 2017). These works are not so much concerned with exploiting popular genre fiction to find new forms of expression beyond realist conventions; instead, they experiment with genres traditionally shelved under nonfiction, such as autobiography, memoir, journalism, and essay, thereby creating hybrid genres like the "fragmentary essay-novel" (Nünning and Scherr 2018) and "autofiction" (see Worthington [2018] for a discussion of US autofiction from Vladimir Nabokov to Ruth Ozeki), as well as the hybrid genre for which Manshel suggests the term "recent historical novel" (2017).

A case in point would be Ben Lerner's acclaimed *10:04* (2014), a novel that tackles a range of thematic issues as diverse as climate change, finance and global capitalism, migration, art, media events, procreation, and, above all else, the writing of fiction itself. A *"making-of* novel" (Voelz 2019, p. 32), *10:04* strategically dilutes all boundaries between protagonist and author, an instantiation of the collision between the fictional and nonfictional, between art and life that is the novel's main theme. To this end, *10:04* incorporates various genres and media ranging from poetry to photographs, as well as an earlier short story by Lerner, entitled "The Golden Vanity," into its plot (if plot is the right term for this uneventful novel). This short story about an author – whose semblance to Lerner is obvious – and his health anxiety was published in *The New Yorker* in 2012 and is reprinted verbatim in the novel; the only difference is that it is presented here as the work of the fictional character/narrator called Ben Lerner. The copying-and-pasting of the short story into the novel's form is a metafictional strategy meant to foreground the artificiality of the literary artwork, part of the author/narrator's attempt at working his "way from irony to sincerity" (Lerner 2014, p. 4). But it is poetry – more specifically, Walt Whitman's prose-poem-memoir *Specimen Days* (1882), itself an example of generic hybridity – that eventually becomes the model for "the book you're reading now, a work that, like a poem, is neither fiction nor nonfiction, but a flickering between them" (2014, p. 194). As the narrator states, "The poem, like most of my poems . . . conflated fact and fiction, and it occurred to me . . . that part of what I loved about poetry was how the distinction between fiction and nonfiction didn't obtain" (pp. 170–171). With the insertion of passages from Whitman as well as his own poetry into the narrative in order to transform the novel form itself, the mixing of genres becomes a central formal strategy as well as one of the novel's major themes.

In her epistolary novel *I Love Dick* (1997), Chris Kraus also suspends the distinction between fiction and autobiographical nonfiction. The novel tells the story of the narrator's infatuation for a character named Dick (later revealed to be the British cultural critic Dick Hebdige). Chris Kraus, the narrator-protagonist and semi-successful film artist and critic, and her husband, the literary theorist Sylvère Lotringer, meet Dick "at a sushi bar in Pasadena" (2016, p. 3) and spend the night at his house. Soon after, Chris and Sylvère begin writing letters in an attempt to come to terms with their feelings ensuing from this encounter. The author summarizes the novel's theme as well as its production in an interview:

> Well, you know, this Dick is real. He is a real person. And I really fell in love with him, I didn't set out to write a book. And I wanted him to love me too so I started writing letters. 200 of them. And then he didn't answer. And correspondence is entirely compulsive, the addressee is a blank screen. And I wanted to tell him everything, and once I started talking I couldn't stop.
>
> (Intra n.d.)

First published in 1997 in *Semiotext(e)*, the novel resulting from this encounter can be understood as the attempt to "fictionalize life a little bit" (Kraus 2016, p. 10). A blend of memoir, art novel, philosophy, and campus novel, *I Love Dick* is emblematic of what Mark McGurl describes as the "acts of authorial self-making" in the program era: "moments in the operation, the autopoiesis, of a larger cultural system geared for the production of self-expressive originality" (2009, p. 49). This autopoiesis of the cultural system provides the context for Kraus's novel, just as it delivers its main theme. Structurally speaking, the free mixing of genres beyond all traditional classifications – literary vs. nonliterary, fiction vs. nonfiction, autobiography vs. philosophy, etc. – becomes the formal correlative of such eclectic self-making. Other novels that oscillate between the poles of fiction and nonfiction include, among many others, Richard Powers's *Galatea 2.2* (1995), Ruth Ozeki's *A Tale for the Time Being* (2013), and Dave Eggers's *What is the What* (2006).

CONCLUSION

In David Shields's *Reality Hunger* (2010), generic in-betweenness is used as a shorthand for the diagnosis of a society in which long-held certainties associated with established forms give way to a new reality:

> I want the contingency of life, the unpredictability, the unknowability, the mysteriousness, and these are best captu.red when the work can bend at will to what it needs: fiction, fantasy, memoir, meditation, confession, reportage... 'Don't mess with Mr. In-Between,' my father would often advise me, but it seems to me that Mr. In-Between is precisely where we all live now.
>
> (2010, pp. 70–71)

If in-between is "where we all live now," then the poetics of genre and genre-mixing might be "indicative, indeed even diagnostic, of shifts in the social conditions in which we live and under which we consume literature" (Lanzendörfer 2016, p. 7). Although by no means a comprehensive survey of mixed-genre fiction, the examples of mashup fiction, speculative realism, literary genre fiction, and autofiction discussed in this entry all attest to such cultural dynamics of generic change (see Basseler, Nünning, and Schwanecke 2013) in recent US literature. Contemporary writers increasingly use strategies of generic hybridization in order to create new forms of expression attuned to a changing reality and capable of creating new narrative possibilities for social criticism. Other popular forms of mixed-genre fiction include "interstitial fiction," "span fiction," "slipstream," or "new weird," generic labels that typically describe the amalgamation of literary fiction and fantasy, as in works by Thomas Pynchon, Mark Z. Danielewski, Jonathan Lethem, Jeff VanderMeer, and China Miéville; the hybrid form of climate fiction (or "cli-fi") as a variety of speculative/science fiction (e.g. T.C. Boyle's *A Friend of the Earth* [2000], Barbara Kingsolver's *Flight Behavior* [2012], and Paolo Bacigalupi's *The Water Knife* [2015]); the intermedial, multimodal mixing of popular genre fiction such as thriller with nonliterary genres and media such as email and Internet websites, for example, Marisha Pessl's *Night Film* (2013) and Danielewski's radically experimental series *The Familiar* (2015–); as well as the blending of textual and visual, literary and popular, fictional and nonfictional genres in the graphic novel (e.g. Joe Sacco's *Safe Area Goražde* [2000], Art Spiegelman's *In the Shadow of No Towers* [2004], and Alison Bechdel's *Fun Home* [2006]).

SEE ALSO: Afrofuturism; After Postmodernism; Butler, Octavia; Egan, Jennifer; Eggers, Dave; Intermedial Fiction; Lerner, Ben; Realism after Poststructuralism; Saunders, George; Whitehead, Colson

REFERENCES

Basseler, Michael, Nünning, Ansgar, and Schwanecke, Christine. (2013). *The Cultural Dynamics of Generic Change in Contemporary Fiction: Theoretical Frameworks, Genres and Model Interpretations*. Trier, Germany: Wissenschaftlicher Verlag Trier.

Behling, Laura L. (2003). "Generic" multiculturalism: hybrid texts, cultural contexts. *College English* 65 (4): 411–426.

Butler, Octavia. (2007). *Fledgling*. New York: Grand Central Publishing; 1st ed. 2005.

Dorson, James. (2017). Cormac McCarthy and the genre turn in contemporary literary fiction. *European Journal of American Studies* 12 (3): 1–16.

Fowler, Alastair. (1982). *Kinds of Literature: An Introduction to the Theory of Genres and Modes*. Oxford: Clarendon Press.

Frow, John. (2010). *Genre*. London and New York: Routledge.

Grahame-Smith, Seth. (2009). *Pride and Prejudice and Zombies*. Philadelphia: Quirk Books.

Grahame-Smith, Seth. (2010). *Abraham Lincoln, Vampire Hunter*. New York: Hachette.

Hassan, Ihab. (1987). *The Postmodern Turn: Essays in Postmodern Theory and Culture*. Columbus: Ohio State University Press.

Hoberek, Andrew. (2007). Introduction: after postmodernism. *Twentieth-Century Literature* 53 (3): 233–247.

Hoydis, Julia. (2015). Fantastically hybrid: race, gender, and genre in Black female speculative fiction. *Anglistik: International Journal of English Studies* 26 (2): 71–88.

Intra, Giovanni. (n.d.). A fusion of gossip and theory. *artnet*. http://www.artnet.com/magazine_pre2000/index/intra/intra11-13-97.asp (accessed July 22, 2021).

Kraus, Chris. (2016). *I Love Dick*. Croydon, UK: Serpent's Tail; 1st ed. 1997.

Lanzendörfer, Tim. (2014). The politics of genre fiction: Colson Whitehead's *Zone One*. *Journal of 21st-century Writings* 3 (1): 39–52.

Lanzendörfer, Tim. (2016). Introduction: the generic turn? Toward a poetics of genre in the contemporary novel. In: *The Poetics of Genre in the Contemporary Novel* (ed. T. Lanzendörfer), 1–16. Lanham, MD: Lexington Books.

Lerner, Ben. (2014). *10:04*. London: Granta.

MacKay, Marina. (2010). *The Cambridge Introduction to the Novel*. Cambridge: Cambridge University Press.

Manshel, Alexander. (2017). The rise of the recent historical novel. *Post45* (September 29, 2017). https://post45.org/2017/09/the-rise-of-the-recent-historical-novel/ (accessed July 22, 2021).

McGurl, Mark. (2009). *The Program Era: Postwar Fiction and the Rise of Creative Fiction*. Cambridge, MA: Harvard University Press.

Nünning, Ansgar and Scherr, Alexander. (2018). The rise of the fragmentary essay-novel: towards a poetics and contextualization of a hybrid genre in the digital age. *Anglia* 136 (3): 482–507.

Pyrhönen, Heta. (2013). Generic stability despite hybridization: the Austenian dominant construction principle. In: *The Cultural Dynamics of Generic Change* (ed. Michael Basseler, Ansgar Nünning, and Christine Schwanecke), 183–200. Trier, Germany: Wissenschaftlicher Verlag Trier.

Rieder, John. (2010). On defining SF, or not: genre theory, SF, and history. *Science Fiction Studies* 37 (2): 191–209.

Rosen, Jeremy. (2018). Literary fiction and the genres of genre fiction. *Post45* (July 8, 2018). http://post45.org/2018/08/literary-fiction-and-the-genres-of-genre-fiction/ (accessed July 22, 2021).

Saldívar, Ramón. (2011). Historical fantasy, speculative realism, and postrace aesthetics in contemporary American fiction. *American Literary History* 23 (3): 574–599.

Saldívar, Ramón. (2013). The second elevation of the novel: race, form, and the postrace aesthetic in contemporary narrative. *Narrative* 21 (1): 1–18.

Salvati, Andrew J. (2016). History bites: mashing up history and gothic fiction in *Abraham Lincoln: Vampire Hunter*. *Rethinking History* 20 (1): 97–115.

Saunders, George. (2017). *Lincoln in the Bardo*. London and New York: Bloomsbury.

Shields, David. (2010). *Reality Hunger: A Manifesto*. London: Penguin.

Sinding, Michael. (2005). Genera mixta: conceptual blending and mixed genres in *Ulysses*. *New Literary History* 36 (4): 489–619.

Todorov, Tzvetan. (1990). *Genres in Discourse*. Cambridge: Cambridge University Press.

Totten, Gary. (ed.) (2016). Crossing borders and genres. *Special issue of MELUS* 41 (2): 1–120.

Voelz, Johannes. (2019). The American novel and the transformation of privacy: Ben Lerner's *10:04* (2014) and Miranda July's *The First Bad Man* (2015). In: *The American Novel in the 21st Century: Cultural Contexts – Literary Developments – Critical Analyses* (ed. Micheal Basseler and Ansgar Nünning), 323–337. Trier, Germany: Wissenschaftlicher Verlag Trier.

Whitehead, Colson. (2011). *Zone One*. New York: Doubleday.

Whitehead, Colson and Selzer, Linda. (2008). New eclecticism: an interview with Colson Whitehead. *Callaloo* 31 (2): 393–401.

Woolf, Virginia. (1958). *Granite and Rainbow*. London: The Hogarth Press.

Worthington, Marjorie. (2018). *The Story of "Me": Contemporary American Autofiction*. Lincoln and London: University of Nebraska Press.

FURTHER READING

Behling, Laura L. (2003). "Generic" multiculturalism: hybrid texts, cultural contexts. *College English* 65 (4): 411–426.

McCracken, Scott. (2004). The half-lives of literary fictions: genre fictions in the late twentieth century. *The Cambridge History of Twentieth-Century English Literature* (ed. Laura Marcus and Peter Nicholls), 618–634. Cambridge: Cambridge University Press.

Nünning, Ansgar. (1993). Mapping the field of hybrid new genres in the contemporary novel: a critique of Lars Ole Sauerberg, *Fact into Fiction* and a survey of other recent approaches to the relationship between "fact" and "fiction." *Orbis Litterarum* 48 (5): 281–305.

Momaday, N. Scott

LYNN DOMINA
Northern Michigan University, USA

N. Scott Momaday is often credited with initiating the Native American Renaissance following publication of his Pulitzer Prize-winning novel *House Made of Dawn* in 1968. Since then, he has published literature in virtually every genre – another novel and short stories, poetry, essays, plays, and even children's books. He is also a visual artist of some renown, and his books occasionally feature his paintings or drawings. Several of his books include material in more than one genre, as well as individual pieces that challenge generic boundaries, emphasizing the fact that many Native American cultural traditions do not place nearly the significance on distinctions among genres that Western literary traditions do. Despite his formal range, however, Momaday has continued to explore some of the thematic obsessions that appear in *House Made of Dawn* and his subsequent book, *The Way to Rainy Mountain* (1969), especially the bear as an important cross-cultural symbolic character, the active and recurrent presence of mythic figures, particularly female ones, and the significance of mythic storytelling time.

Born in 1934 in Oklahoma, Momaday is Kiowa. As a child, he also lived in Arizona and New Mexico, where he became familiar with Navaho, Apache, and Pueblo stories and traditions, supplementing his experience with his own Kiowa traditions. Several of his books incorporate material from these Indigenous traditions, and his nonfiction particularly explores his own identity and position within the Kiowa narrative. After graduating from high school, Momaday earned a Bachelor's degree from the University of New Mexico and continued on to Stanford, where he earned a master's and PhD. His formal education in literature has also influenced his writing. His poetry sometimes takes advantage of classical European forms, and the content of his prose demonstrates familiarity with canonical European literature. He has taught at several universities, including visiting appointments at Columbia and Princeton. He spent much of his academic career within the University of California system. He has won numerous awards for his writing, including not only the Pulitzer Prize for *House Made of Dawn*, but also the National Medal of Arts, a Lifetime Achievement Award from the Native Writers' Circle of the Americas, and many honorary degrees from universities throughout the United States. He returned to Oklahoma in 2007, where he still lives.

Momaday's Kiowa name, Tsoai-talee, translates as "Rock-tree Boy," a reference to Devils Tower (or Bear's Lodge, "Devils Tower" being an unfortunate mistranslation) in Wyoming. This rock tower is an 867-ft upthrust of igneous rock located in the western portion of the Black Hills. It is etched with long grooves that resemble claw scratches. According to the mythic etiological story, a boy, the boy for whom Momaday is named, became a bear. He chased his frightened sisters, who climbed the rock and leapt into the sky, becoming the stars of the Big Dipper. The bear could only attempt to claw his way up the tower. Momaday has explored this story on multiple occasions, from *The Way to Rainy Mountain* to *In the Bear's House* (1999). Many other books also take the bear as a central plot or thematic element.

Although his award of the Pulitzer Prize for his first novel might have suggested a productive career as a novelist, Momaday has published only one other novel, *The Ancient Child*, in 1989. Stylistically, this novel is more conventional than *House Made of Dawn*, but several thematic concerns are explored in both novels. Perhaps the most obvious difference is that the syncretic spiritual explorations, the amalgamation of Christianity with Native practices so central to *House Made of Dawn*, are absent from *The Ancient Child*. Instead, Momaday's second novel centers around a story of a man, Locke Setman, or Set (from Urset, the original bear), becoming a bear, a man recognizing his role within his culture's mythological system – in this sense, Set's task is analogous to Abel's in *House Made of Dawn*. Raised off reservation by an adoptive father, Set has become a painter;

Momaday's own knowledge and experience as a visual artist clearly informs Set's approach to his work. When he returns to the reservation for his grandmother's funeral, he experiences a series of mysterious events, including a vision of a child which others don't see. Set's companions suggest that the child must have been a neighbor, but Set resists this explanation. He meets a much younger woman, Grey, who is herself a visionary and who gives Set a medicine bundle containing bear medicine. Set returns to his life as a successful painter, but after his adoptive father also dies, he is unable to maintain his stability. His long-term romantic relationship disintegrates, and he eventually returns to the reservation. He falls in love with Grey, and she assists Set in recentering himself within his historic and mythic identity.

A subplot of *The Ancient Child* concerns Billy the Kid, the outlaw-hero who has acquired mythic status of his own within American pop culture. Grey imagines Billy's outlaw life, his evasion of capture, and his eventual death, and she imagines herself within those moments. By including such scenes, Momaday complicates the relationships between Indigenous and colonial societies, suggesting, as he also had in *House Made of Dawn*, that mythic stories adapt to new contexts.

These stories, the foundational stories of a given culture, replay themselves in a continually reoccurring cycle, with new individuals incarnated each time to assume the mythic roles. Set, for example, eventually understands himself as a man who becomes a bear, consistent with the story Momaday explores in several of his books, the boy who became a bear, who chased his sisters as they ran from him in fear, the girls climbing a rock and leaping into the heavens, becoming stars.

Momaday successfully incorporates and explores these mythic stories within novels and other prose pieces set in the present or near present through his presentation of time. One standard contrast between cultural conceptions of time is the distinction between linear and cyclic, with modern Western cultures associated with a linear understanding and traditional cultures affiliated with a cyclic understanding. While this distinction can be helpful, it is also too reductive. Momaday's work demonstrates a particular appreciation for narrative, which by definition proceeds linearly, but the linear progression within a given narrative is also affected by that narrative's position within a more cosmic sense of repetition. Stories repeat themselves across time, but the stories are inevitably affected by their specific temporal contexts – it's never quite the same story that is repeated, yet the symbolic nature of characters and events assists people in understanding their roles within these stories. Characters in Momaday's fiction, in other words, rely on these mythic stories in order to choose actions appropriate to their identities.

Following *The Ancient Child*, Momaday published *In the Presence of the Sun: Stories and Poems, 1961–1991* (1992). Primarily poetry, this collection also contains two sections that incorporate prose, "The Strange and True Story of My Life with Billy the Kid," which includes both prose and poetry, and "In the Presence of the Sun: A Gathering of Shields," which consists of short prose pieces that today might be called "flash." The book also reproduces several of Momaday's drawings. The section on Billy the Kid can easily be read in conjunction with Grey's imaginative stories of the outlaw in *The Ancient Child*. Here, Momaday provides a brief outline of Billy the Kid's life, stating that the pieces that follow are all imagined, yet also true. From a factual perspective, the events related in this section are generally plausible, but more interesting than factual truth is Momaday's entrance into Billy's consciousness, which is both fierce and gentle, determined and confused, compassionate and survivalist. The point of view shifts in this section from the first-person personal to the nearly omniscient, but the voice itself remains consistent, characterized by Momaday's quiet insights into the mind of another.

The voice in "In the Presence of the Sun" is quite different, more detached and neutral, perhaps even communal. This sequence relies for its content on traditional stories from Plains tribes, with the shield being a central symbol. Momaday introduces this section by citing details about the surrender of Lakota chief Sitting Bull and then explaining the construction and significance of a warrior's shield. While used for defense in battle, its meaning exceeded its simple use value; it formed part of a warrior's medicine, connecting the visible to the invisible, both a source and an expression of power. In his introduction, Momaday also instructs readers on the significance of the shield stories that follow. They are ritualistic, intended to be told rather than read silently, one each day for sixteen days, with all participants, storyteller and listeners, fasting on each fourth day. Acknowledging the sacred role of the sun in Plains cultures, these stories should be told only at certain times of the day, in – as the title confirms – "the presence of the sun." Each prose piece in this section is accompanied by a drawing of the shield described the piece's title. The titles themselves are descriptive, sometimes almost conclusions to the stories that follow – "The Shield That Died," "Walking Bear's Shield," "The Shield That Was Brought Down from Tsoai" – and the stories themselves are straightforward, the prose style direct, utilitarian, reliant on simple and comparatively short sentences. This style suggests that the "author" in our contemporary sense, the individual creator, is less important than the community through whom and for whom the story is told.

The Man Made of Words: Essays, Stories, Passages (1997) also consists of work in multiple genres, though in this collection nearly all the material is formatted as prose. The book's subtitle is telling, especially its inclusion of "stories" and "passages." Although "stories" implies narratives, they are not necessarily fictional, and the work in this book, as in much of Momaday's other work, challenges Western conceptions of "fiction" and "fact" or "true" and "false" as binary opposites. Even more overtly, "passages" calls attention to the insufficiency of generic labels. The individual pieces in this book could have as easily been described simply as essays and stories, for both of those terms are general and inclusive enough to describe most short prose. By adding "passages" to the subtitle, Momaday suggests that neither of those nouns quite works, for broad as they are, they both create expectations among readers. Even if we cannot always say what an essay or story is, we can often say what it is not. "Passages" is also accompanied by additional connotations beyond simple blocks of writing; a "passage" is a route or corridor leading from one place to another, and it is also a sequence of time. A passage often functions as a transition, through place or time, the portion of a sequence that is often overlooked but should perhaps be granted more rather than less attention. Given Momaday's thematic concerns, "passages" works on all of these levels.

The first section of *The Man Made of Words* includes several essays that are more formal and academic than most of Momaday's work, and it also includes autobiographical material that Momaday has explored in other books, "autobiographical" defined here very broadly – to include his entire cultural past as well as his own individual biological life. The second section consists of essays exploring specific places, in the American Southwest but also in sites widely scattered around the world – Russia, Germany, Grenada. The overarching theme of these essays is spirituality, the relationship of geography to the sacred. For

Momaday, however, the sacred is always linked to language, specifically to storytelling. A person grows into him or herself through telling and hearing stories. A person recognizes his or her belonging, to a community and to a place through story, both historical and mythical.

The final section of this collection consists of brief – generally only a few hundred words each – retellings of traditional stories and considerations of other literary storytellers, Isak Dinesen, Edmund Wilson, Willa Cather. These pieces are frequently structured as impressions illustrated by narratives more than as actual narratives themselves. They illustrate the range of Momaday's interests but are not nearly as developed as the essays in the first two sections. More casual in tone, they read as if the author was briefly intrigued by his topic, interested enough to explore it in writing without feeling compelled to say any more than he wished to. These are likely the "passages" referred to in the book's subtitle, and if so, part of the point is that the passage itself is sufficient – where it leads from or to might also be interesting but is not essential to our understanding.

In the Bear's House is another multigenre collection, also including a final section labelled "passages." In the introduction, Momaday retells the origin of his Kiowa name, Tsoaitalee, and discusses the significance of the bear to him personally and to others who value the idea of wilderness, geographically and also spiritually. (Momaday had earlier published a book-length memoir, *The Names* [1976], that provides a more detailed version of this story.) The longest section of *In the Bear's House* is a dialogue – printed as drama and organized into sections analogous to scenes but lacking the action typical of staged plays – between Urset, the bear, and Yahweh, one of the names the Hebrew scriptures use for God. Here, Momaday associates Yahweh with the Creator, and the dialogue begins with Urset recalling a dream of his creation and Yahweh narrating that moment of creation. In this dialogue, Momaday returns to some of the ideas prominent in *House Made of Dawn*, particularly links between the prologue of the Gospel of John, "In the beginning was the Word," and Momaday's other ideas about language, about being a man formed of words. While the original Greek of John's Gospel does not use "word" exactly as Momaday does, the parallels between these widely divergent cultural stories does offer Momaday the opportunity again to explore the value of language, the ability of breath to become meaning. The two characters speak throughout as near equals, with both Urset and Yahweh highly anthropomorphized. The personification of Bear here is a consistent extension of the presentation of Bear in Momaday's other work. Yahweh, on the other hand, is much more fully – or at least differently – developed than he appears in the Bible. Although *House Made of Dawn* incorporates significant elements of Christian tradition, God himself does not appear as a character. In this sense, then, *In the Bear's House* is more radically syncretic. Yet the purpose of the dialogue is not to radically challenge a master narrative but to continue exploring the power and purposes of language.

Momaday has also written more conventional drama, including "The Indolent Boys," "Children of the Sun," and "The Moon in Two Windows," all collected in *Three Plays* (2007). "The Indolent Boys" was produced as a staged reading at Harvard in 1992, as a full play in Syracuse, New York, in 1994, and as a radio drama on American Indian Radio in 2005. The play tells the highly moving story of boys who, while running away from boarding school, freeze to death in a blizzard. The play reveals the lasting effects of this event on the other children and on their relatives, as well as the effects of guilt and blame on the boarding school staff. It is among Momaday's most accomplished work and should be much more widely known.

Throughout his career, Momaday has also written poetry and published several collections, including *Angle of Geese* (1974), *The Gourd Dancer* (1976), and *Again the Far Morning: New and Selected Poems* (2011). His poetry considers many of the same themes as his prose. Like many other Native American authors, he has also written children's stories, including *Circle of Wonder: A Native American Christmas Story* (1994) and *Four Arrows and Magpie: A Kiowa Story* (2006). Children's stories by Native authors have attained increasing popularity during the past generation, as Indian and non-Indian parents and teachers attempt to provide their children with more diverse views of American history and culture.

One thing *The Man Made of Words*, *In the Bear's House*, and other books illustrate is the ultimate futility of attempting to label much of Momaday's work according to genre. All of his work is equally, if differently, true. Some of it is also, formally, fiction. Nearly all of it – especially the prose but even some of the poetry – takes advantage of the elements of fiction to achieve its effects. A better term than "fiction" for much of his work might be "narrative," though ultimately, he would probably classify his words and all language as story.

SEE ALSO: Ecocriticism and Environmental Fiction; Indigenous Narratives; Mixed-Genre Fiction; Multiculturalism; Religion and Contemporary Fiction

FURTHER READING

Lincoln, Kenneth. (2007). *Speak Like Singing: Classics of Native American Literature*. Albuquerque: University of New Mexico Press.

Rainwater, Catherine. (1995). Planes, lines, shapes, and shadows: N. Scott Momaday's iconological imagination. *Texas Studies in Literature and Language* 37 (4): 376–393.

Rekow, Alec. (1997). Telling about Bear in N. Scott Momaday's *The Ancient Child*. *Wičazo Ša Review* 12 (1): 149–164.

Velie, Alan R. (1994). The return of the native: the renaissance of tribal religions as reflected in the fiction of N. Scott Momaday. *Religion & Literature* 26 (1): 135–145.

Woodard, Charles L. (ed.) (1989). *Ancestral Voice: Conversations with N. Scott Momaday*. Lincoln: University of Nebraska Press.

Moody, Rick

BEATRICE PIRE
University of Sorbonne Nouvelle, France

Rick Moody (b. 1961) belongs to the second generation of American postmodernism, the one that grew up and wrote under the influence of the great postwar metafictionalists John Barth, William Gass, Robert Coover, John Hawkes, William Gaddis, and Thomas Pynchon. Born about the same year as his fellow writers George Saunders (b. 1958), Jonathan Franzen (b. 1959), Jeffrey Eugenides (b. 1960), and David Foster Wallace (1962–2008), he was recognized as early as 1997 by critic R.Z. Sheppard in *Time* magazine as one of "Fiction's New Fab Four" along with Jonathan Franzen, David Foster Wallace, and Donald Antrim: these new authors distinguished themselves not only from the literary "Brat Pack" of Bret Easton Ellis, Tama Janowitz, and Jay McInerney "with modish novels about fast life in the 1980s" but also from their postmodern fathers, whose "irony" they "transcended" (Sheppard 1997). Since then, however, Rick Moody has never gained Jonathan Franzen's media popularity, which has become considerable since *The Corrections* in 2001, nor the academic following of David Foster Wallace, especially since his suicide in 2008.

Hiram Frederick (Rick) Moody III was born in New York City and raised in the Connecticut suburbs, a New England that often serves as the background for his short stories or novels. A student at St. Paul's boarding school in Concord, New Hampshire, where he remembers a teacher who was a Cheever enthusiast, he owes his academic education mainly to Brown University, where he studied in workshops with experimental novelists such as Angela Carter, Robert Coover, and especially John Hawkes, to whom he dedicated his first collection of short stories, *The Ring of Brightest Angels Around Heaven* (1995), and from whom he learned that "the true enemies of the novel were plot, character, setting and theme." Turned down for his MFA by Johns Hopkins, where he wanted to work with John Barth, and by the Iowa Writers' Workshop, he went to Columbia University where he found more "teachers who wrote" than mentors or "writers who taught" and a model of instruction based on "corporate theories" rather than on "the Socratic method" – a place that he felt equally dull and painful, as he recounted in a long piece on "Writers and Mentors" for the *Atlantic Monthly* (Moody 2005b). Graduating from Columbia in 1986, Moody worked for a few years in publishing, first at Simon & Schuster and then at Farrar, Straus and Giroux before the Pushcart Press Editor's Choice Award allowed him to publish his first novel, *Garden State*, in 1992, a first book ironically set in a state that resembles more the place of the Fall than Paradise and is the setting for what was to become Moody's central autobiographical subjects in the last decade of the twentieth century: teenage angst, broken and dysfunctional families, addiction, melancholy, and loneliness. Suffering from drinking and drug problems, Moody even spent a month in the summer of 1987 in a psychiatric hospital in Queens, an episode he described in *The Black Veil: A Memoir with Digressions* (2002): "I had never been in Queens before, that I knew of. I wept. [. . .] I couldn't believe what had happened to me" (p. 191). It was not until the few years that followed the publication of *Garden State* that Moody established himself as one of the most promising and recognized fiction writers, with two novels that remain up to this day his best known and most widely read: *The Ice Storm* (1994) and *Purple America* (1997), which both take place over one autumn weekend.

While *The Ice Storm* was adapted by Ang Lee into a 1997 film starring Kevin Kline, Joan Allen, Sigourney Weaver, and Tobey Maguire, the novel itself begins like this: "So let me dish you this comedy about a family I knew when I was growing up" (p. 3). In composing like *The Catcher in the Rye* (1951) of his generation, Moody has found his tragicomic voice. The voice is cartoonish at times, and accompanies a style influenced by Stanley Elkin or biblical verses: musical, lyrical, harmonious phrases that bellow and swirl, return and repeat, carry and carry away in an ample and anaphoric cadence. Revisiting the domestic malaise, frustrations, inhibitions, betrayals, and divorces that began to shatter marital and family structures in the late 1960s, as John Cheever and John Updike had already described them, *The Ice Storm* recounts a tragic day and night following Thanksgiving 1973 in New Canaan. Infidelities, parental disenchantment, teenage trouble, experimentation, and sexual awakening are dramatized against a backdrop of social, political, and cultural satire in which each of the suburban manners of the WASP privileged classes – dress, music, TV shows, reading, political comment, interior design, cars, private and public rituals – is scrutinized, until an almost biblical storm comes to put an end to the chaos. The storm leaves an atoning victim (an electrocuted teenager) and resounds in prose like a musical ostinato so distinctive of Moody's writing, a fricative note castigating the family institution, here made of two parents and two children: "Fucking Family. Feeble and forlorn and floundering and foolish and frustrating and functional and sad, sad. Fucking family. Fiend or foe. Next month: the end of the Fantastic Four. The Fab Four" (1994, p. 274). Before joining Brown University, Moody had considered attending seminary, and in the puritanical New England tradition, inherited from his ancestors' lineage as well as from his readings, he presents a fictional version of the song "Autumn Love" in a darker, Calvinistic light, himself apparently haunted by the same "Calvinistic sense of Innate Depravity and Original Sin" that Melville had spotted in Hawthorne in his essay "Hawthorne and His Mosses" (1850). As a sign of temptation of the flesh and adultery, the great A that appeared in the Salem sky of *The Scarlet Letter* (1850) is here taken up and parodied through the prism of Marvel Comics into the number 4 that graphically resembles the letter A, "A flaming figure four" that illuminates the last page of *The Ice Storm*, which is visible throughout the country and brings the novel to its end (Moody 1994, p. 279, "Finis"). The book says goodbye to childhood, teenage years, and the moment of parental separation that occurred on the day after the family reunion – a divorce most likely inspired by Moody's own traumatic memory of his parents' separation when he was nine.

Three years later, in 1997, Moody published what remains to this day his masterpiece: *Purple America*. Even David Bowie mentioned the novel on stage at a New York City show while the writer was in the audience, an event that Moody felt as a "moment in the did-I-hallucinate-it, did-that-actually happen category," as he confessed in the online journal *The Rumpus*, where he keeps a monthly music column, being a musician himself, and having written extensively on music (Moody 2013). Released almost the same month as Philip Roth's *American Pastoral*, which brings a father and his stuttering daughter face to face, *Purple America*, in an inverted family structure, features a stuttering son Dexter (Hex) Raitliffe, an NYC freelance publicist in his late thirties, and his mother Billie, who suffers from a degenerative neurological disease which leaves her paralyzed and unable to speak. The book opens with a long incantation, inspired by the Gospel according to John, on a son bathing his mother in a form of baptism or Pietà in reverse: "Whosoever knows the folds and complexities of his own mother's body, *he shall never die*" (1997, p. 3).

As her second husband had just deserted her, the mother calls her son for help on a return trip, just for one single weekend after Halloween. While *The Ice Storm* drilled, even in a parodic guise, in a bare "dirty realistic" vein sometimes reminiscent of Raymond Carver, *Purple America* has a more gothic, almost ghostly dimension. It first unfolds in a family home in Fenwick, Connecticut, furnished with antiques and "Pilgrim-era New England portraits," which have now "taken on the aspect of a clinic" (1997, p. 25), where a suicidal wheelchair-bound or bedridden woman and her alcoholic son wander idly. Were it not for the comic distancing and the stylistic play, the sinister mother–son relationship could resemble that of *Psycho* (1960) or *Suddenly Last Summer* (1959), with Fenwick's most famous former inhabitant, Katharine Hepburn, as the mother. The color purple is not only the prevailing color of the house decoration and Republican America. It defines most of the other places in the book, the red-toned Penelope's Pantry diner where mother and son have dinner or the Aubergine nightclub, set up in a deconsecrated church, where Hex ends the night disastrously. It characterizes above all the "purple prose" of the story, the prose Paul West had earlier defended in *The New York Times*: a style that is ornamental, sophisticated, baroque, virtuosic, drawing attention to itself with its artifices, stylistic inventions, lexical quirks, and extravagant narration (West 1985). Yet if *Purple America* describes the failure of language – a "drama of anguished communication" (1997, p. 9) in which a son stutters, the mother expresses herself with a voice-generating computer, and the parents exchange secrets (such as the father's involvement in nuclear testing) only through letters – writing is there, according to Moody, "as a release from some of the vertiginous anxiety of speaking," reinjecting orality and music into the words (Goldstein 2001). In this prose that seems to go wild and out of control, we hear an external omniscient third-person voice mixed with dialogues, internal voices, stream of consciousness, free indirect speech, bits of idiomatic language, various registers and jargons (cooking, decoration, politics, journalism, education) inlaid through unusual punctuation or fonts, the forsaking of quotation marks and use of italic script. A page by Rick Moody sounds as much as it reads. And flows, following the novel's central liquid metaphor that juxtaposes the mother's incontinent body with the leakage of nuclear waste from a nearby plant into the Long Island Sound. Here again, the destiny of political and collective America meets private and intimate fates, the author having had the project of linking the importance of the A-bomb and the rise of the nuclear family, as he explained to Bill Goldstein: "it was very much the foundation of *Purple America* this idea that the American nuclear family is actually built on nuclear history" (Goldstein 2001).

In those same years, Moody published two collections of short stories that are more experimental than his novels and may have served as writing exercises or training rooms for his longer prose. *The Ring of the Brightest Angels Around Heaven* (1995) brings a new cohort of doomed souls wandering between S&M clubs in the Meatpacking District, porn cinemas around Times Square, and drug joints in the East Village. And most important of all, *Demonology* (2001), which contains some literary jewels such as the title story and "The Mansion on the Hill," both tragically haunted by Moody's older sister Meredith who died accidentally in 1995. In "Primary Sources" – an autobiography in the form of a bibliography with footnotes that closes *The Ring of Brightest Angels Around Heaven* – a note to the *Tales and Sketches* (1900) by Nathaniel Hawthorne offers a brief comment on Joseph Moody (1700–1753) of York, Maine, the minister who wore a handkerchief over his face and was the inspiration for Hawthorne's story "The Minister's Black Veil." This note is the matrix from which Moody then experimented with a hybrid genre he called "A Memoir with Digressions" in the manner of Montaigne's *Essays* (1580) ("I am myself the matter of my book"). Released in 2002, *The Black Veil* is a new interpretation given to the autobiographical or autofictional form. Coming from a long lineage of ancestors settled in Maine that he can trace back to 1680, Moody chose the most famous Moody of New England history – a minister's son and a preacher himself who wrote a diary in code and in Latin – and embroidered the story of his own "black bile" melancholy moody life on an exegesis of Hawthorne's tale and works, the Reverend's book, and numerous historical archives and records (2002, p. 9). If *Purple America* had been a novel of mothers and sons, *The Book of My Mother*, like *The Black Veil*, was rather a *Letter to His Father*, a genealogical investigation and meticulous but fragmentary excavation of fatherland and patrimony that set Rick Moody as a descendant of a name and line going back to the Puritan period as well as the natural son of eminent literary patriarchs. The purple patch of his prose now stood out against a veiled background of black writing, violently decried by some – Dale Peck (2002) wrote an infamous review of it in *The New Republic* – but praised by Thomas Pynchon, who acknowledged Moody's innovative take on the memoir form.

It is at this point, however, that Moody closed his decade-long autobiographical chapter to begin a less critically acclaimed period in his career albeit one that produced much bigger books. In addition to predicting the growing hegemony of the series in American popular culture, as if through a gift for divination, *The Diviners* (2005) drew readers away from New England to the entertainment industry and the Hollywood spotlight. The plot of the 567-page novel, which was even negatively judged for its kitsch cover, revolves around Means of Production, a New York-based independent film company run by "The-Devil-Wears-Prada" or "The-Devil-Eats-Krispy-Kreme" director Vanessa Meandro, who appoints a Sikh cab driver to the office of "theory and practice of TV" and is surrounded by a team of colorful characters including an assistant, a movie star, a wine writer, PR girls, and so on (Moody 2005a, p. 133). The issue at stake is the script of a miniseries on thirst and water diviners from the dawn of humanity up to the founding of Las Vegas. While Moody is probably not on his most familiar ground here, he seems to have taken the ironic tendencies of "the society of the spectacle" (Debord 1967) or David Foster Wallace's critical analysis of television and US fiction at face value, forcing parody, emptiness, and shallow writing. The paratactic juxtaposition of chapters or episodes seems to serve no ambition other than that of displaying the author's infinite capacity to parody any genre, including script writing, and satirize the vain bustle that surrounded the film version of his novel *The Ice Storm*. Metafictional parody conversely worked at its best in the following 729-page novel written in memory of Kurt Vonnegut. Futuristic, dystopian, and hilarious, *The Four Fingers of Death* (2010) is a postmodern story-within-the story with an introduction and an afterword by an author named Montese Crandall, whose wife suffers from lung disease, framing a science fiction novelization of a 1963 horror B-film *The Crawling Hand*. The book dramatizes the NASA mission on Mars of astronauts with an "interplanetary disinhibitory disorder" (2010, p. 134) and the return in the Arizona desert of the only remnant of the spaceship crew, a living arm with a hand missing its middle finger and infected with the fatal *M. Thanatobacillus*. Meanwhile a Korean stem-cell scientist is doing research on the bacterium and apes, one of which is a talking chimp named Morton. The same atmosphere of threat and paranoia combined with critiques of post-9/11 power and nationalism also permeate *Right Livelihoods* (2007), a collection of three novellas published between the two big novels.

So after a quarter century, what has become of one of "Fiction's New Fab Four" (Sheppard 1997)? In the last decade of his already long writing career, Moody's private life has changed a lot. He has become the father of a daughter he wrote about in "The Hazel Effect" for *The New York Times* (2010). He divorced his first wife, Amy Osborne, published a piece in *Salon* entitled "On Fatherhood and Separation" (2014), and married the photographer and video artist Laurel Nakadate, with whom he had a son. This new family breeding ground seems to have brought him back to the origins of his writing, which he had more or less forsaken since the beginning of the millennium. Critics were not mistaken in their unanimous praise for his latest short novel, *Hotels of North America* (2015), an epistolary novel in the digital age or, as Moody says in *The Rumpus*, a "little seventeenth-century tragicomic apparatus" (Krull 2015) built as a series of online hotel reviews, written by a lonely and desperate middle-aged protagonist, Reginald Edward Morse (R.E. Morse), who tells the story of his life. Framed by two other texts – a preface by the director of *The North American Society of Hoteliers and Innkeepers of America* and an afterword by Rick Moody looking for Morse, who has disappeared – the reviews in various tones, "the harsh, the laudatory, the fanciful, the elaborate, the joyful, the melancholy," revisit a conventional literary place, the hotel, in a postindustrial and transnational world where the human condition looks nomadic and homeless (Moody 2015, p. 7).

As in a "second flowering," the latest books unfold like leaves on a new branch of the family tree, growing out of the roots that fueled Moody's novels in the 1990s. To the multivoiced texture of his fiction, he has now added duets with his wife by writing a preface to her photographs, *365 Days: A Catalogue of Tears* (2011) and detailing their marriage in a second memoir, *The Long Accomplishment: A Memoir of Hope and Struggle in Matrimony* (2019). In the past thirty years, Rick Moody's fiction and nonfiction have won numerous awards. He has taught at NYU, The New School, SUNY, Yale, Bennington, Skidmore, and he currently teaches at Brown.

SEE ALSO: Barth, John; Coover, Robert; Eugenides, Jeffrey; Franzen, Jonathan; Gaddis, William; Gass, William H.; Hawkes, John; Pynchon, Thomas; Vonnegut, Kurt; Wallace, David Foster

REFERENCES

Debord, Guy. (1967). *La société du spectacle*. Paris: Buchet-Chastel.
Goldstein, Bill. (2001). An interview with Rick Moody. *The New York Times* (February 25, 2001). https://archive.nytimes.com/www.nytimes.com/books/01/02/25/specials/moody-audio.html?0223bk (accessed August 4, 2021).
Krull, Ryan. (2015). The Rumpus interview with Rick Moody. *The Rumpus* (November 11, 2015). https://therumpus.net/2015/11/the-rumpus-interview-with-rick-moody/ (accessed August 4, 2021).
Moody, Rick. (1994). *The Ice Storm*. New York: Little, Brown.
Moody, Rick. (1997). *Purple America*. New York: Little, Brown.
Moody, Rick. (2002). *The Black Veil: A Memoir with Digressions*. New York: Little, Brown.
Moody, Rick. (2005a). *The Diviners*. New York: Little, Brown.
Moody, Rick. (2005b). Writers and mentors. *Atlantic Monthly* (August 1, 2005). https://www.theatlantic.com/magazine/archive/2005/08/writers-and-mentors/304101/ (accessed August 4, 2021).
Moody, Rick. (2010). *The Four Fingers of Death*. New York: Little, Brown.
Moody, Rick. (2013). Swinging modern sounds #44: and another day. *The Rumpus* (April 25, 2013). https://therumpus.net/2013/04/swinging-modern-sounds-44-and-another-day/ (accessed August 4, 2021).
Moody, Rick. (2015). *Hotels of North America*. New York: Little, Brown.
Peck, Dale. (2002). The Moody Blues. *The New Republic* (July 1, 2002). https://newrepublic.com/article/63251/the-moody-blues (accessed September 9, 2021).
Sheppard, R.Z. (1997). Fiction's new Fab Four. *Time* (April 14, 1997). http://content.time.com/time/subscriber/article/0,33009,986192,00.html (accessed August 4, 2021).
West, Paul. (1985). In defense of purple prose. *The New York Times* (December 15, 1985). https://www.nytimes.com/1985/12/15/books/in-defense-of-purple-prose.html (accessed August 4, 2021).

FURTHER READING

Dewey, Joseph. (2003). Rick Moody. *Review of Contemporary Fiction* 23 (Summer): 7–49.
Millard, Kenneth. (2005). Rick Moody's *Purple America*: Gothic resuscitation in the nuclear age. *Texas Studies in Literature and Language* 47 (3): 253–268.
Ryan, David. (2001). Rick Moody: the art of fiction no. 166. *The Paris Review* 58 (Spring/Summer).
Snider, Zachary. (2014). The popular music experiments of Rick Moody's Connecticut WASPs in *The Ice Storm*. In: *Write in Tune: Contemporary Music in Fiction* (ed. Erich Hertz and Jeffrey Roessner), 111–122. New York: Bloomsbury.
Toal, Catherine. (2003). Corrections: contemporary American melancholy. *Journal of European Studies* 33 (130–1): 305–323.

Moore, Lorrie

JOE KRAUS
University of Scranton, USA

On the strength of her four short story collections and three novels, Lorrie Moore has carved a reputation as one of the leading "writers' writers" of the last four decades. An exemplar of the workshop school, she has experimented with the conventions of the short story at the same time as she has won commercial success. In managing that difficult balance, she has established herself as one of the leading writing professors in the country, having held endowed chairs at both the University of Wisconsin-Madison and Vanderbilt, and she has further balanced an interest in the play of language with the impulse to critique contemporary culture. While much of her work examines individual loss, she suffuses it with a quiet humor and sustained joy. Even as she reinvents herself, her work retains a characteristic tone. As Dave Eggers puts it, "it's important to remember that Moore, while fascinated almost exclusively with broken people, is among the very funniest writers alive" (1998).

Marie Lorena Moore was born in upstate Glen Falls, New York in 1957, and famously burst onto the literary scene at 19 after winning *Seventeen* magazine's short story contest, beating out seasoned writers as a college sophomore. After graduating from St. Lawrence University in 1978, she went to Cornell for her MFA and, widely recognized as a prodigy, joined the faculty at the University of Wisconsin at just 27. She married and subsequently divorced, and she has one child, Benjamin, who survived a bout of childhood cancer. While reviewers have often tried to draw lines between her experience and the situations of her stories, Moore has remained playfully vague about the autobiographical nature of her work. As she told interviewer Angela Pneuman in 2005, "Well, I don't have an interesting enough life for a memoir – unless I get to fudge and exaggerate and lie. But then that's fiction."

As an extension of that disinclination to discuss her own life, Moore has redirected the question of autobiography into the work itself. Characters from throughout her career deal with the question of what it means to write, a condition that has at times had her labeled postmodern. One of the breakthrough stories of her first collection, *Self-Help* (1985), was "How to Become a Writer," a second-person-voiced narrative that seemed as if it could be a recitation of her own adolescent growth into authorship. In *Like Life's* (1990) "Vissi d'Arte," a title drawn from an aria in Puccini's *Tosca* and translated "I lived for art," a struggling playwright refuses to share his work. "The material felt so powerful to him, its arrangement so delicate, that a premature glimpse by the wrong person might curse it forever. He had drawn heavily from his own life for this play" (Moore 1990, pp. 21–22). When he does finally share it, a would-be producer betrays him, acknowledging that he has taken the stuff of the other man's life and turned it into his own fictional creation. As he casually expresses it, "By the way, I have to tell you: I've ripped you off mercilessly" (p. 46).

The publication of *Self-Help* in 1985 marked the culmination of her meteoric rise to acclaim within the academic sphere. *The New York Times*'s influential Michiko Kakutani spoke for many who saw her as someone with the potential to reshape the American short story, praising Moore as "a writer of enormous talent" (1985). Still, such an assessment came with reservation. Kakutani cautioned, "one can only wish that she would release her lyrical gifts more often from her straitjacket of cool decorum, that she would play around a bit more with other narrative forms." Other reviewers were less generous, recognizing Moore's gifts but pushing against what they saw as a too-studied detachment from the everyday. She impressed, the consensus seemed to say, but the technique left some feeling cold. As Carolyn See observed in *The Los Angeles Times*, "there is just one note here, no matter how beautifully sounded" (See 1985).

Self-Help set the pattern for Moore's subsequent work, however, and critics looking back have praised it as a more coherent and ambitious project than it seemed on publication. More than just a collection of stories with virtuosic skill, it offered a scathing commentary on the naive optimism of the Reagan era. As Alison Kelly, Moore's leading biographer, puts it, "The tone of droll irony has since become Moore's trademark; the more painful the experience, the likelier she is to make it the subject of a joke" (2009, p. 1). Reminding us that the collection's title puts it into conversation with the larger self-help and self-improvement "illusion" of the cultural moment, Kelly calls on us to see it as not just a series of character studies but also a sustained and subtle cultural critique. As she puts it, "Already mediated by being set within a parodic self-help framework, the narratives dramatize the main characters' feeling of distance from and lack of control over their own lives – the senses of instability and otherness that mock facile models of life management" (pp. 42–43).

Moore followed up *Self-Help* with *Anagrams* (1986) just a year later. The work, generally considered a novel, deals with three characters – Benna, Gerard, and Eleanor – in a series of five stories that reimagine their respective circumstances. Just as an actual anagram transposes the letters of a word to create a new one, Moore rearranged key elements of the characters' stories in each iteration. Philip Roth did something similar in *The Counterlife*, also published in 1986, but where that novel had an implicit masculine perspective, *Anagrams* featured a feminine self gradually diminishing. In the first iteration, Benna is self-possessed, a singer with modest success, whose glamour overwhelms her next-door neighbor, Gerard. By the final, longer narrative of the book, she is less secure professionally and emotionally, and it is Gerard who has an implicit upper hand in their potential romance.

The central conceit of *Anagrams*, its opening up of the writer's notebook to explore a range of possible futures, brings to mind some of the self-consciousness of writing that runs throughout Moore's career. At the same time, it reveals her philosophical stance toward language itself. Karen Weekes notes that, within *Anagrams*, "language is chiefly used as a bandage to cover the gouged wounds of failing, or failed, relationships. Moore's characters are rarely looking for the 'right' – consoling, helpful – words; they instead choose imaginative wordplay, or imagination itself, as an escape from serious discussion or confrontation" (Weekes 2012). That is, characters – or at least Moore manipulating those characters – seem never to trust language to accomplish what they want. It is always a potentially defective tool, but, like a hammer with a loose head, it's the only tool available.

Moore's critique goes beyond a simple questioning of vocabulary, however. Like the concept of the anagram itself, she pushes for a disassembling and reassembling of individual words. As Robert Chodat puts it, she often engages in "semantic play" that foregrounds the humor of the persistent possibility of misunderstanding (2006, p. 45). In *Anagrams* and elsewhere, she loves puns, inserting them not just as jokes but as a perpetual reminder of the thing-ness of language itself. The final section of *Anagrams*, for instance, is called "The Nun of That" in acknowledgment of Benna's limited opportunities for sex. The nun/none contrast points toward a possible theological digression or meditation on nihilism, but it functions almost entirely as a joke, one that serves the serious purposes of investigating Benna's ever-more limited horizons. Such wordplay runs throughout Moore's career. To take one example from *Self-Help*, a character in "Amahl and the Night Visitors" talks about an aversion to "discussing sex" which another hears as "disgusting sex" (1985, p. 105). Or, in her most recent story, 2020's "Face Time," a meditation on talking long distance with a father dying from Covid, two sisters break the tension by describing him as a potential "Typhoid Murray" should he return from the hospital to his nursing home. In each case, the humor destabilizes the language of the narrative without interrupting it.

Anagrams came in for mixed reviews, however, and Moore acknowledged in at least one interview that she "had to stop reading" the ways critics felt she had shortchanged her promising premise and undiminished skill (Lee cited in Kelly 2009, p. 66). By the time 1990's *Like Life*, Moore's second short story collection, appeared four years later, she was both an established literary figure and someone whom critics seemed to feel could go either way in her career. Perhaps as a result, the stories tend to have more traditional structure, and critics in general seemed to feel she had returned to the trajectory they expected of her.

In "You're Ugly, Too," perhaps the strongest story in *Like Life*, a college professor living in the Midwest returns East to visit her just-engaged sister. She's had a string of failed relationships and is keeping private some potentially troubling news about her health. Moore brings her characteristic skill to the story, drawing Zoe's unfulfilled sense as a teacher and a newcomer in just a few strokes, and she retains much of her detachment and self-awareness as a writer. For instance, Zoe reflects on herself, "Often, when she spoke to men at parties, she rushed things in her mind. As the man politely blathered on, she would fall in love, marry, then find herself in a bitter custody battle for the kids" (1990, p. 83). At the same time, Moore seemed willing to explore the possibility of such a point-of-view character emerging from her preoccupations into a healthier engagement with the world. It ends on an ambivalent note. Her sister has set her up with a man to whom she is not initially attracted. After some banter suggesting that he might also share her sense of irony – an exchange in which she perhaps pushes him too far – we see a glimmer that she might yet find someone for a real and sustained relationship.

In the same way that *Like Life* seemed to tame some of the experimental edges of *Self-Help*, Moore's second novel, 1994's *Who Will Run the Frog Hospital*, proved a more conventional narrative than *Anagrams*. It tells the story of Berie, a woman in a decaying marriage, reflecting on her adolescent friendship with Sils, a local teenage beauty. Each half – the present tense of her marriage and the more prominent flashback of her experience with Sils – deals with the way our most intense relationships don't quite deliver what we need from them. At the same time, there's a sweet sadness that runs throughout. Her husband is a decent guy, someone with whom she has a mostly positive marriage, but he's finding that his love for her has slowly dried up. And Sils, while fun and inspirational even, remains wrapped in herself. Berie eventually steals for Sils, helping her fund an abortion and then to underwrite a lavish-by-small-town-standards lifestyle, and Sils never fully appreciates the sacrifice. The dual perspective of the now/then structure, while providing Moore's fullest coming-of-age narrative, delivers a measured irony, proposing that we find happiness in pursuit of dreams rather than in fulfilling them.

With the 1998 publication of *Birds of America*, widely recognized as her masterpiece, Moore achieved a rare merger of academic acclaim and commercial success. Reviewers saw it bridging the gap of the writing program world, which tends to value precise language and innovative structure, and the can-it-generate-buzz world of traditional publishing. Dwight Garner, for instance, argued that the book demonstrated that Moore was "America's sexiest writer" at the same time as she was one of our "most important writers" (Garner 1998). It made *The*

New York Times Best Seller list, and critics lavished praise, placing it on multiple best-of-the-year lists.

"People Like That Are the Only People Here: Canonical Babbling in Peed Onk," the longest story in the collection and likely the best known of all Moore's work, stands as the quintessential expression of her ironic humor in the midst of brokenness. A couple discovers that their toddler son has cancer, and they have to navigate the world of the local hospital as they see to his treatment. The point-of-view Mother can't help critiquing and disassembling everything she sees. "Pediatric Oncology" becomes "peed onk," a phrase that sounds like a four-year-old's idea of a dirty animal-sounds joke yet one that's rendered at the precise moment that her own child is too sick to appreciate it. She contemplates bargaining for the life of her son, promising to accept his immediate survival even if it means death in a car crash at the age of 16. She bargains, though, not with God but in the *Let's Make a Deal* language of an American game show as part of an imagined conversation with a department store manager. Her husband, equally overwhelmed by all he sees and also fearing financial ruin, suggests at one point that she plan to write about the experience. He tells her, "Take notes. We are going to need the money" (2010, p. 219).

Each moment of the story, as its setting suggests, depresses and bewilders, yet, somehow, Moore produces a comforting note. As James McManus notes in his discussion of the story, "Like Beckett, [Moore] accepts that nothing is funnier than unhappiness; that the more horrible a scenario, the more humor a few literary artists are able to wring from it" (McManus 1998). There's no promise at the end, just the hope that they are leaving the hospital with the recovering child and then the cynically funny concluding sentences, "There are the notes. Now where is the money?" (Moore 2010, p. 250). If nothing else, they have survived, and they can still almost laugh, but they are still part of a story that may or may not reflect the experience of real people.

Moore followed *Birds of America* with 2009's *A Gate at the Stairs*, her most acclaimed novel. In it, a first-year student at a Wisconsin university becomes nanny to a mixed-race child adopted by an older, professional couple. As Tassie settles into her new responsibilities, she's exposed to a simmering local racism, to her vulnerability as a young woman, and to an Islamophobia that's become institutionalized in a post-9/11 world. Moore then puts her characteristic spin on such conventional literary fiction material by undermining one element after another. The couple turn out to have been obscuring their past parenting, when their mutual neglect killed their first child. The boyfriend Tassie thought was Portuguese turns out to be a New Jersey-born Muslim radicalized by what he's finding online. And, while she has to deal with the creepiness of an older man's attentions, she deflects them.

As much as the novel is more plot-driven than anything else Moore has written, she still refuses to bow to the conventions of narrative. Many of the threads go unfollowed; we never learn, for instance, what becomes of the boyfriend or the adoptive mother, and baby Emmie just fades away. And then, in a metafictional moment, she concludes with a nod to the famous line from *Jane Eyre* (1847), "Listener, I did not even have coffee with him. That much, I learned in college." The characters and the situation matter, Moore seems to say, but she nevertheless feels compelled to break the fourth wall and remind us of the fictive, language-based nature of the work.

Moore's 2014 short story collection, *Bark*, represented both a return to experimental form and an extension of her typical characters. The protagonists of "Debarking," "Referential," and

"Wings" find themselves in conversation with others who might be mentally ill, and each pushes forward into spaces that border on magical realism. From there, they launch into what become, effectively, modern-day soliloquies full of Moore's characteristic verbal play. At the same time, Moore seemed to answer some of her earliest critics in the way she developed protagonists very different from her own self: an aging rocker who may or may not be perpetrating elder abuse, a man in love with a woman who's lied about her recent mental breakdown, and a one-time peacenik who's developed near violent feelings for her soon-to-be ex-husband.

The publication of *Bark*, as well as two different editions of her collected stories, one in 2009 and another in 2020, demonstrate that Moore remains a leading literary voice. As an academic presence and an author whose new books come as literary events, she continues to shape her legacy, and she remains a model for a generation emerging under her influence. She stands, without question, as one of the most acclaimed short story writers in America today, and it's likely she has some of her most compelling work yet to share.

SEE ALSO: After Postmodernism; Eggers, Dave; Roth, Philip

REFERENCES

Chodat, Robert. (2006). Jokes, fiction and Lorrie Moore. *Twentieth Century Literature* 52 (1): 42–60.
Eggers, Dave. (1998). This funny book has nothing to do with feathers. *Salon* (October 2, 1998). http://edition.cnn.com/books/reviews/9810/02/birds.america.salon/index.html (accessed September 9, 2021).
Garner, Dwight. (1998). *Birds in America* finds the lighter side of ordinary madness. *Salon* (October 27, 1998). https://www.salon.com/1998/10/27/cov_27int/ (accessed September 9, 2021).
Kakutani, Michiko. (1985). Books of the times. *The New York Times* (March 6, 1985). https://www.nytimes.com/1985/03/06/books/books-of-the-times-070266.html (accessed September 9, 2021).
Kelly, Alison. (2009). *Understanding Lorrie Moore*. Columbia: University of South Carolina Press.
McManus, James. (1998). The unbearable lightness of being. *The New York Times* (September 20, 1998). https://www.nytimes.com/1998/09/20/books/the-unbearable-lightness-of-being.html (accessed September 9, 2021).
Moore, Lorrie. (1985). *Self-Help*. New York: Knopf.
Moore, Lorrie. (1990). *Like Life*. New York: Knopf.
Moore, Lorrie. (2010). *Birds of America*. New York: Vintage Books.
Pneuman, Angela. (2005). An interview with Lorrie Moore. *The Believer* 28 (October 1, 2005). https://believermag.com/an-interview-with-lorrie-moore/ (accessed September 9, 2021).
See, Carolyn. (1985). Festival of sadness from novelist Lorrie Moore. *The Los Angeles Times* (June 3, 1985).
Weekes, Karen. (2012). Words are all you need: speech acts in Lorrie Moore's *Anagrams*. *Journal of American Studies* 46 (3): 551–563.

FURTHER READING

Brauner, David and MacPherson, Heidi S. (2012). Lorrie Moore: Mo(o)re than an interim assessment. *Journal of American Studies* 46 (3): 541–602.

Morrison, Toni

UBARAJ KATAWAL
Valdosta State University, USA

In *Playing in the Dark*, Toni Morrison asks, "Why should a young country [the United States] repelled by Europe's moral and social disorder, swooning in a fit of desire and rejection, devote its talents to reproducing in its own literature the typology of diabolism it wanted to leave behind?" (1992, p. 36). This entry argues that this is one of the central questions underpinning Morrison's oeuvre. It should be important to note, however, that this question becomes more complicated because "the typology of diabolism" is inherent not only within a white culture, but also within an all-Black community, as shown in her novel *Paradise* (1998). What this means is that, much like her literary influence, William Faulkner, Morrison is interested to explore the question of fear, and the attendant quest for purity, when it comes to our relationship with the unknown, whether it is the different nation, culture, or even temporality. Morrison explains the purpose of her work thus: "The kind of work I have always wanted to do requires me to learn how to maneuver ways to free up the language from its sometimes sinister, frequently lazy, almost always predictable employment of racially informed and determined chains" (1992, p. xi). A dramatization of the history of group identity, and the accompanying predicament of those that are outside of the group identity, informs Morrison's works, in which human rights, social justice, crimes, vengeance and forgiveness, care and carelessness all intersect to create a complex literary world.

But first, brief background information on Morrison is in order. Morrison was born on February 18, 1931, as Chloe Wofford in Lorain, Ohio. In 1957, she married Harold Morrison, a Jamaican architect, but the couple divorced in 1964. She first went to Howard University for a bachelor's degree in English and then to Cornell University for a master's degree in American literature. She worked as an educator and editor until her first novel, *The Bluest Eye*, was published in 1970. Her third novel, *Song of Solomon* published in 1977, catapulted her into national fame after it won her the National Book Critics Circle Award. Among numerous other awards, Morrison won the Nobel Prize for Literature in 1993. She also received the Presidential Medal for Freedom in 2012. Besides novels, short stories, and plays, Morrison also wrote numerous children's books. *God Help the Child* was her last novel, published in 2015. She died in 2019 at the age of 88.

As the famous psychiatrist and political thinker from Martinique, Frantz Fanon, had shown before her, Morrison explores how people internalize identity constructs, especially, those that are excluded (Fanon 1967). This mentality develops in the mother country, where a colonized subject is imbued with a Manichean worldview, a worldview that extols the colonizer's culture and lifestyles at the expense of his people and culture. In *The Bluest Eye* and *Song of Solomon*, Morrison encapsulates a phenomenon akin to Fanon's in showing a self-loathing and the attendant desire for the oppressor's physical and philosophical attributes. In their attempt for acceptance by other members in their family and community, Hagar in *Song of Solomon* and Pecola in *The Bluest Eye* desire for an appearance that they can never have. However, Morrison goes beyond a demonstration of Manichean worldviews. Using language both as a creative tool and as metaphor for the complex dynamic of life, she hints at a possibility of life beyond the constraints that the Enlightenment enforced upon the world even as it strived to dismantle them in Europe and the Americas. This possibility of life beyond constraints will be discussed in depth later in the examination of *Paradise*. First, her other works are briefly discussed.

In *Tar Baby* (1981), Morrison demonstrates how Black folks were living in a different social order from the white people, who both nurtured and constricted their upward mobility. In a literal sense, the Streets provide shelter and food for Ondine and Sydney, who serve as cooks to them. But, Ondine and Sydney are also constrained to live and believe in their oppressor's worldview. On a metaphorical level, the novel demonstrates a rupture in Black folks' mental and physical health through a rupture in Jadine and Son's relationship, a rupture that originates in Jadine's nurturing from the Streets, and her subsequent low opinion of Son. Similarly, *Jazz* (1992), which – unlike *Tar Baby*, in which events take place both within and outside of the United States – is set in Harlem, New York, forms a more focused scene of turmoil in a Black community. The fateful triangular relationship between Joe, Violet, and Dorcas stems not just from a community mired by violence, but from the dominant world that compels them to live in that condition in the first place. Their failures in life, thus, cannot be adequately examined without understanding the larger social force that both nurtures and limits their possibilities.

If there is one thing that the Euro-American Enlightenment could live without, it would be love and compassion. After all, in the world where reason and objective classification reign supreme, there is no room for emotion and passion. Morrison calls readers to face this issue head on in her novel *Love* (2003). If characters suffer heartache and confusion, that is because they have allowed little room for care and reflection in their relationships. Romen Gibbons, an outsider figure in the novel, allows others to see what difference a proper communication, filled with care, can bring in people's everyday lives and relationships. Morrison continues this theme of love in *A Mercy* (2008). Even though Florens might seem to be besotted with lust and jealousy for the free Black man, who comes to build Jacob Vaark's gate, the novel ultimately asks Florens, and, by extension, readers, to begin loving themselves first: "Own yourself, woman, and leave us be," as the smith chides Florens (2008, p. 166).

Love and care play a central role in Morrison's works in the backdrop of unhomely homes and racial injustices. In *Home* (2012), Frank Money's traumatic experiences in the Korean War do not stop him from trying to save Ycidra, who is about to undergo a terrible experience at a white doctor's house. The unlikely bond between Bride and Rain in *God Help the Child* (2015) suggests the possibility of something positive despite carelessness, child abuse, and abandonment that both characters experience.

As I have argued in detail in "An Administered Life in *Paradise*" (Katawal 2017), the Enlightenment legacy of knowledge based on systematic classification and stratifications of society impacts the way we view our world, both imaginative and real. Morrison, however, is interested in human problems, rather than in certain groups of people, as critics tend to believe. It is true that many, if not all, of her works are set in a Black community in the United States. This should not lead us to conclude that she speaks for only Black people. Instead, her works pose questions on larger problems facing human beings in general, such as racism, sexism, and other sundry forms of othering, both within a community and outside. More importantly, Morrison's works of fiction stage a condition refashioned out of intersectionality, especially when it comes to race, gender, and nationality. While identitarian epithets have become a necessity in a post-Enlightenment world, Morrison nudges readers to imagine a world free of racialized and gendered systems of classification, however difficult it may be.

In her short story "Recitatif" (1983), Morrison explores this possibility of exploring a character's relationship with the other community members without knowing her racial marker. Readers are privy to the fact that Twyla and Roberta shared a room in an orphanage when they were eight. They also know that one of them is Black and the other is white. However, readers cannot tell for sure who is Black and who is white. In a nutshell, "Recitatif" demonstrates Morrison's idea of using language and fiction to reimagine a world outside racist assumptions. The story speaks to people's emotional experiences as well as shallow misunderstandings, which nonetheless could easily fester into bigger issues in relationships if not properly addressed as it plays out between Twyla and Roberta. Readers notice that Twyla and Roberta share more commonalities than differences when it comes to their childhood experiences. However, they allow their minor misunderstandings to develop into major problems in their relationship.

Paradise goes beyond what "Recitatif" started to do, namely examining how the legacy of instrumental classifications of human beings pervades us, even though deep within such classification markers as race, gender, and nationality do not make a substantial difference in terms of how we feel about and experience our everyday reality. More precisely, in *Paradise*, Morrison is able to recreate a community of Black folks, reeling from and fleeing persecution and discrimination, that ends up ultimately judging and exterminating a group of women.

Similarly to "Recitatif," Morrison raises perennial human issues in *Paradise* such as the fear of the outsiders, the attraction and loathing of pleasure-inducing entities in society, and the quest for racial purity and its devastating consequences on the weak, the defenseless, and the different. Not surprisingly, these issues find a strong energy boost, if not their origin, in the Age of the Enlightenment in Europe and the Americas. Not denying it some credit for bringing about positive changes for social justice and equality, the Enlightenment also exacerbated a culture of inclusion and exclusion, even as it promoted, and still promotes, knowledge based on experience, experiment, and, most potently, classification.

As Morrison argues in *Playing in the Dark*, "We should not be surprised that the Enlightenment could accommodate slavery; we should be surprised if it had not. The concept of freedom did not emerge in a vacuum. Nothing highlighted freedom – if it did not in fact create it – like slavery" (1992, p. 38). In other words, the dialectic of Enlightenment is most prominent only when there is a binary relationship between freedom and slavery. For the freedom to be actualized, there must also exist what freedom is not, that is, the institution of slavery. This rather curious contradiction marked the Age of Enlightenment and it continues to define the post-Enlightenment age to date. Morrison both deploys and dismantles this underlying contradiction of Western modernity in her works, more prominently in *Beloved* (1987).

In *Beloved*, Sethe lives at a time when the United States is going through throes of change. She posits a challenge to the Enlightenment's assumption for a rational progress of human being structured in a preconceived classification. She redefines the antinomy of freedom and slavery by rupturing the divide between them, as she fights for the freedom of her Black children. Inhabiting a liminal space of life and death, history and the present reality, Sethe wrests her right over her children from the white world around her deploying the principle of life and liberty, which is central to the Enlightenment. While the European Enlightenment ascribes freedom as an idea to the white people only, Morrison's novel demonstrates that it is more important than life to Black people as well. Through this demonstration, Morrison does not try to romanticize the effects of racism and slavery on the body and mind of the Black people, however. Morrison is fully aware of this mistake as a writer when she states, "My vulnerability would lie in romanticizing blackness rather than demonizing it; vilifying whiteness rather than reifying it" (1992, p. xi). With this statement, Morrison seeks to walk a fine line both within and outside of the black-and-white social divide, which she must both inhabit and challenge at the same time.

Of all her works, her first novel, *The Bluest Eye*, dramatizes the damage that slavery and racism wreak in the souls of Black folk. Pecola Breedlove's obsession for the bluest eyes and the subsequent psychological breakdown, her father's alcoholism, the hopelessness pervading the Black community all stem from the history of difficult race relations within the United States. So, while some people like Sethe – who also becomes mentally unstable at the end – fight back against unjust social practices and make the powers-that-be uncomfortable, others like Pecola succumb to the psychological trauma that the Enlightenment's othering has caused in the Western literary and cultural histories. The worst that can happen as a result of psychological trauma is when the victim blames herself for what happened to her. Pecola, for example, blames her ugliness for how both her family and the outside world treat her. Her longing for the bluest eyes originates in the dominant white group's anointment of a white woman's physical attributes as the standard to measure one's beauty and, indeed, worth. Needless to say, Pecola's condition is symptomatic of the human condition in general in the sense that she internalizes dominant ideologies of inclusion and exclusion, and the attendant processes of othering. She is simply overwhelmed by society's pressure to accept what is in reality the selective and subjective construction of beauty and truth.

Morrison is at her best in her artful writing, in which she uses language to free social and psychological pressures that her readers experience. The following passage from *Paradise* is an example of how writing can help make a positive change in the world:

> Suddenly Richard Misner knew he would stay. Not only because Anna wanted to, or because Deek Morgan had sought him out for a confession of sorts, but also because there was no better battle to fight, no better place to be than among these outrageously beautiful, flawed and proud people. Besides, mortality may be new to them but birth was not. The future panted at the gate. Roger will get his gas station and the connecting roads will be laid. Outsiders will come and go, come and go and some will want a sandwich and a can of 3.2 beer. So who knows, there will be a diner too.
>
> (1998, p. 306)

In context, Ruby, a new town founded based on the idea of racial purity, has seen the first death, even after routing out the Convent women, whom the founding fathers blame for the town's atrophy. Richard Misner, the town's preacher, and Anna Flood, Misner's friend, are a few of the people that the town's stewards, Deek Morgan and Steward Morgan, consider as rabble-rousers. In fairness, Misner and Anna oppose the town's policy of shutting out the rest of the world to preserve the town's purity. They organize the town's young people to challenge such a policy, an activity that does not sit well with the founding fathers. The passage above coming toward the end of the novel shows Misner's reflection as to how he could help the town by staying because, despite their mistakes, Deek Morgan and Steward Morgan are willing to listen to his advice. Consequently, he changes his initial plan to leave the town and decides to work with the people who need him the most. In displaying Misner's care toward his community, Morrison nudges readers to envision a better future, which is more inclusive and welcoming of the outsiders, in both the literal and metaphorical sense of the term.

Finally, Morrison's works locate the human condition in the future of possibility, even though the past does not appear very remarkable. With the creative deployment of words executed with imaginative dexterity, she is able to refashion human relationships marked by hope and forgiveness. Of course, not all works follow the same path, as some of her works such as *Beloved* end on a sad note. Even *Beloved* forces readers to reckon with their traumatic past so that past mistakes do not repeat. Exhuming minority history from American cultural memory, her works challenge American readers to reevaluate uses and misuses of instrumental classification and stratification of nations and cultures. At the same time, she shows the dangers of either romanticizing or simplifying minority cultures, not least because exclusionary practices exist within each culture and community that need to be opposed and challenged. In a nutshell, Morrison's works continue the robust African American literary heritage to which her predecessors including W.E.B. Du Bois, Richard Wright, Langston Hughes, James Baldwin, and Ann Petry have contributed in the twentieth century.

SEE ALSO: Bambara, Toni Cade; Black Atlantic; Book Clubs; Contemporary Regionalisms; Minimalism and Maximalism; Program Culture; Trauma and Fiction

REFERENCES

Fanon, Frantz. (1967). *Black Skin, White Masks* (trans. Charles Lam Markmann). New York: Grove Press; 1st ed. 1952.
Katawal, Ubaraj. (2017). An administered life in *Paradise*. *South Central Review* 34 (1): 32–52.
Morrison, Toni. (1992). *Playing in the Dark: Whiteness and the Literary Imagination*. Cambridge, MA: Harvard University Press.
Morrison, Toni. (1998). *Paradise*. New York: Knopf.
Morrison, Toni. (2008). *A Mercy*. New York: Vintage International.

FURTHER READING

Denard, Carolyn C. (ed.) (2008). *Toni Morrison: Conversations*. Jackson: University Press of Mississippi.
Goulimari, Pelagia. (2011). *Toni Morrison*. Abingdon, UK: Routledge.
Peterson, Nancy J. (ed.) (1997). *Toni Morrison: Critical and Theoretical Approaches*. Baltimore, MD: Johns Hopkins University Press.
Roynon, Tessa. (2013). *The Cambridge Introduction to Toni Morrison*. Cambridge: Cambridge University Press.
Smith, Valerie. (2012). *Toni Morrison: Writing the Moral Imagination*. Oxford: Wiley Blackwell.

Mosley, Walter

DEREK C. MAUS
State University of New York at Potsdam, USA

Walter Mosley's extraordinary writing career began comparatively late; he published his first novel at the age of 38. He had been working as a computer programmer for more than a decade when he began taking creative writing courses at night at City College of New York in 1985. Although much of Mosley's early work corresponds fairly closely to the tradition of "hardboiled detective fiction" exemplified by such writers as Dashiell Hammett and Raymond Chandler, he has continually extended, transcended, and at times even toppled the conventions of crime fiction in the twenty-nine books he has published within that broad category over the course of his illustrious career. Mosley has also thwarted attempts to pigeonhole him as a writer of mysteries or crime fiction in part by the fact that – as of early 2021 – he has published seven books of science fiction; eight widely divergent books of "literary" fiction; a young adult novel; three works of erotica; and five nonfiction books, including lengthy essays on political philosophy and advice about writing. He has also staged two full-length plays. Despite this variation within Mosley's body of work, Jennifer Larson nevertheless perceives some common – if also fairly expansive – themes: "While Mosley's nonfiction texts seem to engage larger social questions most directly, all of Mosley's texts, regardless of genre, might be read as treatises on race, class, gender, politics, history, and even the act of writing" (2016, p. 5). An earlier attempt at characterizing Mosley's oeuvre also still pertains, even though he has published twenty-three additional books since it appeared: "Mosley is seeking a 'home' for himself in terms of (sub)genre, language, social justice, politics, and even ontology at the same time that he tries to imagine meaningful constructions of home for his pantheon of characters within the various worlds they inhabit" (Brady and Maus 2008, p. xvii).

Walter Ellis Mosley was born in the Watts neighborhood of Los Angeles on January 12, 1952. Like Ezekiel "Easy" Rawlins, his son's most famous fictional character, Leroy Mosley had moved to Los Angeles from the Jim Crow South after serving in the military during World War II. As part of the Second Great Migration, he sought both greater economic opportunity and freedom from racial persecution in Southern California, but found only partial measures of each. While working as a school custodian, Leroy met a Jewish woman named Ella Slatkin, who was herself a relatively recent arrival from the Bronx and worked as a clerk at the same school. The couple soon intended to marry and received the blessing of each of their extended families. However, they were repeatedly denied a marriage license until after Walter's birth, despite the fact that interracial unions had been legal in California since 1948 (it was only in 1967 that the *Loving v. Virginia* Supreme Court decision struck down all such state laws). Walter and his family lived in Los Angeles throughout his childhood and adolescence, moving to West Los Angeles roughly six months before the week of violent unrest that shook Watts in August of 1965.

Despite both the discrimination his mixed-race family faced and the racial turmoil of Los Angeles and the country as a whole, Mosley recalls his early years in starkly personal terms, telling interviewer Harold Heft that "I had an easy time. My parents loved me very much and protected me from most bad stuff" (Heft 2013). He also noted in an earlier interview that he felt somewhat rootless and alienated after his family moved away from Watts when he was 13: "I was very unhappy . . . It seems to me like I wanted something, but the something was intangible; I didn't know how to get it. In L.A., that big middle portion of L.A., people don't walk on the streets, people don't come from the same background or the same area, so your connection with people is very tenuous at best" (George 2011, p. 38). Charles E. Wilson asserts that Mosley derived a complex sense of identity and self-expression from his youthful experiences: "Mosley insists that when he crafts dialogue, he thinks of having a simple conversation with regular people, or he recalls the language he often heard as a child . . . What Mosley finds himself creating in adulthood is the culmination of a variety of imaginary explorations beginning in childhood and extending well beyond adolescence" (Wilson 2003, pp. 2, 6).

Mosley explained his sense of identity to Joanna Neumann in 2010: "People say to me, 'Well, Walter, you're both black and *white*.' And I go, 'No, I'm black, and I'm *Jewish*. Jews are not white people'" (2010, p. 28). Owen E. Brady notes that although Mosley "identifies himself as a black male, he quickly notes that this identity is socially constructed, imposed on him and other African American men by the larger American society." This assertion does not, however, dilute the sense of his own Blackness as "a rich literary resource full of fascinating stories and characters [and] also as a sort of home . . . Mosley's fiction paints a caring but realistic and complex picture of the African American community infused with an intuitive sense of history" (Brady 2011, p. xiii). This connection helps explain his prolific dedication to remedying the perception that "[h]ardly anybody in America has written about black male heroes" (Neumann 2010, p. 30).

Eager to leave Los Angeles after graduating from high school, Mosley initially wandered around the United States and Europe for several years. Although he was nominally enrolled at Goddard College in Vermont, Mosley has stated that, "They kind of kicked me out. I kept hitchhiking back and forth across the country, and eventually my adviser said, You're really not getting much out of this experience. Your parents are spending all this money – maybe you'd better do something else" (Gebremedhin 2017, p. 247). He eventually returned to Vermont and settled in at Johnson State College long enough to earn a BA in politics in 1977. Mosley briefly undertook graduate study in political science at the University of Massachusetts in Amherst, where he met his future wife, Joy Kellman (they were married from 1987 to 2001). Moving first to Boston and then to New York, Mosley embarked on a lengthy stint as a computer programmer for such companies as Mobil, IBM, and Dean Witter.

Mosley began work on what eventually became his debut novel at the age of 34, before which he had shown scant evidence of the copious literary talent that has emerged since. Mosley has frequently retold an anecdote about the dawn of his writing career: "I was working as a consultant programmer. It was a Saturday, and nobody else was there. I was writing programs. I got tired of it, so I started typing on the computer ... I typed: 'On hot sticky days in southern Louisiana, the fire ants swarmed ...' I said – 'Hey, this is cool. This means I could be a writer.' So I start writing" (George 2011, p. 38). In 1985, he enrolled in night classes in creative writing at CUNY City College and soon produced a set of interlinked short stories that featured a pair of streetwise figures from rural Louisiana named Ezekiel "Easy" Rawlins and Raymond "Mouse" Alexander.

Mosley "sent [the manuscript] out to a lot of agents, and they all said, It's wonderful writing, but it's not commercial" (Gebremedhin 2017, p. 249). Mosley was encouraged by several of his teachers – most notably Edna O'Brien, William Matthews, and Frederic Tuten – to rework it as a book of detective fiction, and after he did so, the manuscript for *Devil in a Blue Dress* (1990) was enthusiastically accepted for publication by Norton. It unexpectedly became a bestseller and was made into a film starring Denzel Washington in 1995. Between the advance he received on his next two books and the earnings from his debut, Mosley was able to quit his programming job and has devoted himself entirely to his writing – which he stridently insists upon doing every day – ever since.

Each of Mosley's first four books through *Black Betty* (1994) featured the factory-worker-turned-private-eye Easy Rawlins in plots that demanded he step out of the primarily Black world in which he lives and negotiate various white-dominated realms in which he is perceived as an interloper. This quartet collectively established Mosley's reputation as a gifted writer of "hardboiled" detective fiction in the tradition of such authors as Dashiell Hammett, Raymond Chandler, and Ross Macdonald, each of whom Mosley readily acknowledges as influential (cf. Gebremedhin 2017, p. 252). Another important precursor is Chester Himes, whose gritty "Harlem Detective" novels from the 1950s and 1960s are among the few Black-authored ancestors within this genre. Scott Bunyan notes that Easy Rawlins recalls Himes's "Coffin Ed" Johnson and "Gravedigger" Jones in needing to "operate in liminal spaces, between white and black worlds, between the world of criminals and that of police." Bunyan adds that they depart from Philip Marlowe, Chandler's quintessential hardboiled protagonist, in "struggl[ing] to combat the disempowerment and marginalization in these liminal spaces ... Chandler's hero relies on an exteriority to the legal system, an extra-legal space which is only open to racially privileged white men" (Bunyan 2003, pp. 339–340). Agustín Reyes-Torres contends that all three characters are nevertheless "black sleuths who obtain recognition for their work in American society. In a way, they reverse the system; society needs them to maintain order. Not only does this reversal of order represent racial uplift but also gradual empowerment based on their competencies, a reappropriation of knowledge, and the possibility of each being his own man" (2010, p. 54).

Between 1994 and 2007, Mosley published five more novels and two collections of stories featuring Easy Rawlins before trying to kill him off at the conclusion of *Blonde Faith* (2007). He subsequently revived the character, though, telling interviewer Thomas Gebremedhin that "I realized that I'd reached the border of my father's life and was entering into the world of my life. I decided ... I could write the novels exactly the same way but with my experience forming it, rather than the experiences [of] my father and his generation ... The world has changed, and people have changed. So those two things – his aging and the world getting older – make it a little easier" (Gebremedhin 2017, pp. 264–265). The fifteen total books in the series – *Blood Grove* (2021) being the most recent – have gradually shifted in temporal setting from the late 1930s to the late 1960s, resulting in "a unique perspective on race, class, and masculinity in the mid-twentieth century ... that is just as enigmatic as the mysteries [that Easy] solves" (Larson 2016, p. 3).

Although somewhat less popular among both commercial and scholarly audiences than the Easy Rawlins books, Mosley's other works of crime fiction still resonate with them thematically and stylistically. Overlapping in time, place, and occasionally cast with the Easy Rawlins series, *Fearless Jones* (2001), *Fear Itself* (2003), and *Fear of the Dark* (2006) all depict the vigilante justice dispensed by the unlikely duo of bookstore owner Paris Minton and his violent friend Tristan "Fearless" Jones. Terrence Tucker argues that these characters address two longstanding tropes of African American literary and cultural history: "While Paris's standing as a working class intellectual questions the class politics of W.E.B. Du Bois's 'The Talented Tenth,' Fearless is a prescient interrogator of the amoral badman ... Mosley's interrogation of the intellectual and the badman recovers a time and culture, the American Negro of the 1950s, so that he can redefine heroism and highlight the efforts of African Americans in overcoming racist oppression" (2008, p. 98).

Socrates Fortlow, the protagonist of *Always Outnumbered, Always Outgunned* (1998), *Walkin' the Dog* (1999), and *The Right Mistake* (2008), is from roughly the same generation as Rawlins, Minton, and Jones. However, Fortlow has spent nearly three decades imprisoned prior to his release in 1995, which is when the first book in the series is set. His observations of Los Angeles in the aftermath of the Rodney King and O.J. Simpson cases are framed by his first-hand experience with the American penal system. Ronda C. Henry Anthony argues that "By naming a black rapist, murderer, and ex-convict Socrates, Mosley dares us not to judge Socrates Fortlow as American society, culture, and juridical systems encourage us to [do] ... Through his ethical philosophies and practices, Socrates is poised to transgress our expectations as he teaches us what he has to offer to himself and his community" (2014, pp. 128–129). Mosley's novel *Parishioner* (2012) focuses on a character named Xavier "Ecks" Rule who presents readers with even greater moral challenges, having brutally killed his siblings before seeking redemption decades later in a small California town.

Mosley's most recent crime fiction outside of the Easy Rawlins series is set in contemporary New York. In the six-book series bracketed by *The Long Fall* (2009) and *Trouble Is What I Do* (2020), a former boxer and private detective named Leonid McGill is trying – with mixed results – to walk the straight and narrow after a lengthy career as a "fixer" for a series of shady, yet powerful, figures. Larson suggests that Mosley's choice of setting somewhat mitigates the "stifling backdrop of unrelenting racist oppression" of his other series, allowing "ruminations on post-9/11 New York life and expanded personal and familiar story lines [to] dominate ... complemented by commentary on detective fiction and detective craft" (2016, p. 41). In 2018, Mosley also published *Down the River Unto the Sea*, a novel about a Black former NYPD officer named Joe King Oliver who is falsely imprisoned for raping a white woman and seeks to exonerate himself.

Regardless of their protagonists, Mosley's crime fictions "feature a wide range of formerly and currently nefarious characters ... [who] nevertheless eventually find redemption and community in their texts, revealing the impressive resilience of human nature" (Larson 2016, p. 6). Mosley's Black heroes are never saints, but they are also never in situations that would allow them to be. Instead, they improvise moral codes that allow them to do good for others – particularly those that may not have any other champions available to them – despite their own failings.

Starting with *RL's Dream* (1995), Mosley began his frequent departures from the crime fiction that made him a household name. Mosley has insisted that the fact that a "lot of people want [him] to be a mystery writer" (Brown 2011, p. 116) has not led to him feeling "trapped within a genre or way of writing" (McDonald 2011, p. 127). He declares that the defining trait of one of his books – regardless of form or genre – is that "there is going to be a black man at the center of [it], and he's going to be struggling for identity, for redemption, for some kind of comprehension of who he is in a world which doesn't really care about that" (quoted in Wilson 2003, p. 19).

He has applied this principle to a variety of contexts in the various "literary" books he has published. *RL's Dream* and *The Last Days of Ptolemy Grey* (2010) both deal with older African American men facing up to the realities of their decline and impending death. *A Man in My Basement* (2004) and *Fortunate Son* (2006) are both moral fables told within fairly realistic contemporary settings; set in the posh eastern Long Island town of Sag Harbor, *A Man in My Basement* asks pointed questions about the abuse inherent to racial and economic privilege, whereas *Fortunate Son* depicts the divergent and racially preordained fates of a pair of stepbrothers, one white, one Black. Mosley's *Tempest Tales* (2008) and *The Further Tales of Tempest Landry* (2015) are darkly comic homages to Langston Hughes and his "Simple" vignettes. Finally, *John Woman* (2018) and *The Awkward Black Man* (2020) are a novel and collection of stories, respectively, in which Mosley extends his inquiry into idiosyncratic representations of Black masculinity even further.

Mosley's books of speculative fiction include *Blue Light* (1998), *Futureland* (2001), *The Wave* (2006), *Inside a Silver Box* (2015), and the paired novellas that comprise his three-book "Crosstown to Oblivion" series (2012/13). His young adult novel *47* (2005) also borrows plentifully from science fiction conventions in telling the story of a young runaway slave. Mosley has frequently commented on how his speculative works relate to his other books: "My writing's a lot about relationships and also about politics ... On one hand, I'm interested in atomic signatures and that kind of stuff, and on the other hand, I'm interested in what happens to poor people and to people of color, and how their lives get organized as we advance; what things we leave behind and what we carry on, like our prejudices etc. I can have my adventures, and I can also talk about social relations" (Brown 2011, p. 117).

Although *Killing Johnny Fry* (2006), *Diablerie* (2008), and *Debbie Doesn't Do It Anymore* (2014) have each been characterized as erotica, Mosley coined the term "sexistential novel" to describe *Killing Johnny Fry*. The last of these three novels is also distinctive for featuring Mosley's only female protagonist, an African American porn star named Debbie Dare who is trying to cope with life beyond her unconventional form of celebrity. Finally, he has published five books of nonfiction, ranging from lengthy philosophical essays expressing his personal brand of leftist politics to self-help guides for aspiring writers.

Mosley has received numerous literary awards throughout his career, including several lifetime achievement awards in recent years. He is the first African American recipient of the Mystery Writers of America's Grand Master Award (2016) and the first African American man to receive the National Book Foundation's Medal for Distinguished Contribution to American Letters (2020). Mosley has both advocated for greater opportunities for writers – particularly African American writers – to follow his example, and personally funded the establishment of a certification program in publishing at CCNY, his graduate alma mater. Although his status as an exemplary author of crime fiction seems cemented, the lasting influence of his other works remains less clear.

SEE ALSO: Ellroy, James; Post-9/11 Narratives; Urban Fiction

REFERENCES

Anthony, Ronda C. Henry. (2014). *Searching for the New Black Man: Black Masculinity and Women's Bodies*. Jackson: University Press of Mississippi.

Brady, Owen E. (2011). Introduction. In: *Conversations with Walter Mosley* (ed. Owen E. Brady), ix–xix. Jackson: University Press of Mississippi.

Brady, Owen E. and Maus, Derek C. (2008). Introduction. In: *Finding a Way Home: A Critical Assessment of Walter Mosley's Fiction* (ed. Owen E. Brady and Derek C. Maus), ix–xxiii. Jackson: University Press of Mississippi.

Brown, Charles N. (2011). Walter Mosley: a seat at the table. In: *Conversations with Walter Mosley* (ed. Owen E. Brady), 112–121. Jackson: University Press of Mississippi.

Bunyan, Scott. (2003). No order from chaos: the absence of Chandler's extra-legal space in the detective fiction of Chester Himes and Walter Mosley. *Studies in the Novel* 35 (3): 339–365.

Gebremedhin, Thomas. (2017). The art of fiction, no. 234: Walter Mosley. *The Paris Review* 220: 242–267.

George, Lynell. (2011). Walter Mosley's secret stories: a ride with a mystery writer who evokes the unclichéd. In: *Conversations with Walter Mosley* (ed. Owen E. Brady), 29–41. Jackson: University Press of Mississippi.

Heft, Harold. (2013). America's Blackest Jewish writer. *Tablet* (May 13, 2013). https://www.tabletmag.com/sections/arts-letters/articles/americas-blackest-jewish-writer (accessed July 10, 2021).

Larson, Jennifer. (2016). *Understanding Walter Mosley*. Columbia: University of South Carolina Press.

McDonald, Craig. (2011). Walter Mosley: fearless and easy. In: *Conversations with Walter Mosley* (ed. Owen E. Brady), 127–135. Jackson: University Press of Mississippi.

Neumann, Joanna. (2010). The curious case of Walter Mosley. *Moment* 35 (5): 26–31, 76.

Reyes-Torres, Agustín. (2010). Coffin Ed Johnson, Grave Digger Jones, and Easy Rawlins: Black skins and Black psyches. *Clues: A Journal of Detection* 28 (1): 51–60.

Tucker, Terrence. (2008). American Negroes revisited: the intellectual and the badman in Walter Mosley's Fearless Jones novels. In: *Finding a Way Home: A Critical Assessment of Walter Mosley's Fiction* (ed. Owen E. Brady and Derek C. Maus), 97–108. Jackson: University Press of Mississippi.

Wilson, Charles E., Jr. (2003). *Walter Mosley: A Critical Companion*. New York: Greenwood.

FURTHER READING

Ford, Elisabeth A. (2005). Miscounts, loopholes, and flashbacks: strategic evasion in Walter Mosley's detective fiction. *Callaloo* 28 (4): 1074–1090.

Lock, Helen. (2001). Invisible detection: the case of Walter Mosley. *MELUS* 26 (1): 77–89.

Ruíz-Velasco, Chris. (2010). "Lost in these damn white halls": power and masculinity in Walter Mosley's fiction. *Midwest Quarterly* 51 (2): 135–151.

Soitos, Stephen F. (1996). *The Blues Detective: A Study of African American Detective Fiction*. Amherst: University of Massachusetts Press.

Stein, Daniel. (2008). Walter Mosley's *RL's Dream* and the creation of a blutopian community. In: *Finding a Way Home: A Critical Assessment of Walter Mosley's Fiction* (ed. Owen E. Brady and Derek C. Maus), 3–17. Jackson: University Press of Mississippi.

Mukherjee, Bharati

IZABELLA KIMAK
Maria Curie Skłodowska University, Poland

Bharati Mukherjee, an American author of South Asian background who passed away in 2017, made a name for herself as one of the major writers – if not the major writer in the singular – of the South Asian diaspora in the United States. Having been born in Kolkata, India, in 1940 and having moved to the United States to study at the University of Iowa, after a period of residing in Canada with her husband and fellow writer Clark Blaise, Mukherjee moved permanently back to the United States and became a spokesperson for the first generation of South Asian Americans, giving voice in her fiction to the experiences of migrants crossing borders of not only geographical but also mental and emotional character. If one were to use a single key term which most aptly characterizes and encompasses Mukherjee's oeuvre, that would certainly be the word migration. In her novels and short stories, essays and nonfiction, Bharati Mukherjee repeatedly returned to the topic of migration and probed the impact that migration exerts on the subjectivities of the migrants, mostly female ones. It is my intention in this entry to map out the major routes and trajectories, both literal and figurative, that Mukherjee portrays in her fiction to argue that she indeed is a writer of (multiple) migration(s).

Bharati Mukherjee is perhaps best known for her compelling novel *Jasmine*, published in 1989, which has been widely read and discussed across the United States and included in the syllabi of American ethnic literature in numerous colleges and universities. *Jasmine* was not Mukherjee's debut, though, as it was preceded by two other novels, two short story collections, and two nonfiction books, which – collectively – already signaled the major interests of the budding writer: the portrayal of two zones that had the greatest influence on her own life and development, namely India and North America, and the various ways in which mobility between these two zones alters their perception in the mind of the mobile subject. Mukherjee's debut novel, *The Tiger's Daughter*, published in 1971, reads like a semi-autobiographical text. Even though it is advertised as a novel, that is, a purely fictional text, one finds it hard to resist the temptation to read the protagonist, Tara Banerjee Cartwright, as the author herself. The similarities between the two are indeed striking: the same family background in India, the experience of studying in the United States, the fact of being married to an American, and so on. The novel narrates the summer that Tara spends revisiting her home in Calcutta (now politically correctly named Kolkata) and extending a critical gaze towards the politics of her own Brahmin family and the chasm separating the wealthy castes from the unrest of the city's poor and disenfranchised inhabitants. It is clear that Tara is distancing herself from the lifestyle and values of her beloved family and Indian school friends on account of her experience of life elsewhere; in other words, she views India through a lens already colored by her American experience.

The two short story collections that Mukherjee published within three years of each other, *Darkness* in 1985 and *The Middleman and Other Stories* in 1988, the latter winning the National Book Critics Circle Award, both contain texts that offered Mukherjee an opportunity to further explore the literary terrain signaled in her early novel and two nonfictional texts, the memoir *Days and Nights in Calcutta* (1977) and *The Sorrow and the Terror: The Haunting Legacy of the Air India Tragedy* (1987), both co-written with her husband Clark Blaise, in which she oscillated between South Asia and North America. In *Darkness*, the majority of her characters are North America-based South Asians – residing in the United States or Canada – who need to come to terms with their status as exotic outsiders. This is poignantly visible in one of the most famous stories of the collection, "The Lady from Lucknow," in which an affluent Muslim woman living in Atlanta with her IT-specialist husband and two children engages in a love affair with a much older white American as a way to grow roots into the American soil. The affair finds a bitter ending when the American's enraged wife mocks the lovers' passion by attributing her husband's interest in the Indian woman to the exoticism of her brown body, thereby reminding the protagonist of her non-belonging and her status as an ethnic other. In *The Middleman and Other Stories*, Mukherjee broadened the scope of her thematic interests to encompass new arrivals to North America from other parts of the world as well, including Uganda, Latin America, and the Middle East. Throughout the collection, migration functions as a factor uniting individual stories and characters into a larger process that is reshaping the face of America. In one of the stories, "Jasmine," the eponymous character is a domestic helper from Trinidad who begins to harbor romantic feelings for her employer. The story finds its development and dénouement in the famous novel bearing the same title, whose protagonist is not Trinidadian, however, but comes from India.

The novel *Jasmine* can be read alongside two other texts by Mukherjee, her early novel *Wife* (1975) and her latest novel *Miss New India*, published in 2011. All three texts feature young migrant women as protagonists; even though their journeys may stem from various reasons and follow various routes, all of these female characters experience migration as a corporeal phenomenon, one that both has a bearing on and is influenced by their young brown female bodies. *Wife* stands out in this respect, presenting a rather dismal picture of migration, unlike many other South Asian diasporic texts, criticized by scholars for perpetuating the existence of binary differences between Asia and America and for painting a celebratory picture of migration to the West rendered in terms of liberation from a constricting, patriarchal Eastern culture. Moving to the United States with her husband in pursuit of a better life, the young protagonist of *Wife* finds her uprootedness from her familiar surroundings to impact heavily on her sense of being in touch with reality. The shock of arrival – to use the title of the memoir by Mukherjee's compatriot, the poet and fiction writer Meena Alexander (1996) – literally breaks Dimple, as her alienation and sense of cultural detachment make it impossible for her to come to terms with her new life in the United States. Staying in a rented apartment, surrounded by personal items belonging to a white American family, and binge-watching shows on American TV for hours on end, Dimple progressively slides into madness. What exacerbates Dimple's precarious state is her being torn between two models of womanhood, that of a submissive Indian wife and that of an Americanized feminist. Being unable to choose either of the two paths, Dimple transforms the quintessential space of wifely devotion, namely the kitchen, into a scene of murder, killing her husband with the use of a kitchen knife. Overlooked for some reason by many scholars, *Wife* complicates an easy categorization of Mukherjee as an author who dabbles in what Inderpal Grewal terms Asian women's immigrant narratives that are "framed in the binary oppositions between the United States as first world site of freedom and 'Asia' as third world site of repression" (2005, p. 63). *Wife* romanticizes neither America nor Asia, presenting both geographical areas as posing threats to women.

Among Mukherjee's oeuvre, *Jasmine* has received by far the most scholarly attention, spawning dozens of articles and book chapters analyzing Mukherjee's structurally complex novel from a number of scholarly stances and theoretical perspectives. Frequently, the novel has been used as an example to illustrate general comments about the essentializing nature of South Asian diasporic women's literature, in a manner elucidated above with the example of Inderpal Grewal's argument. It is my contention, however, that even if there are certain shortcomings, both in *Jasmine* and in Mukherjee's other texts, the body of works the late writer produced – when read collectively – testify both to the complexity of migratory processes and to the fraught relation between the native and adopted lands. In *Jasmine*, the eponymous character embarks on a perilous journey to the United States as an illegal immigrant in the wake of her husband's death in a terrorist attack. Violence functions both as the reason for Jasmine's journey and as its inescapable element. Jasmine experiences the ferocity of migratory processes on her own body when she is raped on her entry to the United States by the man who helped smuggle her in, and when she ends up murdering her oppressor, performing as Kali, the Hindu goddess of revenge. Trained subsequently to "walk and talk American" (Mukherjee 1989, p. 120) by a woman aiding illegal aliens, Jasmine learns a hard lesson that her exotic body may be both her liability and her asset in the new land. Performing a number of housekeeping jobs and responding to American males' fantasies about her as an Oriental beauty, Jasmine learns how to put her limited assets to her advantage. The novel has been criticized by many scholars for presenting the protagonist's physical attractiveness as her ticket to prosperity, but looking at the issue from another perspective, one may argue that such a state of affairs can likewise by read as the novel's critique of America for positioning new arrivals as outsiders and for forcing them to take advantage of whatever leverage they may have at their disposal to be able to survive, in this case the leverage in question being the protagonist's beauty.

The Holder of the World, a novel published in 1993, in turn, offers a corrective to the migratory route most often presented in works by Mukherjee and other South Asian diasporic writers. In this striking postmodern and postcolonial novel, Mukherjee asserts her place as a genuinely American writer, rewriting one of the classics of American Romanticism, that is, Nathaniel Hawthorne's *The Scarlet Letter* (1850). In Mukherjee's version of female rebellion in the seventeenth century, her protagonist, Hannah Easton, known also as the Salem bibi, travels from Salem, Massachusetts, via England to India's Coromandel Coast as a wife of an East India Company factor. What many critics view as an attempt to dismantle the myth of America's monolithic Puritan beginnings may also be seen as Mukherjee's more personal project of reworking her own literary mythology established with her earlier texts. By reversing the route in which her characters migrate, the novelist simultaneously reverses the associations generated by specific geographical spaces: it is now Puritan America that functions as a space of female imprisonment, while India offers Hannah liberation – sexual and otherwise – and a possibility of self-fashioning. Interestingly, the story of Hannah is narrated by a late-twentieth-century white woman, who is conducting research to locate the most precious jewel in the world, the Emperor's Tear. It is the narrator and the protagonist of the frame tale, Beigh, who presents the story of Hannah's passionate love affair with a Hindu raja at the time when he is waging a war against Aurangzeb, the Mughal emperor of India. In the wake of her lover's death in combat, Hannah returns to the American colonies and gives birth to an illegitimate child, Mukherjee's equivalent of, and answer to, Hester Prynne's daughter, called Pearl, like her literary predecessor. Structurally and conceptually complex, making use of various modes of travel – including virtual reality techniques – to move back and forth in time and space, *The Holder of the World* is a dazzling literary achievement, with which Mukherjee certainly achieves what she sets out as her goal in her essay "Beyond Multiculturalism: Surviving the Nineties": to be "an American without hyphens" (Mukherjee 1997, p. 460), or in other words, to go beyond her status as an Asian American author.

In *Leave It to Me*, a novel published in 1997, Mukherjee explores the ramifications of one's ethnic identity for one's sense of self, as her protagonist, Devi Dee, adopted and brought up by an Italian American family, embarks on a search for her biological parents to ease her sense of permanent non-belonging and to find her roots. Mukherjee's subsequent two novels, *Desirable Daughters* (2002) and *The Tree Bride* (2004), share the narrator, Tara Chatterjee, and the story they offer of Tara's predecessor and namesake, Tara Lata, married by her Western-educated father to a tree to avert bad luck after her bridegroom dies of a snake bite. While the former novel focuses on the lives of three sisters, two living among the South Asian communities in the United States and one remaining in India, and addresses, among others, the question of the validity of rigid cultural norms, in the latter novel the narrator delves into the story of her ancestor Tara Lata, positioning her within the history of India's struggle for independence from British rule. The female protagonists of all three novels mentioned here find it imperative to establish their family histories as part of the process of making sense of their subjectivities in an ever more complex and interconnected world.

Finally, in *Miss New India*, her last novel, published in 2011, Mukherjee further complicates the picture of migration offered by her literary oeuvre. Unlike her predecessors in other Mukherjee texts, the protagonist of *Miss New India*, Anjali Bose, engages in internal migration from the north to the south of India. Her decision to flee her natal home in Gauripur is spawned by sexual violence to which she falls victim at the hands of the suitor selected by her father. With the financial aid of her American teacher, Peter Champion, a lover and scholar of Indian architecture and languages, Anjali makes her way to the sprawling metropolis of Bangalore, which is undergoing a rapid development as a result of the forces of globalization: the city functions as a locus of call centers outsourced from the United States. By situating her final novel exclusively within India, Mukherjee succeeds in disproving earlier critique of her works as being framed within the dynamics of binary opposites (the East versus the West) to showcase the interconnectedness of the two both in a spatial and in a temporal sense.

Bangalore is literally growing on the remains of old Raj-era buildings that are being demolished to make way for the glossy and non-culture-specific edifices.

From her early texts on both ruptures and opportunities inherent in migration from India to North America, through her remarkable revision of Nathaniel Hawthorne's *The Scarlet Letter* in *The Holder of the World*, which functions at the same time as a certain revision of her own literary map, to the concerns of her final novels and her authorial gaze extended ever more probingly towards Indian history and present, Mukherjee can without a doubt be treated as a literary voice of the first generation of South Asian Americans. Although her works coincided with a whole surge of other South Asian American literary texts, especially at the turn of the century, the structural complexity of her texts and the maturity of her thoughts, as well as the power of her female characters, all contribute to make Bharati Mukherjee an unparalleled literary voice.

SEE ALSO: Jen, Gish; Kingston, Maxine Hong; Lahiri, Jhumpa; Multiculturalism; Tan, Amy

REFERENCES

Alexander, Meena. (1996). *The Shock of Arrival: Reflections on Postcolonial Experience*. Cambridge, MA: South End Press.
Grewal, Inderpal. (2005). *Transnational America: Feminisms, Diasporas, Neoliberalisms*. Durham, NC: Duke University Press.
Mukherjee, Bharati. (1989). *Jasmine*. New York: Fawcett Crest.
Mukherjee, Bharati. (1997). Beyond multiculturalism: surviving the nineties. In: *MultiAmerica: Essays on Cultural Wars and Cultural Peace* (ed. Ishmael Reed), 454–461. New York: Viking.

FURTHER READING

Kimak, Izabella. (2013). *Bicultural Bodies: South Asian American Women's Literature*. Frankfurt am Main: Peter Lang.

Lau, Lisa and Mendes, Ana Cristina. (eds.) (2011). *Re-Orientalism and South Asian Identity Politics: The Oriental Other Within*. London: Routledge.
Maira, Sunaina and Srikanth, Rajini. (eds.) (1996). *Contours of the Heart: South Asians Map North America*. New York: The Asian American Writers' Workshop.
Nelson, Emmanuel S. (ed.) (1993). *Bharati Mukherjee: Critical Perspectives*. New York: Garland.
Srikanth, Rajini. (2004). *The World Next Door: South Asian American Literature and the Idea of America*. Philadelphia: Temple University Press.

Multiculturalism

CYRUS R.K. PATELL
New York University, USA

The debates over "multiculturalism" offer a useful starting point for an understanding of the state of US fiction at the beginning of the 1980s. The widespread institutional acceptance of the idea that resulted from that decade's so-called culture wars in the United States was a crucial development for fiction-writers and scholars, but by 2020 "multiculturalism" as a critical category had largely outlived its usefulness. In fact, what is at stake in those US literatures that were identified with multiculturalism during the 1980s becomes clearer if they are seen not as "multicultural literatures" but, rather as "emergent literatures," a term adapted from the work of neo-Marxist theorist Raymond Williams. These dynamics are, in turn, further illuminated if they are mapped against the development of theories of cosmopolitanism, away from critiques of nationalism and toward critiques of both universalism and multiculturalism. Cosmopolitan theory at the start of the twenty-first century sought to find ways to balance the competing claims of sameness and difference in accounts of culture. Like cosmopolitan theorists, US emergent writers after 1980 understood that storytelling was a crucial way that cultures make meaning. These authors were committed to staging difficult conversations in which fundamental values associated with the ideas of self, identity, community, and nation were open to question.

As an institutional practice, multiculturalism in the United States arose as a response to the failure of the universalism that animated the nation's founding ideals to protect the rights and interests of women and minorities. The authors of *The Great Republic* (1977), a widely used textbook during the 1980s, offered an argument on behalf of the universalism of the liberal principles enshrined in the founding documents of the United States: "The Declaration of Independence set forth a philosophy of human rights that could be applied not only to Americans, but to peoples everywhere. It was essential in giving the American Revolution a universal appeal" (Bailyn et al. 1992, p. 190). Two decades after the Civil Rights movement, however, the evident disjunction between the theory and the practice of the principles outlined in the Declaration demonstrated that the nation's utopian aspirations had yet to be realized because the United States had not yet fully emerged from the oppressive patterns of reasoning that were dominant in the slaveholding patriarchal mode of culture from which US liberalism emerged. Multiculturalism was a way of calling attention both to the importance of the idea of human difference, which universalist thinkers tend to de-emphasize as they seek common denominators among people, and to the historical injustices suffered by women and minorities in the United States throughout its history.

The idea of multiculturalism was by no means an invention of the 1980s – or even of the United States. Susan L. Mizruchi reminds us that the term *multiculturalism* "was not coined until the 1940s" and that "most historians place the advent of multiculturalism in the 1960s." She argues, however, that the roots of US multiculturalism lie in "the late nineteenth century as the extremes of social diversity met an accelerating capitalist system." Noting that "this was a period of widespread literacy, when best-selling works of literature and magazines reached vast readerships and immigrants could find newspapers and magazines in their native languages," Mizruchi contends that writers "assumed an unparalleled cultural authority" as "mediators of modernization" (2008, p. 3–4). Werner Sollors argues that "multiculturalism as an '-ism' word apparently originated in discussions about Africa, Australia, and Canada" (2017, p. 146). By the end of the 1980s, however, the view expressed in 1972 by the American Association of Colleges and Teacher Education that cultural diversity was not only "a fact of life in American society," but also a valuable resource that should be preserved and extended" (1973, p. 264) had become dominant in the United States. Educational activist Diane Ravitch noted in a 1990 essay that "as a result of the political and social changes of recent decades, cultural pluralism is now generally recognized as an organizing principle of this society. In contrast to the idea of the melting pot, which promised to erase ethnic and group differences, children now learn that variety is the spice of life. . . . that differences among groups are a national resource rather than a problem to be solved" (1990, p. 339).

In *We Are All Multiculturalists Now* (1997), sociologist Nathan Glazer argued that African Americans played a decisive role in the victory of multiculturalism during the 1980s: "blacks are the storm troops in the battles over multiculturalism. [T]heir claim that they must play a larger role in the teaching of American literature and history, indeed should serve to reshape these subjects, has a far greater authority and weight than that of any other group" (1997, p. 94). As a result, Glazer suggested, "we all now accept a greater degree of attention to minorities and women and their role in American history and social studies and literature classes in schools" (p. 14) Although Glazer regarded the presence of women's studies within multiculturalism as counterintuitive, he argued that when women's studies came to prominence as a field of scholarly inquiry, "both women's studies and the new ethnic and racial studies could trace a common history, arising in the same decades, drawing on similar resentments, and a common new awareness of inequality." Indeed, Glazer claimed, women's studies has become "so large a part" of multiculturalism "that it often outweighs the rest" (p. 17). Glazer's analysis suggests why Toni Morrison emerged as the uber-canonical US novelist of the late twentieth century.

In Glazer's view, multiculturalism was a response to the "universalistic demand" that "all groups should be recognized," but built, paradoxically, on the ideas of pluralism and toleration of difference (1997, p. 14). Intellectual historian David Hollinger argued that multiculturalism, as institutionalized in the United States, promoted the goal of cultural diversity by advocating a pluralism that "respects inherited boundaries and locates individuals within one or another of a series of ethno-racial groups to be protected and preserved." According to Hollinger, this kind of pluralism "endows with privilege particular groups, especially the communities that are well established at whatever time the ideal of pluralism is invoked" (2000, p. 84). At the root of multiculturalism is an implicit acceptance of the idea that the maintenance of cultural purity is desirable – if the culture in question belongs to one of what Hollinger calls the privileged minority groups.

In literary scholarship, the embrace of multiculturalism was accompanied by a move away from the formalism epitomized by the New Criticism toward contextually oriented forms of critique such as Marxism, feminism, deconstruction, New Historicism, and postcolonialism – and, in the field of "American Studies" a paradigm-shift away from the frontier and toward the borderlands. In "What We Know That We Don't Know: Remapping American Literary Studies" (1994), Carolyn Porter argued that the lines and boundaries that had long structured the field were being "remapped," the result of scholarship energized by identity politics: "Once compartmentalized by historical periods, American literature has been remapped first by African-Americanist and feminist critics and then by the flourishing scholarship on Asian American, Native American, and Chicano literatures." What made this remapping exciting if unnerving was the fact that "these emerging fields" promised new vantage points from which to survey the "American" scene, vantage points that are gained in part by severing the commonly accepted synecdochic identification of "America" with "the United States" (1994, p. 468). What was wrong with the old compartmentalization was its unstated reliance upon "frames . . . dictated by the national, and nationalist, narrative of the US" (p. 468). According to Porter, a work such as José David Saldívar's *The Dialectics of Our America* (1991) made manifest the possibilities of a new American studies because it saw American identities as plural and sought to provide alternative histories of the Americas. For example, Saldívar dared to ask what the literary and cultural history of the Americas would look like if we were to locate its "political and artistic capital" not anywhere in the United States but in Havana, Cuba (1991, p. xv).

In contrast to Glazer, Porter saw the remapping of the field as the work not only of African Americanists, but also of scholars like Saldívar who were working in what was frequently described as "minority discourse." In the introduction to *Ideology and Classic American Literature* (1986), an anthology to which Porter was a contributor, Myra Jehlen wrote that the collection was "inspired" by "an increasing recognition that the political categories of race, gender, and class enter into the formal making of American literature such that they underlie not only its themes, not only its characters and events, but its very language" (Bercovitch and Jehlen 1986, p. 1). In his afterword to the volume, Sacvan Bercovitch traced the "adversarial stance" adopted by most of its essays to the work being done in "Black Studies and Women's Studies." Scholars working in these fields, Bercovitch argued, "have contributed in many ways to American literary scholarship," but their "most important contribution has been ideological." Never again, according to Bercovitch, will we "be able to feel so pure about our acts of canonization, or so innocently to claim that our models of literary development embody the American spirit" (p. 423).

Ideology and Classic American Literature was among the texts that led Frederick Crews to coin the term "New Americanism" in an essay published in *The New York Review of Books* in 1988. Crews's essay made it clear that the "adversarial" stance to which Bercovitch refers had already spread well outside the disciplines of "Black Studies and Women's Studies" by the mid-1980s. The triumph of the New Americanism that Crews predicted at the end of his essay did indeed come to pass by the end of the 1990s, but proved ultimately to create an equally oppressive set of boundaries, which were in turn challenged by the need to create what Gregory Jay called a "multicultural and dialogical model for the study of writing in the United States" (1997, p. 172). Like many scholars who were then seeking to revise the academy's conception of "American Literature" in the light of multiculturalism, Jay found a useful conceptual tool in the idea of the "borderlands," which soon replaced the "frontier" as the dominant site within American Studies.

In the introduction to the collection *Cultures of United States Imperialism* (1993), Amy Kaplan called for a "multicultural critique of American ethnocentrism" that links the "internal categories of gender, race, and ethnicity to the global dynamics of empire-building." The goal of this critique is to deconstruct "the binary opposition of the foreign and the domestic," an opposition reinforced within American Studies by the field's early obsession with the idea of "the Frontier" in the aftermath of Henry Nash Smith's landmark study, *Virgin Land: The American West as Symbol and Myth* (1950). Describing "the Frontier" as "a major conceptual site in American studies," Kaplan noted that it has "undergone revision from the vacant space of the wilderness to a bloody battlefield of conflict and conquest, and more recently to a site of contacts, encounters, and collisions that produce new hybrid cultures." These accounts were limited by their reliance upon "a model of center and periphery, which confront one another most often in a one-way imposition of power." Kaplan found an alternative model in the field of Chicano studies, which had brought attention to writers like Oscar Zeta Acosta, Rudolfo Anaya, Gloria Anzaldúa, Sandra Cisneros, Rolando Hinojosa, Américo Paredes, and Tomás Rivera in order "to redress the conceptual limits of the frontier, by displacing it with the site of 'the borderlands'" (Kaplan and Pease 1993, p. 16).

Part of the problem with multiculturalism in the 1980s was that it often downplayed the importance of hybridity, which plays an outsized role in the literary imaginations of US writers associated with multiculturalism. In her contribution to *Poetics of the Americas* (1997), Mireille Rosello noted that "too often, when borders are conceived as 'frontiers,' they "continue to reproduce the binary fight between the colonizer and the colonized even if the opposition has become anachronistic." As a result, "the principle of the border" can serve to police essentialist conceptions of identity and "successfully pretends that hybridity is an exception to the rule of national homogeneity" (1997, p. 106). Developed most robustly by theorists of postcoloniality like Homi Bhabha, the concept of hybridity was a leap forward for theorists of minority discourse, addressing the "one-way imposition of power" that Kaplan identified and opening up what Bhabha called "the Third Space of enunciation" (1993, p. 54). In *The Location of Culture* (1994), the most influential account of cultural hybridity to appear during the 1990s, Bhabha himself points to the link between hybridity and the idea of the border by beginning with a section entitled "Border Lives" and pointing to "in-between" spaces that "provide the terrain for elaborating new strategies of selfhood ... that initiate new signs of identity, and innovative sites of collaboration, and contestation" (1994, pp. 1–2). Bhabha uses Mikhail Bakhtin's conception of hybridization as "a mixture of two social languages within the limits of a single utterance" (Bakhtin 1982, p. 358) to redescribe a binary relationship in which the two opposed terms are unequal in force: the colonial situation.

The concept of hybridity allows us to see that what appeared to be an either/or situation is in reality a situation of both/and. It thus breaks the constraints of the binary logic of hyphenation, which was frequently dramatized by early twentieth-century US ethnic writers. Writers like Sui Sin Far or Abraham Cahan sought to understand and represent how they and those like them were portrayed as different, incomprehensible, inscrutable, uncivilized – as "others" who could not be assimilated. They sought a solution to what might be called *the impasse of hyphenation*, the idea that the American who belongs to a minority group is caught between incompatible identities, the minority (ethnic or racial) and the majority ("American"). The writer Frank Chin called this phenomenon, in the Asian American context, the "dual personality" (1991, p. 27), as if somehow all Asian Americans were split down the middle and made schizophrenic by US culture. Identity thus becomes a matter of either/or: either "American" or whatever it is that precedes the hyphen, an idea expressed most famously in a 1915 speech in which Theodore Roosevelt asserted that "there is no such thing as a hyphenated American who is a good American. The only man who is a good American is the man who is an American and nothing else" (1923, pp. 457–458).

As Rosello points out, US mainstream culture has often sought to portray hybridity as "an exception to the rule of national homogeneity" (1997, p. 106). In contrast, emergent writers have understood hybridity to be a defining part of the subjectivities they sought to portray. But all too often, hybridity itself, with its reliance on binary modes of thinking, proves to be incapable of describing the ontological richness of emergent writing. For example, the account of identity offered in Anzaldúa's *Borderlands/La Frontera* (1987) moves beyond hybrid identity to a more complex model of heterogeneous identity. Anzaldúa describes herself as a "border woman": "I grew up between two cultures, the Mexican (with a heavy Indian influence) and the Anglo (as a member of a colonized people in our own territory). I have been straddling that *tejas*-Mexican border, and others, all my life" (2012, p. iii). The phrase "and others" is suggestive, for though the border is a powerful metaphor for Anzaldúa and other Latinx writers, it is still a metaphor that describes crossing from one cultural space into another: it is still a binary system. Anzaldúa describes herself as "*mestiza, mulata,* half-breed" (p. 194), yet these terms do not do justice to Anzaldúa's ethnic background, let alone her sexuality: elsewhere, she calls herself "a Chicana *tejana* lesbian-feminist poet and fiction-writer" (Aunt Lute n.d.).

Anzaldúa's landmark text uses the model of the borderlands to powerful metaphorical effect, even as it strains against the limitations of that model. *Borderlands/La Frontera* suggests that to understand emergence in US culture, we must move beyond the duality implicit in late-twentieth century theorizations of hybridity. What happens when two or more emergent categories are located in a single identity or text? To understand hybridity fully, imaginative writers and scholars had to make a transition from an understanding based on "either/or" to an understanding based on "both/and." The next stage, however, in the conceptualization of US emergent literatures, was to move beyond the duality implicit in the hybrid model of "both/ and" to a model that captures the interplay of multiple hybrid states.

This kind of heterogeneity is what appealed to Kaplan in the borderlands model that emphasized the "multidimensional and transterritorial"; for Chicano theorists, the borderlands "not only lie at the geographic and political margins of national identity but as often traverse the center of the metropolis. . . . The borderlands thus transform the traditional notion of the frontier from the primitive margins of civilization to a decentered cosmopolitanism" (Kaplan and Pease 1993, pp. 16–17). In retrospect, Kaplan's invocation of cosmopolitanism was an acknowledgment of some of the shortcomings of the ways in which multiculturalism was beginning to be institutionalized in the US. The philosopher Kwame Anthony Appiah has described multiculturalism as a "shape-shifter" that "often designates the disease it purports to cure" (2006b, p. xiii). If, as Glazer suggested, multiculturalism began as a corrective to universalism intended to add the values of diversity, pluralism, and tolerance to the universalism that serves as the foundation for US liberalism, when it became institutionalized in US educational institutions in the late twentieth century, it shifted towards an over-emphasis on pluralism. Ravitch described this shift in 1990 as a move away from "pluralistic multiculturalism" to a "new, particularistic multiculturalism," cautioning that "the pluralists seek a richer common culture; the particularists insist that no common culture is possible or desirable" (1990, p. 340).

The extent to which the particularistic view became enshrined in the academy is evident in the response given by the National Endowment for the Humanities to a proposal made by the literary scholars Abdul JanMohammed and David Lloyd, who had applied in 1986 for a conference on "The Nature and Context of Minority Discourse." Their application was rejected on the basis of one reviewer's argument that "the proposed conference would almost certainly devolve into an academic tower of Babel. It is not clear that a specialist on Native American literature, for example, will have much to say to someone specializing in African literature" (1991, p. 3). In recommending against funding a conference designed to provoke scholarly conversation among scholars of ethnic literatures, the reviewer both identified and perpetuated the problem with particularistic constructions of multiculturalism. The conference took place anyway, but without funding from the NEH.

Particularistic multiculturalism has the odd effect of replicating the divide-and-conquer strategy that the dominant culture of the United States (long-oriented around white Anglo-Saxon male Protestantism) has pursued to keep minority groups at loggerheads with one another. The central insight behind JanMohammed and Lloyd's conference proposal and the collection of essays to which it ultimately led was that "cultures designated as minorities have certain shared experiences by virtue of their similar antagonistic relationship to the dominant culture." For this reason, a productive way of understanding the work of writers who were identified with multiculturalism in the 1980s and 1990s is to see them as "emergent" writers.

Raymond Williams characterizes culture as a constant struggle for dominance in which a hegemonic mainstream seeks to defuse the challenges posed to it by both residual and emergent cultural forms. According to Williams, residual culture consists of those practices that are based on the "residue of … some previous social and cultural institution or formation," but continue to play a role in the present, while emergent culture serves as the site or set of sites where "new meanings and values, new practices, new relationships and kinds of relationships are continually being created" (1977, pp. 122–123). Both residual and emergent cultural forms can only be recognized and indeed conceived in relation to the dominant: each represents a form of negotiation between the margin and the center over the right to control meanings, values, and practices. The idea of the emergent thus offers a way of conceptualizing the literatures produced by "multicultural" writers during the late twentieth century. Inspired but also antagonized by a dominant "American" literary tradition that seems to exclude them and their writings, these writers find themselves with one foot inside and one foot outside of the US literary mainstream.

An emergent literature is therefore the literary expression of a cultural group that defines itself either as an alternative to or in direct opposition to a dominant mainstream. What makes the literature "emergent" is the fact that it portrays beliefs and practices that are taken to be "new" by the dominant culture, though in some cases they may in fact be thousands of years old, as in the case of the representations of Indigenous belief-systems in the work of writers like Sherman Alexie, Rudolfo Anaya, Louise Erdrich, Linda Hogan, N. Scott Momaday, Leslie Marmon Silko, or Gerald Vizenor. I want to emphasize, however, that an emergent literature is the expression of a cultural identity: avant-garde literatures are also literatures that identify themselves with the "new," but an avant-garde literature that is not the expression of a cultural identity, that orients itself, for example, around a set of formal practices or a philosophical stance, is not what I am describing as an "emergent literature."

What makes these Indigenous novelists – or writers like Maxine Hong Kingston, Toni Morrison, Ishmael Reed, and Karen Tei Yamashita – "emergent" is not their adoption of formally challenging narrative strategies, but rather their interest in remaking the idea of "the American" by filtering it through their own cultural experiences. In the case of a writer like Kingston, this experience is marked as much by California as it is by China. "I want my audience to include everyone," she wrote in an essay entitled "Cultural Mis-Readings by American Reviewers" (1982). Her audience, she claimed, included "everyone" – not only Chinese Americans, but also her "old English professors of the New Criticism school in Berkeley," for whom she embeds references "to Virginia Woolf, Elizabeth Barrett Browning, [and] Shakespeare." But she also writes for "those who are not English majors and don't play literary games" (1982, pp. 64–65). Aware that her writing deals with a culture that has not adequately been portrayed before, Kingston described the difficulty of bridging the gaps among these different audiences: "Sinologists have criticized me for not knowing myths and for distorting them; pirates correct my myths, revising them to make them conform to some traditional Chinese version. They don't understand that myths have to change, be useful or be forgotten. Like the people who carry them across oceans, the myths become American. The myths I write are new, American" (1991, p. 24).

Emergent writers like Kingston set themselves against the idea of cultural purity that lies behind contemporary US multiculturalism and identity politics. Emergent writing demonstrates the power of what Appiah calls "cosmopolitan contamination." Cultures, in Appiah's account, never tend toward purity: they tend toward change, toward mixing and miscegenation, toward an "endless process of imitation and revision" (2006a, p. 52). For Appiah, the term "cultural purity is an oxymoron" (2006b, p. 112). To keep a culture "pure" requires the vigilant policing often associated with fundamentalist regimes or xenophobic political parties. Like Williams's account of the interaction of dominant, residual, and emergent cultures, Appiah's description of culture is about "conversation across boundaries." Such conversations, Appiah writes, "can be delightful, or just vexing: what they mainly are, though, is inevitable" (2006b, p. xxi). Emergent writing conducts conversations with the dominant literary cultures of the United States – the culture of "Virginia Woolf, Elizabeth Barrett Browning, [and] Shakespeare" – that are both an inspiration and a source of antagonism.

The late-twentieth century theories of cosmopolitanism developed by Appiah and other thinkers, such as Craig Calhoun, Martha Nussbaum, Bruce Robbins, and Bryan Turner, offer a way of moving beyond the impasses created by particularist multiculturalism, particularly its tendency to adopt a stance of moral relativism. Originating in the idea of the "world citizen" and conceived in contradistinction to nationalism, cosmopolitanism has more recently been understood as an alternative to universalism, pluralism, and multiculturalism, ideas from which it draws but with which it also takes issue. By 2020, cosmopolitanism had become understood as a perspective that regards human difference as an opportunity rather than a problem to be solved. Cosmopolitanism is a structure of thought, a perspective that embraces difference and promotes the bridging of cultural gaps. This perspective underlies emergent writing from 1980 to 2020, which asks its readers to experience otherness by opening themselves up to another person's words and thoughts – a perspective that we might argue is a fundamental characteristic of the literary imagination generally.

In embracing cosmopolitanism, US emergent writing points to an untapped cultural resource, which, according to historian Thomas Bender, originates in the Dutch prehistory of New York City: "Very early in the city's history, difference and conflict among interests were acknowledged as not only inevitable but perhaps of positive value" (2002, p. 190). This perspective, however, has sometimes made New York City seem to be the most un-American place in the nation. "It is puzzling but true," Bender writes, "that the outlook associated with New York's cosmopolitan experience has been unable to establish itself as an American standard." That failure is linked to the continuing power of what Bender identifies as "the most influential myths of America … In spite of the narrowness and purity of the Puritan dream of a 'city upon a hill' and of agrarian Jeffersonianism, these myths have come to be associated with the essential America, evoking the virtues of the small town and the agricultural frontier" (p. 185). To characterize US multicultural writing as both emergent and cosmopolitan is to highlight how it sets itself against the grain of mainstream US cultural mythologies and historical narratives.

Multiculturalism became an unavoidable part of US higher education in the 1980s, a rejoinder to the universalist narratives of "American identity" like Theodore Roosevelt's 1915 diatribe against "hyphenated Americanism" (1923, pp. 457–458). But if US progressives seemingly won the culture wars of the late twentieth century, conservatives won the political war, with the election of Reagan in 1980, which triggered a massive redistribution of wealth upward and ultimately led to the election of Donald Trump. Speaking in 2016, novelist Rabih Alameddine argued, however, that "no matter how bleak things look these days, what with Trump and other racists yelling on the airwaves and committing overt acts of violence, we are living in a time of greater inclusivity than any other. More people are being allowed into the dominant culture, more people are being allowed to talk, maybe not all at the same volume, and there are still not enough voices, but things are quite a bit better than [they were in the 1960s], and that is reflected in our literature" (2018, p. 69). And yet, as Alameddine acknowledges, this development has been a mixed blessing, because publishers have sought to publish the work of emergent writers who are "safe, domesticated, just exotic enough to make our readers feel that they are liberal, not parochial or biased" (p. 71).

At the same time, the increasing diversity of publishable voices led to a resurgence of identity politics in the cultural sphere. In her National Book Award-winning collection of essays, *Minor Feelings: An Asian American Reckoning* (2020), Cathy Park Hong writes:

> At the time of my writing, this country has seen a retrenchment of identities on both sides of the political spectrum. The rise of white nationalism has led to many nonwhites defending their identities with rage and pride as well as demanding reparative action to compensate for centuries of whites' plundering from non-Western cultures. But a side effect of this justified rage has been a "stay in your lane" politics in which artists and writers are asked to speak only from their personal ethnic experiences. Such a politics not only assumes racial identity is pure – while ignoring the messy lived realities in which racial groups overlap – but reduces racial identity to intellectual property.
>
> (2020, pp. 101–102)

Like most of the "emergent" writers invoked in this essay, Hong believes that there is an "immeasurable value" in "cultural exchange," even as she recognizes that cultural exchange in the United States is driven by the logic of the market: "If the work of art circulates, it circulates for profit, which has been grossly reaped by white authorship." Hong is referring to the controversies over "cultural appropriation," which represent the return of particularistic multiculturalism to the fore in the US cultural sphere. "In reacting against the market economy," Hong writes, "we have internalized market logic where culture is hoarded as if it's a product that will depreciate in value if shared with others; where instead of decolonizing English, we are carving up English into hostile nation-states. The soul of innovation thrives on cross-cultural inspiration. If we are restricted to our lanes, culture will die" (2020, p. 102). Writers like Hong know that what US culture needs in the decades after 2020 is to embrace its identity as a heterogenous nation, to understand the claims of both universalism and multiculturalism, and to mediate between those claims by adopting a cosmopolitan perspective.

SEE ALSO: Border Fictions; The Culture Wars; Globalization; Indigenous Narratives; Kingston, Maxine Hong; Literature of the Americas; Morrison, Toni; Post-Soul and/or Post-Black Fiction; Queer and LGBT Fiction; Third-Wave Feminism

REFERENCES

Alameddine, Rabih. (2018). Comforting myths: notes from a purveyor. *Harper's Magazine* (June): 67–72.

American Association of Colleges for Teacher Education, Commission on Multicultural Education. (1973). No one model American: a statement on multicultural education. *Journal of Teacher Education* 24 (4): 264–265.

Anzaldúa, Gloria E. (2012). *Borderlands/La Frontera: The New Mestiza*. San Francisco: Aunt Lute Books; 1st ed. 1987.

Appiah, Kwame Anthony. (2006a). The case for contamination. *New York Times Magazine* (January 1, 2006): 30–37, 52.

Appiah, Kwame Anthony. (2006b). *Cosmopolitanism: Ethics in a World of Strangers*. New York: Norton.

Aunt Lute. (n.d.). Gloria Anzaldúa. auntlute.com/gloria-anzaldua (accessed September 24, 2021).

Bailyn, Bernard, Dallek, Robert, Davis, David Brion, et al. (1992). *The Great Republic: A History of the American People*, vol. 2. Boston: D.C. Heath; 1st ed. 1977.

Bakhtin, Mikhail M. (1982). *The Dialogic Imagination: Four Essays* (ed. Michael Holquist; trans. Caryl Emerson and Michael Holquist). Austin: University of Texas Press.

Bender, Thomas. (2002). New York as a center of difference. In: *The Unfinished City: New York and the Metropolitan Idea*, 185–197. New York: New Press.

Bercovitch, Sacvan and Jehlen, Myra. (eds.) (1986). *Ideology and Classic American Literature*. Cambridge: Cambridge University Press.

Bhabha, Homi. (1994). *The Location of Culture*. New York: Routledge.

Chin, Frank. (1991). Come all ye Asian American writers of the real and the fake. In: *The Big Aiiieeeee! An Anthology of Chinese American and Japanese American Literature* (ed. Jeffery Paul Chan, Frank Chin, Lawson Fusao Inada, and Shaw Wong), 1–93. New York: Meridian.

Crews, Frederick C. (1988). Whose American renaissance? *New York Review of Books* (October 27, 1988): 68–81.

Glazer, Nathan. (1997). *We Are All Multiculturalists Now*. Cambridge, MA: Harvard University Press.

Hollinger, David. (2000). *Postethnic America: Beyond Multiculturalism*, 10th anniv. ed. New York: Basic Books.

Hong, Cathy Park. (2020). *Minor Feelings: An Asian American Reckoning*. New York: One World.

JanMohammed, Abdul and Lloyd, David. (1991). *The Nature and Context of Minority Discourse*. New York: Oxford University Press.

Jay, Gregory S. (1997). *American Literature and the Culture Wars*. Ithaca, NY: Cornell University Press.

Kaplan, Amy and Pease, Donald. (eds.) (1993). *Cultures of United States Imperialism*. Durham, NC: Duke University Press.

Kingston, Maxine Hong. (1982). Cultural misreadings by American reviewers. In: *Asian and Western Writers in Dialogue* (ed. Guy Amirthanayagam), 55–65. London: Macmillan.

Kingston, Maxine Hong. (1991). Personal statement. In: *Approaches to Teaching Kingston's The Woman Warrior* (ed. Shirley Geok-lin Lim), 23–25. New York: The Modern Language Association of America.

Mizruchi, Susan L. (2008). *The Rise of Multicultural America: Economy and Print Culture, 1865–1915*. Chapel Hill: University of North Carolina Press.

Porter, Carolyn. (1994). What we know that we don't know: remapping American literary studies. *American Literary History* 6: 467–526.

Ravitch, Diane. (1990). Multiculturalism: e pluribus plures. *The American Scholar* 59: 337–354.

Roosevelt, Theodore. (1923). Americanism. Address to the Knights of Columbus, given at Carnegie Hall in New York on October 12, 1915. In: *Works of Theodore Roosevelt*. Memorial Edition, vol. 20, 457–458. New York: Scribner.

Rosello, Mireille. (1997). Interviews with the bridge-keeper: encounters between cultures as phantasmagorized in *Monty Python and the Holy Grail*. In *Poetics of the Americas: Race, Foundin, and Textuality* (ed. Bainard Cowan and Jefferson Humphries), 105–122. Baton Rouge: Louisiana State University Press.

Saldívar, José David. (1991). *The Dialectics of Our America: Genealogy, Cultural Critique, and Literary History*. Durham, NC: Duke University Press.

Sollors, Werner. (2017). *Challenges of Diversity: Essays on America*. New Brunswick, NJ: Rutgers University Press.

Williams, Raymond. (1977). *Marxism and Literature*. Oxford: Oxford University Press.

FURTHER READING

Calhoun, Craig. (2007). *Nations Matter: Culture, History, and the Cosmopolitan Dream*. New York: Routledge.

Cheah, Pheng and Robbins, Bruce. (eds.) (1998). *Cosmopolitics: Thinking and Feeling beyond the Nation*. Minneapolis: University of Minnesota Press.

Nussbaum, Martha J. et al. (1996). *For Love of Country: Debating the Limits of Patriotism* (ed. Joshua Cohen). Boston: Beacon.

Okin, Susan Moller et al. (1999). *Is Multiculturalism Bad for Women?* (ed. Joshua Cohen, Matthew Howard, and Martha C. Nussbaum). Princeton: Princeton University Press.

Turner, Bryan. (2008). *Rights and Virtues: Political Essays on Citizenship and Social Justice*. Oxford: Bardwell.

Nava, Michael

DANIEL ENRIQUE PÉREZ
University of Nevada, Reno, USA

Michael Nava (b. 1954) is a celebrated author who is most known for creating Henry Rios, the iconic gay Chicano criminal defense lawyer who serves as the leading protagonist of the acclaimed Henry Rios Mystery Series. The original series spans fifteen years and includes seven mystery novels: *The Little Death* (1986), *Goldenboy* (1988), *How Town* (1990), *The Hidden Law* (1992), *The Death of Friends* (1996), *The Burning Plain* (1997), and *Rag and Bone* (2001). Nava's life and work have been dedicated to advocating for social justice and human rights, especially as they pertain to LGBTQ communities and people of color. He has been instrumental in reconfiguring the detective fiction genre, and his work has been lauded for providing alternative literary heroes for marginalized people.

In 2013, the books in the Henry Rios Mystery Series were made available as e-books, and in 2016, Nava published a reimagining of the first novel of the series under the title *Lay Your Sleeping Head*. The remaining novels are slated to be reimagined and revised in order to capture the era in which they were written while addressing contemporary LGBTQ issues in US society. Moreover, *Lay Your Sleeping Head* was adapted into an audio drama podcast, the first of the Henry Rios Mysteries Podcasts, which the author continues to write and produce. These iterations of the Henry Rios Mystery Series underscore how relevant the topics and themes developed in the original series remain, especially to LGBTQ communities. Throughout the series, the leading protagonist struggles with several challenges: racism, homophobia, substance abuse, failed relationships, low self-esteem, health issues, and the death of a lover to AIDS. However, as David William Foster suggests, "the greatest form of margination Rios must deal with is homophobia" (2006, p. 74). Certainly, Rios engages in a seemingly never-ending battle against homophobia, both internalized and from external forces. Nevertheless, the protagonist has several redeeming personal characteristics and engages in actions that can be associated with heroes: he is smart, kind, and dedicated to helping others; he is committed to solving difficult crimes, especially those that directly impact members of the LGBTQ community; he remains steadfast in combatting homophobia and other forms of oppression; and he is a social justice advocate who continually works to address the social, legal, and personal injustices he witnesses or experiences. The novels document other forms of oppression that have shaped LGBTQ communities and Queer and Trans People of Color (QTPOC). What makes the series unique is that readers will find a gay Chicano hero at the center. Henry Rios is adept at handling difficult cases and solving mysterious crimes. He is an advocate for social justice, fights evildoers, exposes corruption, defends victims of violence and discrimination, and challenges patriarchy and homophobia. Rios is a necessary hero, portrayed in his full complexity. During a time when queer people had access to few, if any, representations of queer heroes of color, Henry Rios was there to save the day. The significance of his presence in American literature during the AIDS crisis, during a time when positive representations of queer people in popular culture was scant, and during a time when positive representations of queer people of color was even more scant, cannot be emphasized enough.

Nava's Henry Rios Mystery Series was also instrumental in redefining the detective fiction genre. As Garth Greenwell contends, Nava queers noir conventions by not portraying an outsider hero who embodied mainstream virtues: "In Nava's novels, sex scrambles the usual categories of whodunit: victim and assailant, suspect and investigator, and, above all, underbelly and élite. Eros is the great leveller, at least for a moment or two" (2015). In the novels, Rios's sexuality functions to disrupt the tropes prevalent in mystery novels, with the hero himself often at the center of unconventional and complicated homoerotic relationships.

In many ways, Nava has been a renegade throughout his career. Besides defying conventions regarding the detective fiction genre, his life and work have been grounded in social justice and social transformation. These are recurring themes in his nonfiction as well. The author is clearly invested in telling the stories of marginalized people who are powerful in their own right and who deserve to be treated with respect and dignity. Nava's nonfiction includes personal essays and essays advocating for LGBTQ rights. In 1994, for example, he co-authored *Created Equal: Why Gay Rights Matter to America*, which was among the first published works to advocate for marriage equality. Essays in this collection make arguments for advancing other LGBTQ rights and for the treatment of queer people as first-class citizens. Nava's commitment to advancing LGBTQ rights has been unyielding and remains a central theme in his life and work. His written works have also been lauded for exploring complex issues related to identity, especially as they pertain to the intersections of race, class, gender, and sexuality.

Nava has written poetry, short stories, and essays. For example, his autobiographical essays – "Gardenland," "Abuelo," "Coming Out and Born Again," "The Marriage of Michael and Bill," and "Boys Like Us" – appear in *Hometowns: Gay Men Write About Where They Belong* (1991), *A Member of the Family: Gay Men Write About Their Families* (1992), *Wrestling with the Angel: Faith and Religion in the Life of Gay Men* (1995), *Friends and Lovers: Gay Men Write About the Families They Create* (1996), and *Boys Like Us: Gay Men Tell Their Coming Out Stories* (1997), respectively. These essays give insight into Nava's childhood and young adulthood. He writes candidly about his tumultuous childhood, his vexed relationships with family members, and his relationships with men. The essays are heartfelt and inspiring. In them, one will note similarities between Nava's life and the lives of some of his protagonists. Nevertheless, his personal essays tell a unique story that help readers to understand Nava's formative years, which have shaped him and his writing to this day.

In 2014, Nava published *The City of Palaces*. Set in Mexico before and during the Mexican Revolution, the novel is the first of what is slated to be a series of four works of historical fiction that explore themes the author also explores in the Henry Rios Mystery Series: identity, oppression, and the struggle for human liberation. For Nava, identity and difference shape his characters in ways that help readers to understand the actions in which protagonists engage. His central characters face tremendous challenges in their lives. However, they also exhibit a remarkable amount of strength and resilience. His work adeptly cultivates empathy for individuals who are marked as different due to their appearances or the unconventional acts in which they engage. He portrays LGBTQ people as human beings in their full complexity and in opposition to some of the negative stereotypes that have been prevalent in US literature and popular culture for decades. His central characters are not flawless, but what is most significant and unique about them is that they are not tragic characters or a source of comedic relief. In them, readers will find authenticity, intelligence, strength, resilience, beauty, and hope. For LGBTQ and QTPOC communities, finding queer characters with such traits in US cultural production in the late twentieth and early twenty-first century was uncommon.

Nava's characters often inhabit liminal spaces and confront issues like poverty, racism, and homophobia. They also struggle with complex identity issues. For example, the name of the protagonist in his mystery series reflects the borderland identity of the leading character, with an English first name and a Spanish surname combined. Furthermore, although the last name "Ríos" is spelled in Spanish with an accent on the "i," in the Henry Rios Mystery Series, the accent is omitted. These cultural variances and nuances are indicative of the unique experiences of Chicanx and Latinx individuals living in the United States. Gender and sexual variances add another layer of complexity to this matrix. As Gloria Anzaldúa suggests, a *borderland* is "a vague and undetermined place created by the emotional residue of an unnatural boundary. It is in a constant state of transition. The prohibited and forbidden are its inhabitants" (2007, p. 25). Henry Rios's identity and experiences reflect this phenomenon. He is an outlier in most of the spaces he inhabits. His Chicano identity often conflicts with his gay identity; his working-class social background also clashes with the privileged spaces to which he is privy. Moreover, although his mystery novels are works of fiction and *City of Palaces* is historical fiction, Nava keenly embeds elements of his own life and his family in his works. Besides being an award-winning writer, Nava worked as a gay Chicano lawyer for most of his adult career; he also has roots in Mexico. Nava's ancestors fled the Mexican Revolution and serve as a basis for some of the characters in *City of Palaces*. These key aspects of his own identity shape his writing and his characters in complex and meaningful ways. Henry Rios, for example, experiences many challenges and goes through several transformations throughout the mystery series. A brief comparison between the first novel of the series – *The Little Death* – and the last one – *Rag and Bone* – will reveal stark differences in the leading character. Rios matures and ages throughout the series. Whereas the first novel has few references to Chicano/Latino/Mexican culture, the last one is almost entirely dedicated to this theme. Moreover, whereas in early novels in the series the leading protagonist falls in love with and exhibits desire for white men and pursues relationships that are typically unattainable or fleeting, the last novel in the original series contains a lasting romantic relationship between the main protagonist and another Chicano male.

The novels in the mystery series highlight important and necessary processes that some gay men of color experience while living in the United States, where they often confront racism and homophobia on a daily basis while dealing with past traumas. As David William Foster suggests, when Rios is the victim of homophobia, "he returns to the brutality of his father, fully aware that the latter was only blindly, fearfully enacting the wide-ranging discourse of homophobia" (2016, p. 76). Foster also believes Rios's memories of a childhood plagued by homophobia are what help him develop the strategies to survive living as an openly gay man and give him "privileged information necessary to solve the murders with which he comes into contact" (p. 77). In other words, Rios's experience confronting homophobia as a child and in the present-day context of the narrative provide the crime fighter with the ability to identify with other victims of homophobia in order to help him solve difficult cases, which is why the author's own identity remains vital to a discussion of his work.

Nava's great-grandparents migrated to the United States from Mexico during the Mexican Revolution; they eventually settled in Sacramento, California. Born on September 16, 1954, as an illegitimate child, Michael Angel Nava experienced a tumultuous and unhappy childhood. He was raised by his mother and stepfather in Gardenland, a working-class Mexican neighborhood in the Sacramento, California, area. Nava's stepfather was an alcoholic, abusive, and domineering. The author describes his childhood as a form of imprisonment; he was an introverted child who lived in isolation. At the age of 11 years, he was molested. He found solace in books, learning, and writing and began writing poetry at the age of 14. He left home at the age of 17 years to go to college. Nava was the first in his family to attend and graduate from college. He obtained a BA in history from Colorado College in 1976 and his JD from Stanford Law School in 1981. Nava developed his careers as a writer and lawyer simultaneously.

He began writing as a way to deal with his sexuality. He eventually established himself as a pioneer and advocate for LGBTQ rights in both professions. Inspired by the mystery novels of Joseph Hansen and the Dave Brandstetter series, Nava began writing the first novel of his Henry Rios Mystery Series when he was in law school. As he developed his literary and legal careers, he remained invested in advocacy work centered on advancing civil and human rights for the LGBTQ community. From 1981 to 1984 he served as a deputy city attorney in Los Angeles. He worked in private practice from 1984 to 1986 and on the California Court of Appeals from 1986 to 1995. From 1996 to 1999, he returned to private practice primarily representing criminal defendants on appeal. He was a judicial attorney for the California Supreme Court in San Francisco from 1999 to 2016 and served on the staff of Justice Carlos Moreno until Moreno retired. In 2010, he was a candidate for a judicial position on the San Francisco Superior Court but lost by a narrow margin. Nava worked exclusively on death penalty appeals until he retired from his legal career in 2016. He has remained active in literary, legal, and political projects that advance civil and human rights for LGBTQ, QTPOC, and other marginalized communities.

Nava has received several awards recognizing his contributions and achievements. In 2002, he was awarded an honorary doctorate from Colorado College. His works have garnered six Lambda Literary Awards and several nominations for Lambda Literary Awards. The author also received the Bill Whitehead Lifetime Achievement Award from The Publishing Triangle in 2001. *City of Palaces* was awarded an International Latino Book Award in 2015. His work has been lauded for empowering LGBTQ communities and for tackling difficult and important subjects that mainstream writers tended to avoid, like homosexuality, poverty, racism, and AIDS. His novels are skillfully crafted and provide readers with a unique experience and perspective, which have distinguished the author and his work.

Nava resides in the San Francisco Bay Area with his partner. In 2017, he published *Street People*, a novella that centers on the lives of people Gloria Anzaldúa would describe as *atravesados*: "the squint-eyed, the perverse, the queer, the troublesome, the mongrel, the mulatto, the half-breed, the half dead; in short, those who cross over, pass over, or go through the confines of the 'normal'" (2007, p. 25). These are the people whose stories Anzaldúa and Nava are committed to telling, and they comprise a community to which both have dedicated their lives and works. In 2019, for example, Nava founded Persigo Press, which is committed to publishing genre fiction written by LGBTQ writers and writers of color. His contributions to letters and to the advancement of LGBTQ rights continue to inspire and directly impact others. He has a special interest in recounting historical narratives from diverse perspectives. As indicated above, his work is being disseminated in various formats and genres: historical fiction, revised editions of his mystery series, and podcasts, for example. Whether Nava is writing fiction, historical fiction, or nonfiction, he remains committed to social justice and social transformation. Although Henry Rios is a character that was created for a mystery series, for several of his readers, Nava remains the embodiment of the character – a true and necessary hero in nature and deed.

SEE ALSO: Border Fictions; Multiculturalism; Queer and LGBT Fiction; Trauma and Fiction; Urban Fiction

REFERENCES

Anzaldúa, Gloria. (2007). *Borderlands/La Frontera: The New Mestiza*, 3rd ed. San Francisco: Aunt Lute Books; 1st ed. 1987.

Foster, David William. (2006). *El Ambiente Nuestro: Chicano/Latino Homoerotic Writing*. Tempe, AZ: Bilingual Press/Editorial Bilingüe.

Greenwell, Garth. (2015). A gay mystery novelist who chronicles the aftermath of AIDS. *The New Yorker* (September 11, 2015). https://www.newyorker.com/books/page-turner/a-gay-mystery-novelist-who-chronicles-the-aftermath-of-aids (accessed July 10, 2021).

FURTHER READING

Baker Sotelo, Susan. (2005). *Chicano Detective Fiction: A Critical Study of Five Novelists*. Jefferson, NC: McFarland.

Day, Frances Ann. (2003). *Latina and Latino Voices in Literature: Lives and Work*. Westport, CT: Greenwood Press.

Ortiz, Ricardo L. (1993). Sexuality degree zero: pleasure and power in the novels of John Rechy, Arturo Islas, and Michael Nava. *Journal of Homosexuality* 26 (2–3): 111–126.

Pérez, Daniel Enrique. (2009). *Rethinking Chicana/o and Latina/o Popular Culture*. New York: Palgrave Macmillan.

Pérez, Daniel Enrique. (2010). La búsqueda de la justicia social: la lucha contra la homofobia y el racismo en la novela negra de Michael Nava. *Revista Iberoamericana* 76 (231): 409–424.

Rodríguez, Ralph. (2003). A poverty of relations: on not "Making *Familia* from Scratch," but "Scratching *Familia*." In: *Velvet Barrios: Popular Culture and Chicana/o Sexualities* (ed. Alicia Gaspar de Alba), 75–78. New York: Palgrave Macmillan.

Rodríguez, Ralph. (2005). *Brown Gumshoes: Detective Fiction and the Search for Chicano/a Identity*. Austin: University of Texas Press.

Naylor, Gloria

LESLEY LARKIN
Northern Michigan University, USA

Gloria Naylor was the author of six novels and the editor of a fiction anthology; she also published stories and essays in venues such as *The New York Times*, *Essence*, and *Yale Review*. Like Alice Walker and Toni Morrison, she was a key figure in the 1980s "renaissance" of Black women's writing (Gates 1993, p. x). Her debut novel, *The Women of Brewster Place* (1982), won the National Book Award for First Novel (the same year that Walker's *The Color Purple* nabbed the Fiction prize) and was adapted into a television miniseries in 1989. Naylor envisioned her first book and the three that followed – *Linden Hills* (1985), *Mama Day* (1988), and *Bailey's Café* (1992) – as a "quartet" in which she would build a richly imagined physical and spiritual world (Bonetti 2004, p. 54). This vision ultimately extended to a fifth novel, *The Men of Brewster Place* (1999), and an unfinished manuscript, *Sapphira Wade*. The complexity of Naylor's imaginative world, the richness of her archive, the remarkable blend of formal experimentation and emotional resonance in her works, and her facility in recording the diversity and fullness of Black lives make her one of the most accomplished and important fiction writers of the twentieth century.

Naylor was born in New York in 1950 to parents who had been sharecroppers in Mississippi and migrated just ahead of Gloria's birth so that their daughter could have opportunities they were denied in the Jim Crow South. Her mother, in particular, wanted her children to have access to a public library. Naylor explains, in the semi-autobiographical novel *1996*: "I inherited my love of books from my mother, who was never able to completely satisfy her hunger for reading" (2005, p. 3). As a teenager, Naylor found herself drawn to Victorian fiction which, later, she identified as sharing a "strong narrative drive" and "moral point of view" with her own work (Rowell 2004, pp. 152–153). Naylor's mother gave Gloria her first diary, and the constant writing that followed created a "pattern . . . that shaped the rest of [her] life: if you can't say it, write it" (Naylor 2005, p. 5). Naylor was, by her own account, a quiet child but an avid listener, which perhaps explains her keen ear for both vernacular language and the emotional undercurrents of dialogue – or, borrowing a metaphor from Naylor's jazz-inspired *Bailey's Café*, what we hear when we take it "one key down" (Naylor 1992, p. 34).

After she graduated from high school in 1968, Naylor became an evangelist for the Jehovah's Witnesses; amidst the turmoil of the 1960s, she felt drawn to the promise of a new world. She left the church in 1975 and enrolled at Medgar Evers College with plans to become a nurse; however, she was drawn to the study of literature and eventually transferred to Brooklyn College, where she graduated with an English degree in 1981. Naylor's transformative encounter with the works of Toni Morrison, Zora Neale Hurston, Ntozake Shange, and other Black women writers led her to believe she, too, could become an author. During her undergraduate studies – while working and, briefly, marrying – she wrote *The Women of Brewster Place*, published the same year she received her BA. She followed these dual accomplishments with an MA in African American Studies from Yale in 1983. Her second novel, *Linden Hills*, developed from her master's thesis – an indication of the scholarly aspect of her creative work, the "research that give her fictional creations indisputable factual credibility" (Edwards and Harris 2019, p. 323).

In her novels, Naylor "signified" on the writings of several Black forebears, including Hurston and Morrison, as well as James Baldwin, Ralph Ellison, Ann Petry, Jean Toomer, and Richard Wright (Gates 1993, p. x). In her critical work, she helped shape the Black literary canon. In 1995, she edited *Children of the Night: The Best Short Stories by Black Writers, 1967 to the Present*, a companion volume to Langston Hughes's *The Best Short Stories by Black Writers* (1969). Naylor's investments are clear: she organizes the volume thematically, rather than chronologically, with major sections ("Remembering...," "Affirming...," "Revealing the Self Divided...," and "Moving On...") that invite readers to draw connections on subjects such as slavery, the family, class divisions, and the future. *Children* is also impressively diverse. Well over half of the stories are written by women and several by queer writers; Southern, Northern, and Caribbean perspectives are included; and approaches range from the realist to the speculative. This range is also found in Naylor's oeuvre, which includes elements of naturalism, magical realism, historical fiction, the gothic, and the romance; traverses the Americas and beyond; and offers nuanced renderings of both women and men, including queer characters. In her critical and creative work, Naylor enacted a principle articulated in the Editor's Note that precedes *Children*: "We are not a monolithic people" (1995, n.p.). And the emphasis not only on "survival" but also on "affirmation" that Naylor, the editor, sees as an important development in contemporary Black fiction is evident in the scenes of healing and renewal found in her novels (p. xx).

Diversity, survival, and affirmation are all on display in Naylor's first book, *The Women of Brewster Place*. A series of connected short stories that evoke a specific place and community, *Brewster* calls to mind Sandra Cisneros's novel in vignettes, *The House on Mango Street* (1984), and Sherwood Anderson's "composite novel," *Winesburg, Ohio* (1919) (Jones 2020, p. vii). The title also signals, as novelist Tayari Jones writes, that the novel is "audaciously female" (p. vii). Naylor focuses on the "hard-edged, soft-centered, brutally demanding, and easily pleased" women who end up in the building at the end of Brewster Place, a street cut off from the rest of the city by a wall that represents the limitations enforced by racism and sexism (p. 4). Miss Mattie has lost her home because of a debt incurred bailing her son out of jail; Etta is alone after years of moving from city to city – and lover to lover; Kiswana has given up her middle-class life in neighboring Linden Hills (the setting of Naylor's second novel); Ciel and Cora Lee are single mothers; Lorraine and Theresa are a lesbian couple who were outed in their last neighborhood.

Despite its many struggles, Naylor also offers an "affirming" vision of this community of women. Mattie is its loving godmother, the "home" that Etta returns to, when her dreams of marriage are dashed, and the fierce godmother who, when Ciel's young daughter dies, intervenes in a powerful enactment of maternal care. Kiswana also has a salutary effect: by introducing Cora Lee to Shakespeare, she sparks an internal transformation, and her efforts to organize the residents against their negligent landlord are promising. At the end of the novel, Mattie dreams of the women of Brewster Place symbolically dismantling racism and sexism by tearing down the wall behind their building. When Mattie wakes up, readers don't know what will happen, but the possibility of transformation remains open.

By focusing so "audaciously" on women, Naylor has sometimes been misunderstood as "anti-male," a misreading frequently aimed at Black women writers. (One reviewer, for example, wrote that Naylor "has few kind words to waste on members of the other sex" [Wickenden 1993, p. 5]). In fact, *Brewster* offers sympathetic, though not exculpatory, treatments of male characters, including Ben, who drinks to cope with memories of his daughter's sexual abuse, and Eugene, who grapples with white patriarchal expectations. In *The Men of Brewster Place*, Naylor offers portraits as diverse and rich as those of its sister volume. Here, Naylor does not reduce Black men to their "[struggle] with the white world"; rather, she focuses on their family relationships and offers further context for their lives (Rowell 2004, p. 159). (Eugene, for example, is revealed to be gay.) Echoing Toni Morrison's motivation for writing *Song of Solomon* (1977), another book focused on Black men by an author often (mis)understood as writing primarily about women, Naylor wrote *The Men of Brewster Place* in honor of her father. But complex portrayals of men figure prominently in each of her novels. In the unfinished *Sapphira Wade*, Naylor's humanizing characterization extends to white men; the extant section focuses on a European man who becomes a slave owner in America.

Henry Louis Gates, Jr., argues that much of Naylor's work can be described as *"lyrical naturalism,"* in its pairing of social critique with psychological portraits and poetic language (1993, p. x). Many of her novels can also be described as speculative. Take, for example, *Linden Hills*, a gothic novel that also advances an economic critique. Naylor's focus is the privileged residents of the tony title neighborhood that, in its descending circular roads, resembles Dante's circles of hell. At the bottom lives real estate mogul and undertaker Luther (read: Lucifer) Nedeed, the last in a long line of Luther Nedeeds and, by some vague spiritual machination, the exact replica of his forefathers – the first of whom is the Faulknerian founder of the community. In addition to profiting from the lives and deaths of those who have given up "the mirror in [their] soul" to reside in his neighborhood, Luther has locked his wife in the basement with their dead son, whom he deems illegitimate (1985, p. 59). The series of Luthers that control Linden Hills are the embodiment of "survival" (rather than "affirmation") taken to its pathological extreme; the founder's desire to put a "beautiful, black wad of spit right in the white eye of America" is funded by the sale of his own wife and child and leads to generations plagued by illness, depression, divorce, suicide, and torture (p. 9).

The residents of Linden Hills struggle with the spiritual fall that accompanies their economic rise. For example, Xavier Donnell is disturbed by his love for a Black woman who does not fit into his plans for advancement, and Maxwell Smyth leads such a self-controlled life that he has virtually no sex drive and produces odorless bowel movements. (*Linden Hills* has less overt humor than most books by Naylor, but here we must chuckle at her literalization of the old saw, "he thinks his shit don't stink.") Narrative coherence is provided by Willie and Lester, young poets who, like Dante and Virgil in *The Divine Comedy*, travel through Linden Hills bearing witness to its ills and, finally, to a fire that promises to cleanse the neighborhood of the evils – acquisitiveness, individualism, exploitation – at its heart.

Naylor's pairing of social critique with metaphysical elements continues in the following two novels. Indeed, the "quartet" that begins with *The Women of Brewster Place* evinces layers of interconnected reality. The gothic *Linden Hills* is linked to *Brewster Place*, the most "realistic" of the narratives, by Kiswana – and to the magical realist *Mama Day* through Willa, Luther's wife and Mama Day's grand-niece. While trapped in her basement, Willa explores an archive of diaries, letters, and recipes that help her to construct a genealogy of the women who married into the Nedeed family and were cut off from their roots. Mama Day represents those roots; Willa (mis)remembers her as a "toothless" and "almost illiterate" backwoods relative, but in *Mama Day* she is shown to be smart, funny, strong, and a formidable healer (1985, p. 147). Mama Day's ancestral tree reaches back to Sapphira Wade, a mysterious matriarch who, as local lore has it, forced her white husband to deed Willow Springs, the fictional Sea Island where most of the novel takes place, to his slaves. (Naylor described Sapphira, the subject of her unfinished novel, as the "muse" who guided her work for decades, hinting at the scope of her unrealized vision [Edwards and Harris 2019, p. 325].)

Willow Springs is defined by this story of independence. Belonging to no US state and connected to the mainland by a bridge regularly destroyed by storms, the island is largely self-sufficient. It also bears strong links to the past without being stuck there: the residents mix traditional and modern medicine, and they practice customs, such as the annual Candle Walk, that change with each generation. Cocoa, Mama Day's other grand-niece, maintains her island roots even while pursuing a career in New York, where she meets and eventually marries George, a businessman whose lack of ancestral connection is literal: he is an orphan. When visiting the island, George begins to experience a powerful transformation in the context of Black community, though he remains skeptical toward traditional beliefs. When Cocoa becomes the victim of a spiritual attack, he is slow to accept supernatural explanations, a shortcoming that leads to his death even while he manages to save his wife. (Naylor intended the love story in *Mama Day* to echo *Romeo and Juliet*, but many critics have also seen parallels to *The Tempest* – the island setting, the climactic storm – though Naylor's Miranda, Mama Day's given name, is not the daughter of the sorcerer but the sorcerer herself.)

Ill-fated George also provides a link to *Bailey's Café* which, like *The Women of Brewster Place*, focuses on a single street, but this time the street is a version of limbo, a halfway point between life and death. The titular café can be entered from anywhere in the world, and its backdoor leads to an endless void (rather than a wall). The café's neighbors include a pawn shop and a boardinghouse/brothel whose respective proprietors, like the unnamed owner of the café, play undefined spiritual roles (though Gabe's and Eve's roles might be hinted at by their biblical names). *Bailey's Café* is grounded in the "real": it takes place in 1948 and 1949, its characters discuss Negro baseball leagues and the formation of the state of Israel, and it includes detailed accounts of its residents' (often traumatic) experiences. But it is also grounded in the spiritual: Judaism and Christianity figure prominently, not least in the culminating story of Mariam, an Ethiopian Jewish girl who appears to re-enact the biblical virgin birth. Her baby is George, who points out Bailey's Café, in *Mama Day*, as the location of his birth. The fact that the café can be, at once, a real place on a real street and a supernatural place-that-is-no-place suggests that the layering of the supernatural and the real might also characterize Brewster Place, Linden Hills, and Willow Springs.

Reality's layered complexity is also apparent in Naylor's depiction of complex interior realities shaped by memory and time. "Time's passage through the memory," the narrator of *The Women of Brewster Place* tells us, "is like molten glass that can be opaque or crystallize at any given moment at will: a thousand days are melted into one conversation, one glance, one hurt, and one hurt can be shattered and sprinkled over a thousand days" (2020, p. 35). Just a few pages later, we see the effects of memory not just on a character but on narration itself, as Mattie watches her son transform, in a single paragraph, from a baby whose legs "only reached the top rung of his chair" into a "man who was gulping coffee and shoveling oatmeal into his mouth" (p. 40). This breathtaking passage (which literalizes the maternal cliché, "they grow up so fast") is in the middle of a very long memory brought on, the day the elderly Mattie moves into Brewster Place, by the aroma of sugar cane. The fact that this aroma can only be imaginary, given Mattie's surroundings, adds another layer to this Proustian moment, for it is the memory itself that produces the olfactory sensation that brings it to consciousness, while also drawing Mattie's – and the reader's – attention to the expansion and contraction of time.

When readers later encounter examples of Mattie's maternal strength, their memory of Mattie's memories will also remind them that this powerful figure was once herself a young woman in need of help. That Black women, who, all too often, are expected to be strong in the face of impossible obstacles and who live in the shadow of myths of maternal pathology, are a mix of strength and vulnerability is a crucial point for Naylor. Even Mama Day, the embodiment of feminine spiritual power, was once a girl who lost her mother and became "Little Mama" while she was still a child. Late in the novel, Mama Day encounters the spirit of her great-grandmother Sapphira, who dispenses the maternal care she desperately needed in her youth – and still needs as an old woman. In this moving encounter, Naylor evokes what it feels like to slip out of survival mode and into affirmation.

Naylor, creator of characters who offer and receive care in community with others, was both strong and vulnerable herself. In her last published novel, *1996*, she blends an autobiographical account of disturbing experiences of surveillance with a fictional account of the entities she believed responsible for that surveillance, a group that extends from a disgruntled neighbor to the National Security Agency (NSA). Naylor evokes the long history of federal surveillance of Black writers and intellectuals as well as experiences of local and interpersonal harassment familiar to Black Americans. Naylor's claims that she was the victim of mind control techniques are hard to accept as literally factual, but the truth of her experience – of a mind made vulnerable to unwelcome thoughts and scrutiny in the context of powerful agents of oppression – aligns with a truth illustrated throughout her works, and heightened for those who live with the daily realities of racism and sexism: that human beings are subject to the vagaries of a life lived across time, space, and memory; in a body that ages and breaks; with a spirit that needs the love and support of others while being vulnerable to the hurt others can cause; shaped and constrained by forces beyond our control and perception. Naylor died in 2016, but her works remain, not only as complex and beautiful examples of literary art but also as a map for surviving the human experience and affirming one another on the journey.

SEE ALSO: Afrofuturism; Bambara, Toni Cade; Cisneros, Sandra; Cleage, Pearl; Jones, Gayl; Morrison, Toni; Multiculturalism; Story Cycles; Walker, Alice; Ward, Jesmyn; Williams, Sherley Anne

REFERENCES

Bonetti, Kay. (2004). An interview with Gloria Naylor. In: *Conversations with Gloria Naylor* (ed. Maxine Levon Montgomery), 39–64. Jackson: University Press of Mississippi.

Edwards, Suzanne M. and Harris, Trudier. (2019). Gloria Naylor's "Sapphira Wade": an unfinished manuscript from the archive. *African American Review* 52 (4): 323–340.

Gates, Henry Louis, Jr. (1993). Preface. In: *Gloria Naylor: Critical Perspectives Past and Present* (ed. Henry Louis Gates, Jr. and K.A. Appiah), ix–xii. New York: Amistad Press.

Jones, Tayari. (2020). Foreword. In: *The Women* (by Gloria Naylor), i–vii. Boston: Little, Brown.

Naylor, Gloria. (1985). *Linden Hills*. New York: Ticknor & Fields.

Naylor, Gloria. (1992). *Bailey's Café*. New York: Harcourt, Brace, Jovanovich.

Naylor, Gloria (ed.) (1995). *Children of the Night*. Boston: Little, Brown.

Naylor, Gloria. (2005). *1996*. Chicago: Third World Press.

Naylor, Gloria. (2020). *The Women of Brewster Place*. London: Penguin. Kindle ed; 1st ed. 1982.

Rowell, Charles H. (2004). An Interview with Gloria Naylor. In: *Conversations with Gloria Naylor* (ed. Maxine Lavon Montgomery), 151–167. Jackson: University Press of Mississippi.

Wickenden, Dorothy. (1993). Review of *The Women of Brewster Place*. In: *Gloria Naylor:*

Critical Perspectives Past and Present (ed. Henry Louis Gates, Jr. and K.A. Appiah), 4–6. New York: Amistad Press.

FURTHER READING

The Gloria Naylor Archive. (n.d.). https://wordpress.lehigh.edu/naylorarchive/

Harris, Trudier. (1996). *The Power of the Porch: The Storyteller's Craft in Zora Neale Hurston, Gloria Naylor, and Randall Kenan.* Athens: University of Georgia Press.

Montgomery, Maxine Lavon. (2010). *The Fiction of Gloria Naylor: Houses and Spaces of Resistance.* Knoxville: University of Tennessee Press.

Stave, Shirley A. (ed.) (2001). *Gloria Naylor: Strategy and Technique, Magic and Myth.* Newark: University of Delaware Press.

Whitt, Margaret Early. (1999). *Understanding Gloria Naylor.* Columbia: University of South Carolina Press.

The New Experimentalism/The Contemporary Avant-Garde

FLORE CHEVAILLIER
Texas State University, USA

In many ways, new experimental fictions do not diverge vastly different from the experimental tradition that precedes them – both question the nature of fiction writing. The works of William H. Gass, Raymond Federman, John Barth, Ronald Suckenik, Thomas Pynchon, Donald Barthelme, Ursula Le Guin, Robert Coover, Harry Mathews, Susan Sontag, and Clarence Major, to name only a few who were still completing important work during this period, ask us to ponder what literary forms can do. They deconstruct plot, character, and narrative or authorial voices to oppose narrative reliability and closure. Although the fictions of the authors listed above are uniquely different, they all propose to unsettle writing and reading techniques. The texts discussed in this entry continue to ponder the role of literature, but they do so from an emphasis on materiality: the literary materials engaged in the production of fiction themselves are a source of creation and questioning.

As Alexander Starre points out in *Metamedia: American Book Fictions and Literary Print Culture After Digitization* (2015), this rediscovery of the book as an artistic medium stems from the popularization of e-books and from the development of digital literature in the late 1990s. Starre thinks of reflexive fictions that highlight the relationship between narrative and design elements as "metamedia" because they invite readers to rediscover printed books as artistic media, while creating new modes of reading of the printed format. This research on materiality continues to question formal elements – language, genre, plot, and character – but they do so more radically. This is the case in the works of Carole Maso, R.M. Berry, Percival Everett, Christina Milletti, Karen Russell, and Renee Gladman, for example. For other writers, the page, as a locus of literary existence, becomes the object of interrogation. The works of Theresa Hak Kyung Cha, Debra Di Blasi, Lee Siegel, Mark Z. Danielewski, and Steve Tomasula, for instance, call for an exploration of the printed text – the white space on the page, its design elements, as well as the arbitrary and overlooked components of printed works. Finally, others invite readers to examine the physical existence of fiction: books' packaging, marketing, and even the "author" who writes them become part of this question. Michael Martone's play with the notion of author, plagiarism, and the boundaries of fiction and nonfiction are good examples of the manipulation of the materials of authorship. The work of Bhanu Kapil proposes to posit the process of writing itself as a literary material. Other writers take fiction outside of the fixed reality of the printed codex, breaking the boundaries of life, performance, and storytelling. Shelley Jackson's *Skin* (2003) and *SNOW* (2014), for example, bend the structures of narratives, making skin and snow the materials of composition. In short, fictions of the new avant-garde ask us to reconsider the materials of fiction in ways that other fictions, within realist frameworks, do not. It should be noted here that digital literature provides exciting avenues of research in the manipulation of the literary medium: *afternoon, a story* (1990) by Michael Joyce explores the participatory foundation of reading; Shelley Jackson's *Patchwork Girl* (1995) examines the monstrous patching elements of its electronic medium. Tomasula's *TOC* (2009), a story about time, uses time as a material of fiction in its digital existence. While these digital experiments are a part of the discovery of the literary material that concerns the new avant-garde, the focus here is strictly on experiments in printed works.

Understanding the criticism that has framed the foregrounding of materiality in new experimentalism clarifies its evolution and importance. Until about the last decade, literary criticism framed experimental literature within privative terms, highlighting the many fruitful ways in which fictions written by Kathy Acker, William Burroughs, and Gilbert Sorrentino, for example, have defied the arbitrariness of traditional fiction writing and resisted the oppressive messages that it conveys. Formal innovation has been perceived to negate social and literary conventions in its subversion of the notions of character or setting, in its opposition to hierarchical structures of plot, in its resistance to racist uses of themes and images, and so on. This often results in unstable, polyphonic, ironic, ambiguous, and contradictory texts that undermine traditional reading practices, break down the boundaries between high and low culture, or engage in pastiche and parody. In other words, literary experimentation has been interpreted as a response to modes of writing that have become accepted and habitual, but whose "normal" status is problematic.

These critical depictions, influenced in part by fiction writers' own manifestos, shaped experimental writing within an oppositional tradition – a reaction against conventional modes of storytelling. New experimental writing's research on textual materiality has invited readers to reconsider formal practices not as mere responses to oppressive models but as productions of alternative systems of knowledge and power, tangible in their physical presence. Thus, new experimental fictions are not limited to pushing back against restrictive models and messages. In addition, they are not distant from reality, lost in a self-regarding realm, as they are materially real in the world. Framing recent literary innovations this way implies that they do not just aim at contesting dominant modes of writing; they also aim at configuring different realities in their material presence. As fiction writer R.M. Berry explains, "the aim of experimental writing is not to disrupt conventions. Its aim is to find out what writing is. [. . .] I write as I do, not because I want to disrupt anything, but because I want to discover the literary medium" (Chevaillier 2017, pp. 20–21). In their discovery of the literary medium, writers like R.M. Berry reshape new experimentalism as a positive production, one that does not merely respond to past literary traditions and social models.

In line with the development of innovative writing's positive production, recent criticism has re-embedded the new avant-garde within progressive political movements. Marcel Cornis-Pope's *Narrative Innovation and Cultural Rewriting in the Cold War Era and After* (2001), Alex Houen's *Powers of Possibility: Experimental American Writing since the 1960s* (2012), Anthony Reed's *Freedom Time: The Poetics and Politics of Black Experimental Writing* (2014), Ellen

Berry's *Women's Experimental Writing: Negative Aesthetics and Feminist Critique* (2016), and Tyler Bradway's *Queer Experimental Literature: The Affective Politics of Bad Reading* (2017) have stressed new experimental writing's affirmative production of alternative models, realities, and norms as opposed to a negation of oppressive systems of power. As Bradway points out, recent research on experimental writing gives justice to the ways "new experimentalisms force a new reckoning with the category of 'the experimental' itself, attending to what it has failed to include," as these new experiments "embrace a politics of liveliness – in which words bring new worlds into being" (2019, pp. 26, 9). This being, this materially present mode of experimentation, is what the new avant-garde concerns itself with.

In R.M. Berry's *Frank* (2005), for instance, the exploration of the materials of writing takes the form of an "unwriting" Mary Shelley's *Frankenstein* (1818). Full of "unwrit[ing]" (2005, p. 13), "undoing" (p. 14), "unplot[ting]" (p. 15), "unfolding" (p. 19), and "unburden[ing]" (p. 181), the novel tells (or untells?) the story of Frank Stein, distant cousin of Gertrude, whose linguistic research interweaves Frank's contemporary preoccupations with Shelley's monster and Stein's linguistic research. Rife with absurd episodes, surprising juxtapositions, exaggerations, and impossible situations, the novel questions its own existence, asking what writing is and what unwriting is, and why novel writing needs unwriting. Because Berry asks these questions through the materials that traditionally craft fiction (words, plot, character, dialogue, etc.), he implies "that narratives [aren't] just representations of actions; they [are] actions themselves" (Chevaillier 2017, p. 14). Other new experimentalists have explored the matter of representation in their adventurous treatment of the materials of narration.

Percival Everett's novels, for example, redefine writing and interpretive categories, while pointing to the limitations of so-called difference, uniqueness, and innovation. In fact, most of Everett's fictions mock the pretenses of the very forms that they explore, probing the act of formal invention itself. When he writes a parody of poststructuralist discourses in *Glyph* (1999), for example, he also adopts a parodic stance to reveal the limitations of parody. In questioning the stability of the forms and genres he employs, Everett reveals that our reading techniques constrain us. Thus, he invites us, through the experience of unsettling modes of reading, to open the categories of form, genre, fiction writing, and reading.

Other writers of the new avant-garde have also explored these categories, especially in relation to narrative stability: the short stories of Karen Russell and Christina Milletti, for instance, create tension between everyday situations and impossible scenarios. This tension results in a back-and-forth between trust in the narrator, setting, and plot structure and a puzzlement about what seemed to fit, to make sense, to be effortless. In Russell's "Orange World" (2019), fearing to lose her son, a mother makes a deal with a devil that she breastfeeds in the middle of the night, while attending during the day a breastfeeding support group whose discussions are so poignantly realistic that we come to question their stability too since they effortlessly join the fantastic. In Milletti's "Parcel Post" (2006), a woman and the deliverer of a parcel leave each other notes to arrange the delivery. While the delivery is delayed for months, notes accumulate to create Post-it-yellow paper doors stuck to the walls of the protagonist's house, "and through them, she would often come and go" (Milletti 2006, p. 99). In playing with the stability of the categories of real, fictional, and truth, Russell and Milletti invite readers to rethink the literary components that create or disrupt the literary contract between reader and text.

In other works, the exploration of the fictional materials addresses the impossibility of expression. Consider, for example, the premise of Renee Gladman's trilogy – *Event Factory* (2010), *The Ravickians* (2011), and *Ana Patova Crosses a Bridge* (2013): in the city of Ravicka, speech is performed by bodily movements so that communication becomes an odd choreography of gestures, bows, and dances. In such a language, expressing oneself can be challenging: the impact of having to perform deep knee bends for three minutes as part of a daily conversational regimen is an interesting factor to contemplate. In this world, how does the life of one's body infiltrate communication? How does one convey implied or partial meanings? How does one render language's multiplicity? These fascinating interrogations about the corporeal nature of any oral communication also ask questions about the linguistic materials of the novels: the three Ravickian volumes wrestle with the ways in which a text using the printed codex can give justice to Ravic communication. The trilogy also ponders how movement can appear in the fixed reality of the novels. That is, Gladman explores language's movements through the themes of dislocation, translation, writing, and poetry reading, thereby problematizing the notion of communication.

Other new avant-garde writers ground their exploration of the fictional material in the page's relationship to words. In Carole Maso's *AVA* (1991) the poetic and the fictional intermingle in ways that foster a nonmasculine form of writing, materially present in the treatment of the page the novel lays on, much like the body of the protagonist, Ava Klein, on her death bed. She is a 39-year-old professor of comparative literature, who is dying of a rare cancer. The fragmented narrative offers variations on key themes that wander through Ava's mind – her miscarried pregnancy, the books she taught, her lovers and her three husbands, her family's experience of the Holocaust, her travels in Europe, and so forth – on August 15, 1990, the day of Iraq's invasion of Kuwait. The last moments of Ava's life, which escape more and more her control, organize the white page, fragmented by large expanses of unwritten text: the narrative invites poetic line-breaks into the world of fiction, thereby making spatial arrangement expressive.

This material preoccupation is in line with Maso's conception of writing as an open, fluid, and physical activity, which has led her to research the ways in which writing can be expressive both intellectually and sensually. She sees writing as "an experience that exists as heat or light, friction, dissolution, as spirit, as body, as a world that overflows the covers of the book, and crosses into a kind of derangement, a kind of urgency, waywardness, need – a pulsing, living, strange thing" (Evenson 1997). Such an approach to fiction asks that we reconsider the material existence of each word on the page, as well as the white page on which they are printed, as they become part of an embodied approach to language and knowledge. In *AVA*, the disconnected lines of writing take on an importance not available in works of literature where the text exists as a block of words readers go through and consume with no further thought about the page they appear on.

This exploration of the page's materiality is also central to the writing of Theresa Hak Kyung Cha, whose work calls attention to the trauma of dislocation, torture, and the participation of language in these traumas. The page of *DICTEE* (1982) bears the marks of colonization and of Western empires intermingled with gender oppression. The hybrid text is written in English and French, as well as Japanese, Chinese, and Korean whose physical existence calls attention to the domination of Western models and exoticism. This is not expressed linguistically but through the arrangement of the ink of the page of *DICTEE* – the black ink of the handwritten drafts of the book, the painted black ink of the calligraphic pages, and the pages entirely covered in black ink. The collage of verbal and visual texts – images, stills from movies, obscure photographs, and diagrams – bears no caption, nor are translations provided. Thus, Cha forces her readers to experience, through the materials of her fiction, the layers of oppression she presents in the hybrid novel. The material presence of the book in our hands ironically documents physically the impossibility to document the personal and historical trauma it calls attention to, thereby questioning our relationship to language and narrative, which is unavoidably exclusive.

Other writers have considered the surface of writing beyond its white expanses. In *Love in a Dead Language* (1999) by Lee Siegel, *House of Leaves* (2000) by Mark Z. Danielewski, and *Skin of the Sun: New Writing* (2017) by Debra Di Blasi, the materials of books are revisited through visual designs that break the boundaries between literature and visual arts. *S.* by J.J. Abrams and Doug Dorst (2013) pushes the limits of written fiction to the extent that the novel must be recognized on two levels – its physicality and its narrativity. The reviews of the work attest to this dual qualification, considering the novel "both as literature and as a physical object" (Everin 2013) and "a celebration of the book as a physical thing" (Tsouderos 2013). *S.* (2013) is made of *Ship of Theseus* by V.M. Straka, published in 1949, about the enigmatic life of S. *Ship of Thesus*, a text also written by J.J. Abrams and Doug Dorst, appears as a traditionally printed narrative that the characters of the novel pick up from the shelf of the library. This narrative takes the most physical space in the novel – it is the book we hold in our hands – but it functions as a holding place, quite literally, since another story evolves in it through the handwritten marginal comments of Eric and Jen. Eric is a graduate student in English; Jen is an undergraduate student who works at the library and discovers the book with Eric's margin notes. Their conversation generates a third level in the story – the unsolved mystery of Straka's life and writing. Different colors materialize the various stages and timeframes of their relationship, so that page design functions as a narrative tool. The metafictional activity of the narration is also displayed in the physicality of *S.* whose pages are worn and yellowed with library stamps, stains on the pages, and inserts from Eric and Jen (postcards, newspaper clippings, maps, photographs, and other mementos).

These inserts create a nonlinear narrative that readers generate in making connections between the "main" and marginal texts. As Dorst explains, "since we knew that our book was going to purport to be the very book that the two were passing back and forth, it made sense for those additional texts – the ones in the physical world, anyway – to be tucked between pages," in order to "embrace the feeling of play that it offered as fully as possible," enabling readers to "enjoy the idea of reading the exact copy that the two characters possessed" (2020, personal correspondence). These experiments with the construction of the book and its artifacts "in the physical world" call attention to the hierarchical visual presentation of any book. The inserts and the elaborate design elements of *S.* are involved in the telling of the story to the point that they take on narrative responsibilities.

In a similar vein, the work of Steve Tomasula explores the body of books that we often overlook. As Tomasula states, "I try to use the book as both metaphor *and* material – language as material, of course, but also its embodiment. [. . .] I tried to use the book that is *VAS* as a metaphor for the body and the body as a metaphor for the book. That is, *VAS* is very much about making the metaphor of the 'body as a text' literal: we're literally editing the ABCs – the AGCTs – of DNA and creating a type of writing that is an entity in itself"

(Chevaillier 2017, p. 202). *VAS* (2004) is the result of the collaboration between Tomasula and graphic designer Stephen Farrell. The novel is composed of a collage of documents about eugenics; tables of comparisons of cranial measurements and Miss America measurements since 1921; medical imaging; egg and sperm commercialization websites; IQ tests; biology patents; excerpts from anatomy, history, and natural history books; aesthetic surgery advertisements; newspaper articles; and a 25-page reproduction of chromosome 12 code. These documents interrelate with the life of Square, a writer whose wife suggests that he have a vasectomy after she has a miscarriage and an abortion. *VAS*, and many of Tomasula's novels, including *The Book of Portraiture* (2006), of which *VAS* should have been the last chapter, focus on questions of embodiment and materiality in the physical realm of the body and in the intellectual realm of writing and reading while exploring the relationship between textual and visual productions.

VAS: An Opera in Flatland, *The Book of Portraiture*, and *Once Human: Stories* (2014) present fictions that would not exist without their unique physical components. This allows readers to be aware of the material complexities of fiction that they usually take for granted; it also creates a new space for narrating stories that does not solely exist in the linear printed codex. In other words, Tomasula generates new modes of storytelling that do not merely respond to traditional writing frameworks, but also open avenues for fictional possibilities vibrant in the physical existence of texts.

These new possibilities expand the limits of fiction writing outside of the "writing" activity: Michael Martone works within this context, inviting readers to consider fiction not only in his printed books but also in the processes that surround their existence. He is interested in exploring textual materiality through the very existence of the book. This is evident in *Michael Martone* (2005), where the "Contributor's Notes" paint the story, at times funny, at times tragic, of the contributor, Michael Martone. The narrative is conceived out of a collage of voices that are all expressions of "Michael Martone," the author of *Michael Martone*. Yet, the "real" Michael Martone is probably not quite the Michael Martone of *Michael Martone*, though he is also that. Thus, for Martone, the writerly constraints that shape such notes are parallel to the construction of the authorial persona.

Furthermore, Martone's exploration of what surrounds fictional publications has ventured outside the parameters of the book the reader holds: when playing with the concepts of fact and fiction in *The Blue Guide to Indiana* (2001), Martone published fictive parts of the book as nonfiction. Indiana newspapers published sections of the book guiding people on things to explore while in Indiana. The publication of these fictional pieces as nonfiction performed, in the act of publication itself, the blurring of the line between fact and fiction that *The Blue Guide to Indiana* explores.

Martone's exploration of self-plagiarism and usurpation of authorship are further examples of his questioning of the context of literary delivery and distribution as part of fictional productions. In *Fort Wayne is Seventh on Hitler's List* (1990), Martone republished all of *Alive and Dead in Indiana* (1984), with the exception of three new short stories. Martone has also written as Neal Bowers, a poet who described the theft of his poetry, then republished by another author in *Words for the Taking: The Hunt for a Plagiarist* (2007). These experiments with authorship disrupt the frames of writing, so that – as in more mainstream examples by Dave Eggers and other *McSweeney's* writers – elements of texts that we usually disregard as unimportant – the cover pages, the marketing materials, the authoring tools, the promotions tools, and so forth – become part fiction. In addition, such experiments open the field of fiction to "the real world," thus blurring the separation between literature and everyday life.

This intrusion of the "outside" materials in fiction is also at stake in the work of Bhanu Kapil, for whom the writing process becomes part of the writing materials: it is as important as the "final" printed draft. An obvious example of this mode of performance/writing is *Schizophrene* (2011), a book whose draft was sealed in a Ziploc bag and thrown in the garden to spend months outdoors in the Colorado winter. The text, full of gaps created by the erased parts of the "winterized" manuscript, documents "Partition and its *trans-generational* effects: the high incidence of schizophrenia in diasporic Indian and Pakistani *communities*" (2011, p. i). The decaying process of the book in Kapil's garden allowed the creation of a void in her writing – a nonbeing of the work as it was left unwritten – while also impacting the narrative's own exploration of white space, gaps, syntactic experimentation, and fragmentation. The initial "failed" document, the pages of which became "curiously rigid" (p. i), sculpted the "fragments" that "attract each other" in the hybrid text (p. 22). In this case, the practice of generating fiction is equally if not more important and materially present than the published artifact, so that readers have to reconsider the process of writing while considering the process of generating new borders between India and Pakistan.

The stretching of the fictional boundaries in Kapil's work evokes other, perhaps more extreme, experiments with the material support of fiction that Shelley Jackson has explored in *Skin*, a project launched in 2003, involving the tattooing of Jackson's short story word by word on the skin of 2095 volunteers. This writing asks obvious questions about the nature of narrative, as it cannot be "read," will "die," and resists the linearity and closure that are the essence of printed fictions. Ironically, *Skin* makes a permanent mark on the volunteers' skin while it transforms writing into an impermanent product. The unfinished, living status of *Skin* implies the co-presence of multiple and different temporalities, narratives, and frames that underscore the materiality of literature while playing with the immaterial realities of contemporary dissemination of information. Jackson's next project, *SNOW*, started in 2014: it is a story written and designed word by word in snow and documented on Instagram. The site reads, "SNOW: A story in progress, weather permitting. (Read in reverse order.)" The photograph of each word presents an isolated visual story – a portrait of each word. In an age of climate anxiety, this work on snow combines matters of global warming, experimental story writing, digital reading practices, and visual materials. The merging of these elements asks questions about what literature is in today's political and physical contexts: in inviting the weather to control the progression of her work and define its existence, Jackson partially outsources authorial control, collaborating with a nonhuman entity that delineates the pace of her writing, as well as its physical shape and texture. Furthermore, the slow development of the story calls into action various mediums that help negotiate our understanding of time in storytelling. In using the anchoring nature of words in correlation with the melting elements of snow, Jackson situates *SNOW* as a locus of tension between permanence and ephemerality. In fact, in *SNOW*, the tension between the material reality of the work and its immaterial nature makes the short story improbable and contradictory, yet visually present in the photograph of each word, which stands on its own as a visual narrative.

These experiments with the many elements that constitute fiction call attention to their material presence, and it is in this presence – this manifestation in our life, physical and visceral – that new experimentalism generates novel structures of writing and reading. As such, new experimental fictions challenge readers to rethink aesthetic categories, especially as they relate to traditional ideas about narrative. Thus, new experimentalism makes fiction an active and contested concept, deliberately establishing its cultural significance. Yet, instead of merely responding to orthodox modes of fiction writing, new experimental works create innovative pathways to enlarge storytelling in the twenty-first century. In doing so, these works bring fiction to the limit, not only by activating and criticizing dominant literary and cultural codes, but also in creating dynamic forms that incorporate new realities. Indeed, their deviant material presence allows readers to reimagine how to conceive of writing and reading practices and to engage differently with the basic and more extreme components of fiction. As this entry has shown, writers' research in textual materiality encompasses multiple forms, modes, and materials, attesting to the depth and breadth of these alternative paths of storytelling. These writers perturb each other or resonate or contradict each other in their modes of experimentation, but ultimately each author incorporates textual materiality in ways that call for a reconsideration of the potential of fiction today. In other words, in providing open-ended ways to consider fiction, the works discussed here agitate against limiting categories. Through their material liveliness, these new avant-garde approaches strive to offer components for new ecosystems, semantic structures, as well as aesthetic, social, and political schemas.

SEE ALSO: Barth, John; Burroughs, William; Coover, Robert; Danielewski, Mark Z.; Everett, Percival; Federman, Raymond; Gass, William H.; Hypertext Fiction and Network Narratives; Maso, Carole; Mixed-Genre Fiction; Pynchon, Thomas; Russell, Karen; Siegel, Lee; Sorrentino, Gilbert; Tomasula, Steve

REFERENCES

Berry, Ralph M. (2005). *Frank*. Portland, OR: Chiasmus Press.

Bradway, Tyler. (2019). Introduction: the promise of experimental writing. *College Literature: A Journal of Critical Literary Studies* 46 (1): 1–31.

Chevaillier, Flore. (2017). *Divergent Trajectories: Interviews with Innovative Fiction Writers*. Columbus: Ohio State University Press.

Evenson, Brian. (1997). An interview with Carole Maso. *Rain Taxi* 2 (4). https://www.raintaxi.com/an-interview-with-carole-maso/ (accessed July 18, 2021).

Everin, Andrew. (2013). *Miami Herald/S*. by J.J. Abrams and Doug Dorst (review). https://andrewervin.com/2013/12/miami-herald-s-by-j-j-abrams-and-doug-dorst/ (accessed July 18, 2021).

Gass, William H. (1989). *Willie Masters' Lonesome Wife*. Normal, IL: Dalkey Archive Press.

Jackson, Shelley. (2003). *Skin*. https://ineradicablestain.com/skindex.html (accessed July 18, 2021).

Jackson, Shelley. (2014). *SNOW*. https://www.instagram.com/snowshelleyjackson/?hl=en (accessed July 18, 2021).

Kapil, Bhanu. (2011). *Schizophrene*. Callicoon, NY: Nightboat Books.

Martone, Michael. (2005). *Michael Martone*. Normal, IL: FC2.

Milletti, Christina. (2006). *The Religious and Other Fictions*. Pittsburgh: Carnegie Mellon University Press.

Tsouderos, Trine. (2013). Review: *S*. by J.J. Abrams and Doug Dorst. *Chicago Tribune* (November 28, 2013). https://www.chicagotribune.com/entertainment/books/ct-xpm-2013-11-28-chi-jj-abrams-s-review-20131128-story.html (accessed July 18, 2021).

FURTHER READING

Berry, Ellen. (2016). *Women's Experimental Writing: Negative Aesthetics and Feminist Critique*. London: Bloomsbury.

Bradway, Tyler. (2017). *Queer Experimental Literature: The Affective Politics of Bad Reading.* New York: Palgrave Macmillan.

Chevaillier, Flore. (2013). *The Body of Writing: An Erotics of Contemporary American Fiction.* Columbus: Ohio State University Press.

Houen, Alex. (2012). *Powers of Possibility: Experimental American Writing since the 1960s.* Oxford: Oxford University Press.

Reed, Anthony. (2014). *Freedom Time: The Poetics and Politics of Black Experimental Writing.* Baltimore: Johns Hopkins University Press.

Ng, Celeste

ROBERTA WOLFSON
Stanford University, USA

After graduating with a BA in English from Harvard in 2002, Celeste Ng took a fiction writing class at the Harvard Extension School that inspired her to pursue a lifelong dream: turning her side hobby of writing into a career. Ng's decision marked the beginning of a journey that has led her to become one of the most critically acclaimed American authors of the twenty-first century. Ng has published dozens of stories in major newspapers and literary journals, including *The New York Times, The Guardian, TriQuarterly, The Bellevue Literary Review,* and *The Alaska Quarterly Review,* as well as two best-selling novels, *Everything I Never Told You* (2014) and *Little Fires Everywhere* (2017). She has won numerous awards, including the Pushcart Prize and a fellowship from the National Endowment for the Humanities. Ng's debut novel, *Everything I Never Told You,* was named a *New York Times* bestseller, a *New York Times* Notable Book of 2014, and Amazon's #1 Best Book of 2014. The book also won several awards, including the Massachusetts Book Award, the Asian/Pacific American Award for Literature, the American Library Association's Alex Award, and the Medici Book Club Prize. Her second novel, *Little Fires Everywhere,* was named a *New York Times* bestseller, Amazon's Best Fiction Title of 2017, and the recipient of the 2017 Goodreads Choice Award in Fiction. Both novels have been slated for cinematic adaptations; *Little Fires Everywhere* first aired as a mini-series starring Reese Witherspoon and Kerry Washington on Hulu on March 18, 2020, and *Everything I Never Told You* is currently in development to become a limited television series. Ng's notable success as a novelist can be attributed to the widespread appeal of her writing, which considers universal themes like the complexities of parent–child relationships, the growing pains of adolescence, and the impact of race, gender, and class on social interactions.

Ng was born in 1980 in Pittsburgh, Pennsylvania, the second daughter of immigrants from Hong Kong who had moved to the United States in 1968. When Ng was 10 years old, her family moved to Shaker Heights, Ohio, where she lived until moving to Boston to attend college. Both of her parents were scientists; her father worked as a physicist for NASA until passing away in 2004, and her mother was a chemist who taught at Cleveland State University. Ng's older sister eventually became an engineer, making Ng the only member of her family to choose a profession in the humanities. While growing up, Ng attended Shaker Heights High School, where she was the co-editor of the literary magazine, *Semanteme.* After graduating in 1998, she studied English at Harvard, where she recalls developing "an interest in where I had come from" (quoted in Weik 2017). She sought to explore her heritage by taking Asian American literature classes and studying Mandarin for a year. After deciding to pursue a literary career, she enrolled in the University of Michigan's MFA program, where she won the Hopwood Award for her short story "What Passes Over" (2007). During her graduate program, she met her agent, Julie Barer, and wrote a collection of short stories and two early chapters of the manuscript that would eventually become *Everything I Never Told You*. After spending six years to complete this novel and find a publisher, Ng was launched into the literary spotlight when she published the book in 2014, establishing herself as an important new voice in American fiction. By the time she was ready to find a publisher for her second novel, her reputation for crafting moving, page-turning, and thought-provoking fiction helped *Little Fires Everywhere* sell for seven figures. In addition to writing fiction, Ng has taught creative writing at the University of Michigan and GrubStreet, a creative writing center in Boston, and has served as an editor for the online literary journal *Fiction Writers Review*. Presently, Ng lives in Cambridge, Massachusetts, with her husband and son.

Everything I Never Told You explores the devastating consequences of being excluded on the basis of one's race or gender, a phenomenon that Ng herself experienced as a young Chinese American girl growing up in predominantly white neighborhoods in Pennsylvania and Ohio. As one of only a few Asian American households on the block, Ng's family was often subjected to harassment by the neighborhood kids, who would make prank calls to their house and put cherry bombs in their mailbox (Begley 2017). As a result of these experiences, Ng reflects that she became "interested in outliers" due to the experience of "feeling I was the only Asian or person of colour" and thus feeling "out of place but also conspicuous . . . continually other" (quoted in Laity 2017). Ng's experience as a highly visible outlier informs the tragic premise of *Everything I Never Told You*, which begins with three striking words: "Lydia is dead" (Ng 2014a, p. 1). Lydia is the 16-year-old middle daughter of an interracial family living in an Ohio college town in 1977 whose short life comes to a tragic end when she drowns in the local lake. Lydia is survived by her Chinese American father, James, her white American mother, Marilyn, and her two siblings, Nathan and Hannah. As these surviving family members struggle to make sense of Lydia's passing, the unspoken and unresolved complexities of being the only interracial family living in a majority white town begin to rise to the surface, much like Lydia's deformed corpse when it is eventually found floating in the lake's water. As Donna Miscolta argues in her review of this novel, "the root of the tragedy that the family suffers" is not only the loss of their precious middle daughter, but also the alienation of "being 'the other'" (2014, p. 11).

Since the reader knows Lydia is dead from the first page, the plot of *Everything I Never Told You* is centered on unraveling the circumstances that have led to her demise. To explore this history, the novel features two timelines: one that begins on the day of Lydia's disappearance and moves forward in time as her surviving family members struggle with the fallout of this disruption, and another that begins on the day of James and Marilyn's first meeting in 1957 and continues up to the night of Lydia's passing. As these two timelines weave together under the direction of an omniscient third-person narrator, it gradually becomes clear that Lydia was driven to her premature death by a complex web of unspoken secrets within the family. Both Marilyn and James suffer from feelings of shame based on their gender (for Marilyn) and race (for James), but refuse to vocalize such feelings out of fear that doing so will make them undesirable in the eyes of the other. Marilyn's shame is rooted in her failure to fulfill her dream of becoming a medical doctor due to her status as a woman and a mother, while James's shame is rooted in his internalized racism as the US-born son of Chinese immigrants raised in an American society that views Asians as perpetually foreign. Plagued by these insecurities, both Marilyn and James seek to live vicariously through Lydia, who offers them the possibility of indirectly realizing their failed dreams (for James of becoming accepted by white society and for Marilyn of becoming a doctor). This possibility exists because Lydia, out of all three of their children, looks the most phenotypically European, sharing Marilyn's "same elfish chin and high cheekbones and left-cheek dimple, the same thin-shouldered build" and "blue eyes" (Ng 2014a, p. 3). Unfortunately, the burden of being expected to single-handedly fulfill her parents' dreams places Lydia under extreme stress. To satisfy her father's desperate yearning for one of his children to be popular, Lydia pretends to have friends at school, despite being entirely socially isolated. At the same time, in order to fulfill her mother's frantic desire for her to become a doctor, Lydia pretends to love and excel at science and math, despite earning failing grades in both subjects. After years of attempting to maintain this facade, Lydia begins to collapse under the weight of her parents' desires. At the height of her desperation, she sails a boat into the middle of the town's lake and jumps into the water, where she sinks to her death, turning her metaphorical drowning under the pressure of her parents' dreams into a literal tragedy. In this way, the weight of the family's many secrets – which were formed in the shadow of racism and sexism – constitute a cross-generational burden that ultimately drags Lydia's body under water.

Ng's second novel, *Little Fires Everywhere*, continues to explore similar themes found in *Everything I Never Told You*, such as the dynamics of intergenerational conflict, the destructiveness of family secrets, and the social tensions fueled by racial prejudices and class hierarchies. While water is a central motif in Ng's first novel, fire is a central motif in her second, which opens with an enormous house burning to the ground. This house belongs to the Richardson family, which consists of parents Bill and Elena and their four children, Trip, Lexie, Moody, and Izzy. This last family member, the narrator reveals, is suspected of having committed arson by deliberately lighting small fires in the middle of each bed in the house. After opening with this striking scene, the novel moves backwards in time to the previous June to recount the events that have led up to this conflagration, following a similar pattern found in *Everything I Never Told You* of using an omniscient narrator to unravel the secrets of the family's past. As the events of the previous year unfold, it becomes clear that this opening conflagration is the final culmination of several smaller fires that have been smoldering steadily throughout the year, ever since the Richardson family first acquired new tenants for their rental property on Winslow Road, the single artist Mia Warren and her teenage daughter Pearl.

One of these smoldering fires centers around the relationship between the two matriarchs of these families, Elena Richardson and Mia Warren. Elena embodies the white liberal spirit that reigns supreme in 1990s Shaker Heights, Ohio, a suburb of Cleveland that serves as the setting of this novel. Having grown up in Shaker Heights, Ng writes about the community with convincing clarity. Two railroad mogul brothers founded the town in 1911 to fulfill their vision of a perfectly planned alternative to Cleveland's city living. In an effort to promote what Ng calls "rule-oriented wholesome progressivism" (quoted in Laity 2017), these brothers designed Shaker Heights to be a regimented space, with rules that persist today about how residents are allowed to mow their lawns, where they are supposed to place their garbage bins, and when they are allowed to go trick-or-treating on Halloween. A third-generation Shaker resident,

Elena Richardson is more than happy to abide by these rules, which she believes has made the town an idyllic haven of morality and liberalism. Convinced that Shaker Heights is "the best community in America" (Ng 2017, p. 157), Elena has little reason to believe that she does not lead "a perfect life in a perfect place" (p. 158) until she meets Mia Warren, a woman who reminds Elena of the road not taken. Mia is, in many respects, Elena's opposite – a single mother who lives in poverty and leads an eccentric lifestyle by moving from place to place in order to create politicized works of art. For Elena, who once chose not to pursue her dream of becoming a Pulitzer Prize-winning journalist in order to lead a stable suburban life in Shaker Heights, Mia is profoundly disturbing because she demonstrates that it is possible to live contentedly in the midst of unpredictability and disorder. Mia lacks a routine, is driven by passion, and interprets the world in shades of gray, rather than according to clear-cut boundaries. As Elena grows increasingly threatened by Mia's free-spiritedness, "the hot speck of fury that had been carefully banked within her burst into flame" (p. 162), and she finds herself incensed by Mia's presence in her life and community. Fueled by this rage, Elena decides to dig into Mia's past and uncovers a disturbing secret about Pearl's origins that she uses to drive Mia and Pearl out of town. Elena's expulsion of her tenants in turn prompts Izzy (who has grown deeply fond of Mia) to burn down the Richardsons' house in protest against what she perceives to be her mother's selfishness. In representing the devastating consequences of Elena and Mia's relationship, the novel explores the lengths to which one will go to avoid examining one's own failures, suggesting that it is often more tempting to condemn others for their shortcomings than to take a hard look at one's own inability to live up to an imagined ideal.

Another smoldering fire that drives the plot of the novel centers around a custody battle for a baby named May Ling, the child of a woman named Bebe Chow who has recently immigrated to the United States from Guangdong and works with Mia at a local Chinese restaurant. Suffering from post-partum depression and desperate after being abandoned by her baby's father, Bebe decides one day to leave her months-old infant at a fire station. May Ling is eagerly taken in by a white couple, Linda and Mark McCullough, who rename the baby Mirabelle. When Bebe recovers from her post-partum depression and realizes that she has made a grave mistake in giving up her child, she endeavors to regain custody, igniting a highly publicized legal battle over who should have the rights to raise the infant – the impoverished and seemingly unstable birth mother or the wealthy and well connected McCulloughs. This plotline draws attention to the ethical complexities of transracial adoption, a practice that was becoming increasingly popular in the United States in the 1990s. Ng's interest in this topic can be traced back to the early 2000s, when a friend forwarded her a website featuring local resources for parents of children adopted from China. Ng recalls noting that this website was filled with "so many good intentions running smack into the brick wall of privilege, cultural differences, and assumptions" (quoted in Chung 2017). In response, Ng eventually wrote a short story, "How to Be Chinese" (2014b), which explores the perspective of an 18-year-old girl who was adopted from China by a single white American mother and raised without any connection to her Chinese heritage. In *Little Fires Everywhere*, Ng continues to explore the intricacies of transracial adoption by considering how both the logic of colorblindness and assumptions about white cultural superiority influence the custody battle over May Ling Chow/Mirabelle McCullough. During one of the courtroom scenes related to this battle, Bebe's lawyer, Ed Lim, questions Linda McCullough about her plans to nurture May Ling's/Mirabelle's connection to her Chinese heritage. When Linda admits that she knows little of Chinese culture, the novel raises questions about the ethical consequences of denying May Ling/Mirabelle knowledge of her cultural background, especially given that she will most certainly be treated as a racial other in the predominantly white suburb of Shaker Heights. Many of the town's residents, however, do not seem to recognize these concerns, including Linda, who insists on the witness stand, "It's not a requirement that we be experts in Chinese culture. The only requirement is that we love Mirabelle" (Ng 2017, p. 265), and Elena, who later tells her husband, "Honestly, I think this is a tremendous thing for Mirabelle. She'll be raised in a home that truly doesn't see race" (p. 269). Such remarks give voice to the ideology of colorblindness that has become the dominant racial dogma of the post-Civil Rights era. The flawed logic of this ideology is exposed through the plotline of the custody battle, as the basic premise of the McCulloughs' legal argument is that love and resources, rather than ethnic identity and biological ancestry, should be the main factors in determining one's right to parent, a premise that discredits the child's birth mother on the grounds that her poverty and foreignness as a Chinese national make her an unfit mother. The plotline of this custody battle allows the novel, then, to explore both how colorblind ideology can negatively impact the lived realities of people of color and how heteropatriarchal, racist narratives in US society establish the wealthy white woman as the prototypical standard for ideal motherhood.

Across all of her works of fiction, Ng seeks to understand the motivations behind human behavior and how such behaviors are informed by intersecting systems of oppression like racism, sexism, and classism. Ng has commented that her writing is "not always an intentionally political act, but it is often politicized by others, because my very existence – as a woman, as a mother, as an Asian, as a child of immigrants, as someone in an interracial relationship, and on and on and on – is politicized" (quoted in *TLS* n.d.). Ng's inherent politicization as one of the most successful Asian American woman writers of the twenty-first century is evident in the popularity of her Twitter account, which has hundreds of thousands of followers and routinely seeks to amplify the works of other writers of color and promote civil liberties. After the 2016 US presidential election, Ng popularized the hashtag #smallacts on Twitter, in which she called on her followers every Tuesday to make small but impactful gestures to combat intolerance and promote kindness, such as donating to Civil Rights efforts, volunteering at nonprofit organizations, calling state officials to advocate for inclusive legislation, or writing letters of solidarity to organizations targeted by hate crimes. The response to this call to action was, as Ng describes it, "overwhelming" (quoted in Laity 2017) and reflects Ng's notable influence among readers, activist, thinkers, and community members who view her not only as an important literary voice but also as an inspiring role model for promoting empathy and social justice.

SEE ALSO: Fiction and Affect; Kingston, Maxine Hong; Lahiri, Jhumpa; Lee, Chang-rae; Mukherjee, Bharati; Ozeki, Ruth; Suburban Narratives; Tan, Amy; Trauma and Fiction; Truong, Monique

REFERENCES

Begley, Sarah. (2017). Celeste Ng tackles race in the rust belt in *Little Fires Everywhere*. *Time* (September 14, 2017). https://time.com/4941018/celeste-ng-novelist/ (accessed July 10, 2021).

Chung, Nicole. (2017). "I've always been political": Celeste Ng and Nicole Chung in conversation. *Literary Hub* (September 12, 2017). https://lithub.com/ive-always-been-political-celeste-ng-and-nicole-chung-in-conversation/ (accessed July 10, 2021).

Laity, Paul. (2017). Celeste Ng: "It's a novel about race, and class and privilege." *The Guardian* (November 4, 2017). https://www.theguardian.com/books/2017/nov/04/celeste-ng-interview-little-fires-everywhere (accessed July 10, 2021).

Miscolta, Donna. (2014). *Everything I Never Told You* inviting to readers. *International Examiner* (July 16, 2014): 11.

Ng, Celeste. (2007). What passes over. *One Story* 86. New York: Maribeth Batcha.

Ng, Celeste. (2014a). *Everything I Never Told You*. New York: Penguin.

Ng, Celeste. (2014b). How to be Chinese. *Gulf Coast Magazine* 26 (1). http://gulfcoastmag.org/journal/26.1/how-to-be-chinese/ (accessed July 10, 2021).

Ng, Celeste. (2017). *Little Fires Everywhere*. New York: Penguin.

TLS. (n.d.). Twenty questions with Celeste Ng. *The Times Literary Supplement*. https://www.the-tls.co.uk/articles/twenty-questions-celeste-ng/ (accessed July 10, 2021).

Weik, Taylor. (2017). In *Little Fires Everywhere*, author Celeste Ng explores "Asianness" and family. *NBC News* (September 7, 2017). https://www.nbcnews.com/news/asian-america/little-fires-everywhere-author-celeste-ng-explores-asianness-family-n799391 (accessed July 10, 2021).

FURTHER READING

Bonilla-Silva, Eduardo. (2017). *Racism without Racists: Color-Blind Racism and Racial Inequality in Contemporary America*, 5th ed. Lanham, MD: Rowman & Littlefield.

Eng, David L. and Han, Shinhee. (2018). *Racial Melancholia, Racial Dissociation: On the Social and Psychic Lives of Asian Americans*. Durham, NC: Duke University Press.

Lamy, Nicole. (2018). Celeste Ng is more than a novelist. *The New York Times* (December 20, 2018). https://www.nytimes.com/2018/12/20/books/celeste-ng-everything-i-never-told-you-little-fires-everwhere.html

Milne, Leah. (2020). Inseparable suburbia. *Indiana Humanities* (March 16, 2020). https://indianahumanities.org/news/inseparable-suburbia/

Ng, Celeste. (2010). Why I don't want to be the next Amy Tan. *The Huffington Post* (March 18, 2010; updated May 25, 2011). https://www.huffpost.com/entry/why-i-dont-want-to-be-the_b_342340

Ng, Fae Myenne

YOUNGSUK CHAE
University of North Carolina at Pembroke, USA

Fae Myenne Ng, born on December 2, 1956, in San Francisco, is a Chinese American author, known for her highly acclaimed first novel *Bone* (1993), a finalist for the 1994 PEN/Faulkner Award, and her second novel *Steer Toward Rock* (2008), winner of a 2008 American Book Award. Ng's father emigrated from Guangzhou, China, in 1940 as a "paper son" to a legal Chinese immigrant living in San Francisco; it cost him US$4000 to buy his fake US citizenship (Ng 1993a, p. 12). Ng, the oldest of four siblings, grew up in San Francisco's Chinatown, spoke Cantonese at home, and, after her regular school, attended a Chinese school, writing her first stories in Chinese there. Ng received her BA in English from the University of California, Berkeley, and received her MFA at Columbia University in 1984. She lived in New York City for many years and teaches creative writing and literature at UC Berkeley and UCLA.

Ng's novels and short stories thus far are all set in San Francisco's Chinatown and reflect her own experience as well as her parents' lives there. Growing up among old Chinese bachelors, who ended up not being able to return home due to the immigration laws that limited the reentry of Chinese laborers, Ng was keenly aware of the adverse impact on the Chinese of US immigration laws and miscegenation laws (Ng 2019). In an interview with Noah Adams, Ng said she tried to write about Chinatown – the "insular" ethnic enclave – from the insider's perspective. She wanted to write about her parents' economic struggles, their frustrations, and their fear of stepping outside Chinatown. Ng's father worked as a dishwasher, cook, laborer, and merchant seaman, while her mother worked at sweatshops in Chinatown. Ng remembers the grueling work her mother endured as a seamstress, and she was often "called down to the shops to turn interfacing or iron pockets" (Adams 1993). Ng's experiences and memories of her mother as a seamstress and of her father as a merchant seaman are depicted in her short stories, "The First Dead Man" (1986), "A Red Sweater" (1986), "Last Night" (1987), and "Backdaire" (1989). Ng grew up hearing her father lamenting about his "bitter, no-luck life" and watching old Chinese men spending their days in Portsmouth Square. Ng acknowledges that her stories about Chinese immigrants, old Chinese bachelors, and her experiences in Chinatown are her way of repaying her own "unpayable emotional debt" for her father's sacrificing journey (Ng 1993a, p. 12).

Ng's first novel, Bone, which incorporates parts of her short stories "A Red Sweater" and "Backdaire," garnered critical attention from literary scholars. The novel interweaves the history of Chinese immigrants from the past to the present through the stories of Grandpa Leong, his paper son Leon, who works as a merchant seaman, and Mah, a seamstress in San Francisco's Chinatown, with a plot revolving around the suicide of Leila's half-sister Ona. Foregrounding Ona's tragedy in the late 1980s in San Francisco's Chinatown, Ng unfolds her story in reverse order, drawing attention to the causes of her death, Leon's and Mah's hardships and their enduring marriage for their daughters, as well as the lives of old and new immigrants confined in ethnic enclaves. Ng remarks in an interview, "I wanted to write about what it felt like to live in worlds of contrasts. Speaking Chinese but needing English. Mah and Leon came to this country for a better life, but they are shut inside a ghetto. What it felt like for their daughters to live in a glass globe, looking out at the world and sensing all the possibilities but not being able to leave" (Shaw 1993).

In Bone, Leila's stepfather, Leon, experienced social and economic exclusion against Chinese immigrants. Born in 1924 when the Chinese Exclusion Act was enacted, he came to the United States in 1942, claiming to be the son of Leong, who somehow had acquired US citizenship. The Chinese Exclusion Acts of 1882 and 1924 limited Chinese immigration to 105 persons per year and prohibited the reentry of those who left the United States, which created the overcrowding of old Chinese bachelors into Chinatowns – ethnic enclaves historically established in the 1850s when Chinese laborers entered the United States as gold miners, and which provided both physical protection and jobs when antagonism toward cheap Chinese laborers became intense in the 1870s. Leon had to buy a fake identity in order to immigrate during the time when the Exclusion Act prevented the Chinese from entering the United States, and he owed $5000 to his paper father Leong and promised to return Leong's bones to China after his death. Regarding the creation of paper sons, Ronald Takaki, in his book Strangers from a Different Shore (1989), explains that the 1906 earthquake in San Francisco and the accompanying fire destroyed most municipal records and birth certificates. Many Chinese laborers forged themselves birth certificates, falsely claiming that they were born in the United States, and they created slots for their paper sons and wives (Takaki 1989, pp. 234–235). In Bone, Leong's forged citizenship and his claim of Leon as his son on paper enabled Leon to come to the United States. After passing the interrogation at Angel Island, Leon reminds himself about keeping his fake identity on paper: "In this country, paper is more precious than blood" (Ng 1993b, p. 9).

Despite his "legal" citizenship, Leon finds himself segregated and excluded from mainstream society and cannot find any other jobs except to work as a cook, temporary laborer, and merchant seaman. His suitcase is full of rejection letters saying, "We don't want you" (Ng 1993b, p. 58). For Leon, "going back to China, only a bowl of bitterness to show for his life as a coolie" (p. 148), is a humiliation, and he realizes that his situation is not much different from Leong's, whose bones were not returned to China, because he was out at sea when Leong died. Leon's first child, Ona, who had a close relationship with him, bears the consequences of Leon's failed life. Ona's suicide is partly the result of her father's failure in his business partnership, Ong & Leong Laundry, in which Leon put his lifetime savings, and of her father's disapproval of her relationship with Ong's son Osvaldo after Leon was cheated by Ong. Although the question of why Ona killed herself is investigated from the beginning of the novel, Ng does not reduce Ona's death to a case of personal misjudgment; rather the reader is led to understand the tragic incident in terms of the broad social and economic circumstances that Leon's family has faced. Ona's suicide is her own way of escaping from the consequence of her family's deadlocked situation in Chinatown; Ona could not find any other way of escaping. Her broken bones, resulting from jumping off a building in Chinatown, implicate Leon's broken hope and the sense of loss in his life. Although Leon has lived in the United States for almost fifty years, his citizenship, in fact, has not given him any economic security or stable jobs, and his life has been socially confined to Chinatowns. When Leon applies for social security for retirement, he is questioned for having many aliases, which he made up out of fear of being caught for his false papers and on account of his distrust of the government. It is Leila who looks through Leon's papers and finds documents to prove his legal eligibility for social security. Just as Ng feels something owed to her father and pays her emotional debt in her writing, Leila comes to understand Leon's paper history and claims his rightful citizenship: "Leon had paid; Leon had earned his rights. American dollars. American time" (p. 58).

Ng's second novel, *Steer Toward Rock*, published fifteen years after *Bone*, is set in San Francisco's Chinatown from the early 1950s to the late 1970s and highlights the Chinese Confession Program for the paper sons during the McCarthy era. The novel follows the protagonist, Yuo Seen Leung, who bought the name Jack Moon Szeto in order to enter the United States at age 19 as a paper son to Yi-Tung ("Gold") Szeto, who had also entered the country as a paper son to a gold miner. Jack owes $4000 to Gold Szeto for the forged document and works as a butcher at Gold Szeto's Universal Market to pay off his debt; he feels that he lives "as if in a chicken cage" (Ng 2008, p. 8). Moreover, Gold Szeto has listed Jack not only as his paper son but also as married to Ilin Cheung – making him a paper husband for Ilin, who will come to the United States in order to be Gold Szeto's mistress, replacing his barren first wife in China. Besides the loss of his original identity, Gold Szeto's arrangement for Jack as a married man affects Jack's future and love life. Centering on Jack's dilemma as a paper son, the novel begins with his confession: "The woman I loved wasn't in love with me; the woman I married wasn't a wife to me. Ilin Cheung was my wife on paper. Indeed, she belonged to Yi-Tung Szeto. In debt, I also belonged to him. He was my father, paper, too" (p. 3). The woman Jack loves is Joice Qwan, born in San Francisco, working at the Underground Bathhouse, and he wants to create a new life with her.

Jack decides to enter the Chinese Confession Program in order to confess his falsified entry to the country, hoping that Joice would interpret his act as his declaration of love, once he was no longer a married man bound to his paper wife Ilin. He voluntarily surrenders his certificate of identity and passport to the Immigration and Naturalization Services (INS). The Chinese Confession Program, instituted by the INS in 1956, was presented as an amnesty program for the Chinese who had entered the country under false identities in exchange for permanent resident status. However, the Confession Program, according to Takaki, "gave the government a weapon to target certain Chinese residents" deemed to be involved in supporting the Chinese communist government, and the program created "poisonous divisions and distrust within the Chinese community" (Takaki 1989, p. 416). Ng, born in 1956, calls herself a "Confession baby" and remembers the paranoia and fear among the paper sons during the Confession era, as "deport is the first English word she heard her father spoke"; her father entered the Confession Program in 1966 so that her mother could become a naturalized citizen, but her father "lamented Confession, which ruined his already fragile marriage" (Ng 2019). Similarly, in *Steer Toward Rock*, Jack's exposure to the Confession Program backfires on him. As a result of Jack's confession of his false identity, his paper father, Gold Szeto, gets arrested and is deported to China. Although Jack is not being deported, his citizenship is revoked as a consequence, and Gold Szeto retaliates against him: his right hand is cut off by Gold Szeto's messenger as retribution. Moreover, Joice declares she has no desire to marry Jack and leaves San Francisco after giving birth to their daughter, Veda. Despite his effort to create a new life with the woman he loves, Jack's confession only creates more devastation and frustration, causing the loss of his citizenship, his right hand, his livelihood as a butcher, and Joice.

After Joice leaves, it is Jack's paper wife, Ilin, who helps him take care of Veda, and Jack and Ilin begin a love affair and find comfort with each other. Ironically, Jack and Ilin's fake marriage is actualized in their companionship, and they offer mutual support in their artificially created relations. Veda also trusts Ilin as if she is her real mother. Just as Leila in *Bone* embraces Leon's paper history, Veda learns about Jack's paper history and finds the coaching book about the Szeto family that he memorized in order to pass interrogation at Angel Island: "This book is my father's story. He memorized every lie in it and became another man's son. Now these lies have become his truth and his only truth is his love" (Ng 2008, p. 220). Veda realizes that the stories of paper sons are common and that she should break free of shame; she wants to inherit her father's loss of identity and his struggling life in Chinatown. It is Veda who completes Jack's life in America by applying for his naturalization, and she offers to accompany him as a translator for his naturalization interview. The novel ends with Veda choosing her father's paper son name, Jack Moon Szeto, for him to keep at the end of the interview: "I chose his fake name, the name he lived half his life with, the name he made with his own sweat, the name he surrendered for love, the name that made him true" (p. 255). Veda's help with Jack's naturalization is her way of repaying and showing her trust in Jack, who risked "steering toward rock" (p. 112) – thereby breaking free from fear and finding the courage he needed to reinvent a new life in the United States.

As depicted in *Bone* and *Steer Toward Rock*, Ng's San Francisco Chinatown is replete with immigrants suffering unstable legal and economic conditions while socially confined in their ethnic enclaves. The popular myth of Asian immigrants as a "successful minority" who quickly moved away from the ethnic ghetto and settled into the middle class outside Chinatown is not found in Ng's novels. Ng makes working-class immigrants visible and accentuates their legally vulnerable lives confined in ethnic communities. It is in Chinatown where paper sons Leon and Jack live with their fake identities. Leon's and Jack's struggles to survive in Chinatowns cannot be ascribed simply to their personal failure or to their paper son status. Rather, racial and legal exclusions and the structural inequality working against the Chinese and other minority immigrants are the main reason that their lives have been put in such a difficult situation. Chinatown bears the history of the Chinese Exclusion Acts and racial discrimination against the Chinese and Asians. In short, Chinatown as a historical space exemplifies a broader US history of racial minority workers who have been economically and ideologically exploited in domestic labor markets.

Moreover, Ng, through her novels, reexamines the history of Chinese immigrants in a manner that connects the immigrant past to renewed social and economic exclusion experienced by recent immigrants. Although several decades have passed since the Chinese Exclusion Act was repealed in 1943 and legal restrictions against Asians were abolished in 1964, bare life conditions for many recent immigrants reveal that they are still socially and economically marginalized. In *Bone*, Leila, who works as a community specialist and liaison between her school and recent Chinese immigrants, finds hardships and economic struggles continuing for recent immigrants: "Being inside their cramped apartment depresses me. I'm reminded that we've lived like that, too. The sewing machine next to the television, the rice bowls stacked on the table, the rolled-up blankets pushed to one side of the sofa" (Ng 1993b, p. 17). Through this highlighting of the poverty and need-driven life of recent immigrants working at sweatshops in Chinatowns, Ng discloses the manner in which immigrant workers have become the convenient target of contractors for exploitation as cheap labor. For Ng "the sewing machine is almost a metaphor" (Adams 1993) for the strenuous experience of immigrants from China. In the ongoing restructuring of Chinatown in the 1980s, the hiring of mostly female workers in labor-intensive areas renews the exploitation of immigrant laborers and seamstresses in San Francisco's Chinatown.

Ng's depictions of Chinatown and of immigrants confined in their ethnic enclaves underscore the pattern of the labor exploitation of racial minorities that has been continuously functioning with dividing lines between race, ethnicity, and gender. The ideological justification for stratifying the labor force in accordance with racial and ethnic differences has served to maintain class division and structural inequality. Ng's exposures of discriminatory legal restrictions against Chinese immigrants and underrepresented working-class Chinese immigrants show her critical awareness of the contradictory US policies against racial and ethnic minorities. *Bone* and *Steer Toward Rock* convey her dissident voice against oppressive legal and economic mechanisms with respect to racial minority immigrants in American society.

SEE ALSO: Hagedorn, Jessica; Jen, Gish; Kingston, Maxine Hong; Lahiri, Jhumpa; Lee, Chang-rae; Mukherjee, Bharati; Nguyen, Viet Thanh; Ozeki, Ruth; Tan, Amy; Yamashita, Karen Tei

REFERENCES

Adams, Noah. (1993). Chinese American novelist takes reverential look back. *NPR: All Things Considered* (February 4, 1993).

Ng, Fae Myenne. (1993a). False gold: my father's American journey. *The New Republic* (July 19/26, 1993): 12–13.

Ng, Fae Myenne. (1993b). *Bone*. New York: Harper Perennial.

Ng, Fae Myenne. (2008). *Steer Toward Rock*. New York: Hyperion.

Ng, Fae Myenne. (2019). Orphan bachelors. *Harper's Magazine* (February 5, 2019). https://harpers.org/archive/2019/02/orphan-bachelors-chinese-exclusion-act/ (accessed July 22, 2021).

Shaw, Angel V. (1993). Fae Myenne Ng. *BOMB* (April 1, 1993). https://bombmagazine.org/articles/fae-myenne-ng/ (accessed July 22, 2021).

Takaki, Ronald. (1989). *Strangers from a Different Shore*. Boston: Little, Brown.

FURTHER READING

Chang, Yoonmee. (2010). *Writing the Ghetto: Class, Authorship, and the Asian American Ethnic Enclave*. New Brunswick, NJ: Rutgers University Press.

Eng, David L. (2001). *Racial Castration: Managing Masculinity in Asian America*. Durham, NC: Duke University Press.

Koshy, Susan. (2004). *Sexual Naturalization: Asian Americans and Miscegenation*. Stanford: Stanford University Press.

Li, David L. (1998). *Imagining the Nation*. Stanford: Stanford University Press.

Lowe, Lisa. (1996). *Immigrant Acts: On Asian American Cultural Politics*. Durham, NC: Duke University Press.

Nguyen, Viet Thanh

THAOMI MICHELLE DINH
University of Washington, USA

Vietnamese American novelist, professor, and essayist Viet Thanh Nguyen was born on March 13, 1971, in Ban Mê Thuột (now known as Buôn Ma Thuột), Vietnam, and came to the United States as a refugee in 1975. Initially separated from his parents and older brother and placed with a sponsor family in Pennsylvania, Nguyen describes this experience as one of his first indelible moments in America (Harvard University 2018). His family reunited after two months, and they moved to San Jose, California, in 1978. Nguyen graduated from UC Berkeley with an English and ethnic studies degree in 1992. He continued his studies at Berkeley and graduated with a PhD in English in 1997. In 2002, Nguyen published his first scholarly book, *Race and Resistance: Literature and Politics in Asian America*, which discusses the heterogeneity of Asian America and the uncomfortable position that Asian American literature occupies in the literary marketplace and academic institutions. In 2016, Nguyen was awarded the Pulitzer Prize for Fiction for his debut novel, *The Sympathizer*, published in 2015. Later in 2016, Nguyen released *Nothing Ever Dies: Vietnam and the Memory of War*, a study on ethical memory and remembrance of the wars in Southeast Asia. In 2017, he received the MacArthur "genius grant" and published *The Refugees*, a short story collection that he worked on collectively for seventeen years (Nguyen, Fung, and Nguyen 2017). In 2018, Nguyen edited *The Displaced: Refugee Writers on Refugee Lives*, a collection of essays written by refugee writers around the world. Throughout his career, Nguyen has written numerous articles that have appeared in academic journals, such as *American Literary History*, *positions: East Asia cultures critique*, and *MELUS: Multi-Ethnic Literature of the United States*. He is also a contributing opinion writer on immigration, refugees, politics, culture, and Southeast Asia for *The New York Times*. He currently serves as University Professor, the Aerol Arnold Chair of English, and Professor of English, American Studies and Ethnicity, and Comparative Literature at the University of Southern California. He lives in Los Angeles with his wife, Professor Lan Duong, and their two children.

After his family moved to California in the late 1970s, Nguyen's parents opened the second Vietnamese grocery store in downtown

San Jose, where his family experienced racism and gun violence. Nguyen recalls a sign he saw outside their grocery store front's window, "Another American driven out of business by the Vietnamese," which helped him understand the precarious position that refugees and immigrants occupy in the United States (Nguyen 2018c). As a young child, Nguyen remembers being eager to watch Hollywood films about different wars and their battlefields, but it was movies about the Vietnam War from the American military's point of view that gave him pause. Films like *Full Metal Jacket* (1987) and *Apocalypse Now* (1979) focused on the battlefield from American soldiers' perspectives, creating violent and sensational representations of war and death. While these movies were heralded for their genius and antiwar commentary on the Vietnam War, they wholly lacked Vietnamese voices, as Vietnamese characters were relegated to the background and treated as secondary characters in both the film and the larger narrative around the war. Nguyen, grappling with his identity, was unsure of who to cheer for: the white American soldiers committing violence and fighting for their country, or the silent Vietnamese on the receiving end of the violence, who looked like him and his family? Recognizing that these films centered a Western perspective and ignored the stories he had heard from his family and the Vietnamese American community in San Jose, Nguyen was determined to one day tell a different version of Vietnamese American history.

Understanding a wider lens of American ethnic history became important for Nguyen to understand the afterlife of the Vietnam War and its legacies in American culture and memory. When he entered college as an English major, Nguyen soon found that most of the literature he was assigned did not consider Asian American voices. After taking a class in the ethnic studies department on Asian American history, Nguyen became a dual-major in both English and ethnic studies. Through his involvement in both departments, he was able to comprehend the ways in which war histories are written by those in power, and how minority literature was viewed in literary studies and the marketplace. Continuing his studies with a PhD in English, Nguyen was told in his first year of graduate school that he would not get a job on the academic market with a dissertation on Vietnamese American literature (Nguyen 2018a). Taking the advice of his advisers, Nguyen decided to write his dissertation on Asian American literature.

This led to his first scholarly monograph, *Race and Resistance*, which addresses the heterogeneity of Asian America, demographically and ideologically. Describing how the Asian American intellectual class unified under "Asian America" as a political front in the struggle for racial equality, Nguyen writes that Asian immigration post-1968 complicated the goals, methods, and ideologies of Asian America. Because ideological diversity "threatens the ability of Asian America to represent itself in a unified fashion," Nguyen proposes that Asian American communities are "capable of exercising the same rhetoric of pluralism that the American state does, promising equality but practicing hierarchy when it comes to dealing with various Asian ethnic groups with conflicting interests" (2002, p. 15). Citing Yen Le Espiritu's panethnic entrepreneurship and Lisa Lowe's discussion of heterogeneity in Asian America, *Race and Resistance* argues that different ethnic groups may enter into Asian America under a politically unequal partnership of representation, leadership, and power. This becomes significant in the literary marketplace and capitalist economy, which seek to commodify ethnic literature and identity politics by flattening Asian American identity for American consumption. In a society that is capable of transforming "acts of cultural and political resistance into commodity," Nguyen urges readers to recognize the "dissensus rather than consensus" in Asian America (pp. 17, 24). Examining novels written by a diverse range of Asian American writers, such as Le Ly Hayslip, Carlos Bulosan, the Eaton sisters, and Jessica Hagedorn, *Race and Resistance* highlights the importance of understanding the different histories, motivations, and goals of Asian America.

In both Nguyen's academic and fictional work, he critiques American imperialism, the erasure of Southeast Asian voices, and the flattening of Asian American experiences in the United States. Though he was an avid reader of Vietnamese American literature throughout his academic career, Nguyen felt that a more critical approach to the United States' involvement in Vietnam was missing, and this became his motivation for writing *The Sympathizer*. The first instinct of the book, Nguyen shares, was to be "very critical of the role of the Americans in Vietnam and not adopt the usual position of Vietnamese Americans, which is either to be grateful to be rescued by Americans, or conciliatory, not directly confrontational in the literature" (Tran 2015). In addition to critiquing the United States, Nguyen wanted to be critical of all sides: "I didn't want to let anybody off the hook, so the book is also very critical of South Vietnamese culture and politics and Vietnamese communism. Instead of choosing its targets selectively – only being critical of one group – it decides to hold everyone accountable" (Tran 2015).

Described by Nguyen as a spy and anti-American novel, *The Sympathizer* considers what it means for an individual, soldier, or community to hold multiple and contested allegiances. The unnamed, mixed-race narrator works for both the South Vietnamese and the American army while also playing the role of an informant for the North Vietnamese military during the Vietnam War. The narrator escapes Vietnam at the Fall of Saigon and ends up in California, where he begins teaching at a college and working on the Hollywood set of a new Vietnam War film, not unlike *Apocalypse Now*. As the title of the novel signals, the narrator is sympathetic to but also extremely critical of all sides, refusing to fully commit or align himself with one arm of the military or a singular ideological frame of thinking. Holding roles such as a government spy, double agent, "Oriental studies" instructor, movie script reviewer, and prisoner in a reeducation camp, the narrator grapples with different dimensions of the wars in Southeast Asia that are widely ignored in dominant American histories and popular culture.

Resisting binary ways of thinking about the war and its supposed end, *The Sympathizer* becomes an interesting novel in the context of Nguyen's work in *Race and Resistance*. Because of its prize-winning status, the novel has circulated within institutions that determine literary value. In addition to winning the Pulitzer Prize for Fiction, *The Sympathizer* has also been awarded the Dayton Literary Peace Prize, an Edgar Award for Best First Novel from the Mystery Writers of America, the First Novel Prize from the Center for Fiction, the Carnegie Medal for Excellence in Fiction from the American Library Association, le Prix du Meilleur Livre Étranger (Best Foreign Book in France), a California Book Award, and the Asian/Pacific American Award for Literature in Fiction from the Asian/Pacific American Librarians Association (Nguyen n.d.). Nguyen himself has asked what it means for *The Sympathizer* to be called Asian American literature in a world that holds certain expectations and demands for minority writers. In an interview with literary scholars Marguerite Nguyen and Catherine Fung, Nguyen considers how minority writers, such as Toni Morrison and Junot Diaz, "simultaneously subvert society but also represent society" in order to "affirm an America that can acknowledge its sins" (Nguyen, Fung, and Nguyen 2017, p. 211). Joining other politically conscious writers of color who are pushing American literature in "more progressive, possibly even radical directions," Nguyen aims to rethink what multicultural literature can be in the literary marketplace (p. 210). While *The Sympathizer* has been lauded and circulated in institutionalized spaces, its radical potential lies in its explicit critique of American imperialism and refusal to historicize the war within the context of winners or losers.

Published in 2016, *Nothing Ever Dies*, Nguyen's second scholarly monograph, focuses on the afterlife and memory of war in Vietnam and the diaspora. As Nguyen writes eloquently in the introduction, "all wars are fought twice, the first time on the battlefield, the second time in memory" (2016, p. 4). Engaging with memory scholars such as Maurice Halbwachs, James Young, and Paul Ricoeur, Nguyen argues that just memory and ethical remembrance includes remembering one's humanity and inhumanity; that is, the inhumane and violent acts that are committed during war, on both sides, must be acknowledged. While it is easier to remember one's own and forget others, we must confront the inhumane parts of war and ourselves to engage in more ethical ways of remembering. As memories are often facilitated through capital and nationalism, Nguyen argues that the fight over what is remembered becomes fueled by who holds the most power to circulate and implicate memory. Hollywood films and the American narrative of the war have permeated the industry of memory and fuel the sensationalism of violence and Western heroism during war, leading to video games and TV series that allow "the horrors of history [to be] transformed into entertainment" (p. 174). Examining different forms of cultural remembrance, he considers how cultural production from Cambodian, Laos, Hmong, Vietnamese, and Korean artists reveal alternative histories and memories that disrupt the dominant American narrative around the wars.

Nguyen describes silence and selective memory in *Nothing Ever Dies* as fundamental parts of American narratives of the Vietnam War and nationalism. Strategic forgetting and the erasure of refugee voices becomes essential to remembering the Vietnam War as a victorious one. Outside of his scholarly work, Nguyen's fiction and essays contribute to the larger intellectual and political project of ethical remembrance and historiography of the Vietnam War. In 2017, Nguyen published *The Refugees*, a stunning collection of short stories about Vietnamese refugees in the diaspora. Dedicating the book "to all refugees everywhere," Nguyen has shared that the book's intention was to "humanize Vietnamese refugees, to look at their domestic lives, to look at how they were suffering and how those emotions were similar to what we all feel" (2018c). Similar to how Asian Americans have been viewed or portrayed as a homogeneous political identity, Vietnamese refugees have also been characterized as a monolithic group, rather than one that holds individuals with different lived experiences based on intersections of class, sexuality, and gender. The short story collection features diverse characters, including a young man in San Francisco who begins asking questions around his sexuality after being sponsored by a queer couple, an aging man with dementia who calls his wife by another woman's name, and a married couple who visit their daughter in Saigon, where she teaches English. Through the diversity of characters and settings, *The Refugees* writes against the flattened narrative given to the Vietnamese diaspora, revealing the varied ways the war is lived and experienced within Vietnamese communities and how collective and individual memory changes within and across national borders.

"Black-Eyed Women," the first short story in the collection, is a moving and haunting depiction of silence, storytelling, and ghosts. Written from the perspective of a 38-year-old ghostwriter, the narrator and her mother escape Vietnam on a heavily overcrowded fisherman's boat. Neither the narrator nor her mother speaks about the violence or trauma of their escape, and the silence throughout the story becomes a means to survive, revealing the double-edged silence that exists in both American narratives and Vietnamese American communities. After being visited by her brother's ghosts and forced to confront the silences in their family, the narrator shifts from being a silent ghostwriter to a writer of her own stories. As Nguyen writes, "storytelling allows us to tell a different story about war and its relationship to our identity. In this way, storytelling changes how we remember and forget the war" (2016, p. 292). Writing herself and her family into history, the narrator reclaims some form of agency over the dominant history that overwrites Vietnamese voices, shifting her relationship to the war and to herself.

Continuing to amplify the many and diverse voices of refugees, in 2018, Nguyen edited *The Displaced*, a short essay collection written by refugees. The displaced, Nguyen writes, are those who are "mostly unwanted where they fled from; unwanted where they are, in refugee camps; and unwanted where they want to go" (2018b, p. 17). Nguyen reminds former refugees in the United States that they were welcome when American politics happened to align with welcoming refugees, whereas many refugees, such as Haitian or Syrian refugees today, are not. Because "the people we call voiceless oftentimes are not actually voiceless," these stories aim to create a just world in which refugees would be listened to as individuals rather than those who speak for a whole community of refugees (p. 20). Working against a framing of refugees as objects or problems to be solved, the collection features work from artists and writers from around the world, including Fatima Bhutto, Thi Bui, Porochista Khakpour, and Kao Kalia Yang.

In 2021, Nguyen published *The Committed*, the sequel to *The Sympathizer*. Set in France, *The Committed* explores French colonialism, Vietnamese diasporic history, and the global legacy of war.

With Isabelle Thuy Pelaud, Nguyen serves as the co-director of The Diasporic Vietnamese Artists Network (DVAN), a community that supports and promotes the voices of diasporic Vietnamese writers, poets, and artists and connects them to other cultural producers, diasporic communities, and audiences abroad. Highlighting the multifaceted voices of the diaspora, across national borders and generations, DVAN empowers and gives creative agency to diasporic Vietnamese communities. DVAN also publishes *diaCRITICS*, a blog that celebrates multifaceted identities across Vietnamese and Southeast Asian diasporas. While *diaCRITICS* makes space for cultural producers to address the afterlife of the Vietnam War and its numerous legacies, the blog emphasizes the importance of narrative plenitude, arguing that "a wide range of voices, perspectives, stylistic approaches and all types of stories (even those not explicitly dealing with "Vietnamese" or "diasporic" topics) – is vital and necessary in order to make evident the complexities within our communities" (DVAN n.d.).

Nguyen's wide, public-facing reach is unusual not only for an Asian American novelist but even more so for an Asian American academic. It is rare that an Asian American academic appears on *Late Night with Seth Meyers* or *The Charlie Rose Show*. As both a scholarly and a public writer, Nguyen often shares that he is careful to think about how his writing can be more accessible and reach a wider readership, rather than only catering to an academic audience. This is evident in his opinion articles in *The New York Times*, *The New Yorker*, and *The Washington Post*, which address contemporary issues such as immigration restrictions, Southeast Asian deportation, and affirmative action. With America's rising interest in revisiting, understanding, and narrating the Vietnam War, Nguyen is an insightful voice and figure who amplifies the work of other writers who call out and speak against American imperialism. He has noted that his writing relies heavily on the work of other Asian American writers and scholars, including Trinh T. Minh Ha, Le Ly Hayslip, lê thị diễm thúy, and Maxine Hong Kingston. Nguyen's contributions to American literature and cultural studies are invaluable, and he continues to be an important public scholar through his insightful commentary on politics, war, refugees, and Asian American studies.

SEE ALSO: Contemporary Fictions of War

REFERENCES

DVAN (Diasporic Vietnamese Artists Network). (n.d.). Mission. https://dvan.org/mission/ (accessed 13 July, 2021).

Harvard University. (2018). *Viet Thanh Nguyen, History, Identity, Politics, and the Art of Writing*. Radcliffe Institute (February 20, 2018). https://youtu.be/aiIKTkGFK7s (accessed 22 July 2019).

Nguyen, Marguerite and Fung, Catherine. (2017). On writing, radicalism, and literary value: an interview with Viet Thanh Nguyen. *MELUS* 42 (3): 201–221.

Nguyen, Viet Thanh. (2002). *Race and Resistance: Literature and Politics in Asian America*. Oxford: Oxford University Press.

Nguyen, Viet Thanh. (2016). *Nothing Ever Dies: Vietnam and the Memory of War*. Cambridge: Harvard University Press.

Nguyen, Viet Thanh. (2018a). Cannon Fodder. *The Washington Post* (May 3, 2018). https://www.washingtonpost.com/news/posteverything/wp/2018/05/03/feature/books-by-immigrants-foreigners-and-minorities-dont-diminish-the-classic-curriculum/?noredirect=on&utm_term=.6e0f545bfad9 (accessed July 13, 2021).

Nguyen, Viet Thanh. (ed.) (2018b). *The Displaced: Refugee Writers on Refugee Lives*. New York: Abrams Press.

Nguyen, Viet Thanh. (2018c). Viet Thanh Nguyen's stories of "refugees." Viet Thanh Nguyen (September 27, 2018). https://vietnguyen.info/2018/viet-thanh-nguyens-stories-of-refugees (accessed July 13, 2021).

Nguyen, Viet Thanh. (n.d.). Biography. Viet Thanh Nguyen. https://vietnguyen.info/author-viet-thanh-nguyen (accessed July 13, 2021).

Tran, Paul. (2015). Viet Thanh Nguyen: anger in the Asian American novel. *Asian American Writers' Workshop* (June 29, 2015). https://aaww.org/viet-thanh-nguyen-anger-asian-american-novel/ (accessed July 13, 2021).

FURTHER READING

LeMahieu, Michael and Naimou, Angela. (2017). An Interview with Viet Thanh Nguyen. *Contemporary Literature* 58 (4): 438–461.

Oates, Joyce Carol

ERIC KARL ANDERSON
Independent scholar, London, UK

Joyce Carol Oates (b. 1938) has the rare distinction of being not only one of America's most distinguished authors but also one of its most notoriously prolific. Oates first established her writing career in the early 1960s and by 1980 had published two dozen novels and collections of short stories. Oates's Wonderland Quartet (*A Garden of Earthly Delights* [1967], *Expensive People* [1968], *them* [1969], and *Wonderland* [1971]) explored the social and political landscape of modern-day America. This early work earned her widespread recognition and many awards, including a special O. Henry Award for continuing achievement, a National Book Award for her novel *them*, and her collection *The Wheel of Love and Other Stories* (1970) was a finalist for the Pulitzer Prize. As a university professor, Oates had also published a number of books of academic essays and anthologies that consider form and style through the work of particular authors. This amount of acclaim and productivity would be sufficient for the entire span of most literary writers' careers. Yet, for Oates, this served as a jumping off point for even more ambitious and experimental work.

In 1980 she published the novel *Bellefleur*, the first in a series of five "postmodern gothic" novels, and it was also her first bestseller. Oates's plan for the series was to provide perspectives on nineteenth- and twentieth-century America viewed through the prismatic lens of its most popular genres. This series of books was a dramatic departure from Oates's early starkly realistic novels in the way they imaginatively blend fantastical elements into their historical stories. The first in the series is written in a magic realist style that utilizes elements of a traditional family saga. It follows six generations of the wealthy and influential Bellefleur family who live in an expansive haunted house set within a region not unlike the Adirondacks. Since the author was born and raised in Lockport, New York, Oates has frequently reimagined different fictional areas of upstate New York for the purposes of her stories throughout her career. Oates incorporated into *Bellefleur* real events such as the War of 1812, John Brown's abolitionist activities, and the building of the Erie Canal into this wondrous family story which also includes a time-bending garden, a female vampire, and a supernatural cat. In mingling the real and the extraordinary, she provided a new perspective on issues such as economic disparity, political corruption, and racial divisions within society.

The Encyclopedia of Contemporary American Fiction 1980–2020, First Edition. Edited by Patrick O'Donnell, Stephen J. Burn, and Lesley Larkin.
© 2022 John Wiley & Sons Ltd. Published 2022 by John Wiley & Sons Ltd.

A Bloodsmoor Romance (1982), the second novel in the gothic quintet, consciously parodies the conventions of nineteenth-century romance novels by following the stories of young women looking for love and marriage, but also incorporates elements of melodrama, science fiction, and ghost stories. It tells the story of a late-nineteenth-century inventor's five daughters as they grow, marry, or reject marriage. This novel was Oates's most overt critique of the patriarchy since her earlier novel, *Do With Me What You Will* (1973). But, in *A Bloodsmoor Romance*, Oates also shows how the very form of romance novels is complicit with the idea that women must shape themselves to fit into social expectations. *Mysteries of Winterthurn* (1984), the third novel in the gothic quintet, utilizes elements of the detective novel to explore three separate mysteries within a fictional community. Xavier Kilgarvan, the idealistic and philosophical hero of the novel, becomes an embodiment of late-nineteenth-century American dreams of progress. His quest is both thrilling and horrific, but the cases he endeavors to solve also represent the virulent misogyny as well as the class and race warfare which is endemic to American society. These first three novels in the series all share strong thematic links as well as stylistic flourishes, but stand as distinct independent novels.

After enthusiastically pursuing this ambitious series at a rapid pace, Oates only completed drafts of two further novels for the gothic quintet in the 1980s but did not fully revise and publish them until much later. The fourth book, *My Heart Laid Bare* (1998), differs from the previous three novels in that it doesn't contain any explicit supernatural elements and doesn't overtly seek to imitate a particular genre. Rather, it is a historical novel which utilizes elements of melodrama and autobiographical forms of storytelling. The novel recounts the journey of con-man Abraham Licht and his sons and daughters from the early twentieth century through the Great Depression. Every member of the family is a scheming imposter who swindles people for a living. In following the adventures and dramatic downfall of this family of tricksters, Oates probes questions about the true meaning of personality and identity as well as America's obsession with money. Although the fifth book in the series, *The Accursed* (2013), wasn't published until fifteen years after the fourth, it is in many ways a stylistic return to the earlier novels in how creatively it mingles historical and supernatural elements. Similarly, it heavily imitates elements of a particular genre – in this case, gothic horror. The story follows the rise and fall of the Slade family who are part of the upper-class Princeton society of 1905 and 1906, but it also heavily features Woodrow Wilson who was president of Princeton University prior to becoming president of the United States. The demons which are unleashed upon this privileged society enact a chaotic revenge for certain injustices. Together, Oates's sequence of gothic novels uses genre to examine America's social history from distinct angles. Their gothic elements allow an understanding of the nation's past which may not be true, but express a truth which cannot be accessed in historical accounts.

Following this extended foray into ingenious postmodern experimentation, Oates returned to a more traditionally realistic form of storytelling with her novels *Marya: A Life* (1986) and *You Must Remember This* (1987). The author also described *Marya: A Life* as one of her most "personal" in its similarity to the time and place of her early life. It follows the development and search for self-understanding of Marya Knauer who emerges from an impoverished, violent youth in a rural community to succeed at university and become a writer (although Marya eventually abandons writing). Although this novel isn't strictly autobiographical, it is perhaps significant how it expresses the plight one feels at reaching a certain stage of adulthood when it is challenging to reconcile one's past with one's present state of being. *You Must Remember This*, which appeared the year after, could be viewed as a companion novel in its examination of 1950s American conservative culture. It recounts a family's dramatic, emotionally entangled story as they are caught in the era of McCarthyism and backyard fallout shelters.

While Oates continued producing a diverse range of literary novels in her customary style of psychological realism, her gothic novels emboldened her to write more overt genre novels as well. *Lives of the Twins* (1987) is a psychological thriller which she published under the pseudonym Rosamond Smith. This tale of a wayward woman caught between twin brothers who are both psychiatrists has a different tone from Oates's previous novels. With its swift narrative style it resembles both a prose movie and a romance mystery. Oates hoped to elicit fresh critical opinion by using a pseudonym but her identity was immediately uncovered before the novel's publication. This didn't deter her from continuing to use the pen name and she wrote several more novels about doppelgangers published under the name Rosamond Smith. Although Oates eventually put this pseudonym to rest, she later published three suspense novels using another pseudonym, Lauren Kelly. Oates has also published many collections of short stories (under her own name) which are classified under the genres of mystery, suspense, or horror. They demonstrate the author's ongoing fascination with the effects of genre and the challenges that accompany different forms of storytelling.

Oates's novel *Because It Is Bitter, and Because It Is My Heart* (1990) is primarily concerned with racial divisions in America. A young girl named Iris Courtney is the only witness to a murderous street fight between Jinx Fairchild and a white man who has threatened her. The novel is an example of Oates's ongoing exploration of the way racial conflict affects individuals and communities in modern-day America. Many of her novels such as *Black Girl/White Girl* (2006), *The Sacrifice* (2015), and *My Life as a Rat* (2019) are similarly concerned with assumptions and misunderstandings that occur on both sides of racial divisions and how inherited societal notions about other races inevitably cause great tension and often sadly result in violence. Though these novels explicitly deal with this subject, it is an issue that is also referenced throughout a large amount of Oates's fiction. One of Oates's most significant works of nonfiction, *On Boxing* (1987), is, in part, a feminist perspective on the sport. But it also considers the history of boxing in regard to many famous Black boxers and the sport's importance within the African American community as well as wider American society.

Oates's novella *Black Water* (1992) is based on the Chappaquiddick scandal of 1969 when Senator Ted Kennedy accidentally drove his car into a pond and his young female passenger, Mary Jo Kopechne, drowned. Oates relates the story from the female point of view in the final moments of her life as she's drowning. The novel *What I Lived For* (1994) describes a very different set of circumstances but takes the viewpoint of a charismatic up-and-coming male politician who uses a long list of women. These novels consider the damaging effects of male political power and how these domineering attitudes often lead to women being victimized. Both books were nominated for the Pulitzer Prize for Fiction. *Black Water* is also notable in how it takes a significant recent event from American history and fictionally reimagines it from the perspective of the victim. This became a strategy which Oates used in a number of subsequent novels: *The Falls* (2004) was inspired by the notorious Love Canal scandal; *My Sister, My*

Love (2008) was inspired by the tragic case and sensational media surrounding JonBenét Ramsey's death; *The Sacrifice* is a fictional reimagining of the Tawana Brawley case; *A Book of American Martyrs* (2017) is inspired by many violent conflicts that have occurred at clinics between pro- and anti-abortion groups.

Although there are many notable exceptions, much of Oates's fiction is told from the perspective of adolescent girls or young women whose voices aren't often heard in popular discourse. One of the most significant examples is *We Were The Mulvaneys* (1996), which describes how a sexual assault upon 16-year-old Marianne leads to her being expelled from her own family. However, Oates demonstrates in the story that, despite this tragedy, there are still many different opportunities for her to grow and thrive in life. The novel found a significant widespread readership when it was chosen for Oprah's Book Club in 2001. Shortly before this, Oates published *Blonde* (2000), one of her longest and most significant novels. The novel was originally conceived as a novella in the style of *Black Water* describing the early life of orphaned Norma Jeane Mortenson and the development of her acting/modeling career up until the point a Hollywood studio assigns her the name Marilyn Monroe. However, Oates persisted with fictionalizing her story past this point and chronicled her complicated career to the point of her tragic death. In its radical reimagining of the life of one of the most famous American icons of the twentieth century, Oates gives nobility to the point of view of a vulnerable girl and talented young woman intent on honing her craft as an artist as distinct from the blonde bombshell she was turned into. The novel was nominated for both the Pulitzer Prize for Fiction and a National Book Award.

Oates has always been interested in conversing with the lives and works of her literary contemporaries and forebears. As an academic Oates has published a substantial body of nonfiction including *Where I've Been, And Where I'm Going* (1999), *Uncensored: Views & (Re)views* (2005), and *In Rough Country* (2010). These include essays and reflections about particular works of fiction and a diverse range of authors such as Christina Rossetti, Henry Melville, Joseph Conrad, Flannery O' Connor, Jack Kerouac, Elizabeth Hardwick, Jean Stafford, Vladimir Nabokov, Emily Brontë, Paul Bowles, Shirley Jackson, Sylvia Plath, Willa Cather, Patricia Highsmith, Richard Yates, and Muriel Spark. She also critiques the work of many of her contemporaries such as John Updike, William Trevor, Anita Brookner, Kazuo Ishiguro, Alice Sebold, Valerie Martin, Hilary Mantel, Pat Barker, Cormac McCarthy, Annie Proulx, Salman Rushdie, Jim Crace, Susanna Moore, Anne Tyler, Ann Patchett, Alice Munro, and Don DeLillo. However, Oates has also written a number of fictional works which are both tributes and critiques of influential writers. An early short story collection, *Marriages and Infidelities* (1972), demonstrated imaginative reworkings of several classic short stories. Oates's more recent fiction has conversed more directly with the lives of canonical authors. *Wild Nights!* (2008) fictionally reimagines the final days of Edgar Allan Poe, Emily Dickinson, Mark Twain, Henry James, and Ernest Hemingway. These daring tales use genre in fascinating and surprising ways to give a different perspective on these writers' literary achievements and legacy. For instance, "EdickinsonRepliLuxe" is a science fiction story which imagines a future point where a couple purchases a mechanized Emily Dickinson doll. Short stories in other collections such as "Lovely, Dark, Deep" about an imagined interview with Robert Frost and "Night-Gaunts," which radically reimagines the life of H.P. Lovecraft, provide a sharper critique of these authors' misogynistic and/or racist conduct and values.

Quite a significant novel in Oates's oeuvre is *The Gravedigger's Daughter* (2007). It describes the story of Rebecca, the only surviving member of an immigrant family who lost their lives in a terrible domestic tragedy. It is a homage to women of a certain generation whose stories of personal strife were kept hidden. It is also a tale of endurance, self-reinvention, and mythic realism which embodies many of the author's major themes concerning identity, survivor's guilt, and the long-lasting effects of trauma. It utilizes her most commonly used and idiosyncratic narrative style where a character's thoughts or heightened feelings will appear in italics. It also draws upon the author's own family history by reimagining the life story of Oates's beloved grandmother. Interestingly, many of Oates's later books have become much more candid about the author's family life and personal story. *The Journal of Joyce Carol Oates: 1973–1982* (2007) provides a firsthand look at the author's daily process of writing, the challenges of particular books she was working on at the time, experiences in the literary world, and reflections on the artistic process. A more sustained account of the author's origins and development as a writer is described in the memoir *The Lost Landscape* (2015).

A number of personal tragedies in Oates's life have led to the creation of several grief-driven books and works of fiction. When the author's mother Carolina Oates died, Oates was inspired to write the novel *Missing Mom* (2005) about the challenges an independent young woman experiences following the abrupt loss of her mother. The style of the novel is quite different from Oates's other fiction and the author has remarked she wanted to write the kind of novel she knew her mother would have enjoyed reading. When Raymond Smith, Oates's husband of nearly fifty years, unexpectedly died in 2008, Oates eventually published the uncharacteristically candid memoir *A Widow's Story* (2011), which reproduces the writer's journal entries and exchanges with friends. Several notable short stories in collections such as *Dear Husband* (2009), *Sourland* (2010), and *Lovely, Dark, Deep* (2014) describe grief from the perspective of a widow. After Smith's death, Oates eventually married Charlie Gross, a photographer and professor of psychology and neuroscience. However, Gross died in 2019 and the following year Oates published *Night. Sleep. Death. The Stars.* (2020), which is her most sustained and lengthy fictional meditation on the process of grief. It is a significant novel which also considers the subject of police brutality through a family tragedy.

After 36 years as a professor at Princeton University, Oates officially retired from teaching in 2014. However, she continues to participate in seminars and teaches occasional courses for students within universities, online writing platforms, and the prison system. Oates has taught many well-known authors during their university years, including Jonathan Safran Foer, Jodi Picoult, and Clare Beams. *The Faith of a Writer: Life, Craft, Art* (2003) includes a number of informed, instructive, and inspiring essays about the writing process. The essay collection *Soul at the White Heat: Inspiration, Obsession and the Writing Life* (2016) provides a number of other moving reflections about writing as well as criticism about several classic and contemporary works of literature. Oates has not only provided a substantial legacy of diverse and brilliant books, but has inspired and influenced future generations of writers. Having been awarded a National Humanities Medal and numerous lifetime achievement awards, Oates's extensive contribution to literature has been widely recognized and cemented her place as one of the most important American writers of the past forty years.

SEE ALSO: After Postmodernism; DeLillo, Don; Foer, Jonathan Safran; Literary Magazines; McCarthy, Cormac; Minimalism and Maximalism; Mixed-Genre Fiction; Patchett, Ann; Proulx, Annie; Trauma and Fiction; Updike, John

FURTHER READING

Anderson, Eric K. (2019). What you need to know about Joyce Carol Oates. YouTube (June 16, 2019). https://www.youtube.com/watch?v=ullbHQheCmc.

Celestial Timepiece: A Joyce Carol Oates Patchwork. (n.d.). https://celestialtimepiece.com/.

Cologne-Brookes, Gavin. (2005). *Dark Eyes on America*. Baton Rouge: Louisiana State University Press.

Daly, Brenda O. (1996). *Lavish Self-Divisions*. Jackson: University Press of Mississippi.

Johnson, Greg. (1999). *Invisible Writer: A Biography of Joyce Carol Oates*. New York: Plume.

O'Brien, Tim

JO LANGDON
Independent scholar

William Timothy "Tim" O'Brien is the award-winning author of nine books, in addition to essays and short stories that have appeared individually in publications such as *The New York Times*. Informed by the writer's experiences as a conscripted soldier in the Vietnam War, his prose fiction often defies simple categorization, and – while ostensibly comprising, for the most part, works of fiction – can be situated vis-à-vis the genres of life writing, historical fiction, and magical realism. Postmodern in their playful and ambiguous engagement with referential history and biography, O'Brien's novels also resonate with Linda Hutcheon's notion of historiographic metafiction (1989): that is, they are self-reflexive, allusive, and artful, pointedly problematizing their own claims to historical and biographical veracity.

O'Brien's first book, *If I Die in a Combat Zone, Box Me Up and Ship Me Home* (1973), is journalistic and the most overtly "factual," autobiographic, and straightforward of his works, made up of a collection of literary essays about his experience of the war. Some extracts were published as magazine and newspaper articles during O'Brien's enlistment. His next book, *Northern Lights* (1975), is a novel exploring the after-effects of the Vietnam War via two brothers: Harvey, who has returned from the war, and Paul, who has remained home with his devoted wife, Grace. Described in *Kirkus Reviews* (1975) in terms of its "earnestness and clapboard verisimilitude," and as "a long, slow trek, but worth going the distance," *Northern Lights* is not as formally experimental or as playful as O'Brien's later works, but it does establish many key themes and preoccupations relating not only to the war experience but to questions and representations of familial relationships, masculinity, and the idea of courage.

Winner of the 1979 National Book Award for Fiction, his novel *Going After Cacciato* (1975) is a magical realist narrative in which the titular Cacciato deserts the war with the goal of walking from the conflict, through Southeast Asia, to Paris (an ironic choice of destination, given Vietnam's colonial history under French rule, and also in that the Vietnam War was itself an imperialist war). It is followed by *The Nuclear Age* (1985) – described by Mark A. Heberle as "O'Brien's first deliberately comic novel" (2001, p. 259) – in which protagonist William Cowling, increasingly consumed by the threat of nuclear warfare and emotionally estranged from his family, begins to dig a fallout shelter in his backyard. Cowling is adamant that "the facts are these": "The world is in danger. Bad things can happen. We need options, a safety valve" (O'Brien 1985, p. 5). Like many of O'Brien's texts, however, *The Nuclear Age* is explicit in signaling the unreliability of its narrator (indeed, this is also a feature of characters such as the focalized protagonist Paul Berlin in *Going After Cacciato*).

The Nuclear Age opens: "Am I crazy?" (1985, p. 3), with variations on this refrain recurring throughout the opening scene, which depicts Cowling rising from his bed during the night to begin digging: "A crackpot? Maybe, maybe not"; "Crazy? Not likely, not yet"; "It isn't madness" (p. 3); then, once he is in the yard: "*Dig*, the hole says" (p. 7). Also, characteristic of O'Brien's work broadly, the novel places equal emphasis on dreams and the imaginary, depicting them as being just as immediate and tangible as the physical, actual, and objective events and experiences that populate the text and his characters' lives. Early on, Cowling reveals his childhood anxieties, stating: "In dreams, in imagination, I watched the world end" (p. 9).

This attention to the potency of dreams and the illusory also extends into O'Brien's fifth book. First published in 1990 and a finalist for the Pulitzer Prize and the National Book Critics Circle Award, *The Things They Carried* is a short-story cycle: a collection of interrelated stories centering on the soldiers of an infantry platoon, the Alpha Company, during the Vietnam War. Pointed details that work to obfuscate the lines between "fact" (biography and/or memoir) and "fiction" include a "fictional" version of the author Tim O'Brien, along with the book's front-matter, which "lovingly" dedicates the collection to "the men of the Alpha Company, and in particular to Jimmy Cross, Norman Bowker, Rat Kiley, Mitchell Sanders, Henry Dobbins, and Kiowa" – all of whom are named "characters" in the book. Notably, these details are teasingly set vis-à-vis a disclaimer at the beginning of the text – on the page proceeding the book's dedication – that "This is a work of fiction. Except for a few details regarding the author's own life, all the incidents, names and characters are imaginary" (O'Brien 1991). This ambiguity is consistent throughout the collection, and at times particularly heightened and explicit, calling attention to the stories' fabrications and to the author's ambivalent attitude towards questions of truth and authenticity.

Indeed, one of the collection's key concerns is with the art of fiction and storytelling. A central story, self-consciously titled "How to Tell a True War Story," includes detailed metafictional commentary on the preceding stories – and O'Brien's writing practice more broadly – which works to cast doubt over the "truth" of these stories and their events, while simultaneously averring their authenticity. The story opens emphatically with the single line: "This is true" (1991, p. 67). As he unpacks and develops the narrative, O'Brien continues to remind the reader that "It's all exactly true" (p. 69), only to soon flout these earlier refrains with cautions such as: "In many cases a true war story cannot be believed. If you believe it, be skeptical" (p. 70).

In reconciling these apparent incongruities, O'Brien insists:

> In any war story, but especially a true one, it's difficult to separate what happened from what seemed to happen. What seems to happen becomes its own happening and has to be told that way. The angles of vision are skewed. When a booby trap explodes, you close your eyes and duck and float outside yourself. When a guy dies . . . you look away and then look back for a moment and then look away again. The pictures get jumbled; you tend to miss a lot. And then afterward, when you go to tell about it, there is always that surreal seemingness, which makes the story seem untrue, but which in fact represents the hard and exact truth as it *seemed*.
>
> (1991, pp. 69–70)

In stories such as "Good Form" – which spans just two pages – O'Brien returns to this idea, writing: "I want you to feel what I felt. I want you to know why story-truth is truer sometimes than happening truth" (1991, p. 179). This idea of "story-truth" resonates across his works – and across critical approaches to his oeuvre in scholarship on his texts.

The indeterminacy that characterizes the individual stories of *The Things They Carried*, and the collection as a whole, also resonates with understandings of literary trauma – specifically, how trauma might be represented in literary depictions of violence and extremity, given that the traumatic experience and its memory are understood to resist or test the limits of language and challenge narrative chronology. According to trauma theorists such as Cathy Caruth (1995, 1996), trauma is fundamentally unreachable: an experience and memory that can only be understood in incomplete and belated ways, via flashbacks and other symptoms of repetition and dissociation that make distinctions between the past and the present difficult.

While Caruth's understanding of trauma emphasizes absence and obliqueness, suggesting that textual lacunae must be recognized as evidence of trauma's paradoxically amnesiac and intrusive symptoms, the critic Joshua Pederson contends that, rather than being "elusive or absent," traumatic memories are in fact "potentially more detailed and more powerful than normal ones," meaning that "authors may record trauma with excessive detail and vibrant intensity," such that "readers looking for representations of trauma may turn not to textual absence but to textual overflow" (2014, p. 339). This understanding of trauma certainly speaks to O'Brien's textual embellishments and departures. It also characterizes the metaphoric intensity and predilection for hyperbole and transformation for which magical realist fiction is known, as O'Brien's third novel, *Going After Cacciato*, exemplifies.

Indeed, the scholar Eugene L. Arva uses *Going After Cacciato* as a case study for "felt" trauma. In *The Traumatic Imagination: Histories of Violence in Magical Realist Fiction* (2011) – a monograph of literary scholarship significant for its focus on the connection between magical realist fiction and trauma narratives – Arva contends that the magical realist image is "capable of bringing the pain and horror home into the readers' affective world; while it might not need to explain the unspeakable . . . it can certainly make it felt and re-experienced in a vicarious way" (2011, p. 9). Arva describes the "intrinsically uncanny reality of traumatic events – histories that were and were not at the same time" (p. 6). This duality accords with much of O'Brien's own commentary on writing trauma; however, O'Brien himself earnestly maintains that his writing is not magical realist: "I see myself as a realist in the strictest sense," he argues. "That is to say, our daydreams are real; our fantasies are real. They aren't construed as otherwise in any of my books" (quoted in Herzog 1997, p. 80). As Arva contends, this paradoxically confirms rather than denies O'Brien's use of magical realist strategies (2011, p. 265). Indeed, O'Brien's fantasy-filled historical fiction is invested in precisely the kind of incongruity that characterizes the magical realist narrative mode, which compels the reader to doubt what has taken place, and to acknowledge the potency of the fantasy that obfuscates reality, as well as their engagement and belief in this obfuscatory magic.

O'Brien's rejection of the term magical realism arguably also misunderstands or misconstrues the mode of writing and its historical and political engagement – that magical realism is typically ironic and artful in its refusal to distinguish between the believable and the outrageous, which also aptly describes O'Brien's works. As I have argued elsewhere (Langdon 2017), O'Brien's emphasis on authenticity neutralizes his writing's importantly pointed and provocative qualities; that "[t]he ironic charge of many of the fantastic elements of his work, along with the repetition of certain tropes and archetypes – references to other texts and popular cultural icons – work to highlight the cultural status of O'Brien's trauma narratives as literary texts, rather than apparent symptoms of trauma" (2017, p. 342). As Stefania Ciocia writes, accordingly: "even when his intertextual connections are not as easily discernable," O'Brien is "very much a writers' writer and a committed craftsman, conscious of his literary and cultural influences" (2012, p. 29).

In *Going After Cacciato* O'Brien again highlights how unreliable trauma narratives are – while simultaneously engaging the reader in a soldier's fantastical journey from the Vietnam War to Paris: an impossible expedition which is potently rendered as a textual "reality." The event of the titular Cacciato's desertion spurs the novel's initial departure from the "reality" of war, and the novel continually and self-consciously emphasizes the imbrications of fantasy in the realities of traumatic experience. The remaining members of Cacciato's squad, including the focalized protagonist, Paul Berlin, are sent after him, and it is during their pursuit that the destination of Paris becomes a dissociative fantasy for the traumatized Berlin, even while the distinctions between the real and imagined remain conspicuously irresolute.

Narrative indeterminacy also characterizes *In the Lake of the Woods* (1994), which engages with the genre conventions of a "missing person" mystery or literary thriller. The central narrative takes place at a lakeside cabin, where, following a landslide election loss, the recently defeated politician John Wade and his wife Kathy have retreated before Kathy goes missing. The novel gradually reconstructs John's experience of the My Lai massacre – his involvement in which he had kept concealed even from Kathy until his participation in the war crime was revealed during the primary election.

In numerous chapters titled "Hypothesis," the novel teasingly offers readers various narrative resolutions – speculative accounts of what *might* have happened to Kathy, which include the possibility that John has killed her. (Disturbing context that suggests the potential for John's violence against her includes his stalking of Kathy since the beginning of their relationship.) Other chapters are titled "Evidence," and comprise various textual and visual materials from both real and fictional sources. For Barbara Kowalczuk, "By tempting the reader to reach beyond the lines . . . and connect with transtextuality, O'Brien opts for liminality as a creative space" (2014, p. 10) – a creative methodology that again characterizes his works collectively, and can be theorized vis-à-vis trauma studies.

Published in *The New York Times* in the same year as *In the Lake of the Woods*, "The Vietnam in Me" (1994) is a personal essay that alternates between O'Brien's 1994 return to Vietnam with his then girlfriend, Kate, and the ensuing breakup of their relationship on their return to the United States. Its candid account of O'Brien's poor mental health and explicit references to suicide shocked many readers, with lines such as "Last night suicide was on my mind. Not whether, but how" (O'Brien 1994).

Notably, as Lisa Ferguson details, Kate's depiction also belies a current of misogyny that extends across many of O'Brien's representations of his female characters, with Kate mirroring women in *The Things They Carried* and *In the Lake of the Woods* as a "prototype of the typical unsympathetic woman" in "her inability to feel/heal his [O'Brien's, and his characters'] trauma" (2016, p. 88). Ferguson points out that "Kate is never really known as anything more than some sort of virginal flower-child, blissfully unaware of the evils all around her and poorly equipped to deal with the shock of Vietnam – reminiscent of all the major American female characters in O'Brien's narratives" (p. 79). As with the character of Martha in *The Things They Carried* and Kathy in *In the Lake of the Woods* – with the latter text ultimately culminating in Kathy's probable homicide – "the so-called love disintegrates into a feeling that can best be described as a hybrid of lust, obsession, and hate" (p. 88).

Tomcat in Love (1998) would seem to depart in many ways from O'Brien's usual subject matter and tone: it follows Vietnam veteran and linguistics professor Thomas "Tomcat" Chippering, an aspiring womanizer and "antihero" protagonist, as he stalks his ex-wife in the wake of their divorce. As Heberle suggests, "*Tomcat* is the most formally 'plotless' and 'pointless' of O'Brien's trauma narratives, its employment of fragmentation, truncation, repetition, recovery, and re-covering even more extensive than in previous books" (2001, p. 264).

His penultimate book to date, *July, July* (2002), centers on a thirty-year college reunion for the class of 1969, and includes a war veteran and a draftee who fled to Canada among its collection of characters. A composite, multivocal novel made up of various points of view, *July, July* is structurally similar to earlier texts such as *The Things They Carried* in its interlinking of narratives. Moving between the titular Julys of the years 1969 and 2000, the novel traverses the lives of its characters during and before the night of the reunion – including two classmates who have died: Karen Burns, who has been murdered, and Harmon Osterberg, who has drowned.

Although only two of the characters have in fact faced being drafted to Vietnam – and only one actually served in the war – Claire Stocks calls *July, July* "possibly O'Brien's most comprehensive and sustained investigation of the consequences and effects of the Vietnam war" (2006, p. 176). For Glenn Dayley, however, what marks this novel as exceptional for O'Brien is its number of key female characters, who are notable for being clearly, carefully delineated as developed characters – something O'Brien has not achieved or attempted in his earlier books (2003, p. 319). Dayley also notes the political neutrality of the characters of *July, July* in the year the reunion takes place, pointing out that "[t]heir college years were drenched in politics, but 30 years later their worlds have shrunk down to a few essential, personal and human concerns and emotions ... They aren't draft dodging to Canada; they're trying to escape the monotony of their suburban lives" (p. 320).

As noted, given their incorporation of historical and biographical events and details, O'Brien's texts also constitute works of life writing – a category that, as David McCooey contends, is continually concerned with limits: "between literary and factual writing; between narrative as a literary device and narrative as lived experience; and between autobiography and fiction" (2018, p. 1). The fact that many details and experiences are repeatedly represented across O'Brien's works also resonates with understandings of trauma, and with the compulsion to return to or repeat the traumatic experience – something O'Brien shares with authors such as Kurt Vonnegut who have written recurrently on the traumatic events which they have witnessed firsthand (see Wicks 2014).

His most recent work is an epistolary memoir, *Dad's Maybe Book* (2019), comprised of letters to his sons, Timmy and Tad. In an early review of this latest text – published seventeen years after his preceding novel, *July, July* – *Time* book reviewer Matt Gallagher defines O'Brien as the "reluctant bard of the Vietnam War and soldier-poet of the baby boomers" (2019). Tongue-in-cheek though this description might be, it certainly does no justice to O'Brien's rich and dynamic opus; his complexity as a formally experimental author of serious and rigorous commitment to his craft and to the power of storytelling.

SEE ALSO: Contemporary Fictions of War; Fiction and Affect; Mixed-Genre Fiction; Story Cycles; Trauma and Fiction; Vonnegut, Kurt

REFERENCES

Arva, Eugene L. (2011). *The Traumatic Imagination: Histories of Violence in Magical Realist Fiction*. Amherst, NY: Cambria Press.
Caruth, Cathy. (ed.) (1995). *Trauma: Explorations in Memory*. Baltimore: Johns Hopkins University Press.
Caruth, Cathy. (1996). *Unclaimed Experience: Trauma, Narrative and History*. Baltimore: Johns Hopkins University Press.
Ciocia, Stefania. (2012). *Vietnam and Beyond: Tim O'Brien and the Power of Storytelling*. Liverpool: Liverpool University Press.
Dayley, Glenn. (2003). Familiar ghosts, new voices: Tim O'Brien's July, July. War, Literature, and the Arts: An International Journal of the Humanities 15 (1–2): 316–322.
Ferguson, Lisa. (2016). "Dumb coozes" and damaged men: female stereotypes, male victimization, and manipulative narration in The Things They Carried and In the Lake of the Woods. *Journal of Research in Gender Studies* 6 (1): 76–120.
Gallagher, Matt. (2019). The Things They Carried author Tim O'Brien returns to contemplate fatherhood and America at war. *Time* (October 21, 2019). https://time.com/5696948/life-after-wartime/ (accessed July 15, 2021).
Heberle, Mark A. (2001). *A Trauma Artist: Tim O'Brien and the Fiction of Vietnam*. Iowa City: University of Iowa Press.
Herzog, Tobey C. (1997). *Tim O'Brien*. New York: Twayne.
Hutcheon, Linda. (1989). Historiographic metafiction: parody and the intertextuality of history. In: *Intertextuality and Contemporary American Fiction* (ed. Patrick O'Donnell and Robert Con Davis), 3–32. Baltimore: Johns Hopkins University Press.
Kirkus Reviews. (1975). Northern Lights by Tim O'Brien (posted online October 2, 2011). https://www.kirkusreviews.com/book-reviews/tim-obrien/northern-lights-7/ (accessed July 15, 2021).
Kowalczuk, Barbara. (2014). My Lai's "fucking flies!": the stigmata of trauma in Tim O'Brien's In the Lake of the Woods. *War, Literature, and the Arts: An International Journal of the Humanities* 26: 1–14.
Langdon, Jo. (2017). "A thing may happen and be a total lie": artifice and trauma in Tim O'Brien's magical realist life writing. *Life Writing* 14 (3): 341–355.
McCooey, David. (2018). Introduction: the limits of life writing. In: *The Limits of Life Writing* (ed. David McCooey and Maria Takolander), 1–4. Abingdon, UK: Routledge.
O'Brien, Tim. (1985). *The Nuclear Age*. New York: Knopf.
O'Brien, Tim. (1991). *The Things They Carried*. London: Flamingo; 1st ed. 1990.
O'Brien, Tim. (1994). The Vietnam in me. *The New York Times* (October 23, 1994). https://www.nytimes.com/1994/10/23/magazine/l-the-vietnam-in-me-596205.html (accessed July 15, 2021).
Pederson, Joshua. (2014). Speak, trauma: toward a revised understanding of literary trauma theory. *Narrative* 22 (3): 333–353.
Stocks, Claire. (2006). Acts of cultural identification: Tim O'Brien's July, July. *European Journal of American Culture* 25 (3): 173–188.
Wicks, Amanda. (2014). "All this happened, more or less": the science fiction of trauma in Slaughterhouse-five. *Critique: Studies in Contemporary Fiction* 55 (3): 329–340.

FURTHER READING

Evans, Robert C. (ed.) (2015). *Tim O'Brien*. Ipswich, MA: Salem Press.
Herzog, Tobey C. (2018). *Tim O'Brien: The Things He Carries and the Stories He Tells*. New York: Routledge.
Lee, Don. (1995). About Tim O'Brien. *Ploughshares* 21 (4): 196–201.
Smith, Patrick A. (2005). *Tim O'Brien: A Critical Companion*. Westport, CT: Greenwood Press.
Young, John K. (2017). *How to Revise a True War Story: Tim O'Brien's Process of Textual Production*. Iowa City: University of Iowa Press.

Ortiz Cofer, Judith

CARMEN HAYDEE RIVERA
University of Puerto Rico, USA

Judith Ortiz Cofer is a prolific and award-winning author whose life and works have paved the way for new generations of writers, scholars, and educators. Not only are her works taught on different scholarly levels, from middle school to higher education, but they have also been included in renowned anthologies and literary journals as well as in curricula across disciplines and languages. To speak of Ortiz Cofer is to speak of the process of transnationalization and linguistic hybridity. Understanding Ortiz Cofer's works implies understanding her birthplace, Puerto Rico, as a "nation on the move" (Duany 2002, p. 2) and the United States, her adopted land, as a nation of (im)migrants (Morales 2019). Both coalesce in her literary representation of diasporic Puerto Rican experience. Ortiz Cofer's literary repertoire reflects the duality of her bilingual, bicultural upbringing in diverse genres (poetry, essay, memoir, fiction) and also in intrinsically mixed-genre texts that defy literary categorization. In essence, Judith Ortiz Cofer's legacy is multifaceted and interdisciplinary.

Ortiz Cofer was born on February 24, 1952, in Hormigueros, a small town in the western part of Puerto Rico. As a child, Ortiz Cofer was exposed to the natural scenery of the island as well as to its customs and traditions in an era of social turmoil and change. Her parents, Jesus Ortiz Lugo and Fanny Morot Ortiz, met and married in Puerto Rico. Shortly after their marriage, Ortiz Lugo, who had already enlisted in the US Navy, was assigned to duty at the Brooklyn Navy Yards in New York City, and thus began the family's constant traversing between Puerto Rico and the United States.

Ortiz Cofer's parents settled in Paterson, New Jersey, in 1956 during the second wave of Puerto Rican migration to the United States, an era historically known as the Great Migration, when the largest exodus of Puerto Ricans left the island before the massive migration caused by Hurricane Maria in 2017. However, Puerto Rican migration initially began prior to the 1898 US occupation of the island, increased with the concession of US citizenship through the Jones Act of 1917, and peaked during the industrialization era on the island between the 1940s and the 1950s (Acosta-Belen and Santiago 2018). According to recent statistics, there are currently more self-proclaimed Puerto Ricans living outside of the island (Krogstad and Noe-Bustamante 2019). Ortiz Cofer comes from this lineage and her negotiations between two cultures, traditions, languages, and belief systems are at the heart of her writing.

Much of her cultural and linguistic synergy originated with her father's extended military assignments overseas. While Ortiz Cofer's father was away, her mother shuffled her children (Ortiz Cofer and her brother Ronaldo) back to Puerto Rico, at times for stays up to six months. This constant shifting between Puerto Rico and the United States marked Ortiz Cofer's life in a number of ways and eventually sparked her literary creativity. Upon her return visits, Ortiz Cofer became acquainted with island folklore and oral tradition, primarily instilled by her maternal grandmother. She came from a strong matrilineal line of storytellers. Through this oral legacy Ortiz Cofer came to value island customs and traditions and to realize that storytelling was a form of empowerment for the women in her family.

Her trips back and forth from Paterson to the island also broadened her perspective and allowed her to see how aspects of Puerto Rican culture were perpetuated in Spanish-speaking communities in the United States. At the same time, her experience on the island allowed her to witness a gradual Americanization process that increased with industrialization, mass media, technological advances, and frequent air travel. Life in Paterson, New Jersey, and later in Augusta, Georgia, where her family moved when she was 15, became the frame of reference from which to analyze contrasting realities in her bilingual, bicultural existence.

Ortiz Cofer often referred to herself as a cultural chameleon, learning how to adapt to both island and US environments. Social, political, and economic ties between Puerto Rico and the United States facilitated Ortiz Cofer's awareness of how aspects of both cultures emerged and flourished in both places.

In her early years, Ortiz Cofer's education alternated between public schools in Paterson and in Hormigueros, Puerto Rico. She eventually graduated from Butler High School and later attended Augusta College in Georgia, receiving a bachelor of arts degree in 1974. Here she met and married Charles John Cofer. After the birth of their daughter, Tanya, the family moved to West Palm Beach in Florida, where she completed a master of arts degree in English literature from Florida Atlantic University in 1977. Ortiz Cofer also obtained fellowships and grants that allowed her to pursue studies in creative writing at institutions such as Oxford University and the Bread Loaf Writer's Conference at Middlebury College.

With the encouragement and editorial advice of her first English Department director at Augusta College, Ortiz Cofer submitted a poem, "Latin Women Pray," to the *New Mexico Humanities Review* in 1981. The *Review* accepted and published the poem and requested additional submissions. From that moment on, Ortiz Cofer continued to submit her poems to literary journals. In 1984, she joined the faculty of the English Department at the University of Georgia in Athens, having previously lectured for a few years in the English Department at the University of Miami in Coral Gables. By the time of her retirement from the University of Georgia in 2013, Ortiz Cofer held an honorary position as Regents' and Franklin Professor of English and Creative Writing.

In 1986, Ortiz Cofer's first publication appeared, a small chapbook titled *Peregrina*, published in the Poets of the Foothills Arts Center series by Riverstone Press. The pamphlet included a selection of poems previously published in literary journals and magazines. This early work was followed by a collection of poems titled *Terms of Survival*, released by Arte Publico Press in 1987. Ortiz Cofer published two additional poetry collections: *Reaching for the Mainland* in 1987 (later re-edited as *Reaching for the Mainland and Selected New Poems* in 1995) by Bilingual Press, and *A Love Story Beginning in Spanish* in 2005, published by the University of Georgia Press.

Ortiz Cofer's poetry displayed the influences of her bilingual, bicultural upbringing in carefully crafted imagery that focused on cultural icons, Puerto Rican and US customs and traditions, and, most importantly, on rites of passage from young adolescence into womanhood. Some are written as cautionary advice; others focus on the fate of particular women gone astray or women carrying life's burdens. She delved into the recesses of memory for these images, particularly those associated with her childhood visits and exposure to her family's storytelling traditions. In one of her early memoirs, Ortiz Cofer provides an image of her fascination with her mother, aunts, and cousins huddled around her grandmother, mesmerized by her stories:

> They told . . . *cuentos*, the morality and cautionary tales told by the women in our family for generations: stories that became a part of my subconscious as I grew up in two worlds, the tropical island and the cold city, and which would later surface in my dreams and in my poetry.
>
> (1990, p.15)

Without necessarily relinquishing her poetic voice, Ortiz Cofer's next projects can be described as creative nonfiction. These works consisted of mixed-genre texts that included poetry, prose, memoir, and testimonial essays that often displayed folk legends, songs, and certain elements of magical realism in the telling of events and in character portrayals. Fact and fiction, reality and imagination, lived experience and the spirit world coexist with one another in similar ways to the writing of other Latin American authors of the time.

In 1990, Ortiz Cofer published *Silent Dancing: A Partial Remembrance of a Puerto Rican Childhood*, a mixture of verse and narrative forms that not only reflected her development as a writer but also enhanced the literary representation of historical, cultural, and linguistic hybridity. The work begins with a preface that reveals how writer Virginia Woolf's selective process of memory in reconstructing the past enabled her to grasp "precious moments of being" in literary representation of her life's history. Ortiz Cofer writes, "I wanted to try to connect myself to the threads of lives that have touched mine and at some point converged into the tapestry that is my memory of childhood" (1990, p. 13). Other works followed in the same vein: *The Latin Deli: Prose and Poetry* (1993) and *The Year of Our Revolution: New and Selected Stories and Poems* (1998).

In her mixed-genre works, and more prominently in her novels and short stories, Ortiz Cofer's main concerns are the portrayal of the process and effects of migration, the meaning of loss, and the importance of oral tradition in the construction of a cultural legacy. She also highlights the constant negotiation between patriarchal gender roles and female emancipation through the development of a female consciousness; the tenderness and spirituality of her spiritist grandfather; the tenacity of her maternal grandmother; as well as the celebration of communal life, friendship, and the courage to continue living through life's adversities.

Ortiz Cofer's first novel was *The Line of the Sun*, published in 1989 by the University of Georgia Press. Hailed as one of her major works, the novel is set in the 1950s and 1960s in the fictional town of Salud, Puerto Rico, reminiscent of her hometown, but later depicts life in a tenement apartment in Paterson, New Jersey. The novel blends factual and fictional elements in a convoluted portrayal of the mysterious life of her uncle Guzman and the family legend woven around him. The narrator positions herself as a family chronicler by weaving the story of the main characters with her own physical and emotional development. In the novel's epilogue, an adult narrator looking back at the events portrayed concludes that "the only way to understand a life is to write it as a story, to fill in the blanks left by circumstance, lapses of memory, and failed communication" (1989, p. 290). What the narrator ultimately gains from her interaction with family members is the conviction that the power of storytelling can transform her life from one of sorrow and seclusion into one of inspiration and accomplishment.

Works categorized as young adult fiction are also an important part of Ortiz Cofer's literary repertoire. Some titles include: *An Island Like You: Stories of the Barrio* (1995), *The Meaning of Consuelo* (2003), *Call Me Maria* (2004), *If I Could Fly* (2011), *A Bailar! Let's Dance!* (2011), *Animal Jamboree/La Fiesta de los Animales* (2012), and *The Poet Upstairs* (2012). These works still rely on the portrayal of bicultural, bilingual characters but at the same time include universal themes of acceptance, self-discovery, forgiveness, perseverance, and a sense of belonging. Most protagonists are young girls straddling two cultures and languages. Some of these works include legendary fables that form part of Puerto Rican folklore. And several highlight the writing process as a means to cope with harsh environments. These works are not only limited to a young adult reading audience, since they often include evocative and poetic language, psychological searches, and beautiful imagery that reveal intricate portrayals of human experience.

Perhaps one of the most important aspects of Ortiz Cofer's literary career is her contribution to the discussion of the art of writing. Three publications, in particular, focus on how to engage with the written text: *Sleeping with One Eye Open: Women Writers and the Art of Survival* (1999), *Woman in Front of the Sun: On Becoming A Writer* (2000), and *Lessons from a Writer's Life: Readings and Resources for Teachers and Students* (2011). These co-edited collections depict Ortiz Cofer's early aspirations to become a writer; her ritualistic work schedule (rising every day at 5:00 a.m. to write); and her strong commitment to writing as a discipline and teaching as a vocation. The works also include the inspirational repertoire of stories and folklore she built upon since early childhood; her experience teaching writing workshops and classes; and the difficulties of balancing the demands of a home with her writing. Most importantly, with these collaborations Ortiz Cofer helped encourage other women to write and to protect and preserve their artistic space, to challenge the limitations of time, and to realize their own creative potential. Writing became the mechanism through which they could save the images, events, and emotions of their lives as well as create new ones. For Ortiz Cofer, the space of the printed page became a sanctuary for perceptions and imagination, a blank canvas before the artist, both inspiring and rewarding. Her lectures and book presentations across the country and abroad helped to transmit a message of cultural inclusion, of perseverance and tenacity that inspired her audiences for more than three decades.

The last work Ortiz Cofer published was her most autobiographical and, at the same time, emotionally moving. *The Cruel Country*, published by the University of Georgia Press in 2015, a year prior to her death, depicts her mother's illness and eventual passing but became, in the process, a manifesto on loss, sorrow, and bereavement. The work also portrayed how she grappled with the fragility of life and transcendence. The title comes from a quote in the introductory section of Roland Barthes's *Mourning Diary* (2010): "Mourning: a cruel country where I am no longer afraid." Ortiz Cofer contemplates her life alongside her mother's life and how their interconnectedness forms the essence of her ties to the island and lies at the heart of her writing process. Still mourning her mother's death in Puerto Rico, while they prepare for the Catholic ritual of rosaries and prayers, Ortiz Cofer ponders:

> I have a hunger to connect with the power source that fed my mother's passion for life . . . Now I realize how much her life, her energy, made my own life possible. I have no more conduits to the culture and language and costumbres of the place of my birth . . . Without her to guide me, I feel like a denaturalized citizen of my native land.
>
> (2015, p. 184)

Through the writing of this tribute to her mother, Ortiz Cofer also paid tribute to her own diasporic experience, to her family and life in Puerto Rico and in the United States, with its losses and gains, its turmoil and rewards. She finally realized that she belonged in the house she built with her husband in a remote Georgia landscape, surrounded by the English language, yet at the same time she admitted not feeling her mother's or husband's passion for house and place. In the end, Ortiz Cofer claims: "I believe that I will forever feel that I exist in between places. For me, home is a state of mind more than a location. It is how my history shaped me. I am at home where the people I love want and need to be, and where I can function at my best potential" (2015, p. 209).

Judith Ortiz Cofer passed away on December 30, 2016, in her home in Georgia at the age of 64 from a rare type of liver cancer, only three years after her retirement from the University of Georgia. Throughout her productive writing career, she received numerous awards, among them: the PEN/ Martha

Albrand Special Citation in Nonfiction, the Pushcart Prize, the O. Henry Prize, the Pura Belpre Award, the Americas Award, a Pulitzer Prize nomination, and various awards from the University of Georgia for her writing and mentorship. She also received over thirty fellowships and grants, including those from the Rockefeller Foundation, the National Endowment for the Arts, the University of Georgia Research Foundation, and the University of Georgia Center for the Humanities and Arts. On May 31, 2007, Lehman University granted her an honorary doctorate in humane letters. In 2010, she was inducted into the Georgia Writers Hall of Fame and in 2013, upon her retirement, the University of Georgia granted her the Southeastern Conference Faculty Achievement Award in recognition of her literary works and her teaching.

Through her poetry, nonfiction, novels, and mixed-genre works, Judith Ortiz Cofer created a rich array of literary voices and scenarios that celebrate diversity, inclusion, history, culture, and language. Her work is rooted in the migrant Puerto Rican experience, yet her thematic concerns appeal to a wide range of reading audiences, from different generations and backgrounds. Her solidarity with women and the circumstances that affect their lives as artists influence her evolving feminist consciousness. Discipline and persistence inform her writing, while memory and creativity bring forth powerful literary images, in both verse and narrative in Spanish and English. Her unique essence as a writer who crosses geographic, cultural, and linguistic boundaries allowed her to uncover the fragility and beauty of the human condition, and to become a vibrant and enduring voice in the American literary tradition.

SEE ALSO: The Culture Wars; Fiction and Affect; Literature of the Americas; Mixed-Genre Fiction; Multiculturalism; Urban Fiction

REFERENCES

Acosta-Belen, Edna and Santiago, Carlos E. (2018). *Puerto Ricans in the United States: A Contemporary Portrait*. Boulder, CO: Lynne Rienner.

Barthes, Roland. (2010). *Mourning Diary: October 26, 1977–September 15, 1979* (annotated by Nathalie Leger; trans. Richard Howard). New York: Hill & Wang.

Duany, Jorge. (2002). *The Puerto Rican Nation on the Move*. Chapel Hill: University of North Carolina Press.

Krogstad, Jens Manuel and Noe-Bustamante, Luis. (2019). *Pew Research Center*. https://www.pewresearch.org/fact-tank/2019/10/14/facts-for-national-hispanic-heritage-month (accessed August 18, 2021).

Morales, Ed. (2019). *Fantasy Island: Colonialism, Exploitation, and the Betrayal of Puerto Rico*. New York: Bold Type Books.

Ortiz Cofer, Judith. (1989). *The Line of the Sun*. Athens: University of Georgia Press.

Ortiz Cofer, Judith. (1990). *Silent Dancing: A Partial Remembrance of a Puerto Rican Childhood*. Houston: Arte Público Press.

Ortiz Cofer, Judith. (2015). *The Cruel Country*. Athens: University of Georgia Press.

FURTHER READING

Encyclopedia of Puerto Rico. (n.d.). Judith Ortiz Cofer. https://en.enciclopediapr.org/judith-ortiz-cofer

Georgia Writers Hall of Fame. (n.d.). Hall of Fame honorees. https://georgiawritershalloffame.org/honorees/judith-ortiz-cofer

Jimenez Garcia, Marilisa. (2018). A Tribute to Judith Ortiz Cofer. Special issue of *Label Me Latina/o*. https://www.academia.edu/37026040/_Tribute_to_Judith_Ortiz-Cofer

Ocasio, Rafael. (2017). Judith Ortiz Cofer: a valediction. https://repeatingislands.com/2017/01/09/judith-ortiz-cofer-a-valediction-by-rafael-ocasio

Poetry Foundation. (n.d.). Judith Ortiz Cofer. https://www.poetryfoundation.org/poets/judith-ortiz-cofer

The New Georgia Encyclopedia. (n.d.). https://www.georgiaencyclopedia.org/articles/arts-culture/judith-ortiz-cofer-1952-2016

Ozeki, Ruth

ELEANOR TY
Wilfrid Laurier University, Canada

The daughter of a Japanese mother and a Caucasian American father, Ruth Ozeki is an award-winning novelist and filmmaker, a professor of creative writing at Smith College, and a Zen Buddhist priest. Born in New Haven, Connecticut, she is a dual citizen of Canada and the United States, and divides her time between Cortes Island, British Columbia, and New York City. She studied English and Asian Studies at Smith College, and then pursued graduate studies in classical Japanese literature in Japan. Her three novels, *My Year of Meats* (1998), *All Over Creation* (2003), and *A Tale for the Time Being* (2013) reflect the bicultural and transnational influences in her life, and her concern for the environment, our food industry, and women's issues. Ozeki has also made independent documentary films, including *Halving the Bones* (1995), an autobiographical story of her journey to bring her grandmother's remains home from Japan, which was nominated for the Grand Jury Prize at the Sundance Film Festival.

Ozeki's first novel, *My Year of Meats*, won the Kiriyama Prize and Imus/Barnes & Noble American Book Award in 1998. Its narrative structure reveals the connections between women in the United States and Japan in the 1990s. Told from the perspective of Jane Takagi-Little, a biracial feminist TV documentary filmmaker, and Akiko Ueno, a manga artist/housewife in Japan, with chapter epigraphs from the musings of eleventh-century poet and court lady Sei Shōnagon, the novel presents a strong indictment of the meat production industry, of advertising and media, fertility drugs, domestic violence, and racism. Jane, hired to produce episodes of *My American Wife*, a television show designed to feature "middle-to-upper middle class white American women" (1998, p. 13) cooking their favorite beef recipes, challenges cultural beliefs about who is a typical and attractive "American" housewife through her choice of women to feature in the show. She observes that her job is to sell beef and the "vast illusion of America" (p. 9) to the show's Japanese audience. Although she initially complies with the producers and chooses white middle-class families to feature in the show, over the course of the year, she begins to disrupt expectations of who is a typical "American" family by including a Mexican American family; a white couple who adopted Black and mixed-raced children; and a vegetarian lesbian couple.

Critic Monica Chiu notes that the novel questions "many related binaries, including . . . white/Other, purity/pollution, production/consumption, true/false, natural/artificial, and fertile/infertile" (2004, p. 135). Jane's own hybrid identity seems to suggest a breaking down of racial binaries, but Ozeki encourages readers to question other binaries as well. As Jane begins to do research, she discovers that some truths are not so clear, that good/bad, healthy/unclean are largely ideological and subject to manipulation by the media and advertising. For example, beef, which has been advertised as good and healthy to eat, contains synthetic hormones, such as DES (diethylstilbestrol), that were given to cows to stimulate cattle growth and speed up production. This same drug was also prescribed to women because doctors were led to believe that it would produce "bigger and stronger babies" (1998, p. 125). However, they later discovered that DES caused cancer and irregular menstrual cycles in women and difficult pregnancies for daughters of mothers who had taken the drug. After the government banned DES for use in livestock production, "95 percent of feedlot cattle in the US still receive[d] some form of growth-promoting hormone or pharmaceutical in feed supplements" (p. 126), which ended up on our plates. Critic Emily

Cheng notes that "meat in the novel serves multiple functions: a metaphor for womanhood, the locus of anti-capitalist politics, an object through which the violence of capital upon the body is played out, and a subject of public health and environmental concern" (2009, p. 192). In the novel, meat production is shown to be connected to the medical industry and, ultimately, has an adverse effect on Jane's own body.

Although the novel presents a strong indictment of the meat industry, it is also a romance, a collection of recipes, and a tribute to America in the form of a travelogue. Jane's tender, but casual, relationship with the urban musician and masterful storyteller Sloan contrasts with Joichi Ueno's abusive relationship with Akiko. Sloan is Jane's "tall dark stranger in cowboy boots" (1998, p. 53) and she eventually realizes that she loved him. The television show that Jane produces features some zany recipes, including Coca Cola roast, Texas-style beefy burritos, kudzu, beef fudge, and Hallelujah lamb chops. While traveling to various locations to do their filming, Ozeki's narrator remarks that Colorado was "one of the most beautiful states in the country" (p. 245), and she describes the "deep – blue swamplands cloaked in tattered mists; enormous fields of tobacco and cotton and wheat" as she travels from Louisiana to the Carolinas (p. 335). The novel encourages readers to look at things, people, foods, drugs, places, and cultures from different angles and perspectives.

Similarly, Ozeki's second novel, *All Over Creation*, tackles transnational and global issues about agriculture, food production, and the positive effects of America's multiethnic population through the metaphor of seeds. The original meaning of the word "diaspora" was a "scattering away from the homeland" of Jews into "collective exile" (Tölölyan 2007, p. 648). Ozeki's novel is set on a potato farm in Idaho which is owned by an interracial family, a Euro-American potato farmer, his Japanese war bride Momoko, and their biracial daughter, Yumi. It is through Momoko's gardening and exotic vegetable seed-collecting efforts that biodiversity in the county is maintained. As Hsiu-Chuan Lee notes, "although the novel in its most obvious sense is an accusation against potato monoculture, or more precisely a protest against the global capitalist structure behind the demise of biodiversity," *All Over Creation* "delves into the more affirmative life forces that are generated out of the migratory trajectories of people and seeds" (2013, p. 37). Even though Momoko is a marginal character in the novel, an outsider who, by the time the novel opens, suffers from Alzheimer's, Lee reads her as the "epicenter of the novel" (p. 39). Through Momoko and her husband's collecting and planting of seeds for almost half a century, they have become "planetary heroes ... saving these plants from extinction," as one member of the anti-biotechnology activists who call themselves "the Seeds of Resistance" says (Ozeki 2003, p. 162). Significantly, her identity as a Japanese war bride also serves to recuperate the stereotypical and racist depictions of war brides as exotic and treasonous (Lee 2013, p. 41).

Just as *My Year of Meats* criticized the meat production industry, *All Over Creation*'s most important message is the potential destruction of agricultural products through genetic modification, overuse of pesticides, and lack of biodiversity in farming. One of the members of the "Seeds of Resistance," called Geek, says, "We depend on plants. They depend on us . . . Genetic engineering is changing the semantics, the meaning of life itself" (2003, p. 124). Using the example of the potato, he points out that there are "hundreds of different kinds of potatoes" in Peru, but in the United States, there are only "a dozen kinds left" because "engineers have decided that potatoes all have to be the same size" (p. 125). For Ozeki, "monoculture" in plants, as well as communities, "has a sad and hollow ring to it" (p. 125). She draws light-hearted and irreverent parallels between plants and people.

Using the character of Yumi, Ozeki plays with notions of hybridity and Asian American model minority myths. Yumi is the opposite of monoculture as well as the opposite of the stereotype of the model minority. A Japanese American woman, she does not have a successful professional career, but has been a drifter since she ran away from home as a teen. When asked about what she does, she says, "teach a few English classes. Raise kids. Sell a little real estate on the side" (2003, p. 226). Her home in Hawai'i is near a volcano with an "active lava flow" which shows the precarity of her existence (p. 226). While Asian Americans have often been stereotyped as doctors, engineers, and computer geeks, Yumi turns out to be an ordinary woman, sorting out her priorities in life after a misspent youth. She is the prodigal daughter returning home and reconnecting with her family and first lover.

In addition, Ozeki exaggerates the notion of "heterogeneity and hybridity" creating "somewhat comic and ironic effects" (Ty 2010, p. 125). In an oft-quoted article on Asian Americans, Lisa Lowe argues for the heterogeneity of the community in terms of ethnicity, generation, and class. Yumi is biracial, and her own family is a very "heterogeneous" mix of ethnicity and class (see Lowe 1991). Her three children have different fathers of different racial origins – Poo's father is a musician and Hawaiian; Ocean's father sells surfboards in Waikiki and is presumably white; and Phoenix's father is a Japanese plant scientist (Ozeki 2003, p. 96). Ozeki seems to be "self-consciously playing with notions of botany and race" (Ty 2010, p. 125), making analogies between the hybridity of children and plants. The chapter called "The Promiscuity of Squashes" pays tribute to Momoko, and to her skill in preserving and propagating a great variety and mix of zucchinis, tomatoes, beans, and squashes over the years.

Hybridity strengthens the crops and produces tastier vegetables. Instead of taking a moralistic stance regarding Yumi's multiple partners, through the character of the avid gardener Momoko, the novel suggests that the mixed veggies, like her grandchildren, are treasures: "a little bit zuke, and little bit Delicata, and little bit . . . whatchamacallit. Sweet Pumpkin . . . Like them. All mixed up" (Ozeki 2003, p. 118). *All Over Creation* celebrates the wonders and plenty of our earth, suggesting the possibility of regeneration and hope.

In *A Tale for the Time Being*, Ozeki's most ambitious novel to date, she again stresses the theme of global interconnectedness, the dangers of environmental degradation, and the importance of feminist supportive networks. The novel brings out twenty-first-century problems such as the collapse of financial markets, depression, and bullying. Its narrative structure encourages us to see the connections between fact and fiction, to understand that there are personal stories behind official histories, and to show the comforts of following alternative paths to fulfillment. In an interview about the novel, Ozeki says that she was not interested in "a single issue" but "everything that has happened in the past decade, personally as well as globally, in the post-9/11 period and since the turn of the millennium . . . Time itself became the issue that I was exploring" (Ty 2013, p. 161). The novel is told from the point of view of two very different female characters – one is Ruth, a middle-aged writer living in Cortes Island, off the coast of British Columbia, who is modeled after Ruth Ozeki, and the other is 16-year-old Nao, who has been reluctantly uprooted from her home in Sunnyvale, California, to start a new life in Tokyo, Japan. Nao is teased by her classmates because she is older and bigger than them and cannot speak Japanese. So, she writes her thoughts in a diary at a French maid café. While walking along a beach on her island home, Ruth discovers Nao's diary inside a

Hello Kitty lunchbox, probably as debris from the tsunami of March 2011. Thus, we have Ruth and Nao's alternating stories even though they do not happen synchronically.

That places on our Earth are connected across time and space is highlighted at the outset when Ruth finds the lunchbox which contains letters written in Japanese along with a watch and a diary. Oliver, Ruth's husband, modeled after the writer's actual husband, artist Oliver Kellhammer, explains that the package likely floated to the British Columbia coastline as jetsam, through one of the planetary gyres (Ozeki 2013, p. 13). These ocean gyres move at different speeds and carry the sun's heat, but also trash, all across the world. Even though finding Nao's diary becomes a fortuitous way for Ruth to connect to Nao in Japan, it also reveals the proximity, rather than the distance, between North America and Asia. Oliver tells her that there are at least eight large patches of garbage in the world's oceans, containing plastic, "bottle caps, beer cans, Styrofoam, tampon applicators, fishing nets, disposable razors" (p. 36). These are environmental problems that begin locally but impact the world globally, and occur as a consequence of our eagerness to make everything disposable, convenient, and packaged.

The fragility of our oceans and our Earth emphasizes the precarity of our existence in the twenty-first century. In *Cruel Optimism* (2011), Lauren Berlant explains the notion of precarity and argues that we "stay attached to conventional good-life fantasies – say, of enduring reciprocity in couples, families, political systems, institutions, markets, and at work – when the evidence of their instability, fragility, and dear cost abounds" (2011, p. 2). Ozeki's *A Tale for the Time Being* is a "novel about contingency, about people living for 'the time being,' as the title suggests" (Ty 2017, p. 29). Through Nao's family, Ozeki reveals the way we have relied on institutionalized forms of recognition that are shaky at best. Corporations treat people as disposable commodities, to be discarded when no longer useful. Nao explains how her family was radically dislocated: "My dad used to be this hotshot computer programmer, and he was head-hunted when I was three and got this great job in Silicon Valley, and we all moved there" (Ozeki 2013, p. 42). They settle in Sunnyvale, and Nao grows up American, but "we were living in a total dreamland called the Dot-Com Bubble, and when it burst, Dad's company went bankrupt, and he got sacked and we lost our visas and had to come back to Japan, which totally sucked because not only did Dad not have a job, but he'd also taken a big percentage of his big fat salary in stock options so suddenly we didn't have any savings either" (p. 43). In a few paragraphs, Nao illustrates the great reversal of fortune of her transnational family, which leads to her father's depression and multiple failed attempts at suicide, and to her ostracization in an unfamiliar culture.

What saves Nao from complete despair is to have Ruth and us, the readers of the novel, hear her story. Nao tries a variety of techniques to cope with her alienation, including working in a café, Buddhist meditation, and cybertechnology. However, as Marlo Starr points out, "the novel puts forward an alternate model of feminism through its depiction of Ruth and Nao's transnational relationship, one that emphasizes interdependence and communal identity while also preserving individual difference" (2016, p. 100). Ruth becomes a stand-in for the reader. She experiences "a sense of closeness and a reciprocal sense of ownership in her reading of the diary" (p. 116), and this interaction "allows both the writer and reader to participate in narrative creation" (p. 119). Even though the act is implausible if one were to read the novel as realist fiction, Ruth reaches out to Nao's father, crossing geographical and temporal boundaries. In Zen Buddhist philosophy, time and space are lived as integrated, "being-time" to indicate their inseparability (Nagatomo 2020, p. 73). She scolds him for being "selfish" (Ozeki 2013,

p. 352) and manages to convince him to not commit suicide because his daughter needs him. This act averts what might have been a tragic end to the family. This novel, like her previous novels, underscores the importance of human connection across countries, across race and ethnicity, and across generations.

SEE ALSO: After Postmodernism; Ecocriticism and Environmental Fiction; Multiculturalism; Post-9/11 Narratives; Religion and Contemporary Fiction

REFERENCES

Berlant, Lauren. (2011). *Cruel Optimism*. Durham, NC: Duke University Press.
Cheng, Emily. (2009). Meat and the Millennium: transnational politics of race and gender in Ruth Ozeki's *My Year of Meats*. *Journal of Asian American Studies* 12 (2): 191–220.
Chiu, Monica. (2004). Inside the meat machine: food, filth, and (in)fertility in Ruth Ozeki's *My Year of Meats*. In: *Filthy Fictions: Asian American Literature by Women*, 133–166. Lanham, MD: Altamira Press.
Lee, Hsiu-Chuan. (2013). Trafficking in seeds: war bride, biopolitics, and Asian American spectrality in Ruth Ozeki's *All Over Creation*. *Concentric: Literary and Cultural Studies* 39 (2): 33–55.
Lowe, Lisa. (1991). Heterogeneity, hybridity, multiplicity: marking Asian American differences. *Diaspora* 1 (1): 24–43.
Nagatomo, Shigenori. (2020). Japanese Zen Buddhist philosophy. In: *The Stanford Encyclopedia of Philosophy* (ed. Edward N. Zalta). https://plato.stanford.edu/archives/spr2020/entries/japanese-zen/ (accessed July 21, 2021).
Ozeki, Ruth. (1998). *My Year of Meats*. New York: Penguin.
Ozeki, Ruth. (2003). *All Over Creation*. New York: Penguin.
Ozeki, Ruth. (2013). *A Tale for the Time Being*. New York: Viking.
Starr, Marlo. (2016). Beyond machine dreams: Zen, cyber-, and transnational feminisms in Ruth Ozeki's *A Tale for the Time Being*. *Meridians* 13 (2): 99–122.
Tölölyan, Khachig. (2007). The contemporary discourse of diaspora studies. *Comparative Studies of South Asia, Africa and the Middle East* 27 (3): 647–655.
Ty, Eleanor. (2010). Scripting fertility: desire and regeneration in Japanese North American literature. In: *UnFastened: Globality and Asian North American Narratives*, 108–128. Minneapolis: University of Minnesota Press.
Ty, Eleanor. (2013). "A universe of many worlds": an interview with Ruth Ozeki. *MELUS* 38 (3): 160–171.
Ty, Eleanor. (2017). Precarity and the pursuit of unhappiness. In: *Asianfail: Narratives of Disenchantment and the Model Minority*, 27–43. Champaign: University of Illinois Press.

FURTHER READING

Fachinger, Petra. (2017). Writing the Canadian Pacific Northwest ecocritically: the dynamics of local and global in Ruth Ozeki's *A Tale for the Time Being*. *Canadian Literature* 232 (Spring): 47–63.
Lovell, Sue. (2018). Toward a poetics of posthumanist narrative using Ruth Ozeki's *A Tale for The Time Being*. *Critique: Studies in Contemporary Fiction* 59 (1): 57–74.
Poulsen, Melissa. (2011). Hybrid veggies and mixed kids: ecocriticism and race in Ruth Ozeki's pastoral heartlands. *Asian American Literature: Discourses and Pedagogies* 2: 22–29.
Wallace, Molly. (2011). Discomfort food: analogy, biotechnology, and risk in Ruth Ozeki's *All Over Creation*. *Arizona Quarterly: A Journal of American Literature, Culture, and Theory* 67 (4): 155–181.
Wallis, Andrew. (2013). Toward a global ecoconsciousness in Ruth Ozeki's *My Year of Meats*. *ISLE: Interdisciplinary Studies in Literature and Environment* 20 (4): 837–854.

Ozick, Cynthia

LUCY BIEDERMAN
Heidelberg University, USA

Spanning more than half a century, Cynthia Ozick's literary career has included six novels, seven collections of short stories, and seven collections of essays. Although best known for her short fiction, perhaps most notably the "The Shawl" (1980), which depicts the internment of three female characters in a death camp during the Holocaust, Ozick is a prolific essayist who writes frequently about the roles and resonances of authors, authorship, and writing. One of Ozick's major themes, across genres, is the conflict between Western literary traditions and the dictates of Judaism. Her work has earned critical praise through its attention to intellectual, literary, and religious traditions and its stylistic virtuosity, the possible result of Ozick's apprenticeship to Henry James in the first decades of her writing life. Ozick's work has been awarded major national and international literary prizes, including the National Book Critics Circle Award (for *Quarrel & Quandary*, 2000), the PEN/Nabokov Award (2008), the PEN/Malamud Award (2008), and the Rea Award for the Short Story, of which Ozick was the first winner. She has twice been a finalist for the National Book Award, for her novel *The Puttermesser Papers* (1997) and her first collection of short stories, *The Pagan Rabbi and Other Stories* (1971). She has been a finalist for the Pulitzer Prize and the Man Booker International Prize.

Ozick was born on April 17, 1928, in New York City, to Celia and William Ozick, Russian immigrants who owned and operated a neighborhood drug store in Pelham Bay, the Bronx. The Ozicks – Cynthia, her parents, her older brother, and a grandmother – lived in "a little house on Saint Paul Avenue," Ozick writes in the memoiristic essay "A Drug Store Eden" (2001, p. 195). Ozick describes her parents working "monstrously long" hours, struggling through the Great Depression to make rent. "My mother was aflame with ambition, emotion, struggle. My father was reticent, far more resigned to the world as given," Ozick recalls (p. 192). The dynamic and distinctions between her parents perhaps laid the groundwork for some of Ozick's novelistic portrayals of romantic relationships between strong-willed women and passive men, including Allegra and Enoch Vand's marriage in *Trust* (1966) and Ruth and Rupert Rabeeno's affair in *The Puttermesser Papers*.

Education and schooling are frequent themes in Ozick's fictions. Attending both *cheder* (Hebrew school) and public school foregrounded the tension between the principles of Jewish law and Western learning that appears throughout her work. Ozick describes, in a 1985 interview with Elaine Kauvar, an early revelation about gender and education in *cheder*. The rabbi who taught Ozick initially instructed her grandmother to take the five-year-old Ozick home, because girls do not need an education. Soon, however, he came to see Ozick's intelligence: "She has a golden little head," he reported to Ozick's grandmother in Yiddish (Kauvar 1985, p. 385). P.S. 71 was a different story, a school at which Ozick's abilities were never recognized. In both settings, Ozick recalls experiencing different types of outsiderhood: "it was very strange to me to have two lives like this: on the school side, where I was almost always the only Jew, and in *cheder* where I was almost always the only girl" (p. 385).

In *The Cannibal Galaxy* (1983), the tension between Ozick's two types of early schooling is embodied in the protagonist, Joseph Brill, who oversees a dual curriculum school where Jewish and Western beliefs are taught side by side, in an unsteady accord. A young female student, Beulah Lilt, who Brill dismisses readily as "not one of the bright ones" (Ozick 1983, p. 45), grows up to be a celebrated painter – her success an indictment on the dual curriculum and Brill's blind allegiance to it. "Absolutely, Beulah is P.S. 71 for me, there's no question about that," Ozick says (Kauvar 1985, p. 389).

Attending Hunter College High School in Manhattan was an act of defiance against P.S. 71, at which Ozick's teachers had suggested she refrain from taking the admittance exam, assuming she would not pass. At Hunter, Ozick says, she began to recover a sense of her intelligence. "In that school they told you were a Hunter girl, a member of an elite, and this began to have an effect," she tells Kauvar (Kauvar 1985, p. 389). Ozick graduated early and matriculated at New York University (NYU) in February 1946, on the advice of her brother, who had recently graduated. The essay "Washington Square, 1946," which appears in Ozick's 1989 collection *Metaphor & Memory*, describes her innocence and ignorance as an NYU freshman traveling among "the sorrowful literary young," and her subsequent discovery of contemporary writers through magazines like *Partisan Review* (Ozick 1991, p. 118).

Ozick went on to Ohio State University (OSU), where she received a master's degree in 1950. "In those distant days, an M.A. was like a mini-Ph.D.," Ozick recalls in the essay "How I Got Fired From My Summer Job" (Ozick 2001, p. 211). "It was important not to go after a Ph.D., though, because it meant you were not in earnest about becoming a writer; it was, in fact, an embarrassment, a cowardly expedient that could shame you" (p. 213). Ozick produced a thesis, "Parable in the Later Novels of Henry James," in which, she later noted, "I tried to catch up all of James in the net of a single idea" ("The Lesson of the Master," Ozick 1983, p. 293). Ozick not only wrote on James, she "became" him: "I was of his cult, I was a worshiper of literature, literature was my single altar; I was, like the elderly bald-headed James, a priest at that altar; and that altar was all of my life" (p. 294). Ozick's religiosity toward James hints at a notion that haunts her future work: the fear that art can replace religion. Ozick's contentious and fruitful relationship to James has extended her entire career, from her master's thesis, to numerous essays, to her most recent fictions, including the novella "Dictation" (the first piece in 2008's *Dictation: A Quartet*) and the 2010 novel *Foreign Bodies*, which riffs on James's *The Ambassadors* (1903).

Ozick's education continued after OSU, extending to seven years spent writing a novel titled *Mercy, Pity, Peace, and Love*, which was never published, followed by seven more years writing *Trust* (1966), her first novel, published when she was 37. Ozick has characterized this period of artistic commitment as a painful one. "I was a worshipper of Literature. I had a youthful arrogance about my 'powers,' and at the same time a terrible feeling of humiliation, of total shame and defeat" (Teicholz 1987, p. 162). Ozick has professed her predilection, in those years of nascency, for art over life, harboring under "the monkish conviction that Literature was all" ("Afterword," Ozick 2004). Even years afterward, in a brief 1985 essay, "Pear Tree and Polar Bear: A Word on Life and Art," Ozick upholds that monkish conviction: "As for life, I don't like it," she writes. "Life is that which – pressingly, persistently, unfailingly, imperially – interrupts" (1991, p. 111). Of *Trust*, Ozick recalls, "It was the novel of my prime; I will never again write with so hubristic a passion. It marked the crest of life, the old ambition's deepest bite" ("Afterword," Ozick 2004). In *Trust*, the tale of the unnamed female protagonist's coming of age in America and Europe is set against the horrors and upheaval of the Holocaust.

Although best known for her novels and short stories, Ozick began literary life as a poet. A poem of Ozick's published in *Virginia Quarterly Review* caught the attention of an agent, Theron Raines, who inquired after her novel in progress. Raines shepherded *Trust* to publication. Ozick has described trust as a novel in which "every paragraph [is] a poem" (Ozick 1976, p. 4). Ozick's uncle, Abraham Regelson, was a well-known Hebrew poet. "His poetry was complex, imbricated, hugely erudite, with, here and there, noble biblical resonances and classical turns that recalled, to an eminent literary critic, Milton and Shelley," Ozick recalls ("Afterword," Ozick 2004). Poets and poems appear frequently in Ozick's fiction; in *Trust*, the unnamed protagonist's wealthy mother, Allegra Vand, funds an experimental poetry journal titled *Bushelbasket*. "Envy; or Yiddish in America," depicts the tormented Yiddish-language poet Edelshtein (based on Jacob Glatstein) in his observations of Yankel Ostrover (based on

I.B. Singer), whose cartoonish tales of shetl life have found widespread success in translation. Edelstein's angry, passionate attempts to "save Yiddish" are complicated by his envy for Ostrover and for Ostover's blasé attitude toward both literature and the dying language in which he writes (Ozick 1971, p. 93). As Leah Garrett has shown, the Edelshtein poem that appears in full in "Envy" is a parody of Glatstein's poem "Genesis," one of many Glatstein poems that Ozick translated from the Yiddish in *The Penguin Book of Modern Yiddish Verse* (1988). In her 1983 essay "A Translator's Monologue," Ozick laments the difficulty, even impossibility, of translating Yiddish poetry into English, a task that "means a crossing-over from Jewish concepts to Christian concepts, or at best to a secularized sensibility" (1991, p. 203). As for her own poetry, Ozick says she stopped writing verse "at around age thirty-six" (Teicholz 1987, p. 186).

Reflecting these contradictions, Ozick's characters often have complicated relationships with Judaism and Jewish heritage. In "Envy," the poet Edelshtein's frustrations with Yiddish and Jewish American literature stem from fundamental questions about how to present oneself to readerships when one is both a Jew and a writer. In *The Shawl* (1989), a novella developed from Ozick's short story of the same name, Rosa, born and raised in a bourgeois Polish family, survives the brutality of the Holocaust to struggle with poverty, trauma, and assimilation in Miami. Rosa's struggles are entwined with her Jewishness; she is repulsed both by Jews in Miami who speak Yiddish and by her memories of Orthodox Jews in Poland; and yet, her life and mind are shaped by her experiences as a Jewish victim of the Holocaust. *The Puttermesser Papers*, which depicts the life and afterlife of Ruth Puttermesser, from brilliant young lawyer to mayor of New York to lover to mother to murder victim, offers another vision of Jewish life. Puttermesser's Uncle Zindel offers Hebrew lessons; her parents, as Jewish parents stereotypically do, write from Florida urging marriage; considering a daughter, Puttermesser instead creates Xanthippe, a golem out of Jewish folklore. Ever rational, Puttermesser recalls great, philosophically serious figures throughout Jewish history who made golems: "If Vilna Gaon could contemplate the making of a golem, thought Puttermesser, there was nothing irrational in it, and she would not be ashamed of what she herself had concocted" (1998, p. 49). Puttermesser's experiences with Jewishness are not religious; rather, they are intellectual, folkloric, cultural, and familial.

In her nonfiction, Ozick has explored what, if anything, it means to be a Jewish writer and the moral culpability, from a Jewish perspective, of the imaginative work of the fiction writer. Her 1970 essay "Toward a New Yiddish," advocates for a liturgical, morally engaged Jewish literature, as opposed to the imaginatively inclined lyric. Ozick introduces this essay as a "[s]elf-portrait of a third-generational American Jew . . . perfectly at home and yet perfectly insecure, perfectly acculturated and yet perfectly marginal . . ." (1983, p. 152). That sense of marginality, Ozick writes, can lead writers of the Jewish diaspora to produce texts that, in their effort to move from the margins of literary life, incline toward the lyric, rather than the liturgical. But "nothing thought or written in Diaspora has ever been able to last unless it has been centrally Jewish," Ozick concludes here (p. 168). In "Tradition and (or Versus) the Jewish Writer," however, Ozick argues against a religious vision of the novel, arguing, "[w]hat we want from novels is not what we want from the transcendent liturgies of the synagogue" (2007, p. 125). These contradictory visions of what Jewish literature can and should do suggest an irresolvable tension that animates Ozick's work. Another such tension is "the clash of monotheism with image-making, the poet as God-competitor" (Kauvar 1985, p. 380).

In interviews and essays, and in her fictions, Ozick has set imagination against moral and religious duty, suggesting that the imaginative work of writing fiction is fundamentally at odds with Jewish law. This issue plays out in many of her short fictions, including "An Education," "Usurpation," and "The Pagan Rabbi," which examine, in various ways, the joys and dangers of creating idols. "The Pagan Rabbi" takes place in the aftermath of Rabbi Isaac Kornfield's suicide. Attempting to understand the cause of the brilliant, scholarly rabbi's death, the unnamed narrator pores over Isaac's writings, which are included in the short story. In these writings, Romantic Western thought and texts and pagan myths clash against Jewish law; Isaac writes of a love affair with a dryad named Iripomoňoéià, who leads Isaac to his soul – a fellow Orthodox Jew who castigates Isaac for his disobedience. Unable to reconcile his paganistic passions with Jewish tradition, Isaac hangs himself with the old man's prayer shawl in a public park. Recent scholarship argues that critical attention (e.g. Kauvar, Strandberg) to Ozick's engagement with the tension between Jewish and Western traditions has come at the expense of readings of Ozick as a multicultural writer. Dean Franco argues Ozick's work offers "a compelling presentation of Jewish religion and culture that imagines Jews as radically outside the mainstream" (2008, p. 61).

Despite sharing thematic concerns, Ozick's fictions are formally varied, often within the space of a single text. Ozick's frequent use of intertextuality gestures toward a vast world of texts informing the text at hand. The writings of Isaac Kornfield, which take up large portions of "The Pagan Rabbi," are one such example. *The Puttermesser Papers* is frequently interrupted by "other" texts, both invented and real, from letters from Puttermesser's parents, to memos and documents from Puttermesser's work life, to personal ads in the *New York Review of Books*, to the journals of George Eliot. A section of the novel titled "Puttermesser Paired" depicts Puttermesser's love affair with Rupert Rabeeno, a painter who reproduces great works. Rupert and Puttermesser become obsessed with George Eliot and her two lovers, George Henry Lewes and Johnny Cross, reading aloud from Eliot's *Letters*. Rupert and Puttermesser's relationship ultimately becomes a tragic reproduction of Eliot's and Cross's affair. In *The Messiah of Stockholm* (1987), Lars Andemening, believing himself to be the son of the Polish Jewish writer Bruno Schulz, who was killed during the Holocaust, forms a temporary community around the search for *The Messiah*, a lost text by Schulz. That text's absence, and the flickering possibility of its existence, animate the narrative. *Heir to the Glimmering World* (2004) is also oriented around a text: a wildly popular series of illustrated children's books written by the father of James A'Bair. James's fame, wealth, and misery stem from these books, in which he is centrally featured; as a child, he was internationally known as the "Bear Boy" (*Heir* was released in the United Kingdon under the title *The Bear Boy*). The rootless, impoverished young protagonist of *Heir*, Rose Meadows, comes into possession of a valuable edition of the first "Bear Book" that once belonged to James. Rose's employers, the Mitwissers, an eccentric family of refugees from Nazi Germany, are coincidentally beholden to James, as well, relying on his patronage to survive. The invented "Bear Boy" text is the axis around which the characters in *Heir to the Glimmering World* turn. Characteristically, despite Ozick's use of postmodern tactics like intertextuality and formal innovation, she has insisted that she is driven by traditionalism: "Inventing a secret, then revealing it in the drama of entanglement – this is what ignites the will to write stories. The creation of forms has no part in this; I have no interest in 'the new.' Rupture doesn't attract me: I would rather inherit coherence than smash and start over again with enigma." (1991, p. 111).

Optimism and pessimism, toward both literature and Ozick's place in the literary pantheon, are entwined in Ozick's work. In *The Puttermesser Papers*, Puttermesser dies and goes to heaven, only to find that Paradise ultimately sours. "In Paradise, where sight and insight, inner and outer, sweet and salt, logic and illogic, are shuffled in the manner of a kaleidoscope, nothing is permanent," Ozick writes. "Paradise is a dream bearing the inscription on Solomon's seal: *this too will pass* . . . The secret meaning of Paradise is that it too is hell" (1998, p. 234). But in her literary and personal essays, Ozick locates rich, even paradisical, possibility in her memories. Recalling the drug store her parents owned and operated, Ozick writes, "The Park View Pharmacy lives only in a secret Eden behind my eyes." And, of course, Ozick finds a sense of redemption in "the bliss of American prose" (2001, p. xiii). In her two most recent collections of essays, *The Din in the Head* (2006) and *Critics, Monsters, Fanatics, and Other Literary Essays* (2016), Ozick has attended to the question of "Lastingness" – why some writers endure while others are "plummeted into eclipse" (2016, p. 160). Despite her prolific, prize-winning career, Ozick describes herself as having been "mostly obscure for decades" (Neary 2016). Despite those reservations about her own lastingness, Ozick endures. She writes, because, she says, "I simply must" (Neary 2016).

SEE ALSO: Multiculturalism; Religion and Contemporary Fiction; Trauma and Fiction

REFERENCES

Franco, Dean. (2008). Rereading Cynthia Ozick: pluralism, postmodernism, and the multicultural encounter. *Contemporary Literature* 49 (1): 56–84.

Kauvar, Elaine M. (1985). An interview with Cynthia Ozick. *Contemporary Literature* 26 (4): 375–401.

Neary, Lynn. (2016). Why does Cynthia Ozick write? "I simply must, she says." *NPR* (July 17, 2016). https://www.npr.org/2016/07/17/486172884/why-does-cynthia-ozick-write-i-simply-must-she-says (accessed July 22, 2021).

Ozick, Cynthia. (1971). *The Pagan Rabbi and Other Stories*. New York: Knopf.

Ozick, Cynthia. (1976). *Bloodshed and Three Novellas*. New York: Knopf.

Ozick, Cynthia. (1983). *Art and Ardor*. New York: Knopf.

Ozick, Cynthia. (1991). *Metaphor & Memory*. New York: Vintage; 1st ed. 1989.

Ozick, Cynthia. (1998). *The Puttermesser Papers*. New York: Vintage; 1st ed. 1997.

Ozick, Cynthia. (2001). *Quarrel & Quandary*. New York: Vintage.

Ozick, Cynthia. (2004). *Trust*. Kindle ed. Boston: Mariner; 1st ed. 1966.

Ozick, Cynthia. (2007). *The Din in the Head*. Boston: Mariner; 1st ed. 2006.

Ozick, Cynthia. (2016). *Critics, Monsters, Fanatics, and Other Literary Essays*. Boston: Houghton Mifflin Harcourt.

Teicholz, Tom. (1987). The art of fiction XCV: Cynthia Ozick. *Paris Review* 102 (Spring): 154–190.

FURTHER READING

Bloom, Harold. (ed.) (1986). *Cynthia Ozick: Modern Critical Views*. New York: Chelsea House.

Garrett, Leah. (2005). Cynthia Ozick's *Envy*: a reconsideration. *Studies in American Jewish Literature* 24: 60–81.

Kauvar, Elaine M. (1993). *Cynthia Ozick's Fiction: Tradition and Invention*. Bloomington: Indiana University Press.

Kauvar, Elaine M. (1993). An interview with Cynthia Ozick. *Contemporary Literature* 34 (3): 358–394.

Lowin, Joseph. (1988). *Cynthia Ozick*. Woodbridge, CT: Twayne.

Strandberg, Victor H. (1991). *Greek Mind/Jewish Soul: The Conflicted Art of Cynthia Ozick*. Madison: University of Wisconsin Press.

Palahniuk, Chuck

JEFFREY A. SARTAIN
University of Houston-, Victoria, USA

Charles Michael "Chuck" Palahniuk was born in Pasco, Washington on February 21, 1962. His early years as a novelist were propelled by the 1999 David Fincher adaptation of his debut novel, *Fight Club* (1996), which film critic James Berardinelli called "the '90s version of *A Clockwork Orange*" (1999). Plugging into the ennui of the premillennial moment with a haunting prescience, the film adaptation propelled Palahniuk's first novel, already winner of a Pacific Northwest Booksellers' Award (1997) and an Oregon Book Award for Best Novel (1997), to international attention. *Fight Club* established Palahniuk as a force to be reckoned with in American literature, earning him praise for his biting satire of contemporary consumerist culture. Palahniuk originally studied journalism at the University of Oregon, graduating in 1986. Once out of school, the meager salary he was collecting as a journalist was not enough to cover his expenses and student loan payments, so he took a job repairing semi-trucks for Freightliner after quitting his newspaper job in 1988. During this period of his life, Palahniuk drifted from writing for a time, eventually finding his way into Portlander Tom Spanbauer's "Dangerous Writings" workshop which Spanbauer began teaching in 1990 in the tradition of his mentor Gordon Lish's workshops. It was during this period of his early career in which Palahniuk penned *Invisible Monsters* (1999), *Survivor* (1999), *Fight Club*, and *Choke* (2001), though these books were not published in the order they were written.

Palahniuk followed these first four novels with a trio of horror books, *Lullaby* (2002), *Diary* (2003), and *Haunted* (2005), which included his infamous story, "Guts." He continued his impressive literary output with *Rant* (2007), *Snuff* (2008), *Pygmy* (2009), *Tell-All* (2010), and *Damned* (2011). In 2012, Palahniuk released *Invisible Monsters: Remix*, which restored the originally intended order of pages and chapters for the first novel he ever penned. The year 2013 saw the release of *Doomed*, the sequel to *Damned* and second in a promised trilogy, while 2014 brought *Beautiful You* and the co-edited collection *Burnt Tongues*. His most recent novels are *Adjustment Day* (2019) and *The Invention of Sound* (2020). In recent years, Palahniuk collaborates frequently with graphic artists on the *Fight Club 2* (2015–2016) and *Fight Club 3* (2019) graphic novels, as well as two coloring books with accompanying short stories, *Bait* (2016) and *Legacy* (2017), all published by Oregon-based Dark Horse Comics.

As a novelist, Palahniuk utilizes many of the literary techniques Tom Spanbauer taught in the "Dangerous Writings" workshop. In the workshop, Spanbauer taught a craft-oriented curriculum based in part on his scholarship under Gordon Lish, the infamous fiction editor of *Esquire*. From Spanbauer's teachings, Palahniuk adapted many of the techniques utilized by masters of the literary minimalist short story, such as Amy Hempel, Denis Johnson, and Mark Richard, for use in his novels. As a result of his efforts in Spanbauer's workshop, Palahniuk published his first short fiction, "The Love Theme of Sybil and William" (1990) and "Negative Reinforcement" (1990), in the now defunct literary magazine *Modern Short Stories*. He also wrote the initial manuscripts for *Invisible Monsters* and *Survivor* during this period, though neither found success when he sent them to publishers for consideration. After hitting rejection after rejection with his first two books for being "too dark and risky," Palahniuk claims he wrote *Fight Club* as a kind of protest against the publishers' standards for transgressive fiction (Tomlinson 1999). W.W. Norton, however, bought *Fight Club* for a low amount, and within four years David Fincher had directed the film adaptation, starring Brad Pitt, Edward Norton, and Helena Bonham-Carter. Though receiving mixed reviews and falling short of projected box office earnings, the film earned a cult status among viewers and sold very well on home release.

Fight Club tells the story of an unnamed narrator and his split personality, the anarchist revolutionary Tyler Durden. The narrator's disaffected, dispassionate life of work and middle-class materialism were unfulfilling, so his psyche created an alter ego that was able to express all the lust, rage, and violence the narrator's life lacked. Together, they found a men's organization called Fight Club, which spreads quickly among disaffected men all over the city. Tyler notably manifests when the narrator meets Marla Singer, a fellow support-group faker to whom he is attracted. Unable to express his own desire, the narrator's alter ego Tyler seduces Marla and carries on a relationship with her. Fight Club continues to expand across the nation, and eventually evolves into the terrorist movement Project Mayhem. Tyler leads Project Mayhem's anarchist mission, to set the human race back thousands of years. To that end, the members of Project Mayhem infiltrate private and public organizations at key positions. All the members of Project Mayhem are required to kill someone, and one step in their eventual goal is part of the book's climax – to explode buildings onto the Natural History museums, erasing multiple forms of history at once. After he recovers from a self-inflicted gunshot wound, the narrator awakens in a hospital ward, his consciousness clearly medicated. The book ends with hospital orderlies suggesting, through the narrator's drug-induced fog, that Project Mayhem was proceeding with the plans and awaited his return.

When adapted to film, several details of the language, as well as a few plot details, were altered significantly by screenwriter Jim Uhls. These include how the narrator met Tyler, the inclusion of Marla's mother as an important character, the more savage crimes Project Mayhem members commit, the fact that the narrator kills his boss, and the ending of the film. Despite these changes, the film is widely considered a classic of 1990s cinema. Chuck Palahniuk, on the author/screenwriter commentary for the film's home release, praises the film as more coherent and tighter than his book.

On the back of the film's pre-release buzz, W.W. Norton published Palahniuk's first two novels to coincide with the release of the film in 1999. At the turn of the millennium, Palahniuk found himself a long way from the Pasco, Washington desert where he grew up with three siblings, moving to his grandparents' ranch when he was a teenager and his parents divorced. Along with success, tragedy also struck Palahniuk in 1999 when his father, Fred, and Fred's girlfriend, Donna Fontaine, were brutally murdered by her ex-lover. At the subsequent trial, Palahniuk wrote in support of the death penalty for the murderer, which was later reduced to a life sentence (Akbar 2012). In 2001, with the success of *Choke*, which reached number 3 on *The New York Times* Best Seller list, Palahniuk was finally able to quit his job as a mechanic and pursue writing full time.

Since his move to full-time writing, Palahniuk has produced an average of about a book a year and shows no signs of stopping his output. The critical press around Palahniuk's fiction has been interesting and varied. In the trades he tends to garner mixed reviews, though almost all of his fiction has earned critical attention in academic books and journals. Indeed, almost a cottage industry of academic publishing around Palahniuk sprung up in the postmillennial moment, and Palahniuk's fiction has been treated with a depth and seriousness that most similarly popular writers and contemporaries cannot boast.

Of his work, Palahniuk frequently claims the labels minimalist and transgressive. Thematically, Palahniuk's fiction displays a dark sense of humor and irony that he uses to satirize contemporary values and mores. His novels, often portraying the darker sides of violence, fame, sexuality, consumerism, and drug use, utilize social transgression as a liminal space from which to mount the works' social critique. The social statements Palahniuk makes in his novels are grounded in the particular qualities of his characters, and how they negotiate tenuous relationships between their status as outsiders and the mainstream. Palahniuk's work tends to focus on the affective and embodied aspects of language and storytelling, which readers experience through the first-person immediacy of his narrators. This focus allows Palahniuk to deliver language laden with "allusion, implication, and efficiency" (Clark 2014, p. 138) that are critical to minimalist fiction techniques. Palahniuk explained many of the tropes of his minimalist approach to novel-length fiction in a series of craft-oriented workshops that he taught through essays published on his website in 2005/2006, and further explored at length in his book about writing, *Consider This: Moments in My Life after Which Everything Was Different* (2020).

Palahniuk also participates in a postmodern tradition of metafictive storytelling, even experimenting with the materiality of the text itself. For example, *Diary* contained a message related to the story on the inside of the dust jacket, and *Survivor*'s pagination runs in reverse as the airplane carrying the main character runs out of fuel. *Survivor* also boasts a trick ending that is so often overlooked that for twenty years Palahniuk's website maintained a page explaining the ending in the author's own words (Widmyer 1999). Palahniuk's most materially experimental text is *Invisible Monsters: Remix*, in which chapters are presented in a nonlinear order to resemble the article breaks in fashion magazines. There are even chapters that are hidden from the main narrative, as there are no cues to turn to those particular pages as a reader moves through the text. Upon the original publication of *Invisible Monsters* in 1999, Palahniuk bowed to pressures to order the story chronologically, but with his success came the opportunity to restore the original text's wildly experimental form (Weston 2012).

Palahniuk's early novels, the aggressive, punk-influenced, transgressive fiction of his early years, form a distinctive first movement in his career. These works include his first four novels, as well as a good deal of his early magazine journalism, and his earliest short stories from 1990. This phase of Palahniuk's career is what he is best known for, as two of these books, *Fight Club* and *Choke*, have been adapted to major feature films

(*Choke* was released in 2008, directed by Clark Gregg). *Fight Club*, especially, contributed to Palahniuk's breakout literary success, as it is a cult film that has seen massive growth and saturation of the culture since its release in 1999. His magazine writing was collected in *Stranger than Fiction: True Stories* (2004), a remarkable foray into subcultural America and interviews with icons of the counterculture.

The first two novels, *Invisible Monsters* and *Survivor*, also focus on notions of countercultural transgression and repression. *Invisible Monsters* tells the story of disfigured supermodel Shannon McFarland, her mentor Brandy Alexander, and a rogues' gallery of marginalized friends. *Survivor* recounts the tale of Tender Branson, an apocalyptic cult leader who hijacks a plane to tell his side of the story. Both have been wildly popular with Palahniuk's fans, and it is the popularity of *Invisible Monsters* that allowed Palahniuk to restore the text to his originally intended version with *Invisible Monsters: Remix*.

Palahniuk also contracted with the Crown Journeys series to produce the travelogue/memoir *Fugitives and Refugees: A Walk in Portland, Oregon* (2003), which he claims is the closest thing to an autobiography he will ever write. Interspersed between the chapters about the city, the travelogue through Portland's seamy underbelly of strip clubs and haunted tunnels gives the reader "Postcards" from Palahniuk's life in Portland, glimpses back at specific experiences that shaped the author in the city. It is in this volume that the personal legend of Palahniuk was largely built, as it is a tale of independence, exploration, and bad behavior largely, supporting the assertion Palahniuk attributes to author Katherine Dunn: that the dislocated, marginalized, and striving people of the country move west to the Pacific Ocean, eventually depositing all the nation's "fugitives and refugees" in Portland (Palahniuk 2003, p. 14).

The next phase of his career is marked by a turn to the fantastic and the horrific with a three-book contract with Doubleday, resulting in the publication of *Lullaby*, *Diary*, and *Haunted*. This period saw Palahniuk's notoriety skyrocket. When he was touring in support of *Diary* and *Haunted*, the gruesome bodily horror of his story "Guts," which he was reading on tour, caused people to vomit and faint in the aisles of the readings. This was clearly documented in the media coverage and interviews on display in *Postcards from the Future: The Chuck Palahniuk Documentary* (2003), an independent film by Dennis Widmyer, Kevin Kölsch, and Joshua Chaplinski. The three directors were instrumental in Palahniuk's early Internet presence and accessibility to his fans. Soon after meeting Palahniuk at a reading, they set up "The Cult," Palahniuk's official website, in September 1999. A large part of Palahniuk's popularity and accessibility is due to his active fan base centered around the site. Widmyer, Kölsch, and Chaplinski have all gone on to successful film careers since the documentary, and the non-Palahniuk literary activities taking place on The Cult website eventually spun off into their own literary website, LitReactor, in 2011. In 2014, Widmyer co-edited (with Palahniuk and Richard Thomas) *Burnt Tongues: An Anthology of Transgressive Stories*, a collection of stories that had been developed as part of an online writing workshop hosted by Palahniuk's official website.

Much of Palahniuk's later writing includes an emphasis on the themes of media spectacle, a turn in his fiction that certainly seems related to his status as cult author and literary celebrity. *Snuff* is an examination of the pornography industry and its effects on sex workers; *Tell-All* examines celebrity culture and biographies; *Rant* is a pastiche of the oral biography, set in a science fictional apocalyptic near future, and focuses on a messianic figure named Rant Casey. *Damned* and *Doomed* parody the style of Judy Blume's young adult writings while telling a new version of Dante Alighieri's *Divine Comedy* (1320). *Pygmy* is unique in Palahniuk's career, but nonetheless represents some of his most humorous achievements of craft at the sentence-to-sentence, word-to-word level. The book offers a poetry of puns and malapropisms buried in the satire of totalitarian thinking and American pop culture.

Palahniuk has also recently ventured into graphic novels/comic books, as well as coloring books, in collaboration with many talented graphic artists. He wrote the *Fight Club 2* comic book series with artists Cameron Stewart and David Mack, and also released the coloring books *Bait* and *Legacy* with renowned publisher Dark Horse Comics. Palahniuk has also penned the script and began working, in 2016, to bring *Lullaby* to the big screen with director Andy Mingo in a crowd-financed film that has seen continual delays. Palahniuk also published his first anthology of short stories, *Make Something Up*, in 2015. Palahniuk's relationship with the short story is interesting, as his novels almost all start out as short stories, and if the shorter work is productive enough, it will become a novel. His first fiction published were short works, including two early pieces from 1990 that have not been republished. One of Palahniuk's most notorious short pieces, "Guts," caused bodily reactions in audiences all over the world when read aloud, even in translation. "Guts" was published as part of the novel *Haunted*, which originally started as a short story anthology but eventually became a much larger, multifaceted novel that included a frame-tale narrative and works of poetry between every chapter.

Recently, Palahniuk's book tours frequently include other authors from his writers' group in Portland – Chelsea Cain, Monica Drake, and Lidia Yuknavitch often accompany Chuck on book tours that resemble live performances more than classical book readings. Monica Drake describes the tour as one "dream gig" after another, and that their performances "sold out fast" (Drake 2018).

In June 2018, Palahniuk explained on his website and social media that he was "close to broke" (Palahniuk 2018) after it was revealed that he was the victim of a long-term embezzlement performed by the bookkeeper, Darin Webb, at his literary agency, Donadio & Olson, one of the most respected agencies in New York (Flood 2018). Donadio & Olson filed for bankruptcy in December 2018, and Webb received a sentence of two years for the more than $3.4 million he stole over the course of eight years from numerous clients of the agency (Albanese 2018).

Palahniuk has rebounded with *Adjustment Day*, considered by many to be a thematic successor to *Fight Club*. Simultaneously, he released the *Fight Club 3* graphic novel as a series of comics across 2019. The year 2020 saw the release of *The Invention of Sound and Consider This*. Work reportedly continues on the film adaptation of *Lullaby* with director Andy Mingo, and other Palahniuk novels are regularly discussed for development and adaptation to film.

SEE ALSO: Debut Novels; Fiction and Affect; Fiction and Terrorism; The Graphic Novel; Hempel, Amy; Johnson, Denis; Minimalism and Maximalism

REFERENCES

Akbar, Arifa. (2012). Chuck Palahniuk: "I shy away from non-consensual violence." *Independent* (June 16, 2012). https://www.independent.co.uk/arts-entertainment/books/features/chuck-palahniuk-i-shy-away-from-non-consensual-violence-7851425.html (accessed July 5, 2021).

Albanese, Andrew. (2018). Bookkeeper gets two year sentence for scheme that destroyed Donadio & Olson. *Publishers Weekly* (December 17, 2018). https://www.publishersweekly.com/pw/by-topic/industry-news/publisher-news/article/78860-darin-webb-gets-two-years-in-prison-for-embezzlement-scheme-that-destroyed-donadio-olson.html (accessed July 5, 2021).

Berardinelli, James. (1999). Review of *Fight Club*. Reel Views. https://www.reelviews.net/reelviews/fight-club (accessed July 5, 2021).

Clark, Robert. (2014). *American Literary Minimalism*. Tuscaloosa: University of Alabama Press.

Drake, Monica. (2018). Doomed in Nashville. Long Reads (March 2018). https://longreads.com/2018/03/05/doomed-in-nashville/ (accessed July 5, 2021).

Flood, Alison. (2018). Chuck Palahniuk "close to broke" as agent's accountant faces fraud charges. *The Guardian* (May 30, 2018). https://www.theguardian.com/books/2018/may/30/chuck-palahniuk-agent-accountant-faces-charges-fight-club (accessed July 5, 2021).

Palahniuk, Chuck. (2003). *Fugitives and Refugees: A Walk in Portland, Oregon*. New York: Crown.

Palahniuk, Chuck. (2018). The big secret behind everything so far. Facebook post (May 29, 2018). https://www.facebook.com/39860039925/posts/10155782111654926/ (accessed August 5, 2021). (accessed October 6, 2019).

Tomlinson, Sarah. (1999). Is it fistfighting, or just multi-tasking? *Salon* (October 13, 1999). https://www.salon.com/1999/10/13/palahniuk/ (accessed July 5, 2021).

Weston, Hillary. (2012). Chuck Palahniuk on the reissue of "Invisible Monsters." *BlackBook* (June 2012). https://blackbookmag.com/arts-culture/books/chuck-palahniuk-on-the-reissue-of-invisible-monsters/ (accessed July 5, 2021).

Widmyer, Dennis. (1999). *Chuck explains the ending of Survivor*. The Cult: The Official Fan Site of Chuck Palahniuk. https://web.archive.org/web/20180407024537/http://chuckpalahniuk.net/content/chuck-explains-ending-survivor (accessed August 4, 2021).

FURTHER READING

Kuhn, Cynthia and Rubin, Lance. (eds.) (2009). *Reading Chuck Palahniuk: American Monsters and Literary Mayhem*. New York: Routledge.

McCracken, David. (2016). *Chuck Palahniuk, Parodist: Postmodern Irony in Six Transgressive Novels*. Jefferson, NC: McFarland.

Schuchardt, Read M. (ed.) (2008). *You Do Not Talk About Fight Club: I Am Jack's Completely Unauthorized Essay Collection*. Dallas: Benbella Books.

Patchett, Ann

BARBARA KITT SEIDMAN
Linfield College, USA (retired)

Ann Patchett stands among the most successful contemporary practitioners of literary fiction in the United States – in 2012 she was named as one of *Time* magazine's 100 most influential people. She has earned numerous grants and awards, including both the Orange Prize and the PEN/Faulkner Award. Her complicated plots and psychologically compelling characters come alive through lyrical prose infused with gentle humor and an optimistic worldview. Patchett's widely published essays blend autobiography with larger ethical or philosophical themes. She deftly weds entertaining stories to resonant themes and complex questions that make her a favorite of book groups: as the co-owner of Parnassus Books in Nashville, TN, she knows the importance of nurturing an engaged readership.

Born in Los Angeles in 1967, Patchett moved to Tennessee with her mother and sister at age six following her parents' divorce. Though as an adult she has studied, taught, and lived throughout the United States, she has resided in Nashville for decades, where she met and married physician Karl VanDevender. Patchett attended Catholic schools run by the Sisters of Mercy, who exemplified for her "working women who had given every aspects of their lives over to their belief... the kind of singular life I imagined for myself [as a writer] (Patchett 2013, p. 289). She credits creative writing teachers at Sarah Lawrence College for turning her toward a career in fiction. It was at the Iowa Writer's Program that she began the influential friendship with Lucy Grealy that is commemorated in the memoir *Truth and Beauty* (2004).

Irish Catholic households like her own fill Patchett's novels, as do nuns and priests, who function as fellow strivers after goodness with plenty of their own shortcomings. Her Catholic upbringing also explains her recurrent attention to the collision between American affluence and the "burden of things" that oppresses the spirit. In counterpoint she often celebrates selflessness, good works, and forgiveness as avenues for the transcendent workings of grace that can "miraculously" rescue broken souls. Her protagonists typically find themselves at a crossroads when the abrupt fracturing of their lives prompts seemingly irrational choices that ultimately prove redemptive. In so doing she applies gentle humor to the absurdities of the human condition that even the most risk-averse bourgeoisie cannot escape. The mysteries beneath the mundane surfaces of her characters' lives frequently surface in dreams, sometimes through magical realist communication between the living and the dead.

Patchett's most consistent subject involves family – both the blood kin who inhabit her protagonists' origin stories and the alternative communities they enter afterward. Her varied plots depict the unexpected circumstances that pull families apart and the equally unpredictable developments that can heal old wounds. Yet reinvention often provokes characters to craft deceitful narratives to escape a haunting past or stifling present – they warily hide within fictions of their own making while bewildered loved ones stay behind. But Patchett also encourages empathy for these flawed humans who stumble toward unsought moments of grace that liberate them from guilt or myopia. In the fairy tale subtexts beneath her plots, characters are often ejected from seemingly golden worlds as the catalyst toward hard-won self-understanding that just may earn them a "happy ending."

Such is the case for Sabine, title character of *The Magician's Assistant* (1997). Twenty years of unrequited romantic devotion to Parsifal, a gay magician, lead to their unlikely marriage before he dies of AIDS in their elegant Los Angeles home. She discovers from his will that he has lied both about his name and about his backstory: far from being an orphan, Guy Fetters has a devoted mother and sister in Nebraska heartbroken at his defection. They insist on entering Sabine's world and draw her deeply into theirs, where she learns of Guy's traumatic youth and merges her grief at his death with their decades-old loss. Their collective sorrow knits them together and unexpectedly promises Sabine a reciprocal romance at long last. The novel's central motif aligns magic with the fiction-making enterprise itself as welcome illusions that revive one's imaginative capacity for wonder.

The first-person narrator who begins *The Patron Saint of Liars* (1992), Rose Clinton, also constructs a protective disguise after she abruptly flees her 1960s southern California idyll upon discovering she's pregnant. Driving to St. Elizabeth's home for unmarried expectant mothers in rural Kentucky, Rose gives birth and then stays on as the community's kitchen manager, her past unexplained. Wrapped in a carapace of prickly self-sacrifice, Rose asks God to reveal the shape her life should take and regards an unexpected marriage proposal from Son Abbott, St. Elizabeth's handyman, as her answer. The emotional glue of their household resides in the bond between him and Rose's child Cecilia. The mysteriously opaque Rose recedes, not only as narrator but as a presence in her family's daily routines, first moving into an adjacent bungalow and eventually driving away altogether to avoid the pending visit of her first husband. In her stead, Son and Cecilia tell their own stories. Cecilia, age 15, meets her biological father without ever learning his full identity – for her he remains only a poignant marker of her mother's previous life. Nor can Son risk losing Cecilia to a man oblivious to his paternity; instead, he spins his own deceit to sustain the illusion that he and Rose conceived the child. Uniting all three characters as they awkwardly share dinner is their mutual grief at Rose's inability to commit herself emotionally to any of them. Yet Cecilia's openheartedness bespeaks a resilience born of the love invested in her by all who have helped raise her, including elderly Sister Evangeline, a model of compassionate forgiveness in the face of heartbreak.

Failed mothers fill Patchett's work – women whose personal compulsions cause their offspring long-lasting damage. The blended families of *Commonwealth* (2016) draw upon her own biography, and she concedes, "I've been writing the same book my whole life – that you're in one family, and all of a sudden, you're in another family, and it's not your choice and you can't get out" (quoted in Southgate 2019). The inciting event occurs at a baptismal celebration where guest Bert Cousins drunkenly kisses hostess Beverly Keating and ignites a passion that rips apart both families. The novel's fifty-year trajectory moves back and forth in time as various characters reconcile with their history: skillfully rendered moments of domestic comedy alternate with tragedy and loss as the reworkings of memory foster the getting of wisdom. The most sustained vantage point belongs to Franny and describes her cross-country relocation to Virginia with her sister and mother, as well as the summers spent yoked to the four Cousins children sent out east to visit their father. The traumatic core event of those summers involves the accidental death of the oldest Cousins boy during their "free range" wanderings out of sight of the overwhelmed Beverly. In a sly postmodern wink, Patchett subjects Franny to the unscrupulous co-optation of her family stories by an older writer with whom she has an unwise affair: the appearance of his novel, also entitled *Commonwealth*, not only provokes a family uproar but throws into relief the fraught relationship between fiction and the lived experience that inspired it, as well as the many who claim it.

In another half-century family drama, *The Dutch House* (2019), an underlying fairy tale through line positions its sibling protagonists as a modern Hansel and Gretel at the mercy of a wicked stepmother. Yet Andrea Smith would not have gained her power over Maeve and Danny Conroy had not their own mother posed a vexing problem: how does an upwardly mobile American family accommodate the disruptive presence of saintliness in their midst? Elna Conroy's inability to live in the Gatsby-like mansion her husband Cyril purchases in suburban Philadelphia derives from her growing unease with his relentless pursuit of affluence in a world filled with so much suffering. When her charitable work at the convent where she was once a postulant takes her increasingly away from home, Cyril demands that she leave, and divorce opens the door for Andrea to marginalize her stepchildren in their own home and eventually expel them altogether after their father's sudden death.

The shame-filled scars created by orphanhood and dispossession last far into their adulthoods. For years, Danny and Maeve clandestinely visit the Dutch House, making a "fetish out of our misfortune." Yet the adult Danny, the novel's central consciousness, voices his growing unease with their grudge by asking Maeve, its chief architect, "Do you think it's possible to ever see the past as it actually was?" (Patchett 2019, p. 45). In another of Patchett's gentle ironies, each child temperamentally resembles the same-sex parent they have lost. Maeve's nun-like existence is spent in an undemanding job that allows her the time for self-sacrificial dedication to Danny's life and the good works she undertakes in her Catholic parish. Danny jettisons the medical education Maeve had insisted he pursue and devotes himself to property investment and renovation, marrying and raising a family with the same passivity that informs his relationship with his sister. Though Danny asserts at one point that he is telling Maeve's story, in truth he is delineating his own struggle toward a healthy masculine identity despite a father who failed to "tell him what kind of man to be" (p. 85).

When Elna suddenly reenters her middle-aged children's lives after decades of absence, the aloof Danny withholds forgiveness while Maeve embraces her mother's return as "miraculous." But Elna's self-sacrificing compulsion again eclipses her maternal loyalties when she improbably becomes the live-in caretaker for a senile Andrea. Maeve dies within weeks of this second betrayal, but Danny finally reconciles with his past. Following Andrea's death, Danny also finds himself the owner of the Dutch House itself, where he installs his own daughter May, Maeve's namesake and a budding film star eager to return glamor to the mansion that had already presided over the dissolution of the Hoebeekes who built it and the Conroys who bought it.

The most provocative examples of "family" elasticity in Patchett's work involve personal bonds forged by love and compassion that transcend cultural divisions of race, and in both *Taft* (1994) and *Run* (2007) the nature of paternal responsibility invites Patchett's close scrutiny. Despite risking charges of cultural appropriation, she builds *Taft* on the first-person narrative of African American John Nickel, an ex-jazz drummer who runs a bar in Memphis and laments his earlier failure to create a family with his pregnant lover. When she leaves for Miami with their son, the grieving John redirects his energies toward newly fatherless white youths Fay and Carl Taft. Both severely test his compassion, especially when Carl's drug activities lead to violence against John himself. Patchett's layered picture of fatherly devotion, both John's and that of the dead Taft patriarch Leon, climaxes in a dreamscape where accepting the weighty duty to nurture children redeems both men's failures.

In the Boston-based family depicted in *Run*, fatherhood weighs heavily on former mayor Bernard Doyle, a widower still idealizing his dead wife while estranged from their biological son Sullivan and overly demanding of the African American brothers they adopted as toddlers. Tip and Teddy, now young men, embody disciplined achievement that eludes their troubled stepbrother, and Bernard envisions them as political leaders who will assist in healing Boston's grim racist history. But Teddy prefers the study of ichthyology – fish – over people, and Tip aspires to the priesthood. As both struggle with their hybrid identities and opaque origins, a string of unlikely coincidences introduces them to their birth mother one snowy night when she pushes Tip out of the way of a moving car and is fatally injured herself. Already possessing her own narrative within the novel, Tennessee, has long assuaged her guilt for surrendering her boys to a more affluent future with the Doyles by raising Kenya, the child of a deceased friend. A gifted adolescent track athlete, Kenya knows nothing of her actual parentage, and as Tennessee's life winds down, Kenya wrongly "reveals" Tip and Teddy to be her brothers, whose lives she and their mother have shadowed for years. Given this second orphaning, Kenya herself is absorbed into the Doyle family circle. Thus, a magical girl in running shoes unwittingly becomes another of Patchett's miracle workers with the power to crash through culturally divisive binaries through the power of love as the more essential binding agent among humans.

Patchett's most ambitious novels to date – *Bel Canto* (2001) and *State of Wonder* (2011) – expand her fictional canvas beyond the United States. In *Bel Canto* an omniscient narrative transforms a heterogeneous collection of international elites into an unlikely community abruptly suspended in time when the world's grievances violently disrupt their evening entertainment. They have gathered for a private concert by operatic soprano Roxanne Coss given in the presidential palace of a poor Latin American country that is courting investment by Japanese businessman Katsumi Hosokawa. The event becomes a hostage-taking siege when a hapless band of ragged militants discover the absence of their real target, the nation's president. The hostages' initial terror yields to more mundane responses as the weeks drag on, but their anxiety, pettiness, and ennui also make way for more rewarding interpersonal connections, including two romances – one between Coss and Hosokawa, the other between Gen Watanabe, Hosokawa's multilingual translator, and Carmen, a female rebel. A babel of competing languages obstructs communication among the hostages themselves, as well as between them and their captors. But Gen's tireless translations and Coss's singing slowly bridge those divisions and generate a magic circle wherein the power of art inspires other forms of personal transcendence: the enhanced skills of an amateur pianist, the masterful cooking of a would-be chief, the ministering talents of a priest.

The novel's title references the "beautiful singing" style of a specific kind of lyrical operatic performance which mirrors *Bel Canto*'s narrative arc: comic misunderstandings yield to love arias which give way to inevitable tragedy as the government's patience gives way to a bloody assault on the rebels. The numerous victims include Hosokawa, Carmen, and a young militant whom Coss has been teaching to use his exceptional voice. The novel's international success launched Patchett into the top tier of American literary artists, though some critics attack the eclipsing of its global justice themes by melodrama (indeed, its historical antecedent was the 1996/7 siege of the Japanese Embassy in Lima, Peru). *Bel Canto* works as a fantasia, its fabulist spirit initially punctured when the world outside cannot be held at bay indefinitely by art's magic. Yet an epilogue quickly restores the fantasia by extending happy endings to four of the hostages, most notably the surprise coupling of Roxanne and Gen, who have translated their grief into a "love for each other and the love of all the people they remembered" (Patchett 2001, p. 318). The novel has been adapted both into an opera (*Bel Canto*, premiered in 2015) and a film (2018).

State of Wonder resists such fabulist ornamentation and instead tackles its global politics head-on, dramatizing the ethical damage done to medical science by Western capitalism, the destructive commodification of co-opted Indigenous knowledge, and the collision of competing cultural constructions of gender. The novel openly borrows from other literary journeys to "hell" and back, including the Orpheus and Eurydice myth, Joseph Conrad's *Heart of Darkness* (1899), and Werner Herzog's 1982 film *Fitzcaraldo*. Its initiating action involves the quest for a "miracle" fertility drug after decades of academic research among the Lakashi, a fictional Brazilian tribe. Pharmacologist Marina Singh, biracial child of a white Minnesotan mother and an Indian father, travels to Brazil to investigate the death of a colleague and to evaluate the progress of the team funded by her company. She makes the trip despite her vexed history with the head researcher, Dr. Annick Swenson.

Marina's repeated loss of her luggage literalizes her gradual repudiation of the mindset with which she entered the Lakashi world. As the heroine of a feminist adventure tale, she twice explodes into heroic action, killing a massive anaconda that is squeezing a child to death and later rescuing her colleague, not dead at all, from the tribe that has held him captive. These plot twists accompany her complex ethical evolution as she assesses Swenson's fifty-year research project. No simple Kurtzian reboot, Swenson's self-absorbed scientific monofocus coexists with enlightened commitment to the protection of the Lakashi culture itself. Ingestion of a specific tree bark not only produces the lifelong fertility of Lakashi women but also protects them against malaria, due to an intricate chemical symbiosis within the grove's ecosystem. Swenson's true agenda is development of a malaria vaccine, not the fertility drug her employer is paying her to discover, since she rejects the desirability of endless pregnancies for the Western women who are its intended consumers. Swenson herself demonstrates the problems of such reproductive interference by impregnating herself at age 72 and delivering a stillborn, malformed fetus. She and Marina collude to keep their company in the dark about the research team's real focus, knowing that its greatest benefit will accrue to the world's poorest people and will not enrich investors. Left unresolved at novel's end is the likelihood that whatever uses are made of Swenson's discoveries, yet another raid by the Global North on the resources of the Global South will devastate a fragile Indigenous community and its biosphere. Marina's own status as she returns to Minnesota with her "resurrected" colleague proves equally equivocal. As the price of his release, she had to exchange the deaf native boy renamed "Easter" whom Swenson had stolen from his family years earlier and whom Marina had also hoped to steal away to Minnesota with her. This becomes Marina's hardest lesson: the terrifying "otherness" she initially feels threatening her in the Amazon gives way to a self-critical repudiation of the presumptuous "normalizing" of a Western upbringing (Wisker 2017, p. 427). But here too there are qualifiers: 42-year-old Marina, who has herself consumed the "magical" bark during her stay, may herself be pregnant. If so, she will exemplify the marketability of the fertility project she no longer supports.

Patchett's wide-ranging subject matter and settings, rendered in lyrical prose, consistently offer ingenious fictions that have firmly installed her on the global literary scene as a champion of love, compassion, and forgiveness as curatives within the lives of ordinary women and men, if not for the wider world's unresolvable geopolitical and ecological crises.

SEE ALSO: Ecocriticism and Environmental Fiction; Fiction and Terrorism; Globalization; Multiculturalism; Pynchon, Thomas; Realism after Poststructuralism; Religion and Contemporary Fiction; Suburban Narratives

REFERENCES

Patchett, Ann. (2001). *Bel Canto*. New York: HarperCollins.
Patchett, Ann. (2013). *This Is the Story of a Happy Marriage*. New York: HarperCollins.
Patchett, Ann. (2019). *The Dutch House*. New York: HarperCollins.
Southgate, Martha. (2019). Home truths. *New York Times Book Review* (September 29, 2019). https://www.nytimes.com/2019/09/24/books/review/ann-patchett-dutch-house.html (accessed August 17, 2021).
Wisker, Gina. (2017). Imagining beyond extinctathon: Indigenous knowledge, survival, speculation – Margaret Atwood and Ann Patchett's eco-Gothic. *Contemporary Women's Writing* 11 (3): 412–431.

FURTHER READING

Cowart, David. (2015). The aim was song: Ann Patchett's *Bel Canto*. In: *The Tribe of Pyn: Literary Generations in the Postmodern Period*, 124–125. Ann Arbor: University of Michigan Press.
Ferreira, Maria Aline. (2016). Monstrous motherhoods: alternative visions of late pregnancy. *Femspec* 17 (1): 12–36.
Gruber, Eva. (2012). Narrating terrorism on the eve of 9/11: Ann Patchett's *Bel Canto*. In: *Literature and Terrorism: Comparative Perspectives* (ed. Michael C. Frank and Eva Gruber), 87–102. New York: Rodopi.

Periodization

CHRISTIAN MORARU
University of North Carolina, Greensboro, USA

The sea change undergone by the past four decades of American literature has been neither exclusively American nor solely literary.

Since World War II, the country had been moving increasingly with the world and even ahead of it, prompting others to follow suit in a new world-system where, especially after the crumbling of the Soviet Bloc, few actors operate unilaterally. Global leaders such as the United States itself have been no exception to this unprecedented, worldwide condition of interdependence, and so, more extensively than other transformative chapters in US history, the post-1980 mutations in America's novel and society have broadly been part and parcel of processes unfolding on scales larger than the nation-state, the region, and the continent. A major repercussion of this socioeconomic and cultural rescaling and ensuing world scalarity of the US mechanics of renewal is that while these shifts have taken place *in* time, they have been spurred *by* space or spaces within and, more than ever before, without America – by world spaces and ultimately by the world as a geocultural ensemble.

I use the previous sentence's closing word advisedly. No doubt, spatialization can be viewed in all kinds of ways no matter what force one imagines to be behind this phenomenon. For example, one can picture cultures as "spaced out," set apart from each other by and across space, hence the various times they tell, as it were. Or, one can imagine a spatialization where space works like an ontological copula, linking up instead of separating what lies inside it. To quote Amanda Anderson's (2001) title, "the powers of distance" are such that they do more than just reinforce distance. They shorten it too, and it is this lessening of spatial extension and the resulting world assemblage that intrigue me here. For, having made the modern world into what it is, and still carrying us forward despite a whole string of crises and hardships clamoring, seemingly, for a change of course, *de*-distancing has left an indelible imprint on the production of local histories.

This is the premise of my contribution and also something worth reminding ourselves amid the isolationisms, tribalisms, and "first-isms" stoked by the current recrudescence of populist politics and other pandemics. Indeed, it behooves us today to face up to the global strictures of copresence and recognize that the cultural time of the United States during the past forty years has been repeatedly reset in relation to time zones much bigger than the national territory. The obtaining temporality, which concerns me in this entry – recent US history, literary and otherwise – can thus be seen as an upshot of de- and trans-territorializations tying America and its literature in with wider expanses and their traditions. Mapping the latter's horizontal thrust onto the vertical axis of domestic change, this "macro" sort of spatialization has rendered time, in the United States and elsewhere, a function of growingly integrated and integrating transnational space. Depicted as both a compression and a dilation of world space, simultaneously appreciated for its collaborative opportunities and blamed for its sharpening antagonisms, world-scale spatialization picked up speed abruptly in the late 1980s and early 1990s, and so did with it the coming together of humankind. After the Cold War, this spatially driven "worlding" of people, lands, and histories ushered America into a new if atypical period. This is "our" period – "our" *contemporary* period. Several critics have named it "late global." Less satisfied with the accuracy of the "global" family descriptors particularly in aesthetic matters, others have talked about the age of "planetarity" (Moraru 2015, p. 88). Either way, what distinguishes the post-Cold War period is a new, "combined" albeit "uneven" world setup into whose grid US circuitries of change got, and have remained, plugged. Feeding off these vast cultural energies, literary-cultural history has been moving in the country – making it in turn move across time – in sync with world spaces, so much so that, itself worlded in fashions and with implications previously unexperienced, the study of history had to be rethought too. Not only did the new "world order" not sound the death knell of history, but the 1990s opened up a new historical chapter, and this novelty has encouraged unorthodox ways of looking at history as a scholarly pursuit, especially at its basic building block, namely, period.

In joining this scrutiny, I offer a largely theoretical argument for a period-friendly history of the past forty years of the US novel but also for a "soft" period and "flexible" periodization, attributes that, as I elaborate below, characterize history's own modes before becoming the literary historiographer's prevailing theoretical moods. One would be hard pressed, I believe, to do this history without charting the tremendous changes of this time and, further, to tackle such changes by eschewing the inherently periodizing explanation of what has changed into what or when. I do allow that, profoundly reworked by de-distancing world spatiality, American cultural time too had to be remeasured, and, as I will show momentarily, this undertaking could not but revisit the measuring units themselves, period included. I decline, however, to throw this notion out with the bathwater of its critique, as I call out, in my entry's part two, a few of the misconceptions and inconsistencies surrounding the case against period and postmodernism. Not that I am necessarily making one for either. I am less interested in scrapping or defending period than I am in thinking through the bearings of world spatialization on it.

These come into sharper relief, I propose, when one takes a closer look at the volatility, composite structure, and cyclical life – or lives – of contemporaneity. Itself subject to controversies, contemporaneity, or "the contemporary," does have, in my opinion, an epochal component to it; one does not have to be guilty of "'chronic' ageism" (Apter 2016, p. 30) to entertain this hypothesis. Incessantly "drifting" (Martin 2017, p. 2) across history and thus flaunting its impermanence as it does, the contemporary nevertheless repeatedly acquires, leaves behind, and gets itself again, and again temporarily, a historical body and, more often than not, an equally well-defined cultural body also – viz., a time span, a "when," and a formal identity, a "what" (or "how"). Eventually, both end up disputed by later commentators, who no longer see nor appreciate what others noticed or liked before them. For, to be sure, the contemporary is always located and assessed as such by observers inhabiting a certain "now" itself in motion, steadily ebbing away from past nows and their own determinations of contemporariness. Accordingly, I designate as contemporary a "counter-" or, better yet, "paraperiod" that has been slithering across the post-World War II temporal plateau and that – for a while and from *our* perspective – appears to have solidified, and to have become our contemporary, within the banks of the last three quarters of the 1980–2020 interval, also crystalizing, in the process, a number of novelistic forms typical of this moment. David Cowart is right to describe "[c]ontemporary" as a "moving targe[t and] semantic shapeshifte[r]" that "make[s] lexicographers and cultural historians weep" (2015, p. 1). Nonetheless, the closing section of my intervention zeroes in on this paraperiod in hopes that, its mercurial appurtenances notwithstanding, making legible a certain logic of post-1980 American novel history is not beyond our reach. To that effect, I dwell primarily, if succinctly, on Don DeLillo's oeuvre, which is in many ways exemplarily illustrative of this logic. And a final spoiler alert: encrypted in this period's idiosyncratic name itself, in the "para-" prefix, more precisely, is, as I will detail too, spatiality's very signature and also the cypher of the contemporary's historical dynamic. I contend that "[p]rivileg[ing] place," particularly America's among the world's places, "when discussing periodization" (Brooks 2012, p. 309) goes a long way toward limning, by means of a few unavoidably broad brushstrokes and claims, this dynamic while getting period thus recalibrated a new lease on life, theoretically and analytically.

THE TROUBLE WITH PERIOD

If our period is that in which cultural period itself has fallen into disrepute, that too is due to the spatialization of "real" history itself. As David Blackburn writes, "[t]he renewed recognition that history occurs in space as well as time has indeed been a welcome development of recent years" (2012, p. 305). Attesting to the "spatial turn" Blackburn and others have been talking about across the humanities, this realization has affected period both as segment of events that came to pass and as model to group and narrate them. More to the point, what has happened *to* US history as a whole during these forty-odd years has been duplicated *inside* it, bringing about a spatialization or spatial thickening of time, a "lateral" accumulation of cultural times within a given temporal slice, hence what looks like an abundance of period – that is to say, of more or less marked-out period*s* – in the "actual" history of these decades. Yet again, the broad change they have witnessed has been triggered, signaled, and accompanied by incidents, crises, "breaks," and shifts that, from the collapse of Europe's communist regimes and the consolidation of world markets to the birth of the Internet and COVID-19, have made a big difference not only in history but also to historians. For many of them, the time passed since 1980 is not just a period of transition out of the Cold War and subsequently out of postmodernism, but a chain or, better yet, a pileup of periods and subperiods, all of them periodically challenged and even "supplanted" by others. Thus, by most accounts, while the four decades do make up by and large a single, coherent entity, what this historical container purports to contain – all puns intended – is a blur of moving milestones and dimensionally fluctuating stretches. Future historians will likely view the Cold War's wind-up and dragged-out aftermath as one cultural-temporal unit, but to many of those closer to the historical canvas, the image is clear *and* fuzzy; it is well delineated, for so is its frame, whereas the painting itself is pointillistic. Epochal and heterogeneously so, the picture looks like an epoch but also like an epochal hub, a crossroads and contest of periods.

The effort to describe and label this interregnum and its historical stratification has yielded clarifications as well as an excess of clarity and all-too-neat delimitations, and the period-based attempts to tell the story of a period of remarkable change in American and world history became predictable. No wonder generation after generation of scholars, from Marshall Brown's to the even feistier Victorianist Young Turks a.k.a. the V21 network (Dimock 2018), have grown increasingly weary of "periodizing." It has become de rigueur, in fact, to deplore the pitfalls of periodization, discrete "epochality," and the straight-line chronologies presumably underwriting them all. In the same breath, critics have berated the individual and institutional self-complacencies involved in pressing into service – granted, sometimes mechanically – temporal and cultural categories, divides, "turns," "bookends," and other periodizing accoutrements as if they were already there, carved in history's stone. Gradually, all these have come to be seen as peddling Eurocentric chronopolitics (Apter 2016, p. 31), "ideological" and "hegemonic," skewing rather than laying bare the complex workings of history, and betraying a "dominant," inertial intellectual routine that "amounts to a collective failure of [the] imagination and will on the part of the literary profession" (Hayot 2011, p. 740).

Such allegations have added insult to older injuries. Pre-dating this anti-periodism is one that, for lack of a better word, we might call postmodern. It holds that both "conventional," *a posteriori* historiography and the Baudrillardian, "*a priori* history" forged by the media (Hartog 2017, p. 115) presuppose varying degrees and forms of "revisionism." History is not immutable; it moves in a dizzying array of directions successively and concomitantly and morphs into new configurations of events and meanings thereof. As an *object*, it is as fluid and protean as the disciplinary paradigm grappling with it. In that sense, history, *all* history, is contemporary; one need not be Crocean, Borgesian, or a card-carrying postmodern to get all that, although it may help. For the critique of the retrospective manufacturing of the bygones – influences, origins, causality, tradition, Kafka's "precursors" and antecessors generally – and a hyperawareness of the related, provisionally "constructed," and intrinsically evolving nature of the periods and rubrics under which this "Grand Narrative" sort of parading of the past ordinarily takes place mark postmodernism from forerunners such as Friedrich Nietzsche, Walter Benjamin, T.S. Eliot, and Jorge Luis Borges to its Pynchonian-Lyotardian heyday. These postmodern hallmarks have drawn accusations of "relativism" and even "ahistoricism," notoriously trumped-up charges every now and then brought as a "presentist" indictment.

In François Hartog's version, this presentism involves a "regime of historicity" under which "the production of historical time seems to be suspended" while "generat[ing] today's sense of a permanent, elusive, and almost immobile present, which nevertheless attempts to create its own historical time . . . as though there were nothing but the present" (2017, pp. 17–18). Neither identical with nor inseparable from the historical now in which we live after the fall of the Berlin Wall, this bloated omnipresent present tends, says Hartog, to dehistoricize history by recreating past times in its own self-obsessed image. In this "anti-periodist" picture, established periods and their sequential chronology are far less conspicuous than under other "regimes." Like Eric Hayot, Hartog takes note of the ever-heightening pace of existence and correspondingly progressive abbreviation of production-consumption-reproduction cycles. According to Hayot, this quickening of cultural rhythms appears, however, to fuel another kind of presentism, enacting in and *on* our present the periodist fashion in which we treat "historical" time roughly understood as the "past." This historiographic approach is presentist because, as pointed out earlier, and as Hartog himself would underscore, it projects our time's "horizontal," rushed tempo onto the vertical axis of history. Thus, applied on the yesteryear mass, the pressure of now-rhythms, remarks Hayot, makes "[p]eriods get shorter as we get closer to the present [and] expand as we move backwards" (2011, p. 745). We see better, bigger, and more (in) what is adjacent temporally. This, claims Hayot, is not an inevitable perspectivism at all, a "natural" optical condition foreordained by the viewer's physical location; "the entire literary profession results from a self-regarding love for our historical present" (p. 746). But this temporally myopic self-centeredness is presentist, and this presentism is "periodist," not necessarily because it breaks down the past into periods that get tinier and tinier as they near "our" point in time. It is so simply because it is period driven. The analogous, incremental temporal shrinking of scholarly focus, expertise, and description – "historical microscopism" (p. 746) – is just a fallout of betting the farm on period, period.

ANTI-PERIODISM AND ANTI-POSTMODERNISM

Presentism in general and "postmodern" presentism in particular are then, oddly enough, responsible for both the declining and the inflationary use of the period concept. Compounding the inconsistency are critics like Amy Hungerford and Susan Stanford Friedman who, in the same sentence, have professed to be fed up with periodism and have pronounced the postmodern irrevocably dead and "passé," either "supplanted" by a new, "post-postmodern" . . . period or sucked back into the modernism from which, ten or twenty years back, it seemed safely and usefully demarcated. It is not always clear what the reason for the anti-postmodern hostility is, although denying postmodernism its period status would relitigate the issue of the modern–postmodern divide (real? a self-serving postmodern fiction?) and bring back the question as to whether modernism has ever ended or subsided. In any case, one cannot help noticing that, in many revisitations of recent literary-historical periods *and* of period itself, "old" modernism has suddenly overflown its historical banks and has grown into a *longue durée* or "long modernism" eager not just to swallow formerly stand-alone postmodernism whole but also to dehistoricize and ultimately dissolve it by cavalierly reclassifying postmodern aesthetic protocols such as autoironic metafiction and intertextual revision and authors like Gabriel García Márquez as "modernist" (Friedman 2015, p. 72). And vice versa: what appeared for a while to hold as a single cultural-historical age has split, some have suggested, into better-marked "stages." A case in point, "late postmodernism" anticipates the postmodern's more unequivocal, post-2000 "waning" and the mushrooming, under "post-postmodernism," of "metamodernism," "digimodernism," "exomodernism," "performatism," and other "isms" that at least recall if not mirror, at the dawn of the twenty-first century, the similarly avant-garde effervescence of one hundred years ago and by the same movement fold postmodern aftershocks back into modernist history and aesthetics. Also revealing their spatialized, Teflon-like temporality at the hands of literary historians working during and sometimes openly against postmodernism have been periods' own temporal subunits and elements: decades, centuries (wholes or halves), pivotal years or multiyear epoch-making events like world wars and "interwar" respites, what with the proliferation of "long" and "short" centuries and, of late, the mega-"ageism" of a new period player such as the Anthropocene.

Historical signposts have shifted but remain in use, and so beginnings and ends of periods and, with them, entire epochs themselves have vanished from one place only to pop up elsewhere, unchanged in length or not. They have not disappeared even in the work of anti-periodist hardliners, who, in all actuality, have been busy *re*periodizing, thinking up *alternate* periods (Hayot 2011, p. 747) rather than *alternatives* to periodization – what is "post-45," after all, if not a period vision of a broadly conceived, surprisingly dehistoricized "contemporary"? As a thought-provoking anti-periodist such as Friedman concedes, even "V21 affirms the Victorian period as an entity, and Dimock herself filters literary history through the discourse of time as the linear chronology of past, present, and future" (Friedman 2019, p. 387). Thus, "[t]he traditional notion of period," Katie Trumpener has concluded, "may be bankrupt, depleted, a mere placeholder for a truth we know to be more complicated. Yet it is hard to see just how to reorganize curricula, job descriptions, or library cataloging systems using alternative templates" (2012, p. 354). Indeed, it looks like when the rubber of teaching and research hits the road of history, "we cannot not periodize" (Jameson 2012, p. 29).

A MOVING TARGET: THE CONTEMPORARY

Accelerating de-distancing worldwide, the demise of Central and East European totalitarianisms sped up, ironically or not, the world's morphing into a total space. This space is or threatens to become total because, as Andrei Codrescu and others have intimated, it knows no "outside" (Codrescu 2001, pp. 193–207). This suspicion crops up already in DeLillo's 1982 novel *The Names*. Our period, for which *The Names* serves, if not as an actual bookend, then as an eerily prescient allegory, is here defined by ever-amplifying and multidirectional "spatializing" movements toward a new, all-encompassing spatial world order that hardly allows for any places truly external to neoliberal economics, data and other kinds of flows, and so forth. What makes the picture DeLillo drew some forty years ago both uniquely observant and relevant to this very day is precisely the insight into this emerging, self-saturated geototality. As a hero of the novel muses in a famous passage, no "escape" is possible either in or from this "self-referring" space:

> This thing has seeped into the texture of the world. The world for thousands of years was our escape, was our refuge. Men hid from themselves in the world. We hid from God or death. The world was where we lived, the self was where we went mad and died. But now the world has made a self of its own. Why, how, never mind. What happens to us now that the world has a self? How do we say the simplest thing without falling into a trap? Where do we go, how do we live, who do we believe? This is my vision, a self-referring world, a world in which there is no escape.
>
> (DeLillo 1989, p. 297)

This is late-Cold War world space, an advanced phase in the making of the geopolitical sublime. The huge swath of land conquered by Alexander the Great twenty-three centuries ago and across which protagonist Jim tracks a murderous cult provides an apt synecdoche for this concurrently, and quasi-absolutely, limitless and limiting geography. Sometimes international and sometimes postnational – across countries and frequently "over" their sovereignty, regulations, and borders – the "coverage" of this territory has been pushing people inside and outside *The Names*, during the time of the book's plot and ever more so after the Cold War, closer and closer to one another, through the expanses separating them and into an ever-thickening "texture."

A de-distancing vector, *relationality* becomes after 1989 fully the rationality of this world "network," as most critics designate it (Moraru 2011, p. 29). Individuals, cultural practices and sites, styles and their histories, texts and contexts find themselves, under late globalization more than before, *co*related inside the same spaces or over them, effectively or virtually in each other's vicinity if not sharing and at times clashing in the same place. Lengthy excursions through the ontology of the Heideggerian *Mitsein* are not needed to drive home the basic point that the prepositional prefix of correlationality thematizes the existence modality DeLillo and other American novelists deem characteristic of our world and our time in it: being in this world, and being in it now, as being-with. Differently put, to be in and *of* this "spatialized," "worlded" time is to be *with* others, their *con*-temporary. "One is not contemporary; one is contemporary to somebody" (*contemporain de*), Martin Rueff reminds us (2010, p. 94), and this has never been truer than in and of the post-1980s age. Verbalization of the ontological copula mentioned earlier, the *con*-, the "with" (from the Latin *cum*), encapsulates the juxtaposing, relational rationality of the historically unmatched world spatiality that affords our contemporaneousness while making it a period unlike any other – a *paraperiod*.

The term indexes this oddity but is also apposite, on two accounts. Both have to do with this spatiality, which the Ancient Greek adverb and preposition captures quite accurately – *para* signifies, among other things, nearness, being alongside, beside, and next to or in the presence of something or somebody. For one thing, the *para-* morpheme shares in the spatial syntax of the *con-*, reaffirming the being-with as the onto-topological marker of our era. For another, the prefix front-loads the same spatial semantics temporally, working it into the diachronic restlessness of period itself: we are not, *para* hints, just others' *con*temporaries, willy-nilly *beside* them, near them in this "now-" and "with-world" regardless of what the Donald Trumps of this world may tweet; contemporaneity itself is, again and again, *para*, a paraperiod "beside itself," constantly streaming forward, changing places and names. It washes over the post-World War II interval, its schools, movements, and generations of writers, settling in a few decades' riverbed only to brim over and resume its search for its next temporal abode, where it sheds its modernist or postmodern skin only to grow a new one and into a new contemporary altogether.

I call this Viconian *corsi e ricorsi* of sorts the cycle of contemporaneity. As far as I can see, there have been two of them since 1945. *The Names* comes on the scene toward the end of the first, which was also the longest. In 1982, the contemporary period was and it would be for about ten more years, for historians and literary historians alike, the time elapsed since World War II. This is, or was, the "old" contemporary. Its axial, twin development was, culturally speaking, the eclipse – partial or total, depending on whom you ask – of modernism and the birth of postmodernism. The contemporary, *this* contemporary, aged precipitously, and the world began to renew itself once again with and at the end of the Cold War.

The 1980s may have gotten out to a disappointing start, at least for some, what with Ronald Reagan elected into office, but finished with a bang "on or about" November 9, 1989. The bringing down of the Berlin Wall marked the de facto end of World War II (a few anti-periodists would probably agree), of the "short" twentieth century (1914–1989), as well as of "peak postmodernism" (McHale 2015, pp. 62–122). Succeeding what used to be the contemporary for almost half a century – when it successively culminated with, and passed, one by one, high modernism, the onset of postmodernism in the late 1960s, and the rise of postmodernism's avant-pop spin-off in the mid-late 1980s – is the "new" contemporary period, *our* contemporary. This is essentially a post-Cold War affair whose merging financial, commercial, environmental, cultural, and stylistic codes and geographies DeLillo's *White Noise* (1985) further prefigured alongside other landmark novels of the 1980s such as William Gibson's cyberpunk classic *Neuromancer* (1984) and Maxine Hong Kingston's Whitmanian homage *Tripmaster Monkey* (1989), a point of reference in the rapidly swelling and diversifying canon of multiethnic American fiction. At the same time, Louise Erdrich's *Love Medicine* (1984), Alice Walker's *The Color Purple* (1982), Toni Morrison's *Beloved* (1987), Philip Roth's *Zuckerman Bound* (1985), and other Native American, African American, and Jewish American milestones of the 1980s convey a clear sense that the transnational rescaling of US prose cannot occur at the expense of a critical genealogy of national identity's racial, ethnic, or gender- and sex-related stratifications.

Premonitory as some of these fictions are, DeLillo's 1997 masterpiece *Underworld* takes their de-stancing poetics to a whole new level. The meganovel, a genre that thrives in the 1990s – William H. Gass's *The Tunnel* and

David Foster Wallace's *Infinite Jest* came out in 1995 and 1996, respectively – straddles the pre-/post-Cold War divide narratively. On the one hand, the novel chronicles, and symbolically brings to a close, the Cold War's schismatic geopolitics of blocs and ideological antagonisms. On the other, it begins to upgrade *The Names*' spatial perceptiveness for the post-Internet, hyperintegrative cyberenvironments. The most significant stage of the update so far is still the 2003 novel *Cosmopolis*. When, in it, protagonist Eric Packer's "chief of theory" Vija Kinski ventures that "[t]here is no outside anymore" (DeLillo 2003, p. 90), she does more than corroborate Codrescu's or the 1982 book's spatial intuitions. Noteworthy in Kinski's non sequitur is the temporal qualification too, the "anymore": the outside, the not-here, and the "out there" already "in here" are, we gather, spatial features of a *hic* that differentiate our *nunc*, our "now" in time – the post-1980s period – from previous "nows" in history. Eric's "now" is qualitatively different from Jim's. Where *The Names*' hero had to travel physically and resort to antiquated communication technology such as telex, the lead character of *Cosmopolis* is virtually ubiquitous and perpetually "on time" and *in* it, playing in real time in the currency markets of the era of digitally assisted space-time compression. Extremely de-distanced, world space, complete with its no longer external or exotic outside, is "now" condensed, "packed" informatically in Packer's hi-tech stretch limo.

Cosmopolis foregrounds several interrelated developments while conceivably forecasting others. All bound up with recent forms and intensities of spatialization, these set the post-1989 contemporary cycle in motion and also circumscribe the new contemporary in US novel history and beyond. As I conclude, let me enumerate them quickly.

First, digitalization assumes a cardinal role in the shift away from the predominantly disjunctive cultural modes of the 1960s and 1970s and into the spatially conjunctive "worlding" of national cultural times around the turn of the millennium. In this regard, and both literarily and literary-historically, September 11, 2001 only renders tragically concrete what non-nation-state affiliation of terrorist and other networks, unchecked flows of people, cash, information, and "border-crossing" can mean after the deep freeze of the Cold War; the "9/11 novel," another genre formation of the new contemporary, supplies plenty of evidence for this.

Second, the totality in the making of the world *qua* world becomes the ultimate horizon of domestic novelistic production, which is why North Americans, Irish-Turkish Americans, and American Bengalis like DeLillo, Emily St. John Mandel, Jhumpa Lahiri, and Joseph O'Neill, Frenchmen and francophone Algerians like Michel Houellebecq, Frédéric Beigbeder, and Boualem Sansal, Brits, British Indians, and British Pakistanis like Ian McEwan, David Mitchell, Hari Kunzru, and Mohsin Hamid, Austrians like Daniel Kehlmann, South Africans and Australians like J.M. Coetzee and David Malouf, and Japanese like Haruki Murakami, to pick at random from an endless list, author books not only structurally and thematically compatible but also fitting fresh rubrics such as the "global," "geopolitical," or "international" novel.

Third, while these genres may or may not herald the "end of postmodernism" (Adams 2007), they do bear witness once more to nation-states' contemporary predicament as well as to the nation's own, twofold crisis as a traditional locus of writers' imagination, which is now openly enticed by wider vistas, and as an analytic-historiographic operator that, of late, has drawn criticisms similar, and in effect related, to those leveled at period (Hayot 2019, p. 485; Friedman 2019, p. 395).

Fourth, the American novelistic lens's refocusing on the world has continued apace after

September 11, 2001, with world-spatial events such as the "War on Terror," the financial crisis of 2008, and the 2020 pandemic increasingly suggesting that our paraperiod itself may be at the end of its cycle. In literature, this cycle will be completed when the transition out of the postmodern itself will have been effectuated as well.

Fifth, and last, we are not there yet despite postmodernism's protracted twilight (Moraru 2011, p. 11). The postmodern crisis broke out in the 1990s and became chronic – enduring and a marker of our contemporary times – after that. Its symptomatology is complex, but here I single out only two of its aspects. One pertains to aesthetics; the other does too but has an ontological purview to it, speaking to postmodern art's engagement with the present world and possibly accounting for our paraperiod's approaching its final years. What bears highlighting aesthetics-wise is a certain over-the-top self-reiterative narrative routine, with household figures such as Pynchon putting out riffs on their earlier works and with the 1990s generation of novelists in turn rehashing, if sometimes brilliantly, the big names of the 1970s and producing a whole series of Freudian symbiotic pairs – Pynchon, DeLillo, Robert Coover, Roth, and John Barth on one side, and Wallace, Mark Leyner, Richard Powers, William Gibson, Dave Eggers, Bret Easton Ellis, Jonathan Franzen, Jennifer Egan, Michael Chabon, and Mark Danielewski, on the other. As for the twenty-first century "world out there," the intertextually inbreeding protocols, geared as they were self-reflectively toward literary endogeny itself, at least in the works of some newcomers, appeared as a sign of both paradigm exhaustion and poor receptiveness to the world's *real* troubles. Postmodernism had marked an ontological turn, as Brian McHale has so influentially argued in *Postmodernist Fiction* (1987), but one political, financial, racial, ecological, and health crisis after another made jocularly and ironically articulated postmodern ontology look out of touch with a painfully present and urgent world. No wonder Wallace, Powers, Eggers, Franzen, Nicole Krauss, Steve Tomasula, Ben Lerner, St. John Mandel, Colson Whitehead, and others started turning away, sometimes polemically, from postmodern aesthetics to explore new narrative formats like the graphic and born-digital novel and new or newly resurrected styles altogether, such as "new authenticism," "(new) realism," "(new) sincerity," "docufiction," "autofiction," and so forth. Does this sound, as Lionel Ruffel would have it in *Brouhaha: Worlds of the Contemporary* (2016), as one big, loud, and confusing literary hubbub in which the incantations of Afrofuturist novels à la Colson, neo-metafiction à la Jonathan Safran Foer and Percival Everett, and genre-inflected fiction of the kind in which Jonathan Lethem excels in *The Feral Detective* (2018) cut through the static of repetitiveness, pre-modernist false restarts, and awkwardly disguised nostalgias? The cliché notwithstanding, time *will* tell. It will happen, I believe, sooner than we might think.

SEE ALSO: After Postmodernism; DeLillo, Don; Globalization

REFERENCES

Adams, Rachel. (2007). The ends of America, the ends of postmodernism. *Twentieth-Century Literature* 53 (3): 248–272.

Anderson, Amanda. (2001). *The Powers of Distance: Cosmopolitanism and the Cultivation of Detachment*. Princeton: Princeton University Press.

Apter, Emily. (2016). Rethinking periodization for the "now-time." In: *Being Contemporary: French Literature, Culture and Politics Today* (ed. Lia

Brozgal and Sara Kippur), 29–42. Liverpool, UK: Liverpool University Press.

Blackburn, David. (2012). "The horologe of time": periodization in history. *PMLA* 127 (2): 301–307.

Brooks, Lisa. (2012). The primacy of the present, the primacy of place: navigating the spiral of history in the digital world. *PMLA* 127 (2): 308–316.

Codrescu, Andrei. (2001). *The Disappearance of the Outside: A Manifesto for Escape* (with a new Preface). St. Paul, MN: Ruminator Books.

Cowart, David. (2015). *The Tribe of Pyn: Literary Generations in the Postmodern Period*. Ann Arbor: University of Michigan Press.

DeLillo, Don. (1989). *The Names*. New York: Vintage; 1st ed. 1982.

DeLillo, Don. (2003). *Cosmopolis*. New York: Scribner.

Dimock, Wai Chee. (2018). Historicism, presentism, futurism. *PMLA* 132 (2): 257–263.

Friedman, Susan Stanford. (2015). *Planetary Modernisms: Provocations on Modernity across Time*. New York: Columbia University Press.

Friedman, Susan Stanford. (2019). Alternatives to periodization: literary history, modernism, and the "new" temporalities. *MLQ* 80 (4): 379–402.

Hartog, François. (2017). *Regimes of Historicity: Presentism and Experiences of Time* (trans. Saskia Brown). New York: Columbia University Press.

Hayot, Eric. (2011). Against periodization; or, on institutional time. *New Literary History* 42 (4): 739–756.

Hayot, Eric. (2019). Literary history after literary dominance. *MLQ* 80 (4): 479–494.

Jameson, Fredric. (2012). *A Singular Modernity*. London: Verso.

Martin, Theodore. (2017). *Contemporary Drift: Genre, Historicism, and the Problem of the Present*. New York: Columbia University Press.

McHale, Brian. (2015). *The Cambridge Introduction to Postmodernism*. New York: Cambridge University Press.

Moraru, Christian. (2011). *Cosmodernism: American Narrative, Late Globalization, and the New Cultural Imaginary*. Ann Arbor: University of Michigan Press.

Moraru, Christian. (2015). *Reading for the Planet: Toward a Geomethodology*. Ann Arbor: University of Michigan Press.

Rueff, Martin. (2010). La concordance des temps. In: *Qu'est-ce que le contemporain?* (ed. Lionel Ruffel), 93–110. Nantes, France: Cécile Defaut.

Trumpener, Katie. (2012). In the grid: period and experience. *PMLA* 127 (2): 349–357.

FURTHER READING

North, Michael. (2018). *What Is the Present?* Princeton: Princeton University Press.

O'Donnell, Patrick. (2010). *The American Novel Now: Reading Contemporary American Fiction Since 1980*. Oxford: Wiley Blackwell.

Rudrum, David and Stavris, Nicholas. (eds.) (2015). *Supplanting the Postmodern: An Anthology of Writings on the Arts and Culture of the Early 21st Century*. New York: Bloomsbury.

Perkins-Valdez, Dolen

SHARONY GREEN
University of Alabama, USA

Dolen Perkins-Valdez has achieved in the world of fiction what the historian has had a far harder time doing in historical research and writing: allowing readers to not only apprehend, but to see and, if they are fortunate, feel the horrors of our complicated and often brutal racial past. Her first two novels *Wench* (2010) and *Balm* (2015), the former a *New York Times* bestseller, are persuasive and superbly written works set in the years surrounding the Civil War, the deadliest social and military conflict in United States history. It is worth noting that the books were published over fifty years after historian Kenneth Stampp (1956) tackled longstanding agreements about slavery in the historical profession. Indeed, he did as much when he decided slavery was a peculiar institution. How could someone with thoughts and the ability to act on their thoughts be a mere commodity? This is one of the issues on which he invited deliberation.

By 1974, Eugene Genovese broke new ground for historians studying American history when he explained the "world the slaves made." It was a timely task. This publication followed the Black freedom and feminist struggles of the 1950s and 1960s and the founding of various departments and curriculums addressing the experiences of oppressed groups. Genovese had more evidence about just how peculiar slavery was. He also had the same intuition that Perkins-Valdez, a writer who just happens to also be an African American woman, would someday possess.

Born in Memphis, one year before Genovese's *Roll, Jordan, Roll* (1974) was published, Perkins-Valdez sprinted beyond the flat histories still being published. She is the daughter of a FedEx business executive and a hat designer mother. After earning bachelor's, master's, and doctoral degrees at Harvard, the University of Memphis, and George Washington University, and teaching creative writing at Mary Washington College in Fredericksburg, Virginia and American University in Washington, DC, among other institutions, Perkins-Valdez joined the growing number of researchers and laypeople alike who were open to investigating the degree to which enslaved people strategically maneuvered in order to have some say on matters concerning their very existence. By the time *Wench*, for example, was on bookshelves in 2010, dozens of writings, among them several written by women and about enslaved women, were being well received. Key works include Stephanie Camp's 2004 study on enslaved women's everyday resistance in the plantation South and Thavolia Glymph's 2008 investigation of the cranky ways of the so-called Southern belle and the bondage she helped erect in her household. These two works helped readers in and outside of academic circles navigate extremely difficult conversations, and sometimes with just a few pieces of evidence. For instance, before her untimely death at age 46 in 2014, one impressively researched chapter in Camp's 2004 book *Closer to Freedom: Enslaved Women and Everyday Resistance in the Plantation South* relied on just two letters between a plantation manager and a planter to stress the audacity of a woman named California. This Mississippi enslaved woman refused to remove amalgamation prints from her cabin walls. As the manager that she angered said, she had it in her mind that she was "free" and was not the kind to do well in Mississippi.

California was no anomaly. By 2015, Sharony Green encountered, via numerous archives, other such women and presented their stories in her historical monograph *Remember Me to Miss Louisa: Hidden Black–White Intimacies in Antebellum America*. The nerve of seemingly powerless people was presented in Avenia White, an enslaved woman from Virginia who was freed in 1838 on the eve of her master's marriage. Beside her was another enslaved woman and four children, likely their master's progeny, who were also freed. These six were relocated to Cincinnati, a sort of ground zero for freed Black and biracial women and children owing to its position on the Ohio River, the largest branch of the Mississippi River. These two waterways served as a transportation highway that helped people easily travel between the north and south. The abolitionist presence in Ohio and the opportunity for freedpeople to obtain an education there – at Oberlin College, Blacks and women were admitted as early as 1833 – was also attractive to white men who quietly made provisions for freedwomen and children. These men include a Huntsville, Alabama, planter who left the equivalent of $5.1 million to ten enslaved children, nine of them his own produced from relations – coerced or not – with five enslaved women. These children's mothers and next of kin were also listed in his will, which was overseen by a lawyer-turned-Confederate politician who, while consulting powerful white statemen like Illinois Senator Stephen Douglas and New York Senator William Seward, removed the children and their families from the South before the Civil War. Some of the freed children appear in a bellum-era yearbook for Wilberforce University. When looking at the pages of that yearbook, one can see that most of the children are from the South and were almost certainly the children produced by white southern men with enslaved and free women.

Such realities require combing through southern white men's correspondence as well as legal and business papers if they are to be discovered. This was the case if we were to know about the freedwoman White, who sent five letters to her former master that survive at the University of North Carolina at Chapel Hill. In one letter, she told him if he had forgotten her, she hoped he had not "forgotten the children." Another letter closed with the word "love." Whether she was delusional or strategic is worth debating. Just as challenging is the difficulty in sorting through her privilege and tragic moments in two different regions. So difficult was her life in Ohio (the main two paths for employment for African American women in and outside the South were domestic work and sex work), she appears to have returned to slave territory where she died of bloody flux on one of her former master's plantations. A better future was likely had by the children sent north with her and the other freedwoman. Indeed, one of her letters announced that "Elizabeth was in school."

But something else is still needed to fill in the gaps about our quirky past. This is where the work of one of the most skillful and persuasive writers of our age – Dolen Perkins-Valdez – comes in. References to Wilberforce in *Remember Me to Miss Louisa* present the opportunity to at last address her debut novel *Wench*. In this work, the reader is introduced to Tawawa House, a former resort near Xenia, Ohio, an hour northeast of Cincinnati, where slaveholders "vacationed" with Black women they owned. Tawawa means "yellow springs." These medicinal waters were filled with iron sought by seasonal visitors. Perkins-Valdez was made aware of the springs and the resort while reading a biography of W.E.B. Du Bois. The noted intellectual and activist taught at Wilberforce, which opened in 1856 following the closing of the Tawawa House amid escalating tensions between the North and South. It is the country's oldest private historically Black college.

Perkins-Valdez intuits the multilayered significance of this historical site in order to offer up the fictitious young and enslaved Lizzie, a woman who spends time with her master Drayle at the Tawawa House. At one point in her novel, she presents Drayle flipping the script as he bathes Lizzie, instead of being bathed by her. He does as much while still delaying his decision as to whether he will free the two children produced with her. One could never see Thomas Jefferson and Sally Hemings in this fashion. While Jefferson believed that slavery was a "moral depravity" and wrote that "all men are created equal," he enslaved more than 600 people of African descent, shoring him up as a contradictory man. Even as Jefferson freed the children that he fathered with Hemings, she was not exempt from fieldwork chores, not unlike Lizzie. Moreover, as a statesman, he projected a certain air via his words and behavior that arrive as being the antithesis of the intimacy permitted between Lizzie and Drayle. As had many in his day and in days beyond, he said one thing publicly and lived in a manner that, on the face of it, was contrary to the words he uttered. With Perkins-Valdez's creativity and skillful writing, a thought or two about the everyday lives of such contradictory relationships can be momentarily glimpsed.

Perkins-Valdez, to be clear, sketches out both the unbelievable and believable. Before the book ends, Drayle chains Lizzie to a resort cottage. Drayle's barren wife has little empathy for Lizzie and even accompanies them to Ohio one summer. Lizzie is reminded that she is little more than a wench, a word whose origins can be traced to the Middle English term wenchel, for girl or maid. Lizzie is mostly without power, not unlike a maid, like generations of female children and other young women, some in worse condition than others. Three other enslaved women at Tawawa House – Reenie, Sweet, and Mawu – indeed have their own troubles with their white men, who also manage to compartmentalize their evil ways, doling out concessions. In letting the reader see such doling, Perkins-Valdez reminds the reader about how life is often filled with grays and awful realities that are rarely just black and white.

How can white people be only bad if Drayle is sometimes good?

How can white people be only bad when a poor white woman traverses a forest with eggs for the Tawawa House, opening her home to these troubled women whose other joys include repurposing hand-me-down dresses to be worn when they dine like white folk next to their old men?

The same bizarreness literally haunts *Balm*, Perkins-Valdez's second novel, which is set in Chicago right after the war. As is true of *Wench*, themes such as gender, race, religion, class, civility, and waterways emerge. The nuanced past surfaces now in Madge, an African American woman who was born free in Tennessee and raised by a bitter mother. Nevertheless, she has acquired healing abilities. If the yellow springs could not entirely take away Black women's pain, maybe Madge's concoctions can. Perkins-Valdez via Madge offers a balm, in other words.

Around Madge circle two other characters needing her presence. One of them is a freedman from Kentucky named Hemp who has joined countless freedpeople looking for their loved ones, from whom they were earlier separated. He obtained his freedom while fighting for the Union, but longs for his wife who followed the well-documented exodus of Blacks in various migratory waves from the South. But Madge will have his eye. Her company and labor will also be needed by the wealthy white widowed Sadie, who also has gifts after losing her husband during the war. She can talk to the dead. Sadie is most unsettled by this ability, as revealed in the restless spirit of a Union officer. He comes back to life via her. It is not a gift she wants or desires, but in the end, she surrenders to this man possessing her and speaking through her. Other dead people live again through her. A shattered country that had a war that left more than 600,000 people dead is also filled with shattered people. She is one of them. And she reluctantly allows the mourning to commune with those who have passed on. The author has tapped into a historical development which found real-life people wanting to do this very thing after the Civil War. She and Madge seem to be very different kinds of healers. One has herbs. One can hear the dead speaking. They help people in a country that is mourning all kinds of losses and failed hopes. To be clear, African Americans have had a long-lasting yearning even after the passage of the 13th, 14th, and 15th Amendments, to embrace all of the promises of freedom.

In reading this book and *Wench*, one hears alternately lyrical and sometimes sparse writing that helps us look over our shoulders as we try to move forward differently in dire political times. Perkins-Valdez's use of landscape and space (the latter is more political than "place") is a gift that keeps on giving. In *Balm*, we read how "Hemp drove east on Michigan Avenue, past the Dearborn House, across Lake Street, turning south on Randolph" (2015, p. 202). One almost wants to map this Black man's movements given the ironies of such a man's inability to move without being surveilled with dangerous consequences, then and now. He and the women in *Balm* and *Wench* want more than America is willing to give. They snatch at whatever can be had. They take liberty! Lizzie desires to teach Reenie, one of the enslaved women at Tawawa, how to read. She takes a "Small square of slate framed by wood. The cook managed to get her a piece of chalk" that Lizzie planned to take back to her children (she is always thinking about her children) (2011, p. 194). With chalk in hand, as Perkins-Valdez writes,

> Lizzie had thought to begin with A since that was the first letter of the alphabet. But then she changed her mind and began with teaching Reenie how to read and write her own name.
> "How you keep track of them big letters and little letters? How you know which is which?"
> Lizzie smiled. Reenie smelled of lavender. The older woman gripped the sides of the slate until the bones flex over her knuckles.
> "R-E-E"
> "How many E's in my name?"
> "Three," Lizzie answered. "Can you count, Miss Reenie?"
>
> (2011, p. 194)

This private moment is interrupted by Reenie wanting to explain how she lost part of her finger. The violence of slavery is never out of view. But even this confiding must wait as Mawu, another one of the four women "vacationing" with their masters, runs toward them, "face hardened. News was coming their way and whatever she'd had to confide in Lizzie would have to wait" (2011, p. 195).

The four enslaved, "vacationing," women, as well as two enslaved men, are permitted a day of shopping on their own in Dayton. Indeed, their white masters can be generous when they want to be. They allow the women and two enslaved men to have a bit of autonomy. But, it is not long before Lizzie is reminded again of how white folks had their limits with their generosity. Accompanied by a third African American man who kept watch on them, Lizzie and the other enslaved people board an omnibus for the short day trip in Dayton. She and her cohort have a meal and walk freely in ways that would have been impossible to do had they been in slave territory. Lizzie is even selfish for a while, wanting to keep the money that Drayle gives her for herself, rather than share it with anyone else. This brief moment of freedom from her master's oversight apparently shifted something inside of her, placing her in line with other modern people filled with greed the moment they sniffed freedom. She became the very thing that French visitor Alexis de Tocqueville saw when he visited the States in 1831. He observed an "American character," which is to say, a way of being that people in the States possessed (Leeden 2000). They seemed best suited to be competitive. No group like this had been seen prior to the late eighteenth century and no other group like this has been seen since that time. One could be rich or poor in any given moment. The fixed classes of the Old World were a thing of the past. Even an enslaved woman seems positioned, however momentarily, to forget her true status and to even convince the people surrounding her that what she pretended to be she in fact was, at least for a while.

As demonstrated in this passage and elsewhere in *Wench* and *Balm*, Perkins-Valdez emerges as part of a generation of writers/scholars interested in the curling contours of oppression for those living in the African diaspora. She enhances our awareness of slavery and African American history. That such information is offered via the voice of a woman of African descent is especially meaningful given present-day conversations concerning the need for a broader range of voices addressing our shared past. Her particular interest in complex Black–white interaction in the nineteenth century, however, is offered in accessible and compelling ways with rich detail that brings to mind what the late Octavia Butler achieved in *Kindred* (1979) via the tussles between Dana, a modern-day Black woman, and Rufus, the antebellum ancestor she must save. Both *Wench* and *Balm* can be meaningfully paired with this sci-fi work that toggles between the antebellum period and the 1970s, the decade in which Perkins-Valdez's third and in-progress novel takes place in Montgomery, Alabama.

In 2002/3, Perkins-Valdez was a president's postdoctoral fellow at the Center for African American Studies at the University of California at Los Angeles. Her essays and short stories have been published in numerous publications including *The Kenyon Review*, *StoryQuarterly*, *storySouth*, and *African American Review*. A PEN/Faulkner Board Member, she was a 2011 finalist for two NAACP Image Awards and Hurston/Wright Legacy Award for fiction for *Wench*. She was also a finalist for the 2009 Robert Olen Butler Fiction Prize and the winner of the 2011 First Novelist Award by the Black Caucus of the American Library Association. Perkins-Valdez's next book, *Take My Hand*, to be released in 2022, is set in postwar Alabama.

She resides in Washington, DC.

SEE ALSO: Black Atlantic; Butler, Octavia

REFERENCES

Butler, Octavia. (1979). *Kindred*. New York: Doubleday.
Genovese, Eugene D. (1974). *Roll, Jordan, Roll: The World the Slaves Made*. New York: Vintage Books.
Green, Sharony. (2015). *Remember Me to Miss Louisa: Hidden Black–White Intimacies in Antebellum America*. Dekalb: Northern Illinois University Press.
Leeden, Michael A. (2000). *Tocqueville on American Character*. New York: St. Martin's.
Perkins-Valdez, Dolen. (2011). *Wench: A Novel*. New York: Amistad; 1st ed. 2010.
Perkins-Valdez, Dolen. (2015). *Balm*. New York: Amistad.
Stampp, Kenneth. (1956). *Peculiar Institution: Slavery in the Ante-Bellum South*. New York: Vintage Books.

FURTHER READING

Du Bois, W.E.B. (1968). *The Autobiography of W.E.B. Du Bois: A Soliloquy on Viewing My Life from the Last Decade of Its First Century*. New York: International Publishers.
Gordon-Reed, Annette. (1998). *Thomas Jefferson and Sally Hemings: An American Controversy*. Charlottesville: University of Virginia Press.
Metaxas, Eric. (2007). *Amazing Grace: William Wilberforce and the Heroic Campaign to End Slavery*. New York: HarperOne.
Potter, Eliza. (1991). *A Hairdresser's Experience in High Life* (1859). New York: Oxford University Press.

Phillips, Jayne Anne

BRIAN JARVIS
Loughborough University, UK

Jayne Anne Phillips (b. 1952) describes her hometown of Buckhannon in West Virginia as a place where

> everyone knew everyone's stories, but the stories were secret. As the writer in my family, I felt that I was the person who was charged with making sure all these stories and ideas survive, but at the same time you're not allowed to tell anyone. Writing is the telling of secrets. Secrets have to be told. It's terrible if they're not, but if you tell the secrets, they can transform and unite one moment with another, and bridge the gulf between time, distance, difference.
>
> (Gerard 2000)

Over the course of a career spanning almost half a century, Phillips has written five novels and over thirty short stories. Collectively, this work composes an intimate cartography of secret countries and strange connections across space and time, between locations and generations, objects and animals, machines and mythologies, dreams and desires. Her first narrative maps were a series of short prose poems which appeared in the limited edition chapbooks *Sweethearts* (1976) and *Counting* (1978). Further short stories followed in *Black Tickets* (1979) and *Fast Lanes* (1987). In these collections, Phillips experimented with voice and genre ranging from gritty naturalism ("1934") and the colloquial ("How Mickey Made It") to lush surrealism ("Gemcrack") and the densely figurative ("The Patron"), from fairy tale and myth ("Bluegill") to Frostean *Bildungsroman* ("Bess"), from a Southern gothic reminiscent of Flannery O'Connor or Yoknapatawpha County ("El Paso" and "Country") to urban noir and beat homages to Burroughs and Kerouac ("Black Tickets" and "Fast Lanes"). The mercurial stylistics of Phillips's short fiction was mirrored by a geographic restlessness as it migrated between remote farms in West Virginia and inner-city ghettoes, small towns and suburbs, Deep South and West Coast, and the open roads in between. The class contours of this cartography are marked. The reader of Phillips's short fiction often finds themselves in dusty border towns and dirt farms, public toilets and dilapidated motels, strip joints and porn shops, pool halls and rat-infested cinemas, budget supermarkets and run-down shacks.

The presence of the dispossessed in these locations – the rural and urban poor, hookers and drunks, drifters and outlaws – led to her early work being classified as "Dirty Realist," but alongside this affiliation with Carver's fashionable minimalism, Phillips's short fiction also contributed to well-established traditions of regional and domestic fiction. In terms of its sociospatial mapping, Phillips's fiction drifts to the margins, but always gravitates back to the epicenter of family and home in small-town Virginia. In this regard, the perspective of children and in particular daughters is privileged. Mothers appear center stage on occasion whilst fathers feature as mysterious and even menacing figures in the wings. In opposition to the hegemonic fables of the Reagan era, *Black Tickets* and *Fast Lanes* offered a dissident rewriting of the American Family which highlighted problems of separation, divorce, breakdowns in communication, and varieties of abuse. A provocative challenge to conservative values was similarly evident in a frequent and often Freudian engagement with sex and violence that included incest and rape, sadomasochism and homosexuality, pedophilia and prostitution. A foregrounding of the unruly materialism of the sexual body was wedded to a preoccupation with sickness. Around half of the stories in *Black Tickets* and *Fast Lanes* feature ill health: cancer and TB, ulcers and tumors, poisoning and accidental injury, problems associated with periods, pregnancy, and menopause, hysterical blindness, mystery illnesses and deformity. In addition to physical ailments, mental illness and the derangement of the senses through drug use (cocaine, heroin, mescaline, speed, and sleeping pills) are another signature of the short fiction. The sensible is also subverted in dreams. Cryptic dream sequences are the centerpiece to "Lechery," "Bess," "Bluegill," and "El Paso." Whilst Phillips's road map offers dreams as a fast lane to the unconscious, it rarely displays a Freudian faith in the legibility of the signs encountered en route.

The inscrutable power of dreamlife is central to Phillips's debut novel. Published between the two volumes of short fiction, *Machine Dreams* (1984) chronicles three generations in the history of the Hampsons and Danners, American families falling apart together in the West Virginian small town of Bellington. The local community and family units are riven by world history. The everyday lives of parents and their children are fractured by socioeconomic developments on the home front and national involvement in World War II, the Korean War, and Vietnam. This melancholy invocation of loss – broken marriage, illness, and bereavement – is shot through with a hope that the daughter can save herself and the family by taking on the role of storyteller. *Machine Dreams* is Danner Hampson's book. She listens to the stories of her parents, grandparents, and kid brother, collects their letters, imagines their dreams, and pieces them all together alongside her own. The breakdown of her parents' marriage and the loss of her brother in Vietnam act as a catalyst to genealogical curiosity and political sensibility. In the process of telling her family's story, Danner begins to understand and critique aspects of her country's actions in Southeast Asia. The daughter excavates a "secret country" (a chapter title in *Machine Dreams*) buried beneath her nation's history, her family's past and dreams, and on into the secret life of objects. *Machine Dreams* offers an elaborate curation of material history that includes family heirlooms and war memorabilia, cameras and photographs, radio and film, cars and trucks, planes and helicopters. Phillips traces the effects that this ensemble of machines has on physical, social, and psychic landscapes and the novel's evocative title signifies elisions between technology and consciousness. *Machine Dreams* adumbrates an integration between technological forms and the mechanisms of consciousnesses and in a stunning conceit, this process extends into an intersubjective unconscious and mythology. Family members are seen to share memories, fantasies, and dreams which revolve around machines and resonate with ancient legends. So, for example, in one of the novel's most intricate image clusters, several characters encounter the figure of Pegasus in the shape of flying horses, planes from World War II, and a helicopter in Vietnam.

Phillips's second novel, *Shelter* (1994), shares a number of similarities with her debut. The setting, once again, is Virginia and a story focused on family is framed by war. A polyvocal structure produces a lyrical counterpoint between the voices of adults and children. The same events are articulated from different perspectives and then, as in *Machine Dreams*, an intense intersubjectivity blurs epistemological boundaries between memory, fantasy, and dream. There is a dizzying confluence of streams of consciousness in *Shelter*. Family members seem to share each other's experiences, but it is unclear whether this process is psychological (the unconscious transmission of traumatic secrets) or parapsychological (a mode of telepathic bonding). "Shelter" is the ironic misnomer of a girls' summer camp in the Appalachian backwoods where the main events unfold during a sweltering July in 1963. The story is narrated alternately by three children and one adult: 15-year-old Lenny Swenson; her younger sister Alma; eight-year-old Buddy, who is the son of the camp cook and lives a feral existence in the woods; and Parson, who is an escaped convict and snake-handling evangelist obsessed with tracking down a fellow inmate called Carmody (who is also Buddy's stepfather). When the paths of these characters converge at a site called "Turtle Hole," the children's rite of passage reaches a cryptic climax in a bloody ritual. In terms of genre, *Shelter* interweaves strands of the Grimm fairy tale and Southern gothic with religious allegory and Freudian fable. The children are lost in a dark forest where they discover damp caves and forbidden watering holes, animal bones and snakes, shadows and dangerous strangers. There are echoes here in style and subject of Faulkner, Flannery O'Connor, and William Golding's *Lord of the Flies* (1954). Religious colorings are not confined to Parson's fevered fundamentalism. The forest is also a Garden in which innocence is lost and primal evil is encountered in the devilish shape of Parson's nemesis, Carmody. The apocalyptic epiphany at Turtle Hole is both spiritual and sexual. The children's confrontation with Carmody embodies the culmination of an extravagantly Freudian drama packed with haunting hints of taboo desire, incest, and traumatic abuse at the hands of Oedipal fathers.

Phillips's next novel shifted focus from a pernicious relationship between the Oedipal father and his children to bonds between mother and daughter. *Motherkind* (2000) charts a year in the life of a young woman that sees the birth of her child and the death of her mother. There are numerous autobiographical convergences between Phillips and Kate, the figure at the heart of the novel: both are writers who married doctors, had two sons, and became pregnant whilst taking care of a mother during the terminal stages of cancer. There are occasional flourishes of lyrical intensity, but for the most part the stylistic pyrotechnics of Phillips's previous work are sidelined in favor of a voice which is muted and at times unapologetically prosaic. Whilst the local chronicles and family drama in *Machine Dreams* and *Shelter* were framed by war and large-scale historical forces, *Motherkind* eschews the telescope for the microscope. During a family trip to a Kennedy museum, there are fleeting glimpses of the Vietnam War on a video screen, but this is a distant backdrop to the day's unfolding domestic drama. Phillips offers a resolute concentration on details from everyday experience and the private sphere. *Motherkind* is named after a household help service and devoted to a meticulous inventory of domestic labors such as cleaning, cooking, and caring for children and the sick. Such acts are vigorously valorized as the essential preconditions for daily life. Phillips seeks to evoke the poetics of small good things; familiar things which, according to Kate's mother, "*are so intensely themselves. It's almost magical*" (Phillips 2000, p. 291). A genealogy might almost be traced here back to *Uncle Tom's Cabin* (1852) and Harriet Beecher Stowe's paean to the "living gospel" of "*home*" and housework as a "thousand unconscious acts of love and good will" (Stowe 1998, p. 147). *Motherkind* offers homilies to the "mundane, celestial detail of the everyday" in baby clothes, birthday presents, and festive meals, but does not ignore the sexual politics of domesticity (Phillips 2000, p. 118). The closeness of the bond between daughter, mother, and child entails compromises and at times claustrophobia. Kate has to sacrifice her career as a writer and loses much of her autonomous identity as she tends to the needy and sick. Phillips's embrace of domesticity largely manages to avoid the risk of sentimentalism by casting intimate moments as an affective resource in a ceaseless and ultimately unwinnable battle against death. Kate loses her mother as she becomes a mother and the infant's cot lies in the shadow of the deathbed. *Motherkind* sustains a plaintive counterpoint between fetus and tumor, mashed-up bananas and morphine, the first steps of the toddler and the bedridden terminally ill. At the same time, Phillips never discloses the precise moment of birth or death. The music falls silent before the most intimate of human experiences.

In *Lark & Termite* (2009) "death surges in the ground like a bass line" and as in *Motherkind*, cycles of nativity and mortality are conjoined (2009, p. 7). At precisely the moment that an American soldier is dying in the Korean War, his mentally handicapped son is being born back home in the United States. Phillips's fifth novel remains in familiar territory with a setting in the 1950s in West Virginia and a locus of family relations knitted with war, secrets, and dreams. The eponymous Lark and Termite are sister and brother. Lark is 17 years old and has always helped to look after her disabled half-brother who cannot walk and struggles with language. Termite's father is Corporal Robert Leavitt, who dies during the No Gun Ri massacre in the early days of the Korean War. The two other main characters are Lark and Termite's absent mother, Lola, a cabaret singer who commits suicide when she hears of her husband's death, and Lola's sister, Nonie, who raises the children. *Lark & Termite* repeats the structure and core thematic of *Machine Dreams*. Whilst children, women and men seem to inhabit separate spheres at home and at war, the hard lines of a polyvocal narrative dissolve and a delicate tracery of moments and images bridges the gap between streams of consciousness. Self and other are imbricated whilst space and time echo to suggest intense psychological and possibly mystical bonds. The connection between brother and sister at times appears telepathic. Termite repeats not only the words Lark says, but also the words she is thinking. The siblings also appear to share an inviolable connection with their dead father and absent mother. A scene involving Lark and Termite in a tunnel near their home coalesces with their father's death scene in another tunnel in South Korea. During Termite's own uterine passage his mother has visions of her dying husband who in turn hears her labor pains. Robert Leavitt seems to appear to his children both as a mysterious visitor called Robert Stamble and in spirit form as a deer. Termite declares that "Lola is the cat" (the family pet is ginger-colored and the dead mother had red hair). Phillips's rendition of Termite's inchoate consciousness is indebted to Faulkner's Benjy in *The Sound and the Fury* (1929) and its phantasmagorical indeterminacy leaves events and experiences elegantly poised on the cusp between coincidence and magical correspondence.

The jarring juxtaposition of intimate family relations and horrific violence is again pivotal in Phillips's sixth and most recent novel. *Quiet Dell* (2013) also develops the author's interest in blending historical events with fiction since it is based on an infamous incident which took place in Depression-era Appalachia. In interview, Phillips has mentioned that this historical event intersects with her own family history: "[m]y mother told me of holding her mother's hand at age six, walking along a crowded dirt road in the heat and dust of August, past a 'murder garage'" (Gunn 2014). This crime scene was the home of a con man who lived in the small West Virginian hamlet of Quiet Dell. Harry Powers employed the services of matrimonial agencies and "Lonely Hearts" ads to find vulnerable widows whom he proceeded to murder for their money. In 1931 he lured Asta Eicher and her three children (Greta, Harry, and Annabel) to his home before imprisoning and then killing them in a secret basement hidden under his garage. The murders and subsequent trial and execution of Powers received national media coverage for several months. *Quiet Dell* opens with Christmas celebrations at the Eicher house and takes time to imagine the life of the family before their tragic end. After their disappearance, the focalization shifts to a Chicago reporter and her efforts to uncover the stories of the victims and ensure that their killer is brought to justice. Emily Thornhill becomes a surrogate for Phillips herself as she pieces together a tragic narrative. The metafictional subtext supplements a reenactment of true-life crime in the manner of Capote's new journalism. In addition, as in Phillips's other work, there is an element of fairy tale, myth, and the gothic embedded in historical drama. There is an accumulation of references to Andersen and Grimm, to Powers as "Bluebeard," to "trolls" and "crumbs in the woods" (Phillips 2013, p. 180). As she investigates and seeks to bring the Eicher family to life in words, Thornhill increasingly senses the ghostly presence of the little girl, Annabel. Whether the ghost is real, a dream, or a product of the writer's empathy and creative faculty, the story in *Quiet Dell* offers forceful testimony to "the power of [. . .] vanished lives" (p. 236).

Loss lies at the heart of the Phillips's oeuvre, but melancholy is mitigated by a fierce sensitivity to mythic cycles of renewal and the power of the writer to "intervene in the dynamics of loss [and] insist that sorrow not be meaningless" (Phillips 1994). Phillips's own interventions have produced a cohort of diverse, distinctive, and accomplished fictions. Critical responses to Phillips have not been voluminous. There is, to date, only one critical monograph devoted to the author. In *The Secret Country: Jayne Anne Phillips and the Cryptic Evocation of a Region* (2007), Sarah Robertson combines historical materialism with psychoanalysis and linguistics in a series of deft close readings. Robertson foregrounds the importance of the Appalachian setting and mirrors aspects of her subject's own style with evocative explorations of a range of psychological and socioeconomic "secrets." In a similar vein, Richard Godden in "No End to the Work? Jayne Anne Phillips and the Exquisite Corpse of Southern Labor" (2002) offers an eccentric and provocative engagement with Phillips's literary output up to and including *Motherkind* which seeks to unveil cryptic connections between a private realm riven by trauma and the public context of war, economic crisis, and class conflict. An earlier and less densely theoretical contribution to scholarship is provided by Phyllis Lassner in "Jayne Anne Phillips: Women's Narrative and the Recreation of History" (1989). Phillips's work has also been the subject of a number of essays in Southern journals including *Appalachian Heritage* and *Appalachian Journal*. In this regard, readers looking for an introduction to the author might consult Sue Meredith Willis's "Seduced into Consciousness: The Art of Jayne Anne Phillips" (2009).

SEE ALSO: Contemporary Regionalisms; Fiction and Affect; Illness and Disability Narratives; Minimalism and Maximalism; Trauma and Fiction

REFERENCES

Gerard, Nicci. (2000). Building bridges: interview with Jayne Anne Phillips. *The Guardian* (September 24, 2000). https://www.theguardian.com/books/2000/sep/24/fiction.niccigerrard (accessed July 22, 2021).

Godden, Richard. (2002). No end to the work? Jayne Anne Phillips and the exquisite corpse of Southern labor. Journal of American Studies 36 (2): 249–279.

Gunn, Kirsty. (2014). Veering wildly: review of *Quiet Dell* by Jayne Anne Phillips. *London Review of Books* (July 31, 2014). https://www.lrb.co.uk/the-paper/v36/n15/kirsty-gunn/veering-wildly (accessed July 22, 2021).

Lassner, Phyllis. (1989). Jayne Anne Phillips: women's narrative and the recreation of history. In: *American Women Writing Fiction: Memory, Identity, Family, Space* (ed. Mickey Pearlman), 194–206. Lexington: University Press of Kentucky.

Phillips, Jayne Anne. (1994). The writer as outlaw. *The Washington Post* (October 16, 1994). https://www.washingtonpost.com/archive/entertainment/books/1994/10/16/the-writer-as-outlaw/fc048d80-6932-4348-9a37-8f0554ba8267/ (accessed August 5, 2021).

Phillips, Jayne Anne. (2000). *Motherkind*. London: Vintage Books.

Phillips, Jayne Anne. (2009). *Lark & Termite*. London: Vintage Books.

Phillips, Jayne Anne. (2013). *Quiet Dell*. London: Vintage Books.

Robertson, Sarah. (2007). *The Secret Country: Jayne Anne Phillips and the Cryptic Evocation of a Region*. Amsterdam: Rodopi.

Stowe, Harriet Beecher. (1998). *Uncle Tom's Cabin: Or, Life Among the Lowly*. Oxford: Oxford University Press; 1st ed. 1852.

Willis, Meredith Sue. (2009). Seduced into consciousness: the art of Jayne Anne Phillips. Appalachian Heritage 37 (1): 22–28.

FURTHER READING

Amfreville, Marc. (2010). "Born into absence": Jayne Anne Phillips's *Lark and Termite*. *Études anglaises* 63 (2): 161–173.
Bronfen, Elisabeth. (1988). Between nostalgia and disenchantment: the concept "home" in Jayne Anne Phillips' novel *Machine Dreams*. *Arbeiten aus Anglistik und Amerikanistik* 13 (1): 17–28.
Douglass, Thomas E. (1994). Jayne Anne Phillips. *Appalachian Journal* 21 (2): 182–189.
Durrans, Stéphanie. (2009). Of spirals, snakes, and selves: Jayne Anne Phillips's *Black Tickets*. *Appalachian Heritage* 37 (1): 29–44.
Grove, James. (2000). "Because God's eye never closes": the problem of evil in Jayne Anne Phillips's *Shelter*. In: *The World Is Our Home: Society and Culture in Contemporary Southern Writing* (ed. Jeffrey J. Folks and Nancy Summers Folks), 73–92. Lexington: Kentucky University Press.
Jarvis, Brian. (2001). How dirty is Jayne Anne Phillips? *Yearbook of English Studies* 31 (1): 192–204.
Willis, Meredith Sue. (1996). Witness in the nightmare country: Jayne Anne Phillips. *Appalachian Journal* 24 (1): 44–51.

Piercy, Marge

MELANIE A. MAROTTA
Morgan State University, USA

On March 31, 1936, Marge Piercy was born in Detroit, Michigan. Urban spaces are often her setting for her novels, denoting the significance and impact of Piercy's birthplace and place of her childhood on her writings. Piercy attended the University of Michigan, winning a scholarship to attend and, while there, won awards for her poetry and her fiction. She then went on to Northwestern University and earned a master's degree. Notably, Piercy's novels are written in third-person, self-reflective yet the narrator is always at a distance observing events and reporting them to the reader. Many of Piercy's late-twentieth-century novels concentrate on a divorced or widowed woman who must navigate a patriarchal society, deftly carving out an identity separate from male ideals.

A prolific poet and novelist, Piercy's second prose work, *Woman on the Edge of Time* (1976) rocketed Piercy to stardom. As with Piercy's body of work, this novel focuses on the journey of a woman as she fights for a place for herself in a patriarchal society. As with famed feminist novels that came before hers – such as Mary Wollstonecraft's *Maria: or, The Wrongs of Woman* (1798) or Gayl Jones *Eva's Man* (1976) – Piercy concentrates her novel on a cis-woman who is being convinced by the dominant male society that she is mentally unstable, an act meant to discredit her and suppress her voice. Like she did with the inclusion of a new introduction in the 2012 edition of *Vida* (1980), Piercy added a preface to the 2016 edition of *Women on the Edge of Time*, citing her intention to create female utopic space thereby following in the footsteps of writers like Joanna Russ (*The Female Man*, 1975). In the preface, Piercy observes that female utopias are safe spaces for the marginalized in society, for example single mothers and older women. She asserts, "Like most women's utopias, *Woman on the Edge of Time* is profoundly anarchist and aimed at integrating people back into the natural world and eliminating power relationships" (2006, p. viii). Connie (Consuelo) Ramos has been institutionalized before the novel began, and is once her niece Dolly comes in search of a refuge. Dolly, who is pregnant, has been forced into prostitution by her lover (and later pimp), Geraldo, and flees to her aunt after Geraldo physically assaults her. Geraldo comes to Connie's, forcing his way into her space, bringing a "doctor" to perform an abortion against Dolly's will. After Connie strikes Geraldo with a wine bottle, she is committed to an institution as a danger to others. Connie lies strapped to the table protesting the accusation that her assault of Geraldo was unprovoked as the male doctor and pimp decide her fate. After an undetermined period of time, Connie awakens only to be ignored by two female nurses, both of which categorize her as unstable, thereby denigrating her and taking away her self-worth. After she is transported to a mental institution, she is placed in isolation, forced to ingest an overdose of her medication, and left is deplorable conditions. Rather than helping Connie – she downward spiraled after the death of her partner – she is left due to suffer, her punishment after she assaults her child. Over the course of the novel, Connie encounters Luciente, who knows her secrets and who she greatly fears. She claims to be from the future, as part of the group called the Manhattan Project, but Connie is suspicious as only she can see Luciente. Luciente is from a utopic space in the future, Mattapoisett, one that values women and their freedom. The novel mainly centers on Connie's experiences in the institution, including horrific mistreatment of herself and other patients, including shock treatments. After the publication of this novel Piercy is acknowledged for her work in 1978 when she was awarded a National Endowment for the Arts award, which is a major accomplishment for an American writer.

In the new introduction (2011) to the 2012 edition of her novel *Vida*, Piercy discusses how she created her characters, citing her desire to make them not only products of the time but also to make them realistic. She asserts, "The characters are quite human. All the major characters are rounded, possessing both virtues and vices, strengths and weaknesses" (2012, p. v). The novel revolves around Vida Asch, a Leftist activist who was one of many fugitives from the Network being sought by the FBI. Vida, whose real name is Davida Whippletree, has returned to New York with a new name and hair color, attempting to elude capture. As she readies herself to see her husband after a period of absence, she reminisces about her pre-fugitive life, clinging onto her memories of her sister, Natalie, and her second husband, Leigh, in an attempt to reassure herself that she has not really changed since going on the run, even though she has had six additional names. Unlike others in the novel, Vida is stagnant, unable to move on within her life as she is ultimately trapped by her past, namely her part in the bombings as a member of Little Red Wagon. As the novel progresses, Vida reveals that she has an open marriage, that she is bisexual, and that she is exceedingly lonely. She meets Joel in a safehouse, and they become lovers; throughout the novel, Vida asserts her desire for someone in her life, but also that she prefers to be selfish – it is ultimately her and her cause.

Designated as a New York Times Notable Book, Piercy's *Fly Away Home* (1984) centers on Daria Walker, a cookbook author, and the after-effects of the dissolution of her marriage. Piercy plants in their marriage the signs of an affair: separate phones, Ross's mysterious absences, a lull in their sex life, and a gift of lingerie for Daria that is not in her size. Unexpectedly, Ross informs Daria that he wants a divorce; he has been having an affair and later tries to have Daria murdered. One of the reasons for the divorce is Ross's secretive behavior, not only the affair but that Ross has been conducting illegal activity and a death results due to arson. Ultimately in *Fly Away Home*, Daria's story is one that Piercy covers in other novels, that of a woman struggling to find her place in a patriarchal society once her marriage dissolves. Daria seeks to find an identity outside of that of wife and mother and must escape the oppressive actions of Ross, who blames her for his own dissatisfaction with his life.

Gone to Soldiers (1987) focuses on the theme of duality. The novel begins with the duality of a female character; Louise Kahn, who also goes by the name of Annette Hollander Sinclair, is a divorced woman with a fifteen-year-old daughter, Kay, who is living amidst World War II. Her husband, Oscar, left her and when he did so, Louise came to the conclusion that without his patriarchal dominating behavior, she and her daughter were better off. Louise is caught between worlds, working to adapt to her societal structure even though it is discriminatory in many ways. When she was younger, Louise wanted to be a journalist but discovered that her fiction sells. It is through the war that Louise becomes the journalist that she desires. Early in her life Louise establishes a persona once she realizes that there are no female Jewish writers; she creates an image (physical representation is important to Louise/Annette as wardrobe is discussed by her and other characters) that she believes would be acceptable to her readers, and her popularity soars. As a result, Louise begins to live separate lives, a fact observed by her daughter as Kay asserts that the outfit Louise wears is not appropriate for Louise but is for Annette. It is Louise that begins the novel, the first of many intertwined characters to have their stories unfold. Through the course of the novel, the reader learns about – amongst others – Abra from Bath, Maine, Oscar's research assistant who meets her own needs, quickly discarding those who cannot; Jacqueline and Naomi Lévy-Monot, French Jews subjected to discrimination by their friends and others because of their religion; Naomi, who is separated from her immediate family and sent to live with relatives, including Ruthie, in Michigan where it is safer for Jews; and Bernice, who cares for her ailing father the professor while she seeks an identity separate from her father. As the war unfolds, it impacts the characters in the novel, changes their families and their circumstances: Piercy offers readers characters whose continue to live even through the harrowing events of the war, events that include the deaths of families.

Summer People (1989) focuses on Dinah but follows the polyamorous relationship between Dinah, Susan DeWitt, and Willie, who live out on Cape Cod. Dinah Adler, who is the most assertive of the three, dominates the text offering to readers her contentment with the couple, their cats, and the old families of Cape Cod. This satisfaction is surface-level as she is brimming with dissatisfaction, which stems from her domestic relationship – including her lack of a child – and the changes to Cape Cod by new residents. Like Vida, Dinah is sexually fluid, entering into a relationship with Susan initially and then her husband, Willie, after Dinah's poet husband succumbs to illness. As the novel progresses, the narrator's concentration shifts to other characters and their problems. Susan, who is forty-six, has entered a different stage of her life than Dinah, who wants to have a baby with Willie. For Susan, Dinah was an adventure, a thrill that is waning as their lives unfold. Susan's children – Jimmy and Siobhan – are adults with lives of their own and she is passed the point when they consume her – she declares that she is at a point in her life that she gets to concentrate on her own needs – not that of others. Willie's chapters are less emotionally-filled as those of Dinah, Susan, and Laurie, their friend's Tyrone Burdock's daughter. As the novel develops, their relationship breaks due to jealousy and intense need; ultimately Dinah learns not only what fulfills her but also that of a partner.

Piercy was raised by her parents and her grandparents. Both Piercy's mother, Bert Bernice Bunnin who inspired her to become a poet, and her grandmother, Hannah, have a significant role in Piercy's upbringing and as her family is matrilineal, her mother and grandmother are also Jewish. In fact, Hannah bestowed on Piercy her Hebrew name of Marah. Throughout her career, Piercy has held writer-in-residences at numerous Judaic educational spaces and has given copious lectures and readings at Jewish centers of worship and universities. In 1991, Piercy's *He, She and It* was published, demonstrating the integrality that Judaism and matriarchal figures are to Piercy's life. Shira Shipman, Piercy's female protagonist, lives in the Yakamura-Stichen dome, a patriarchal corporate enclave. Shira attempts to adhere to patriarchal guidelines, believing herself to be a good wife, mother, and citizen, loses custody her son once her marriage dissolves. The Y-S system shows that it favors men as not only does her former husband gain custody of her child, but also her lifestyle disintegrates, and she is left socially disadvantaged. Also, under the Y-S dome, Shira must hide her religious beliefs, following "the born-again Shintoism of Y-S" instead (Piercy 1993, p. 2). Disillusioned by the societal guidelines in place for women, Shira leaves the Y-S dome and returns to her family's enclave – Tikva. Once she returns home to her grandmother, Malkah, and Judaism, she is able to obtain physical and mental freedom. Notably, Piercy has opted to utilize the Jewish story of the Golem as a basis for her novel. After Shira can no longer conform to Y-S and the corporate enclave culture, she accepts a job continuing her work in cybernetics. Now, Shira is employed by her friend (and her former love interest's father) Avram, taking the place of her grandmother in the creation of a cyborg named Yod. Channeling the story of the golem in her writing of Yod, the cyborg has been created so that he may protect Tikva and its inhabitants from harm. Through her relationship with Yod and her grandmother, Shira regains her self-worth and rediscovers her religion and her need for community. This novel won the Arthur C. Clark award in 1993.

Suzanne Blume, an attorney and university professor made her appearance in Piercy's *Three Women: A Novel* (1999). Harvard Alum Suzanne's life is offered over the course of the novel, intertwined with that of her friend, Marta, and Suzanne's two daughters. As with Piercy herself, Suzanne is enamored with her cats. In her memoir *Sleeping with Cats* (2002), Piercy delineates her experiences intermingled with her other family members – her cats – much as she does with Suzanne's character. As indicated by the novel's title, and repeating the construction used for *Summer People*, Piercy's late twentieth-century *Three Women* follows the lives of three generations of women: Suzanne; her mother, Beverly; and her daughter, Elena. Unlike her sister Rachel who is going to become a rabbi, Elena is portrayed as lacking direction, is considered by other characters to be a great beauty, and has been sexually active since her early teens. In fact, Elena's sexual power unnerves many characters in the novel; she is conditioned by society to utilize her sexuality to get what she wants. It is her sexual activity that is a point of consternation for her mother; the event that she does not wish to discuss is Elena's polyamorous with Evan and Chad as an adolescent. As Suzanne comes to terms with her daughter's sexuality, she also does so with her own lack of desire for a romantic relationship. Elena is selfish and is shown as being larger than life; her mother worries about her and is intimidated by her as her daughter knows what she wants, she is self-assured, and is impulsive. Some of Piercy's own life has influenced the writing of Elena as both Piercy and Elena had to work a variety of low-wage temporary jobs in order to support themselves. Like Elena, Piercy persisted, continuing to write while in Chicago even though publishers refused her novels. Like Suzanne, Piercy was divorced twice, again her life impacts her novels, thereby asserting their relatability to the reader. After two husbands and ten years alone, Suzanne meets the man she has been corresponding with through email; they have a brief affair and then a familial crisis occurs. Beverly has a debilitating stroke and, as a result, the family bands together to help her on what they believe is a journey of physical healing and self-acceptance. Many of Beverly's scenes show her frame of mind – she wants to die – as the two strokes and her new bodily condition have depleted her. For Suzanne, her life destabilizes after her daughter has an affair with Marta's husband; for Rachel, it is when she learns that Judaism is patriarchal; and for Elena, it is when she learns that she must refrain from having men and sex dominate her life. Each character must come to terms with deaths in their lives, whether they be literal or figurative, so that they may become a functioning family.

In 2014, Piercy's short story anthology, *The Cost of Lunch, Etc.* centers on the lives of women and the inequalities that they face. In the opener, which is titled "The Cost of Lunch," struggling poet Maud has lost her teaching job and is trying to be acknowledged for her skill as a writer. She resents needing men for her success and for Othering women in American society. Piercy' story, set in the 1970s, is a timely expose regarding systemic gender discrimination in the United States. The anthology includes many worthy stories such as "The Border." Here, the unnamed female protagonist narrates her drive to the United States–Canada border, telling readers about how she is transporting a soldier over the border, so he does not have to go back to Vietnam. In a rare change, "I Wasn't Losing My Mind" was written using the first-person point of view. The unnamed narrator tells the story of things, of possessions handed down to her from her mother. Her mother was poverty-stricken and wanted her daughter to have things that held great meaning. Piercy further intertwines the narrator's life with that of her assistant, Jean's life; it is Jean that she learns is stealing these things from her, not caring about the narrator nor the significance of these things, the carefully curated collection of memories handed down through the family.

Piercy lives with her husband, Ira Wood, and their cats in Wellfleet, Massachusetts. They married in 1982 and he, too, is a writer. Together they have written a play, *The Last White Class: A Play about Neighborhood Terror* (1979); a novel, *Storm Tide* (1998); and stared a publishing company – Leapfrog Press. In Wellfleet, Piercy holds and participates in juried poetry workshops. *On the Way Out, Turn off the Light*, Piercy's latest book of verse, was released in October 2020. Piercy's papers are housed at the University of Michigan.

SEE ALSO: The Culture Wars; Debut Novels; Jones, Gayl; Queer and LGBT Fiction; Trauma and Fiction

REFERENCES

Piercy, Marge. (1993). *He, She, and It*. New York: Ballantine. 1st ed. 1991.
Piercy, Marge. (2012). *Vida*. Oakland, CA: PM Press. 1st ed. 1980.
Piercy, Marge. (2016) *Woman on the Edge of Time*. New York: Ballantine; 1st ed. 1976.

FURTHER READING

Barr, Marleen S. (2000). Shutting the bestial mouth: confessions of male clones and girl gangs. In *Genre Fission: A New Discourse Practice for Culture Studies*, 31–69. Iowa City: Iowa Press.
Bickford, Donna M. (2019). *Understanding Marge Piercy*. Columbia: University of South Carolina Press.
Hanson, Elaine Tuttle. (1985). The double narrative structure of small changes. In *Contemporary American Women Writers* (ed. Catherine Rainwater and William J. Scheick), 209–223. Lexington: University Press of Kentucky.
Marotta, Melanie A. (2014). Acceptance of the marginalized in Marge Piercy's *He, She, It* and Melissa Scott's *Trouble and Her Friends*. In: *Environments in Science Fiction: Essays on Alternative Spaces* (ed. Susan Bernardo), 28–45. Jefferson, NC: McFarland Press.
Walker, Sue and Hamner, Eugenie. (eds.) (1991). *Ways of Knowing: Essays on Marge Piercy*. Mobile, AL: Negative Capability Press.

Post-9/11 Narratives

JOSEPH M. CONTE
University at Buffalo, USA

> Burning burning burning burning
> O Lord Thou pluckest me out
> O Lord Thou pluckest
> burning
>
> T.S. Eliot, *The Waste Land* (1922)

The attacks on September 11, 2001, ushered in the Age of Terror, which is an epistemic shift in American polity from the bright lattices of virtual capital that fueled the dot-com boom of the 1990s to a twenty-first century marked by asymmetrical warfare across the globe, not only in New York, Washington, DC, and Shanksville, PA, but also in London, Madrid, Bali, Boston, Beslan, North Ossetia, and Colombo, Sri Lanka. The US prosecution of a so-called War on Terror, in pursuit of a regenerative abstraction, has resulted in indefinite and worldwide conflicts not limited to Iraq and Afghanistan. For those who say that everything was changed, that day marked the termination of a univocal American exceptionalism; and for those who opined that nothing has changed, the globalization of the market state runs on unimpeded. In cultural matters, it's possible to make assertions of periodization like those made for the postwar or postmodern era, that 9/11 either signals a rupture from the narcissistic narratives of an all-American future or a continuity with the past in that the terroristic ground was long sown with the abuses of power. Post-9/11 narratives may turn wholly on the spectacular events of that day, or they may take account of the collective transformation afterward in the social order, politics, psychopathology, or modes of representation in the arts. In either case, these novels register a shock to human consciousness not unlike that described by Virginia Woolf "in or about December, 1910" (1924, p. 91).

It would be inaccurate, however, to describe post-9/11 narratives as a subgenre of the novel because genres have rules of literary style and form, and fictions that reference 9/11 are too diverse to comply with such rules. As examples, William Gibson's *Pattern Recognition* (2003) is a speculative fiction, and on the morning of 9/11 Gibson, writing in Vancouver, BC realized that the event had "changed everything" for his brand-sensitive protagonist, Cayce Pollard, whose father, a Cold War security analyst, disappears in lower Manhattan. Jonathan Franzen's *Freedom* (2010) is a social and coming-of-age novel in which Walter and Patty Berglund's son Joey blames the 9/11 attacks for his failures at college and turns to profiteering in war materiel. Ken Kalfus's *A Disorder Peculiar to the Country* (2006) is a satire in which a divorcing Brooklynite couple are delighted by the prospects of each other's demise in the attacks, as a wave of "Epidemic terror" overtakes the nation. Art Spiegelman's *In the Shadow of No Towers* (2004) is a graphic memoir that offers "notes of a heartbroken narcissist" traumatized by history. And Laila Halaby's *Once in a Promised Land* (2007), in which a Jordanian couple encounter Islamophobia in Arizona after 9/11, incorporates features of the Arabesque tale in the narrative.

Rather than consider post-9/11 narratives as a single genre, this entry will collect prominent examples into four categories according to their modes of address (how the text speaks to its audience), their verbal mood (not strictly grammatically), or modality. First, the Indicative mood, in novels that make a direct address toward the event, in which the representation and experience of the attacks on 9/11 is a pivotal element of the narrative structure, and the protagonist is either a survivor of the fall of the towers or closely related to a victim. In these books, characters exhibit symptoms of profound psychological trauma, or post-traumatic stress disorder. Second, the Subjunctive mood, or indirect address, is used when the event occurs offstage and the characters are proximate witnesses to the attacks. The conditional modality of this group, or what might happen if circumstances were changed, lends itself to works of fabulation, reflexivity, or metafiction. In these books, alternate worlds are entertained and hypotheticals about the causes and repercussions of 9/11, or whether it need have happened at all, are considered. Third, the Interrogative mode is employed, in whose questioning of the nature of the attacks political, judicial, or cross-cultural arguments are broached. In these books, global, transnational, or transversal inquiries of the post-9/11 subject are made, often with regard to xenophobia, Islamophobia, and oppression of the Other. Fourth, the Demonstrative or Imperative mood is used, in books that document that such a thing is (or was) the case; or that such a thing has (or must have) happened. Here are found narratives of historical realism that critique the social order both before and after 9/11. Unlike genres in which the rules of literary style and form are not made to be broken, these four modalities allow for the possibility of more than one address in a given work. So, a novel such as Don DeLillo's *Falling Man* (2007) may feature a protagonist, Keith Neudecker, who is a traumatized survivor of the north tower's collapse (Indicative), but his estranged wife Lianne questions her religious or ideological beliefs (Interrogative). David Janiak, the performance artist known as Falling Man, and the tripartite recursive structure of the narrative, such that the novel ends in the towers shortly before it begins, are reflexive elements of an innovative literary form (Subjunctive).

FALLING (WO)MEN

DeLillo has said that he did not want to write a novel of 9/11 in which the protagonist gazed over his shoulder at the catastrophe but rather that he would place that character directly in the maelstrom (Binelli, 2007). Three novels in the Indicative mood place their protagonist, or a close relative, in the fall of the towers as a victim and/or survivor of the attacks. The direct address toward the character's experience of the event, however, poses the challenge of representing the unrepresentable for the writer. While the fall of the towers was the most widely broadcast event in history, the experience of those trapped in the towers (see the Franco-American Frédéric Beigbeder's novel, *Windows on the World*, 2004) must be unknowable, while the trauma of those who survive a near-death experience is inexpressible. And yet, novelists have brought the power to conjure affective and subjective states in their characters that would not otherwise be accessible in our primarily visual culture. In *Falling Man*, DeLillo focuses his narrative on the traumatic experience of one man, Keith Neudecker, a corporate lawyer who escapes from the north tower. Stunned and injured, Neudecker accepts a ride from a stranger, giving the address of his estranged wife, Lianne, and their son in uptown Manhattan, a decision that temporarily reunites the family. While being treated for his injuries by an emergency-room physician, Neudecker is told that survivors of suicide bombings often develop lesions that are, literally, "tiny fragments of the suicide bomber's body," bits of flesh and bone that become lodged beneath the skin of anyone within proximity of the blast. "They call this organic shrapnel" (2007, p. 16). Forcibly, physically penetrated by the body of his attacker, Neudecker – and the American psyche of which he is a symbolic case – bears in body and mind the internalized scars of this violation. The counternarrative to terror does not, to the consternation of some readers, involve a healing personal epiphany with the aid of his family. Keith seeks out another survivor, Florence Givens, a Black woman whose briefcase Keith carries from the north tower and returns, calling her "out of the blue" (p. 54). Instead, the figure of restitution rests with the performance artist, David Janiak, known as Falling Man, whose plunges from overpasses are intended to shock the New York commuters. Suspended upside down, "Was this position intended to reflect the body posture of a particular man who was photographed falling from the north tower of the World Trade Center, headfirst, arms at his sides, one leg bent, a man set forever in free fall against the looming background of the column panels in the tower?" (p. 221). As in the photograph by Richard Drew, Falling Man emulates the Hanged Man of the Major Arcana in the Tarot, a figure not of death but of contemplative suspension. As terrible as the consequences of 9/11 were, those deaths were not to be avenged in a War on Terror. Rather, the novel bids us to stay retribution, ponder the consequences of our actions, and through selflessness gain illumination.

The youthful author of *Everything Is Illuminated* (2002), Jonathan Safran Foer returned with *Extremely Loud & Incredibly Close* (2005), which features a precocious nine-year-old boy named Oskar Schell who has lost his father, Thomas Schell, Jr., in the collapse of the towers on 9/11. While examining his father's possessions in the aftermath of this tragedy, he discovers an envelope in a vase, on which is written the word "Black." Inside the envelope is a key, and extraordinarily, Oskar sets out to find every person named "Black" in New York City, an impossible task, with the hopes that the key, in the right lock, will reveal the fate of his father. The vase is symbolically a funerary urn, and yet what its blackness does not contain is the ashes of Oskar's father, whose remains, like so many of those lost on 9/11, are undiscoverable, and so represent a haunting, negative, empty sign of trauma and loss. Foer's novel is notably replete with photographs of doors, keys, and other images that appear to illustrate aspects of Oskar's search for the safe-deposit box that the key marked "Black" fits. And yet, the inclusion of these and other graphical elements in the book, especially the concluding "flip book" of manipulated video stills of a person who appears to rise up rather than fall from the towers on 9/11, are not intended as an "illustrated" novel of 9/11 but rather as a multimodal image-text whose visual supplement compensates for the unspeakability of the event. Also included are a series of undelivered letters written by Oskar's grandfather, Thomas Schell, Sr., to his son, "Why I'm Not Where You Are," beginning in 1963 and concluding on "9/11/03" (2005, p. 262). The elder Schell is a survivor of the firebombing of Dresden in World War II, in which he loses his pregnant fiancée, Anna. On arrival as a refugee in New York, he loses the power of speech, beginning with his beloved's name. His mutism takes the form of a book with blank pages on which he writes phrases such as "I don't speak, I'm sorry" (p. 262). Wanting to recapitulate his son's life, a son lost in the cataclysm of 9/11, Thomas needs "an infinitely long blank book and forever" (p. 280). He plunges into graphomania, which is the therapeutic resolution to his mourning, represented by black pages incrementally saturated with print. These pages are both illegible to the reader and filled with Thomas's impassioned address to his lost son.

In the opening chapter of Ken Kalfus's *A Disorder Peculiar to the Country*, Marshall Harriman barely escapes with his life from his office on the eighty-sixth floor of the south tower. As

Marshall struggles to carry a dazed man across the plaza between the two towers, a "woman in a navy business suit" hits the ground nearby and bursts (2006, p. 16), while Lloyd is killed by molten debris falling from the towers. The falling men and women were "colleagues and friends" (p. 14). In fact, Father Mychal Judge, the chaplain to the New York Fire Department, was struck in the head and killed by debris from the collapsing south tower, while praying in the lobby of the north tower. The removal of his body was captured by the documentary filmmakers, Gédéon and Jules Naudet in *9/11* (2002). Marshall learns that United 93 from Newark to San Francisco, on which his wife, Joyce, with whom he has been bitterly feuding, had been scheduled to fly, has crashed in Shanksville, Pennsylvania. Among "the flood of refugees: filthy, dazed, grieved, bereft," he went "nearly skipping" over one of the East River bridges (2006, pp. 19–20). Kalfus remarks that he had arrived at "a grim observation in the aftermath of the terrorist attacks, at a time when, in our grief, we were glorifying the victims of the attacks, calling them heroes, as well as beloved, perfect husbands and wives. My view is that through cliché we were dehumanizing the dead." His "point is satirical, of course, a rebuff to our assumed national piety" (2013). Like Keith Neudecker, Marshall escapes the falling towers with his life, but his life, like Keith's, is not saved by what comes after. In their marital dispute, Joyce and Marshall adopt the very same conspiratorial and terrorist tactics that were employed by al-Qaeda in the attacks. Their children, Victor and Viola, under Joyce's supervision, are injured "playing 9/11," as they jump repeatedly from a porch to the ground: "The World Trade Center was on fire and we had to jump off together! But he let go of my hand!" (2006, pp. 114–115). In this war of domestic terrorism, the two children are "their divorce's civilian casualties" (p. 7). Marshall becomes a self-radicalized martyr, donning a suicide vest under his bathrobe that he has assembled by following a printable diagram downloaded from a website in Arabic. He enters the apartment's kitchen, declares "God is great," and touches the wiring clips together. Nothing happens. Joyce and the kids offer to troubleshoot the wiring, and while they fail to fix the problem, they participate in an ironic exchange of unwitting victims and terrorist conspirators. Joyce declares, "You don't follow through with anything. That's what's wrong with you" (p. 191). Surely the American family should be united in time of crisis, but the Harrimans suffer, as the novel's title alludes, from the "peculiar malady . . . of Epidemic terror" (Klein, 2006).

ALTERNATE WORLDS

The events of 9/11 were, as DeLillo observes, "an extraordinary blow to consciousness, and it changed everything" (Ulin, 2003, p. E1). Writers of post-9/11 narrative, however, have refused to drape themselves in the cloak of national mourning, and recognizing the shock to the political order, turn to formally inventive presentations that acknowledge the event's unpresentability. Such works are most prominently found in the Subjunctive mood, in which fabulation and metafiction are employed to explore the conditional or hypothetical "what ifs." Paul Auster's *Man in the Dark* (2008), as an example, ventures an alternative history of secession and civil war that erupts between Red states and Blue states in response to the illegitimate election of George W. Bush in 2000, instead of the imperial wars waged by his administration. In this counterfactual timeline, possible in a quantum universe or Giordano Bruno's theory of infinite worlds, it is 2006, the "twin towers" are still standing, and "there's no war in Iraq" (2008, p. 31). In this nocturnal narrative, an insomniac book critic, August Brill, invents the story of Owen Brick, who is conscripted to fight in the second civil war. In a piercing of the ontological mantle of the narrative, between a post-9/11 world and one in which the event never occurs, Brick is assigned to terminate the hypnogogic man who has summoned this internecine conflict into existence. The critic's granddaughter, Katya, mourns her fiancé, Titus Small, a military contractor who has been abducted and executed by insurgents in the "phony, trumped-up war" in Iraq, "the worst political mistake in American history" (p. 172). One world collides with another, one war is exchanged for another, and the expression of political affect demands the in(ter)vention of literary form. Auster has said that ever since the presidency of Albert Gore was "taken away from him by political and legal maneuvering ... I've had this eerie feeling of being in some parallel world, some world we didn't ask for but we nevertheless got. In the other world Al Gore is finishing his second term now, we never invaded Iraq, maybe 9/11 never happened" (Flood, 2008).

The mode of address can shift within any post-9/11 narrative, and such is the case with the conclusion of Kalfus's *A Disorder Peculiar to the Country*. The novel's chapters progress chronologically from September 2001 to March 2003, as the drumbeat for war – from Colin Powell at the UN, Tony Blair before Parliament, Hillary Clinton in Congress, Leon Wieseltier in *The New Republic*, and David Letterman on the *Late Show* – grows louder in its "contempt for the doubters" (2006, p. 201). And then the novel, either because it has caught up with events or because of its utter disrespect for such mendacities, makes a proleptic leap into a fantasia in which "*Bush was right*" (p. 202). In its alternative ending to the War on Terror, Saddam Hussein is hanged by freedom-loving Iraqi forces; WMD are discovered in large stockpiles with the medium-range missiles to deliver them to Israel and Europe; Bashar al-Assad flees Syria; Iranian women doff their chadors; Osama bin Laden is captured in the Tora-Bora caves along the Afghan-Pakistani border; and most unlikely of all, the Harrimans reconcile at Ground Zero. The narratological shift into a counterfactual future arrives like "Shock and Awe," obliterating the reader's complicity with the conventions of realism, at least in so far as it is represented in nonfiction narrative and mass media. What is true is false; what is false is true. The formal rupture of the novel – its break with the assertions of realism – underlies its satirical attack on political discourse and social consensus, a "disorder peculiar to the country."

TRANSNATIONAL POLITICS

The domestic political satire of Kalfus's novel can be compared with Jess Walter's *The Zero* (2006), in which Brian Remy, a cop with a possibly self-inflicted headwound, awakens five days after the attacks with episodic amnesia. As Mayor Rudolph Giuliani urges New Yorkers to return downtown and "go shopping" only days after the attacks, Remy passes a signboard that reads, "God Bless America. New Furniture Arriving Every Day" (2006, p. 120). And yet, the Interrogative mode of political inquiry, questioning the 9/11 Commission's report on the origins of the al-Qaeda plot against America and the rationale for war in the Middle East, turns in the hands of American writers to an interrogation of the linkage between non-state terrorism and globalization, xenophobia and transmigration, national populism and cosmopolitanism. Laila Halaby is a multilingual global citizen, born in Beirut, Lebanon to a Jordanian father and an American mother; she grew up mostly in Arizona, where her novel, *Once in a Promised Land*, is set. It's the morning of September 11th, and Jassim Haddad, a hydrologist specializing in water conservation in arid lands, and his wife, Salwa Khalil, a banker, real estate agent, and self-styled Queen of Pajamas, awake in Tucson to a changed world after the destruction of the World Trade Center "by Arabs, by Muslims.... But of course, they have nothing to do with what happened to the World Trade Center. Nothing and everything" (2007, p. viii). Salwa fears "repercussion toward Arabs in this country" and wonders whether Americans are "so ignorant as to take revenge on" Jordanians, Lebanese, or Sikhs "for the act of a few extremist Saudis" (p. 21). Halaby is agitated by a pervasive "American 'jahiliyya,' or generalized ignorance of other cultures" (2008), that under routine circumstances might be expected from the people of a continental nation and a dominant mass culture but which under duress turns into a toxic and indiscriminate Islamophobia. Jassim, who has built a well-respected professional career in water conservation in the desert southwest, suffers a cold-sweat panic attack when he realizes that he is nothing more than a "visitor to this country" (2007, p. 153), one who is no longer welcome. This destabilization of his identity – that he is not an assimilated "Jordanian-American" but remains a Jordanian expatriate – is compounded by an accident in which a young skateboarder swerves in front of Jassim while driving his Mercedes and is killed. The Arabesque design in Jassim's life unravels after an investigation reveals the teen had been "freaked out" by 9/11 and began talking like a racist who "wished he could kill an Arab" (2007, pp. 200–201). Salwa has come under suspicion as an Arab Muslim woman – although she is not veiled – and yet it is America that has become alien to her. As a natural-born American citizen of migrant refugee parents, twice-displaced, once by the Palestinian exodus, "al-Nakba" (the catastrophe), and once by an accident of birth, she pointedly refuses to assert her citizenship, that she is just as American by law as other native Tucsonans. She purchases a single ticket to Amman where she intends to rejoin her family. Salwa realizes that the American Dream she has pursued is a "huge lie," and that "she did not come from a culture of happy endings" (2007, pp. 316–317). By unofficially renouncing her American citizenship, Salwa fully embraces and honors her global, diasporic Palestinian identity.

Islamophobia and remigration are likewise visited in Amy Waldman's novel, *The Submission* (2011). Mohammad Khan, an American-born architect and non-observant Muslim, wins the juried, blind-submission competition for the 9/11 Memorial on the site of the World Trade Center. His selection is opposed as insensitive to the families of the victims, not only by the fictional mayor of New York City but also by a xenophobic hate group called Save America from Islam. As one of the jurors opines, "It's Maya Lin," the Chinese-American architect who designed the Vietnam Veterans Memorial in 1981, "all over again. But worse" (2011, p. 18). When he eventually testifies at a hearing to decide the fate of the memorial, Mo doesn't help his cause with the SAFI (in Arabic, ṣāfī means pure, clear, unmixed; but here the acronym alludes to white supremacist objectives of racial purity and ethnic cleansing) who suspect the Islamicate origins of his design, building a Muslim prayer garden on harrowed Ground Zero. Nor does he satisfy the Muslim advocacy groups who recoil at his blasphemous speculation that "man wrote the Quran" in part to create a "model for paradise" (p. 246), questioning belief in its divinely inspired origin. The cashiering of Khan's design for the memorial has the ironic effect of leading an agnostic, highly-educated Western professional to eventual "submission to God's will" (p. 81), the Arabic meaning of Islam. Unlike the martyrs who refuse to renounce their faith,

Mohammad's trial causes him to reconsider his secularism and disbelief. For their part, the fanatical SAFI foment anti-Muslim hatred, which leads to the stabbing death of an undocumented immigrant, Asma Anwar, the widow of a Bangladeshi man killed in the collapse of the towers. Asma's son, Abdul Karim, who is entitled to birthright US citizenship, is brought to Bangladesh to be raised by relatives. Though his "parents idealized America" (p. 328), and in receipt of his father's 9/11 death benefits, Abdul refuses to return to the US for his education. For his part, Mohammad Khan, unable to recognize himself in the factionalized controversy over the 9/11 Memorial, relinquishes his parents' dream of life in America and "traced his parents' journey in reverse: back to India, which seemed a more promising land" (p. 330).

SOCIAL HISTORIES

As we pass the twentieth anniversary of 9/11 and the 1776-foot-tall Freedom Tower with its blast proof glass has risen over Ground Zero, the events of that day are now decidedly a part of history. But in its aftermath, novelists considered how that transformational moment might be represented in a work of fiction that would combine the imaginative construction of characters with the facts as they were known. Two novels in the Demonstrative mood, Jay McInerney's *The Good Life* (2006) and Claire Messud's *The Emperor's Children* (2006), are works of an immediate history that documents and preserves the sensibility of a nation under assault, of what the world was like both before and after it all changed. Their narrative arcs span the divide between pre- and post-9/11 New York, and their characters dramatize the shock of what sociologist Erving Goffman called a frame-breaking event, in which the conceptual frameworks that bind a particular social group are suddenly inadequate to a rational understanding of what has happened (1974, p. 27). In fact, McInerney abandoned a novel in which a terrorist bombing in New York City is perpetrated by a radicalized Muslim who has taken offense with American cultural imperialism and the extravagances of global capitalism – a premise at once prescient of and insufficient to the enormity of 9/11. Despite his reservations that a novelist's "invention [would] be overwhelmed and overshadowed by the actual catastrophe," he decides that he must be willing to "engage the 'post-9/11 era'" in all its daunting scope and complexity (2005). Russell Calloway, an ambitious "editor at one of the big houses" (2006, p. 53), lives in a refurbished railroad apartment in TriBeCa with his wife, Corrine, who has quit her job to raise their six-year-old twins conceived with ova donated by her younger sister. Russell entertains the literati of New York in their home with gourmet cooking and wine pairings, "all the trappings of the good life" (p. 323). Further up the social register, Luke McGavock, an investment banker on voluntary leave from his firm, his socialite wife Sasha, and neurasthenic daughter, Ashley, occupy a lavish duplex on the Upper East Side, decorated to merit feature treatment in *Architectural Digest*. But then, "That Autumn" (p. 71), these pairings of precious and privileged New Yorkers will intersect beginning on Ash Wednesday – September 12th – as the debris and particulate matter sift down over lower Manhattan. Luke, who "was supposed to meet [his] friend Guillermo at Windows on the World" (p. 74), has spent the day fruitlessly digging for survivors on the pile. Corrine is similarly drawn to Ground Zero where she encounters an exhausted Luke and offers him water. She learns that Russell's friend, the film producer Jim Crespi, is also among the missing. It seems that everyone in

New York, a city teeming with strangers, knows someone who has disappeared in the ashes of the World Trade Center. Luke and Corrine volunteer at an ad hoc relief station on Bowling Green, supplied with donations scavenged by a burly carpenter named Jerry. There they befriend Captain Davies, a policeman from Brooklyn, other first responders, and families displaced by the disaster. Corrine's story, however, is not "part of the narrative of heroic acts, random acts of kindness, last words to loved ones on cell phones, bizarre coincidences, missed planes" (p. 95) and late arrivals that have become the stock devices of 9/11 narrative. In the soup kitchen, the frameworks that define social groups are dissolved and aid to those most in need is rendered by those willing to suspend personal drives. The affair between Luke and Corrine is born of mutual solace and generosity, rather than the aspirations and acquisitions of the self-absorbed class that populates McInerney's New York. Would they "ever feel guilty" (p. 220) that their meeting resulted from such terrible tragedy? Yet nothing can be as it was on September 10th, and their bonding is a counternarrative to a traumatized society in which "everything's falling apart" (p. 83).

Claire Messud's *The Emperor's Children* shares a cast of editors, pundits, producers, and poseurs – the "glitterati" of New York's culture class – with McInerney's *The Good Life*. The plot is triskelion in design, turning on three college friends, Danielle Minkoff, Marina Thwaite, and Julius Clarke who, possessed of a fine Ivy-league education, have come to New York in the 1990s in order "to do something important" (2006, p. 73) with their lives. But at thirty, Danielle is the only gainfully employed musketeer, as a producer of documentary segments for public television (one imagines the investigative journalism of *Frontline*), although her piece on reparations for African Americans through the lens of the Australian government's formal apologies to the Aborigines is killed. Marina, who had been "a young intern at *Vogue*" and "celebrated native beauty" (p. 26), has gotten and spent an advance for a book on the social significance of children's clothing, on which she is now stalled. Julius, gay, Eurasian, libertine, and writing pithy but unremunerative columns for *The Village Voice*, is kept in style by an aspiring young businessman, David Cohen. These three adult children turn in thrall around the famous liberal columnist, Murray Thwaite, who is retreading his best work on Vietnam, civil rights, Iran Contras, Kosovo, and Operation Desert Storm as a distinguished speaker. More disturbingly, he is a sexual predator, made even more monstrous in the era of the #MeToo movement. From March to September 2001, these New Yorkers embody a weak cosmopolitanism – sophisticates, attuned to world culture – yet narcissistic (as satirized by Saul Steinberg's cover for *The New Yorker*, View of the World from 9th Avenue) in their unfulfilled, or in the case of Murray, insatiable desire for personal gratification. Into this eddy drops Ludovic Seeley, an Australian editor who plans to launch a "revolutionary" magazine of literary and cultural commentary, *The Monitor*, "an instrument to trumpet that the emperor has no clothes" (p. 123). Murray's nephew, Frederick "Bootie" Tubb, from Watertown, NY, abjures the fakery of higher education, and though he extols Emerson's "Self-Reliance," insinuates himself into Murray's Central Park West household as amanuensis, only to grievously betray his confidences. Marina finally publishes her book, *The Emperor's Children Have No Clothes*, the title suggested by Ludovic, but it is they and their friends, the children of "entitlement" (p. 401), whose fatuousness is made glaringly plain in the catastrophe that ends the novel. When September 11th comes, it catches them unawares, as was the case for us all. Danielle and Murray are caught in flagrante delicto after spending Monday night together, and Murray abandons her to return to his wife. The launch date for *The Monitor* is to be that very day, but "nobody wanted such a thing in this new world, a frivolous, satirical thing.... So much for revolution. The revolution belonged to other people now, far away from them, and it was real" (p. 449). Apropos, Jonathan Franzen's novel, *The Corrections* (seen on the nightstand in Luke McGavock's Village apartment where he trysts with Corinne in *The Good Life*) was published on September 15th. That "big social novel" is immediately declared "laughably archival," surpassed by a cultural and political cataclysm that it could not have anticipated, by Messud's husband, the literary critic James Wood (2001). Bootie disappears among the missing on 9/11 only to reemerge in Miami, Florida, to live as Emerson advised: "Great geniuses have the shortest biographies. Their cousins can tell you nothing about them. They live in their writings, and so their house and street life was trivial and commonplace" (2006, p. 105). Perhaps Messud's New Yorkers would dare to become stronger cosmopolitans after 9/11, both attentive to revolutionary change in the world and changed in turn by the world beyond themselves.

SEE ALSO: After Postmodernism; Auster, Paul; DeLillo, Don; Fiction and Terrorism; Foer, Jonathan Safran; Franzen, Jonathan; Gibson, William; Globalization; Periodization; Trauma and Fiction

REFERENCES

Auster, Paul. (2008). *Man in the Dark*. New York: Henry Holt.
Binelli, Mark. (2007). Intensity of a plot: an interview with Don DeLillo. *Guernica* (July 17, 2007). https://www.guernicamag.com/intensity_of_a_plot/ (accessed August 2, 2021).
DeLillo, Don. (2007). *Falling Man*. New York: Scribner.
Flood, Alison. (2008). Paul Auster talks: the novelist explains his rage at what the Bush presidency has done to the world. *The Guardian* (October 29, 2008). https://guardian.co.uk/books/2008/oct/29/paul-auster-interview?INTCMP=ILCNETTXT3487 (accessed August 2, 2021).
Foer, Jonathan Safran. (2005). *Extremely Loud & Incredibly Close*. Boston: Houghton Mifflin.
Goffman, Erving. (1974). *Frame Analysis: An Essay on the Organization of Experience*. Cambridge, MA: Harvard University Press.
Halaby, Laila. (2007). *Once in a Promised Land*. Boston: Beacon Press.
Halaby, Laila. (2008). Dare I ask. Beacon Broadside (January 17, 2008). https://www.beaconbroadside.com/broadside/2008/01/dare-i-ask.html (accessed August 2, 2021).
Kalfus, Ken. (2006). *A Disorder Peculiar to the Country*. New York: Harper Perennial.
Kalfus, Ken. (2013). Author interview: Ken Kalfus on *A Disorder Peculiar to the Country*. https://b0f646cfbd7462424f7a-f9758a43fb7c33cc8adda0fd36101899.ssl.cf2.rackcdn.com/book-interviews/BI-9780060501419.pdf (accessed August 2, 2021).
Klein, J. (2006). Interview with Ken Kalfus. *Salon* (December 13, 2006). https://salon.com/2006/12/13/kalfus_int_excerpt/ (accessed August 2, 2021).
McInerney, Jay. (2005). The uses of invention. *The Guardian* (September 17, 2005). https://books.guardian.co.uk/review/story/0,,1570906,00.html (accessed August 2, 2021).
McInerney, Jay. (2006). *The Good Life*. New York: Random House.
Messud, Claire. (2006). *The Emperor's Children*. New York: Knopf.
Ulin, David L. (2003). Finding reason in an age of terror. *Los Angeles Times* (April 15, 2003): E1. https://www.latimes.com/archives/la-xpm-2003-apr-15-et-ulin15-story.html (accessed August 2, 2021).
Waldman, Amy. (2011). *The Submission*. New York: Picador.
Walter, Jess. (2006). *The Zero*. New York: Harper Collins.
Wood, James. (2001). Tell me how does it feel? *The Guardian* (October 6, 2001). https://theguardian.com/books/2001/oct/06/fiction (accessed August 2, 2021).

Woolf, Virginia. (1924). Mr. Bennett and Mrs. Brown. In: *The Captain's Death Bed and Other Essays* (ed. Leonard Woolf) (1950), 90–111. London: Hogarth Press.

FURTHER READING

Conte, Joseph M. (2020). *Transnational Politics in the Post-9/11 Novel*. New York and London: Routledge.

Däwes, Birgit. (2011). *Ground Zero Fiction: History, Memory, and Representation in the American 9/11 Novel*. Heidelberg: Universitätsverlag.

Gray, Richard. (2011). *After the Fall: American Literature Since 9/11*. Malden, MA, and Oxford: Wiley-Blackwell.

Versluys, Kristiaan. (2009). *Out of the Blue: September 11 and the Novel*. New York: Columbia University Press.

Posthumanism

ANDY J. HICKS
Independent scholar, Exeter, UK

The eponymous question of Cary Wolfe's extensive monograph *What is Posthumanism?* (2010) remains, eleven years later, as open as ever. As the old joke goes, if one were to ask three different posthumanist scholars for a definition of "posthumanism," one would receive five different answers in turn. Such are the growing pangs of any bourgeoning critical movement, however, and just as with the poststructuralist/-modernist movement that posthumanism both incorporates and succeeds, heterogeneity and multivocality are integral and inevitable elements of the broad movement. With that said, posthumanist theorists and philosophers of all stripes would nevertheless agree that it is an urgent critical intervention. In a time in which the liberal West has been brought to its knees by a species-hopping virus and humanity faces the distinct (and increasingly proximate) possibility of engendering its own extinction, as algorithms and artificial intelligence come to dominate the dynamics of human social and cultural interaction, and technological prostheses and advances in genetic engineering render the traditional category of "human" itself malleable or even untenable, the methodologies generated, and concerns raised by, posthumanist theorists will only become more relevant. As the prevalence of such themes in works by American writers as diverse as Toni Morrison, Richard Powers, Marilynne Robinson, Neal Stephenson, and Karen Tei Yamashita suggests, it has never been more important to challenge the supposed exceptionality and autonomy of the figure of the "human" that has been handed down to us via the explicitly anthropocentric discourse of Enlightenment humanism. In this entry I will trace the development of, and current state of, the posthumanist theoretical movement, first by defining the humanist (and specifically *liberal* humanist) tradition that provoked its post- variant in the first place, which still remains the ideology *de jour* in Western society; second, by providing an overview of modern posthumanism and its close relatives, anti- and transhumanism; and finally, by considering the ways in which posthumanism may be adapted to serve as literary theory.

As Serenella Iovino notes, the "blueprints" of the modern "posthumanist house . . . were sketched in the last two decades of the 20th century" (2016, pp. 12–13), with arguably the most recognizable early intervention being Donna Haraway's "A Cyborg Manifesto," published in 1985. Haraway's influential essay seeks to "signal three crucial boundary breakdowns" in the late twentieth century regarding the traditional demarcation between the figure of "the human" and other entities. First, she states that science has "thoroughly breached" the boundary between human and animal; since the traditionally exclusively human arenas of "language, tool use, social behavior, [and] mental events" are readily demonstrated in animals, "nothing really convincingly settles the separation." The second "leaky boundary" is between "animal-human (organism) and machine," since "late twentieth-century machines have made thoroughly ambiguous the difference between natural and artificial, mind and body, self-developing and externally designed ... our machines are disturbingly lively, and we ourselves frighteningly inert" (2000, p. 293). As she notes, in "our time, a mythic time, we are all chimeras, theorized and fabricated hybrids of machine and organism" (p. 292). Finally, Haraway takes an even more explicitly ontological tack, arguing that "the boundary between physical and non-physical is very imprecise to us ['cyborgs']" (p. 293); thought, information, culture, consciousness itself – everything traditionally considered transcendental and reified, in some sense separate from brute matter or wild nature – are instead figured as part of the same ontological spectrum. The elision of these boundaries is also explored in another fundamental text of the current posthumanist movement, N. Katherine Hayles's *How We Became Posthuman* (1999). Hayles opts for a substrate-agnostic conception of information ("the posthuman view privileges informational pattern over material instantiation, so that embodiment in a biological substrate is seen as an accident of history rather than an inevitability of life"), and argues that in "the posthuman, there are no essential differences or absolute demarcations between bodily existence and computer simulation, cybernetic mechanism and biological organism, robot teleology and human goals" (1999, pp. 2–3). Once again (and this time explicitly under the rubric of "posthumanism") the figure of the "human" is recontextualized as but one immanent element of the world among many.

With that said, and as we shall see, these are not wholly new insights, though they have rarely been so explicitly formulated; the posthumanist movement works to simultaneously succeed and encompass both its critical antecedents (such as poststructuralism, systems theory, and ecocriticism, to name but a few) and its interlocuter, humanism itself. As Cary Wolfe notes:

> My sense of posthumanism is thus analogous to Jean-François Lyotard's paradoxical rendering of the postmodern: it comes both before and after humanism: before in the sense that it names the embodiment and embeddedness of the human being in not just its biological but also its technological world, the prosthetic coevolution of the human animal the technicity of tools and external archival mechanisms (such as language and culture)... but it comes after in the sense that posthumanism names a historical moment in which the decentring of the human by its imbrication in technical, medical, informatic, and economic networks is impossible to ignore ... a new mode of thought that comes after the cultural repressions and fantasies, the philosophical protocols and evasions, of humanism as a historically specific phenomenon.
>
> (2010, pp. xv–xvi)

It is to those humanistic philosophical protocols (and, indeed, "evasions") that we will now turn.

HUMANISM

If one were to ask even a single humanist scholar for a definition of the term "humanism," one would receive a vertiginous number of answers in turn. Tony Davies alone lists fourteen different varieties, temporally ranging from "the civic humanism of Confucian sages" of ancient China all the way to the bourgeois liberal humanism that characterizes Western modernity (2008, pp. 140–141). The word "humanism" itself is ultimately derived from the Latin *humanitas*, a word that incorporates both proper human *being* and proper human *practice*. From its inception the term has carried both pedagogical and ethical connotations, as several derived English words attest; we still refer to disciplines such as literature, philosophy, rhetoric, linguistics and law as "the humanities," and the word "humanitarianism" denotes an active regard for, and valuing of, human life and wellbeing. For the Romans and their medieval, Renaissance and Enlightenment successors, the word has also stood for the particularity and superiority of the human over other animals. It is remarkable that an idea could be so singularly consistent as to link figures as temporally distant as Cicero (106–43 BCE) and Giovanni Pico della Mirandola (1463–1494), but for all humanism's heterogeneity, anthropocentrism and human exceptionalism have always remained core tenets. As Oscar E. Nybakken notes, according to Cicero, man, although an animal, "is distinguished by being clear-sighted, keen, complex and many-sided, and... possesses the faculties of reason, memory, and prudence." On the other hand, of course, man's animal nature, if indulged, may also lead to his "fall into depths of sorrow and disaster; he may be to himself and to mankind either a god or a wolf" (1939, p. 397). Fifteen hundred years later, Pico would write "On the Dignity of Man" (1496), a dramatization of the encounter between God and Adam in which God tells his new creation that, unlike all other "limited and constrained" beings, man is set "at the world's centre... [and] mayest fashion thyself in whatever shape thou shalt prefer" (1948, pp. 224–225). Pico's oratory, which W.G. Craven has called "the manifesto of Renaissance humanism" (quoted in Davies 2008, p. 95), casts man in the promethean position of complete self-ownership and self-authorship – unlike any other creature, man has *free will*, the ability to choose to be, or to become, anything he so pleases. In this dualistic account, with its poles of divinity or bestiality, virtue or sin, ethereal freedom or slavery to base biological drives (1948, p. 226), man stands alone. There is nothing more important in creation, and existence itself has been built for his benefit. As the centuries wore on and the Enlightenment succeeded the Renaissance, the term "humanism" began to shed its religious cloaking, becoming synonymous with a more rationalistic and scientific perspective; by the twentieth century, "humanist" became almost synonymous with "atheist." So, for instance, the American Humanist Association (AHA) declares that "we strive to bring about a progressive society where being good without a god is an accepted and respected way to live life... humanism is a nontheistic worldview with ethical values informed by scientific knowledge... at the foundation of those values is an affirmation of the dignity of every human being" (AHA, 2021). This aspect of modern humanism has become so dominant that the other assumptions and prejudices embedded within the philosophy – the "repressions," "fantasies," and "evasions" that Wolfe identifies – are often able to largely pass without comment. Indeed, even its express disavowal of supernaturalism can often end up reinscribing that which it seeks to oppose, often by reifying or even deifying humanity itself.

ANTIHUMANISM, TRANSHUMANISM, POSTHUMANISM

Although humanism remains – at least in its bourgeois "liberal" incarnation – the dominant philosophical position in the West, by the start of the twentieth century several of its most central tenets had begun to be critiqued by thinkers skeptical of its claims. Friedrich Nietzsche had already passionately criticized the optimism, universality, and emphasis on rationality that characterized Enlightenment thought. His emphasis on the overriding role of dark, pre-conscious forces in driving human behavior, and on the essentially hostile and ahuman realm of the universe, would prefigure the work of Freud, who, in "A Difficulty in the Path of Psycho-Analysis" (1917), would claim that modern man's narcissistic self-love had been struck "three severe blows from the researches of science." The first, "cosmological" blow had already been struck, in the Renaissance, by Copernicus and his heliocentric model; no longer was mankind the literal center of a universe created for its benefit. The second was the "biological" blow of Darwin, who had proven that the human was but one animal among many, created by the same grinding, mechanistic evolutionary processes as all other life on Earth, no better or worse than any other species. The third, "psychological" blow was Freud's own psychoanalysis, which emphasized the essential limitedness of the conscious, rational ego in perceiving, controlling, or constraining the unconscious impulses that drive all human behavior (2001, pp. 139–141). It would, however, take the dual horrors of World Wars I and II (and the Nazi death camps in particular) to provoke a more sustained and analytic critical attack on the tenets of humanism; an optimistic belief in the power of human rationality and the inevitability of universal human progress appeared grossly untenable to many critics of the mid- to late-periods of the twentieth century. It was the Marxist philosopher Louis Althusser who coined the term "antihumanism" in his 1964 essay "Marxism and Humanism." For Althusser, Marxist humanism – a then popular position – was a gross contradiction in terms, and humanism an expression of bourgeois individualism. Indeed, Althusser was concerned not only with interrogating humanist ideals of rationality, universality, or human exceptionalism, but *of the very idea of human nature itself*. For Althusser, any conception of human "essence" is inherently ideological, and under his schema, ideology is a "system, known not in relation to a reality external to it but in relation to the logic that governs it, the rules according to which its elements are combined . . . [ideology] operates behind the backs of human individuals [who] are not conscious of its existence, let alone of the rules that govern it (and them)" (Montag 2013, p. 107). In Althusser's structuralist perspective, ideology is "transparent" to its participants in the same way as language or culture, ready-to-hand and "given" although it is in fact constructed and historically determined; subjects are always already caught within ideology (including the ideology of universal human essence), and consciousness – one of the jewels in the crown of humanity as figured by humanism – "is no longer at the center, no longer constitutive; instead it is an agent and an element of a system external to it, to which it submits unawares" (p. 115). Suddenly, the figure of the autonomous, rational, and universalized human no longer appears quite so independent, free-thinking, or inevitable. Roughly contemporaneously, Michel Foucault would proclaim, at the conclusion of *The Order of Things* (1966), the "end of Man" (note the capitalization). For Foucault, as for Althusser, the *concept* of "Man" – an assemblage of assumptions about the nature of human consciousness, capacities, and behaviors – is a product of the modern "episteme" (Foucault's term, *very* roughly, for "way of thinking," which includes not only the things thought, but also the historical, cultural, linguistic, psychological, etc. conditions by which things *can* be thought of in the first place). The book ends on a passage now famous for its eerily apocalyptic tone, as Foucault predicts a day when the supposedly essential, universal category of "Man" disappears for the figment of modernity it really is:

> [the] appearance [of Man] was not the liberation of an old anxiety, the transition into luminous consciousness of an age-old concern,

the entry into objectivity of something that had long remained trapped within beliefs and philosophies: it was the effect of a change in the fundamental arrangements of knowledge...If those arrangements were to disappear as they appeared, if some event of which we can at the moment do no more than sense the possibility... were to cause them to crumble, as the ground of Classical thought did ... then one can certainly wager that man would be erased, like a face drawn in sand at the edge of the sea.

(2005, pp. 421–422)

It is very difficult, embedded as we remain in our still mostly modern episteme, to grasp the fact that "man" was not always and not everywhere "the proper study of mankind," as Alexander Pope once said; that (at least according to Foucault) man was once merely one category among many, a polysemous, lived reality rather than a singular, reified ideal. Just as post-Enlightenment modernity displaced God and replaced him with Man, Foucault predicts a day when Man will be displaced by something else again. Perhaps this displacement may be literal, as in the extinction narratives of Cormac McCarthy's *The Road* (2006) or Kurt Vonnegut's *Galapagos* (1986), in which humanity either ceases to exist as a category at all, or is changed beyond all recognition. Perhaps it will be more figurative. Nevertheless, this – whatever it is – is what many of us call the *posthuman*.

Antihumanism and posthumanism are often used interchangeably and both terms remain in use, although there are differences between the two, not least of which is their differing tenors. As Francesca Ferrando notes, while the "deconstruction of the human" is central to both terms, "Antihumanism fully acknowledges the consequences of the 'death of Man' ... In contrast, posthumanism does not rely on any symbolic death: such an assumption would be based on the dualism dead/alive, while any strict form of dualism has been already challenged by posthumanism, in its post-dualistic process-ontological perspective" (2013, pp. 31–32). Antihumanism remains caught within its oppositional dialectic – it is explicitly opposed to humanism, and envisions a time when the Man of humanism is left in the dustbin of history. Posthumanism, by contrast, is rather more haunted; the specter of humanism cannot be so easily exorcised. Just as postmodernism represents a reflexive commentary upon, and extension of, modernism, rather than its simplistically temporal "replacement," so posthumanism recognizes that humanism has always already left its trace and must be continually negotiated and renegotiated. As Rosi Braidotti astutely notes, posthumanism "is the historical moment that marks the end of the opposition between Humanism and anti-humanism and traces a different discursive framework, looking more affirmatively towards new alternatives ... The posthumanist perspective rests on the assumption of the historical decline of Humanism but goes further in exploring alternatives, without sinking into the rhetoric of the crisis of Man" (2003, p. 37). Further, she is perfectly willing to accept that posthumanism and humanism can exhibit significant crossover when it comes to emancipatory principles or ethical judgments, including "the basic principles of social justice, the respect for human decency and diversity, the rejection of false universalisms; the affirmation of the positivity of difference [and] the principles of academic freedom, anti-racism, openness to others and conviviality" (p. 11). The "baby" of humanitarian humanism needn't be thrown out with the admittedly more dubious "bath water" of liberal humanism. Nevertheless, the figure of the human must be recontextualized.

As noted in the introduction, with Donna Haraway's three breached boundaries, modern posthumanism – which has incorporated such diverse fields of study as animal studies, ecocriticism, poststructuralism, feminist criticism, cybernetics, philosophy of science, systems theory, and the New Materialist movement, to name but a few – lays special emphasis on the elision of traditional binaries, in an attempt to gain a more accurate and nuanced understanding of the human as embedded within its environmental, social, and biological contexts. Common binaries that have been interrogated, with various degrees of emphasis, include nature/culture (from whence does "culture" arise if not "nature"?), human/animal (a binary that, as we now know, can only be maintained through religious or otherwise purely chauvinistic means), animate/inanimate (what is so special about living organisms that their functions may not be replicated or shared by other, supposedly "dead" matter?), male/female (it cannot be stressed enough that the "Man" of humanism is almost invariably male, white, and heteronormative) or even, to be bluntly synoptic, human/everything else.

The closely related field of *trans*humanism (which is very often used interchangeably with "posthumanism," at least in specifically transhumanist contexts) similarly relies on the elision of these dichotomies. However, whereas posthumanism tends to follow a more critical, philosophical, and sociological approach to the question of the human and its relation to the nonhuman, transhumanism is more concerned with concrete technological processes, and specifically with the modification of the human itself. Transhumanism tends to be concerned with the potential benefits, dangers, and ethical questions regarding current or near-future "sci-fi" technologies such as cyborgization, genetic engineering, artificial intelligence, or even the uploading of human minds to computers. The "posthuman" of transhumanism is quite literal; what kind of hybridized or modified creatures might succeed humanity as we know it? If strong artificial intelligence is possible, then what relationship will it have with us, and might it replace us? These speculative questions may be answered in the optative mode, as in the case of the famous futurist Ray Kurzweil, who predicts that the exponential development of computing will lead to the "Singularity," a wholly new stage in human evolution in which virtual immortality and superintelligence will be achieved, and humanity will reach new and previously unthinkable ways of thought and being. Alternatively, Francis Fukuyama more pessimistically predicts that the rise and widespread adoption of genetic engineering will lead to new and potentially insurmountable obstacles to happiness and equality, as the rich perfect themselves and their progeny, creating a genetic underclass and undermining the idea of what it is to be "human" in the first place (2002). The exploitative potential of genetic hybridization is a related concern, as dramatized in Karen Russell's short story "Reeling for the Empire" (2013), in which a group of women are spliced with moth DNA in order to produce cheap and plentiful silk. Transhumanists subscribe to the basic interchangeability of information (so as, for instance, to consider a precisely modeled human mind on a non-organic substrate as being equal or even preferable to being contained within an organic body), while many critical posthumanists are more skeptical of the field's more wild-eyed or utopian claims. As the prominent posthumanist Cary Wolfe argues, transhumanism is particularly susceptible to falling into the same traps of humanism, since it can so easily fall into the fantasy of "a triumphant transcendence of embodiment" into pure information, as envisioned by Kurzweil or even N. Katherine Hayles – the twenty-first-century equivalent of the soul's ascension into heaven, or the pure and independent *cogito* of Cartesian philosophy. Instead, Wolfe calls for a posthumanism that instead "requires us to attend to that thing called "the human" with *greater* specificity, *greater* attention to its embodiment, embeddedness, and materiality, and how these in turn shape and are shaped by consciousness, mind, and so on" (2010, p. 120). In many ways, the "post" of "posthuman" has never really been "post" after all; we have always been posthuman, even if we haven't always recognized it.

Materiality is particularly fertile ground in posthumanist circles. Though posthumanists broadly accept, and often utilize, poststructuralist and postmodernist theory, there has nevertheless been a broad consensus that the so-called "linguistic turn" of the twentieth century – in which human psychology, culture, and society are thought to be fundamentally linguistic in nature, and which has often been caricatured as declaring that language literally constitutes reality itself – inadequately accounts for the incredible potency of nonhuman, nonliving forces and objects. For New Materialists, such as Jane Bennett and Karen Barad, or Speculative Realists such as Graham Harman or Levi Bryant, the line between "animate" and "inanimate" is no more stable or sustainable than any other binary. While it may seem odd or even bizarre in traditionally humanistic perspectives, these critics wish to erode the subject/object distinction in order to problematize concepts such as intentionality, agency, or even consciousness, and extend these qualities not only to other, nonhuman living things, but also to *matter itself*. This is not, however, as strange as it may seem; we have not, after all, ever found a "living" molecule that was not "dead" before and afterwards. Levi Bryant argues that subjects (that is, beings with unique consciousnesses and experiences) "are objects among objects, rather than constant points of reference related to all other objects" (2011, p. 22), rather than free-floating, transcendental observers, ontologically separate from base, "dead" material. As Jane Bennett notes in her influential monograph *Vibrant Matter* (2010),

> The quarantines of matter and life encourage us to ignore the vitality *of* matter and the lively powers *of* material formations ... I will turn the figures of "life" and "matter" around and around, worrying them until they start to seem strange, in something like the way a common word when repeated can become a foreign, nonsense sound. In the space created by this estrangement, a *vital materiality* can start to take shape ... By "vitality" I mean the capacity of things – edibles, commodities, storms, metals – not only to impede or block the will and designs of humans but also to act as quasi agents or forces with trajectories, propensities, or tendencies of their own.
>
> (2010, pp. vii–viii)

Living things are objects amongst many, and agency, when figured as the capacity to demonstrate predispositions and to produce effects, is no longer tied tightly to the solely living/organic domain. This is not to say that objects think or feel as we do, or even as animals do; nor does it mean that calls for the recognition of the ontological equality between objects is directly analogous to a call for direct political or ethical equality. As Levi Bryant notes in *The Democracy of Objects* (2011), the democracy which he imagines

> is not a political thesis to the effect that all objects ought to be treated equally or that all objects ought to participate in human affairs. The democracy of objects is the ontological thesis that all objects, as Ian Bogost has so nicely put it, equally exist while they do not exist equally. The claim that all objects equally exist is the claim that no object can be treated as constructed by another object. The claim that objects do not exist equally is the claim that objects contribute to collectives or assemblages to a greater and lesser degree.
>
> (2011, p. 19)

Theorists such as Karen Barad, meanwhile, question the very possibility of inseparable "objects" at all. In *Meeting the Universe Halfway* (2007), Barad utilizes her previous experience as a quantum physicist to develop her theory of agential realism, and makes the startling claim that relations actually *precede* and *create* matter; objects are created by situations ("apparatuses") rather than vice versa, and these apparatuses are "material-discursive" in the sense that they produce the determinate meanings and material beings that we are all familiar with. Barad's work problematizes the very possibility of individual objects (what, after all, counts as an "object" anyway?) or independent observers, and casts meaning and agency as spread across the entire ontological spectrum, rather than confined to the minds of human beings alone. Indeed, as Barad is keen to point out, in the words of Niels Bohr, "we are part of that nature that we seek to understand" (2007, p. 26), and *thinking itself* is a material enactment, entangled in the phenomena it is a part of. The universe that Barad presents is strange indeed – it is a place that does not and never has contained discrete subjects, objects, thoughts, words, minds, agencies, humans, animals, shoes, ships, sealing wax, cabbages, or kings. Barad – and posthumanists in general – are keen to point the way to a more integrated, embedded, immanent understanding of the universe that human beings are in and, most importantly, *of*. How, though, might these insights be adapted in such a way as to produce a textual analysis?

POSTHUMANISM AS LITERARY THEORY

Posthumanist theory has not yet become a codified literary approach. When a writer declares that they are going to perform a feminist, ecocritical, postcolonial, or deconstructive reading of a text, that declaration carries with it the expectation of certain strategies, tropes, and source materials that posthumanism – in its heterogeneity and youth – does not (yet). I believe, however, that it is helpful to remember that there are two ways that posthumanist theory is relevant to the study of literature. Broadly speaking, one might say that there is "posthuman literature," and there is "reading through posthumanism"; that is to say, there is literature that has posthumanist themes or elements in form or content, and there is posthumanist theory as applied methodology. Examples of the former are easy to find in post-1980 American fiction, especially in the genres of science fiction and speculative fiction. Artificial Intelligence, cyborgization, and genetic engineering are transhumanist tropes so common – and science fiction has become, in our hyper-technologized age, the mode de jour for the majority of mass media – that examples scarcely need to be enumerated. As Stefan Herbrechter notes, "What makes science fiction such a powerful genre and, ironically and unintentionally, such a strong ally for critical posthumanism, is the fictional indulgence in the desires and anxieties of "becoming posthuman" while remaining in the ultimate safety of a fictional framework" (2013, p. 130). Even when the treatment of these themes is relatively surface level, their sheer prevalence speaks to the extent to which technologically mediated change has come to dominate contemporary concerns. Examples of posthumanist themes in literary science fiction include Jeff VanderMeer's *Annihilation* (2014), which depicts a strange, posthumanist zone in which the barriers between human, animal, and plant matter breaks down, creating bizarre hybrids according to the designs of an unknown (and possibly unknowable) alien presence. In Peter Watts's *Blindsight* (2006), humanity experiences first contact with an alien species that is hyper-intelligent but completely non-conscious;

the novel's thesis is that consciousness itself is a parasitic accident of natural selection and an evolutionary dead end. The short stories of George Saunders, such as "Escape from Spiderhead" or "The Semplica Girl Diaries" in *Tenth of December* (2013), emphasize the posthuman elements of consumer capitalism, meanwhile, as powerful drugs are used to instantly induce emotions and beliefs in the former and trafficked women are used as living lawn ornaments in the latter. Even the most "conventional" or "realistic" works are amenable to posthumanist criticism; just as Edward Said famously produced a postcolonial reading of *Mansfield Park* (1814), a novel that is not *ostensibly* about slavery, so can the posthumanist critic pay attention to the things that might otherwise be eclipsed by the figure of the traditionally humanist human. The objects, forces, and animals that might otherwise be considered mere "background" for the great human drama can instead be foregrounded, and attention drawn to the Things, with all their power and potency, that all human interactions are inevitably wholly reliant upon. This emphasis is not mere pathetic fallacy (a quintessentially anthropomorphic and humanistic trope) but instead should draw attention to objects in their own right, as mysterious, unique, and ontologically significant as any character. And of course, as critics as varied as Mikhail Bakhtin, Jacques Derrida, and Niklas Luhmann have all pointed out, in their own times and ways, language itself – in its multivocality, its relationality and its stubborn resistance to control – has always challenged the conceit of human independence and autonomy. Overall, the posthumanist project promises to provide a synoptic approach that will merge the insights of its critical predecessors, promote more effective interdisciplinarity, and more acutely, sensitively, and inclusively respond to the questions of our time. It emphasizes the increasingly necessary understanding that human beings are not ontologically separate from the rest of the universe, and that such oppositional binaries were always already false, even if we have for quite some time thought otherwise. Indeed, a posthumanist rubric that erodes the binaries of the discursive and materialistic, the particulate and the systemic, the artificial and natural – *the human and the nonhuman* – is almost limitless in scope.

SEE ALSO: Big Data; Biological Fictions; Cyberpunk; Ecocriticism and Environmental Fiction; McCarthy, Cormac; Morrison, Toni; Russell, Karen; Saunders, George; Stephenson, Neal; Vonnegut, Kurt

REFERENCES

American Humanist Association. (2021). About the American Humanist Association. https://americanhumanist.org/about/ (accessed August 6, 2021).

Barad, Karen M. (2007). *Meeting the Universe Halfway: Quantum Physics and the Entanglement of Matter and Meaning*. Durham, NC: Duke University Press.

Bennett, Jane. (2010). *Vibrant Matter*. Durham, NC: Duke University Press.

Braidotti, Rosi. (2003). *The Posthuman*. Cambridge: Polity Press.

Bryant, Levi. (2011). *The Democracy of Objects*. Ann Arbor: Michigan Publishing.

Davies, Tony. (2008). *Humanism*. Abingdon: Routledge.

Ferrando, Francesca. (2013). Posthumanism, transhumanism, antihumanism, metahumanism and new materialism: differences and relations. *Existenz: An International Journal in Philosophy, Religion, Politics and the Arts* 8 (2): 26–32.

Foucault, Michel. (2005). *The Order of Things: An Archaeology of the Human Sciences*. London: Routledge; 1st ed. 1966.

Freud, Sigmund. (2001). A difficulty in the path of psycho-analysis. In: *The Standard Edition of the Complete Psychological Works of Sigmund Freud*,

Volume 17 (1917–1919): An Infantile Neurosis and Other Works (ed. James Strachey, Anna Freud, Alix Strachey, and Alan Tyson), 135–144. London: Vintage; 1st ed. 1917.

Fukuyama, Francis. (2002). *Our Posthuman Future*. New York: Farrar, Straus and Giroux.

Haraway, Donna. (2000). A cyborg manifesto: science, technology and socialist-feminism in the late twentieth century. In: *The Cybercultures Reader* (ed. David Bell and Barbara M. Kennedy), 291–324. New York: Routledge; 1st ed. 1985.

Hayles, N. Katherine. (1999). *How We Became Posthuman: Virtual Bodies in Cybernetics, Literature, and Informatics*. Chicago: Chicago University Press.

Herbrechter, Stefan. (2013). *Posthumanism: A Critical Analysis*. London: Bloomsbury Academic.

Iovino, Serenella. (2016). Posthumanism in literature and ecocriticism. *Relations: Beyond Anthropocentrism* 4 (1): 11–22.

Montag, Warren. (2013). *Althusser and His Contemporaries: Philosophy's Perpetual War*. Durham, NC: Duke University Press.

Nybakken, Oscar E. (1939). Humanitas romana. *Transactions and Proceedings of the American Philological Association* 70: 396–413.

Pico della Mirandola, Giovanni. (1948). Oration on the dignity of man (trans. Elizabeth L. Forbes). In: *The Renaissance Philosophy of Man: Selections in Translation* (ed. Ernst Cassirer, Paul Oskar Kristeller, and John Herman Randall, Jr.), 223–256. Chicago: University of Chicago Press; 1st ed. 1496.

Wolfe, Cary. (2010). *What is Posthumanism?* London: University of Minnesota Press.

FURTHER READING

Badmington, Neil. (2000). *Posthumanism*. New York: Palgrave.

Coole, Diana H. and Frost, Samantha. (2010). *New Materialisms: Ontology, Agency and Politics*. London: Duke University Press.

Hicks, Andrew. (2020). *Posthumanism in the Novels of Kurt Vonnegut: Matter That Complains So*. London: Routledge.

Strehle, Susan. (1992). *Fiction in the Quantum Universe*. Chapel Hill: University of North Carolina Press.

Varela, Francisco J., Thompson, Evan, Rosch, Eleanor, and Kabat-Zinn, Jon. (2017). *The Embodied Mind: Cognitive Science and Human Experience*. Boston: MIT Press.

Post-Soul and/or Post-Black Fiction

DEREK C. MAUS
State University of New York at Potsdam, USA

In his 2011 book, *What Was African American Literature?*, Kenneth W. Warren declared African American literature to be a thing of the past. He argued that "African American literature was a postemancipation phenomenon that gained its coherence as an undertaking in the social world defined by the system of Jim Crow segregation." In light of the "legal demise of Jim Crow, the coherence of African American literature has been correspondingly, if sometimes imperceptibly, eroded as well" (Warren 2011, pp. 1–2). Warren readily acknowledged that his argument is provocative, but it is also situated firmly within an ongoing critical debate over generational differences in attitude toward the artistic representation of Black identity. Warren (2011, p. 9) wrote that "Whether African American writers of the segregation era acquiesced in or kicked against the label, they knew what was at stake in accepting or contesting their identification as Negro writers. By contrast, the entailments of being regarded or not being regarded as an African American writer at the present moment are comparatively less clear." The idea that contemporary Black artists feel far less obligation to uphold societal expectations about racial representation pervades the scholarly and cultural discourse that has variously been named the post-soul aesthetic, the New Black Aesthetic, and post-Blackness. Neither synonymous nor universally accepted in their denotations, these terms nevertheless all shed light on Warren's (p. 5) contention "that to a great extent something significant has changed" in contemporary literature by Black American authors.

THREE EARLY EFFORTS AT DEFINING THE NEW AESTHETICS

Greg Tate's 1986 essay "Cult-Nats Meet Freaky-Deke: The Return of the Black Aesthetic" was perhaps the earliest effort to define what that "something significant" might be. Tate (1986, pp. 5, 7) noted that although the Black Arts Movement of the late 1960s and early 1970s "produce[d] a post-liberated black aesthetic . . . [that] freed up more black artists to do work as wonderfully absurdist as black life itself," that same aesthetic was being superseded in the mid-1980s by "a generation of bohemian cult-nats [i.e. cultural nationalists] who are mutating black culture into something the old interlocutors aren't ready for yet." Both echoing and updating Langston Hughes's 1926 manifesto, "The Negro Artist and the Racial Mountain," Tate asserted that this new generation consists of:

> artists for whom black consciousness and artistic freedom are not mutually exclusive but complementary, for whom "black culture" signifies a multicultural tradition of expressive practices; they feel secure enough about black culture to claim art produced by nonblacks as part of their inheritance . . . Yet though their work challenges both cult-nats and snotty whites, don't expect to find them in *Ebony* or *Artforum* any time soon. Things ain't hardly got that loose yet.
>
> (1986, p. 7)

Much as Hughes (1926, p. 693) noted that the "Negro artist [of the mid-1920s] works against an undertow of sharp criticism and misunderstanding from his own group and unintentional bribes from the whites," Tate (1986, p. 8) suggested that his contemporaries were compelled "to take on racist representations and black self-hate simultaneously."

Within six years, two writers notably took up Tate's (1986, p. 8) call for "a worldly-wise and stoopidfresh intelligentsia of radical bups [i.e., 'buppies' or black yuppies]." A relatively unknown young novelist named Trey Ellis and Tate's *Village Voice* colleague Nelson George both published influential essays that extend the ideas outlined in "Cult-Nats Meet Freaky-Deke." Each also coined critical neologisms that labeled the shift in the perceptions, expressions, and/or contestations of Blackness by contemporary African American artists.

In outlining a "New Black Aesthetic," Ellis (1989, pp. 234–235) also introduced the term "cultural mulatto" to describe the same generation of young Black artists to whom Tate (1986, p. 7) ascribed "a postnationalist black arts movement, one more Afrocentric and cosmopolitan than anything that's come before." Whereas Tate emphasized visual artists and critical theorists, Ellis (1989, p. 234) widened the aperture by profiling musicians (Fishbone, Public Enemy, and Living Colour), filmmakers (Spike Lee, the Hudlin brothers, and Robert Townsend), dancers (Bill T. Jones), visual/performance artists (Lisa and Kellie Jones), playwrights (George C. Wolfe), and actors (Eddie Murphy and Chris Rock) who responded to "gr[owing] up feeling misunderstood by both the black worlds and the white" by expressing themselves in "an open-ended New Black Aesthetic . . . that shamelessly borrows and reassembles across both race and class lines." Although Ellis (1989, p. 235) insisted that "[t]oday's cultural mulattoes echo those 'tragic mulattoes' critic Sterling Brown wrote about in the Thirties only when they too forget they are wholly black," he also paralleled both Hughes and Tate in asserting that they "no longer need to deny or suppress any part of our complicated and sometimes contradictory cultural baggage to please either white people or black."

Ellis situated the origins of the New Black Aesthetic in the work of a transitional group of artists who rose to prominence during the 1970s, including John Edgar Wideman, Ishmael Reed, August Wilson, Toni Morrison, Clarence Major, George Clinton, David Hammons, and Richard Pryor. Ellis characterizes them as:

> a minority of the black-arts community, branded either counter-revolutionary, too artsy or just not good propagandists [. . .]. Stripping themselves of both white envy and self-hate they produced supersophisticated black art that either expanded or exploded the old definitions of blackness, showing us as the intricate, uncategorizeable folks we had always known ourselves to be.
>
> (1989, p. 237)

Ellis ultimately asserted that the New Black Aesthetic did not reject past conceptions of Blackness outright, but rather insisted on the freedom to choose whether to feel bound by them. Elaborating on Tate's (1989, p. 5) sardonic observation that "if white people weren't around to be mad at, people into being black would be out of a job," Ellis (1989, pp. 239–240) affirmed a relationship to the ongoing reality of racism that is simultaneously aware and aloof: "Neither are the new black artists shocked by the persistence of racism as were those of the Harlem Renaissance, nor are we preoccupied with it as were those of the Black Arts Movement. For us, racism is a hard and little-changing constant that neither surprises nor enrages . . . We're not saying racism doesn't exist; we're just saying it's not an excuse."

George's 1992 essay "The Complete History of Post-Soul Culture: Buppies, B-Boys, Baps & Bohos" provides both a diagnosis and a taxonomy of the modifications in Black aesthetics. Although George expanded his observations on "post-soul" in two subsequent books, this article establishes his fundamental views on how:

> the tenor of African American culture has changed . . . [from] the we-shall-overcome tradition of noble struggle, soul and gospel music, positive images, and the conventional wisdom that civil rights would translate into racial salvation . . . [to] a time of goin'-for-mine materialism, secular beat consciousness, and a more diverse, fragmented, even postmodern black community.
>
> (1992, p. 25)

George's (1992, p. 25) terminology arose from his experience of advocating for the renaming of *Billboard*'s "Soul" music charts in 1982, noting that "Prince wasn't soul, nor was Kurtis Blow or Run-D.M.C. The direction of black music, one of the truest reflectors of our culture, had changed profoundly, as it always does." As the editorial staff considered alternatives, George became aware of the underlying conundrum: "Where 'soul' was once universally accepted, the new era had yielded no new all-purpose catchphrase for the black mood – we couldn't very well call it the funk-disco-hip hop-soul-crossover chart." Although *Billboard* spent a decade searching for a replacement, George argued that their ultimate failure (in his eyes) indicated both "the new African American mentality desegregation has spawned" and "a whole population overwhelmed by the complexity of the present."

While generally sustaining Tate's earlier argument, George added that "there was more than one aesthetic at work" in the "post-soul era," resulting in:

> four new African American character types . . . that began germinating in the '70s and blossomed in the '80s. There is the Buppie, ambitious and acquisitive, determined to savor the fruits of integration by any means necessary; the B-boy, molded by hip hop aesthetics and the tragedies of underclass life; the Black American Princess or Prince a/k/a/ Bap, who, whether by family heritage or personal will, enjoys an expectation of

mainstream success and acceptance that borders on arrogance; and the Boho, a thoughtful, self-conscious figure . . . whose range of interest and taste challenges both black and white stereotypes of African American behavior.

(1992, p. 26)

The wellspring of these new types was the 1971 release of Melvin Van Peebles's film *Sweet Sweetback's Baadasssss Song*, which George (1992, p. 26) called "a renegade work that, like many pivotal expressions throughout history, has only been encountered by a small percentage of the folks it affected." He found the film notable for defying "the positive-image canon of Sidney Poitier, dealing openly with black sexuality, government-sanctioned brutality, and the arbitrary violence of inner-city life. Its refusal to compromise still sparks black artists from Ice Cube to Matty Rich." Like Tate and Ellis, George observed an estrangement from the past, asserting that younger Black artists who were directly or indirectly influenced by *Sweetback* "stroll our streets alienated from if not ignorant of the old soul verities." This attitude helps explain how and why "African American culture evolve[d] (or, as some old jacks argue, devolve[d]) from gospel-and-blues rooted with a distinctly country-accented optimism to assimilated-yet-segregated citified consciousness flavored with nihilism, Afrocentricism, and consumerism" (p. 27).

Anticipating Warren's claims by almost twenty years, George (1992, p. 27) noted that the "unending debate over authenticity, co-optation, and redefinition" is less consequential for those Black artists who have "come of age since the end of the struggle against blatant segregation." Like Ellis's "cultural mulattoes," George's "young-gifted-and-black post-soulers" often:

attended predominantly white schools and took their access to mainstream opportunities for granted. That's not to say they're Uncle Toms or even that they're out of touch with the masses of unassimilated African Americans, but both dangers lurk. Their experience, especially if it was not formed by ghetto life or some romantic ghettocentric identification, makes race consciousness less central to their being.

(1992, p. 27)

This explains why, as of 1992, "[t]he soul world lingers on, but for the current generation it seems as anachronistic as the idea of a National Association for the Advancement of *Colored* People and as technologically primitive as a crackly old Motown 45" (George 1992, p. 27).

THE NEW MILLENNIUM AND THE ARRIVAL OF POST-BLACKNESS

Whereas George's terminology specified that "soul" no longer encapsulated Black aesthetics, the concept of "post-black art" that emerged in the new millennium was widely perceived as a threat to Blackness itself. Tate and Ellis had both argued for a "new" Black aesthetic, but the shared prefix of "post-soul" and "post-black" seemed to suggest abandonment. In the catalogue for the 2001 *Freestyle* exhibition at the Studio Museum in Harlem, curator Thelma Golden (2001, p. 14) wrote that she and artist Glenn Ligon had started using "post-black" a few years earlier as "a shorthand for a discourse that could fill volumes. For me, to approach a conversation about 'black art,' ultimately meant embracing and rejecting the notion of such a thing at the same time." Golden added that it gradually took on "ideological and chronological dimensions and repercussions. It was characterized by artists who were adamant about not being labeled as 'black' artists, though their work was steeped, in fact deeply interested, in redefining complex notions of blackness." By the time of the *Freestyle* show, Golden pronounced that "post-black had fully entered into the art world's consciousness," cheekily adding that "Post-black was the new black."

This final comment troubled several prominent Black artists. For example, visual artist Larry Walker (whose daughter Kara was cited by Golden as a major influence on many of the *Freestyle* artists) insisted that "On the surface . . . the term is an effort to distance the ideological and methodological concerns of a number of effective African American artists from the tired, misused and inadequate term 'Black Art' [. . . but it should not] morph into yet another shortsighted term such as 'the new black'" (quoted in Byrd 2002, pp. 36–37). Similarly, *Freestyle* participant Kojo Griffin found "the use of the term post-black to be somewhat problematic because the word 'black' has so many connotations within society as well as in the microcosm of the art world. As a person who is very proud of being 'black' or of African heritage, I would be reluctant to ever describe myself as 'post-black' in any sense" (quoted in Byrd 2002, p. 38). These artists' uneasiness epitomizes the concerns voiced about each of the aforementioned formulations of generational change. They have all been accused of sacrificing the communal and signifying powers of Blackness in exchange for individual artistic autonomy. Although Tate, Ellis, George, and Golden all forestalled such critiques, the intensification of "colorblind" and "post-racial" rhetoric in the first two decades of the 2000s has frequently blurred the distinctions between their ideas and such overt erasures of racial signification.

THE EVOLUTION OF POST-SOUL AND POST-BLACK DISCOURSE

After *Freestyle*, a three-pronged dynamic regarding the putative divergence of contemporary Black expression emerged. One set of scholars – e.g. Bertram Ashe, Margo Natalie Crawford, Darryl Dickson-Carr, Richard Iton, Mark Anthony Neal, Paul C. Taylor, Touré, Kenneth W. Warren, Ytasha Womack, Kevin Young – continues to refine, revise, and/or expand the concepts that Tate, Ellis, George, Golden, and Ligon introduced. Another set of scholars – e.g. Daphne Brooks, Kimberly Chabot Davis, Soyica Diggs Colbert, James J. Donahue, Bambi Haggins, Candice M. Jenkins, Michael K. Johnson, Cameron Leader-Picone, Derek C. Maus, Barbara McCaskill, Danielle Fuentes Morgan, Derek Conrad Murray, Francesca Royster, Ilka Saal, Christian Schmidt, Richard Schur – has employed these diverse concepts to interpret particular works by contemporary authors, musicians, filmmakers, visual artists, and performers.

A third group that includes Houston A. Baker, Bernard W. Bell, Tera Hunter, Habiba Ibrahim, Randall Kennedy, Stephanie Li, Eric Lott, Riché Richardson, K. Merinda Simmons, and Greg Thomas, has pushed back, often vociferously, against various assertions of a "post-liberated" (Tate 1986, p. 7) Blackness. For example, Ibrahim (2007, p. 23) contended that Ellis's praise of the "cultural mulatto" requires willful ignorance of the "interpretive impasse that lies between an ongoing allegiance to historical, politically based concerns, and a posthistorical present and future . . . [and which reflects] a profound uncertainty over what the political and cultural stakes are of positing 'postmodern blackness' in such a way as to neutralize facets of a complicated past." In a similar vein, Bell included Ellis among a class of:

> contemporary antiessentialist critics and readers who seek to move beyond the label of racial provincialism [and who] seem obsessed with validating and valorizing transcultural literary relationships while neglecting or rejecting an acknowledgment of the core vernacular roots of intracultural relationships and identities in the African American narrative tradition.
>
> (2012, p. 303)

Like most of the other contributors to *The Trouble with Post-Blackness* (2015), Li directed her criticisms towards Touré's *Who's Afraid of Post-Blackness?: What It Means to Be Black Today* (2011), a book that introduced the discourse of post-Blackness to a substantial non-academic audience. Li (2015, p. 45) maintained that, "[w]ith its emphasis on individualist expressions of racial identity, post-blackness threatens to become a dangerous abdication of history . . . Black literature can never be post-black because the signifyin(g) language of black narrative affirms history, even as texts may alter or transform that history."

The divide between advocates and detractors has not, however, been wholly impermeable. Numerous critics have employed these terms while also disputing the contention of a radical departure from the past. For example, even as Neal (2002, pp. 103, 112) echoed "The New Black Aesthetic" in declaring that "the generation(s) of black youth born after the early successes of the traditional civil rights movement are in fact divorced from the nostalgia associated with those successes and thus positioned to critically engage the movement's legacy from a state of objectivity that the traditional civil rights leadership is both unwilling and incapable of doing," he pointed out flaws in Ellis's "negotiat[ion of] his own class sensibilities with those he has come to understand as black." Young (2012, pp. 283–284), whose poetry has occasionally been labeled "post-black," offered both a rebuke and partial concurrence in *The Grey Album: On the Blackness of Blackness* (2012): "[B]lackness is not something I wish to be beyond or past; it is still ever-present and remains unavoidable, and more important pleasurable . . . [yet] black art is whatever art is made by black folks."

Crawford (2017, p. 217) likewise balanced sanction with objection by emphasizing that "[t]he 'post' in black post-blackness is, partially, post-ideological blackness." Arguing that "[s]kepticism about any fixed notion of 'black art' plays a profound role in the 1970s 'second wave' of the BAM [Black Arts Movement]," she both indissolubly linked the present to the Black nationalist past and contested perceived restrictions on representations of Blackness:

> As the BAM became the first cultural movement determined to make art that is specifically and unapologetically black, the artists' search for the specificity of black art led to a wide horizon of shaping and unshaping blackness that I call 'black post-blackness.' . . . [B]lack art (in its most innovative forms) is always a remaking of 'black' and 'post-black' within the layered circle of black post-blackness.
>
> (2017, pp. 1–2)

Melissa Daniels-Rauterkus goes still further, discerning traces of contemporary attitudes throughout African American literary history:

> [W]hat has always defined African American literature is its ongoing dialectic with literary realism. From the truth-telling imperatives of the slave narrative to the flat-out rejection of the concept of racial authenticity that characterizes so many postsoul, postblack, and new black writings, black literature has been shaped alongside and against calls to, in more informal terms, *keep it one hundred* [i.e. authentic or true].
>
> (2020, pp. 173–174)

Morgan (2016, p. 10) similarly intertwined novelty with continuity in arguing that the "real critical application of the post-soul, then, can be found in the ways that it shapes a future understanding of race – not by tearing race asunder, but instead by asserting the ways that its existence as a social construct underscores the fact that it was historically constructed to create a hierarchy that still exists in significant ways."

Few, if any, of the artists, performers, and writers who have been identified using the aforementioned critical nomenclature have actually claimed it for themselves or for their work. Nafissa Thompson-Spires is one of the few authors to explicitly embrace the generational terminology, citing "[p]ost-soul aesthetics" (Wayne 2018) as an influence on her short story collection, *Heads of the Colored People* (2018). Li (2015, p. 46) has suggested that the "glaring omission of black novelists in [Touré's] *Who's Afraid of Post-Blackness?* would seem to imply that literature is the one realm of black artistic production that has been uninfluenced by the rise of post-blackness," but this seems overstated, given the substantial body of well-regarded criticism that employs post-Blackness and its conceptual kin. Nevertheless, her claim buttresses the sense that these terms pertain far more to the *reception* of contemporary Black art than to its *creation*. As Colson Whitehead stated more broadly, "literary theory is great for discussing literature, but hasn't been much help in writing the stuff" (Selzer 2008, p. 398).

EXEMPLARS OF POST-SOUL AND POST-BLACK FICTION

Despite the paucity of either explicit endorsements or condemnations, numerous works by contemporary writers evince an altered relationship to Blackness. Fran Ross's novel *Oreo* was originally published in 1974, but remained relatively obscure until its republication in 2000, when Harryette Mullen (2015, p. 220) praised the novel's prescience: "Ross's novel dazzles by deliberately straining the abilities of its readers, as if she wrote for an audience that did not yet exist. Relatively few people in 1974 would have possessed the linguistic competence, multicultural literacy, and irreverently humorous attitude toward racial and ethnic identity that Ross demonstrates and expects of *Oreo*'s ideal audience." *Oreo*'s opening paragraph alone testifies to Mullen's assertions:

> When Frieda Schwartz heard from her Shmuel that he was *(a)* marrying a black girl, the blood soughed and staggered in all her conduits as she pictured the chiaroscuro of the white-satin *chuppa* and the *shvartze*'s skin; when he told her that he was *(b)* dropping out of school and would therefore never become a certified public accountant – *Riboyne Shel O'lem* – she let out a great *geshrei* and dropped dead of a racist/my-son-the-bum coronary."
>
> (2015, p. 3)

Novelist Danzy Senna mentions both Tate and Ellis on the opening page of her foreword to the novel's 2015 reissue, and their ideas permeate her memory of discovering *Oreo* in the late 1990s while living among:

> a community of people I thought of as "the dreadlocked élite." [. . .] We were authentically nothing. Each of us had experienced a degree of alienation growing up – too black to be white, or too white to be black, or too mixed to be anything . . . *Oreo* came to me in this context like a strange, uncanny dream about a future that was really the past. That is, it read like a novel not from 1974 but from the near future – a book whose appearance I was still waiting for. [. . . Ross's] blackness was our blackness.
>
> (2015, pp. xi–xii)

Thompson-Spires expresses a similar sense of "alienat[ed] blackness" in describing *Heads of the Colored People*:

> I wanted to write about Black people today, at least from the '90s to the present, and the kind of unique struggles they deal with. Because we are one of the first generations post-integration living out everyday problems . . . In some ways, I think the collection is trying to deal with the pressures of all that baggage, which I think we

inherited from the generation before us, and to think about new ways of trying to be Black in spite of that pressure

(Coleman 2018)

Paul Beatty's *The White Boy Shuffle* (1996), Senna's *Caucasia* (1998), Percival Everett's *Erasure* (2001), Whitehead's *Sag Harbor* (2009), and Mat Johnson's *Loving Day* (2015) stand out among the dozens of books of fiction by contemporary African American authors that depict being "marginalized within a marginalized group" and/or being "perceived as the 'wrong' Black" (Coleman 2018).

The White Boy Shuffle features an idiosyncratic narrator named Gunnar Kaufman whose introduction both unsettles his claim to have "managed to fill the perennial void in African-American leadership" (Beatty 1996, pp. 1, 5) and separates him from African American literary history:

> Unlike the typical bluesy earthy folksy denim-overalls noble-in-the-face-of-cracker-racism aw shucks Pulitzer-Prize-winning protagonist mojo magic black man, I am not the seventh son of a seventh son of a seventh son . . . I am the number-one son of a spineless colorstruck son of a bitch who was the third son of an ass-kissing sell-out house Negro who was indeed a seventh son but only by default.
>
> (1996, p. 5)

Prodigiously talented as both a basketball player and a poet, Kaufman eventually becomes a "Negro Demagogue" by offering his audiences "grueled futility [and] unveil[ing] the oblivion that is black America's existence," such as his half-glib suggestion that African Americans kill themselves: "Nothing works, so why suffer the slow deaths of toxic addiction and the American work ethic when the immediate gratification of suicide awaits?" (Beatty 1996, pp. 1, 2).

Thelonious "Monk" Ellison, the narrator of *Erasure*, may have a name that registers as more Black than Kaufman's, but his introduction similarly disrupts racially reductive presumptions:

> I have dark brown skin, curly hair, a broad nose, some of my ancestors were slaves and I have been detained by pasty white policemen in New Hampshire, Arizona, and Georgia and so the society in which I live tells me I am black; that is my race . . . Some people in the society in which I live, described as being black, tell me I am not *black* enough. Some people whom the society calls white tell me the same thing. I have heard this mainly about my novels, from editors who have rejected me and reviewers whom I have apparently confused and, on a couple of occasions, on a basketball court when upon missing a shot I muttered *Egads*.
>
> (Everett 2001, pp. 1–2)

Ellison is horrified by the success of a clichéd novel called *We's Lives in da Ghetto* that is hailed as an "authentic" depiction of Black American life and writes a satirical response called *My Pafology* under the pseudonym Stagg R. Lee. His parodic-satirical intentions remain unnoticed, even after he changes the title to *Fuck*, and the book ends up winning a major literary prize and a lucrative film deal.

Sag Harbor is outwardly a coming-of-age novel centered around a 15-year-old who embodies the concept of the "cultural mulatto." Benji Cooper spends the summer of 1985 at his family's beach house in the African American enclave of Sag Harbor on eastern Long Island. *Sag Harbor* resembles *Erasure* in featuring a Black character whose comparably privileged class-status often clashes with presumptions based on his skin color: "according to the world, we were the definition of paradox: black boys with beach houses. A paradox to the outside, but it never occurred to us that there was anything strange about it" (Whitehead 2009, p. 57). Benji is forced not only to contend with the racial expectations of both Black and white observers, but also to navigate his internalized sense of Blackness, which is confused by being "the only black kid in the room" (p. 7) at his prep school in Manhattan. Coming to Sag Harbor for the summer involves "catching up on nine months of black slang and other sundry soulful artifacts I'd missed out on in my 'predominantly white' private school. Most of the year it was like I'd been blindfolded and thrown down a well, frankly" (p. 29).

Caucasia is a semi-autobiographical expression of Senna's upbringing in an interracial household, as well as a muted homage to *Oreo*. The novel focuses on a pair of mixed-race sisters, Cole and Birdie Lee, growing up amidst the racial tension of Boston in the mid-1970s. Because of her comparatively dark skin and physical features, Cole is invariably perceived as Black, while the lighter-skinned Birdie can pass for white. This fact allows Birdie and her white mother, who believes she is wanted by the FBI, to adopt fictitious Jewish identities upon fleeing from Boston. By the end of the novel, Birdie rejects the conventional logic of the "tragic mulatto" story (which suggests that mixed-race identity is both ill-fated and ruinous) by moving to California to live with her sister. In doing so, Birdie restores Cole's incontrovertible Blackness – and that of their Black nationalist father – to her own mixed-race identity, undoing the self-negation required by passing for white: "It had come so easily to me. I had become somebody I didn't like. Somebody who had no voice or color or conviction. I wasn't sure that was survival at all" (Senna 1998, p. 349).

Loving Day also examines how mixed identity fits uncomfortably, at best, into contemporary American discourses of race. Johnson's protagonist/narrator is an unheralded comic book author named Warren Duffy, who returns to the predominantly Black Germantown neighborhood in his native Philadelphia in order to take possession of a crumbling mansion that belonged to his white father. Not long after his arrival, Duffy also learns that he has a teenaged daughter from a past relationship. He exists both bodily and culturally between whiteness and Blackness, although he is quite direct about his intention to choose Blackness, regardless of how others perceive him: "I'm not white, but I can feel the eyes of the few people outside on me, people who must think that I am, because I look white, and as such what the hell am I doing here? This disconnect in my racial projection is one of the things I hate . . . I hate that because I know I'm black. My mother was black – that counts, no matter how pale and Irish my father was" (Johnson 2015, p. 4). Warren awkwardly navigates between factions – both Black and white – that would dictate both his racial identity and that of his daughter instead of accepting their attempts to "express all of who [they] are culturally," contending that "if you grew up connected to parents of two races, just saying, 'I'm black,' or whatever, negates part of who you are, culturally. As a person" (p. 112).

Other notable authors of fiction whose work has been associated with the aforementioned critical discourses include Nana Kwame Adjei-Brenyah, Jamel Brinkley, James Hannaham, Darius James, T. Geronimo Johnson, Victor Lavalle, Kiese Laymon, James McBride, ZZ Packer, Emily Raboteau, Kiley Reid, Maurice Carlos Ruffin, Chris L. Terry, Michael Thomas, and Jesmyn Ward.

Despite the ongoing dissonance regarding the definitions and the probity of both post-Blackness and the post-soul aesthetic, each of these discourses remains well represented in the scholarly work surveying the literature produced by African American authors as of the start of the 2020s. The combination of critical acclaim and popular recognition earned by Beatty, McBride, Senna, Ward, and

Whitehead will likely extend awareness of exploratory and iconoclastic representations of Blackness still further into the mainstream.

SEE ALSO: Beatty, Paul; Everett, Percival; Johnson, Mat; LaValle, Victor; McKnight, Reginald; Senna, Danzy; Ward, Jesmyn; Whitehead, Colson

REFERENCES

Beatty, Paul. (1996). *The White Boy Shuffle*. New York: Picador.

Bell, Bernard W. (2012). *Bearing Witness to African American Literature: Validating and Valorizing Its Authority, Authenticity, and Agency*. Detroit: Wayne State University Press.

Byrd, Cathy. (2002). Is there a "post-Black" art?: investigating the legacy of the "Freestyle" show. *Art Papers* 26 (6): 34–39.

Coleman, Tyrese L. (2018). Nafissa Thompson-Spires is taking Black literature in a whole new direction. *Electric Literature* (January 8, 2018). https://electricliterature.com/nafissa-thompson-spires-is-taking-black-literature-in-a-whole-new-direction/ (accessed July 20, 2021).

Crawford, Margo Natalie. (2017). *Black Post-Blackness: The Black Arts Movement and Twenty-First Century Aesthetics*. Urbana: University of Illinois Press.

Daniels-Rauterkus, Melissa. (2020). *Afro-Realisms and the Romances of Race: Rethinking Blackness in the African American Novel*. Baton Rouge: Louisiana State University Press.

Ellis, Trey. (1989). The new Black aesthetic. *Callaloo* 38 (Winter): 233–243.

Everett, Percival. (2001). *Erasure*. New York: Hyperion.

George, Nelson. (1992). The complete history of post-soul culture: buppies, b-boys, baps & bohos. *Village Voice* 37 (11): 25–27. https://www.villagevoice.com/2020/01/09/buppies-b-boys-baps-bohos/ (accessed July 20, 2021).

Golden, Thelma. (2001). Introduction. *Freestyle* [exhibition catalogue], 14–15. New York: Studio Museum of Harlem.

Hughes, Langston. (1926). The Negro artist and the racial mountain. *The Nation* 122: 692–694.

Ibrahim, Habiba. (2007). "It's a kind of destiny": the cultural mulatto in "The New Black Aesthetic" and *Sarah Phillips*. *Saint John's University Review* 6 (1): 21–28.

Johnson, Mat. (2015). *Loving Day*. New York: Spiegel and Grau.

Li, Stephanie. (2015). Black literary writers and post-Blackness. In: *The Trouble with Post-Blackness* (ed. Houston A. Baker, Jr. and K. Merinda Simmons), 44–59. New York: Columbia University Press.

Morgan, Danielle Fuentes. (2016). Post what? The liminality of multi-racial identity. *Humanities* 5 (2): 1–11.

Mullen, Harryette. (2015). Afterword. In: *Oreo* (by Fran Ross), 213–230. New York: New Directions.

Neal, Mark Anthony. (2002). *Soul Babies: Black Popular Culture and the Post-Soul Aesthetic*. New York: Routledge.

Ross, Fran. (2015). *Oreo*. New York: New Directions; 1st ed. 1974.

Selzer, Linda. (2008). New eclecticism: an interview with Colson Whitehead. *Callaloo* 31 (2): 393–401.

Senna, Danzy. (1998). *Caucasia*. New York: Riverhead.

Senna, Danzy. (2015). Foreword. In: *Oreo* (by Fran Ross), xi–xvii. New York: New Directions.

Tate, Greg. (1986). Cult-nats meet freaky-deke: the return of the Black aesthetic. *Village Voice Literary Supplement* (December 9, 1986): 5–8. https://www.villagevoice.com/2020/01/10/cult-nats-meet-freaky-deke/ (accessed July 20, 2021).

Warren, Kenneth W. (2011). *What Was African American Literature?* Cambridge, MA: Harvard University Press.

Wayne, Teddy. (2018). 5 writers, 7 questions, no wrong answers. *Literary Hub* (April 10, 2018). https://lithub.com/5-writers-7-questions-no-wrong-answers-3/ (accessed July 20, 2021).

Whitehead, Colson. (2009). *Sag Harbor*. New York: Doubleday.

Young, Kevin. (2012). *The Grey Album: On the Blackness of Blackness*. Minneapolis: Graywolf.

FURTHER READING

Ashe, Bertram D. (2007). Theorizing the post-soul aesthetic: an introduction. *African American Review* 41 (4): 609–623.

Baker, Houston A., Jr. and Simmons, Merinda. (eds.) (2015). *The Trouble with Post-Blackness*. New York: Columbia University Press.

Leader-Picone, Cameron. (2019). *Black and More than Black: African American Fiction in the Post Era*. Jackson: University Press of Mississippi.

Maus, Derek C. and Donahue, James. J. (eds.) (2014). *Post-Soul Satire: Black Identity after Civil Rights*. Jackson: University Press of Mississippi.

Thompson-Spires, Nafissa. (2018). *Heads of the Colored People*. New York: Random House.

Touré. (2011). *Who's Afraid of Post-Blackness?: What It Means to Be Black Now*. New York: Simon & Schuster.

Womack, Ytasha. (2010). *Post Black: How a New Generation is Redefining African American Identity*. Chicago: Lawrence Hill Books.

Power, Susan

VANESSA HOLFORD DIANA
Westfield State University, USA

Soon after Standing Rock Sioux writer Susan Power published her first novel, *The Grass Dancer* (1994), it became a bestseller, winning the 1995 PEN/Hemingway Award for best first fiction, and receiving glowing reviews. The success of her first novel launched Power into the classrooms and book clubs of the United States. Since then she has published *Roofwalker* (2002), a collection of short fiction and autobiographical stories, the novel *Sacred Wilderness* (2014), and essays on writing, visual arts, and the cultural and political elements of Native American identity. In her fiction and nonfiction, Power draws on her own experiences as the daughter of a Sioux mother and Irish American father, growing up in Chicago, where her political activist mother founded the American Indian Cultural Center. Power earned her bachelor's degree from Harvard University and went on to Harvard Law for her JD. Power's decision to switch career paths from law to creative writing was inspired by a dream-vision in which she was visited by a character who would later appear in her first novel. In autobiographical writings, Power credits her mother with teaching her to see the world as full of spirit and creative possibilities and her father with teaching her to love the literature and family stories of her European American ancestors. Both have clearly influenced her creative imagination and sense of identity.

That all Americans can learn from *all* of the stories that make up the nation's history is a theme threaded through Power's fiction and nonfiction work. Power crafts stories that are distinctive for their mix of humorous voice and serious attention to US history's most painful episodes of settler colonial violence as well as ongoing struggles facing Native Americans and women. Her characters are emotionally convincing, demonstrating Power's fascination with complex human relationships. In her depictions of cross-cultural exchanges, Power consistently affirms the rich creative possibilities in reciprocal learning and syncretism in matters of storytelling, education, faith, love, and imagination. In a recent essay titled "Native in the Twenty-First Century," Power critiques Eurocentric traditions of education and literature that have ignored Native perspectives: "[t]hey've been educating us for years, for several lost generations, but we're up-ending that one-sided desk, that one-sided conversation that can only tell stories in a single direction" (Power 2017).

Power's first novel, *The Grass Dancer*, traces the family lines of two Sioux teenagers, Harley Wind Soldier and Charlene Thunder, backwards from the 1980s to the late 1800s, weaving a multigenerational tale of star-crossed lovers and their descendants who navigate war, cultural divides, and family tragedies but also find love and redemption. The novel is equal parts humor and pain, with an emphasis on ancestral spirits and medicine traditions that Susan Power emphatically insists are *not* magical realism.

Ultimately, *The Grass Dancer* offers in its youngest protagonists a pair of coming-of-age stories in which teens can move into their adult lives only after understanding their place in ancestral stories. The ancestors who offer those stories emerge as some of Power's most memorable characters.

Power divides her second book, the collection *Roofwalker*, into short fiction and autobiographical stories mostly featuring women and girls. The fiction explores themes familiar to readers of *The Grass Dancer*. But unlike her first novel, in *Roofwalker* most of the fictional and autobiographical stories explore the lives of Sioux characters in cities. From the Chicago Field Museum of Natural History to Harvard Yard in Cambridge, MA, the city settings often reflect Power's experiences growing up in Chicago or attending Harvard University. While Power herself and many of her fictional characters do find their place in cities and successfully maintain a connection to Native identity in urban landscapes, stories in *Roofwalker* also depict the painful cultural erasure, family fragmentation, intergenerational trauma, and displacement that resulted from the Indian Relocation Act specifically and US policies toward tribal nations more generally.

In her most recent novel, *Sacred Wilderness*, Power returns to themes of syncretism, storytelling, ancestral spirits, and feminism by weaving the stories of four mothers across time. In the early colonial period, Maryam, the Virgin Mary mother of Jesus, is called by Mohawk clan mother Jigonsaseh, mother of another visionary son, Ayowantha, for spiritual conference. In the present day, both spirit mothers serve as guides to a pair of contemporary women living in Saint Paul. Ojibwe-Dakota Gladys, hired as a housekeeper, helps her wealthy Mohawk Jewish employer Candace reconnect to her ancestral roots. Maryam's spirit character visits Candace to share with her Jigonsaseh's story and spur Candace on a journey of healing.

While most of the critical work published on Power's fiction has focused on *The Grass Dancer*, many of the themes and stylistic elements considered are also relevant to *Roofwalker* and *Sacred Wilderness*. Power's white characters often serve to highlight popular misconceptions about Native American people (Winters 2019). In *The Grass Dancer*, missionary priests articulate Manifest Destiny ideology during the years of westward expansion and war while a well-intentioned white teacher on a Sioux reservation in the 1980s sees her students as romanticized noble savages and can scarcely believe they participate in contemporary American culture. White characters are often juxtaposed to Native characters – offering a contrast in worldviews that emphasizes the limitations imposed by one-sided stories. In *The Grass Dancer*, Reverend Pyke, the villain of Fort Laramie in the years of the Indian Wars, espouses Manifest Destiny in his opposition to Red Dress, the ancestral warrior woman who becomes a spirit witness as her people struggle to maintain Dakota culture. In *Roofwalker*, "First Fruits" begins with a campus tour guide at Harvard who doesn't know the history of the seventeenth-century Indian College established at Harvard to convert Native Americans to Christianity. Ultimately, the Sioux protagonist, a freshman at Harvard, comes face to face with the spirit of Caleb Cheeshahteaumuck, a Wampanoag who in 1665 was the first Native graduate from Harvard. In *Sacred Wilderness*, Candace is a stereotype of white success: wealthy, successful, fit and beautiful, living in a mansion chock full of material possessions. But Candace's failure to hear stories of her own Native past have led to depression and disassociation that require spiritual intervention.

In all three works, Power uses museum settings to challenge misrepresentations of Native American people and history. In the autobiographical "Museum Indians," Power recalls a childhood visit with her mother to the Chicago Historical Society where a statue depicts an Indian warrior poised to kill a white woman and children. Her mother complains to museum officials until the statue is removed. Beyond the savage stereotype, museums also depict Native people as dead and Native cultures as frozen in the past. Museums become prisons in Power's work, in which sacred artifacts await repatriation to their people where they can be returned to appropriate use. In both *The Grass Dancer* and "Museum Indians," Power references the Chicago Field Museum, where a beaded dress on display is described as belonging to Margaret Many Wounds, a grandmother character in *The Grass Dancer*, and as belonging to Power's own great-grandmother in "Museum Indians" (Schweninger 2009). In the latter, Power and her mother visit the dress "stand[ing] before the glass case as we would before a grave" (Power 2002, p. 163). The characters share a wish to "rescue" the dress and return it to the descendants of the woman who beaded it. Lee Schweninger notes the dress is described as displaced, evoking the repercussions of Indian Removal and the sense of displacement from home experienced by some urban Native people.

The parallel scenes also allude to the 1990 Native American Graves Protection and Repatriation Act, which requires human remains, funerary objects, and sacred items to be returned to tribes based on their value in kinship, cultural affinity, and continuity. In *Sacred Wilderness*, Candace's character represents the trend among non-Native collectors to display Native artifacts out of context of their ceremonial use. Candace's private collection housed in her personal Indian Arts Museum includes paintings by real contemporary artists whose work Power herself has written about and chosen for cover art on her books, but Candace's appreciation of these contemporary Native artists does not extend to understanding how inappropriate it is to display sacred objects as curios. Hanging on the wall of Candace's private exhibit room is an Iroquois medicine mask, which Gladys immediately recognizes is seething with anger. While Gladys is not Iroquois, she recognizes the mask is intended for spiritual practice: "Gladys wanted to chide the woman for hanging the Face on her wall as if he were nothing more than a lifeless object in a collection. Something acquired. Something owned. This is a living being you've trapped in your house, but you haven't diminished his power, that's for sure" (Power 2014, p. 17). Candace learns over the course of the story that she is participating in the commodification of Native culture and desecration of sacred objects by removing them from their people and disregarding their original ceremonial context.

Foremost in discussions of Power's work is her treatment of spiritual elements as realism, *not* magical realism. Writing about her mother's influence on her creative imagination in an essay, "The Table Loves Pain," Power explains, "I was taught to see the world as a landscape of spirit and story – magic on the air, God (the Great Mystery) in every cell" (Power 2004, p. 115). Power specifically rejects the label "magical realism" as failing to represent Native views of spiritual reality (Carlson *et al.* 2009). In *The Grass Dancer*, reality includes revelations in a Yuwipi ceremony, the workings of spells to control amorous attention, and spirit visitation to the moon. The novel's witch character Anna (Mercury) Thunder repeatedly asserts that she is not a fairy tale – a distinction that has sparked critical analyses of Power's very distinct form of realism (Hearne 2017; Diana 2009). Red Dress, the nineteenth-century ancestor spirit who lingers on Earth to help guide the living, communicates with her descendants through dreams and visions. In *Roofwalker*, Power weaves spirits into familiar urban landscapes, even in autobiographical stories:

Power's mother tells her while walking along the shore of Lake Michigan that stones with holes house "powerful spirits trying to tunnel their way out" (2002, p. 195).

In *Sacred Wilderness*, Power sets the spirit of Maryam, mother of Jesus, in the middle of her twenty-first-century story line where some contemporary characters can see Maryam and others can sense her presence. Grounded in the physical world, Maryam enjoys coffee and takes interest in the domestic dramas of the contemporary characters, sits among guests at a family dinner, admires Gladys's pet cat, and enjoys the poetry of Sherman Alexie while attending a reading by LeAnne Howe at Birchbark Books, the Minneapolis bookstore owned by Louise Erdrich. This is not the first time Power weaves into her fiction references to real Native American authors that function as gestures of tribute. In *The Grass Dancer*, Power similarly mentions Vine Deloria, Jr., an influential Standing Rock Sioux writer whom Power's characters refer to as "our cousin" (1994, p. 59). But in *Sacred Wilderness*, Power overtly places her spirit character Maryam in scenes of hyperrealism involving real figures in Native American arts and set at real locations, demonstrating Power's consistent representation of the magical as the real. When, by the end of *Sacred Wilderness*, Gladys brings Candace the Mohawk medicine mask in a hospital where she is being treated for depression and anxiety, spiritual elements are so central to the text that readers are prepared to accept that the mask has become more than a symbol on the mansion wall of the misguided Candace. The mask communicates with Candace, inviting her to look through its eyes and allowing her to see into the past to access the story of her Mohawk ancestor Jigonsaseh.

Across Power's fiction, characters revel in the joys of cross-cultural storytelling and find balance in syncretism of multiple spiritual and story traditions. Moments of syncretism are often funny in Power's work, and the familiar stories of Western, Judeo-Christian literary and faith traditions become decentered but not devalued. In *The Grass Dancer*, Margaret Many Wounds and her husband, who was educated at Carlisle Indian School, exchange stories. She teaches him the Dakota songs and stories and language forbidden at Carlisle, and he shares with her the classics of British literature, including their favorite, Jane Austen, whose Elizabeth Bennett of *Pride and Prejudice* (1813) Margaret liked because "she had wit and a backbone. I thought she would have made a good Sioux" (Power 1994, p. 107). Elsewhere in the novel, Shakespeare's *Macbeth* delights Red Dress, and the story of witch Anna Thunder draws heavily on fairy tales of the brothers Grimm. Power's characters who are fluent in both Native and Western story traditions are enriched by the dual traditions and draw on both for wisdom, guidance, and enjoyment (Hearne 2017). In "Angry Fish," a Winnebago thrift store volunteer finds a talking statue of St. Jude and embarks on a relationship of cross-cultural creative and spiritual exchange with the Catholic icon. In the autobiographical story "The Attic," Power and her mother search through the attic of her paternal grandmother's New England home to unearth her father's ancestral history. Power's Sioux mother urges her: "Come take a look! This is your heritage too" (2002, p. 176). Similarly, the wise Yuwipi man of *The Grass Dancer*, Herod Small War, counsels the white schoolteacher Jeannette McVay as she cradles her baby, who "looks more Sioux than her Sioux father and without a trace of her mother's lineage," that her baby "needs to know both sides. Otherwise, she'll stand off-balance and walk funny and talk out of one side of her mouth. Tell her *two* stories" (1994, p. 314). While Candace of *Sacred Wilderness* devours literature by Native and Euro-American authors, her healing is only possible once she finally becomes receptive to the stories offered by *both* Maryam and Jigonsaseh.

One critical debate Power has invited about her work centers around how much historical and cultural background her readers need to make sense of her fiction. Power asserts, "what a reader makes of my work is beyond my control. I worry too much that people read my work sometimes as History, Sociology, Ethnography, when it's really fiction, and that's all it's meant to be" (Carlson *et al.* 2009). Yet Power draws deeply on Dakota and other tribal traditions. For example, Deer Woman stories serve as a tool to explore the use and misuse of sexual energy, as is evident in the characters of Red Dress, Anna Thunder, and Charlene Thunder (Van Dyke 2004), and Power's characterization of Herod Small War draws on accurate depictions of the Yuwipi ceremony (Diana 2009). In *Roofwalker*, the title story centers on a Sioux girl in Chicago whose grandmother teaches her not to kill spiders, for they may be Iktome, the traditional trickster character in Dakota stories. In *Sacred Wilderness*, Power incorporates Haudenosaunee traditions such as the Wampum belt and story of Ayowantha to contextualize her characters' Mohawk ancestry. So, while Power's fiction is not ethnography, her incorporation of traditional elements of various tribal cultures encourages readers to learn more about those traditions.

Similarly, while Power claims to be neither a historian nor a sociologist, she does often incorporate history – from pre-contact to recent – involving US–Native conflict, as well as social issues impacting contemporary Native people. In her autobiographical story "Stone Women," Power describes her mother's anger over the mid-twentieth-century construction of the Oahe Dam, for which the US government seized under eminent domain significant portions of the Standing Rock and Cheyenne River Reservations' best agricultural land, displacing many and contributing to persistent poverty. In the same story, Power points to the epidemic of missing and murdered Indigenous women in the example of her Aunt Elsie, murdered by a white boyfriend, the crime never investigated. Power also takes on social issues impacting women in her fictional stories from *Roofwalker*: "Watermelon Seeds" depicts a physically abusive relationship, and the teenaged title character of "Indian Princess" commits suicide when she discovers she has become pregnant from her alcoholic boyfriend. The stories are not without hope, however. A reviewer of *Roofwalker* observes "that the past must be alive in the present in order that people deal with the grim social realities and cultural dilemmas facing urban Native Americans" (Carnahan 2003).

SEE ALSO: Indigenous Narratives; Multiculturalism; Religion and Contemporary Fiction; Story Cycles; Urban Fiction

REFERENCES

Carlson, Mara, Dedinsky, Angi, Duesterhoeft, Jolyn, and Oslos, Shari. (2009). Susan Power. *Voices from the Gaps*. Regents of the University of Minnesota. https://conservancy.umn.edu/bitstream/handle/11299/166308/Power%2c%20Susan.pdf?sequence=1&isAllowed=y (accessed July 15, 2021).

Carnahan, Tim. (2003). *Roofwalker*: submerged spirituality. MN Artists. https://mnartists.walkerart.org/roofwalker-submerged-spirituality (accessed July 15, 2021).

Diana, Vanessa Holford. (2009). "I am not a fairy tale": contextualizing Sioux spirituality and story traditions in Susan Power's *The Grass Dancer*. *Studies in American Indian Literatures* 21 (2): 1–24.

Hearne, Joanna. (2017). I am not a fairy tale: Indigenous storytelling on Canadian Television. *Marvels & Tales* 31 (1): 126–146.

Power, Susan. (1994). *The Grass Dancer*. New York: Penguin Putnam.

Power, Susan. (2002). *Roofwalker*. Minneapolis: Milkweed Editions.

Power, Susan. (2004). The table loves pain. *The American Indian Quarterly* 28 (1–2): 115–117.
Power, Susan. (2014). *Sacred Wilderness*. East Lansing: Michigan State University Press.
Power, Susan. (2017). Native in the twenty-first century. *World Literature Today* 91 (3–4). https://www.worldliteraturetoday.org/2017/may/native-twenty-first-century-susan-power (accessed August 28, 2021).
Schweninger, Lee. (2009). Lost and lonesome: literary reflections on museums and the roles of relics. *The American Indian Quarterly* 33 (2): 169–199.
Van Dyke, Annette. (2004). Encounters with Deer Woman: sexual relations in Susan Power's *The Grass Dancer* and Louise Erdrich's *The Antelope Wife*. *Studies in American Indian Literatures* 15 (3–4): 168–188.
Winters, Kelly. (2019). Critical essay on *The Grass Dancer*. Detroit, MI: Gale.

FURTHER READING

Brogan, Jacqueline Vaught. (2000). Two distinct voices: the revolutionary call of Susan Power's *The Grass Dancer*. *North Dakota Quarterly* 67 (2): 109–125.
Kelsey, Penelope. (2015). Review of *Sacred Wilderness*. *Native American and Indigenous Studies* 2 (2): 199–201.
Richards, Geraldine. (2014). Review of *Sacred Wilderness*. *Foreword Reviews*. https://www.forewordreviews.com/reviews/sacred-wilderness/
Solomon, Christopher. (2002). Review of *Roofwalker*. Books in Brief: Fiction & Poetry. *The New York Times* (October 27, 2002). https://www.nytimes.com/2002/10/27/books/books-in-brief-fiction-poetry-453170.html
Wright, Neil H. (1995). Visitors from the spirit path: tribal magic in Susan Power's *The Grass Dancer*. *Kentucky Philological Review* (10): 39–43.

Powers, Richard

JON ADAMS
Independent scholar, Castle Hedingham, UK

Novels about individuals matter because individuals matter. The rise of the individual and the rise of the novel are aspects of the same process. But things are reaching a head: never before have individuals mattered so much, and never before have there been so many of us.

If the novel provides a form through which our species-level narcissism can be elevated to an art, then the fiction of Richard Powers represents a sustained attempt to repurpose the novel for the opposite goal: to marginalize, or at least recontextualize, the individual not as the supreme object of inquiry but as a single node within a much wider network; a bit player within an ecosystem that includes both the physical environment in which human bodies and brains exist (and from which they are materially constituted), and the information environment – what Thomas Pynchon was able to describe as far back as 1984, long before the Internet, as "flows of data more vast than anything the world has ever seen" (1984, p. 1). For Powers, the novel is a site and (importantly) a *method* for exploring how the self is built and buffeted by those data flows, how ephemeral and transcendent selfhood is always contingent upon the continued operation of the situated and physical brain from which it emerges, and how that embodied brain is in turn yoked to the wider social and ecological system. In a short essay reflecting on his work up to 2008, Powers quotes naturalist John Muir: "When we try to pick out anything by itself, we find it hitched to everything else in the Universe" (Muir 1911, p. 211). "That's the hitch my fiction wants to discover," Powers adds (2008, p. 309).

All of which is not to say that Powers isn't interested in people, or fails to create individuated characters. It is more that he wants to break away from the humanitarian tradition that claims motivation and behavior can be adequately explained by reference to beliefs and desires. Against a literary landscape "overwhelmingly dominated by the psychological" (Hamner 2020), Powers wants to tell stories where the drama isn't wholly solipsistic – the introspective musings of a lonely artist, the anatomizing of middle-class marriage breakdowns. What he resists, as a character in *The Overstory* (2018) puts it, are novels about "privileged people having trouble getting along with each other in exotic locations" (pp. 331–332). Powers's novels explore how the stuff of thought, through being learned and acted upon, comes to alter the world of things.

What results are serious, data-rich works, where artistic effects are often achieved by shuttling between or juxtaposing scales or narrative forms in order to disclose isomorphisms and echoes. The mode is realism, undergirded by copious and diligent research, but set into intricate narrative structures more typical of musical arrangements. In *Gain* (1998), for example, the gradual development over two centuries of a small business into a corporate behemoth, Clare International, is plotted against the rapid devastation of a single human body by a cancer caused by pollutants from Clare's chemical plant. Pages of expository writing about the shift from mercantilism to global trade will be followed by pages about the embodied experience of Laura's chemotherapy-induced nausea. Interleaving those two accounts exposes homologies: the consequences of unchecked growth, corporations as persons, the fallacy of believing the environment is an externality. Taken together, the narrative strands make a murder story: Clare kills Laura.

Virginia Woolf once suggested that women historically wrote novels because they were frustrated scholars of fields from which they were professionally excluded (Woolf 2015, p. 51, et passim). Given the volume of data on show, it is tempting to see Powers as involved in a similar deflection; a popular scientist manqué, someone who really wants to be Carl Sagan (whose quip, "If you want to make an apple pie from scratch, you must first invent the universe" [1995, p. 242], echoes Muir, sounds like something a Powers character might say). But that's a mistake. Powers finds himself in an inverted version of the situation Woolf is describing. He is drawn to the novel because it is the only form that can accommodate his interests. There is no academic field or discipline which caters to the polymath, and never will be. Fiction, as Powers sees it, "has the potential to be the most complex set of experimental networks ever built." He goes on to add that: "Story alone can refract vast, voiced, complex interactions between local and global that no single discipline can know inclusively or pretend to master" (2008, p. 309).

Over the course of twelve novels, he has established himself at the vanguard of contemporary American novelists. Unusually for an author who was embraced almost immediately as the subject for serious academic attention, Powers has enjoyed significant popular success: his novels are widely reviewed and have, from his first book in 1985, *Three Farmers on Their Way to a Dance*, consistently garnered honors and awards. He is a four-time finalist for the National Book Critics Circle Award, a National Book Award winner, in 1991 *The Gold Bug Variations* was *Time* magazine's fiction book of the year, and he has been a finalist and, in 2019, winner of a Pulitzer for *The Overstory*.

If his biography is relevant (and Powers, who refused to give interviews for the first six years of his career, thinks it probably isn't), it is as proof that the type of autodidactic, discipline-hopping characters that often feature in his novels really can exist outside of fiction. Although he has included self-portraits in his books – most fully as the author "Richard Powers" in *Galatea 2.2* (1995) – the young Richard Powers is very much a real-life Richard Powers character.

Born in Evanston, Illinois, on June 18, 1957, Powers is the fourth of five children. A musical family, the siblings performed vocal harmonies and accompanied arrangements for neighbors. At nine years old, he reads Darwin's *Voyage of the Beagle*. He reads Homer, he reads Hardy. At 11, the family moves to Thailand, where his father (a principal back in Lincolnwood, Illinois) heads up the International School. While in Bangkok, he acquires conversational Thai, further develops his talent for music – he plays guitar, cello, and half of the woodwind section. When Powers's father's health declines, the family return to the United States in 1973, settling in De Kalb, Illinois. Powers graduates high school and in 1975 attends university at Urbana-Champaign – initially to study physics, but switching to the Rhetoric program after his second year. Meanwhile, he becomes fascinated by PLATO, a pioneering networked computer system used by the university for coursework, especially music education, and teaches himself coding on weekends. When his father dies in 1978, Powers reconsiders the value of an academic career, and although he subsequently completes his master's degree in English literature, he declines the opportunity to pursue a doctorate. In 1980, paralyzed by the threat of ever-winnowing specialization, and disenchanted by the failure of academic literary criticism to engage with the emotional potential of language, he leaves the university and moves to Boston, where he employs the coding skills he acquired to work as a computer programmer.

The programming jobs provide a mental discipline and allow him flexible working. Freed from the curriculum of the university, he reads intensively: Proust, Mann, Musil, Joyce, Gaddis. It is during his time in Boston that, visiting the art gallery one Saturday morning in 1982, he first encounters a photograph by August Sander, "Young Farmers, Westerwald, ca. 1914." The image captures three men in hats, starched collars, smart suits, each holding canes, caught by the camera as if glancing back. They are apparently dressed up on their way to a dance in the nearby village, but all three will soon be embroiled in the coming war. Powers has spoken of the encounter as a Damascene moment, as he would later recall about first seeing the photograph: "That was a Saturday. On Monday I went in to my job and gave two weeks notice and started working on *Three Farmers*" (Berger 2002/3, p. 111).

Completed three years later and published by William Morrow, his first novel, *Three Farmers on Their Way to a Dance*, was well reviewed and nominated for a National Book Critics Circle Award. The book imagined lives for the three men from the photograph, drawing their stories into the story of how the technological developments that allowed the mass reproduction of their photograph also enabled the mass destruction of the world wars. The historical accounts are intercut with a present-day narrative following a computer magazine journalist. Overseeing it all is a third narrative, written by an author named "P" who is hopelessly beguiled by the photograph.

Much of what would become distinctive of Powers's fiction, certainly in the first phase of his career, is already in place: the obsessive researcher-protagonist, the slight dislocation of history into fiction, the characters who might be portraits of the author, the sweeping history of ideas. Structurally, *Three Farmers* establishes a formal template that Powers would employ for his next seven novels: braided narratives, where total meaning emerges only epiphenomenally, as a superimposition of two or three independent and partial accounts.

Apparently startled by his debut success, Powers retreated to Urbana and subsequently moved to Europe. It was while living in southern Holland that Powers completed his second novel, *Prisoner's Dilemma* (1988), which introduced the theme of simulation and similarity – a problem he will work through repeatedly over several books. Spurred by the postwar promise of game theory to rationalize human irrationality, the simulated worlds of *Prisoner's Dilemma* also represent an attempt to impose order and clean up the messiness of real life. And, metafictionally, the novel is itself such a construction – delivering coherence and structure and closure into a world which usually withholds those things. *Prisoner's Dilemma* can be usefully compared to *Plowing the Dark* (2000), inspired by hearing former Beirut hostage Terry Waite talk of the value of "productive solitude" (Berger 2002/3, p. 111) as a coping mechanism for isolation.

In *Plowing the Dark*, the simulated worlds are virtual: a kidnapped American hostage is alone in the Middle East, locked in a room with only memory and imagination as stimulation; meanwhile, in Seattle, a team of computer scientists, variously disenchanted with the world, are building a fully immersive virtual reality environment called, in a nod to Plato, The Cavern, which enables users to step inside paintings, thus escaping into art as a refuge from life. Like the model worlds of *Prisoner's Dilemma*, the implication is bleak: why build a simulation when you already have the real thing? Answer: because we need a hiding place. Fiction is, as Powers puts it in *Prisoner's Dilemma* (a book written in exile), "a place to hide out in long enough to learn how to come back" (1988, p. 345).

After the publication of *Prisoner's Dilemma*, Powers was named as a MacArthur Fellow and awarded the famously generous "genius grant." He returned to the theme of similarity in *The Gold Bug Variations* (1991), his best known and for a long time most significant work. Huge, and hugely ambitious, *Gold Bug* also saw Powers exploring the possibilities of music as system and structure, but allied to biological self-similarity and recursion – the feedback loops that are the basis of genetic transcription. Taking off from Douglas Hofstadter's bravura *Gödel, Escher, Bach: An Eternal Golden Braid* (1981), Powers finds a stimulating parallel in the contrapuntal music of J.S. Bach, and particularly the thirty-two Goldberg Variations, which, just like DNA, employ a four-note base in sixty-four possible combinations. The numerical coincidence might have veered toward spooky hermeticism – the type of superficial alignments that make the conspiracy novels of Dan Brown so popular. But Powers hangs little on the conceptual rhyme, and everything on the common process: repetition with variation is the same structural device that produces the complexity of the Goldberg Variations and the driving force behind the manifest complexity of evolved life on earth. *Orfeo*, from 2014, will tackle again the analogies and homologies between music and genetics when aging composer Peter Els sets up a homemade laboratory in his garage and finds himself arrested for bioterrorism. And two decades after *Gold Bug*, Powers's fascination with music yielded another novel – *The Time of Our Singing* (2003). Once again, it is the power of music to unite, but the thematic backdrop now is the discord of race in post-Civil Rights America.

He followed up *Gold Bug* with *Operation Wandering Soul* (1993), a grim account of a pediatrics ward in a refracted version of Los Angeles, Angel City, where the history of human suffering and cruelty makes the plight of children under the care of fifth-year resident Richard Kraft in a modern hospital horribly inevitable. It is an unusually pessimistic novel, but a reminder that amid the dazzle of futuristic technologies, the pleasure to be found in music, and his boundless love of learning, there is an undercurrent of gloom in Powers's work. The local goodness of individuals is never quite enough when matched against the tidal force of human greed, abetted by rapacious capitalism, all within a pitiless universe.

Fittingly, then, his next novel would end with a suicide, of sorts. *Galatea 2.2* self-consciously reworks the Pygmalion story, but where in Greek myth the statue came to life, here, life – or at least a functional simulation of consciousness – emerges disembodied from a computerized neural network. A writer called "Richard Powers" is brought in to teach the computer, Helen, how to pass a literature exam. But after absorbing the Western canon, the machine turns herself off. As elsewhere in Powers's fiction, there is the sense that the rational response to life is to get out while you can, that happiness is a delusional state. (Indeed, the premise of 2009's *Generosity* is exactly this: a student is diagnosed with "hyperthymia" – a disorder resulting in excessive happiness: "renewable elation . . . constant mania without the depression, ecstasy without the cyclic despair" [pp. 67–68]. Happiness might be a pathological condition.)

Galatea 2.2 is almost a partner piece to 2006's *The Echo Maker*: both employ contemporary brain science to explore the dependency of consciousness on the distributed network of the mind-brain, both describe the reciprocally therapeutic process of coaxing a self into being. In *The Echo Maker*, brain damage following a car crash leaves a man unable to recognize his own sister. That condition – Capgras syndrome – is real, but in Powers's hands becomes an expansive metaphor for the ways in which identity is always being constructed on the fly. *The Echo Maker* also significantly brings ecology front and center. In the delicate correspondences Powers draws between fragile ecosystems and the fragility of selfhood, much of what he has been circling for the past two decades begins to cohere.

If there's an overall trajectory in his works, it reaches an apex with *The Overstory* (2018), a book that foregrounds the background, inverts the pathetic fallacy to depict a society growing sick because nature is sick – and hence the aim of the environmental movement is also to save humanity. As one character asks, "Who does the tree-hugger really hug, when he hugs a tree?" (2018, p. 238). A novel about the destruction of virgin forests, and a disparate band of activists seeking to save them, it also pulls together so many of Powers's abiding concerns: there is the modulation of timescale from the human to the arboreal, the simulation of an environment within a virtual space, the paranoid pattern-finding that begins to see trees everywhere: the tree of life in evolutionary cladistics, the tree of knowledge in the Internet. It doesn't take the fantasy of Tolkien to get trees talking: biochemically, they already do – exchanging information through a complex language of chemical signals. Structurally, *The Overstory* (a term for the upper canopy of forests) represents a significant shift from his usual technique of braided narratives. An artifact made of paper about the misuse of trees, the novel is arranged as concrete poetry – akin to George Herbert's "Easter Wings" (1633) or cummings's "r-p-o-p-h-e-s-s-a-g-r" (1935). Nine separate characters form the "Roots" whose lives entwine within the middle section of the novel, "Trunk," before being dispersed into the "Crown." A coda, "Seeds," follows.

It's also a site where the subtextual misanthropy and antinatalism of Powers's novels can be tabled. One doesn't have to subscribe wholly to Ian Watt's thesis to agree that the rise of the novel was coincident with the rise of individualism, but both were accompanied by a much more significant human development: global population ballooned exponentially from less than one billion in the eighteenth century to over 7.5 billion in 2020. Such has been the severity and ubiquity of humanity's impact upon the environment that there is now a growing movement (initiated by Paul J. Crutzen) to rename our geological epoch the "Anthropocene," dating from James Watt's invention of the steam engine in 1784. When taken together – the emergence of individualism, the explosion in the global population – the novel's traditional focus on individuals begins to look problematic, at best, and Powers's longstanding resistance to the same prescient. For how to coherently or responsibly argue for the specialness of 7.5 billion souls? The answer is compensatory: uniqueness matters precisely because there are so many of us.

Crowds and crowding had become a subject of increasing concern in Power's preceding work – *Generosity* and *Orfeo* are both haunted by crowds – but it is in *The Overstory* that the welling pessimism that has run below all his works really surfaces: "Humankind is a thug" (2018, p. 313). The modern environmental movement emerged out of the overpopulation movement in the late 1960s, when Norwegian ecologist Arne Næss (whose "deep ecology" urged a revision of the idea that nature existed for human employment) and the American philosopher Garrett Hardin found themselves pilloried for suggesting the root of the environmental problem was us. The obvious solution is Larkin's – "Get out as early as you can/And don't have any kids yourself" (2004, p. 142). There are no children at the end of *The Overstory*, and even the final act of reading is significantly via audiobook, but Powers doesn't think suicide is the answer, if only because suicide is – if the ecological predictions are correct – already the route we are on. Hence he suggests the rather awkward-sounding answer of "unsuicide" – urging that we escape from the simulations and distractions, divest ourselves of post-Enlightenment privilege, quit the fictional game of *let's pretend*: "we need to live where we live, to become indigenous again" (2018, p. 339). *The Overstory* makes the back catalogue of Powers's fiction seem like it might also be a complete structure, the roots and trunk of which this is the crown.

SEE ALSO: Biological Fictions; The Brain and American Fiction; Ecocriticism and Environmental Fiction; Fiction and Terrorism; Kingsolver, Barbara; Pynchon, Thomas; Stephenson, Neal; Vollmann, William T.

REFERENCES

Berger, Kevin. (2002/3). Richard Powers, the art of fiction no. 175. *The Paris Review* 164: 106–138. https://www.theparisreview.org/interviews/298/the-art-of-fiction-no-175-richard-powers (accessed September 6, 2021).

Hamner, Everett. (2020). Here's to unsuicide: an interview with Richard Powers. *Los Angeles Review of Books* (April 17, 2018). https://www.lareviewofbooks.org/article/heres-to-unsuicide-an-interview-with-richard-powers/ (accessed September 6, 2021).

Larkin, Philip. (2004). *Collected Poems* (ed. Anthony Thwaite). New York: Farrar, Straus and Giroux.

Muir, John. (1911). *My First Summer in the Sierra*. Boston: Houghton.

Powers, Richard. (1988). *Prisoner's Dilemma*. New York: Morrow.

Powers, Richard. (2008). Making the rounds. In: *Intersections: Essays on Richard Powers* (ed. Stephen J. Burn and Peter Dempsey), 305–310. Champaign, IL: Dalkey Archive Press.

Powers, Richard. (2009). *Generosity: An Enhancement*. New York: Farrar, Straus and Giroux.

Powers, Richard. (2018). *The Overstory*. New York: Norton.

Pynchon, Thomas. (1984). Is it O.K. to be a Luddite? New York Times Book Review (October 28, 1984): 1.

Sagan, Carl. (1995). *Cosmos: The Story of Cosmic Evolution, Science and Civilisation*. London: Abacus; 1st ed. 1980.

Woolf, Virginia. (2015). *A Room of One's Own and Three Guineas* (ed. and intro. Anna Smith). Oxford: Oxford University Press; 1st ed. 1929.

FURTHER READING

Burn, Stephen J. and Dempsey, Peter. (eds.) (2008). *Intersections: Essays on Richard Powers*. Champaign, IL: Dalkey Archive Press.

Holland, Rachel. (2019). *Contemporary Fiction and Science from Amis to McEwan: The Third Culture Novel*. Cham, Switzerland: Palgrave.

Labinger, Jay. (1995). Encoding an infinite message: Richard Powers's *The Gold Bug Variations*. Configurations 3: 79–93.

Program Culture

LOREN GLASS
University of Iowa, USA

In 2014, Chad Harbach, best-selling novelist, graduate of the UVA Creative Writing Program, and editor of *n+1* magazine, published a collection of essays called *MFA vs. NYC: The Two Cultures of American Fiction*. The collection was prompted by the many responses *n+1* had received to the 2010 publication of Harbach's essay of the same name, which was in turn a response to (and review of) Mark McGurl's magisterial *The Program Era: Postwar Fiction and the Rise of Creative Writing* (2009), which single-handedly inserted the term into our literary-historical lexicon. Before McGurl's paradigm-shifting intervention, most English professors placed postwar American fiction under the loose and baggy umbrella of the term "postmodernism," a word which never sat particularly well with the handful of token creative writers lurking in their midst, who tended to position themselves in opposition to "pomo" and the professors who deployed it. *The Program Era* reminded those professors that, while they had been attending to Thomas Pynchon and Don DeLillo, an entire canon of postwar fiction had been produced by the creative writers right under their noses. By the time McGurl published his book, MFAs were beginning to outpace PhDs in both number and influence on American college campuses, and Harbach's collection indexes this profound change in the demographics of English departments and the culture of American fiction.

Harbach provocatively asks us to read his collection as "a kind of jointly written novel – one whose composite heroine is the fiction writer circa 2014" (2014, pp. 4–5) and insofar as most Program Era fiction is, according to McGurl, a "portrait of the artist" (2009, p. 48) the book can be seen as an example of the topic it engages, which is less about any real combat between the two cultures than it is about the uneasy coordination between them. For the most part, American novelists continue to write what they know, and what they know is the autopoetic culture and precarious economy of the creative writing program, to which writers increasingly retreat when they can't afford to live in New York City, which remains home to the major publishing houses and literary agencies.

McGurl describes the act of authorship in the Program Era as "autopoetic" (2009, p. 18 and passim) because most fiction produced in creative writing programs, even when not directly autobiographical, is both written and read as an instance of creative self-expression whereby personal experience is transmuted into literary art. The pedagogical shibboleths "write what you know" and "find your voice" both reflect this autopoetic understanding of fiction's nature and purpose. And this understanding inflects both the writing and the reading process, insofar as such texts offer readers, according to McGurl, "a mediated experience of expressive selfhood as such" (p. 19). And, in the classic tradition of the *Künstlerroman*, Program Era novels tend to tell the story of their own production, with the protagonist, frequently an avatar of the author, working on a book (or some other form of creative expression) that, literally or allegorically, represents the book we are reading.

Insofar as the Program Era institutionalizes the role of the individual creative subject, it should not surprise us that creative writing programs facilitate an elaborate star system which powerfully inflects the culture, career structure, and subject matter of contemporary American fiction. Complex hierarchies of talent and taste obtain both within and between programs, and celebrity is as much the coin of the realm as content, with literary value accruing to famous writers through prizes, readings, social media platforms, festival appearances and remunerative visiting gigs, and individual programs structured around charismatic figures and their emulative acolytes. And since celebrity is by nature the exception to the rule, Program Era culture is correlatively characterized by visions of failure. Most graduates, even of the most prestigious programs, will not be able to make a living on their writing and will have to fall back on teaching which, though frequently rewarding, can also be exhausting and distracting, especially in the burgeoning ranks of contingent faculty with high teaching loads, low pay, and little job security. The long tail of failure and precarity haunts program culture, whether or not it figures as an explicitly thematic element of any particular work of fiction.

WHEN

McGurl breaks his book down into three chronological sections, but it is worth affirming that only the third can be truly designated as the Program Era proper. Part one, focusing on the first two thirds of the twentieth century, is really a prehistory, presenting the rise of progressive (and expressive) education in the United States and detailing the fitful and uneven movement of novelists and critics into the American university system, alongside the gradual ascendance of literary modernism as an object of study in English departments under the banner of the new criticism. Most aspiring novelists during this era eschewed higher education, preferring Parisian cafés to American seminar rooms, and English departments hardly acknowledged that contemporary American fiction was worthy of academic study, much less academic apprenticeship.

McGurl's second part, on "the pivotal and famously 'expressive' period of the long 1960s" (2009, p. 28), is in fact transitional. While creative writing programs achieved impressive growth during this period, they were still looked upon with skepticism by the American literary establishment, by this point based securely in New York City, which had become a global culture capital rivaling Paris. San Francisco and Los Angeles also rose to literary and cultural prominence in the immediate postwar era, generating their own fertile regional scenes. Bohemian enclaves on both coasts were the center of literary production and cultural experience; creative writing programs (frequently in Midwestern college towns) were condescended to with occasional visits for readings and temporary teaching stints, but were still shunned as permanent gigs. The literary scene was widely perceived as divided between a countercultural avant-garde centered in urban bohemian communities and a traditional establishment housed in university and college English departments.

It really isn't until the 1980s that the MFA becomes a standard component of the American novelist's career path, and teaching a standard mode of professional remuneration. The numbers make this clear. In 1967, when the Association of Writing Programs (AWP) was founded by novelist and Iowa graduate R.V. Cassill, among others, there were only a handful of MFA-granting creative writing programs. After that the growth is rapid, with 79 by 1975, 319 by 1984, 535 by 1994, 719 by 2004, and 880 by 2012 (according to the AWP Guide to Writing Programs). Creative writing majors now predominate, both numerically and culturally, in many American English departments and many undergraduates go to college with the explicit intention of becoming novelists.

WHERE

This development has not only diminished the dominance of New York City as a culture capital, it has also substantially restructured the literary map of the United States, in terms of both where writers live and work and where their fiction is set. The two inaugural programs, at Iowa and Stanford, were far from New York, and their growth in popularity and influence gradually reoriented the regional imaginary of American fiction. The development can be tracked in terms of the changing nature and status of literary regionalism over the course of the twentieth century. If, at the turn of the twentieth century, regionalist writers like Hamlin Garland and Willa Cather wrote about the places they grew up in but subsequently left behind in order to become professional writers, then now, at the turn of the twenty-first, novelists like Marilynne Robinson and Jane Smiley write about the places they went in order to become professional writers. Indeed, at least one short story set in the college town in which they got their MFA is something of a literary rite of passage for aspiring novelists. What we might call "squatter regionalism" has become a subgenre of Program Era fiction, and previously peripheral locations such as Iowa City and Palo Alto have become miniature culture capitals in a radically decentered literary ecosystem. This trend was reinforced by the demographic impacts of the GI Bill and the National Defense Education Act, which democratized the previously elite experience of "going away to college," creating a vast readership that could relate to this form of affective attachment to place.

Prominent programs such as Iowa and Stanford established cultural identities based not only in their regional locations but also in the literary styles and temperaments of their founding members and long-serving directors. Wallace Stegner stamped both his name and his middlebrow realist style on Stanford's program and Iowa, particularly under the directorships of Jack Leggett and Frank Conroy in the 1970s and 1980s, would also become associated with classical realist modes of fiction. Other programs, such as the Johns Hopkins Writing Seminars with John Barth or Brown University's Literary Arts program under Robert Coover, would come to be associated with more experimental postmodern modes. Over time, these tendencies would mature into institutional brands that can be partly understood as routinizing the charisma of the founders and, over time, prominent faculty and graduates. The result is a loose mapping of regions onto stylistic tendencies, with the Midwest tending to be associated with more traditional realist modes and the East Coast tending to be associated with experimentation and innovation.

Publication venues also shifted during this era as university-based journals such as *The Kenyon Review* and *The Iowa Review* replaced the interwar "little magazines" as literary gatekeepers. American colleges and universities had gone from cultural backwaters to cultural capitals, where contemporary American fiction was produced, published, and taught. These journals also enhanced the apprenticeship value of the MFA, insofar as creative writing students could learn about both the process and product of publication through providing editorial assistance and reading slush piles for the editors, who are frequently also creative writing professors. And each journal, of course, enhances the literary reputation of the institution whereby it is named, reminding readers of the degree to which the literary landscape of the Program Era is oriented around college towns as opposed to urban centers.

WHO

In the immediate postwar era most students who attended creative writing programs were veterans, frequently with young families in tow, benefiting from the GI Bill with dreams of Hemingway in their heads. They participated in this new experiment in higher education alongside a cohort of New Critics (some of whom were also novelists) busy canonizing the modernism of the interwar years. And if Hemingway was the model, Henry James was the master, with his famous prefaces providing required reading for young men working to hone their craft. As McGurl affirms, the technical mastery of point of view became the essential marker of literary craft in creative writing pedagogy; it provided an assurance for administrators that writing could be taught in an academic environment and it also provided a mechanism whereby the autopoetic process could expand out into other minds without sacrificing the central authority of the narrative voice. The process was initially highly gendered, insofar as Flaubert's *Madame Bovary* (1856) became a model for the expert navigation between empathetic identification and ironic distance. A minor subgenre of American *Madame Bovary*s, from R.V. Cassill's *Pretty Leslie* (1963) to Wallace Stegner's *A Shooting Star* (1961) to Philip Roth's *When She Was Good* (1967), became proving grounds for a kind of misogynistic mastery of literary point of view.

But if these initial cohorts were overwhelmingly male, it would be the work of a woman that first embodied what would come to be called "workshop fiction." The short stories of Flannery O'Connor, in their disciplined mastery of Jamesian limited omniscience (as well as Flaubertian irony), were the first fiction explicitly celebrated in terms of the creative writing program in which their author was trained. Almost single-handedly she put Iowa on the literary map of the United States, and Paul Engle, the workshop's tireless director and promoter in this crucial era of growth, in turn would use her success to leverage its reputation during a period when most writers were skeptical of such programs. It didn't hurt that O'Connor was also championed by the New Critics, many of whom did teaching stints at Iowa, as exemplifying precisely the masterful literary craft that close readings are designed to explicate.

She was also a pioneer for the handful of (predominantly white) women who studied creative writing in these years, a trickle that would grow to a flood in the wake of the women's liberation movement that transformed both the demographics and the sexual politics of American college campuses. By the late 1970s, women would numerically equal men in creative writing cohorts and classrooms, and their presence and power would alter the culture and aesthetics of American fiction. Women such as Gail Godwin and Jane Smiley introduced a new generation of sexually active female protagonists and emotionally complex (frequently multigenerational) family sagas, while for men the domestic abjection of Raymond Carver replaced the cosmopolitan stoicism of Ernest Hemingway. And, in the wake of the sexual revolution and the Stonewall uprising, gay and lesbian authors came out of the closet and into the seminar rooms, as both subjects and students, permanently diversifying and complicating the range of sexual expression and experience in American fiction. Many of these authors would in turn come to teach creative writing, contributing to the growth of the discipline and permanently altering the demographics and dynamics of the workshop.

Like the English departments in which they were housed, writing workshops were overwhelmingly white in the immediate postwar era, with only a handful of writers of color, such as Margaret Walker at Iowa and Ernest Gaines at Stanford, managing to navigate the many impediments to success in a system shaped by both structural and personal racism. The new social movements of the 1960s altered this situation somewhat, but racism both subtle and overt continues to constitute the experience of writers of color in creative writing programs up to the present day. That said, the prize-winning rise of Toni Morrison and other ethnically marked

American writers such as N. Scott Momaday, Gish Jen, and Sandra Cisneros, altered the landscape of Program Era fiction in the later twentieth century. Many of these writers returned to and revised histories of slavery, racism, and colonialism, resulting in such subgenres as the "neo-slave narrative," which frequently deployed institutional formations of the past, such as the plantation or the slave trade, as allegories for institutions of the present, such as the creative writing program or the publishing industry. Morrison's own career arc, from editor at Random House to professor at Princeton, can be seen as symptomatic of the gradual and uneven absorption of writers of color into what had heretofore been overwhelmingly white institutions.

HOW

The primary mode of instruction in the creative writing program was and for the most part remains the so-called "Iowa model," in which one student submits a draft of a story and then remains silent while the rest of the class critiques it. As McGurl confirms, one result of this pedagogical model was to thematize shame and pride and map them in turn onto the minimalism and maximalism of postwar fiction. The brevity and precision of the short story became a disciplinary mode for mastering the shame of the workshop experience, while the magisterial achievement of an encyclopedic novel came to express the pride of post-workshop success. More subtly, the collective social experience of the workshop and its ancillary institutions (such as festivals and conferences) slowly became incorporated into both the form and content of American fiction. Recent American novels such as John McNally's *After the Workshop* (2010), which satirically details the abject career of a recent Writers' Workshop grad as a media escort for successful visiting writers, or Andrew Sean Greer's *Less*, which chronicles the frenzied flight of a gay male novelist who responds to every speaking invitation he receives in an attempt to get over the loss of his lover, are increasingly situated in relation to creative writing programs and the global literary event network that subtends them. These novels are not only about creative writing, they are also formal experiments that reflect the opportunities and constraints of the workshop process, especially in terms of point of view, the control of which remains the principal sign of technical mastery for Program Era fiction.

WHAT

McGurl breaks Program Era fiction down into "three relatively discrete but in practice overlapping aesthetic formations" which he calls technomodernism, high cultural pluralism, and lower-middle-class modernism (2009, p. 32). The first term roughly correlates to what we used to (and sometimes still do) call postmodernism, as it refers to those novels, usually very long and usually written by white men, that engage information-age technology and science as their principal context and formal corollary. While these novels, ranging from John Barth's *Giles Goat Boy* (1966) to David Foster Wallace's *Infinite Jest* (1996), are invariably ambitious and magisterial, they have ironically become a minor genre, sustained by a dedicated (and mostly white male) fan base.

The somewhat surprising fate of these novels, and the term once unanimously used to categorize them, indicates a larger transformation in the scholarly periodization of the postwar era. In order to describe this transformation, we can refer to David Harvey's landmark study, *The Condition of Postmodernity* (1989), which provided a whole generation of scholars with a vocabulary for describing postmodernism. Chapter six of Harvey's study is entitled "POSTmodernism or postMODERNISM," and in it he notes that "there is much more continuity than difference between the broad history of modernism and the movement called postmodernism. It seems more sensible to me to see the latter as a particular kind of crisis in the former, one that emphasizes the fragmentary, the ephemeral, and the chaotic" (1989, p. 116). One might speculate that this crisis was "resolved," so to speak, by the institutionalization of modernist imperatives in the American university, containing and domesticating the more chaotic and opaque strains of postmodernism within a larger culture in which modernist ideas about form, subtended by romantic convictions about the artistic vocation and realist protocols of character and plot, predominate. In essence, the Program Era subordinates postmodernism into a minor instance of a larger culture of institutionalized modernisms.

High cultural pluralism, the most consequential and expansive of McGurl's three formations, refers to the powerful postwar merger between ethnic identity and modernist complexity, a combination that covers a range of prominent American novelists from Toni Morrison and Sandra Cisneros up through Viet Thanh Nguyen and Tommy Orange. All of these figures have deep allegiances to canonical modernist figures such as Joyce and Faulkner, and all retain strong institutional associations which are democratizing and diversifying access to Program Era culture. Sometimes this involves transforming traditional institutions such as Princeton and USC, and sometimes it inspires inventing new ones, such as the Macando Writers Workshop and the Institute of American Indian Arts.

Finally, lower-middle-class modernism refers more discretely to the work of Raymond Carver and other "Kmart realists" whose topic is economic precarity and emotional anomie and whose form is the minimalist short story. Of the three formations, this last is the most symptomatic of the workshop experience, insofar as the short story is the coin of the realm during the Program Era and economic precarity is usually the price to be paid for pursuing a literary career in the postwar United States. The three modes together indicate the degree to which the creative writing program can be seen to have institutionalized literary modernism, demoting so-called postmodernism from a cultural dominant to a minor strand of a much larger late modernist formation.

The Program Era has become the basis of all subsequent critical work on the rise of creative writing in the United States, but it is worth noting that McGurl neglects to fully consider or account for the persistence of traditional literary realism, not only during the Program Era but across the entire twentieth century leading up to it. While English departments gradually adopted modernist innovation and complexity as the key criteria for the canonization of American fiction, the popular literary marketplace continued to be dominated by middlebrow realists such as Edna Ferber and Sinclair Lewis. And to the degree that Program Era novelists wanted to make money, releasing them from the necessity to teach, they mastered this mode, which also tended to situate them outside the circle of academic consecration. The division is deeply gendered, as Curtis Sittenfeld succinctly expresses in her recent short story, "Show Don't Tell" (2017), in which her narrator, a female student at a prominent creative writing program clearly based on Iowa, drives a famous visiting alumnus to the airport, musing that, "He's the kind of writer . . . about whom current students in the program have heated opinions; I'm the kind of writer their mothers read while recovering from knee surgery."

In other words, Program Era fiction straddles what Pierre Bourdieu calls the restricted and general fields of cultural production, with the more modernist (and masculine) formations keyed toward an audience of creative writing teachers and students and the more middlebrow (and feminine) formations geared toward a mainstream audience composed predominantly of women. Unlike poetry, fiction is a resolutely heterotopic literary mode, circulating across fields of cultural production and appealing to audiences both large and small. This contradictory cultural situation is loosely contained under the banner of "literary fiction," a category that hovers between high cultural cachet and mainstream popular appeal.

Not surprisingly, Program Era fiction has recently come to thematize this conflict in the form of realist novels that, either directly or allegorically, engage the problem of irony and complexity as a measure of literary value. What Donal Harris (2016) has usefully called "peripheral realism," associated most prominently with white male writers such as Jonathan Franzen and Chad Harbach, has emerged as a rebuke, frequently couched in tones of sincerity and humility, of the more encyclopedic ambitions and ironic postures of technomodernism and its variants. This paradoxically postmodern brand of realism is both a critique of modernist complexity and a testimony to the persistence of realism. It is also a symptom of the unease and insecurity that has descended on white men writing in the wake of figures such as Philip Roth and John Updike, whose masculine posture and practice of mastery have come under increasing scrutiny.

"Literary fiction" could be considered coterminous with Program Era fiction. More than modernism or realism, it describes the cultural ambition of creative writing students to produce novels and short stories that aspire to the canonicity of the literature syllabus and reflect the level of learning expected of English majors. Like all categories, it as useful for what it excludes as for what it includes, and what it excludes is genre fiction. Science fiction, horror, mystery, Western, and, especially and symptomatically, romance were resolutely shunned in the curriculum of creative writing in its inaugural decades. Unlike literary fiction, these genres don't straddle cultural fields; they circulate exclusively in the general field and are neither read nor written by teachers and students of creative writing.

Until recently. Starting with science fiction, genre fiction has gradually been entering the academy, both as a field of study and as an acceptable professional aspiration for creative writers. This development began with white male writers such as Jonathan Lethem, who grew up reading comic books and genre fiction and then incorporated them into both the content and form of their fiction. But the trend rapidly spread, with Program Era writers such as Junot Díaz and Chang-rae Lee incorporating various subgenres of science fiction into their novels. The trend was further amplified by the unprecedented popularity of so-called Young Adult (YA) literature like the Hunger Games series, which formed the adolescent reading habits of many Americans who would go on to major in creative writing. Many prominent creative writing programs now include courses on graphic novels and genre fiction at both the undergraduate and graduate level.

McGurl's last chapter is called "Miniature America: The Program in Transplanetary Perspective," and the new millennium has indeed witnessed a globalization of what had initially been a parochially American institutional formation. This globalization has been both individual and institutional. On the one hand, creative writing programs have begun to crop up across the world, from Asia to Latin America to Africa to Europe; on the other hand, individual writers are more likely to have highly itinerant lives, making it more difficult to include them in a specific national tradition. For example, Rachel Cusk, widely considered a British novelist, was in fact born in Canada and grew up in Los

Angeles; Teju Cole was born in Michigan but grew up in Lagos, Nigeria; Ling Ma was born in China but grew up in the United States and received her MFA from Cornell. The examples proliferate, with the cosmopolitan and multicultural upbringings and itineraries of the novelists amply reflected in their fiction, which still bends toward the form of the Künstlerroman.

After the economic collapse of 2008 and now with the COVID-19 pandemic, many are predicting the end of the Program Era. And it is certainly true that a college education is becoming less affordable and teaching jobs less available. That said, creative writing remains a highly popular major, generating large cohorts of underemployed literary artists eager to cobble together careers in and out of academia. As long as they continue to write about their experiences, American fiction will remain grounded in the portrait of the college-educated artist seeking to survive in a literary field shaped by economic precarity.

SEE ALSO: After Postmodernism; Carver, Raymond; Contemporary Regionalisms; Coover, Robert; Fictions of Work and Labor; Globalization; Literary Magazines; Minimalism and Maximalism; Momaday, N. Scott; Periodization; Pynchon, Thomas; Realism after Poststructuralism; Robinson, Marilynne; Smiley, Jane; Viet Thanh Nguyen

REFERENCES

Harbach, Chad. (ed.) (2014). *MFA vs. NYC: The Two Cultures of American Fiction*. New York: Faber.
Harris, Donal. (2016). Getting real: from mass modernism to peripheral realism. In: *After the Program Era: The Past, Present, and Future of Creative Writing in the University* (ed. Loren Glass), 219–232. Iowa City: University of Iowa Press.
Harvey, David. (1989). *The Condition of Postmodernity*. Oxford: Blackwell.
McGurl, Mark. (2009). *The Program Era: Postwar Fiction and the Rise of Creative Writing*. Cambridge, MA: Harvard University Press.
Sittenfeld, Curtis. (2017). Show don't tell. *The New Yorker* (May 29, 2017). https://www.newyorker.com/magazine/2017/06/05/show-dont-tell (accessed September 14, 2021).

FURTHER READING

Bennett, Eric. (2015). *Workshops of Empire: Stegner, Engle and American Creative Writing during the Cold War*. Iowa City: University of Iowa Press.
Dowling, David. (2019). *A Delicate Aggression: Savagery and Survival in the Iowa Writers' Workshop*. New Haven: Yale University Press.
Glass, Loren. (ed.) (2016). *After the Program Era: The Past, Present and Future of Creative Writing in the University*. Iowa City: University of Iowa Press.
Myers, D.G. (2006). *The Elephants Teach: Creative Writing Since 1880*. Chicago: University of Chicago Press.

Proulx, Annie

BENEDICTE MEILLON
University of Perpignan Via Domitia, France

Annie Proulx's contribution to contemporary literature is characterized at once by her inimitably mordant humor and poetic prose, her erudite, dense style, packed with metaphors and innuendos, her often grotesque and tragicomic characters, and her postmodernist challenging of the myths that form the fabric of society in North America. Reflecting Proulx's academic training in history and her interest in geography, economics, and environmental sciences, her writing exhibits a thorough understanding of the multiple, deterministic processes at play in the evolution of a particular place and of the individuals enmeshed within it. She is a writer of long and short fiction as well as nonfiction. She achieved literary acclaim as the first woman to earn the Pen/Faulkner Award, for her 1992 novel, *Postcards*. Proulx's second novel,

The Shipping News (1993) – later adapted into a film by Lasse Hallström – won her prestigious prizes, amongst which a National Book Award for Fiction and the Pulitzer Prize for Fiction in 1994. She is well known as an incisive short story writer, a genre in which she excels. Her story "The Half-Skinned Steer" was included in John Updike's best-selling anthology *The Best American Short Stories of the Century*, published in 1999. "Brokeback Mountain" was propelled to international fame by the faithful, award-winning movie adaptation directed by Ang Lee in 2005. Some of Proulx's idiosyncrasies lie in her rural settings and mostly inarticulate characters struggling with brutal living conditions, while submitting to relentless fates. Her wry narrative voices are also typical of her craft. Her writing displays a mixture of bleak realism with postmodernist play and sardonic caricature, with increasingly frequent incursions into magical realism.

Edna Annie Proulx was born in Norwich, Connecticut, on August 22, 1935, to George Napoleon Proulx, the vice president of a textile mill, and Lois Nellie Gill Proulx, a painter and amateur naturalist. Annie Proulx credits her mother for passing on to her the love and art of storytelling, as well as for teaching her "to see and appreciate the natural world, to develop an eye for detail" (quoted in Rood 2001, p. 2). While she first published under the name E. Annie Proulx, she dropped the E., for Edna, in 1997 and has since been referred to simply as Annie Proulx. The eldest of five daughters, she is of French Canadian descent on her father's side – the Proulxs left France for Quebec in 1637 – and of British origins on her mother's, the Gills having emigrated to New England in 1635. In the 1860s, her father's grandparents moved to New England, where Annie Proulx grew up and lived a great part of her life, mostly in Vermont and Maine. She went through college in those two states, before moving to Montreal as a graduate student in history. After earning her MA in 1973, she started on a doctoral path, which she dropped two years later as she decided against an academic career. While she had regularly published short stories in magazines since 1970, it is only as she quit graduate school and moved back to Vermont that she established herself as a freelance journalist and writer. By then, Annie Proulx had been through three marriages and divorces. Her daughter from her first marriage was raised by her father while Annie Proulx took care of her three sons born from the last two marriages. Proulx is sometimes referred to as a New Englander, as much of her earlier writing is set in New England, but she has also often been associated with the West. Indeed, much of her fiction dramatizes the West, following her move to Saratoga, Wyoming, in 1995. She also spends time yearly in her second home in Newfoundland, where her novel *The Shipping News* is set, and has traveled much across North America.

There are many aspects of Annie Proulx's fiction that distinguish it from other contemporary writers in the United States. A staple of her writing has to do with the historical sweep her fiction covers, as it often includes several generations. Simultaneously, it often rests on significant details anchoring her fiction in a particular place and time. Her training as a historian visibly sharpened her outlook onto the present, making her question the many, entangled sociohistorical and economic forces at work in orienting one's development. "I like stories with three generations visible," she told an interviewer. "Geography, geology, climate, weather, the deep past, immediate events, shape the characters and partly determines what happens to them. [...] The characters in my novels pick their ways through the chaos of change. The present is always pasted on layers of the past" (*The Missouri Review* 1999, p. 1). During her studies, Proulx was especially interested in the approach developed by the *Ecole des Annales*: "I was attracted to the French *Annales* school, which pioneered minute examination of the lives of ordinary people through account books, wills, marriage and death records, farming and crafts techniques, the development of technologies. My fiction reflects this attraction" (pp. 1–2). The local color of her fiction is obtained from a careful blending of creativity, reliance on observation, and dedicated studies of the actual lives of locals living in the places she sets her fiction in: "I read manuals of work and repair, books of manners, dictionaries of slang, city directories, lists of occupational titles, geology, regional weather, botanists' plant guides, local histories, newspapers. I visit graveyards, collapsing cotton gins, photograph barns and houses, roadways. I listen to ordinary people speaking with one another in bars and stores, in laundromats. I read bulletin boards, scraps of paper I pick up from the ground" (p. 4).

Proulx first started writing short stories during her college years. They were initially published in the teenage magazine *Seventeen*. As Karen Rood (2001) observes, some of her favorite subjects that run through her later fiction can already be traced in these earlier stories, in particular environmental concerns, matters of cultural and socioeconomic heritage, and dealing with isolated young women growing up with few opportunities in poor, rural communities. When Proulx turned to journalism, she wrote many articles, essays, and books on subjects tied to the rural lifestyle, such as cooking, making cider, the local fauna and flora, landscape design, or outdoor activities such as gardening, fishing, and hunting. These subjects remain under scrutiny in her fiction as most of her characters engage in such activities. During that same period, Proulx kept up her fiction-writing, publishing short stories in outdoor magazines such as *Esquire Magazine* and *Gray's Sporting Journal*. Proulx first considered herself a short story writer. She has confided that she finds it a superior art form – at once more interesting and more difficult to write than novels. In 1988, her first collection of short stories, *Heart Songs and Other Stories*, set in New England, was published by Charles Scribner's Sons. It garnered much praise, making Proulx perceived as a promising, début writer. Her inimitable, poetic prose, her dry sense of humor, her unsentimental tone, violent plots, and tragic endings are already in place in those tightly written stories. So too are the metonymical relationships between characters and the inhospitable places they inhabit.

Prompted by her editor, Proulx then wrote her first novel, *Postcards*, dealing with the disintegration of the American Dream as New England dairy farmers must confront the harsh economy of the twentieth century. It was published in 1992, with reviews propelling Proulx amongst the best American novelists of the time. The novel tackles inherited violence as male fits of rage on children, women, and animals get passed down from one generation to another. The question of responsibility – and in this case one's blind, utter incapacity to acknowledge and own up to it – lies at the heart of the plot. Indeed, the main character, Loyal Blood, travels the country in an attempt to flee the rape and murder he commits at the beginning of the novel. Threading epistolary exchanges into the novel, nearly each chapter is headed by a handwritten postcard, the only remaining communication between Loyal and his family over the years after his sudden departure from the farm. Most are made to look handwritten, translating the characters' sociolects and idiolects, including grammar and spelling mistakes. In line with the French *Annales* school approach, these provide the illusion of bearing testimony to authentic documents at the level of ordinary people. They translate the local characters' voices – unmediated by the third-person, omniscient narrator otherwise in charge of the storytelling. Sometimes the postcards have to do with orders, medical appointments, bills, and other ordinary business. By then, some of the traits characteristic of Proulx's writing are salient, that is, her ruthless plotting of implacably dark fates for arrogant or ignorant characters, often depicted as brutal and moronic, intellectually or emotionally maimed, and given to betrayal; the contrasting, caustic tone and shrewd insight of her narrators; the unforgiving roughness of both characters and places; and lurid violence, mostly carried out by men, with rampant outbursts of aggression, rape, incest, and murder.

Proulx's second novel, *The Shipping News*, set in Newfoundland, was published the following year, attracting even more enthusiastic reviews and promptly becoming a bestseller. The novel dramatizes a family and community subsisting from fishing in inclement weather and economies – the intensive evolution of the fishing industry coupled with oil drilling again endangering traditional lifestyles and skills. Instead of postcards as epigraphs to each separate chapter, this novel foregrounds sketches and descriptions of knots reproduced from *The Ashley Book of Knots* (1944), alternating with definitions from *The Mariner's Dictionary* (1952) that echo the chapter titles. This paratext often serves as a metatextual comment, casting light on the intricate weaving at play in the novelistic craft, as well as on the entanglements between the characters and their natural and cultural environments. Of all Proulx's novels this may be the one with the happiest ending.

Growing even more epic in scope, *Accordion Crimes* came out in 1996. Spanning a historical background that extends from the late nineteenth century to the late twentieth, the novel travels in both space and time. The title refers to the musical instrument that moves across the country as it constantly changes owners over a period of a century, first landing on the American continent together with a Sicilian immigrant. As such, the accordion symbolizes the folk culture that was progressively swallowed up via decades of immigration and assimilation into the melting pot and fabric of American culture. Again mixing novelistic prose with a form of archives, Proulx has included pictures of many different types of accordions and related instruments. Grappling with the failure of the American Dream myth, the novel offers a bleak vision of the history of the United States. Written as a novel, it however contains multiple stories, with eight separate sections and different characters. Some critics have argued that the novel's fragmentary composition likens it to a collection of short stories.

Proulx then returned to the short story genre, with a collection that was to be the first of three *Wyoming Stories* books. Published in 1999, *Close Range* included some stories that had first been published in *The New Yorker*, winning her wide acclaim. Two of those stories earned Proulx the year's best short story O. Henry Prize, namely "Brokeback Mountain" in 1998 and "The Mud Below" in 1999. With the following two collections, titled *Bad Dirt* (2004) and *Fine Just the Way It Is* (2008), Proulx's created a cycle, or sequence, of Wyoming stories, with many an overarching theme, motif, and even sometimes recurring characters and places.

In 2002, Proulx published her fourth novel, *That Old Ace in the Whole*. Taking place in the Texas and Oklahoma panhandle, the novel recounts the slow waning of small hog farms as they get gobbled up by the intensive farming industry. As with most of her fiction, this novel is both amusing and disturbing, written in colorful, taut prose. Once again, characters strive to make it in extremely harsh landscape and weather. As with her Wyoming stories, the novel takes place in tough ranch country. While retracing the grim development of the hog industry in the United States, the novel also winds through many laces as it focuses now and then on secondary characters whose backstories lead to meandering analepses, traveling back in time and often through different parts of the country too.

As Proulx was working on the last of her three collections of Wyoming stories, she simultaneously edited a coffee table book with photographs by Martin Stupich. Devoted to one of the then least developed places in the United States, the book represented an effort to protect this central and southwest Wyoming wildness, endangered by industries seeking to exploit the area's natural resources. The book was published in 2008, under the title *Red Desert: A History of Place*. Proulx and Stupich called on a transdisciplinary group of scientists and scholars to write chapters dealing with the history and value of the Red Desert from the standpoint of anthropology, archeology, botany, climatology, geology, history, hydrology, ornithology, paleontology, sociology, and zoology.

Proulx's most recent and longest novel, *Barskins*, was published in 2016. It has been announced as her last piece of fiction. In this novel in particular, Proulx's environmental concern occupies the front stage. She has even confided that she would from now on dedicate herself solely to nonfiction environmental writing. Covering over 700 pages and a timeline of 320 years, *Barskins* is the most ambitious of all of Annie Proulx's works. If some critics, as with her previous novels, have found that the novel rambled at times while some characters may have deserved more development and detail, Proulx's epic novel sweeps through the history of deforestation in North America. As much of her other fiction, this book lends itself to an ecofeminist reading – here with beautiful, contemporary, forest ecopoetics. Her ecological saga is also a postcolonial one, as the novel follows the bloodlines of one couple of European descent and one of mixed European and First Nations descent. Proulx's novel starts with the arrival of French immigrants hired as indentured servants in the woodcutting business in New France, now Quebec, in 1693. The two characters follow widely different destinies that speak worlds about American values, dreams, and somber realities. They thus tease out many of the entangled processes of social and environmental exploitation embedded in capitalism, of gender and ethnic discrimination and oppression throughout centuries, and the long, natural, and cultural devastation and extraction processes we now refer to as colonialism and the Anthropocene. The story takes us from France, to Canada, to the United States, New Zealand, and Greenland, thus tackling those interrelated issues on a global scale too. Rooting the origins of climate change in New World ideologies and values, the novel ends with a vision of melting glaciers in 2013, revealing the planetary scale of Proulx's hard look at the history of the depletion of natural resources. One of the family storylines, that of the Duquets, follows a rags-to-riches plot – a typically American story of individual hard work and success. Embodying the mobility, rootlessness, and individualism that are often the flip of the coin of the American Dream, Duquet runs for his freedom from his master, survives through the wilderness, and eventually builds a fortune reaped from the fur and lumber trades. He then passes on an East Coast empire to a greedy dynasty of descendants. Meanwhile, the other family, the Sels, tell the tragic story of the erasure of First Peoples, together with their cultures and understanding of the more-than-human world. With her Indigenous knowledge about the forest and medicine, Sel's Mi'Kmaq wife, Mari, serves to braid the postcolonial and ecofeminist strands of the novel which border on magical realism, as with many of her *Wyoming Stories* or *Postcards*.

Proulx's constant dabbling with history and geography has kindled much academic interest. Alex Hunt collected brilliant essays on the subject in *The Geographical Imagination of Annie Proulx: Rethinking Regionalism* (2009), tackling her short stories as well as her novels. Some of these scholars have dwelled on the postmodernist dimension and the regional focus of Proulx's landscape writing. Others have paid much attention to her rewriting of the West in her treatment of landscape and male characters. Katie Arosteguy homes in on the cowboy myth and masculine stereotypes of virility in *Close Range* (2010), while Mark Asquith's monograph *The Lost Frontier: Reading Annie Proulx's Wyoming Stories* (2014) uses the frontier myth as a reading lens. Shifting attention to Proulx's female characters to nonhuman nature, as well as to the pervasive use of magical realism in Proulx's short fiction, Bénédicte Meillon has written multiple essays exploring Proulx's playful rewriting of myths, legends, folktales, and fairy tales. Meillon's work sheds light on the intertextual connections that can be traced through Proulx's short story collections. She focuses on the feminist and ecopoetic drives of Proulx's omnivorous, mythopoeic writing, intimating the overall ecofeminist work of deconstruction at play in Annie Proulx's self-reflexive, provocative craft.

SEE ALSO: After Postmodernism; Contemporary Regionalisms; Ecocriticism and Environmental Fiction; Fiction and Affect; Minimalism and Maximalism; Mixed-Genre Fiction; Queer and LGBT Fiction; Realism after Poststructuralism; Story Cycles

REFERENCES

Rood, Karen L. (2001). *Understanding Annie Proulx*. Columbia: University of South Carolina Press.
The Missouri Review. (1999). An Interview with Annie Proulx (March 1, 1999). https://www.missourireview.com/article/an-interview-with-annie-proulx/ (accessed July 22, 2021).

FURTHER READING

Arosteguy, Katie. (2010). "It was all a hard fast ride that ended in the mud": deconstructing the myth of the cowboy in Annie Proulx's *Close Range: Wyoming Stories*. *Western American Literature* 44 (2): 116–136.
Asquith, Mark. (2014). *The Lost Frontier: Reading Annie Proulx's Wyoming Stories*. New York: Bloomsbury.
Hunt, Alex. (2009). *The Geographical Imagination of Annie Proulx: Rethinking Regionalism*. Lanham, MD: Lexington Books.
Meillon, Bénédicte. (2014). Unreal, fantastic, and improbable "flashes of fearful insight" in Annie Proulx's *Wyoming Stories*. *Journal of the Short Story in English* 62: 111–130.
Meillon, Bénédicte. (2014). Inheriting "bad dirt," white trash, and "dump junk": the art of recycling in Annie Proulx's *Wyoming Stories*. In: *Thy Truth Then Be Thy Dowry: Questions of Inheritance in American Women's Literature* (ed. Stéphanie Durrans), 53–72. Newcastle upon Tyne, UK: Cambridge Scholars.
Meillon, Bénédicte. (2018). Silent nature as "a claw in the gut": shock therapy epiphanies in Annie Proulx's *Wyoming Stories*. *Revista Canaria de Estudios Ingleses* 77: 105–125.
Meillon, Bénédicte. (2019). Deconstructing gender roles and digesting the magic of folktales and fairy tales in Annie Proulx's omnivorous *Wyoming Stories*. *L'Ordinaire des Amériques* 224. http://journals.openedition.org/orda/4868

Pynchon, Thomas

DIANA BENEA
University of Bucharest, Romania

Thomas Pynchon's oeuvre has been central to the canonization, the changing contours, and the afterlives of postmodernism. While his first three novels became the epitome of postmodernism in the 1980s, the later works have nonetheless exceeded the frames of that early corpus, bringing to the fore a subtly different imagination that has been argued to gesture *through* and *beyond* postmodernism. Through their signature narrative complexity, interdisciplinary scope of reference, pastiche, linguistic virtuosity, and quirky humor, Pynchon's works focus on such wide-ranging themes as capitalism; colonialism; science and technology; domination and resistance; conspiracy and paranoia – in their various incarnations from early modernity to the contemporary age. While continuing such explorations, the post-*Gravity's Rainbow* (1973) novels illustrate a more transparent and pressing concern with questions of social justice, ethical relationality, and the viability of (political) communities, thus significantly reorienting our understanding of Pynchon's entire body of works.

Pynchon was born on May 8, 1937, in Glen Cove, New York in a family whose roots can be traced back to magistrate and theologian William Pynchon, one of the founders of the Massachusetts Bay Colony. In 1953 Pynchon enrolled in the Engineering Physics major at Cornell University, but left the program in 1955 to serve in the US Navy. Two years later, he returned to Cornell and graduated from the BA program in English in 1959. He then published several short stories through the mid-1960s: "The Small Rain" and "Mortality and Mercy in Vienna" (1959), "Low-Lands" and the widely anthologized "Entropy" (1960), "Under the Rose" (1961), and "The Secret Integration" (1964). The year 1963 saw the publication of Pynchon's first novel, *V.*, which received the Faulkner Foundation Award for the best debut novel of the year, as well as a nomination for the National Book Award. He received a Rosenthal Foundation Award for his second novel, *The Crying of Lot 49* (1966), and shared a National Book Award (with Isaac Bashevis Singer) for his monumental *Gravity's Rainbow*. The seventeen-year silence between his third and fourth novel, *Vineland* (1990), was broken only once, with the publication of his collected short stories, except for "Mortality and Mercy in Vienna," in *Slow Learner* (1984), which also featured an autobiographical introduction about his apprenticeship as a writer and retrospective comments on the stories. In 1988 Pynchon was awarded a five-year MacArthur Foundation Fellowship. *Mason & Dixon* appeared in 1997, followed by the massive *Against the Day* in 2006, *Inherent Vice* in 2009, and *Bleeding Edge* in 2013, which was also nominated for the National Book Award. Over the years, Pynchon has also published essays on the Watts riots (1966), Luddism and technology (1984), and sloth and "the rise of evil regimes" (1993); a review of Gabriel García Márquez (1988); forewords to a posthumous collection by Donald Barthelme (1992) and to reprints of works by Richard Fariña (1983), Jim Dodge (1997), and George Orwell (2003); letters of support; liner notes. A notoriously private figure, Pynchon lived in Seattle in the early 1960s while working as a technical writer for Boeing, then in Mexico until 1964, and mostly in California through the 1980s. Since around 1989, he has lived in NYC with his wife and son (Krafft 2012).

Pynchon's first three novels famously thematize the postmodern condition through the lens of two concepts that have ever since been associated with his work: entropy, or, "the progression towards inanimateness" (Pynchon 1963, p. 442), and paranoia, or, the cognitive mode in which "*everything is connected*, everything in the Creation" (Pynchon 1973, p. 703). While the paranoid hermeneutic at the heart of these quest narratives is meant to expose the ways in which various interlocking power structures join efforts in order to shape the course of history, the opposite anti-paranoid stance, holding that "nothing is connected to anything, a condition not many of us can bear for too long" (p. 434), emerges as an equally undesirable scenario. The only alternative to Herbert Stencil's paranoid search for the ever-shifting female figure

V. of the eponymous novel, which takes him through various scenes of conflict and massacre in Europe and Africa between 1898 and 1943, is Benny Profane's random yo-yoing and the solipsism of the Whole Sick Crew in the narrative present of the novel, the mid-1950s. Named co-executrix of the estate of an ex-lover, Oedipa Maas of *The Crying of Lot 49* navigates an ever-multiplying network of historical and political phenomena seemingly associated with the subversive mailing system Tristero, arriving at the conviction that there is either "another mode of meaning behind the obvious," inherent in Tristero's existence, "or none" (1966, p. 150). Through Oedipa's quest, the novel also narrativizes entropy in its communication theory sense – the more signifiers she discovers (or "projects," like the tower maidens in Remedios Varo's painting), the less coherent is the signified. Likewise, the only alternative to the They-system of *Gravity's Rainbow* is a Counterforce that eventually proves "as schizoid, as double-minded" (1973, p. 712) as its supposed antagonist; in such circumstances, the quester of the novel, American lieutenant Tyrone Slothrop, ends up "scattering" across the German landscape, in an ambivalent act suggesting either his liberation from, or inescapable subjection to, the conglomerate of state and corporate powers responsible for his conditioning. Holding the promise of a grand epiphany about historical patterns and the interrelated workings of political, economic, and technological power, these quests remain inconclusive, while the possibility of individual resistance is equally unresolved.

On the strength of these three canon-forming novels, Pynchon has been traditionally read as the postmodern fabulist of a world in decline and a central figure of the paranoid tradition in American fiction, alongside William Gaddis and Don DeLillo; however, starting with his fourth novel, scholars have suggested that we might be witnessing a shift of sensibility and a turn towards an "attenuated postmodernism" (Cowart 1990) in his work. This critical argument has been reinforced with each new novel, as part of broader reflections aligning late Pynchon with an emerging cultural mode variously designated as post-postmodernism, late postmodernism, or metamodernism.

Set in 1984, *Vineland* charts America's transformation from the revolutionary energies of the 1960s to the Reaganite backlash – even more ominously, to the "pre-fascist twilight" (1990, p. 371) – of the 1980s, through the stories of complicity and co-optation of one-time countercultural figures like Frenesi Gates, the absent center of the novel. While early reviewers lamented the waning of Pynchon's historical depth and narrative complexity, *Vineland* engages with thematic concerns only marginally addressed hitherto. Departing from the circularity of the epistemological quests and the social atomization of the first three novels, the narrative is structured around a radically different quest, that of teenager Prairie Wheeler for her mother, Frenesi Gates, and for a broader sense of community. The novel features the first detailed genealogy in Pynchon's work, comprising the previous two generations of Frenesi's line – a family history which overlaps with that of the twentieth-century American Left, from Eula and Jess' life in the service of Wobbly principles, to Sasha and Hubb's unionism in the blacklist 1950s, to young Frenesi's New Left agenda, to Prairie's emerging political *Bildung*, with its distinctly feminist orientation cultivated via her apprenticeship at the Sisterhood of Kunoichi Attentives, one of the particularly sustainable communities of the novel. While none of these strands is idealized, in a fictional universe otherwise saturated by the Tube, the annual gathering of the trans-generational Becker-Traverse family on the pasture of Vineland functions as the remnant of a viable historical and political consciousness – and a reminder that antagonists like federal prosecutor Brock Vond might be defeated after all, if only in a *deus ex machina* move. The narrative strand centered on the ghostly Thanatoids also enhances the thematic focus on the question of working through the ambivalent legacy of leftist "revenants" in recent American history, and the possibility of their "karmic" readjustment with a present that, as the self-reliant Prairie suggests, is still rife with political potential.

Narrated in 1786 by the Rev. Wicks Cherrycoke (and occasionally by an extra-diegetic narrator), *Mason & Dixon* mixes historical accuracy and dazzling fabulation in its chronicle of the surveying and drawing of the boundary line between Pennsylvania and Maryland between 1763 and 1767, which later came to be regarded as the demarcation between the North and the South of the United States. The trope of "America" becomes the vehicle for an exploration of the complicated legacy of modernity through the lens of three intersecting phenomena: nation-making (and the correlative "ghosting" of communities that do not fit with the idea of the nation), early global capitalism (and its problematic reliance on practices of enslavement and oppression), and scientific rationalism (and its tensions with anti-rationalist forms of knowledge, such as the many instances of "magic" encountered by the two protagonists in their American adventures). In the early modern America of the 1760s, the boundary marker unwittingly promotes an agenda of rational nationalism, performing an act of material and symbolic violence upon a space that was by no means blank but actually inscribed by Native American spatialities and temporalities. The line therefore stands for a series of conversions: from wilderness to order, from openness to enclosure, from "nature" to "civilization," and from "the Subjunctive World" of Native spirituality to the "dreamless Indicative" (1997, p. 677) of the Age of Reason. The novel also offers Pynchon's first sustained exploration of an intersubjective relationship, tracing the vagaries of the friendship between the self-proclaimed rational Dixon and the more mystical Mason, portrayed as "Twins, ever in Dispute" (p. 689), forever oscillating between fusion and separation. In the homogenizing context of an embryonic America where the Native American population is systematically "ghosted" into non-existence, Mason and Dixon's communion across difference (also suggested by the ampersand in the title) might serve indeed as a model for a more hospitable stance towards Otherness. Narrated in mock eighteenth-century English by a self-consciously "untrustworthy Remembrancer" (p. 8) and full of playful yet thought-provoking anachronisms, the novel is a veritable historiographic metafiction, sharing affinities with other examples of the genre coined by Linda Hutcheon, such as works by Kurt Vonnegut and E.L. Doctorow. As such, *Mason & Dixon* invites reflection not only on the inescapable textuality of history-writing, but also on the different paths the New World could have taken to avoid the devastating effects of a "Bad History" (p. 615) of divisions and dispossessions.

Against the Day interweaves several plotlines and a cast of more than four hundred characters in its exploration of a wide range of political crises spanning from the 1890s to the years after World War I, such as the labor conflicts in Colorado, anarchist activities in Europe, and the Mexican revolution, among others. The most prominent of these storylines is the Traverse saga, which focuses at first on Webb Traverse, the prime anarchist of the novel and father of *Vineland*'s Jess Traverse, and his clash with plutocrat Scarsdale Vibe. In line with the post-*Gravity's Rainbow* emphasis on family ties, the latter sections of this strand orbit around Webb's sons' attempts to avenge the murder of their father at the hands of Vibe's mercenaries, highlighting questions of ethical obligation. The anarchists of the novel emerge as the locus of an alternative vision of society, founded on ideals of freedom and social justice, thus interrogating an America that has delivered itself "into the hands of capitalists and Christers" (2006, p. 643). The book is at the same time an unorthodox 9/11 fiction, infrequently referenced in the 9/11 canon, which not only allegorizes the scene of the attacks (in the Vormance episode), but also reveals the ways in which previous historical periods can function as distant mirrors for our present, by displacing the phenomenon of terrorism onto a different era. Shifting the emphasis to an earlier incarnation of "terrorist" violence in the domestic late nineteenth-century conflict between plutocrats and anarchists, the novel thus destabilizes the newness of the terrorist narrative prompted by 9/11, calling attention to similarities in the rhetorical construction of the terrorist, then and now. Frequently referencing topoi, motifs, and imagery from the previous works, *Against the Day* is also an anthology of popular genres, incorporating and rewriting the conventions of genres that were in vogue during its narrated time, such as the boys adventure series, the Western, the spy novel, or the scientific romance à la H.G. Wells (McHale 2011).

Inherent Vice offers yet another pastiche of (and homage to) a popular genre, hard-boiled detective fiction, while returning to the chronotope of Pynchon's more strictly American novels, namely, California and the 1960s. As the third part of what has been referred to as his California trilogy, the novel builds upon some of the thematic concerns of *Vineland*, particularly the corruption of the 1960s ideals of social change. Furthermore, it consolidates the ethical and political imagination of Pynchon's later novels by bringing to the fore two particularly productive sites of analysis: the urban space of LA and the profile of private eye Doc Sportello. Prefaced by a translation of the famous graffito of the Paris uprisings of May 1968, *Inherent Vice* is a meditation on the equivalence of spatial and social justice and the possibility of reforming or at least re-envisioning urban space away from the capitalist logic of unsustainability and social stratification. Pynchon's environmental critique is more transparent than ever before in a novel whose plot revolves around the spoilage of American land – dramatized through real estate mogul Mickey Wolfmann's failed moral conversion from greedy developmental drive to environmentally-friendly housing à la visionary Buckminster Fuller. In line with the ambivalent construction of Vineland at the intersection of utopian and dystopian frames, the novel juxtaposes the critique of a depleted California caught in the clutches of unsustainable development, environmental hazards, and displacement through urban renewal, with an irrepressible longing for the "subjunctive" and possibly redeeming space of the mythical Lemuria. Through his unwavering allegiance to a code of honor that self-consciously opposes the climate of paranoia and "moral ambiguity" (2009, p. 7) of the late 1960s, Doc emerges as the most decidedly ethical figure in the Pynchon canon, his construction as a stock character notwithstanding. Through truth-telling practices reminiscent of the *parrhesiastes* of ancient Greece, he also functions as a counterweight to the politics of *Gleichschaltung* (literally translating as "bringing into the same line") and systematic repression of resistance that pervades the world of the novel (Benea 2017).

Another iteration of the detective story in quotation marks, *Bleeding Edge* begins in New York City, in the spring of 2001, and focuses on fraud specialist Maxine Tarnow's investigation into the operations of a company that has survived the dotcom crisis. The novel takes forward the environmental concerns of *Inherent Vice*, and, more broadly, Pynchon's enduring interest in the spatial transformation of America – from the colonial times of *Mason & Dixon* to the turn of the millennium in his latest work. Mapped onto a "Disneyfied" metropolis from which "the unkempt and unhoused and unspoken-for have been pushed out" (2013, p. 51), Maxine's quest serves as a vehicle for another mournful critique of the inherent or perhaps acquired vices of the American real estate system. Furthermore, this quest unfolds not only in the physical space, or "meatspace," of NYC, but also in cyberspace – more specifically, in Deep Archer, a bleeding-edge program whose promising beginnings are seemingly informed by a collaborative, de-hierarchized, and non-commercial ethos. The novel interrogates, however, the utopian potential and even the neutrality of such new technologies and the communities formed around them, which turn out to be as liable to appropriation by governmental and corporate interests as the almost-forgotten ancestor of the Internet, the Cold War DARPAnet. In the wake of the destabilizing experience of 9/11, the narrative locates more authentic and viable spaces of relationality in the "meatspace" community of Maxine's extended circle of family and friends. Departing from the allegorical mode of *Against the Day* to engage with 9/11 in a straightforward manner, the latest novel is nonetheless organized around a similar imaginary of the event, which emerges as a "privileged little window" (2013, p. 432) onto a more empathetic understanding of the humanity of the Other, as well as onto the global interconnectedness of the United States. Significantly, in the post-9/11 part of the novel, Maxine's inquiries morph into a quest for connectivity and care, not only within the private sphere of the family (via a narrative focus on parenting reminiscent of *Vineland*'s Prairie and Zoyd Wheeler), but also beyond it, as illustrated at one point by her particularly poignant encounter with a transient community of fellow subway passengers. While both her predecessor Oedipa Mass and Maxine have to navigate entropic labyrinths of clues, the latter not only exhibits a more nuanced moral profile, but is also invested with more agency in her quest, as well as in matters of negotiating gender roles within and beyond her family.

Reflecting the encyclopedic character of the oeuvre itself, the vast scope of Pynchon criticism has examined the novels through the diverse lenses of their representations of history and history-writing; scientific paradigms; religion and myth; political visions, from liberal to anarchist; gender and sexuality; spatiality and temporality; as well as, more recently, through approaches informed by ecocriticism, posthumanism, or new materialism, to name only some of the critical tools that have been brought to bear on this challenging yet immensely rewarding corpus and its vibrant imagination.

SEE ALSO: After Postmodernism; DeLillo, Don; Doctorow, E.L.; Ecocriticism and Environmental Fiction; Fiction and Terrorism; Gaddis, William; Periodization; Post-9/11 Narratives; Vonnegut, Kurt

REFERENCES

Benea, Diana. (2017). *The Political Imagination of Thomas Pynchon's Later Novels*. Bucharest: Ars Docendi – University of Bucharest Press.

Cowart, David. (1990). Attenuated postmodernism: Pynchon's *Vineland*. *Critique* 32 (2): 67–76.

Hutcheon, Linda. (1988). *A Poetics of Postmodernism: History, Theory, Fiction*. London: Routledge.

Krafft, John M. (2012). Biographical note. In: *The Cambridge Companion to Thomas Pynchon* (ed. Inger H. Dalsgaard, Luc Herman, and Brian McHale), 9–15. Cambridge: Cambridge University Press.

McHale, Brian. (2011). Genre as history: Pynchon's genre poaching. In: *Pynchon's "Against the Day": A Corrupted Pilgrim's Guide* (ed. Jeffrey Severs and

Christopher Leise), 15–28. Newark: University of Delaware Press.

Pynchon, Thomas. (1963). *V.* Philadelphia: Lippincott.

Pynchon, Thomas. (1966). *The Crying of Lot 49*. Philadelphia: Lippincott.

Pynchon, Thomas. (1973). *Gravity's Rainbow*. New York: Viking.

Pynchon, Thomas. (1990). *Vineland*. Boston: Little, Brown.

Pynchon, Thomas. (1997). *Mason & Dixon*. New York: Henry Holt.

Pynchon, Thomas. (2006). *Against the Day*. New York: Penguin.

Pynchon, Thomas. (2009). *Inherent Vice*. New York: Penguin.

Pynchon, Thomas. (2013). *Bleeding Edge*. New York: Penguin.

FURTHER READING

Chetwynd, Ali, Freer, Joanna, and Maragos, Georgios. (eds.) (2018). *Thomas Pynchon, Sex, and Gender*. Athens: University of Georgia Press.

Dalsgaard, Inger H. (ed.) (2019). *Thomas Pynchon in Context*. Cambridge: Cambridge University Press.

Freer, Joanna. (ed.) (2019). *The New Pynchon Studies*. Cambridge: Cambridge University Press.

Herman, Luc and Weisenburger, Steven. (2013). *"Gravity's Rainbow," Domination, and Freedom*. Athens: University of Georgia Press.

Krafft, John M., Tölölyan, Khachig, and Duyfhuizen, Bernard. (eds.) (1979–2009). *Pynchon Notes*. https://pynchonnotes.openlibhums.org/

Queer and LGBT Fiction

E.L. MCCALLUM
Michigan State University, USA

We cannot fully appreciate the proliferation of LGBTQ+ American fiction in the past forty years without a clear sense of the social changes that drove this cultural flowering, many of which were set in motion decades before the 1980s. The 1969 Stonewall uprising, which now retrospectively is widely taken to mark the start of the gay liberation movement and the emergence of modern LGBTQ+ civil rights activism, happened in the context of considerable social upheaval. There was an ongoing foreign war and a military draft – when being homosexual in the armed forces could get you dishonorably discharged. At home, vibrant civil rights movements advocating for equality for Black, Latinx/Chicanx, and Indigenous Americans had been gaining traction in transforming society, while the feminist movement was similarly changing minds and laws about the role of women in society. The student movement's protests of the draft and the Vietnam war converged with these other progressive movements for racial, ethnic, sexual, and gender equality. The election of Ronald Reagan in 1980, however, marked a starkly conservative turn in mainstream US politics, a backlash to the liberal optimism of prior decades. This conservative turn coincided with the first clinical reports in 1981 of the syndrome that came to be known as HIV/AIDS, and whose deathly shadow loomed large over the next two decades within queer cultures and – eventually – the mainstream.

In the face of this crisis of representation in the 1980s – that is, the refusal of those in power in our representative democracy to address the needs of all their constituents – came a turning point in representation – that is, innovation in not only fiction's content, but the strategies and styles for fiction's depiction of worlds. As LGBTQ+ folks fought for increased visibility and reduced homophobia in the social world, many felt a need for stories centering lesbian or gay characters. But how do we tell these stories? Do LGBTQ+ characters need different forms of narrative, different modes of representation?

We can start to answer this question by looking at three defining books published in 1982: *Zami: A Biomythography* by Audre Lorde; *The Color Purple* by Alice Walker; and *A Boy's Own Story* by Edmund White. It is striking that two of these push the limit between life and literature. *Zami* invents a new genre, biomythography, to tell a life story by lesbian icon and poet Audre Lorde, while White's book, often

The Encyclopedia of Contemporary American Fiction 1980–2020, First Edition. Edited by Patrick O'Donnell, Stephen J. Burn, and Lesley Larkin.
© 2022 John Wiley & Sons Ltd. Published 2022 by John Wiley & Sons Ltd.

considered semi-autobiographical, focusing on an unnamed narrator, inaugurates a trilogy of novels (*The Beautiful Room is Empty* [1988], and *The Farewell Symphony* [1997]). The close proximity of life to page touches on the fact that LGBTQ+ fiction is particularly predisposed to readers seeking it out in search of connection and identity. Moreover, all three books herald how so much LGBTQ+ fiction comes to contest the practices of conventional genres, suggesting we do need new ways to tell queer stories.

We often read fiction to see ourselves in a world, even – or especially – if our actual world fails to find room for us. LGBTQ+ fiction historically has enabled queer readers to forge a self, to bridge the sense of isolation they may feel in reality by reading how someone like themselves navigates a fictional world, or to indulge in more imaginative explorations of how those in a fully queer world relate to one another. In short, fiction both provides key lessons in how to be gay and transmits LGBTQ+ cultural knowledge, as quite a few critics have observed. Prefacing her 1994 anthology, Lilian Faderman reflects that "In 1956, as a teenager, I began to consider myself a lesbian. Almost as soon as I claimed that identity, being enamored of books, of course I looked around for literary representations that would help explain me to myself" (1994, p. vii). Yet not all novels provide a mirror to the world or offer a place of self-identification for every reader. While a number of white gay or lesbian readers found solace, community, or even respectability in canonical English-language literature, the overwhelming whiteness of the Western literary canon meant that "queer and trans of color readers tend . . . to continue to search for, and ultimately construct, something else," (Ponce 2018, pp. 319–320) than the canon, although as Martin Joseph Ponce acknowledges, "it would be impertinent to assume that queer readers of color cannot lay claim to canonical traditions or identify with certain representations on specious grounds of 'cultural difference'" (p. 320). In short, there is leeway in how readers lay claim to LGBTQ+ fiction to negotiate their sense of self or community, and likewise the question of what constitutes LGBTQ+ fiction is not as, er, straightforward – as these three 1982 books attest.

Zami has proved the book with the strongest staying power – indeed, it has become foundational in discussions of LGBTQ+ writing across genres. One key to *Zami*'s longevity is the intersectionality of Lorde's work: her biomythography not only elucidates a range of ways of expressing same-sex desire, but also refracts these experiences through lenses of ethnicity, class, race, (dis)ability, and gender. For Lorde, such differences afford connections across communities – feminist activists in New York, factory workers in CT, family and school life growing up, Caribbean immigrant experience, etc. The book celebrates the love of Black women by Black women, depicting them as desirable as well as desiring. Yet the negotiation of interracial same-sex relationships also comes into focus, illustrating some of the gaps as well as overlaps in women's lived experiences. In an important sense, *Zami* anchors the main strands in the trajectory of LGBTQ+ fiction: it is a life-based story, so it deploys strategies of realism, but it's also a poet's novel, a book which is consciously inventing a new form, the biomythography. Setting this prose masterpiece alongside the work of LGBTQ+ fiction is essential to understanding the field because of the power of the genre of autofiction and realist, character-driven works in this period; yet *Zami* is also important for how it imagines the world otherwise, even as it draws on a lived, actual world of a particular poet in a particular place to support that vision.

Zami was published by Persephone Press, an independent feminist press founded in 1976 by a lesbian collective; it is rooted in precisely the cultural efflorescence made possible by the liberation movements in US society in the 1960s and 1970s. Its provenance contrasts with *The Color Purple*, Alice Walker's epistolary novel centering a lesbian narrator/protagonist, which was published the same year by Harcourt Brace Jovanovich (HBJ). HBJ at the time was a mainstream press with a pedigree of literary prestige – such canonical authors as Virginia Woolf, James Thurber, Sinclair Lewis, and Robert Penn Warren published with them. Thus, Walker's book was well-positioned to win both the National Book Award and Pulitzer Prize, as it did in 1983. The broad visibility of *The Color Purple* brought a Black lesbian-centered story into the hands of many who might not otherwise have turned to this tale set in rural Georgia and Africa. Like *Zami*, *The Color Purple* imagines a range of ways that Black women love each other and form communities: not just the central pair of lovers, Celie, the lesbian narrator/letter-writer, and Shug Avery, the bisexual blues singer who brings Celie into her world, but also Celie's sister Nettie, Celie's (step)daughter-in-law Sofia, and Squeak, who succeeds Sofia in Celie's stepson's bed and emerges as a singer in her own right, among several others. While this range of familial and quasi-familial relations may not look like a particularly lesbian or queer community, Celie's love for Shug – and Shug's reciprocity of that love – is the fulcrum of the novel, bolstered by Celie's love for her sister. The acceptance of Celie's and Shug's relationship among their intimate community – at least, as accepted as any romantic coupling that disrupts other pairings is – shifts the novel into new terms of engagement that remain uncommon for a mass audience even now, much less in 1982. Insofar as it weaves among lesbian and heterosexual relationships and is published by a mainstream rather than LGBTQ+-oriented press, *The Color Purple* also sharpens the question of how do we define LGBTQ+ fiction – is this a lesbian novel? Beyond pondering whether LGBTQ+ fiction is simply about same-sex desire, foregrounds LGBTQ+ characters no matter who writes it, or must be stories by self-identified LGBTQ+ writers (Walker identifies as bisexual), we should consider whether there are particular styles of storytelling or plot that gay or lesbian fiction engenders? How does LGBTQ+ content require reconsideration of conventional form?

Walker's epistolary form, a centuries-old genre of the novel, adds a different dimension to the realist orientation of LGBTQ+ fiction than Lorde's and White's autofictional approaches; the letter form feels intimate and authentic yet it remains autonomous from the author's life. Care is the dominant mode of Walker's novel's ethical advocacy, and the epistolary form fortifies that affirmative connection. While *The Color Purple* depicts abusive relationships and devastating oppressions (sexist, racist, and colonialist), its parsing of the ways Black women love sets the novel alongside *Zami* as fundamental texts in exploring how queer passions and same-sex desire might be represented as part of counter-patriarchal and antiracist activist strategies. Both *Zami* and *The Color Purple* set the stage for progressive and intersectional politics of LGBTQ+ fiction.

A conflicted alignment with white patriarchy also structures White's *A Boy's Own Story*, although the limited degree to which it questions whiteness or class privilege in its focus on negotiating being gay in a homophobic world seems dated now. Recounting a life before Stonewall, *ABOS* tells of an upper-class adolescent boy struggling with the knowledge of his sexual attraction to other men and how it locates him in the world. While *ABOS* depicts a number of different sexual encounters the protagonist has, these moments of bodily intimacy occur in a context of alienation and isolation; no other gay or lesbian characters provide community or even solace, and the unnamed narrator confronts his homosexuality largely alone. This is not to say that he doesn't find other gay individuals – he does, although the boys he shags are at pains to distance themselves from identifying as homosexual (as the time would term them). Rather, the gay men he meets are also closeted and conflicted by their sexuality. It's quite a contrast to the worlds of Walker or Lorde, where despite episodes of loneliness or alienation, the protagonists do ultimately find connection and community. Notwithstanding its limitations, White's novel became a classic in the gay canon; its poetic language transcends the confined world of 1950s homophobic America and its provincial privilege while the nonlinear unfolding of the plot begins to chafe at dominant narrative convention.

White's novel might be instructively contrasted with David Levithan's *Boy Meets Boy* (2003), a vitally out, proud, and even utopian view of those same high school years some three decades after Stonewall. Levithan's novel opens with the inscription on the narrator's kindergarten report card "Paul is gay, and has a very strong sense of self"; the level of acceptance in Levithan's diegetic world is inspiring. Arrayed around Paul are friends gay, straight, trans, queer, and lesbian – in short, precisely the community that is lacking in *ABOS*. Of course, not all is well in this novel's world; Paul's good friend Tony, son of a fundamentalist-religious family the next town over, is closeted with his family though out to Paul and his friends. But the broad acceptance – not just tolerance, but embrace of LGBTQ+ people and cultural practices – means that *BMB*'s plot conflicts can focus on the machinations of high school romance angst – and its queer possibilities – rather than on inner struggle or opposition to society. The utopian disposition of *BMB* veers it sharply away from the autofiction genre, even as it remains in the vein of realist fiction.

And while twenty years later the world has still not fully caught up with *BMB*'s vision, its own two-decade distance from *ABOS* marks a significant change in what is possible in the realist genre.

If *BMB* offers one example of how LGBTQ+ fiction builds on *Zami*'s desire to imagine the world otherwise, fiction genres that outright embrace fantasy offer a whole other set of possibilities. Although usually based in realist narrative styles, speculative fiction helps us imagine the world otherwise. Such genres as science fiction, fantasy, gothic, and Afrofuturism have been spaces where writers of color and women find audiences and construct that "something else" that Ponce points to beyond the canon. Speculative fiction – from Ursula LeGuin's *The Left Hand of Darkness* (1969), to Samuel Delany's sci-fi novels like *Stars in My Pocket Like Grains of Sand* (1984) – has found ample space to explore and experiment with imagining queer desires and genders. LGBTQ+ speculative fiction could be its own chapter, but it is notable that recent Afrofuturist novels, like N.K. Jemisin's *Inheritance Trilogy* (2010–2011) or her Hugo Award-winning *The Fifth Season* (2015), smoothly incorporate queer and trans characters, even if not centering them in a predominantly heterosexual world. Vampire stories, such as Jewelle Gomez's lesbian vampire in *The Gilda Stories* (1991), have proved to be especially hospitable for queer imagining, since as critics note the vampire's marginalized social situation resonates with the closeted queer. This is perhaps not surprising, given that the classic stories of the gothic, rooted in late eighteenth- and early nineteenth-century fiction, were penned by gay writers or even used the vampire trope as a way to represent same-sex desire. Gomez's modern treatment of the vampire foregrounds questions of sexuality, kinship, and Blackness over the ages, adroitly recasting the gothic with deeper considerations of history, belonging, exchange, and identity in ways that transcend the genre. Similarly, Randall Kenan's vividly gothic novel *A Visitation of Spirits* (1989) – set in the fictional community of Tims Creek NC, a rural African American Christian town – may follow the convention of ending with the gay character's death, but its blurring of real, imaginary, and psychotic spaces sets a new standard for how to queer realist fiction through speculative genres.

The life-based fiction trend continued into the 1990s with landmark novels like Leslie Feinberg's *Stone Butch Blues* (1993), which hews closely and powerfully to the author's own experience. *SBB* gives a compelling account of gender-nonconfomity and queer desire, through lenses of butch dyke or trans man (there's interpretative flexibility). The first-person narrative of Jess Goldberg, a working-class butch, spans growing up in the 1950s, working in a factory in the 1960s, and passing as a man in the 1970s isolated from a queer or feminist community. The novel bracingly confronts the violence – sexual and physical – visited upon Jess for presenting masculine, and it starkly lays out the risks LGBTQ+ people faced before Stonewall even just gathering in a bar where they could build community and be themselves. The economic precarity of blue-collar workers, particularly those who don't have union jobs or who lack access to licenses, diplomas, or degrees when the certifying institutions police gender norms, is a key concern as well, laying out the challenges for being able not only to get by but to access gender-supporting health care (like breast reduction surgery or hormones). As difficult as some moments are, the novel also shares the affirmative aspects of queer and trans life – the alternative kinship models and ways of transmitting queer culture, the satisfactions of finding love and intimacy that aligns with one's deepest sense of self, and the triumphs of being able to be oneself out in the world (Jess is thrilled to be passing as a man in a barbershop). *SBB* is very much a Bildungsroman, focused on an individual's development, but it is also a novel of community and cultural formation. Like *Zami*, *SBB* launched a new mythos or set of coordinates to navigate LGBTQ+ lives and cultures, beyond a middle-class, normatively-gendered mainstream.

Maggie Nelson's *The Argonauts* (2015) takes up this lineage of queer/trans fiction that skims the surface of life, but shifts to full-on queering of genre and life through its combination of autofiction and queer theory. The narrator reflects on her family – her own child and experience of pregnancy in begetting that child, her nonbinary partner and his son, her mother and stepfather – as well as engages with a wide range of heady intellectual texts, from Judith Butler's *Gender Trouble* (1990) or D.W. Winnicott's object-relations theory, to Eve Kosofsky Sedgwick's queer theory or Audre Lorde's *Cancer Journals* (1980). How queer is it when one repeats the configurations of heteronormativity with a family photo mug featuring two differently gendered parents and two kids, the narrator ponders. Praised as a brilliant and groundbreaking text, *The Argonauts*' exploration of gender, kinship, marriage, genre, and commitment challenges conventions both conceptual and formalist, of identity and fiction. Rather than plot, the drive of the narrator to figure things out, to question relentlessly but also striving to express precisely, holds this text together.

That effort to narrate the full range of LGBTQ+ experience impels some writers to answer our earlier question, do LGBTQ+ characters need different forms of narrative, different modes of representation?, with an unequivocal yes. Alongside realism and speculative genres, experimental modes of fiction emerged that afforded new ways of representing same-sex desire. Experimental fiction investigates how to break through conventions of representation, through formal innovation at the level of syntax, narrative structure, or finding new routes for pleasure in reading, even embracing displeasure. While experimental fiction may do some of the work of facilitating queer readers' identification, and may even share similar political and identitarian commitments that realist LGBTQ+ fiction explicitly foregrounds, experimental fiction's use of identity and sexuality has a different orientation. Nelson's book presents one such example; its veering between domestic narrative and philosophizing and intellectual reflection in a pastiche of genres is comparable to Delany's *The Mad Man* (1994), which integrates even more sexually explicit stories and undomesticated relations among philosophical reflections, or Eileen Myles's *Inferno* (2016), which proclaims itself as a poet's novel but as reviewer Heather Cromarty (2012) notes, "[t]he narrative, while substantial, functions as foundation for rumination and philosophy. It too is about pulling pieces together."

Experimental fiction is often keen to push beyond the depth subjectivity of selfhood or provide an outlet for the bad affect(s) that contestatory politics requires. Acknowledging the negative – shame, cruelty, exploitation, the pornographic – can be a powerful aesthetic practice. Within experimental fiction, the legacy of New Narrative offers particularly queer examples of rule-breaking fiction to consider, as early practitioners like Robert Glück (*Jack the Modernist* [1985; republished 1996]) openly embraced forms like pornography considered beyond the pale of polite society.

New Narrative originates in the San Francisco poetry scene during the turn from the 1970s to the 1980s as a reaction to the mores of avant-garde American writing of the time, "when 'self' and 'story' were arguably considered retrograde" as Rob Halpern and Robin Tremblay-McGaw note (2017, p. 7). As Steve Abbot editorialized in 1981, "New Narrative is language conscious but arises out of specific social and political concerns of specific communities. . . . [It] makes political and emotional (as well as linguistic) connections. . ." While not every New Narrative writer identifies as LGBTQ+, the mode has been especially hospitable to new queer writing. Kevin Killian's *Shy* (1989) pushes the autofictional to hyperbolic extreme, plagiarizing from its paired memoir, *Bedrooms Have Windows* (1989) and opening up new possibilities for first-person narration. Dennis Cooper's *Frisk* (1991) draws on porn films both in form and content to push its sexually explicit and violent exploration of men's bodies, blurring the boundaries between desire and the death drive, evacuating its characters of subjective depth even as it aims to peel back and penetrate the surfaces of the body – only to reveal more surfaces. Story collections, such as Killian's *Impossible Princess* (2009) or Sam D'Allessandro's *Wild Creatures* (2005), assemble a range of approaches to first-person narration but also, in D'Allessandro's case, juxtaposes short story alongside prose poem or other experimental fiction. Kathy Acker's lesbian novel *Pussy King of the Pirates* (1996) offers a parodic rewriting of the adventure tale, demonstrating that women concoct sexually explicit romps as well as any of the porn-influenced New Narrative instigators, and trenchantly critique patriarchy while doing so. In the second wave, Megan Milks's *Kill Marguerite and Other Stories* (2014) returns us to repurposing popular genres with a fresh take on queer gendering.

Second-wave New Narrative writers include Renee Gladman, whose Ravicka trilogy of four short books (*Event Factory* [2010], *The Ravickians: A Novel* [2011], *Ana Patova Crosses a Bridge* [2013], *Houses of Ravicka* [2017]) explores an invented city, with a vaguely Eastern European patina and African American cultural mores, ensnared in some unspecified social/political/environmental crisis. Pamela Lu's *Pamela: A Novel* (1995) traces relations among a coterie of young folks, all designated by a letter rather than a name. These two more overtly fictionalizing approaches turn against the earlier tendency to hyperbolize the author's life. They also move towards a less sexually explicit but no less erotically tense mode of writing, where the beauty of the language burnishes the text's surface and the play with the novel form simultaneously foregrounds and queers the conventions of story itself.

New York has long served as an epicenter for a good deal of LGBTQ+ writing, and lesbian fiction flourished here in the 1990s. Jane deLynn's *Don Juan in the Village* (1990) delineates a series of lesbian conquests in the city in a realist style. In the experimental vein, Eileen Myles's *Chelsea Girls* (1994) brings New Narrative to New York. Sarah Schulman's *Empathy* (1992) experiments with therapeutic dialogue, although her novels like the critically acclaimed post-breakup jeremiad *After Delores* (1988) tend towards realism. Schulman's attention to the HIV/AIDS crisis decentered gay men: *Rat Bohemia* (1995) vividly illuminates the networks of lesbians and gay men in the 1980s while *People in Trouble* (1991), hinging on a bisexual woman and her straight male partner, shows how the margins are not so distant from the center as AIDS and queer activism permeated New York lives. *People* presages the problem of gentrification that devastated New York's vibrant arts/literary scene as much as HIV/AIDS did.

As Schulman's oeuvre shows, the crisis in representation – both political and aesthetic – is undoubtedly fueled by the unprecedented experience of the outbreak of HIV/AIDS. An entirely new genre of AIDS literature emerged in the 1980s and 1990s in response to the crisis – science struggled to understand how the illnesses that HIV/AIDS induces were being activated in the body, while elected representatives refused to approve funding for scientific research or take steps to assist patients in need or the communities and institutions supporting them in the face of decimating illness. Life stories took on a certain urgency in this genre, exemplified by how memoirist Paul Monette crossed over into novels (*Afterlife* [1990] and *Halfway Home* [1991]).

In the darkest days, HIV+ was a death sentence rather than a chronic condition (now manageable with good health insurance and antiretroviral drugs available by the mid-1990s). The crisis exploded not only the social and cultural worlds of LGBTQ+ folks, but also the genres/styles of writing. Edmund White and Adam Mars-Jones collected short stories on living with HIV (*Darker Proof* [1987]) because a novel was problematically linear and predictable in its ending. David Wojnarowicz's *Close to the Knives* (1991) recasts the AIDS memoir in a sexually explicit and innovatively experimental vein that provides an important comparison to the edgier fiction work being done at that time, such as Carole Maso's *The Art Lover* (1990) or Delany's *The Mad Man*. Maso uses a story-within-a story to blur the boundary between art and reality, life and its representation, from the vantage point of a recently bereaved writer whose good friend is dying of AIDS; the novel she's writing is framed by her grieving, her caretaking, and her reflecting on relationships. Working across word and image, the novel incorporates pictures by Gary Falk and skymaps from the *New York Times*. Delany's novel follows protagonist John Marr, philosophy student and sexually active gay man who engages in the very assignations safer-sex activists warn against – casual hookups with strangers in parks, restrooms, or porn theaters. The novel offers an explicit catalogue of the variety of ways that men give one another pleasure and the subcultures of erotic exchange among men in New York at this time, yet its protagonist remains HIV–. While the descriptions indulge in pornographic detail, the exchange of bodily fluids is embedded among a number of other social exchanges – buying someone a beer or food, offering them shelter, advice, conversation, affirmation – in a way that equalizes the activities, emphasizing the generosity of exchange over the specific materials of that generosity.

Melvin Dixon's 1991 *Vanishing Rooms* offers an interesting counterpoint to the novel in the age of AIDS. A multinarrator book set in New York City in the early 1970s, *Vanishing Rooms* alternates first-person narration chapter by chapter among Jesse, a Black dancer whose white lover, Metro, is murdered on the street by a gang of Italian youth; Ruella, another Black dancer in Jesse's class; and Lonny, one of the Italian working-class boys who is part of the murderous gang. The untimely death of Jesse's lover resonates with the contemporaneous deaths of gay men's lovers in the early 1990s, even if the former is an unexpected loss through street violence rather than the state and institutional violence of the early years of the epidemic. *Vanishing Rooms* offers a potent reminder that HIV/AIDS is not the only threat to LGBTQ+ people; queer-baiting remains a danger. The novel's rich diegetic world offers an incisive parsing of the ways that class, race, region, and sexuality converge within the larger systems of racism, white supremacy, homophobia, and class. The shifting lenses of *Vanishing Rooms* and how truth keeps evolving over the course of the novel as it simultaneously unwinds the events that led to Metro's murder and moves us forward in the linear progression of the lives of those who are living on – that dynamism is moving us towards queer.

If in Dixon's hands, the multinarrator form serves to reveal social encounters and intimate relationships across a largely synchronic experience, in Craig Womack's *Drowning in Fire* (2001) the multinarrator form facilitates a more expansive historical sweep. *Drowning* focuses on a gay Muskogee Creek man, Josh Henneha, but uses the vantage of other characters, from Josh's great aunt to his childhood friend Jimmy, to bring to life Muskogee Creek history in Oklahoma and integrate tradition with the characters' visions, dreams, and lived experiences under contemporary settler colonialism and its homophobia.

As Womack's novel indicates, not every queer novel focuses on urban spaces or takes its politics only from queer movements. Carole LaFavor's lesbian mystery, *Evil Dead Center* (1997), set in northern Minnesota Ojibwe reservation Red Earth and surrounding towns, is influenced by its protagonist's history with the American Indian Movement and exemplifies how the political upheaval/activism of the late 1960s and 1970s resonates in LGBTQ+ literature two decades later. *Evil Dead Center* is the second of the two mystery novels driven by Renee LaRoche (*Along the Journey River* [1996] is the first). Its story navigates among several threads: discrimination against and exploitation of Native communities, the interracial relationship between Ojibwe Ren and her white lover Samantha, the return of Ren's former Ojibwe lover and fellow Movement activist Caroline Beltrain, the role of alcoholism and drug use in rural life and among Native Americans, the struggle to sustain Native families and tribal culture in the face of poverty, marginalization, and discrimination under settler colonialism. To appreciate a fuller range of Native LGBTQ+ and Two-Spirit literature, look to Qwo Li Driskoll et al.'s anthology, *Sovereign Erotics: A Collection of Two-Spirit Literature* (2011), with its mix of stories, essays, and poems that reflect the complexity of identities within Native LGBTQ+ communities. Prior to that, Beth Brant's groundbreaking anthology *A Gathering of Spirit: A Collection by North American Indian Women* (1984) was the first to focus entirely on Native writers, although its scope included women beyond lesbian, queer, and two-spirit folks and genres beyond fiction.

We should look to multigenre anthologies to grasp the extensive range of LGBTQ+ fiction in the last forty years, particularly for writers of color; frequently these collections encompass writers from a wide variety of backgrounds. A foundational multiracial and multigenre collection, *This Bridge Called My Back: Writing by Radical Women of Color* (1981), established its editors, Cherrie Moraga and Gloria Anzaldúa, as major figures in lesbian and queer studies as well as Chicanx/Latinx studies. Moraga's own multigenre *Loving in the War Years* (1983) was an early queer Chicanx classic. *Ambientes: New Queer Latino Writing* (Lázaro Lima and Felice Picano, eds., 2011) and Carmen Machado's short story collection *Her Body and Other Parties* (2017) extend this lineage. Five years after *This Bridge*, the first anthology of Black gay men's writing, Joseph Beam's *In the Life* (1986), was published; five years later, Essex Hemphill completed Beam's sequel anthology *Brother to Brother: New Writings by Black Gay Men* (1991). Most recently, Quang Bao and Hanya Yanagihara's *Take Out: Writing from Queer Asian Pacific Americans* (2000) stakes a claim for the diverse range of linguistic and cultural heritages of Asians in its selection of short fictions.

As this brief sketch shows, LGBTQ+ fiction pushes many limits of conventional literature – not only in representing overtly desires that had often been relegated to margins or subtext of stories, but also in blurring boundaries of genres, butting up against the limits of fictionality or hyperbolizing realism, mixing fiction and philosophy, history and story. Do queer stories need different forms of narrative? We see a rich range of responses to the question, as writers strive to depict histories, lives, loves that unfold under this rainbow, holding close the telling of queer desire with race, ethnicity, class, or sexual differences.

SEE ALSO: Cooper, Dennis; Delany, Samuel; Feinberg, Leslie; Indigenous Narratives; Maso, Carole; Mixed-Genre Fiction; The New Experimentalism/The Contemporary Avant-Garde; Queer and LGBT Fiction; Walker, Alice; White, Edmund

REFERENCES

Abbot, Steve. (1981). Introduction. *Soup* 2: 1.

Acker, Kathy. (1996). *Pussy King of the Pirates*. New York: Grove.

Cromarty, Heather. (2012). Review of Eileen Myles' *Inferno*. Lemon Hound (September 21, 2012). https://lemonhound.com/2012/09/21/review-of-eileen-myles-inferno-a-poets-novel/ (accessed August 2, 2021).

Faderman, Lilian. (1994). *Chloe Plus Olivia: An Anthology of Lesbian Literature from the Seventeenth Century to the Present*. New York: Viking.

Feinberg, Leslie. (1993). *Stone Butch Blues*. Ithaca, NY: Firebrand Books.

Halpern, Rob and Tremblay-McGraw, Robin. (2017). *From Our Hearts to Yours: New Narrative as Contemporary Practice*. Oakland, CA: One Contemporary Practice.

Hemphill, Essex with Beam, Joseph. (1991). *Brother to Brother: New Writings by Black Gay Men*. Boston: Alyson Publications.

Ponce, Martin Joseph. (2018). Queers read what now. *GLQ* 24 (2–3): 315–341.

FURTHER READING

Bradway, Tyler and McCallum, E.L. (eds.) (2019). *After Queer Studies: Literature, Theory and Sexuality in the 21st Century*. Cambridge: Cambridge University Press.

Carbado, Devon W., McBride, Dwight A., and Weise, Donald. (eds.) (2002). *Black Like Us: A Century of Lesbian, Gay, and Bisexual African American Fiction*. Jersey City, NJ: Cleis Press.

McRuer, Robert. (1997). *Queer Renaissance: Contemporary American Literature and the Reinvention of Lesbian and Gay Identities*. New York: NYU Press.

R

Realism after Poststructuralism

MARY K. HOLLAND
State University of New York at New Paltz, USA

Contemporary American fiction works hard to differentiate itself from the late-nineteenth-century realism that long seemed the standard for literary prose. Its metafictive techniques are more diverse and extreme than those that first prompted critics to coin "anti-realism" in the 1960s, and advances in digital production have allowed its experiments in textual layout and physical form to reshape text and books altogether. And yet, critics over the last thirty years have proffered more than twenty new "realisms" to describe this same body of work and to characterize the new period of literature it ushers in. Contemporary fiction's transformation of the techniques of late-nineteenth-century fiction, and critics' insistent enlistment of the term that names that fiction, demonstrates how indebted today's fiction remains to the mode it is often seen as rejecting. The repetition of "realism" reimagines the movement from realism to modernism, postmodernism, and beyond as continuous evolution rather than fragmented revolution. Meanwhile, the modification of these "realisms" by terms including "postmodern," "metafictive," and "material" illustrates how contemporary fiction mediates "realism" through post-realist ideas about language, reality, and the relationship between the two. Taken together, contemporary realisms raise questions about how "realism" has been used as a term in the past, how we might understand it today, and how we might think about periodizing more productively as we move forward into the literary history to come, while aiding in our contemporary project of characterizing literature after postmodernism.

The most fundamental question this post-postmodern proliferation of realisms raises is, "what, after all, is realism?" A look at theory and criticism demonstrates that, as St. Augustine said of time, we know what it is until we try to explain it. Shall we define "realism" according to one historical or cultural period? a set of literary techniques? themes or moral concerns? a text's ability to represent the real world faithfully? (And what do "real world" and "faithful" representation mean, exactly?) Critics and practitioners of realism have taken this variety of tacks for well over a hundred years, resulting in a collection of theories on realism that is at least as motley as are definitions of postmodernism. Core writers and theorists of realism in the late

The Encyclopedia of Contemporary American Fiction 1980–2020, First Edition. Edited by Patrick O'Donnell, Stephen J. Burn, and Lesley Larkin.
© 2022 John Wiley & Sons Ltd. Published 2022 by John Wiley & Sons Ltd.

nineteenth century, namely William Dean Howells, Mark Twain, Henry James, and Edith Wharton, defined "realism" as a literary mode that depicted the truth of the world and its everyday events in "natural" ways. But often their fiction did not agree with their theory, instead exposing the limits of what we can know, the contradiction inherent in every truth, and the artifice of much of what we take to be natural. Eric Auerbach's influential *Mimesis* (1946) acknowledged realism's ability – and intention – to represent such complexity, through developments in techniques such as point of view. But by arguing that technical evolutions past what he considered realism's peak in his own time (late modernism) were killing it, Auerbach also exposed the unconscious historical bias of every critical act of defining. Other mid-century critics, such as René Wellek and Georg Lukács, attempting to be more historically specific than a formalist analysis like Auerbach's tends to be, defined realism according to ideas or thematic agendas, often resulting in a loss of literary and generic specificity.

Rather than clarifying realism, the arrival of poststructural theory in the American academy during the postmodern period – and its quick domination of critical practices – significantly intensified the definitional problem. By conceiving of language as fundamentally disconnected from reality while also shaping it in ways we cannot control, poststructuralism called into question not only the criteria by which we might define realism as literary mode but also our understanding of reality itself, and the presumption that language could in any way stand in for it. Such a major shift made it all the more difficult to establish criteria for defining realism that could make sense over time and across philosophical and literary periods. Critics informed by Lacan's poststructural ideas about slippery language and subjectivity, and Derrida's deconstructive concept of endlessly indeterminate meaning, reacted to the professed certainty of the nineteenth-century realists in two equally unhelpful ways: some viewed realism as hopelessly naive in comparison with poststructural and postmodern ideas and therefore no longer useful (e.g. J.P. Stern), while others saw it as presciently doing all along the representational sleight of hand we have come to associate with poststructuralism (e.g. Eric Sundquist) – in which case, how is it any longer discernibly "realist"? Both of these rereadings amounted to rewritings of realism that essentially erased its usefulness as a distinguishing literary term.

More recent attempts to find a place for the empirically minded "realism" in our decidedly non-positivist poststructural world wind up weakening the term further, by making it overly inclusive rather than meaningfully exclusive. By its 1993 edition, M.H. Abrams's widely consulted *A Glossary of Literary Terms* attempts to account for poststructural reconsiderations of realism by pointing out that even traditional realism is only representation, then offering a problematically broad definition of realism as "a recurrent mode, in various eras and literary forms, of representing human life and experience in literature" (1993, p. 174). In her 2003 *Realism*, Pam Morris makes a similar gesture, defining realism as "any writing that is based upon an implicit or explicit assumption that it is possible to communicate about a reality beyond the writing" (2003, p. 6). Such definitions raise thorny questions: is there any writing that *doesn't* qualify as realism? If a text assumed it could not communicate with us about the real world, how would we – its readers, who are dutifully interpreting it in some way that feels like communication – know?

Steven Moore's recent redefinition of realism in *The Novel: An Alternative History* (2010) avoids such looseness while simultaneously opening up our concept of the mode past its traditional roots: Moore identifies in thirteenth-century Icelandic sagas many specific qualities of late-nineteenth-century realism. And yet, such backwards defining of an earlier literature according to characteristics of a later one raises its own questions about the validity of ahistorically applying a literary mode that is always produced historically. In *The Antinomies of Realism* (2013), Fredric Jameson explores what he calls the "dialectic of realism" in terms of the generic and formal devices authors invent and then reject in their constant attempts to articulate affect and escape the strictures of aesthetic form. And yet his theory of realism has it killing itself off during the same contemporary period in which over twenty new versions are flourishing. So we find ourselves, at the cusp of the third decade of the twenty-first century – with multiple contemporary versions of realism vying to characterize a new literary period that itself remains in need of characterizing – more unclear than ever before about what "realism" is or was, much less what it might become.

These new realisms, proposed by critics as early as 1983 but beginning in earnest in 1992 as postmodernism began to end, include the following: dirty realism, neorealism, postmodern realism, British postmodern realism, traumatic realism, tragic realism, figural realism, hysterical realism, meta-realism, speculative realism, agential realism, disquieting realism, capitalist realism, post-postmodern realism, poststructural realism, metonymic realism, ecocritical realism, relational realism, metafictive realism, material realism, and quantum realism. Some of these concepts remain enamored with traditional realism (Bill Buford's dirty realism), mourn its displacement by supposedly inferior literary developments (James Wood's hysterical realism), or remain primarily interested in postmodern themes or theories (Hal Foster's traumatic realism). But quite a few of them reimagine realism *productively* for our current poststructural, "post-postmodern" period.

And though the fiction that inspired this slew of realisms is as diverse as are the terms coined to describe it, its common features point to helpful ways of understanding how contemporary American fiction works and what it aims to say about the world, as well as how realism in general works and how we might rethink the relationship between nineteenth-century realism and the realisms exploding today. These shared qualities of new realisms are metafiction, as a tool for bending traditional realism toward poststructural ends; and materiality, in terms of texts' attention to the material world, to their own materiality, and to reminding us of our embodied experiences of literature and of the world.

Metafiction may be as old as fiction itself, appearing at least as far back as *Don Quixote* (1605), but the explosion of metafiction in 1960s America remains unprecedented. Characterizing the writing of many of our most prominent early postmodern writers, including John Barth, Donald Barthelme, Robert Coover, Ishmael Reed, and William H. Gass (who coined the term in 1970), metafiction quickly became a defining feature of postmodern fiction, and one that set it at sharp odds with its predecessor, realism. Whether in an attempt to claim new territory or to paint metafiction as a threat to the status quo and so to the future of literary fiction, critics produced a slew of competing terms for self-reflexive fiction that is perhaps only rivaled by today's pile-up of new realisms. The postmodern prospects – "anti-realism," "anti-novel," "introverted novel," "irrealism," "fabulation," and "surfiction" – eventually gave way to today's less overtly negative offerings ("experimental" and "conceptual" fiction). But all of these terms ghettoize overtly self-reflexive fiction as a reaction to or negation of "standard" fiction, identifying metafiction as realism's "other."

At the same time, metafiction was being theorized by some as an integral part of all fiction.

While Robert Alter saw nineteenth-century realism as temporarily eclipsing fiction's inherent self-reflexivity (*Partial Magic* [1975]), Linda Hutcheon described the evolution of novelistic mimesis from realism to self-reflexivity as a steady progression of metafiction from covert to overt, acknowledging (as Aristotle pointed out long before) that the act of narration is always part of the story being told (*Narcissistic Narrative* [1980]). Likewise, Patricia Waugh saw metafiction as a "tendency *within* the novel" that holds in tension fiction's opposing impulses toward "construction and deconstruction of illusion" (1984, p. 14, original italics). Indeed, we find this dialectical relationship between realism and metafiction – construction versus deconstruction of the illusion of narrative – at the heart of one of our founding theories of literary studies, Boris Eichenbaum's "The Theory of the Formal Method" (1926), which uses the "unmotivated" techniques of *Don Quixote* – those elements uncalled for by plot – as evidence of why formalist analysis is necessary in the first place.

The sudden prominence of self-reflexivity in American fiction of the 1960s and beyond, however, signaled a change not only in fictional technique but also in ideas about the world that the fiction was aiming to represent. Waugh argues that metafiction exploded in the 1960s precisely because the worldview that had supported realism – empiricism – profoundly shifted. Of course, many significant historical, cultural, scientific, and technological changes have occurred since the 1960s, the dissemination of poststructuralism in America prominent among them. Once again, changes in metafiction – or in fiction's technical, structural, and formal methods of deconstructing the illusion of verisimilitude – accompany these changes in the world. Likewise, metafiction's representational aims transform as well.

David Foster Wallace, a central influence on literature in and after postmodernism, developed several new techniques – dialogism of perspective, the endless binary, and contrapuntal metafictive realism – that demonstrate the interdependence of metafiction and realism and establish the metafictive realism that will shape much of fiction from the late twentieth century forward. Wallace created a dialogism of perspective in two ways: by shifting, multiplying, and at times hiding the text's technical *point of view* (first, second, or third person); and by splitting and layering *perspective* (the focalizing point from which the reader receives information, regardless of technical point of view). "Good Old Neon" (in *Oblivion* [2004]) exemplifies the first type: initially we think we are reading the first-person point of view of a living Neal; next, we realize we are actually getting the first-person point of view of dead Neal addressing his live self; but near the story's end, we are asked to reconstrue the entire story as imagined from the perspective of Neal's friend, David Wallace, whose impressive ability to empathize with his friend, dead by suicide, teaches him how to stop his own suffering of the crippling self-doubt that killed Neal. "My Soul Is Not a Smithy" (in *Oblivion* [2004]) illustrates the second type by incorporating not only multiple perspectives over different times but also multiple texts and textual registers, to generate multiple narratives and subnarratives, all of which are necessary to reveal the story's central trauma: not the mental breakdown of the substitute teacher, but the narrator's intense fear that he will become his self-alienated father. Wallace's uses of these techniques suggest that all truth, meaning, and identity require that we negotiate multiple selves – our own and others' – from multiple perspectives, and at multiple points in time and space, in a process that is never complete. His metafictional techniques thus depict a reality that has moved beyond the skepticism of Woolf's experiments with point of view and time, as described by Auerbach, to reflect the total epistemological and ontological indeterminism of poststructuralism.

Wallace's endless binary accomplishes a similar radical skepticism by asking us to evaluate a story or character in opposing ways that never resolve into a singular truth. "Brief Interview #20" and (the second) "The Devil Is a Busy Man" (both from *Brief Interviews with Hideous Men* [1999]) ask us to read their narrators as alternately selflessly sincere and pathologically narcissistic; the stories' only ultimate truth is that it is impossible to tell which is ultimately true, and that truth and sincerity always exist in tandem with deception of the self and the other. In this way, Jorge Louis Borges, whose fiction often chased the impossible aleph – or the point from which one can see all points – is a crucial ancestor to Wallace and to the metafictive realism that has come to characterize contemporary fiction.

If realism is best understood as existing in dialectic with metafiction, then Wallace's posthumous *The Pale King* (2011) must be his most realistic work of all. Indeed, a note included at the end by his editor Michael Pietsch describes what Wallace considered to be the novel's "Central Deal: Realism" (2012, p. 546). Like *Brief Interviews*, Wallace's last novel achieves that realism by mixing overtly metafictive pieces with formally realist ones, which depend upon each other to create the book's overall verisimilitude. The novel's realist sections are undermined by its metafictive ones, as when we are forced to reconsider the seeming clarity and directness of the section published separately as "Good People" – written in pitch-perfect Hemingway style – once we find that it is our manipulative narrator who has polished it to its high sheen. Likewise, the author-narrator reveals that the moving *Bildungsroman* of the Chris Fogle section is the result of significant editing and excerpting. Read in this light, the psychic ability of Claude Sylvanshine, whose mind is constantly flooded with impossible knowledge about the world around him, satirizes traditional realism by pointing out the absurdity of every omniscient third-person narrator who has ever gained our trust.

The novel as a whole enacts such contrapuntal metafictive realism on the largest level by positing a form of realism that is the opposite of traditional realism, critiquing it, and then enacting it. Like many of the films described in James Incandenza's filmography in *Infinite Jest* (1996), *The Pale King* imagines realism as narrative in which nothing happens, as rarely broken monotony. Though dismissed by the author-narrator, this is exactly the realism the novel overall produces, both in discrete moments (such as §25, comprising only descriptions of wigglers turning pages) and as a massive, nonlinear whole, which creates through language the conditions in which awareness might arise, and thus an embodied experience of being that – as Fogle proposes – may be our most powerful avenue to reality. This desire to invoke reality not by painting a visual picture of it but by *instantiating* aspects of it, or of our embodied experience of it, describes many of the new techniques of contemporary realist fiction. We might say that metafiction, or fiction's drawing attention to itself as a linguistic or physical thing in itself, is the primary tool used to achieve contemporary fiction's thematic goal of forcing us to encounter and consider the material world.

Like metafiction, foregrounding materiality as literary technique dates back beyond the twentieth century, characterizing works as diverse as Laurence Sterne's image-laden *Tristram Shandy* (1759), William Blake's engraved plates of *The Marriage of Heaven and Hell* (1790), and the late-nineteenth-century manuscripts of Emily Dickinson's sprawling poetry. Also like metafiction, literary materiality erupted in the late 1960s, as modernist interest in the thingness of language (as in work by Gertrude Stein, Ezra Pound, James

Joyce, and Samuel Beckett) encountered postmodern suspicion of textual authority and authorial control. We might see the resulting materiality of works such as William H. Gass's *Willie Masters' Lonesome Wife* (1968) and Ishmael Reed's *Mumbo Jumbo* (1971) as a subset of metafiction, but one that depicts the text's awareness of its own material form or of the materiality of its language, rather than simply its awareness of itself as text. Their "antirealist" strategies sought to alter the form of traditional realism in order to use the literary text to do new work – to remind us of the intimate connection between language and literature and the real world, and of our own fundamentally physical existence in that world. In this way, materiality as a contemporary realist technique begins to move literature away from the estrangement of word from world insisted upon by poststructuralism.

From the end of the twentieth century on, such material techniques grew so common as to become characteristic not of a subset of a subset of literary fiction, but of much of literary fiction in general. One of the reasons for this increase in the use of material techniques is the rapid development of digital technologies and literature that began in the 1990s. Electronic lit reimagined all formal elements of realism, becoming resolutely nonlinear and hypertextual (moving between multiple points, screens, or fragments of text), often eschewing closure, requiring the reader's interaction, and blurring or erasing lines between text and reader, text and world, text and other texts. Some print literature, influenced by elit, adopted these approaches as if to remain relevant in a literary world of such suddenly abundant possibility; other texts exhibit these innovations on realism even though their authors claimed to have no interest in elit. Still other texts pushed against the development of elit and digital technology by emphasizing their materiality and their strategic uses of the print medium over electronic (while taking advantage of advances in technology that made their material techniques possible).

These reactions to the rise of digital technology resulted in an identifiably new kind of realism, material realism, that draws attention to and uses materiality in two ways: to emphasize the physical properties of printed texts as things in the world that act on the world; and to emphasize the materiality of language itself as marks in and on the world. In a prime example of the first type, one narrator of Mark Danielewski's *House of Leaves* (2000), Johnny Truant, materializes the academic study contained in the novel by editing and assembling a textual mess left behind by another, Zampanò. Meanwhile, the novel as a whole materializes the text's ability to become material, as the "Labyrinth" chapter visually concretizes the thematic labyrinth of the novel, and its ability to shape the material world, as we witness one narrator's imposition on the diegetic space of another, with the check mark on page 97 signifying Pelafina's intrusion into Zampanò's (or Johnny's?) narrative. Many diverse texts at the end of the twentieth century accomplish the second type of materiality, including Carole Maso's *The Art Lover* (1990), Gass's *The Tunnel* (1995), and Lee Siegel's *Love in a Dead Language* (1999), using words, images, and documents to make present the tangible world and bodies implied by their narrators' linguistic attempts to slake their bodily desire.

The intensification of material realism in the early twenty-first century coincides with the development of a theory of "new materialism" in philosophy, social sciences, and physics. Uniting the multidisciplinary approaches to new materialism is the mandate to turn our attention back to material reality rather than language and discourse – which, through linguistic and poststructural theories, had been seen as dominating the real in the postmodern period. Karan Barad's quantum physics-based new materialism connects materiality and ethics using empirically generated information about the quantum world, which reveals that all matter exists necessarily in relation to and continuous with all other matter (Barad 2007). Such a redefinition of reality from representational (in which acts of observation and consideration, including linguistic, are seen as external and separate from reality) to relational (in which all observers and acts of observation, including linguistic, are fundamentally continuous with and implicated in the reality being observed) requires a similarly bold rethinking of our chief linguistic "representational" method, realism.

Unlike traditional realist literature, whose formal aspects are purely linguistic and intangible, material realist fiction materializes the core ideas from new materialism using the physical structures of the print text and of language on the page, foregrounding literature's physicality as instrumental to its acts of meaning-making while demonstrating the agency of matter. It also materializes the relationality of matter and observer, book and reader, resulting in books that act as changing interactions with the reader rather than dead objects. Steve Tomasula alters the shapes, page colors, font styles and colors, and typesetting of his books to reveal the dangerous power of art – and of all ideology – to physically shape our behavior (as in *VAS: An Opera in Flatland* [2002]; *IN&OZ* [2003]; and *The Book of Portraiture* [2006]). Lily Hoang's *Changing* (2008) configures language on the page to materialize the sixty-four hexagrams that signify the world in the ancient Chinese philosophy text *I Ching*, thus embodying her own Jack-and-Jill story in the shape of the universe and of one of our oldest stories about it. Salvador Plascencia's *The People of Paper* (2005) features a black box that initially aligns with characters' blocked thoughts but begins to float freely around the surface of the text, moving up from the level of language to occupy the physical space of the page itself, and so to mark a diegetic layer we cannot identify. All of these material realist techniques construct contemporary American literature as antidote to the linguistic eclipse of the real and poststructural evasion of meaning threatened by postmodern literature.

Contemporary American fiction also uses material realism to counter another postmodern danger: the loss of historicity (as theorized by Fredric Jameson in "Postmodernism and Consumer Society" [1988]). While William Gibson's material realist *Agrippa (A Book of the Dead)* (1992) – which resembles an unearthed box and contains a disappearing poem – represents the "death of history" anxiety that characterizes postmodernism, early-twenty-first-century fiction often uses material realist practices to construct books as witnesses to and makers of history. Anne Carson's *Nox* (2010) reproduces the scrapbook made by Carson in response to her brother's death and invites the reader to join her in piecing together the brother's lost life while translating a memorializing poem from its original Latin. The book reminds us throughout that its reproduced photos, marks, and indentations are as unreal and inaccurate as our attempts at translating the poem: all memory and history are translation, a kind of building we all do using narrative and/as the material remnants of a life. J.J. Abrams and Doug Dorst take this notion of reading as an act of building even further with their novel *S.* (2013), which greets the reader as a stolen library book in a box with notes, postcards, and even a decoder swelling its pages. We might consider *S.* to be the extreme materializing of the state in which Johnny Truant finds the materials he uses to produce part of *House of Leaves*, as reading *S.* requires our own physical manipulation of the pieces of narrative in ways that *House* only asks us to imagine. Like the fictional encyclopedia of Borges's "Tlön, Uqbar, Orbis Tertius" (1940), which begins to alter the real world as soon as it is read there, *S.* presents the book as artifact of history and memory, not only materially standing in for experience and empathetic connection but physically placing the reader in a position from which she must reconstruct and inhabit those experiences.

The impact of quantum physics on realism illustrates how profoundly literature of the late twentieth century and after reflects not just changing philosophies about how we think, know, communicate, or represent, but new concepts of reality itself. Quantum theories of physical reality date back to the early twentieth century and show up in science fiction by the 1960s (as in Samuel Delany's *Babel 17* [1966]), but American literary fiction did not begin to register quantum concepts of reality in earnest until the mid-1990s. Core elements of quantum theories – uncertainty (a particle's location and speed may not be measured accurately at the same time), superposition (a particle exists at multiple points in spacetime simultaneously until measured), observer effect (we inevitably change everything we measure and are part of the measurement), entanglement (acting on one entangled particle affects another light years away), and many worlds (what we experience as reality is only one of infinite universes existing simultaneously) – influence the themes and plots of fiction by diverse writers including Jonathan Lethem (*As She Climbed Across the Table* [1994]), John Updike (*Toward the End of Time* [1997]), Helen Dewitt (*The Last Samurai* [2000]), Jennifer Egan (*A Visit from the Goon Squad* [2010]), and Paul Auster (*4321* [2017]). But still other writers challenged themselves to use the tools of traditional realism – which arose out of and are best suited to depicting the linear, causal, measurable world of Newtonian physics – to represent a fully quantum world not simply thematically but formally as well. The resulting quantum realism thus generates a whole new body of technical, formal, and structural innovations, much as our post-empirical worldview produced an explosion of metafiction in the 1960s.

Ruth Ozeki's *A Tale for the Time Being* (2013) uses quantum concepts to materialize the ethical principles of Buddhist belief. According to the novel's main characters – a writer and a reader, the latter of whom learns from the former – Buddhism's oneness and unresolvable paradoxes of being/not-being are spiritual versions of the physical concepts of entanglement, spacetime, and the observer effect, or two different ways of expressing the paradoxical truth of the universe: light is a wave and a particle; form is emptiness and emptiness is form. Ozeki uses multiple and changing points of view, second-person address, nonlinearity, intertextuality, and circular structures to give her narrative the complex form of her quantum/Buddhist world, depicting entanglement between characters as a result of empathic connection and illustrating the ethical implications of every act of language. *Tale* also conceives of language itself as the material of spacetime, through which one character moves to save the life of another, in the ultimate blending of language, material, and ethics.

Don DeLillo's 2001 *The Body Artist* is less formally "anti-realist" than Ozeki's quantum realism, while asking most overtly what happens when humans try to access and art tries to represent quantum reality. Like Ozeki, DeLillo uses mixed verb tenses, multiple points of view and perspectives, and intertextuality to illustrate a clash between Newtonian and quantum realities and realisms. But *The Body Artist* ends not in circularity or many worlds, but in the closure of flat, past-tense narrative. By constructing this final surrender into realism in relation to the novel's repeated efforts to escape it through formal innovations, as its main character attempted (and failed) to escape linear time through her body art, the novel offers its own version of *The Pale King*'s dialectical realism: both quantum reality and quantum realism become visible only in relief against the contrasting structures of Newtonian reality and traditional realism. Thus *The Body Artist* ends in paradox, illustrating both the limits of realism to invoke the quantum world, and the necessity of realism to articulate these limits.

This shared reliance on paradox – awareness that language both is and is not reality, that realism both is and is not capable of invoking the truth of reality – demonstrates that contemporary realisms remain inherently poststructural. Their reliance on metafiction, itself in dialectical relation to traditional realism, to depict materiality and its paradoxes should finally exorcise the realism/metafiction split from our critical vocabulary. Contemporary realisms demonstrate the core truth of storytelling as articulated from Aristotle to Waugh and Jameson: how we tell the story is always part of the story. As our ideas about ourselves and the universe continue to change, so will our stories and the ways in which we tell them. All of these ways will be realism. But, just as our stories are no longer straightforwardly empirical or Newtonian – orchestrated by linear revelation – so might they one day no longer be strictly material. How will realism change should we and our stories one day leave our bodies? Such a leap of selves and stories out of the material might signal the next epochal shift in realism, beyond the empirical realism of the late nineteenth century and the poststructural realism of the last half century or so, to a virtual realism yet to be imagined. As our vision of the universe grows larger and our ways of living in it more complex, so must our perspective on our methods of representing that universe to ourselves do the same. The recent explosion of contemporary realisms, alongside literature's embracing of not only global and anthropocenic perspectives but also cosmic ones, suggests that rather than debating various definitions and end dates for realism, we might more productively chart its methods of continually remaking itself in response to our endless conceptual, linguistic, material, and technological reinventions of our world.

SEE ALSO: After Postmodernism; Danielewski, Mark Z.; Delany, Samuel; DeLillo, Don; Egan, Jennifer; Gass, William H.; Gibson, William; Hypertext Fiction and Network Narratives; Maso, Carole; The New Experimentalism/The Contemporary Avant-Garde; Ozeki, Ruth; Reed, Ishmael; Siegel, Lee; Tomasula, Steve; Wallace, David Foster

REFERENCES

Abrams, M.H. (1993). *A Glossary of Literary Terms*, 6th ed. New York: Harcourt.
Barad, Karan. (2007). *Meeting the Universe Halfway: Quantum Physics and the Entanglement of Matter and Meaning*. Durham, NC: Duke University Press.
Jameson, Fredric. (2013). *The Antinomies of Realism*. London: Verso.
Morris, Pam. (2003). *Realism*. New York: Routledge.
Wallace, David Foster. (2012). *The Pale King: An Unfinished Novel*. New York: Back Bay Books; 1st ed. 2011.
Waugh, Patricia. (1984). *Metafiction: The Theory and Practice of Self-Conscious Fiction*. New York: Routledge.

FURTHER READING

Auerbach, Erich. (1953). *Mimesis: The Representation of Reality in Western Literature* (trans. Willard Trask). Princeton: Princeton University Press.
Chiang, Ted. (2016). Story of Your Life. In: *Stories of Your Life and Others*. New York: Vintage Books.
Holland, Mary K. (2020). *The Moral Worlds of Contemporary Realism*. London: Bloomsbury.

Reed, Ishmael

VINCENT PÉREZ
University of Nevada at Las Vegas, USA

On May 23, 2019, Ishmael Reed's latest work, *The Haunting of Lin-Manuel Miranda*, premiered at the Nuyorican Poets Café in Manhattan. The origin, content, context, and style of this play reflect key elements of Reeds's body of fiction over the last forty years of his extraordinary career. These include his works' engagement with history, the contemporary political moment, race and ethnicity (multiculturalism), language and popular culture, thematic elements woven into narrative and satiric form through the author's engaging and uproarious trickster voice. Like all great satirists, Reed sees his role as a writer as that of a comic provocateur who uses humor to expose hypocrisy, ignorance, greed, injustice, and any other social or human shortcoming that opposes truth. Most importantly, unlike other contemporary satirists, Reed draws as much, or more, from non-Western, non-European cultures as he does from US and European literary and cultural sources. He embraces global culture in his fiction in ways that distinguish him from almost all contemporary US writers, and even from most US ethnic minority authors. He views African American, Latinx, Native American, Asian American, and other minority cultures as homegrown conduits of global culture and as foundational sources of US cultural identity.

From the inception of his career in the 1960s, Ishmael Reed (b. 1938) has been one of the leading proponents of multiculturalism, just as this now octogenarian founding father of the movement continues to be in the twenty-first century. His early writings inspired the radical critique of Eurocentric discourses about US culture and identity and called for the inclusion of the histories and cultures of racial and ethnic minorities in all social, educational, and media institutions. His post-1980 works continue and expand on this project, addressing how the historically specific social ills that have plagued the United States during this period – racism, class inequality, greed, and jingoism – originated in the Reagan administration reactionary response to the cultural and political liberalism of the 1960s. Reed has called out racism in the US news and entertainment media and especially in the publishing industry. As right-wing news media and the corporate dominance of the publishing industry – which have expanded in the postmodern era as predicted in Reed's novel *The Terrible Twos* (1982) – have come to define contemporary US culture, Reed's contemporary works continue to engage this subject. Though identified with his pre-1980 works, Reed's multicultural (postmodernist) Neo-Hoodoo aesthetic, modeled after the cultural syncretism of the vodoun religion of the African diaspora, continues to shape his later and contemporary writings, including the novels *The Terrible Twos*, *Reckless Eyeballing* (1986), *The Terrible Threes* (1989), *Japanese by Spring* (1993), *Juice!* (2011), and *Conjugating Hindi* (2018). With his extensive pre-1980 body of work, Reed's oeuvre, spanning fiction, nonfiction, poetry, and drama, places him alongside canonical writers such as Mark Twain and Kurt Vonnegut as one of the most prolific, insightful, and entertaining satirists in US literary history. Today there are few other US writers of his stature as a novelist, satirist, and social critic. His recent collections of nonfiction both mirror and illuminate key themes in his fiction. They include *Going Too Far: Essays About America's Nervous Breakdown* (2012), *The Complete Muhammad Ali* (2015), and *Why No Confederate Statues in Mexico* (2019).

The Haunting of Lin-Manuel Miranda highlights a number Reed's ongoing preoccupations, including the ways in which the corporate publishing and media industries co-opt writers of color. Reed's play mounts a scathing critique of the musical *Hamilton* for its portrait of Alexander Hamilton as a progressive-minded founding father whose legacy transcends the issues of race and slavery. After Hamilton opened on Broadway in 2015 and before it became a mass cultural sensation, Reed had written an essay, titled "'Hamilton: The Musical': Black Actors Dress Up Like Slave Traders . . . and It's Not Halloween." In it, he takes Miranda to task for depending on Ron Chernow's adulatory biography of Hamilton to the exclusion of contemporary works by historians who repudiate Chernow's portrait for its dismissal of Hamilton's family ties to slavery. Reed compares the current historical moment to "the heady times during the slave revolt of the 1960s," when "the rebels boasted about how they were using the enemy's language and how they were 'stealing his language.'" But today, "things have been turned upside down. Now the masters, the producers of this profit hungry production, which has already made 30 million dollars, are using the slave's language: Rock and Roll, Rap and Hip Hop to romanticize the careers of kidnappers, and murderers. People, who, like Jefferson, beat and fucked his slaves" (Reed 2015).

The 1960s remains a pivotal theme and subtext in much of Reed's fictions. From *The Terrible Twos* to *Conjugating Hindi*, his post-1980 novels collectively comprise a critical interrogation of the legacies, contradictions, and betrayals of the sixties generation as it sacrificed its revolutionary ideals in the 1980s and beyond. After *Hamilton* had achieved blockbuster status, Reed published a second essay on the musical, "Hamilton and the Negro Whisperers: Miranda's Consumer Fraud" (Reed 2016), in which he criticized Hamilton mania and the myopic entertainment industry which had enabled and profited from the work's distorted and racist rendering of early US history. Just as Reed draws from scholarly sources in his fictions, in this essay he cites historians who identify the exclusions and biases in Miranda's musical. Miranda, Reed advises half-facetiously, "should have consulted [these] other sources that challenge [his] high school notion that Hamilton was some sort of abolitionist. But that would have been a real turn off for the feel good version of the Founding Fathers . . . which has drawn largely white audiences, who can afford tickets that sell for as much as $700" (2016).

As in the farcical novel *The Terrible Twos* and its sequel *The Terrible Threes*, together perhaps the most eloquent representation in fiction of the cruel and corrupt character of the Reagan presidency, in *The Haunting of Lin-Manuel Miranda* Reed uses ghosts as central players. A procession of apparitions, slaves owned by Hamilton's in-laws, Native Americans victimized by the founding fathers' racism, Harriet Tubman, and even Alexander Hamilton himself, confront a naive Miranda with their own perspectives on his famous musical. Together, they jolt Miranda into recognizing his own miseducation. Near the end, Hamilton, the ghost, congratulates Miranda for the musical's flattering portrait, free of his family's slave-owning past, to which an outraged Miranda responds, "This is all Ron Chernow's fault!" (quoted in Hsu 2019). The play also reminds us that Miranda did a commercial for the American Express card, another cardinal sin in Reed's anti-corporate, anti-elite worldview. Writers of color who achieve mainstream success pose a special concern for Reed, who remains justifiably suspicious of the mostly white mainstream publishing industry and the corporate interests that drive it. Although he has not criticized the blockbuster superhero movie *Black Panther* (2018), which has an all-Black cast and Black director, in an interview Reed said that he is "suspicious of a film where Walt Disney and all those people cut all the checks" (Lucca 2018).

The Haunting of Lin-Manuel Miranda exemplifies Reed's steadfast fealty to his responsibility as a satirist to rebuke works and figures for their falsehoods even when the public embraces and elevates them or simply regards them as beyond criticism. At the same time, Reed's satire differs dramatically from lesser works in this genre for its attention to historical and cultural accuracy, a realism that strengthens the satire and derives from the author's wide-ranging research and erudition. For example, a cursory reading of *The Terrible Twos*, in which Reed parodies two iconic US cultural traditions – the celebration of Christmas and the glorification of the American presidency – might lead one to believe that Reed's absurdist farce contains little historical depth. In the novel, a Christian sect, the Nicholaites, have embraced St. Nicholas, the fourth-century bishop from Asia Minor, as their deity. Influenced by the sixties counterculture and the teachings of Christ, they replace a celebrity Santa Claus with a Manchurian candidate Santa who calls for an end to the commercialization of Christmas and the overthrow of the corporate and capitalist system that promotes it. The president, a puppet of the corporations, has Santa Claus arrested and cracks down on the anti-corporate social movement his speeches have inspired. At their marches, the followers of the Nicholaite Santa Claus wear white berets to express their solidarity. The ghost of St. Nicholas visits the president and, like the ghost of Christmas past in Dickens's *A Christmas Carol* (1843), transports him to see the outcomes of sins committed by previous presidents now condemned to purgatory. Dwight D. Eisenhower is there for approving the CIA's 1961 assassination of Prime Minister Patrice Lumumba of the Republic of the Congo. Scrooge-like, the president undergoes a transformation, preparing a speech to the nation in which he will speak the truth publicly for the first time in his career. His speech targets his corrupt presidential cabinet and the moneyed interests that control it and calls for a new era in which Americans embrace the true spirit and ideals of Christmas: charity, generosity, love, and compassion.

A postmodernist version of *A Christmas Carol*, Reed's novel teaches readers much more about the origins of Christmas, and of saints such as St. Nicholas, than Dickens's novel and prompts readers to appreciate the real virtues that Christmas embodies. Beneath the Christian "master" narrative handed down in the West since late antiquity, Christmas in *The Terrible Twos* is the product of a network of historical, religious, cultural, and political filiations reaching back centuries and transcending the pagan and Christian eras. Early Nordic and Moorish, and ancient Roman, influences play as important a role in the history of Christmas in the novel as do English, Dutch, or Christian. Black Peter, in early European narratives St. Nicholas's dark-skinned, Moorish/African porter, appears in Reed's work as a central character, a Harlem street hustler who becomes a leader of the Nicholaites. Black Peter criticizes the Nicholaites' Eurocentricism, hoping to incorporate Afro-Caribbean (Rastafarian) religion into its theology. His namesake's historical exclusion from US Christmas celebrations derived, according to Reed, from nineteenth-century racism; in parts of Europe, where Black Peter never fell out of favor, he appears today alongside Sinterklaas at Christmas. As Reed does in much of his fiction, in *The Terrible Twos* he unmasks a seemingly monolithic US cultural tradition, revealing its complex multicultural origins. Few Americans today would associate Santa Claus with an olive-complected St. Nicholas from Turkey, or Christmas customs such as the Christmas tree and mistletoe with Northern European pagan rituals and myths. Nor would many believe, as mentioned in the opening pages, that Ronald Reagan's family name was "O'Reagan," identifying his ancestors as members of one of the most despised and persecuted immigrant groups of the nineteenth century.

Reed's critical engagement with institutional power defines much of his contemporary fiction. His novels operate at several levels, some focusing on how power corrupts the government and (news) media at the national level and others examining similar failings in institutions such as academia and the publishing industry. His eleventh and most recent novel, *Conjugating Hindi*, the first written during the Trump presidency, in many ways recalls his 1980s novels written during the Reagan administration, two of which fall into the first category. *The Terrible Twos* and *The Terrible Threes* parody presidential politics and expose the news media's culpability in government corruption, identifying the incestuous relationship between the two. Like these novels, *Conjugating Hindi* portrays a contemporary US society dominated by reactionary political elites who have polluted its media-saturated culture with xenophobia, racism, and crass materialism. Along with *The Terrible Twos*' deconstruction of US Christmas customs, Reed's 1982 novel also presciently portrayed the rise to the presidency of a TV celebrity much like Donald Trump. Dean Clift, a former model, first becomes a vice presidential running mate because of his TV fame and "sex appeal." He assumes the presidency after the death of the president. Like Trump, Clift has no background or experience whatsoever in politics, and possesses the emotional and intellectual maturity of a toddler. The "terrible twos" captures his condition, a running motif in the novel for both the president and an American individualism run amok. As one of the Nicholaites observes, "I keep thinking of a two-year-old when I think of an appropriate metaphor with which to describe this sour, Scroogelike attitude which began with the Scrooge Christmas of '80 . . . Two years old, that's what we are, emotionally – America, always wanting someone to hand us some ice cream, always complaining, Santa didn't bring me this and why didn't Santa bring me that" (Reed 1999, p. 95).

Although Reed engages Trumpism in *Conjugating Hindi* differently than he does Reaganism in *The Terrible Twos* and *The Terrible Threes*, he similarly sets its African American protagonist against representatives of the reactionary right-wing elite, in this case people of color (Indian Americans), some of whom paradoxically embrace its ideology despite its racism. As in many of his fictions, Reed portrays ethnic minority characters such as this as tragic souls, though he also finds them richly enigmatic. *Conjugating Hindi* condemns Trump's racism and nativism indirectly through its depiction of violent anti-Indian hysteria provoked suddenly by the shooting down of an American airliner by India after political disputes with England. Peter "Boa" Bowman teaches at a community college in Oakland and cultivates a position as a public intellectual. Invited to participate in a series of debates with a right-wing Hindu intellectual on the subject, "Was Slavery All That Bad?," he reluctantly accepts out of financial exigency. Boa knows that the contrived debates favor the right-wing perspective and that he will be publicly humiliated in the process. But he desperately needs the money. His adversary, Shashi Paramara, a darling "model minority" embraced by the conservative establishment, makes the case that slavery wasn't that bad, winning accolades from white right-wing audiences. Boa grins and bears the humiliation as the debates travel across the country. After the downing of the airliner, anti-Indian xenophobia intensifies to include mob attacks against Indians and congressional bills that target this group for persecution. The name of the US president in the novel is Kleiner Fuhrer. Boa finds himself taking in Shashi to protect him, which gives the two an opportunity to talk freely. As in *The Terrible Twos*, in which many of the characters, like Scrooge, learn to embrace the true spirit of Christmas and renounce their former selfishness, Boa convinces Shashi to reflect on the history of white supremacy in the United States and colonial India and to interrogate his views. Shashi slowly comes around to Boa's perspective, and begins to understand how the white right-wing establishment has used him as a "model minority" to further their own racist views.

As many critics and scholars note, jazz music heavily influenced Reed's literary aesthetic and idiosyncratic style of writing. What is often overlooked is that Reed draws from post-Bebop jazz artists more than from earlier, more well-known (Bebop) musicians. The experimental nature of his aesthetic and writing style points to figures such as Sun Ra, Ornette Coleman, Albert Ayler, Don Cherry, and Cecil Taylor over traditional Bebop music. Sun Ra especially offered a mythology and persona as an artist that appealed to Reed. Not only do Reed's novels often structurally and stylistically echo post-Bebop music, but his language and metaphors do as well. For example, Reed uses the term "Conjugating Hindi" as a metaphor for the convoluted amalgamation of social contradictions and ills that characterize the postmodern United States, entangled and unresolved because of our collective failure to address them in earlier eras. The title also serves as a critique of monolingualism and monoculturalism in the United States. In the end, Boa decides to learn more about Indian history and culture and begins studying Hindi. As the narrator explains, "Maybe he needed a vacation from English. Maybe it's unhealthy for one language to have a patent on one's brain" (2018, p. 69). The same line could have appeared in *Japanese by Spring*, in which the protagonist, Benjamin "Chappie" Puttbutt, a professor at a college in Oakland, decides to learn Japanese as a hedge against the growing influence of Japanese corporate money in academia.

Reed's 1970 "Neo-Hoodoo Manifesto" provides a useful framework for interpreting his contemporary fictions. The Neo-Hoodoo aesthetic decenters European and US literary and artistic models by embracing the syncretic cultures of the Afro-Caribbean, a "contact zone" long identified with spirits (loas), magic, nature, and music, and which Reed, following the work of other scholars and writers, further associates with history, creativity, and freedom. Reed's landmark essay recalls the Cuban writer Alejo Carpentier's 1949 literary manifesto, "On the Marvelous Real in America," which rejected European surrealism in favor of the organic "magical reality" of the Afro-Caribbean. Similarly, Reed's Neo-Hoodoo aesthetic criticizes the reified and monocultural nature of Eurocentric traditions. Like Carpentier, Reed does not reject European literary and cultural traditions out of hand; rather, he calls for the creation of new kinds of writing based on multivocal and multicultural sources and traditions. While Neo-Hoodooism emerged at the "confluence of African-Haitian vodoun and the music and dance of slave culture," Reed envisions it as a cultural movement through which new artist-priests "are building our own American 'pantheon'" or "loas [spirits]" from the resources of all people, not just African Americans (1972, p. 23). Among the many characters in Reed's fictions who embody Neo-Hoodooism, the most obvious is Black Peter, the Rastafarian Nicholaite leader in *The Terrible Twos*. The multivalent linguistic and cultural polyphony portrayed in novels such as *Conjugating Hindi*, *Japanese by Spring*, and *Reckless Eyeballing* also exemplifies Reed's Neo-Hoodoo aesthetic.

Reckless Eyeballing and *Japanese by Spring* satirize the publishing (theater) industry and academia respectively. The first exposes the cynical gender and racial politics behind publishers' and producers' decisions to embrace some authors over others; the second, the ingrained corruption that plagues the unequal power dynamics in academia. *Reckless Eyeballing* addresses one of Reed's recurring themes, the portrayal of Black men in literature and in the media as violent criminals. It expresses his belief that some African American women writers financially benefit from their depiction of Black male characters as such. Reed's riposte to the portrayal of Black men in Alice Walker's best-selling work *The Color Purple* (1982), the novel was the subject of much criticism by feminist writers and critics. In it, the Black playwright Ian Ball tries to curry favor with feminist producers who have "sex-listed" him. His new work, "Reckless Eyeballing," a play with mostly women characters, exploits the title's metaphor to comment on the misconduct of men's unrelenting sexual gaze. Ball soon discovers that his director, Tremonisha Smarts, whose play "Wrongheaded Man" depicts a crime spree by a Black man who commits rape and incest, plans to revise her work. A series of crimes follows in which several well-known feminists, including Smarts, have their heads shaved by an unknown Black assailant. As detectives try to solve the crimes, through contentious relationships with Ball and others, Smarts begins to understand how whites might co-opt her depiction of Black men to support and rationalize their own racial biases. Disillusioned, she leaves the New York theater scene.

Ball's character represents not only Black men who must contend with various types of racism, including the indirect type transmitted unintentionally by some Black feminists, but also a broad Neo-Hoodoo outlook. Ball is from the West Indies, and throughout he moves between his home there and New York. In *Reckless Eyeballing* this Afro-Caribbean cultural legacy proves to be both more complex and more problematic than in Reed's other novels. Ball's struggles as a Black male playwright stem from a curse placed on him at birth by a Voodoo priestess, which condemned him to "be born a two-head, of two minds, the one not knowing what the other was up to" (1986, p. 146). This division, an obvious echo of W.E.B. Du Bois's concept of the double-consciousness, remains unresolved at the end of the novel. Like Reed's best novels, *Reckless Eyeballing* captures the author's absurdist vision of the African American experience in the contemporary United States and pushes comically against all of the forces and institutions in the country that would diminish or confine this group.

SEE ALSO: After Postmodernism; Black Atlantic; Realism after Poststructuralism; Vonnegut, Kurt; Walker, Alice

REFERENCES

Hsu, Hua. (2019). In "The Haunting of Lin-Manuel Miranda," Ishmael Reed revives an old debate. *The New Yorker* (January 9, 2019). https://www.newyorker.com/culture/cultural-comment/in-the-haunting-of-lin-manuel-miranda-ishmael-reed-revives-an-old-debate (accessed July 10, 2021).

Lucca, Violet. (2018). Interview: Ishmael Reed. *Film Comment* (March 30, 2018). https://www.filmcomment.com/blog/interview-ishmael-reed/ (accessed July 10, 2021).

Reed, Ishmael. (1972). *Conjure: Selected Poems, 1963–1970*. Amherst: University of Massachusetts Press.

Reed, Ishmael. (1986). *Reckless Eyeballing*. New York: St. Martin's Press.

Reed, Ishmael. (1999). *The Terrible Twos*. Normal, IL: Dalkey Archive Press; 1st ed. 1982.

Reed, Ishmael. (2015). "Hamilton: The Musical": Black actors dress up like slave traders … and it's not Halloween. *Counterpunch* (August 21, 2015). https://www.counterpunch.org/2015/08/21/

hamilton-the-musical-black-actors-dress-up-like-slave-tradersand-its-not-halloween/ (accessed July 10, 2021).

Reed, Ishmael. (2016). Hamilton and the Negro whisperers: Miranda's consumer fraud. *Counterpunch* (April 15, 2016). https://www.counterpunch.org/2016/04/15/hamilton-and-the-negro-whisperers-mirandas-consumer-fraud/ (accessed July 10, 2021).

Reed, Ishmael. (2018). *Conjugating Hindi*. Victoria, TX: Dalkey Archive Press.

FURTHER READING

Gates, Henry Louis. (1988). *The Signifying Monkey: A Theory of African-American Literary Criticism*. Oxford: Oxford University Press.

Nazareth, Peter. (1994). *In the Trickster Tradition: The Novels of Andrew Salkey, Francis Ebejar and Ishmael Reed*. London: Bogle-L'Ouverture.

Reed, Ishmael, Singh, Amritjit, and Dick, Bruce. (eds.) (1995). *Conversations with Ishmael Reed*. Jackson: University Press of Mississippi.

Rushdy, Ashraf H.A. (1999). *Neo-Slave Narratives: Studies in the Social Logic of a Literary Form*. Oxford: Oxford University Press.

Soitos, Stephen F. (1996). *The Blues Detective: A Study of African American Detective Fiction*. Amherst: University of Massachusetts Press.

Religion and Contemporary Fiction

RAY HORTON
Murray State University, USA

BEYOND DISENCHANTMENT

"I tried to find a kind of radiance in dailiness," Don DeLillo explains in his oft-cited 1988 interview with *Rolling Stone*. Asked why characters in *White Noise* (1985) experience "the supermarket as a sacred place," DeLillo elaborates: "Sometimes this radiance can be almost frightening. Other times it can be almost holy or sacred. Is it really there? Well, yes . . . I think that's something that has been in the background of my work: a sense of something extraordinary hovering just beyond our touch and just beyond our vision" (DeCurtis 1998, p. 330). To summarize the importance of religion for American fiction since 1980 is to plumb the theological depths beneath the "radiance in dailiness" to which so many of the period's writers are drawn, but it is also to skim the surfaces of such fiction's complicated entanglements with the historical and ideological forces attributable to what Charles Taylor (2007) calls "a secular age." In the work of writers as varied as Don DeLillo, Octavia Butler, Marilynne Robinson, and James McBride, religious thought and practice resist the simplistic categorization one finds in binaries such as "religious" and "secular," "sacred" and "profane," "transcendent" and "immanent." Instead, novels such as *White Noise*, *Parable of the Sower* (1993) and *Parable of the Talents* (1998), *Gilead* (2004), and *The Good Lord Bird* (2013) draw upon a range of religious and spiritual traditions in ways that serve to cultivate what we might call secular faith: a fidelity to the finitude of the material world that acknowledges the fragility and vulnerability of our experience, bearing faithful witness to the ephemerality that characterizes the everyday.

If the twentieth century began with premonitions of the "disenchantment of the world" (Weber 1919, p. 139), with theories of the novel as "the epic of a world that has been abandoned by God" (Lukács 1915, p. 88), and with histories of American literature that mapped neatly onto a narrative of progressive secularization (from R.W.B. Lewis's *The American Adam* [1955] to Perry Miller's *Errand into the Wilderness* [1956]), then the twentieth century concluded, somewhat surprisingly, with a rekindled interest in what DeLillo aptly qualifies as the "almost holy or sacred." For many of the most prominent American novelists since 1980, the world's "disenchantment" has been far from total. For such writers, the novel, even when it depicts "a world . . . abandoned by God," nevertheless retains an inexhaustible preoccupation with the "sense of something extraordinary hovering" in the space where traces of divinity might linger.

Although American fiction since 1980 has exhibited a persistent fascination with the "almost holy or sacred," literary critics took a decade or two to catch up. In her 1995 essay "Invisible Domain: Religion and American Literary Studies," Jenny Franchot articulates the problem that scholars of religion and literature would spend the subsequent decades working to resolve. "The country," Franchot observes, "is in the midst of a conservative revolt. . .an angry controversy about religious issues and, indeed, about whether religion has any legitimate place in American culture" (1995, p. 833). Unfortunately, she laments, "Americanist literary cultural critics have little to say" in response. If, for DeLillo, contemporary fiction remains preoccupied with the "sense of something extraordinary hovering just beyond our touch," then according to Franchot, most literary critics of the period preferred to keep it there, safely out of reach. "For many," she quips, "the Inquisition or the Holocaust is always just around the corner . . . for we are all dangerously prone to force our beliefs upon others." Resisting this fear, Franchot asks "whether we want to persist in evading the larger culture's religious concerns. . .as a subject of serious inquiry" (p. 834).

If the developments in American literary studies over the past two decades (including the presence of an entry on "religion and contemporary fiction" in this encyclopedia of contemporary American literature) tell us anything, the discipline has largely answered Franchot's question with a resounding "no." From special issues of flagship journals such as *American Literature* (Coviello and Hickman 2014) and *American Literary History* (Ebel and Murison, 2014) to influential monographs such as John McClure's *Partial Faiths* (2007), Amy Hungerford's *Postmodern Belief* (2010), and Christopher Douglas's *If God Meant to Interfere* (2016), scholars of religion and American literature have increasingly come to agree that, as Coviello and Hickman explain: "The secularization thesis is dead" (2014, p. 645). Consequently, we have grown far more adept at recognizing the ways in which "religious expression invites dynamic analysis" beyond reductive gestures of "demystification" (Franchot 1995, p. 840).

To understand one key reason literature scholars since the turn of the century have grown more attentive to what DeLillo calls the "almost holy or sacred" in the texts they study, we must acknowledge an important development throughout the humanities and social sciences during this period: the collapse of the secularization thesis, which resulted in a growing recognition that the "disenchantment of the world" by way of modernity and postmodernity can hardly be taken as axiomatic. Writing in 2007, Michael Kaufmann invites us to rethink the discipline of literary studies itself in light of recent scholarship on secularism and secularization. The secularization thesis, he argues, shaped the "generally accepted" histories of literary studies" (2007, p. 607). Drawing on the work of Talal Asad, José Casanova, Vincent Pecora, and others whose work has challenged us to reconsider "whether the present is as secular as we now think" (p. 608), Kaufmann explains that "the secular and the religious depend on *each other* for meaning." In literary studies, as much as in other discourses and disciplines, "what counts as 'religious' and what counts as 'secular' . . . will change according to setting and time" (pp. 610–611). Indeed, he continues, for contemporary scholars of religion, terms like "'religion' or the 'religious'" are hardly "stable, universal concepts," just as terms like "literature" or "literary" have proven to be fluid, malleable categories for the discipline of literary studies. By understanding the religious and the secular not as a linear teleology (as we grow less religious, we become more secular), but as provisional, mutually constitutive categories which depend on each other for their significance, scholars of American literature have become better equipped to give serious attention to the claims of a writer like Don DeLillo, secular postmodernist *par excellence*, to be writing with a sense of the "almost holy or sacred" shimmering "in the background" of virtually all his work.

There are many ways to classify the role of religion in contemporary American fiction, too many to enumerate in these pages. For the purposes of this overview, however, I will take Kaufmann's discussion of the religious and the secular as my cue, and to his religious/secular binary I will add two others: the secular and the postsecular, as well as the postsecular and secular faith, terms that I will define at greater length in my discussion of *White Noise*. While far from comprehensive, these three pairs of concepts – all of which, we must remember, carry multiple and contested meanings for numerous academic disciplines – will serve as an organizing principle for comparing four of the most intriguing examples of religion's persistence in contemporary American fiction.

In these examples, different offshoots of Christian thought and practice serve as the predominant religious tradition in question, albeit some (DeLillo and Butler) prove much more heterodox and syncretic than others (Robinson and McBride). My reasons for focusing on texts that draw principally upon Christian allusions and imagery are twofold. First, as religious studies scholars routinely remind those who work on the subject of "religion" in other disciplines, the word "religion" itself betrays a fraught, Christocentric history, and the academic study of "religions" has a long history of grafting a tacitly Christian understanding of the word "religion" onto other spiritual and cultural traditions for which the term may not be entirely appropriate. Second, by maintaining a relatively consistent focus within a single tradition, one that is itself quite diverse and wide ranging, we can better concentrate on the way categories like religion, secular, postsecular, and secular faith define and redefine each other across the writing of four very different contemporary novelists.

DON DELILLO, *WHITE NOISE*

Toward the end of the penultimate chapter of *White Noise*, an atheistic nun named Sister Hermann Marie disavows her belief in the traditional religious dogma that the narrator, Jack Gladney, sentimentally supposes her to hold. Instead, she expresses a commitment to something like the "dailiness" that DeLillo describes in his *Rolling Stone* interview, insisting that although her "pretense is a dedication," her life is "no less serious than if [she] professed real faith, real belief" (DeCurtis 1998, p. 319). "If we did not pretend to believe these things," she tells Jack, "the world would collapse" (p. 318). Although critics routinely interpret this scene as yet another iteration of the novel's postmodern pastiche, its endless procession of insubstantial simulacra, there are other ways of reading this exchange that highlight the novel's sophisticated engagement with the religious, the secular, the postsecular, and secular faith – categories that persist across a wide array of contemporary American fiction.

By admitting that she does not believe in what Jack calls the "great old human gullibilities," such as God, angels, and the afterlife,

Sister Hermann Marie provides many of DeLillo's readers with justification to classify *White Noise* as a postmodern apotheosis of secular disenchantment. Christopher Douglas, for instance, begins his groundbreaking study of American literature and the Christian right by citing this very scene as a way to explain the secularization thesis I have outlined above. "Recasting religious belief in terms of pretense," Douglas argues, "the nun portrays religion in the final stages of secular decline...a vivid literary snapshot of American religion in the 1980s, but one that was spectacularly wrong" (2016, p. 2). Likewise, despite including DeLillo's later work as part of her study of "belief in belief" in postwar American literature, Amy Hungerford exempts *White Noise* from her argument, describing it only in passing as "a standard text of the old postmodernism" and an "aberration within DeLillo's oeuvre" (2010, p. xx), citing Jack's encounter with the atheist nun as her principal example. By interpreting *White Noise* as a novel committed to an inverse relationship between the religious/secular binary, where the latter expands as the former wanes, Douglas and Hungerford overlook Sister Hermann's central claim in exactly the same manner as Jack Gladney. Jack asks, "You've been praying for nothing all these years?" To which the nun retorts, "For the world, dumb head...We take vows. Poverty, chastity, obedience. Serious vows. A serious life. You could not survive without us" (DeLillo 1998, p. 320). The content of Sister Hermann's belief may not fit neatly within conventional Christian theology. "You would talk about heaven," she tells Jack, "you must find another place" (p. 318). But her "vows," her "serious life," and her lifetime of prayers "for the world" hardly reveal a "religion in the final stages of secular decline" (Douglas 2016, p. 2). To better grasp how DeLillo's atheist nun honors the traces of the "almost holy or sacred" that she finds in the "dailiness" of her dedicated life, we must look beyond the religious/secular binary and consider two concepts that might prove more illuminating: the postsecular and secular faith.

By maintaining the forms of religious practice while eschewing its dogmatic content, Sister Hermann Marie's dedication to pretense, her "serious life" of "vows" and prayers without God, closely resembles the condition of religious faith in the late twentieth century that John McClure and others call the "postsecular." Applying the term to postmodern American fiction, including and perhaps especially DeLillo's novels, McClure explains that, in postsecular fiction, "stories ... trace the turn of secular-minded characters back toward the religious," that the "ontological signature" of such fiction "is a religiously inflected disruption of secular constructions of the real," and that "its ideological signature is the rearticulation of a dramatically 'weakened' religiosity with secular, progressive values" (2007, p. 3). Examples of what McClure calls "postsecular" spirituality are not hard to find in *White Noise*. Jack's wife, Babette, teaches classes on proper posture in the basement of a Congregational church, where "the sweetness of their belief" strikes Jack as "the end of skepticism" (DeLillo 1998, p. 27). Withdrawing cash from the ATM, Jack experiences the "relief and gratitude" of an invisible system that "had blessed my life" (p. 46). Listening to his daughter Steffie mutter in her sleep during the airborne toxic event, Jack hears "words that seemed to have a ritual meaning, part of a verbal spell or ecstatic chant," only to discover that the phrase she keeps repeating is the name of an automobile: "Toyota Celica" (p. 155). The "white noise" of postmodern mass culture, far from furthering the "disenchantment of the world," produces a steady influx of enchanting disruptions of mundane, secular life, with product names and posture classes taking the place of prayer and liturgy.

Appropriate as the term "postsecular" might be for categorizing such scenes in *White Noise*, however, it does not quite capture the iconoclastic conviction with which the novel's atheistic nun rejects all images of the divine – including, one must assume, the postsecular spiritualities of quasi-mystical consumerism. To better understand the importance of DeLillo's heretical nun to the conclusion of Jack's spiritual search, I propose the term "secular faith." Martin Hägglund defines secular faith as dedication "to persons or projects that are *worldly* and *temporal*. . .the form of faith that we all sustain in caring for someone or something that is vulnerable to loss" (2019, p. 6, original emphasis). And although Hägglund, with some reliance on the secularization thesis, defines this term in opposition to religious faith, which he takes to be faith in the eternal, transcendent, or otherworldly, DeLillo's fiction – and, indeed, the fiction of many contemporary American writers – serves to complicate this binary. In novels like *White Noise*, the persistence of religious faith, in some form or another, provides a vehicle for, rather than an obstacle to, the sustained fidelity toward finitude and fragility that Hägglund and others describe when defining secular faith.

In *White Noise*, the nun's continued religious commitment – her dedication to the pretense of belief, which leads her to continue wearing the habit, serving the poor, and caring for the sick – is precisely what grounds her secular faith. Remaining faithful despite (or, perhaps, because of) her atheism is what animates her commitment to the "faith that we all sustain in caring" for what is "vulnerable to loss," as Hägglund puts it, to the "dailiness" that DeLillo describes when speaking of its "radiance." "Our lives are no less serious," Sister Hermann Marie reminds Jack, "than if we professed real faith, real belief" (1998, p. 319). She is, to invert the popular phrase, religious but not spiritual, embodying a form of life and a manner of coping with death diametrically opposed to the spiritual shopping that Murray Jay Siskind, the novel's postmodern, postsecular false prophet, recommends when he lists the world's spiritual traditions and glibly advises Jack to "pick one" (p. 286). Indeed, one might argue that this superfluity of belief, the supermarket of spirituality recommended by Murray, is precisely what the nun is rejecting when she crushes Jack's naïve, sentimental spiritual yearnings. By associating the consumer culture of late capitalism with a form of postsecular spirituality, and by giving the most vigorous rejection of all spiritualities to the novel's most explicitly religious, non-secular character, *White Noise* offers a sacramental attention to the everyday, a secular faith grounded in one of the most orthodox of religious traditions, as an alternative to the otherworldly escapism of ATM blessings and "Toyota Celica" chants.

OCTAVIA BUTLER, *PARABLE OF THE SOWER* AND *PARABLE OF THE TALENTS*

Where DeLillo appeals to secular faith by means of an atheistic nun, Octavia Butler's *Parable* novels respond to the intersecting crises of racial injustice and climate collapse by contrasting a new, fictional, syncretic sect called Earthseed as an expression of secular faith against the growing dominance of a nationalistic Christian right. Early in *Parable of the Talents*, protagonist Lauren Olamina explains her fears about her "least favorite presidential candidate, Texas Senator Andrew Steele Jarret" (1998, p. 19). Jarret, Lauren observes, "insists on being a throwback to some earlier, 'simpler' time." A powerful voice in the "Christian America" movement, he "wants to take us all back to some magical time when everyone believed in the same

God." Even worse, his followers "have been known, now and then, to form mobs and burn people at the stake for being witches." These acts elicit only the mildest disavowal from Senator Jarret (p. 19). Familiar as these patterns sound, there is one statement which today, more than two decades removed from the novel's publication, seems almost uncanny: "Leave your sinful past behind," Jarret says on the campaign trail, "and become one of us. Help us to make America great again" (p. 20). Unsurprisingly, he wins the election and inaugurates a regime dedicated to separating the faithful from the apostate, the obediently religious from the defiantly secular.

In contrast to President Jarret's frighteningly prescient Christian America movement, Butler's protagonist proposes an alternative rooted not in disenchantment or secularization, conventionally understood, but in a new form of religious community. In *Parable of the Sower*, Lauren begins to devise Earthseed, first as a personal creed that sustains her as she braces herself for the inevitable social and ecological catastrophes she anticipates, later as the series of spiritual teachings and rituals that guide a new form of beloved community through its attempts to survive in exile while a post-apocalyptic California burns. The principal injunction of Earthseed, which borrows from a diverse array of religious traditions ranging from American Protestantism to Yoruba spirituality, is formal rather than doctrinal: "Shape God" (1993, p. 17). This emphasis on shaping God through ritual and community praxis, as opposed to believing in the God of a preordained theological system, makes Butler's *Parable* novels a prime candidate for the kind of analysis McClure and Hungerford provide in their studies of postmodern religiosity in contemporary fiction. Countering a resurgent, anti-secular religious fundamentalism with what, at first glance, seems to be a postsecular experiment in "partial faith" (McClure) or "belief in belief" (Hungerford), Butler's *Parable* novels ultimately champion a project of "Shaping God" for the purpose of secular faith. By devising a new religious movement that strives to care for and preserve whatever is most vulnerable to the interlocking violence of racism and climate change, Butler's characters affirm the "radiance in dailiness" described by DeLillo and his nuns, not through dedication to the pretense of traditional belief, but by establishing religious liturgies, practices, and communities that can take better care of a world facing unprecedented civilizational crises.

Although Earthseed evolves throughout the novels as a counterpoint to Jarret's Christian America movement, a political project eerily reminiscent of the forceful advances made by the Christian right in the United States from the Reagan era onward, Lauren's new religion begins not as an ambitious attempt at building a robust counterhegemonic bloc, but as a deeply personal response to her own family's Evangelical beliefs. Lauren's God, she explains, is not "a big-daddy-God or a big-cop-God or a big-king-God." Disentangling the notion of God from institutions of patriarchy ("daddy"), state violence ("cop"), and sociopolitical authority ("king"), her God is not a "superperson" or "an ultimate reality" (1993, p. 15). Rather, "God" in Earthseed is the name given to the most immanent of natural phenomena: Change. In one of her first entries into "Earthseed: The Book of the Living," Lauren writes:

> We do not worship God.
> We perceive and attend God.
> We learn from God.
> With forethought and work,
> We shape God.
> In the end, we yield to God.
> We adapt and endure,
> For we are Earthseed
> And God is Change.
>
> (1993, p. 17)

In Earthseed, God is not an immutable and omnipotent supreme being, and God is most certainly not the authoritarian patriarch who licenses Christian America's mission to "make America great again." Rather, her God is the very contingency and finitude which inheres in all experience of being in the world. To know God is both to attend with care to the material world as it perpetually changes, and to shape the world oneself, to contribute constructively to its open ended, non-teleological processes of endless change.

MARILYNNE ROBINSON, GILEAD

Unlike DeLillo, whose attention to the "radiance in dailiness" emerges through the dedicated pretense of an unbelieving nun, or Butler, whose counterpoint to the binary between religious fundamentalism and the disenchantment of the world involves the fictional creation of a syncretic new religious movement, Marilynne Robinson's fiction draws primarily upon a familiar form of orthodox Christianity: Calvinism. Turning theological discourse into the material of characterization and conflict, Robinson's Gilead anchors an aesthetics of the quotidian within a background replete with religious belief. In Gilead, as I have argued elsewhere, "the creedal orientation that Ames inhabits…constitutes a background and a system of thought that sharpens his aesthetic perception of the mundane, visible world" (Horton 2017, p. 120). The religious and the secular coexist rather amicably in Robinson's fiction, and John Ames, the narrator, embodies the pluralist, cosmopolitan erudition one comes to expect from characters who are "living in Charles Taylor's secular age" (Hungerford 2010, p. 114). Yet despite her work's investment in helping characters and readers "negotiate the difficult terrain where the spiritual and secular meet in our time" (McClure 2007, p. 25), the doctrinally specific and historically grounded religiosity of Robinson's Gilead novels leaves them somewhat less amenable to the label "postsecular." Rather, by situating characters within a religious background that prompts them to pay closer attention to the textures of daily life, to the "radiance in dailiness," Robinson's work offers yet another example of contemporary American fiction which draws upon religious thought and practice in order to explore a form of secular faith.

Reflecting on what he has learned from his father (who, like Ames, was a minister), which his father learned, in turn, from Ames's grandfather (also a minister), John Ames explains to his son: "When you encounter another person … it is as if a question is being put to you … What is the Lord asking of me in this situation?" (2004, p. 124). Explaining the weighty responsibility provoked by the "encounter" with another, Ames continues, turning to a somewhat unconventional reading of Calvin:

> Calvin says somewhere that each of us is an actor on a stage and God is the audience. That metaphor has always interested me, because it makes us artists of our behavior, and the reaction of God to us might be thought of as aesthetic rather than morally judgmental in the ordinary sense. How well do we understand our role? With how much assurance do we perform it? I suppose Calvin's God was a Frenchman, just as mine is a Middle Westerner of New England extraction. Well, we all bring such light to bear on these great matters as we can.
>
> (2004, p. 124)

While it would be easy enough to understand Ames to be making the familiar observation one is likely to find in much postsecular thought – that our images of God are socially constructed, byproducts of custom and convention rather than universally binding truths – I would argue that it is Ames's emphasis on the aesthetic itself which captures the principal focus of Robinson's fictional engagement with religion as a model for secular faith. The difference between Calvin's "Frenchman" God and Ames's "Middle Westerner" God is not merely the difference between historical and cultural circumstances; rather, Ames is making a point about how a Calvinist picture of God, cobbled out of whatever imaginative resources are ready to hand, pivots around the questions of aesthetic judgment and interpersonal encounter. Where one comes by one's image of God is, for Ames, a peripheral matter; what counts is how one's faith in that God serves to shape one's perception of both the "aesthetic" and the "encounter." To believe in God, in other words, is for Ames to live one's life as though one is an artwork with a divine audience; it is, moreover, to encounter others with the same "aesthetic rather than morally judgmental" disposition; finally, it is to attend to every surface of the material world, as Ames goes on to reflect, from the assumption that "the world exists for God's enjoyment, not in any simple sense, of course, but as you enjoy the *being* of a child even when he is in every way a thorn in your heart" (2004, pp. 124–125).

Insofar as Robinson invites her reader to consider her narrator with the same "aesthetic rather than morally judgmental" perspective that Ames ascribes to Calvin's understanding of God, however, it is difficult to avoid a certain amount of ethical reflection. For despite the extraordinary attention Ames is able to direct toward the material world and its most quotidian elements, he periodically proves to be an unreliable narrator, prone to significant lapses in attention with regard to the experiences of others. The inattention in some areas that results from his remarkable perceptiveness in others interferes with his ability to comprehend the needs of his godson, Jack. More troubling, it blinds him to the crisis of racial injustice facing his own church and community in rural Iowa during the 1950s. For if the call to encounter the other as if "a question is being put to you" by God himself is a family tradition passed through Ames's grandfather, the other significant legacy of the elder John Ames is that of the abolitionist struggles in Bleeding Kansas, during which Ames's grandfather proudly took up arms alongside John Brown. And this legacy, as we discern from observing how Jack reacts when Ames responds to his questions about Gilead's history, proves to have been less faithfully preserved.

When Jack asks Ames about the radical history behind his family and town, Ames comes across as amiable but somewhat oblivious. "When I was growing up," Jack recalls, pressing the issue more pointedly, "there were some Negro families in this town." Ames replies, "Yes . . . but they left some years ago." Jack suggests that this might have something to do with a fire at their church, and Ames reflects, "yes, but that was *many* years ago," downplaying the fire's seriousness by noting that "it was only a small fire" which caused "very little damage." Unlike Ames, Jack is quick to recognize the injustice and hypocrisy of the situation: "So they're all gone now," Jack remarks, leading to a long, awkward silence that lingers until Jack encourages Ames to talk about a subject on which he is considerably more garrulous: the theologian Karl Barth (Robinson 2004, p. 171). While religion, for Ames, serves as the impetus to a kind of secular faith, a committed attention to and care for that which is finite and familiar, immanent and ordinary, it nonetheless shapes intellectual and ethical barriers that Ames never quite manages to overcome. As one critic observes, readers are left uncertain "whether to bless the town or exercise our judgment upon it" (Vander Weele 2010, p. 232), and for many readers, the same seems to be true of Ames and the theological sources that prompt his secular faith.

JAMES MCBRIDE, *THE GOOD LORD BIRD*

Where John Ames's memory of the fire at the local Black church in *Gilead* seems frustratingly fuzzy, a similar fire sets the stage for the narrative frame of James McBride's *The Good Lord Bird*, a fictional retelling of the events prior to and during John Brown's raid on Harper's Ferry. The novel begins with a prologue, dated June 14, 1966, describing the novel that follows as a document recovered from a fire at the First United Negro Baptist Church of the Abyssinia. "Fire officials blamed a faulty gas heater," the report explains (2013, p. 1). The story recovered from the "charred notebooks" tells the story of John Brown's abolitionist struggle from the perspective of an adolescent ex-slave named Henry Shackleford. Early in the novel, we learn that Brown's physical and spiritual eyes remain fixed so doggedly on his mission – "to deliver the Redeemer's justice to free His people" and "to exact the Lord's revenge" on all who sustain the institution of slavery (p. 53) – that he initially mistakes Henry's name for "Henrietta." Not wanting to offend the white man who simultaneously liberated and kidnapped him, Henry never corrects Brown's error until very late in the novel, when Brown is in prison awaiting his execution.

Brown's inattention to worldly matters – mistaking "Henry" for "Henrietta," praying for hours over a dinner that is beginning to spoil, and reciting long passages of scripture in the middle of a gun fight – paints a picture of Brown's Christianity that seems, at first glance, utterly otherworldly, entirely unconcerned with the "radiance in dailiness" that DeLillo and other contemporary writers tend to privilege. "Old John Brown could work the Lord into just about any aspect of his comings and goings in life," Henry recalls, "including using the privy. That's one reason I weren't a believer, having been raised by my Pa, who was a believer and a lunatic, and them things seemed to run together" (2013, p. 24). This contrast between the "lunatic" believer and the more reasonable, discursive unbeliever would seem to reestablish the religious/secular binary characteristic of the secularization thesis, but Henry's narration, as the novel progresses, presents something far more nuanced. "The Old Man's prayers was more sight than sound, really, more sense than sensibility" (p. 37), Henry observes, describing John Brown's spiritual practice with the sympathetic yet ironic distance one comes to expect from the literature that McClure and others call "postsecular." But in Henry's manner of describing Brown's prayer, if not necessarily in Brown's own perspective on his religious practice, we find the same sort of sensitive attention to the everyday that we have seen in novels as wide ranging as *White Noise*, *Parable of the Sower* and *Parable of the Talents*, and *Gilead*.

> You had to be there: the aroma of burnt pheasant rolling through the air, the wide, Kansas prairie about, the smell of buffalo dung... Just when he seemed to wrap up one thought, another come tumbling out and crashed up against the first ... and after a while they all bumped and crashed and commingled against one another till you didn't know who was who and why he was praying it, for the whole thing come together like the tornadoes that whipped across the plains, gathering up the sagebrush and boll weevils and homesteads and tossing them about like dust.
>
> (2013, p. 37)

Caught up in John Brown's boisterous, endless prayers, Henry turns the reader's attention back to the sensory experience of Bleeding Kansas – the hunger, the smells, and most of all, the tumult of righteous violence, rumblings of a brewing storm that, as John Brown predicts, will crash suddenly upon the nation like a tornado on the plains, "tossing [those guilty of upholding slavery] about like dust." Throughout *The Good Lord Bird*, Henry explores the religious conviction undergirding John Brown's secular struggle, a commitment to "caring for someone or something that is vulnerable to loss" (Hägglund 2019, p. 6) with few parallels in American history.

If, as Marilynne Robinson writes, "Literature and religion seem to have come into being together" (2012), then we should not be surprised by how thoroughly the fusion of fiction and faith has persisted into the twenty-first century. From the unbelieving nuns who devote themselves to caring for the world in *White Noise* and the new religious movement devised in Butler's *Parable* novels, to the extraordinary moments of aesthetic vision (and, at times, of ethical blindness) granted to John Ames in *Gilead* and the clever narrative reframing of John Brown's holy wrath in *The Good Lord Bird*, one finds throughout the past four decades of American fiction a lingering fascination with religion's capacity to shape how we look and what we see. "Wherever you turn your eyes," John Ames explains at the end of *Gilead*, "the world can shine like transfiguration. You don't have to bring a thing to it except a little willingness to see" (2004, p. 245). This art of transfiguration is but one of the many ways by which contemporary American fiction responds to the disenchantment of the world.

SEE ALSO: Afrofuturism; After Postmodernism; Butler, Octavia; DeLillo, Don; Ecocriticism and Environmental Fiction; Multiculturalism; Realism after Poststructuralism; Robinson, Marilynne

REFERENCES

Butler, Octavia E. (1993). *Parable of the Sower*. New York: Grand Central Publishing.

Butler, Octavia E. (1998). *Parable of the Talents*. New York: Grand Central Publishing.

Coviello, Peter and Hickman, Jared. (2014). Introduction: after the postsecular. American Literature 86 (4): 645–554.

DeCurtis, Anthony. (1998). Matters of fact and fiction. In: *White Noise: Text and Criticism* (ed. Mark Osteen), 329–330. New York: Penguin; 1st ed. 1985.

DeLillo, Don. (1998). *White Noise*. In: *White Noise: Text and Criticism* (ed. Mark Osteen), 3–326. New York: Penguin; 1st ed. 1985.

Douglas, Christopher. (2016). *If God Meant to Interfere: American Literature and the Rise of the Christian Right*. Ithaca: Cornell University Press.

Franchot, Jenny. (1995). Invisible domain: religion and American literary studies. American Literature 67 (4): 833–842.

Hägglund, Martin. (2019). *This Life: Secular Faith and Spiritual Freedom*. New York: Pantheon.

Horton, Ray. (2017). "Rituals of the ordinary": Marilynne Robinson's aesthetics of belief and finitude. PMLA 132 (1): 119–134.

Hungerford, Amy. (2010). *Postmodern Belief: American Literature and Religion since 1960*. Princeton: Princeton University Press.

Lukács, Georg. (1915). *The Theory of the Novel* (trans. Anna Bostock). Cambridge, MA: MIT Press; 1st ed. 1915.

McBride, James. (2013). *The Good Lord Bird*. New York: Riverhead Books.

McClure, John. (2007). *Partial Faiths: Postsecular Fiction in the Age of Pynchon and Morrison*. Athens, GA: University of Georgia Press.

Robinson, Marilynne. (2004). *Gilead*. New York: Picador.

Robinson, Marilynne. (2012). Reclaiming a sense of the sacred. *The Chronicle of Higher Education* (February 12, 2012). https://www.chronicle.com/article/reclaiming-a-sense-of-the-sacred/ (accessed August 4, 2021).

Taylor, Charles. (2007). *A Secular Age*. Cambridge, MA: Harvard University Press.

Vander Weele, Michael. (2010). Marilynne Robinson's *Gilead* and the difficult gift of human exchange. Christianity and Literature 59 (2): 217–239.

Weber, Max. (1919). Science as a vocation. In: *From Max Weber: Essays in Sociology* (ed. C. Wright Mills and Hans Gerth, 1946), 129–156. New York: Routledge.

FURTHER READING

Fessenden, Tracy. (2014). The problem of the postsecular. American Literary History 26 (1): 154–167.

Furani, Khaled. (2015). Is there a postsecular? Journal of the American Academy of Religion 83 (1): 1–26.

Garton-Gundling, Kyle. (2019). *Enlightened Individualism: Buddhism and Hinduism in American Literature from the Beats to the Present*. Columbus: Ohio State University Press.

Haddox, Thomas. (2013). *Hard Sayings: The Rhetoric of Christian Orthodoxy in Late Modern Fiction*. Columbus: Ohio State University Press.

Knight, Mark. (ed.) (2016). *The Routledge Companion to Religion and Literature*. New York: Routledge.

Revoyr, Nina

MONICA CHIU
University of New Hampshire, USA

Issues relative to race and space consistently intertwine themselves across Nina Revoyr's six novels. Place resonates through Revoyr's work, as it does in her American regional literary predecessors: Sarah Orne Jewett's rural Maine, Mary Wilkins Freeman's pastoral New England, William Faulkner's Southern Yoknapatawpha County, and Cormac McCarthy's beautiful but brutal West. Revoyr's sympathies lie predominantly in and around Los Angeles, never allowing her readers to forget that race informs space. She plunges us into the low-income neighborhoods of South Los Angeles' Crenshaw district and the predominantly white and wealthy gated communities of Beverly Hills; she introduces us to theater spaces where Asian Americans attempted to reinvent themselves, to mixed-race basketball courts as safe racial spaces, and to California's mountain canyons, dangerous ravines because they might conceal Mexican drug cartels and white nationalists. Beauty and violence converge in Revoyr's racial spaces.

As a theoretical approach, I turn to Sherene H. Razack's introduction, "When Place Becomes Race," in her edited collection *Race, Space, and the Law: Unmapping a White Settler Society* (2002). "Unmapping" in Razack's work implies taking a critical look at how we divide, name, and use spaces, from land stolen through settler colonialism to current enclaves still divided by racism and therefore often bereft of essential resources. Razack incisively asks, "What is being imagined or projected on to specific spaces and bodies, and what is being enacted there?... How are people kept in their place... how does place become race?" (2002, p. 5). These questions become statements in Revoyr's work in that space is raced, and (darker) bodies are enacted upon because they are perceived as less privileged in that space, the latter defined as both physical locations and figurative arenas.

Revoyr was born in Tokyo to a Japanese mother, a survivor of World War II, and a Polish American father. After her parents divorced, she spent some time as the only biracial child in Marshfield, Wisconsin, living on her paternal grandparents' farm – the lived racism and its psychological discomfort inform aspects of her novel *Wingshooters* (2011) – before moving with her father to Culver City, California, in Los Angeles County (see Revoyr 2003). She later earned a bachelor's degree at Yale University and an MFA in creative writing at Cornell University. She has been honored with an Edgar Award and a Lambda Literary Award (Gilmartin 2004). In addition to being an acclaimed author, Revoyr also is an administrator in an institute aiding youth traumatized by violence in their Los Angeles locations (Gilmartin 2004).

It is no surprise, then, that the city in which she lives, writes, and works – the city of angels – serves as the predominant catalyst for Revoyr's focus on anger, race riots, and resistance in five of her six novels. Race for Revoyr is an element of friction and anger as well as attachment, unification, and alliance. Los Angeles has a history of both harmonious and contentious race relations, outlined in studies by Scott Kurashige on the history of race and Mike Davis on issues related to water and resources. Into these histories, steps Revoyr.

In her second novel, *Southland* (2003), wherein *land* and thus the occupation of *space* persist in the title and throughout the work, Revoyr describes how Crenshaw was a racially diverse neighborhood in the 1930s, but after its Japanese American residents were interned, became heavily occupied by predominantly Black residents (see Chiu 2014). In *Southland*, the revelation of this history of race relations unfolds through an unsolved racist crime. Japanese American protagonist Jackie Ishida, in paying tribute to her recently deceased grandfather, discovers a mystery involving several Black boys locked and frozen to death in a grocery freezer during the 1964 Watts riots of South Central LA. A white police officer is the novel's racist perpetrator who accuses the boys/victims of being "two-bit hoodlums" only because they are Black (Chiu 2014, p. 238). According to Caroline H. Yang, the store – passed from Black hands to Jackie's Japanese American father, bequeathed to his (deceased) Black-Japanese son, operated by Korean owners by novel's conclusion – suggests an "ongoing war against blacks" (2018, p. 188). The store ultimately is not a coalitional space, as Jackie's grandfather views it, but a racial war zone and "a site of death only for the black characters" (p. 189). "*Southland*," Yang argues, "concedes to the limits of solidarity in and through the store," wherein Blackness is always incomparable to, or less than, whiteness and Asianness, yet the latter is still inferior to whiteness (p. 189).

Revoyr never lets us forget that race relations are entangled in economic class issues, as evident in her latest novel, *A Student of History* (2019). Protagonist and biracial graduate student Rick Nagano, of Japanese and Polish heritage, accompanies his prosperous employer, Mrs. W—, to an event at an opulent residence: white fashion models dressed in impractical outfits yet able to walk on water provide a visual image by which to understand the different kind of (shaky) ground on which her raced characters often traverse: facing daily discrimination, the latter must tread carefully in daily life while the former seemingly walk on water. The models are supported by a thin but buoyant strip of carpet stretched across a sparkling swimming pool of a gated Hollywood Hills estate, channeling how property secures and secludes the wealthy, obstructs and rejects those without equivalent financial means. That the models are dressed in impractical outfits suggests the fun and frivolity of everyday life enjoyed by those who hire and admire them. Fabric of the finest weave or softest cashmere, such as that worn by Mrs. W—, also channels difference, as it contrasts with the coarse and utilitarian fabrics donned by the estate's cooks, gardeners, and servers. The latter are grounded in a reality of hard and constant work in order that their employers may float and glide seemingly effortlessly in public.

Such are the relevant contrasts evident to 22-year-old Rick, himself dressed in a practical Gap button-down and khakis, when he unearths an unpublicized history of LA's wealthy white inhabitants, but at the destruction of his self-respect. When Rick ascends to Mrs. W—'s mansion, not inappropriately named Casa del Cielo (Heaven's House), where he will type scores of her handwritten journals kept from girlhood onward, it's as if he is driving "into a new country" (Revoyr 2019, p. 19). "All the way up the canyon, the hills had been green from the winter rains, but inside the gates, everything was even brighter, cleaner, as if the ever-present filter of LA smog was not permitted on the premises" (p. 19). The imperious Mrs. W— is un/identified through the use of an em-dash after the first initial of her last name. Is she so well known that she need not be fully named? Her wealth also is both hidden (in a gated environment nestled in the Hollywood Hills, even though to reside in that community always already publicizes wealth) and visible (she is a publicly well-known philanthropist).

Locations of affluence lay the foundation for *A Student of History*. Charity events and social affairs, all by invitation only, are attended by community members whose attire makes visible their abundance while money works simultaneously as an element that conceals ugly secrets. Mrs. W—'s clothes, for example, are "expensive-looking and elegant" (2019 p. 22), and even her bones had a "fineness" about them. Her fashion is au courant, but it does not necessarily serve attire's basic functions: Rick observes that she wore a shawl that "looked more fashionable than warm" (p. 39). Looking (fashionable) and being so are commensurate for Mrs. W—, while for Rick "looking" becomes a metaphor for seeming other than you are: "Funny, you don't look Japanese," comments Mrs. W— upon first meeting Rick (p. 23). Or Rick becomes other than she thought: "You look like an earnest young man" (p. 23). He certainly is part Japanese, and he begins his work with earnest sincerity. But cloaked in the corruption of his environs, he acts in contrast to the confidentiality contract he signs for Mrs. W—, becoming devious, like her, only to topple from his post, lose his graduate funding, and forgo his degree.

If "farther back in the hills was an entirely different world," according to Rick, one "hidden from the rest of the city" (2019 p. 18), the characters in Revoyr's *Lost Canyon* (2015) find themselves in a secluded world of the Sierra mountains, a land of feuding Mexican drug cartels and of white nationalists, the latter of whom chase the protagonists across crests and valleys, intent on killing them. For Black protagonist Gwen Foster, employed in a Watts-based agency supporting vulnerable youth, an appealing backpacking venture turns into a sickening survival game. At first, the hike beckons: a physical venture by which to stretch her corporeal capabilities as well as a psychological adventure to refresh her flagging emotional state after years of working in a neighborhood where one "had to be prepared for the worst" (2015, p. 18). Nature, she assumes, will be invigorating and nonjudgmental, as Gwen seeks relief from the daily negative assumptions and struggles, many the result of racism, that she and her young charges face.

The war on the mountain top between Mexican drug lords and white nationalists mirrors the racial wars at the mountain's foot in LA. Gwen's group sets off on a breathtaking path to a little-traveled place called Lost Canyon. Gwen's notion of losing herself in the wilderness becomes Revoyr's ironic twist: Gwen's Black body is exposed to more raw racism in this remote location in confrontation with the white supremacist gun-toting character AJ than in LA's crowded neighborhoods. The hiking group's accidental discovery of a large acreage of marijuana and the men who tend to and guard it, exacerbates the racial challenges Gwen expected to leave behind in the valleys. "You're a pretty one for a darky," AJ says, after touching her all over; later he tries to rape her (2015, p. 172). Similar to Mrs. W—, AJ possesses extreme power in his aerial territory, not with financial and social capital, but with a gun and intimate knowledge of the terrain.

Gwen survives. The ordeal ultimately strengthens her psychologically, but the trek to Lost Canyon costs the group the disappearance of Irish Japanese Tracy, who "just vanished" (2015, p. 311). That her body is never found allows for speculation about her possible existence elsewhere, a biracial woman powerful in spirit and body whose gifts of strength, positive persuasion, and survival are perhaps needed in another place. Is she a victim of AJ's or cartel violence, or is she a hero? These are questions Revoyr asks but does not herself answer for us.

She takes up similar questions in *The Age of Dreaming* (2008), where protagonist Jun Nakayama, a former 1920s silent film star, conceals a shameful past whose revelation is both a tribute to his success as a Japanese star in a white-dominated industry and a mark on his otherwise impeccable, principled character. The stage space invokes his ability to perform a fiction of himself – as innocent, pure, uncorrupt – in order to conceal a shameful personal history. At the novel's start, Jun presents his humble self, ironically, in highly embellished language. Its overwrought quality suggests a hidden depth to which readers have no access. We sense deception amid his pride, fear despite steady tranquility. Jun acts as if his alarming move from albeit short but scintillating notoriety in silent films to "my present state of invisibility" is one of current acceptance (2008, p. 15). Jun's comment on "the completeness of my erasure from public memory" in the same sentence as his claim to "have learned to take comfort in my obscurity" is jarring (p. 15). Something is intentionally shrouded between the formerly revered star and his current obscurity, a missing link replicated here: "Moreover, the fact that I even appeared in such prominent roles was itself an indication of racial progress . . . It is also a mistake to assume that the waning of my career was attributable to prejudice" (p. 18). Jun claims that nobody or nothing encouraged him to retire early in his maturing career, for "It was I who made that decision" (p. 18). Who is this "I" whose narrative voice and mannerisms are equivalent to the artifice of the screen? The screen is a space in which the public consumes a fantasy, one played by actors who become other than who they are. But can this be true for Jun, whose Japanese racial features are always already socially scripted, thus confining him to narrow roles? From Jun's confinement to playing particular characters because of rising anti-Japanese sentiment and laws (the Gentleman's Agreement, Alien Land Laws, etc.) to his possible contributions to the murder of a popular director to the prohibition against his openly loving white actress Nora Minton Niles, all are related to race. Image, not words, drives his reputation and his quiet conclusion: a 73-year-old has-been, dreaming of another age and perhaps a better time, when race did not prove a barrier to love and success.

In Revoyr's essay about the impetus for *The Age of Dreaming*, "Silent Dreams" (2013), she maps the novel's connection between fictional Nakayama and real-life Japanese American silent film actor Sessue Hayakawa. (Real-life connections also exist between Revoyr's fictional Nora Minton Niles and actor Mary Miles Minter, as well as between Revoyr's Ashley Bennett Tyler and director William Desmond Taylor.) Hayakawa was well known for his appearance in Cecil B. DeMille's hit silent film *The Cheat* (1915), starring Fanny Ward cast as white socialite Edith Hardy. In both of Revoyr's *A Student of History* and *The Age of Dreaming*, as well as in DeMille's *The Cheat*, a young white and wealthy woman serves as a catalyst between an Asian man and entry into Western elite culture from which he is racially and socially barred. All of the Japanese men, on and off screen, are driven to act against their better moral judgment. In *A Student of History*, Rick's eventual exposure of Mrs. W—'s financial payoffs to protect her son also uncover how young, wealthy Fiona, whom Rick thinks he loves, has used him. Mrs. W— and Fiona survive the public revelation unscathed, while Rick abandons his dissertation, forfeits his graduate school fellowship, and returns, we assume, to a less "rich" life without a job or a degree. Jun reveals his involvement, in the 1920s at the apex of his career, in the disappearance of Nora Minton Niles, a talented white actress half his age. In a moment of forbidden passion, they have sex, her subsequent pregnancy removing her from the screen, the cover-up devastating Jun's career. Returning to the resonance between *The Cheat* and *The Age of Dreaming*, the financial relationship between the former's Hishuru Tori, a Burmese trader of Oriental goods played by Hayakawa, and Edith (played by Ward), who borrows money from him, concludes in Tori's brutal sexual violation of her, the "cost" of her inability to repay him in cash. That Tori's ruthless behavior is scripted and managed by Hollywood resonates with the same culturally produced narratives circumscribing Jun in *The Age of Dreaming*. Race, sex, and the screen-as-stage collide in Revoyr's mystery.

If the screen is Jun's initial success and eventual failure, the basketball court figures largely in Revoyr's *The Necessary Hunger* (1997), about girls' high school games in LA in the 1980s, and within a blended Black and Japanese American family. Nancy Takehiro and her crush, Black Raina Webber, play ball within and without institutionalized settings: at school, in parks, on the streets. Basketball unites the young women of different ethnic heritage, but it also encourages unhealthy personal competition between them (see Markels 2000 and Yamamoto 2002).

Finally, an aching for acceptance, not competition, and the early revelation of the brutality of race rejection are eight-year-old Japanese American Michelle Le Beau's public and private challenges in Revoyr's novel *Wingshooters*. Michelle moves in with her white grandparents, who live in predominantly white rural Deerhorn, Wisconsin, a location that is far removed from Revoyr's Los Angeles, but also rife with race issues. Racism plays out in Michelle's adopted home, including her grandparents' objection to their son's marriage to a Japanese woman (hence implicating their disapproval of Michelle herself, their biracial granddaughter), and encompassing the rural community's unwelcoming attitude toward a newly arrived Black couple to Deerhorn, of whom one is murdered by a white resident, leaving issues of race unsettling and unsettled (see Sohn 2019). That the interplay of location and race marks Revoyr's work indicates that, from the most diverse of cities to the paucity of diversity in America's rural Midwest, her Asian American characters must navigate race within their place.

SEE ALSO: Jen, Gish; Kingston, Maxine Hong; Lahiri, Jhumpa; Lee, Chang-rae; Mukherjee, Bharati; Multiculturalism; Ng, Celeste; Ng, Fae Myenne; Tan, Amy; Urban Fiction

REFERENCES

Chiu, Monica. (2014). The conspicuous subjects of interracial spaces in Nina Revoyr's *Southland*. In: *Scrutinized! Surveillance in Asian North American Literature* (ed. Monica Chiu), 48–67. Honolulu: University of Hawai'i Press.

Gilmartin, T.A. (2004). Nina Revoyr's *Southland*: a Los Angeles love story. *Lesbian News* 29 (9): 22.

Markels, Robin Bell. (2000). The conduct and culture of women's basketball in *The Necessary Hunger*. *Aethlon* 17 (2): 143–157.

Razack, Sherene. (2002). Introduction: when place becomes race. In: *Race, Space, and the Law: Unmapping a White Settler Society* (ed. Sherene Razack), 1–20. Toronto: Between the Lines.

Revoyr, Nina. (2003). Foreigner in Marshfield. In: *Dream Me Safely Home: Writers on Growing Up in America* (ed. Susan Richards Shreve), 172–178. Boston: Houghton Mifflin.

Revoyr, Nina. (2008). *The Age of Dreaming*. New York: Akashic Books.

Revoyr, Nina. (2015). *Lost Canyon*. New York: Akashic Books.

Revoyr, Nina. (2019). *A Student of History*. New York: Akashic Books.

Sohn, Stephen Hong. (2018). Inscrutable belongings in hunting: interracial surrogates in Nina Revoyr's *Wingshooters*. In: *Inscrutable Belongings: Queer Asian North American Fiction*, 159–195. Stanford: Stanford University Press.

Yamamoto, Traise. (2002). An apology to Althea Connor: private memory, public racialization, and making a language. *Journal of Asian American Studies* 5 (1): 13–29.

Yang, Caroline H. (2018). The Asian-owned store and the incommensurable histories of war in narratives of the city. *MELUS* 43 (2): 172–195.

FURTHER READING

Kennedy, X.J., Gioia, Dana, and Revoyr, Nina. (2013). *Literature for Life*. Boston: Pearson.

Kurashige, Scott. (2010). *The Shifting Grounds of Race: Black and Japanese Americans in the Making of a Multiethnic Los Angeles*. Princeton: Princeton University Press.

Robinson, Marilynne

LUCAS THOMPSON
University of Sydney, Australia

Marilynne Robinson is one of the most original and important figures in contemporary US literature. A deeply religious writer, Robinson's liberal Protestant worldview informs her entire body of work, which comprises five novels and six works of nonfiction, along with countless essays and occasional addresses. She has spent her career rethinking many of the animating assumptions of American cultural and intellectual life, and is as surprised as anyone by the extraordinary success and diverse audience she has found. A profoundly eccentric writer and thinker, Robinson occupies an unlikely space within US literature, as a wise and generous contrarian whose profoundly Christian voice is compelling to both religious and secular readers. Her literary reputation rests largely on her elegant prose style, elaborate extended metaphors, complex portraits of characters' inner lives, and her unmistakably American, regional vision of literature.

Born in Sandpoint, Idaho in 1943, Robinson was raised a Presbyterian, though she has said that her earliest experiences of religion came more as an "inherited intuition than an actual fact." Even as a child, she had an unorthodox intellectual life, drawn to various unfashionable and outmoded books, and inclined to follow her own interests and enthusiasms without any regard for contemporary intellectual trends. She was influenced early on by various ancient and Classical texts, learning, for instance, a "good deal about Constantinople and the Cromwell revolution and chivalry" (2012, p. 105). She left Idaho for an undergraduate degree at Pembroke College, now part of Brown University, from which she graduated with a Bachelor of Arts in 1966. Among her teachers was the celebrated postmodern novelist John Hawkes, who saw promise and potential in her work. It is hard to think of two more stylistically and thematically divergent writers, yet Hawkes's encouragement stuck with Robinson, who has since praised him as a "perfect" teacher (Voss 1992, p. 26) and credited him as providing a crucial early nudge in the direction of finding her vocation as a novelist.

Robinson spent the next decade working on a PhD at the University of Washington, which she completed in 1977 with a dissertation on the second part of Shakespeare's *Henry VI*. While working on her dissertation, she married Fred Miller Robinson, a professor of English, with whom she had two sons. (The two divorced in 1989 and Robinson has not remarried.) It was during her time as a graduate student that she began writing fiction: her first story, "Connie Bronson," was written a decade or so before her first novel and contains many stylistic and thematic elements of her later work. She also began experimenting with extended metaphors, an experiment that gradually evolved into her first novel, *Housekeeping* (1980). Written predominately in rural France, and set in the rural Idaho of her youth, Robinson assumed at the time that her deeply eccentric novel was unpublishable. However, a friend sent it on her behalf to a literary agent, who enthusiastically championed it to publishers, and the novel was subsequently released to great critical acclaim. On its release, it was ushered in to a new wave of feminist fiction by North American women, and taken by readers as a cerebral and lyrical antidote to the literary minimalism then in vogue. The narrative tracks the development of two young girls, Lucille and Ruth, cared for by their idiosyncratic aunt Sylvie in mid-century Idaho. But the real power of the novel resides in the complex portrait of Ruth's intense interiority, and her idiosyncratic vision of reality. It was championed early on by both Anatole Broyard, in *The New York Times Book Review*, and the novelist Doris Lessing. In 1987, it was adapted into a feature film directed by Bill Forsyth.

After completing her PhD and publishing *Housekeeping*, Robinson moved to the East Coast, where she lived for twenty years, teaching at Amherst College and in the Creative Writing Department at the University of Massachusetts Amherst (together with short-term appointments in England), before moving to Iowa City to take a position at the Iowa Writers Workshop. Robinson taught here for almost thirty years, from 1991 to 2016. For much of this mid-career period, Robinson published very little. The long stretch from the publication of her first novel, in 1980, to her first major nonfiction work, *The Death of Adam: Essays on Modern Thought* (1998) was almost twenty years, and it was not until 2004 that she reemerged as a novelist once more with *Gilead*. The only other publication in the intervening years was *Mother Country* (1989), a jeremiad against the use of nuclear power in the UK, with Robinson taking aim at Sellafield, a notorious government-operated nuclear reprocessing plant on the Irish Sea that had polluted the surrounding landscape and community. The book was mostly well-received, and was a finalist for the National Book Award for Non-Fiction. But it also led to Robinson being sued by Greenpeace for alleged libel. Refusing to recant, Robinson's book was banned in the UK, where to this day it cannot legally be sold. Her long publishing hiatus, with the exception of this unexpected piece of investigative journalism, is almost unheard of in the contemporary literary world, where young writers feel immense pressure to follow up a successful debut with another novel as quickly as possible. Of course, Robinson was raising children in these years, and teaching in various settings, but her disappearance from the US literary scene puzzled many readers at the time, particularly those enamored with *Housekeeping*, her extraordinary debut.

It was in these intervening years that Robinson embarked on a rigorous reading regiment of her own making, tracking down obscure and forgotten texts and immersing herself in theology, economics, and history, tracking down neglected and forgotten texts, and spending time with the kinds of primary documents – such as the writings of Karl Marx and the early Puritans – that are often mentioned by historians and intellectuals but rarely studied in their entirety. Considering her university education to have ultimately consisted in nothing more than "a kind of annotated bibliography," her ambition seems to have been to try and clear up certain blindspots and incomplete understandings in her own understanding of various matters. It was also clearly motivated by her guiding intuition that many widely accepted narratives – both those by intellectuals and those operating within the culture more broadly – rested on either misunderstandings or else lazy or ungenerous misreadings. Her polymathic program of self-education in these years has enabled her to speak authoritatively on many topics in her essays and addresses, both abstruse and mainstream. She has made important interventions in the understanding of canonical thinkers such as Freud, Marx, and Darwin, for instance, along with compelling arguments for reassessing the work of lesser-known figures, whom she takes to have been either unfairly neglected or mischaracterized, including William McGuffrey, J.F. Oberlin, and Marguerite de Navarre. The one figure, though, on whose behalf Robinson has most consistently and passionately advocated is the sixteenth-century Reformation theologian John Calvin – or as Robinson sometimes like to refer to him, in a gesture of deliberate defamiliarization, Jean Cauvin. Robinson is surely the foremost apologist and defender of Calvin's thought, retrieving his reputation and thought from what she considers to be unfair characterizations. She has written extensively on Calvin's significance to Christian theology (particularly Mainline Protestantism) and European humanism, and shown how his conceptions of such theological ideas as grace and forgiveness can be rehabilitated and used within the lives of modern Christians. Alongside this decades-long recovery mission, Robinson has also offered countless reappraisals of the American Puritans who were so heavily influenced by Calvin's thought, and has gone to great lengths in order to make their thinking both intellectually and theological respectable to modern readers. (She has also written a long preface to a new edition of Calvin's *Selected Writings* [2006].)

As one might expect from a writer with such intellectual preoccupations, Robinson's novels are concerned with weighty theological questions, concerning the nature of grace, for instance, and the possibilities of spiritual redemption, all of which are worked out in tangible, eminently physical forms. *Gilead*, for instance, weaves the history of American slavery and western expansion into a narrative of a troubled son's homecoming. Written as a gloss on the Parable of the Prodigal Son, the novel is fundamentally concerned with forgiveness and grace, and the possibilities for wayward and wearied souls to find peace and rest. Set in 1956, at the dawn of the Civil Rights movement, and articulating a complex historical account of midwestern Christians committed to the Abolitionist cause, the novels in the *Gilead* series offer a self-consciously revisionist history of US racial politics. They do so by giving readers a generous portrait of how faith can inspire a demanding vision of social justice, and by documenting the profound sacrifices and hardships endured by progressive nineteenth-century Christians, who set up churches and institutions across the Midwest to act both as bulwarks against the spread of Southern slavery and to help slaves to freedom. Many of the historical anecdotes Robinson includes – of the Underground Railroad, for instance, and of figures such as John Brown – are by no means readily accessible within the cultural understanding of slavery, and her account adds considerable complexity and nuance to this crucial period of US history. *Home* (2008) and *Lila* (2014) further flesh out this world, as does her latest novel, *Jack* (2020), as well as offering complex and tender character portraits of the kind found in *Housekeeping*. These novels are all concerned with the same characters and inhabit roughly the same time period, though they are not sequels or prequels in any straightforward sense. Instead, they each jump around in time, with many overlaps and scenes described from different points of view. With the exception of *Jack*, which is set in St. Louis, Missouri, the novels in this series take place in Gilead, Iowa – a fictionalized version of Tabor, in the state's southwest. Gilead is Robinson's version of Yoknapatawpha County (indeed, she has written a critical introduction to Faulkner's *The Sound and the Fury* [1929]), a setting within which she explores the various cultural and historical forces at play in this period of US history.

It is no accident that Robinson's novels all take place in the middle decades of the twentieth century. Characteristically, Robinson's portrait of this period fits neither the nostalgic tropes beloved of US conservatives nor those that have been endlessly lampooned and satirized by liberals. Here as elsewhere, Robinson asks readers to reconsider a historical period that has been mischaracterized, searching for nuances and complexities that have profound implications for how we understand the present moment.

In interviews and elsewhere, she has been forthcoming about her own literary influences, which include mostly nineteenth-century US writers such as Henry David Thoreau, Ralph Waldo Emerson, Emily Dickinson, Herman Melville, Edgar Allen Poe, and Walt Whitman. She regularly cites such authors in her essays (particularly in *When I Was a Child I Read Books* [2012] and *Absence of Mind* [2010]) and has also praised Wallace Stevens and William James. All of these influences have a palpable presence within her fiction and prose, but perhaps none more than Melville. (Robinson has quipped that an alternate title for *Housekeeping* might be *Moby-Jane*.) Revealingly, Robinson's list of influences are exclusively American, and she has made very few mentions of novelists from outside the United States. She is by no means a cosmopolitan in her literary tastes, and may in fact be the most purely American novelist writing today, seeing herself in relation to a long tradition that extends back to Jonathan Edwards and the first Puritan writers, through to the nineteenth-century New England Transcendentalists and beyond. Synthesizing many of these influences and traditions within her own work, she effectively transposes them into the Midwest of the 1950s. As many critics have noted, she is an emphatically regional writer, concerned with local customs, practices, and traditions, and with no desire whatsoever to participate within global literary traditions. Fundamentally, Robinson is an American writer and intellectual – not a world novelist in the least, but instead emphatically insisting on the importance of region and nation in an era far more focused on the global and international. Indeed, rehabilitating terms like *region* and *nation* is part of Robinson's broader intellectual project, and she constantly offers generous and historically nuanced programs for how this might be achieved.

Several critics have noted Robinson's antipathy toward the formal strategies and underlying assumptions of modernism – with the exception of Faulkner and Stevens. Instead, she writes with what she describes as a "democratic esthetic" that, in trying to be generous to all her characters, shares more in common with certain liberal Victorian novelists, such as George Eliot and Anthony Trollope, than other twentieth-century figures. Such an aesthetic points to an unmistakable dimension to Robinson's prose that is difficult to analyze: her respect – indeed, reverence – for her readers. All of her novels find subtle ways to communicate a lofty conception of readers, and Robinson has spoken in many interviews of her own recurring advice to creative writing students, to "write as if people who are smarter than you are will read [your work]" (Mulkerrins 2014). Robinson sees such a strategy as encompassing a properly spiritual ambition for fiction, as well as a way of avoiding the "air of falsity" that can "creep in" to prose that does not conceive of its future audience in such lofty terms.

Her novels each find different ways of exploring the sacramental nature of ordinary experience, and they take seriously the aspirations and strivings of various characters' souls. "Ordinary things have always seemed numinous to me" (Fay 2008), Robinson has said, in a statement that offers a kind of credo for her entire fictional method. For all of these reasons, particularly because of the central presence of Christianity within all her fiction, there are very few contemporary or twentieth-century writers with whom Robinson can be compared. Yet as idiosyncratic as her novelistic project is, she might be placed within a tradition of American Christian novelists that includes mid-century writers such as Flannery O'Connor and Walker Percy, as well as Annie Dillard, Brian Doyle, Madeleine L'Engle, and Frederick Buechner (in fact, Robinson delivered the 2012 Annual Buechner Lecture at The Buechner Institute at King University). Robinson shares certain thematic territory and in some cases even stylistic affinities with such writers, though her wide-ranging autodidacticism and provocative nonfiction ultimately mean that she has more in common with the nineteenth-century American writers she admires.

If she is often a generous, kind, and loving presence in her fiction, her prose writing offers readers a slightly different version of Marilynne Robinson. In such pieces, she resembles nothing so much as a prophetess, railing against the follies of contemporary culture and making intellectual provocations of various kinds. She is intent on pulling the rug out from underneath comfortable assumptions and supposed certainties, whether those relating to economic rationalism or the kinds of science-inspired worldviews that she takes as hubristic parascience. In all her essays, but particularly in late-career collections such as *Absence of Mind*, *The Givenness of Things* (2015) and *What Are We Doing Here?* (2018), Robinson is a true contrarian, heedless of offending either liberals or conservatives. A genuine eccentric, she has nonetheless found a place as a respected public intellectual, offering theologically inspired perspectives on a range of contemporary issues.

While in lesser hands such an approach might seem that of a mere crank or curmudgeon, Robinson's rigorous approach to research, along with her sophisticated lines of argument, have proved compelling to countless readers who would seemingly have little in common for her intellectual approach. She is an impossibly erudite and rigorous in her essays, ranging over almost all of the pressing questions – whether political, cultural, religious, or otherwise – of twenty-first century life for mainstream publications such as *The New York Times*, *The Guardian*, and *The New York Review of Books*. Such work brings together the prophetic voice of the personal essayist with that of the nineteenth-century lyceum lecturer, and her immense productivity in recent years shows no signs of abating.

Both her nonfiction and her novels have been praised and celebrated by the most influential critics in the United States, and Robinson has received countless awards for her work, including the 2004 Pulitzer Prize for Fiction, for *Gilead*, and, in 2012, a National Humanities Medal in 2012 presented by President Obama, with whom she subsequently struck up a friendship. In fact, in an unprecedented collision of US politics and literature, Obama interviewed her in a lengthy and wide-ranging conversation that was published in *The New York Review of Books* in 2015. Robinson's work has been translated into countless languages and she is routinely spoken of as a candidate for the Nobel Prize in Literature. (In 2019, the British betting company Nicer Odds gave her 10/1 odds.) Rowan Williams, the former Archbishop of Canterbury, extolls Robinson as "one of the world's most compelling English-speaking novelists," and she has taught and influenced many noteworthy contemporary US writers in her creative writing classes, including David Foster Wallace, Paul Harding, Lan Samantha Chang, Ayana Mathis, and Fatima Farheen Mirza. Robinson embodies countless paradoxes that render her a true original – she is at once liberal and conservative in her perspectives on culture and theology; deeply learned but eminently accessible; morally serious but also slyly and subversively funny. A liberal humanist and an unapologetically devout Christian, Robinson's work has made a certain vision of liberal theology respectable and compelling to a largely non-religious reading public. She holds a unique position and reputation within US literature, and will surely continue to expand her devoted readership in coming decades.

SEE ALSO: Contemporary Regionalisms; Debut Novels; Literature of the Americas

REFERENCES

Fay, Sarah. (2008). Marilynne Robinson: the art of fiction no. 198. The Paris Review 186 (1). https://www.theparisreview.org/interviews/5863/the-art-of-fiction-no-198-marilynne-robinson (accessed September 17, 2021).
Mulkerrins, Jane. (2014). Marilynne Robinson: the Pulitzer Prize-winning author on her new book. *The Telegraph* (October 18, 2021). https://www.telegraph.co.uk/culture/books/author interviews/11158670/Marilynne-Robinson-the-Pulitzer-Prize-winning-author-on-her-new-book.html (accessed July 23, 2021).
Robinson, Marilynne. (2012). *When I Was a Child I Read Books*. New York: Farrar, Straus and Giroux.
Voss, Anne E. (1992). Portrait of Marilynne Robinson. The Iowa Review 22 (1): 21–28.

FURTHER READING

Cunning, Andrew. (2020). *Marilynne Robinson, Theologian of the Ordinary*. New York: Bloomsbury.
Engebretson, Alex. (2017). *Understanding Marilynne Robinson*. Columbia: University of South Carolina Press.
Larsen, Timothy and Johnson, Keith L. (eds.) (2019). *Balm in Gilead: A Theological Dialogue with Marilynne Robinson*. Downers Grove, IL: Varsity Press.
Mariotti, Shannon L. and Lane, Joseph H., Jr. (eds.) (2016). *A Political Companion to Marilynne Robinson*. Lexington: University Press of Kentucky.
Stevens, Jason W. (ed.) (2015). *This Life, This World: New Essays on Marilynne Robinson's Housekeeping*. Boston: Brill.

Roth, Philip

JOE KRAUS
University of Scranton, USA

By 1980, Roth was already one of the best-known and most controversial novelists in the United States. He had achieved renown and notoriety in his middle 20s with the publication of *Goodbye, Columbus and Other Stories* (1959) which won the 1960 National Book Award. At the same time, it brought him criticism when senior figures in the Jewish American community read his interrogation of Jewish tribalism as an instance of self-hatred. His fame, and its counterbalanced criticism, rose dramatically with the 1969 publication of *Portnoy's Complaint*, a novel narrated by a successful young man speaking to his psychoanalyst about his sexual exploration and conflicted relationship to his Jewish family, with his wanting, as Portnoy puts it, to "put the id back in yid" (1969, p. 124). While *Portnoy's Complaint* has come to be regarded as a seminal work of American literature, some outspoken critics of the time – most notably Irving Howe – saw it as a self-indulgent, even dangerous departure from literature as a tool of broad social critique.

Roth published a handful of additional novels in the 1970s, but they are less well regarded in retrospect than the work that first emerged in 1979 with the publication of *The Ghost Writer*, the opening volume in what eventually became known as the first of the Zuckerman trilogies. Like Roth himself, Nathan Zuckerman is a Jewish American novelist, one concerned with locating his identity between poles of tradition and modernity. In *The Ghost Writer*, Zuckerman makes a visit to the home of E.I. Lonoff, a distinguished older novelist often seen as a fictionalized version of Bernard Malamud. While there, he meets a young woman, Amy Bellette, who may or may not be Lonoff's mistress and whom Zuckerman comes to imagine as Anne Frank, survived to adulthood but unwilling to acknowledge herself as the author of the famous Holocaust diary. The novel was well received – it was a finalist for the 1980 Pulitzer Prize in fiction – and it set in motion the slow transformation in his reputation from provocative young bad boy to more contemplative and mature author. His next novels, 1981's *Zuckerman Unbound* and 1983's *The Anatomy Lesson*, dealt with Zuckerman's sudden fame as a consequence of having published a novel seemingly reflective of *Portnoy's Complaint* and the first inklings of the physical and emotional toll that middle age would bring.

Taken as a whole – indeed, published as a whole with an additional novella under the title *Zuckerman Bound* in 1985 – the trilogy established perhaps the central theme of Roth's mid- and late career: the calculated commingling of his lived and written lives. Perhaps in response to widespread speculation that he "was" Zuckerman – and perhaps as a reflection of his exposure to authors of communist Europe such as Milan Kundera and Bruno Schulz, whose suppressed work he daringly helped promote in the West – Roth followed up the trilogy with *The Counterlife* in 1986, an experimental narrative that asserted the fictionality of his literary alter ego. *The Counterlife* begins with Zuckerman considering the experience of his brother, a man preparing to risk his life on an operation that might restore his sexual vitality. Then, in a series of "re-sets," the novel explores several different potential outcomes, or "counterlives." In some of those, Henry Zuckerman dies; in others he lives. In at least one, it is Zuckerman himself who is forced to contemplate the choice of the operation. While Roth has other novels in which he foregrounds fictionality – most notably 1972's *The Breast* which features a man who, something like Gregor Samsa of Frank Kafka's "The Metamorphosis," transforms into a woman's breast – it marked a clear contrast to the verisimilitude of most of his later work. At the same time, it was highly regarded, winning The National Book Critics Circle Award and remaining perhaps the high-water mark of his middle career.

As part of his continuing exploration of the line between the lived and the written life, Roth would, over the next decade, write two memoirs – 1988's *The Facts* and 1991's *Patrimony* – as well as two novels that closely reflected the facts of his own life. In *Deception* (1990), he wrote about a protagonist named "Philip Roth" who was married to an upper-class British woman. At the time, Roth was himself married to the Anglo-Jewish actress Claire Bloom and living with her in London. The novel is almost frighteningly intimate, consisting largely of pillow talk between husband and wife as their marriage unravels. Even though he and Bloom were a high-profile couple, Roth denied that *Deception* was an autobiography. At the same time, in *The Facts*, which was subtitled *A Novelist's Autobiography*, he included a letter purportedly from his fictional creation Nathan Zuckerman critiquing other parts of the memoir. The effect is to keep his readers guessing, to blur the line between that which happened and that which he invented.

In many respects, *Patrimony* represents a transition from that mid-career experimentation into the late-middle period that seems, from this vantage at least, the most successful sustained stretch of Roth's career. In *Patrimony*, likely his finest nonfiction work,

Roth explored his relationship with his dying father. One result was that he focused all the more clearly on the theme of mortality, on the experience that he would refer to in the title of a later novella as "the dying animal." Another was that, through his meditations, he stripped away elements of the metafiction he had constructed in the preceding work to obscure his lived experience. He worked toward a candor that, powerful in its own right, seemed to authorize him to undertake the fiction that would follow and, living alone in rural Connecticut, he became staggeringly prolific. His five novels over the succeeding seven years constitute as fertile a period as any American author has known.

Operation Shylock (1993) also featured a protagonist named Philip Roth, but it complicated the experience by providing him with a doppelganger claiming the same name. As he reports it, Roth is recruited by the Israeli government to help counter the efforts of that other "Philip Roth," whom Roth christens "Moishe Pipik" after a trickster figure from Yiddish folklore. The tangling of those two narratives, while playing on the themes of his middle career, extended the exercise into a more sustained social critique than he'd earlier managed. On the one hand, he echoed some of the "bad-boy" posture of his youth, giving to Moishe Pipik a series of sustained complaints about the effects of Jewish tribalism. On the other, in his own person, he spoke of a Jewish historical sensibility remaining relevant in the increasingly complicated politics of the Middle East as well as in the moral imagination of American Jews and Americans at large. And yet, he presented the entire discussion as a clear fictional exercise; though he was at times playful in interviews, it was apparent that he had never actually worked as an undercover agent for the Mossad.

Sabbath's Theater from 1995 showed Roth returning to the manic quality of *Portnoy's Complaint* with a harrowing and hysterical account of Mickey Sabbath, an uncompromising and never-to-be-appreciated puppeteer consumed in equal parts by his quest for artistic truth and his unrelenting sexual urges. Unsettled by the death of his longtime lover, his already unconventional life unravels, and he sets out to excavate elements of a past he had often fled. Sabbath is perhaps Roth's most fully realized holy fool, a man who, despite being named for the Jewish day of rest, can never find peace of his own. Sabbath stands, in many respects, as the necessary failure of the artistic imagination, a figure whom it is easy to imagine the younger Roth both drawn to and repelled by. Sabbath refuses to make peace with the forces of moral piety and facile patriotism, and he simultaneously finds himself unable to embrace the suicide that seems so appropriate to his situation. Nevertheless, at his own pace, he acts on an ethics all his own, honoring his country and those he has loved through actions others see as transgressive. The book won the National Book Award and was a finalist for the Pulitzer, marking it as among Roth's most lauded works even as it has come to be overshadowed in popularity by the novels that followed.

Roth cemented his career renaissance from 1997 to 2000 when he brought out the second of the Zuckerman trilogies. *American Pastoral* (1997), *I Married a Communist* (1998), and *The Human Stain* (2000) all explored broad and relevant questions of American identity in ways that few contemporary authors of the time accomplished. Implicitly answering the charge that his work was self-absorbed for presenting so many seeming iterations of himself, Roth came to employ Zuckerman as a point-of-view character rather than as a central protagonist. In each of the stories, the aging Zuckerman stands as the friend of a figure in the midst of a larger narrative. His own griefs and frustrations about aging pale next to the experiences of Swede Levov, Ira

Ringold, and Coleman Silk, yet his perspective amplifies the drama of their stories. Each of the centrally observed characters of the trilogy emerges as a cultural type, a figure representative of the best of which America is capable. Each is also tragic in the classical sense, brought low by the very strengths that raised him.

In *American Pastoral*, Swede Levov begins as a boyhood hero of Zuckerman's – a onetime star athlete who succeeded in the glovemaking industry. Zuckerman is reminded of his story when he encounters Levov's younger brother at a high school reunion and, from a combination of first-hand recollections and literary speculation, he recreates the story of Levov and his daughter Merry, a 1960s militant activist. Through the course of the narrative Roth simultaneously brings the Zuckerman story forward fifteen years, hones his career-long exploration of the nature of fictionality, and reopens the deep wound of the sometimes violent youth movement of Roth's own young adulthood. As part of a Weather Underground-like organization, Merry Levov committed acts of political violence that resulted in multiple deaths. As a consequence, at least in Zuckerman's reconstruction, she has drifted into paralyzing emotional illness, putting her experience into direct conflict with the seeming all-American success of her father. The effect is a simultaneous presentation of the twentieth-century American dream in the Jewish American context and, in the spirit of *The Great Gatsby* (1925), the wreckage that can follow in its wake. *American Pastoral* won the 1998 Pulitzer Prize and stands for many readers as Roth's most enduring single work.

In *I Married a Communist*, Zuckerman encounters another figure from his youth in Ira Ringold, a one-time radio actor whose career and then life are ruined by the accusations of right-wing culture warriors and the devastating break-up of his marriage to a fellow actress. In form, the novel echoes *American Pastoral*'s retrospective reconstruction of a fallen hero's life while it shifts its focus from the legacy of the 1960s to the earlier cultural wound of the McCarthy era. Effective as the novel often is in conjuring a character who bridged the "new left" of the 1960s and the "old left" of the 1930s, it loses some of that critique in the way it invests so much in the family politics of the marital breakdown. Some critics have expressed concern over the parallels between the failure of Ringold's marriage and the dissolution of Roth's to Bloom in 1994, and some discussion around it has descended to unpacking the ways it serves as an answer to a memoir in which Bloom condemned Roth's conduct. Despite that controversy, *I Married a Communist* sustains the later Zuckerman narrative, and other critics have argued for its standing within the second trilogy.

In *The Human Stain*, Roth ended that phase of his career with a stinging indictment of cultural sensitivity and with a direct inquiry into the question of race. The novel opens with purportedly Jewish professor Coleman Silk asking of a pair of students who have yet to attend a meeting of his class, "are they spooks?" (2000, p. 6). Although he intends it innocuously, the comment inflames the campus when the young men turn out to be African American. Charged with racism, Silk has to defend himself and slowly reveals his own history to Zuckerman: he was born a light-skinned African American himself and managed, through a lengthy self-reinvention, to present himself to the world as a Jew. As an extended consequence, Silk's life falls to pieces; he engages in an affair with an apparently illiterate woman and is ultimately killed in what Zuckerman suspects was not an accident. Zuckerman is so troubled by the experience that he determines to leave the Connecticut site of the second trilogy, marking the fictional end of his life there and, for Roth, marking the end of his late-middle career.

Roth's sustained success from 1993 to 2000 produced the widespread expectation that he would receive the Nobel Prize for literature, and it became a source of literary gossip that he was disappointed every year. Whether that was the case, Roth seemed determined to write at least one more novel that would strike like a cultural broadside, and the result was 2004's *The Plot Against America*. A vision of what might have happened if Charles Lindbergh had been elected President in 1940 and had kept the United States out of World War II, the novel is full of foreboding and evocative of a latent American anti-Semitism and racial intolerance. While generally admired, it struck many reviewers as less inspired than Roth's recent work. It featured a young protagonist named Philip Roth, part of a family identical to Roth's own, yet the extent of its alternate history made it perhaps less effective than, for instance, *Operation Shylock*, which foregrounded the playfulness of the speculative experiment. Recent years have seen a reevaluation of the novel – particularly in the wake of the effectiveness of Donald Trump's divisive political messaging – for its sensitivity to a strain of the American temperament few others saw so acutely. He never did win the Nobel Prize, a disappointment for his legion of fans if not for himself, but, having written *The Plot Against America*, he seemed to retreat from the "big" novel.

That said, Roth had a final, extensive chapter before him. Including *The Dying Animal* (2001), which appeared between *The Human Stain* and *The Plot Against America*, he wrote six short novels, one a year from 2006 to 2010, the cumulative effect of which critics are still just beginning to grapple with. As is clear only in retrospect, Roth was suffering from greater physical illness than was publicly known. Each of those final novels is a meditation on how an individual filled with vitality and called to the same sexual urgency of the young Alexander Portnoy confronts the inevitability of death. Few aging novelists have explored such difficulties while still retaining their full skill, and none have done so as repeatedly as Roth. As the narrator of *Everyman* puts it, "Old age isn't a battle; old age is a massacre" (2006, p. 157), and Roth powerfully sets up a succession of compelling protagonists whom he proceeds to "massacre" without sentimentality.

As part of that end-career exploration, Roth returned to his own childhood, working in details of Jewish Newark, New Jersey, more carefully than at any time outside his memoirs. The protagonists of most of the late novels recall their experiences growing up in the area, and there is a wistfulness, a sense of irrecoverable loss, hovering over all of them. Reviews of the novels were mixed – *Everyman* won the 2007 PEN/Faulkner Award while 2009's *The Humbling* (2009) came in for the worst reviews Roth had seen since the middle 1970s – but collectively they constitute his valediction from writing and life, two dimensions he had spent a career conflating. In that light, 2007's *Exit Ghost* was memorable for the way it provided a final glimpse of Nathan Zuckerman who, in New York, stumbles across the same Amy Bellette he met in *The Ghost Writer*, confronting the real woman he had imagined into the persona of Anne Frank. In even rawer fashion, *Indignation* (2008) presents Marcus Messner, a promising young writer who, caught up in the now almost-forgotten Korean War, dies before he has the opportunity to live the life Roth himself has known. And then, in *Nemesis* (2010), he imagines Bucky Cantor as an idealist who may inadvertently have spread polio to an idyllic summer camp. Across them, Roth showed a fearlessness about confronting old age and disappointment. If, as some critics charged, they departed from the larger critiques of American life of his late-middle period, they nevertheless interrogated the aging self with unprecedented clarity of mind.

Roth announced that *Nemesis* would be his final novel, but many of his admirers held out hope that he was, for a final occasion, telling fictions around his own life. Instead, his career seems complete and unusually well-documented. All thirty-one of his books remain in print; indeed, he was the first (and so far the only) living writer to have his complete work brought out by The Library of America. While Roth failed to win the Nobel Prize, and while he himself championed writers such as Bernard Malamud and Saul Bellow, he is on a short list of candidates for the most important American novelists since World War II. Few writers had a cultural impact comparable to his, and, of those that did, none matched him for critical acclaim. While known in some circles as the ultimate chronicler of Jewish American life from the twentieth century, he regularly insisted that he be seen instead as simply "an American novelist." Given the powerful mixture of humor, irony, and insight that he brought to his task – given the range of his concerns from the nature of sexuality to the intertwining of art and life, the violent side of pastoral America, and the toll that aging takes – he succeeded.

SEE ALSO: The Culture Wars; Realism after Poststructuralism

REFERENCES

Roth, Philip. (1969). *Portnoy's Complaint*. New York: Random House.
Roth, Philip. (2000). *The Human Stain*. New York: Houghton Mifflin.
Roth, Philip. (2006). *Everyman*. New York: Houghton Mifflin.

FURTHER READING

Parrish, Timothy. (2007). *The Cambridge Companion to Philip Roth*. Cambridge: Cambridge University Press.

Pierpont, Claudia Roth. (2013). *Roth Unbound: A Writer and His Books*. London: Vintage Books.
Royal, Derek Parker. (ed.) (2005). *Philip Roth: New Perspectives on an American Author*. Westport, CT: Praeger.
Schechner, Mark. (2003). *Up Society's Ass, Copper: Rereading Philip Roth*. Madison: University of Wisconsin Press.

Russell, Karen

CHRISTOPHER RIEGER
Southeast Missouri State University, USA

Karen Russell is an American fiction writer, author of three short story collections and one novel, all of which fall into the broad category of speculative fiction. Russell's work blends the realistic and the fantastical in narratives that often focus on child or adolescent protagonists. Her debut collection, *St. Lucy's Home for Girls Raised by Wolves* (2006), garnered praise for its surrealism, humor, and style. Her first and only novel, *Swamplandia!* (2011), was a finalist for the Pulitzer Prize, and her short story collection *Vampires in the Lemon Grove* (2013) was named to many best books of the year lists. She published *Sleep Donation: A Novella* in 2014, and her latest book of short stories, *Orange World and Other Stories* (2019), mixes elements of speculative fiction with realistic character portraits and was named one of the year's best short story collections by *Library Journal*.

Russell was born July 10, 1981 in Miami, Florida and says she knew she always wanted to be a writer. She graduated from Coral Gables Senior High School in 1999, graduated *summa cum laude* from Northwestern University in 2003 with a BA in Spanish, and received her MFA from Columbia University in 2006. As of 2020, she lived in Portland, Oregon with her husband, Tony Perez, an editor at Tin House, her son and daughter. In 2010 Russell spent time as a visiting writer at the Iowa Writers' Workshop and was a 2011

Guggenheim Fellow and a 2012 Fellow at the American Academy in Berlin. She served as an artist in residence at Yaddo in Saratoga Springs, New York, in 2013, and in the fall of 2013, Russell was a distinguished guest teacher of creative writing in the MFA program at Rutgers University-Camden. That same year, she received a MacArthur Fellowship "genius grant." Russell has been the Endowed Chair in Creative Writing at Texas State University's MFA program since 2017, where she teaches in the fall semesters.

Among her primary influences Russell cites Flannery O'Connor, Virginia Woolf, Stephen King, Ray Bradbury, Gabriel García Márquez, Italo Calvino, Carson McCullers, Mary Gaitskill, Katherine Dunn, and George Saunders. One might detect the influence of Saunders in the weird and abandoned theme parks of *Swamplandia!*, while the dark vibes and weird characters of O'Connor's and McCullers's versions of Southern gothic, and even King's horror, resonate throughout Russell's work. The interior lives of her female characters suggest Woolf's influence, and García Márquez's or Calvino's inspiration is felt most keenly in stories that blend the fantastic and the real. Russell's world-building, even in short stories, is reminiscent of Bradbury's, as well as Kurt Vonnegut's or even Haruki Murakami. Readers may find Russell's work similar in some ways to that of contemporary writers like Jennifer Egan, Lauren Groff, Kevin Brockmeier, and Marisha Pessl.

Child and adolescent protagonists are prominent in her work, often as first-person narrators, which Russell commented on in an interview: "A lot of my protagonists are stuck between worlds, I think, coming alive to certain adult truths but lacking the perspective to make sense of them. There's something about that blend of adult knowingness and innocence that I find incredibly compelling" (BookBrowse n.d.). Russell is close to her own siblings (one brother and one sister), and her first two books feature numerous sibling relationships. Landscapes, especially the swamps, forests, and other natural environments of south Florida, also figure prominently in her fiction. *St. Lucy's Home for Girls Raised by Wolves* features stories (among others) about two brothers who search for their dead sister in underwater sea caves, encountering ghost children, glowing worms, and a dinosaur along the way ("Haunting Olivia"); children at a summer camp for those with sleeping disorders ("ZZ's Sleep-Away Camp for Disordered Dreams"); a junior astronomer stealing sea turtle hatchlings ("The Star-Gazer's Log of Summertime Crime"); a family migrating to the West on a wagon train with their father – a Minotaur – pulling the wagon ("*from* Children's Reminiscences of the Westward Migration"); a high school junior sentenced to visit an elderly amputee in a retirement home made of houseboats ("Out to Sea"); and the title story about nuns who care for a pack of feral girls. In these stories, the actual landscapes and ecosystems blend with the apocryphal ones of Russell's imagination. Special goggles allow the brothers in "Haunting Olivia" to see the ghosts of dead sea creatures alongside the living in the ocean: "There are ghost fish swimming all around me. My hands pass right through their flat bodies. Phantom crabs shake their phantom claws at me from behind a sunken anchor. Octopuses cartwheel by, leaving an effulgent red trail. A school of minnows swims right through my belly button. Dead, I think. They are all dead" (2006, p. 35). The setting of "The City of Shells" is equal parts natural wonder and tourist attraction, foreshadowing the setting of her debut novel:

> It isn't technically, a city: it's a megalithic formation of Precambrian Giant Conchs. The brochures make it look like some Neptunian version of Easter Island. The cover illustration

shows a dozen of the Giant Conchs, arrayed in a weird half-moon formation along the beach. Each of the shells is a swirly, pearly licorne, some the height of a house.

(2006, p. 158)

The book won the Bard Fiction Prize and led to Russell being named a National Book Foundation "5 under 35" young writer honoree.

Swamplandia! expands on the story "Ava Wrestles the Alligator" from her debut collection, revisiting the Bigtree family who operate and live in the alligator theme park of the novel's title. The novel is more in the magic realism genre than the fantastic and speculative worlds of Russell's short story collections. The child protagonists, strange characters, and counterpointed stories suggest the inspiration of Katherine Dunn's *Geek Love* (1989), a novel Russell has praised (she thanks Dunn in the Acknowledgments). When the mother – the alligator-wrestling star attraction of the park and center of the Bigtree family – dies, the three children, Ava, Osceola, and Kiwi, are forced to navigate their ways through adolescence toward adulthood alone. Their father, "the Chief," leaves them alone in the family-run "Gator-Themed Park and Swamp Café" on islands only accessible by boat when he heads to the mainland for a job he hopes will save the theme park and home that the children both want to leave and feel compelled to inhabit: "Every rock on the island, every swaying tree branch or dirty dish in our house was alike a word in a sentence that I could read about my mother. All objects and events on our island, every single thing that you could see with your eyes, were like clues that I could use to reinvent her" (2011, p. 71). The two sisters' encounters with ghosts, a mysterious Bird Man, and a journey to the Underworld leave readers unsure at first if the characters exist in a speculative reality, as in Russell's first book, or if Ava's narrative perspective presents the mundane as supernatural:

Each night he [the Chief] burned our garbage in a ditch behind the coop . . . Columns of thick smoke rose behind the red wall at dusk, and frantic clucks rose from the chicken coop like rainfall reversing itself, spraying up into the cumulus puffs in the night sky. From the kitchen window, I would watch the Chief build his midweek pyre: leftovers and little bones and milk cartons, eggshells and newspapers, a grab bag of detritus. Whatever we couldn't use or sell before nightfall, our chieftain struck a match against and sent to the stars.

(2011, pp. 51–52)

Counterpointed to the sisters' adventures is Kiwi's sojourn to the mainland to work at a rival theme park, the World of Darkness. His isolated upbringing in the swamps causes him to be an outcast in the mainstream culture he encounters for the first time and provides much humor to balance the more serious, even dangerous, travails of his sisters. Convinced he will save his family, Kiwi endures the indignities of community college night school and menial jobs, such as cleaning a giant whale attraction called the Leviathan at the World of Darkness: "Weekends, inside a whale: Kiwi worked the nine-hour Friday shift inside the Leviathan and for that period he forgot all about Swamplandia! He dragged his wheelie bucket through the Flukes and he forgot his mother, his sisters, . . . his anger, his mission, his genius burning inside him all day like a grounded rocket" (2011, p. 226). The sections following Kiwi are highly realistic and told by a third-person narrator, while Ava is the first-person narrator of the sections focused on her and her sister, Osceola, that employ more of the surreal touches of Russell's short stories. One of the novel's strengths is Russell's ability to move adeptly between different perspectives, styles, and even genres. Reviewers praised the book's spin on Southern gothic, Russell's language and characterization, and her evocative depictions of the swampy settings of Florida.

The New York Times named the novel as one of the "10 Best Books of 2011" and it was longlisted for the Orange Prize, as well as being a finalist for the Pulitzer Prize (which was not awarded that year).

The stories in *Vampires in the Lemon Grove* feature more use of third-person narrators, less focus on adolescent protagonists, and a wide variety of settings spanning the globe. The title story is narrated by an elderly vampire narrator in Italy who does not drink blood, "Proving Up" follows Nebraska homesteaders guarding an extremely valuable window, and "Dougbert Shackleton's Rules for Antarctic Tailgaiting" is set in a version of Antarctica where natural contests between whales and krill are treated like football games. Fantastic and speculative elements are prominent in stories like "Reeling for the Empire," winner of the 2012 Shirley Jackson Award for best novelette, which follows young Japanese women being lured to a factory and turned into human-silkworm hybrids. "The Barn at the End of Our Term" finds President Rutherford B. Hayes reincarnated as a horse (alongside quite a few other ex-presidents). More realistic stories (always with at least a touch of the surreal) include "The New Veterans," set in a Wisconsin massage therapy office with flashbacks to Baghdad, and "The Graveless Doll of Eric Mutis," set in urban New Jersey. Similarly, in "The Seagull Army Descends on Strong Beach, 1979," an invasion of seagulls coincides with a particularly fraught period of 14-year-old Nal's life, leading to this seagull-infused nightmare that exemplifies Russell's singular style:

> Millions of them flew out of a bloodred sunset and began to resettle the town, snapping telephone wires and sinking small boats beneath their collective weight. Gulls covered the fence posts and rooftops of Athertown, drew a white caul over the marina, muffled every window with the static of their bodies – and each gull had a burgled object twinkling in its split beak. Warping people's futures into some new and terrible shapes, just by stealing these smallest linchpins from the present.
>
> (2013, p. 73)

Reviewers noted Russell's imaginative storytelling, humor, and emotionally charged narratives as hallmarks of the collection. "The New Veterans" combines these traits in a story about a massage therapist who is somehow able to manipulate the back tattoo of a war veteran so that his traumatic war memories shift into her mind: "She stops wasting her time debating whether she's harming or helping him. Each time a session ends without any reappearance of the wire, she feels elated. That killing story, she excised from him. Now it's floating in her, like a tumor in a jar. Like happiness laid up for the long winter after the boy heals completely and leaves her" (2013, p. 182). Themes of suffering and redemption connect the stories at least as much as Russell's style and fantastic world-building.

The 2019 collection *Orange World and Other Stories* is described by Russell "as being primarily a collection of long landscape stories, where setting is not a static, painted backdrop for human dramas but where nonhuman nature intersects with a character's interior world" (Gresko 2019). This emphasis on the natural environment is often tinged with ecological anxiety so that trauma and pain become avenues for humans' connections to nature. In the book's opening story, "The Prospectors," an avalanche buries Civilian Conservation Corps workers in the Oregon mountain lodge they were building, though their ghosts continue to party with human visitors. "The Bad Graft" finds a visitor to Joshua Tree National Park being invaded by the spirit of a Joshua tree, human and natural merging into something new. The desert terrain both reflects and molds the inner lives of the young couples seeking to escape themselves and their problems in nature:

> People think of the green pastoral when they think of lovers in nature. Those English poets used the vales and streams to douse their lusts into verse. But the desert offers something that no forest brook or valley ever can: distance. A cloudless rooming house for couples. Skies that will host any visitors' dreams with the bald hospitality of pure space. In terms of an ecology that can support two lovers in hot pursuit of each other, this is the place; everywhere you look, you'll find monuments to fevered longing. Craters beg for rain all year long. Moths haunt the succulents, winging sticky pollen from flower to flower.
>
> (pp. 41–42)

"Madame Bovary's Greyhound" explores a deep bond between human and dog, Gustave Flaubert's famous character and her companion, while wind farmers lead a precarious existence breeding tornados in "The Tornado Auction," and "The Gondoliers" is set in a post-apocalyptic (though perhaps not far-fetched) flooded landscape of south Florida that is almost completely underwater: "New Florida is composed of grassy water, the bleached reefs of submerged and abandoned cities, and dozens of floating villages. It's illegal to live here, although thousands of us do" (2019, pp. 197–198). The death-in-life theme of the opening ghost story is continued in "Bog Girl: A Romance," when teenage Cillian Eddowis falls in love with a 2000-year-old corpse that he uncovers in a peat bog, and in "Orange World," which conveys the horrors of new parenthood through the story of a new mother who agrees to provide a demon with her breast milk. It is in moments like these where Russell conjures horror from the routine and the everyday that the influence of Stephen King is seen in her fiction: the shocks of motherhood expressed through supernatural and gothic horror the way King milks terror from the trials of owning a house, car, or pet.

Russell's highly original stories blend elements of realism, the supernatural, the gothic, science fiction, magic realism, and tall tales in ways that keep readers off balance. Blending humor and horror, her stories are often effective and affecting character studies told in a dense, engaging style that draws from a variety of genres and influences to create a style unique to Russell.

SEE ALSO: Contemporary Regionalisms; Debut Novels; Ecocriticism and Environmental Fiction; Egan, Jennifer; Groff, Lauren; King, Stephen; Saunders, George; Trauma and Fiction; Vonnegut, Kurt

REFERENCES

BookBrowse. (n.d.). An interview with Karen Russell. *BookBrowse*. https://www.bookbrowse.com/author_interviews/full/index.cfm?author_number=1367 (accessed July 6, 2021).

Gresko, Brian. (2019). Orange world, elastic space: an interview with Karen Russell. *Poets & Writers* (May 13, 2019). https://www.pw.org/content/orange_world_elastic_space_an_interview_with_karen_russell (accessed July 6, 2021).

Russell, Karen. (2006). *St. Lucy's Home for Girls Raised by Wolves*. New York: Vintage Books.

Russell, Karen. (2011). *Swamplandia!*. New York: Vintage Books.

Russell, Karen. (2013). *Vampires in the Lemon Grove*. New York: Knopf.

Russell, Karen. (2019). *Orange World and Other Stories*. New York: Knopf.

FURTHER READING

Graham, Sarah. (2013). Unfair ground: girlhood and theme parks in contemporary fiction. *Journal of American Studies* 47 (3): 589–604.

Rieger, Christopher. (2015). From childhood to the underworld: native American birdman iconography and Karen Russell's *Swamplandia!*. *Mississippi Quarterly* 68 (3): 399–414.

Saunders, George

MARSHALL BOSWELL
Rhodes College, USA

Like his fellow Syracuse University colleague Raymond Carver, George Saunders is primarily a short story writer who focuses on the struggles and deferred hopes of white workers caught in the absurdities of contemporary capitalist America. While his work, like Carver's, is minimalist in many respects – the terse dialogue, the elliptical interiority, the brief brushstroke setting descriptions – Saunders eschews Carver's gritty realism for a flamboyant comic absurdity that is equal parts Kurt Vonnegut and Monty Python, both of whom he has cited as influences. His stories can take place in quirkily conceived theme parks, futuristic suburban neighborhoods, sci-fi laboratories, or cock-eyed corporate motivational seminars. For all its whimsy and postmodern play, however, his work remains firmly grounded in an ethics of empathy and kindness. His fanciful settings, no matter how far-flung from the real, always point back to, and diagnose, contemporary discontent. Writer Junot Díaz observes, "There's no one who has a better eye for the absurd and dehumanizing parameters of our current culture of capital," adding that "the cool rigor" of Saunders's fiction is "counterbalanced" by the "capacious[ness of] his moral vision" (Lovell 2013, p. 25). Meanwhile, Joel Lovell, in a *New York Times Magazine* profile promoting Saunders's acclaimed 2013 story collection *Tenth of December*, defines that "moral vision" as a desire "to be as open as possible, all the time, to beauty and cruelty and stupid human infallibility and unexpected grace" (2013, p. 24).

Like his down-on-their-luck protagonists, Saunders had a very unliterary background. Born in Amarillo, Texas in 1958, he spent most of his life in the exurban environs of Chicago, Illinois, where his father ran a series of chicken restaurants. After his 1981 graduation from Oak Forest High School in Oak Forest, Illinois, he studied geophysical engineering at the Colorado School of Mines. By this time, his parents had moved back to Amarillo, where his father owned a pizza restaurant. When the restaurant burned down, and the family was denied any insurance compensation, they moved to New Mexico and lived in a mobile home while his father worked on local oil rigs. Following his graduation from the School of Mines, Saunders worked as a seismic prospector in Sumatra (Lovell 2013, p. 26). It was during this time in Indonesia that Saunders began to read widely in the literary canon. As he told Joel Lovell,

The Encyclopedia of Contemporary American Fiction 1980–2020, First Edition. Edited by Patrick O'Donnell, Stephen J. Burn, and Lesley Larkin.
© 2022 John Wiley & Sons Ltd. Published 2022 by John Wiley & Sons Ltd.

"I'd been a kind of Ayn Rand guy before that," referring to the author of *The Fountainhead* (1943) and *Atlas Shrugged* (1957), books beloved by libertarians and free-market absolutists. "And then you go to Asia and you see people who are genuinely poor and genuinely suffering and hadn't gotten there by whining" (Lovell 2013, pp. 26–27).

Of the books he discovered while in Asia, the most formative was Kurt Vonnegut's *Slaughterhouse-Five* (1969), an encounter he details in his essay "Mr. Vonnegut in Sumatra," included in his 2007 essay collection, *The Braindead Microphone*. Describing himself at the time as "an untrained reader," he explains that, in those early years, he understood "great writing was hard reading" and "was done in a language that had as little as possible to do with the one I spoke" (Saunders 2007, pp. 73–74). What's more, he subscribed to the Ernest Hemingway idea that "great writing required a Terrible Event One Had Witnessed" (p. 75). Conversely, Vonnegut, who had been a prisoner of war during the Allied firebombing of Dresden in 1945, wrote about that Terrible Event via absurdist science fiction, all of it cast in an accessible language ever conscious of its own shortcomings. Saunders describes the reading experience as a revelation: "*Slaughterhouse-Five* seemed to be saying, our most profound experiences may *require* this artistic uncoupling from the actual"; what's more, rather than bear stoic witness to the Terrible Event, à la Hemingway, "Vonnegut's goal seemed to be to soften the heart, to encourage our capacity for pity and sorry" (p. 79). In many respects, this experience with Vonnegut's classic novel planted the seeds for Saunders's unusual artistic project.

Upon his return from Indonesia, he committed himself to becoming a writer, supporting himself by living in his aunt's basement and working as a roofer. In February 1986, having returned to his parents' home in Amarillo, he learned that Tobias Wolff had admitted him into the famed Masters of Fine Arts program at Syracuse University, where his hero Raymond Carver – sober, sainted, and married to poet Tess Gallagher, the writing program's legendary coordinator – finished out his remarkable career. In a characteristically generous and self-effacing account of his time at Syracuse excerpted in *The New Yorker*, Saunders reveals that he spent his time at the program trying to wean himself off the "silly humorous crap I applied to the program with, i.e., the stuff that had gotten me into the program in the first place" (Saunders 2015). When he told Wolff about this decision to produce more serious work, his genial mentor gave him a worried look and said, "Well good! Just don't lose the magic." And so, as Saunders explains, "I go forward and lose all of the magic, for the rest of my time in grad school and for several years thereafter" (Saunders 2015). Nevertheless, even as he was losing all this magic, he met and fell in love with fellow writer Paula Redick, whom he met during his first week at the program and married three weeks later. Their first child, Caitlin, was born in March 1988.

In 1989, he and Redick moved to Rochester, where Saunders worked as a technical writer for the Radian Corporation and continued to hone his craft. During this period, he and Redick welcomed a second daughter, Alena, born in August 1990. In an expansive "Author's Note" included in a 2012 reprinting of his debut collection, Saunders reveals that he spent the early years post-Syracuse writing a novel titled "La Boda de Eduardo," which, perhaps owing to its Mexican setting, was deeply influenced by Malcolm Lowry's *Under the Volcano* (1943). He claimed the original manuscript was "seven hundred pages," which he whittled down to "a very very efficient 250, rendering it even more difficult to understand" (Saunders 2012, p. 188). Redick's negative appraisal of the draft compelled him to shift tracks and return to the "humorous crap" that had originally secured his admission to Syracuse. What's more, his experience as a wage-worker in contemporary corporate America recalled the lesson he'd learned while reading Vonnegut, namely that "absurdism wasn't an intellectual abstraction, it was actually realism" (Lovell 2013, p. 27). The stories that emerged from this seven-year period would eventually make up his first story collection, *CivilWarLand in Bad Decline* (1996), the title piece of which first appeared in *The Kenyon Review* in Fall 1992.

Read in the light of the rich run of stories that would follow it, "CivilWarLand" serves as a concise microcosm and prophetic harbinger of Saunders's unique literary project. Set in a dying theme park, a premise Saunders would return to several times in his subsequent career, the story focuses on its compromised protagonist, a middle-management schlub trapped between the unethical demands of his desperate and disreputable boss, Mr. Alsuga, and his need to support his wayward wife and children. After the narrator agrees to hire a mentally unstable Vietnam vet to exterminate a group of teenagers who have been vandalizing the park, the narrator finds himself implicated in a mass murder only to discover that his wife has left him anyway. Written in Saunders's characteristic elliptical minimalism, the story boasts a number of additional features that would become hallmarks of his fiction, including a ghost family, a sustained parody of bureaucratic double-speak and pop psychology, and a violent ending resulting in a finale written from some undenominational afterlife. Even the Civil War backdrop anticipates his one and only full-length novel, *Lincoln in the Bardo* (2017), which is set in 1862 and dramatizes the purgatorial suspension of Abraham Lincoln's deceased 11-year-old son, Willie. Although the story lacks the emotional impact and formal lucidity of the work that would follow it, "CivilWarLand" succeeded in announcing Saunders as a new and original voice in the American literary landscape.

While the collection's remaining stories similarly invoke a range of themes and modes that would become touchstones throughout his career, *CivilWarLand in Bad Decline* is unique in Saunders's corpus for its unremitting cruelty. "Isabelle" asks the reader to empathize with a racist cop who senselessly murders a Black man but who nevertheless cares for his paraplegic daughter, while the narrator of the "The 400-Pound CEO" is exactly as advertised, a relentlessly abused 400-pound office worker who accidentally murders his boss, serves as company CEO for a day, and ends his miserable life in prison as the plaything for his sadistic cellmate. The collection's concluding novella, "Bounty," imagines a post-apocalyptic United States where people with birth defects, called "Flaweds," are routinely sold into chattel slavery. The narrator, while on a mission to save his sister from a life as a sex worker, gets rounded up by slave traders and undergoes unremitting torture before escaping to freedom. In all these stories, the depicted horrors rub shoulders with scenes of whimsical satire, while Saunders's prose remains rapid fire and deadpan throughout. What keeps the collection – and Saunders's art more generally – from collapsing under the weight of its purposeful contradictions is its unashamed sentimentality, which, in the context of the work's postmodern self-consciousness, emerges as heartfelt sincerity. At the nadir of his humiliation and failure, the 400-pound CEO observes, "If only I could say: Give up. Be alone forever . . . But no. My heart's some kind of idiotic fish bobber" (2012, p. 53). Taken out of context, the passage sounds mawkish and maudlin; encountered in the onrush of the story's catalogue of cruelty, the narrator's admission reconfigures the story's moral trajectory.

CivilWarLand in Bad Decline was rapturously received when it first appeared in 1996. The notoriously competitive novelist David Foster Wallace, fresh from the contemporaneous publication of his magnum opus, *Infinite Jest* (1996), famously declared Saunders to be "the most exciting writer in America," a pronouncement that helped cement the perception that Saunders and Wallace are, in Saunders's own terms, "like two teams of miners, digging at the same spot but from different directions" (Lovell 2013, pp. 25, 26). A finalist for the PEN/Hemingway Award, the book earned Saunders a coveted teaching position at his beloved Syracuse, where he has continued to teach ever since. Critics struggled to describe the stories' unique blend of high-handed satire and heartfelt seriousness. Both Jay McInerney, in his *New York Times* review, and David Gates, writing in *Newsweek*, hesitated to call Saunders a "visionary," but even these disavowals introduced the possibility, which Saunders's subsequent status among his contemporaries has amply confirmed. In his "Introduction" to *CivilWarLand*, Joshua Ferris, armed with sixteen years of hindsight, argues that Saunders's debut collection "established a new template for the short story . . . as influential as Raymond Carver's was to his generation, and even Hemingway's to his" (Ferris 2012, p. xv). In describing that template, Ferris explains, "while Saunders does satirize, or, in other words, render the real absurd, he also carefully and lovingly and artfully renders the absurd real" (p. xiv).

Saunders's second collection, *Pastoralia* (2000), closely follows that original template, even to the extent of opening the volume with yet another theme-park parody. The title-piece protagonist works as a "caveman" in a prehistoric theme park, where patrons get to "experience" life in the Paleolithic era. The heart of the story focuses, yet again, on the tested loyalties of its narrator, another compromised "middle-manager" who must balance his employee responsibilities with his desire to protect his threatened co-worker, a frazzled woman named Janet whose son is a self-proclaimed "Inadvertent Substance Abuser" (2000, p. 30). Although the mock Paleolithic setting serves as a fairly heavy-handed, but no less pertinent, parody of contemporary office life, the story generates deep empathy for the narrator, who, like the country's vast population of service employees, must endure humiliation not only from unfeeling supervisors but from entitled customers as well.

"Sea Oak" similarly addresses the plight of service employees, in this case a male waiter at a Hooter's-type restaurant called Joysticks. By ingeniously flipping the gender dynamic, Saunders highlights the exploitative nature of such places without also participating in it. The story occasioned one of the earliest scholar studies of Saunders's work, David P. Rando's "George Saunders and the Postmodern Working Class," which concludes, "Saunders's fiction responds to the state of current theory regarding class as a differential category and suggests a way of moving beyond the formal impasse for representing these complexities by setting up the tendencies of realism and postmodernism to shock one another" (2012, p. 459).

The collection's concluding story, "The Falls," ends with an act of selfless, self-annihilating heroism that marks a shift from the early work's cruelty to the more expansive and humane aspirations of his subsequent work. Saunders himself, in his author's note to his debut, notes, with some surprise, that those early stories "are mean, in places. They're occasionally nasty . . . Sometimes the author seems to be rooting for the cruel world to go ahead and kick his characters' asses" (2012, p. 196). Starting with his second collection, and with "The Falls" in particular, Saunders's work becomes increasingly more redemptive, to his many champions, and more cloying to his detractors. This trend is amplified in his third collection, *In Persuasion Nation* (2006), which does not include a novella, as did the earlier two volumes, but rather offers ten concise stories, many of which take place in a dystopian future.

The earlier collection's focus on the service economy is exchanged here with a new interest in commercialism, media, and consumerism broadly understood. Saunders litters the collection with trademarks and brand names and capitalized self-help slogans. The opening story consists of a company representative's reply to a customer complaint letter regarding a product called "I Can Speak!" that creates the illusion that one's infant is fluent in German. The title character of "Brad Carrigan, American," is an actor in a doomed television program that, on the cusp of cancellation, must resort to increasingly absurd and repellent shock tactics. The title story starts out as a series of "vignettes" presented as parodies of commercials before expanding out into a broader invocation of the Book of Job, in which the indifferent God of suffering is "the green symbol" – that is, money, consumerism. At the story's conclusion, a polar bear shouts, "The green symbol is a false GOD . . . obsessed with violence and domination! Reject him! Let us begin anew! Free your minds! Free your souls and live! There is a gentler and more generous GOD within us, if only we will look!" (2006, p. 179). As is characteristic of Saunders's late work, that final admonition earns its moral heft paradoxically because of, rather than in spite of, its placement in the story's absurd, satirical setting.

Tenth of December, published in 2013, is his most accomplished collection to date, containing three of his most celebrated pieces, "Victory Lap," "Escape from Spiderhead," and "The Semplica Girl Diaries." In the first of this trilogy, a teenage cross-country runner rushes to save a guilelessly optimistic neighbor from being raped. Upping the ethical stakes, Saunders assumes the perspective of all three characters, including the rapist, forcing readers to test the capaciousness of their powers of empathy. Similarly, in "Escape from Spiderhead," a convicted murderer participates in a drug-test trial. Early drugs in the trial include Verbaluce, which grants the user uncharacteristic eloquence, and ED289/290, which makes the user fall instantly and temporarily in love. Late in the story, the narrator is asked to administer a drug called Darkenfloxx, which induces a state of depression so severe that the user will commit suicide to escape the drug's debilitating effects. Despite the fact that the narrator and his other participants are all murderers, Saunders forces his readers again to test the scope of their empathy.

"The Semplica Girl Diaries" is perhaps Saunders's most audacious and capacious story to date. Here he imagines a suburban neighborhood in which genuine prosperity includes a yard display of Semplica Girls, literally female Asian immigrants who are strung together along a cord that runs through holes drilled into their necks. The narrator, a struggling father failing to keep up with the Joneses, unexpectedly wins the lottery and purchases a Semplica-Girl display for his own yard. The story's extraordinary premise invites a number of allegorical interpretations: the SGs, as they are called, invoke the plight of both immigrant workers and victims of sex trafficking. More importantly, their escape from the narrator's front yard with the help of anti-SG activists connects the SGs to the United States' slaveholding past. The story dramatizes the ease with which our current-day consumerism not only normalizes exploitation but also builds upon the country's original and unpaid sin, chattel slavery.

Given this interest in the Civil War and slavery that has run through his work from its inception, it is not surprising that Saunders's first, and thus far only, novel takes place in the midst of that crisis. Winner of the Man Booker Prize, *Lincoln in the Bardo* takes place in the Buddhist version of purgatory, the "bardo" of the title. Comprised primarily of disembodied voices, the novel dramatizes 11-year-old Willie Lincoln's time in this suspended realm between life and the afterlife following his death in 1862. With the help of his fellow "bardo" inhabitants, he struggles against various forces keeping him in limbo, chief among them being his famous father's reluctance to accept his son's death. As with so much of Saunders's work, a thumbnail description of the novel fails to convey the genuinely moving reading experience the novel provides, one that, also characteristically, combines humor, absurdity, and sentimentality to address such major themes as guilt and repentance, grief and familial attachment, and the United States' long history of exploitation and Puritan intolerance.

George Saunders is a singular voice in American fiction. Although his canvas is often small, his emotional and thematic reach is broad and deep. He has developed a wide range of original narrative modes, from his theme-park parodies to his consumerist sci-fi satires, that he has returned to over and over again to a degree that, in a lesser writer, would be repetitive were it not for his resourcefulness and, even in the face of his reliance on humor, seriousness of purpose. In the words of Joshua Ferris, "Saunders writes like something of a saint. He seems in touch with some better being" (2012, p. xviii).

SEE ALSO: After Postmodernism; Carver, Raymond; Díaz, Junot; Ferris, Joshua; Fictions of Work and Labor; Minimalism and Maximalism; Vonnegut, Kurt; Wallace, David Foster

REFERENCES

Ferris, Joshua. (2012). Introduction. In: *CivilWarLand in Bad Decline* (by George Saunders), xi–xviii. New York: Random House.

Lovell, Joel. (2013). "Stay open, forever, so open it hurts": the beautiful, brutal vision of George Saunders. *The New York Times Magazine* (January 3, 2013): 22–27, 46–47. https://archive.nytimes.com/www.nytimes.com/2013/01/06/magazine/george-saunders-just-wrote-the-best-book-youll-read-this-year.html (accessed August 4, 2021).

Rando, David P. (2012). George Saunders and the postmodern working class. *Contemporary Literature* 53 (3): 437–460.

Saunders, George. (2000). *Pastoralia*. New York: Riverhead Books.

Saunders, George. (2006). *In Persuasion Nation*. New York: Riverhead Books.

Saunders, George. (2007). Mr. Vonnegut in Sumatra. In: *The Braindead Microphone*, 73–84. New York: Riverhead Books.

Saunders, George. (2012). *CivilWarLand in Bad Decline*. New York: Random House; 1st ed. 1996.

Saunders, George. (2015). My writing education. *The New Yorker* (October 22, 2015). https://www.newyorker.com/books/page-turner/my-writing-education-a-timeline (accessed July 10, 2021).

FURTHER READING

Coleman, Philip and Ellerhoff, Stephen Gronert. (eds.) (2017). *George Saunders: Critical Essays*. New York: Palgrave Macmillan.

Schwartz, Lynne Sharon

JAMES PEACOCK
Keele University, UK

> . . . it dawned on me that I had to make a choice: "be good" or be a writer.
>
> (Quoted in Pearlman and Henderson 1990, p. 194)

A typical Schwartz protagonist is "a sensitive family-oriented semibohemian whose tastes are literary but refreshingly unstuffy" (Cole 2000, p. 23). Schwartz chronicles the lives of intelligent, artistic, middle-class people who conform to many expectations of bourgeois life – mortgages, marriages, parenthood, witty dinner parties – but whose greatest fear is of succumbing to unquestioning conventionality and unoriginality – becoming "good." Examples abound: Alison, the teenage protagonist of *Balancing Acts* (1982), is an aspiring writer who resists the suburban normality of her parents and forms an attachment to an elderly circus performer. *The Fatigue Artist* (1995) tells the story of Laura, a writer who eschews "politeness or discretion" (p. 58). In her memoir, *Ruined by Reading* (1996), Schwartz adopts similar values in justifying her childhood love of literature: "In books I found explicitly, flamboyantly, everything censored in life" (p. 44).

Though in terms of consumer choices and their neighborhoods her characters display the privileges of postwar gentrification, they resist, often through creative activities, what Sarah Schulman calls "the gentrification of the mind," by which Schulman signifies a homogenization of attitudes, a denial of the middle-class individual's role in social change, and a collective loss of imagination and memory among baby boomers who participated in the postwar transformation of American cities (Schulman 2012). Schwartz leads the resistance through forensic satire of bourgeois attitudes and reflections on the relationship between memory and self-invention, "authentic" selfhood and fictionalization. Writing, therefore, has a crucial role to play.

As she observes in her essay collection *Face to Face* (2000), Schwartz is fixated on "the presentation of self in everyday life" (2000a, p. 6). Her work investigates what Lionel Trilling calls "manners": "a culture's hum and buzz of implication" (1948, p. 12), anxieties about class, taste, worries about invasions of difference into settled lives. Such themes are reflected in the formal qualities of Schwartz's prose. Her writing resides primarily in a realist mode reminiscent of Henry James, with the emphasis less on plot than on consistency of character, point of view, and social discourse – as she describes James's work, "a world of the mind" rather than "a reflection of physical realities" (1996, p. 93). Inevitably, then, she also includes, particularly in her most complex novel, *Leaving Brooklyn* (1989), self-conscious reflections on writing, the role of language and the possibility that society functions most successfully when "character" is understood as performative gestures or convincing fictions.

Thus, Schwartz's novelistic examinations of middle-class mores, which are also explorations of bohemian creative impulses, sometimes frustrated, are as much *self*-examinations as her memoirs, and to both she applies an anthropological gaze. In her debut novel *Rough Strife* (1980), an unsentimental portrayal of the marriage between Ivan, a business executive, and Caroline, a mathematician, the shifting dynamics of the relationship are prompted, in part, by instincts that are deep, tribal, and mythic. When Caroline first encounters Ivan at a party in Rome, she appraises him as "a noble savage" (1980, p. 21). Her initial reluctance to tell him her name is driven by her internal reflection that "[p]eople of primitive tribes [...] do not give their names away; they cannot so readily entrust that emblem to strangers" (p. 22). Soon afterwards, his insistence that she visit Rome's historical treasures feels "overwhelming, like the ritual labors assigned in mythology" (p. 26). Much later in their relationship, after affairs, arguments, and childbirth, the family, including daughters Isabel and Greta, is described as "a primitive clan, bound by the markings of hallowed tradition" (p. 187), and the parents as being "like ancient, bickering neighbor nations of common descent" (p. 188). Incapable of serenity they might be but, "hammer and chisel to each other" (p. 18), they are functionally and spiritually inseparable.

In addition to "primitive" civilizations, Schwartz frequently compares the characters in *Rough Strife*, a novel fascinated by power and potential violence, to animals. Ivan, in particular, is visualized this way from Caroline's perspective. Taking her on their first date to see a caged wolf on Capitoline Hill in Rome, he is thereafter referred to in predatory terms as "a wolf in sheep's clothing" (1980, p. 47), "a creature of such unimpeded instinct" (p. 154). Caroline, unaccustomed to company, feels that she and Ivan are "yoked together like animals in harness" (p. 52). On the one hand, Schwartz's deployment of animalistic and primitivist metaphors contributes to the "stripping away of civility to show the nakedness beneath" (p. 34) which is an important aspect of her work. The final scene, in which wife and husband cut themselves on the glass from a smashed champagne bottle and Caroline initiates a blood bonding ritual, causing Ivan admiringly to call her "wild" (p. 200), shows how precarious the barrier between bourgeois manners and savagery might be.

On the other hand, Schwartz's characters are never merely atavistic in their behavior, driven by ancient, unconscious, unchanging impulses about which they have no understanding. Rather, their behavior is historicized; there is a productive friction between drives and attitudes regarded simply (and problematically) as "human nature" – sexual appetites, the desire to create a home, the love of one's children – and the historical, political, and economic circumstances that reveal the very notion of human nature to be contingent and shifting. *Rough Strife*, for example, stages its black comedy against a backdrop of sixties and early seventies radicalism and second-wave feminism. Finding herself burdened with domestic duties, which she is forced to balance with the chairmanship of her math department, Caroline bitterly reflects on the irony that Ivan has time to protest against the Vietnam War while she, "an anarchist at heart" (1980, p. 175), is too busy. Furthermore, she feels guilty that her preference for "quick and uncomplicated" sex "with a minimum of talk" runs counter to the prevailing feminist "literature of sexual discontent" that demands more sensitivity and respect from men (p. 177). In an argument excited by his burning of some cooking pots, Caroline accuses Ivan of oppression and justifies her outburst with the slogan, "the personal is political." He in turn responds, "Did I ever once stop you from doing what you want?" and insists that the personal "is just that, *personal*" (p. 179).

The tensions and ironies of this scene are characteristic. First, its specific historical context is filtered through Caroline's perspective, which hears "ancestral voices prophesying war" (1980, p. 175) and sees "a malevolent ancient scheme" at work in gender inequality (p. 181), to suggest a consciousness simultaneously embracing radical change and attributing that change to timeless impulses. Secondly, both Caroline and Ivan's language and actions in this scene indicate that the division Caroline perceives between radicalism and "raising a family in the conventional way" (p. 175) is murkier than she might admit: in conducting an argument full of clichéd sloganeering and familiar gendered role-playing, the antagonists confirm that radicalism and dissent, bourgeoisified, can also slip into conventionality.

Schwartz's puncturing of baby boomers' complacent self-regard reaches its apotheosis in *In the Family Way* (2000), a farce set primarily in an Upper West Side apartment building presided over by Anna, a formidable matriarch who has lived there for 50 years. In the building live Anna's daughter Bea, her ex-husband Roy, his second and third wives Serena and Lisa, Bea's sister May (who becomes Serena's lover), and various children from the different relationships, most importantly Tony and Jane, who are mixed race, Roy's first wife being a Vietnamese woman called Lien. This bizarre, incestuous arrangement constitutes a utopian experiment, with Bea as orchestrator, a collective dedication to the unconventional rather than "the good": a bewildered Tony, employing his author's anthropological language, describes it as "that tribe my mother's running" and, disparagingly, as an attempt to "relive her hippie youth" (2000b, p. 22). His assertion is absolutely correct: his family's perpetuation of "the spirit of the sixties" (p. 25) represents a self-gratifying and nostalgic attempt to arrest historical change, one which requires the cultivation, as far as possible, of endogamous relationships confined to the tribe's ancestral home. This is rudely illustrated in the opening scene, in which Serena persuades Roy to impregnate her to provide a child for her and May. But it is more disturbingly apparent in Roy's "socially irresponsible" tendency to view the Vietnam War in which he served "in purely personal terms" as the vehicle for the birth of his kids (p. 178). Worse, he now regards his wartime experiences as a means to impress women, "especially young ones, even if they deplored war" (p. 178). As in *Rough Strife*, the self-serving tendency to separate the political and historical from the personal is frequently gendered as masculine.

Nobody is obliged to be traumatized, of course, but Roy's is typical of the adult characters' selective attitude toward the sixties. Memory, which might be employed to critique present behavior, deliquesces into a nostalgia which necessitates not only the willed forgetting of the traumatic political and social upheavals that defined Bea and Roy's generation (and partly enabled their "alternative" living arrangements), but also the freezing of time, the denial of historical change. The building is the spatial manifestation of this nostalgic temporality. It represents a last bastion of supposed sixties liberalism as the world, signified by the construction sites surrounding the building and the jackhammers that comically accompany Roy and Serena's sexual activity at the start of the novel (p. 7), embraces capitalist expansionism. On the one hand, the fact that parts of the building – the elevator, for example – keep malfunctioning, and that Anna's increasing forgetfulness leads to a torrent of water gushing through the ceiling into the other apartments (p. 217), shows the fragility of the residents' nostalgic vision. On the other, Schwartz makes it clear that it is precisely their middle-class economic security that enables this lifestyle: that the desire to keep the family under one roof is a form of investment, of capital accumulation. In a moment of perspicacity, Anna observes: "We used to hate the landlords, but that's what we became. You're on one side or the other, and whichever side you're on, that's who you become. Self-interest, we used to call it" (p. 229). Ultimately, the author demonstrates that the building itself dictates human interactions: "Intimate relations in New York are governed by real estate" (p. 32). Of all Schwartz's fictions, this is the one most pointedly concerned with what she describes in her nonfiction as "the palpable boundaries drawn by race and class and money, cutting across the landscape of delicate feelings" (2000a, p. 102).

Despite being labeled "an urban comedy," *In the Family Way* shows the potentially tragic consequences for the younger generation of the baby boomers' self-interest and gentrifying psychology. The closing chapters see the breakdown of relationships between Tony and his girlfriend Melissa as well as another young couple, Danny and Coral; the abortion of Magenta, a friend of Bea and Roy's daughter Sara (2000b, p. 261); and finally Tony's departure to Vietnam in search of his true identity (p. 299). That we see the collapse of youthful optimism occurring during a climactic family party held in the building only serves to highlight the gap between the parents' complacency, born of denial, and the suffering and material difficulties of their kids. As Melissa reflects, echoing Anna's thoughts on self-interest: "The hell with family. You were on your own. She had always known it" (p. 290). Tony's escape to his roots reveals the true legacy of the sixties and the Vietnam War: a young generation suspicious of authority, lacking the relative affluence of their parents and the solace of nostalgia. The resistance to conventional family units espoused by people like Roy and Bea, the desire not to be good, is a luxury their children cannot afford.

Trauma, either experienced or fantasized about, is a recurring theme in Schwartz's work. In *The Fatigue Artist*, Laura's chronic tiredness is provoked partly by ennui, but also by the death of her first husband, Ev. The short story "Hostages to Fortune" features a suburban couple who, for unspecified traumatic reasons, argue over two imaginary children. *The Writing on the Wall* (2005) uses the events of 9/11 as a catalyst to exploration of the protagonist's traumatic history, including the deaths of her father and sister and her mother's institutionalization. In the title story from *Referred Pain* (2004), Richard Koslowski regards the escalating problems with his teeth as both an analogy of his parents' suffering during World War II and a punishment for his failure to suffer in the same way as them, for enduring only pain "so small in the scheme of things" (2004, p. 45). Root canal work thus becomes a deep metaphor for Richard's pathetic attempts to emulate the trauma of the true "aristocrats of pain" such as "the women in Bosnia" (p. 104) and particularly Holocaust survivors like his parents. Dispensing wisdom as well as expensive dentistry, one of his consultants, Dr. Fisher, explains the phenomenon of referred pain: "the place where it hurts is not the source of the trouble" (p. 76). Richard's pain is existential and based on guilt that he is "the designated beneficiary of his parents' investment of pain" (p. 80), and thus able to live a relatively comfortable, middle-class life after their traumas.

If Richard's conjuring of his father's image, "skeletal in the striped uniform of the camps" (2004, p. 49), echoes the "photographs of skeletal figures in striped pyjamas clawing at barbed wire" deliberately ignored by the postwar residents of Brooklyn at the start of *Leaving Brooklyn* (1989, p. 13), it is also a reminder that images of Jewish trauma occupy an ambiguous position in Schwartz's work. She claims that: "I have no mission, only language [. . .] I wouldn't set out to rectify something" (quoted in Rubin 2001, p. 82). Rather than directly confronting traumatic Jewish experience, Schwartz employs it as she does all forms of trauma: to interrogate authenticity and the power of language. Richard's pain, he feels, is essentially *inauthentic* in not being tethered to a wider communal history of suffering. Likewise, the willful amnesia of the Brooklynites among whom Audrey, the first-person narrator of *Leaving Brooklyn*, comes of age, is a form of psychological gentrification, a refusal to confront the vicissitudes of lived experience, and a way of appearing "good."

If, throughout Schwartz's oeuvre, it is writing that allows one to be authentic, it is nonetheless a deeply ironic authenticity. The protagonist of *Disturbances in the Field* (1983), a story which also pivots on a traumatic event, reflects: "The novel was imbued with that deepest and most treasured of middle-class notions: that life should, and would, reward good behavior" (1983, p. 102). The irony of this metafictional statement is that it appears in a novel which not only questions what good behavior is, but sets about forensically detailing the pain arising from a good, semibohemian life. What Schwartz's characters discover is that modes of creativity, especially writing, encourage authenticity precisely because they allow one not only to address painful experiences, but also to test different identities, to fictionalize oneself (which is, for Schwartz, a human impulse). Renata, protagonist of *The Writing on the Wall*, considers that she cannot change the facts of her life "but maybe she could change the way she told them to herself [. . .] Would that make a new story? Would it make her someone else?" (2005, p. 11). Audrey's interpretation of her mother's mantra – "to thine own self be true" – is to reinvent herself through the book she writes – *Leaving Brooklyn*. Audrey's defective right eye is a rich metaphor for her ability to deconstruct the smooth, gentrified surface of her parents' world, to reassemble it in new configurations. In Schwartz's most metafictional tale, the eye represents the writerly impulse to seek authenticity in stories, the endlessly generative tools of language, the blurring of the boundaries between memoir and fiction, and the (re)creation of identity. Given the centrality of creativity for selfhood in Schwartz's work, it follows that inauthenticity becomes malignant when one attempts to pass off somebody else's art as one's own: this is the scenario at the heart of the novel *Two-Part Inventions* (2012).

Perhaps the biggest irony of Schwartz's work is that a writer whose reputation is founded on dissections of middle-class society is invested most passionately in privacy. Her memoirs reveal a commitment to the solitary acts of reading and writing as the best means of understanding the world; in *Not Now, Voyager* (2009) she admits to a lifelong reluctance to travel because she would rather be writing. In "Only Connect," the first essay in *Face to Face*, she confesses: "The world's approach, for me at any rate, is an interruption of the inner dialogue" (2000a, p. 7), and "the uninterrupted flow of consciousness is our true life, maybe our only entitlement" (p. 20). What we learn from reading Schwartz is that the world must, of course, be engaged with – relationships formed, groceries purchased, houses renovated – but to offset its banal exigencies, one needs the private space of literature to be unconventional, thus truly oneself. As she writes in her long poem, "In Solitary," retreat into the creative solitude is a "long journey from fear to magic" (2002, p. 23).

SEE ALSO: Debut Novels; Post-9/11 Narratives; Suburban Narratives; Trauma and Fiction; Urban Fiction

REFERENCES

Cole, Diane. (2000). *Face to Face: A Reader in the World* by Lynne Sharon Schwartz. *New York Times Book Review* (May 21, 2000): 23.

Pearlman, Mickey and Henderson, Katherine Usher. (1990). *Inter/View: Talks with America's Writing Women*. Lexington: University of Kentucky Press.

Rubin, Lois. (2001). Growing up Jewish in Rapoport and Schwartz: two different stories. *Studies in American Jewish Literature* 20: 81–87.

Schulman, Sarah. (2012). *The Gentrification of the Mind: Witness to a Lost Imagination*. Berkeley and Los Angeles: University of California Press.

Schwartz, Lynne Sharon. (1980). *Rough Strife*. New York: Perennial.

Schwartz, Lynne Sharon. (1983). *Disturbances in the Field*. New York: Counterpoint.

Schwartz, Lynne Sharon. (1989). *Leaving Brooklyn*. London: Mandarin.

Schwartz, Lynne Sharon. (1995). *The Fatigue Artist*. New York: Scribner's.

Schwartz, Lynne Sharon. (1996). *Ruined by Reading*. Boston: Beacon Press.

Schwartz, Lynne Sharon. (2000a). *Face to Face: A Reader in the World*. Boston: Beacon Press.

Schwartz, Lynne Sharon. (2000b). *In the Family Way*. New York: Perennial.

Schwartz, Lynne Sharon. (2002). *In Solitary: Poems by Lynne Sharon Schwartz*. Riverdale-on-Hudson, NY: Sheep Meadow Press.

Schwartz, Lynne Sharon. (2004). *Referred Pain and Other Stories*. New York: Counterpoint.

Schwartz, Lynne Sharon. (2005). *The Writing on the Wall*. New York: Counterpoint.

Trilling, Lionel. (1948). Manners, morals, and the novel. *The Kenyon Review* 10 (1): 11–27.

FURTHER READING

Field, Robin E. (2015). The traumatic past in Schwartz's "The Opiate of the People." *The Explicator* 73 (3): 187–191. https://doi.org/10.1080/00144940.2015.1058227

Mellard, James M. (1997). Resisting the melting pot: the Jewish back-story in the fiction of Lynne Sharon Schwartz. In: *Daughters of Valor: Contemporary Jewish American Women Writers* (ed. Jay L. Halio and Ben Siegel), 175–193. Cranbury, NJ: Associated University Presses.

Schwartz, Lynne Sharon. (1991). The opiate of the people. In: *Imagining America: Stories from the Promised Land* (ed. Wesley Brown and Amy Ling), 175–190. New York: Persea.

Scott, Joanna

MICHAEL LACKEY
University of Minnesota, Morris, USA

Recipient of the MacArthur Fellowship, often referred to as the "genius grant," Joanna Scott has been recognized as one of America's most prominent writers since the 1980s. Startling about Scott is her ability to excel in so many genres. American novelist and founding editor of the journal *Conjunctions*, Bradford Morrow praises Scott's 1996 novel *The Manikin*, a finalist for the Pulitzer Prize for Fiction. Specifically, Morrow admires the "Gothic sensibility" (Morrow 2020, p. 47) in the work, which is why he compares her to writers like Edgar Allen Poe and Charlotte Brontë. Maureen Howard won the National Book Critics Circle Award, and she praises Scott's use of the ballad form in her 2009 novel *Follow Me*. American novelist Bruce Bauman marvels at Scott's ability to write "philosophical and politically inspired works" (Bauman 2020, p. 118), which is why he compares her to Iris Murdoch. Scott's extraordinary range explains why English novelist Nick Hornby says in a *New York Times* (2000) review that "Joanna Scott is a Michael Jordan: she has talent to burn," and the poet Daniel Nester refers to her as a "writer's writer" (2020, p. 77).

Mining history for lost stories and transvaluing and repurposing those stories for the contemporary world are dominant ideas in Scott's most effective and successful fiction. For instance, Scott's second novel, *The Closest Possible Union* (1988), is set in the nineteenth century, and it charts the inner life of a 14-year-old who works on his father's slave ship. What makes this novel so freakishly powerful, according to Morrow, is Scott's uncanny ability to use such a story to illuminate the inner life of a young person. As he says to Scott in an interview: "You have a gift for conjuring childhood consciousness, of depicting the many nuances of not-yet-knowing as it graduates toward knowledge" (Morrow 2020, p. 43).

This engagement with and usage of history takes center stage in what many regard as Scott's best novel, *The Manikin*. From the outside, Manikin – the big house at the center of a large estate in western New York, purchased shortly before his death by Henry Craxton, "the Henry Ford of natural history" (Scott 1996, p. 9) – appears to be a stately and dignified residence. But Scott takes readers inside, and what they find is a Darwinian drama "of rough-and-tumble congregations" (p. 174) among the Craxton family and the servants, rife with casual sexual assaults, tortured domestic intimacies, overbearing and thwarted wills to power, and perpetually deferred dreams.

Given Scott's range, originality, and talent, there are many ways to characterize her enduring appeal and her contribution to the world of letters, but I will focus on only one: biofiction. Different from both biography and historical fiction, biofiction is literature that names its protagonist after an actual historical figure, and Scott has significantly advanced studies of the aesthetic form as both a practitioner and a critic. The first example in her oeuvre is *Arrogance*, a biographical novel about the Austrian artist Egon Schiele. Published in 1990, this novel foregrounds Schiele's upbringing as a son of an abusive father, his near-incestuous relationship with his sister, his desire and drive to become an artist, his shifting relationship with and allegiance to Gustav Klimt, and his trial and imprisonment for pornography. Critically acclaimed when first released (it was a finalist for the PEN/Faulkner Award), this work continues to receive attention and to enhance Scott's reputation. The timing of the publication of this novel in part accounts for its continued significance, for it was in the 1990s that the biographical novel started to become a dominant literary form. Michael Cunningham, Margaret Atwood, and Thomas Pynchon are just a few celebrated writers who published stellar biographical novels during the decade. But Scott innovated with this literary form before all of them, and she has also done much to answer some questions that have perplexed scholars. For instance, many scholars treat the biographical novel as a form of biography, which means that fidelity to the biographical record is one of the primary criteria for determining a work's effectiveness and quality. But in her 2016 essay "On Hoaxes, Humbugs, and Fictional Portraiture," Scott set the scholarly record straight about the biographical novelist's usage (not representation) of the biographical subject by claiming: "I was not pretending that my Schiele was the real Schiele. I just wanted him to be real" (2017, p. 103). The aesthetic objective of the biographical novelist is not to accurately represent the biographical subject. It is to fictionalize the life of the historical figure in order to project into being the author's own aesthetic vision.

This is exactly what Scott did in many of the short biofictional stories (about Francis Huber, Madame Couteiler de Bretteville, and Dorothea Dix) from her 1994 collection, *Various Antidotes*. Nominated for a PEN/Faulkner Award, this book won the *Southern Review*'s Short Fiction Prize and was named among twenty-five best books of the year by *Voice Literary Supplement*. Moreover, the collection includes two award-winning stories: "A Borderline Case" won the Aga Khan Award for the best story published in the *Paris Review* in 1992, and the story "Convicta et Combusta" won the Pushcart Prize, which "honors the best 'poetry, short fiction, essays or literary whatnot' published in the small presses over the previous year." The collection's opening story, "Concerning Mold Upon the Skin, Etc.," which was included in the 1993 anthology of *Best American Short Stories*, is vintage biofiction. The protagonist is Antonie van Leeuwenhoek, a Dutch scientist and businessman who is considered today one of the founding fathers of microbiology. Driven by an obsession that alienates and even destroys his family to some degree, Leeuwenhoek is overjoyed when he realizes the potential impact of his discoveries with his microscope: "This was the lasting consequence of his invention: he had forever changed the nature of belief. Nothing visible to the naked eye could be trusted anymore, for everything had a secret microscopic life. He, the master of magnification, had made visible the unimaginable" (Scott 1994, p. 11). On the surface, this story is about Leeuwenhoek. But if we understand the uncanny power and the ambiguous semiotics of biofiction, these lines tell us as much about Scott's ideas about art as they do about the Dutch inventor. In essence, the story uses Leeuwenhoek not to get to his consciousness but to clarify what the artist does. Accordingly, what Leeuwenhoek did in the world of science, Scott does in the world of fiction. As one of the narrators from *Arrogance* says, "it is the artist's responsibility to educate" the "eyes" (Scott 1990, p. 68) of the audience, and for Scott, this means that the fiction writer's ability to expose the "secret microscopic life" of consciousness would lead people to distrust what is "visible to the naked eye," an act of literary "magnification" that makes "visible the unimaginable." Put more succinctly, surface projections belie the more complex and shadowy realities of human interiors. Such is the stuff that Scott's fiction is made of.

Readers get much more insight into Scott's view of biofiction through her 2014 novel *De Potter's Grand Tour*, which is about her great-grandfather, Armand de Potter. This work was the Editor's Choice of *The New York Times Book Review* and a *Chicago Tribune* Best Book of the Year. In the novel, de Potter leads world tours and glories in his collection of ancient Egyptian art. But there are problems. To establish a reputable and successful tourist agency, de Potter deceives everyone, including his wife, into believing that he is much more than he really is. In essence, de Potter plays a big hoax on everyone. But ultimately, the hoax is on him, because he eventually discovers that some of his ancient Egyptian antiquities, for which he paid a fortune and went into considerable debt, are forgeries.

When Scott was working on *De Potter's Grand Tour*, she did an interview with me titled "The Masking Art of the Biographical Novel" (Lackey 2020). While that interview focuses mainly on *Arrogance*, what she says in it clearly relates to *De Potter's Grand Tour*. At the time, Scott was "thinking about the artificial nature of fiction," and to define it, she realized the value of "the metaphor of the mask." As a novelist, Scott claims, "I'm probably closer in spirit to a masked performer wandering through the fog of Venice during Carnivale than to a historian." Notice how Scott distances herself from history. The scholarly tendency has been to define the biographical novel as a subgenre of the historical novel, but Scott indicates why this is a mistake. For the author of a biographical novel, the emphasis is not on the actual "historical figure." Rather, it is on the artist's vision as expressed through "the dynamic relationship between the mask wearer [novelist] and the mask [fictionalized figure] itself," which is why Scott concludes that "it is the ingenuity of the performance rather than the precision of the resemblance that counts." Therefore, instead of asking whether biographical novelists accurately represent the biographical subject or his/her time period, readers should be asking how the authors use the historical figure (the way "the mask is put into action") in order to project something new into being. As Scott says: "The deeper I got into writing *Arrogance*, the more my attention went to creating something new rather than repeating what was already known" (Lackey 2020, p. 97).

The same principle applies to *De Potter's Grand Tour*. In a crucial moment in his life, de Potter shares his philosophy of art with others. The great artist is not the one that persuades "us that the false thing is real" but rather convinces "us to forget reality altogether" (Scott 2014, p. 182). This is the case because reality is not a pre-existent Platonic Form waiting to be discovered. It is a provisional conceptual formation that "some influential artist has given us" (p. 183). Is this an accurate representation of de Potter's philosophy of art? In other words, did he really make such claims? Given Scott's aesthetic approach, which is to take de Potter "out of history, out of the factual swamp, and to reinvent him as a fictional character" (Lackey 2020, p. 106), these are misguided questions. Here are some more suitable questions: How did Scott fictionalize and alter de Potter's life in order to express her view of the artistic construction of conceptual reality? How does she use de Potter's life to illuminate the negotiation between an individual's projected sense of reality and the projected realities external to self? In short, *Arrogance* and *De Potter's Grand Tour* are not biographical works about Schiele and de Potter. They are novels that use Schiele and de Potter to express Scott's view of life and the world.

The most recent novel, *Careers for Women* (2017), gives us new and deeper insight into Scott's craft as well as the biographical novel more generally. The novel tells the story of the fictional character Pauline Moreau, whose life is determined in large measure by two business executives. The fictional Robert Whittaker Jr. works for Alumacore, a company that puts profits above people and poisons the environment through illegal dumping and emissions. Whittaker, who is married, impregnates the 17-year-old Pauline and gives her hush money to relocate. After working some odd jobs in New York City and descending into poverty and then prostitution, Pauline meets Lee K. Jaffe, an actual person who served from 1944 through 1965 as director of public relations at the Port Authority in New York City. Jaffe hires Pauline, giving her the opportunity to salvage a happy and meaningful life for herself and her daughter, but Whittaker's toxic lifestyle eventually leads to Pauline's death.

What makes *Careers for Women* so important is the degree to which it reveals Scott's aesthetic commitments. In 1937 Georg Lukács published *The Historical Novel*, which treats the biographical novel as a subgenre or version of the historical novel. But many contemporary biographical novelists, such as Bruce Duffy, Colm Tóibín, Olga Tokarczuk, and Rosa Montero, reject the historical novel and insist that they do not write historical fiction. In a recent public forum, Scott locates herself within the biofiction literary tradition by saying that she is "not alone in sharing some deep skepticism in terms of what we used to call the historical novel" (Lackey, Kildegaard, and McCumber 2020, p. 133). The logical product of the Enlightenment's valorization of science and reason, history was increasingly treated as a hard science during the nineteenth century, which resulted in the historical novel's privileging of the way environmental conditions and historical forces shape and determine human subjectivity, an aesthetic act that subordinates at best and eliminates at worst human autonomy and individual agency. To counter the historical novel, there was a shift in emphasis from history to biography, from scientific determinism to individual autonomy. While Scott deeply respects science and history, she has a deeper commitment to human mystery and individual autonomy, and this in part explains her reservations about historical fiction and her propensity to author biofiction.

It is important to note that for Scott we do not have to choose between science and literature, facts and the imagination. At stake for her is the intrusion of science or history-as-science into the world of art. Scientists should do science, and historians should do history, and Scott respects and values both as such. But neither should demand that artists subordinate the literary to the scientific or the historical, because literature is and does its own thing, which is oftentimes in irreconcilable conflict with what science and history do. This explains why Scott resists the contemporary impulse to turn to the empirical to legitimize fiction: "Imagination does not need to be made legitimate. The creative work that the mind does when it is leaving behind verifiable information won't be saved and made newly legitimate if it is imbued with facts" (Lackey *et al.* 2020, p. 133). As a devout Enlightenment rationalist, Lukács formulates a science-based approach to history and then demands that authors incorporate that approach into aesthetics. But for Scott, while she frequently uses history and biography in her fiction, the fiction is of primary and ultimate importance, and thus cannot be subordinate to either science or history.

Given Scott's privileging of autonomy over history, what readers get in *Careers for Women* is less an accurate representation of history than a historical person converted into a symbolic figure that models human autonomy. This explains why Jaffe "creates a kind of center for the novel" (Lackey et al. 2020, p. 130), as Scott claims, for she is a figure that embodies "strength and vision" (Bauman 2020, p. 119). In an interview with Lisa Tschernkowitsch, Scott specifies the kind of effect she hopes her Jaffe will have on her audience: "I want to absorb readers, but I want them to come away with a sense of heightened possibility, of imagination that's perhaps lit up a little bit more, a sense of their own creative powers" (Tschernkowitsch 2020, p. 127). Lukács (and historical novelists more generally) thinks that the author should create a fictive protagonist that functions as a symbol to accurately represent the past as it really was, an aesthetic feat that would deterministically clarify for us in the present how we have come to be as we currently are, while Scott (and biographical novelists more generally) thinks that authors should use figures from the past in order to model the process of human autonomy, thus empowering readers in the present to activate their imagination in order to create new ways of thinking and being for the future. For Scott, literature has an uncanny power to enable people to engage and experience the world in new, fresh, and meaningful ways. As she says in her interview with Martin Naparsteck: "I have always appreciated the power of fiction to make us responsive, not just to get us absorbed imaginatively, but then to give us the ability to go out and see the world with a freshness and intensity" (Naparsteck 2020, p. 117).

That Scott would reject a Lukács-inspired aesthetic form and turn to something like biofiction makes perfect sense given her intellectual and aesthetic commitments. The nineteenth century witnessed the rise of positivism, a deterministic system of thought which defined everything according to the strict and mechanistic laws of cause and effect. Many intellectual disciplines were heavily impacted, but artists and thinkers like Edouard Manet, Arthur Rimbaud, Friedrich Nietzsche, and Oscar Wilde, to mention only a notable few, committed themselves to the intellectual and aesthetic project of safeguarding the human interior, that part of the individual that endlessly creates meaning and sense. Scott fits comfortably within this latter intellectual tradition. Indeed, Scott is very clear in distancing herself from the Lukács literary tradition in her interview with me. After noting that "Lukács was reacting against" "the modernist immersion in individual subjectivity," Scott says that she "was nurtured by that immersion and it is absolutely what I love. I came to be a writer because I was reading Woolf and Faulkner and Conrad, all good distorters who remind us of the value of individual existence" (Lackey 2020, p. 101).

In her 1998 interview with Howard, Scott, discussing Howard's work, reveals how literature functions to illuminate the human inner life: "I feel in your work and especially in this new novel [*Bridgeport Bus*] that I am very much seeing myself holding the book. There's an intense self-consciousness that makes me think about where I am in my life" (Scott 2020, p. 31). Readers may be reading about historical or fictional figures, but great literature enables them to see something inside themselves that had previously been hidden. This is not always a pleasant experience, for sometimes people are in thrall to sick or twisted systems of thought. For instance, in *Careers for Women*, Scott uses the character of Whittaker "to trace how violence can result from a slow-burning corruption, a way of thinking that involves weird, contorted logic" (Bauman 2020, p. 120). In a sense, Scott sees the literary author as a cultural diagnostician, as someone who can "keep the [cultural] problems visible" (Morrow 2020, p. 50). Understanding the near-implacable logic and compulsion of systems of thought, what Scott refers to as "that tug of inevitability"

(Naparsteck 2020, p. 110), explains her appreciation and usage of psychology. As she says in an interview with Anne Panning and Ralph Black: "There is definitely room to be skeptical of the simplistic cause-and-effect psychology that diminishes the intricacy of behavior. But we can't give up on psychology" (Black and Panning 2020, p. 67).

Scott is committed to exposing and defining specific psychologies, no matter how contorted or perverse, which is why she values so highly the study of psychology and the usage of it in literature. But what matters most to her is that uncanny ability to evade psychological determinism and to originate a new way of thinking and being. As she says in her 2010 interview with Howard: we "need literature to keep teaching us how meaning can be made" (Scott 2020, p. 89). For Scott, novelists do not use established systems of knowledge in order to illuminate what Lukács refers to as "objective reality." To the contrary, novelists picture how systems of knowledge are produced. The emphasis here is on the autonomous creation rather than the mechanical usage of knowledge. As Scott claims, "the fundamental joy" in literature "is in the act of invention" (Lackey 2020, p. 102). And what she does in literature is what she hopes to impart to her reader. In short, Scott is obsessed with the originating power and creative potential of the mind: "To watch the artist in action, working on or responding to something – I learn from that, I learn about what we can do and what we can think and what we haven't thought before. Every new sentence teaches me something new about the potential of the mind" (p. 105).

SEE ALSO: After Postmodernism; Banks, Russell; Cunningham, Michael; Ecocriticism and Environmental Fiction; Gass, William H.; Hawkes, John; Mixed-Genre Fiction; Oates, Joyce Carol; Trauma and Fiction; Vidal, Gore

REFERENCES

Bauman, Bruce. (2020). An interview with Joanna Scott (2017). In: *Conversations with Joanna Scott* (ed. Michael Lackey), 118–124. Jackson: University Press of Mississippi.

Black, Ralph and Panning, Anne. (2020). Joanna Scott: novelists (2003). In: *Conversations with Joanna Scott* (ed. Michael Lackey), 57–71. Jackson: University Press of Mississippi.

Hornby, Nick. (2000). Review of *Make Believe*. The *New York Times* (February 20, 2000). http://movies2.nytimes.com/books/00/02/20/reviews/000220.20hornbyt.html (accessed July 16, 2021).

Howard, Maureen. (2020). A conversation with Maureen Howard (2010). In: *Conversations with Joanna Scott* (ed. Michael Lackey), 82–90. Jackson: University Press of Mississippi.

Lackey, Michael. (2020). The masking art of the biographical novel (2014). In: *Conversations with Joanna Scott* (ed. Michael Lackey), 94–107. Jackson: University Press of Mississippi.

Lackey, Michael, Kildegaard, Athena, and McCumber, Corinne. (2020). A roundtable forum with Joanna Scott (2018). In: *Conversations with Joanna Scott* (ed. Michael Lackey), 129–148. Jackson: University Press of Mississippi.

Lukács, Georg. (1983). *The Historical Novel*. Lincoln: University of Nebraska Press; 1st ed. 1937 (in Russian).

Morrow, Bradford. (2020). Joanna Scott: an interview by Bradford Morrow (2000). In: *Conversations with Joanna Scott* (ed. Michael Lackey), 43–53. Jackson: University Press of Mississippi.

Naparsteck, Martin. (2020). An interview with Joanna Scott (2015). In: *Conversations with Joanna Scott* (ed. Michael Lackey), 108–117. Jackson: University Press of Mississippi.

Nester, Daniel. (2020). Catching up with Joanna Scott: a profile. In: *Conversations with Joanna Scott* (ed. Michael Lackey), 77–81. Jackson: University Press of Mississippi.

Scott, Joanna. (1990). *Arrogance*. New York: Picador.

Scott, Joanna. (1994). Concerning mold upon the skin, etc. In: *Various Antidotes*, 1–11. New York: Henry Holt.

Scott, Joanna. (1996). *The Manikin*. New York: Picador.

Scott, Joanna. (2014). *De Potter's Grand Tour*. New York: Farrar, Straus and Giroux.

Scott, Joanna. (2017). On hoaxes, humbugs, and fictional portraiture. In: *Biographical Fiction: A Reader* (ed. Michael Lackey), 98–103. New York and London: Bloomsbury.

Scott, Joanna. (2020). Joanna Scott interviews Maureen Howard (1998). In: *Conversations with Joanna Scott* (ed. Michael Lackey), 27–37. Jackson: University Press of Mississippi.

Tschernkowitsch, Lisa. (2020). Interview with Joanna Scott (2017). In: *Conversations with Joanna Scott* (ed. Michael Lackey), 125–128. Jackson: University Press of Mississippi.

FURTHER READING

Lackey, Michael. (2016). Locating and defining the bio in biofiction. In: *a/b: Auto/Biography Studies* 31 (Winter): 3–9.

Rabinowitz, Paula. (1999). Pulp theory: on literary history. In: *Poetics/Politics: Radical Aesthetics for the Classroom* (ed. Amitava Kumar), 83–100. New York: St. Martin's.

Tissut, Anne-Laure. (2002). Wonder-working "antidotes": the storyteller's paraphernalia. *Revue Française d'Études Américaines* 94 (December): 85–90.

Senna, Danzy

MELISSA DENNIHY
Queensborough Community College, CUNY, USA

Danzy Senna is the author of five critically acclaimed works of literature: novels *Caucasia* (1998), *Symptomatic* (2004), and *New People* (2017); short story collection *You Are Free* (2011); and memoir *Where Did You Sleep Last Night?* (2009). Senna's best-selling debut novel, *Caucasia*, won the Stephen Crane First Fiction Award and the American Library Association's Alex Award. Senna was also the recipient of the 2002 Whiting Award in Fiction, awarded annually to emerging writers, and the 2016 John Dos Passos Prize for Literature, awarded annually to a contemporary American writer with a substantial and significant body of work. Senna's writing explores the complexities of mixed-race identities, as well as the ways race intersects with other facets of identity, including class, gender, culture, religion, language, and family history. Initially recognized for her contribution to a long history of US passing literature with her first novel, *Caucasia*, Senna's literary career has burgeoned over the past twenty years. Her oeuvre has established Senna as a prominent contemporary American writer and one of the defining voices within the growing field of mixed-race American literature.

Senna was born in Boston, Massachusetts in 1970, one of three children of Irish-English-American poet, novelist, and short story writer Fanny Howe and African Mexican American writer and editor Carl Senna. Herself a prolific author, Howe has published over two dozen works of poetry and fiction and was a recipient of the prestigious Ruth Lilly Poetry Prize. Carl Senna has authored *The Black Press and The Struggle for Civil Rights* (1993), among other works. Both Howe and Senna were involved in Civil Rights era activism.

As a child, Danzy Senna attended Boston public schools as well as the Elma Lewis School of Fine Arts, an institution focused on instilling racial pride in Black students through an alternative arts education (Senna's *Caucasia* is also set in Boston, and its protagonist also transfers from a public school to an alternative "Black power" school – where she finds herself lacking acceptance among her peers because she looks too white). Originally intending to avoid the literary professions of her parents and become a doctor, Senna enrolled at Stanford University for her undergraduate degree, where her literary interests and talents nonetheless prevailed. She founded *Enigma: The Stanford Journal of Black Expression* as an undergraduate before going on to pursue an MFA from UC-Irvine. *Caucasia* was written during Senna's years at UC-Irvine and published in 1998.

After completing her graduate degree and her first novel, Senna lived and worked in Fort Greene, Brooklyn, which is also the setting of her third novel, *New People*. She later moved to Los Angeles, where she currently lives with her husband, novelist Percival Everett (also a recipient of the John Dos Passos Prize), and their two children. A former Cullman Center Fellow at the New York Public Library, Senna is currently a professor of English at the University of Southern California.

Caucasia, published by Riverside Books in 1998 and subsequently translated into ten languages, won the Stephen Crane First Fiction Award and the American Library Association's Alex Award and was a finalist for the International Dublin Literary Award. The novel attracted the attention of literary critics and scholars as a work of mixed-race literature as well as a passing story. Set in Boston and New Hampshire in the 1970s, *Caucasia* depicts the disintegration and eventual breakup of the Lee family: Deck, Sandy, and their biracial daughters, Cole and Birdie. Protagonist Birdie is, like Senna herself, the light-skinned daughter of a Black man and a white woman. When Deck and Sandy separate, Cole, who looks much darker than her sister, moves with her father to Brazil, while Birdie, the "white(r)" child, lives with her mother, passing for white when she and Sandy resettle in a virtually all-white New Hampshire town. Birdie's passing has led critics to situate *Caucasia* within a long tradition of US passing literature, including early-twentieth century works such as James Weldon Johnson's *Autobiography of an Ex-Colored Man* (1912), Walter White's *Flight* (1926), Nella Larsen's *Passing* (1929), and Fannie Hurst's *Imitation of Life* (1933), as well as more contemporary passing novels such as Colson Whitehead's *The Intuitionist* (2000) and Philip Roth's *The Human Stain* (2001).

While the racial dynamics within the Lee family might seem to suggest that the novel treats matters of race rather simplistically – Birdie passes as white because she looks more like her white mother, while Cole is identified as Black because she looks more like her Black father – *Caucasia* actually presents racial identity as much messier and more complex than merely a matter of appearances. Indeed, the novel demonstrates how difficult it is for Birdie to consistently claim or identify with any racial identity, white or Black. Although Birdie may look white (or, at least, white*r* than her sibling), *Caucasia* emphasizes that race is constructed of more than what is inferred by the body: Birdie learns how to claim, affirm, or hide blackness and whiteness to varying degrees by modifying other aspects of her identity, such as her forms of dress and self-expression; affiliation with cultural practices and social circles; and uses of language. The narrative portrays race and racial identity as defined not only by physical characteristics, but through a myriad of facets of identity, making race mutable and dynamic even in its permanence. In this sense, *Caucasia,* like its protagonist, refuses easy categorization: it is a work of passing literature, but the novel also broadens and supersedes the boundaries of the passing genre, presenting race as more than a black-white dichotomy and emphasizing the plurality and multifariousness of racial identity.

Symptomatic, Senna's second novel, was published in 2004. Like *Caucasia*'s Birdie, *Symptomatic*'s protagonist is a young woman of mixed race who struggles with feelings of displacement and isolation, particularly in relation to her racial identity. After landing her dream job, she moves to New York City, where she develops an increasingly intense relationship with an older woman of similarly ambiguous racial origins, whose obsession with the young protagonist has led readers to draw parallels to Nella Larsen's *Passing*, in which two biracial women form a similar relationship that includes elements of the erotic and obsessive. Described by some critics as a psychological thriller, *Symptomatic* is a darker, more suspenseful novel than Senna's debut novel, even as it explores many of the same themes.

Though primarily recognized as a novelist, Senna made her mark as a memoirist with *Where Did You Sleep Last Night?: A Personal History*, published in 2009. Written and researched while Senna was a fellow at the New York Public Library's Cullman Center for Scholars and Writers, this intensely personal autobiographical and familial history looks at Senna's upbringing in a mixed-race household and her contentious relationship with her father, Carl Senna. It also travels further back in time to uncover the history of Carl's childhood in the rural South and his volatile marriage to Fanny Howe – the latter a white Bostonian of established lineage; the former a Black man born to a poor, single mother and an unknown father. Carl and Fanny's marriage, which occurred one year after the landmark *Loving v. Virginia* Supreme Court case legalizing interracial marriage in the US, was vehemently opposed by family and friends, and the couple spent years trying to overcome opposition to their union before ultimately divorcing. In this sense, the memoir not only explores Senna's own family history, but also offers insight into some of the autobiographical elements of *Caucasia*, as the parents of protagonist Birdie seem to be loosely based on Senna's own parents, and the problems in their marriage very similar to those faced by Fanny and Carl.

While *Where Did You Sleep Last Night?* is a nonfiction work, it has been described as a genre-crossing text, blending elements of memoir, family history, travel narrative, and detective story. Senna takes us with her from Boston, where her maternal lineage is literally written into the public landmarks of the city, to the rural South, where she does the emotionally wrenching work of seeking to recover some of her undocumented paternal history as she travels throughout Alabama and Louisiana. Senna has noted in an interview that this memoir is not just about race but also class: she describes her parents' marriage as an "interclass" as well as interracial one, and considers herself mixed in terms of class and race (Gautier 2009). In seeking to learn more about her father's childhood and parents' marriage, Senna learns a good deal about herself, too – but her memoir resists a redemptive or healing narrative and does not offer resolution in the form of a happy ending. In this sense, *Where Did You Sleep Last Night?* continues the trajectory of Senna's earlier fiction works in resisting many of the conventions and expectations imposed on writers and literary genres.

In 2011, Senna published the short story collection *You Are Free*. The collection marked not only a new genre for Senna but also a shift in her oeuvre's thematic focus: race and racial identity are somewhat less prominent in this text than in her other works. Instead, the eight stories in *You Are Free* focus more on gender, specifically women's identities, experiences, and relationships with other women. However, one thematic thread that carries over from her previous works is the messiness and multifariousness of identity, whether racial or gender identity. In *You Are Free*, the difficult questions being asked are less about the murkiness of mixed race than about the various forms of freedom – or lack thereof – available to different women: women who are single or married; longing or refusing to become mothers; raising their own children or nurturing others. As Senna notes in an interview, the book's title comes from a phrase used by a character in the eponymous story who has just had an abortion. Leaving the clinic, she repeats "you are free" to herself over and over. Yet, as Senna points out, *who* is free remains ambiguous and open to interpretation: "Is she referring to herself or the fetus she has just aborted? . . . In an odd way, that dead fetus is the only character in this collection that is truly 'free.' Once we are born, we are encumbered by 'identity'. . . Our bodies – the meanings they speak to the world – will always be encumbered. So then how do we make choices? Where, if anywhere, do we feel free?" (2011). The experience of being "encumbered by 'identity'" – and seeking freedom from it – is portrayed again and again throughout Senna's body of work, explored through the angle of race most frequently, but also through other lenses such as gender, sexuality, socioeconomic class, and culture.

Explorations of identity – its constraints, possibilities, permanence and mutability – emerge again in Senna's novel *New People*. Like *Caucasia*, *New People*'s protagonist is a light-skinned, mixed-race woman, but the setting has shifted from New England in the 1970s to New York City in the 1990s – specifically, the neighborhood of Fort Greene, Brooklyn, where Senna herself lived and wrote following the completion of her MFA degree. *New People*'s protagonist Maria and her partner Khalil live in a pre-gentrified mixed-race bohemian artist's neighborhood, and the alienation and displacement they experience in a place where they should easily fit in is not dissimilar from the experiences of the young protagonist newly arrived in New York City in Senna's *Symptomatic*. A work that has enjoyed considerable critical acclaim since its recent publication, *New People* was named a Best Book of the Year by the *New York Times Book Review*, *Time* magazine, and *NPR*.

In addition to her major works, Senna has written essays for the *New Yorker*, the *New York Times*, and *Vogue*. Senna also wrote the foreword to a new edition (2015) of Fran Ross's 1967 mixed-race novel *Oreo*. This is apt given the similarities in their work. Senna's characters are often racialized but also racially ambiguous: they aren't Black or white, but rather blackish or whitish, not-quite-Black-enough or not-quite-white-enough – they are, like Ross's protagonist, "oreos," who destabilize constructions of racial identity through their inability to neatly fit into racial categories. And, like Ross, Senna is also interested in what she has called the "comedy of race." Writing about *Oreo*, Senna describes how the text works against the literary trope of the "tragic mulatto," instead presenting readers with "a comic mulatto, turning the world on its head with a verbal precocity and wit that sharpen her ability to shape-shift and pass" (2015). Though Senna is describing Ross's protagonist here, she could just as easily be describing her own characters, many of whom are also (tragi-)comic mulattos who use "verbal precocity and wit" to "shape-shift and pass." Senna, like Ross before her, offers keen insights into the ironies and absurdities of racial identity in America; by highlighting these through incisive wit and satirical humor, her works ask readers to re-engage with the very concepts of race and racial identity from a more critical, subversive perspective.

While race is central to Senna's work, she also emphasizes through her writing and in interviews and speaking engagements that identity is comprised of much more than race, and that racial identity is always intersectional with other facets of identity such as class, gender, religion, language, and sexuality. In a discussion of her short story collection *You Are Free*, perhaps the work in her oeuvre that is least focused on race and racial identity, Senna describes the role of race as "an unspoken presence": "sometimes it seems not to matter at all and sometimes it seems like everything revolves around it," adding that, "in these stories race is just one of many different identities that the [characters] are struggling to understand – but it is certainly not the whole picture" (2011). Indeed, in all of Senna's works, she invites us to consider the lasting significance of race in contemporary America, while also revealing a bigger picture of identity and individuality – one in which racial identity is shaped by and intersectional with many other complexities of selfhood and society.

Like its mixed-race characters, Senna's literature is not easily categorized. While Senna has self-identified as Black in at least one essay (2015), her work has been categorized as American literature, mixed-race literature, passing literature, biracial literature, African American literature, and even postracial literature. *Caucasia*, in particular, has been categorized as a contemporary passing novel, joining works like Philip Roth's *The Human Stain* and Colson Whitehead's *The Intuitionist*, modern-day takes on the traditional passing story as seen in century-old texts like Nella Larsen's *Passing* and James Weldon Johnson's *Autobiography of an Ex-Colored Man*. What seems most significant, however, is that Senna has been increasingly recognized for her seminal contributions to a now burgeoning field of mixed-race American literature, which includes works like Barack Obama's *Dreams from My Father* (1995), James McBride's *The Color of Water* (1996), Toi Derricotte's *The Black Notebooks* (1999), Rebecca Walker's *Black, White, and Jewish* (2002), Matt de la Peña's *Mexican WhiteBoy* (2008), and Celeste Ng's *Everything I Never Told You* (2014) – all of which join earlier but lesser-known mixed-race narratives such as Ross's *Oreo*. This recent proliferation of mixed-race literature, including both the publication of new stories and the re-release of older ones, is significant given that the categorization of American literature along racial lines has often come at the cost of inattention to and exclusion of literature by mixed-race authors and about mixed-race characters. Scholars, critics, booksellers, and readers frequently designate contemporary American fiction as belonging to one racial group or another – for example, we read African American literature and Mexican American literature, but rarely find anthologies or bookstore sections devoted to Afro Mexican American literature. Senna not only belongs to a new era of writers bringing attention to the complexities of race, both in literature and in lived experience, but is also taking part in the revival of earlier works of mixed-race literature, such as Ross's *Oreo*, that were under-recognized or unrecognized at the time of their initial publication. Discussing *Oreo*, Senna writes, "[Ross's] novel is multifaceted and multilingual, making it an awkward presence on the landscape of American fiction, where 'ethnic' literature can be put in kiosks like dishes at a food fair, and consumed just as easily" (2015). When it was first published over twenty years ago, *Caucasia* arguably occupied a similarly awkward space within the landscape of American fiction, but Senna's debut novel and others like it have since helped to establish a field of mixed-race literature that has successfully pushed the boundaries of how we think about the categorization of American literature along racial lines.

With a literary career that has already spanned twenty years and four genres, readers and critics can look forward to what is yet to come from Senna. Still a relatively young writer, her oeuvre will likely continue to expand and evolve as Senna explores new subjects and forms. Her work as a novelist and short story writer have earned her a notable place in the canon of contemporary American fiction, while also helping to transform the landscape of that fiction in the process.

SEE ALSO: Mixed-Genre Fiction; Ng, Celeste; Post-Soul and/or Post-Black Fiction; Roth, Philip; Whitehead, Colson

REFERENCES

Gautier, Amina. (2009). Interview with Danzy Senna. *The Rumpus* (July 7, 2009). https://therumpus.net/2009/07/the-rumpus-original-combo-with-danzy-senna/ (accessed July 18, 2021).

Senna, Danzy. (2011). Author Q&A. https://www.amazon.com/You-Are-Free-Danzy-Senna/dp/1594485070 (accessed September 16, 2021).

Senna, Danzy. (2015). An overlooked classic about the comedy of race. *The New Yorker* (May 7, 2015). https://www.newyorker.com/books/page-turner/an-overlooked-classic-about-the-comedy-of-race (accessed July 18, 2021).

FURTHER READING

Arias, Claudia M. Milian. (2002). An interview with Danzy Senna. *Callaloo* 25 (2): 447–452.

Dennihy, Melissa. (2017). Talking the talk: linguistic passing in Danzy Senna's *Caucasia*. *MELUS* 42 (2): 156–176.

Elam, Michele. (2011). Passing in the post-race era: Danzy Senna's *Caucasia*, Philip Roth's *The Human Stain* and Colson Whitehead's *The Intuitionist*. In: *The Souls of Mixed Folk: Race, Politics, and Aesthetics in the New Millennium* (ed. Michele Birnbaum), 96–124. Stanford: Stanford University Press.

Harrison-Kahan, Lori. (2011). Passing for white, passing for Jewish: mixed race identity in Danzy Senna and Rebecca Walker. *MELUS* 30 (1): 19–48.

Jerkins, Morgan. (2017). The old problems of *New People*. *The New Republic* (June 22, 2017). https://newrepublic.com/article/143452/old-problems-new-people

St. Félix, Doreen. (2017). Danzy Senna's new Black woman. *The New Yorker* (August, 7, 2017). https://www.newyorker.com/books/page-turner/danzy-sennas-new-black-woman.

Serros, Michele

VERÓNICA QUEZADA
Soka University of America, USA

Michele Serros (b. February 10, 1966, d. January 4, 2015) was born and raised in Oxnard, California, a fourth-generation Mexican American. She was the second and youngest child of George R. Serros and Beatrice Ruiz Serros. In interviews, she recounted her need to stay at the public library to pass time before heading home, which in turn fostered her love for reading and books and her desire to become a writer. Both her parents and Oxnard, especially her neighborhood, El Rio, had a significant influence on her and her writing, as becomes apparent in their prominence in her literary works. Mike Sonksen, in *L.A. Letters*, describes her as having a compassionate personality and an incomparable sense of humor, which also resonates throughout her writings (Sonksen 2015).

As is well known, Serros was inspired by the American children's author Judy Blume to become a writer at the age of 11 years. She wrote to Blume for advice on how to deal with her parents' divorce. The author answered her letter and advised her to keep a journal to express her emotions, which she did from that age, and which later influenced or became the source of her writings.

In terms of her writing career, Serros studied journalism in Ventura College before moving to Los Angeles. She first attended Santa Monica College and then transferred to the University of California, Los Angeles, where she graduated *cum laude* with a BA in Chicano Studies in 1996. She published her first literary work, a poetry collection, *Chicana Falsa and Other Stories of Death, Identity, and Oxnard* (1993) while still an undergraduate. It was first published by Lalo Press; after the press closed down, she would sell it herself in her garage and after performances in any place that allowed her. She had great success with her poetry; the band *Rage Against the Machine* even featured her poetry collection in one of their album's liner notes (Sonksen 2015). That same year, she was chosen as one of twelve "Road Poets" to tour with Lollapalooza, an iconic music festival based in Chicago, Illinois, which features renowned and popular artists. In addition, in 1998, the Poetry Society of America selected Serros's poetry to be featured on MTA buses throughout Los Angeles County in a program called "Poetry in Motion" (Pool 1998).

Two years after its publication, *Chicana Falsa and Other Stories* was out of print. However, the spoken word label Mouth Almighty became interested in Serros's work and launched an audio version of some of her poems. Riverbooks bought the rights to the title in 1998, after high schools and colleges had started adding it to their curricula. Her poems had also been included in the anthology *New World: Young Latino Writers* (1997), edited by Ilan Stavans.

In 2000, Michele Serros published her remarkable novel *How to Be a Chicana Role Model* with the same press, Riverbooks, which instantly placed on the *Los Angeles Times* bestseller list. This work sealed her popularity and recognition after literary critics and reviewers agreed she was "a woman writer to watch for in the new century," as *Newsweek* described her. With her characteristic wit, she positioned herself as a Chicana writer with a revisionist approach to a Chican@/x identity. (Note: I use "Chican@," used during Serros's time, to reflect the inclusion of women, and "Chicanx" as a current all-inclusive term.)

Michele Serros was not only a poet and novelist, she was also an essayist, performer, motivational speaker, social commentator, script writer, young adult writer, and entrepreneur too. She was a contributor to *The Washington Post*, the *Los Angeles Times*, *Ms. Magazine*, *CosmoGirl*, *The Huffington Post*, and National Public Radio. In 2002, Serros was hired by George Lopez and ABC to write for his television sitcom's first season. Despite advice to the contrary, she did not renew her contract for the second season, claiming she missed writing fiction. However, in an interview with David Starkey for "The Creative Community," she mentioned not agreeing with producers who modified her writing or proposals with comments like, "is the person from Missouri going to understand this" (Starkey 2009). In 2005, she immersed herself in the young adult genre when she was approached by Alloy Entertainment to create a "Latina version" of their successful Gossip Girl series. In 2006, her first young adult novel, *Honey Blonde Chica*, was published, followed by its sequel, *¡Scandalosa!* (2007). Her entrepreneurship line included a T-shirt brand called "Medium Brown Girl," representing her Chican@ ideology, which she sold via her official website: www.miralamichele.com.

In 2013, she was diagnosed with a rare disease, adenoid cystic carcinoma of the salivary gland. The cancer had metastasized and while she endured chemotherapy she passed away two years later. Serros's contribution to the Chican@/x and American literary canon has been felt and her literary legacy has continued in different universities and literary venues. Recently, California State University, Channel Islands – which received a posthumous donation from her – has opened a permanent exhibition in her honor that includes her memorabilia and a mural of her.

The Chican@/x literary movement of the 1960s and 1970s and the Chicana feminist revival of the 1980s equipped Serros with a post-political consciousness and awareness. Even though writers like John Rechy and Cecile Pineda had begun the bifurcation of the Chican@/x writing scene by exploring taboo or nontraditional Chican@/x topics in their writings, she seems closer to them in ideology and style than to the constantly mentioned point of reference, Sandra Cisneros. Serros represents a younger generation of American writers of Mexican descent who "refused to become a barrio stereotype" (Cano 2017). She belongs to the Generation X writers (those born between 1965 and 1979), or the "hybrid fiction" writers included in Daniel Grassian's *Hybrid Fictions: American Literature and Generation X* (2003). However, Serros was not fond of labels and would have preferred to be considered a multidimensional writer who happened to be of Mexican descent.

A recapitulation of the sociohistorical context helps us understand Serros's position in the Chican@/x literary realm. After the turbulent years of the Chicano Movement in pursuit of civil rights in the 1960s, the Mexican American community's new struggle became the establishment of a literary corpus that reflected their presence in the hegemonic discourse of the nation. The majority of the pioneer Chicanx activists, artists, and writers were first-generation Americans and/or immigrants. The spatial and sociopolitical settings of the literature of this era occurred in neighborhoods (*barrios*), relegated to the Mexican and Mexican American communities, many infested with violence, poverty, discrimination, and other social issues. Nevertheless, by the next decade, Chicanos had accomplished a foundational narrative (including *Bless Me Ultima* [1972] by Rudolfo Anaya and *Y no se lo tragó la tierra...* [1971] by Tomás Rivera), which focused on Chicano or Mexican communities living in the Southwest United States. Consequently, representative Chicanx literature, studied in higher and secondary education, portrayed exclusively the segment of politically committed writers creating a necessary sociopolitical and cultural awareness about an emerging identity – one politically charged, which was not Mexican or American, but was complemented by both. In the 1980s, the literary production emanated from Chicanas, women writers and theorists, such as Gloria Anzaldúa and Ana Castillo. The first generation of Chicana writers revised female archetypes and, just like their male counterparts had done a decade before, constructed their own encyclopedia and identity much influenced by the new *mestiza* consciousness coined by Anzaldúa. Even though it was, and has been, a struggle to include Chican@/x literature in the public and educational spheres, and have it accepted as part of the American narrative, nonetheless by the early 1990s, a corpus and canon had been accomplished and was perceptible. Finally, there was a vivid Chican@ encyclopedia of symbols which constructed a cultural community, but which also indirectly formed paradigms about Chicanx literature that future generations would have to question and/or challenge.

It is in this literary and sociopolitical atmosphere that Michele Serros's *Chicana Falsa* is born. Serros's poetry portrays the narrative of Mexican Americans who do not fit the community and parameters created by the first Chican@/x writers. She is the voice of a generation of Mexican Americans who are no longer first generation, who were discouraged from learning Spanish, encouraged to assimilate, and who did not have to confront many of the struggles Chicanos faced in the fields or *barrios*, with immigrant parents, in the preceding decades. Therefore, she questions this early identity as she simultaneously revises or rewrites both Chican@/x and American discourses about ethnicity, identity, and gender.

While other writers and critics acknowledge Serros's distancing from traditional or canonical Chican@/x literatures, less attention has been paid to her wit and writing style. Her writing is characterized by her greatest tools: humor and sarcasm. The poetry collection *Chicana Falsa* illustrates the ingenuity with which she writes about everyday situations in a succinct manner, but with keen cultural or sociopolitical comments that mainly question identity but also problematize other topics, such as friendship, sexuality, ethnicity, and racism. The title, "Chicana falsa" (or fake Chicana), highlights the revisionist stance, signaling the absence of the "real" Chicana in these poems. However, her first poem, "La Letty," blurs the dichotomy of real versus fake Chicana. Leticia or "la Letty" accuses and labels the speaker for not acting Chicana enough, "you know what you are? / A Chicana Falsa" [. . .] "HOMOGENIZED HISPANIC, / that's what you are" (Serros 1993,

p. 1). However, Serros immediately counteracts with the description of Letty, who has become the stereotypical media's representation of a Chicana, a "raccoon eyed beauty [...] the whole-creased-khaki / pressed-flannel / medallion-wearing scene" (p. 2), that is the constructed image of a *chola* (gang member).

There is also the narrator's aunt, in "Annie Says," who discourages her from pursuing a writing career because she was not "born in no barrio / No tortilleria down your street / Bullets never whizzed past your baby head" (Serros 1993, pp. 5–6) and finally labeling her "a Chicana Without a Cause" (p. 6). Leticia and Aunt Annie corroborate Serros's internalized oppression; she did not fit the parameters defining a Chican@/x and what qualifies as Chican@/x literature. However, Serros challenges them and constructs her own identity, a Chicana falsa, one who cannot speak Spanish fluently, as in "Mi problema," and one who can perceive racism even in the packing of frozen vegetables, as in "Attention Shoppers." Serros's unapologetic approach to taboo topics also makes her writing distinct, as in "Planned Parenthood: Age Sixteen," where a teenage Chicana resists becoming another number in the teenage-pregnancy statistics and becomes once again "the minority in a sea of blond and green eyes" (p. 65) because family and religion impede Chicanas from using contraceptives. In an interview she confessed, "I relished the fact that I was a fourth-generation Californian, but not looking like the stereotypical blond beach girl [...] I always felt like an outsider" (Quintero-Flores 2013); manifesting the ambivalence in her identity, she felt Californian, yet the stereotypes imposed on her made her feel an "outsider." She did not fit the white or the brown mold.

By the time she wrote *How to be a Chicana Role Model*, Serros had acquired sufficient popularity to be considered a Chicana writer and role model. Thus, this novel is semi-autobiographical and narrates her journey from an aspiring writer to a Chicana role model with her characteristic sarcasm. The novel is a manual on how to be a role model, composed of thirteen chapters, each headed by a rule. However, the reader soon discovers it to be a parody; after every rule, the story reveals an ironic twist contradicting the apparent teaching. The main targets of her sarcasm and critique are those who claim to be Chican@s/x or represent the community. In "Role Model Rule Number 1: Never Give Up an Opportunity to Eat for Free," for example, the narrator is invited to a Chicana writers' conference, which she gladly accepts, thinking she would have an opportunity to read her poems. However, once at the conference, she discovers the invitation was to serve food and not to read with the "real" Chican@/x writers. She soon learns the disdain writers and attendees have for individuals like her, who "look" Chicana, but cannot speak Spanish fluently and who serve croissants instead of *pan dulce* (sweet bread). However, inadvertently, this also becomes the opportunity to promote her poetry when she meets a publisher. Serros ends the lesson of the chapter with the determination to express her ideology through her writing. In "Role Model Rule Number 2: Seek Support from Sistas," the narrator quickly learns that Chicana or Latina solidarity is an illusion. When she reaches out to another Latina for help at work, "a brown woman supporting another brown woman [...]" (Serros 2000, p. 23), she realizes that she cannot always expect another Latina to be her ally. This incident exposes the imagined (or fake) community created along ethnic labels.

Furthermore, along the same lines as *Chicana Falsa*, Serros challenges the concept of ethnicity. "Role Model Rule Number 8: Reclaim Your Right as a Citizen of Here, Here" complicates the categorization of individuals into ethnicities, especially in the narrator's case, "it's like [Americans] are uncomfortable not being able to categorize things they're unfamiliar with and so they need to label everything as quickly and neatly as possible" (Serros 2000, p. 124), thus making assumptions, such as asking the narrator where she "really" is from because she does not look Californian. Serros also revisits and resists typical female representations, for example nontraditional grandmothers. The narrator admits the reason why she ends up at her father's work place on "Take Our Daughters to Work Day" is not due to a learning opportunity, but due to lack of money for babysitting because "unlike what so many people think of Mexican grandmothers, ours really disliked children" (p. 172), thus leaving her parents no options. In addition, in "Role Model Rule Number 11: Honor Thy Late-Night Phone Calls from Abuelita," her Grandmother Socorro becomes a go-between; whenever she receives phone calls from fans of the narrator, she gives them personal information. The narrator, on the other hand, cannot resist a relationship with fans and falls for them, jeopardizing the moral of her lesson. When asked about her novel, Serros said, "I use the term 'Chicana' in such a tongue in cheek manner; I actually feel unworthy of the title, as I haven't really done anything worthy to earn it" (Quintero-Flores 2013). However, after analyzing and scrutinizing topics affecting the Chican@/x community, she earned the title, even when she preferred to add an adjective: Chicana falsa.

On the other hand, the two young adult novels Michele Serros wrote, *Honey Blonde Chica* (2006) and *¡Scandalosa!*, have been overlooked and dismissed as light, non-academic literature. Nonetheless, even in these novels Serros's legacy is undeniable. She not only created the Chicana version of *Gossip Girl*, but she also managed to revise the portrayal of social standing in Chican@/x literature and to draw attention to the upper-class group, that is, business owners or descendants of powerful Mexican and Mexican American families. This is a community that has been completely imperceptible in both Chican@/x and American narratives because the lower- and middle-class Chicano fit the parameters better. The protagonist of both novels, Evelina (Evie) Gomez, is the daughter of a Mexican businessman, owner of a chain of bakeries, which allows her family to live a privileged life and to mingle with Chicanx and Mexican families from the upper class. Evie and her friends are entirely bicultural, and they embrace both their American and their Mexican culture, blurring borders between the two. These novels are far away from the traditional young adult novels, but they reveal hidden realities: there are rich Mexicans and Mexican Americans, and not all immigrants from Mexico live in poor neighborhoods. There are prosperous Chicanx who have benefitted from capitalism and trading agreements between the two countries. Therefore, although many claim Serros's novels are depoliticized, referring to the expected continuous participation of literature in the Chicano struggle (*La causa*), not only is she political and committed to the Chican@/x community, but her literary work is exhaustive, analytical, and deserves more attention.

SEE ALSO: Alarcon, Daniel; Álvarez, Julia; Anaya, Rudolfo; Braschi, Giannina; Castillo, Ana; Chick Lit and the New Domesticity; Cofer, Judith Ortiz; García, Cristina; Hinojosa, Rolando; Urrea, Luis Alberto

REFERENCES

Cano, Daniel. (2017). Remembering Michele Serros: a writer's journey. *La Bloga* (December 14, 2017). https://labloga.blogspot.com/2017/12/remembering-michele-serros-writers.html (accessed July 16, 2021).

Grassian, Daniel. (2003). *Hybrid Fictions: American Literature and Generation X*. Jefferson: NC: McFarland.

Pool, Bob. (1998). MTA buses adding rhyme to the ride. *Los Angeles Times* (October 2, 1998). https://www.latimes.com/archives/la-xpm-1998-

oct-02-me-28555-story.html (accessed July 16, 2021).
Quintero-Flores, Isabel. (2013). An interview with Michele Serros. *Orange Monkey Publishing* (April 20, 2013). https://orangemonkeypublishing.wordpress.com/2013/04/20/an-interview-with-michele-serros-april-2013 (accessed July 16, 2021).
Serros, Michele. (1993). *Chicana Falsa and Other Stories of Death, Identity, and Oxnard.* New York: Riverhead Books.
Serros, Michele. (2000). *How to be a Chicana Role Model.* New York: Riverhead Books.
Sonksen, Mike. (2015). Remembering Michele Serros. KSET (January 14, 2015). https://www.kcet.org/history-society/remembering-michele-serros (accessed July 16, 2021).
Starkey, David. (2009). The creative community: Michele Serros. *The Creative Community* (October 14, 2009). https://vimeo.com/7523850 (accessed July 16, 2021).

FURTHER READING

Anzaldúa, Gloria. (2003). *Borderlands/La Frontera. The New Mestiza.* San Francisco: Aunt Lute Books; 1st ed. 1987.
Hernandez, Guillermo E. (1991). *Chicano Satire: A Study in Literary Culture.* Austin: University of Texas Press.
Ibarraran Bigalondo, Amaia. (2007). How to be a Chicana role model, or how to be a 21st century Chicana. *ES. Revista de Filología Inglesa* 28: 97–106.
Ibarraran Bigalondo, Amaia. (2011). Sandra Cisneros, Yxta Maya Murray, Michelle [sic] Serros: three decades, three ways, some examples of the "Chicana Youth Experience" in literature. *ES. Revista de Filología Inglesa* 32: 147–160.
Mize, Ronald L. (2019). *Short Introductions: Latina/o Studies.* Cambridge: Polity Press.

Shteyngart, Gary

MARTYNA BRYLA
Universidad de Málaga, Spain

The story of Gary Shteyngart starts in Leningrad, where the author spent his early childhood. Shteyngart recalls being a frail, asthmatic boy whose parents, a piano teacher and a mechanical engineer, were determined to secure a better life for their only child. When the opportunity arose to take advantage of the political accord between the Soviet Union and the United States, the Shteyngarts left the country with a one-way ticket to the West. From the point of view of the communist state, the decision was commensurate with "the act of treason and meant severing one's links with other 'good citizens,' becoming an outcast," and as such involved a series of administrative and professional "rituals of punishment" (Remennick 2012, p. 38). From a personal perspective, it meant leaving at least part of the family behind and undergoing professional devaluing in the host country. The story of the family's immigration to the United States and the process of their cultural adjustment is the subject of Shteyngart's memoir, *Little Failure* (2014), which spans the author's life from his Soviet childhood until his literary debut at the age of 30. The memoir, described by Shteyngart as "an unhappy love letter to my parents" (Chicago Humanities Festival 2014), is also a bitter-sweet record of coming to terms with one's hyphenated heritage and struggling to find a voice of one's own in a foreign language and reality.

Little Failure reveals real-life inspiration behind fiction, allowing the reader to trace back the origin of some of the running motifs of Shteyngart's earlier works. Since the beginning of his literary career, Shteyngart has sourced his Russian Jewish background to produce literature which crosses languages and cultures, responding to the global interconnectedness of the contemporary world but also pointing out the traps and limits of liquid modernity.

Symptomatically, Shteyngart's characters are usually migrant males trying to make it in a world which preaches multiculturalism but practices ethnocentricity, and where one's hyphenated status can be an asset and a drawback at the same time. Shteyngart's preferred mode of writing is a comic-mordant satire, reminiscent of the tradition of Jewish and Jewish American humor, where irreverent laughter is a value in itself but also a means of exposing certain uncomfortable or perturbing social dynamics. Shteyngart's characters, such as Vladimir Girshkin, Misha Vainberg, or Lenny Abramov, are part *schlemiel*, part trickster. As insecure and vulnerable as they appear to be, they are nevertheless determined to fulfill their dreams and ambitions, often outwitting those who stand in their way by means of their cross-cultural credentials. These dreams range from fitting in (Vladimir Girshkin), becoming American (Misha Vainberg), or being loved in a society where getting old is commensurate with becoming disposable (Lenny Abramov). In Shteyngart's fiction, a sense of not-fitting-in is aggravated by vulnerable masculinity: Shteyngart's males are on the quest for a father figure and romantic love, looking for protection and redemption from their own flaws and inadequacies. The fear of being neglected is often a driving force behind their fantastical exploits, making them cross national and cultural borders in search for meaning, acceptance, and social acclaim.

Shteyngart's works tend to straddle at least two locales and temporal dimensions, moving between continents and countries, whether real or imaginary, and looking back to the protagonists' childhood, which is where many of their personal issues originate. Most of the time, the sociopolitical realities and others' expectations of what they should be interfere with the characters' aspirations and desires. Thus, in Shteyngart's debut novel, *The Russian Debutante's Handbook* (2002), Vladimir Girshkin, a Russian American of Jewish origins, is plunged into the midst of post-communist transition from the state-controlled economy to Western-style capitalism. The novel moves from New York to East-Central Europe, with the bulk of the work taking place in Prava, the capital of the post-Soviet Republic of Stolovaya, or *Cafeteria Republic*, named in reference to throngs of American youths colonizing the bars and cafés of the city, hoping to turn it into their "Paris of the 90s" (Shteyngart 2004, p. 66). The name Prava is a thin disguise for Prague, which Shteyngart visited in the 1990s. The novel belongs to a wave of "post-communist expat safari novels" (Borenstein 2003) written by young authors with a first-hand experience of touring East–Central Europe in the aftermath of the collapse of communism. True to the name, Prava is a veritable safari ground torn between the side effects of the transition, embodied by the post-Soviet mafia, and wild capitalism, which is gradually devouring the urban landscape and transforming the city in the image of the West.

Written in Shteyngart's trademark style of mixing the East and the West into a cultural and linguistic hybrid, where references to American pop culture blend in with passionate Russian interjections, the novel explores the migrant's condition as a state of in-betweenness in which a belief in social determinism coexists with the narrative of the self-made man. With his Soviet upbringing and American know-how, Vladimir Girshkin finds himself caught between the East and the West, striving to convince both the Mafiosi and the young American expats that he is authentic enough to play the role of an insider in both worlds. In the process, he outwits both parties, playing trickster in the disguise of a *schlemiel*, and mocking every nationality involved in this post-communist imbroglio.

The novel gives an ample taste of Shteyngart's emblematic reliance on national and ethnic stereotypes as a source of laughter. While the novel has been generally warmly received by American reviewers, some Russian critics have found fault with Shteyngart's treatment of their country, claiming that his extensive use of clichés may reinforce prejudice (Wanner 2011, pp. 120–121).

Shteyngart did not take this criticism to heart, as evidenced by his second novel, *Absurdistan* (2006), which surpasses the debut in terms of unabashed, politically incorrect humor and extravagant storyline. Like Vladimir Girshkin, the protagonist, Misha Vainberg, takes after his creator in that he is a young man of Russian Jewish origins. Girshkin even makes a passing appearance in the novel, as does Jerry Shteynfarb, a caricature of the writer himself. The ambivalence which characterized Girshkin, who was neither Russian nor American to those around him, is shared by Misha, whose very existence is suspended between the two countries. Although Misha is in love with American democracy and multiculturalism, it does not prevent him from living the lifestyle of a nineteenth-century nobleman in post-communist Russia. Outwardly, he is said to resemble an American rap star, but his lordly ways (he does not work and keeps a manservant) bring to mind Ivan Goncharov's Oblomov, a nineteenth-century symbol of idleness and sluggishness. *Absurdistan* attests to Shteyngart's appreciation of classic Russian literature, manifested also in his other novels. In addition to Goncharov, the novel makes intertextual references to Fyodor Dostoyevsky and Nikolai Gogol. Thus, Misha thinks of himself as part Oblomov, part Prince Myshkin, while a section of the novel is a reworking of Gogol's "The Portrait" (1835). Importantly, Gogol's influence is also visible in Shteyngart's portrayal of post-Soviet St. Petersburg (Wanner 2011, p. 120) as absorbing the most garish and vulgar elements of Western-style consumerism.

Like Shteyngart's debut novel, *Absurdistan* carries the tradition of social satire off into the twenty-first century though the "portrayal of the vicious, rampant capitalism stripping the life out of Putin's Russia and of the band-aid of multiculturalism on the gaping wound of sectarianism" (Ness 2007). But the novel is as much about the East as it is about the West. The post-Cold War world of *Absurdistan* is intersected by deep social divisions, provoking some uncanny parallels as far as the social malaise tormenting both the United States and Russia is concerned. No one puts it more succinctly than Misha's streetwise girlfriend, Rouenna, when she observes that "'all of you Russians are just a bunch of nigaz.' ... '[Y]our men don't got no jobs, everyone's always doing drive-bys whenever they got beefs, the childrens got asthma, and y'all live in public housing'" (Shteyngart 2008, pp. 11–12). The separation of Russian society into oligarchs and the poor, or the winners and the losers of the great political transition of the century, is clear to Rouenna but eludes Misha, who is the product of this very system and too obsessed with his own ego to notice what is going on around him. To do so, he has to be plunged into the midst of a civil war in Absurdsvanï, another imaginary locale which, in a manner similar to Prava, serves to illustrate the side effects of the post-Cold War politics of economic exploitation and the social burden of undigested historic legacies in the former Soviet colonies. While hilarious and upbeat until the very end, *Absurdistan* is nevertheless a bitter comedy of social determinism where the rich get off with a slap on the wrist, while the rest suffer the consequences of the political system and the historical era they must live in.

In a change of pace, Shteyngart's third, critically acclaimed work, *Super Sad True Love Story* (2010), is set almost entirely in America, albeit the United States of the future. In this dystopian novel, the country is in decline: the economy is crumbling, violence breaks out, and artificial intelligence reigns supreme. Shteyngart depicts a world where emotions have been replaced by data, and relationships of any kind are formed on the basis of ratings provided by omnipresent *äppärät* – personal devices which stream people's thoughts and feelings, continuously churning out information about their potential social attractiveness.

Glued to their screens, the novel's characters live their lives mostly virtually, willingly offering their lives for scrutiny and rejecting anything that used to be "the real thing" in the days of yore: from falling in love to the musty smell of a printed page, both of which are regarded as relics of the past, since love is entirely commodified and pornified while even the sight of books provokes disgust. It is thus no wonder that in this dictatorship of the visual, preserving youth and beauty becomes the utmost value and aspiration, while anyone who cannot afford to renew their cells is considered expendable. In creating a world where individuals constantly assess others and undergo endless assessment themselves, Shteyngart might be responding to the popularity of such social media as Instagram, where the visual attractiveness of the feed determines the value of an account, or even predicting the rise of dating applications like Tinder, whose photo-driven design allows the user to endorse or reject another person in a matter of seconds. Stylistically, Shteyngart alternates between the diary of Lenny Abramov, the novel's protagonist, and the email correspondence between his girlfriend, Eunice Park, and her friends and family. Full of abbreviations and culture-specific linguistic codes, the emails mimic contemporary teenage slang while at the same time approximating the language of the future in which communicability and vividness are achieved at the expense of correctness and elegance of expression.

If the other two novels pointed to the potential pitfalls of rampant capitalism and excessive consumerism, *Super Sad True Love Story* shows a world where progress has gone awry to the point of reversing some of the twentieth century's gains. Shteyngart's ultramodern society may be the most advanced so far, but it is also deeply socially flawed, as patriarchy is having a comeback (the female body is commodified and most women only aspire to work in *retail*), while anyone who does not live up to the prescribed social standards of popularity, affluence, and attractiveness is publicly ostracized.

Nevertheless, Shteyngart does inject a dose of hope into this grim picture through the novel's main focus: the eponymous love story between Lenny, the son of Russian Jewish immigrants, and his young girlfriend of Korean origin, Eunice Parks. Separated by almost everything, from cultural and family background to age and attractiveness, the two make an unlikely couple who defy the differences that divide them, erecting a common bastion against the loneliness inscribed in commodity culture. Although ultimately the relationship does not survive, moments of tenderness and passion that occur between Lenny and Eunice cancel out the antiseptic and artificial reality around them, promising, if only momentarily, that love is indeed all we need.

With its emphasis on family dynamics and its influence on the individual's adult choices, *Super Sad True Love Story* seems to foretell Shteyngart's next work, *Little Failure: A Memoir* (2014), where he uses his and his parents' migrant stories as literary material. The work is at once a writer's *Bildungsroman*, charting Shteyngart's initiation into storytelling, and an example of migrant literature par excellence, focused on the process of negotiating descent and consent to reconstruct a sense of self in the host culture. Narratively, the memoir is characterized by Shteyngart's trademark blend of Russia and America, interlocked with elements of Jewish culture and tradition, resulting in a narrative which embodies hybridity. Much of it is written from the retrospective point of view of the child migrant, which makes it heart-breaking and disarmingly funny at the same time: the very title of the memoir references Gary's Russian American nickname, *Failurchka*, which he was given by his mother. The work explores family dynamics in a migrant household, and especially the challenging task of fitting in the new reality while at the same time preserving a sense of continuity with the pre-emigration life. Shteyngart does not shy away from writing about his parents' personal traumas, inevitably related to the historic circumstances under which they had been brought up, to sketch a poignant family portrait of tough love and unresolved personal issues, which, in hindsight, have left an imprint on all of his work so far.

In the light of Shteyngart's most recent work, *Lake Success* (2018), *Little Failure* constitutes an apt "coda" to his Russian American novels with a Jewish cultural accent. As the author himself admitted, "[r]elying on the Russian-American background was always an easy way for me to differentiate my work, but I wanted to write an American novel without the Russian part" (Farwell 2018). Not only is *Lake Success* set entirely in the United States on the eve of Donald Trump's election to president, but it also reaches back to the classics of the American canon, *The Great Gatsby* (1925) and *On the Road* (1957). The result is a work in which a novel of manners and road fiction come together to respond to Shteyngart's ongoing concern with the country's condition under Trump's presidency, and provide an updated commentary on the issues which run through his oeuvre. Barry Cohen, the protagonist of the novel, is a wolf-from-Wall-Street type of character, a hedge fund manager whose "net worth" has earned him a coveted position among the higher echelons of Manhattan's financial elite. Underneath the glamorous facade, including an attractive younger wife and a ritzy apartment, there is, however, a personal drama spurred by his son's autism and Barry's unethical business doings. Unable to cope with the pressure of both, Barry embarks on his private on-the-road experience on the Greyhound bus, idealistically hoping to encounter a sense of self and the meaning of life in the vastness of America. As the journey progresses, it becomes increasingly clear that many of Barry's problems result from his own inability to form mature relationships with others and take responsibility for his actions. It is implied that Barry's difficulty at relating and responding to others may suggest a degree of autism spectrum disorder, but may also stem from the character's early trauma: losing his mother in a car accident at the age of three. At the same time, Barry's unethical business decisions reveal him to be an unscrupulous individual for whom empathy ends where personal profit begins. The character's strength lies thus in his complexity, which evades easy categorizations: Barry is at once reprehensible and worthy of sympathy. This nuanced treatment of the main character is extended onto America through which Barry travels. By zooming in on Barry's encounters with others, who are often dramatically less privileged than himself, Shteyngart explores contemporary America in cross-section, exposing the ever-present social divisions within the country where the aggressive culture of self-development commands an incessant pursuit of the American Dream, which, however, remains feasible only for some. That said, the novel is ultimately an uplifting one, particularly in its emphasis on the significance of communication and relationality in difficult times, and its defense of human difference, one of the essential if somewhat obliterated premises of the American Dream.

Lake Success has revealed Shteyngart's versatility as an author for whom comedy is not the only means of literary expression. No matter what direction his fiction takes next,[1] there is no doubt that he has established himself firmly on the American literary scene, compelling popular and critical attention with his sharp transnational satire on the many absurdities and pitfalls of the globalized world.

Shteyngart's protagonists are the flawed heroes of our times, challenging the contemporary culture of self-optimization with their weaknesses and imperfections, while at the same time striving to live their (American) dreams on their own terms.

NOTE

1 Shteyngart's new novel, *Our Country Friends*, published in November 2021, is set during the COVID-19 pandemic.

SEE ALSO: Big Data; Debut Novels; Globalization; Hemon, Aleksandar; Multiculturalism; Roth, Philip

REFERENCES

Borenstein, Eliot. (2003). Was it sexy, or just Soviet? The post-communist expat safari novel has its day. *Nation* (February 3, 2003): 33–36.

Chicago Humanities Festival. (2014). *Little Failure*: Gary Shteyngart in conversation with Aleksandar Hemon (January 27, 2014). https://www.youtube.com/watch?v=vnm4pvt7_Jg (accessed July 11, 2021).

Farwell, Eric. (2018). "There are incredible reservoirs of anger sloshing around our country": an interview with Gary Shteyngart. *Hazlitt* (September 4, 2018). https://hazlitt.net/feature/there-are-incredible-reservoirs-anger-sloshing-around-our-country-interview-gary-shteyngart (accessed July 11, 2021).

Ness, Patrick. (2007). Absurd person singular: review of *Absurdistan*. *The Guardian* (June 9, 2007). https://www.theguardian.com/books/2007/jun/09/featuresreviews.guardianreview4 (accessed July 11, 2021).

Remennick, Larissa. (2012). *Russian Jews on Three Continents: Identity, Integration, and Conflict*. New Brunswick, NJ: Transaction.

Shteyngart, Gary. (2004). *The Russian Debutante's Handbook*. London: Bloomsbury.

Shteyngart, Gary. (2008). *Absurdistan*. London: Granta Books.

Wanner, Adrian. (2011). Gary Shteyngart: the new immigrant chic. In: *Out of Russia: Fictions of a New Translingual Diaspora*, 95–133. Evanston, IL: Northwestern University Press.

FURTHER READING

Bryla, Martyna. (2018). Tracking the transnational trickster: Gary Shteyngart and his protagonists. *Nordic Journal of English Studies* 17 (2): 1–28.

Hamilton, Geoff. (2017). *Understanding Gary Shteyngart*. Columbia: University of South Carolina Press.

Shteyngart, Gary. (2016). Living in Trump's Soviet Union. *The New Yorker* (November 21, 2016). https://www.newyorker.com/magazine/2016/11/21/living-in-trumps-soviet-union

Siegel, Lee

JASON SHRONTZ
Klamath Community College, USA

A quick Internet search for Lee Siegel, the writer – not the musician or medical doctor – would reveal a list of articles about a controversial cultural critic with a long list of bestselling books. This Lee Siegel is not the subject of this entry. And yet, so much of what this entry has to say about the Lee Siegel who *is* the subject of this entry (the author of four experimental novels and multiple genre-bending scholarly works, and erstwhile professor of religion), is revealed in this strange alignment of identities. While Siegel the critic often writes about the intersection between people, books, and the Internet, Siegel the novelist creates this same intersection within his novels through patchworks of clipped web pages, unfinished books, and characters who navigate the spectrum of truth and fiction therein. The Siegels' identities overlap frequently in the digital world. When Siegel the cultural critic wrote an op-ed piece about why people should default on their student loans, Siegel the religion professor received hate mail. In a short documentary video about the mix-up, the novelist was optimistic that the popularity of the other Siegel would result in higher book sales for him due to Google and Amazon's inability to distinguish between the writers (Blalock 2015). This confusion is fitting for Siegel the novelist, whose corpus of work grapples with questions of identity and illusion, truth and fiction. So, in 2006 when Siegel the critic was suspended from *The New Republic* for creating a fake online identity and picking fights with his critics on *The New Republic*'s blog, while vehemently denying that he was Lee Siegel, the layers of fiction and truth seem little more than a plot arc from a work by the novelist, Lee Siegel.

Lee Siegel, the novelist, and henceforth, the sole Siegel of this entry, is the author of four novels that persistently exploit the novelty of the novel. At times, this exploitation is performed through formal innovation. *Love in a Dead Language* (1999), for example, is presented as a translation of the *Kamasutra*, but the protagonist's story unfolds through a maze of footnotes, reprinted web pages and letters, upside-down text, and images. *Love and Other Games of Chance* (2003) is organized around the classic game of Snakes and Ladders, with a corresponding chapter for each square on the game board. The reader is instructed to roll a die and read the book as one would play upon the included game board. His continual efforts to exercise the limitations of the novel situate him in the tradition of postmodern writers such as William Gass, B.S. Johnson, Italo Calvino, and Kathy Acker. For these writers, the novel is an artifice always in the process of becoming. Yet, blurring the lines between truth and fiction is also central to Siegel's fiction. His third novel, *Who Wrote the Book of Love* (2005), for example, follows a young Lee Siegel through his efforts in adolescent love. An author's note at the beginning explains that even though many of their experiences are "identical," the character "should not be confused with Lee Siegel, the adult author of this book." Siegel's fourth novel, *Love and the Incredibly Old Man* (2008), begins with a letter from Juan Ponce de Leon, claiming that the fountain of youth has run dry, and in his final days he needs a ghostwriter to tell his life story. Through the layering of literary and historical references, Siegel aligns more closely with eighteenth-century novelists – Sterne, Richardson, Defoe – who frequently passed off illusions as testimony, while steeping historical references in myth and folklore.

Siegel's fascination with illusion and reality seemed inevitable, given his upbringing in the shadow of mid-century Hollywood. He was born in Los Angeles in 1945 to Noreen Nash and Lee Siegel Sr. His mother was a well-known film actor and his father was a doctor who ran a medical practice. Though his mother retreated from acting soon after his birth, their family remained closely connected to the film industry, especially through the work of his father, who was also a medical director for 20th Century Fox. Siegel grew up in a world where the illusions of film and the reality of the writers and actors who sustained these illusions coexisted. On Sunday afternoons, Siegel explains, his childhood home "had a salon feeling to it," with "people who often came by who also influenced me substantially – lots of writers and movie people" (Burn 2006). Among them were the writer and director Jean Renoir, as well as novelist Henry Miller. Miller, a close family friend of the Siegels, married his fifth wife at their home, and would play ping-pong with them on Sunday afternoons. Since Miller didn't know how to drive, Siegel would pick him up. It was during these drives that Miller would talk about books and writing. These experiences had a profound impact on Siegel as he went on to study comparative literature at UC Berkeley and pursue an MFA at Columbia University. Eventually Siegel earned his doctorate at Oxford University, where he studied Sanskrit, and later became a professor of religions at the University of Hawaii.

Prior to his first novel, *Love in A Dead Language*, Siegel had already published six academic books about ancient India and its traditions of comedy, illusion, and storytelling. Through them, he developed the formal and comedic style that would later define his work as a novelist. During his research for *Net of Magic: Wonders and Deceptions in India* (1989), Siegel studied with street magicians in India. This experience, he explains, "taught me much more than he could ever imagine about writing. In attempting to evoke his performances for my book, I realized that each trick made sense as a story in the larger narrative of the magic show" (Burn 2006). Siegel began using narrative elements – narrators, plots, characters – in his scholarly work. He explains: "my scholarly writing had been getting more and more like fiction. My previous academic book, *City of Dreadful Night* [1995], had started as a scholarship on the history of horror and the macabre in Indian literature, but I ultimately adopted the techniques of narrative fiction to make my argument" (Burn 2006). With *Love in a Dead Language*, he "flipped the experiment over and decided to write narrative fiction using the techniques of scholarly writing. It has footnotes, a bibliography, epigraphs, and index – all of it fabricated" (Burn 2006). Even after his fourth novel, Siegel's work continues to explore themes of illusion while defying categorization. His most recent book, titled *Trance-Migrations* (2014), is equal parts narrative, how-to guide, and academic research. Described by its publisher as "one of the most playful experiments ever put between two covers," the book is designed to be read with a partner in order to experience hypnotism as Siegel explores the traditions of love and hypnosis, reader and text. Throughout his entire corpus, writing is an act of simultaneously sustaining and dismantling illusion.

Siegel's fiction is about the process of writing. Each of his novels features a text under construction, always on the precipice of coming together or falling apart. Leopold Roth's translation of the *Kamasutra* in *Love in a Dead Language*, for example, is quickly hijacked as the misguided protagonist determines to experience the sacred text through the seduction of an Indian American student, Lalita. Their story, which draws frequent parallels to Nabokov's novel *Lolita* (1955), unfolds in the commentary of the translation. As Roth misreads the original text in order to justify his illicit affair, his translation becomes yet another iteration of the *Kamasutra*, one that simultaneously reifies and rewrites the original. The tension between this iteration and the original is stressed in the maze of footnotes written by Anang Saighal, a graduate student who helped prepare the manuscript for publication after Roth's death. The footnotes stress the many authors – both alive and deceased – attempting to take control of these iterations: Roth's attempts to mold Vātsyāyana's text to his own means, Saighal's attempts to wrest it back, Lee Siegel's attempt to give it narrative form by borrowing the work of Nabokov. In one note, as Roth uses anagramic charades (where the spaces between words are moved to create new meanings) to show the relationship between "Am I able to get her" and "Amiable Together," Saighal adds the footnote "take note of the 'old rot' in 'Leopold Roth'" (Siegel 1999, p. xvi). Later, when Lalita is described as wearing a Sari at a party, Saighal's footnotes explain that "Lalita was not wearing a sari, but rather khakis and a red cardigan over a white blouse" (p. 47). The tension intensifies when a fictional Lee Siegel writes to Saighal (note the phonetic similarities in their names) to advise him against annotating Roth's translation. He writes: "I think it would be just as well if we are spared this incriminating evidence of the existence of Leopold Roth" (p. x). The constant maze of rewritings and misreadings characterizes the endless possible iterations of the original text.

The epigraph of the translation is taken from a work of literary criticism about fictional author Nathaniel Lee. It is written by Roth's wife, Sophia White-Roth. She writes, "Lee, drinking even more gin than usual, was trying to use writing as a method of dealing with the failure of his erotic impulses ... And while it may be tempting to look for autobiographical reference and indeed outright confession in Lee's work, the text is ultimately not so much either about love or about Lee as it is about the process of writing" (1999, p. 1). The reader is left wondering to whom Sophia (from the Greek root of "wisdom") refers. Is it the author or character Lee Siegel? Leopold Roth? Nathaniel Lee? This open-ended conclusion is consummate of so much of Siegel's work. Rather than resting with a single outcome, Siegel's work holds lightly to the possibility of all outcomes simultaneously.

Siegel's second novel, *Love and Other Games of Chance*, reprises many elements of *Moby-Dick* (1851). The novel opens with the line "Call me Isaac," and later, when Isaac is introduced to a character named Ishmael, he is instructed to "Call him Ishmael" (Siegel 2003, pp. 11, 141). The novel is an account of a treacherous journey from the Dead Sea to the summit of Mt. Everest, though in this novel, the white whale is Isaac Schlossberg, the narrator's father, who is composed mostly of myth. Like *Moby-Dick*, the novel comprises frequent expository elements on any matter of subjects, including the techniques of illusion, tightrope walking, and snake charming. This novel also begins with the discovery of a text when a fictional Lee Siegel learns that his real father, whom he never met, was a traveling vaudeville performer. He was left a Snakes and Ladder game board with 100 squares as well as 100 large pages of text, which correspond to the novel's 100 chapters. The text is designed to be read nonsequentially as one would play the game, by rolling the dice, climbing the ladders, and descending the serpents until one finally reaches square 100 and finishes. Siegel explains:

> To play the game ... is to become acquainted with the author in the same way we get to know a person in real life. We don't meet people at birth and follow them chronologically ... We encounter people in one square of their life at one time in one place, and then we run into them again in another square at another time in another place ... That different people know us in different ways and understand in us different characters is determined by which and how many squares of our life they happen to have landed in.
>
> (2003, p. 5)

Each alternative reading of the text, then, reveals a different composite of the writer. Some stages of the writer's life are omitted, others repeated. No reading of the text is privileged over another; rather, all are simultaneously, though often contradictorily, true.

Identity, in Siegel's fiction, is equally multiplicitous. Many characters embrace new identities as they move from one phase of their lives to another. After introducing Isaac in the opening chapter of *Love and Other Games of Chance*, he continues: "Years ago, when I was a child, I was known as Samoo, Samoo the Snake Boy. And, although I've been called many things – Little Chief Magpie, Swami Balakrishna, Professor Solomon Serpentarius, Doctor Bungarus, and Leroy Lestrange, to name a few – Samoo the Amazing Snake Boy of Hindustan ... is the first identity I remember" (2003, p. 11). Each identity marks a specific phase in the character's life, but the character never moves entirely out of that phase; rather, he accumulates versions of himself. Perhaps this is why so many of his novels contain a fictional character named, Lee Siegel. This fictional character figures most prominently in his third novel, *Who Wrote the Book of Love*, which follows a young Siegel navigating the identity-bending territory of adolescence. As he attempts to woo the girls in his class, he assumes many identities, including Dick Steele, the hero of a contraband romance novel, and Elvis Presley. Throughout Siegel's corpus, identity is plural, a composite of endless iterations, whether real or false, performed or belied. As described in *Love and Other Games of Chance*, "we come to know that person better when we hear of their past, when the serpents of their memory reveal what has gone on before, even if that past is imagined or fabricated. A person's lies always reveal some truth about them" (2003, p. 5). And the genre of the novel, with its tradition of obfuscating the boundaries between truth and fiction, is a suitable stage for this exploration.

The relationship between truth and fiction is perhaps most evident in his fourth novel, *Love and the Incredibly Old Man*. This novel opens with a letter addressed to a fictional Lee Siegel. It begins, "Dear Mr. Siegel, I introduce myself here with no expectation that you will believe me, but with some hope that you might be inclined to trust in my sincerity. Incredible as it may seem, I am, in fact, none other than Juan Ponce de León" (2008, p. 1). According to the letter, the fountain of youth has run dry and Mr. León, facing mortality, wants Siegel to ghostwrite his memoir. The novel follows Siegel as he attempts to draft de León's incredible autobiography while wrestling with its implausibility. He finally confesses to the explorer: "it's hard for me to imagine that any editor, at any respectable publishing house, will be willing to accept the claim, true or not, that our manuscript . . . is the actual autobiography of a five-hundred-and-forty-year-old Juan Ponce de León" (p. 220). Instead, he decides to "write a true story about a man in Florida claiming that he was Ponce de León" (p. 219). It would "be a truthful book about truth and lies, about history and fiction." At this idea, de León draws his sword, calls Siegel a traitor, and shrieks: "It is *my* book. *My* story. *My* TRUTH!" (pp. 220–221). For Siegel, however, texts, like truth, are not proprietary; rather, truth is approached only in its plurality. Falsity, on the other hand, is a reduction of this plurality. In a conversation between Isaac and Angel near the end of *Love and Other Games of Chance*, Isaac asks, "do you actually sleep with him? And I don't mean 'sleep' in the literal sense. What I mean is, do you actually make love with him? And I don't mean 'make love' in a philosophical sense. What I mean is, do you do *it* with each other?" To which Angel responds, "I don't know what you mean by *it*" (2003, p. 354). As Isaac tries to pinpoint a singular understanding of her love life, he moves further and further away.

In *The City of Dreadful Night* (1995), Siegel's final scholarly publication before writing his first novel, he uses the conventions of narrative to write about the tradition of horror and macabre in India. Near the end of the book, a storyteller becomes aware of, and frightened by, the ways the stories have molded him. Siegel writes: "The storyteller shivered with the uncanny feeling that he was, like the figures in his own stories . . . being composed, made up, fabricated not of flesh and bone but of borrowed words and phrases, sentences, paragraphs, and plots" (1995, p. 177). Locating Siegel in American fiction is a matter of understanding the palimpsest of identities in his work and understanding that a palimpsest is always in the process of becoming. The plurality of Siegel – a scholar of ancient India, a novelist, a recurring character in four books about love – is never a contradiction, though they often contradict. Rather, it is a view of the writer in the process of being written. In this view of Siegel, we see not only the American novelist at the turn of the century, but a tradition of writers who have continuously tested the limits of the novel, borrowing and rewriting ad infinitum. It is no wonder that so many of Siegel's novels leave their central texts unfinished. In *Love in a Dead Language* Leopold Roth is killed before he can complete his translation. In *Love and Other Games of Chance* chapter 100 is left blank. *Who Wrote the Book of Love* concludes with the line "A new life was about to begin" (2005, p. 235). *Love and the Incredibly Old Man* ends when Ponce de León refuses to tell any more stories to his ghostwriter, and though Siegel completed "decent drafts of chapters one, three, and six," he ultimately "didn't have the time to finish Mr. De Leon's book" (2008, p. 226). In several of these books, the unfinished texts were left to another to write, whether to the grad student Anang Saighal or to the fictional Lee Siegel. They are a testament to the continued novelty of the novel.

SEE ALSO: Coover, Robert; Egan, Jennifer; Gaddis, William; Gass, William H.; Hypertext Fiction and Network Narratives; Maso, Carole; Mixed-Genre Fiction; Powers, Richard; Wallace, David Foster

REFERENCES

Blalock, Jason. (2015). Author and professor Lee Siegel on the dangers of writing. https://vimeo.com/132873216 (accessed July 13, 2012).
Burn, Stephen J. (2006). Anatomizing the language of love: an interview with Lee Siegel. *electronic book review* (September 28, 2006). https://electronicbookreview.com/essay/anatomizing-the-language-of-love-an-interview-with-lee-siegel/ (accessed July 13, 2012).
Siegel, Lee. (1989). *Net of Magic: Wonders and Deceptions in India*. Chicago: University of Chicago Press.
Siegel, Lee. (1995). *City of Dreadful Night*. Chicago: University of Chicago Press.
Siegel, Lee. (1999). *Love in a Dead Language*. Chicago: University of Chicago Press.
Siegel, Lee. (2003). *Love and Other Games of Chance: A Novelty*. New York: Penguin.
Siegel, Lee. (2005). *Who Wrote the Book of Love?* Chicago: University of Chicago Press.
Siegel, Lee. (2008). *Love and the Incredibly Old Man*. Chicago: University of Chicago Press.

FURTHER READING

Moraru, Christian. (2018). Revisionary strategies. In: *American Literature in Transition, 1990–2000* (ed. Stephen Burn), 199–213. Cambridge: Cambridge University Press.
Ruthven. K.K. (2001). *Faking Literature*. Cambridge: Cambridge University Press.

Silko, Leslie Marmon

KYOKO MATSUNAGA
Hiroshima University, Japan

Since her debut novel *Ceremony* was published in 1977, Leslie Marmon Silko (b. 1948) has been widely regarded as one of the most compelling American writers and among the most influential Indigenous voices of the twentieth and twenty-first centuries. Born in Albuquerque, New Mexico, on March 5, 1948, to Leland (Lee) Howard Marmon and Mary Virginia Lee Leslie, Silko grew up in Laguna, one of the Keresan-speaking Pueblo Nations in New Mexico. Being of mixed ancestry (Indigenous American, Mexican, and Anglo-American), Silko has been acutely conscious since childhood of her peripheral positions in both Laguna and American societies. In a video, *Running on the Edge of the Rainbow: Laguna Stories and Poems* (Carr 1978), Silko says, "Look where all the Marmon houses are, down below the village here. We are closer to the river than the rest of the village. I always thought there was something symbolic about that placement, sort of putting us on the fringe of things." While the sense of being "on the fringe of things" is reflected in her writings, Silko often places Laguna Pueblo worldviews, stories, and land at the center of her narratives. The old Pueblo cosmology, according to Silko, celebrates differences, rejects conventional boundary systems, and appreciates communal connections and continuance through stories which are deeply connected to the land, and these Pueblo values resonate in Silko's writings.

Often crossing conventional boundaries of literary and artistic genres – by merging stories with poetry or juxtaposing visual images and written words – Silko conjures up the topography, living beings, and Indigenous presence of places such as Laguna Pueblo (*Ceremony*, 1977; *Almanac of the Dead*, 1991), the tundra of Bethel, Alaska ("Storyteller," 1975), the Sonoran Desert (*Gardens in the Dunes*, 1999; *The Turquoise Ledge*, 2010), and the Gulf Coast of Mexico (*Oceanstory*, 2011). Silko's portraits of these places do not ignore the history of the colonial violence and its memories. Between the 1950s and 1980s, the Jackpile-Paguate uranium mine was operated on Laguna land, and it has greatly impacted the psyches, culture, environment, and sociopolitics of the Laguna people. Silko sees the atomic bomb as an unprecedented threat to human existence. At the same time, she views nuclearism in the American Southwest as one episode in the long history of colonialism affecting the Pueblos and other Indigenous nations. In her works, Silko subverts apocalyptic narratives by envisioning the potential of global Indigenous movements and by recognizing that the history of the Earth not only predates the Anthropocene but will outlast it.

Silko's complex and provocative vision is shaped by her belief in the power of stories and by her sense of justice. She grew up listening to the stories of her paternal great-grandmother, Marie Anaya, who lived next door, as well as to the stories of her paternal great-aunt, Susie, who taught school at Old Laguna after attending Carlisle Indian School and Dickinson College in Pennsylvania. Silko herself attended the local Laguna day school run by the Bureau of Indian Affairs until she started to attend a Catholic school in Albuquerque.

Her first published story, "The Man to Send Rainclouds" (1969), was written when she took a creative writing course at the University of New Mexico. The story was inspired by a similar incident that she heard about from her grandmother in Laguna. After receiving a BA in English, Silko enrolled in the American Indian Law School Fellowship Program at the University of New Mexico. Since childhood, the land claims lawsuit, which was filed when her father was elected treasurer of Laguna Pueblo, had made a strong impression on her. Laguna elders, with the help of Aunt Susie who translated English for them, testified against the state of New Mexico with their stories. Disappointed in the result of the lawsuit and realizing how "injustice is built into the Anglo-American legal system," Silko "decided the only way to seek justice was through the power of the stories" (Silko 1996, pp. 19–20). By the 1980s, Silko had achieved literary acclaim as a poet and writer of fiction. Before publishing her much lauded novel *Ceremony* in 1977, she had published a book of poems, *Laguna Woman*; a short story, "Lullaby," in *The Chicago Review*; and several stories in *The Man to Send Rain Clouds* – all in 1974.

Silko's fascination with visual images is no less important than her belief in the power of stories, and this is most evident in *Storyteller* (1981), an experimental book incorporating photographs and cross-genre writings. After leaving law school, Silko took an introductory photography class along with a couple of graduate courses in the English department at the University of New Mexico. During this time, she started to take photographs and to envision combining them with written narrative to tell stories. Silko's interest in creating works that pair visual images with written words goes back to primary school. In the sixth grade she handprinted two copies of a self-made joke magazine, *Nasty Asty*, in which she pasted silhouette images from *Playboy* magazine next to a "dirty joke." In the "Author's Notes" to *Sacred Water* (1993), another exploratory self-published book with photographs, Silko refers to that experience and explains how, as a sixth grader, she already recognized the balance of power between visual images and written words: "I knew the color magazine photographs of bare breasts would over-power and take too much attention away from the text" (1993, p. 81). In *Storyteller*, Silko merges autobiographical narratives, stories she heard as a child, poetry, short stories, and notes with photographs taken by her paternal grandfather, Hank, and her father, who is a professional photographer. Beyond offering her most celebrated short stories, including "Storyteller" and "Yellow Woman," *Storyteller* presents a new creative space where photographs of the land and people are fused to stories of the land and people. This work blurring the boundaries of visual arts and written words reveals the impacts of modernity such as her own mixed-blood heritage, Indian boarding schools, and an open-pit uranium mine. *Storyteller* reaches beyond the limits of the photographs and the written word to evoke stories much older than what had been captured by the images and narratives.

Completing *Storyteller* was not an easy task for Silko. While working on it, she wrote letters to the poet James Wright, expressing the difficulties of her second divorce, including the child custody hearing. The correspondence with Wright between August 28, 1978, and March 25, 1980, provided Silko moral support as well as literary encouragement, and she thanks him for his letters in the acknowledgment to *Storyteller*. Wright's letters expressed his appreciation of her writing, reported progress on his work, and encouraged her to apply for a Guggenheim Fellowship. In response, Silko reported on her surroundings, conveyed her feelings about the American writing and publishing scenes, and shared her ideas and pieces of her published and unpublished work. Silko sent Wright a photocopy of "Storyteller" and poems, which were later included in *Storyteller*, and told him about her excitement at working on a Laguna film project, *Arrowboy and the Witches* (1981), part of her unfinished *Stolen Rain* series. In these lyrical letters (and postcards), we see two artists connecting, supporting, and inspiring each other's creative expression. Six years after Wright died of cancer, their correspondence was published as *The Delicacy and Strength of Lace* (1986), and this collection of letters eventually won the Boston Globe Book Prize for nonfiction.

As she expressed in letters to Wright on June 16 and September 12, 1979, Silko decided to quit her teaching job at the University of New Mexico to allow herself more flexible time to work on her projects. She noted that an art or humanities teacher was not permitted more than one-year leave, while laser and atomic scientists were allowed to spend many years for their projects (the institution relied heavily on money from the Atomic Energy Commission and the Defense Department). In 1981, Silko received a five-year MacArthur Fellowship. She used the first year to work on the film project *Arrowboy and the Witches* and started to write notes and sections for her second novel, *Almanac of the Dead* (1991). Vast in volume, content, and time span, *Almanac of the Dead* depicts dystopian landscapes of the modern world reflected in illegal organ selling, child pornography, nuclear weapons, drug-related violence, political corruption, and resource extraction. Into the narratives of destruction and violence that permeate the novel, Silko dexterously weaves the threads of Indigenous prophecies and calendars that predict the eventual disappearance of "things European." Because of its stark contrast to her celebrated first novel *Ceremony*, *Almanac of the Dead* met with some negative reviews. Soon, however, critics began to recognize the revolutionary nature of the novel and its powerful political innuendos. Focusing on the multicultural, cross-cultural, and transnational alliances among characters in the text, some critics view *Almanac of the Dead* as a work that reflects the environmental justice movement. Recent scholarship salutes Silko's prophetic narrative for presaging global Indigenous movements calling for the restoration of Indigenous lands and rights. Publication of *Almanac of the Dead* coincides with the First People of Color Environmental Leadership Summit held in 1991, and it precedes the 1994 Indigenous uprising in Chiapas, Mexico, where an Indigenous people's protest march to Tucson also takes place in the novel.

Another prominent feature of *Almanac of the Dead* is the reference to a giant stone snake found near a pile of uranium tailings on Laguna land. In her collection of essays, *Yellow Woman and a Beauty of the Spirit* (1996), Silko explains how two Laguna Pueblo workers at the Jackpile mine found a stone snake formation near the open-pit mine in 1979. Silko writes, "I realized that the giant snake had been a catalyst for the novel from the start. In a way, one might almost say that I had to write this novel in order to figure out for myself the meaning of the giant stone snake that had appeared near the uranium mine in 1979" (1996, p. 144). Snakes play an important role in many of Silko's writings. In *Almanac of the Dead*, while the spirits of snakes are a catalyst to connect Indigenous people of the Americas and Africa, the giant stone snake provides a vision that goes beyond the history of human beings. At the end of the novel, Sterling, one of more than seventy characters, comes to a realization near the giant stone snake on Laguna land that even if the use of uranium kills human beings, humans destroy only themselves, not the earth.

After the book tour of *Almanac of the Dead*, Silko decided to keep distance from big publishers for a while, and she rekindled her desire to work on handmade publications. Silko's *Sacred Water* is an experimental project juxtaposing photographic images with written text. In this work incorporating photographs printed with a laser copier, Silko depicts interconnections between water and the fauna and flora in places she lives or has lived such as the Sonoran Desert, Laguna Pueblo, and Ketchikan, Alaska. Balance between photographs and written words is again carefully crafted. Silko composed the book so that the impact of photographic images is minimal and the text does not drown out the nuance of the visual images. In contrast to the apocalyptic images and dark tone of *Almanac of the Dead*, *Sacred Water* explores the symbiosis of living beings. Like *Rain* (1997), another creative project combining essays and photographs, *Sacred Water* has not received much critical attention so far, most likely because of its limited availability. The few who have examined the text see it contrasting the Earth's longevity with the brief lives of human beings. Referring to the purifying effect of datura on irradiated soil, Silko repeats the message included in *Almanac of the Dead*: "humans desecrated only themselves with the mine, not the earth" (1991, p. 762).

Eight years after her controversial second novel, Silko published her third novel, *Gardens in the Dunes* (1999). Much different from *Almanac of the Dead* in tone and setting, Silko explains how *Gardens in the Dunes* came out of *Almanac of the Dead*. In 1994, to promote the German translation of *Almanac of the Dead*, Silko visited Europe where she encountered European gardens as well as the old European cultures and spirits. In *Gardens in the Dunes*, Silko illustrates the fundamental similarities between old European connections to the land and the Southwestern "home" of two young Indigenous sisters. While depicting historical violence against Indigenous communities such as the massacre of the Ghost Dancers, Indian boarding schools, and the damming of the Colorado River, *Gardens in the Dunes* explores Indigenous ties between Europe and America, alliances among women at the turn of the century, and cross-cultural reciprocity through the ideas of gardens and gardening. The novel narrates the stories of two sisters, Indigo and Sister Salt, from a fictional clan (the Sand River clan) of the actual Colorado River Indians, but it is as much a story of Hattie, a Euro-American "guardian" of Indigo, who recognizes the importance of women in gnostic heresies and learns at the end the deceptive nature of the modern and capitalistic way of life. In essence, *Gardens in the Dunes* reflects Silko's worldview that breaks down spiritual boundaries between Indigenous and Western cultures.

In an interview with Ellen L. Arnold, Silko explains how she tried to write something apolitical before launching *Gardens in the Dunes*, but soon she came to realize the highly political nature of gardens (Arnold 2000). Similarly, when she was going to write a nonfictional work, *The Turquoise Ledge: A Memoir* (2010), Silko attempted to steer clear of "unpleasantness and strife and politics as much as possible" (Silko 2010, p. 170). Again, it turned out not to be so easy. *The Turquoise Ledge* is a memoir depicting her everyday life in the Sonoran Desert. In this work, Silko weaves poetic prose (depicting turquoise, snakes, and rocks), historical and geological knowledge, and stories she heard while growing up. Silko mostly celebrates the beauty and richness of the desert life, but on a few occasions she could not avoid referring to the damage done by a man and his bulldozer to the boulders and sandbars in the big arroyo near her house. *The Turquoise Ledge* also dedicates a whole chapter to explain the history of the Jackpile uranium mine and the giant stone snake discovered near the tailings. Silko does not ignore the violence wrought by capitalism and modernization in *The Turquoise Ledge*. On the whole, however, the text envisions pre-Columbian Indigenous history and culture and resonates with the representations of indigeneity in *Gardens in the Dunes*. Silko's vision in *The Turquoise Ledge* is no less planetary than *Almanac of the Dead*. In conjecturing about the existence of the ancient turquoise ledge, she reimagines the geological history of turquoise, which predates the age of human beings.

In the penultimate chapter of *The Turquoise Ledge*, Silko pictures the immense history of the Sonoran Desert, which had been flooded before and will be returned to the sea eventually. It is not surprising then that Silko's following work, *Oceanstory* (2011), focuses on the power of the ocean. Set in Mexico (and partially Tucson) after the September 11 attacks, *Oceanstory* returns to the dark tone of *Almanac of the Dead*. The narrator, who is an Indigenous person from Tucson, witnesses intrigue and violence brought about by capitalism and technology in the wake of the 2001 attacks, and the ensuing war and torture. In stark contrast to these human trials is the vast scale of the history of the ocean. Incorporating the stories of Comcaac and O'Odom sorcerers as well as the geology of the Gulf of Mexico, the narrator of *Oceanstory* not only envisages the Indigenous people's reclamation of the land, but also reclamation of the land by the ocean.

Since the 1980s, Silko's significance in the Indigenous, American, and global literary scenes has been affirmed and reaffirmed as her texts have been read through the lenses of various fields including Indigenous studies, ecology, ecocriticism, environmental justice, transnational studies, feminism, (post)colonialism, Marxism, and psychoanalysis. Silko's literary vision has routinely been at the forefront of social and environmental concerns. Her writing, for example, has prefigured or coincided with developments in the global Indigenous movement, climate change activism, and the field of blue humanities. Waves of acclaim and backlash vary in size and shape, but Silko's cosmology is as solid and inclusive as the Earth.

SEE ALSO: Ecocriticism and Environmental Fiction; Indigenous Narratives; Mixed-Genre Fiction; Momaday, N. Scott; Vizenor, Gerald

REFERENCES

Arnold, Ellen L. (2000). Listening to the spirits: an interview with Leslie Marmon Silko by Ellen L. Arnold. In: *Conversations with Leslie Marmon Silko* (ed. Ellen L. Arnold), 162–196. Jackson: University Press of Mississippi.
Carr, Dennis. (dir.) (1978). *Running on the Edge of the Rainbow: Laguna Stories and Poems*. Produced by Larry Evers. In cooperation with the University of Arizona Radio-TV-Film Bureau. https://parentseyes.arizona.edu/node/889 (accessed July 11, 2021).
Silko, Leslie Marmon. (1991). *Almanac of the Dead*. New York: Simon & Schuster.
Silko, Leslie Marmon. (1993). *Sacred Water*. Tucson: Flood Plain Press.
Silko, Leslie Marmon. (1996). *Yellow Woman and a Beauty of the Spirit*. New York: Simon & Schuster.
Silko, Leslie Marmon. (2010). *The Turquoise Ledge: A Memoir*. New York: Viking.

FURTHER READING

Arnold, Ellen L. (ed.) (2000). *Conversations with Leslie Marmon Silko*. Jackson: University Press of Mississippi.
Barnett, Louise K. and Thorson, James L. (eds.) (1999). *Leslie Marmon Silko: A Collection of Critical Essays*. Albuquerque: University of New Mexico Press.
Moore, David L. (2016). *Leslie Marmon Silko: Ceremony, Almanac of the Dead, Gardens in the Dunes*. London: Bloomsbury.
Salyer, Gregory. (1997). *Leslie Marmon Silko*. New York: Twayne.
Tillett, Rebecca. (ed.) (2014). *Howling for Justice: New Perspectives on Leslie Marmon Silko's Almanac of the Dead*. Tucson: University of Arizona Press.

Simpson, Mona

AMBREEN HAI
Smith College, USA

Acclaimed fiction writer Mona Simpson has won numerous awards, including a Whiting award (1986), a Princeton University Hodder Fellowship (1987), a Guggenheim Fellowship (1988), a Lila Wallace Reader's Digest Prize (1995), and an American Academy of Arts and Letters Literature award (2008). Her six published novels (1986–2014) offer a range of themes and techniques, but all share an interest in charting the emotional contours and complex micro-dynamics among families, biological or constructed, and small tight-knit communities, located in vividly evoked places, over sustained periods of time. They mainly focus on parent–child relationships, friendships, the effects of abandonment, particularly on women and children, and the psychological consequences of both staying in place and moving away. Powerful for their realism and emotional impact, deeply rooted in a sense of history and place (mainly Wisconsin and California), the novels deploy accumulation of detail, deadpan dialogue, and frequent alternation of multiple perspectives and voices, to build insightful, nuanced portrayals of an array of human relationships. Simpson's work overall has drawn surprisingly little scholarly attention, with the exception of her first novel, which especially evoked interest among feminist literary critics. However, more recently, ethnic and gender studies literary scholars have (re)discovered Simpson either as an "invisible ethnic" author of part-Arab origin (Naaman 2013, p. 363), or as a writer interested in migration, race, and class as well as gender dynamics (Hai 2016), and more scholarly articles about her fiction have begun to appear.

Simpson was born in 1957 in Green Bay, Wisconsin, to a European American mother (Joanne Schieble Simpson) and Syrian immigrant father (Abdulfattah Jandali) who returned to Syria when Simpson was very young. After her parents divorced and her mother remarried, Simpson took the last name of her stepfather. As a teenager, after her mother's second divorce, Simpson moved to Los Angeles with her mother. She received her bachelor's degree from the University of California, Berkeley, an MFA from Bard College, and attended the MFA program at Columbia University in New York, where she completed her first novel and worked as an editor at *The Paris Review*. She is the younger sister of Apple Inc. co-founder Steve Jobs, whom she met in her twenties, and who was given up for adoption before their parents were married. Simpson was married to Richard Appel, writer of *The Simpsons*, who named the show after her, and with whom she has two children. She lives in Santa Monica, California, teaches creative writing at UCLA and Bard College, and, as of January 2020, has been appointed publisher of *The Paris Review*.

Anywhere But Here, Simpson's 535-page debut novel (1986), was a tour de force. Spanning the lives of four generations of women in fictional Bay City, Wisconsin, over the course of a century, it focuses on the youngest, Ann August, as she learns about her Midwestern family's past, and copes with her dysfunctional, twice-divorced single mother, Adele Diamond, who drives the unwilling Ann from Wisconsin to California in hopes of independence for herself and child-stardom for Ann in television. Scholars have focused on how, in the context of second-wave feminism, the novel highlights the complexity of mother–daughter relations (Morse 1989), particularly of daughters "charged with mothering their mothers" (Rogers 1992, p. 177), the possibility of female agency, the novelty of the female road narrative as an overturning of masculine and patriarchal norms (Heller 1989), the subjectivity of mothers, and women's rejection of domesticity (Smyth 1999). In focusing on Ann and Adele, however, these readings overlook the extent to which the novel is also concerned with a family of women, with the intergenerational shifts, experiences, and hence contrasts and gaps, as well as overlaps, between worlds and perceptions within the same family, to which it calls attention through its unusual architecture. (A 1999 film adaptation starring Susan Sarandon and Natalie Portman also leaves out the other women, and softens the novel's portrayal of Adele.)

The novel has a complex, dischronological, multi-perspectival narrative structure. Divided into nine parts, it alternates between past and present, and between the first-person narration of Ann and three of her female relatives who reflect on their lives and pasts to help Ann understand herself, her family, and their history. *Anywhere But Here* begins in the late 1960s with Ann's attention-catching account of how, after repeated disagreements during their road trip to Los Angeles, Adele kicks 10-year-old Ann out of the car and abandons her on the highway. It moves forward to how (after her mother returns to pick Ann up again) the pair drive through Arizona and Nevada, arrive in California, and then (as if echoing the characters' movements forward and backward) moves back to the home and family they left behind in Wisconsin. While Ann narrates the first four odd-numbered sections (Parts One, Three, Five, and Seven), describing her longing for her grandmother, her life in California, and eventual departure for Brown University, the even-numbered sections are narrated by Ann's relatives (Part Two by Lilian, Ann's maternal grandmother, and Parts Four, Six, and Eight by Carol, Adele's older sister) recounting their pasts and divergent lives subsequent to Ann and Adele's departure. Simpson breaks this pattern in the brief final section (Part Nine), which gives us access for the first time to Adele's perspective, who, now living alone in Beverly Hills, congratulates herself on having done well by her daughter, and contests Ann's account of her as a problem mother. The novel's structure of juxtaposition and alternation thus emphasizes how Ann's story is inextricably interconnected with those of her grandmother, aunt, and mother, and how the connections and disjunctions between their narratives highlight both what they share and what they do not see or know about each other.

Simpson's style throughout is simple, spare, unvarnished, yet each woman's voice is distinctive. If teenage Ann's voice is at once laconic, poignant, and occasionally snarky, and Adele's whiny, self-pitying, self-justifying, and self-deluded, Lilian comes across as gentle, wise, and calm, attempting to provide guidance and support for her granddaughter, while Carol, in contrast to her family's perception of her, suggests both deep pain and hidden strength. Throughout, the novel also offers a history of a place, Wisconsin, and the differences between the experiences of generations of women who have lived there. Lilian's account of her childhood and of Ida, her mother, reveals a world more elemental, rugged, and tough, and women with more resilience and capacity for sustaining loss and hardship, than the more cushioned, seemingly adventurous but volatile and fragile Adele. Carol, a stay-at-home mother subservient to a crude, sexist husband, reveals unexpectedly to Ann her experiences as a nurse in Europe in World War II, and the untimely death of a first husband of whom her family has no knowledge. Adele, though self-styled as the smart one, the first in her family to complete college and permanently leave their hometown, is ironically the one overdependent on men, who sees advancement as possible only through sex, marriage, and the use of women's bodies, not brains, and sexualizes her daughter as well as herself. Gradually it becomes clearer that Adele is mentally ill, subjecting her daughter alternately to abuse, negligence, and excessive indulgence. What remains shadowy in this novel is the figure of Ann's Arab father, Adele's first husband, who has abandoned both wife and child. The novel focuses directly on women, who survive despite knocks, impediments, and losses, and indirectly presents their men, who disappoint, fail, betray, or die untimely deaths.

If *Anywhere But Here* centers on Ann and her mother, its sequel, *The Lost Father* (1991), explores how damaged Ann is by the absence of her father. A sequel that is not sequential, but both a continuation and a filling in of Ann's story, Simpson's second novel picks up with Ann, who has reverted to her given name, Mayan Atassi, and is now living in New York City, a medical student at Columbia. But even as the narrative moves forward in time to track Mayan's obsessive journey in search of her father, it keeps returning, in a recursive structure, to excavate the past, memories of which haunt and shape her every move. It becomes clearer how the dysfunctionality, not only of Mayan but also of her narcissistic mother, is linked to Mayan's father's disappearance, though it remains unclear whether he left because Adele was impossible to live with, or whether she became consequently (more) impossible. The problem is not just that he left, but that he left them not knowing when, or if, he would return. Mayan remembers as a child endlessly waiting for him to return, setting "an extra place for every supper" (1992, p. 139). For adult Mayan, the world is divided into those (daughters) who are "fathered" and those who are not; her entire sense of self is unbuilt, not because she is fatherless, as if he were merely deceased, but because she was abandoned, or, as she sees it, "unwanted" (p. 131). Unable to date, work, or study, she hires a private investigator who defrauds her. She drops out of medical school, and spends all her money pursuing her own Odyssey, driving from Wisconsin, through Minnesota, to North Dakota, even flying to Egypt, until she finally finds him, herself, through the telephone directory, in California. "Disappearing was all you had to do to become somebody's god. And maybe being found was all it took to be mortal again," Mayan reflects drily (p. 444). Of course, when found, he is both a disappointment and a relief; it was not her father per se that she needed, but the fact of having found him, of laying to rest the not-knowing. Now she can start to build her own life, to claim an identity, to say "I'm half Arab" (p. 505), to be someone with an anchor in the world. Revealing that lifelong sense of insecurity and instability, she concludes poignantly, "I still haven't found what I'm looking for. But I am more like anybody else" (p. 506).

The Lost Father, unlike its prequel, offers no alternating perspectives, but instead presents instead 506 pages narrated entirely in Mayan's first-person voice (except for a brief letter from Mayan's father at the end). This formal choice risks tedium, the monotony of a prolonged single perspective, but it enables Simpson to portray well the almost pathological condition of deprivation, insecurity, and obsession of a girl trapped in her own head. Stylistically, this older narrator's voice is more lyrical and figurative, more poetic and poignant, and more wistful than the plainer, blunter, sardonic style of Ann. In this novel, Simson addresses more fully Mayan's father's ethnic and religious otherness, and Mayan's own inchoate sense of her own ambiguous positionality, perceived both as white and yet as somehow different. Attentive to prejudice, Simpson suggests sympathetically how Mayan's father faced racism, both at the institutions where he taught and from his wife's family, how even Mayan wonders if he is a terrorist (1992, p. 131), and how Mayan is touched inevitably by a sense of alterity, by how white Midwesterners see her. "She's part whatever he is, isn't she?" she remembers hearing an acquaintance say to her grandmother (p. 392).

Yet Mayan is also aware that she is "invisible in the world," and knows next to nothing about being Arab or Muslim (p. 390). Ironically, to try to learn about Arabness, she sits through *Lawrence of Arabia*, itself a Western Orientalist construction. However, Simpson unfortunately also reaffirms stereotypes about Arab Muslim men as dishonest and unreliable. She presents Mayan's father as a scandalous scam artist, fired from his job as a college professor because he stole money from the American tourists he took to Egypt; and as a self-absorbed ladies' man, who cheats and lies to the white women he is with. That said, however, Simpson implicitly (and rightly) also criticizes some sexist, patriarchal norms of Arab cultures: Mayan's father is happy to see Mayan again but is more interested in his nephews, or in Mayan's imagined wedding, than in her.

"He was a man too busy to flush toilets. More than most people Jane had known, he was oblivious to the issuance from his body that might offend" (1996, p. 3). With this emblematic opening to *A Regular Guy* (1996), her third novel, Simpson proceeds to build a portrait of brilliant but quirky Tom Owens, an inventor, oblivious to others, secure in his success and privilege, who finally learns to be a father, committed to wife and children – but who still remains oblivious to others. Though often presented from the perspective of Jane, the illegitimate daughter he will eventually accept as his, this is Simpson's only novel narrated by a third-person omniscient narrator, allowing an ironic, distanced perspective, as well as point-of-view shifts between various characters who comprise Owens's unconventional community, of people who orbit around Owens as their magnetic center.

Simpson's first three novels are often seen as a trilogy, but only the first two have continuities of plot or character. *A Regular Guy*, set in the Silicon Valley, elaborates on the theme of a daughter raised by negligent parents, but presents an entirely new family and community. It offers primarily an attempt to understand a man much like Steve Jobs (or a composite of Simpson's brother and father). All three novels revolve around a single mother, a daughter, and difficult or absent father, but each takes a different approach. In an interview, Simpson admits that "twenty-five percent" of her fiction is autobiographical, but says she finds fiction a more conducive medium for telling greater truths than memoir: "all writers are probably trying to get at some core truth of life, at some configuration that is enduring and truthful" (Bing 1996, p. 51). Her focus remains on uncovering truths about relationships, about the contemporary American family – non-nuclear, non-normative, and extended. As she observes laughingly: "[W]hat else is there but families?" (p. 51).

Shifting away from the parent–child focus in her unusually slim fourth novel, *Off Keck Road* (2000), Simpson returns to Green Bay, Wisconsin, this time to track, over the course of half a century, the lives of two single women who return to or stay in their insular Midwestern hometown. Bea Maxwell, affluent, capable, kind and enterprising, a college graduate who gives up a career in Chicago to look after her arthritis-stricken mother, and Shelley, six feet tall, working class, physically strong but disabled by childhood polio, an outcast who trains to become a nurse, hail from opposite ends of their town social strata. Both are strong, independent women, successful in their own ways, both survivors who are considered pitiable failures by their conventional families and communities because they remain unmarried and childless. Mesmerizing, moving, quietly powerful, and deeply evocative, this novel beautifully charts seemingly disparate lives lived in the physical and emotional harshness of a particular place and time, the emotional contours of each individual and her relationships, and the unexpected connections between them.

Taking over ten years to write, *My Hollywood* (2011) is Simpson's first novel published after 9/11. References to Arabs, however, are hard to find as Simpson focuses differently on issues of migration, otherness, gender, and servitude. Even more of a departure from her first three novels, this substantial novel centers on the relationship – and connections and disconnections – between two mothers in Santa Monica, California: one, Claire, a musician struggling to balance a career and a newborn, unsupported by her Hollywood writer-husband; the other, Lola, Claire's undocumented migrant nanny, who supports her children in the Philippines with the earnings she sends home. Powered by Simpson's acute observations, characteristic psychological astuteness, and emotional insights, *My Hollywood* innovatively explores the micropolitics of domestic work, gender, and cross-racial and cross-class intimacy and interdependence. Again, Simpson alternates perspectives and different voices to elucidate the contrasts, similarities, and unexpected bonds between women built, despite conflict and difference, as they cope with the challenges that life throws at them over long stretches of time.

Simpson's most recent novel, *Casebook* (2014), also set in southern California, also interested in the narrative of a family that spans two decades, in this case a divorced mother with three young children, attempts for the first time the voice of a young adolescent boy, from whose partial perspective the entire novel is narrated. Obsessed with eavesdropping on his unsuspecting mother through a variety of self-made contraptions, Miles, the absurdly Oedipal young protagonist, seems at first neither interesting nor healthily preoccupied until his espionage reveals that Eli, his mother's new boyfriend, is in fact a married man, and a gratuitous, compulsive, pathological liar. With deft humor and emotional punch, Simpson constructs powerfully and intricately the world of a family whose linchpin, the mother, falls apart twice, first when the father leaves, and second when the man she trusts and believes she will marry, so gratuitously deceives her and her children. In this novel, the mother is sweet, pathetic, and gullible – Simpson presents no strong-minded feminist – but it is the son, Miles, who emerges as the stalwart caregiver of his mother and two younger sisters, a counter, perhaps, to the portrayals of failed fathers that litter Simpson's work. A continuing strain in Simpson's work thus is her interest in plumbing the impact on children as well as women, differently vulnerable to and damaged by men who betray, break promises, or fail to fulfill the responsibilities of fatherhood.

An astute and compelling writer, Simpson charts, over the course of her career, the changing shapes and intricacies of the American family from the early twentieth century into the twenty-first, exploring the ways that families are both made and unmade. With skill, insight, and emotional punch, she expands into questions of gender, class, and race, and power, migration, and movement, tied to particular regions in the West and Midwest. As herself both an (invisible) outsider and insider, Simpson explores with sensitivity the experiences of those who exist on and around such borders, and who help us (re)define and understand more deeply a variety of contemporary American lives.

SEE ALSO: Abu-Jaber, Diana; Alameddine, Rabih; Contemporary Regionalisms; Globalization; Illness and Disability Narratives; Jarrar, Randa; Multiculturalism; Millennial Fiction; Realism after Poststructuralism; Suburban Narratives

REFERENCES

Bing, Jonathan. (1996). Mona Simpson: return of the prodigal father. *Publisher's Weekly* 243 (45): 50–51.

Hai, Ambreen. (2016). Motherhood and domestic servitude in transnational women's fiction: Thrity Umrigar's *The Space Between Us* and Mona Simpson's *My Hollywood*. *Contemporary Literature* 57 (4): 500–540.

Heller, Dana A. (1989). Shifting gears: transmission and flight in Mona Simpson's *Anywhere But Here*. *University of Hartford Studies in Literature* 21: 37–44.

Morse, Deborah D. (1989). The difficult journey home: Mona Simpson's *Anywhere But Here*. In: *Mother Puzzles: Daughters and Mothers in Contemporary American Literature* (ed. Mickey Pearlman), 67–75. Westport, CT: Greenwood.

Naaman, Mara. (2013). Invisible ethnic: Mona Simpson and the space of the ethnic literature market. In *The Edinburgh Companion to the Arab Novel in English* (ed. Nouri Gana), 363–385. Edinburgh: Edinburgh University Press.

Rogers, K.L. (1992). The autobiographical Anna: Mona Simpson's *Anywhere But Here* and Susanna Moore's *My Old Sweetheart*. In: *The Anna Book: Searching for Anna in Literary History* (ed. Mickey Pearlman), 177–185. Westport, CT: Greenwood.

Simpson, Mona. (1992). *The Lost Father*. New York: Vintage; 1st ed. 1991.

Simpson, Mona. (1996). *A Regular Guy*. New York: Vintage.

Smyth, Jacqui. (1999). Getaway cars and broken homes: searching for the American Dream *Anywhere But Here*. *Frontiers: A Journal of Women's Studies* 20 (2): 115–132.

FURTHER READING

Ahmed, Riham. (2019). Half Arab, half American: searching for cultural roots in Mona Simpson's *The Lost Father*. *Advances in Language and Literary Studies* 10 (1): 9–16.

Majaj, Lisa S. (2000). Arab-Americans and the meanings of race. In: *Postcolonial Theory and the United States: Race, Ethnicity, and Literature* (ed. Amritjit Singh et al.), 320–337. Jackson: University Press of Mississippi.

Smiley, Jane

JASON S. POLLEY
Hong Kong Baptist University, Hong Kong

Though born in Los Angeles, Jane Smiley grew up in Webster Groves, Missouri. Her 1971 BA in literature from Vassar College was followed by an MA, an MFA, and a PhD, all awarded in the 1970s, and all from the University of Iowa, an institution distinguished for its 1967-founded International Writing Program. For the first fifteen years of her writing career, Jane Smiley was a professor of English at Iowa State University (1981–1996). Her first novel, *Barn Blind*, was published in 1980. Just over a decade (and four novels) later she garnered wide acclaim for *A Thousand Acres* (1991), which won both the National Book Critics Circle Award and the Pulitzer Prize. The near 400-page novel adapts *King Lear* to the advent of the Midwestern farm crisis in the 1980s.

Set primarily in the summer of 1979, *A Thousand Acres* is a first-person, recollective narrative that intimately details the dissolution of two neighboring families in rural Iowa. Since 1991, Smiley has published another nine novels, including her latest encyclopedic work: the 2100-page The Last One Hundred Years Trilogy: A Family Saga (2014, 2015, 2015). Though renowned for her regional representations of farms, property, and luck, her career might best be defined by her experiments with genre and narration. For instance, *Duplicate Keys* (1984) is an urban crime fiction; *The Greenlanders* (1988) is a medieval Nordic epic; *Moo* (1995) a campus social comedy; *Lidie Newton* (1998) a bellum romance; *Horse Heaven* (2000) a compendium of racetrack life; *Good Faith* (2003) a 1980s real-estate boondoggle pastoral; and *Ten Days in the Hills* (2007) a Hollywood celebrity-culture satire. Her longest fictions are her most compelling. This is due to Smiley's refined narrative strategies, strategies that solicit intimate reader alignment with a host of wide-ranging characters.

A Thousand Acres provides a source of Smiley's sophisticated narrative acts. Not unlike *King Lear*, the family drama centers on a patriarch's selfish bequest, one that exposes a legacy of incest while moving through rancor, seduction, duplicity, death, blindness, madness, reconciliation, suicide, and attempted sororicide. These Shakespearean tropes are complicated not only by focusing on how women are the victims of the carcinomata and miscarriages associated to chemical run-off in farm well water, but also by delivering the narrative through the sympathetic perspective of the Goneril-modelled "Ginny." The noun phrase "point of view" recurs in *A Thousand Acres*, most notably at the novel's midpoint (Smiley 1991, pp. 175, 176, 182, 212). Smiley thus bestows a female-centered perspective to *King Lear*, one that integrates contexts, backstories, and interiorities absent in Shakespeare's play. The "oil and blood and muck" of Iowa farm life (p. 121) provides a poignant backdrop to the regional realities of Middle America. Everyday persecutions – of children, of women – remain unspoken. After all, "appearances are everything" (p. 284). This applies especially for small, family-run farms, which depend upon seed loans from Big Agriculture. It applies even more so to families engaged in litigation, so *A Thousand Acres* illustrates.

The *tranche de vie* that *A Thousand Acres* offers folds into a small portion of Smiley's most recent, and most accomplished, oeuvre. The Last One Hundred Years Trilogy includes the novels *Some Luck* (2014), *Early Warning* (2015), and *Golden Age* (also, incredibly, 2015). *Early Warning* briefly returns readers to the "grain embargo" that sets the Middle America-stage for *A Thousand Acres*. Whereas farm life in the last summer of the 1970s is at the heart of *A Thousand Acres*, which makes reference to then-President Carter three times in its first 100 pages (1991, pp. 7, 23, 102), President "Carter's response to the crisis" in *Early Warning* (2015, p. 592) is only one of myriad events occurring in a period also remembered for the rise of Rupert Murdoch (p. 535), the "mass suicide" of the 900 Peoples Temple worshippers who relocated to Jonestown, Guyana (p. 561), Russia's invasion of Afghanistan (p. 592), the "Iran hostages" (p. 592), presidential candidate Ronald

Reagan's "trouble" over a racial joke (p. 593), the hi-tech advent of the Kirby vacuum cleaner (p. 595), "Mossadegh's . . . courting of the Soviets" (p. 599), the surprising cinematic reversals in *American Gigolo* (p. 602), and the Environmental Protection Agency's cost-cutting "Bubble Policy" allowing industry managers flexibility to clean up air pollution (p. 618), as well as Iowa being "one of the first states to grant no-fault divorce" in 1971 (p. 624). (New York didn't ratify this law, which finally granted married women a measure of personal and legal autonomy, until 40 years later!)

The above list of world-historical events, ones crucial to the American imaginary, is selected from a mere five-year period of *Early Warning*, a 750-page novel chronologically unfolding from 1953 to 1986. The epic quality of the abbreviated catalogue accentuates the range and depth, the variety and gravity, of Smiley's unique, encyclopedic fiction. Certainly, she is best known for her intimate portrayals of farming families. The bevvy of scholarly treatments of *A Thousand Acres* disseminates this appreciation of regional realism far beyond literary circles, so Jack Temple Kirby's 1996 *Agricultural History* article "Rural Culture in the American Middle West: Jefferson to Jane Smiley" evidences. Yet Smiley's most ambitious fiction transcends the regionalist parameters that popularly define her.

In the mode of Jane Austen, *A Thousand Acres* focuses on a handful of characters. The author applies the same narrow, detailed lens to her first novel, as well as to her second novel, the three-generation domestic drama *At Paradise Gate* (1981). Smiley redeploys this rural inclination, however, in her third fiction. *Duplicate Keys* finds six friends from the Midwest relocated to New York City. They share an apartment, one with, so the title implies, countless copies of the door key, allowing for a rotating cast of crashers. Yet the novel quickly develops into a double-murder mystery, thus plumbing the locked secrets that even longtime friends harbor.

Smiley's scope expands as her career develops. Her three encyclopedic works include large, Dickensian collections of characters (Smiley admits to idolizing both Dickens and Trollope) whose experiences extend to the international stage. Her fourth novel remains critically overlooked. Partly researched over the year she spent as a Fulbright scholar in Iceland during her doctoral candidacy, Smiley's saga *The Greenlanders* details the demise of what Jared Diamond referred to as "European civilization's most remote outpost" (Diamond 2005, p. 212). Neil Nakadate, whose *Understanding Jane Smiley* (1999, 2010) remains the only monograph entirely dedicated to Smiley, recalls how the novelist's Nordic saga was personally inspired by the singularity of the Greenlander's decline: "One of the first things that intrigued me about [the fate of the colony] was that it was the only attested case of an *established* European civilization falling apart and vanishing" (quoted in Nakadate 1999, p. 106).

Nakadate also quotes Smiley's description of the Greenlanders as having "fall[en] through a whole in history and disappeared" (1999, p. 106). As noted in the book *Jane Smiley, Jonathan Franzen, Don DeLillo: Narratives of Everyday Justice* (Polley 2011), which features these Nakadate appropriations, Jane Smiley's "narrative technique is as merciless as the Greenlandic way of life was harsh" (2011, p. 33). *Jane Smiley, Jonathan Franzen, Don DeLillo* furthermore observes how "Smiley congratulates herself for the remorseless style of her saga" (p. 33). At her 1996 talk "Shakespeare in Iceland," a title accenting her early career indebtedness to Shakespeare, Smiley divulges the source of her first epic text: "After writing *The Greenlanders*, I rather prided myself on my cruelty to my characters. I was pleased at how readily I could sacrifice them to principle. Sudden, accidental death, for example, is a prominent feature of the Icelandic Saga" (Smiley 1998, p. 53).

Captivatingly, and counterintuitively, it's this very remorselessness that appears to make her characters so compelling. Smiley's most accomplished works – *The Greenlanders*, *Horse Heaven*, and The Last One Hundred Years Trilogy – begin (and end) with a focus on characters. *The Greenlanders*, for instance, opens with a "List of Characters" following a verse from the Icelandic "The Sayings of the Prophetess." In the mode of Shakespeare, each of Smiley's "players" is briefly defined, usually in terms of kinship, employment, and social relationships, such as, "Gunnars Stead Folk," "wealthy farmer," "mother of Ketil the Unlucky," "caretaker of the Episcopal See of Gardar," "a teller of tales," "Asgeir's neighbor and rival," and "Erlend's wife or mistress." Not unlike Dickens, famous for the variety and number of his fictional figures, Smiley includes over fifty characters in this "List." Only ten of these, all of whom are second or third generation in the arc of the saga, are supplied with birthdates.

Horse Heaven, "a comic epic poem in prose," so the copyright page qualifies it, likewise opens with a "Cast of Characters." These fifty-plus "actors" include one dog and six horses. Beyond the brief racing and breeding history for each horse ("stakes winner in France, bred in Germany"), human characters are ascribed half-comedic descriptors like "Checker at Wal-Mart," "owner, industrialist," "toy magnate, racehorse owner," "Elizabeth's boyfriend, futurologist," "racetrack aficionado, theorist of track life," and "small-time owner, former Red Guard." "Book One," subtitled "1997," starts with a "Prologue," one itself subtitled "Who They Are." Setting up Smiley's signature character-driven encyclopedic style, one grounded in free-indirect narration, the "They" of *Horse Heaven*'s prologue are the six "*Horses*" in the "Cast of Characters," which ought not to surprise Smiley fans, given the devotion to horses she divulges in her nonfiction *A Year at the Races* (2004). This list of players moves through eight increasingly large, and less specific, zones. The first concrete character affiliations occur under the subheading "*New York and Florida (Aqueduct, Belmont, Saratoga, Calder, Gulfstream).*" The next three are similar, detailing first "*Maryland*" then "*Chicago and New Orleans*" then "*California*," and the respective racetracks servicing each of these American places. The final four zones, however, are ever more ambiguous: "*Texas,*" "*France,*" "*Everywhere,*" and, fittingly, "*Horses.*" Heaven or transcendence in *Horse Heaven*, as elsewhere in Smiley's best work, comes in the form of the author's unique ability to produce an interiority so visceral, so unique, so realist, that readers experience the world through the eyes, words, feelings, and impressions of her distinctive characters – even if these characters are not fully self-aware human beings. Not too unlike Orwell in *Animal Farm* (1945), Richard Adams in *Watership Down* (1972), and Art Spiegelman in *Maus* (1980), Smiley compels readers to deeply identify with the interiority of horses, dogs, pigs, and infants alike.

Some Luck is the first novel of the Last One Hundred Years Trilogy. The title *Some Luck* evokes the first book of *The Greenlanders* saga: "Riches." The two books that follow in *The Greenlanders* are "The Devil," and, ironically, "Love." After all, as Smiley herself admits, "One of the first things that intrigued [her] about [the fate of the colony] was that it was the only attested case of an *established* European civilization or culture falling apart and vanishing" (quoted in Nakadate 1999, p. 106). In parallel with *The Greenlanders'* saga, the second and third novels of The Last One Hundred Years Trilogy are *Early Warning* and *Golden Age*. These interconnected titles rightly suggest that Smiley's long, encyclopedic sagas – *The Greenlanders* measures almost

600 prose-stuffed pages; the manuscript, however, was over 1100 pages – follow traditional narrative arcing, in the standard form of introduction, complication, and resolution. The momentum of these accomplished texts, including *Horse Heaven*, itself measuring 600 pages, also follows the chronological logic of modern, realist representation.

The Greenlanders starts after the death of the Western Settlement in 1345 and concludes at an undefined time nearing the collapse of the Eastern Settlement some seventy years later. The tale frames the birth and death of heroine Margret Asgeirsdottir, herself born in 1345, the first birth year indicated in the "List of Characters." *Horse Heaven* begins in late 1997, and moves forward typically in terms of the calendar months of the racing seasons. The novel concludes at an undefined time in the winter following the millennial turn. That the end-of-the-millennium *Horse Heaven* covers a period lasting no longer than two and a half years is testament to the novelist's Tolstoyan gift of clearly conveying interiority. Unlike her mostly male encyclopedic, maximalist contemporaries, including luminaries like Gaddis, Gass, Pynchon, Wallace, Danielewski, and Lucy Ellmann, Smiley's longest works are as much about interiority as they are about internationalism. Though also a stylist, Smiley remains indebted to modernism (with a modicum of postmodernist flourishes, which Jonathan Franzen admittedly emulates) – and one dedicated to engaging with the minds, the impressions and memories, of her complex characters.

Smiley's career-long devotion to a pure form of reliable realism is most remarkable in The Last One Hundred Years Trilogy. *Some Luck* starts in 1920 with the chapter heading "1920." The book's last chapter is "1953." Every chapter in between, each measuring around 20–30 pages, is duly titled according to the year in which its events take place. The same holds true for the indicatively titled *Early Warning* and *Golden Age*. The former commences in "1954" and concludes in "1986." The latter, respectively, in "1987" and "2019."

Each novel in the family saga, which is a crowning achievement in a career marked by literary accolades, starts with a family tree. The first novel has forty-five characters, the second seventy-one, and the third, now eight generations down the Langdon family line, 100. It is not until the third novel that the family tree includes some birthdates. Certainly, assiduous readers have already filled in the birth years, and lamentably, almost always lamentably, the death years, of key characters. As we learn in Smiley's fellow Iowa Writers' Workshop alumnus Kevin Brockmeier's *A Brief History of The Dead* (2006), characters only die once there's no one left to remember them, no one left to circulate, to adapt, and to lionize their stories. Such is the case with problematic hero Frank Langdon (b. 1920, d. 1994) in The Last One Hundred Years Trilogy.

Notwithstanding his four decades of gallivanting following his return from Italy in World War II, a flitting that included covert arms trade in the Middle East, as well as innumerable paramours, and amassed fortunes, it is the enigmatic Frank whose cherished name concludes the family saga in 2019. So exacting, so principled, so cruel is Smiley, that Frank's eventual passing increasingly haunts readers from the get-go of The Last One Hundred Years. Smiley devotees know that, like the fated co-hero Kollgrim in *The Greenlanders*, and unlike the transcendent claim horse Justa Bob in *Horse Heaven*, Frank is destined to leave readers bereaved before trilogy's end. And the haphazard, unlucky way in which he suddenly dies, and this after finally being recuperated, after finally becoming affectionate and likable, after a lifetime of cool, impressive detachment, is all the more discomfiting, nay, heartbreaking, for readers – just as it is for a large portion of the Langdon family in

The Last One Hundred Years Trilogy. Frank's sudden death does not leave the Langdons. It's just as present, if not even more present, by virtue of family member stories, stories of stories, and impressions of stories of stories (some openly shared, others kept confidential) in 2019 as it is in 1994. By 1994, readers have spent seventy-four years enveloped in/by Frank's own interiority, not to mention innumerable considerations of this son's, this brother's, this husband's, this father's, this grandfather's actions, reactions, and inactions.

Jane Smiley's signature style is her magician-like mastery of detailing the inner lives of her characters. Though The Last One Hundred Years Trilogy is hyperrealist, there's no single, straight description of person, place, or thing. Every event, minute or momentous, personal or public, is described through the sentiments, the aggravations, the arguments, and/or the ebullitions of a unique character. Smiley's career-long commitment to character, and to a wealth of diverse characters, as the casts of players detailed above ideally illustrate, really is the stuff of life – not simply fiction. In many ways, her detailed, encyclopedic work can be understood as a long-developing empathetic Exercise in Ordinary Love & Grief, which is something the titles of her two short story collections intimately anticipate: *The Age of Grief* (1987) and *Ordinary Love & Good Will* (1989).

SEE ALSO: Contemporary Regionalisms; Ecocriticism and Environmental Fiction; Fictions of Work and Labor; Periodization; Realism after Poststructuralism; Third-Wave Feminism; Writers' Collectives

REFERENCES

Diamond, Jared. (2005). *Collapse: How Societies Choose to Fail*. New York: Viking.
Nakadate, Neil. (1999). *Understanding Jane Smiley*. Columbia: South Carolina University Press.
Polley, Jason. (2011). *Jane Smiley, Jonathan Franzen, Don DeLillo: Narratives of Everyday Justice*. New York: Peter Lang.
Smiley, Jane. (1991). *A Thousand Acres*. New York: Knopf.
Smiley, Jane. (1998). Shakespeare in Iceland. In: *Shakespeare and the Twentieth Century: The Selected Proceedings of the International Shakespeare Association World Congress* (ed. Jonathan Bate, Jill L. Levenson, and Dieter Mehl), 44–59. Newark: Delaware University Press.
Smiley, Jane. (2015). *Early Warning*. New York: Pan Macmillan.

FURTHER READING

Bergman, Ingmar. (dir.) (1957). *The Seventh Seal*. Svensk Filmindustri.
Polley, Jason S. (2013). Race, gender, justice: storytelling in *The Greenlanders*. *Amerikastudien/American Studies* 58 (1): 27–50.
Shakespeare, William. (1980). *King Lear*. New York: Random House.
Smiley, Jane. (2002). *Charles Dickens*. New York: Penguin.
Smiley, Jane. (2004). *A Year at the Races: Reflections on Horses, Humans, Love, Money, and Luck*. New York: Knopf.

Sontag, Susan

SCOTT J. JUENGEL
Vanderbilt University, USA

As the story goes, Susan Sontag was 14 in 1947, a year before matriculating at the University of Chicago and thus still in her astonishingly precocious Southern California girlhood, when she and a friend looked up Thomas Mann in the local phonebook and gave him a call. The aging German Nobel laureate – "a god in exile who lived in a house in Pacific Palisades" – invited the two awkward teens to tea, where they discussed Mann's *Doktor Faustus* while the novel's English translation was still in manuscript (Sontag

2017, p. 29). It is one of those origin stories that retains a tenacious hold on the mythology surrounding a contemporary author, even as some parts of the story were fabricated when Sontag published "Pilgrimage" in the December 1987 issue of the *New Yorker*. The giant of European modernism sharing exilic knowledge with a promising young woman who will arguably become America's foremost cultural critic is almost too good to be true.

And "too good to be true" offers just the kind of lazy aesthetic standard Sontag would despise, even as it proves useful when considering Sontag herself, a figure of dizzying contradictions, prodigious intellect, and literary star power. While she may have only published two novels after 1980, it is difficult to discuss America and its literary culture at the end of the twentieth century without accounting for Sontag. The publication of *Against Interpretation and Other Essays* in 1966 set in motion a decades-long reign as arguably America's most inimitable public intellectual. One can without much exaggeration make the case that Sontag had a hand in the importing European theory into the American mainstream by championing figures like Claude Lévi-Strauss, Roland Barthes and Walter Benjamin; laid early groundwork for queer theory with her oft-cited essay "Notes on 'Camp'" (1964); anticipated elements of narrative medicine with *Illness as Metaphor* (1978), *AIDS and Its Metaphors* (1988), and short stories like "The Way We Live Now" in the *New Yorker* (1984); and advanced our cultural literacy in fields ranging from photography to pornography, art house cinema to ethnic cleansing. Moreover, Sontag was President of PEN America when the Ayatollah Ruhollah Khomeini issued a *fatwa* against Salman Rushdie after the publication of *The Satanic Verses* in 1989. In support of her beleaguered compatriot, Sontag gathered many prominent novelists catalogued in this encyclopedia (e.g. Don DeLillo, Norman Mailer, E.L. Doctorow, and others) to participate in public readings of Rushdie's novel as a show of first amendment solidarity. "[W]hipped into line by Susan," writes Rushdie in his witness protection memoir, *Joseph Anton*, "almost all of them had found their better selves and stood up to be counted" (2013, p. 150).

Such a defense of art in the age of terror isn't surprising coming from Sontag, who famously staged a performance of *Waiting for Godot* in war-torn Sarajevo while the city was under siege and without electricity. From early essays like "The Artist as Exemplary Sufferer" (1962) to her final stand-alone volume, *Regarding the Pain of Others* (2003), Sontag's career restlessly returned to the correspondences between suffering, moral seriousness and aesthetic judgment. In arguing that the artist has replaced the saint in our secular age, Sontag remarks that "the sensibility we have inherited identifies spirituality and seriousness with turbulence, suffering, passion . . . [I]t has been spiritually fashionable to be in pain. Thus it is not love which we overvalue, but suffering – more precisely, the spiritual merits and benefits of suffering" (1966a, pp. 47–48). Sontag's frequent recourse to the question of pain is hardly a matter of philosophical abstraction. Born Susan Rosenblatt in 1933, Sontag lost her father to tuberculosis at age five and endured an unhappy childhood with a cold, indifferent mother; she married sociologist Philip Rieff at age seventeen after a ten-day courtship, divorcing him eight tumultuous years later; she was first diagnosed with breast cancer in 1975, enduring a mastectomy and chemotherapy, and lived with a recurrence of cancer the last six years of her life. Early in her landmark *On Photography* (1977), Sontag describes a sensibility profoundly shaped by photographs of Bergen-Belsen and Dachau glimpsed in a Santa Monica bookstore in

1945: "Nothing I have seen – in photographs or in real life – ever cut me as sharply, deeply, instantaneously. Indeed, it seems plausible to me to divide my life into two parts, before I saw those photographs (I was twelve) and after... When I looked at those photographs, something broke" (1977, pp. 19–20).

"What good was served by seeing them?" Sontag asks of those concentration camp images; "[t]hey were only photographs – of an event I had scarcely heard of and could do nothing to affect, of suffering I could hardly imagine and could do nothing to relieve" (1977, p. 20). This issue of the questionable "good" of our images arguably structures much of Sontag's career as a public intellectual, for the simple query opens onto matters of modern aesthetics and anesthetics, our collective moral education, and the escalating power of technology to create, and then photochemically capture, our suffering. Notably, Sontag would revise her thesis about the relationship of photography and sympathy between *On Photography* and *Regarding the Pain of Others*: "People don't become inured to what they are shown – if that's the right way to describe what happens – because of the *quantity* of images dumped on them. It is passivity that dulls feeling" (2003, p. 102). In other words, our exposure to the world's anguish isn't a matter of feeling compassion or its desensitization, for "[o]ur sympathy proclaims our innocence as well as our impotence"; rather, horrors are made palatable because we refuse to recognize that "our privileges are located on the same map as their suffering" and we don't dare examine our complicity (pp. 102–103).

To her credit, Sontag traveled that map, accepting an invitation to visit North Vietnam in May 1968 at the height of the conflict (a journey that produced the long essay, "Trip to Hanoi" [1969]); flying to Israel in the final days of the 1973 Yom Kippur War to film her documentary, *Promised Lands* (1974); encamping in Sarajevo during the siege to stage Beckett's famous play; and writing unflinchingly about 9/11 and the Abu Ghraib torture photos, bearing the brunt of public outrage for doing so. Indeed, Sontag's candor about America's outsized place in the world order and its concomitant history of white supremacy often made her a lightning rod for conservatives. In the mid-1960s Sontag used a questionnaire about American values in *Partisan Review* as the catalyst for a blistering essay entitled "What's Happening in America" (1966). There she calls the United States a "passionately racist country" founded on genocide, and delivered one of her more memorably acerbic lines: "The white race is the cancer of human history; it is the white race and it alone – its ideologies and inventions – which eradicates autonomous civilizations wherever it spreads, which has upset the ecological balance of the planet, which now threatens the very existence of life itself" (1969, pp. 198, 203). According to her biographer, Sontag later apologized for the line about the white race as a cancer, but "more for the metaphor than for the underlying sentiment" (Moser 2019, p. 274).

Despite her lasting fame and cultural authority as an essayist, critic and polemicist, later in life Sontag would insist that she was first and foremost a fiction writer. At the start of her career this was something of a distinction without a difference for Sontag, who drew inspiration from the French *nouveau roman* and figures like Maurice Blanchot, Nathalie Sarraute, and Michel Butor whose philosophical fictions often eschew readerly pleasure for critical exposition. In the early 1960s Sontag viewed the contemporary novel as "intransigently *arrière-garde*" compared to other arts, unserious as a vehicle for ideas because beholden to its nineteenth-century realist heyday (1966b, p. 101). Consequently her first publication was *The Benefactor* (1963), a novel that reads like a cross between

Candide and notes from a psychoanalytic session, but one weighed down by a sobriety of purpose. Indeed, both *The Benefactor* and her follow-up, *Death Kit* (1967), suffer from the burden of their self-importance and Sontag's French curriculum: each concocts hallucinatory dreamscapes pointedly designed to blur any attribution of the real and the unreal, then coldly analyzes that which they've rendered unresolvable. Like Albert Camus's *The Stranger* (1942) or Alain Robbe-Grillet's *The Voyeur* (1955), Sontag's first two novels intimate that their heroes commit a murder, only to trouble not only whether a crime occurred or not, but what constitutes an act of killing in fiction: "Imagine to yourself, reader, that you are a murderer. What is it that makes a murderer?" (1963, p. 141). Reflexivity of this kind makes conspicuous Sontag's desire to deploy the genre for philosophical ends, and as a result her early novels unwittingly made the case for her stature as an essayist.

Twenty-five years had passed since *Death Kit* when Sontag published *The Volcano Lover* (1992), a historical novel set primarily in late-eighteenth century Naples and the diplomatic circles of the British envoy, Sir William Hamilton. Sontag's lifelong desire to write a novel of ideas found its proper form in historical fiction, where her prodigious erudition is channeled into narrative world-building and any high modernist irony is subordinated to the occasional wink at the self-consciousness of it all. *The Volcano Lover* has some of the historical nonchalance of Doctorow's *Ragtime* (1975), giddily filling out its world with a veritable who's who from the European enlightenment, including Goethe, Danton, de Sade, Reynolds, Piranesi, Marat, Mozart, Lessing, Gibbon, Napoleon, Walpole, and perhaps most notable of all, Admiral Horatio Nelson, British naval hero. Known throughout the novel by his Italian sobriquet, the Cavaliere, Hamilton is a collector of art and antiquities, an amateur volcanologist, and an occasional ambassador. He also became one of the age's most distinguished cuckolds when his young wife Emma became Nelson's mistress. Over the course of the narrative, Emma Hamilton's story gradually emerges as the novel's central concern.

Stationed in the shadow of Mount Vesuvius, a live volcano, the Cavaliere and the Neapolitan court indulge in such gaudy privilege and rank dissipation that the coming revolution seems as inexorable as the next eruption. Sontag clearly relishes portraying the reckless intemperance of a Europe in need of toppling: the first half of her novel is stuffed with secret cabinets of erotica, pet monkeys, a horrific "mountain" of just-slaughtered meats for the king, and the general waggery of unchecked aristocrats. Famous for burying Pompeii and Herculaneum in volcanic ash and lava in 79 CE, Vesuvius looms over these scenes of debauchery as a retributive force and a ready metaphor for sociopolitical tumult: "Both to the revolution's partisans, and to the horrified ruling class of every European country, no image for what was happening in France seemed as apt as that of a volcano in action – violent convulsion, upheaval from below, and waves of lethal force that harrow and permanently alter the landscape" (1992, p. 161). But Sontag's interests are less concerned with historical eruptions and more with the role that art and connoisseurship play in our historical consciousness.

For *The Volcano Lover* is a novel of collecting. The predilections of Sontag's hero allow her to indulge her essayistic side, peppering the narrative with aphoristic riffs on taste, aesthetic appraisal and acquisition. "Collecting expresses a free-floating desire that attaches and re-attaches itself," we're told, "it is a succession of desires" that alters how one views the physical world (1992, p. 24). Hamilton and other wealthy connoisseurs seek to rescue beautiful things from time's onslaught, for "[e]very collector feels menaced by all the imponderables that can bring disaster"

(p. 201). And there is disaster at every turn in *The Volcano Lover*, from madmen who slash paintings and shipwrecks that engulf whole libraries, to the ravages of "that insatiable art predator, Napoleon" pillaging all of Europe (p. 214). Notably, the novel bears the influence of German thinker Walter Benjamin on Sontag's thinking. *Under the Sign of Saturn* (1980), Sontag's third volume of essays, takes its title from her study of Benjamin's melancholia, and observes that "[i]f this melancholy temperament is faithless to people, it has good reason to be faithful to things" (1980, p. 120). Benjamin is modernism's great theorist of collecting, and Sontag found in his writings both the epigrammatic style and the melancholic view of history that pervade *The Volcano Lover*. Losing his first wife to ill health and his second to the arms of a national hero, the Cavaliere finds solace in his treasures, a "Don Juanism of objects" that promise mute fidelity (Sontag 1992, p. 202).

Significantly, Emma Hamilton begins to demand narrative attention once she renders herself an object of art. While still the Cavaliere's "protégé," Emma gains fame with her "Attitudes" or poses, a talent for representing "a figure from ancient mythology or drama or history" in tableau vivant (1992, p. 148). Have mastered impassioned expression, stillness, and a sense of the narrative weightiness, Emma performs a "gallery of living statues" – "a kind of Pygmalion in reverse" – changing from Ariadne to Dido to Medea to Iphigenia, much to the delight of her courtly audience (pp. 144, 145). This parlor trick grimly mimics the casts of Pompeii's victims, the in-situ figures frozen in agonizing postures that have become icons of sudden death and the fragility of life on earth. Again and again in *The Volcano Lover* the virtuosic unfolds in the shadow of destruction, and scenes of vitality are weighed down by their finitude.

Emma Hamilton's peculiar form of theatricality anticipates the concerns of Sontag's fourth and final novel, *In America*, which won the National Book Award in 2000. The novel is inspired by the 1876 emigration to America of Helena Modrzejewska, Poland's most celebrated actress and a Victorian-era diva now recognizable in stylized *carte de visites* of her most famous roles, such as Ophelia or Desdemona. Modrzejewska, who performed under the name Helena Modjeska, becomes Maryna Zalezowska in Sontag's novel, and provides the novelist with an opportunity to explore the performative nature of identity. Maryna's star power lies in playing the tragic heroine, whether in Shakespeare or the more melodramatic fare popular with nineteenth-century audiences, especially in backwater America. This means playing things big: "Authority on the stage is tantamount to the ability to project continuously, fluently, piercingly, a character's essence.... (Anything else would be trivial, unfocused; oozing instead of signaling and shaping.) To act a role is to show what is emphatic in a person, what is sustained" (2000, p. 305). Like Emma before her, Maryna has mastered the art of commanding attention by slipping in and out of personas and personalities, although Maryna is the sturdier, more principled character of the two. However, as one contemporary review of *In America* points out, Maryna's celebrity may soon give way to a historical shift in tastes, for "in a few decades Maryna may be regarded as a high priestess of dreck" (Kerr 2000).

Indeed, this sense of expiring fame is one of the subplots of *In America*, as Sontag's heroine feels ambivalent about the profession which has given her so much. Maryna uproots her family and her entourage to move to the American West, eager to constitute a utopian agrarian community near Anaheim. Sontag's portrait of late nineteenth-century California and environs is part of the charm of the novel: a relatively new state filled with prospectors and visionaries, criminals and cult leaders, all praying to the minor gods of opportunity. Where her native Poland understands that "the past is a fate," America seems to live in a perpetually optimistic now: "Here the present does not reaffirm the past but supersedes and cancels it," for Americans "do not feel dwarfed by *anything*" (2000, p. 223). However, within this bustling historical landscape Sontag's eye, as always, is on the function of art. Once she recommits to acting, Maryna's itinerary takes her from gaudy opera houses in booming mining towns to the theatrical circuits of "Bradford, Warren, Scranton, Wilkes-Barre, Easton, Oil City" and other minor burghs (p. 329), where the great European diva shares the playbill with juggling acts, minstrel shows, academic lectures, and medleys of Wagner and Verdi. The persistence of art in the cultural backwater provides the novel with an occasion to glimpse the American experiment from the perspective of Old World cosmopolitanism, Henry James in reverse.

Fittingly then, James turns up in Sontag's novel. Late in the narrative Maryna travels to England to return to her roots in Shakespeare, and begins to acknowledge the shallowness of her recent success: "It had taken this sojourn in England to understand how much easier it was (*hadn't* it been easy?) to prevail in America: a whole country of people who believe in the will" (2000, p. 342). Luckily for her, the next night finds her at a posh dinner party seated next to "the formidable American novelist and theatre critic, Henry James, recently settled in London." James is a fan of Maryna – which he admits "with circuitous bluntness" – and Sontag relishes the opportunity to experiment with some Jamesian stylings as the two discuss the difference between American and English audiences; or as James puts it, "For all the want of *spread* in these compact isles there is much more *surface* here, one thing is said while another is meant, they are cautious, they can be suspicious, they are not keen on making a great effort, they would rather be thought a bit slow than too clever, they, how can I put it, *withhold*" (p. 342). While *In America* is replete with celebrity cameos – Henry Wadsworth Longfellow, Alfred Tennyson, Ellen Terry, Oscar Wilde, Edwin Booth and more – the novel is Jamesian in its sensibility, if not its pretensions.

Sontag died in late December 2004 after a recurrence of her cancer, leaving behind an prodigious corpus of critical and imaginative work, from essays and monographs, to films, plays and works of fiction. While at times the public celebrity – her controversies, her style, her provocations, her romances, including a decades-long relationship with photographer Annie Leibowitz – threatened to outshine the sober, serious prose of the intellectual, every new offense to human dignity reminds us how badly we need a Susan Sontag to remind us of our precarity and our promise.

SEE ALSO: DeLillo, Don; Doctorow, E.L.; Mailer, Norman

REFERENCES

Kerr, Sarah. (2000). Diva. *The New York Times* (March 12, 2000). https://archive.nytimes.com/www.nytimes.com/books/00/03/12/reviews/000312.12kerrlt.html (accessed August 9, 2021).

Moser, Benjamin. (2019). *Sontag: Her Life and Work*. New York: Harper Collins; 1st ed. 2017.

Rushdie, Salman. (2013). *Joseph Anton: A Memoir*. New York: Random House.

Sontag, Susan. (1963). *The Benefactor: A Novel*. New York: Farrar, Straus and Giroux.

Sontag, Susan. (1966a). The artist as exemplary sufferer. In: *Against Interpretation and Other Essays*, 39–48. New York: Farrar, Straus and Giroux; 1st ed. 1962.

Sontag, Susan. (1966b). Nathalie Sarraute and the novel. In: *Against Interpretation and Other Essays*, 100–111. New York: Farrar, Straus and Giroux; 1st ed. 1962.

Sontag, Susan. (1969). What's happening in America. In: *Styles of Radical Will*, 193–204. New York: Farrar, Straus and Giroux; 1st ed. 1962.

Sontag, Susan. (1977). *On Photography*. New York: Farrar, Straus and Giroux.
Sontag, Susan. (1980). *Under the Sign of Saturn*. New York: Farrar, Straus and Giroux.
Sontag, Susan. (1992). *The Volcano Lover: A Romance*. New York: Farrar, Straus and Giroux.
Sontag, Susan. (2000). *In America: A Novel*. New York: Farrar, Straus and Giroux.
Sontag, Susan. (2003). *Regarding the Pain of Others*. New York: Farrar, Straus and Giroux.
Sontag, Susan. (2017). Pilgrimage. In: *Debriefing: Collected Stories* (ed. Benjamin Taylor), 1–29. New York: Farrar, Straus and Giroux.

FURTHER READING

Kaplan, Alice. (2013). *Dreaming in French: The Paris Years of Jacqueline Bouvier Kennedy, Susan Sontag and Angela Davis*. Chicago: University of Chicago Press.
Mitrano, Mena. (2016). *In the Archive of Longing: Susan Sontag's Critical Modernism*. Edinburgh: Edinburgh University Press.
Nelson, Deborah L. (2017). *Tough Enough: Arbus, Arendt, Didion, McCarthy, Sontag, Weil*. Chicago: University of Chicago Press.
Nunez, Sigrid. (2014). *Sempre Susan: A Memoir of Susan Sontag*. New York: Riverhead Books.

Sorrentino, Gilbert

EMMETT STINSON
Deakin University, Australia

Gilbert Sorrentino (1929–2006) was an experimental writer and poet, who wrote nineteen novels, ten collections of poetry, a book of essays, a collection of stories, and a novella. He is particularly known for his use of formal constraints and metafictional conceits. Sorrentino was born in Brooklyn on April 7, 1929, and went to public schools there. Although he had two stints at Brooklyn College in the 1950s, he never completed his degree, and is usually considered an autodidact. He served in the medical corps of the US army, and, upon leaving in 1953, decided to become a writer. Sorrentino's first marriage, to Elsene Wiessner, ended in 1960 after a cross-country road trip, which he fictionalized in *The Sky Changes* (1966). They had two children, Jesse and Delia. Sorrentino subsequently married Victoria Ortiz and had another child, the novelist Christopher Sorrentino. Sorrentino achieved some early renown as a poet with links to Robert Creeley and the Black Mountain school. He founded the journal *Neon* with Hugh Selby, Jr. and others and served as its editor until 1960. During this period, William Carlos Williams included a small piece of Sorrentino's writing in Book Five of the long poem *Paterson* (1958). He then edited the journal *Kulchur* in the early 1960s and worked as an editor at Grove Press under Barney Rossett through the end of the 1960s. Sorrentino also had a long friendship with John O'Brien, and encouraged him to create *The Review of Contemporary Fiction* and Dalkey Archive Press.

Sorrentino worked at a variety of different universities, including Columbia University, Sarah Lawrence, The New School for Social Research, and the University of Scranton, before taking a position at Stanford University in 1982, where he worked until his retirement in 1999. Sorrentino received many awards and honours, including two Guggenheim Fellowships (1973, 1987), a National Endowment for the Arts grant (1975), the John Dos Passos Prize for Literature (1981), the American Academy of Arts and Letters Award for Literature (1985), the Lannan Literary Award for Fiction (1992), and the Lannan Lifetime Achievement Award in 2005. He was also twice a finalist for the PEN/Faulkner Award (1981, 2003). He died on May 18, 2006.

Sorrentino's work is difficult to classify, because it traverses so many genres and forms. He is often considered a comic writer, due to such novels as *Mulligan Stew* (1979), which self-consciously employs metafictional techniques, including parabasis, aporia, and pastiche. This might seem to make him a contemporary of fabulist writers like Robert Coover and John Barthes. But Sorrentino produced starkly different works whose content, if not exactly realist or naturalist, certainly focuses on the lives of everyday people. Moreover, Sorrentino's "novels" typically lack key features associated with the form: they often have no clear plot, character development, rising tension, or thematic resolution. Many of his later works present alternating, obliquely linked vignettes that inhabit a space between the story cycle and the novel. Finally, Sorrentino's works are rigorously formal, usually applying constraints in the manner of writers associated with Oulipo. As Sorrentino stated, his writing employs "a structure or series of structures that can, if one is lucky enough, generate 'content,' or, if you please, the wholeness of the work itself. Almost all of my books are written under the influence of some sort of preconceived constraint or set of rules" (Conte 2002, p. 78). Sorrentino is renowned for his love of lists, which often take the form of Rabelaisian catalogues that comically highlight the incongruity of the listed items. While Sorrentino has been frequently identified as a postmodern author based on his techniques, he has expressed doubts about this label, calling postmodernism an "imprecise term" and suggesting that "maybe a better term would be late-late modernism, or contemporary modernism" (Laurence 1994).

Despite these differences, however, Sorrentino almost obsessively returns to the same topics and themes. Sexuality is frequently depicted in forms that are simultaneously scatological and satirical in order both to criticize the notion of sexual liberation and to affirm the degree to which lives are shaped by sexuality. Similarly, his novels frequently examine divorce, infidelity, and emotional, physical, and sexual abuse within families and relationships. Artistic pretensions, failures, and fraudulence are also a recurrent fixation. His novels foreground clichéd language, particularly when used in emotionally charged situations. These topics reflect Sorrentino's studied refusal of sentimentality, and his desire to view lives as the product of their material constituents; as the narrator of *Imaginative Qualities of Actual Things* (1971) notes, "It is difficult to accept a life as nothing more or less than the pattern it makes" (1991, p. 118). Here, Sorrentino's interest in the "pattern" of a life mirrors his interest in formal patterns as the basis for creative composition. Fittingly, he often revisits his own work, recycling characters, plots, settings, formal devices, although in unexpected ways. Sorrentino also advocated a particularly strong mode of formalism, arguing against claims that literature should be useful, idea-driven, or readily intelligible.

Sorrentino first attained recognition as a poet in the 1960s and had published eight books of poetry by the end of the 1970s. But he increasingly turned his attention to novels, publishing thirteen of them between 1980 and 2006, and no new volumes of poetry aside from an edition of selected poems. This transition may have been partially the result of the success of *Mulligan Stew*, which sold well enough to go into second printings in both hardcover and paperback editions. *Mulligan Stew* is a hypertrophic reenvisioning of Flann O'Brien's metafictional *At Swim-Two-Birds* (1939) that incorporates other novelists' characters. It was famously rejected by "nearly thirty" different publishers before being accepted by Grove Press (McPheron 1991, p. 37); the novel dramatizes this process with a series of fictional rejection letters that appear before its title and imprint pages. The novel ranges across modes of discourse, including avant-garde poetry, an experimental play, an academic essay about mathematics and projectile physics, an imaginary publisher's catalogue, and an interview with an art collector. It remains Sorrentino's best-known work as a result of its exuberant invention and absurd humor.

Sorrentino's next novel, *Aberration of Starlight* (1980), seems to depart radically from this metafictionality. The novel tells a coherent story about an incident at a bordering house in rural New Jersey in 1939 through four different perspectives, belonging to 10-year-old Billy, his mother Marie, her prospective lover, Tom Thebus, and her father, John. Robert McLaughlin has noted that all four sections contain ten chapters with the same content described from different perspectives such that the novel examines "its own method of composition and interpretability" (2001). While *Aberration of Starlight*'s composition may be rigorously formal, it remains comparatively conventional in narrative, characterization, setting, and style. The novel was published by Random House in hardcover and by Penguin in paperback, and again sold well without going into a second printing (McPheron 1991, pp. 43–46).

Crystal Vision (1981) returns to explicitly avant-garde territory, while also revisiting material from Sorrentino's second novel, *Steelwork* (1970). Opening in what appears to be a bar and presided over by an author-surrogate known as the Magician, the novel presents seventy-eight vignettes with a recurring cast of characters. As Louis Mackey notes, the novel is structured like a tarot deck with the first twenty-two chapters representing the "trumps of the Greater Arcana" while the "remaining 56 chapters traverse the four suits of the lesser arcana – Wands, Cups, Swords, and Pentacles – moving within each suit from King through Ace" (1997, p. 6). The title simultaneously suggests a fortune told in a crystal ball, a prismatic view of the world, and an unflinching way of looking at things. The novel criticizes notions of the American dream (the novel's final section is entitled "Red White and Blue"), but also undermines any potential didacticism; as one character notes on the final page, "Yes, yes, the whole thing turns out to be so subtlelishly and unerredly American" (1982, p. 289).

The composition of *Blue Pastoral* (1983) was determined by a series of destinations plotted on the "transcontinental route" its characters traverse (McPheron 1991, p. 58), a method that also recalls *The Sky Changes*. The novel depicts the story of Serge Gavotte (aka "Blue"), who quits his job at a university and sets off on a quest for a perfect musical phrase; his means of transport is a piano on top of a cart. The novel appears to end with the cart falling into the San Francisco Bay, where the splash accompanies the discovery of Blue's ideal music. The novel incorporates many pastoral tropes and different genres of writing for comedic effects, not unlike *Mulligan Stew*. Although the novel's premise is intentionally absurd, it is grounded in autobiographical detail, since Sorrentino had just taken up a position at Stanford University and undertaken a similar journey from New York to California.

Perhaps Sorrentino's most significant work of the 1980s comprises a "trilogy" of novels: *Odd Number* (1985), *Rose Theatre* (1987), and *Misterioso* (1989), which would subsequently be repackaged in one volume as *Pack of Lies* (1997). But the entire trilogy might be productively thought of as a sequel to Sorrentino's third novel, *Imaginative Qualities of Actual Things* (1971), since both focus on the same ensemble cast of characters. *Imaginative Qualities* – which was heavily influenced by Wyndham Lewis's *Apes of God* (1930) – is a frequently brutal satire of artists and writers in the Greenwich Village scene of the 1950s and 1960s, and is also, as David Andrews notes, a thinly veiled *roman à clef* of such writers as Joel Oppenheimer, Fee Dawson, Tony Weinberger, Basil King, John Chamberlain, and Joe and Anna Early (Andrews 2003, p. 17). But despite this, the narrator of the novel repeatedly insists upon the complete fictionality of these characters: "These people aren't real. I'm making them up as I go along" (1991, p. 27).

Odd Number, whose title comes from a line in Flann O'Brien's *At-Swim Two Birds* (McPheron 1991, p. 63), might be thought of as an attempt to operationalize this latter statement by wholly fictionalizing the cast of *Imaginative Qualities*. The novel comprises three sections in which an unnamed investigator interrogates three different characters about the death of Sheila Henry (who, as it turns out, may not be dead). The first two sections present the same thirty-three questions in reverse order, while the third section moves on to different questions (Mackey 1997, p. 19). The use of interrogation invokes the detective novel, but the three respondents' claims contradict each other, as well as information originally presented in *Imaginative Qualities*. The novel frequently seeks to blur the line between fiction and reality: a party at Horace Rossette's house, which originally appears in *Imaginative Qualities*, appears to form the basis for a film called *The Party*, which is later revealed to be an adaptation of a French novel, *La Soiree Intime*, which is "about a group of people who go to a party in order to talk about making a film about the very party that they're attending" (Sorrentino 1985, p. 16; see also Mackey 1997, pp. 20–21). Leo Kaufman's (fictional) *roman à clef* satire *Isolate Flecks* resembles *Imaginative Qualities*, but in *Imaginative Qualities*, the narrator, who is not Leo, imagines writing a satire called *Isolate Flecks* after a poem by William Carlos Williams. Fittingly, *Odd Number* ends with a reference to a stack of papers that appears to contain the text of *Odd Number* itself (Mackey 1997, p. 28).

The complex allusions, illusions, claims, and counterclaims of *Odd Number* are further ramified in *Rose Theatre*. Sheila Henry, for example, appears once again to be alive, although she imagines three instances in which she could have died. The novel's fifteen chapters derive from items in "an inventory made by Philip Henslowe of the Rose Theatre's props in 1598 in London, when he moved the company to a new location" (McPheron 1991, p. 62). The novel focuses on "seven women or pairs of women" who appear in two sections each and then together in a final section (Mackey 1997, p. 39). Here, they are described by the narrator as "Women he has been given to think of as actual" (Sorrentino 1987, p. 282), a sentence that recalls *Imaginative Qualities of Actual Things*, while highlighting the complex ontological status of fictional characters, who are *thought of* as actual, without necessarily being so. *Rose Theatre* was also the first of Sorrentino's novels to be published by Dalkey Archive Press.

Misterioso takes its title from a Thelonius Monk song, and has an alphabetical organization. The text is not broken up into sections; instead specific letters clearly predominate over the text, which proceeds from A to Z. Sorrentino stated that the novel's "constraint was that all the proper names used in *Odd Number* and *Rose Theatre* must, on their first occurrence in *Misterioso*, appear in alphabetical order" (Mackey 1997, p. 67). The novel, however, is missing the letter X, which may be an Oulipian "clinamen," though Mackey has suggested a complex formal reason for its absence (p. 64). Ultimately, *Misterioso* does not answer the questions in the earlier novels, but multiplies them; as Conte states, the novel is "a complex mixing of recognizable elements into an entirely new pattern" rather than a conclusion (2002, p. 97).

Under the Shadow (1991) produces a series of fifty-nine interlinked and often comic vignettes that are "based upon the drawings done for Raymond Roussel's *Nouvelles Impressions D'Afrique*" which have "nothing to do with the text, but which, oddly enough, make a text of their own" (Laurence 1994). But while the different sections of the novel are linked in tantalizing ways, a coherent narrative never quite emerges.

Red the Fiend (1995) is perhaps one of the most unusual novels in Sorrentino's catalogue and one of his strongest. It might be thought of as a naturalist work not thematically dissimilar in style to works by Sorrentino's friend Hugh Selby, Jr. The book unites two of Sorrentino's earlier novels in an odd way: the protagonist, Red Mulvaney, is taken from *Steelwork*, but his family situation is nearly identical to Billy's in *Aberration of Starlight*. There is one essential difference, however; his grandmother (again a character from *Steelwork*), is not deceased like Billy's, but is instead a brutal abuser who tortures Red both physically and emotionally. The novel is unrelenting in depicting this abuse, but the reader is given little space to sympathize with Red, who has also assaulted a young girl in the neighborhood. Related with a characteristic ironic detachment, the novel is arguably Sorrentino's most emotionally affecting. It is also the final work that he published with Dalkey Archive.

Gold Fools (2001) is a comic take on the Western that consists entirely of questions spread across twenty-five chapters. The novel's characters and plot are allegedly based on a real boys' adventure novel from the 1920s. Although Sorrentino novels are often thought of as plotless, *Gold Fools* arguably has an excess of plot: each chapter brings wild developments that are almost as insistent as the relentless interrogatives, which also recall the ninety-nine questions that structure *Odd Number*. While *Gold Fools* clearly satirizes both older Westerns and idealized notions of US history, it has more contemporary targets, as well, including Cormac McCarthy's *Border Trilogy* (1992, 1994, 1998): "Did this authentic Western speech pattern accurately reflect Bud's disturbed mental state? Was it somewhat Faulknerian? Melvillean? Conradian? Hemmingway-esque? Or a little of each, i.e. McCarthyan?" (Sorrentino 2001, p. 90).

Sorrentino published his last four novels with Coffee House Press, and they share similarities in length, structure, constraint, and content, since all four comprise loosely connected vignettes. *Little Casino* (2002) was shortlisted for the PEN/Faulkner Award for Fiction and is comprised of fifty-two sections, which apparently are modeled on the weeks of the year, as was his 1968 poetry collection *The Perfect Fiction*. Each story is followed by a "commentary" on that story. *Lunar Follies* (2005) consists of fifty-three descriptions of modern works of art, which take their names from geographical features of the moon; its satire recalls *Imaginative Qualities of Actual Things*, but its critique is comparatively distant and laconic. *A Strange Commonplace* (2006) takes its title from William Carlos Williams's poem "The Forgotten City." Its two sections each consist of twenty-six stories that share many details or reappearing objects, such as a pearl-gray Homburg (itself a recurring item in Sorrentino's bibliography). The names of the first twenty-six stories are repeated in a shuffled order in the second half of the collection, though the connection between these linked vignettes is tangential. Thematically, all of the stories deal with infidelity, divorce, or the break-up of couples, which seems to be the "strange commonplace" to which the title refers, and, of course, is a key fixation of Sorrentino's going back to *The Sky Changes*. Sorrentino's final and posthumously published novel, *The Abyss of Human Illusion* (2009), takes its title from Henry James's story "The Middle Years" and consists again of two sections. Section one contains fifty vignettes which get progressively longer, from 130 words to over 1300, and which share key details without explicitly overlapping. These vignettes are mostly realist stories about lost illusions or broken dreams. The second section then presents a set of commentaries on specific words or phrases from the initial vignettes. These commentaries might be seen to reflect a key point in James's story that would appeal to Sorrentino: novelists' creative works provide insights into their own lives, but these same insights cannot be retrospectively applied.

SEE ALSO: Davis, Lydia; Ducornet, Rikki; Elkin, Stanley; Everett, Percival; Federman, Raymond; Gaddis, William; Gass, William H.; McElroy, Joseph

REFERENCES

Andrews, David. (2003). Of love, scorn, and contradiction: an interpretive overview of Gilbert Sorrentino's *Imaginative Qualities of Actual Things*. *The Review of Contemporary Fiction* 23 (1): 9–44.

Conte, Joseph M. (2002). *Design and Debris: A Chaotics of Postmodern American Fiction*. Tuscaloosa: University Alabama Press.

Laurence, Alexander. (1994). Gilbert Sorrentino interview. The Write Stuff. http://www.altx.com/int2/gilber.sorrentino.html (accessed July 20, 2021).

Mackey, Louis. (1997). *Fact, Fiction, and Representation: Four Novels by Gilbert Sorrentino*. Columbia, SC: Camden House.

McLaughlin, Robert. (2001). A teacher's guide to Gilbert Sorrentino's aberration of starlight. Center for Book Culture. https://web.archive.org/web/20070204060057/http://www.centerforbookculture.org:80/dalkey/teachersguides/teachersguide_Aberration.html (accessed July 20, 2021).

McPheron, William. (1991). *Gilbert Sorrentino: A Descriptive Biography*. Elmwood Park, IL: Dalkey Archive Press.

Sorrentino, Gilbert. (1982). *Crystal Vision*. London: Marion Boyars; 1st ed. 1981.

Sorrentino, Gilbert. (1985). *Odd Number*. San Francisco: North Point Press.

Sorrentino, Gilbert. (1987). *Rose Theatre*. Elmwood Park, IL: Dalkey Archive Press.

Sorrentino, Gilbert. (1991). *Imaginative Qualities of Actual Things*. Normal, IL: Dalkey Archive Press; 1st ed. 1971.

Sorrentino, Gilbert. (1997). *Pack of Lies*. Normal, IL: Dalkey Archive Press.

Sorrentino, Gilbert. (2001). *Gold Fools*. Los Angeles: Green Integer.

FURTHER READING

Andrews, David. (2001). Gilbert Sorrentino. *The Review of Contemporary Fiction* 21 (3): 6–59.

Booker, M. Keith. (1991). The dynamics of literary transgression in Sorrentino's *Mulligan Stew*. In: *Techniques of Subversion in Modern Literature: Transgression, Abjection, and the Carnivalesque*, 72–101. Gainesville: University Press of Florida.

Miller, Tyrus. (2003). Fictional truths: Gilbert Sorrentino's *Imaginative Qualities of Actual Things* between image and language. *The Review of Contemporary Fiction* 21 (10): 45–68.

O'Brien, John. (1981). Every man his voice. *The Review of Contemporary Fiction* 1 (1): 62–80.

Spiotta, Dana

STEPHEN J. BURN
University of Glasgow, UK

The twinned terms that comprise the title of Dana Spiotta's fourth novel – *Innocents and Others* (2016) – introduce the reader to the dyadic structures that govern her storyworlds. Her acute novels shuttle between different pairs of characters (especially brother-sister pairings, and close female friends); strategically juxtapose stretches of first- and third-person narration; and are structured to oscillate between two disparate moments in time. They also seem to pair different aesthetics, as Aliki Varvogli noted in the first academic article devoted to Spiotta's work. Her novels, Varvogli argued, "offer a corrective to the ironic, cynical tones" of much postmodern fiction, but they do so by employing "a number of familiar postmodernist techniques such as multiple points of view, unreliable narration, nonlinear storytelling, merging of fact and fiction, and interactions between fictional and 'real' characters" (2010, p. 660). Spiotta's attempt to correct postmodernism has often seen her work categorized alongside novels by Jennifer Egan, Rachel

Kushner, and David Foster Wallace. But that her contrasting tendency to mix the fictional and the real might put a reader in mind, specifically, of the Don DeLillo of *Libra* (1988) and *Underworld* (1997) is not coincidental, since Spiotta is, as Kasia Boddy has noted, a writer who is frequently identified as one of DeLillo's "heirs" (2019, p. 323).

Spiotta – who has published a new novel every five years since her millennial debut – was born in New Jersey in 1966, to parents who attended Hofstra University with Francis Ford Coppola. Her father eventually relocated the family to the West Coast, when he left Mobil Oil to manage Coppola's LA studio, before going on to form his own production company. When the company collapsed, the 19-year-old Spiotta's life was thrown into disarray: her parents split up; the family home was lost; and Spiotta dropped out of Columbia University. She moved to Seattle, supporting herself by working at a record store while attending Evergreen State College, but her formative connections as a young writer were forged back on the East Coast, when she took a job with Gordon Lish, who introduced her to Don DeLillo, "who became a mentor and friend" (Burton 2016). Much of this biographical material clearly survives into her novels, which crisscross between coasts, often take place on the fringes of the movie industry, and document delicately poised marriages. But these books also concentrate on young characters whose intense engagement with works of art borders on obsession: in each novel, a character fixates on a single work, experiencing it again and again and again, until it either empties out all meaning or renders up its secrets. "If you watched a movie enough," Mina – the first of these characters – contends, "it became a funnel for the entire universe" (2001, p. 74).

Spiotta describes her first novel, *Lightning Field* (2001), in terms of a sequence of pairings: it is a book "about Los Angeles and alienation. Adultery and loneliness" (Meyer 2008). The novel is told via a series of short takes that variously circle around Mina (a former movie director's daughter, whose mind constantly seeks cinematic precedents), Lorene (her older friend, whose high concept restaurants ride the frivolous surf of LA excess, and provide much of the book's satirical thrust), Michael (Mina's neurodiverse brother and Lorene's ex-lover, who has recently left hospital), and – more briefly – Lisa (Lorene's working-class cleaner). As these paired L and M names suggest, the book's structure is, in part, a matrix designed to move the characters into different couplings and contexts that probe similarities and differences amid their various passions and relative privileges. This design throws up nuances in any single personality as they are moved between these pairings, but Mina – as the book's central character – is stretched further than most. Mina believes truth lies in "in-between places" and she exists "at the seams of things" (Spiotta 2001, p. 20), a tendency that's encapsulated in the balancing act she carries on between the dwindling embers of her marriage and the "alternate fictions" (p. 200) of two separate affairs.

The book's title is taken from an example of "Earth Art," a movement that combined human ingenuity with a yearning for the sublime qualities of nature, and whose key works (appropriately for Spiotta's simulacra-filled novel) were normally exhibited not as objects themselves, but only as photographic reproductions. *Lightning Field*, itself, was designed by Walter De Maria, and completed in the New Mexico desert in 1977, and Spiotta has Michael gloss it as involving: "stainless-steel rods, four hundred of them, equidistant, precise, in a field ... So the delineated space, this grid, is exactly a mile long and a kilometer wide. Four hundred rods out there to attract lightning" (2001, p. 99). As such, the title stands, in part, for the book's characters who are similarly shaped both by the Western spaces they occupy, and the human technologies that have been placed there (especially cinematic technologies), but it also works in more subtle ways, as we can see in the novel's opening sentences:

> Her hands are white and long and lithe. They make elusive, fleeting frames – flirtations of shapes, really – on anything they touch. Anything in the world. I would follow those hands out to the desert.
>
> (2001, p. 7)

De Maria's design is invoked by the desert location and the lightning-like description of Lorene's hands, and such passages establish associative chains that extend the title's resonance outwards, likening the power of another human's touch to a momentary bolt of lightning. Assessing the aftermath of the (often ambivalent) lightning strikes that happen when two characters come into contact becomes a key part of the book's investigation, but Spiotta's initial description of the "fleeting frames" (and her later reference to "lightning edit[s]" [2001, p. 19]), also remind the reader of the ways that our constant exposure to photographic and cinematic technologies have become as crucial to understanding relationships as they have to appreciating De Maria's earth art. This is especially important in terms of the book's probing account of female sexuality, and Mina's gradual discovery of her "need to be filmed" as a subset of the way that "women were in a way programmed to be animated by the attention of others" (pp. 196–197).

Lightning Field was blurbed by DeLillo, and reviews in high-profile publications noted its style and sophistication, but offered more lukewarm assessments of Lisa's role in the book, with the *New York Times* finding her sections "less successful, verging on working-class cliché" (Casey 2001). But if Spiotta's debut prompted measured praise, her second novel – *Eat the Document* (2006) – elicited more fulsome notice. The book was a finalist for the National Book Award (losing out to Richard Powers's *The Echo Maker* [2006]), and it remains her most critically acclaimed work.

On one level, *Eat the Document* clearly borrows its chronological design from *Lightning Field*, inasmuch as both books begin by pairing a scene set relatively near the book's present with one that dives backwards into the past, before spending the rest of the book gradually filling in the gaps between these two moments. This kind of temporal patterning is a common strategy across Spiotta's generation: Wallace famously relies on the same device in *Infinite Jest* (1996), while Jonathan Franzen does something similar in *The Corrections* (2001), and Egan's *A Visit from the Goon Squad* (2010) builds most of its narrative momentum through sudden time leaps that repeatedly pose and complicate the apparently straightforward question "what happened between A and B" (Egan 2011, p. 101). In each of these examples, the temporal gap partly acts as a narrative hook – teasing the reader to keep turning the pages, to find out what happened in the unnarrated gap (why can't Hal communicate? What happened to the ageing Lamberts? Why is Sasha in therapy?) – and this is certainly also true of Spiotta's books. But beyond generating suspense, Spiotta uses these holes in narrative time to throw key moments of change into particular relief. "In all my books," she told *Publisher's Weekly*, "I'm interested in characters who are trying to change, or even just trying see themselves with clarity, because I think change is so hard." Balancing her timelines to present another key pairing – before and after the critical moment of change – helps make the tipping points of her characters' lives particularly apparent as her narratives probe the legacy of key decisions.

In the case of *Eat the Document*, the temporal gap is between the early 1970s and the millennium, as Spiotta juxtaposes the lives of Mary Whittaker and Bobby Desoto – young seventies radicals protesting the military-industrial complex, who accidentally kill a housekeeper when their collective bombs a summer home – with the identities that Mary and Bobby have adopted after decades of being separated and on the run: Caroline (suburban mother to Jason, a Beach Boys fanatic) and Nash (an ineffectual manager of an alternative bookstore). This temporal scope allows Spiotta to both trace the legacy of 1960s counterculture in corporate America, and to complicate questions of intent, responsibility, and guilt, largely through her efforts to limn large systems (in a fashion that recalls Agent Orange in *Underworld* and Orfic in *The Corrections*) by dramatizing the growth of Allegecom, an octopus-like company with tentacles reaching from psychopharmaceuticals to managed communities, and which "put dioxin in everything from PVC pipes to Agent Orange" (2006, p. 206).

This supple dual timeline makes the book a key example of what Mark West calls "the contemporary sixties novel" (2020, p. 210), a vibrant strand of post-1990s American fiction (West identifies forty examples) that return to the past to interrogate the 1960s and its legacy, but it also suggestively overlaps and diverges from DeLillo's example in the 1980s and 1990s. Where DeLillo has turned to the historical record to reimagine interior lives for Lee Harvey Oswald or J. Edgar Hoover, so Spiotta found a template for Whittaker in the life of Katherine Ann Power, who evaded arrest for twenty-three years after a police officer was killed during a bank robbery in 1970. Yet while many of DeLillo's compromised male characters follow their author's ambition in trying to move "out of the realm of the domestic and into that of history" (2005, p. 115), Spiotta follows Whittaker as she makes the opposite move, retreating from history to hide out in the "amnesiac everyday" (p. 198). The task of filling in the gap between the two moments in time falls to Jason – Mary's son, and the character most immersed in domestic suburbia – as he gradually detects that his mother's life contains "eleven years I know nothing about" (p. 88).

Eat the Document's triple braid of central characters across two timelines allows Spiotta to separate out three obsessions that recur through her work: Mary works as a chef; Nash is a filmmaker; and Jason is immersed in music. The latter two subjects carry forward to her third novel, with Spiotta assigning them to Nik and Ada, the two characters whose lives encircle Denise Kranis, *Stone Arabia*'s (2011) 47-year-old protagonist. Denise is one of Spiotta's porous characters; without edges, she flows into the terrible news stories she consumes in 2004 (thanks to this, she's considerably ahead of her time in her fears of a "corona virus" [2012, p. 62]), while the rising tides of the lives of those around her seep in and drown her own concerns. She describes herself as neither "an observer" nor "a participant," but "an absorber of events" (p. 38), and, beyond the 24-hour newsfeed, the events she absorbs are primarily those created by her older brother, Nik. While his day-to-day life is made up of debts and addiction, Nik exists in an alternate reality that's half-driven by the music he records (he is "stuck in some dead-ended wrong-turn rut where experimental music met art met folk met acoustic rock and roll" [p. 96]), and half by the documentary record he fabricates around that music (a chronicle of fake interviews, reviews, and even obituaries). Denise has spent much of her life following (and covering for) her brother, and so the book revives and extends *Lightning Field*'s focus on the brother-sister dynamic. But Nik's eminence in Denise's affections is offset by the return of her daughter, Ada, who begins a documentary devoted to her musician uncle. While Ada's film gradually comes together, Nik writes his own obituary and disappears. As such, Nik acts as a double for his and Denise's father, who "randomly appeared and then one day he was just gone" (p. 5), and these two calculated male disappearances, in turn, serve as a counterpoint to the book's lost females, particularly the young girl who disappears from the Amish community that provides the novel's title, and whose story Denise is entranced by when she watches the cable news.

Denise is left trying to make sense of both her brother's and the girl's disappearance. To try to understand her brother, she must follow the quintessential Spiotta pattern of closing the gap between the present and the past, so she sets out to write an account of their relationship designed to "inch. . . her way back to this exact moment" (Spiotta 2012, p. 200). The bulk of the novel is made up of Denise's "counterchronicle," which attempts to offset Nik's fabulations with an account that locates more honest moorings. This attempt makes much of the book both an experiment in, and an investigation of, narration, simultaneously posing questions about whether saying "something important" is only possible when surrounded by "cynical equivocations" (p. 72), experimenting with different forms (letters, documentary transcripts, fake articles, first- and third-person accounts), and invoking a diary format only to abandon the "sequential, linear, chronological" (p. 105).

Early in the novel, Denise senses that the Internet has replaced memory, and Spiotta's fourth novel extends and historicizes the relationship between changing technologies (videos, phones, internet essays) and bodily capabilities, focusing, in particular, on the senses. *Innocents and Others* contrasts two friends and filmmakers, Meadow Mori (the high art cinéaste, whose films are designed to point back to the filmmaker, and get "her inventiveness noticed" [2016, p. 66]) and Carrie Wexler (the more mainstream artist, who works via genres, "not breaking the form, but pushing it in subtle ways" [p. 69]). But if this suggests that the book is wholly about vision (and it does prominently allude to Laura Mulvey's work on narrative cinema, in its exploration of the female filmmaker's gaze), that assumption is challenged by the soundings of the book's deceptively simple title, which encourages us to think about the senses both in isolation and in combination. The book's title doesn't just carry a sonic pun about what it means to view something through a single sense (*In-a-sense and Others*), but the title's initials also offer a suggestive pairing joining a visual homophone (I/eye) with a sonic exclamation (O/oh). This sonic focus may partly be explained by the fact that Spiotta started using a hearing aid while working on the novel, but while aural puns recur in the book (Meadow Mori is, of course, meant to echo Memento Mori), the importance of sound is most directly explored in the story of Jelly, who temporarily loses her vision following a meningitis infection. Partially modeled on Miranda Grosvenor, the "proto-catfisher" (Treisman 2015) who cold-called famous Hollywood men in the 1980s, Jelly relies on her unusually seductive voice to create intense but unsustainable relationships with the men she calls.

Toward the end of *Lightning Field*, Mina edges toward the title of Spiotta's fourth novel when she reflects that "reality was much more complex than innocence and culpability" (Spiotta 2001, p. 204), and much of the later book is dedicated to probing the interrelated questions of what *innocence, guilt,* and *responsibility* mean in an interlinked society. The book uses its multiple narrative strands to move from the ethics of private relationships – how should we judge Jelly for deceiving the men she calls? – through questions of public exploitation – what is the human cost for the people Meadow films for larger audiences? – to larger historical interrogations of America's culpability – especially in the book's focus on the Kent State Massacre. These tiered investigations, in fact, animate all of Spiotta's novels – whether the focus is on a marriage, a family, or the historical guilt of radicals – as her dyadic fictions look to join the personal and the historical.

SEE ALSO: After Postmodernism; DeLillo, Don; Egan, Jennifer

REFERENCES

Boddy, Kasia. (2019). Making it long: men, women, and the great American novel now. *Textual Practice* 33 (2): 318–337.
Burton, Susan. (2016). The quietly subversive fictions of Dana Spiotta. *The New York Times Magazine* (February 21, 2016). https://www.nytimes.com/2016/02/21/magazine/the-quietly-subversive-fictions-of-dana-spiotta.html (accessed August 24, 2021).
Casey, Maud. (2001). Material girl. Review of *Lightning Field*, by Dana Spiotta. *The New York Times* (September 30, 2001). https://www.nytimes.com/2001/09/30/books/material-girl.html (accessed August 24, 2021).
DeLillo, Don. (2005). *Conversations with Don DeLillo* (ed. Thomas DePietro). Jackson: University of Mississippi Press.
Egan, Jennifer. (2011). *A Visit from the Goon Squad*. New York: Anchor-Random; 1st ed. 2010.
Meyer, Angela. (2008). Interview with Dana Spiotta. *Literary Minded* (July 6, 2008). https://literaryminded.com.au/2008/07/06/dana-spiotta-interview/ (accessed August 24, 2021).
Spiotta, Dana. (2001). *Lightning Field*. New York: Scribner.
Spiotta, Dana. (2006). *Eat the Document*. New York: Scribner.
Spiotta, Dana. (2012). *Stone Arabia*. Edinburgh: Canongate; 1st ed. 2011.
Spiotta, Dana. (2016). *Innocents and Others*. London: Picador.
Stefanakos, Victoria Scanlan. (2021). Dana Spiotta is finding her way – interview with Diana Spiotta. *Publisher's Weekly* (April 30, 2021). https://www.publishersweekly.com/pw/by-topic/authors/profiles/article/86225-dana-spiotta-is-finding-her-way.html (accessed August 24, 2021).
Treisman, Deborah. (2015). Dana Spiotta on the inner lives of con artists. *The New Yorker* (December 7, 2015). https://www.newyorker.com/books/page-turner/fiction-this-week-2015-12-14 (accessed August 24, 2021).
Varvogli, Aliki. (2010). Radical motherhood: narcissism and empathy in Russell Banks's *The Darling* and Dana Spiotta's *Eat the Document*. *Journal of American Studies* 44 (4): 657–673.
West, Mark. (2020). The contemporary sixties novel: post-postmodernism and historigraphic metafiction. *21st-Century US Historical Fiction* (ed. Ruth Maxey), 209–227. Cham, Switzerland: Palgrave.

FURTHER READING

Colton, Aaron. (2019). Dana Spiotta and the novel after authenticity. *Arizona Quarterly* 75 (4): 29–51.
Vermeulen, Pieter. (2015). Analog agency: Dana Spiotta's *Eat the Document*. *Contemporary Literature and the End of the Novel*, 116–125. London: Palgrave.

Stephenson, Neal

ANNA McFARLANE
University of Glasgow, Scotland

Neal Stephenson made his name as one of the most significant writers to come out of the cyberpunk movement in science fiction, a movement that combined the cybernetic order offered by the Internet and the anarchy of its punk, DIY potential for hackers. At the birth of cyberpunk, the Internet was a tool that had only recently emerged from secretive development by the USA's Defense Advanced Research Projects Agency (DARPA) to be opened up to civilian users, and the potential of the Internet to change social structures was being imagined and explored by these writers at the forefront of a new wave of science fiction. Stephenson has continued to explore the ways in which technological breakthroughs might alter society, though he has not confined himself to the potential of the Internet or of artificial intelligence. The son of a professor in electrical engineering, and with a degree in geography and a minor in physics himself, Stephenson is fascinated by the development of individuals with specialist skills, whether those skills be in the arena of coding, engineering, robotics, astrophysics, or theoretical mathematics. His novels tend to explore such scientific specialisms, combining detailed descriptions of real and theoretically possible scientific endeavors (working within the genre known as "hard sf") with explorations of the cultures that grow up around specialist fields working under high-pressure conditions. He has settled in Seattle, giving him a first-hand view of the ways in which technology and its subcultures shape the environments beyond; Seattle is a center for Internet start-ups and tech development, leading some to name it "Silicon Valley North." As well as publishing under his own name, Stephenson has co-authored a number of books with his uncle, the historian George Jewsbury (also known by the pseudonym J. Frederick George). The two have published under the pseudonym Stephen Bury.

Stephenson made his name with *Snow Crash* (1992), which captured cyberpunk's spirit, combining cybernetic society with the cool of punk music. With the possible exception of William Gibson's *Neuromancer* (1984), *Snow Crash* had greater influence in tech circles than any other cyberpunk novel. Where Gibson coined the term "cyberspace" and showed the space of the matrix as a dark night lit up by the neon glow of visualized data, Stephenson imagined an environment rendered more realistic by generations of computer programmers flaunting their skills in the simulation of ever more complex virtual worlds. Stephenson populated his virtual worlds with "avatars," a term which describes the visual representation of a computer user within the game or the virtual space. Taken from Sanskrit by way of Hindi and Urdu, avatar became the standard term for a person's online representation. Stephenson's innovation was also in drawing connections between how people choose to present themselves in cyberspace and their real-world socioeconomic position; this offered a framework for thinking about how socioeconomic inequalities and disadvantages might be replicated, reinscribed, and even reinforced by the Internet. At its birth, techno-utopianism led many to hope that the Internet might be a place of pure, direct democracy where all voices were heard equally and the visual markers that led to discrimination in the real world (sex, race, ability) might be erased, ushering in an egalitarian space that might redress some of the power imbalances of the real world. Stephenson's vision warned against such simplistic correlations between connectivity and equality, showing a virtual world where the rich, or tech savvy, could represent themselves via baroque, unique avatars while those less fortunate have to make do with off-the-shelf images, amalgamations of popular celebrities, that immediately mark them out as an underclass in cyberspace.

As well as having influence through the popularization of the term avatar to denote one's online representation, Stephenson's novel acted as a catalyst for software development. Philip Rosedale, the creator of the online platform *Second Life* developed through Linden Lab, credits *Snow Crash*'s Metaverse with inspiring his vision (Maney 2007). While *Second Life* is now a relic of a bygone Internet era, at the height of its popularity it was considered original and successful, trailblazing some of the features now available to us through social media. The online space was a cross between the computer game *The Sims* (in which users operate characters as they live mundane lives) and modern-day social media, providing a space for people to interact through avatars. The combination of video game and social space ultimately became outdated, but *Second Life* was an important chapter in the development of online spaces toward the social media landscape we now recognize, and *Snow Crash*'s influence on that space is an important example of the two-way street of inspiration between science fiction and science itself, particularly in the tech world.

After the success of *Snow Crash*, Stephenson turned to steampunk, a genre that combines Victorian settings and aesthetics with anachronistic technologies. The relationship between cyberpunk and steampunk was already a close one as William Gibson and Bruce Sterling had co-written *The Difference Engine* (1990) a few years previously, which described the development of a mechanical computer by Charles Babbage and Ada Lovelace, an invention that remained theoretical in our reality. Stephenson's steampunk novel, *The Diamond Age: or, A Young Lady's Illustrated Primer* (1995), continued this trend, helping to establish steampunk as a distinct literary genre while also showing Stephenson's developing interest in the interstices of technology and feminism. *The Diamond Age* imagines the development of an artificially intelligent book that makes use of nanotechnology, designed to teach a young girl how to survive in any environment. Meant for a young aristocrat, the book falls into the hands of Nell, a young girl from a troubled background who finds herself homeless with nothing but her wits, and the primer, to survive. The book leads Nell toward an "interesting" life, which tends to be one based on an independence and pragmatism that allow the primer's reader to deviate from the conformity enforced by society. Nell is Stephenson's first main female protagonist, but the first of many, and the book directly deals with the theme of rape as an occupational hazard for a woman navigating a patriarchal world. While feminism had been explored via cyberpunk, this was primarily through the work of lesser-known feminist writers such as Melissa Scott, whose *Trouble and Her Friends* appeared in 1994. Stephenson's investigation of these themes was unusual in the mainstream, and successfully satirized the concept of a young lady's guide to life by situating Nell in a society that demands "unladylike" behavior to ensure her survival.

Stephenson followed *The Diamond Age* with *Cryptonomicon* (1999), which gives an account of encryption and cryptocurrency through two narrative threads, one featuring Alan Turing and set in the era of World War II, the other set against the backdrop of the Internet bubble of the late 1990s. *Cryptonomicon* explores its scientific and mathematical ideas via historical fiction, while giving the reader a deep dive into the politics of cryptography through detailed explanations of key technical concepts. Stephenson went on to develop his interest in historical science fiction through his Baroque Cycle (2003–2004), a three-volume mash-up of science fiction and historical fiction set primarily between 1660 and 1714. This series gives the deep history of some of the characters and situations he had explored in *Cryptonomicon*, and featured the ancestors of some of the characters from that novel. *Cryptonomicon* and the Baroque Cycle were well received, being awarded the Locus Award (for *Cryptonomicon* and Baroque Cycle volumes 2 and 3) and the Arthur C. Clarke Award (for *Quicksilver* [2003], Baroque Cycle volume 1).

While exploring the possibilities of science, technology, and virtual environments in his fiction, Stephenson also acted as a commentator on technological issues, most significantly through his essay *In the Beginning Was the Command Line*, published as a short book in 1999. The essay traces the origins of the famous antagonism between users of Apple's Macintosh computers and those of Microsoft's personal computers, showing the political and aesthetic considerations that shaped the reception of the operating systems and hardware in different user groups. Stephenson gives a snapshot into the politics of computer use in America at the turn of the millennium. For much of the corporation's history, Apple software could only be run on Apple products, making the company primarily a hardware company. This trend has continued today through the market dominance of the iPhone with its exclusive software packages, non-universal hardware, and operating system, as opposed to the more generic Android products. By contrast, Windows software was not restricted to one make of hardware, so the company did not maintain control over the image of their product as it was experienced by users, through the hardware. The lasting influence of these issues makes Stephenson's essay central to understanding the development of computing and the importance of the social and historical context in shaping the ways we use and think of smartphones today. Stephenson's essay shows how the messy entanglement of market pressures with political and aesthetic ideals shape the adoption of new technologies. In providing this account – by turns personal, historical, and technical – Stephenson shows the talent of the science fiction writer in teasing out the human stories that shape our technologies, and in turn the worlds in which we live. Playing this role as the Internet developed from a new frontier to a centralized system dominated by monopolies (in terms of software, hardware, and the social media companies that have come to dominate online space since the development of Web 2.0), Stephenson played a role that would later fall to post-cyberpunk writer Cory Doctorow, who combines writing novels with activism against Digital Rights Management (DRM) and advocacy for reclaiming the Internet as a commons.

Following the terrorist attacks on the Twin Towers and the Pentagon on September 11, 2001, and the resultant political atmosphere in the USA in the following years, Stephenson moved to address some of the concerns of the contemporary age through *REAMDE* (2011). The novel reads as a techno-thriller, combining corporate espionage with intercontinental travel, kidnapping, and terrorism with North American survivalism. The novel can be read as an example of what Veronica Hollinger refers to as "science fiction realism" (2006, p. 453); while the novel does not contain any imagined technological innovations such as we might expect to see in a science fiction novel, elements of the science fictional bleed into the narrative. Some of the novel's action is set in the virtual game-world of *T'Rain* and, in an aside, Stephenson jokes about his own role in the development of *Second Life*. In China, sweatshops have been set up to mine the virtual gold found in the video game – virtual gold that can then be traded for real currency. Hollinger has said that science fiction realism has taken place in a world where technology is always catching up to reality, and Stephenson seems to recognize this phenomenon in his own writing: in an interview he comments that a phenomenon like gold farming is the kind of thing that makes him want to give up writing science fiction (Sinclair 2011). Once again, Stephenson builds his narrative around a smart female protagonist, an Eritrean refugee named Zula who has been raised in the USA by an independent family of survivalists and entrepreneurs. The novel also introduces Richard "Dodge" Forthrast, who would appear in Stephenson's 2019 novel *Fall, or Dodge in Hell*.

Politically, Stephenson's interest in specialist knowledge has encouraged his novels to explore libertarianism and technocracy. In *REAMDE*, the independence of Zula's family, which includes survivalists in rural America, gives her the skills she needs to protect herself from terrorists and manipulative boyfriends. She is competent in her physicality, whether through hand-to-hand combat or electrical engineering. In *Seveneves* (2015), the destruction of the moon by an unknown "Agent" puts in motion a series of difficult problems that are solved by the crew of the International Space Station (ISS) and a team of scientists launched up to join them, including a fictionalized version of astrophysicist and science communicator Neil deGrasse Tyson. Upon the destruction of the Earth by the hail of moon fragments, a civilian population is also launched into space and the US president, who has traveled into space against international accords, begins to foment rebellion in her search for power. The attempts to establish some form of democracy are met with eye rolls by the scientists in power, who see the practical challenges facing the human race in their exposed orbital position, and the reader's sympathies are with these characters who sacrifice their lives and put all the power of their intellects into planning a realistic, viable future for the population that has been placed in their hands. In portraying the minutiae of the practical problems being solved by the crew of the ISS and the camaraderie developed between these elite specialists, the novel positions democracy as an inappropriate political structure for a tiny population living in a deadly environment.

As well as writing about science and technology, Stephenson has investigated ways in which technology can be put into the service of storytelling, and has been a consultant on the ways in which literature can inform technological development. As the co-founder of the Subutai Corporation, Stephenson oversaw the collaborative writing project eventually published as *The Mongoliad* (2012), which featured fellow science fiction author Greg Bear, recognized as one of the founding authors of cyberpunk through his inclusion in Bruce Sterling's landmark collection *Mirrorshades: A Cyberpunk Anthology* (1986). The Subutai Corporation was formed to explore new ways of using technology to build multi-author multimedia franchises and *The Mongoliad*, set against the backdrop of the Mongol invasions of the thirteenth century, was the first text to be produced under its auspices, being released on a digital platform followed by a print version. The shared universe of the novel encouraged fans to add to the narrative's epic sweep with fan stories published digitally as additions to the main novels. The project also led to a more traditional output, the publication of *The Rise and Fall of D.O.D.O.* (2017) with fellow-*Mongoliad* contributor Nicole Galland, a time-traveling adventure. While experimenting with the use of digital applications to widen the possibilities of literary forms, Stephenson has also acted as an adviser to Blue Origin, an aerospace company founded by Amazon's Jeff Bezos, and is a futurist for virtual reality company Magic Leap.

Stephenson's use of science in his novels and his willingness to act as a commentator on scientific issues, an adviser on science-based start-up companies, and his use of technology in developing experimental works of fiction have led Jay Clayton to describe his work as a means of bridging the cultures of the arts and the sciences. Drawing on C.P. Snow's diagnosis that the academy had split science from the humanities, acting as a barrier to holistic imaginative thinking, Clayton claims that Stephenson's work goes some way to redressing those problems (Clayton 2002). However, Mark McGurl has gone on to argue that Stephenson's work shows the tension between science and the humanities in institutional spaces. Pointing out Stephenson's close associations with the academy, McGurl quotes the biographical blurb from *Snow Crash* – "Neal Stephenson issues from a clan of rootless, itinerant hard-science and engineering professors (mostly Pac 10, Big 10, and Big 8 with the occasional wild strain of Ivy)" – and points out that his first novel, *Big U* (1984), is set on a fictional American university campus (McGurl 2005, p. 122). McGurl's analysis identifies Stephenson's work as part of a wider postwar trend in American literature that saw an ever-strengthening relationship between literature and the academy. McGurl goes so far as to argue that Stephenson's commitment to science and technology is a kind of "technicity as ethnicity," the use of technology as a way of identifying and celebrating a cultural group – that of the white nerd (p. 123). This observation is taken to an extreme conclusion via Stephenson's *Seveneves* in which the seven "eves," the women who will give their genetic material to restart humanity, end up developing seven different races defined by the scientific specialisms and personality traits of their respective eves. Reading this as simply a means of dramatizing the antagonism, or the possibility of bridging, the "two cultures" of the humanities and the sciences ignores the ways in which Stephenson's work engages with the American culture wars that are ongoing, arguably reaching an unfortunate apotheosis in the presidency of Donald Trump. The polarized politics that has seen part of American society succumb to a rabid anti-intellectualism must be read as the backdrop for Stephenson's work which, as McGurl rightly argues, identifies with an academic, scientific sensibility. This sensibility is depicted as aspirational, in that those who belong to it have the skills and independence lacking in the rest of society. This class is qualified to take the role of the adult in the room, shepherding the rest of society through dark and dangerous times. Stephenson's science is, in some ways, intolerant of views and lifestyles that do not conform to its apparent pragmatism, but also offers hope that rationality (inextricably associated here with technical skill) will triumph in humanity's long history.

SEE ALSO: The Culture Wars; Cyberpunk; Gibson, William; Post-9/11 Narratives

REFERENCES

Clayton, Jay. (2002). Convergence of the two cultures: a geek's guide to contemporary literature. *American Literature* 74: 807–831.

Hollinger, Veronica. (2006). Stories about the future: from patterns of expectation to *Pattern Recognition*. *Science Fiction Studies* 33 (3): 452–472.

Maney, Kevin. (2007). The king of alter egos is surprisingly humble guy. Creator of *Second Life*'s goal? Just to reach people. *USA Today* (February 5, 2007).

McGurl, Mark. (2005). The program era: pluralisms of postwar American fiction. *Critical Inquiry* 32 (1): 102–129.

Sinclair, Brendan. (2011). *Snow Crash* author on the state of storytelling in games. *Gamespot* (October 11, 2011). https://www.gamespot.com/articles/snow-crash-author-on-the-state-of-storytelling-in-games/1100-6339423/ (accessed July 11, 2021).

Stephenson, Neal. (1992). *Snow Crash*. New York: Bantam Books.

Stephenson, Neal. (1999). *In the Beginning Was the Command Line*. New York: Avon Books.

FURTHER READING

Haney, William S. (2006). Neal Stephenson's *Snow Crash*: humans are not computers. In: *Cyberculture, Cyborgs and Science Fiction: Consciousness and the Posthuman*, 113–130. Amsterdam: Rodopi.

Lewis, Jon. (ed.). (2006). *Tomorrow Through the Past: Neal Stephenson and the Project of Global Modernization*. Newcastle, UK: Cambridge Scholars Publishing.

McFarlane, Anna. (2016). Neal Stephenson's REAMDE: a critique of gamification. *Foundation: The International Review of Science Fiction* (March): 24–36.

Vint, Sherryl. (2007). Jack Womack and Neal Stephenson: the world and the text and the world in the text. In: *Bodies of Tomorrow: Technology, Subjectivity, Science Fiction*, 138–170. Toronto: University of Toronto Press.

Stone, Robert

CHRISTINE GROGAN
University of Delaware, USA

During a half-century career, Robert Stone published eight well-received novels – two of which spawned feature-length films – two collections of potent short stories, a memoir of the 1960s, and a body of journalism. Questioning the role of man in contemporary American society, these works hold up a mirror to the changing social, political, and moral milieu of the second half of the twentieth century, from the tumultuous 1960s Vietnam era to the dawn of the twenty-first, with its uncertainties of post 9/11. His literary reputation rests on his novels, which are often opuses, peopled with America's underclass: surprisingly well-read and versed in classical music, these alcoholics, schizophrenics, murderers, psychopaths, drifters, drug smugglers and addicts, corrupt cops, and clergyman converge, collide, and sometimes crash right into each other. In the dense, ambitious, and oftentimes violent plots, the main characters seek out or find themselves engrossed in extreme experiences in exotic lands, from drug trading in Vietnam and gun running in Central America to solo circumnavigation and voodoo trance rituals in the Caribbean. An artist of the grand scale, Stone took for his canvas the topics they say one should never talk about – religion and politics. He discussed them at length, oftentimes together. A rolling Stone, he made it a point to be at the places where history was being made, capturing in his literature the dangerous external environments which often paled in comparison to the threatening battlegrounds of one's own imagination. The human condition, according to Stone, is plagued with corrupting forces in a flawed world absconded by God. A contemporary of Raymond Carver and writing in the narrative lineage of Melville, Conrad, and Hemingway, Stone acknowledged literary debts to such forebears as Fitzgerald, Steinbeck, and Dos Passos. His commanding fiction, almost always rendered from a third-person point of view and casting male protagonists, is written in the realist mode with surreal, at times hallucinogenic, elements. Riffs of drunken and drugged musings punctuate the narratives. His rigorous craftsmanship is marked by a sharpness of characterization, sure use of dialogue, and elegiac descriptive passages. To accomplish such technical masterpieces, he devoted years to writing each novel. Like Conrad, Stone was a firm believer that "fiction must justify itself in every line" (Woods 1985, p. 49).

Before becoming an internationally respected author, Stone hailed from humble and rather desperate origins. Born on August 21, 1937, in Brooklyn, New York, Robert Anthony Stone was raised by a mentally-ill mother, Gladys Catherine Grant, who worked for a time as a schoolteacher and who had him when she was forty-three years old; his father, C. Homer Stone, a New Haven Railroad worker, was wholly absent. His parents never married. Admitting that his "early life was very strange" (Woods 1985, p. 34), Stone attributes his narrative impulse to the "curious luck to be raised by a schizophrenic" (p. 43). It gave him a "tremendous advantage in understanding the relationship of language to reality" (p. 43); "life wasn't providing [coherent] narrative so [he] had to" (p. 43). During the years his mother was institutionalized, Stone was placed at the mercy of St. Ann's school at Lexington and Seventy-Seventh Street in Manhattan, being a boarder from just after his sixth birthday until he was almost ten. There he read widely, studied Latin, and started to write sci-fi. His experience in the Roman Catholic orphanage run by the Marist Brothers, where even the military could not compete with Prefect Brother Francis when it came to violence, had a far-reaching impact on Stone's work. This formative and scarring experience is fictionalized in his 1987 "Absence of Mercy," the most autobiographical piece he authored along with a nonfiction piece he wrote for the *Architectural Digest* (1996). Despite a period of intense Catholic devotion during his early teens, Stone claimed to have converted to atheism at the age of 17. His ambivalent moral outlook and Catholic guilt permeate almost all of his novels and short stories in which his characters, some of whom are lapsed Catholics, embody the religious longings of their creator. And, like Stone, they are men in which the flesh is weak but the spirit is willing. These characters, many of whom embark on physical and spiritual journeys, sometimes use politics as a vehicle to express moral vision.

Upon being released from the hospital, Stone's mother lost her teaching job, and subsequently was no longer able to get a lease. The two embarked on many trips that lasted until money ran out (to Chicago twice, New Mexico, and Montreal), introducing a wanderlust that would persist well into his adult years. In addition to initiating a desire for travel and a romance with bus stations, Stone's mother also instilled in him a respect for literature. In fact, she sent one of his earliest stories, "The City Is the Night," out for publication. Although *The New Yorker* rejected it, they encouraged him to send more of his writing. In *Prime Green* (2007), Stone's memoir of the 1960s, he calls that rejection slip his "proudest possession": "It was the form demurrer sent out to disappointed contributors to *The New Yorker*, as elegantly worded as anything the magazine published at that time. What made that familiar totem of obscurity an artifact of such sweet promise to me was the fact that some unknown hand had inscribed a three-word message in one corner of the standard slip: 'Try us again.' That brief extra message would serve me as an anthem for many years to come" (2007, p. 29).

It was not, however, until quite some time had passed that Stone would try his hand at publishing again. A member of a West Side, mostly Irish, street gang, he was expelled from St. Ann's in May of his senior year because of his atheism and earned his GED while in the Navy. During his three-year cruise, Stone's journeys ranged from Western Europe to Africa and Antarctica. He saw combat when working as a radioman assigned to the Suez Canal to protect and extract American civilians during the crisis there. After military service, he worked at various, low-paying jobs while taking classes at New York University, notably the narrative writing workshop taught by M.L. "Mack" Rosenthal. At the age of 24, while writing copy for low-end furniture, Stone reread *The Great Gatsby* (1925) and was inspired to write his own novel: "I understood patterns in life. I figured, I can't sell this understanding, or smoke it, so I will write a novel" (Woods 1985, p. 27). In short order, he got married in 1959, ventured with his bride to New Orleans, had a daughter, and then moved cross-country to California on a Stegner Fellowship at Stanford. Although defined apart from all groups, he befriended Ken Kesey and other beatniks and partook in the merry prankstering, psychedelic, and countercultural scene while in San Francisco. From 1962–1964, Stone was a regular at the Perry Lane parties in Menlo Park. In 1963, he had exploratory surgery; instead of finding a brain tumor, however, a minor neurological disorder that affected his vision was discovered. By 1964, he returned to New York with his wife and two children, Deidre and Ian, to write his novel. Because they were married and had children very young, Stone and wife Janice (née Burr) were permissive, even encouraging, of extramarital affairs. One of his such liaisons resulted in a daughter, Emily Burton, who remained behind in California. She may have served as a model for the illegitimate Christopher Lucas in his sixth novel *Damascus Gate* and the neglected Rowan Smart in the novella "Bear and His Daughter" (1997).

The fellowship to Stanford was awarded to Stone on the basis of the beginning of what would become his debut novel, *A Hall of Mirrors*, published on his 30th birthday (August 21, 1967). Stating he learned how to be a novelist during the course of writing the novel, Stone drew inspiration for his plot from the nine months he and Janice lived in the French Quarter. Set on the brink of the Civil Rights Movement in the segregated Deep South, his first novel questions America's claims to being the land of opportunity as so many live in deplorable conditions. Made into the film *WUSA* (1970) starring Paul Newman, it also established themes that would characterize his work, namely that the promises of life, liberty, and the pursuit of happiness are mere illusions.

After the publication of *A Hall of Mirrors* and a move to London, Stone went to Vietnam in mid-1971 for a couple of months, in part as a correspondent for an English countercultural weekly named *Ink*. While there, he gathered material for his second book, *Dog Soldiers* (1974) as he witnessed Vietnamization and investigated the thriving drug trade and black market. Although a Vietnam novel, only the first chapters are set in southeast Asia; the others take place in California and the fantasy terrain of the American Southwest. This drug-trade-gone-wrong proves to be as unsuccessful as the Vietnam War. The motive of all the main actors is striking: profit, at best, no reason, at worst. But if the causes are unclear, the effects are palpable. Even the noncombatants contain latent criminal capacities and are shells of the men and women they could have been. *Dog Soldiers*, made into the film *Who'll Stop the Rain* (1978) starring Nick Nolte and Tuesday Weld, reveals that fighting a war to stop the spread of communism and to preserve democracy were a front for the real reason the war was fought: a few gained at the expense of many.

Shortly after the fall of Saigon, Stone went to Central America, a region he returned to on several occasions, on somewhat of an impulse: in March 1976, he was in Tuscaloosa giving a reading at the University of Alabama; the next day, he caught a plane to Honduras. There he witnessed ill-governed countries whose people were exploited and infected by American influence. Set in Tecan, a fictional Central American country on the eve of a revolution, *A Flag for Sunrise* (1981), covers ten days in late January and early February of 1976. Considered to be emblematic of Stone's oeuvre, his third novel shows that even the good guys are bad and tainted by transnational corporate capitalism. Launched with front-page coverage in *The New York Times Book Review*, *A Flag for Sunrise* cemented Stone's reputation as a preeminent voice of his time.

For his fourth novel, Stone turned his gaze to the hills of Hollywood, whose deceptions he knew firsthand from his misadventures in movie making. Covering three days in the life of a cocaine-addicted film writer in the throes of a midlife crisis, *Children of Light* (1986) follows his brief but intense time on the set of a screenplay he wrote based on Kate Chopin's *The Awakening* (1899). He ushers in the final descent into madness of a schizophrenic actress who has recently stopped taking her medicine in the hopes of delivering a more convincing performance. The novel ends with a dizzying display of life imitating art. In this perhaps least characteristic work, Stone seems to draw from his mother's illness, in which the actress's hallucinations, endearingly called "Long Friends," he was well acquainted with. In this work, Stone expresses his uncertainty that an artist can represent the truth while inherently flirting with artifice.

If Stone's *Children of Light* gestures towards questions of authenticity, his fifth novel,

Outerbridge Reach (1991) explicitly meditates on the nature of the real. Following in the footsteps of the real-life Donald Crowhurst, the Naval-Academy graduate – but sorely underqualified sailor – Owen Browne embarks on a maiden voyage around the world in an effort to satiate his heroic longings, which trace their origins to his years in Vietnam. In an unfortunate series of events, both the boat and Browne begin to come unhinged. He spends a few days literally and figuratively going in circles, radioing in false coordinates but keeping score in his log. A novel which on one level is about a sailboat race reveals deeper, darker truths about the human psyche: losers are left with little in the race to succeed in a winner-take-all, materialistic society. The commercial underpinnings of the American Dream are exposed as false promises predicated on greed and fraud.

The search for Truth (capital T) persists in Stone's sixth novel, *Damascus Gate* (1998), set in the political and religious hotspot of fin de siècle Jerusalem. For this research-intensive tour-de-force, Stone took two extended trips to the Middle East. He spent time in the Mishkenot Sha'ananim, a cultural center in the Israeli section of the city, and a few days on the Palestinian side; toured the Gaza Strip; visited where the Jordan River flows into the Sea of Galilee; went to Golan Heights and the Syrian border; climbed Masada, a mountaintop fortress in the Judean Desert; and swam in the Dead Sea. Roaming the complex terrain and labyrinth of the land more hostile than holy, most of Stone's large cast are afflicted with the "Jerusalem Syndrome," a condition used to describe religious extremists who go to the Middle East on largely delusional divine missions. When a conspiracy to blow up the mosque on the Temple Mount comes to a head, spiritual unrest and political violence erupt. Despite its potential to unite humanity, religion is shown to be a divisive force responsible for death and destruction. Questions of identity and fidelity loom large, and, even though the main character comes to doubt his doubt by the novel's end, there is no sense of reconciliation or redemption as the curtain closes on twentieth-century apocalyptic Jerusalem.

Stone takes a more literal interpretation of lost souls in his *Bay of Souls* (2003), as the main female character thinks she actually lost hers. This novel takes the reader to the fictionalized Caribbean island of Saint Trinity, which bears an uncanny resemblance to Haiti, a place Stone visited with one of his mistresses. In the fictionalized version, an unhappily married professor of English has an affair with a poly-sci professor whose brother has recently died. The plot is set in motion when she invites him to join her in Saint Trinity, her hometown, to take care of her brother's affairs. As in *A Flag for Sunrise*, this mission proves to be another foray into corrupt Latin American politics. *Bay of Souls* reinforces Stone's theme of misconceptions: as the veil lifts on the femme fatale, the male lead realizes that without a soul, "everything between us would be illusion" (2003, p. 121).

Continuing his exploration of adultery, Stone's last novel, *Death of a Black-Haired Girl* (2013), attests that he had command of his craft to the very end. In this psychological thriller set in New England, another seemingly happily married professor who is about to welcome a second child has been entertaining an affair with one of his students who recently wrote an article attacking pro-lifers. As foreshadowed in the title, the girl is murdered – right outside of the professor's house shortly after he tried to end the relationship. Regardless of who was driving the car that killed her, Stone implies that many carry the guilt. Stone inflicts the girl's father with terminal COPD, contracted when responding to the World Trade Center on September 11. Like his creator at this time, the bereaved father is dealing with a terminal lung disease and seems helpless in the face of guilt and grief.

One of the last American authors to be paid a salary by his publishers, Stone garnered many literary accolades, notably the National Book Award, a Guggenheim Fellowship, and the Mildred and Harold Strauss Living from the American Academy of Arts and Letters. He taught at a number of US universities, including Johns Hopkins, University of Hawaii, Manoa, Princeton, and Amherst College, the last of which granted him an honorary degree, the only college degree he ever received. Despite his many accomplishments, Stone acknowledges in one of the last pieces he wrote that his readership, although faithful, has been rather small and scholarly attention, rather sparse. In his final *ars poetica* addressed to his beloved readers, "Coda" (2020) is a portrait of an artist accepting his imminent death, seemingly going gentle into that good night after a life of hard living. Longing for the divine grace that escapes so many of his characters, Stone admits that he has nothing to offer but "dread reverence" (2020, p. 360). He states that he has hope and that "the promise of hope, of life against death, of edges and surviving, were what I wanted to write about" (p. 360). Wishing he had done more, Stone regrets the time he wasted on drugs and alcohol. A long-time chain-smoker, drinker, and drugger, he spent four stints in rehab, his longest sobriety, six months. Although he kicked his smoking habit in 1982, too much damage had been done to his lungs. He succumbed to chronic obstructive pulmonary disease on January 10, 2015, at the age of 77. Despite his many affairs, he was still married to Janice, his "first reader." Her voice is central to Madison Smart Bell's 2020 *Child of Light: A Biography of Robert Stone*. And yet, as Bell himself admits, if one really wants to know about Stone's inner life, one should read his fiction.

SEE ALSO: Carver, Raymond; Contemporary Fictions of War; Millennial Fiction; Post-9/11 Narratives

REFERENCES

Stone, Robert. (2003). *Bay of Souls*. Boston: Houghton Mifflin.
Stone, Robert. (2007). *Prime Green: Remembering the Sixties*. New York: Harper Perennial.
Stone, Robert. (2020). Coda. In: *The Eye You See With: Selected Nonfiction* (ed. Madison S. Bell), 359–362. Boston: Houghton Mifflin Harcourt.
Woods, William C. (1985). Robert Stone: the art of fiction no. 90. *The Paris Review* (Winter): 26–57. https://www.theparisreview.org/interviews/2845/the-art-of-fiction-no-90-robert-stone (accessed August 9, 2021).

FURTHER READING

Bell, Madison S. (2020). *Child of Light: A Biography of Robert Stone*. New York: Doubleday.
Heath, William. (ed.) (2016). *Conversations with Robert Stone*. Jackson: University Press of Mississippi.
Solotaroff, Robert. (1994). *Robert Stone*. New York: Twayne.
Stephenson, Gregory. (2002). *Understanding Robert Stone*. Columbia: University of South Carolina Press.

Story Cycles

JENNIFER J. SMITH
North Central College, USA

The short story cycle – also called the novel-in-stories, linked stories, short story sequence, and short story composite – has been a richly generative genre for contemporary American writers. The short story cycle is, at its most essential, a volume of stories that are simultaneously interrelated and independent. These volumes are cyclical in so far as themes, situations, characters, and/or settings recur and resonate across disparate stories. Writers – diverse in artistic styles and backgrounds – including Julia Alvarez, Sandra Cisneros, Stuart Dybek, Jennifer Egan, Louise Erdrich, Tim O'Brien, Annie Proulx, Elizabeth Strout, and Amy Tan have all published cycles, and these story cycles are often their most famous and studied works. However, within literary criticism and the popular imagination, the story cycle remains on the margins as these works tend to get read as novels or collections, as their subtitles (for instance, Erdrich's *Love Medicine: A Novel* [1984]) often reveal. The recent proliferation of cycles is an extension of a longstanding tradition of such volumes that dates to the nineteenth century and includes Caroline Kirkland, Sarah Orne Jewett, Sherwood Anderson, Eudora Welty, and many others. The cycle's loose structure, characterized by a tension between stories' individual autonomy and their relation to the whole, allows the form to explore the contingency that characterizes so much of modern and contemporary life in the United States and beyond. The gaps that occur within cycles reflect the uneasy but persistent pulls of pluralism and individuality that shape contemporary American culture and expression.

Scholars of the short story cycle have debated the meaning and limits of the genre since Forrest Ingram's 1971 monograph, *Representative Short Story Cycles of the Twentieth Century: Studies in a Literary Genre*. In attending to the composition history of the stories and cycles, as well as their effects on readers, Ingram's study remains foundational in scholarship on the genre, especially in US literary studies. He initiated the term shortstory cycle, which scholars Susan Garland Mann, Rocío Davis, James Nagel, Mark Whalan, Michelle Pacht, and Benjamin Forkner continue to use. Some opt for the hyphen, suggesting the constitutive element of the short story to the larger cycle. Others have argued for composite novel (Dunn and Morris 1995), short story sequence (Luscher 1989 and Kennedy 1995), and short story composite (Lundén 1999). If genre exists on a spectrum, as Cathy Day, author of the story cycle *The Circus in Winter* (2004), has suggested, each of these terms privileges landing closer on that spectrum to novel or short story (Day 2011). Looking at a particular author's cycles illuminates the ways in which the elements of the genre cohere and create gaps.

When Elizabeth Strout released *Olive, Again: A Novel* in 2019, the book was a highly anticipated and well-received sequel to the best-selling and acclaimed 2008 cycle *Olive Kitteridge*, which was turned into a lauded HBO miniseries in 2014. Each book contains thirteen standalone yet interdependent short stories. *Olive Kitteridge* and *Olive, Again* are archetypal short story cycles in many ways. Strout often published the stories separately in magazines and journals prior to their inclusion in the cycle. She writes in a realist tradition, mirroring the characters' plain-spoken manner and drawing compassion from quotidian tragedies and triumphs. The stories are set largely but not exclusively in the small town of Crosby, Maine. They feature moments and characters that gain resonance as the reader encounters those same scenes or characters across discrete stories. The temporal settings span the title character's life, creating a portrait of late-twentieth-century American life. The stories center on a protagonist whose point of view sets a tone for the pieces throughout, and yet several stories feature the title character as only a minor character and occasionally not at all. The stories focus on the internal lives of characters who often have trouble verbalizing their needs and desires. Stifled communication and emotional repression within a tight-knit community and even family are common themes within cycles that extend from the realism of not just Jewett and Anderson but also mid-century cycles including Evan S. Connell's *Mrs. Bridge* (1959) and *Mr. Bridge* (1969), also a sequel of short story cycles, and the short stories of Raymond Carver.

Strout's cycles are atypical in several ways too. First, they sold well, and the subtitle of novel suggests the conventional wisdom that novels sell better than short stories. The reality of the marketplace, which often requires categorizing by genre, helps account for the number of subtitles that appear alongside story cycles in general (novel in stories, stories, and fiction are other common subtitles). Second, the central figure is a middle-aged and then elderly math teacher; more commonly, cycles center on a young person's coming of age, whether that be Ernest Hemingway's Nick Adams or Sandra Cisneros's Esperanza Cordero. Olive is smart, often ungenerous and petty, pudgy, sexual without being sexy in a conventional sense, and opinionated without apology. Olive is also vulnerable, kind, and desperate for connection. Olive is not the typical protagonist of story cycles or most other popular narratives. Strout's cycle also diverges from many others by being funny. The stories – and Olive's judgments and behaviors – offer sustained hilarity in a way that few books of fiction, of any genre, do. In an essay on Olive Kitteridge, Rachel Lister builds on Sara Ahmed's theory that although happiness is often imagined as teleological, it is, in reality, often momentary and provisional. Lister argues that "The short story cycle is in many ways the ideal form for subverting hegemonic notions of happiness. By presenting readers with a series of beginnings and endings, it disconcerts preconceptions of character, time, and plot, decentering protagonists" (2016, p. 50). Lister traces how Olive is happy in ways that do not conform to conventional ideas of happiness; she is not giddy or even satisfied. Instead, she is contemplative, serious, and open to growth, even if it is incremental.

Most significantly, Strout's cycles diverge from many other story cycles in that they are paired; a larger narrative emerges across the two volumes, which troubles the primacy of a single book, a subtitle, or the marketing of a text. There is precedent for this: William Faulkner's Yoknapatawpha novels and stories form a cycle; Louise Erdrich's *Love Medicine* initiates a linked tetralogy of books; and Cristina García considers her story cycle *Dreaming in Cuban* (1992) the first of a trilogy on Cuban lives in exile. In a 2016 special section in the *Journal of the Short Story in English* called "Roundtable: Affect, the Short Story, and the Cycle," Jane Thrailkill relates,

> I've been thinking about a short story mode that includes a significant "pause" that exists outside the diegetic frame: I refer to the sequel. Pairing two stories in this way produces an intriguing extra-textual gap, in which a single work – which upon initial publication is presented as complete, giving no indication of an impending follow-up – is then finished or concluded by a second. The appearance of a sequel creates a "bookend" effect, with the production of new, temporal spaces between the two, existing both in the reader's world (e.g. one year between publication dates) and, discrepantly, in the story world . . . To put this a slightly different way: a sequel doesn't just conclude the original story; it produces a phantom novel.
>
> (Hogan *et al.* 2016, pp. 176–177)

Strout's cycles create phantom narratives not just within the intervening years between cycles but also the years that predate both cycles, as the stories sometimes flash to previous figures and encounters that do not take place in the narrative present of any story. For Olive and her husbands, they often flashback to moments from earlier relationships that shape the current ones. Between stories and across these volumes, phantom novels and stories appear, replicating the way memories of the past intercede in the present. The story cycle is especially attuned to capturing the temporality of memory with its gaps and connections.

Paul Ardoin and Fiona McWilliam (2016) outline how critics are still questioning what makes the genre distinct: "Is it the repeated appearance of a character across stories that makes a collection a cycle? Is it a unifying theme or location?" (2016, p. 22) Strout's cycles nicely demonstrate this challenge; most of the stories concern Olive but not all, and most are set in Crosby but not all. Instead, Ardoin and McWilliam turn to the affective work of the cycle: "perhaps a short story cycle can be defined by its stickiness. Perhaps the stories of a cycle impress upon the reader and upon each other. Perhaps this brand of impression is depicted inside a story. Perhaps an impression is created at the meeting of the reader and a character, or a theme, or a location. Perhaps the trace left by that meeting gains in meaning through repetition – another story, another instance, another meeting" (p. 22). As we encounter Olive again and again, her characterization gains layers and complexity. Her prickliness and her depth stick with us between and beyond the stories. In the same "Roundtable," Justine Murison examines "the intricate relation of the short story form to affect," arguing that "The affective work in the narrative, including its humor, and the generic work of the short story are inextricably linked. To put this differently, in its very shortness, a short story often depends upon affective loops and leaps in place of exhaustive detail: there simply is no room to spin a totality" (Hogan et al. 2016, p. 168). *Olive Kitteridge* and *Olive, Again* do not aim for totality but take pleasure in the loops and leaps between stories.

Thrailkill identifies such gaps as the particular narrative province of the short story and the cycle: "The short story is good at leveraging gaps ... The interspersing of slices, pauses, snapshots, and places of rest is arguably the sine qua non of this short narrative form" (Hogan et al. 2016, p. 176). Gerald Lynch, whose prolific scholarship often focuses on the story cycle in Canadian fiction, agrees: "such gaps throughout short story cycles enable much creative work between writer and reader (contra the continuities of the conventional novel) and ... imply a metafictive strategy at work in such a narrative structure" (Hogan et al. 2016, p. 179). Readers of story cycles often trace how the action or motivation in one story can be linked to another; sometimes this connection is made explicit by author and sometimes not. For Lynch, "each story gains meaning in the context of the whole cycle, which does not imply any lack as a discrete story but rather highlights the advantage of the story cycle form." As is often the case when trying to describe the particularities of the genre, Lynch turns to an analogy: "The stories of the cycle, like plucked guitar strings responding to others of its strings, gain much distinctively in resonating not only within the whole cycle but from proximity to – in relation to – the other stories, individually and collectively, whatever their place in the cycle" (Hogan et al. 2016, p. 191). In scholarship and reviews, other analogies abound: reading story cycles is like putting an iPod on shuffle, playing a game, completing a puzzle, looking through a kaleidoscope, or making a quilt.

Strout's cycles use one of the most common linking devices: a shared setting. Sometimes these settings are a shared urban geography, as in the neighborhoods of Chicago mapped out in Sandra Cisneros's *The House on Mango Street* (1984) and *Woman Hollering Creek* (1991) or Stuart Dybek's *The Coast of Chicago* (1990) and *I Sailed with Magellan* (2003). In these cycles, Cisneros and Dybek restrict the geographic terrain of the city to a street or neighborhood, and they focus on the experiences of Mexican and Polish immigrants, respectively. For instance, *I Sailed with Magellan* follows Perry Katzek through the turbulent decades of the mid-twentieth century. A modern-day George Willard or Nick Adams – complete even with a typewriter in a near-empty city loft – Perry eulogizes a vanishing industrialism that brought his family and so many Polish immigrants to the city. These Chicago-based cycles often use an artist's coming of age as a linking device making them akin to the *Künstlerroman*, with the cycle's form implying the fits and starts that distinguish an artist's maturation. The vignettes of Cisneros's cycle trace how the setting of this Mexican American community shapes Esperanza Cordero's artistic and personal development. The setting and character interconnect to create cohesion but not unity across stories. Bill Savage locates the power of Dybek's stories in their spatial and temporal setting: "His characters inhabit and interpret the landscape of ethnic urban villages transformed by postwar deindustrialization, white flight, neighborhoods obliterated for urban renewal, and familiar streetscapes bulldozed for expressways" (2007, p. 536). A similar sentiment characterizes Cisneros's Mango Street, which seems a snapshot in an ever-changing urban topography. Other cycles that focus on a shared urban geography include Gloria Naylor's *The Women of Brewster Place* (1983), Edward P. Jones's *Lost in the City* (1992), and Mark Chiusano's *Marine Park* (2014).

More common than city settings are small towns. Following in the tradition of Anderson's *Winesburg, Ohio* (1919) are a number of authors who explicitly cite the influence of that modernist archetypal cycle on theirs: Russell Banks's *Trailerpark* (1981), Cathy Day's *The Circus in Winter* (2004), Rebecca Barry's *Later, at the Bar: A Novel in Stories* (2007), and Donald Ray Pollock's *Knockemstiff* (2008). In these story cycles, the authors explore small-town spaces and the characters that occupy them. Main Streets, dive bars, and local newspapers recur, and these cycles often depict characters whose economic livelihoods have been diminished because of deindustrialization and the rise of substance abuse. Following in Anderson's footsteps, these cycles address the frustrated dreams and unexpressed desires that haunt these small-town characters. Although these writers all cite Anderson as an influence, the tradition of small-town cycles begins much earlier with the regionalist sketchbooks of the nineteenth century, which includes works by Washington Irving, Caroline Kirkland, Eliza Buckminster Lee, and others. Annie Proulx's *Close Range: Wyoming Stories* (1999) and Ann Beattie's *The State We're In: Maine Stories* (2015) take the state as their spatial settings and, following in the sketchbook vein, explore everyday life and internal conflicts through local language and cultural practices.

Another common linking device in contemporary story cycles is linking the volume through a single family. Susan Minot's *Monkeys* (1986) follows the children of a large Catholic family in a series of chronological stories. According to James Nagel, Minot "insisted on having the word 'novel' deleted from her contract." He describes the book as "a brilliant series of minimalist stories about salient moments in the lives of the Vincent family" (2001, p. 9). Linking stories through the experiences and points of view of a particular family allows these writers to paint portraits of the time and experiences of subsets of American culture, as in Minot's cycle, which explores Irish Catholic life in South Boston during the 1960s and 1970s. Julia Alvarez's semi-autobiographical *How the Garcia Girls Lost Their Accents* (1991) explores the same time period but through the lens of a Dominican Catholic family fleeing Rafael Trujillo's regime. Alvarez presents the stories in reverse chronological order so that the stories begin with the title characters as political exiles living middle-class lives in the United States and then traces backward to their time as the affluent members of a prominent family in the Dominican Republic. Stephanie Lovelady argues that the "gaps and loops" of the cycle's temporal structure reflect "the fractures and messy overlaps in their narrators' attempts to make sense of the crossing between childhood and adulthood and between one country and another, either their own or someone else's" (2005, p. 20). Cycles centered on family often explore pivotal moments that transform their family members and affect them in divergent, often contradictory ways. In so doing, these cycles mirror how families experience the same situations and relationships but perceive and reckon with them very differently.

This conflict between shared experiences and its individual effects is especially pronounced in cycles about migrations. In these, family remains a prominent linking device. Amy Tan's *The Joy Luck Club* (1989), for instance, structures the stories around four pairs of mothers and daughters who are all experiencing the move from China to the United States in profoundly distinct ways between generations. Generational conflict is often central to story cycles that focus on family and migration. However, Lisa Lowe cautions that generational readings tend to universalize ethnic literatures:

> interpreting Asian American culture exclusively in terms of the master narrative of generational conflict and filial relation essentializes Asian American culture, obscuring the particularities and incommensurabilities of class, gender, and national diversities among Asians. The reduction of the cultural politics of racialized ethnic groups, like Asian Americans, to first-generation/second-generation struggles displaces social differences into a privatized familial opposition.
>
> (1996, p. 63)

Instead of privileging the vertical, hierarchical model of family, Lowe looks to horizontal affiliations to show individual responses to larger patterns of migrations within a generation.

The five interconnected stories that constitute Maxine Hong Kingston's *The Woman Warrior: Memoirs of a Girlhood among Ghosts* (1975) make inter- and intra-generational conflict in the context of migrations a theme but do not structure the stories around individual family members, as Alvarez and Tan do. In his book *The Contemporary American Short-Story Cycle: The Ethnic Resonance of Genre*, Nagel contends that "The short-story cycle in modern American fiction is patently multicultural, deriving, perhaps, both from ethnic cross-fertilization within the literary community and from a shared legacy reaching back to ancient oral traditions in virtually every society throughout the world" (2001, pp. 4–5). The cycle's form, with its multiple (and often competing) narrative points of view, mirrors divergent responses to migrations. No two characters experience the moves to and from the United States the same, and the cycle's form makes this explicit by giving us their accounts. Rocío G. Davis, in *Transcultural Reinventions: Asian American and Asian Canadian Short-Story Cycles*, argues that "the story cycle offers formal possibilities that allow its practitioners the freedom to challenge . . . the totalizing impression of the traditional novel of social and psychological realism" (2002, p. 6). Gish Jen's *Typical American* (1991) exemplifies this resistance to totality, as the cycle explores how three members of the Chang family respond to American culture. The title is a cheeky nod to the presumption that there might be a typical American. This tension about how characters from the same or interconnected families respond to immigrating to the United States recurs in semi-autobiographical cycles including Denise Chávez's *The Last of the Menu Girls* (1986), Sara Suleri's *Meatless Days* (1989), Cisneros's cycles, the Hema and Kaushik trio of stories in Jhumpa Lahiri's *Unaccustomed Earth* (2008), and the story cycles of Junot Díaz – *Drown* (1996) and its sequel *This Is How You Lose Her* (2012). Notably, writing in 1995, Margot Kelley notes that since 1980, "about 75 percent of the current writers [of the genre] are women, often women who live in positions of double marginality as members of visible minorities or lesbians" (p. 296). This is not, however, a new phenomenon. Writers have long turned to the cycle form to narrate the experiences of being ethnically and racially marked in the United States, including Alice Dunbar Nelson's *The Goodness of St. Rocque, and Other Stories* (1899), Sui Sin Far's *Mrs. Spring Fragrance* (1912), and Zitkála-Šá's *American Indian Stories* (1921).

García's semi-autobiographical *Dreaming in Cuban* (1992) demonstrates how writers use family as a linking device to show individual responses to shared experiences. The cycle begins with paired stories that narrate the death of the patriarch from family members' points of view. In many ways, the death of the father is the gap around which the other stories are built. The parallel structure of the opening stories, with the narrative point of view shifting within each story, announced by the character's name at a break, shore up the parallel themes and motifs within these and later stories. In the opening stories, the father, Jorge, is established as a deeply fastidious man, committed to cleanliness and decorum, in an effort to "be a model Cuban, to prove to his gringo boss that they were cut from the same cloth" (p. 6). His career, which requires that he travel five weeks out of six, is selling electric brooms, a symbol of cleanliness and bespeaking his faith in innovation. The fact that he travels so much means that he was already a gap in the children's lives, and many of the stories are concerned with reconciling how to grieve someone who was already gone. Beginning with a death that the stories return to throughout, this cycle is similar to Erdrich's *Love Medicine*, to which it was often compared in reviews and scholarship. García's cycle likewise explores the affinities and fissures within and between generations. A sense of affirming kinship is strongest between Jorge and his first daughter, Lourdes, and then between the matriarch, Celia, and her first granddaughter, Pilar. *Dreaming in Cuban* begins with a family tree, a paratextual element in common with *How the Garcia Girls Lost Their Accents*, *The Joy Luck Club*, and Antonio Ruiz-Camacho's *Barefoot Dogs: Stories* (2015), among others.

If García's cycle has a connecting plot, it is how each family member responds to the Cuban revolution. The family's disparate interpretations of Castro's Cuba set them at odds with each other, until Pilar and Celia's reunion brings some measure of peace. They share such a spiritual connection that they can speak to each other even after Pilar goes to New York. They are both artists, they are atheists and rebellious, they struggle with being understood by their families, and they share a love and longing for Cuba. Throughout the cycle are interludes composed of letters that Celia wrote on the 11th of every month for years to her lover before Jorge. In this way, the cycle also shows a gap in the family history as love precedes and exceeds marriage. The final story is just one letter: the letter Celia wrote to her long-departed lover following Pilar's birth and her own fiftieth birthday. The last letter takes place some twenty years before the narrative present of Celia and Pilar's reunion, which is the subject of the penultimate story. When Pilar returns to Cuba, she gives meaning and life to Celia. The stories celebrate this but also mourn it, because the same love is not shared with Lourdes or Celia's other children and grandchildren. One connecting theme is that love takes circuitous routes. The cycle's form captures these detours and diversions as the family members find their ways back to each other and to uneasy reconciliations. There are other common threads in the cycle – the cancers that run through the family, the varying degrees of faith in Santería, the conflicting political sentiments of the family, and recurring sea imagery, among others. The cycle's loose form allows these currents to rise to the top and recede without resolution. One of the chief advantages of the form is that it resists totalizing or teleological narratives in favor of openness, ambiguity, and multiplicity.

For these reasons, the cycle – and, more broadly, fragmented narrative forms – has been a compelling form for rendering war experiences. From Hemingway's *In Our Time* (1923) to Tim O'Brien's *The Things They Carried* (1991), to Phil Klay's *Redeployment* (2014), authors use the cycle to render war experiences. These cycles represent experiences of coming of age in a time of war. In flashing back to the past, these cycles remind us that the characters' loss of innocence and acculturation to death often begins much earlier at home and that the effects of conflict far exceed the temporality of the stories. In blending personal and fictive experiences, these cycles arrive at a mosaic of individual and collective violence. In writing about Operation Iraqi Freedom (2003–2010), Klay, himself a veteran, drew on research to create twelve distinct voices to show a range of experiences and responses to war. Writers turn to story cycles and fragmented long narrative to relate war experiences because these forms resist the impulses toward totalizing narratives that prompted the United States into wars in the late twentieth and early twenty-first centuries. These authors assert that war must be described in ways that make individual actors and moments of connection meaningful but not in ways that begin or end from some sense of inevitability. They seek a form more open, because as the narrator of O'Brien's fragmented story, "Spin," puts it, "Stories are for joining the past to the future. Stories are for those late hours in the night when you can't remember how you got from where you were to where you are. Stories are for eternity, when memory is erased, when there is nothing to remember except the story" (2009, p. 36).

This openness of the story cycle invites formal experimentation, as is evident in Jennifer Egan's innovative and widely acclaimed *A Visit from the Goon Squad* (2010). Egan's story cycle is a long-form meditation on time, music, and change. In interviews, Egan explains that she resists the story cycle label because, in her view, story cycles tend toward tonal monotony (Wambold 2010). Instead, she mapped out three principles that would inspire tonal diversity and generic hybridity. She relates these rules in an interview:

> One of them was that each piece had to stand strongly on its own: it had to be forceful individually. I wanted the whole to be more than the sum of its parts, but I didn't want them to lean on each other: I wanted them to enhance each other. The second was that each piece had to be completely different in terms of mood and world and voice. It ranges from sad to outright farce, and I really wanted to encompass all that in one book. And the third rule was that each piece had to be about a different person. There could be overlapping people, but there's only one chapter in which we look through a particular person's set of eyes.
>
> (Luckin 2010)

These rules resulted in a story cycle that tests the idea of what constitutes a short story. While some resemble the realist bent of Carver, Strout, and others, many of the volumes' nonlinear stories test the limits of genre. One resembles a celebrity profile in a literary magazine. One integrates anthropological asides from its graduate student protagonist. Most famously, the penultimate story is a bittersweet coming-of-age diary story told in PowerPoint. The book has an A and B side suggesting that we read it the way one might listen to a concept album, which was a major inspiration to Egan along with Proust and *The Sopranos*. Even as much of the cycle concerns the passage of time, which is the ultimate Goon, the final story turns to the short story to examine what happens when people attempt to morph and condense language.

A preoccupation with the power of brevity animates a subgenre of the story cycle, which is the cycle told through flash fiction. Here too labels and names proliferate: the flash fiction novel, the novella-in-shorts, the flash novella, the vignette novel, and novella-in-flash (Beckel and Rooney 2014, p. vii). In 2014, Rose Metal Press published an anthology of five cycles told in flash; individual cycles in the anthology range from 5000 to 12,000 words. The novellas-in-flash that make up *My Very End of the Universe* are "composed entirely of standalone flash fiction pieces organized into a full narrative arc" (Beckel and Rooney 2014, p. vii). As with longer-form story cycles, "many gaps and separations and new-yet-continuing stories force the reader to play closer attention – to not get lulled – while also creating a whole fictional reality" (p. xiii). Flash fiction expands upon the power of brevity in constructing a story cycle. Other flash cycles include Justin Torres's *We the Animals* (2011), Matthew Salesses's *I'm Not Saying, I'm Just Saying* (2013), Mario Alberto Zambrano's *Lotería* (2013), and Jenny Offill's *Dept. of Speculation* (2014). These flash cycles also examine family relationships in the context of migrations as is so often the case of cycles since 1980. Precursors to these recent cycles-in-flash are Joan Didion's *Play It as It Lays* (1970), *The House on Mango Street*, and Mary Robison's *Why Did I Ever* (2001), which was originally drafted on hundreds of notecards (Pokrass 2014, p. 52).

Story cycles are one of the most popular and widely taught genres in fiction of the twentieth and twenty-first centuries. They might be confused "with those twentieth century novels that fragment narrative point of view to project multiple versions of complex experience" (Kennedy 1995, p. x) or, when individual stories get anthologized or taught independently, they may appear a part of the short story tradition of distilling singular experiences. This paradox portends the future of the genre: story cycles will experiment with long and short forms, multiple points of view, cohesion and fragmentation, recurrence and singularity, the local and global. Fittingly, there is no single narrative that captures the range of the contemporary story cycle.

SEE ALSO: Banks, Russell; Beattie, Ann; Carver, Raymond; Contemporary Fictions of War; Díaz, Junot; Egan, Jennifer; Erdrich, Louise; García, Cristina; Jen, Gish; Kingston, Maxine Hong; Lahiri, Jhumpa; O'Brien, Tim; Proulx, Annie; Strout, Elizabeth; Tan, Amy

REFERENCES

Ardoin, Paul and McWilliam, Fiona. (2016). Introduction: on the stickiness of the short story and the cycle. *Journal of the Short Story in English* 66: 21–29.

Beckel, Abigail and Rooney, Kathleen. (2014). Introduction. In: *My Very End of the Universe: Five Novellas-in-Flash and a Study of the Genre* (by Tiff Holland, Aaron Teel, Meg Pokrass et al.), vii–xx. Brookline, MA: Rose Metal Press.

Davis, Rocío G. (2002). *Transcultural Reinventions: Asian American and Asian Canadian Short-Story Cycles*. Toronto: TSAR Publications.

Day, Cathy. (2011). Linked stories workshop. The Big Thing (February 6, 2011). https://cathyday.com/2011/02/linked-stories-workshop/ (accessed July 16, 2021).

Dunn, Maggie and Morris, Ann. (1995). *The Composite Novel: The Short Story Cycle in Transition*. New York: Twayne.

García, Cristina. (1992). *Dreaming in Cuban*. New York: Penguin Books.

Hogan, Patrick Colm, Lynch, Gerald, Murison, Justine et al. (2016). Roundtable: affect, the short story, and the cycle. *Journal of the Short Story in English* 66: 163–213.

Kelley, Margot. (1995). Gender and genre: the case of the novel-in-stories. In: *American Women Short Story Writers: A Collection of Critical Essays* (ed. Julie Brown), 295–310. New York: Garland.

Kennedy, J. Gerald. (1995). *Modern American Short Story Sequences: Composite Fictions and Fictive Communities*. Cambridge: Cambridge University Press.

Lister, Rachel. (2016). "Preposterous adventures": affective encounters in the short story cycle. *Journal of the Short Story in English* 66: 49–66.

Lovelady, Stephanie. (2005). Walking backwards: chronology, immigration, and coming of age in *My Ántonia* and *How the García Girl Lost Their Accents*. *Modern Language Studies* 35 (1): 28–37.

Lowe, Lisa. (1996). *Immigrant Acts: On Asian American Cultural Politics*. Durham, NC: Duke University Press.

Luckin, Joshua. (2010). Part of us that can't be touched. *Guernica* (July 1, 2010). https://www.guernicamag.com/egan_7_1_10/ (accessed July 16, 2021).

Lundén, Rolf. (1999). *The United Stories of America: Studies in the Short Story Composite*. Amsterdam: Rodopi.

Luscher, Robert M. (1989). The short story sequence: an open book. In: *Short Story Theory at a Crossroads* (ed. Susan Lohafer and Jo Ellyn Clarey), 148–167. Baton Rouge: Louisiana State University Press.

Nagel, James. (2001). *The Contemporary American Short-Story Cycle: The Ethnic Resonance of Genre*. Baton Rouge: Louisiana State University Press.

O'Brien, Tim. (2009). *The Things They Carried*. Boston: Mariner Books.

Pokrass, Meg. (2014). Breaking the pattern to make the pattern: conjuring a whole narrative from scraps. In: *My Very End of the Universe: Five Novellas-in-Flash and a Study of the Genre* (by Tiff Holland, Aaron Teel, Meg Pokrass et al.), 47–53. Brookline, MA: Rose Metal Press.

Savage, Bill. (2007). Stuart Dybek. In: *The Encyclopedia of Twentieth-Century Fiction*, vol. 2 (ed. Brian W. Shaffer, Patrick O'Donnell, David W. Madden et al.), 536–537. Oxford: Blackwell.

Wambold, Sarah. (2010). *A Visit from the Goon Squad*. Texas Book Festival interview. *The Austinist* (October 16, 2010).

FURTHER READING

Ardoin, Paul and McWilliam, Fiona. (eds.) (2016). Affect and the short story and cycle. Special section of *Journal of the Short Story in English* 66.

D'hoker, Elke. (ed.) (2013). The short story cycle. Special issue of *Short Fiction in Theory and Practice* 3 (2): 17–213.

Kennedy, J. Gerald. (1995). *Modern American Short Story Sequences: Composite Fictions and Fictive Communities*. Cambridge: Cambridge University Press.

Strout, Elizabeth

REBECCA CROSS
Study Group, Australia

Elizabeth Strout is a North American author who publishes both books (novels and short story cycles) and short stories, many of which are set in and around a cluster of small towns in Maine. She has published seven books: *Amy & Isabelle* (1998), *Abide With Me* (2006), *Olive Kitteridge* (2008), *The Burgess Boys* (2013), *My Name is Lucy Barton* (2016), *Anything is Possible* (2017), and *Olive, Again* (2019), which form the main focus of this entry. Her writing is characterized by its stark, emotion-eliciting content, the interlinked web of characters woven across several books, and the sense of community this creates between the characters. Characters and places are repeated across Strout's oeuvre, creating links between books and stories. These repetitions portray different perspectives and sides of familiar characters, highlighting the complexity of human existence and the resilience of everyday people through the mundanity and overwhelming nature of quotidian life. A key feature of Strout's writing is the authentic sense of vulnerability that is conveyed through her characters' exploration of their desire to be understood.

Strout's writing has received scant academic attention to date. Book reviews and author profiles can easily be located and Strout has many short stories published in short fiction-based journals, but very little academic scholarship exists focusing on her work. However, she has received critical acclaim for her writing: her short story cycle *Olive Kitteridge* won the Pulitzer Prize for Fiction in 2009, *My Name is Lucy Barton* was longlisted for the Man Booker Prize in 2016, among other recognitions. The popularity of Strout's works expanded further with the adaptation of *Amy & Isabelle* into a 2001 film produced by Harpo Films and HBO's 2014 mini-series based on *Olive Kitteridge*.

Strout's books evoke a closeness of subject matter and of character type. *Amy & Isabelle* is Strout's debut novel and features a young single mother named Isabelle who moves to Shirley Falls with her infant daughter Amy. The story focuses on one particular summer when Amy is 16 and spends her holidays working at the mill office where Isabelle is the boss's secretary. Amy has an intimate affair with her high school math teacher and it is eventually revealed that Isabelle had a similar affair with a much older married friend of her father that resulted in Amy's birth when she was also a teenager in high school. The story explores the fraught relationship between mother and daughter as Amy comes of age and the sense of loneliness caused by the secrets they each keep from the other.

Abide With Me is set in the small town of West Annette, Maine and follows the story of Tyler Caskey, the town's minister, whose wife has recently passed away. His five-year-old daughter Katherine struggles to adjust to the loss of her mother. Like *Amy & Isabelle*, this book focuses on the power of secrets and the complexity of relationships, exploring the dynamics of small-town gossip cycles and the rewards that can come from breaking down barriers of perception and mistrust.

Olive Kitteridge is a short story cycle comprised of thirteen short stories which center on the small town of Crosby, Maine, the next town over from Shirley Falls, and explore the interconnected relationships of Olive and those around her. Olive has three significant relationships: her husband Henry, her son Christopher, and her lover Jack, whom she meets after she becomes a widow. Throughout the stories Olive struggles to articulate clearly her enduring sense of yearning and loneliness in her life.

The Burgess Boys focuses on two brothers, Jim and Bob Burgess. The brothers originate from Shirley Falls but leave the small town as soon as they become adults to move to New York, where they both become lawyers. The book follows the brothers as they come to their nephew Zach's aid, returning to Shirley Falls to assist their sister with her troubled teenage son. Zach becomes embroiled in a hate crime – which he views as a racist prank gone wrong – against the Somali community of the town. Jim and Bob untangle their relationship, while they are helping their sister, to discover that their perceptions of, and assumptions about, each other do not reflect reality, and each brother realizes the other is not as carefree and happy as he appears.

My Name is Lucy Barton follows the journey of the eponymous Lucy as she recovers from an operation in a hospital in New York. It is written from Lucy's first-person perspective, which contrasts with Strout's other works, which are written in third person. The sudden appearance of her mother, whom she has not seen in years, by her bed sparks Lucy to recall her unstable and troubled childhood in rural Amgash, Illinois, where she suffered abuse at the hands of her parents, and the thoughts and feelings she has been avoiding as she went about her life with her husband and two children in New York.

Anything is Possible is a short story cycle. The nine interlinked stories provide perceptions of Lucy Barton from other people who live in the same small town of Amgash where she grew up. The crossover ties with *My Name is Lucy Barton* provide more information and different perspectives on Lucy, and give an insight into the upbringing she touches on in *My Name is Lucy Barton*. Like Strout's other short story cycles, *Anything is Possible* is written in third person, providing contrast with the first-person narration of *My Name is Lucy Barton*.

Olive, Again is another short story cycle that returns to the characters of *Olive Kitteridge*, with thirteen stories that focus closely on Olive as she navigates life as a senior citizen, finding happiness and comfort in her new marriage to Jack Kennison, before experiencing further loss and again facing a feeling of inescapable loneliness that pervades her body. With Jack, Olive has found the sense of intimacy and connection she was searching for in *Olive Kitteridge*. Throughout these stories Olive is in her seventies and eighties, and is portrayed as a much more likable character than in *Olive Kitteridge*; this could be attributed partly to the closer narration of more of her innermost thoughts rather than descriptions of her surface thinking and corresponding actions. Olive is portrayed as a deeply misunderstood woman who is still trying to find acceptance with herself and the world in which she lives.

Strout's characters demonstrate the myriad ways in which presumptions, prejudice, and preconceptions can influence the way a person's actions are received. They highlight the importance of empathy and compassion and illuminate the interconnectedness of human life and the need for community.

There is a common sense of loneliness that permeates Strout's books. For example, in *My Name is Lucy Barton*, Lucy finds herself alone in a hospital room considering the different relationships in her life; a sense of darkness pervades her memories from her past and she struggles to hold on to a semblance of happiness in her present life. Lucy tries to hide her sadness from those closest to her but admits "had anyone known the extent of my loneliness I would have been embarrassed" (2016, p. 6). In *Abide With Me*, Tyler is grieving his wife: "Anyone who has ever grieved knows that grieving carries with it a tremendous wear and tear to the body itself, never mind the soul. Loss is an assault; a certain exhaustion, as strong as the pull of the moon on the tides, needs to be allowed for eventually" (2006, p. 283). Olive has a proclivity for solitude in *Olive Kitteridge* but after her first husband Henry dies, she finds her life is lacking meaning. In *Olive, Again* she finds a sense of solace and solidarity in the company of her new husband Jack, and with that a sense of fulfillment and contentment but also honesty with herself. When Olive again feels a pervading sense of loneliness she is able to identify the emotion but still feels overwhelmed: "Loneliness. Oh, the loneliness! . . . It may have been the terror finally wearing off and gibing way for this gaping bright universe of loneliness that she faced, but it bewildered her to feel this" (2019, p. 260).

Strout's characters demonstrate loneliness in different ways; however, one of the consistent messages throughout her writing is the significance of human connection and its ability to overshadow or deplete feelings of loneliness. The relationship between Olive and Jack in *Olive, Again* gives a sense of hope and a place for Olive to be fully understood and accepted that did not exist in her life until their marriage. When Jack thinks of this new and unexpected development in his late life, he reflects that "his marriage to Olive had been surprisingly wonderful in many ways, to go into old age with this woman who was so–so Olive" (2019, p. 168). In *Abide With Me*, Tyler, who assisted his terminally ill wife to end her suffering and her life by leaving a bottle of pills next to her bed, is told by his old theology professor, "I suspect the most we can hope for, and it's no small hope, is that we never give up, that we never stop giving ourselves permission to try to love and receive love" (2006, p. 283).

My Name is Lucy Barton also explores loneliness and a desire to find a comfortable and secure place within the world, but diverges from Strout's typical style of richly constructed characters and detail-driven storylines with interlinking characters. Each word is carefully considered and the tone is stark and emotionally raw. In this book Lucy's mother visits her in hospital, which sparks Lucy to think back to certain times in her childhood. The first-person narration provides a directness and a vulnerability to Lucy's introduction that encourages a sense of tenderness toward her. For example, "[w]e were oddities, our family, even in that tiny rural town of Amgash, Illinois, where there were other homes that were run-down and lacking fresh paint or shutter or gardens, no beauty for the eye to rest upon" (2016, p.11). However, despite the change in writing style, the exploration of Lucy's relationships, both those from her present life and those she recalls from her past, is consistent with Strout's other writing through the focus on the interconnections between people and the distinction between intent and reception within relationships.

Although there are great differences in style between *My Name is Lucy Barton* and Strout's other books, the complex and raw insight into Lucy's life is similar to the central premise of Strout's fictions as a whole. Her writing highlights the complexity of human existence in many different forms: Isabelle Goodrow became pregnant with her daughter Amy to a much older man while she was still in high school and spends her life fearing she is not good enough as a mother; Olive Kitteridge is a small-town teacher who struggles to accept and love herself, especially as she grows older, and she simultaneously feels abandoned by and pushes away her only son; Jim and Bob Burgess's brotherly relationship is based on the understanding that Bob was responsible for their father's death through an accident when he was four years old, but Jim later reveals some information that reshapes Bob's entire understanding of his life.

The sense of familiarity and an ability to empathize with the characters is another common feature of Strout's writing. Strout's characters intersect in each other's lives; the small towns in which they live become epicenters of this interlinked web from which a vast network of characters and events slowly unfolds. The interconnection of Strout's works instigates a process of apperception in the reader, where each new work is assimilated into a larger community or sense of understanding of Strout's writing, adding more richness and meaning to the whole. David Herman argues that the process of closely analyzing texts provides "a finer-grained account of textual patterns discoverable in the story" (p. 427); this viewpoint can be extended to Strout's entire storyworld: the presence of links encourages a search for further links, thus perpetuating a process of searching for and finding patterns and links between stories and books, which in turn provides a sense of fulfillment and emotional engagement when they are found.

The repetition of characters and places throughout Strout's work becomes a spatial and thematic anchor that draws her stories together and gives them a sense of authenticity and ingenuity. For example, in *Amy & Isabelle*, one Saturday afternoon while having coffee with her daughter, Isabelle mentions that while she was growing up she knew a man whose wife was a school teacher who shot himself in the hallway of their house while she was at work (1998, pp. 54–55). In *Olive Kitteridge*, Olive reveals to her former student Kevin Coulson, a young man who grew up in Crosby but moved away when he was 13, that her father committed suicide by shooting himself in the kitchen of the house he shared with her mother. Olive tells Kevin, whose mother died by suicide in the same way when he was a child, that it is "[u]nusual for a woman to use a gun" (2008, p. 40). In *Olive, Again*, when Olive is having breakfast with Andrea L'Rieux, another former student, Olive tells her about her father's death and Andrea notes, "I think it's unusual for a woman to use a gun" (2019, p. 202). Olive's father's death becomes solidified through these mentions of the event and the repetitions of the phrase. While it is not certain that these comments relate to the same person – Isabelle refers to the father being found in a hallway whereas Olive remembers her mother finding her father in the kitchen – the similarity between the comments and their repetition across different books creates connections between stories, characters, and lives, linking them together. This encourages a search for other connections throughout the books.

Strout's strength lies in the way that she engages her reader, and encourages a search for connection through the repetition of characters and places throughout many of her works. The family trauma that is hinted at by Lucy in *My Name is Lucy Barton* is further explored in *Anything is Possible* in the story "Sister," which focuses on Lucy and her difficult return to the town of Amgash, Illinois, where she grew up. Similarly, in *Olive, Again* a connection is formed between Olive and Isabelle, the mother from *Amy & Isabelle*, when Olive and Isabelle move into the same nursing home (2019, p. 275). Small moments like this occur throughout Strout's works. They encourage a search for links and foster a sense of connection between Strout's books and stories. The links become small ties that grow in significance as more and more ties are revealed. The connections between stories are boosted by the sense of community fostered through the repetition of familiar characters throughout the books. These repetitions encourage a search for further connections, triggering a sense of engagement and increasing the sense of authenticity of the small towns and the descriptions of their people.

Strout has written several of her books in the form of short story cycles. *Olive Kitteridge*, *Anything is Possible*, and *Olive, Again* can all be read as a set of interconnected short stories, although they are frequently referred to as novels in reviews. In addition, her other books also contain snippets of connections with one other, some more significant than others, but all working to tie her fictions together. The connections have the potential to spark a search for further links. These moments of connection that can be experienced throughout Strout's works strengthen the veracity of the communities she creates and the sense of comfort brought forth through repetition of familiar characters and places. Strout's works consistently portray characters who are searching for a sense of their place in the world and the contentment they believe will come with that; the interconnected nature of her stories reinforces the sense of truth and reality within the storyworld she has created, which in turn increases the believability of her characters and their lives.

SEE ALSO: Fiction and Affect; Story Cycles

REFERENCES

Herman, David. (2013). Narrative theory and the sciences of the mind. *Literature Compass* 10 (5): 421–436.

Strout, Elizabeth. (1998). *Amy & Isabelle*. London: Simon & Schuster.
Strout, Elizabeth. (2006). *Abide With Me*. London: Simon & Schuster.
Strout, Elizabeth. (2008). *Olive Kitteridge*. London: Simon & Schuster.
Strout, Elizabeth. (2016). *My Name is Lucy Barton*. Harmondsworth: Penguin Books.
Strout, Elizabeth. (2019). *Olive, Again*. London: Viking.

FURTHER READING

Cross, Rebecca. (2016). Yearning, frustration, and fulfillment: the return story in *Olive Kitteridge* and *Kissing in Manhattan*. *Journal of the Short Story in English* 66: 67–84.
Ingram, Forrest L. (1971). *Representative Short Story Cycles of the Twentieth Century*. The Hague: Mouton.
Lynch, Gerald. (2001). *The One and the Many: English-Canadian Short Story Cycles*. Toronto: University of Toronto Press.
Tager, Michael. (2019). Divided America in Elizabeth Strout's *The Burgess Boys*. *Critique: Studies in Contemporary Fiction* 60 (4): 432–446.

Suburban Narratives

KRISTIN J. JACOBSON
Stockton University, USA

Post-1980 American suburbs are a paradox: dream and nightmare, place and placeless, region and global. They continue to invoke white privilege due in part to a legacy of redlining and other discriminatory policies while concurrently "more immigrants and people in poverty now live in the suburbs than in urban areas" (Knapp 2011, p. 501). American suburbs are increasingly diverse. A 1980 Census Bureau report outlined emerging trends with "the potential for halting or even reversing" white flight to the suburbs (Spain, Reid, and Long 1980, p. 1). A 2020 study confirms the suburbs' increased racial and ethnic diversity: the real estate company Refin analyzed Census Bureau data alongside their own housing data and found "People of color made up 28% of the suburban population nationwide in 2018, up from 26.2% in 2010, driven by 15.3% more people of color living in the suburbs over that time period" (Anderson 2020). Post-1980 suburban narratives reflect these demographic changes, concurrently portraying American domesticity as a bastion of white privilege and a battering ram that breaks longstanding stereotypes. The post-1980 suburban narrative houses these contradictions.

Recent scholarship further confirms the suburban narrative's paradoxical status. Notably, this enigmatic status is not new: "In the popular imagination, postwar suburbia exists simultaneously as the ultimate icon of American values and a horrific signifier of conformity and excess" (Banash and Enns 2003, p. 2). The suburb's dual role as authentic American icon and gross signifier of consumerism reveals fissures in the ideal home and family's conventional definitions. Suburban criticism has focused on noting the dominance of the white, middle-class everyman suburban narrative while rectifying any reification of it as the only narrative. Television adaptation of recent suburban literature by and primarily about women, such as *Little Fires Everywhere* (Celeste Ng, 2017) and the young adult series *Pretty Little Liars* (Sara Shepard, 2006) suggests a contemporary appetite for more female-centered suburban stories told through multiple perspectives rather than the singular "everyman."

Recent criticism focuses on the dominance (waning or not) of the white, middle-class heteronormative narrative and the narrative's increasing diversity. Catherine Jurca, for example, describes the contemporary suburban narrative as characterized by "sentimental dispossession," emphasizing how the narrative maintains a focus on white middle-class ennui, despite the characters' economic security (2001, pp. 7–14). Martin Dines argues, however, "suburban environments are less places of alienation and dispossession than of attachment" (2015, p. 82). He rejects the notion that contemporary suburban fiction is "the same as it ever was." Kathy Knapp similarly argues the suburban narrative changes after 9/11: "uncertainty... provides the basis for a new suburban literary tradition" in the twenty-first century (2011, p. 503). She argues 9/11 prompts a "reconsideration" of "the suburban literary tradition" (p. 500). Rather than offering a "retreat," post-9/11 suburban fiction "suggest[s] instead that the world has come to the suburbs" (p. 501). The literature, as we see in the discussion that follows, illustrates how the characters' race, gender, class, and location inflect their particular forms of alienation and attachment. Their glocal settings, moreover, emphasize the suburb's dual status as both regionally unique and nationally uniform homes.

Post-1980 cultural and historical contexts play key roles in understanding the narratives set in this environment. The 1980s tip off a third wave of US suburban development characterized by gated technoburbs, McMansions, and the rapid growth and then burst of the 2005 housing bubble and 2008 stock market downturn. This era of suburban development is distinguished by the "exurban gated community that has proliferated across the United States since the 1980s" (Dines 2015, p. 85). In addition to the rapid growth of exurbs, the period is also defined by the savings and loan crisis, mortgage fraud, failed housing developments, and – as will be discussed shortly – the climate crisis.

The previous suburban housing stock from the first late-nineteenth-century wave and the postwar period second wave of suburban development remain as key settings, while also undergoing changes that renovate their narrative significance, especially in the wake of 9/11. Change and evolution broadly define the postwar suburb, as Knapp argues, and this holds true for the new wave of gated technoburbs:

> Yet despite their reputation as soulless buffer zones, the postwar suburbs have been steadily evolving since their inception, and the novels that represent them have duly registered the various social changes that have shaped and reshaped territory where more Americans now live than in cities and rural areas combined. Suburbia has indeed become a complex environment that presents varied, vexing social, ethical, and political challenges.
>
> (2011, p. 501)

For Catherine Jurca, the postwar suburban narrative also indicates change. She traces "the systematic erosion of the suburban house as a privileged site of emotional connection and stability" while highlighting the "paradox that is fundamental to" suburban narratives: "white middle-class characters are homeowners... who are plagued by the problem of 'homelessness'" (2001, p. 4). Late-twentieth-century and twenty-first-century suburban fiction continues this evolution and rehearses earlier themes that demonstrate suburbia's dual grounding and instability. The post-1980s, therefore, are distinguished by the new forms the suburb takes, their distinct cultural and economic contexts, and the increasingly diverse residents who inhabit them. Suburban narratives reflect such changes in their settings and protagonists.

Lan Cao's *Monkey Bridge* (1997) offers a case in point. *Monkey Bridge* tells the story of suburban Vietnamese refugee renters. Mai lives in a suburban apartment, is a Vietnamese refugee, and is a young woman, all characteristics that set her apart from the conventional white, middle-class suburban male homeowner protagonist. The inclusion of Thanh (Mai's mother) as a second narrator also shifts the typical singular "everyman" narrative focus to multiple narrators. Suburban fictions with a singular narrative focus often convey "a national ethic that favors privacy and the rights of the individual over the community," as opposed to the arguably more democratic "multiple perspectives employed by contemporaneous postmodern writers" (Knapp 2011, p. 507). Shifting the narrative structure from singular to multiple perspectives further opens the suburban narrative. The postmodern *House of Leaves* (Mark Z. Danielewski, 2000) likewise diversifies the suburban narrative through its experimental form. Like Stephen King's *It* (1986) and Jack Ketchum's *The Girl Next Door* (1989), moreover, *House of Leaves* connects the horror and suburban genres. Formal experimentation and generic innovation are also part of the contemporary suburban narrative.

Yet, Mai also experiences her own characteristically suburban dispossession. Mai explains how she "adopt[s] the anthropologist's eye" and "step[s] back and watch[es] with a degree of detachment the habits and manners of Little Saigon," the refugee community where she lives with her mother (Cao 1997, p. 146). Mai's "detachment" offers important texture to the theme of alienation that has long characterized white male-focused suburban fiction. She notes, for example, how she is both part of and separate from her community: "Detached, I could see this community as a riot of adolescents, obstreperous, awkward, out of sync with the subscribed norms of American life, and beyond the reach of my authority. I could feel for them, their sad shuffles and anachronistic modes of behavior, . . . their foreigners' ragged edges" (p. 146). Mai feels empathy, suggesting that that they are not "aware of their differences. They had never managed, nor had the desire to manage, the eye-blinking, arm-folding maneuvers needed for a makeover. Here, in a walk-up apartment in a suburban neighborhood thirty minutes from Washington, D.C., they continued to present themselves as reproductions from the tropics" (p. 146). These suburban residents have no interest in reproducing the "subscribed norms of American life." Rather than reproduce (white) American domesticity, they work to maintain a semblance of their Vietnamese life. They are the residents of what Kristen Hill Maher calls the "global suburb," which erode "traditional patterns of segregation" while new ones emerge (2004, p. 782).

Even as the global influences the suburb, the suburb arguably constitutes its own region and reflects its local setting. As Keith Wilhite argues, suburban narratives offer "the endgame and final outpost of US regionalism" (2012, p. 618). In many ways, the East and West Coasts provide the iconic settings for the chronicling of and commentary on post-1980 suburban development. Notable East Coast suburban fictions include the Connecticut-based *Falling in Place* (Ann Beattie, 1980), *The Ice Storm* (Rick Moody, 1994), *Goodnight Nobody* (Jennifer Weiner, 2005), and *The Cosmopolitans* (Nadia Kalman, 2010). They also include the Maryland-based *The Amateur Marriage* (Anne Tyler, 2004) and *The Development* (John Barth, 2008), and a host of New York-based novels, including Alice McDermott's *That Night* (1987), Chang-rae Lee's *A Gesture Life* (1999) and *Aloft* (2004), and Mary Beth Keane's *Ask Again, Yes* (2019) as well as the Boston suburbs in which Anthony Giardina's *Norumbega Park* (2012) and *White Guys* (2006) and Tom Perrotta's *Little Children* (2004) are set. These novels read differently than their West Coast counterparts.

Don DeLillo's *White Noise* (1985) offers a representative example. Eunju Hwang notes *White Noise* is "set in a fictional college town named Blacksmith, presumably located in the Northeastern United States," and "has been considered a suburban novel by not a few critics despite its lack of reference to any metropolitan area nearby" (2015, p. 339). As a result, "Critics tend to more broadly define Blacksmith as a prototype of the American suburb" (p. 339). The novel, in this sense, presents the suburb as a "non-place," which is everywhere and nowhere at once. Its consumer culture filled with Chinese food (DeLillo 1985, p. 16), a supermarket that resembles a global bazaar (p. 169), and newspaper delivery "by a middle-aged Iranian" (p. 184) signify it as a prototypical global suburb that could be located anywhere.

The suburb's placelessness challenges regional readings, yet post-1980 suburban narratives highlight the ways regional characteristics still play key roles in shaping the suburban narrative amid the seeming national uniformity. As the fictional place names Blacksmith and Iron City invoke, the novel is set in postindustrial America. Regional location has not been completely stripped from the novel. Vestiges of regionalism remain. While "New York émigrés" (1985, p. 65) might be found anywhere outside of NYC, the expensive "College-on-the-Hill" (p. 41), snow-frenzied, postindustrial landscape (p. 167), and "most photographed barn in America" (p. 12) invoke the Northeast.

Of course, the East and West Coasts are not the only significant settings for the post-1980 suburban narrative. Therese Anne Fowler's *A Good Neighborhood* (2020) is set in North Carolina, and Frederick Barthelme's *Natural Selection* (1990) is set southwest of Houston. Set in 1990 in Houston's suburbs, Alicia Erian's *Towelhead* (2005) chronicles Jasira's recent move to live with her Lebanese father, just as the Gulf War begins. Jonathan Franzen is perhaps the best-known chronicler of the suburban Midwest with his novels *The Corrections* (2001) and *Freedom* (2010), despite the fact these novels are not exclusively set there. Other Midwest suburban novels include Jeffrey Eugenides's *The Virgin Suicides* (1993), set in Grosse Pointe, Michigan, and Celeste Ng's *Little Fires Everywhere*, which is set in Shaker Heights, a suburb of Cleveland. Again, regional location colors suburban narratives in specific ways.

Part of Michael Cunningham's *A Home at the End of the World* (1990), for instance, is set in the suburban track development Woodlawn near Cleveland. While *A Home at the End of the World* is not strictly a suburban novel, Bobby and Jonathan's Midwestern suburban origins highlight the "hegemony of heterosexuality," which shapes their expectations for home and family (Dines 2010, p. 3). As Wilhite argues in regard to the Lambert children in *The Corrections*, Midwest suburban childhoods shape the homes they build elsewhere (2012, p. 626). *A Home at the End of the World*'s chosen family queers the suburban family narrative. The home's boundaries and family ethics are especially tested when Jonathan's lover Erich tests positive for AIDS. Cunningham's novel highlights how even as the nuclear family continues to model home, the American family is multiple: queer, blended, divorced, multigenerational, childless.

Attention to region, thus, uncovers the ways the post-1980 suburban narrative invokes both place and placelessness. In part two of Donna Tartt's *The Goldfinch* (2013), for example, Theo Decker moves from New York City to live with his dad and his dad's girlfriend Xandra in suburban Las Vegas. Theo shifts from visiting museums – an urban world of art and culture – to listening to "Ladies of the Eighties Lapdance lunch" on the radio. His home is the half-completed Canyon Shadows: "Desatoya Ranch Estates, on 6219 Desert End Road, where lumber was stacked in some of the yards and sand blew in the streets" (2013, p. 223). Named after the Desatoya mountain range in Nevada, the homes there have no garbage collection

(p. 232) and are mostly abandoned (p. 240). This suburban desert wasteland serves as the backdrop for Theo's initiation into substance abuse.

Suburban Las Vegas as depicted in the novel is both stereotype and type. While a stereotypical wasteland, suburban Las Vegas is not uniform – at least in its population. It, too, is a global suburb. Theo's school is full of foreigners and students who "had lived in nine or ten different states in as many years, and many of them had lived abroad" (2013, p. 234). Notably, "The suburbs of Las Vegas diversified most out of the 100 most populous U.S. metro areas over the last decade, with people of color making up 40.2% of the suburban population in 2018, up from 30.5% in 2010" (Anderson 2020). While *The Goldfinch* focuses on white Theo, Theo inhabits a global suburban world defined by "transience" and where popularity is determined by "who'd lived in Vegas the longest" rather than "money, or even good looks" (Tartt 2013, p. 234). Canyon Shadows, thus, embodies what Robert Beuka argues is a core "paradox" that defines the postwar suburb: it is "a paradox" because it is "both a 'place' and a 'noplace'" (2004, p. 20).

Canyon Shadows is anonymous while at the same time its architecture invokes, if not a distinct place, then an amorphous Southwestern atmosphere: "we turned into the driveway of a large Spanish-looking house, or maybe it was Moorish, shuttered beige stucco with arched gables and a clay-tiled roof pitched at various startling angles. I was impressed by the aimlessness and sprawl of it, its cornices and columns, the elaborate ironwork door with its sense of a stage set, like a house from one of the Telemundo soap operas" (2013, p. 223). Theo's description uncovers the home's theatrical staging and precariousness. The unfinished Desatoya Ranch Estates invokes "placelessness," or the loss of a distinctive regionalism or "placeness" due to the "homogenization of American life," especially as embodied in the suburb's uniform architecture and design (Beuka 2004, p. 2). At the same time, the architecture invokes an imaginary Spanish/Moorish heritage. This "fantasy topography" is the "mystified Southwest that real estate developers sell" (Comer 1999, pp. 147, 148). This transient, unreal place causes the students at Theo's school to reward "placeness," as measured in real time, with popularity.

Jane Smiley's *Good Faith* (2003) and Eric Puchner's *Model Home* (2010) both focus on failed Reagan-era housing development schemes, offering East and West Coast perspectives on the status of the American dream. Set in the Northeast during the savings and loan crisis, *Good Faith* follows real estate agent Joe Stratford from 1982 to 1990 during his involvement in and the aftermath of a shady land development attempt. While the property ultimately is developed successfully by another investor, Joe ends the novel much as he begins. Joe is now "as good as fifty," yet he is "still at square one. Still living in my parents' duplex, still selling housing, still spending a fair amount of time at the Viceroy," the local bar (Smiley 2003, p. 416). While Joe is a poor "sucker" (p. 415), he also ends the novel skiing and chasing after a woman, which he sees as "the operation of grace in the material world" (p. 417). As his love interest and similarly "poor" Felicity states, "this is what it's like not having to pay taxes ever again" (p. 416). The irony of being too poor to pay taxes and still enjoying downhill skiing as a leisure activity highlights Joe and Felicity's privileged survival. He ends the novel still game for another run on the slopes as well as love – determined in his pursuit of "felicity" or happiness.

Model Home like *Good Faith* examines the launch and aftermath of an unsuccessful mid-1980s housing scheme. This California novel opens in the summer of 1985 and concludes in the winter of 1986. Warren Ziller increasingly doubts his decision to leave Wisconsin and move his family to Southern California. He sees the failed development as punishment for his risky, unethical economic decisions:

> Just as Dante's sinners had their own punishments in hell, Warren had this putrid block of vacant homes. It was demonically tailored to his own sins. First he'd moved his family to California, to a house they couldn't afford. Even when he might have pulled out, he'd pushed through with the project anyway, investing money intended for his children's future. He'd lied to honest people about the dump. Now he'd gotten what he deserved, the same home he once tried to con others into buying.
>
> (Puchner 2010, p. 208)

Warren ends up a knife salesman trying not to think about "the idea of living in an empty house, waiting for the bank to kick him out" (2010, p. 358). Yet, the novel also offers some hope, a glimmer that love and family – "the face in your dream" – will appear and "darkness undone" (p. 360). Thus, while both *Good Faith* and *Model Home* are tragedies, tracing the downfall of their suburban white male protagonists, both also keep some vestige of the American dream alive.

The status of the American dream and the suburbs' role in housing it thus remains a perennial theme among post-1980 suburban narratives. The white male protagonist also continues to provide a significant "everyman" perspective on this pursuit. The narrator of Philip Roth's *American Pastoral* (1997), for example, is both "everyman" (as made evident by Roth's 2006 novel with that title) and individual, a bit like the suburbs themselves in their uniform individuality. As I argue in *Neodomestic American Fiction*, suburban literature is often read as the more masculine – if not always more muscular – domestic literary tradition. Its most recognized authors and protagonists tend to be male. Like their nineteenth-century suburban counterparts, these often-alienated white male characters seek suburban security, "a solidification of homeland security amidst change and cultural diversity" (Jacobson 2010, p. 123). Suburbia also seems to soften them – emasculate them due to their association with domesticity. These men are heads of household, but their domestication also paradoxically contributes to their inability to enjoy the comforts of home – the earned and unearned rewards of their (white) male heteronormative privileges.

Frank Bascombe is perhaps the most celebrated contemporary fictional Northeast real estate agent who struggles to enjoy his privileges. Richard Ford's New Jersey-based *The Sportswriter* (1986), *Independence Day* (1995), *The Lay of the Land* (2006), and *Let Me Be Frank with You* (2014) chronicle Frank Bascombe's life. As Kathy Knapp argues, the Bascombe novels also chronicle a key shift in suburban literature, especially for the literature focused on white male protagonists following 9/11. Knapp argues Bascombe specifically changes from a character hamstrung by "his stunted growth" (2011, p. 509) to one that promotes reflection and community: "individual experience, which in the first two novels provided the neoliberal argument for personal advancement over the common good, is here [in *The Lay of the Land*] reconceived as the first step along a makeshift bridge to a flexible but meaningful sense of collective identity" (p. 516). Rather than offer a "retrograde return" to "stasis, angst, alienation," as Knapp explains in her study *American Unexceptionalism: The Everyman and the Suburban Novel after 9/11*, the novels that "center on such old, square, white middle-class male protagonists" share a "determined open-endedness" (2014, pp. xi, xiii). More ambivalent in this regard than *Good Faith*, the final two Bascombe books offer perspective on the American dream, if not clear-cut hope or pessimism.

The fates of several characters in the California-based *House of Sand and Fog* (Andre Dubus III, 1999) are more overtly tragic. And, like *Model Home* and *Monkey Bridge*, this novel expands the suburban narrative perspective beyond the singular "everyman" white, middle-class male protagonist. Two sides vie for ownership and reader empathy in *House of Sand and Fog*. An uncorrected clerical error means Kathy Nicolo has been evicted from the San Mateo county home she inherited from her father. The Iranian immigrant Behrani family purchases the California bungalow in a sheriff's sale, an opportunity to reverse their fortunes. The older suburban home symbolizes Kathy's struggle to maintain her white middle-class status and the Behrani family's last chance to salvage what remains of their wealth and status after living beyond their means in the United States. As seen in other suburban fictions such as A.M. Homes's *Music for Torching* (1999) and Richard Russo's *Empire Falls* (2001), violence breaks the suburban facade of respectability. The pursuit of the American dream becomes a blood sport. Where Elaine and Paul set fire to their own house in *Music for Torching*, in *House of Sand and Fog*, class and ethnic tensions fuel the dispute over the home, which leads to the death of nearly all the Behrani family and lands Kathy in jail. Such dysfunctional family narratives constitute another important, largely dystopian approach to the American dream in post-1980 suburban narratives.

The climate crisis provides another context and force of change for post-1980s dystopian suburban fiction. Suburbia's environmental consequences are addressed obliquely in *The Goldfinch* when the students at Theo's school discuss Thoreau (Tartt 2013, pp. 235–236) and in the descriptions of the desert reclaiming Canyon Shadows (p. 237). "The Airborne Toxic Event" section in *White Noise* directly addresses white suburbia's assumed privileged position where issues of environmental justice are concerned. Jack, for example, is not initially worried about the toxic cloud because "Society is set up in such a way that it's the poor and the uneducated who suffer the main impact of natural and man-made disasters.. . . These things don't happen in places like Blacksmith" (DeLillo 1985, p. 114). Disaster, however, does come to Blacksmith, causing Jack and his family to flee. While they are able to return home after nine days (p. 163), Jack's exposure to the toxic cloud may or may not have long-term health implications, further emphasizing his position in society was not enough to protect him. Irrevocable environmental disaster takes center stage in T.C. Boyle's *A Friend of the Earth* (2000).

Like *The Goldfinch*, *A Friend of the Earth* is not, strictly speaking, a suburban novel. The near-future novel moves between the years 2025 and 2026 and events that primarily occur from 1989 to 1997. While it is not exclusively set in the suburbs, *A Friend of the Earth* offers a telling example of post-1980 fiction's portrayal of suburbia as a mode of environmental critique. The novel's environmental monkey-wrencher protagonist is a self-described "criminal." While Ty has served time in jail, he assigns his criminal behavior and identity to his former suburban lifestyle and implicates the reader as party to these criminal acts as well: "Just like you. I lived in the suburbs in a three-thousand-square-foot house with redwood siding and oak floors and an oil burner the size of Texas" (Boyle 2000, p. 42). Ty goes on to explain, "I caused approximately two hundred fifty times the damage to the environment of this tattered, bleeding planet as a Bangladeshi or Balinese, and they do their share, believe me. Or did" (p. 43). *A Friend of the Earth* maps a different type of dystopian suburban fiction – one that highlights what the future of the United States might look like if such suburban criminality does not stop.

A Friend of the Earth is one of several near-future novels set on the West Coast that highlight the suburban narrative's role in imagining possible futures as well as its role in understanding America's present and past. Notably, during the 1989 period Ty landscapes his family's suburban rental home. Ty replaces the non-native plants with natives and turns the pool into "a marsh where waterfowl could frolic side by side with the red-legged frog and the common toad" (2000, p. 236). Changing his home, however, proves unsatisfying for Ty, who seeks bigger, bolder, and more direct environmental interventions. In the end, his environmental monkey-wrenching accomplishes "Nothing . . . Absolutely nothing" (p. 270). *Parable of the Sower* (Octavia Butler, 1993) and *California* (Edan Lepucki, 2014) similarly imagine the suburb's role in the dystopian environmental futures depicted.

Parable of the Sower opens in a multiethnic walled suburban community, Robledo, which is located twenty miles from Los Angeles. When violence finally bridges the community's walls, those who survive are forced to find and make a new home outside. Their gated community is destroyed and so the characters must adapt to the changes forced upon them. *California* includes flashbacks to living in a similarly brutal Los Angeles, which the white protagonists decide to leave due to its "chewed-up streets," "people starving on the sidewalks, covered in piss and crying out," and its "crime" (Lepucki 2014, p. 12). The characters end the novel "safely" trapped in a Stepford-wives-like enclave called The Pines. Both novels offer critiques of post-1980 gated enclaves. The walls ultimately fail to provide safety in *Parable of the Sower* and The Pines' gates may provide physical safety – at least for now – but at the cost of conforming to retrograde gender roles, eating poor quality food, and wearing substandard clothing. The novels' distinct spatial politics highlight the ways race and gender inflect the suburban narrative as well as key differences in what the characters are willing and forced to give up in order to have a safe home.

In keeping with the suburb's multiplicity, not all post-1980 suburban narratives are so deadly serious. Sandra Tsing Loh's *If You Lived Here You'd Be Home By Now* (1997), Jean Kyoung Frazier's *Pizza Girl* (2020), and Lauren Weisberger's *When Life Gives You Lululemons* (2018) constitute representative West and East Coast suburban fictions that focus more on humor than tragedy to render their portraits of suburban life. The satiric and highly allusive *The Sellout* (2015) by Paul Beatty also uses humor to render a biting critique of both the institutionalized racism that prevents African Americans from achieving the American dream and the culturally imposed authenticity markers that exclude Blacks from enjoying middle-class respectability: "Beatty's depiction of place enables his dual-pronged critique of identity politics and postracialism and proposes simultaneously anti-identitarian and antiracist thinking" (Lutenski 2019, p. 15). Like Gloria Naylor's *Linden Hills* (1985), by focusing on a Black suburban community *The Sellout* breaks a key stereotype associated with suburban narratives: its foundational whiteness.

Older, more densely populated non-white suburbs are not often seen as suburbs or read as suburban narratives. Emily Lutenski corrects this misreading by outlining the suburban development, decay, and subsequent rebranding of Compton, which is the basis for Beatty's fictional Dickens. Like its real counterpart, "The Los Angeles-area community at the heart of the novel, Dickens, is transforming due to encroaching gentrification and neoliberal divestment, leading to a crisis of identity as the town literally disappears" (Lutenski 2019, p. 22). Disputed boundaries play a key role in *Linden Hills*, too: "There had been a dispute for years over the exact location of Linden Hills . . . But it patiently bore the designation of Linden Hills as its boundaries contracted and expanded over the years" (Naylor 1985, p. 1). Naylor's tony Linden Hills and Beatty's ghetto Dickens in many ways could not be more different settings, and yet both trace their suburban roots to the first wave of nineteenth-century suburban development. In *Linden Hills* Luther Nedeed allegedly "sold his octoroon wife and six children for the money that he used" to purchase Linden Hills (p. 2). "Founded in 1868," Dickens's "original charter" was exclusionary toward "Chinamen, Spanish of all shades, dialects, and hats, Frenchmen, redheads, city slickers, and unskilled Jews" (Beatty 2015, p. 27). Both Black suburban narratives uncover the exploitative, exclusionary practices that provide the foundation for both suburban development and the American dream.

Understanding the suburban narrative involves examining structures beyond the detached single-family home as well as narratives not exclusively set there. Along these lines, Christian Long's "Mapping Suburban Fiction" examines how "commuting offers chances for reflection and self-knowledge for the middle-class suburbanite's psyche" (2013, p. 194). Long emphasizes driving and roadways – not walking and sidewalks – characterize the suburban landscape and fiction. Thus, it is especially fitting that Lauren Groff's short story "Ghosts and Empties" from her collection *Florida* (2018) follows a woman walking around her dilapidated Victorian neighborhood at night. Her walking – as opposed to driving – signals the story's and the protagonist's anti-suburban narrative.

The story's opening describes northern Florida's suburban development and its impact on the protagonist's Victorian neighborhood; she traces outward, from her Victorian home to the "1920s bungalows, then mid-century modern ranches at the edges." Her family's ability to own their centrally located dilapidated Victorian is due to 1970s suburban development, which caused "the historic houses in the center of town . . . [to be] abandoned" (Groff 2018, p. 2): "We moved here ten years ago because our house was cheap and had virgin-lumber bones, and because I decided that if I had to live in the South . . . at least I wouldn't barricade myself with my whiteness in a gated community" (p. 3). Like Walter and Patty Berglund in Franzen's *Freedom*, who similarly capitalize on homeownership in the city center, Groff's protagonist is part of the reversal of white flight to the suburbs and subsequent city center gentrification. The post-1980 suburban narrative, thus, moves against itself: its associated whiteness, now a liability, prompts white liberal characters to make home elsewhere.

The suburban narrative's paradoxical representations of American domesticity arguably grant the narrative unique power and insight: "The extremism of critically polarized images of suburbia in critical texts, and the ironic sublation of those images in our fictional imagination, testifies to the power of these planned communities, their utopian aspirations, and their often horrifying reality" (Banash and Enns 2003, p. 3). The post-1980s era notably includes the final two novels in John Updike's iconic, postwar white male suburban Rabbit series, *Rabbit is Rich* (1981) and *Rabbit at Rest* (1990). The period also includes non-white and multiperspectival narratives, such as *Monkey Bridge*, that depict the suburb's global multiplicity and formal innovations. As such, post-1980s suburban narratives exceed the familiar suburban tropes of alienation and uniformity, telling new stories, offering fresh twists on familiar themes, and reinventing the suburb and its representative family for its increasingly diverse inhabitants.

SEE ALSO: Boyle, T.C.; Butler, Octavia; Chick Lit and the New Domesticity; Contemporary Regionalisms; DeLillo, Don; Ecocriticism and

Environmental Fiction; Ford, Richard; Franzen, Jonathan; Groff, Lauren; Lee, Chang-rae; Ng, Celeste; Post-9/11 Narratives; Smiley, Jane; Tartt, Donna; Updike, John

REFERENCES

Anderson, Dana. (2020). The suburbs have become more diverse, more liberal and more dense in the past decade. *Redfin Real Estate News* (November 23, 2020). https://www.redfin.com/news/suburbs-demographics-more-diverse-liberal/ (accessed July 17, 2021).

Banash, David and Enns, Anthony. (2003). Introduction: suburbia. *Iowa Journal of Cultural Studies* 3 (1): 1–7.

Beatty, Paul. (2015). *The Sellout*. New York: Picador.

Beuka, Robert. (2004). *SuburbiaNation: Reading Suburban Landscape in Twentieth-Century American Fiction and Film*. New York: Palgrave Macmillan.

Boyle, Thomas Coraghessan. (2000). *A Friend of the Earth*. New York: Bloomsbury.

Cao, Lan. (1997). *Monkey Bridge*. New York: Viking.

Comer, Krista. (1999). *Landscapes of the New West: Gender and Geography in Contemporary Women's Writing*. Chapel Hill: University of North Carolina Press.

DeLillo, Don. (1985). *White Noise*. New York: Penguin Books.

Dines, Martin. (2010). *Gay Suburban Narratives in American and British Culture: Homecoming Queens*. New York: Palgrave Macmillan.

Dines, Martin. (2015). Metaburbia: the evolving suburb in contemporary fiction. In: *Making Suburbia: New Histories of Everyday America* (ed. John Archer, Paul J.P. Sandul, and Katherine Solomonson), 81–90. Minneapolis: University of Minnesota Press.

Groff, Lauren. (2018). *Florida*. New York: Penguin Books.

Hwang, Eunju. (2015). The geography of non-places in Don DeLillo's *White Noise*. 영미문화 (*English-American Cultural Studies*) 15 (2): 337–367.

Jacobson, Kristin J. (2010). *Neodomestic American Fiction*. Columbus: Ohio State University Press.

Jurca, Catherine. (2001). *White Diaspora: The Suburb and the Twentieth-Century American Novel*. Princeton: Princeton University Press.

Knapp, Kathy. (2011). Richard Ford's Frank Bascombe trilogy and the post-9/11 suburban novel. *American Literary History* 23 (3): 500–528.

Knapp, Kathy. (2014). *American Unexceptionalism: The Everyman and the Suburban Novel after 9/11*. Iowa City: University of Iowa Press.

Lepucki, Edan. (2014). *California*. New York: Little, Brown.

Long, Christian. (2013). Mapping suburban fiction. *Journal of Language, Literature and Culture* 60 (3): 193–213.

Lutenski, Emily. (2019). Dickens disappeared: Black Los Angeles and the borderlands of racial memory. *American Studies* 58 (3): 15–35.

Maher, Kristen Hill. (2004). Borders and social distinction in the global suburb. *American Quarterly* 56 (3): 781–806.

Naylor, Gloria. (1985). *Linden Hills*. New York: Penguin Books.

Puchner, Eric. (2010). *Model Home*. New York: Scribner's.

Smiley, Jane. (2003). *Good Faith*. New York: Knopf.

Spain, Daphne, Reid, John, and Long, Larry. (1980). Housing successions among Blacks and Whites in cities and suburbs. *Current Population Reports*, Bureau of the Census, P-23, No. 101 (January). https://www2.census.gov/library/publications/1980/demographics/p23-101.pdf (accessed July 17, 2021).

Tartt, Donna. (2013). *The Goldfinch*. New York: Little, Brown.

Wilhite, Keith. (2012). Contested terrain: the suburbs as region. *American Literature* 84 (3): 617–644.

FURTHER READING

George, Joseph. (2016). *Postmodern Suburban Spaces: Philosophy, Ethics, and Community in Post-War American Fiction*. London: Palgrave Macmillan.

Hayden, Dolores. (2000). *Building Suburbia: Green Fields and Urban Growth, 1820–2000*. New York: Pantheon.

Jurca, Catherine. (2011). The American novel and the rise of the suburbs. In: *The Cambridge History of the American Novel* (ed. Leonard Cassuto, Clare Virginia Eby, and Benjamin Reiss), 879–892. New York: Cambridge University Press.

Low, Setha. (2004). *Behind the Gates: Life, Security, and the Pursuit of Happiness in Fortress America*. New York: Routledge.

Tan, Amy

SUSANNA HOENESS-KRUPSAW
University of Southern Indiana, USA

Amy Tan's memoir *The Opposite of Fate: A Book of Musings* (2003), written while she was recovering from Lyme disease, includes pieces unified by the theme of hope. Having battled a serious illness, Tan concludes that she is no longer subject to "fate and fear"; on the contrary, she will change what is "not right" through her storytelling (2003, p. 398). This ability to create hybrid characters through narratives that intertwine the multiple subjectivities of mothers and daughters engaged in recovering the past and rewriting history has been a hallmark of Tan's six novels, two children's books, and two collections of creative nonfiction.

Hope and fate constitute only one of the many binaries encountered by Tan's characters. In *Between Worlds: Women Writers of Chinese Ancestry* (1990), Amy Ling mentions that Tan's characters experience a "feeling of being between worlds, totally at home nowhere" (1990, p. 105). Ling highlights the comic touches tinged with sadness and ambivalence in the Chinese American daughters' attempts to seek a self and a place apart from their mothers and their motherland and their final recognition that the old Chinese ways must also be respected (p. 141). Like Ling, E.D. Huntley, in *Amy Tan: A Critical Companion* (1998), views "the tensions" of living between worlds as a major concern of Tan's works (1998, p. 143).

Born to first-generation Chinese immigrant parents, John and Daisy Tan, Amy Tan grew up in California. The 15-year-old Tan experienced serious trauma when both her father and her older brother were diagnosed with brain tumors and passed away. Distraught, her mother moved Tan and her younger brother John to Switzerland where Tan attended a prestigious boarding school. At the University of California at Santa Cruz, she earned a master's degree in linguistics. Subsequently, she worked first as a language development specialist for disabled children and then as a technical writer. After attending a writers' workshop, she started writing the short stories that would eventually be fused into her first novel, *The Joy Luck Club* (1989). Tan has received many prestigious awards, such as the Commonwealth Gold Award and the Golden Plate Award from the American Academy of Achievement, and nominations for the National Book Award. Moreover, she starred as herself in the TV show *The Simpsons* and performed with Stephen King and others in the rock band The Rock Bottom Remainders. Amy Tan lives with her husband, the tax attorney Lou DeMattei, and two dogs in San Francisco and New York.

The Joy Luck Club, published at a time when audiences were receptive to emergent minority voices, amazed both literary critics and casual readers alike. Focused on the life of June Woo, whose mother Suyuan has just passed away, the text both reconstructs the deceased mother's life story and analyzes the American daughter's life crises. Interweaving of character biography and verifiable historical facts, as well as Chinese myths, ghost world, and folklore and use of multiple narrative voices have been a hallmark of Tan's fiction. The novel also became a successful Wayne Wang directed movie (1993), co-produced and co-written by Tan herself.

In addition to June and Suyuan's carefully braided narrative, three further mother–daughter narratives complete the novel. In these interwoven narratives, several binary patterns immediately become apparent: the mothers want their daughters to be highly successful independent Americans while remaining obedient traditional Chinese daughters. This conflict drives a wedge into their relationship that increases the daughters' rebelliousness. Estrangement from the mother and the Chinese side of their identity, however, leaves such a void in the daughters' lives that they attempt to reconnect both to their mothers and to their Chinese ancestry by reconstructing the mothers' pasts. Creation of common ground, eliminating the painfully divisive binaries, occurs in the novel through the telling of stories within a circle of trusted women friends and family members.

Tan renders the world of Chinese Americans so realistically that some readers misinterpret her novels as sociological studies. In interviews, she has strongly objected to this kind of ethnic labeling. Nonetheless, some critics have pointed out Tan's supposed stereotyping of Chinese characters. Other critics even find the novel too tightly structured and neatly composed. Similar criticism alleging Tan's orientalism (i.e. presumed catering to Western readers' clichéd and exotic notions of the East) was leveled against Tan's children's books (both illustrated by Gretchen Schields) *The Moon Lady* (1992) and *The Chinese Siamese Cat* (1994). Despite these complaints, the cat Sagwa became the center of a successful *PBS Kids* program.

In *The Kitchen God's Wife* (1991), the theme of a daughter recovering her mother's past persists. Again the mother's embrace of traditional Chinese beliefs contrasts starkly with the daughter's avowed rationalism. While mother–daughter narratives alternate in *The Joy Luck Club*, in *The Kitchen God's Wife*, the daughter's, Pearl Louie's, narrative begins the novel, followed by her mother Winnie's narrative, which constitutes the greater part of the novel. Winnie comes to see her life as paralleling that of the kitchen god's wife in an ancient tale, for she, too, bravely endured her first husband's cruelties. To furnish the house shrine for her daughter, Winnie later purchases an unnamed new deity whom Pearl can then worship as the Lady Sorrowfree. Symbolically, at the end of the novel, after Winnie and Pearl have exchanged their innermost secrets and overcome many years of misunderstandings, it appears that the deity also serves as validation of the mother's wisdom. Reconstruction of memories and past events confirms that characters must learn to deal with the uncertainty and ambiguity in their lives to be able to embrace hope for the future. Says Pearl, "I can taste it too. I can feel it. Only a little amount and it is enough to remember – all the things you thought you had forgotten but were never forgotten, all the hopes that can still be found" (Tan 1991, p. 526).

The Hundred Secret Senses (1995) reveals Tan's increasing reliance on the presence of the ghost world by juxtaposing not a mother and daughter but two sisters, one raised in China and one raised in the United States. As the biracial American-born Olivia Bishop recovers her Chinese sister Kwan's past, she even engages in time travel. In an interview with *Entertainment Weekly*'s Erica Cardozo (1995), Tan says that she had help writing *The Hundred Secret Senses* from "yin people," whom she describes as guardian angels or ghosts and who have been with her for a long time. In this novel, the older sister Kwan adopts the place of the mother by caring for and nurturing her younger sister. It is she who puts her sister in touch with her Chinese roots and represents a link to the ghost world.

More than in preceding works, in this novel, Tan emphasizes the fluidity of time and memory, making it impossible to determine what is historical fact or Kwan's fabulation. To create this effect, Tan masterfully handles flashbacks to enhance the effect the past has on the present. She also counterpoints events in twentieth-century San Francisco and Changmian, China, through the sisterly bond that connects Olivia and Kwan. In another layer of time, in nineteenth-century China, the pair consisting of Nelly Banner and Nunumu lives through the final years of the Taiping Rebellion.

Readers even gain a different perspective on the history of the Taiping Rebellion as described by the one-eyed Nunumu. Only after the narrator grasps this concept of multiplicity, of multiple perspectives and multiple possibilities, can she understand how she connects to various characters in her experience. Her conflicts appear, at least temporarily, resolved by her acceptance of reincarnation as an explanation for the bizarre coincidences in her life. Finally, she can reestablish the bond with her sister. When Olivia has her own little girl after Kwan's disappearance and considers her Kwan's last gift to her, a gift of both hope for the future and connection to the past, she says: "I now believe that truth lies not in logic but in hope, both past and future" (Tan 1995, p. 357).

Inspired by Tan's mother Daisy's diagnosis with Alzheimer's disease and questions about Daisy's mother's suicide, *The Bonesetter's Daughter* (2001), features yet another daughter who reconstructs her mother's past. Tan worked with composer Stewart Wallace on an operatic adaptation of the novel which premiered in San Francisco in 2008. The novel focuses on the 82-year-old Chinese immigrant LuLing and her daughter Ruth and the bonesetter's daughter Bao Bomu, known as Precious Auntie, now deceased, who took care of LuLing during her childhood in China. In Tan's characteristic multivoiced format, Ruth's chapters alternate with her mother's told in first person. The parts dedicated to each woman's story unfold chronologically in the narrative present with deep layers of flashbacks to the narrator's childhood. Ruth's Part One is preceded by LuLing's first chapter and ends with Ruth's resolve to finally translate a manuscript written in Chinese given to her by her mother who is beginning to experience memory loss.

Part Two narrates LuLing's somewhat selective memories of her childhood and youth in China and the reconstruction of her own mother's identity whom she first knew only as Precious Auntie. In this manner, Part Two echoes and clarifies some of the persons and events already alluded to in the first part. The short Part Three returns to Ruth, who must remand her mother to a care facility and reluctantly accepts a role reversal that puts her in charge of her mother. The novel's epilogue shows Ruth in her study, beginning to write, with her grandmother's ghost by her side, a story, which "is for her grandmother, for herself, for the little girl who became her mother" (Tan 2001, p. 353). This scene, coupled with the revelations at the end of the novel, forces Ruth to reassess some of her own beliefs about ghosts.

While earlier novels had emphasized the power gained by the mother's China narratives over the daughter's education, Tan explores the daughter's power in this novel. Initially, "By using Chinese words, LuLing could put all kinds of wisdom in Ruth's mind. She could warn her away from danger, disease, and death" (2001, p. 68), but later Ruth is the one who explains American life to her aging mother and eventually comes to frame her own narrative – out of the broken pieces of her mother's memories. Again mother's and daughter's experiences mirror each other. As in past novels, resolution arrives in the form of Ruth's rewriting of the past and thus claiming her own space within her maternal history.

In *The Bonesetter's Daughter*, Tan closely links language development and thought to the Name of the Mother. Tan's essay "Mother Tongue" (included in *The Opposite of Fate*) sheds light on the many autobiographical linguistic elements in this novel. In validating her mother's language, often identified as "broken English" by outsiders, Tan asserts, "That was the language that helped shape the way I saw things, expressed things, made sense of the world" (2003, p. 273). In the end, Tan's ability to employ "all the Englishes" she had grown up with led to the composition of *The Joy Luck Club*.

While Amy Tan's first four novels highlighted mother–daughter plots, *Saving Fish from Drowning* (2005), pays more attention to "the tensions of living between worlds" explored in E.D. Huntley's book. The omniscient narrator, named Bibi Chen, is already dead and tells her story from a liminal space between life and death. Bibi, a Chinese American art dealer from San Francisco, died under mysterious circumstances just shortly before a trip to Burma. When her friend Bennie Trueba y Cela replaces her as the trip leader, she recognizes the advantages of her ghostly state for being able to read the other characters' minds.

In addition to Bibi Chen, Tan introduces a large group of ethnically diverse characters who journey together to Burma for many different reasons and speak to each other in many different voices. Tan depicts humans as possessing social selves by examining very carefully the social relationships among her characters. Abducted by the politically oppressed Karen minority group, the tourists have to adjust to their new environment and reassess their beliefs and values.

In addition to Bibi retelling the events of the tourists' abduction, she is also recollecting her past, the loss of her mother, and the family's departure from Shanghai during World War II. Bibi's struggle to make sense of memory fragments parallels the other characters' attempts to come to terms with events in their lives. The experience at the Karen's home "No Name Place" contributes significantly to their growing awareness that human nature is not finite and independent, but that humans are social creatures that need to rely on each other. During a singing and drumming ritual performed by the Karen, the group experiences a moment of transcendental ecstasy. In this moment, all barriers among them are removed and they finally understand each other completely, without misunderstandings or complications. Their admission that such miracles can occur eventually becomes a liberating experience, an experience that Tan describes with the very simple term "love" (2005, p. 412).

Published in 2013, *The Valley of Amazement* revisits many of Amy Tan's most familiar motifs. An excerpt of the novel published as the tale "Rules for Virgins" (2011) offered a sneak preview of the novel itself. Inspired by several works about courtesans' influence in bringing Western culture to Shanghai – and, possibly, an eponymous painting by Carl Blechen – this novel is Tan's first to emphasize women's sexuality. In an interview with Bridget Kinsella (2013) writing for *Publishers*

Weekly, Tan jokingly refers to her novel as "Fifty Shades of Tan." While still anchored in her customary mother–daughter plot, this novel involves several acts of betrayal and focuses on the power of the imagination to transform history. Hybrid characters and hybrid places abound with a shift from contemporary American daughters of Chinese ancestry to early twentieth-century mixed-race characters in the culturally diverse Chinese city of Shanghai.

The novel centers on the colorful experiences of Violet Minturn, known as Vivi, who grows up in her mother Lucretia "Lulu" Minturn's brothel in Shanghai, thinking that, like her mother, she is Anglo-American. As the Ching dynasty ends in 1912 and the Manchu mount a campaign against foreigners, Vivi must realize that her Chinese father Lu Shing took no interest in her and, instead, abducted her baby brother Teddy to San Francisco. When Lulu and Vivi try to leave together to find him, they are separated, and Vivi is sold as a virgin courtesan. Tan pairs Vivi with another courtesan named Magic Gourd, who serves as both mirror and advisor to Vivi.

As Vivi trains for her future profession, she realizes that with enough makeup, she can cover her European heritage enough to turn her Eurasian looks into an asset. Tan writes a veritable guidebook for courtesan behavior, including sexual elements that she shunned before. Indeed, Vivi employs all her wiles to enchant Loyalty Fang, a wealthy but unreliable merchant who buys her virginity. It is through him that she meets the American Edward Ivory with whom she has a daughter Flora. When Edward dies of the Spanish Flu, his wife Minerva kidnaps Flora. Somewhat unexpectedly, Vivi simply returns to her life as – now a lesser – courtesan. After a short stint as concubine, she escapes this drudgery via a mountain path that leads her to the Valley of Amazement, the subject of a painting that Vivi inherited from her mother.

This is when the novel shifts to the narrative perspective of Vivi's mother, Lucretia Minturn, an American from San Francisco, who fell in love with the Chinese art student Lu Shing in 1897 and followed him to China when she realized that she was pregnant with his child. When he, however, obeys his family and offers Lucretia the status of second wife, she is torn between her American pluck and his Chinese acceptance of fate. Lulu sets out on her own and becomes a successful entrepreneur when she and Magic Gourd first open lucrative pubs, which they consolidate into the highly successful courtesan house "Hidden Jade Path," where businessmen from East and West can meet to discuss business and be entertained.

From there, the braided narrative again shifts to Vivi's point of view, now in 1926, when Vivi manages to reconnect with Lulu. As they begin to establish a relationship, the ending seems strangely rushed. It is Lulu who keeps an eye on Flora, who also knows nothing about her Chinese ancestry. After Flora and Vivi meet for the first time in Shanghai, the two part knowing full well that the looming World War II may make it impossible for them to ever meet again. In their journey toward self-knowledge, the three generations of women must come to terms with their past and must acknowledge maternal ties.

In her 2017, *Where the Past Begins: A Writer's Memoir*, Tan elaborates not just some of her own childhood memories, especially of her father whom she idealized, but also the circumstances of writing *The Valley of Amazement*, including an email exchange with her editor, David Halpern, that sheds light on her composing process.

The tensions experienced by Tan's hybrid characters who live between worlds, ideologies, and value systems, often create pain, but, as Tan's novels show, being vested in several cultures may also be a positive and enriching experience. In an April 2019 *LitHub* article, Amy Tan comments that "[f]iction is a portal to a deeper understanding of myself, and when I went through it the first time, I knew I would write fiction the rest of my life" (Tan 2019). The profusion of multicultural experiences and interactions in Tan's novels offers readers a portal to a deeper understanding of our ever more globalized world.

SEE ALSO: Fiction and Affect; Globalization; Kingston, Maxine Hong

REFERENCES

Cardozo, Erica K. (1995). The spirits are with her. *Entertainment Weekly* 298 (October 27, 1995): 84.
Huntley, E.D. (1998). *Amy Tan: A Critical Companion*. Michigan: Greenwood Press.
Kinsella, Bridget. (2013). Fifty shades of Tan. *Publishers Weekly* (August 9, 2013): 26–27. https://www.publishersweekly.com/pw/by-topic/authors/profiles/article/58667-fifty-shades-of-tan-amy-tan.html (accessed July 15, 2021).
Ling, Amy. (1990). *Between Worlds: Women Writers of Chinese Ancestry*. Oxford: Pergamon.
Tan, Amy. (1991). *The Kitchen God's Wife*. New York: Putnam.
Tan, Amy. (1995). *The Hundred Secret Senses*. New York: Putnam.
Tan, Amy. (2001). *The Bonesetter's Daughter*. New York: Putnam.
Tan, Amy. (2003). *The Opposite of Fate: A Book of Musings*. New York: Putnam.
Tan, Amy. (2005). *Saving Fish from Drowning*. New York: Putnam.
Tan, Amy. (2019). Amy Tan reflects on 30 years since *The Joy Luck Club*: writing fiction that's truer than memoir. *LitHub* (April 23, 2019). https://lithub.com/amy-tan-reflects-on-30-years-since-the-joy-luck-club/ (accessed July 15, 2021).

FURTHER READING

Bloom, Harold. (ed.) (2000). *Amy Tan: Modern Critical Views*. New York: Chelsea House.
Borus, Audrey. (2017). *Reading and Interpreting the Works of Amy Tan*. Berkeley Heights, NJ: Enslow.
Ho, Wendy. (1999). *In Her Mother's House: The Politics of Asian American Mother-Daughter Writing*. Walnut Creek, CA: Altamira Press.
Redford, James. (dir.) (2021). *Amy Tan: Unintended Memoir*. PBS American Masters and KJPR Films.
Snodgrass, Mary Ellen. (2004). *A Literary Amy Tan Companion*. Jefferson, NC: McFarland.
Tan, Amy. (n.d.). Personal webpage. http://www.amytan.net/about.html
Yuan, Yuan. (1999). The semiotics of China narratives in the con/texts of Kingston and Tan. *Critique* 40 (3): 292–303.

Tartt, Donna

HANNA MÄKELÄ
University of Tartu, Estonia

Donna Louise Tartt was born on December 23, 1963, in Greenwood, Mississippi. She attended the University of Mississippi in 1981–1982, before transferring to Bennington College, a prestigious liberal arts college in Vermont. Tartt's northern move was inspired by her literary mentors in Mississippi, Willie Morris and Barry Hannah. It was at Bennington where Tartt began working on her debut novel, *The Secret History* (1992) (Kuiper 2019).

The Secret History, enjoyed an unusual amount of attention, both in the publishing business and with readers. Michiko Kakutani, the revered *New York Times* arbiter, wrote a glowing review where she aptly encapsulated the various intertexts of Tartt's work and the skill with which these canonical influences were absorbed: "Imagine the plot of Dostoyevsky's 'Crime and Punishment' crossed with the story of Euripides' 'Bacchae' set against the backdrop of Bret Easton Ellis's 'Rules of Attraction' and told in the elegant, ruminative voice of Evelyn Waugh's 'Brideshead Revisited'" (Kakutani 1992).

Kakutani's analysis notes so many traits of Tartt's that it works as a miniature portrait of the then twenty-eight-year-old writer and is quite prescient as to how her oeuvre would develop over time, as demonstrated by her subsequent novels, *The Little Friend* (2002) and *The Goldfinch* (2014). Dostoevsky's psychologically complex and morally compromised characters, as well as his existential plots are also the bread and butter of Tartt's later writings, as are the more or less explicit allusions to the Russian master. As is so often the case with Dostoevsky, Tartt's fictional crimes also have their accomplices and "doubles": Richard Papen and Henry Winter in *The Secret History*, Harriet Dufresnes and Hely Hull in *The Little Friend*, and Theo Decker and Boris Pavlikovsky in *The Goldfinch*. The Euripides tragedy that plays out its contemporary version in the story world of *The Secret History* has its counterparts in the anachronistic nostalgia the protagonists of *The Little Friend* and *The Goldfinch* experience vis-à-vis the Old South and the Dutch Golden Age, respectively. Brett Easton Ellis, though much more breezily self-conscious and "meta" than Tartt, is nevertheless a solid reference point to a literary writer come of age in the postmodern 1980s who fuses popular genre fiction with art prose. Ellis and Tartt know each other from their student days at Bennington College and are both associated with the so-called "literary brat pack," together with Jay McInerney, Tama Janowitz, and Jill Eisenstadt (Diamond 2016). Finally, as for Tartt's affinity with Waugh, it is not merely stylistic, but also thematic: Tartt is a practicing Catholic, and although theology is less conspicuously present in her novels and short stories than those of Waugh's, it is not inconsequential either. This is not to say that her spiritually tortured protagonists are destined for any fully orthodox conversion. Tartt herself puts it best when she writes in her essay, "The spirit and writing in a secular world" (2000):

> As a Roman Catholic, my faith is a viewpoint which is universally applicable to all questions in life; but if I, as a novelist, set out with the attitude that *any* view – Catholicism, Freudian psychology, what-have-you – is an unfailingly correct solution to all dilemmas within my novel, then my novel will seem predetermined and dull at best, and quite ridiculous and unbelievable at worst.
>
> (2000, p. 26)

There are some affinities here between Tartt and her fellow Southerner, Flannery O'Connor, who similarly disavows didactic religiosity in creative writing in her posthumously published essay collection, *Mystery and Manners* (1969). Whatever the interpretation or degree of adherence, religion and spirituality point towards an existential realm that is important to Tartt's characters, affected as they are by traumatic transgressions of either their own or someone else's making. Psychological trauma and moral transgression, the two major narrative engines driving Tartt's character motivation and plot development, are always tied up with a more thoroughly existential alienation and ontological questioning.

Tartt's debut novel, *The Secret History*, came out in what could be characterized as a particularly postmodern moment in anglophone literature. However, despite its mixture of "high" (philosophical novel, social satire, *Bildungsroman*) and "low" (crime thriller, melodrama, campus novel) genres, as well as certain moderately metafictional elements in the first-person narrator's pursuit to create his identity through the act of writing his "secret" memoir, the book is also deliberately traditional. *The Secret*

History is driven by plot, character, and theme rather than self-referential parody. Literature is one of the subjects of Tartt's novel, and in that way at least *The Secret History* could be seen as a postmodernist case of textuality imitating textuality. Then again, the main characters' inability to distinguish between fact, fiction, and myth and thus engage with unvarnished reality is precisely their ethical failure. Despite their superior language skills and expensive education, the Classics students are essentially *bad readers*.

Through its many intertexts, *The Secret History* slyly unmasks the contemporary Western intellectual's anachronistic longing for a supposedly more authentic and holistic being-in-the-world. Ironically, the students' Nietzschean preoccupation with self-flattering immoralism is one characteristic the ancient Greeks decidedly lacked in their own collectively religious feasts. In order to revitalize the social hierarchy beneficial to them, the over-compensating students fetishize the age-old religiosity they otherwise have little use of.

Moreover, it is the students' studied manner of engaging with their subject matter at an intellectual distance that gives the lie to their murderous field trip. It is because the students initially fail to see their Dionysian re-enactment for the textbook-scripted live-action role play that it is that the orgy turns murderous. Pragmatically enough, the second murder is dictated by a need for witness elimination, though also fused with petty resentments and grudges against a former friend.

As the crime story at the heart of the novel unravels, the character-narrator Richard Papen comes to realize how his complicity in the second murder does not make him an unconventional hero of Nietzschean proportions after all, but that his deep-seated inferiority complex compelled him to belong in the seductive Classics group simply because it seemed so different from him and thus had to be better than him. When his fundamental similarity with the four accomplices begins to dawn on him, Richard is no longer flattered by the in-group status he once so eagerly sought (Mäkelä 2014, pp. 230–231). While strangeness inspires fascination, familiarity merely breeds contempt:

> At one time I had liked the idea, that the act, at least had bound us together; we were not ordinary friends, but friends till-death-do-us-part. This thought had been my only comfort in the aftermath of Bunny's death. Now it made me sick, knowing there was no way out. I was stuck with them, with all of them, for good.
>
> (2002a, p. 519)

What makes Richard's position in the group unique is his willingness to identify with the perpetrators after the first murder – a murder that cannot be legally attributed to him. Once the second murder is carried out with Richard's help, he has an actual violent event haunting him, thus fusing psychic trauma with moral guilt.

Published between the precocious debut that was *The Secret History* and the mature fulfillment that was *The Goldfinch*, Tartt's second novel, *The Little Friend*, can easily come off as somewhat underwhelming by comparison. However, while falling short of its predecessor's success, it still won the W.H. Smith Literary Award in 2003 and was shortlisted for the Women's Prize for Fiction (at the time still called the Orange Prize).

As she told her interviewer at *The Guardian* (Viner 2002), Tartt wrote *The Little Friend* as a conscious departure from *The Secret History*. In many ways the novels really are each other's direct opposites. The protagonist of *The Little Friend* is not only female, but a pre-teen child, who furthermore is not the narrator, this role being taken up by a third-person omniscient voice.

The Little Friend is set in 1970s Mississippi where Tartt herself spent her formative years. Although the book is fictional, its depiction of a "Southern gothic childhood" resonates with an autobiographical essay of Tartt's that recounts how a De Quincey-reading great-grandfather prescribed for her "glasses of whiskey at my bedtime and regular and massive doses of some red stuff which I now know to have been codeine cough syrup" (Tartt 1992). Perhaps this endearingly anachronistic family influence partly explains two of Tartt's major preoccupations: a nineteenth-century epic scale of her prose, as well as characters who suffer from some form of substance abuse or other addictions. Besides these two, another theme that *The Little Friend* shares with *The Secret History* is that both are books about books and the potentially pernicious ways to read them. The main character of *The Little Friend*, the twelve-year-old Harriet Cleve Dufresnes, immerses herself in the exotic adventure tales by Stevenson and Kipling but is unable to distinguish between those fictional works on the one hand and her family lore of violent tragedy on the other. Despite, or rather because, she is precociously intelligent, Harriet is, like the undergraduates of *The Secret History*, both bookish and bloodthirsty.

The setting of *The Little Friend* is not the only aspect to parallel the Southern gothic canon. The genre is famous for its preoccupation with psychological and moral coming-of-age stories, often contrasting themes of innocence and decay, perceived past greatness and present impoverishment. Collective nostalgia as a moral problem is also something that Tartt's first and second novel have in common.

That children so often are at the center of Southern gothic narratives is an additional intertextual layer picked up by *The New York Times* critic A.O. Scott who, among other influences, singles out William Faulkner's *The Sound and the Fury* (1929), Carson McCullers's *The Member of the Wedding* (1946), and Harper Lee's *To Kill a Mockingbird* (1960) (Scott 2002). Unlike many of the child characters of the preceding Southern canon, Tartt's protagonist is not so much the deceptively innocuous observer as she is a full-fledged (anti)heroine of her own story. This strength of agency means that Harriet is no mere innocent, but that her precociousness makes her transgressive adventure – a quest to solve and avenge her brother's murder – almost as callous as the one undertaken by the Dionysian revelers of *The Secret History*. Harriet's precociousness is supposedly downright supernatural, since she claims to remember her brother despite being quite literally still a baby at the time of his death:

> Though she'd been less than six months old when Robin died, Harriet said she could remember him; and Allison and the rest of the Cleves believed that this was probably the truth. Every now and then Harriet came out with some obscure but shockingly accurate bit of information – details of weather or dress, menus from birthday parties attended before she was two – that made everyone's jaw drop.
>
> (2002, p. 24)

Ironically, Harriet's ego is much more robust than that of the adult male protagonists of *The Secret History* and *The Goldfinch*. What all the main characters in all of Tartt's novels have in common, though, is a sense of alienation in relation to one or several parental figures, as well as a varying degree of moral ambivalence that makes them both victims of circumstance and willing transgressors at the same time. In the end, Harriet is redeemed by her relief of having failed in her murderous pursuit of justice.

Following Tartt's by now familiar pattern of spending a decade, give or take, writing her novels, *The Goldfinch* was published in 2013. After the relative disappointment that accompanied *The Little Friend* – even Tartt's champion, Michiko Kakutani, described the second novel as "ungainly" (Kakutani 2002) – *The Goldfinch* was treated as a return to form. This time around Kakutani's review was more than favorable, complimenting the book's "finely drawn" characters and "narrative verve" and taking notice of Dickens's influence, especially of *Oliver Twist* (1838) and *Great Expectations* (1861) (Kakutani 2013). In 2014 Tartt's third novel was awarded the Andrew Carnegie Medal for Excellence in Fiction, as well as the Pulitzer. It furthermore gained her a place among *Time* magazine's list of that year's 100 most influential people (Patchett 2014).

Not all reactions from the major literary review outlets were positive, however. The overall reception of *The Goldfinch* was more polarizing than that of the author's previous works (Peretz 2014). Though the 2019 film adaptation directed by John Crowley was mostly negatively received, Tartt's novel would have benefited from the film's narrative clarity and precise articulation. The film's main weakness is its inevitably hurried pace, as in its faithfulness to Tartt's story the screenwriters had no chance of developing the plot and the characterization to an equal degree. Tartt's writing is weighed down with an unbalanced structure of its own that has nothing to do with the book's epic length. The novel's dialogue sequences are more repetitive and verbose than per usual, and the text relies too much on impressionistic and catalogue-like descriptive passages that at times appear unnecessarily confusing to the reader who already knows to expect a certain amount of incoherence from the traumatized and drug-addicted narrator. That said, *The Goldfinch* is even more psychologically nuanced and its characters more rounded than is the case with *The Secret History*, while the latter is stylistically more compact.

The Goldfinch signals a return to the familiar territory of *The Secret History* also in that both their stories are told in the first person, in a private written confession that is not meant for any flesh-and-blood narratees. The confessional mode allows the character-narrators to not only experience, but also articulate their guilt.

The novel takes its name from a real-life work of art, a 1654 painting by the Dutch Golden Age master, Carel Fabritius. In reference to the actual Fabritius, who died in a gunpowder plant explosion near his studio, Tartt's fictional story of where and in whose possession his painting travels also begins with an explosion. The main character, Theodore "Theo" Decker and his art-loving mother fall victim to a terrorist bombing at the New York Metropolitan Museum of Art. Theo's adored single mother Audrey perishes, while Theo survives, having "saved" Fabritius's work before finding his way back out of the rubble. By linking circumstances of Fabritius's and Audrey's deaths, as well as his painting and Audrey's memory in Theo's mind, *The Goldfinch* ties together two of its author's favorite themes, namely psychological trauma and moral guilt. A third favorite theme, that of complicity between friends, comes into play as Theo meets his best friend, Boris Pavlikovsky, a lovable rogue and future gangster whose underworld contacts produce the most crucial plot twists.

Instead of Tartt's usual ethical mirroring between *literary* texts and their fictional readers, *The Goldfinch* is first and foremost a book about man-made *visual* artifacts and their preservation, often with moral compromise involved (the adult Theo deals in counterfeited antique furniture, in addition to having stolen the eponymous painting). A framed picture can hold a mirror to the flesh-and-blood viewer's hidden self-image:

Because: if our secrets define us, as opposed to the face we show the world: then the painting was the secret that raised me above the surface of life and enabled me to know who I am. And it's there: in my notebooks, every page, even though it's not. Dream and magic, magic and delirium. The Unified Field Theory. A secret about secrets.

(2014, pp. 856–857)

When the mirroring process is benign and enhances rather than obscures a deeper knowledge of the self, it ceases to be doubling in the sense of mere replication and becomes a form of genuine communication.

Although the long silences between the publications of her novels tend to receive most of the attention, Tartt has produced other, shorter texts mostly published in magazines. These include four short stories ("A Christmas Pageant," 1993; "Tam-O'-Shanter," 1993; "A Garter Snake," 1995; "The Ambush," 2005) that echo the styles and themes of her novels, namely childhood insecurities, awareness of death, the unexpected threat of violence, as well as confessional tones in recounting past events. Tartt's non-fiction is equally short in length and encompasses various genres (memoir, eulogy, sports writing, book introduction).

Apart from prose, Tartt has also written poetry, and her first publication, at the age of thirteen, was a sonnet (Kuiper 2019). Her short prose poem, "True Crime" (1996), has all the thematic markings of a psychological thriller, regardless of the format that is atypical of the author. Still, Tartt is quite open about her special affinity with the novel, especially the medium's immersive narrative potential that comes from sheer length, but also the aesthetic "craft" involved in the writing process (Manufacturing Intellect 2016).

It is thus fair to summarize that Tartt's novels make up the bulk of her legacy. At their best, they strike a fine balance between epic scale and dramatic intensity, sensuously lyrical style and psychologically nuanced characterization, plot-driven action, and cerebral contemplation. All these narrative virtues combined contribute to Donna Tartt's firm standing as an ambitious, yet accessible, literary artist.

ACKNOWLEDGMENTS

Research for this entry was supported by the European Regional Development Fund (Mobilitas Pluss, MOBJD282) and the Estonian Research Council (Grant 1481).

SEE ALSO: After Postmodernism; Contemporary Regionalisms; Debut Novels; Erdrich, Louise; Hannah, Barry; Hustvedt, Siri; Morrison, Toni; Oates, Joyce Carol; Trauma and Fiction; Wolfe, Tom

REFERENCES

Crowley, John. (dir.) (2014/2013). *The Goldfinch*. Warner Bros. Pictures.
Diamond, Jason. (2016). Sex, drugs, and bestsellers: the legend of the literary brat pack. *Harper's Bazaar* (November 2, 2016). https://www.harpersbazaar.com/culture/art-books-music/a18422/literary-brat-pack-donna-tartt-jay-mcinerney/ (accessed July 13, 2021).
Kakutani, Michiko. (1992). Students indulging in course of destruction. *The New York Times* (September 4, 1992). https://www.nytimes.com/1992/09/04/books/books-of-the-times-students-indulging-in-course-of-destruction.html (accessed July 13, 2021).
Kakutani, Michiko. (2002). In a Mississippi town, a little boy's murder spells the death of a family. *The New York Times* (October 17, 2002). https://www.nytimes.com/2002/10/17/books/books-times-mississippi-town-little-boy-s-murder-spells-death-family.html (accessed July 13, 2021).
Kakutani, Michiko. (2013). A painting as talisman, as enduring as loved ones are not. *The New York Times* (October 7, 2013). https://www.nytimes.com/2013/10/08/books/the-goldfinch-a-dickensian-novel-by-donna-tartt.html (accessed July 13, 2021).

Kuiper, Kathleen. (2019). Donna Tartt: American author. In: *Encyclopedia Britannica*. https://www.britannica.com/biography/Donna-Tartt (accessed July 13, 2021).

Mäkelä, Hanna. (2014). "Narrated Selves and Others: A Study of Mimetic Desire in Five Contemporary British and American Novels." Doctoral dissertation, University of Helsinki. http://urn.fi/URN:ISBN:978-952-10-9754-6 (accessed July 13, 2021).

Manufacturing Intellect. (2016). Donna Tartt interview (1992) (November 9, 2016). https://www.youtube.com/watch?v=7oo-wNuP9tU (accessed July 13, 2021).

Patchett, Ann. (2014). Donna Tartt. *Time* (April 23, 2014). https://time.com/70819/donna-tartt-2014-time-100/ (accessed July 13, 2021).

Peretz, Evgenia. (2014). It's Tartt – but is it art? *Vanity Fair* (June 11, 2014). https://www.vanityfair.com/culture/2014/07/goldfinch-donna-tartt-literary-criticism# (accessed July 13, 2021).

Scott, Anthony O. (2002). Harriet the spy. *The New York Times* (November 3, 2014). https://www.nytimes.com/2002/11/03/books/harriet-the-spy.html?auth=login-facebook&login=facebook (accessed July 13, 2021).

Tartt, Donna. (1992). Sleepytown: a Southern Gothic childhood, with codeine. *Harper's Magazine* (July 1992) 286, pp. 60–66. http://www.languageisavirus.com/donna_tartt/nonfiction-sleepytown.php#.YV2jDtrMKU1 (accessed September 19, 2021).

Tartt, Donna. (2000). The spirit and writing in a secular world. In *The Novel, Spirituality and Modern Culture: Eight Novelists Write about their Craft and their Context* (ed. Paul S. Fiddes), 25–40. Cardiff: University of Wales Press.

Tartt, Donna. (2002). *The Secret History*. London: Penguin Books; 1st ed. 1992.

Tartt, Donna. (2014). *The Goldfinch*. London: Abacus; 1st ed. 2013.

Viner, Katharine. (2002). A talent to tantalise. *The Guardian* (October 19, 2002). https://www.theguardian.com/books/2002/oct/19/fiction.features (accessed August 2, 2021).

FURTHER READING

Arkins, Brian. (1995). Greek themes in Donna Tartt's *The Secret History*. *Classical and Modern Literature: A Quarterly* 15 (3): 281–287.

Clements, Mikaella. (2019). The secret herstory: what happened to Donna Tartt's women? *The Guardian* (September 25, 2019). https://www.theguardian.com/books/2019/sep/25/secreted-history-what-happened-to-donna-tartt-women

Corrigan, Yuri. (2018). Donna Tartt's Dostoevsky: trauma and the displaced self. *Comparative Literature* 70 (4): 392–407. https://www.academia.edu/32939634/Donna_Tartts_Dostoevsky_Trauma_and_the_Displaced_Self

Hargreaves, Tracy. (2001). *Donna Tartt's The Secret History: A Reader's Guide*. London: Continuum.

Melvin, Barbara A. (1996). Failures in classical and modern morality: echoes of Euripides in *The Secret History*. *Journal of Evolutionary Psychology* 17 (1–2): 53–63.

Third-Wave Feminism

JUSTYNA WŁODARCZYK
University of Warsaw, Poland

Third-wave feminist fiction is by no means a universally accepted designation. However, it has been proposed by several scholars (Drake 2006; Włodarczyk 2010) as a useful grouping of emerging American writers who were starting their careers in the 1990s and creating fiction exploring issues of gender identity, while employing what could be termed third-wave sensibility and aesthetics. Aware of the problems related to establishing formal categories for what counts as feminist writing, this entry assumes Rita Felski's broad definition of feminist literature as "texts that reveal a critical awareness of women's subordinate position and of gender as a problematic category" (1989, p. 14). It should be emphasized that third-wave literature has overwhelmingly consisted of nonfiction – personal essays and memoirs – and that boundary-blurring, especially of the boundary between fiction and life writing, has been an important political strategy for feminist writers. Some scholars argue that chick lit can be seen as having a strong relationship to the "girlie" strand within third-wave feminism (Genz and Brabon 2009), although others – probably the majority of critics – see this type of genre fiction as postfeminist (McRobbie 2004). Eve Ensler's 1996 play *The Vagina Monologues* is usually listed as a feminist text that emphasizes both body positivity and the significance of combatting violence against women for third-wave feminism; stagings of the play were also significant events integrating feminist activists in the 1990s and 2000s. Some scholars see a connection between third-wave feminism and memoir/fiction that explores writings in which young female protagonists negotiate their intersectional identities, usually focusing on the interplay of race and gender or class and gender; for example, Sapphire's *Push* (1996), novels by Edwidge Danticat and Danzy Senna, and Rebecca Walker's memoir *Black, White and Jewish: Autobiography of a Shifting Self* (2001). Some suggest that fiction and graphic novels building on the post-punk (and often queer) aesthetics of the "Riot Grrrl" movement can be read as one of the literary expressions of third-wave feminism (for example, memoir/fiction/poetry by Michelle Tea, and the *Naughty Bits* comic book series by Roberta Gregory). While third-wave writings incorporated an intersectional feminist perspective, their overtly feminist agenda was much less explicit than the agenda of, for example, consciousness-raising novels associated with the second wave of feminism. Even though third-wave writers usually self-identified as feminists, their work was not explicitly marketed as "third-wave feminist" by the publishing industry, which may have contributed to the waning of this label. Because of the inherent intersectionality of these texts, many entered other (nonfeminist) canons; some texts have been marketed as voices of Generation X, others have entered the canon of queer literature. The designation generally waned in the second half of the first decade of the 2000s, as feminist organizing entered the online era.

The emergence of third-wave feminism in the United States is usually dated to the early 1990s, when a confluence of high-publicity events, such as the Anita Hill–Clarence Thomas hearings and increased restrictions on access to abortion in several US states, and their media coverage evoked both an activist response from young women and an outburst of activist-based writings related to these events (Baumgardner and Richards 2000; Heywood 2006). The key issues for young feminists in the 1990s also included the persistence of gender-based violence (highlighted through, among other activities, Take Back The Night marches, which were gradually replaced with Slut Walks; a symbol of how second-wave solemn seriousness was replaced with third-wave shameless playfulness). This outburst of activity followed a decade of decreased media visibility of feminist activism during the Reagan administration, also referred to as a period of backlash (Faludi 1991). Genealogies of feminism often point to three strands – sometimes referred to as "nodes" (Garrison 2000) – that can be seen as contributing to the emergence of third-wave feminism: the notion of "power feminism" associated with the writings of Naomi Wolf, the rise of intersectionality as embodied in the writings of Rebecca Walker and the agenda of the Third Wave Foundation Walker founded, and, finally, the influence of the Riot Grrrl movement, centered around the punk music scene in the Pacific Northwest region of the United States. The aesthetics and politics associated with these three nodes can, in turn, be detected in three strands of fiction that appeared in the 1990s.

THIRD-WAVE POLITICS OF THE PERSONAL

Before discussing these three strands of third-wave feminist fiction, it is important to note that the narrative mode unquestionably linked to third-wave activism is not fiction but first-person life writing. This in itself should not be surprising: life writing and the women's movement have had a close relationship since the beginning of feminist writing in the Western sphere. Drawing out the political dimension of women's personal lives through depictions of personal experiences has been both a literary and a political strategy for bringing to life the "personal is political" slogan of second-wave feminism. Feminist writers have used first-person narratives to speak of their own experiences of gender-based oppression and to establish bonds with their readers, using their texts as vehicles of so-called consciousness-raising, a term adopted from Marxist activism (Hogeland 1998). Rita Felski has memorably written of "the feminist confession," a mode of writing based on the promise of establishing a close affective relationship with another woman through the act of writing. Felski sees this task as somewhat contradictory – the building of community through the solitary act of writing (1989, pp. 86–88). Defining the feminist confession more as a mode than a literary genre, Felski focuses on how it brings together politics and aesthetics: the seemingly unadorned, unmediated, and honest mode of direct expression, in which the writer bares her soul and increases the reader's emotional investment in the protagonist's story, thus facilitating the reader's acceptance of the book's political premise.

The texts most explicitly identified with the third wave of feminism have come in the form of essays, largely published in anthologies bearing the word feminism in the title. These include: Rebecca Walker's *To Be Real: Telling the Truth and Changing the Face of Feminism* (1995), Barbara Findlen's *Listen Up! Voices from the Next Feminist Generation* (1995), and the slightly more academic *Third Wave Agenda: Being Feminist, Doing Feminism*, edited by Leslie Heywood and Jennifer Drake (1997), or Rory Dicker and Allison Piepmeier's *Catching a Wave: Reclaiming Feminism for the 21st Century* (2003). The essays in these collections largely follow the narrative and aesthetic conventions of second-wave feminist essays, with several modifications. There is most definitely greater emphasis on ethnic, class, and sexual diversity among the authors and a greater diversity of concerns identified as feminist. In fact, the unifying feature of many of these texts is the possibility of being a feminist while not conforming to what the young authors see as second-wave criteria of feminist identity. Consequently, the stories include testimony by both fitness instructors and overweight women; young women who argue that interest in fashion and beauty is an element of self-care and those who reject mainstream beauty practices; religious women and those who seek spirituality outside of organized religion. The goal of these texts is to elicit empathy and "raise the consciousness" of the reader, convince her – the implied reader is clearly female – that because the stories she is reading are so diverse, she, too, can identify as a feminist. Many of the narratives contain elements of a secularized version of the "conversion narrative," that is, they recount a period of internal struggle followed by a moment of revelation. In these cases, the struggle often has to do with what is perceived as a conflict between one's various identity positions – Can I be both an Asian American and a feminist? – and the resolution is ultimately a positive one. While the exploration of such themes confirms that intersectionality is indeed one of the key issues in the third wave, in other words, that young women want to understand how their overlapping and sometimes contradictory subject positions can be negotiated in ways that turn them into sources of strength and knowledge, it also points to the fact that feminism is not defined in these texts through standard political activism but through lifestyle choices. In other words, the authors decide to practice feminism through self-acceptance; by not dieting, not succumbing to the pressure to perceive themselves as ugly, and so on.

It is important to note that already second-wave feminist writers have – with various degrees of self-awareness – attempted to blur the boundary between life writing and fiction. Many of the well-known feminist texts marketed as fiction use first-person narration and are, at least to some extent, based on the authors' lives. The fictional genre most closely tied to second-wave feminism, the consciousness-raising novel – as practiced by, for example, Marge Piercy or Alix Kates Shulman – is actually based on a premise somewhat similar to that of the confession; through the establishment of a representative female character, an "everywoman," such fiction aims to encourage the reader to make connections between the fictional protagonist's life and the experiences of the individual reader. This blurring of boundaries becomes even more pronounced in feminism's third wave. As a result, in third-wave feminist writings it sometimes becomes impossible to draw the line between memoir and novel.

NAOMI WOLF AND CHICK LIT

The term third-wave feminism was used for the first time by Naomi Wolf in her 1991 nonfiction book *The Beauty Myth*, where Wolf wrote of the "feminist third wave" to speak of a younger generation of women who came of age in a world that had benefited from the achievements of the feminist movement of the 1970s, yet who still felt that further activism – coupled with an update of activist strategies – was necessary for true gender equality to be achieved. The main argument of Wolf's book was an updated version of the classic argument from Simone de Beauvoir's *The Second Sex* (1949), which claimed that encouraging women's efforts to take care of their physical appearance is an intrinsic element of patriarchy; women's time-consuming preoccupation with their looks is a distraction from becoming engaged in other issues. Wolf's update of Beauvoir came in the form of recognition that women's increased presence in the public sphere is coupled with further pressure related to physical appearance, often exerted through constant scrutiny by the popular media. In her second book, *Fire with Fire* (1993), Wolf coined the term "power feminism," which she saw as underlying the generational divide within feminism. According to Wolf, in second-wave feminism the subject position of women was that of victims of patriarchal oppression, a strategy that disqualified the movement in the eyes of the younger generation, who grew up thinking of themselves as strong and empowered. Wolf encourages younger women to redefine feminism in ways that make it possible for them to speak from a position of power rather than victimhood. In this book, Wolf also is much more sympathetic to traditionally feminine beauty-related practices; she sees the need to reclaim them as a source of female strength and not a bowing down to patriarchal pressure. Wolf wrote in a highly reader-friendly format, using nonacademic language, and her books, published by trade publishers, quickly became bestsellers and attracted the attention of the media. Wolf became the face of third-wave feminism, creating the impression that her agenda was the movement's agenda. Critics have argued that Wolf's version of third-wave feminism was "apolitical, individualistic, self-promotional and applicable only to white, middle-class women" (Heywood 2006, p. xvi). In light of Wolf's explicit critique of second-wave feminism, though also because of her praise of the individualist ethic which can be easily co-opted by consumerism, her version of third-wave feminism is sometimes equated with postfeminism. Because one of the ways of challenging the sociohistorical associations of femininity with weakness suggested by Wolf is through a reclamation of typically feminine attributes as attributes of power, Wolf's ideas have sometimes been linked with sub-labels such as "girlie" feminism or "lipstick" feminism. These positions, in turn, have been aligned with the popular genre of "chick lit."

What ties chick lit to Wolf's version of third-wave feminism is the figure of the heroine, a single professional woman in her thirties whose struggles with self-acceptance are coupled with a usually heterosexual romance plot, albeit one with a twist because it is the woman who plays the active role in ensnaring a husband. The founding text for this genre is Helen Fielding's bestseller *Bridget Jones's Diary* (1996), written using first-person narration and a confessional tone, established largely through what appears to be a very candid depiction of the heroine's slightly comic struggles with improving her imperfect appearance, fulfilling professional aspirations, and finding a husband. The popularity of Fielding's book sparked the growth and international expansion of the genre in the early 2000s. Some well-known American titles include Lauren Weisberger's *The Devil Wears Prada* (2003), Jennifer Weiner's *Good in Bed* (2001) and *In Her Shoes* (2002), and Emma McLaughlin and Nicola Kraus's *The Nanny Diaries* (2002). While the self-identification of these authors with feminism varies – Weiner being the most outspoken feminist of the group – their novels all share a focus on young, urban, single heroines. Genz and Brabon claim that the singleton heroine was "appealing for a 1990s generation of women who are unwilling to renounce their joint aspirations for job and romance, their feminist and feminine values" (2009, p. 86). Meanwhile, Imelda Whelehan, who classifies *Bridget Jones's Diary* as a feminist bestseller, argues that "chick lit has clear links with the tradition of the consciousness-raising novel in seeming to tell it like it is and to raise individual awareness of shared personal concerns" (2005, p. 186). However, many critics suggest that chick lit actively undermines the feminist agenda by recycling the old romance plot, encouraging women's excessive preoccupation with body image, consumerism, and promoting "retail therapy as a means of personal fulfillment" (Ferriss and Young 2006, p. 11). Most definitely, the debate surrounding chick lit brings to the forefront uneasy distinctions between third-wave feminism and postfeminism. This distinction plays a key role for the second "node" of third-wave genealogy, one in which third-wave feminism is defined in opposition to postfeminism.

REBECCA WALKER AND THIRD-WAVE INTERSECTIONALITY

Another famous declaration of third-wave identity was articulated in Rebecca Walker's essay, originally published in *Ms.* magazine in 1992, titled "Becoming the third wave." Walker's article was a direct response to the Anita Hill–Clarence Thomas hearings, which forced the young writer to acknowledge that despite the gains of the 1970s, women's experiences of sexual harassment were still taken lightly in the public sphere. Acknowledging young women's disconnection from the movement defined by their mothers – here, not only metaphorical mothers, as Rebecca Walker is the daughter of feminist and novelist Alice Walker – Walker argued for the need for sustained activism in an era sometimes referred to as postfeminist. She famously announced: "I am not a postfeminism feminist. I am the Third Wave" (2006, p. 5). Walker understood postfeminism not in the sense in which it had been sometimes used in academia in the 1990s, that is, to signal the critique of essentialism and the recognition of the dismantling of the individualist subject (Fraser and Nicholson 1990; Wright 2000), but in the popular understanding of a time when feminism is no longer necessary, slightly similar to the more theoretical definition proposed by Angela McRobbie in her by now classic article "Post-Feminism and Popular Culture" (2004). According to McRobbie, postfeminism is "an active process by which feminist gains of the 1970s and 1980s come to be undermined" (2004, p. 255). Walker's essay, her subsequent writings, and her activism – she started the Third Wave Foundation – foreground a focus on intersectionality, which became a trademark of third-wave activism. This term, first coined by Kimberlé Crenshaw (1991) to speak of the need to recognize how overlapping social identities contribute to systemic oppression, reshaped feminist activism and theory in the 1990s. In "Becoming the third wave" Walker brought to the forefront the dynamics of race and gender, just as Kimberlé Crenshaw initially had done in her article "Mapping the margins" (1991), but other third wavers took on other intersectional dynamics, including the linking of feminist positions to nonheteronormative sexualities, environmentalism, anti-capitalism (or, more broadly, issues of class privilege). Ironically, the linking of multiple issues and the recognition of intersectionality may have also contributed to the decreased visibility of feminist activism in the public sphere in the 1990s and 2000s. The kind of third-wave sensibility associated with Walker's writings can be linked with works of fiction and memoir that foreground issues of intersectionality.

Walker herself authored the memoir *Black, White and Jewish: Autobiography of a Shifting Self*, which dramatizes examples of the issues encountered by young women trying to navigate the multiple strands forming their constantly shifting identities. After the divorce of her parents, mixed-race Walker is placed in a joint custody arrangement and spends time with her Jewish father in an upper-class suburban environment and her womanist activist African American mother, who lives on the West Coast. Walker's memoir, while presenting the individual experiences of the writer, suggests that these experiences are somehow typical for members of her generation: young women whose adolescence has been marked by various disruptions (frequent moves, divorces, shifting family dynamics) and the resulting need to constantly redefine oneself in perpetually changing circumstances. For a memoir written by a feminist activist, it is also surprisingly nonpolitical and does not even use the word feminism. Still, the author presents herself as shaped by a plethora of forces that have to do with social expectations related to gender, ethnicity, and social class. Because the author is a mixed-race subject, the memoir also tropes on the classic passing narrative, subverting it in ways that turn mixed-race identity from stigma and shame to a source of power and, most certainly, a position that by default results in a more nuanced understanding of social dynamics in the United States. Similarly to Walker's memoir, some novels and short stories by young ethnic female writers also embrace a comparable position; turning minority ethnic positions into sources of strength, resilience, and sensitivity, while exploring the particularity of the situation of young women in these nonwhite ethnic groups. These include Danzy Senna's *Caucasia* (1998), the fiction of Edwidge Danticat, Lois-Ann Yamanaka, and the short stories of ZZ Packer. However, it must be mentioned that none of the three writers listed above self-identified as third-wave feminists.

A very popular novel that can also be linked to the "intersectional" strand within third-wave feminism is Sapphire's *Push*. The novel recounts how the main protagonist, Precious, a pregnant teenage African American girl from a disadvantaged inner-city neighborhood, struggles with the consequences of a childhood filled with physical abuse, sexual exploitation, and incest. The novel is written using first-person narration and critics have noted how it tropes on other stories of incest and abuse by African American writers and on the legacy of incorporating nonstandard language into African American novels. Alice Walker's *The Color Purple* (1982) is an obvious example here, both in terms of theme and form. In *Push*, the protagonist's writing style evolves similarly to the evolution of the style of Celie's letters in Walker's novel. Push is written from an undeniably feminist perspective and aimed at a young readership, carrying a rather clear message about the interdependence of racial, class, and gender-based oppression. The author (Ramona Lofton) had been a performance poet and feminist/queer rights activist before debuting with her first work of fiction. It should be emphasized that both the narrative style and the subject matter of the novel became the matter of much criticism from more established writers. Percival Everett's *Erasure* (2001) can be read as a parodic response to this novel.

The topic of gender-based violence was a significant issue for third-wave activists: Rebecca Walker identified the need for further feminist activism while witnessing hearings related to charges of sexual harassment voiced by Anita Hill against Clarence Thomas. The book that best epitomized the third wave's focus on preventing violence against women and which managed to achieve huge international success was Eve Ensler's play *The Vagina Monologues*. In 2006, the *New York Times* called the play "probably the most important piece of political theater of the last decade" (Isherwood 2006). While Ensler, just like Sapphire, is not generationally part of the third-wave age cohort (both Ensler and Sapphire were born in the 1950s), the strategies employed by *The Vagina Monologues* embody the third-wave mixture of political and aesthetic strategies. The short pieces, grouped thematically via their focus on women's bodies, attempt to reclaim pejorative terms used to stigmatize women and their bodies. At the same time, while rejoicing in the potential pleasures of sexuality, the monologues also offer a very direct critique of sexual violence. Stagings of the play often served as a way of third-wave feminist organizing and the structure of the play amplified its consciousness-raising message: the individual experiences of the characters make the audience aware of the political dimensions of female experience.

RIOT GRRRL AND POST-PUNK QUEER AESTHETICS

A third genealogical thread for third-wave feminism is the punk and grunge music scene in Olympia, Washington and Washington, DC, in the early 1990s. In 1991, a group of young women active in the punk scene on the West Coast organized to protest sexism in the music underground and named themselves "Riot Grrrls." The word "grrrl" was coined by Kathleen Hanna, lead singer in the band Bikini Kill, as a reclamation of the derogatory use of the word "girl" (Garrison 2000). The reclaiming of the word "girl" by the Riot Grrrl movement took the form of skillful and playful manipulation of cultural images: the combination of pink skirts and combat boots, knee-high "girly" socks and body piercings. This rejection of mainstream beauty standards through the use of mockery, irony, and parody was, of course, taken over from the broader punk movement. The lyrics of Riot Grrrl songs spoke of both female power and the experience of gender-based oppression, bringing out issues often deemed taboo, such as sexual violence. Many Riot Grrrls were non-heteronormative and their song lyrics sympathetically presented the experiences of queer youth. In its reluctance to become involved with mainstream media, the Riot Grrrl movement, in addition to the women-only punk bands and a girl-positive concert scene, also spawned a do-it-yourself (DIY) publishing scene, initially focusing on fanzines of various bands and later expanding to include overtly political issues. In terms of its politics, Riot Grrrls, similarly to other youth countercultural movements, openly rebelled against conspicuous consumption and capitalism through ways of dressing and behaving, but also through the establishment of alternative media, record distribution networks, and the use of DIY technologies. The significance of the zine cottage industry definitely decreased with the popularization of the Internet in the late 1990s and early 2000s. Many scholars argue that, in general, the third wave of feminism ended with the emergence of the dot.com era and the kind of activism associated with the #MeToo movement, that is, activism that incorporates skillful use of new social media and is so different from the organizing of the 1990s that it deserves to be called the fourth wave of feminism (Chamberlain 2017).

Even though Riot Grrrls did not spawn a literary movement, some of the activists dabbled in poetry and fiction, while some writers, who for various reasons were not members of the movement, adopted the post-punk aesthetic as a literary strategy. The first group includes Lynn Breedlove, founder and lead singer of Tribe 8, whose 2002 novel *Godspeed* is loosely based on the author's experiences as a drug addict. Michelle Tea's largely autobiographical writings – including *Valencia* (2000) and *The Chelsea Whistle* (2002) – also explore sexuality and violence in ways that seem indebted to both the Riot Grrrl music scene and writers like Sarah Schulman and Kathy Acker, who formed the literary wing of the 1970s and 1980s New York queer punk scene. Michelle Tea is also a spoken word performer and the founder of Sister Spit, a lesbian-feminist performance art collective. Together with illustrator Lauren McCubbin, Tea co-authored the graphic novel *Rent Girl* (2002) about the life of a sex worker. While the problems faced by the queer and poor protagonist are presented in gritty detail and lead to a more complex understanding of sex work, the book turns into neither a tear-evoking victimology nor an optimistic tale of overcoming obstacles. Like other writings by Tea, it is characterized by a dose of irony and socially grounded awareness of the character's marginal positioning. This dive into the genre of the graphic novel (and graphic memoir) can also be linked to the DIY aesthetics of Riot Grrrl zines. Other examples of comics/graphic novels published in the 1990s espousing a feminist/queer sensibility include Roberta Gregory's *Naughty Bits* series (1991–2004). Many of the texts mentioned above are usually classified as belonging to the canon of queer writing, even though they are also grounded in a feminist sensibility.

While it is impossible to speak of one feminist genre or to impose some kind of uniformity on the writings mentioned above, the features these very diverse texts share include a focus on young protagonists, coming-of-age narratives, a focus on the body, on women's sexuality, and on the fluidity of identity categories. They also share a very fluid distinction between fiction and life writing: the memoirs are often based on similar narrative patterns as the novels (e.g. Walker's and Senna's books); some authors pen multiple books marketed as memoirs yet presenting differing recollections of the same time period in the author's life (e.g. Michelle Tea's works). While the texts often contain elements of the consciousness-raising narrative, the "feminist" content of the texts is usually not explicit; it serves as a certain grounding but – unlike the second-wave consciousness-raising novel – rarely does it become the main theme. The intersectionality of these texts contributed to their incorporation into other canons: African American, queer, and so on. The diversity of thematic concerns and literary genres and modes employed by third-wave writers also contributed to the waning of the use of the term "third-wave fiction" among critics of literature.

SEE ALSO: Acker, Kathy; Chick Lit and the New Domesticity; Danticat, Edwidge; Everett, Percival; The Graphic Novel; Piercy, Marge; Queer and LGBT Fiction; Senna, Danzy; Walker, Alice; Yamanaka, Lois-Ann

REFERENCES

Baumgardner, Jennifer and Richards, Amy. (2000). *Manifesta: Young Women, Feminism, and the Future*. New York: Farrar, Straus and Giroux.

Chamberlain, Prudence. (2017). *The Feminist Fourth Wave: Affective Temporality*. London and New York: Palgrave Macmillan.

Crenshaw, Kimberlé. (1991). Mapping the margins: intersectionality, identity politics, and violence against women of color. *Stanford Law Review* 43 (6): 1241–1299.

Dicker, Rory and Piepmeier, Allison. (eds.) (2003). *Catching a Wave: Reclaiming Feminism for the 21st Century*. Boston: Northeastern University Press.

Drake, Jennifer. (2006). Fiction, third wave. In: *The Women's Movement Today: An Encyclopedia of Third-Wave Feminism* (ed. Leslie L. Heywood), 145–148. Westport, CT, and London: Greenwood.

Faludi, Susan. (1991). *Backlash: The Undeclared War Against American Women*. New York and London: Doubleday.

Felski, Rita. (1989). *Beyond Feminist Aesthetics: Feminist Literature and Social Change*. Cambridge, MA: Harvard University Press.

Ferriss, Suzanne and Young, Mallory. (2006). Introduction. In: *Chick-lit: The New Woman's Fiction* (ed. Suzanne Ferriss and Mallory Young), 1–13. New York and London: Routledge.

Findlen, Barbara. (ed.) (1995). *Listen Up! Voices from the Next Feminist Generation*. New York: Seal Press.

Fraser, Nancy and Nicholson, Linda J. (1990). Social criticism without philosophy: an encounter between feminism and postmodernism. In: *Feminism/Postmodernism* (ed. Linda J. Nicholson), 19–38. New York and London: Routledge.

Garrison, Ednie K. (2000). U.S. feminism-grrrl style! Youth (sub)cultures and the technologies of the third wave. *Feminist Studies* 26 (1): 141–170.

Genz, Stephanie and Brabon, Benjamin A. (2009). *Postfeminism: Cultural Texts and Theories*. Edinburgh: Edinburgh University Press.

Heywood, Leslie L. (ed.) (2006). *The Women's Movement Today: An Encyclopedia of Third-Wave Feminism*. Westport, CT, and London: Greenwood.

Heywood, Leslie and Drake, Jennifer. (eds.) (1997). *Third Wave Agenda: Being Feminist, Doing Feminism*. Minneapolis and London: University of Minnesota Press.

Hogeland, Lisa M. (1998). *Feminism and its Fictions: The Consciousness Raising Novel and the Women's Movement*. Philadelphia: University of Pennsylvania Press.

Isherwood, Charles. (2006). The culture project and plays that make a difference. *The New York Times* (September 3, 2006). https://www.nytimes.com/2006/09/03/theater/03ishe.html (accessed September 15, 2021).

McRobbie, Angela. (2004). Post-feminism and popular culture. *Feminist Media Studies* 4 (3): 255–265.

Walker, Rebecca. (ed.) (1995). *To Be Real: Telling the Truth and Changing the Face of Feminism*. New York: Anchor Books.

Walker, Rebecca. (2001). *Black, White and Jewish: Autobiography of a Shifting Self*. New York: Riverhead Books.

Walker, Rebecca. (2006). Becoming the third wave. In: *The Women's Movement Today: An Encyclopedia of Third-Wave Feminism* (ed. Leslie L. Heywood), 3–4. Westport, CT, and London: Greenwood.

Whelehan, Imelda. (2005). *The Feminist Bestseller: From Sex and the Single Girl to Sex and the City*. New York and London: Palgrave Macmillan.

Włodarczyk, Justyna. (2010). *Ungrateful Daughters: Third Wave Feminist Writings*. Newcastle upon Tyne, UK: Cambridge Scholars.

Wolf, Naomi. (1991). *The Beauty Myth: How Images of Beauty Are Used Against Women*. Toronto: Vintage Books.

Wolf, Naomi. (1993). *Fire with Fire: The New Female Power and How It Will Change the 21st Century*. New York: Random House.

Wright, Elizabeth. (2000). *Lacan and Postfeminism*. Cambridge: Icon.

FURTHER READING

Gillis, Stacy, Howie, Gillian, and Munford, Rebecca. (2004). *Third Wave Feminism: A Critical Exploration. Expanded Second Edition*. New York: Palgrave Macmillan.

Henry, Astrid. (2004). *Not My Mother's Sister: Generational Conflict and Third-Wave Feminism*. Bloomington: Indiana University Press.

Zahava, Irene. (ed.) (1996). *Feminism3: The Third Generation in Fiction*. Boulder, CO: Westview Press.

Tomasula, Steve

DAVID BANASH
Western Illinois University, USA

The novels, short stories, and critical essays of Steve Tomasula mark and respond to the vast changes in computing, biotechnology, consumerism, and economic globalization that revolutionized everyday life at the turn of the millennium. Through four experimental novels, a collection of short stories, and series of critical reflections on writing, art, and technology, Tomasula has created a body of work that reimagines the possibilities and necessities of fiction in our unprecedentedly mediated world. While the physical forms of his novels challenge the limits of both the page and the codex, his plots trace the forces of time, biology, and technology on the human body.

Tomasula's most important and influential work is the experimental novel *VAS: An Opera in Flatland* (2002). The book tells the story of Square, a middle-aged, middle-class Midwesterner in "Flatland." His life is thrown into chaos when his wife, Circle, asks him to get a vasectomy so that she will no longer carry all the physical and emotional weight of regulating their sexual pleasure and reproduction. This conventional narrative of everyday familial anxieties and antagonisms grounds the novel, and it follows closely the exact kinds of narratives, focused on reproduction, family, politics, and inheritance, that are at the center of the history of the novel, from *Clarissa* (1748) to *Howard's End* (1910). Like these earlier novels, Tomasula uses the length and open form of the novel to plot the context in which his characters live, the histories that inform the broad social antagonisms, and the possible futures that await them. While the plot of *VAS* thus belongs firmly to the history of the novel, the form of *VAS* is a radical departure. The decision to undergo the vasectomy leads Square into an overwhelming research project that opens the archive of eugenics, the cutting edge of genetics, and the emerging Internet.

Where traditional novels rely almost exclusively on prose forms with occasional illustrations tied to the action of the narrative, *VAS* develops its story through a vast and often overwhelming collage of materials in a multitude of forms: medical illustrations, web pages, quotations from eugenicists and politicians, bureaucratic forms, images of scientific equipment, the entire sequence of a gene, and so on. These thick archival materials are combined with original illustrations, inventive typography, and even a chapter presented as a comic that enacts an opera of biological evolution. Where the traditional realist novel would use a narrator to unify all this material in a coherent voice and perspective, *VAS* presents a multidimensional collage in which the reader is tasked to make the connections and draw out the implications. *VAS* thus puts the reader into our contemporary situation, where even the smallest domestic and seemingly personal questions quickly force us to confront emerging technologies and a vast archive of materials in a bewildering array of forms, almost all available with just a few clicks on the Internet.

Working through the story of Square and the archives of eugenics and genetics, *VAS* reenacts an event in our evolving definition of the human. *VAS* argues that where life was once imagined as a part of divine and sacred mystery, developments in genetics make it clear that our biology is a literal form of writing, one that we are now capable of manipulating and changing with our own direct interventions – just as we might revise a sentence, we can now edit our DNA. Tomasula drives this point home by binding the book in a facsimile of human skin – the book and the body the same. For Tomasula, the human must now be understood through the history and technologies of writing.

VAS was originally meant to be only a chapter in Tomasula's *The Book of Portraiture: A Novel* (2006). This book takes the portrait as its key figure, skipping through time and forms, with each chapter charting critical technological and discursive moments when our collective self-portraits of the human change. *The Book of Portraiture* begins by imagining the invention of writing as a myth in which a fictional Moses invents a phonetic alphabet. He sees the power of writing to change reality and consciousness, recognizing it as something new entering the world, but also intuiting it as one of many dangerous forces that influence human life: "And he trembled to find himself among their number, for he could see this curse for the power it held, a spell or a power he could multiply" (2006, p. 10). The myth of Moses is followed by the fictional diary of Diego Velázquez, the golden-age Spanish court painter. Heavily illustrated with sketches, the diary dramatizes how representation and power are enmeshed and how technological changes in representation – in this case the invention of one-point perspective – place the individual at the center of the world. This power brings Velázquez face to face with the Inquisition, where he must defend and evade the ways his paintings challenge medieval orthodoxies. The diary gives way to the case history in the invention of psychoanalysis, marking changes in the theory of mind and sexuality, while pointing out historically obvious occlusions. The corporate surveillance state ties together a chapter told as an investigation of theft, adultery, and terrorism, unfolding on security camera screens, digital files, and Internet logs. In the final chapter, the story of a feminist bioartist intersects with the story of a terrorist. While the terrorist inflicts violence and death through bodies to send a political message, the feminist artist harvests one of her own eggs and uses techniques of artificial insemination to give a potential embryo an impossible parentage. Both the artist and the terrorist literally write through the body, making the point that our physical embodiment and our manipulation of it are also acts of signification. N. Katherine Hayles notes that most of these chapters unfold first at the level of human scale, in face-to-face everyday dramas, but that the forces of technological developments and the span of time across the chapters create something more. Hayles writes: "the work as a whole is emergently posthuman, weaving patterns that do not make conventional sense but that hint at webs of connections too vast to grasp in their entirety, too tangled to represent directly. Insofar as the text can be read as a history of representation, this emergent effect suggests that such a history is impossible to represent" (Banash 2015, p. 134). Here, the forces of time, technology, and biology are registered as the sublime, and indeed, like much of Tomasula's work, the book strives to produce emotions of terror and wonder at our apprehension of inaccessible but nonetheless overwhelming and determining forces of history on our present.

These forces are at the heart of Tomasula's shortest and most accessible work, *IN&OZ* (2003). Written in an allegorical style, the short novella tells the story of Mechanic, his romantic pursuit of Designer, and his coming to consciousness as an artist with the help of his friends Sculptor, Photographer, Composer, and Poet. The book takes place in urban industrial corridors of IN and the gleaming urban core of OZ, a thinly veiled Chicago and Gary, Indiana. Its central character is a humble automobile mechanic, living in IN and fixing cars for a living. Mechanic's life is changed when, working on a transmission one day, he suddenly perceives not just the mechanical problem before him but forces of time, biology, and technology that brought the car and himself into existence. Tomasula writes:

> Though he has seen gears like this thousands of times before, it had never once occurred to him how eloquently their polished metal teeth explained his life: their mesh and power ratios may as well have been engineers, and foundry men, all on a shaft, with machinists, and mechanics, as his father had been, and the farmers, and cooks, as his mother had been, who fed the factory workers, and highway builders who made it possible for everyone to get jobs that brought into existence the need for marvels such as cars which needed transmissions which needed gears which needed him.
>
> (2003, p. 19)

In this epiphany, the ordinary car is no longer a utilitarian means of transportation but a text opening the sublime history that brought it into being. Unable any longer to merely repair the cars of his customers, Mechanic begins to alter their cars with unnecessary and perceptually disruptive repairs. Through the baffled and angry reactions of his customers and the insights of his new friends, he slowly comes to realize that he is not a mechanic but an artist himself. Rather than Christian salvation, the allegory at the heart of *IN&OZ* is Victor Shklovsky's concept of defamiliarization, in which the role of art is to challenge habits of mind in order to heighten perception of the world as an act of value and meaning in its own right. This aesthetic is opposed to slick corporate design that seeks to quell the perceptual and ethical difficulties at the heart of defamiliarizing art. Throughout, the battle between perceptual ease and challenge is played out across the geography of the slick OZ and the gritty IN as the characters engage in a series of philosophical dialogues on labor, consumption, and the role of art as a life practice in the contemporary world.

Tomasula's most extreme experiment is *TOC: A New Media Novel* (2009). Though called a novel, this work is readable only on a screen. Like *VAS*, the work is a vast collage, here including animations, paintings, photographs, music, voices, and written words. However, unlike the pages of a codex, reading *TOC* means both reading texts, seeing images, and listening to music, voices, and sound effects while also interacting to navigate the complex and not always intuitive interfaces. *TOC* in many ways resembles the evolving worlds of video games, in which different levels are opened by the reader's actions. All these sections grapple with the problem of time. In N. Katherine Hayles's formulation, "*TOC* creates a rich assemblage in which the conflicts between measured and experienced time are related to the invention, development and domination of the Influencing Engine, a metaphoric allusion to computational technologies" (Hayles 2012). Thus *TOC* opposes different subjective experiences of time and a multitude of clocks, from the rising and setting sun to the gestation period, the life span, and the big bang, as well as all the mechanical and digital apparatuses we use to measure time. At the heart of the work is the reader's experience of time, for it is the reader who dictates the pace of the movement and chooses a direction through *TOC*'s levels. The work thematizes this, sometimes capturing the reader in a long animation that must be watched from beginning to end, while at other points, the reader can simply browse through materials quickly or distractedly, or with the slowest and most complete attention. However, even with such attention, some texts are deliberately illegible. In *TOC*, Tomasula seems to take his aesthetics to its most extreme. The reader, rather than the plot, is most fully empowered, undertaking a search of meaning that demands the synthesis of a wealth of multimedia texts.

In his essay "Visualization, Scale, and the Emergence of Posthuman Narrative" (2014), Tomasula lays out a critical argument for experimental literature and particularly for the aesthetics of his own work. The essay begins by invoking the globalized world of trade, consumption, biohacking, digital communication, terrorism, and surveillance. Given the vast, impersonal, and often invisible forces at work in the world, how can they possibly be represented, especially when they simply cannot be grasped directly? Taking Napoleon's Russian campaign as an example, he frames this as a problem of scale in nineteenth-century works like Adolphe Northern's painting *Napoleon's Retreat from Moscow* (1851) and Tolstoy's novel *War and Peace* (1867), writing, "the scene is at the scale at which humans interact as individuals, so let us call this the Human Scale with its title character and shared concerns of the realist novel: individual feeling or emotion, authenticity, mimetic representation through sensory detail, especially visual detail of individuals" (Tomasula 2014). The human-scale focus on central characters and individual emotion eclipses the inhuman forces at work that exist at scales too large or too small for direct perception, scales that reframe and decenter subjective, individual experience and suggest that factors other than human fear or desire might be paramount in the world. For literature to grasp and attempt to represent these forces, new scales are needed. Tomasula writes: "To study the stars, goes the unconsidered logic, one must use a telescope; to study a flea, a microscope – instruments that allow us to see our subjects comfortably at the Human Scale. But it must also be true that the selection of scale determines subject – as well as what can be said – and this has ramifications for how we use literature to view our world" (Tomasula 2014). To write at human scale is to put subjectivity and emotion at the center of the story, but this might well not be the best way to discover the truth, and Tomasula follows N. Katherine Hayles and Gerald Bruns in looking for a posthuman literature, one that creates scales that reveal the larger patterns of historical forces (such as time, evolution, technology, and finance) as key to the posthuman plot.

While all of Tomasula's work has characters enmeshed in face-to-face human-scale conflicts that keep his work more firmly rooted in the history of the novel than many other experimental writers, the collage of thick archival materials, narrative asides and shifts in perspective, and innovative typography that surround Tomasula's characters are set at scales from microscopic DNA to globe of the Earth, from the intimate experience of time in a romance or a sick room to the cosmic scales for time's emergence as a force at the big bang. In "Visualization, Scale, and the Emergence of Posthuman Narrative" Tomasula offers a kind of negative gesture toward the definition of the posthuman novel by questioning the limits of the modernism it seeks to transcend:

What might an emerging posthuman narrative look like? A narrative that does not, like its Modernist precedents, feel a blurring of the self's boundaries as an existential crisis? That simply takes this new status of the human as a state of nature? A narrative that turns the page on the modernist novel with its dream of the individual soaring above history as James Joyce ends his *Portrait of the Artist as a Young Man*, or the despair of not being able to escape history, the nihilism at the end of Hemingway's *Farewell to Arms*? A narrative that is at home with a larger-than-human scale? That not only does not mourn the loss of the first person narrative, but privileges absence over presence, pattern over detail, that takes as a given the fact that the body, the last firewall to the individual, is in the end as permeable as other barriers between "I" / "others"?

(Tomasula 2014)

Each of Tomasula's novels should thus be seen as attempts to answer these questions, to write a newly posthuman literature that better reflects our emerging senses of the biological, technological, financial, and cosmic sublime.

SEE ALSO: After Postmodernism; Big Data; Biological Fictions; Fiction and Terrorism; Globalization; Hypertext Fiction and Network Narratives; Intermedial Fiction; The New Experimentalism/The Contemporary Avant-Garde

REFERENCES

Banash, David. (ed.) (2015). *Steve Tomasula: The Art and Science of New Media Fiction*. New York: Bloomsbury.

Hayles, N. Katherine. (2012). Tech-TOC: complex temporalities in living and technical beings. *Electronic Book Review* (June 28, 2012). https://electronicbookreview.com/essay/tech-toc-complex-temporalities-in-living-and-technical-beings/ (accessed July 11, 2021).

Tomasula, Steve. (2003). *IN&OZ*. Chicago: University of Chicago Press.

Tomasula, Steve. (2006). *The Book of Portraiture: A Novel*. Normal, IL: FC2.

Tomasula, Steve. (2014). Visualization, scale, and the emergence of posthuman narrative. *Sillages Critiques* 17. https://doi.org/10.4000/sillagescritiques.3562 (accessed July 11, 2021).

FURTHER READING

Benzon, Kiki. (2015) An interview with Steve Tomasula. *Electronic Book Review* (May 3, 2015). https://electronicbookreview.com/essay/an-interview-with-steve-tomasula/

Chevaillier, Flore. (2013). *The Body of Writing: An Erotics of Contemporary American Fiction*. Columbus: Ohio State University Press.

Stephens, Paul. (2018). The bioinformatic sublime: the life of data and the data of life in conceptual writing. In: *Postscript: Writing After Conceptual Art* (ed. Andrea Andersson and Nora Burnett Abrams), 270–289. Toronto: University of Toronto Press.

Tomasula, Steve. (2002). Genetic art and the aesthetics of biology. *Leonardo* 35 (2): 137–144.

Tomasula, Steve. (2012). Information design, emergent culture, and experimental form in the novel. In: *The Routledge Companion to Experimental Literature* (ed. Joe Bray, Alison Gibbons, and Brian McHale), 435–451. London: Routledge.

Trauma and Fiction

DAMJANA MRAOVIĆ-O'HARE
Carson-Newman University, USA

Trauma has been an inherent element of American literature since its beginnings, but not until the emergence of trauma studies in the 1990s did trauma fiction became a focus of American letters. A relatively new field, trauma studies examine the ways in which psychological trauma is represented in language and explore ethical, cultural, and political implications of individual and collective traumas manifested in literary texts. Theoretical premises of trauma studies are indebted to Sigmund Freud's psychoanalysis, Jacques Derrida's deconstruction, and Theodor Adorno's metaphysics, while its roots are in the medical recognition of post-traumatic stress disorder (PTSD). Trauma literature, on the other hand, is defined as texts that are influenced by trauma studies, and in which a traumatic experience is presented through a series of stylistic innovations such as disrupted causative and temporal narration, iteration, and characters' doubling. Trauma fiction and trauma studies are closely related, while trauma fiction authors explore a wide range of issues such as race, feminism, violence, and postcolonialism.

ORIGINS OF TRAUMA FICTION

The origins of trauma studies can be traced to the 1980s and to a medical and scientific discourse: the American Psychiatric Association (APA) classified PTSD in the *Diagnostic and Statistical Manual of Mental Disorders* in 1980 as a psychological disorder that is initiated by a "psychologically distressing event outside the range of usual human experience," which triggers "intense fear, terror, and helplessness" and causes "significant distress in most people." PTSD was officially recognized by the medical community as both environmentally induced and with potential long-lasting psychological consequences. Such a formal recognition of PTSD was a result of a campaign of Vietnam War veterans who, in addition to opposing the military conflict, argued for counseling of veterans and "also commissioned research into the impact of wartime experiences on combatants. This resulted in a five-volume study on the psychological legacies of Vietnam, which clearly delineated the syndrome of PTSD and demonstrated its direct relationship to combat exposure" (Whitehead 2004). Trauma studies developed a decade later at Yale University as an attempt to explore manifestations of the traumatized self in literary works, as well as the consequences such a self has on a literary text. Subsequently, the scientific premise of the origins of trauma is transferred to a humanistic concern about trauma's ethical, social, and historical effects. Cathy Caruth, Shoshana Feldman, Dori Laub, and Geoffrey Hartman are thought to be the pioneers of trauma studies, whose work was embodied in theories of Sigmund Freud and Jacques Lacan (latency, memory), as well as theories of deconstruction by Jacques Derrida and Paul De Man (rupture, absence, aporia). Trauma, which derives from the Greek word that means wound, was first used in English in the seventeenth century by physicians to refer to a bodily injury that is caused by external means. Nowadays, however, trauma usually indicates mental and psychological scars, even though it is still used in medicine to denote bodily injuries. The change from the physical to mental hurt started happening in the late nineteenth century: in 1895, *Popular Science Monthly* published that "We have named this psychical trauma, a morbid nervous condition" (Luckhurst 2008, p. 2). In the twentieth century, such a shift was assisted by the developments in psychiatry and psychology, and culminated in 1980 by a recognition of PTSD as a mental disorder caused by a traumatic experience.

Trauma Fiction

Trauma studies scholars argue that contemporary trauma fiction is inspired by the development of trauma studies and the dissemination of its theory into culture. The "traditional model," as the first generation of trauma studies scholars are commonly described, insists that because of the belatedness of a traumatic experience, trauma is unpresentable in language and therefore is frequently manifested in a text as a series of formal innovations. Its unrepresentability is rooted in the fact that trauma ruptures one's psyche and as such cannot be effectively represented or retrieved. It cannot be manifested in traditional genres, or traditional narration, but in a style that corresponds with traumatic experiences in the period after World War II. Trauma fiction is also expressed through a revision of a realist mode that requires the reader to accept the supernatural, or embrace the illogical.

The "traditional" trauma theorists of the 1980s and 1990s are particularly interested in examining personal trauma caused by a collective event, such as the Holocaust or slavery, therefore linking the individual and collective and, consequently, suggesting a connection between the personal, cultural, and political. They operate within the concepts of memory and identity. Trauma fiction, which is sometimes identified as the "trauma genre," is associated with avant-garde and postmodernism because those poetics enable traumatic experiences to be presented as fragmented and disjointed in a literary text.

Toni Morrison's *Beloved* (1987) is considered one of the earliest trauma narratives, but is also noted for providing a supposed paradigm for future trauma novels: *Beloved* is the most analyzed narrative in trauma studies. In 2008, there were more than 500 articles on academic databases dedicated to the book (Luckhurst 2008); in 2020, there are more than 1600 articles on academic databases published in academic journals discussing only trauma in *Beloved*. The book, which won the Pulitzer Prize in 1988, is partially based on the biography of Margaret Garner from Kentucky who escaped her owner in 1856 across the frozen Ohio River to Cincinnati, but who cut the throat of her own daughter – best loved – when faced with the possibility that she would be captured and returned to slavery under the 1850 Fugitive Slave Law. Garner wounded her other three children but did not manage to kill them and herself before being captured. Her trial turned into somewhat of a sensation because it lasted four weeks, at the time when fugitive trials lasted a day. In the end, the judge decided that the federal law, according to which she should be recaptured, superseded the state murder charges for which her defense lawyer wanted her to be charged, and she and her husband, with other captured fugitives, were returned to slavery.

Morrison voiced the experience of a slave, and of a woman, while its "formal and conceptual links reinforced its influence to the trauma paradigm, reinforced its influence on American culture" (Luckhurst 2008, p. 90). Dedicated to "Sixty Million and more" who died as a consequence of the Atlantic slave trade, *Beloved* starts in post-Civil War Cincinnati, Ohio, where Sethe, a formerly enslaved woman, lives with her daughter Denver. Since the house is haunted by presumably a ghost of Sethe's oldest dead daughter, whom Sethe killed, Denver is timid and housebound even though she likes the ghost, while Sethe's two sons run away, supposedly after an encounter with the ghost. Years of the family's disruptive daily routine are normalized for a short time, with the arrival of Paul D, because of whom the ghost disappears. However, with the appearance of a young woman who calls herself Beloved, the family dynamics are yet again problematized. Sethe is convinced that Beloved is her long-lost daughter and becomes submissive to her wishes and desires, while Beloved takes advantage of Sethe's grief and guilt. Paul D is manipulated and seduced by Beloved even though there is an apparent animosity between the two of them, and a sexual encounter with Beloved prompts horrifying memories of Paul D's time as a plantation slave. Beloved becomes an incarnation of evil that the local community tries to exorcise. Even when Beloved leaves, in a confusion created by a white man coming to offer a job to Denver whom Sethe mistakes for her previous owner and attacks to kill, Sethe is heartbroken and ready to die, claiming that Beloved was her "best thing" (Morrison 1987, p. 321). Morrison finishes the novel with the notion that presents the trauma of slavery through a series of flashbacks, nonlinear narration, and readdressing episodes that add little to the general narrative line of the text but illuminate the characters' perspectives and allow the reader to engage with the characters. Morrison presents the collective trauma of slavery as imposing deeply damaging multigenerational, individual psychological effects; trauma, in Morrison's text, not only dehumanizes but also triggers the death drive by severely disrupting one's psyche.

Disruption of linear narrative, figuration of trauma as a ghost, and the complex, ethical issues associated with traumatic history are three paradigmatic elements of *Beloved* that influenced future trauma narratives. The reader is expected to make sense of the narratological omissions and reiterations, and establish a chronological line through the process of reading. For instance, Sethe's trauma is manifested both as a physical (Beloved) and a psychological ghost; the presence of Beloved in her house is as troubling for Sethe as is her psychological, traumatic torment. Beloved's presence obliterates memory of the traumatic event, while the presence of Denver, who was born in freedom, is linked to mourning. However, both of the daughters are melancholy, which is caused by the traumatic event. The narrative is purposely repetitive to indicate the lack of coherence induced by trauma, both for Sethe and the characters closest to her, which culminates in the reiteration of a sentence and creation of one of the most memorable chapters of the book: "I am Beloved and she is mine" (1987, p. 210). The main traumatic event is not explained until halfway through the narrative, whereas certain details are defamiliarized in such a way that once their identity is revealed, they are shocking and appalling for the reader. The tree on Sethe's back, for instance, is actually scar tissue from whipping at the plantation during her life as a slave. Sethe cannot fully remember the traumatic event that caused her trauma, exactly because trauma is haunting, unexplainable, and unreachable, and memory of it transitory: "Sethe knew that the circle she was making around the rook, him, the subject, would remain one. That she should never close in, pin it down for anybody to who to ask. If they didn't get it right off – she could never explain" (p. 163). The rewriting of official history, in this case the history of slavery and providing a voice to a female African American character, as well as the use of the supernatural in order to recount the traumatic past, are elements unique to *Beloved* but transformed into characteristics typical of trauma fiction.

Art Spiegelman's *Maus* (1991) is one of the most effective examples of "traumatic realism" (Rothberg 2000, p. 27): it is a graphic novel that presents the Holocaust as a conflict between mice (Jews), cats (Nazis), and pigs (Poles). Spiegelman presents the Holocaust, an event that made Theodor Adorno question the existence of any thought after its occurrence, through a low-art genre (graphic novel), while transforming a deeply traumatic personal experience into an allegorical story about grief and trauma. In the process, *Maus* became a critical and commercial success and yet the trauma contained within it is not diminished or simplified. *Maus* is described as a memoir, autobiography, history, and fiction – a combination of different genres – and is still the only graphic novel that won a Pulitzer Prize (Special Award in Letters, 1992).

Maus, subtitled *A Survivor's Tale: My Father Bleeds History*, is a narrative seemingly about two distinctive stories: one is about Vladek, the father of *Maus*'s author, an Auschwitz survivor, and his and his family's horrific experiences that they encounter as Polish Jews during the 1930s and 1940s in Adolf Hitler's Europe. The other storyline is about Art, Vladek's son, a

New York graphic artist, who tries to understand his father's trauma, but also somewhat removes himself from it because it is a defying element of his identity that causes contradictory reactions. While Art is respectful of his family history, and interested in recording his family's sufferings over the span of about fifteen years because of their historical, ethical, and private significance, he is also easily annoyed by his bitter and emotionally distant father. Art says that "One reason I became an artist was that he [father] thought it was impractical – just a waste of time . . . it was an area where I wouldn't have to compete with him" (Spiegelman 1991, p. 97). The narrative timeline is also twofold, and nonlinear. Vladek narrates to Art past events in a series of flashbacks, through which the Nazi systematic abuse and mistreatment of Jews is presented as a gruesome family history, while Art focuses on daily activities of his aged, cantankerous father.

Vladek says that at the end of the war, only Vladek and his wife Anja are alive from the entire, big, middle-class family. Even their child, Richieu, dies in 1944, in a manner that recalls the traumatic real-life account behind *Beloved*. Richieu was sent to live with his Aunt Tosha and two cousins in hopes of surviving the Nazi terror. However, when the Nazis order an evacuation of a town in which his aunt lives, and therefore a relocation of all town Jews to Auschwitz, she poisons all three children and herself because "I won't go to their gas chambers! . . . And my children won't go to their gas chambers" (1991, p. 109). Even though Art's parents never talked to him about Richieu, and he learns about his brother's tragic death only as an adult, the trauma associated with his brother has haunted Art his entire life. Richieu's photo was kept in Art's parents' bedroom throughout his upbringing, contributing to the traumatic reaction caused by, specifically,

his father's response to trauma. For instance, Art tries to justify his father's paranoia, stinginess, and emotional detachment by his prolonged traumatic experience, but dismisses such an attempt in a conversation with Mala, Vladek's second wife with whom Vladek does not get along. Art says that, "I used to think the *war* made him that way," to which Mala dismissively responds: "Fah! *I* went through the camps . . . *All* our friends went through the camps. *Nobody* is like him" (p. 131, all emphases original). Even though Spiegelman does not provide an admiring portrait of his father, he interestingly argues that to define him only through his trauma would be reductive, dehumanizing, and incorrect.

With his graphic novel, Spiegelman as well suggests that the traumatic experience is horrifying and disorienting not only for survivors of the traumatic event, but also for their immediate family members and their identity formations. Art suffers from postmemory, the concept that Marianne Hirsch describes as the relationship that children of Holocaust survivors have to their parents' traumatic experiences. Art's relationship with his father is complicated and damaged, and the graphic novel culminates and closes with Art accusing his father of being a murderer because the father burnt Art's mother's diaries after she had committed suicide. Born after the Holocaust, Art did not experience its terrors, but he feels displaced in his own family because his parents' existence is deeply marked by the trauma of the Holocaust and therefore his childhood; his mother did not want to discuss the past, while Art found his father cold and controlling. Typical of first-generation survivors, Vladek is reluctant to share his experience and claims that nobody would be interested in traumatizing stories such as his. Consequently, his story is marked by gaps and omissions, he is often distracted by details that disrupt his chronological narrative, and he is emotionally and physically exhausted after sessions with his son. Art, on the other hand, feels burdened and disturbed by his parents' trauma even though he adopts a role of a family chronicler, and is understanding of his parents' pain. Spiegelman presents the Holocaust trauma as a transgenerational issue, but complicates that notion by arguing that the trauma is not only perceived differently by survivors and their offspring, second-generation survivors, but that such a discrepancy causes a generational misunderstanding. Coping mechanisms and existential tactics that were beneficial during the Nazi regime and the Holocaust often become damaging in the postwar period, causing yet another trauma. Currently, the third and fourth generations of the Holocaust survivors maintain the history behind the trauma of the Jewish people.

While "traditional" trauma studies scholars insist on unrepresentability of trauma that is demonstrated in disrupted traditional narration, the second generation of scholars, "pluralists," argue the opposite: trauma's multifaceted presentability forms new relationships between language and experiences, changing the comprehension about the self and the self's environment. "Pluralistic" trauma studies scholars claim that trauma is variable and transitional, and not fixed and unapproachable. In the early 2000s, Michelle Balaev, Ann Cvetkovich, Greg Forter, Amy Hungerford, and Naomi Mandel write that trauma does not always need to trigger a pathological disruption of one's self – which is associated with trauma's scientific recognition – but that trauma can activate and form new relationships with the external world. These scholars argue that trauma can be theorized through various approaches and not reduced to the idea of the unrepresentable, whereas memory can be fluid and is open to interpretations that are conditioned by social, political, or cultural contexts.

In 2013, Karen Joy Fowler published *We Are All Completely Beside Ourselves*, a novel about an atypical dysfunctional family that is representative of the "pluralist" approach to trauma. The novel introduces a new type of trauma and raises a set of concerns that enrich and problematize the notion of trauma through a provocative narrative about the nature of humans and animals. Amy Whitehead writes in her *Trauma Fiction* (2004) that postmodernism, together with postcolonialism and a postwar legacy of consciousness, contributes to the rise of trauma fiction, while postmodern poetics lends it an approach that mimics psychological manifestations of trauma and, consequently, disrupts traditional narration and genres. Trauma fiction is therefore characterized by intertextuality, repetition, and a dispersed narrative voice. All these elements are masterfully utilized in Fowler's novel, which is narrated in first person by Rosemary Cook, the youngest of three siblings. Rosemary is a college student, deeply upset by the childhood traumatic experience of losing her sister that also caused her family to fall apart: the mother became depressed, the father turned into an alcoholic, while the older brother, Lowell, left home before ever graduating high school, only to become an animal rights activist wanted by the FBI. However, the trauma of losing one's sibling becomes even more complex – and the narrative provided with an unusual twist – when, about one quarter through the novel, Rosemary reveals that her sister is actually a chimpanzee named Fern. The delay in revealing the crucial element about Rosemary's sister is explained by reducing the trauma of losing a sister to losing a pet: "I tell you Fern was a chimp and already you aren't thinking of her as my sister" (Fowler 2013, p. 77). Narratologically, however, this is consistent with trauma narratives in which the identification of a trauma is delayed because it causes a belated emotional response, as is the narrator's insisting that the narrative starts "in the middle," and the characters' repeated inability to verbalize the traumatic event (p. 37).

And yet, things are even more complicated. Rosemary's father was a psychologist studying animal behavior in 1970s Indiana, and as part of a scientific experiment, Fern and Rosemary are raised together as twins from birth to the age of five. The mother explains to the adult Rosemary that she wanted her to have an extraordinary life, by introducing Fern as her sister, while the father was solely focused on his potential scientific achievements. Rosemary claims that as much as Fern believed she was human, Rosemary mirrored her behavior as well: "Mom warns me to stay upright. No loping through the snow on my hands and feet.... Most home-raised chimps, when asked to sort photographs into piles of chimps and humans, make only the one mistake of putting their own picture into the human pile. That is exactly what Fern did" (2013, p. 101). The family is exceedingly happy, which is signaled ironically by the title of the book, until one summer day Rosemary is sent to her grandparents for three weeks, and when she returns home, she finds no Fern and the entire family in disarray. More importantly, she blames herself for Fern's disappearance, even though the traumatic experience of losing a sister erases any memory of behavior that could have caused such an outcome. Previously extremely verbal and precocious, Rosemary gradually becomes quiet and reticent, socially awkward, and cautious. The trauma of losing a sister – and a daughter – albeit an animal, so significantly damages the entire family and every family member's mental health that the reader is prompted to continuously pose questions about, for instance, ethics and parenthood, ethics in relation to scientific research, ethics in relation to animals, their treatment by humans and their rights, as well as about the animalistic nature of humans, animals'

memory, emotions, and consciousness. While Fowler offers a somewhat comforting ending that allows Rosemary and her mom to soften the consequences of the childhood trauma and reestablish their relationship with each other and Fern, she emphasizes the credibility of the concerns raised by *We Are...* by including historical overviews of cross-fostering and language experiments with chimpanzees. Fern is removed from the home not because of her twin sister's behavior, which Rosemary presumed for almost two decades, but because she becomes too big and too dangerous for the humans around her. Fern's fate replicates exactly the fate of the chimpanzees who were adopted by human families, while the traumatic narrative offers a moral consolation supported by a legal ruling: since 1999, twenty-nine countries have banned experiments on nonhuman apes for ethical reasons, whereas in 2015, the US National Institutes for Health decided that all federally owned chimps would be permanently retired from research.

Similarly to Fowler who exposes ethical origins of trauma, Imbolo Mbue in *Behold the Dreamers* (2016) critically examines the trauma of immigration through a revision of the American Dream, reevaluating the common tropes associated with immigrant fiction. Herself an immigrant from Cameroon, Mbue situates her narrative in the 2007 New York City that is characterized by the collapse of Lehman Brothers and an impending global economic crisis. Jende Jonga, his wife Neni, and their six-year-old son Liomi come to the United States from Cameroon in hopes of a more prosperous life; Neni wants to become a pharmacist and climb the social ladder, while Jende attempts to become a permanent resident using a false asylum claim. But Jende is a taxi driver, Neni a home health aide, and they can barely make ends meet. Unexpectedly, Jende becomes a chauffeur for a senior Lehman Brother executive, which allows him to finance his wife's education and support his family back home. That is, until the company is bankrupted, the asylum claim is denied, and the fissures already present in their version of the American Dream become even more obvious. For instance, in order to study, Neni needs to hire a babysitter for Liomi and a newborn girl; she also works as a housekeeper for Jende's boss's wife, while the cost of living in New York City, even in Harlem, is so exorbitant that it seems impossible to ever escape their class. At the same time, Neni and Jende are privy to their employees' lifestyle, which includes spending summers in the Hamptons and marital problems, and whose friends are terrified of the potential crisis because "It's scary how bad this could get ... When people start talking about flying coach and selling vacation homes" (Mbue 2016, p. 180). And yet, Jende and Neni are in love with the United States despite their daily traumas of immigrant living that are emotionally and mentally exhausting. Neni is especially fond of America which, notwithstanding its flaws related to class and race, can offer her a professional accomplishment that is out of her reach in Cameroon. When they decide to go back home, it is because "it's just not easy for a man to enjoy his life in this country if he is poor" (p. 373). Unusual for an immigrant novel, the main characters willingly give up their American Dream because it is unattainable. The trauma associated with it is quotidian and recurring but also conceivably eliminated if the couple relocates again, to their home country. As Nene explains at the end of the novel, with $21,400 that they saved in the United States, their children would grow up in a spacious house, would go to elite private schools, and she and Jende would be respected members of the upper class. The trauma of immigration in Mbue's interpretation is temporal; the novel closes with a sense of relief.

Cormac McCarthy, in *The Road* (2006), offers a much broader understanding of trauma that is associated with ethical and political concerns of our contemporary world. *The Road* is an apocalyptic novel in which a father and a son attempt to survive after an undefined catastrophe wiped out most of the United States and turned its residents into cannibals. The trauma, here, is ecological in nature, and projected into the future. Ann Kaplan in *Climate Trauma: Foreseeing the Future in Dystopian Film and Fiction* (2015) introduces the idea of pre-traumatic stress disorder (PreTSS), trauma associated with future catastrophic events. Such trauma, as in *The Road*, is centered around dystopian narratives that have become a global phenomenon induced by the contemporary environmental issues. The novel is written as a combination of sparse descriptions and simplified dialogues without conventional punctuation, in which first- and third-person point of view mix unexpectedly, as well as dream and realistic sequences. Fragments and run-on sentences are common. The disruptive narrative style is suggestive of the novel's helpless world: although aware of his fatal sickness, the father starts a journey to the warmer south in an attempt to save his son's life. Even more so, the trauma of apocalypse is dehumanizing: the boy's mother committed suicide because she could not bear the horrific environment; the father carries a gun and teaches the son how to kill him if he becomes too weak; the father kills and maims in self-defense multiple times; and the duo repeatedly witnesses cannibalism, which culminates in a scene of an infant roasted on a spit at an abandoned campsite.

And yet, the man consistently insists to the boy that they are "good guys," while the boy reiterates that idea by asking his father to treat kindly those they meet, even when they obviously pose a threat to their existence. When at the end the father dies, and after three days of guarding him a group of people shows up and asks the boy to join them, their leader claims he is one of the good guys, and that they do not eat people. The boy is interested whether the man's group carries the fire with which his father identified him. The ambiguous ending does not offer an answer to that question despite McCarthy's invocation of the religious theme of the messiah throughout the narrative. The quest of the novel is to preserve basic human ethics, while raising philosophical questions about the justifiability of violence, community, and life drives. In essence a travel narrative, *The Road* offers a speculative trauma that is as haunting as actual historical or physical traumas.

Kaplan claims that dystopian narratives have a dual function: they are warnings about our potential future as a species, and they also offer "'memory *for* the future,' less a disabling anxiety than a productive warning to bring about needed change" (Kaplan 2015, p. 18). In such an interpretation of trauma, the concept that was initially associated with passivity and involuntary randomness turns into an invitation for a radical social and political transformation because of its upsetting nature. *The Road*, with its graphic details and factual style, creates discomfort and distress. In that sense, *The Road* is an encouragement to move beyond focusing on memory and past traumatic experiences, and an encouragement to prevent potential calamities by presenting extreme consequences of globally flawed environmental and governmental policies.

In 2012, the University of Nebraska founded the *Journal of Literature and Trauma Studies* (*JLTS*), acknowledging a wide breadth of trauma fiction and reflecting the plurality of trauma studies. The peer-reviewed journal "aims to foster a broad interrogative dialogue between philosophy, psychoanalysis, and literary criticism and develop new approaches to the study of trauma in literature and the trauma of literature," while the journal's goal is to "encourage philosophical, political, and historically oriented research that takes literature as the primary site for investigations into trauma in all its forms and manifestations" (*Journal of Literature and Trauma Studies* n.d.). According to this approach, trauma is multifaced, ubiquitous, and deeply theoretical.

In more recent contemporary fiction, trauma and poetic elements associated with its presentation in writing can be identified in race, ethnic, war, 9/11, and dystopian narratives, to name just a few, as well as in comics, graphic novels, and sci-fi film. Such narratives are, for example, Alice Walker's *The Color Purple* (1982), Colson Whitehead's *The Underground Railroad* (2016) and *The Nickel Boys* (2019), Octavia E. Butler's *Kindred* (1979), Louise Erdrich's *Love Medicine* (1984), Sherman Alexie's *Reservation Blues* (1995), Téa Obreht's *Inland* (2019), Ben Fountain's *Billy Lynn's Halftime Walk* (2012), Phil Klay's *Redeployment* (2014), Khaled Hosseini's *Kite Runner* (2003), Jonathan Safran Foer's *Extremely Loud & Incredibly Close* (2005), Don DeLillo's *Falling Man* (2007), Mohsin Hamid's *Reluctant Fundamentalist* (2007), Veronica Roth's *Divergent* (2011), Margaret Atwood's *Handmaid's Tale* (1985), and Susan Collins's *The Hunger Games* (2008). The clear line of distinction between a trauma and a nontrauma text seems to be diminished, most likely because trauma and stress are the key qualifiers of the contemporary way of living, while stylistic innovations are not exclusively associated with trauma fiction. In the twenty-first century, the understanding of trauma has expanded beyond the notion of a singular, piercing event (rape, assault) that disrupts one's psyche to include issues associated, for instance, with class concerns that are typical of the contemporary way of living in the time of global migrations, fluid politics, and highly polarized economies.

SEE ALSO: After Postmodernism; Alexie, Sherman; Contemporary Fictions of War; DeLillo, Don; Ecocriticism and Environmental Fiction; Erdrich, Louise; Foer, Jonathan Safran; The Graphic Novel; Hosseini, Khaled; McCarthy, Cormac; Morrison, Toni; Post-9/11 Narratives; Third-Wave Feminism; Walker, Alice; Whitehead, Colson

REFERENCES

American Psychiatric Association. (1980). *Diagnostic and Statistical Manual of Mental Disorders*. Washington, DC: APA.
Fowler, Karen Joy. (2013). *We Are All Completely Beside Ourselves*. New York: Putnam's.
Journal of Literature and Trauma Studies. (n.d.). About the journal. https://www.jlts.stir.ac.uk/about/ (accessed September 21, 2021).
Kaplan, Ann. (2015). *Climate Trauma: Foreseeing the Future in Dystopian Film and Fiction*. New Brunswick, NJ: Rutgers University Press.
Luckhurst, Roger. (2008). *The Trauma Question*. London: Routledge.
Mbue, Imbolo. (2016). *Behold the Dreamers*. New York: Random House.
McCarthy, Cormac. (2006). *The Road*. New York: Knopf.
Morrison, Toni. (1987). *Beloved*. New York: Knopf.
Rothberg, Michael. (2000). *Traumatic Realism: The Demands of Holocaust Representation*. Minneapolis: University of Minnesota Press.
Spiegelman, Art. (1991). *Maus*. New York: Pantheon.
Whitehead, Amy. (2004). *Trauma Fiction*. Edinburgh: Edinburgh University Press.

FURTHER READING

Bényei, Tamás and Stara, Alexandra. (eds.) (2014). *The Edges of Trauma: Explorations in Visual Art and Literature*. Newcastle upon Tyne, UK: Cambridge Scholars.
Davies, Dominic and Rifkind, Candida. (2020). *Documenting Trauma in Comics: Traumatic Pasts, Embodied Histories, and Graphic Reportage*. London: Palgrave Macmillan.
Davis, Colin and Meretoja, Hanna. (eds.) (2020). *The Routledge Companion to Literature and Trauma*. London: Routledge.

Gibbs, Alan. (2014). *Contemporary American Trauma Narratives*. Edinburgh: Edinburgh University Press.
Kurtz, Roger. (ed.) (2018). *Trauma and Literature*. Cambridge: Cambridge University Press.

Truong, Monique

MARGUERITE NGUYEN
Wesleyan University, USA

Monique Truong is best known as a novelist, but she is also a prolific short story writer and essayist whose works have significantly contributed to Asian American and American cultural studies. Her three novels – *The Book of Salt* (2003), *Bitter in the Mouth* (2010), and *The Sweetest Fruits* (2019) – have all won or been nominated for prestigious awards, while her nonfiction covers topics ranging from the emergence of Vietnamese American literature to local and global dynamics of migration and foodways, particularly as shaped by hierarchies of race, gender, and labor. One thread that ties Truong's works together is the literary question of narration. All three novels are written from first-person perspectives, in turn raising questions of the self and self-representation. These topical concerns often manifest in Truong's nonfiction as more explicit interrogations of who gets to tell stories, who is left out of them, and what historical factors contextualize those inclusions and exclusions. Truong's writings meditate on the social, economic, and geopolitical factors that shape the literary "I" while undoing the logics that determine American authorship and the broader category of American literature.

In *The Book of Salt*, Truong enters one of the most famed literary households of the modernist era – GertrudeStein (as renamed by Truong) and Alice B. Toklas's Parisian salon – and turns it inside out, hypothesizing that the presence of colonized Vietnamese in imperial

France shaped modernism's development. Main character Binh is a queered composite of several Vietnamese cooks whom Stein and Toklas historically employed and who are depicted as memorable, yet childlike, servants in Toklas's *The Alice B. Toklas Cookbook* (1954). In *The Book of Salt*, Binh is a wordsmith and cultural observer who understands how his inventive, imperfect French feeds Stein's radical plays with language. In one scene, Binh's attempt to name a pineapple results in stuttered speech – "Madame, I want to buy a pear . . . not a pear" (Truong 2003, p. 35) – that becomes an appropriative moment for GertrudeStein – "my Madame was amusing herself with my French. She was wrapping my words around her tongue, saving them for a later, more careful study of their mutations" (p. 35). Binh's first-person perspective reveals the incongruity between his simplified speech and elaborate interiority and indexes how GertrudeStein repackages his linguistic struggles and colonial abjection into Steinian expression. GertrudeStein, Toklas, and Binh may align in terms of queer affiliations, but race and empire position them unevenly, cutting unequal domains of desire, work, and literary recognition.

Scholars often praise *The Book of Salt*'s conjecture that colonized Vietnamese servants shaped modernist art for its purposeful *in*authenticity. History's possibilities show that we cannot "know" history and historical figures fully. Indeed, we find out that Binh is not Binh's real name, and Binh's lover for a few pages, "the man on the bridge," is more compelling because of the mystery and queer desire he embodies rather than his historical stature as the future Ho Chi Minh. Yet *The Book of Salt* does not advance an untethered view of fiction. Rather, it is very much invested in the factual aspects of French Indochinese history and the bodily experiences of colonized subjects – material realities that are often made to disappear from American literary history. Binh's first-person primacy releases a linguistic, emotional, and somatic life that breaks open typical modernist genealogies. *The Book of Salt* posits that we have yet to contend with the full scope of colonialism's impact on modernist creation and American culture, particularly as related to US–Southeast Asian connections across the long twentieth century.

In *Bitter in the Mouth*, Truong's interest in US–Southeast Asian ties is brought to Boiling Springs, North Carolina, where Truong's family also first resettled after the Vietnam War. Here, protagonist Linda Hammerick's auditory–gustatory synesthesia directs attention to the embodied, experiential effects of language, while her transracial adoption questions the foundations of how kinship and community are formed. Synesthesia is represented in the novel by cleaved words that depict how Linda processes heard speech, as in "Linda*mint*" and "God*walnut*," an onslaught that Linda calls "incomings." *Bitter in the Mouth* is more plot-driven than *The Book of Salt* and is organized around two central conceits: Linda's withholding of her synesthesia from friends and family and the novel's withholding of her Vietnamese American background from readers; the novel's overall trajectory works toward the gradual revelation of both.

In Linda's Boiling Springs, ideals of whiteness, purity, and heteronormativity are givens of the social fabric. Certain motifs and practices give rise to Southern culture and ecology, such as the languid pace of speech, blossoming magnolias, and Southern Baptist influence on daily life. Transnationalism manifests as the occasional Asian restaurant, while Linda's many attempts at assimilation fail, evident in how Iris, Linda's grandmother and the Hammerick family matriarch, treats her adopted relative: "Iris ignored me altogether when I started growing my hair long again, wearing gloss on my lips, and carrying a purse full of feminine protection. I had disappeared because I had disappointed." (Truong 2010, p. 133). The region's prominent families aim to leave "no stain" behind, thus Linda is an undesirable mark on idealized notions of Southern family and genealogy (p. 110).

But *Bitter in the Mouth* exposes Southern ideals for the gendered and racist myths that they are. Linda's adoptive great-uncle, Harper Burch ("Baby Harper"), is gay, making him an outsider to both the family and the broader community. Thomas, Linda's father, still harbors feelings for his former love Mai-Dao, who is Linda's mother. Horrific violation is committed by Kelly's cousin Bobby, a high schooler who molests Kelly and rapes Linda when they are girls – which Linda understands as a racially motivated act – destroying their childhood and sense of the future: "He wasn't how we had imagined the boys in our lives to be. Forced hands, eyes shut, blood" (2010, p. 37). Stains, contaminations, and crimes abound in *Bitter in the Mouth*'s Southern families, their suppression and secrets shaping the novel's Southern Gothic frame.

Scholars point out that *Bitter in the Mouth*'s focus on the Southeast Asian ties that make up the US South expands the conceptual horizons of Asian American studies, which typically focuses on the West Coast and urban areas, and Southern studies, which is not always in touch with its transpacific ties. Indeed, Linda's story is tightly interwoven with regional history and lore to make these strands inseparable. In addition to the novel's incorporation of Southern writers and genres such as Harper Lee and the Southern Gothic, chapters that reimagine the life of fellow orphan Virginia Dare, slave poet George Moses Horton, and the Wright brothers' feats of flight are threaded throughout, placing Linda's perspective and history on par with these Southern narratives. But *Bitter in the Mouth* does not simply privilege or exceptionalize the South as a category of analysis. The rhizomatic tree of Southern culture and history that emerges is both regionally specific and *relational*, more broadly interested in how exclusionary dynamics of home and belonging echo across space. This is especially apparent in how the North is as parochial as the South in *Bitter in the Mouth*. Linda's fiancé, Leo, is a Beacon Hill Bostonian whose family traces its American roots back to 1795. He is a grating embodiment of New England elitism, "a man fixated on provenance" who eventually leaves Linda after a surgery leaves her unable to have children (2010, p. 169).

That those with whom Linda most closely identifies are Harper, Kelly, and a global community of synesthetes questions the biological, ethnic, and legalized foundations of kinship (such as the family or nation). Synesthesia becomes key to this inquiry, requiring readers to follow Linda's complex experiences with language as taste on her own terms and, thus, enabling an associative, non-automatic thinking that reshapes how we read and perceive. Synesthesia functions as also a formal device – a structure of language that breaks with straitjacketed habits of communication and paves the way for rethinking how language denotes core categories of intimacy, family, Southernness, and, by extension, Americanness.

The Sweetest Fruits continues Truong's exploration of social hierarchies and secret histories embedded in the American "I" but forges intersubjective narration out of multiple first-person voices. Imagining three women from around the world who were all intimates of writer Lafcadio Hearn but did not directly know each other, the novel shows how the women who substantially shaped Hearn's life then disappear in writings about Hearn as well as in Hearn's own writings. Returning to the prior novels' structure of juxtaposing a marginalized character's perspective with that of major American figures and histories, the dynamic women of *The Sweetest Fruits* – Rosa Antonia Cassimati (Greece), Alethea Foley (Ohio), and Koizumi Setsu (Japan) – carve out a storytelling space for those who have been edited out.

One of America's most established and popular writers of the nineteenth century, Hearn was born on the island of Lefkada, Greece, to an Ionian mother and Irish father and was educated in Wales and France. His itinerancy took him to Cincinnati, New Orleans, Martinique, and Japan, where he eventually married and lived. He worked in a range of genres, including journalism, novels, and essays, and covered a variety of topics, from Cincinnati crime to the origins of an early eighteenth-century Malay fishing village in New Orleans, to Japanese ghost stories. Hearn is one of America's earliest self-appointed white brokers of American multiculturalism, and it was his liaisons with women, many of whom were socially and/or economically marginalized, that helped him gain access to the "underground" environments that he typically exoticized in his works.

If Hearn is the ostensible center of *The Sweetest Fruits*, he gets no chapters of his own. Rather, the lives and voices of Rosa, Alethea, and Setsu take center stage as *The Sweetest Fruits* elaborates on their day-to-day experiences as women who perform invisible labor, make unconventional choices, and are discriminated against by patriarchal and other societal norms. Each of the three sections operates under the conceit that the character is telling her story to someone else. In the first chapter, Rosa, Hearn's mother, is in transit on the seas and pregnant with her third son while she narrates her life to a traveling companion in hopes that Lafcadio Hearn will eventually read the tale. Rosa has been shipped home to Greece from Ireland, where she has been living with husband Charles Hearn, whom she met on Cerigo island while he was an Irish surgeon serving the British occupation. Hearn's family asks Rosa to leave Ireland and the young Lafcadio Hearn behind so that he can be raised as a Catholic and future heir. Used to Charles's abandonments, Rosa accepts the proposal: "I know Charles, upon learning of my departure from Dublin, will fold up the letter from his aunt and let out a sigh of relief" (Truong 2019, p. 63). Rosa's excision from the Hearn family, which she sees as an act of Anglo theft, is just one of many losses. Her mother dies young, she suffers sexist condemnation throughout her life for her relationship with Charles, and she loses her first son in infancy. Rosa's chapter roots Hearn's lifelong wanderlust in the Hearn family's ethnocentric and gendered separation of kin.

Alethea Foley inhabits the second, longest chapter. Hearn's first wife whom he abandons when he takes off for New Orleans, Alethea is a former slave who works as a cook in the boarding house where Hearn lives during his time in Cincinnati. This section takes place after Hearn's death, as Alethea discusses her marriage with a reporter in order to lay claim to part of his estate. The key effect of Alethea's narration is to capture her influence on two things that defined Hearn's career – cooking and storytelling.

One of Hearn's most famous books, *La Cuisine Creole* (1885), was the first printed book of Creole recipes and helped to establish New Orleans' reputation as a unique multicultural hub and Hearn's overall literary reputation. While Hearn credits the book's recipes to "leading chefs and notable creole housewives," in *The Sweetest Fruits*, it is Alethea who teaches Hearn what he knows. She reveals that Hearn had "very particular ideas about how foodstuff should be prepared," yet he "never went into the kitchen except to tell me a story" (Truong 2019, p. 129). Alethea also tempers Hearn's self-aggrandizement as a storyteller, charging, "Pat was a terrible storyteller" who "would sometimes miss the heart of the story, which I could hear" (pp. 107, 123). She works hard to help Hearn better discern the core of a narrative. The fact that her food knowledge and storytelling skills stem from slave history, which has separated her family and sends her on an eternal quest for her mother, reconnects the culinary and narrative expertise Hearn claims and miscredits back to the slave economies that are subsumed in his multicultural celebrations. Hearn completely ignores the risks Alethea takes as an African American woman who decides to share her life with him. As she fights for recognition of her marriage and her rights as his widow, Alethea knows that in the eyes of whites, "there was no marriage, no house, no bond except for labor or something sordid" (p. 120). Her labor and influence remain unpaid and unrecognized.

The last section of *The Sweetest Fruits* introduces Setsu, Hearn's second wife, as she writes her memoir of "Lafcadio Hearn and how he became Koizumi Yakumo" (2019, p. 184). The daughter of a samurai, Setsu is hired by Hearn to be a live-in maid and Japanese-language instructor. After marrying him, she serves as his constant cultural guide, easing the conflicts that arise as he proudly travels to places "where [his] Western face was the first" (p. 244). Like Alethea, Setsu helps Hearn hone his storytelling craft – "I was the storyteller and you the listener" (p. 220) – and, like Rosa and Alethea, she comes to expect her husband's departure and the ensuing sense of alienation: "we were each other's country . . . When you departed, I was left an exile in the country outside" (p. 202). Hearn's physical abandonment is exacerbated by his literary erasure of Setsu, similar to his literary deletion of Alethea. In his many works about Japan, traces of Setsu are barely detectable, as she is often recast as a series of fictionalized native informants, her knowledge appropriated to create Hearn's persona of multicultural authority. Even son Kazuo struggles to comprehend these literary absences: "Kazuo then wanted to know why I was nowhere else in your book. He asked this of me as if it were proof that I did not exist, that this body was not of bones, of flesh, and of his same blood" (p. 254).

Collectively, Rosa, Alethea, and Setsu critically comment on Hearn's career, rooting his dreamy and mythic stories in material circumstances. Rosa's story is also a story of the British Empire, Alethea's also a narrative of slavery's ongoing effects, Setsu's also a personalized account of how Japan transitioned into the Meiji era. These women not only record Hearn's masculinist abandonment of the women who loved him, they take risks and cross borders of their own. Yet, as in Truong's other novels, the hypothetical recovery of silenced voices is not idealized. Interlocutors in each section do not always catch or understand what the narrator says, or they question the significance or veracity of what they hear. Rosa chides her traveling companion, "You do not have to believe me in order to write what I say" (2019, p. 32); Alethea questions the journalist, "You're not writing this down either, Miss?" (p. 118); and Setsu notes of Kazuo, "He doubted me" (p. 254). This dialogic structure is layered with yet another mediating frame formed by excerpts from Elizabeth Bisland's *The Life and Letters of Lafcadio Hearn* (1906), the first biography of Hearn, which shaped Hearn's iconic status yet depicted Rosa, Alethea, and Setsu dismissively. Bisland's air of third-person objectivity precedes each chapter, indicating the entrenched power that dominant literary voices still have; even when they do tell their stories, devalued women continue to be disbelieved and erased. Across Truong's fiction, then, first-person perspectives affirm that marginalized subjects' memory, orality, and writings must be valued alongside widely accepted versions of who constitutes and narrates the literary self. Only then can we discern the intersubjectivity of the literary "I," the unequal conditions that frame it, and the tensions and lacunae that shape the archival record.

In addition to Truong's significant contributions to the world of fiction, Truong's nonfiction is equally important, with numerous publications in a range of print and online venues, including *The New York Times, dia-CRITICS, Time, Town & Country, Gourmet, Southern Foodways Alliance*, and a number of newspaper columns, including "Ravenous," which appeared monthly in *T Magazine*. Truong has co-edited the anthology *Watermark: Vietnamese American Poetry & Prose* (1998) and edited a collection of reportage by Lafcadio Hearn titled *Vom Lasterleben am Kai* (2017), demonstrating her efforts as a literary curator invested in widening the range of what global audiences read. Truong is also a lyricist and librettist. In interviews, Truong often references her geographically and professionally expansive background as a refugee and intellectual property attorney, which may speak to the combined aesthetic, political, historical, and institutional questions consistently raised in her works.

Of particular note are Truong's critical writings that challenge embedded habits of writers and scholars and ask what new directions Asian American and American studies can take. The essay "The Emergence of Voices: Vietnamese American Literature 1975–1990" (1993) was an important attempt to define this body of work as it was then emerging and offer an appropriate interpretive model. Truong argues that because emergent Vietnamese American narratives often take less canonical forms, readers need to enlist flexible notions of the literary to account for forms such as interviews and collaborative autobiographies. Analytical approaches must also be attuned to the mediation and inauthenticity inherent to such texts, whereby Vietnamese diasporics narrate their stories to a white interviewer or transcriber, resulting in a multiply mediated text.

In "The Reception of Robert Olen Butler's *A Good Scent from a Strange Mountain*: Ventriloquism and the Pulitzer Prize" (1997), Truong extends her investigation of literary collaboration with a scathing critique of the "ventriloquism" of Butler's 1992 Pulitzer-Prize winning story collection. The book is a collection of fifteen short stories, all told from first-person Vietnamese American perspectives. Truong asks why these acts of appropriation garnered little attention from Asian American scholars at the time, confronting Asian American studies' neglect of Vietnamese American works and contexts. Truong's criticism helped to advance the eventual emergence of Southeast Asian American studies as a field and to illustrate how Vietnamese American literary texts can push the conceptual foci of existing disciplines.

Truong's fiction and nonfiction need to be interpreted together to appreciate their collective contributions to Asian Americanist and Americanist critique. If Truong's novels question who gets to speak, who gets to tell stories, and who gets to write, her nonfiction works do so as well. Truong's intersectional concerns with long histories of colonialism and racialized and gendered contexts of migration contribute to broader questions of whose literature receives what kind of public and critical attention and who gets to lay claim to this thing we call American literature.

SEE ALSO: Apostol, Gina; Contemporary Regionalisms; Fictions of Work and Labor; Kingston, Maxine Hong; Lahiri, Jhumpa; Lee, Chang-rae; Multiculturalism; Nguyen, Viet Thanh; Ozeki, Ruth; Yamashita, Karen Tei

REFERENCES

Truong, Monique. (1997). The reception of Robert Olen Butler's *A Good Scent from a Strange Mountain*: ventriloquism and the Pulitzer Prize. *Viet Nam Forum* 16 (Fall): 75–94.

Truong, Monique. (2003). *The Book of Salt*. Boston: Houghton Mifflin.

Truong, Monique. (2010). *Bitter in the Mouth*. New York: Random House.

Truong, Monique. (2019). *The Sweetest Fruits*. New York: Viking.

FURTHER READING

Cruz, Denise. (2014). Monique Truong's literary South and the regional forms of Asian America. *American Literary History* 26 (4): 716–741.

Eng, David. (2010). *The Feeling of Kinship: Queer Liberalism and the Racialization of Intimacy*. Durham, NC: Duke University Press.

Hearn, Lafcadio. (2017). *Vom Lasterleben am Kai* (ed. Monique Truong). Munich, Germany: C.H. Beck.

Tran, Barbara, Luu, Khoi Truong, and Truong, Monique. (eds.) (1998). *Watermark: Vietnamese American Poetry & Prose*. New York: Asian American Writers' Workshop.

Truong, Monique. (1993). The emergence of voices: Vietnamese American literature 1975–1990. *Amerasia Journal* 19 (3): 27–50.

Truong, Monique. (2018). A rejected "travelogue" of Singapore, the Philippines, and Vietnam. *diaCRITICS* (October 22, 2018). https://dvan.org/2018/10/se-asia-imagined-travelogue-by-monique-truong/ (accessed July 16, 2021).

U

Updike, John

MATTHEW SHIPE
Washington University in St. Louis, USA

Over the course of a career that spanned six decades and over thirty books, John Updike established himself as one of the most prolific and significant writers of his generation, his work meticulously tracing the contours of middle-class American life, what he termed in his autobiography *Self-Consciousness* (1989) as "the whole mass of middling, hidden, troubled America" (p. 103). In his foreword to *The Early Stories: 1953–1975* (2003), Updike noted that as a writer his "only duty [has been] to describe reality as it had come to me – to give the mundane its beautiful due" (p. xv). Throughout his twenty-three novels and numerous short story collections, he endeavored to do just that and, in the process, amassed a body of work that renders the complexities and the contradictions of sixty years of American life. Born in 1932 in Shillington, Pennsylvania, Updike spent the bulk of his fiction depicting the textures of small-town American life. In his Rabbit Angstrom tetralogy, the quartet of novels chronicling the life and times of Harry "Rabbit" Angstrom, a high school basketball star turned Toyota salesman, Updike constructed a history of the United States during the Cold War, from the conservatism of the Eisenhower fifties to the uncertainty of the Reagan/Bush years. Even as his fiction frequently explored the implications and contradictions of male sexuality, with novels such as *Couples* (1968) bringing a new level of explicitness to literary depictions of sex, Updike's fiction more broadly was devoted to chronicling American domestic life during the second half of the twentieth century and the opening decade of the new millennium. Much like Philip Roth, who was Updike's contemporary and chief literary rival, Updike set out to render an intimate history of his nation during his lifetime, his immense body of work capturing the transformation of American life from the Depression and World War II to the War on Terror.

Updike's standing as one of the most prominent American writers of his generation was established early in his career. After the initial promise of his first novel, *The Poorhouse Fair* (1959), he found more commercial and critical success with *Rabbit, Run* (1960), which would be adapted into a motion picture in 1970, and *The Centaur* (1962), the latter of which was awarded the National Book Award, the first major recognition that Updike would receive as a writer. However, it would be the publication of *Couples* in 1968 that would establish Updike as a literary celebrity. The

---

The Encyclopedia of Contemporary American Fiction 1980–2020, First Edition. Edited by Patrick O'Donnell, Stephen J. Burn, and Lesley Larkin.
© 2022 John Wiley & Sons Ltd. Published 2022 by John Wiley & Sons Ltd.

novel, which features a group of adulterous young adults during the waning days of John Kennedy's presidency, would land Updike on the cover of *Time* magazine – under the tagline "The Adulterous Society" – and would make him, alongside Roth and Erica Jong, one of the most prominent (and explicit) relators of the sexual revolution.

While *Couples* marked the pinnacle of his commercial fortunes, much of the fiction that he produced in the subsequent decade pursued the consequences of the cultural and political upheavals that *Couples* had anticipated. In *Rabbit Redux* (1971), the second installment of the Rabbit tetralogy, Updike returned to the character of Harry Angstrom to explore the political and social upheaval of the 1960s; the novel, by far the most political and violent in the series, remains one of the most brilliant documents of the turmoil that pervaded American life during those years – the troubled "O.K.?" that concludes the novel serves as a fitting epilogue for the uncertainty of those years (1995, p. 619). Indeed, the late 1960s would prove crucial to shaping Updike's political perspective and the trajectory of much of his subsequent fiction as Updike felt himself acutely out of step with many of his literary peers for the resentment he felt toward (from his perspective) the radical rhetoric of the New Left and the antiwar movement. "The protest," Updike observed twenty years later in his memoir *Self-Consciousness*, "from my perspective, was in large part a snobbish dismissal of [Lyndon] Johnson by the Eastern establishment; Cambridge professors and Manhattan lawyers and their guitar-strumming children thought they could run the country and the world better than this lugubrious bohunk from Texas" (1989, p. 120). Sentiments such as this would lead some critics to classify Updike as a conservative writer. In *A New Literary History of America* (2009), Updike's only mention comes in an article entitled "The Plight of Conservative Literature" – an assessment that both misreads his politics – Updike consistently supported the Democratic party and one of his final poems expresses his excitement over Barack Obama's presidency – and flattens out the complex critique of American culture that would inform much of his subsequent fiction (Kimmage 2009, p. 949).

Indeed, Updike's novels of the 1970s reflected the pessimism and sense of exhaustion that has now come to characterize our sense of the post-Watergate, post-Vietnam moment in US history. He would, however, enter the 1980s with a sense of rejuvenation that would propel his fiction of the next decade. The novels and stories that Updike would produce in the nine-year span that separates the final two Rabbit novels – 1981's *Rabbit is Rich* and 1990's *Rabbit at Rest* – would in many ways mark his most ambitious and successful work as a novelist. Taken together, the final two novels in the tetralogy chronicle the final decade of the Cold War, and in both we see Rabbit grapple with his past – a past that often seems more substantial than his present moment – and the uncertainties of American life as it entered a new point in its history. Set in the final year of the Carter administration, *Rabbit is Rich* finds Harry Angstrom enjoying the comforts of his newly secured middle-class existence, his fortunes running counter to the nation's economic stagnation under Carter. "The fucking world is running out of gas," Updike writes in the novel's brilliant opening paragraph. "But they won't catch [Rabbit], not yet, because there isn't a piece of junk on the road gets better mileage than his Toyotas, with lower service costs" (1995, p. 623). Indeed, there is a sense of fullness to *Rabbit is Rich* that makes it one of the most satisfying novels that Updike would produce: not only is it the happiest entry in the series but it is also a book that is deliciously awash in the texture of American life during those years. "A dreamy mood pervades the book,"

Updike noted in his introduction to the tetralogy, "Rabbit almost has to keep pinching himself to make sure that his bourgeois bliss is real" (p. viii).

If *Rabbit is Rich* captures Harry Angstrom at his happiest, then its sequel is a far less sunny affair as Rabbit, now bloated from a life of overconsumption, approaches an early death from heart disease and his only son, Nelson, squanders the family's Toyota dealership due to his cocaine addiction. The novel reflects both the uncertainty and promise of this moment in US history: Rabbit finds himself fixated by the news reports of the terrorist bombing that exploded the Pan Am flight over Lockerbie, Scotland and he finds himself missing Reagan and the sense of security that the Cold War offered. Dressed as Uncle Sam for his town's Fourth of July parade, "Harry's eyes burn and the impression giddily – as if he had been lifted up to survey all human history – grows upon him, making his heart thump worse and worse, that all in all this is the happiest fucking country the world has ever seen" (1995, pp. 1386–1387). The moment not only offers one final moment of triumph for Harry Angstrom before he falls victim to a second heart attack, but also captures the tetralogy's interest in Americans' impulse to strive for happiness, a pursuit that is often self-defeating and unsatisfactory.

Between the final two Rabbit books, Updike produced a pair of novels, *The Witches of Eastwick* (1984) and *Roger's Version* (1986), that demonstrated his ambition and dexterity as a novelist with both books explicitly moving away from the realism that until then had characterized the bulk of his work as a novelist. Along with *The Coup* (1978), *The Witches of Eastwick* and *Roger's Version* would signal the more experimental approach – the Nabokovian narrative gamesmanship and unrepentant (and sometimes morally dubious) narrators – that Updike would employ in many of his later novels. In *The Witches of Eastwick*, one of the few Updike novels to be adapted for the big screen, he imagines a group of suburban witches who end up destroying one of their own against the backdrop of the late 1960s; the novel is Updike's response both to magical realism – a mode he would return to less successfully in *Brazil* (1994) – and to second-wave feminism as he considered the implications of female power, coming to the somewhat cynical conclusion that women can be just as destructive and self-interested as their male counterparts. *Roger's Version*, the second installment in the *Scarlet Letter* trilogy, remains one of Updike's most ambitious and successful novels as it threads together ecclesiology, particle physics, computer science, Hawthorne, a critique of neoliberal policies, and pornography. Set against the backdrop of the 1984 presidential election in an unnamed but clearly recognizable Boston, the novel offers a grim view of Ronald Reagan's "Morning in America" as it captures the devastating effects, the widening gap between rich and poor, that the Reagan administration's economic and social policies had on US inner cities.

Continuing the ambition that propelled *Roger's Version* and *The Witches of Eastwick*, the short stories that Updike produced during this period – collected in *Trust Me* (1987) and *The Afterlife* (1994) – stand as some of his most compelling work. A sense of belatedness hangs over the middle-aged male protagonists who populate many of the stories in *Trust Me*. Themes of aging and time become even more prominent in *The Afterlife*; in stories such as "A Sandstone Farmhouse" (1990), "The Other Side of the Street" (1990), and "The Brown Chest" (1992), Updike returns to the Pennsylvania landscape and the childhood memories that had been at the heart of his earliest fiction, a move partially inspired by his mother's death in 1989. Revisiting the character of Allen Dow, who had been the teenaged protagonist of "Flight" (1959), Updike in "His Mother Inside

Him" (1992) reassesses the familial relationships – the only child in a home of mismatched parents – that had been the subject of his earliest fiction. "[Allen's mother] was in him not as he had been in her, as a seed becoming a little male offshoot," Updike writes in the story, "but as the full tracery of his perceptions and reactions; he had led his life as an extension of hers" (2013, p. 517). During this same period, Updike's prominence as a critic also expanded. His third volume of criticism, *Hugging the Shore* (1983), won the National Book Critics Circle Award for Criticism; he would publish four more massive volumes of criticism – *Odd Jobs* (1991), *More Matter* (1999), *Due Considerations* (2007), and the posthumous *Higher Gossip* (2011) – as well as three volumes of art criticism, a book on golf, and a memoir, the aforementioned *Self-Consciousness*.

With the exception of *In the Beauty of the Lilies* (1996) – a multigenerational epic that considers the intersection of faith and entertainment in the American consciousness during the course of the twentieth century – Updike's post-Rabbit fiction was frequently less expansive than his most successful work, as his aging male narrators frequently turn their attention to a past that now seems more substantial, more real, than their current situation. Unlike Philip Roth, who wrote his most ambitious novels during the 1990s – most notably the American trilogy that revisited US history in the post-1945 era – Updike's novels of this period were more idiosyncratic and narrow in their focus. Of these novels, the most significant are *Memories of the Ford Administration* (1992) and *Toward the End of Time* (1997). In the former, Updike revisits the period of domestic disorder that he had chronicled in *A Month of Sundays* (1975) and the stories of separation and divorce gathered in *Problems* (1979) as well as the research that he had conducted on President James Buchanan for his only play, *Buchanan Dying* (1974). But more than just a recycling of old material, *Memories of the Ford Administration* offers Updike's argument for the historical significance of his largely private fiction, as the novel's narrator, the historian Alf Clayton, rails against the ways in which history – the academic study of the past – always gets that past, at best, slightly wrong. Published five years after *Memories of the Ford Administration*, *Toward the End of Time* imagines the United States in the year 2020 after the nation has been devastated by a nuclear war with China. Yet the novel is less interested in detailing the dystopian potential of its setting than in exploring the implications of the aging male consciousness as it grapples with the loss of sexual potency. The novel ranks as one of Updike's strangest, but also most ambitious late novels, as it ultimately offers his most astringent portrait of a United States in decline.

Updike ended the century by returning to two of his most enduring and successful characters, Henry Bech and Harry Angstrom. In "Rabbit Remembered," a novella included in the story collection *Licks of Love* (1999), Updike revisits the Angstrom clan as they face the uncertainties of American life in the waning days of the century and as they cope with the memory of Harry Angstrom. More successful is *Bech at Bay* (1998), the final book chronicling the travails of the Jewish American writer Henry Bech, whose misadventures Updike had chronicled in *Bech: A Book* (1970) and *Bech is Back* (1982). In many respects, *Bech at Bay* remains one of the more satisfying of his late works as the book allows Updike to humorously consider both his own legacy – in the wonderfully bizarre "Bech Noir" the writer hunts down and kills the critics who have been cruel to him throughout his career – and the waning status of literature in American culture as the century reaches its conclusion. In "Bech and the Bounty of Sweden," Bech wins the Nobel Prize that eluded Updike and gives the address that Updike never had the opportunity to give. "[B]ut what, my distinguished friends, do I know of the world," Bech asks toward the end of his speech. "My life has been spent attending to my inner weather and my immediate vicinity" (1998, p. 239). And while Updike could certainly have been accused of largely "attending to [his] inner weather," his meticulous recording of the historical and personal circumstances that shaped his lifetime yielded one of the most substantial bodies of work of the post-1945 era, his work providing an intimate history of American life in the second half of the twentieth century and the opening decade of the new millennium.

Updike's novelistic output in the final decade of his career continued the idiosyncratic approach that had characterized his work in the 1990s. Perhaps not surprisingly the past looms large in many of these novels: whether it is the more removed history covered in *Gertrude and Claudius* (2000) or the more recent past chronicled in *Seek My Face* (2002), a delightful (and underrated) consideration of mid-twentieth-century art that is loosely based on Lee Krasner's career and life, and *Villages* (2004), a final reconsideration of the suburban adultery that had been the subject of so much of Updike's early fiction. The late work, however, that has received the most critical attention is *Terrorist* (2006), a portrait of Ahmad Ashmawy Mulloy, a teenaged son of an Irish American mother and Egyptian father, who gets embroiled in a jihadist plot to blow up the Lincoln tunnel. While Updike received criticism from some corners for attempting to write from the perspective of a Muslim American teenager, his depiction of Ahmad remains largely sympathetic – in many ways, he seems to be a rewriting of the young David Kern in "Pigeon Feathers" (1960) whose faith is challenged by the adults who surround him – as Ahmad's faith is consistently challenged by a culture that seemingly undermines any attempt to maintain religious belief. The novel, while ending peacefully, would in some ways anticipate the 2013 Boston Marathon bombing, and the book as a whole offers Updike's sharpest critique of American life in the new century.

His final novel, *The Widows of Eastwick* (2008), a sequel to *The Witches of Eastwick*, was published a few months before his death from lung cancer in January 2009. Shortly after his death, *Endpoint* (2009), a collection of poetry, much of which was composed in the aftermath of Updike's cancer diagnosis in 2008, and a final volume of short stories, *My Father's Tears* (2009), were published. Many of the stories in *My Father's Tears* revisit Updike's memories of a childhood and adolescence spent in small-town Pennsylvania. A final volume of criticism, *Higher Gossip*, would appear in 2011. All three of the volumes are fine additions to Updike's oeuvre – in many ways, *Endpoint* stands as his most successful volume of poetry and the title story of *My Father's Tears* is one of his most affecting – as they offered one final reminder of Updike's immense gifts as a writer and chronicler of life in the United States. His dexterity and his accomplishments in so many different forms make his career exceptional in American letters and his oeuvre ultimately stands as one of the more remarkable and revealing bodies of work to come out of the post-1945 period.

SEE ALSO: Fiction and Terrorism; Roth, Philip; Suburban Narratives

REFERENCES

Kimmage, Michael. (2009). The plight of conservative literature. In: *A New Literary History of America* (ed. Greil Marcus and Werner Sollors), 948–953. Cambridge, MA: Harvard University Press.

Updike, John. (1989). *Self-Consciousness*. New York: Knopf.

Updike, John. (1995). *Rabbit Angstrom: The Four Novels*. New York: Everyman's Library.

Updike, John. (1998). *Bech at Bay*. New York: Knopf.

Updike, John. (2003). *The Early Stories: 1953–1975*. New York: Knopf.
Updike, John. (2013). *Collected Later Stories* (ed. Christopher Carduff). New York: The Library of America.

FURTHER READING

Bailey, Peter. (2006). *Rabbit (Un)Redeemed: The Drama of Belief in John Updike's Fiction*. Madison, WI: Farleigh Dickinson University Press.
Boswell, Marshall. (2001). *John Updike's Rabbit Tetralogy: Mastered Irony in Motion*. Columbia: University of Missouri Press.
Miller, D. Quentin. (2001). *John Updike and the Cold War: Drawing the Iron Curtain*. Columbia and London: University of Missouri Press.
Pritchard, William. (2000). *Updike: America's Man of Letters*. South Royalton, VT: Steerforth Press.
Schiff, James A. (1998). *John Updike Revisited*. New York: Twayne.

Urban Fiction

KEENAN NORRIS
San José State University, USA

This article chronicles the development of urban fiction from 1980 through to the present day. Late twentieth-century and early twenty-first-century urban fiction is a subgenre of African American literature which is sometimes referred to by the narrower monickers of "street lit" and "hip-hop fiction." Linked to hip-hop by its unstinting focus on the lives of socially marginalized Black people living in American inner cities, the subgenre is inseparable from hip-hop. The urban fiction novelists that emerged in the early and mid-1990s were African American writers who did not seek validation from the traditional mainstream publishing industry nor the network of MFA programs across America. Instead, an audience for urban fiction emerged in the 1990s from a primarily urban African American readership. Sister Souljah, Terri Woods, Vickie Stringer, Shannon Holmes, and K'wan Foye are among the African American writers who came to prominence in the 1990s and 2000s. Along with Latino/x and Afro-Latino/x writers such as Aya de Leon, these authors continue to produce novels for a devoted readership.

Urban fiction's location of a Black urban readership in the 1990s can be seen as of a piece with the cultural sea change wrought by hip-hop. Like hip-hop, urban fiction centered the Black urban experience while allowing often disenfranchised Black urbanites to monetize their culture to a greater degree than ever before. As hip-hop became a global, billion-dollar industry in the 1990s, urban fiction became increasingly popular. While the height of its popularity passed with the decade of the 2000s, urban fiction's continued presence in the literary landscape is testament to the necessity of the narratives characteristic to the subgenre.

The popular novelist Omar Tyree's debut book *Capital City* (1993) would inaugurate a new era for urban literary narrative. The novel, which is set in Washington, DC, in the early 1990s, is a portrait of Black male urban youth culture in that era, with specific focus on how the crack cocaine trade and hip-hop's emergence have fundamentally separated these youth from Black people of past generations. Told through the alternating first-person narratives of a trio of main characters, Butterman, Shank, and Wes, the novel foregrounds the slang, style, and bravado of the streets, as well as the quieter, more nuanced aspects of each man. Their narratives also suggest the three are living in post-Civil Rights Movement America where they are much more influenced by the disintegration of the American inner city, as well as by the rivalrous intraracial class politics of Black America, than by the solidarity of social justice movements. The stories of the three young men form a Black urban dialectic, each character representing a different response to life conditions in early

1990s DC. Shank, as his street moniker suggests, is a hard case; emotionally erratic, quick to anger and to act out violently, he serves as the enforcer for Butterman's drug-dealing enterprise. Shank represents the roughest elements of Black hood life in the early 1990s. He is the product of a volatile single-parent home. He harbors deep resentment toward his mother, who brought an abusive stepfather into their home when he was a child. Shank is also highly sensitive, despite his rough exterior. He reads Maya Angelou's *I Know Why the Caged Bird Sings* (1969) in order to better understand his girlfriend and Black women in general. Yet he regularly pays the bitterness he feels toward his mother forward to the Black men he contends with in the streets, leaving a trail of destruction that predictably follows him as the novel develops. At the opposite pole is Wes, a Howard University student possessed of a militant, intellectual, Afrocentrist worldview. Despite being from modest economic circumstances, Wes engages the world of the streets with disarming, dangerous naivete. His heady Afrocentrist politics compel him to connect with Black street figures like Shank and Butterman. In fact, it is Butterman who manipulates Wes into working for his clandestine enterprise, using Wes's learnedness to help with the business end of his drug trafficking. Wes is torn between his idealistic Afrocentrist worldview, which does not include cocaine dealing, and the urge to connect with young Black men whose backgrounds are more troubled and whose opportunity horizons are more limited than his own. Spanning the vast divide between Shank and Wes is Butterman, who represents the back-slid children of the hip-hop generation. Raised for a time in an upper-class section of Washington, DC, he earned enrollment to an elite university several years before the book's beginning. Uninterested in matriculating due to social alienation and other race-based factors, Butterman returns home and finds his way into the most lucrative business available to him. By the book's outset, he's a successful drug dealer who manages a small crew. Intent on making as much money as possible, he draws Shank and Wes into his orbit, setting the stage for a saga of the streets.

Taken in sum, *Capital City* is a vivid period piece about an era and a culture that elevated both hip-hop and urban fiction upon closely related tracks. While urban fiction hasn't gone global the way hip-hop has, it has become a major subcategory within African American literature of the late twentieth and twenty-first centuries.

Tyree's first major commercial success, the urban romance novel *Flyy Girl* (1993), centers the Black female experience of late 1980s urban America. "I traveled back home to Philadelphia just in time to catch a traveling Expo event," Tyree writes in his foreword to the critical anthology *Street Lit: Representing the Urban Landscape* (2013). "I made $1500 that weekend and was practically forcing my book down people's throats for $13, $12, $10, $8, and even $5, depending on how many people were around and how badly you wanted the book at a discount. The bottom line for me was moving the product, like a drug dealer would. So I was even willing to give away free samples to help spread the word if I had to . . . The next thing I knew, I was selling multiple boxes of *Flyy Girl* books to the stores and distributors up and down the East Coast" (2013, pp. viii–ix). While Tyree reasonably likens his salesmanship strategy to that of a drug dealer, he could as credibly liken it to the Do It Yourself, out-the-trunk ethos of such iconic hip-hop acts as the Wu-Tang Clan, who originally marketed their music without major record label backing, instead pressing the albums themselves and distributing them at the shows that they played. In their marketing methodologies, urban fiction and underground hip-hop are closely connected, which is no surprise given that they arise from the same era and the same urban locales. Tyree's entrepreneurial model, with its echoes in hip-hop and the drug trade, is one that numerous Black writers in the urban fiction category went on to follow in the 1990s and 2000s.

In Tyree's wake would emerge many writers whose books took on the often harrowing experiences of young Black hustlers in urban America, but this time rather than an almost exclusively male experience as had been the case with the subgenre's previous vogue in the 1960s when Iceberg Slim and Donald Goines were its chief exemplars, many of the most popular urban fiction novels of the 1990s and 2000s would be penned by women. Sapphire's novel *push* (1996) was published to significant commercial success and critical plaudits as well as stiff criticism from within the Black literary intelligentsia, setting the template for a pattern of popular success and intraracial rebuke that has marked the subgenre ever since. Percival Everett's satirical novel *Erasure* (2001) concerns the life and work of a Black professor and writer of little-read literary fiction who, after witnessing the success of a *push*-like novel by a literary upstart, pens an overwhelmingly stereotypical depiction of Black ghetto life to dubious but widespread acclaim. Despite its detractors, *push* would eventually be adapted for the screen as the award-winning *Precious* (2009).

Most famous among the female urban fiction novelists would be the New York-based activist Sister Souljah, who had come to prominence during Bill Clinton's 1992 presidential run when the candidate used his invitation to a NAACP event to publicly castigate Souljah, a fellow speaker at that event, after Souljah had been quoted in *The Washington Post* as saying "If black people kill black people every day, why not have a week and kill white people?" Souljah has consistently stated that the inflammatory statement was a journalist's fabrication (Mills 1992, p. 1).

Souljah's debut novel *The Coldest Winter Ever* (1999) became the most famous urban fiction text of the late twentieth and early twenty-first century. Told from the perspective of Winter Santiaga, the benighted and abandoned daughter of a jailed drug kingpin, the novel explores myriad themes archetypal to urban fiction. Hip-hop's hypermaterialism and misogyny, as well as the drug trade in America and mass incarceration, are among the novel's central topics.

In the novel, Winter's mother teaches her daughter an ethic of hypermaterialism and relationship manipulation. Mrs. Santiaga fetishizes brand name clothing and models for her daughter how to manipulate a man into having her as a kept woman by manipulating her husband, referred to in the novel simply as Santiaga. Santiaga models a version of manhood for Winter that is even more negative: his occupation attracts violence and police investigations. Ultimately, his family is left with nothing when he is imprisoned. Winter spirals out of control, searching through a gauntlet of flashy, dangerous men for someone who can provide for her the life that Santiaga provided for her and her mother prior to his imprisonment. Even as she hurtles toward self-destruction, her first-person narration makes the novel more than a stereotypical gangster drama: Winter is self-styled and self-willed, wild, chippy, sarcastic and bitterly hilarious, a Black teen female antihero in the American tradition of Huckleberry Finn, Holden Caulfield, and Harley Quinn.

While Winter pursues an increasingly self-destructive life path, her doomed way lit by the failures of her parents, the characters Midnight and the eponymous Sister Souljah present a counternarrative of honor, responsibility, right manhood and womanhood, and Afrocentric identity formation. The novel ends with brutal determinism: Unable to attract the interest of Midnight due to her incorrigible immaturity, Winter instead pursues a relationship with a brutish drug dealer named Bullet. Bullet takes psychological control over Winter by isolating her in the bedroom of his Brooklyn apartment without food until she is completely compliant. At his beck and call, she allows him to rent a car under her name for the purpose of a drug run. The caper eventuates in Winter's arrest and imprisonment. Several years into a long prison sentence, Winter learns that her crack-addicted mother has finally died from her demons. Winter is allowed to attend the funeral. Also in attendance is Santiaga. ". . . [My father] wanted to hug me," Winter recalls, "but his hands were chained, and so were mine" (Souljah 1999, p. 426). At book's end, father and daughter find themselves state property, barely able to mourn their dead, no different than if they were slaves.

In her seminal urban fiction analysis "Reading Street Literature, Reading America's Prison System," Kristina Graaff observes that "A particular important facet of the genre is how it is inextricably linked to the US penal system on multiple levels . . . Imprisonment is also a central theme in most storylines" (2010, p. 1). *The Coldest Winter Ever* opens and closes in the shadow of incarceration. In her essay, Graaff identifies as fundamental to contemporary urban fiction a "stagnation narrative" wherein the characters oscillate permanently between incarceration and the low-opportunity environs of the inner-city streets. Tightly bound to their urban confines, they are fundamentally unfree. Prison, thus, becomes symbolic of the intractable systemic limitations that have been imposed upon the Black poor for centuries.

In subsequent years, Sister Souljah has gone on to author a trilogy of novels about Midnight, the character that *The Coldest Winter Ever* figures as the symbol of right manhood. The subsequent novels *Midnight: A Gangster Love Story* (2008), *Midnight and the Meaning of Love* (2011), and *A Moment of Silence: Midnight III* (2015) complete Midnight's character arc. The novel *A Deeper Love Inside: The Porsche Santiaga Story* (2014) is narrated by its eponymous heroine, Winter's younger sister Porsche, who at the close of *The Coldest Winter Ever* seems just as enthralled as was Winter with the trappings of ghetto fabulousness. *A Deeper Love Inside* not only allows Porsche to tell her own story but continues the narratives of Winter and Midnight.

Following in Sister Souljah's wake, Terri Woods and Vickie Stringer took their places among the most powerful and prolific figures in the history of urban fiction. Woods self-published *True to the Game* (1998) and over the next two years sold copies of the novel out of the trunk of her car. The novel became a street lit classic, so much so that Woods made of it a trilogy with the subsequent releases *True to the Game II* (2007) and *True to the Game III* (2008). In the midst of completing that trilogy, Woods authored a second trilogy, *Deadly Reigns I* (2005), *Deadly Reigns II* (2006) and *Deadly Reigns III* (2009). Caleb Alexander has since carried on the *Deadly Reigns* franchise with the publication of an additional six *Deadly Reigns* novels. Stringer was serving a seven-year prison sentence in Ohio for drug trafficking and money laundering when she wrote *Let That Be the Reason* (2001), a novel about a female drug dealer. Upon her release from prison in 2001, Stringer found that she was unable to find a publisher for the novel. She instead self-published *Let That Be the Reason* and used her earnings from it to found the street lit publishing company Triple Crown Publications. Stringer's next novel, *Imagine This* (2004), was published by Simon & Schuster and spent two full years on the *Essence* magazine bestseller list. Her subsequent five-novel *Dirty Red* series has garnered popular attention, cementing Stringer's legacy as among the most impactful of all street lit novelists.

Shannon Holmes, K'wan Foye, Carl Weber, and Jihad are among the African American male writers who came to prominence in the 2000s and continue to produce novels for a devoted readership. Foye's prolific bibliography includes over twenty novels, including *Eviction Notice* (2011) and *Animal* (2012), both of which were awarded the Street Lit Book Award Medal in 2012 and 2013, respectively. Holmes has been nearly as prolific, authoring ten books over the past two decades. Like Vickie Stringer, Holmes penned his first novel, *B-More Careful* (2001), while imprisoned. Since then, his novels, among them *Bad Girlz* (2005), *Never Go Home Again* (2007), and *Dirty Game* (2007), have attained bestseller status and have sustained a devoted readership. *Never Go Home Again* in particular is exemplary of several of the archetypal tropes of urban fiction, including the journey from a life in the streets, to incarceration, then personal renaissance and redemption. These key narrative movements are also present in famous pre-street lit African American autobiographical narratives like Claude Brown's *Manchild in the Promised Land* (1965), Piri Thomas's *Down These Mean Streets* (1967), and Malcolm X's and Alex Haley's *The Autobiography of Malcolm X* (1965). Meanwhile, Weber's literary success allowed him to establish Urban Books, a publisher that specializes in urban fiction titles. In his tenure at Urban Books, Weber has signed several dozen urban fiction novelists and seen their work through the process to completion and publication, making Urban Books among the most – if not the most – successful publishers of contemporary urban fiction. Among the major titles published by Urban Books is Jihad's autobiographical debut novel *Street Life* (2004). The novel takes as its outline the classic redemption arc from the dangerous streets (in this case with Atlanta, Georgia, as its setting), to imprisonment, and eventually on to self-willed uplift.

It is a cautionary tale wherein the protagonist, Lincoln Jackson, a reformed former hustler-turned-small business owner, is ambushed by some young hoodlums. After subduing and handcuffing the robbers, Lincoln shares with them his story rather than calling the police. Lincoln's life story is in the tradition of pre-street lit era texts like *The Autobiography of Malcolm X* and Iceberg Slim's *Pimp: The Story of My Life* (1967) as well as street lit-era novels such as *The Coldest Winter Ever* that make highly intentional claims on the morality of their readership, seeking to guide socially marginal readers away from lives of crime and unnecessary hardship. Since the publication of *Street Life*, Jihad has capitalized on the novel's success by branching off on his own in archetypal street lit style, publishing more than ten titles under his own publishing imprint.

Late twentieth- and early twenty-first-century urban fiction not only serves as a genre of mass-produced pulp crime fiction for Black Americans, it has changed the dynamic between Black American writers and the publishing industry. Whereas Holloway House, the original publisher of Iceberg Slim, Donald Goines, and other writers of urban literature during the 1960s and 1970s, was owned by white businessmen whose experience of African American life was minimal, the more recent iteration of urban fiction has featured more Black-owned publishing concerns and more female leadership helming those outfits. Where Holloway House's founders Bentley Morris and Ralph Weinstock have come under deserved criticism for underpaying authors and promoting African American novels through sensationalist, often stereotypical means, by contrast publishers such as Urban Books, Triple Crown, and Terri Woods Publishing center the Black authors themselves in the production and marketing process. Cash Money Content, the publishing arm of the hip-hop empire Cash

Money Records, has, likewise, seen success through publishing urban fiction novels. Owned by hip-hop mogul Birdman, Cash Money Content bought the rights to all of Iceberg Slim's novels; it also serves as the publisher for K'wan's widely popular novels.

Black ownership has not immunized the subgenre from the criticism that it is an amoral capitalist enterprise that trades in stereotypes harmful to communities of color. Omar Tyree, the self-proclaimed progenitor of urban fiction in its modern iteration, in 2008 announced his retirement in an open letter published online, "An Urban Street Literature Retirement" (2008). Tyree's rationale was largely a repudiation of what he alleged urban fiction had become: a field of writing that trafficked in harmful representations of disenfranchised Black urbanites. Tyree's open letter heralded a backlash against street lit/urban fiction in the mid-2000s. Nick Chiles's *New York Times* editorial "Their Eyes Were Reading Smut" (2006) is among the most well-known arguments lodged against urban fiction's often stereotypical, salacious, and degrading depictions of African American life. Perhaps most notable in the backlash against the subgenre was Terry McMillan's widely circulated email to Simon & Schuster editors which criticized the publishing industry's prioritization of stereotypical and degrading fiction about African Americans over books by more skillful and intellectually ambitious African American writers like Toni Morrison and Barack Obama. While the letter was long ago scrubbed from the Internet, Karen Grigsby Bates's National Public Radio *All Things Considered* episode (2007) chronicles the conflict.

Omar Tyree's *The Last Street Novel* (2007), a metanarrative about a hapless romance novelist whose attempt to take up street lit ends in mayhem, marked the beginnings of a shift in the genre from the portrayal of stereotypes and archetypes of twentieth-century Black inner-city life to an updated narrative of the early twenty-first-century inner-city that enfolds into its plot the issues of gentrification, toxic masculinity understood as such, and complex metanarrative.

The title of Tyree's novel was widely panned by street lit readers at the time of its publication for it seemed to speak to an unbecoming level of hubris on the part of a romance writer who had long since disconnected from the urban fiction genre. In this way, the novel's metanarrative of a Tyree-like novelist disconnected from the streets who journeys back to his Harlem hometown to do research for the urban fiction novel he intends to write seemed to overflow the book's pages and enter real life. Interestingly, however, Tyree actually intended to title the novel *The Writer*, not *The Last Street Novel*, but was informed by his publisher that his chosen title was simply not edgy enough (Tyree 2008). Here, too, Tyree's real-life predicament provides the conceptual frame for his fictional creation, the novel's protagonist Shareef Crawford. Harassed by Harlem street criminals who fear that Crawford's upcoming urban fiction novel will associate them with the crimes depicted in his book, thus opening them to law enforcement investigation, the writer only finds sanctuary with his childhood nemesis-turned-gangster-going-legit Jurell, who protects Crawford in exchange for control over Crawford's writing career. Recasting himself as The Street King, Crawford at the novel's end has been manipulated into literary servitude. At Jurell's behest, he labors through one formulaic street lit novel after the next. *The Last Street Novel* is, at core, not a hubristic assertion of Tyree's control over the urban fiction genre, but rather a subtler statement on the writer's bondage to controlling corporate and audience demands. Those demands are perhaps particularly cordoning for urban fiction writers since they are operating under the double boundary of genre typecasting and stereotypes typically affixed to African American life.

In the 2010s, academia took up the formal analysis of urban fiction. Many scholars did the work of historical recovery by looking to the writers of the 1960s and 1970s whose works presaged the emergence of urban fiction decades later. LaMonda H. Stallings's *Word Hustle: Critical Essays and Reflections on the Works of Donald Goines* (2011) and Justin Gifford's *Street Poison: The Biography of Iceberg Slim* (2015) chronicle the life and analyze the works of Donald Goines and Robert Beck (pen name: Iceberg Slim), respectively. Looking to the urban fiction of the 1990s–2010s, the scholar Kristina Graaff's monograph *Street Literature: Black Popular Fiction in the Era of U.S. Mass Incarceration* (2016) focuses on the advent of urban fiction as it is connected to the era of mass incarceration in America. Scholarly guides to contemporary urban fiction include Megan Honig's *Urban Grit: A Guide to Street Lit* (2011), Vanessa Irvin Morris's *The Readers' Advisory Guide to Street Literature* (2011), and *Street Lit: Representing the Urban Landscape*, the first multi-author critical text about the genre.

In recent years, pioneering urban fiction authors have sought to expand the genre's themes. Aya de Leon's debut novel *Uptown Thief* (2016) is a heist drama about a woman, Marisol, who has seemingly escaped a life of prostitution and abuse and has opened a shelter in Spanish Harlem for women in the same predicament. The shelter is constantly on the brink of economic ruin, which provides the pretext for Marisol to use the shelter as a front for her own prostitution ring, which she oversees. Catering to a wealthy Wall Street clientele, Marisol uses the funds both to pay the shelter's rent and to provide the young women in the shelter a variety of educational and employment opportunities well beyond high-end prostitution. As the widely different prostitution experiences of Marisol's women are detailed, what emerges is a dialectic around sex work, its roots in economic necessity, and its tenuous financial rewards and ever-present physical dangers. When, late in the novel, Marisol vacations to Cuba and has a brief affair with a handsome male prostitute there, the novel's examination of the complexities of prostitution crosses genders and national borders, making clear just how wide is the lens that de Leon seeks to train upon this street life mainstay.

As financial pressures mount in gentrifying Harlem, Marisol is compelled to use the prostitution scheme in ever more inventive and reckless ways to cover costs. Meanwhile, she reunites with her childhood friend Raul, eventually beginning a relationship with him. Raul is an ex-cop, jettisoned by the NYPD after blowing the whistle on a case of police brutality. Much as Omar Tyree's intent in *Capital City* is to show the diversity of perspective and experience in the Washington, DC, Black community, in *Uptown Thief* de Leon shows the differing relationship to the law and to elicit business that these two prominent Puerto Rican characters exhibit. Genuine altruism and feminism are at the heart of Marisol's criminal enterprise, so that even the elaborate heists the women perpetrate on unsuspecting moguls take on the air of righteous defiance. This narrative logic speaks to de Leon's intent to use the street lit form to popularize radical forms of feminism that foreground the needs of poor women in urban environments, in particular Black and Brown women in inner-city environments. A politics of prostitution decriminalization, wealth redistribution, and uncompromising female empowerment is core to de Leon's first novel.

De Leon's subsequent novels *The Boss* (2017), *The Accidental Mistress* (2018), and *Side Chick Nation* (2019) take on similar themes, including the diverse experiences of sex work in America and abroad, the critical examination of race and class within the context of impoverished, crime-ridden communities of color, the institutionalization of misogyny, and the expression of diverse Afro-Latina identities. De Leon, Daniel Serrano, and other Afro-Latin writers have somewhat diversified the street lit genre, bringing to the fore powerful narratives of the lives of Latino/x and Afro-Latino/x persons in urban America.

Urban fiction underwent a renaissance in the early 1990s, reemerging in Black popular sphere culture in direct relation to the rise of its musical equivalent, hip-hop music. Both artistic forms center the Black urban experience, with particular focus on the lived experiences of the incarcerated and the socially marginalized. In fact, urban fiction more than any other artistic form, depicts America's age of mass incarceration, a carceral system more extensive than any other system of detention in the history of the Western world, the self-evident extension of slavery and Jim Crow into the twenty-first century. Diverging from the vast body of hip-hop narratives, urban fiction has uniquely provided a platform for Black and Afro-Latina women to share their urban experiences in story form. In this sense, urban fiction is important for its panoramic portrayal of Black urban life in the 1990s and 2000s. Often autobiographical in nature, urban fiction narratives continue the autobiographical tradition of archetypal African American literature from the slave narratives, to the autobiographies of Richard Wright, Malcolm X, and Maya Angelou. Often branded as stereotypical and bad for Black America, urban fiction narratives have trod hyperviolent narrative ground made familiar by both the gangster rap of the 1990s and 2000s and the street literature of the 1960s and 1970s. Often cautionary in nature, urban fiction narratives sharply critique hypermaterialism, misogyny, pimping, retributive violence, and the like. A unique business phenomenon in the literary marketplace, urban fiction has empowered African American businesswomen and men who have established their own publishing imprints. A uniquely ethnic form of pulp fiction dependent primarily on a reliable African American readership, urban fiction once and for all has demolished the myth that Black people are not readers. Ultimately, urban fiction is an important literary phenomenon without which any history of American literature, let alone African American popular culture, in the late twentieth and early twenty-first century is incomplete.

SEE ALSO: Everett, Percival; McMillan, Terry; Mosley, Walter; Multiculturalism; Post-Soul and/or Post-Black Fiction; Trauma and Fiction; Urban Fiction

REFERENCES

Chiles, Nick. (2016). Their eyes were watching smut. *The New York Times* (January 4, 2006). https://www.nytimes.com/2006/01/04/opinion/their-eyes-were-reading-smut.html (accessed July 20, 2021).

Graaff, Kristina. (2010). Reading street literature, reading America's prison system. PopMatters (February 11, 2010). https://www.popmatters.com/119786-reading-street-literature-reading-americas-prison-system-2496156823.html (accessed July 20, 2021).

Grigsby Bates, Karen. (2007). Publishing company called out over "Ghetto Lit." *NPR: All Things Considered* (October 12, 2007). https://www.npr.org/transcripts/15236974?storyId=15236974?storyId=15236974 (accessed July 20, 2021).

Mills, David. (1992). Sister Souljah's call to arms. *The Washington Post* (May 13, 1992). https://www.washingtonpost.com/archive/lifestyle/1992/05/13/sister-souljahs-call-to-arms/643d5634-e622-43ad-ba7d-811f8f5bfe5d/ (accessed July 20, 2021).

Souljah, Sister. (1999). *The Coldest Winter Ever*. London: Atria Books/Simon & Schuster.

Tyree, Omar. (2008). An urban street literature retirement. *The Daily Voice* (June 19, 2008).

Tyree, Omar. (2013). Foreword. *Street Lit: Representing the Urban Landscape* (ed. Keenan Norris). Lanham, MD: Scarecrow Press.

FURTHER READING

Foye, K'wan. (2012). *Animal*. New York: Cash Money Content.
Graaff, Kristina. (2016). *Street Literature: Black Popular Fiction in the Era of U.S. Mass Incarceration*. Heidelberg, Germany: Universitätsverlag Winter.
Irvin Morris, Vanessa. (2011). *The Readers' Advisory Guide to Street Literature*. Chicago: American Library Association Editions.
Norris, Keenan. (ed.) (2013). *Street Lit: Representing the Urban Landscape*. Lanham, MD: Scarecrow Press.
Stringer, Vicki. (2009). *Let That Be the Reason*. New York: Atria Books; 1st ed. self-published, 2001.

Urrea, Luis Alberto

AMY T. HAMILTON
Northern Michigan University, USA

Luis Alberto Urrea was born in 1955 in Tijuana to a Mexican father and an American mother, a reality that he says has shaped his identity and his writing. As a young boy he moved with his parents to San Diego where he spent his childhood with frequent trips back across the border to visit family. As he recounts in *By the Lake of the Sleeping Children: The Secret Life of the Mexican Border* (1996), "[m]y father raised me to be 100 percent Mexican, often refusing to speak English to me, tirelessly patrolling the borders of my language, watching for any error in diction, inflection, grammar, or accent. And my mother raised me to be 100 percent American: she never spoke Spanish, and she never pronounced my name correctly once in my entire life." He describes himself in that book as having "a barbed-wire fence nearly bisecting my heart" (1996, p. 4). Later, in his memoir *Nobody's Son: Notes from an American Life* (1998), he mentions how a reporter misquoted the earlier passage, changing it to: "If you were to cut Urrea's heart open, you would find a border patrol truck idling between his ribs" (1998, p. 12). This bifurcated identity, rooted in the fraught history and contested present of the US–Mexico border, informs much of Urrea's prolific writing career, both fiction and nonfiction. However, Urrea's written archive is less focused on the wounds and divisions the border represents than on what he asserts it reveals about the deep truth of our time: "we miss each other" (Tippett 2018).

Notable for his versatility as a writer, Urrea has published nonfiction, poetry, novels, essays, and short stories. Among his many awards and honors, Urrea won an American Book Award for his memoir *Nobody's Son*, his poetry was included in the 1996 edition of *Best American Poetry*, and his short story "Amapola" won an Edgar Award for mystery writing. *The Devil's Highway: A True Story* (2004) won the 2004 Lannan Literary Award and was a finalist for the Pulitzer Prize. His novel *Into the Beautiful North* (2009) was selected by the National Endowment for the Arts for their Big Read series, and *The House of the Broken Angels* (2018), in addition to being on the Best Books of the Year lists for many organizations and publications, was a National Book Critics Circle Award finalist. In 2000, Urrea was voted into the Latino Literature Hall of Fame.

Urrea asserts, "As a writer, I am drawn to the liminal space – the human borders which divide us all. Yes, I am most attracted to a literature of witness . . . It is my form of prayer, it is my form of praise, it is my form of battle" (Goodman 2018). This emphasis on the literature of witness infuses Urrea's fiction and nonfiction, creating a larger body of work in which the imagined and the lived are closely intertwined; the harsh realities that are laid bare in his nonfiction are further explored and exposed in his novels and short stories.

In two of his nonfiction texts, *Across the Wire: Life and Hard Times on the Mexican Border* (1993) and *By the Lake of the Sleeping Children*, Urrea writes about the experiences of working with missionaries in one of Tijuana's municipal garbage dumps. He details the despair that haunts these spaces, zeroing in on the physical, mental, and emotional impact of desperate poverty. He describes in straightforward detail "lice, scabies, tapeworm, pinworm, ringworm, fleas, crab lice . . . diphtheria, meningitis, typhoid, polio, *turista* (diarrhea), tuberculosis, hepatitis, VD, impetigo, measles, chronic hernia, malaria, whooping cough . . . madness and 'demon possession'" that marked the lives of the people he worked with (1993, p. 10).

In *By the Lake of the Sleeping Children*, Urrea tells a story that is particularly illustrative of his work as a witness. He writes that on a particular day he sat by the missionary van in the Tijuana dump, writing in his journal. A man working in the trash notices him and asks what he's writing about. "This," Urrea replies. The man is initially perplexed and continues to question Urrea. Finally he understands: "You're writing about me." The man wants to know if people will read what is written. Urrea cautiously answers in the affirmative, worried that the man is angry or offended. But the man nods and says, "Good! You write it down. Write it all down. Because I live in the garbage, and I'll die in the garbage, and I'll be buried in the garbage. And nobody will ever know that I lived. So tell them about me. Tell them I was here" (1996, p. 22). Urrea's version of the literature of witness fulfills this man's desire to be seen and heard. He provides readers with characters and settings that are fully embodied. Whether drawn from life or created in fiction, the people in his texts have life beyond the story; one can imagine them stepping from the page into another adventure that we are not privy to witness.

One of Urrea's great gifts as an author is the palpable compassion with which he tells stories. As he chronicles the maggots in the head wounds of an inhabitant of Tijuana's dump or the emptying bowels of men dying in the desert in *The Devil's Highway*, his spare and unwavering descriptions are deeply compassionate. He imbues all of his characters with dignity, including the most down-trodden. Even his descriptions of truly malevolent figures contain within them explanations about how economic, structural, cultural, and religious realities can come together to nurture evil. What becomes abundantly clear through all of Urrea's work is a world in which the material and the affective are deeply intertwined; readers are drawn into relationships with the characters and events depicted because they are so fully material, so fully fleshed.

Nobody's Son is the final installment of a three-part series that includes *Across the Wire* and *By the Lake of the Sleeping Children*. While the first two of those texts are primarily outward facing, telling the stories of the people he met in the *colonias* (colonies/neighborhoods) and *dompes* (garbage dumps) of Tijuana, *Nobody's Son* is crafted as a more personal memoir. In this text, Urrea tells his own story and the stories of his parents, standing witness for their triumphs and tragedies and compassionately examining the sometimes severe damage they do to themselves, each other, and to Urrea. The memoir opens with his mother waking an adult Urrea and his wife at 7:30 a.m. by declaring, "I'm so sick of your God-damned Mexican bullshit!" (1998, p. 5). Urrea does not indicate if any particular event or circumstance prompted this attack, rather he frames it as a not-so-surprising outgrowth of her anti-Mexican prejudice. Yet his portrait of his mother does not end with her racism. Urrea explores the story of his mother's youth as a Red Cross volunteer in World War II. The horror and violence she saw haunted her for the rest of her life. She tells Urrea, "I saw 10,000 die" (p. 26). Urrea remembers that "[l]ike many soldiers, she kept a clutch of atrocity pictures. She didn't know what to do with them. She couldn't bear to throw them away. That would be like killing those innocent people again. But she couldn't bear to look at them either" (p. 25). Urrea's act of honest witness reveals that his mother's racism exists alongside her own complex history of witness. Her experiences, both those she shares and those she keeps in the shadows, have shaped her identity.

Urrea produces a similarly candid and yet compassionate portrait of his father, a man he describes as "my hero and my greatest source of terror" (1998, p. 33). A volatile and sometimes cruel man, Urrea's father's "memories were full of ghosts, natural catastrophes, demons, miracle, weird sex, weirder pranks, floods, appalling deaths, flying saucers, Indian spirits, and tall tales" (p. 31). A prodigious storyteller, there was still something he held back, a mysterious and terrible experience that Urrea only glimpsed in rumors of lost love, death, murder, and betrayal. The specters of his father's unspoken experiences created "a nightmare of silence" (p. 58).

Urrea's own act of witnessing attempts to make sense of the silence, to use language to imagine those things his parents lived through and cannot speak. Yet it would be a mistake to believe that Urrea mitigates or excuses his parents' faults by presenting them as complex figures. Rather he illustrates how multiple realities can coexist at the same time. He can hold compassion and love toward his parents while also recognizing their errors. "[S]ometimes you can't escape from home," he writes, "no matter how far you go" (1998, p. 157).

Urrea's layered storytelling continues in one of his most celebrated books, *The Devil's Highway*, which chronicles the journey of a group of twenty-six Mexican men who crossed the US–Mexico border into the Arizona Sonoran Desert in 2001. Fourteen of those men never walked out of that desert. Urrea's depiction of their experience draws from border lore, medical discourse, border patrol procedures, Indigenous and colonial histories, religious iconography, personal interviews, newspaper articles, and more. It tells a story that is both uncompromisingly honest and deeply empathetic. One particularly impactful passage details the final minutes of several of the men who died from dehydration and exposure. Urrea shares the words of José Bautista, one of the survivors: "When we got sick . . . there was no shade. So I crawled up to hide in the rocks. One of the boys went crazy and started jumping up and down. He started screaming, 'Mama! Mama! I don't want to die!' He ran up to a big cactus and started smashing his face against it. I don't know what his name was." Urrea writes, "A voice carried on the still air, crying, 'Mother, save me!'" (2004, p. 166). Urrea presents the physical and mental deterioration of the walkers in a way that highlights the relatability of their suffering and fear. In their moments of distress and terror the men call out for their mothers, a primal call that speaks to the earliest need for safety and comfort.

As I have written about elsewhere, Urrea roots the narrative of the men's walk in the complex stories of the border; however, the material experience of the crossing continually intrudes. The agential power of the desert writes the experiences of the men rather than their experiences defining the land. Urrea draws attention to the physical reality of bodies and desert spaces, creating a deeply layered narrative and embedding readers in the narrative. Urrea reinforces this connection by sliding from third person to second person in his descriptions of the physical experience of heat stroke: "They choke to death, their throats filled with rocks and dirt . . . [Their] muscles, lacking water, feed on themselves. They break down and start to rot . . . The system closes down in a series. Your kidneys, your bladder, your heart. They jam shut. Stop. Your brain sparks. Out. You're gone" (2004, pp. 128–129). Urrea starkly illustrates the merciless way the desert acts upon the walkers' bodies, and in so doing encourages readers to imagine that physical experience themselves. The entanglement of readers' bodies and walkers' bodies centers materiality and creates a multilayered experience of witness.

The work of witness does not stop with Urrea's nonfiction work; rather, it flows through his fiction as well, which to date includes two collections of short stories (*Six Kinds of Sky* [2002] and *The Water Museum* [2015]), five novels (*In Search of Snow* [1994], *The Hummingbird's Daughter* [2005], *Into the Beautiful North, Queen of America* [2011], and *The House of Broken Angels* [2018]), and a graphic novel (*Mr. Mendoza's Paintbrush* [2010]). In these texts, Urrea braids together a clear-eyed look at historical and present realities of the US–Mexico border and the lives of Chicanx peoples rooted in family histories and the stories and experiences he gathered living and working on both sides of the US–Mexico border. For example, *Into the Beautiful North* draws characters and places from Urrea's volunteer work recorded in his earlier nonfiction. Urrea writes in the acknowledgments of the novel: "Although everyone in this novel is fictional, anyone with roots in or near Rosario, Sinaloa, will recognize names, personalities, locations, and addresses" (Urrea 2009). In addition, one of his most beautiful novels, *The Hummingbird's Daughter*, imagines the life of Urrea's ancestor Teresita, the Saint of Cabora. Drawing on extensive research into family stories, Mexican history, Yaqui and Mayo history and culture, and Jesuit history and customs, as well as Indigenous Mexican spiritual and healing traditions, the novel is in conversation with Urrea's nonfiction work. Urrea explains, "I hunted her story down all over the US and Mexico, and even found some interesting roots for the novel in France. I learned things in sweat lodges, in kitchens, in desert outbacks and tumbledown ranchos as much or more than I learned in libraries and museums." Yet, he continues, "[f]or all its history, I am no historian, I am a story-teller. My goal was to write a story, big and wild. Those who have a more cosmic bent can see embedded in the adventure a guidebook into the mysteries of sacredness" (Urrea 2020). In his fiction, Urrea expands the possibility of witness by putting flesh on a figure of both family and cultural lore, imagining her life and in so doing providing a more complete invocation of place, politics, and miracles.

Urrea's most recent work is *The House of Broken Angels*. Inspired by the death of his older brother, the novel chronicles two days in the life of the de La Cruz family, the funeral of the matriarch and the last birthday party of the dying elder brother. The novel is capacious with multiple characters – some sharing names – reaching across several generations, multiple decades, and two countries. Though he began the book several years ago, Urrea says that the rise in hate crimes and the normalizing of racism and sexism following the election of Donald Trump to the US presidency transformed the novel from a deeply personal story of family to "a cry against all of this ugly disrespect that tarnished not only all of us, but the memory of my own sibling, the lives of my ancestors" (Goodman 2018).

Thematically, the novel lives in the borderlands, exploring borders between countries, languages, family members, and what initially appears to be the most consequential border of all, that between life and death. Told by his doctors that he has weeks or perhaps only days of life remaining, the elder brother, Big Angel, is struggling to accept his approaching death. His birthday party is actually a "living wake," an opportunity for the family to join together a final time to reminisce, reconnect, and say goodbye. The novel begins with Big Angel wondering, "How can a man out of time repair all that was broken?" (2018, p. 3). He strives to find a way to make amends and voice those things that have festered in the background, while also keeping certain memories veiled. The memories that have created the family are "a swirl. [Little Angel, Big Angel's half-brother] caught small flashes of family history like shreds of colored paper spinning in the wind. Until massive assaults of revelations and confessions came out of nowhere and destroyed whatever drinking party they threw" (p. 116). Readers are caught in a similar swirl of stories as the characters examine some memories very carefully, others partially, and still others not at all. Later in the novel, Urrea tries another metaphor for capturing the fragmentary memories that construct any family: "So many imperfect scenes. It felt as though they had opened a box of photographs, each of the pictures torn and tattered" (p. 277). In the novel the act of bearing witness is frustratingly and beautifully fractured.

In his memoir *Wandering Time* (1999), Urrea recalls his decision to devote himself to writing:

> This is the real world, you see. This. This here. These words. These feelings. This magic. This love which I cannot contain. Yes, these troubles. But this glory, this hope. This work, these days, these hikes, this desire, these smoky erotic nights, this expectation, this literature, this landscape, these publications, these friends, this blaring music, these movies, this house. This journal. This small, yet growing, feeling of hope.
>
> (1999, p. 39)

Urrea's literature of witness is clear-eyed and honest. Urrea holds himself and his readers still, shows us what we need to see, even if we don't want to see it. But there is also a deep sense of care and empathy in the way Urrea lays bare hard truths – care and empathy that extend to all involved. In *The House of Broken Angels* that empathy is for an extended family that has failed one another time and again and yet still is held together by love and memory. In *The Devil's Highway* that empathy is directed toward the border walkers, the border patrol, and even the coyotes who lead the walkers across the border for monetary profit. In *Nobody's Son* that empathy is for his family, himself, and for all of us.

As a still-growing body of work, Luis Alberto Urrea's writing presents readers with a complex picture of historical, national, and personal relationships. Working within and between fiction and nonfiction, he complicates narratives about the US–Mexico border and Chicanx families in part by exploring how memory functions as an imperfect witness to personal and national histories. Urrea ends Part One of *Nobody's Son* with the contention that it is through language and story that we can find connection. "Words are the only bread we can really share," he writes.

> When I say "we," I mean every one of us, everybody, all of you reading this. Each border patrol agent and every trembling Mexican peering through a fence. Every Klansman and each NAACP office worker. Each confused mother and every disappointed dad.
>
> For I am nobody's son.
> But I am everyone's brother.
> Some come here to me.
> Walk me home.
>
> (1998, p. 59)

SEE ALSO: Border Fictions; Contemporary Regionalisms; Globalization; Literature of the Americas; Mixed-Genre Fiction; Multiculturalism; Trauma and Fiction

REFERENCES

Goodman, Brianna. (2018). The PEN Ten with Luis Alberto Urrea. *PEN American: The Freedom to Write* (March 8, 2018). https://pen.org/pen-ten-luis-alberto-urrea/ (accessed 16 July 2021).

Tippett, Krista. (2018). Luis Alberto Urrea: what borders are really about and what we do with them. *On Being* (July 12, 2018). https://onbeing.org/programs/luis-alberto-urrea-what-borders-are-really-about-and-what-we-do-with-them-jul2018/ (accessed 16 July 2021).

Urrea, Luis Alberto. (1993). *Across the Wire: Life and Hard Times on the Mexican Border*. New York: Anchor Books.

Urrea, Luis Alberto. (1996). *By the Lake of the Sleeping Children: The Secret Life of the Mexican Border*. New York: Anchor Books.

Urrea, Luis Alberto. (1998). *Nobody's Son: Notes from an American Life*. Tucson: University of Arizona Press.

Urrea, Luis Alberto. (1999). *Wandering Time: Western Notebooks*. Tucson: University of Arizona Press.

Urrea, Luis Alberto. (2004). *The Devil's Highway: A True Story*. New York: Back Bay Books.

Urrea, Luis Alberto. (2009). *Into the Beautiful North*. New York: Back Bay Books.

Urrea, Luis Alberto. (2018). *The House of Broken Angels*. New York: Back Bay Books.

Urrea, Luis Alberto. (2020). *Luis Alberto Urrea: The Hummingbird's Daughter*. http://luisurrea.com/books/the-hummingbirds-daughter/ (accessed 16 July 2021).

FURTHER READING

Hamilton, Amy T. (2018). *Peregrinations: Walking in American Literature*. Reno: University of Nevada Press.

Vidal, Gore

HEATHER NEILSON

UNSW, Canberra, Australia

After the death of Gore Vidal had been reported, the marquee lights of theaters on Broadway were dimmed in respectful acknowledgment of the event. At that time, the latest revival of his play about a presidential election, *The Best Man* (1960), was underway, having been nominated for two Tony Awards earlier in the year. A memorial service subsequently took place at the Gerald Schoenfeld Theater, where *The Best Man* was running. Given that the connection between politics and performance was one of the central themes of his oeuvre, and indeed of his life, the timing and location were apposite. Vidal was a prolific writer in several genres, but was also an actor, a politician, and a polemical critic of the United States. The fact that for over forty years he and his partner, Howard Austen, lived for part of every year in Italy was interpreted by his critics as further evidence that he did not love his country. Although always popular with readers, Vidal's work received noticeably more attention amongst scholars from the year 2005, in which he turned 80, and his "relevance" as a public intellectual continues to be recognized.

Vidal's literary career began in the 1940s, and by the end of the 1970s he was well established as a novelist, essayist, playwright, screenwriter, and often controversial media personality. However, some of his most significant work was produced in the last two decades of the twentieth century and beyond. His most ambitious historical novel, *Creation*, was first published in 1981 and the revised version in 2002. Four volumes of the seven-part fictional chronicle of the United States – which Vidal collectively entitled *Narratives of Empire* – appeared after 1980. A volume of Vidal's collected essays, *United States: Essays 1952–1992* (1993), won the National Book Award for Nonfiction in 1993. Subsequent collections include *The Last Empire: Essays 1992–2001* (2001) and *Gore Vidal's State of the Union: Nation Essays 1958–2005* (2013). The first and most substantial of Vidal's memoirs, *Palimpsest* (1995), was published in his seventieth year. His two most notable cinematic performances also occurred in the 1990s: as Senator Brickley Paiste of Pennsylvania in Tim Robbins's *Bob Roberts* (1992); and as the villainous Director Josef in Andrew Niccol's *Gattaca* (1997).

Eugene Luther Gore Vidal was born at West Point, where his father was then a football coach and instructor. Eugene Vidal, Sr. would become a pioneer of the aviation industry, and served as Franklin Roosevelt's Director of Air Commerce from 1933 to 1937. Gore Vidal's mother, Nina, was the daughter of the first senator from the state of Oklahoma, Thomas Pryor Gore, who had been blinded as a result of two accidents in childhood. Vidal always acknowledged his grandfather as the most important influence upon his life – he assumed the first name "Gore" in adolescence. Nina's second husband was the lawyer and stockbroker Hugh D. Auchincloss. Following the end of that marriage, Auchincloss married Janet Bouvier, the mother of the future Jacqueline Kennedy Onassis. It was through his membership in Auchincloss's complexly blended family that Gore Vidal became acquainted with two figures in American political history who would become significant in his own life. John F. Kennedy was the 35th president of the United States: Aaron Burr was its third and most infamous vice president. Although Burr left no known direct descendants, Auchincloss was descended from a close relative.

After graduating from Phillips Exeter Academy in 1943, the 17-year-old Vidal enlisted in the army. His first novel, *Williwaw* (1946), drew upon his experience as first mate on a supply ship stationed in the Aleutians. His third novel, *The City and the Pillar* (1949), would make him notorious. This work (which Vidal would substantially revise in 1965) created a sensation because of its dispassionate portrayal of an ordinary American boy's homosexuality. After the publication of his eighth novel, *Messiah* (1954; revised edition, 1993), Vidal turned for financial reasons to the writing of television plays. In the late 1950s he also wrote screenplays for Metro-Goldwyn-Mayer, his best-known work from that period being his contribution to *Ben-Hur* (1959). Although he resumed the writing of novels in the 1960s, Vidal continued intermittently to write scripts for television, cinema, and stage. In 1989, *Billy the Kid*, based on his screenplay, was broadcast on the TNT cable channel. An expanded and updated version of an early play, *On the March to the Sea*, which had originated in one of his television scripts, was performed in Hartford, Connecticut and at Duke University in 2004/5.

Although thoroughly educated in literature, history, and the classics, Vidal was also a child of the movies, as he elaborated in a personal reflection entitled *Screening History* (1992). The protagonist of *Myra Breckinridge* (1968) is a post-operative transsexual woman who is obsessed with the Hollywood movies of the 1940s, and who embarks on a quest to effect population control and the subversion of traditional gender roles. This novel further entrenched Vidal's reputation as a provocateur. Although a staunch supporter of civil rights and an advocate for the decriminalization of victimless crimes, Vidal was a reluctant icon for the gay liberation movement, and always resisted attempts to label him. He insisted that the adjectives "homosexual" and "heterosexual" were applicable to sexual acts but not to people.

In public Vidal was dismissive of the concept of love. However, he maintained an incongruously nostalgic affection for a classmate who had been killed at the age of 19 on Iwo Jima. There had been intimations of Jimmie Trimble in Vidal's oeuvre from the start of his career, but it was in *Palimpsest* that Trimble was first openly discussed. In the novel *The Smithsonian Institution* (1998), an adolescent mathematical genius, known only as "T" (who embodies both Trimble and Time itself), invents a form of time travel which should enable him to preempt the outbreak of World War II. However, the plan does not succeed – T still dies at dawn on Iwo Jima in 1945. *The Smithsonian Institution* can thus be read as a companion piece to *Palimpsest*, but also to *The Golden Age* (2000), the last of the *Narratives of Empire*. Both novels commence in 1939 and manifest the author's enduring wish that history could be rewritten, and war thus avoided.

Vidal regarded himself as the political heir of his grandfather, who had cherished an unfulfilled ambition to become president of the United States. Senator Gore was an isolationist when such a position was unpopular, and his grandson would largely maintain that stance. Although Vidal averred that there was no real difference between the two major political parties in the United States, he sought political office twice as a Democrat. In 1960, he was a candidate for the 29th Congressional district in New York and campaigned with John F. Kennedy. Although defeated in that election, Vidal significantly reduced the majority of the Republican incumbent. After Kennedy's assassination, Vidal would critique the Kennedy family's dynastic ambitions in the novel *Washington, D.C.* (1967) and in an essay, "The Holy Family," first published in *Esquire* in the same year. Nonetheless, he maintained affection for Kennedy himself, recalling him in some detail in *Palimpsest*. In 1982, Vidal campaigned for nomination as the Democratic candidate for senator from California. Despite attaining a respectable vote, he lost to Jerry Brown, then Governor of California. The last six months of Vidal's campaign are encapsulated in Gary Conklin's documentary, *Gore Vidal: The Man Who Said No* (1983).

After this second blow to his political aspirations, Vidal retreated to Italy to work on *Lincoln* (1984), the fourth in his series of novels on American history. Throughout these *Narratives of Empire*, significant figures from history interact with the invented Sanford dynasty, descended from a fictional illegitimate son of Aaron Burr. The iconoclastic novel *Burr* was published in 1973 and was a finalist for the National Book Award the following year. The sequel to *Burr*, *1876* (1976), depicts the ignominious end of the administration of Ulysses S. Grant and the controversial election of the Republican Rutherford B. Hayes over the Democrat Samuel Tilden. *Lincoln* (1984) offers a generally respectful and sympathetic portrait of its eponymous protagonist. Nonetheless, as a self-declared Southern writer, Vidal emphasizes that Abraham Lincoln's foremost concern in the conduct of the Civil War was not the abolition of slavery but rather the metaphysical concept of the Union itself. *Empire* (1987) begins in the aftermath of the Spanish–American War of 1898. The novel continues Vidal's exploration of the expanding power of the media within American politics, exemplified by the rise of William Randolph Hearst. Of the historical politicians who populate the text, the central character is John Hay, who had been one of Lincoln's secretaries and later the American ambassador to Great Britain. He served as Secretary of State in the administrations of William McKinley and Theodore Roosevelt, in which role he would exert enduring influence upon American foreign policy. Although Hay was an enthusiastic proponent of American expansionism, the affinity which Vidal clearly felt with this dedicated public servant is evident in the novel.

Hollywood (1989) moves the *Narratives of Empire* into the administrations of Woodrow Wilson and Warren G. Harding, and explores the interrelationship between the burgeoning cinema industry and American political culture. Despite Vidal's personal disdain for Wilson as a president who led his country into war, the characterization of Wilson in *Hollywood* is predominantly benevolent. So, too, is the portrait of Harding, whose term in office was abruptly curtailed by his sudden death. After the posthumous revelation of the extensive corruption of several of his appointees, Harding's reputation sharply declined, although the novel intimates that his only major flaw was the naivete with which he trusted his friends. *The Golden Age* concludes the series, Vidal reworking material from *Washington, D.C.* but also extending the saga to bring together his principal fictional cast with their historical counterparts at the start of the new millennium. Underscoring his centrality in Vidal's imagination, Aaron Burr himself is reincarnated at the end of the twentieth century, still pursuing power in the form of an invented descendant, the enigmatic "A.B."

The most provocative aspect of *The Golden Age* was arguably Vidal's allegation that Franklin Roosevelt had had prior information that the Japanese were preparing an assault on Pearl Harbor. In Vidal's view, Roosevelt was complicit in the attack, wanting a rationale for the United States to become involved in the war. (Vidal elaborated on the assertion in an essay entitled "Japanese Intentions in the Second World War" in *The Times Literary Supplement* [2000]). His main source appears to have been a Gore relative, Admiral James O. Richardson, who had been appointed Commander-in-Chief of the Pacific Fleet early in 1940. Although Roosevelt had regarded himself as the heir of Woodrow Wilson, and had also led the United States into war, Vidal wrote far more critically about Harry Truman, whom he held responsible for transforming the American republic into a "National Security State."

A considerable proportion of Vidal's writing in all genres was devoted to American presidents. The slim volume entitled *The American Presidency* (2002) was based on a British television miniseries narrated by Vidal, which was broadcast in 1996. That booklet concluded with William Jefferson Clinton. Vidal's most bitter invective was reserved for Clinton's successor, as exemplified in what he referred to as "pamphlets" (actually collections of essays, some previously published). The titles are self-explanatory: *Perpetual War for Perpetual Peace: How We Got To Be So Hated* and *Dreaming War: Blood For Oil and the Bush-Cheney Junta* (both 2002). Thomas Pryor Gore had been born during the period of post-Civil War Reconstruction: his grandson spent his last years railing against the Iraq War. One of Vidal's favorite invented characters, Senator James Burden Day, begins in the *Narratives of Empire* as a representation of Senator Gore but would evolve into Vidal's mouthpiece. At one point in *Hollywood*, listening to President Harding's emotive rhetoric following the conclusion of World War I, Senator Day reflects: "But all it took was a generation to forget war's horrors in order to hunger, yet again, for war's thrills and profits. How stupid the human race was. . ." (1989, p. 453).

Although he openly craved political influence, Vidal was apparently immune to the lure of religious belief. The essay entitled "Monotheism and Its Discontents" concisely summarizes his objections to religions premised on belief in a "sky-god" (1992, reprinted in Vidal 1993). Five of his novels predominantly focus on the human impulse to create deities, but also on the inevitable distortions of an original, benign message by a prophet's successive followers. *Messiah* satirized the establishment of Christianity in the fourth century CE by depicting the rapid rise of a global death-cult in the twentieth century. *Julian* (1964), a fictional biography of the last pagan Roman emperor, is a noticeably more mature and accomplished work. In *Kalki* (1978), an American veteran of the Vietnam War, who believes himself to be the tenth avatar of the god Vishnu, manages to effect the annihilation of the entire human race. *Creation* (1981), set in the fifth century BCE, is narrated retrospectively by the fictional Cyrus Spitama, who had represented first Darius the Great and then his son Xerxes on trading missions in India and Cathay. A grandson of Zoroaster, Cyrus is perplexed by the various belief systems which he encounters in other lands. Of all those he meets during his travels, Confucius has the most lasting and illuminating impact. *Creation* thus indirectly continues the demystification of Christianity which was central to both *Messiah* and *Julian*. Vidal's most overtly inflammatory challenge to Christianity is represented in *Live From Golgotha* (1992). NBC in the late twentieth century has acquired the technology to transport a camera crew back in time, so that the crucifixion of Jesus can be broadcast live on television. The novel concludes with the acquisition of Christianity – the corporation – by Japanese investors based in Hollywood.

In the essay "Armageddon?" (1987, reprinted in Vidal 1993), Gore Vidal rejected the concept of life after death. Presciently concerned about the environment, he declared that "because there is no cosmic point to the life that each of us perceives on this distant bit of dust at galaxy's edge, all the more reason for us to maintain in proper balance what we have here. Because there is nothing else" (1993, p. 1006). Since his death, however, he has entered the version of an afterlife that is reserved for a particular echelon of celebrity. Whereas Vidal's work has continued to be the subject of academic scholarship, he himself has been dissected in memoirs and reanimated as a character in works of fiction and film. Nicholas Wrathall's engaging documentary, *Gore Vidal: The United States of Amnesia*, was released in 2013. The notorious television debates of 1968 between Vidal and William F. Buckley, in which Buckley impetuously exposed Vidal as a "queer," have been analyzed in another documentary, *Best of Enemies*, released in 2015 (Gordon and Neville 2015). When Fred Kaplan's substantial biography of Vidal appeared in 1999, it was repudiated by its subject. Vidal's friend and protégé, Jay Parini, prudently waited until after Vidal's death to bring out his own biography (2015). Although depicting Vidal with sympathy and gratitude, Parini represented his late mentor as a complex man, capable of both extraordinary generosity and destructive paranoia, in denial about his sexuality and finally the victim of his own alcoholism. This portrait largely accords with those in other memoirs published since Vidal's death, such as Michael Mewshaw's *Sympathy for the Devil: Four Decades of Friendship with Gore Vidal* (2015), Fabian Bouthillette's *Gore Vidal's Last Stand: Part One* (2014), and Tim Teeman's "tell-all" biography, *In Bed With Gore Vidal* (2013).

Parini had previously portrayed Vidal in cameo in *The Apprentice Lover* (2002). A few years later, Edmund White aroused Vidal's ire by portraying in his play *Terre Haute* (2007) a celebrated writer, obviously modeled on Vidal, who falls in love with a convicted killer, clearly based on the Oklahoma bomber, Timothy McVeigh. After Vidal's death, Parini returned to the theme of ambivalent relationships between renowned writers and their ephebes in a screenplay co-written with Michael Hoffman. The resulting film, featuring Kevin Spacey as Vidal and Michael Stuhlbarg as Howard Austen, was in postproduction in 2017 when allegations against Spacey, of historical sexual harassment, became public knowledge. Netflix, which had produced the film, cancelled its release. At the time of this writing, therefore, it is doubtful whether the film will ever be screened. John Boyne's novel *A Ladder to the Sky* (2018) also addresses the theme of predatory writerly relationships, portraying a ruthlessly ambitious and charismatic young writer who serially steals the work of more talented writers. The only uninvented characters in the novel are Gore Vidal and Howard Austen, who appear in one brief section. The portrait of Vidal is unexpectedly flattering – he is the only character who can discern the malevolent young man's true nature.

The real Gore Vidal's life and work defied categorizing in conventional terms. Although born into privilege, he consistently argued for a more equitable taxation system and increased funding for education. While he would remain vehemently opposed to American intervention in conflicts between other nations, and the American defense budget, Vidal respected servicemen and took pride in the fact of his own military service. A proponent of civil rights, he nevertheless supported greater restrictions on both gun ownership and population growth. Scholars have variously predicted that he will be best remembered either for the incisive wit of his essays or for the historical novels. Perhaps his greatest bequest is what he offered his nation as its self-appointed educator, who persistently warned his compatriots against confusing myths with truths.

SEE ALSO: Contemporary Fictions of War; Doctorow, E.L.; Mailer, Norman; Queer and LGBT Fiction; White, Edmund

REFERENCES

Bouthillette, Fabian. (2014). *Gore Vidal's Last Stand: Part One: My American Initiation*. Self-published.
Boyne, John. (2018). *A Ladder to the Sky*. London: Doubleday.
Conklin, Gary. (dir.) (1983). *Gore Vidal: The Man Who Said No*. Mystic Fire Video.
Gordon, Robert and Neville, Morgan. (dirs.) (2015). *Best of Enemies*. Magnolia Pictures.
Kaplan, Fred. (1999). *Gore Vidal: A Biography*. New York: Doubleday.
Mewshaw, Michael. (2015). *Sympathy for the Devil: Four Decades of Friendship with Gore Vidal*. New York: Farrar, Straus and Giroux.
Niccol, Andrew. (dir.) (1997). *Gattaca*. Columbia Pictures.
Parini, Jay. (2002). *The Apprentice Lover*. New York: Harper Perennial.
Parini, Jay. (2015a). *Empire of Self: A Life of Gore Vidal*. New York: Random House.
Parini, Jay. (2015b). *Every Time a Friend Succeeds Something Inside Me Dies: The Life of Gore Vidal*. London: Little, Brown.
Robbins, Tim. (writer and dir.) (1992). *Bob Roberts*. Twentieth Century-Fox.
Vidal, Gore. (1989). *Hollywood*. New York: Random House.
Vidal, Gore. (1993). *United States: Essays 1952–1992*. London: André Deutsch.

White, Edmund. (2007). *Terre Haute*. London: Methuen.
Wrathall, Nicholas. (dir.) (2013). *Gore Vidal: The United States of Amnesia*. IFC Films.

FURTHER READING

Altman, Dennis. (2005). *Gore Vidal's America*. Cambridge: Polity Press.
Baker, Susan and Gibson, Curtis S. (1997). *Gore Vidal: A Critical Companion*. Westwood, CT and London: Greenwood.
Bram, Christopher. (2012). *Eminent Outlaws: Gay Writers Who Changed America*. New York: Twelve.
Frank, Marcie. (2005). *How to be an Intellectual in the Age of TV: The Lessons of Gore Vidal*. Durham, NC: Duke University Press.
Kaplan, Fred. (ed.) (1999). *The Essential Gore Vidal*. London: Little, Brown.
Raw, Laurence. (ed.) (2012). Remembering Gore Vidal. *Journal of American Studies of Turkey* 35–36.
Wiener, Jon. (2012). *I Told You So: Gore Vidal Talks Politics. Interviews with Jon Wiener*. Berkeley: Counterpoint.

Viramontes, Helena María

PAULA M.L. MOYA
Stanford University, USA

Helena María Viramontes is the author of several richly metaphorical fictional narratives about Mexican Americans in mid-to-late twentieth century Los Angeles and in the fields of California. Her work has proved enormously generative for Chicanx/Latinx readers, as well as for scholars working in Chicanx/Latinx, Gender, Narratological, Environmental, Disability, Religious, Urban, and Food Studies. The author of a short-story collection, *The Moths and Other Stories* (1985), and two acclaimed novels, *Under the Feet of Jesus* (1995) and *Their Dogs Came with Them* (2007), Viramontes is also the co-editor of two collections containing cultural production and scholarship: *Chicana Creativity and Criticism – Charting New Frontiers in American Literature* (1987) and *Chicana (W)rites: On Word and Film* (1996). Acclaimed as much for her densely lyrical language as for her facility in representing an impressively wide range of characters, Viramontes exhibits a deft touch when it comes to incorporating into her fiction critiques of Catholicism, Aztec symbolism, patriarchy, capitalism, and structural racism. Throughout her work, these writerly and critical skills are put to use in order to imagine alternative and more just ways of being in the world. An activist, teacher, and valued mentor to younger writers, Viramontes's literary output and mentorship together have established her as one of the most influential Latina writers working today. She is the recipient of a USA Ford Fellowship in Literature, the John Dos Passos Prize for Literature, a Sundance Institute Fellowship, a National Endowment for the Arts Fellowship, and the Luis Leal Award for Distinction in Chicana/Latino Literature awarded by the University of California, Santa Barbara.

Viramontes's strong Chicana feminist outlook was shaped by the economic duress, racial subordination, and patriarchal character of her childhood family life, and by the circumstance of growing into womanhood during a time and place of intense political activism. She was born fifth to the youngest of a sprawling Mexican American family of nine children in East Los Angeles, California on February 26, 1954. Viramontes's father supported his growing family by working in construction as a hod carrier and by occasionally enlisting his children in seasonal agricultural work picking grapes (Viramontes 2010). Facing systemic racism and stressed with the responsibility of supporting a growing family, he "drank and was mean." Because he was "impatient, screaming a lot of the time," Viramontes and her siblings often found themselves "trembling in his presence" (Viramontes 1990, p. 292). Viramontes's mother, by contrast, was a homemaker and a woman of "total kindness" and "relentless energy" whose care and domestic inventiveness made her "the fiber that held [the] family together" (p. 291). Viramontes herself was an "invisible" middle child, an unremarked witness to the chaotic goings-on of her vibrant, busy, crowded, and ultimately loving and stable childhood home (Viramontes 2008). Listening in from the other side of the door to "late night kitchen meetings where everyone talked and laughed in low voices, played cards, talked of loneliness, plans for the futures, [and] of loves lost or won," Viramontes was privy to the dreams, fears, and joys of those around her. It is perhaps this exposure that has allowed her to represent an impressively wide range of characters, from the deeply depressed 50s-something housewife in "Snapshots," to the troubled transgender character of Turtle in *Their Dogs Came with Them*, to the profoundly responsible elderly Perfecto Flores in *Under the Feet of Jesus*, to the romantically yearning but tough young women (Estrella and Ermila) in each of her novels. Thus, it was as a child that Viramontes began her "apprenticeship" as a writer "without even knowing it" (1990, p. 291).

A product of the East LA public schools, Viramontes was a student at James A. Garfield High School during the infamous 1968 "Chicano Blowouts" in which primarily Chicano students staged a series of planned walk outs to protest unequal funding and racial discrimination in the Los Angeles School District. Her proximity to the walk outs and the marches sponsored by the National Chicano Moratorium Committee Against the Vietnam War (NCMC) – especially the August 29, 1970 antiwar march involving approximately 30,000 people in East LA that ended with police violence and the death of the award-winning Chicano journalist Rubén Salazar – greatly impacted her orientation toward social justice (Chávez 2002, pp. 61–79; Oropeza 2005, pp. 145–160). After graduating from high school in 1971, Viramontes matriculated at Immaculate Heart College, a private nonprofit liberal arts college located in the hills of Los Angeles. Two years before she arrived, 90% of the nuns had renounced their vows to Rome in accordance with a spiritual renewal and curricular reorganization that had been encouraged by the reforms of Vatican II but condemned by Los Angeles Archbishop Cardinal James McIntyre. The result was a feminist-inspired social justice curriculum that featured readings by Latin American liberation theologians and a focus on combating structural oppression (Viramontes 2020, pp. 24–25). One of her fellow students at the college was the Chicana poet, playwright, and essayist Cherríe Moraga. After graduating from college in 1975 with a BA in English, Viramontes began working as co-coordinator of the Los Angeles Latino Writers Association and as the literary editor of an avant-garde magazine *XhismeArte*. In 1979, she entered the MFA program in Creative Writing at the University of California, Irvine, but left shortly after a negative interaction with a faculty mentor, who complained about her propensity to write about "Chicanos" instead of "people" (Viramontes 2007, pp. 9–10). Years later, after she published her first short-story collection and was invited by Gabriel García Márquez to participate in his 1989 Sundance Institute Storytelling Workshop, Viramontes returned to UC-Irvine to complete her MFA, which she received in 1994.

After graduating from college and while working in Chicanx literary circles, Viramontes started a family with Eloy Rodriguez, a biochemist, with whom she has two children, Pilar and Eloy Francisco. She also engaged in a productive collaboration with scholar María Herrera-Sobek to coordinate three major conferences at UC-Irvine, resulting in the publication of the two aforementioned volumes, *Chicana Creativity and Criticism* and *Chicana (W)rites on Word and Film* (Viramontes 2020, p. 27). In 1994, Viramontes and her family left for Ithaca, NY where she and her husband were hired as faculty members at Cornell University – she in Creative Writing and he in Plant Biology. Viramontes spent one year as a visiting professor at the University of Miami and a semester as the Visiting Mary Routt Chair of Creative Writing at Scripps College. She was promoted to full professor at Cornell in 2007 and named the Distinguished Professor of Arts and Sciences in English in 2018. From 2015–2020 she directed Cornell's Program in Creative Writing.

Viramontes's first book, a short-story collection entitled *The Moths and Other Stories*, was published in 1985 by Arte Público Press. A small press founded in 1979 by Nicolás Kanellos for the explicit purpose of bringing Hispanic-authored books to the market, Arte Público was responsible for launching the careers of writers such as Denise Chávez, Sandra Cisneros, Rolando Hinojosa, and Tomás Rivera. Viramontes's collection quickly emerged as one of the most significant and challenging works by a Chicana writer published to that point. It contains stories told from the perspectives of girls and women, all of whom wrestle with gender-based restrictions and lives of unfulfilled potential. Naomi in "Growing," for example, is on the cusp of womanhood and resentful of her father's suspicion, even as she confronts her sexual desires and struggles against the unwanted attention her body elicits from men. Finding momentary relief in a game of stickball – thus returning briefly to a place of relative gender-freedom – Naomi ends the story by reflecting on the unfair obligations she faces as a result of her impending womanhood. "Snapshots," by contrast, treats a woman at the other end of her reproductive life. When the story opens, Marge's daughter has grown up and her husband has abandoned her for another woman. Having been taught that sex is for reproduction and passion should be bounded, Marge is left alone – postmenopausal – to confront the lie that "good women" will always be rewarded for their goodness. Having been deprived for years of her bodily desires, Marge has lost touch with the sensual, emotional, and feeling part of herself. Experiencing a crisis of meaning and suffering from depression, she becomes indulgent and nostalgic, refusing to do what others expect of her – eat dinner, clean the house, "do something" productive. A beautifully written story, "Snapshots" stands as a stark warning to women who devote themselves to others at the expense of developing their sexual and intellectual selves. The title story, "The Moths," is a widely anthologized mother-daughter story that also features a protagonist whose impending womanhood brings gendered obligations and a father's distrust. An important element of this exquisitely written short story is how Viramontes's symbolism involving the sun and the moon at the story's climax evokes the Aztec legend of Coyolxauhqui. The story re-members (both in the sense of bringing to mind, and also of putting back together) the moon goddess/ sister/daughter, whose physical dismemberment by her brother/sun god Huitzilopochtli inaugurated Aztec warrior society and affirmed an ideology of male dominance. Its plot narrates a reconciliation between mother and daughter, even as its symbolism enacts that same operation (Moya 2016, pp. 79–107). The story in the collection that Viramontes considers to be her "most personal" is "The Cariboo Café" (Viramontes 2020, p. 23). In it she tests out a narrative technique that is perfected in her first novel. Seeking to bring attention to the human toll exacted by US covert military intervention into Central America during the Reagan years, Viramontes writes about a poor washerwoman in an unnamed Central American country whose son is kidnapped and killed by the Contras. Driven mad by grief, poverty, and desperation, the woman migrates to the United States where she takes custody of a young boy she mistakes for her son. Wanting to move her readers away from a voyeuristic viewing of the woman's suffering and to implicate them in the death-dealing international policies enabled by their tax dollars, Viramontes experiments with narrative perspective. Switching narrative and focalizing perspectives among three different characters, all of whom are involved in the death of the washerwoman, Viramontes makes an abrupt shift in narration at the end of the story from third person to first person as the woman defends herself, and the boy she imagines is her son, from what she believes is certain destruction. In effect, Viramontes positions her reader within the woman's emotional and physical reality as the woman is shot point-blank in the forehead. Difficult for a first-time reader, this powerful story is best read, re-read, unpacked, and subjected to historical and cultural contextualization to be fully appreciated. Still in print after thirty-five years, stories from the collection have been translated into Hindi, German, Japanese, and Czech.

Viramontes's first novel, *Under the Feet of Jesus*, is an exquisitely written and moving account of the lives and struggles of a California-based migrant farmworker family and their interaction with a young man who, after being poisoned by pesticides, is left in their care. The novel's focus is on the daughter, Estrella, who is on the brink of both womanhood and a consciousness of herself and her family as exploited workers. Narrated entirely in the third person, the novel has a distinctive narrative structure in which the focalization shifts among the four major characters (13-year old Estrella, Estrella's mother Petra, her stepfather Perfecto, and the young man Alejo), often from one paragraph to the next. Although they all occupy the same physical world, each character experiences and perceives that world differently, in ways consistent with their ages, genders, and social roles. As a result, the fictional world portrayed in the novel changes according to which character is orienting the narrative, effectively emphasizing the partiality of perspective (Moya 2002, pp. 175–214). Each character thus contributes to the competing ideologies that structure the novel's sustained meditation on the nature of love, life, work, and obligation to a larger community. Viramontes's use of variable character-bound focalization in *Under the Feet of Jesus* is unusual and together with other late-twentieth century writers like Louise Erdrich and Toni Cade Bambara, prefigures a shift toward multifocality in the narrative structure of later novels by twenty-first century writers like Bernardine Evaristo, Marlon James, Tommy Orange, and Jennifer Egan.

Currently in its thirty-eighth printing, *Under the Feet of Jesus* has garnered significant attention from everyday readers, curriculum planners at both the high school and college level, and literary critics. In the fall of 2019, the Jordan Schnitzer Museum of Art at the University of Oregon launched "Resistance as Power: A Curatorial Response to *Under the Feet of Jesus*," in connection with the novel's selection as the university's "common reading" for its first-year students. The exhibit featured visual art works by artists such as Ester Hernandez, Betty LaDuke, Emanuel Martinez, and Victor Maldonado, among others. Scholars who write about the novel address a wide range of topics. It has proved compelling to critics working in Environmental Studies, Race Studies, Chicanx and Marxist Literary Studies, and has attracted attention from others working in Food Studies, Sound Studies, Immigration Law, and Bilingualism. Articles about the novel discuss its sensitive representations of the precarious lives of migrant farmworkers, who are subject, in a systemic way, to labor exploitation, food insecurity, and the risks associated with environmental degradation and pesticide poisoning. Some critical essays focus on Viramontes's craft, such as her masterful use of figural language, including metaphor, metonymy, and simile. Others explore the novel's conception of literacy (conceived of as the ability to more accurately "read" the social and material world) and its representation of the power of language to shape reality and serve as a medium of communication between people. Those who situate the novel within the larger tradition of Chicanx literary studies frequently read it alongside Tomás Rivera's novel . . . *y no se lo tragó la tierra* (1971), Cherríe Moraga's play *Heroes and Saints* (1992), and Ester Hernandez's visual images of migrant farmworkers.

Viramontes's second novel, *Their Dogs Came with Them*, is a beautiful character-study of sundry types of people living together in a complex community, and also a profound exploration of the dynamics of subordination that reveal the socioeconomic and ideological forces that keep Latinx peoples from achieving full citizenship in the United States. Set in East Los Angeles during the 1960s and 1970s, the novel portrays the contiguous, and occasionally intersecting, daily lives of a large range of characters who populate the neighborhood around the Long Beach and Pomona freeway interchange at a time of intense social, political, and geographic upheaval. The novel's opening shows how those people most adversely affected by the building of the LA freeway system first encounter the coming upheaval. It then jumps forward ten years into the future to show how the neighborhood's dismemberment has negatively impacted its residents' already limited transportation and employment options. Over the course of the novel, Viramontes concretizes in readily perceptible forms (freeways, rabid dogs, gendered dynamics, the Quarantine Authority) the environmental forces that subordinate a community. The freeways, for example, destroy homes, disappear neighbors, displace businesses, cut off important neighborhood travel routes, introduce traffic gridlock, bring pollution, and trap the neighborhood residents into an area that had been envisioned by city planners not as a place to live but rather as a space to travel through on the way to somewhere else. Taken as a whole, the novel explores what happens to the relatively powerless people who live in a community that, because of how its residents are situated within the prevailing racial and socioeconomic order, is subject to a range of externally produced and pernicious structural forces. It represents the lives of the ignored and the marginalized in a way that humanizes but does not sentimentalize them. Scholars of the novel write about Viramontes's masterful use of figural language; her critique of environmental racism; her use of religious discourse and meditations on faith; the way she connects older and newer forms of spatial control as an exploration of the legacy of colonialism; and how she plumbs the political and psychological effects of urban transformation on those whose neighborhoods are decimated by urban renewal.

Their Dogs Came with Them has also been extraordinarily generative for other artists. Virginia Grise, an award-winning writer and playwright, was commissioned by Tucson's Borderlands Theatre to adapt the novel for the stage. After workshopping and producing the adaptation in the Perryville Women's Prison in Goodyear, Arizona in February 2019, Grise produced an open-air site-specific performance at the Julian Wash Archeological Park located underneath the I-19 freeway in Tucson. A todo dar productions in Austin, Texas is publishing a page-to-stage documentation of the process. Grise has also partnered with musical director Martha Gonzalez from the Grammy Award-winning band Quetzal to produce a concept album and concert adaptation of the novel. The planned album, *Riding the Currents of the Wilding Wind*, was awarded a 2020 Creation Fund Grant from the National Performance Network and has garnered additional support from arts organizations across the country.

Viramontes is currently writing a novel in triptych called "The Cemetery Boys" that further expands the geographic and temporal reach of her fiction. The planned historical novel spans three wars and runs from the turn of the twentieth century up to the Iraq War. It includes characters from the fields of California to Punjab, India; from Germany to Haiti; and from the Philippine island of Luzon to the city streets that make up ethnic Los Angeles. It explores the trauma of several interconnected families whose lives are impacted by their loved ones entering, surviving, or dying in wars. In part because Viramontes grew up around several cemeteries in East Los Angeles, she has been inspired by their cryptic engravings to attend to, rather than ignore, the buried lives and hidden legacies that rarely make it into official histories. Several excerpts from the novel have been published in journals and edited collections.

SEE ALSO: Álvarez, Julia; Bambara, Toni Cade; Castillo, Ana; Cisneros, Sandra; Ecocriticism and Environmental Fiction; Erdrich, Louise; Fictions of Work and Labor; Kingston, Maxine Hong; Literature of the Americas; Silko, Leslie Marmon

REFERENCES

Chávez, Ernesto. (2002). *"¡Mi Raza Primero!" My People First!: Nationalism, Identity, and Insurgency in the Chicano Movement in Los Angeles, 1966–1978*. Berkeley: University of California Press.

Moya, Paula M.L. (2002). *Learning from Experience: Minority Identities, Multicultural Struggles*. Berkeley: University of California Press.

Moya, Paula M.L. (2016). *The Social Imperative: Race, Close Reading, and Contemporary Literary Criticism*. Stanford: Stanford University Press.

Oropeza, Lorena. (2005). *¡Raza Sí! ¡Guerra No!: Chicano Protest and Patriotism During the Viet Nam War Era*. Berkeley: University of California Press.

Viramontes, Helena María. (1990). Nopalitos: the making of fiction. In: *Making Face, Making Soul – Haciendo Caras: Creative and Critical Perspectives by Women of Color* (ed. Gloria E. Anzaldúa), 291–294. San Francisco: Aunt Lute Books.

Viramontes, Helena María. (2007). Marks of the Chicana corpus: an intervention in the universality debate. In: *A Companion to Latina/o Studies* (ed. Juan Flores and Renato Rosaldo), 3–14. Oxford: Blackwell.

Viramontes, Helena María. (2008). Beach blanket Baja. *The New York Times* (August 17, 2008). https://www.nytimes.com/2008/08/17/opinion/17iht-edviramontes.1.15360697.html (accessed August 9, 2021).

Viramontes, Helena María. (2010). Scripted language: writing is the only way I know how to pray (June 17, 2010) https://www.cornell.edu/video/helena-viramontes-scripted-language/s542 (accessed August 9, 2021).

Viramontes, Helena María. (2020). My insurgent heart. Keynote address to the AWP's 2020 Annual Conference. *The Writer's Chronicle.* Riverdale Park, MD: Association of Writers and Writing Programs.

FURTHER READING

Alarcón, Norma. (1988). Making "familia" from scratch: split subjectivities in the work of Helena María Viramontes and Cherríe Moraga. In: *Chicana Creativity and Criticism: Charting New Frontiers in American Literature* (ed. María Herrera-Sobek and Helena M. Viramontes), 147–159. Houston: Arte Publico Press.

Franco, Dean. (2015). Metaphors happen: miracle and metaphor in Helena María Viramontes's *Their Dogs Came with Them. Novel: A Forum on Fiction* 48 (3): 344–362.

Gutiérrez y Muhs, Gabriella. (ed.) (2013). *Rebozos de Palabras: An Helena María Viramontes Critical Reader.* Tucson: University of Arizona Press.

Hsu, Hsuan L. (2011). Fatal contiguities: metonymy and environmental justice. *New Literary History: A Journal of Theory and Interpretation* 42 (1): 147–168.

Lawless, Cecelia. (1996). Helena María Viramontes' homing devices in *Under the Feet of Jesus.* In: *Homemaking: Women Writers and the Politics and Poetics of Home* (ed. Catherine Wiley and Fiona R. Barnes), 361–382. New York: Garland.

Muñoz, Alicia. (2013). Articulating a geography of pain: metaphor, memory, and movement in Helena María Viramontes's *Their Dogs Came with Them. MELUS* 38 (2): 24–38, 157.

Wald, Sarah D. (2013). "Refusing to halt": mobility and the quest for spatial justice in Helena María Viramontes's *Their Dogs Came with Them* and Karen Tei Yamashita's *Tropic of Orange. Western American Literature* 48 (1–2): 70–89.

Vizenor, Gerald

CRISTINA STANCIU
Virginia Commonwealth University, USA

Gerald Vizenor is one of the most prolific and versatile writers of his generation, inhabiting simultaneously multiple spaces of creativity, from poet, novelist, essayist, and playwright to autobiographer, journalist, literary critic, teacher, and scholar. A mixed-blood author of Anishinaabe (Ojibwe/Chippewa), French, and Swedish ancestry, he was born on October 22, 1934, in Minneapolis to a mixed-blood father, Clement William Vizenor (Anishinaabe and French), and a Swedish American mother, LaVerne Lydia Peterson. He traces his descent from the Crane clan of the White Earth Anishinaabe and is an enrolled member of the White Earth Chippewa tribe in Minnesota. Author and editor of over forty books in many genres over a half century of creative work, he is the recipient of many awards and honors, including two American Book Awards, for *Griever: An American Monkey King in China* (1986) in 1988 and for *Shrouds of White Earth* (2010) in 2011, as well as the PEN Oakland–Josephine Miles Award in 1990, a Lifetime Literary Achievement Award from the Native Writer's Circle of the Americas in 2001, a Distinguished Achievement Award from the Western Literature Association in 2005, and the MELUS Lifetime Achievement Award in 2011. Vizenor has taught and lectured at prestigious universities in the United States and across the world, redefining both Native American writing and literary criticism.

From his first published volume, *Two Wings The Butterfly* (1962), a privately published collection of haiku poetry, to his most recent nonfiction work, *Native Provenance: The Betrayal of Cultural Creativity* (2019), Vizenor continues to challenge and educate his readers on Indigenous matters, from form to method, from politics to hermeneutics, from the local to the international. Before he became a creative writer, Vizenor was a journalist for the *Minneapolis Tribune*, where he wrote about Indigenous issues. Among his many achievements is the rewriting of the White Earth Nation constitution, ratified in 2009 – the first Indigenous democratic constitution on a reservation in Minnesota – for which he was principal writer. The open access academic journal *Transmotion* (2014–) is inspired by his work and vision for Indigenous studies, and has been dedicated to Vizenor studies as well as theoretical, experimental, postmodernist, and avant-garde writing by Native American and First Nations authors. Writing about the concept of "Native Transmotion" in *Fugitive Poses*, Vizenor defines it in the context of what he calls "the sovereignty of motion," or "the ability and vision to move in imagination and the substantive rights of motion in Native communities" (1998, p. 182). A main concern of his artistic and activist work in all genres is the relation between Native and non-Native worlds.

Although he navigates skillfully across many genres and writing registers, challenging conventions of literary genres, Vizenor started his creative work as a haiku poet, which Anishinaabe poet and literary critic Kimberly Blaeser attributes to similarities between the Japanese haiku form and the Ojibwe dream songs (Blaeser 1996, p. 110). He studied Japanese literature, including haiku practitioners Matsuo Basho and Kobayashi Issa, with Edward Copeland. His first volume of poetry, *Two Wings The Butterfly* (1962), inspired by life in Japan – where he served in the US army after World War II – was followed by five books of haiku: *Raising Moonvines* (1964) and *Seventeen Chirps* (1964), *Slight Abrasions: A Dialogue in Haiku* (with Jerome Downes) (1966), *Empty Swings* (1967), *Matsushima: Pine Islands* (1984), and *Cranes Arise* (1999), as well as a new edition of *Raising the Moon Vines* (1999). Louis Untermeyer praised his volume *Seventeen Chirps* on the book cover as "haiku in the best tradition." Vizenor has been recognized for his fine haiku poetry, his works being included in the *Haiku Anthology*, and he was invited to deliver a keynote address at the Haiku North American Conference in 1999. His later poems revisit favorite themes, such as the lives of contemporary urban Native people.

Vizenor's creative and personal investment in Ojibwe culture and history permeates his entire oeuvre, with early forays into Ojibwe stories and songs in volumes such as *Summer in the Spring: Lyric Poems of the Ojibway* (editor, 1965), reissued as *anishinabe nagamon: Songs of the People* (1970) and *Summer in the Spring: Ojibwe Lyric Poems and Tribal Stories* (1981). He credits Frances Densmore for her insights into the dream songs of the Ojibwe that she translated; to those translations, Vizenor adds his own vision, rewriting and revising, inserting episodes from the Ojibwe trickster cycle. *Anishnabe adisokan* (1970) is a collection of traditional stories about Ojibwe life, religion, and customs, published originally in the White Earth Reservation newspaper, *The Progress* (1887/8), edited by Vizenor's great uncle, Theodore Baulieu. The collection introduces tropes and stories Vizenor incorporates in his later writing, from the origin story of the most sacred Ojibwe ceremony (the midewiwin) to the Ojibwe culture hero and trickster (Manabozho). In the notes accompanying the Native stories in *Summer in the Spring* (1981), Vizenor also engages the critical tradition of reading Ojibwe oral stories. He de-emphasizes the role of the ego in his renditions of the dream songs, writing against previous anthropologists' misconceptions and representations.

In his fictive autobiography, *Interior Landscapes: Autobiographical Myths and*

Metaphors (1990), Vizenor reveals his writing process, which entails the inclusion of the autobiographical self into the narrative, resulting in an imaginative process of self-creation and self-presentation. This concern with authorial or narratorial personas – the voices of his writing – informs much of his prose and poetry, as well. And there is much postmodern playfulness in preparing the reader for understanding autobiographical personas and their constructedness, as Vizenor moves swiftly between first- and third-person narrators: "This is a mixedblood autobiographical causerie and a narrative on the slow death of a common red squirrel. The first and third person personas are me. Gerald Vizenor believes that autobiographies are imaginative histories; a remembrance past the barriers; wild pastimes over the pronouns" (1987, p. 99). His meditations on the genre of autobiography are interweaved with the narration of the slow death of a squirrel, an incident which prompted the narrator to never hunt animals again. Writing in a detached third person, Vizenor ponders his life while interspersing stories of his family and community: "The mixedblood autobiographer is a word hunter in transitive memories" (p. 108).

Just as he pushes the boundaries of experimentation and imagination in other genres, Vizenor's novels combine the inventive with the experimental to tell stories of belonging, identity, Native sovereignty, human remains, violence, sexuality, genetic therapies, education policies, corporate greed, environmental disaster, and the postmodern culture of simulation and celebrity. Throughout his novels, Vizenor returns to the oral tradition, weaving traditional stories into his works. One of the most radical and revolutionary contemporary Native American writers, Vizenor's novels challenge his readers through both form and content. Characters from earlier novels (such as *Bearheart* [1978], *Griever*, or *The Trickster of Liberty* [1988]) make new appearances in later novels (such as *The Heirs of Columbus*[1991]), connecting readers intertextually to his earlier works through humor, satire, and breaks with conventional narrative forms and critical conventions used by the literary market to assess Native American literatures.

Vizenor's use of satire conveys his critique of the ongoing assaults on Native people (whom he refers to as "tribal" rather than "Indian" to suggest his emphasis on community). To wit, the novel *Bearheart* is set in the future, following a group of mixed-bloods who break out of a pattern condemning them to destruction. These "Circus pilgrims" (a familiar Western intertext, reminiscent of Chaucer or Bunyan, yet placed in a hyperreality in Vizenor's novel) escape the Third World to become vision bears in another world, the Fourth. Here Vizenor combines traditional Anishinaabe and other Native references with contemporary social and political satire, implicitly critiquing the relegation of Indian reservations to the Third World. Inspired by canonical authors (from Dante and Chaucer to Fielding and Swift), as well as contemporary authors (such as Pynchon and Vonnegut), *Bearheart* became the first postmodern novel by a Native American writer, opening new literary spaces for Vizenor and other Native authors.

Griever: An American Monkey King in China, the author's most conventional novel in terms of narrative structure and character development, won Vizenor his first American Book Award. The novel's mixedblood protagonist, Griever de Hocus, also a trickster character, is a university professor. Unlike many Native American novels at the time, *Griever* is set in China and has a Native professor as a protagonist. Based on Vizenor's own experiences as a visiting professor at Tianjin University, the novel uses political satire and creative parody to criticize post-Mao China. It brings together

Chinese mythology (Sun Wukong, the Mind Monkey or The Monkey King) and Native American trickster figures to show that, despite repressive political environments (colonialism in North America and communism in China), the tricksters ultimately survive. Although lukewarm about the novel's pro-American undertones, critics have found the interpretation of the Monkey King as a trickster figure "an innovative and provocative step" in connecting two very different cultures (Hochbruck 1992, p. 275). The identities of the characters multiplying rapidly in the novel – for instance, China, both the name of Griever's friend from his reservation and the name of the country he writes to her about in his letters – point to the instability of the concept of identity itself, in true post-structuralist and Vizenorian fashion.

The novel *The Trickster of Liberty*, a prequel to both *Bearheart* and *Griever*, returns to stories of mixed-blood characters on the White Earth Reservation. The novel takes political aim at the American reservation system by having a monument named *Trickster of Liberty* – the counterpart to the Statue of Liberty in New York Harbor – erected on Indian land. Similarly, *The Heirs of Columbus*, a novel published during the quincentenary observance of the arrival of Columbus in America, reimagines Christopher Columbus as a descendant of Mayans and Sephardic Jews. In this novel, the discovery of healing genes in the bones of Columbus (which belong to the Anishinaabe as his legal "heirs") reverses the story of genocide and colonialism to healing and survival. By appropriating this colonial historical figure, Vizenor rethinks and reimagines the master narrative of "discovery" and settlement. His subsequent novels continue to expose and disrupt both stereotypes about Native people and local and global political myths: *Dead Voices: Natural Agonies in the Word Wars* (1992), *Hotline Healers: An Almost Browne Novel* (1997), *Chancers* (2000), *Hiroshima Bugi: Atomu 57* (2003), *Father Meme* (2008), *Shrouds of White Earth, Chair of Tears* (2012), *Blue Ravens* (2014), *Treaty Shirts: October 2034 – A Familiar Treatise on the White Earth Nation* (2016), and *Native Tributes: Historical Novel* (2018).

Besides fiction, activist writer Vizenor has also written about the rights of Native people of mixed descent, Indian child welfare, land claims, hunting and fishing rights, and Native education. In *Tribal Scenes and Ceremonies* (1976), a collection of articles from his time as a journalist for the *Minneapolis Tribune* and a Civil Rights organizer in Minnesota, Vizenor writes about contemporary Native life, both on the reservation and in urban areas, including pieces about the American Indian Movement. Several of his books portray various forms of assault against Native people. In "Sand Creek Survivors," a story in the volume *Earthdivers* (1981), Vizenor connects the death of a 13-year-old Sioux boy, Dane Michael White, with the massacres of the Cheyenne at Sand Creek (1864) and the Blackfeet at the Marias River (1870). (These are two of the bloodiest massacres in US history, where the US cavalry killed hundreds of Indigenous people, the majority of them women and children.) Vizenor's allusions to these massacres emphasize the continued attacks on Native people's bodies. More recently, his involvement in the constitutional reform work of the Minnesota Chippewa Tribe as a lead writer and delegate to the constitutional convention of the White Earth Reservation reveals his dedication to protecting the rights of mixed-blood family members. As the tribe rethinks tribal membership away from an antiquated, colonial blood quantum system, and toward a traditional tribal membership based on adoption, kinship, and family ties, Vizenor has been at the center of debates over Native identity and its definition. As many

Native American constitutions were written by the federal government, the White Earth democratic constitution Vizenor co-wrote with Anishinaabe scholar Jill Doerfler – *The White Earth Nation: Ratification of a Native Democratic Constitution* (2012) – offers a Native perspective on Indigenous sovereignty and traditional leadership, as well as individual and human rights.

As Vizenor continued to publish his fiction, he also wrote two plays thematically connected to much of his fiction and creative nonfiction. Vizenor's play, *Harold of Orange*, became the screenplay for a movie by the same title, awarded the Film-in-the-Cities Award in 1983 and the Best Film award at the San Francisco Film Festival for American Indian Films. Starring Oneida actor Charlie Hill as the central trickster character, the film playfully confronts issues at the heart of his other works. The 30-minute film *Harold of Orange*, directed by Richard Weise, tells the story of Harold Sinseer, founder of the New School of Socioacupuncture, tribal leader, and trickster extraordinaire. It follows Harold and his "Warrior of Orange" as they scheme for charitable foundation money to assist them in growing pinchbean coffee on their reservation in Minnesota. As Harold had been previously awarded a similar grant to raise miniature oranges on the reservation (with questionable results), the new project is suspect. The screenplay and movie delve deeper into 1980s white liberal concerns for minorities and economic assistance grants, as well as the ironies of funding creative work (Vizenor's project having been funded by foundation money). Harold's criticism of anthropologists, a recurrent theme across Vizenor's work, is sobering: "The rivers are dead near the universities, fish are poisoned, even the carp yawn near shore ... Birds are stalled in flight ... Interstates uproot our families ... These anthropologists invented us and put our parts in museum cases ... now we come around our parts here like lost and lonesome animals" (Vizenor and Sainte-Marie 1993, pp. 73–75).

Vizenor's later play in four acts, *Ishi and the Wood Ducks* (1995), first performed in 1996, revisits these concerns by centering the story around the life and post-life of Ishi, "the last" Yahi (the southernmost group of the Yana tribe in California), and subject of a study at the UC Berkeley Museum of Anthropology in the early 1900s, where he lived for five years. Vizenor's Ishi is far from the "primitive man" the anthropologists studying him from 1911 till 1916 made him to be; instead, he is at the center of a contemporary trial for having violated the Indian Arts and Crafts Act of 1990, in a play which mixes compassion and humor to showcase the character's humanity.

A theorist of Native expression of postmodernity who has engaged post-structuralist theory in much of his creative work, Vizenor has coined popular concepts (which Kimberly Blaeser calls "Vizenorese"; Blaeser 1996, p. 71), from "trickster consciousness" and "postindian warriors" to "survivance" and "manifest manners." *Manifest Manners: Postindian Warriors of Survivance* (1994) historicizes what he calls the simulations of Native representation from American writers such as James Fenimore Cooper to Native activists like Russell Means. Native Americans have been long misrepresented in the literature of dominance through what Vizenor calls "manifest manners" – a cultural legacy of Manifest Destiny – representations or simulations produced by both Natives and non-Natives. In *Fugitive Poses: Native American Indian Scenes of Absence and Presence* (1998), Vizenor defines yet again the concept at the heart of his theoretical and creative work: "the indian" (author's lower case). To Vizenor, "the indian is a simulation, the absence of natives; the indian transposes the real, and the simulation of the real has no referent, memories, or native stories. The postindian must waver over the aesthetic ruins of indian simulations" (1998,

p. 15). According to Vizenor, "indian" represents the sum of simulations central to writing and thinking about Native Americans, with no referent in real life, therefore an empty signifier. He remains, in Thomas King's words, "a coyote with a word processor" (quoted in Hochbruck 1992, p. 278). Always the trickster, Vizenor continues to navigate these worlds of representation, illuminating the distortions of contemporary "Indianness" in both popular and academic contexts, and pointing his readers to tribal values and stories with wit and humor, irreverence, and imagination.

SEE ALSO: Indigenous Narratives; Multiculturalism; Periodization; Story Cycles

REFERENCES

Blaeser, Kimberly M. (1996). *Gerald Vizenor: Writing in the Oral Tradition*. Norman: University of Oklahoma Press.

Hochbruck, Wolfgang. (1992). Breaking away: the novels of Gerald Vizenor. *World Literature Today* 66 (2): 274–278.

Vizenor, Gerald. (1987). Crows written on the poplars: autocritical autobiographies. In: *I Tell You Now* (ed. Brian Swann and Arnold Krupat), 99–110. Lincoln: University of Nebraska Press.

Vizenor, Gerald. (1998). *Fugitive Poses: Native American Indian Scenes of Absence and Presence*. Lincoln: University of Nebraska Press.

Vizenor, Gerald and Doerfler, Jill. (2012). *The White Earth Nation: Ratification of a Native Democratic Constitution*. Lincoln: University of Nebraska Press.

Vizenor, Gerald and Sainte-Marie, Buffy. (1993). Harold of Orange: a screenplay. *Studies in American Indian Literatures* 5 (3): 53–88. https://www.jstor.org/stable/20736752

FURTHER READING

Blaeser, Kimberly M. (2005). Gerald Vizenor: postindian liberation. *The Cambridge Companion to Native American Literature* (ed. Joy Porter and Kenneth Roemer), 257–270. Cambridge: Cambridge University Press.

Madsen, Deborah L. (2009). *Understanding Gerald Vizenor*. Columbia: South Carolina University Press.

Madsen, Deborah L. (ed.) (2012). *The Poetry and Poetics of Gerald Vizenor*. Albuquerque: University of New Mexico Press.

Madsen, Deborah L. and Lee, A. Robert. (eds.) (2010). *Gerald Vizenor: Texts and Contexts*. Albuquerque: University of New Mexico Press.

Owens, Louis. (guest ed.) (1997). Gerald Vizenor. Special issue of *Studies in American Indian Literatures* 9 (1).

Vollmann, William T.

THEOPHILUS SAVVAS
University of Bristol, UK

The first thing to note about William T. Vollmann is his prodigious output. Since the early 1990s he has published at a rate of roughly a book a year; several of these books are over a thousand pages long. While Vollmann has met with considerable success – being listed in *The New Yorker*'s 1999 feature on the top "20 under 40," for instance, and winning the National Book Award and the American Book Award – the formidable size and difficult subject matter of his books means that he has not received the readership or critical attention that he deserves. Vollmann's corpus includes fiction and journalism, but most of his books defy easy categorization. He frequently blends novelistic technique and reportage to produce hybrid works that destabilize and challenge any epistemological distinction between fact and fiction. As Larry McCaffery has noted: Vollmann's "devotion to literary aestheticism" is co-existent with his urge to document "grim, often horrific social and political realties" (McCaffery 2004, p. xiv). This is evident in Vollmann's first novel, *You Bright and Risen Angels: A Cartoon* (1987), the story of power struggles between insects and the inventors of electricity. The fantastical nature of the plot, and the wide-ranging subject matter, which includes entomology, ecology, computer science, and physics, meant that the novel inevitably drew comparisons with the encyclopedic postmodernist fiction of the second half of the twentieth century. While the influence of writers such as Thomas Pynchon, William Gaddis, and Joseph McElroy is palpable, *You Bright and Risen Angels* has a stronger commitment to representing the lives of drug users, prostitutes, and other representatives of what the FBI, in their report on the author, labeled "the seamy, underside of life" (Vollmann 2013). In hindsight, then, the novel can be seen as anticipating both the shift towards the "new sincerity" of post-postmodernism and the emergence of the major theme of Vollmann's mature work: empathy for those marginalized from mainstream society.

William Tanner Vollmann was born in Santa Monica, California, on July 28, 1959, to Thomas and Tanis. Bookish from the start, the young Vollmann was a keen reader of science fiction – the influence of which can be seen in *You Bright and Risen Angels* – and has commented that he wanted to write "ever since [he] was six or seven" (Vollmann 2004a, p. 3). After graduating from high school in 1977, Vollmann attended the prestigious all-male Deep Springs College situated on a cattle ranch and alfalfa farm in the high desert of California. The college offered a nonstandard curriculum which combined rigorous academic education with manual laboring duties. After going to Cornell University, where he graduated *summa cum laude* in comparative literature in 1981, Vollmann chose to defer a fellowship to do graduate work at Berkeley so that he could travel to Afghanistan in an attempt to join the Mujahedeen. The experience was documented in *An Afghanistan Picture Show, or, How I Saved the World*, which was eventually published in 1992. The title acknowledges the naivete with which the trip was undertaken, but the self-reflexive frankness of the book is also part of its success. As Steven Moore wrote in the *Washington Post Book World*: "the book succeeds not only in achieving its original goal – to bring attention to the plight of Afghan refugees [...] but also in dramatizing the limitations of altruism and activism, the difficulty of understanding the context of any culture other than your own" (Moore 1992). Vollmann himself has suggested that his failure to "confront this foreign other," meant that his book ultimately ended up being about "the unknowability of their experience" (Hemmingson 2009, p. 86).

Through most of the 1980s and 1990s Vollmann worked on a project which deals with themes similar to those in *Picture Show*, and which took even longer to come to fruition: *Rising Up and Rising Down: Some Thoughts on Violence and Urgent Means* (2003/4). In their original form these thoughts were published by McSweeney's in a seven-volume slip-cased edition with a single print run of just 3500 copies (which roughly equates to the number of pages of the project); a year later an abridged version of the work was published by Ecco, an imprint of HarperCollins. The first part of the book is an attempt to devise a "moral calculus" to decide when violence might be acceptable; the rest of the work consists of case studies exploring historical figures and examples taken from Vollmann's own experience and research. Vollmann sums up his findings in the preface to the distilled edition:

> The ultimate position of *Rising Up and Rising Down* is that moral values can be treated as absolutes in some respects, as relative quantities in other. I believe that every violent act refers itself back to a rational explanation. To the extent that the explanations are irrational, they can be quickly disposed of. To the extent that they are rational, they do enjoy the *possibility* of absolute status, provided that ends, means and the intellectual-moral logic in between have all been correctly assembled.
>
> (2004b, p. xi; author's italics)

An Afghanistan Picture Show and *Rising Up and Rising Down* are nuanced exercises in empathic understanding. The former recognizes that while empathy is always required, it may not always be enough; the latter highlights that to understand the reasons for an act of extreme behavior is not necessarily to excuse the act itself.

Vollmann's meditation on violence is not the only seven-volume enterprise of the author's career. "Seven Dreams: A Book of North American Landscapes" is an extraordinarily ambitious attempt to retell the narrative of North America. Five books of the series have so far been published. *The Ice-Shirt* (1990) conflates *The Saga of Greenlanders* and *Eirik's Saga* to tell the "Symbolic truth" of the early contact between Europeans and "Vinland" and spans a period of about five years. *Fathers and Crows* (1992) has a larger time frame and draws heavily on the 73-volume Jesuit Relations to recreate the clashes between the French settlers and the Huron and Iroquois peoples during the first half of the seventeenth century. In 1994, the sixth volume was published (as with another famous fictive interpretation of American history, James Fenimore Cooper's "Leatherstocking Tales," Vollmann's series has not been published in chronological order). *The Rifles* (1994) chronicles Sir John Franklin's quest for the Northwest Passage in the first half of the nineteenth century and juxtaposes it with the tragic effect of the introduction of mechanized weaponry to the Inuit of the area. If publishing the books out of sequence was not the best decision commercially, Vollmann's fears that writing the next volume, *Argall: The True Story of Pocahontas and Captain John Smith* (2001), in florid Elizabethan-style prose, would prove the final straw for his publisher proved unfounded. Viking have stuck with the project and *The Dying Grass*, which begins with General Oliver Otis Howard's attempt in the late nineteenth century to confine the Nez Percés to a much smaller reservation than previously agreed upon, was published in 2015.

"Seven Dreams" is an attempt to give equal weight to the experiences of native inhabitants and European settlers, so origin stories and myths sit alongside rigorously researched historical narrative and copious paratextual documentation, including hundreds of pages of notes, glossaries, and maps. No privilege is afforded to either way of understanding the past. One of Vollmann's rules for writing, as described in his piece "American Writing Today," helps explain this methodology: "We should strive to feel not only about Self, but also about Other. Not the vacuum so often between Self and Other. Not the unworthiness of Other. Not the Other as a negation or eclipse of Self. Not even about the Other exclusive of Self, because that is a trickster-egoist's way of worshipping Self secretly. We must treat Self and Other as equal partners" (2004c, p. 332). Vollmann includes both native and European epistemologies to establish the dialogic relationship between self and other that is the ultimate aim of all his writing.

This desire to create such a relationship explains why Vollmann considers it necessary to visit the places he writes about (however dangerous) and why he puts himself in potentially compromising positions – traveling through the United States in the boxcars of freight trains in *Riding Towards Everywhere* (2008), for instance – in order to meet the subjects of his books; it also explains why he inserts himself, or a version of himself, in so many of them. This produces a conflation of the biographical and the literary which gives the impression that Vollmann conceives of his life and work as part of the same ethical project. The drive to rescue the "other" from the margins of the text is surely the same as that which led him to purchase a 12-year-old Thai prostitute in order to smuggle her to a rescue operation in Burma. In turn, that drive itself seems intimately related to the death by drowning of one of his sisters while under his supervision, something which he has described as a formative experience of his childhood (and which is explored most vividly in "Under the Grass," in *The Atlas* [1996]). Whatever the merits or demerits of biographical criticism in general, Vollmann is consistently so present in his texts that it is both inevitable and necessary that he too becomes the object of ethical enquiry. The need to develop a subtle understanding of the nature of Vollmann's relationship with his subject is particularly acute when it comes to sex workers. They feature prominently in Vollmann's life and writing. *Whores for Gloria* (1991), *Butterfly Stories: A Novel* (1993), and *The Royal Family* (2000) all detail the pursuit of prostitutes by solitary men. For Daniel Lukes, these works downplay the role of exploitation in sex industries and provide evidence of Vollmann's "sometimes passive-aggressive relationship with feminism" (2015, p. 248); but Melissa Petro has lauded Vollmann's writing because it "clearly acknowledges multiple perspectives and plural industries – not falling into the trap of inadvertently re-enforcing the notion that sex workers are either empowered or oppressed" (2015, p. 245). The more general question of the nature of the feminine is considered in *Kissing the Mask: Beauty, Understatement and Femininity in Japanese Noh Theatre* (2010) and *The Book of Dolores* (2013), a series of self-portraits of Vollmann's eponymous female alter ego.

Imperial (2009), Vollmann's longest single volume book to date, is part history, part psycho-geographical investigation of Imperial County, California, and the Imperial Valley, a border zone of California and Mexico. Vollmann makes it clear that this rough Eliotic wasteland, which has the highest unemployment of any county in the United States, serves a broader function: it is a synecdoche for America as a whole. *Imperial* is thus a literalization of Vollmann's interest in other sorts of borderlands – the fluidities of identity, for instance, and the margins of society may be understood in such fashion. So, too, may his experimentations in form. Generic distinctions as well as the boundaries of fiction and fact are dissolved by Vollmann's work. *The Rainbow Stories* (1988), *Thirteen Stories and Thirteen Epitaphs* (1991), and *The Atlas* all experiment with the short story form, with the last of these being inspired by the "palm-of-the-hand" stories of the Japanese writer Yasunari Kawabata. More recently, *Last Stories and Other Stories* (2014), with its air of the supernatural, reads like a foray into genre fiction.

Europe Central (2005) is also technically a series of interlinked stories but is more usually described as a historical novel. It is a magisterial book about Germany and the Soviet Union between 1914 and 1975 – although it is centered on the years of World War II – and features a wide range of historical figures, including Hitler ("the realist"), Stalin ("the sleepwalker"), Anna Akhmatova, and most prominently, Dimitri Shostakovich. The novel intertwines the themes of sex and violence through an imagined love triangle between Shostakovich, Roman Karmen, and Elena Konstantinovskaya, and the graphic rendering of the details of the death camps. *Europe Central* is the most successful of Vollmann's books in critical and commercial terms, winning the National Book Award and extending the writer's readership beyond the cult following of the 1990s. Such success afforded no occasion for rest. In the following two years, Vollmann published *Uncentering The Earth: Copernicus and the Revolution of the Heavenly Spheres* (2006), an attempt to explain the findings of the sixteenth-century astronomer for the lay reader, and *Poor People* (2007), an investigation into the lives of those who struggle to subsist and a reflection upon the nature of poverty itself.

Perhaps it was inevitable that an author so interested in human nature and the human condition would turn to the biggest existential threat to the species. *Carbon Ideologies* – winner of the American Book Award – is a suitably (and characteristically) massive response to climate change. It was published in 2018 in two volumes (a rare accession on behalf of Vollmann to the requests of an editor) and runs to 1264 printed pages with a further 129,000 words of sources and footnotes available online at the publisher's website (Penguin Random House n.d.). The work may be read as a lengthy riposte to "Carbon Capture," a 2015 *New Yorker* piece by Vollmann's friend Jonathan Franzen. Franzen bemoaned the fact that climate change has come to dominate the ecological agenda on the grounds that it has had the effect of marginalizing the more immediate goals of conservation. For Franzen, the abstraction of climate change – the way in which any individual's effort to improve the situation has no discernible effect – works against our intuitive logic: "the human brain evolved to focus on the present, not the far future" so that climate change "deeply confuses" it (Franzen 2015). Vollmann's book is specifically addressed to the "far future," to an imaginary reader who is living in the devastated world that we have left behind, and it is marked by Vollmann's familiar methodology: the use of "induction to generalize from subjective case studies into analytical categories of the phenomenon under investigation" (Vollmann 2018, p. ix). In other words, the author draws on interviews from individuals already affected by our need for power: coal workers in Bangladesh, oil workers in Abu Dhabi, those living near the Fukushima nuclear plant in Japan, to make his overall case. Familiar, too, is his own presence. Vollmann calculates in immense detail his personal energy consumption: "coal, oil, natural gas, even nuclear – haven't I consumed them all? Better an honest muddler than a carbon-powered hypocrite," he explains in his preface (p. ix). This helps clarify the practice elsewhere. For Vollmann, these insertions of self function as acknowledgments of his complicity, and all our complicity, in the "horrific historical and political realities" which he documents.

Focusing on individual experience does not produce a hopeful book. For one reviewer Vollmann has written "the most honest book about climate change yet" (Rich 2018); for another, he has unhelpfully gone "full Cormac McCarthy" (Schwartz 2018). What really fascinates Vollmann about climate change, perhaps, is not the existential threat that it poses, but the fact that it is an existential threat of our own making. It thus dovetails the main thematic interests of his career so far and allows him to pose the ultimate question of empathy: can we understand and forgive ourselves for a series of behaviors which will most likely marginalize each and every one of us?

SEE ALSO: After Postmodernism; Border Fictions; Ecocriticism and Environmental Fiction; Franzen, Jonathan; Mixed-Genre Fiction; Wallace, David Foster

REFERENCES

Franzen, Jonathan. (2015). Carbon capture. *The New Yorker* (April 6, 2015). www.newyorker.com/magazine/2015/04/06/carbon-capture (accessed July 13, 2021).

Hemmingson, Michael. (2009). *William T. Vollmann: A Critical Study and Seven Interviews*. Jefferson, NC: McFarland & Co.

Lukes, Daniel. (2015). "Strange hungers": William T. Vollmann's literary performances of abject masculinity. In: *William T. Vollman: A Critical Companion* (ed. Christopher K. Coffman and Daniel Lukes), 247–280. Newark: University of Delaware Press.

McCaffery, Larry. (2004). Introduction. In: *Expelled from Eden: A William T. Vollmann Reader* (ed. Larry McCaffery and Michael

Hemmingson), xvii–xxxvi. New York: Thunder's Mouth Press.
Moore, Steven. (1992). William Vollmann: an artist in the American grain. Review of *Fathers and Crows* and *An Afghanistan Picture Show*. *Washington Post Book World* (August 2, 1992). www.stevenmoore.info/vollmannrevs1.shtml (accessed July 13, 2021).
Penguin Random House. (n.d.). William T. Vollmann's *Carbon Ideologies*. https://www.penguinrandomhouse.com/carbonideologies/ (accessed July 17, 2021).
Petro, Melissa. (2015). The shattered object: on representation versus self-representation and becoming whole. In: *William T. Vollmann: A Critical Companion* (ed. Christopher K. Coffman and Daniel Lukes), 241–246. Newark: University of Delaware Press.
Rich, Nathaniel. (2018). The most honest book about climate change yet. *The Atlantic* (October 2018). www.theatlantic.com/magazine/archive/2018/10/william-vollmann-carbon-ideologies/568309/ (accessed July 13, 2021).
Schwartz, John. (2018). William Vollmann would like a word or two about climate change. Or 1200 pages. *The New York Times* (August 11, 2018). www.nytimes.com/2018/08/06/books/review/william-t-vollmann-carbon-ideologies-no-immediate-danger-no-good-alternative.html (accessed July 13, 2021)
Vollmann, William T. (2004a). Biographical statement (c. 1989). In: *Expelled from Eden: A William T. Vollmann Reader* (ed. Larry McCaffery and Michael Hemmingson), 3–6. New York: Thunder's Mouth Press.
Vollmann, William T. (2004b). *Rising Up and Rising Down: Some Thoughts on Violence and Urgent Means*. New York: Ecco.
Vollmann, William T. (2004c). American writing today: diagnosis of a disease. In: *Expelled from Eden: A William T. Vollmann Reader* (ed. Larry McCaffery and Michael Hemmingson), 229–332. New York: Thunder's Mouth Press.
Vollmann, William T. (2013). Life as a terrorist: uncovering my FBI file. *Harper's Magazine* (September 2013). https://harpers.org/archive/2013/09/life-as-a-terrorist/ (accessed July 13, 2021).
Vollmann, William T. (2018). *No Immediate Danger. Carbon Ideologies*, vol. 1. New York and London: Viking.

FURTHER READING

Hemmingson, Michael. (2012). *William T. Vollmann: An Annotated Bibliography*. Lanham, MD: Scarecrow Press.
Lukes, Daniel. (ed.) (2020). *Conversations with William T. Vollmann*. Jackson. University of Mississippi Press.
Malvestio, Marco and Carrara, Giuseppe. (2019). William T. Vollmann. Special issue of *Enthymema* 23. https://riviste.unimi.it/index.php/enthymema/index
Özcan, Işil. (2019). *Understanding William T. Vollmann*. Columbia: University of South Carolina Press.
Qian, Cheng. (2012). *A Study on William Vollmann: Transgression in the Postmodern Context*. Xiamen: Xiamen University Press.

Vonnegut, Kurt

CHRISTINA JARVIS
State University of New York at Fredonia, USA

Best known for his wildly imaginative fiction, accessible style, dark humor, and unflinching critiques of American culture, Kurt Vonnegut was one of the most iconic writers of the late twentieth century. During a career spanning more than five decades, Vonnegut published fourteen novels, three short story collections, five nonfiction volumes, a children's book, two plays, and several television dramas. Although his early years as a novelist were marked by financial instability, minimal critical attention, and a largely underground readership, the publication of *Slaughterhouse-Five* (1969) launched his career as a literary celebrity. While his status as a cultural icon provided a larger stage for his pacifist, social justice, environmental, and humanist views and freed him to experiment with a broader range of creative forms, it also brought increased critical scrutiny and a complicated, sometimes contentious relationship with reviewers.

Kurt Vonnegut, Jr. was born on November 11, 1922, in Indianapolis, Indiana, where he grew up surrounded by a large extended family of free-thinking German American architects, business owners, civil servants, musicians, and artists. Although his two older siblings, Bernard and Alice, went to private schools and enjoyed a comfortable childhood, Vonnegut was raised more modestly because of his family's financial struggles during the Great Depression. His time in Indianapolis's public schools influenced his civic values and early experiences as a writer. At Shortridge High School, he wrote for and edited *The Daily Echo*, and he continued working as a journalist for *The Cornell Daily Sun*, despite majoring in biochemistry at Cornell University.

Those literary apprenticeships shaped the accessible, lean prose that would become a hallmark of Vonnegut's writing style and confirmed his desire to become a writer. Vonnegut brought a portable typewriter to army basic training, planning to chronicle his World War II adventures. After surviving the Battle of the Bulge, intense hardships as a prisoner of war, and the February 1945 firebombing of Dresden, he realized that recounting the devastation, inhumanity, and absurdity of war would require new approaches to writing.

Shortly after his repatriation, Vonnegut married Jane Marie Cox, a brilliant Swarthmore English major, who served as his first editor and unflaggingly supported his writing career and graduate coursework in anthropology at the University of Chicago. The birth of their first child, Mark, prompted Vonnegut to leave Chicago without a degree in 1947 to obtain more lucrative employment in the News Bureau at General Electric in Schenectady, New York. Nonetheless, his anthropology studies of cultural relativity and ethnography inspired the defamiliarizing views of culture, invented religions, and big questions about humanity that became signature elements of his fiction.

Many of these elements appeared in Vonnegut's first novel, *Player Piano* (1952), which drew upon his experiences at General Electric to question the ethics, social implications, and human costs of automation. Depicting a near-future "utopian" society of peace and prosperity, where virtually all labor and decisions have been outsourced to machines and a super computer, *Player Piano* raises questions about human dignity, the meaning of work, and "what people are for?" The novel, along with his next three, had weak sales, forcing Vonnegut to concentrate on short fiction for popular periodicals, such as *Collier's* and the *Saturday Evening Post* between 1952 and 1963.

During that period, Vonnegut published three novels that responded to the increasingly deadly technologies, scientific irresponsibility, and uncritical patriotism he saw in Cold War America. Incorporating science fiction elements, *Sirens of Titan* (1959) satirized the US–Soviet space and weapons races while balancing interplanetary adventures with inward-focused musings on fate, luck, and free will. A dark comical take on the spy novel genre, *Mother Night* (1961) offered the fictionalized confessions of Howard W. Campbell, Jr., an American secret agent who became a writer and radio broadcaster for wartime Nazi propaganda efforts, to investigate the dangers of nationalism and the complexities of determining guilt and innocence. Tapping into fears about nuclear war, *Cat's Cradle* (1963) paired the story of an apocalypse caused by the release of ice-nine, a crystal that freezes all the liquid water it encounters, with explorations of an invented religion called Bokononism. A postmodern novel par excellence, *Cat's Cradle* loops together multiple narratives, black humor, and religious, environmental, and literary apocalyptic traditions to explore the negative consequences of blind faith in science and religion.

With *God Bless You, Mr. Rosewater* (1965) and *Slaughterhouse-Five*, Vonnegut returned to his own war experiences while simultaneously addressing economic disparities and violence, cultural fragmentation, and trauma connected to the Vietnam War. In the former, protagonist Eliot Rosewater turns to science fiction, alcohol, and philanthropy to assuage his guilt over accidentally killing three civilian German firemen during World War II. Embodying progressive mid-1960s political leanings, Rosewater rejects his family's conservative, aristocratic lifestyle to undertake the radical experiment of loving "discarded Americans." After a personal prologue chapter about Vonnegut's decades-long failure to tell his "Dresden story," *Slaughterhouse-Five* combines science fiction and a disorienting, fragmented narrative to convey the wartime and postwar experiences of Billy Pilgrim. While Billy's trips through time and experiences in captivity on the planet Tralfamadore mirror symptoms associated with post-traumatic stress disorder, the novel yokes together specific historical moments to encapsulate the broader cultural upheaval of the 1960s and to challenge narrative structures that foster war.

Following the tremendous commercial and critical success of *Slaughterhouse-Five*, Vonnegut became a public spokesman and worked in a wider variety of genres during the 1970s. His play *Happy Birthday, Wanda June* (1970), a strongly pacifist contemporary retelling of *The Odyssey*, was produced on and off Broadway, which hastened a move from his home and family on Cape Cod to New York City and a relationship with photographer Jill Krementz. As a literary celebrity, Vonnegut was invited to speak at and report on major events, such as the first Earth Day, the Biafra–Nigeria conflict, and the 1972 Republican National Convention, and the popularity of his nonfiction pieces led to the publication of *Wampeters, Foma & Granfalloons: Opinions* (1974).

Like his earlier six novels, the three Vonnegut published during the 1970s continued to respond to the pressing political, social, environmental, and economic issues of the day; however, they incorporated more explicitly personal and experimental elements. In *Breakfast of Champions* (1973), he included a personal preface, punctuated the text with his own irreverent felt-tip drawings, and playfully turned himself into a character who interacted with his fictional creations, including Kilgore Trout, a failed science fiction writer and Vonnegut's alter ego. Beyond these formal innovations, he used his fictional Midland City to tell a broader national story about environmental pollution, racism, economic disparities, and the plasticization of American culture.

With *Slapstick* (1976), Vonnegut continued his satirical critiques of environmental devastation and fraying political and social institutions, but turned to fantastic elements in the story of Wilbur and Eliza Swain, physically grotesque "neanderthaloid" twins who possess a "single genius" together but limited intellects separately. Reviews of *Slapstick* were terrible, and some critics began to attack Vonnegut's canon as a whole. Shaken by the scathing criticism, Vonnegut shifted to a more realistically textured style in *Jailbird* (1979). Blending real historical events and figures with fiction, *Jailbird* recounts the misadventures of Walter F. Starbuck, a minor figure in the Watergate scandal, who also has ties to organized labor movements, economic justice idealists, the Sacco and Vanzetti trial, and 1950s McCarthy hearings.

Bolstered by *Jailbird*'s strong critical reception and an ever-widening fan base, Vonnegut continued to explore new creative forms in the early 1980s. In collaboration with artist Ivan Chermayeff, he published the children's book *Sun Moon Star* (1980), a humanist retelling of Christ's birth from the perspective of the infant. The following year, Vonnegut published *Palm Sunday* (1981), an "autobiographical collage" that merged personal stories with speeches, essays, reviews, sermons, a television play, and his final short story, "The Big Space Fuck."

Despite these ventures into other literary forms and a growing body of visual artwork, Vonnegut returned to the novel as his preferred artistic medium to address concerns about weapons development, human-caused environmental devastation, legacies of war, and global inequalities in the 1980s. Although the decade saw a tapering off of reviews in major periodicals, with critics noting repeated themes, characters, and techniques in Vonnegut's work, scholars recognized important new directions, such as the inclusion of more complex female characters and optimistic, resilient views of humanity.

As *Deadeye Dick* (1982) demonstrates, Vonnegut's return to his fictional Midland City and its inhabitants from *Breakfast of Champions* allowed him to add nuance, complexity, and deep personal meaning to earlier critiques of American culture. Taking aim at the military–industrial complex, *Deadeye Dick* places a pair of two seemingly disconnected accidents at its center – protagonist Rudy Waltz's Mother's Day 1944 shooting of a pregnant woman and the detonation of a neutron bomb near an interstate exit that depopulates the entire city. While responding to Ronald Reagan's 1981 reauthorization of the production of neutron warheads, Vonnegut connects the events to larger patterns of violence-prone models of masculinity and the disposability of human life. As a prequel to *Breakfast of Champions, Deadeye Dick* also explores the backstory of Celia Hoover, whose addiction to amphetamines leads to a tragic decline that parallels the much larger epidemic of substances destroying individuals, communities, nation, and planet.

Vonnegut's concerns as a planetary citizen came to the forefront in *Galápagos* (1985), his most explicitly environmental novel. Set in the year 1,001,986 AD, *Galápagos* examines the evolutionary fate of humanity, which has evolved into amphibious "fisher folk" with a silky seal-like pelt, arm flippers, streamlined skulls, and much smaller brains. Narrated by the ghostly Leon Trout, the story focuses on the "lucky" accidents of 1986 AD that bring a tiny band of colonists to the fictional Galápagos island Santa Rosalia. Escaping the rioting, looting, warfare, and other catastrophes unfolding in Ecuador, a new Adam, six Eves, "Mother Nature Personified," and two other women travel on the *Bahia de Darwin* to a new Eden, the cradle of humanity's future. Intertwining Darwin's theory of natural selection and biblical allusions, the story is a parable about the potential apocalyptic damages human beings are inflicting on themselves and the planet through warfare, neoliberal trade policies, overconsumption of resources, species extinction, global economic inequalities, and pollution. Ultimately, this anthropogenic damage is kept in check by microorganisms, which attack human ova and wipe out everyone except for the isolated Santa Rosalia colonists. Despite this apocalyptic warning, *Galápagos* is a remarkably optimistic book, which encourages readers to learn the vital ecological lesson of Santa Rosalia: "Just in the nick of time they realized that it was their own habitat that they were wrecking – that they weren't merely visitors" (Vonnegut 2009, p. 106).

With *Bluebeard* (1987), Vonnegut shifted from geological timeframes and fantastic fables to historically grounded reflections on the Abstract Expressionist Movement, the Armenian Genocide, World War II, and late-1980s US capitalism. *Bluebeard* is ostensibly the autobiography of Rabo Karabekian, an Armenian American, artist, wounded World War II veteran, and wealthy widower, who is rescued from a failed art career and spiritual depression by the lively, bestselling writer Circe Berman. A more complex and fully developed version than the abstract expressionist painter who appears in *Breakfast of Champions*, Rabo Karabekian's character allows Vonnegut to revisit his own wartime experiences and meditate on the redemptive, healing powers of writing and the visual arts. Through the strong female characters of Circe Berman and Marliee Kemp, Karabekian's first artistic supporter, friend, and lover, Vonnegut specifically explores the gendered dimensions of warfare. In their 1950 reunion in Florence, Kemp helps Karabekian see the horrific violence toxic masculinity and warfare inflict on women, children, the elderly, and male soldiers themselves. A gifted realistic illustrator, Karabekian embraces abstract expressionist painting because it negates standard forms of meaning, representing "The End" of the traditions that promote cycles of war. Loosely alluding to the mythological goddess who magically turns Odysseus's warriors to swine, Circe Berman sparks Karabekian's artistic rejuvenation through writing and inspires him to display his artistic masterpiece, "Now It's the Women's Turn," which he had locked away in an old potato barn. Drawing on scenes Vonnegut witnessed, the painting realistically depicts 5219 World War II survivors in a lush valley on May 8, 1945, to capture individual human stories of civilians and combatants from all nations involved in the war.

As Vonnegut started a new decade, the optimistic, redemptive tone of his mid- to late-1980s novels yielded to a more scathing one in *Hocus Pocus* (1990), which biographer Charles Shields dubbed "his most depressive" novel (2011, p. 383). Like *Mother Night*, *Hocus Pocus* is a first-person prison memoir that explores issues of war guilt, but it addresses a wider range of social issues via narrator Eugene Debs Hartke's experiences teaching at Tarkington, a college for the super wealthy, and Athena, a racially segregated prison. Hartke is falsely imprisoned for supposedly masterminding a prison break and attack on the local town, but he wrestles with his real unpunished sins – the people he killed while serving in Vietnam and his numerous extramarital affairs. Set only eleven years in the future from its 1990 publication date, the novel's near futuristic setting invites readers to examine the social, racial, and economic injustices and other trends Vonnegut saw plaguing America. These trends include "foreign investment in America," the "privatization of formerly public or even governmental institutions," and the question of "how to come to terms with the legacy of Vietnam" (Klinkowitz 2009, pp. 102–103). While Hartke's narrative explores a broad sweep of American history, the novel specifically challenges the revisionist representations of the Vietnam War that flourished in the Reagan era. Reacting to 1980s political transformations of the Vietnam War into "a noble cause" and an excuse for rearmament, *Hocus Pocus* exposes sites of personal and national trauma to promote frank recollections and accountability.

When Vonnegut published his last novel, *Timequake* (1997), he intended it to be the final chapter of his writing career. Innovative in metafictional technique, *Timequake* combines the "fillet" remnants of a failed novel by the same name with Vonnegut's personal reflections from 1996 as he revised the manuscript. Driving the nominal plot is a timequake, "a sudden glitch in the space-time continuum" that transports everyone back a decade and forces them to repeat everything they had done until free will kicks in again (1998, p. xiv). Anchored in the relationship between Vonnegut and his alter ego, Kilgore Trout, *Timequake* blurs the lines between fact and fiction, art and life, past and future, and explores profound subjects from Friedrich Nietzsche's ideas about eternal recurrence to Isaac Newton's and Albert Einstein's views of time to the unique place of human beings in the cosmos. Culminating in a clambake that brings together Vonnegut's fictional characters and stand-ins for editors, agents, critics, family members, and close friends who supported his writing career, *Timequake* is ultimately about the creative joys, imagination, healing potential, and community-making possibilities of writing and reading.

Despite his promise that *Timequake* would be his last book, Vonnegut continued a strong and steady creative output until his death on April 11, 2007. In 1999, Vonnegut published *Bagombo Snuff Box*, a collection of short stories that, with one exception, did not appear in his previous compilations, *Canary in a Cat House* (1961) and *Welcome to the Monkey House* (1968). That same year, he also published, *God Bless You, Dr. Kevorkian* (1999), a slim volume of brief pieces based on radio broadcasts Vonnegut did for WNYC's fundraising drives. Imagining a fictional scenario where Dr. Jack Kevorkian facilitates controlled near-death experiences, Vonnegut interviews twenty individuals just outside Heaven's gates, bringing back comments from famous figures, such as William Shakespeare, Mary Shelley, and John Brown, and seemingly random individuals. The sketches offered Vonnegut a late-career outlet to capture his signature concerns: human rights activism, public service, social justice, an "Edenic" love of nature, romantic love, scientific curiosity, the joy of writing, creativity, and "resolve in the face of tragedy" (Leeds 2016, pp. 268–270).

In addition to giving speeches and publishing brief opinion pieces in magazines and newspapers, Vonnegut continued to create artwork in collaboration with artist Joe Petro III, who turned the writer's drawings into individually handcrafted silk screen prints. Together they produced a series of largely text-based silk screen Confetti prints that responded to the wars and policies of the Bush administration and allowed Vonnegut to leave his fans with pearls of wisdom, reprieves of laughter, sobering critiques, and stark reflections on life in the early twenty-first century. Some of these reflections and images appeared in Vonnegut's final book, *A Man Without a Country* (2005), a collection of essays and autobiographical anecdotes edited by Dan Simon of Seven Stories Press. With Confetti prints interspersed throughout its twelve chapters, *A Man Without a Country* captures Vonnegut's outrage over America's preemptive war in Iraq, addiction to fossil fuels in the wake of worsening climate change, the erosion of civil liberties and civil discourse, the dehumanization of people based on religion and race, and political tribalism. Although despairing in tone and outlook, Vonnegut encouraged readers to embrace the arts, human connections and communities, and common decency.

With all his major works in print, a steady stream of posthumous publications, renewed scholarly attention, and dozens of foreign language translations, Vonnegut's popularity remains steadfast – especially as his critiques of warfare, gun violence, the pharmaceutical industry, environmental pollution, consumerism, and isolating digital technologies become more prescient.

SEE ALSO: Contemporary Fictions of War; The Culture Wars; Ecocriticism and Environmental Fiction; Fictions of Work and Labor; Globalization; Trauma and Fiction

REFERENCES

Klinkowitz, Jerome. (2009). *Kurt Vonnegut's America*. Columbia: University Press of South Carolina.
Leeds, Marc. (2016). *The Vonnegut Encyclopedia, Revised and Updated Edition*. New York: Delacorte.
Shields, Charles J. (2011). *And So It Goes: Kurt Vonnegut: A Life*. New York: Henry Holt.
Vonnegut, Kurt. (1998). *Timequake*. New York: Berkley Books; 1st ed. 1997.
Vonnegut, Kurt. (2009). *Galápagos*. New York: Dial Press; 1st ed. 1985.

FURTHER READING

Farrell, Susan. (2008). *Critical Companion to Kurt Vonnegut: A Literary Reference to His Life and Work*. New York: Facts on File.

Morse, Donald E. (2003). *The Novels of Kurt Vonnegut: Imagining Being an American*. Westport, CT: Praeger.

Strand, Ginger. (2015). *The Brothers Vonnegut: Science and Fiction in the House of Magic*. New York: Farrar, Straus and Giroux.

Tally, Robert. (ed.) (2013). *Critical Insights: Kurt Vonnegut*. Ipswich, MA: Salem.

Vonnegut, Kurt. (2017). *Complete Stories*. Collected and introduced by Jerome Klinkowitz and Dan Wakefield. New York: Seven Stories.

W

Walker, Alice

CHERYL R. HOPSON
Western Kentucky University, USA

African American writer Alice Walker won the Pulitzer Prize and National Book Award for her signature novel, *The Color Purple* (1982), adapted into an Emmy-nominated film, directed by Steven Spielberg, in 1985, and a Tony Award-winning Broadway musical in 2005.

Born in Eatonton, Georgia, in 1944, Walker was the eighth and youngest child of parents Willie Lee and Minnie Lou Walker, both sharecroppers. Additionally, Walker's mother worked as a domestic for forty years. According to the late scholar Rudolph P. Byrd, though Walker's parents worked six of seven days a week, the family's income never exceeded $300 annually. As Angela Davis has written, sharecropping reduplicated US slavery. Walker grew up then at an economic level beyond poverty, what she has referred to as peasant class. However, and as Walker has stated, she "never confused" herself "with the poverty." Rather, Walker identified "with the grandeur, the beauty," of Eatonton and her surrounding community (Byrd 2010, p. 174).

In 1961, after graduating high school valedictorian, Walker left Eatonton to attend Spelman College, an elite African American women's college in Atlanta, Georgia. A student on scholarship, Walker studied with the late historian Howard Zinn and the late writer and philanthropist Charles E. Merrill, Jr. It was also at Spelman that Walker began her activities as a student participant in the Civil Rights movements of the mid-to-late 1960s. In 1963, Walker transferred to Sarah Lawrence College in New York, an elite primarily white women's college, where she studied with the late poets Muriel Rukeyser and Jane Cooper, and from where she matriculated in 1966. The years following graduation were prolific for Walker as a writer. Since the year 1967, and with the publication of her award-winning essay "The Civil Rights Movement: What Good Was It?" in *American Scholar*, Walker has published in every genre, including children's literature.

The discussion to follow concerns Walker's five novels published after 1980. Those novels include the award-winning *The Color Purple*, *The Temple of My Familiar* (1989), *Possessing the Secret of Joy* (1992), *By the Light of My Father's Smile* (1998), and *Now Is the Time to Open Your Heart* (2004). In discussing Walker's post-1980s fiction, it is important to note Walker's self-defining as a Womanist, a term she coined to mean "a Black feminist or feminist of color" (1993,

p. xi) and further expounded on in her groundbreaking collection of essays *In Search of Our Mothers' Gardens: Womanist Prose* (1983). In a four-part definition that prefaces *In Search of Our Mothers' Gardens*, Walker provides that a Womanist, in addition to being a Black feminist, is a woman who "love[s] women, sexually and/or non-sexually," and appreciates women's emotional flexibility.

Walker continues that a Womanist has an appreciation and preference for women's culture, creative compelling, and curiosity (1993, p. xi). Thus, Womanism as an ideological framework is central to Walker's aesthetics as a novelist. Characters such as Shug Avery in *The Color Purple*, Miss Lissie in *The Temple of My Familiar*, and Kate Talkingtree in *Now Is the Time to Open Your Heart* bear this out. They prove Black women characters who are, ultimately, self-directed, artistic, independent-minded, and aspiring; and who like Walker herself represent and embrace culturally and sexually pluralistic identities and existences. In addition, these characters seem to embody, imagine, and embrace an earth-centered, polytheistic spirituality – similar to Walker's Womanist.

Finally, in her choice of topography and time in the development of her post-1980s novels, Walker complicates any idea of Blackness, and Black femininity, as monolithic, or even monolingual. Walker creates fictional diasporic Black (African, African American, Afro-Indian, and Afro-Mexican) characters who occupy simultaneously singular and multiple racial/ethnic identities, *as well as* sexualities. Thus, in her post-1980s novels Walker subverts heterosexuality, in the words of scholar June Pamelab, by writing Black women characters who are lesbian as well as bisexual, and without need of remark. In this way, Walker suggests that lesbianism and bisexuality in *Black women* perhaps especially is endemic to Black communities, as well as to the Black experience. Finally, Walker's post-1980s fictional characters, and situations, span historical time, continents (e.g. Africa, North America, South America), and, in the case of Lissie in *The Temple of My Familiar*, lifespans. Walker's novelistic compelling seems to be the creation of a more democratic, more just, more sexually liberatory and culturally pluralistic society, culture, and literature – all of which she provides in her post-1980s novels.

Walker's third novel, *The Color Purple*, brought the already known writer greater national and world acclaim and, significantly, economic solvency. An epistolary novel co-written by Celie, the novel's 14-year-old protagonist, and Celie's younger sister, Nettie (12 at the novel's opening), *The Color Purple*, like much of Walker's post-1980s fiction, develops from a question in the character/narrator's mind. "What is happening to me?" writes Celie, at 14, and to a God she imagines as white and deaf. What is happening is that Celie's "Pa," Alfonso, actually her stepfather, a fact unknown to Celie for thirty years, is raping and has twice impregnated Celie – and sold the babies, a boy and a girl, off. At the death of Celie's mother, Pa marries Celie off to Mr.___/Albert, a brutalizing, adulterous, and widowed Black man with four unruly children, who, too, rapes and brutalizes Celie – and out of spite keeps Nettie and Celie apart for thirty years by confiscating their letters to one another. It is in the community of her Black and Black-identified sisters (i.e. Sofia, Shug Avery, Nettie, and Mary Agnes) that Celie, over the course of the novel, transforms from a brutalized, victimized, and beholden isolated Black girl, to a liberated, enterprising, loved, and loving *sexual* Black woman in the community. With her sister and children returned to her, and her lover become friend Shug Avery by her side, an aged Celie feels the youngest she has felt in years. Celie has also replaced her image of God as an aloof white man with the idea of God as Everything, which is to say she is now free in mind and spirit of (white) heteropatriarchy-informed Christian theology. *The Color Purple* brought attention to the reality of abuse, physical, sexual, and otherwise, within Black communities, and Black families, especially. Widely celebrated as well as criticized for the novel, in 1996 Walker published *The Same River Twice: Honoring the Difficult* an essay collection detailing the alternately joyful and bewildering experience of writing the novel and seeing it into film.

In her follow-up novel, *The Temple of My Familiar*, Walker centers the character and narrative of African American male intellectual Suwelo, a history professor and the former husband and lover of Fanny, Miss Celie's granddaughter from *The Color Purple*. Significantly, and in an uncharacteristic move for Walker, it is Suwelo, Black male intellectual elite, who links every narrator and character in the novel. Through artistic license, Walker gifts Celie a granddaughter through Olivia, the daughter born to Celie through rape. Fanny, born of an African American mother and an elite African father, represents diasporic Blackness in the novel, even though she grew up in Georgia and in a home with her "Big Mama" Celie, her Big Mama's special friend, "Mama Shug," her mother Olivia, and in the company of Miss Sofia, her grandmother's friend. What Fanny knows from the Black women who raised her is strength, a necessity for autonomy, as well as the value of women and some men's company. Because of this, Fanny, a former discontented college professor become masseuse, deeply values herself and trusts her own way of thinking.

Fanny's struggle, however, is in her marriage to, and later divorce from, Suwelo. Walker suggests through Suwelo's and Fanny's challenging, shifting, and ultimately loving relationship, that is, not marriage – the two must divorce – that men, through blind exercising of patriarchal thinking, feeling, and actions, can kill women's love for them. Fanny divorces Suwelo because she comes to see his regard for everything feminine or suggestive of the feminine as beneath him; his conviction, even, that intellectual thought is the domain of Western men alone. However, and as *The Temple of My Familiar* suggests, while Suwelo is not the man for Fanny at the novel's opening, once he has engaged with and been transformed by his interactions with other characters/narrators in the novel, including Miss Lissie and Fanny, he is closer to being the man for Fanny by the novel's end.

Fanny, too, must grow, however. Part of her growth comes from her understanding through Suwelo that it is impossible to love someone without sometimes contradicting yourself. Walker's *Temple* does not end in a marriage knot. In fact, by the close of the novel, none of the married couples remains so. *Temple* thus demonstrates through the character of Suwelo and his relationship to others, most especially his former wife, the diminishing effects of internalized *and* embodied patriarchy in our most intimate of relationships. The novel demonstrates as well Suwelo's as well as our own ability to actively imagine and create a liberatory, womanist, and Afrocentric life and imagining and, Walker would add, literature – if only we are willing.

In *Possessing the Secret of Joy*, Walker's fifth novel, the author again refers back to *The Color Purple*, and in particular to the minor character Tashi Johnson, the young African (Olinkan) wife of Celie's son, Adam (Adam, too, was born of rape). Tashi's timeline of life events, however, is ahead of and differs from that of the historical setting and time of *Color*. *Possessing the Secret of Joy* is set in 1990s Berkley, California, 1960s "Africa" or Olinkan society, and in Switzerland, at the home of a fictionalized Carl Jung, who, until his death, is Tashi's psychotherapist. The novel opens with an eight-year-old Tashi in tears. Tashi's beloved older sister, Dura, at 11, and a known hemophiliac, has bled to death following the Olinkan tradition of female genital mutilation (FGM). Dura's FGM was performed by a Tsunga, or "the circumciser" (Walker 1992, p. 204), a poor aged African woman called M'Lissa. This same woman would later perform the procedure on Tashi, a situation and experience so dire it will compel Tashi to murder the Tsunga, and so face the firing squad as a result. Seduced by Olinkan (male) elders, as well as by a desire for acceptance by her own people, Tashi undergoes FGM as an adult. Tashi nearly dies from the experience; the Tsunga used broken, unsterilized glass, and no anesthesia, to remove Tashi's clitoris, labia minora and majora, and to scrape off any remains of Tashi's vulva. The Tsunga then sewed Tashi up so tight that Tashi could barely pass urine, sex was painful if near impossible, and giving birth led to Tashi and Adam's son being born with a birth defect.

Walker suggests in the novel that *resistance* to cultural practices, that is, traditions that harm, oppress, and at worst kill the spirit if not the bodies of women, and more directly women as sexual beings, is the secret of joy. In fact, it is not until Tashi decides to murder the Tsunga, and thus to figuratively put an end to the cultural practice of FGM, that Tashi is joyful for the first time perhaps ever. Despite criticism, and following the publication of *Possessing the Secret of Joy*, in 1993 Walker published *Warrior Marks: Female Genital Mutilation and the Sexual Blinding of Women*, also a documentary directed by filmmaker Pratibha Parmar.

In *By the Light of My Father's Smile*, Walker's sixth novel, the author takes on the subject of fathers' responsibility and relationship to their daughters' sexual selves, and sex lives. It is told in multiple voices, the primary of which is that of the deceased Señor Robinson, an African American male intellectual, husband, father, and anthropologist with a PhD in the 1940s United States. When Robinson and his wife, Langley, a pedigreed Black woman and also an anthropologist, cannot secure funding for their work in the United States, they beseech their church to underwrite their studies of an Afro-Mexican people in the mountains of Mexico, the Mundo people. The Robinsons accept the funding which comes with the condition that Señor Robinson introduce Christianity to the remote village and people, and serve as the minister. This means then that at the center of the Robinsons' life and research (and thus family) is a lie about who and what they are. In fact, Señor Robinson initially identifies as atheist.

The Mundo regard, believe in, and celebrate sex as pleasurable, and the most intimate of connections. This way of thinking regarding sex and sexuality is what Magdalena and Susannah are introduced to at ages 10 and eight, respectively. However, when their father discovers 14-year-old Magdalena making love with a 13-year-old Mundo boy named Manuelito, the father falls upon her with a belt (and silver buckle) and brutally beats Magdalena; he does not stop even after he draws blood. Susannah, the younger daughter, witnesses her father's transformation to a monster, in her eyes, from the keyhole of the bedroom door. The novel suggests that the damage done to Magdalena mirrors, to a degree, the damage done to the father and Susannah's relationship. In fact, Magdalena, always a curious and free-spirited girl, cannot understand her father's anger, rage, hypocrisy, and brutal beating of her. As Magdalena says of herself as a girl, "I knew I was wild. Disobedient. Wayward and headstrong. But I did not understand [father's] violence, after I had experienced so much pleasure" (Walker 1998, p. 64). Whereas Magdalena expects understanding, approval, and love from her father, similar to what she sees among the Mundo, her father instead is raging, violent, and silent as her beats her. Señor Robinson's violence leaves lifelong visible as well as invisible wounds that the father must return after death to try to mend.

As Byrd writes in his review of the novel, "Walker challenges fathers to assume a prominent role in the expansion of their daughters' knowledge and understanding of their sexuality" (1999, p. 722). *By the Light of My Father's Smile* does many things, including highlight what Walker regards as the hypocrisy of anthropologists who assume they know better than the people they study. Walker suggests as well through the story of Magdalena and Susannah, the Robinson's daughters, 10 and eight respectively when the family leaves New York for Mexico, that anything premised on a lie is bound to fail. Finally, *By the Light of My Father's Smile* serves as a cautionary tale that violence(s) of fathers enacted on the bodies and psyches of daughters, out of blindness, hypocrisy, or forgetfulness, can cause inalterable lifelong physical, emotional, and psychological damage to all involved, most of all, however, to daughters.

Walker's seventh novel, *Now Is the Time To Open Your Heart*, introduces readers to Kate Nelson, a 54-year-old Black female character who has recently changed her name to Kate Nelson Talkingtree, signaling an internal shift. Kate, a successful novelist, is a six-time divorced mother of adult children who, by now is marriage-averse. Kate is instead in a committed relationship with a male musician a decade or more her junior. At 54, Kate is suffering an existential malaise that compels her to seek out its source. Add to this the fact that Kate's knees have begun to creek, her home has begun to show signs of shabbiness to which she has turned a blind eye, and she, a writer by profession, cannot seem to write anything of substance.

Now Is the Time to Open Your Heart takes on the subject of spousal rape and violence against women, as well as loss, and the lasting impacts of these traumas. Readers learn that when Kate, then a young mother and wife, who had recently lost her parents in an automobile accident, asks her then husband for a divorce, this man, who is also the father of her children, attempts to push Kate off a cliff, abandons her so that she has to hitchhike home, and later rapes her. The book is ultimately about Kate's coming to full consciousness about the traumas and bewilderment of her past, which she does in the company of a supportive group of women, and where she can safely vent and release finally the pent-up rage and silenced words that have made her spiritually sick. Having faced down, felt, and ultimately jettisoned a past that no longer serves her, Kate, at the book's end, now occupies a present in which she is autonomous, loved, *as she is*, in a community of diverse (age, race, ethnicity, socioeconomic class, sexuality) women, has Yolo (her younger male lover), and is creatively reawakened.

In all of Walker's fiction discussed here, the author, a self-defined Womanist, challenges readers to imagine a sexually and culturally pluralistic society, culture, and literature in which the creativity, life experiences, preoccupations, loves, and concerns of Black and Black-identified women, primarily, but also *some* men, are centered, considered, and affirmed. It is this very literature, this very artistic compelling and imagining, that Walker demonstrates in her five novels written and published between 1982 and 2004.

SEE ALSO: Allende, Isabel; Allison, Dorothy; Bambara, Toni Cade; Butler, Octavia; Castilla, Ana; Danticatt, Edwidge; Erdrich, Louise; Everett, Percival; Marshall, Paule; Whitehead, Colson

REFERENCES

Byrd, Rudolph P. (1999). Review of *By the Light of My Father's Smile*. African American Review 33 (4): 719–722.

Byrd, Rudolph P. (ed.) (2010). *The World Has Changed: Conversations with Alice Walker.* Atlanta: Georgia State University Press.

Walker, Alice. (1982). *The Color Purple.* Orlando, FL: Harcourt Brace Jovanovich.

Walker, Alice. (1992). *Possessing the Secret of Joy.* San Diego: Harcourt Brace Jovanovich.

Walker, Alice. (1993). *In Search of Our Mothers' Gardens: Womanist Prose.* Orlando, FL: HBJ Book; 1st ed. 1983.

Walker, Alice. (1998). *By the Light of My Father's Smile.* New York: Random House.

FURTHER READING

Davis, Angela. (1981). *Women, Race, and Class.* New York: Random House.

Hopson, Cheryl. (2017). Alice Walker's womanist maternal. *Women's Studies: An Interdisciplinary Journal* 46 (3): 221–233.

Hopson, Cheryl. (2018). "Tell nobody but God": reading mothers, sisters, and "the father." In: Alice Walker's *The Color Purple. Gender and Women's Studies* 1 (1): 3. https://doi.org/10.31532/GendWomensStud.1.1.003

Palmelab, June. (2011). Subverting heteronormativity: another look at Alice Walker's *By the Light of My Father's Smile. Women's Studies* 40 (5): 600–619.

Sanders, Joshunda. (2013). What greater gift: Alice Walker's legacy continues to bloom. *Bitch Magazine: Feminist Response to Popular Culture* (Fall): 55–57.

Walker, Alice. (1997). *Anything We Love Can Be Saved: A Writer's Activism.* New York: Ballantine.

White, Evelyn C. (2004). *Alice Walker: A Life.* New York: Norton.

Wallace, David Foster

JEFFREY SEVERS
University of British Columbia, Canada

David Foster Wallace, perhaps the most celebrated contemporary avatar of experimental fiction, grew up in Illinois in the 1960s and 1970s, the eldest child of professors who specialized in moral philosophy and grammar, subjects he would take up as a writer. Wallace attended Amherst College, where he studied analytical philosophy and wrote his first novel, *The Broom of the System* (1987), as one of two senior theses. Higher education marked his life from then on: he earned an MFA at the University of Arizona; did a short stint as a philosophy doctoral student at Harvard; and in 1993, moved from Boston to his home state to teach English at Illinois State (including some involvement with its *Review of Contemporary Fiction*), followed by a move west for a job at Pomona College in 2002. In 1996 the publication of his 1079-page novel of tennis, addiction, depression, and deadly entertainment, *Infinite Jest*, made him famous, drawing comparisons to Pynchon, Barth, Coover, and Burroughs. Over the ensuing decade Wallace published two short story collections (*Brief Interviews with Hideous Men* [1999] and *Oblivion* [2004]) and two books of essays (*A Supposedly Fun Thing I'll Never Do Again* [1997] and *Consider the Lobster* [2005]), the latter volumes showcasing his lengthy reportorial works on cruises, political campaigns, and films. In September 2008, having struggled with intense depression for much of his life, Wallace, age 46, died of suicide, leaving behind the unfinished manuscript for *The Pale King*, a novel of bureaucracy, the IRS, and rural Illinois, which was eventually published in 2011.

How to tie together Wallace's multifaceted oeuvre? His self-announced break with postmodern predecessors ("patriarch[s] for my patricide" [Burn 2012, p. 48]) has led to prominent critical accounts by Lee Konstantinou (2016) and others centered on his rejection of irony. More recently critics have begun to focus on his representation of the body, cognition (Burn 2014), and spirituality (McGowan and Brick 2019). Here I propose stillness and stasis as the Wallace tropes that unite all three of these categories of experience. I am interested in unifying his work around what *Infinite Jest* – a book that risks long, climactic stretches in which its two central characters lie on the floor and in a hospital bed – calls the "hero of *non*-action, the catatonic hero, the one beyond calm, divorced from all stimulus" (Wallace 2006, p. 142). States of physical immobility and statuehood, and their associations with both deathly stasis and productive contemplation, draw Wallace's innovative fictions together.

Since the patient lying on the couch to talk is the classic scene of Freudian analysis, Wallace could interweave supine characters with his often parodic exposure of psychiatry's limits. Moreover, Wallace's defiance of his realist teachers at Arizona led not only to manifesto-like essays such as "E Unibus Pluram: Television and US Fiction" (1993), but also to the hero of non-action, his way of honoring influences such as Beckett and existentialist fiction and a means of valuing what those Arizona teachers would have ridiculed as "the bathtub story," in which confined characters contemplate much but never act (Stern 1991, p. 70). Always more than experimentation for its own sake, though, Wallace's stillness and stasis, never singular in their meanings or moral valences, served his varied explorations of psychology, spirituality, and media awareness. Especially early in his career, Wallace needed states of arrest to explore people who were stuck, frozen into routines of consumption, solipsism, and tired rhetorical maneuvers, most famously irony, which he called one of the key "agents of a great despair and stasis in US culture" (1997, p. 49). On the more palliative side, though, increasingly so after *Infinite Jest*, depicting immobility and slowing life to creeping speeds led Wallace to examine efforts to make a willed *choice* to remain still in a world hostile to contemplation, supporting Krzysztof Piekarski's claim that Wallace "intuit[ed] that Buddhist practices offered much of what he was struggling to embody as an artist" (2019, p. 175).

His first novel, *The Broom of the System*, begins Wallace's investigation of loops, cycles, and whole cultures in a rut by having the two main characters, Ohioans Lenore Beadsman and Rick Vigorous, meet at their psychiatrist's office, where they pass in seat-belted chairs pulled by a chain on a circular track. The psychiatrist, Dr. Curtis Jay, simultaneously ridiculous, villainous, and illuminating, is Wallace's first attempt to use fiction to both send up therapy and expand mightily on its traditional remit. Lenore, deeply unsure about her very existence and in denial about an abusive childhood, would ideally break away from her doctor, her father, and many other tracks to confront what one character calls "a world ... stripped of any static, understandable character by the fact that it changes, radically, all the time" (1987, p. 143). But her romantic pursuers offer nothing but control and sadism, while other characters model the act of becoming thing-like. The most extreme example is Norman Bombardini, who wants to eat not only all available food but people as well – an absurd portrait of American consumerism and monstrous immobility. Lenore's brother, caught up in drugs and the nihilism Wallace often derided, is named Stonecipher like his father, but among his nicknames is "Stoney," a joke about both his marijuana habit and his unfeeling nature (p. 161). Submitting to the corporate-familial dictates of Stonecipheco, the Beadsmans' baby food company, entails joining a line of statues, the "smooth, heavy wooden sculptures of ... Stoneciphers I, II, and III" seen in an artificial garden (p. 38). Family and business mimic their community: Ohio's governor has fulfilled his own nihilistic agenda by creating the Great Ohio Desert, or G.O.D., an unlikely tourist attraction featuring a giant statue of himself – as though he "was trying to set himself up as god of the Desert," Lenore says (p. 424). The obscure, conspiratorial plot seems designed to hound her toward this unenlightening G.O.D.

Wallace's early short stories, most written in opposition to those realist teachers at Arizona and collected in *Girl with Curious Hair* (1989), mine the discontented of media-saturated culture. These include Edilyn, the David Letterman guest who narrates "My Appearance" and finds a suspect epiphany in a stunt involving a ring of explosives: despite her marriage being ruined, Edilyn "survived in the stillness created by great disturbance from which I, as cause, perfectly circled, was exempt" (1989, pp. 200–201). Another TV critique, "Little Expressionless Animals," begins with the trauma of Julie Smith and her autistic brother being abandoned by a mother who tells them to touch a roadside post until she returns; it ends with Julie a sad *Jeopardy!* champion, staring blankly at the audience. This story's moments of blankness and being "transfixed" (p. 18), as well as lyrical analysis (drawing on John Ashbery's poetry) of slight facial movements, are Wallace addressing an entertainment-obsessed culture that risks falling into the gape-mouthed stasis of "expressionless" emptiness. In the ending novella, "Westward the Course of Empire Takes Its Way," TV again recapitulates trauma when adman J.D. Steelritter plans an apocalyptic McDonald's commercial that will kill all the participants and leave him lying in the road: "He'll relax and feel the great heavy earthspin beneath him" (pp. 310–311). "Westward," responding by complicated means to Barth's self-conscious denial of reader pleasures, is Wallace's first attempt at a narrative of stalling and slow time, a technique he would deploy to greater effect in *Oblivion* and after. In "Westward," stalling the characters' trip allows the story to end on a note of calm, countering J.D.'s perverse relaxation: "Relax. Lie back. I want nothing from you. . . . You are loved" (p. 373).

This ending seems, in hindsight, only a momentary reprieve, since when Wallace returned to publishing in 1996, *Infinite Jest* depicted corpses lying on couches and literalized Neil Postman's 1985 title, *Amusing Ourselves to Death*. Wallace's title film, a Macguffin linking the terrorists and spies who want to control it, kills viewers by causing them to stop all functioning in favor of endless watching, producing the "rictus of a face" (2006, p. 79). This film's "recursive loop" (p. 54) dictates the logic of other thoughtless pursuits: students at Enfield Tennis Academy suffer through mind-numbing repetitions and watch a film in which "Stan Smith's follow-through loops seamlessly into his backswing" (p. 112); the United States is addicted to waste-to-energy recycling based on annular fusion; and drug and alcohol addicts live in the grimmest ruts of all, including, in an early scene, a man who ritually quits with one last binge. The Shakespearean title for novel and film suggests endless pleasure paired with the *memento mori* evoked by Yorick's skull, and Wallace casts this video-age dystopia into centuries-long traditions of the danger in sublimity, beauty turned into monstrosity able to freeze its viewer. The Medusa's face turning witnesses to stone turns up as an analogue to the film, and Joelle van Dyne, probably the film's star (much remains unresolved), wears a veil as though she is a medieval maiden, either because she is hideously deformed, astonishingly beautiful, or deformed *by* her beauty. Joelle's first long scene involves her overdosing on crack in a misguided attempt to achieve the ecstatic look of Bernini's sculpted St. Theresa. There are also nightmares involving a "face in the floor" (p. 254), but the truly horrific face throughout is that of depression. As a character observes after a tale of a lobotomy, mental illness can produce an urge for the worst stasis of all: the face of "anhedonia, complete psychic numbing. I.e. death in life" (p. 698).

The best art, Wallace knew, acknowledges the stillness, stasis, and mortality at the heart of existence while still communicating dynamically with its audience, but the balance is tricky. The avant-garde films of James Incandenza are justly accused of being "narratively dull and plotless and static" (2006, p. 911), and though *Infinite Jest* shares his work's "anticonfluential" (p. 65) qualities, the novel wants active reader minds, the opposite of the passivity films here inspire. James, his skills in quantum physics, optics, and filmmaking having led to murder and dangerous energy production, returns after death as a "wraith" seemingly punished by having to reckon with slow time, in ways that embody Wallace's ideas about the intertwining of stillness, truth, and communication (p. 829). Wraiths "move at the speed of quanta," he explains on hospital visits to Don Gately, and so "it took incredible discipline and fortitude and patient effort to stay stock-still . . . long enough" to be visible and communicative (p. 831). As the wraith describes these trials floating in "a strange cross-legged posture" (p. 832), Wallace uses a unique gothicism and a version of Buddhism to encourage meditative stillness and patient listening in living readers.

Wallace's fame in the wake of *Infinite Jest* intensified his use of the statue image, a countervailing trope to the wraith's effortful stillness. A coach warns of young players becoming "slaves to the statue," meaning slaves to "entertainment and personality" (2006, p. 661). D.T. Max's biography shows how often Wallace employed the image to describe his fears: in 1997 Wallace "was wondering whether he hadn't become a literary statue, 'the version of myself' as he wrote a friend . . ., 'that I want others to mistake for the real me . . . a Mask, a Public Self'" (Max 2012, p. 240). This statue-self is portrayed by the poet (like Wallace, the winner of a MacArthur "genius grant") who lies languidly poolside in "Death is Not the End," near the start of *Brief Interviews with Hideous Men*. The "Brief Interview" stories, scattered throughout, are not technically therapy sessions but constantly evoke their atmosphere, continuing Wallace's testing of psychiatry's limits, as do stories of unprocessed childhood suffering like "Signifying Nothing" and "The Depressed Person." One story, rendered as a playscript, features a Lear-like father raving from his hospital bed, while a Hideous Man also speaks from a bed (in an asylum) about a masturbatory childhood fantasy of stopping time itself. This satirized, grotesque man, though, is humanized in "Forever Overhead," about a boy ("you") anxious about the high dive. As the boy delays diving, Wallace writes what could be an epigraph for his paradoxical narratives in which voluminous thought and meager action seem out of sync: "There's been time this whole time. You can't kill time with your heart" (1999, p. 15).

Oblivion takes its title from a story about sleep but names a blank state that haunts, in Wallace's account, almost all waking life. Having largely left behind his relentless satire of slack-jawed audiences, Wallace turns most often in *Oblivion* to a more general examination of attention and trauma, topics considered by the narrator of "The Soul is Not a Smithy," who remains in his school desk, daydreaming, during a hostage situation. As Stephen J. Burn argues, Wallace's decades-long interest in popular neuroscience arises most vividly in *Oblivion* and *The Pale King*, books he developed in tandem. No scene is ever actually static, every moment bursting, Burn writes, with "sensory overload" managed by a "nonconscious filter" (2014, p. 164). Still, the effort to gain spiritual benefit from meditative stillness remains paramount in *Oblivion*. In "Good Old Neon," Neal crystallizes the dual possibilities in stillness for Wallace when describing his meditation class: his teacher gives him an award reading "CHAMPION MEDITATOR, MOST IMPRESSIVE WESTERN STUDENT, THE STATUE" (2004, p. 160). Treating spirituality as though it were sports, Neal converts stillness from training for mindfulness into mere show. Another anecdote from Max is relevant here: in 2001 Wallace attended a meditation retreat in France under Zen master Thich Nhat Hanh but "left early." Max summarizes, "He found that writing about [meditative bliss] and achieving it for oneself were two different things" (2012, p. 262).

The Pale King marked Wallace's most ambitious attempt at a novel of stillness and stasis. The boredom of IRS tax accounting, often noted in reviews as the book's major theme, defines characters' relationship to time and work, but just as prominent are concomitant states of stillness, often suggesting a sacredness in the civic service of tax examination. The word "stillness" occurs in the book's 540 pages more than seventy times, particularly when the monk-like examiners are described. Wallace refashions old techniques (a long political dialogue occurs in a stalled elevator; there is a detailed consideration of a traffic jam) within the larger context of repetitive work and slow-moving government. One way of understanding the book, assembled by editor Michael Pietsch in 2011 from Wallace's discontinuous manuscript, is as a response to nervous airplane passenger Claude Sylvanshine's mind near the start: "nothing would hold still in his head in all the confined noise" (2012b, p. 8). Holding still, mentally and physically, might be the antidote to the "Total Noise" of an information-saturated culture Wallace bemoaned in a 2007 essay (2012a, p. 301). Concentration seems a superpower of sorts throughout *The Pale King*, but in this paranoid plot it is trauma that has mysteriously and ironically led to this skill. Toni Ware's accounting prowess, for instance, seems tied to her ability to stare unblinkingly and "play dead" during childhood sexual abuse (2012b, p. 66).

Wallace is more keen than ever to explore the palliative effects of stillness in this final work, but often, as in "Good Old Neon," characters pervert Buddhist principles in practice. An unnamed boy in §36 uses body-contorting yogi techniques to kiss every inch of his skin, an ironic quest for self-love amid parental neglect. The dissolute Chris Fogle becomes a convert to the vocation of tax-examining, but earlier his various accidentally meditative tools consist of an appetite-suppressing drug, staring at the wall, and twirling a soccer ball while watching soap operas. Shane Drinion, the most hopeful case (because his meditative acts are inherently social?), takes the efforts of *Infinite Jest*'s wraith to sit stock-still and listen and achieves a powerful empathy in the real world, if also with magical levitation: while he focuses intently on a co-worker's suffering, Drinion's backside rises "1.75 inches off the chair seat" (2012b, pp. 497–498). Pietsch places last in *The Pale King* an appropriate destination for the Wallace of stillness, the Wallace so restless over the practice's frequent failure. The second-person scene offers advice from a quasi-therapist who seems untrustworthy. "The way we start is to relax and become aware of the body," she says to a reclining worker ("you"). "It is at the level of the body that we proceed . . . Do not try to relax" (p. 540). This moment of attempted relaxation, like so many others created by Wallace, places its reader on edge, about to learn even more about the important challenges arising from trying to lie still.

SEE ALSO: After Postmodernism; Barth, John; Fiction and Affect; Fictions of Work and Labor; Franzen, Jonathan; Hypertext Fiction and Network Narratives; Minimalism and Maximalism; Pynchon, Thomas; Realism after Poststructuralism; Saunders, George

REFERENCES

Burn, Stephen J. (ed.) (2012). *Conversations with David Foster Wallace*. Jackson: University Press of Mississippi.

Burn, Stephen J. (2014). A paradigm of the life of consciousness: *The Pale King*. In: *David Foster Wallace and "The Long Thing": New Essays on the Novels* (ed. Marshall Boswell), 149–168. New York: Bloomsbury.

Konstantinou, Lee. (2016). *Cool Characters: Irony and American Fiction*. Cambridge, MA: Harvard University Press.

Max, D.T. (2012). *Every Love Story is a Ghost Story: A Life of David Foster Wallace*. New York: Penguin Books.

McGowan, Michael and Brick, Martin. (eds.) (2019). *David Foster Wallace and Religion: Essays on Faith and Fiction*. New York: Bloomsbury.

Piekarski, Krzysztof. (2019). Zen Buddhist philosophy lurking in the work of David Foster Wallace. In: *David Foster Wallace and Religion: Essays on Faith and Fiction* (ed. Michael McGowan and Martin Brick), 175–185. New York: Bloomsbury.

Stern, Jerome. (1991). *Making Shapely Fiction*. New York: Norton.

Wallace, David Foster. (1987). *The Broom of the System*. New York: Avon Books.

Wallace, David Foster. (1989). *Girl with Curious Hair*. New York: Norton.

Wallace, David Foster. (1997). *A Supposedly Fun Thing I'll Never Do Again: Essays and Arguments*. New York: Little, Brown.

Wallace, David Foster. (1999). *Brief Interviews with Hideous Men*. Boston: Little, Brown.

Wallace, David Foster. (2004). *Oblivion*. New York: Little, Brown.

Wallace, David Foster. (2006). *Infinite Jest*, 10th anniv. ed. New York: Back Bay Books; 1st ed. 1996.

Wallace, David Foster. (2012a). *Both Flesh and Not: Essays*. New York: Little, Brown.

Wallace, David Foster. (2012b). *The Pale King: An Unfinished Novel*. New York: Back Bay Books; 1st ed. 2011.

FURTHER READING

Boswell, Marshall and Burn, Stephen J. (eds.) (2013). *A Companion to David Foster Wallace Studies*. New York: Palgrave Macmillan.

Clare, Ralph. (ed.) (2018). *The Cambridge Companion to David Foster Wallace*. Cambridge: Cambridge University Press.

Hayes-Brady, Clare. (2016). *The Unspeakable Failures of David Foster Wallace*. New York: Bloomsbury Academic.

Severs, Jeffrey. (2017). *David Foster Wallace's Balancing Books: Fictions of Value*. New York: Columbia University Press.

Wallace, David Foster. (2014). *The David Foster Wallace Reader*. New York: Little, Brown.

Ward, Jesmyn

AGNIESZKA TUSZYNSKA
Queensborough Community College/CUNY, USA

Jesmyn Ward is an African American novelist, memoirist, and essayist, whose lyrical prose has garnered a slew of literary prizes, including the MacArthur "Genius Grant" and two National Book Awards, as well as comparisons to Nobel Prize winner Toni Morrison. Although she was born in Oakland, California, it is more accurate to say that Ward is from DeLisle, Mississippi, a small Gulf Coast town to which her parents returned when she was three, after their youthful sojourn in the West. The oldest of her parents' four children, Ward grew up surrounded by a community where most people share not only ancestors – close to 200 of DeLisle's residents are related to Ward's parents – but also transgenerational poverty and racism. As Ward's writing illustrates, rural Mississippi became inescapable for her, both as the setting of her major works and as the home from which she tried to run yet to which always returned.

Ward's mother struggled to support her family after her separation from her husband, and made a living cleaning white people's houses. One of her employers, a wealthy lawyer, offered to send her oldest daughter to the private Episcopalian school where his own children went. Then 12-year-old Ward, who was an avid reader and motivated student, was thus exposed both to an educational opportunity and to the racist prejudice of her mostly white classmates. Not allowing the bullying to dampen her drive, Ward resolved to do what no one else in her family had done before: go to college, and thus escape. Escape she did, although not permanently. Ward went to Stanford University where she earned a BA in English and a Master's in communication, and where she also discovered being away from Mississippi made her feel lonely and homesick. Having completed her studies in 2000, she returned to DeLisle. However, she was soon forced to confront the joblessness of her home region. Unable to find work in her hometown, in October 2000, Ward made a trip to New York City to interview for a job in the publishing industry.

While she was away, her brother Joshua was killed in an accident caused by a drunk driver. The white driver would later be ordered to pay restitution, which he never paid, and was sentenced to five years in prison, of which he served three (Ward 2013, p. 235). Her brother's death and its aftermath left Ward deeply traumatized. Her 2013 memoir, *Men We Reaped*, explores the circumstances of Joshua's death, her own feelings about it, and the grim legacy of devaluing young Black men's lives in Mississippi. As Ward said in an interview, she is always "writing towards" her brother (Bowean 2018).

After a brief time living and working in New York City following her brother's death, Ward was accepted into an MFA program at the University of Michigan. The writing she completed while she was there laid the foundation for her first novel, *Where the Line Bleeds* (2008). Throughout her time in Michigan, she spent winter, spring, and summer breaks in Mississippi and longed to go back home. It was homesickness that brought her to DeLisle after completing her MFA in 2005, and that made her postpone a return to Ann Arbor where she was supposed to start a teaching position. As a result, Ward was caught up in Hurricane Katrina, barely surviving the storm with her family, a haunting experience that inspired her second novel, *Salvage the Bones* (2011).

Ward moved back to Mississippi again, and worked as a composition instructor, commuting daily from DeLisle to New Orleans while trying to find a publisher for her first novel. Just as she started considering that the book might never see the light of day, and was looking into nursing as a career path, *Where the Line Bleeds* found a home with Agate, a small publishing house focused on African American authors. Following her first novel, Ward was made a Stegner Fellow in Creative Writing at Stanford from 2008 to 2010. She returned to her home state as the John and Renée Grisham Writer in Residence at the University of Mississippi for 2010/11. Next came a position as a creative writing professor at the University of Alabama leading up to her most recent, and likely permanent, return to DeLisle in 2014 and a faculty position in Tulane University's English Department. While she continues to perceive her bond with Mississippi as a love–hate relationship, she no longer plans to escape, recognizing that she is bound "by a love so thick it choked me," as she writes in her memoir (2013, p. 195).

That love has made place a defining feature of Ward's writing. Her hometown provides the setting for all her books, including the memoir and the three novels in which DeLisle is fictionalized as Bois Sauvage. Little can be understood about Ward's characters without understanding where they live and how foundational that place is in the formation of their identities, social relations that nurture or limit them, the ways that history affects their present, and their resulting vision of the future. Within that setting, the motif of family bonds – the struggle to protect them and the damage they suffer – recurs in Ward's writing. Family is both a source of sustenance and a structure bound to suffer under the weight of devastating poverty, racist violence, and addiction driven by hopelessness. Ward's emphasis on the price her characters pay for being Black, poor, and Southern manifests in the sense of loss present in all her books. That loss often comes from death, or from the lack of viable reason to maintain hope. Her exploration of the lives – and deaths – of young Black men in the South is matched by her attention to the plight of young Black girls whose voices have often gone unheard not only by the white world but also by those closest to them. But equally important to her characters' experiences of loss and struggle is Ward's insistence on their survival, and the value and wonder of lives lived against the odds. Blood, a frequent element in Ward's writing, symbolizes suffering as much as life, a proof of the characters' staying alive.

Ward's commitment to representing her community has direct implications for her stylistic choices. When Betsy Burton of the American Booksellers Association called Ward "the new Toni Morrison," at least in part the comparison had to do with the lyrical quality of Ward's prose, which contrasts sharply with the bleak reality of the world she writes about. But her poetic language has not always met with praise; in an interview, Ward recalled the critical responses she received during her years in a creative writing program when a more spare writing style was the trend (Ramsey 2019). The main objection has been grounded in the idea that the uneducated characters she writes about in the first person are unlikely to use the lavish language with which she equips them. But to Ward, giving her characters sophisticated language to express their thought processes, while their speech remains colloquial, allows her to render the complexity of their inner lives. She credits William Faulkner with the origin of her distinction between the way her characters speak and the language that expresses their interior lives. The poetry of Ward's prose, then, is another way she illustrates the humanity of people who are often perceived solely through the prism of the material scarcity of their lives.

Originating in the thesis Ward submitted for her MFA, her first novel, *Where the Line Bleeds*, introduces Bois Sauvage, the fictional counterpart of DeLisle, and centers on twin brothers Joshua and Christophe, whose graduation from high school coincides with post-Katrina despair and joblessness. Raised by their grandparents, the boys navigate early adulthood and the world of drugs and dead-end jobs, while trying to balance loyalties to their family and each other. Ward (Berry 2009) has said that Jean Toomer's Harlem Renaissance novel, *Cane* (1923), was a strong influence on her novelistic debut. To her, Toomer's book captured the fascinating quality of the South that she too felt inspired by and compelled to render. *Where the Line Bleeds* was a 2009 Essence Book Club Selection, a recipient of a 2009 Honor Award from the Black Caucus of the American Library Association, and a winner of the 2009 Hurston/Wright Legacy Award for fiction. Yet, retrospectively, in a gesture of startling self-criticism, Ward would write in her memoir that the boys she created in *Where the Line Bleeds* "weren't *real*" (2013, p. 70). The twins in her first novel are composites of the different young men she knew in her hometown, including her brother, friends, and cousins. Writing in 2013, she admits that the love she felt for those characters prevented her from exposing the full reality of their lives, rendering them less multidimensional. The characters in Ward's next two novels would not be granted the same protections.

Ward's second novel, *Salvage the Bones*, tells a story of familial love and community bonds that spans the ten days preceding

Hurricane Katrina, the day of the storm, and the day after. To a reader familiar with Ward's first novel, *Salvage the Bones* may read like an earlier chapter of a larger collective saga, with some of the same characters populating both novels. At the center of the narrative is Esch Batiste, a pregnant 15-year-old girl, surrounded by men – father, three brothers, and friends – and so lonely and wanting for affection that her brother Skeetah's love for his pit bull inspires her envy. Her name, with its onomatopoeic likeness to a shushing sound (at one point, Esch is unsure whether Skeetah is calling her name or quieting her), points to the novel's goal to give voice to young Black women in the rural South, to empower the kinds of characters that Ward herself as a young girl could not find in the books she was reading. In recognition of that effort, Ward won the 2012 Alex Award, which recognizes books written for adults that have special appeal to young adults. This is also the novel that led to Ward's first National Book Award for Fiction in 2011. In her acceptance speech, Ward said: "I wanted to write about the experiences of the poor, and the Black and the rural people of the South, so that the culture that marginalized us for so long would see that our stories were as universal, our lives as fraught and lovely and important, as theirs."

Ward's memoir, *Men We Reaped* (2013), recounts the lives and deaths of five young men, including Ward's brother Joshua, who grew up in the author's coastal community and died between 2000 and 2004. The book's title and one of its epigraphs come from a quotation from Harriet Tubman: "We saw the lightning and that was the guns; and then we heard the thunder and that was the big guns; and then we heard the rain falling and that was the gun falling; and when we came to get in the crops, it was dead men that we reaped." With this reference, Ward draws attention to the fact that, even if not linked in an immediate way, all five deaths involved a degree of violence – getting hit by a drunken driver, being killed by a train, a suicide, a murder, and a heart attack probably linked to cocaine – and were connected by the Southern legacy of perceiving the lives of poor Black people as devoid of value. The book met with critical acclaim, winning the 2014 Chicago Tribune Heartland Prize for Nonfiction, being named a finalist for the 2013 National Books Critics' Circle Award for Autobiography and the 2014 Hurston/Wright Legacy Award for Nonfiction, and being included on the New York Times Notable Books list.

Speaking about the emotional implications of writing her memoir, Ward called it "the hardest task that I've undertaken in my life because it required me to sit with my grief" (Bowean 2018). Apart from the necessity to face her own pain up front, Ward was confronted with other difficulties while working on *Men We Reaped*. While her community in DeLisle welcomed her previous books with pride, the publication of the memoir evoked a more complicated response, with some people resenting Ward's frankness in portraying the young men as both beautiful and flawed. While her community's response to losing young people has traditionally been to "sanitize" their memory and preserve them as "angels," Ward's memoir did "the exact opposite" (Bowean 2018). As with the humanizing work of her fiction, in her autobiographical writing Ward refuses to reduce people to their simplified versions.

Sing, Unburied, Sing (2017) is the first novel Ward has written since moving back to Mississippi. Yet again, Ward returns to Bois Sauvage and focuses on a family. Of the three first-person narrators, Jojo, a 13-year-old boy living with his sister Kayla and his maternal grandparents, is the one to open the novel. His Black mother, Leonie, who had him at age 17, struggles with drug addiction, and his white father, Michael, whose cousin killed Leonie's brother years earlier, is completing his sentence at the notorious Parchman prison. Inspired by another Mississippi-based novel, William Faulkner's *As I Lay Dying* (1930), Ward centers the main events of *Sing* around a road trip that Jojo's mother takes with her children and a friend to bring her husband home after his release. But while the family in Faulkner's novel travels across Mississippi with a body, Ward's characters are accompanied by two ghosts of Black boys who died violent deaths and cannot find peace. The spirits allowed Ward to make literal what her fiction often communicates in other ways: that the past lives on in the present, especially in the South. Ward writes, "Mississippi is the memory America invokes whenever it wants to convince itself that racial violence and subjugation are mostly lodged in the past, that they have no space in our present moment" (Ward 2018). But the novel uses the simultaneity of the past and present and the haunting presence of ghosts to show that there is no escaping the racist history of the American South, or America in general; rather, the past needs to be accounted for and faced squarely. Ward won the National Book Award for the novel, thus joining Faulkner and a handful of others who have been awarded the prize twice, and making her the first woman and the first African American to join the ranks of two-time winners. *Sing* also won an Anisfield-Wolf Book Award and that same year Ward became the recipient of a MacArthur Fellowship.

The focus on forgotten or silenced voices in *Sing, Unburied, Sing* and Ward's other works is also an integral component of her writing process. Ward says that she is "not a plotter" (Bowean 2018). Rather than asking herself *what* she should write about next, she tries to figure out *who* to write about next – whose story needs to be told. Over the years, that process has led her to delve into lives and histories with which she was less familiar. While her first novel required no research, and the research for her second focused mostly on the hurricane season, in *Sing* she felt challenged by a territory she knew little about, particularly regarding the history of Parchman Penitentiary, and research played an important role in her process. This trajectory continues, as Ward's next novel will deal with New Orleans' past as the hub for the domestic slave trade.

While almost all of her writing focuses on her Mississippi coastal community, Ward gave voice to her broader concerns about racial relations in America by editing an anthology of essays and poems on race by Black American writers, *The Fire This Time* (2016). With her usual attention to the complicated relationship between the past and the current moment, Ward's title references James Baldwin's 1963 essay *The Fire Next Time*. With its nod to Baldwin's nuanced scrutiny of American race relations, and with its dedication "To Trayvon Martin and the many other black men, women, and children who have died and been denied justice for these last four hundred years," the anthology delivers a set of sobering reflections on the failings of the American progress narrative with respect to race, while at the same time reinforcing Black Americans' perseverance and determination to continue hoping. While harrowing, the contributions to the collection also celebrate love, family, and survival, a balance Ward maintains in her own novels and memoir. Ward has pointed out that Black people are "often reduced to our trauma but we're more than that" (Bowean 2018).

Now a mother of two, Ward lives with her children in DeLisle, the place that has given her as much as it has taken away. Her daughter goes to the same school that Ward once attended as a result of a wealthy white benefactor's generosity. Her decision to move back and to raise her children in this home-place riddled with hardship has been a source of internal conflict and worry. The grief that permeates her writing translates also into fear of future loss. But, as always, fear for Ward is coupled with hope. True to that balance, she writes:

> I like to think that after I die, my children will look at that place and see a place of refuge, of rest. I hope they do not flee. I hope that at least one of them will want to remain here in this place that I love more than I loathe, and I hope the work that I have done to make Mississippi a place worth living is enough. I hope they feel more themselves in this place than any other in the world, and that if they do leave, they dream of that house, that clearing, those woods, when they sleep.
>
> (Ward 2018)

SEE ALSO: Contemporary Regionalisms; Ecocriticism and Environmental Fiction; Trauma and Fiction

REFERENCES

Berry, Nico. (2009). Getting the South right: a conversation with Jesmyn Ward. *Fiction Writers Review* (August 19, 2009). https://fictionwritersreview.com/interview/getting-the-south-right-an-interview-with-jesmyn-ward/ (accessed July 16, 2021).

Bowean, Lolly. (2018). Interview with Jesmyn Ward for the Chicago Humanities Festival (May 16, 2018). https://www.chicagohumanities.org/media/jesmyn-ward-sing-unburied-sing/ (accessed July 16, 2021).

Ramsey, Marshall. (2019). Interview with Jesmyn Ward. *PBS Conversations* (January 20, 2019). https://www.pbs.org/video/jesmyn-ward-uqgzjb/ (accessed July 16, 2021).

Ward, Jesmyn. (2013). *Men We Reaped*. New York: Bloomsbury.

Ward, Jesmyn. (2018). My true South: why I decided to return home. *Time* (July 26, 2018). https://time.com/5349517/jesmyn-ward-my-true-south/ (accessed July 16, 2021).

FURTHER READING

Brown, Holly Cade. (2017). Figuring Giorgio Agamben's "Bare Life" in the post-Katrina works of Jesmyn Ward and Kara Walker. *Journal of American Studies*, 51 (1): 1–19.

Choi, Sodam. (2018). The haunted Black South and the alternative oceanic space: Jesmyn Ward's *Sing, Unburied, Sing*. *Journal of English Language and Literature/Yŏngŏ Yŏngmunhak* 64 (3): 433–451.

Clark, Christopher W. (2015). What comes to the surface: storms, bodies, and community in Jesmyn Ward's *Salvage the Bones*. *The Mississippi Quarterly* 68 (3–4): 341–358.

Marotte, Mary Ruth. (2015). Pregnancies, storms, and legacies of loss in Jesmyn Ward's *Salvage the Bones*. In: *Ten Years after Katrina: Critical Perspectives of the Storm's Effect on American Culture and Identity* (eds. Mary Ruth Marotte and Glenn Jellenik), 207–2020. London: Lexington.

Washburn, Frances

MARTHA L. VIEHMANN
Retired

Frances (Franci) Washburn is the author of three novels – *Elsie's Business* (2006), *The Sacred White Turkey* (2010), and *The Red Bird All-Indian Traveling Band* (2014) – all of which tell stories about Native women in twentieth-century South Dakota. Washburn (Lakota/Anishinaabe) grew up in the places where her novels are set, on the Pine Ridge Reservation and in nearby small towns. Lakota lifeways and beliefs, US Indian policy and its impacts, the ordinary dramas of rural life, and observations of the land and its other-than-human inhabitants infuse her work. Washburn has also contributed to the field of Native American studies as a scholar and a mentor. She and her former student Billy J. Stratton proposed a new theory and methodology for critical analysis of Native American literature in 2008; while the specific method they proposed has not yet been widely adopted, Stratton and Washburn's assertion of the importance of grounding criticism in Indigenous perspectives has become a significant thread in twenty-first-century approaches to Native American literature.

Washburn is an emeritus professor of English and American Indian studies at the University of Arizona, where she served as Director of Graduate Studies in the American Indian studies program. Growing up on the Pine Ridge Reservation and in nearby towns, Washburn was hungry for something to read, but the library was often far away. So, she turned to hand-me-down comic books for a steady supply of reading materials. Washburn was a working mother before she enrolled in college at age 45. She received a bachelor's degree from the University of New Mexico and continued her studies there, earning a PhD in American studies in 2003. She published her first novel in 2006, when she was in her 50s. Dr. Washburn is an expert at transforming a difficult situation into something positive, or, as she put it in an interview, "Out of the seeds of something horrendous, you get something good . . . As we say in Native-American societies, it's the trickster at work. He starts out to pull some rotten stunt on somebody and it backfires and turns into something good" (Willett 2014). Washburn faced many challenges before she learned that she could get financial support to attend college and fulfill a lifelong dream.

Washburn is a scholar and educator as well as a novelist. Her contributions to the field of Native American studies are small yet noteworthy. Her book reviews are incisive and contain the kind of constructive criticism that is the hallmark of a demanding and supportive teacher. Washburn has contributed to the development of Indigenous literary studies by holding students and other scholars to high standards. This scholarly work also provides insight into how readers can productively approach Washburn's own fiction.

In her 2006 introduction to Luther Standing Bear's (Dakota) collection *Stories of the Sioux* (1934), Washburn affirms the ubiquity as well as the social and cultural significance of stories. She asserts that stories "convey information," "delight, entertain, and enlighten," and "connect us to each other, to our individual spiritual beliefs, and to our place in the world" (2006, pp. v, vii). This introduction also notes that European American readers frequently bring to their reading expectations that differ from the perspective and aims of Native authors, which is in effect a warning to non-Native readers to reflect upon the expectations they bring to reading Washburn's own works.

That distance between worldviews is also an important element in her preface to Billy J. Stratton's monograph *Buried in Shades of Night: Contested Voices, Indian Captivity, and the Legacy of King Philip's War* (2013). There, Washburn notes that her own education, even in college and graduate school at the turn into this century, included material that "so often negates and demonizes important historical American Indian figures . . . while simultaneously glorifying white colonialist oppression and cultural suppression" (Washburn 2013, p. xiii). She praises Stratton for "giv[ing] voice to the silenced Narragansett, Pokanoket, and Nashaway/Nipmuk people . . . and to all American Indian people who only want our side of the story told objectively with grace, dignity, and respect" (p. xiii).

Like Stratton's *Buried in Shades of Night*, Washburn's novels highlight the significance of storytelling and present Native perspectives "with grace, dignity, and respect." Washburn's work therefore shares themes with other, earlier works of Native American literature such as Leslie Marmon Silko's *Storyteller* (1981) and Louise Erdrich's *Tracks* (1988). Silko's and Erdrich's works receive abundant scholarly attention; however, Washburn's works have so far been neglected, except for one piece of criticism (written in Korean) on *Elsie's Business*.

Washburn's critical approach, however, is not always consistent with her fiction. Her article "The Risk of Misunderstanding in Greg Sarris's *Keeping Slug Woman Alive: A Holistic Approach to American Indian Texts*" (2004) cautions that Sarris's "attempt to incorporate aspects of oral tradition within the written word and . . . to make the traditions and lessons of story-telling understandable" may take a "catastrophic" risk by explaining too little to "the more usual Eurowestern reader" (2004, pp. 70–71). In this essay, Washburn urges those who write about oral literature to explain cultural references, and yet Washburn's first novel fits her description of Sarris's work: They both "enigmatically answer a story with another story" and "invite the reader to participate . . . and interpret" (p. 70). It seems that Washburn began with a desire to teach white readers and other outsiders what they need to know in order to understand specific cultural references. But her views apparently shifted to expecting readers to make the effort to teach themselves about the cultures in their reading, just as readers today must learn about Puritan practices and thought to understand the Rowlandson text that Stratton dissects and contextualizes.

Washburn's contribution to critical theory in the field of American Indian studies is a collaborative essay written with Billy J. Stratton, a graduate of the University of Arizona's American Indian studies program. In their article, Stratton and Washburn assert that "the Peoplehood Matrix, as advanced by Tom Holm, J. Diane Pearson, and Ben Chavez" in an earlier article also published in *Wičazo Ša Review*, is a valuable "unifying theory for American Indian Studies" (Stratton and Washburn 2008, p. 51). They argue that the four components of the matrix – "language, sacred history, place or territory, and ceremonial cycle" – are also integral to Native literature, and they demonstrate how the Peoplehood Matrix can be used as an "interpretive tool" for American Indian Literatures "that enriches meaning through a culturally grounded point of view" of American Indian literatures (pp. 51, 54–55). Stratton and Washburn claim that the Peoplehood Matrix is broader than other theories advanced by scholars of American Indian literature, which tend to focus on only a few of the components included in the matrix. They assert that the Peoplehood Matrix allows for local, culturally specific interpretation within a broadly applicable framework.

Stratton and Washburn demonstrate the flexibility of this method in their discussion of language, noting that "the very absence of a Native language within a given literary text can reveal much about the sociohistorical context of the work" and that any language, Native or not, employed "to emphasize the power of the word" is in keeping with Indigenous ways of knowing (2008, p. 58). Likewise, texts that do not explicitly reference sacred history or ceremony may convey the cultural knowledge that is expressed in daily life, such as "the importance of family, of hard work and cultural pride" (p. 64). Finally, the authors assert that the Peoplehood Matrix is also useful in exploring the absence of the four components in contemporary Indigenous life and "what those absences reveal about a given community" (p. 69). Although their application of the Peoplehood Matrix has not yet caught on, Stratton and Washburn's emphasis on interpretations rooted in Indigenous knowledge systems has become a major approach in the decade since the article's publication.

Of all Washburn's works, her first novel, *Elsie's Business*, most explicitly references the cultural components of the Peoplehood Matrix, especially storytelling and ceremony. In this novel, the arrival of an outsider in Jackson, South Dakota, results in the recounting of the story of Elsie Roberts's life and death. Elsie, a young woman of Lakota and African American parentage, grew up in another South Dakota town, but after recovering from a vicious gang rape and the death of her mother, Elsie is offered a new home and a job through the kindness of white people associated with law enforcement and the Catholic Church. That is, the white people who step up to help Elsie are from institutions that wield colonial power, raising questions about their expectations about and projections onto Elsie. In Jackson, Elsie remains an outsider, underestimated by white neighbors and largely ignored by the local Native population. The novel incorporates themes of missing and murdered Indigenous women, racial prejudice, projection, and the figure of the Deer Woman from Lakota stories. Most of her story is recounted by Oscar DuCharme, a Lakota elder who invites the stranger and the readers into the Lakota cultural matrix. Elsie's weak ties to the local community and the centrality of the outsider character to the framing of Elsie's story underscore the significance of the flexibility of Stratton and Washburn's methodology; readers may be challenged to see the novel as a work of Native American literature if their expectations are too narrow. As in Silko's *Ceremony* (1977), this novel attends as much to cultural transformations and the impacts of settler culture as it does to the continuity of Indigenous culture. *Elsie's Business* also employs the most experimental style of all Washburn's novels. The narrative point of view shifts from second person to third-person omniscient, with the omniscient viewpoint standing in for stories implicitly related by two characters. The narrative strategy raises questions about the relationship between knowledge and narrative and about the meaning of stories. Indeed, the challenge of understanding traditional Lakota narratives is underscored by the outsider's inability to grasp the lessons Oscar DuCharme proffers in the Lakota stories he recounts along with Elsie's story.

Washburn's other novels center the perspectives of the women protagonists. Her second novel, *The Sacred White Turkey*, features Lakota characters and a reservation setting. Hazel Latour and her granddaughter Stella narrate this novel about strange events in 1963 that begin on Easter Sunday with a white turkey knocking, or pecking, on their door. Stella is convinced that this bird is *wakan* – translated as sacred but also acknowledged as meaning something that cannot be explained. Hazel, who is skilled in using herbs for healing and is recognized as a medicine person (someone who performs ceremonies), scoffs at the idea that the turkey is sacred, but it attracts visitors whose requests for healing or ceremonies provide a windfall of offerings in exchange for Hazel's services. When Hazel returns from the Sun Dance to find all her chickens slaughtered and the white turkey nailed to her door by its wings, she assumes that her main rival, George Wanbli, directed the violence out of jealousy over her popularity and increasing, though still modest, wealth. But Hazel soon uncovers something bigger tied to Wanbli's role in the Oglala Lakota Nation leasing office. Hazel seeks a form of justice that will stop the corruption without exacerbating the factionalism of the tribe, and sacrifices her own livelihood as a medicine person to bring it about.

Washburn writes in an unsentimental style that resists stereotypes attached both to reservation communities (especially Pine Ridge) and to Native American medicine people. Readers find neither poverty porn nor mystical magic tricks. Hazel believes in the power of spirits and traditional ceremonies, but her plant knowledge is purely practical. There is nothing occult about her practice. From the land and her garden, Hazel gathers medicinal plants and food, which she preserves with care and hard work. She longs for running water to ease that work and eliminate winter trips to the outhouse, and as soon as she can afford to do so, she installs indoor plumbing. Likewise, Washburn represents a sense of community through close relationships with other families who watch over each other's children, through events that bring the people together, and in the web of gossip and mutual concern that connects the Lakota people. While Stella and the other children live with few amenities, they are not victims to be pitied and rescued. Instead, determination and care for others resolve the conflicts within the novel and make Hazel a complex and admirable protagonist.

Washburn includes a mystery in all of her works, leading to book jacket descriptions and reviews that reference solving a crime, yet the novels are fundamentally about characters and relationships, not crime solving. This is especially true of her most recent work, *The Red Bird All-Indian Traveling Band*, a coming-of-age story that explores community life and gender expectations. Sissy Roberts is a young woman without a plan. She works as a waitress, plays and sings in a band with three men, lives with her parents in Jackson, South Dakota, and wonders how she can escape the usual path of marriage and children that all the girls from her 1960s-era high school graduating class typically follow. In addition to dreaming of escape, Sissy is set apart by her one remarkable talent: people come to her to air their problems, and she usually helps them. Since everyone in town talks to her, Sissy draws the attention of the FBI agent who arrives to investigate a suspicious death. Sissy eventually figures out who killed Buffalo Ames (and so does the FBI agent), and she also figures out how to break free of the local norms. She moves to Kearney, Nebraska, lives with her aunt and uncle to establish residency and save for college, and earns her degree from the local branch of the state university. Sissy both forges an independent path and retains her ties to her family, making her story both American and Lakota, like Charles Eastman's assertion about his own life path two generations before her. Charles Eastman, MD, lost his position as the doctor at Pine Ridge following the Wounded Knee massacre because his ability to speak directly to his Lakota patients made the federally appointed Indian agent suspicious. Eastman turned to writing and concluded his autobiography with the words "I am an Indian . . . I am an American" (1977, p. 195).

Although Lakota culture plays only a slim role in *The Red Bird All-Indian Traveling Band* (one chapter includes a brief description of a powwow; there's a smattering of Lakota words), the novel is steeped in the importance of relationships and of caring for one another, although most people most of the time do not treat each other well. Sissy becomes the voice for the Lakota concept of *mitakuye oyasin* ("We are all related") (2014, p. 121). After witnessing an angry man brutally beat another man without anyone stepping in to stop the fight, Sissy bemoans, "Makes me wonder what the hell is the matter with people around here . . . No one tries to fix anything" (p. 123). Sissy attempts to fix some of the problems, often by admonishing men about their selfish views of women and encouraging women and girls to take time for themselves. Thus, Sissy becomes a voice for a budding feminist consciousness that is consistent with Lakota values.

Throughout the novel, Sissy seems to be stuck in a state of stasis, like the plains landscape with a gathering storm in the distance (see 2014, p. 49). She is a young adult who still lives with her parents in a town that is "not quite Pine Ridge, not quite Rosebud" (p. 19). She worries about her future but resists making plans. Finally, a freak accident gives Sissy a rest from the incessant demands of daily life, and she realizes that the advice she keeps giving to others suits her as well. In an epilogue that reverts to the first-person narration used in the opening chapter, we learn the fruits of her epiphany and the continuity of her role as listener people come to in order to tell "the terrible things they did or thought" (pp. 3, 178). While initially Sissy feels that her role as a "human wailing wall" is "a curse," in the end, she realizes it is "a blessing . . . a gift" (p. 178). Like Hazel, Sissy is often prickly and practical, yet her love of the land and of her family provides a clear example of a life lived in the understanding that "We are all related" (p. 121).

Washburn's work is significant for her focus on modern women and girls and her attention to themes that resonate with contemporary issues. For example, like Louise Erdrich's *The Round House* (2012), *Elsie's Business* alludes to the complex criminal legal system in Indian Country where the location of the crime determines whether the tribe or the federal government has jurisdiction, although state and county law enforcement may also claim a role. Washburn also centers contemporary Indigenous perspectives without sentimentality, countering the expectations that readers may have established through their encounters with representations of Native people throughout popular culture and narratives about US and state history. Her first two novels have occasional lapses in narrative economy that pull the reader out of the story. For example, in *Elsie's Business* the inner thoughts of the characters disrupt the pretense of direct narration converted to the third person. In *The Sacred White Turkey*, Hazel provides background information about reservation politics for the reader's benefit, but there is no motivation within the text itself for these details. *The Red Bird All-Indian Traveling Band* avoids these pitfalls. The bulk of the novel relies on a third-person narrator, and the FBI agent's presence justifies any backstory Sissy provides. Focused on one small person in one small town during the summer of 1969, *The Red Bird All-Indian Traveling Band* is a gem of a novel that can sit beside other works of Native American, women's, and regional literature. This novel, indeed all of Washburn's work, deserves the attention of literature scholars.

SEE ALSO: Contemporary Regionalisms; Erdrich, Louise; Glancy, Diane; Hogan, Linda; Indigenous Narratives; Silko, Leslie Marmon

REFERENCES

Eastman, Charles. (1977). *From the Deep Woods to Civilization: Chapters in the Autobiography of an Indian*. Lincoln: University of Nebraska Press; 1st ed. 1916.

Stratton, Billy J. and Washburn, Frances. (2008). The peoplehood matrix: a new theory for American Indian literature. *Wičazo Ša Review* 23 (1): 51–72.

Washburn, Frances. (2006). Introduction. In: *Stories of the Sioux* (by Luther Standing Bear), v–vii. Lincoln: University of Nebraska Press; 1st ed. 1934.

Washburn, Frances. (2013). Foreword. *Buried in Shades of Night: Contested Voices, Indian Captivity and the Legacy of King Philip's War* (by Billy J. Stratton), xi–xiii. Tucson: University of Arizona Press.

Washburn, Frances. (2014). *The Red Bird All-Indian Traveling Band*. Tucson: University of Arizona Press.

Washburn, Franci. (2004). The risk of misunderstanding in Greg Sarris's *Keeping Slug Woman Alive*: a holistic approach to American Indian texts. *Studies in American Indian Literature* 16 (3): 70–82.

Willett, Johanna. (2014). Local voices: Native American author and UA professor Frances Washburn. *Arizona Daily Star* (March 13, 2014). https://tucson.com/entertainment/books-and-literature/local-voices-native-american-author-and-ua-professor-frances-washburn/article_bfe5bc87-dba0-5423-a46c-ce5c4fab2694.html (accessed July 22, 2021).

FURTHER READING

Erdrich, Heid and Tohe, Laura. (eds.) (2002). *Sister Nations: Native American Women Writers on Community*. St. Paul: Minnesota Historical Society Press.

Erdrich, Louise. (1988). *Tracks*. New York: Henry Holt.

Erdrich, Louise. (2012). *The Round House*. New York: HarperCollins.

Goeman, Mishuana. (2013). *Mark My Words: Native Women Mapping Our Nations.* Minneapolis: University of Minnesota Press.

Green, Joyce. (ed.) (2017). *Making Space for Indigenous Feminism*, 2nd ed. Winnipeg: Fernwood Publishing.

Silko, Leslie Marmon. (1977). *Ceremony.* New York: Viking Press.

Silko, Leslie Marmon. (1981). *Storyteller.* New York: Arcade Publishing.

Welch, James

ANDREA OPITZ
Stonehill College, USA

James Phillip Welch, Jr., was born on November 18, 1940, in Browning, Montana (headquarters of the Blackfeet Indian Nation) and was an enrolled member of the Blackfeet tribe. His father was Blackfeet and Irish, and his mother was Gros Ventre and Irish. Welch, along with N. Scott Momaday (Kiowa) and Leslie Marmon Silko (Laguna Pueblo), launched the rebirth of Native American literature in the late 1960s and early 1970s, a movement the critic Kenneth Lincoln termed the "Native American Renaissance." Welch, Momaday, and Silko were joined by historian and activist Vine Deloria Jr. (Standing Rock Sioux), writers and critics Gerald Vizenor (Anishinaabe) and Paula Gunn Allen (Laguna Pueblo), and poets Simon Ortiz (Acoma Pueblo) and Joy Harjo (Muscogee Creek) in exploring the stories of Indian Country, past and present. Since this second generation, contemporary authors – most prominently Louise Erdrich (Anishinaabe), Sherman Alexie (Spokane-Coeur d'Alene), David Treuer (Ojibwe), and Tommy Orange (Cheyenne-Arapaho) – have continued writing about Native communities in the context of their own traditions as well as the legacy of US colonial history.

Welch began his writing career as a poet, publishing *Riding the Earthboy 40*, in 1971. He published five novels, *Winter in the Blood* (1974), *The Death of Jim Loney* (1979), *Fools Crow* (1987/1986), *The Indian Lawyer* (1990), and *The Heartsong of Charging Elk* (2000). He co-wrote the script for *Last Stand at Little Big Horn* (with Paul Stekler, American Experience, PBS, 1993), which, eventually, he turned into a book-length "meditation on a particular historical event" (Catsoulis 2014), *Killing Custer: The Battle of Little Big Horn and the Fate of the Plains Indians* (1994).

Highly praised for his work, Welch received public recognition for his contributions to literature and the wider understanding of Native Americans. Among his many awards are the Indian Council Fire National Achievement Award, the American Book Award, and the Pacific Northwest Book Award. He received honorary doctorates from the University of Montana, Montana State University, and Rocky Mountain College. Especially praised in France, in 1995 Welch was made a Chevalier de l'Ordre des Arts et des Lettres, one of the highest honors the French government presents to foreign writers and artists.

Welch grew up on the Blackfeet and Fort Belknap reservations in Montana, before moving, with his family, to Minneapolis, where he finished high school and briefly attended the University of Minnesota before transferring first to Northern Montana College and then to the University of Montana, Missoula, from which he graduated in 1965 with a BA in liberal arts. The following fall semester Welch enrolled in the Creative Writing MA program at the University of Montana, where he studied under Richard Hugo, the great poet of the Pacific Northwest, and Madeline DeFrees. It was Hugo who became an enduring influence on the budding writer. Hugo encouraged Welch to write about what he knew: life on the reservation and the plains and being Indian in a predominantly white world. Welch would later write that, while too much of the country, reservations were "bleak" and "hopeless," to "a kid growing up, they weren't bad at all. You had friends, your parents loved you, you loved your culture, you rode horses, you put up hay, you fished and hunted" (Welch 1997).

In 1968 Welch married Lois Monk, then professor of Comparative Literature and English at the University of Montana in Missoula, where they made their home. Welch occasionally accepted invitations to teach creative writing and Native American literature at the University of Washington and Cornell University, led workshops and short writing seminars, and gave readings all over the country and abroad. From 1979 to 1990 Welch served on the Montana State Board of Pardons, work that inspired *The Indian Lawyer*. He died in August 2003 after a year-long battle with cancer.

Riding the Earthboy 40 – abstract, surreal, and ironic – is admired for its imagery, precision, and measured rhythms. Many of Welch's poems express desperation, but at times they also voice an urgent longing for a belief in hope, evident in poems like in "In My Lifetime," where the speaker says that even if he is "desperate in my song" he also is "rhythm to strong medicine." Welch stopped writing poetry after *Earthboy* because he felt like he needed fiction's wider canvas to explore his subjects; however, many readers still detect poetry in his fiction. For Poet Laureate Joy Harjo, the collection is "the touchstone for a generation who were figuring out a poetry that had to be assembled from broken treaties, stolen lands, the blues, horses, fast cars and long rough nights" (Harjo 2021). The poet and writer Sherman Alexie has proclaimed the book to be the most important volume of poems in the Native American literary canon.

Welch remained true to his poetry origins throughout his career, as what is most distinct about Welch's writing is the care he takes with language, the precision with which he imagines ordinary as well as extraordinary lives. To everything he wrote about, Welch took an unsentimental eye that, stripped of even the hint of fluff by a poet's sense of economy, critically challenged the romanticized ideas of American Indians populating American mainstream imaginations.

Riding the wave unleashed by the critical acclaim and Pulitzer Prize win of N. Scott Momaday's novel *House Made of Dawn* (1969) and the growing public interest in Native issues following the founding of the American Indian Movement (AIM) in 1968, Welch published his own first novel, *Winter in the Blood* in 1974. The novel established him as a leading voice in Native American literature. *Winter in the Blood* takes an unromantic look at Native/White relations and Native life on the Eastern Montana Plains. The unnamed 32-year-old protagonist lives on the Fort Belknap Reservation in Montana and gradually comes to terms with the haunting memory of his brother's death, learning to put together fragments of stories into a cohesive understanding of the past and his identity in relation to that past. The novel received national attention with a front cover review in the *New York Times Book Review*, in which Reynolds Price described it as "an almost flawless novel" (1974, p. 399). The novel's humor, sometimes not noted by first readers, is seen by some critics as its distinguishing characteristic. Welch himself reads the novel's humor as countering "that vision of alienation and purposelessness, aimlessness" often associated with Native American novels (McFarland 1986, p. 9). In her introduction to the 2008 reissue of *Winter in the Blood*, Louise Erdrich asserts that the novel should have won the 1974 Pulitzer Prize for Fiction, and describes it as a "touchstone" for her when she herself began to write. The 2013 movie adaptation, written and directed by Andrew and Alex Smith, who knew Welch as a close family friend, and starring the Lakota actor

Chaske Spencer (*Twilight Saga*), received mixed reviews. The reviewer for the *New York Times* concludes, "The journey from page to screen may have battered Mr. Welch's novel, but its lamenting heart beats loud and clear" (Catsoulis 2014).

Welch's much bleaker second novel, *The Death of Jim Loney*, features a protagonist who is haunted by the past and disconnected from both his Indian and his white heritage. Unlike the narrator of *Winter*, Loney is unable to interpret the signs that disrupt his life because he lacks the necessary cultural references. Some readers find hope in the fact that Loney actively orchestrates his own death, after rejecting the lure of white assimilation (always already doomed by failure) and moving onto the reservation.

Welch's early work concerns itself with questions of what it means to be an American Indian in a predominantly white world and focuses on the search for identity through the excavation of a meaningful past in the face of the devastating effects of colonialism on tribal cultures. Some later projects increase in historical and geographical scope in order to examine and critique major narratives of American history – such as the myths surrounding the Battle at the Little Big Horn. Welch deconstructs historical representations of American Indians and reimagines US history from the "other side" in order to celebrate the perseverance of Native American peoples.

The 1986 publication of the historical novel *Fools Crow* marks this shift in Welch's writing. No longer content to explore what contemporary Native life is like, the novel imagines what life must have been like for the Blackfeet on the plains of the late 1860s. Welch uses a mix of straightforwardness and surrealism, creating a text that aims to approximate the way the Blackfeet perceived the particular western landscape around and within them. In order to achieve this approximation, Welch, himself not a native speaker of Blackfeet, created a language that can be read as a translation of verbal Blackfeet into written English. One aspect that Welch captures in written English is the formality of the Blackfeet language, often seen in dialogue ("Yes, you speak true, Fast Horse!" [1987, p. 8]) or newly created descriptive terms for the natural environment, such as "Cold Maker" (winter), "Backbone of the World" (Rocky Mountains), or "Seven Persons" (Pleiades). In the colonizer's language, one could say, Welch created a narrative that imagined the soon-to-be colonized culture of the Blackfeet from within. The Choctaw-Cherokee writer Louis Owens called the novel "the most profound act of recovery in American literature" (1992, p. 166). In Owens's reading, the text creates a "conceptual horizon – or 'map of the mind'" through which the reader must pass (p. 157). And indeed, for non-Indian readers, the novel produces an initial sense of alienation, forcing readers to readjust their expectations, and to occupy, if only for a while, an experience altogether "other" from a mainstream American perspective. Much of the novel is informed by the stories that Welch's great-grandmother told his father – who then passed them on to him. She survived the Marias River Massacre of 1870 with which the novel ends. Despite the well-known history lying in wait for the plains tribes, the novel has an optimistic ending, reinforcing an argument underlying much of Welch's work: despite conquest, alcoholism, suicide and unemployment ravaging reservations today, Native Americans are resilient and will persevere.

In his fourth novel, *The Indian Lawyer*, Welch experimented with the mystery genre, portraying a more contemporary and successful model of the American Indian. Published in 1990, the novel has a more conventional, genre-oriented, structure and style than his other works. The protagonist, a successful attorney, gets caught up in a blackmail scheme while serving on the Montana State Board of Pardons. Indian identity is much less important to Sylvester Yellow Calf than to Welch's earlier protagonists. Primarily focused on what it means to be a successful American Indian in white America, *Indian Lawyer* also portrays the increasing distance felt by the successful Indian from his native community. In his analysis of the novel, Sidner Larson describes this shift as "the transformation from insider to outsider" that triggers an identity crisis, "reflecting the complexity of modern life" (1994, p. 495). At the end of the novel, Yellow Calf returns "home" to his Indian community; Welch has commented that he intentionally left Yellow Calf's motivation for returning ambiguous: is he "returning wholeheartedly or [is his return] partly a retreat from the white world" (Lupton 2005, p. 201).

Killing Custer, Welch's only nonfiction work, developed out of Welch's collaboration with filmmaker Paul Stekler on the documentary *Last Stand at Little Bighorn*. In this book, Welch explores from an Indian perspective the history and mythology surrounding the Battle at the Little Bighorn, where Sioux and Cheyenne defeated Custer and the 7th Cavalry. Welch found this project nothing short of intimidating, considering that the battle "may be the most depicted event in our nation's history" (Welch with Stekler 1994, p. 22). His book makes no claims to be a historical textbook but instead is meant to provide an alternative understanding of American Indians through a mix of personal reflection and reinterpretation of historical documents. Richard White, a prominent historian of the American West, reads *Killing Custer* as "both an evocative work of rediscovery and a multilayered examination of how we tell contested stories." In White's assessment, Welch is "one of the finest writers in the current renaissance of western fiction" (1995). The book is Welch's most overt criticism of US government policies and the military's treatment of America's Indigenous population, a legacy still felt today.

The Heartsong of Charging Elk, Welch's final novel, is about a young Lakota who travels to France as a performer in Buffalo Bill's Wild West show in 1889. His story of being stranded in Marseilles, where no one speaks his language, is based on historical incidents that Welch researched on trips to France in the 1990s. Welch here explores how someone finds their way in a radically foreign environment and against great odds. Thematically, the novel complicates questions of home and national belonging and also challenges romanticized images of the vanishing Indian produced by Buffalo Bill's Wild West show (along with Edward Curtis's photographs and countless dime novels) during the late nineteenth century.

Early drafts of the novel, tentatively titled "Marseille Grace," had a rather conventional contemporary frame: the protagonist, Jack, was, similar to Welch's "Indian lawyer" Sylvester Yellow Calf, disconnected from his Native community and heritage. It is through research and his own journey to Marseille that Jack, a professor, discovers the story of Charging Elk's travels in Europe and his eventual life in Marseille. In these early versions of the novel, the narrative foregrounded contemporary issues of Indian identity, loss of culture, and, essentially, an academic path to uncovering a deeply Native story, albeit in Europe, that would help the protagonist discover something meaningful about his own cultural heritage. Following his editor's advice, Welch decided to drop the contemporary frame and reimagine the story to focus not on recovering an Indigenous identity lost in contemporary American life but on "looking for a way back" (Shanley 2015, p. 167) while remaining in an alien, but ultimately safe place: while Charging Elk creates a life for himself in France, his family and the Lakota community he left behind suffer through starvation, the Massacre at Wounded Knee in the winter of 1890, and government policies that would make life increasingly difficult, if not impossible, for Native communities in the United States.

At this time, US government policy and public sentiment followed some version of General Richard H. Pratt's notion that the only imaginable future for Indigenous peoples in the United States was complete assimilation, and thereby to "kill the Indian, but save the man." (In 1879 Pratt founded the Carlisle Indian Industrial School in Carlisle, Pennsylvania, one of the first of many non-reservation boarding schools designed to separate Native children from their families and communities.) The novel suggests that while, within the US context, the Indian has become "nonexistent, a ghost you might say," Charging Elk remains in France and thus, ironically perhaps, has found a place where he can stay alive, and also where he can create a Lakota identity on his terms. Welch imagines a protagonist who escaped Euroamerican notions of Indians as a vanishing people, as better dead than alive, as seemingly incompatible with a nation that imagines itself moving full steam ahead into a future in which Indigenous populations have no place. Welch was working on a sequel to *Heartsong* at the time of his death. In this novel, to be set in 1916, he intended to have Charging Elk take his young son back to America. Thus he would explore both the joy and difficulty of returning to a culture as changed for the Indians as Europe had been by World War I.

In 2002 Welch reflected on the survival of the Lakota, how despite "all they have endured, [they] will always remain Lakota" (Welch 2002, p. 5). Native communities in general have shown great resilience in the face of US colonialism. Today over five million Americans identify as American Indian, Alaska Native, or Native Hawaiian, and there are over 570 federally recognized Indian tribes in the United States. Some of these communities suffer greatly the impacts of colonialization and count among the poorest communities in the Western world, while others have revitalized their economies and cultures, moving through the twentieth and now into the twenty-first century. Welch suggests that contemporary discussions of Native American communities and identity often emphasize poverty, desolation, and loss, over other, equally important, qualities of Native life in America: an enduring sense of community and family, inner strength and great pride in each individual, and a strong sense of maintaining tribal, as well as, individual identities.

Poet Laureate Joy Harjo describes Welch as being "among the best storytellers, those that keep the stories alive" (Harjo 2021). The "taut poeticism" of Welch's language invents narratives through "small gestures," full of humility, humor, and "natural grace" (Erdrich 2008). His work was grounded in the places that he knew, the Native reservations at the Hi-line in Montana, inspiring writers like Harjo and Erdrich to imagine those places for themselves, whether in Oklahoma or Minnesota. Echoing the advice that Welch had received from Richard Hugo years earlier, Erdrich explains that Welch's first novel "helped me to understand that I came from the place I was supposed to write about" (2008, p. xiii).

Welch's work clearly evokes a sense of place – David Treuer has said that "no other writer I know has ever given so much life to the north-central plains of America" (2006, p. 79) – while not necessarily reflecting "real life." Writings by non-white writers often are burdened by reader expectations of delivering authentic portrayals of non-white people's lives to counter white, mainstream representations and stereotypes. Some non-white writers may even lay claim to doing this type of anthropological "repair" work. However, Treuer argues, readers would "miss Welch's genius altogether" if we thought of his work merely in terms of offering a window, unmediated and authentic, onto contemporary reservation life, the material culture of the 1870s Plains Indians, or the cultural narratives propagated by Buffalo Bill's traveling Wild West show. Treuer encourages readers to drop the "Native American" from the fiction of writers like Welch, to avoid readings that search for authenticity, accuracy, and, above all else, "cultural insight," and instead to analyze and appreciate the *literary* nature of his work, work that conjures rhetorical pasts and worlds, not actual ones. Welch's language has had a deciding influence on the younger generation, to writers like Treuer, Tommy Orange, and the poet Layli Long Soldier. Orange writes about his first encounter with the Native American literary canon – *Winter in the Blood* – and how the content and setting were less important to him than "how well the sentences in it are crafted." He calls it "brilliant, brutal" (Orange 2018). Long Soldier, in her award-winning collection *Whereas* (2012), reflects on the guiding presence Welch has on her writing: "be/cause/ when I/sweat over/diction James/Welch guides me/his angle a marginal/slope corner arrange/ment" (p. 17).

SEE ALSO: Alexie, Sherman; Erdrich, Louise; Hogan, Linda; Indigenous Narratives; Momaday, N. Scott; Power, Susan; Silko, Leslie Marmon; Vizenor, Gerald

REFERENCES

Catsoulis, Jeannette. (2014). Montana skies, childhood wounds. *The New York Times* (August 20 2014). https://www.nytimes.com/2014/08/20/movies/8216winter-in-the-blood8217-a-drama-about-alcoholism.html (accessed September 10, 2021).

Erdrich, Louise. (2008). Introduction. *Winter in the Blood* (by James Welch), ix–xiv. New York: Penguin, 1st ed. 1974.

Harjo, Joy. (2021). Foreword. *Winter in the Blood* (by James Welch), xiii–xvi. New York: Penguin, 1st ed. 1974.

Larson, Sidner. (1994). The outsider in James Welch's *The Indian Lawyer*. *American Indian Quarterly* 18 (4): 495–506.

Long Soldier, Layli. (2012). *Whereas: Poems*. Minneapolis: Graywolf.

Lupton, Mary Jane. (2005). Interview with James Welch (1940–2003). *American Indian Quarterly* 29 (1/2): 198–211.

McFarland, Ron. (1986). Interview with James Welch. *James Welch* (ed. Ron McFarland), 1–19. Lewiston, ID: Confluence.

Orange, Tommy. (2018). Why Thanksgiving isn't necessarily a celebration: a Native American writer's take. *The Washington Post* (November 16, 2018). https://www.washingtonpost.com/entertainment/books/why-thanksgiving-isnt-necessarily-a-celebration-a-native-american-writers-take/2018/11/14/c4516a2a-e2d8-11e8-ab2c-b31dcd53ca6b_story.html (accessed September 10, 2021).

Owens, Louis. (1992). Earthboy's return: James Welch's acts of recovery. In: *Other Destinies: Understanding the American Indian Novel*, 128–166. Norman: University of Oklahoma Press.

Price, Reynolds. (1974). Review of *Winter in the Blood*. *New York Times Book Review* (November 10, 1974): 399. https://www.nytimes.com/1974/11/10/archives/winter-in-the-blood-by-james-welch-176-pp-new-york-harper-https://www.nytimes.com/1974/11/10/archives/winter-in-the-blood-by-james-welch-176-pp-new-york-harper-row-695.html (accessed September 10, 2021).

Shanley, Kathryn. (2015). "Looking for the way back": displacement, diaspora, and desire in *The Heartsong of Charging Elk*. In: *Companion to James Welch's* The Heartsong of Charging Elk (ed. Arnold Krupat), 167–195. Lincoln: University of Nebraska Press.

Treuer, David. (2006). *Native American Fiction: A User's Manual*. Minneapolis: Graywolf.

Welch, James. (1987). *Fools Crow*. New York: Penguin; 1st ed. 1986.

Welch, James. (1997). Introduction to our third catalog of Native American literature. Ken Lopez Bookseller. https://lopezbooks.com/articles/welch/ (accessed July 22, 2021).

Welch, James. (2002). Preface. *Rêveurs-de-Tonnerre: à la rencontre des sioux lakotas* (by Maurice Rebeix). Paris: Albin Michel.

Welch, James. (2004). *Riding the Earthboy 40*. New York: Penguin. 1st ed. 1971.

Welch, James with Stekler, Paul. (1994). *Killing Custer: The Battle of the Little Big Horn and the Fate of the Plains Indians*. New York: Norton.

White, Richard. (1995). Last stands. Review of *Killing Custer*. *The New York Times* (April 30, 1995). https://www.nytimes.com/1995/04/30/books/last-stands.html (accessed August 9, 2021).

FURTHER READING

Coulombe, Joseph L. (2008). Writing for connection: cross-cultural understanding in James Welch's historical fiction. *Studies in American Indian Literatures* 20 (3): 1–28.

Krupat, Arnold. (ed.) (2015). *Companion to James Welch's* The Heartsong of Charging Elk. Lincoln: University of Nebraska Press.

McFarland, Ron. (2000). *Understanding James Welch*. Columbia: University of South Carolina Press.

Opitz, Andrea. (2009). A haunted nation: cultural narratives and the persistence of the Indigenous subject in James Welch's *The Heartsong of Charging Elk*. In: *All Our Stories Are Here: Critical Perspectives on Montana Literature* (ed. Brady Harrison), 160–179. Lincoln: University of Nebraska Press.

Shanley, Kathryn. (2006). Remembering James Welch. Special issue of *Studies in American Indian Literatures* 18 (3).

White, Edmund

NICHOLAS F. RADEL
Furman University, USA

Edmund White is primarily important for his formative influence on the fundamentally new genre of gay fiction that emerged in the United States in the last decades of the twentieth century. Starting in the 1970s, White began publishing a series of novels and stories of extraordinarily high literary merit that helped define an emerging, new gay voice in American literature. During this period, White was also a prolific writer of nonfiction, producing masterpieces of autobiography, biography, and ethnography in addition to voluminous occasional essays on sociological and literary topics – all of which helped document gay subculture and sensibility at the turn of the century. Unlike many gay and lesbian American writers of his generation who remained reluctant to identify their sexualities publicly, White saw his sexuality as central to his work. Hence, even his writings not specifically about gay lives or people explore American life within the difference visible from a gay perspective. And the key to his success, White is a man of letters who holds his own among the learned and enlightened voices in recent American and European culture. He is, without doubt, the most significant gay author the United States has yet produced.

Edmund Valentine White III was born on January 13, 1940, into a prosperous upper middle-class family in Cincinnati, Ohio. His parents divorced when he was seven years old, and White subsequently spent much of his adolescence in Evanston, Illinois, outside Chicago. In 1962, he graduated from the University of Michigan and moved to New York City. White relocated to Paris in 1983 (early in the AIDS crisis), and he lived there for the next fourteen years. He returned to New York in 1997 to accept a position at Princeton University, where he taught creative writing until retiring in 2018. Unsurprisingly, New York and Paris serve as settings for much of White's work, and both cities figure into White's exploration of the ways gay lives flourished – differently in Europe and America, of course – within urban cultures at the turn of the century.

White is a virtuoso writer who rarely repeats himself in terms of theme or form. So, his large and varied body of fiction cannot be easily categorized. But his most important achievement may be the gay autobiographical fictions he wrote in the last two decades of the twentieth century. These works are unprecedented in American letters, in part because they movingly document the ways American homophobia shaped and misshaped their gay characters' experiences. They represented that time in the United States when homosexuality was transformed from a criminal or medical malformation into a vital, and at the least semi-legitimate, subcultural community. As good fiction has done for other groups in the United States, White's writings helped give identifiable public shape to a little-known minority constituency.

Of particular significance was a group of novels White consciously fashioned as a trilogy. *A Boy's Own Story* (1982), *The Beautiful Room is Empty* (1988), and *The Farewell Symphony* (1997) narrate the first-person experiences of an unnamed gay narrator much like White himself. The trilogy begins with the narrator's adolescence in the American Midwest in the 1950s, moves through his relocation to New York City in the 1960s and 1970s, and then proceeds into the worst of the AIDS crisis in the 1980s and early 1990s. This story was in a sense continued in *The Married Man* (2000), a third-person narrative in which White explored the life of a named character, Austin (who is not unlike the author himself), and his relationship with Julien, a young French man dying of AIDS in the 1990s (who recalls White's real-life partner, the architect Hubert Sorin).

The shift from first- to third-person and the change from an unnamed to a named narrator in this group of novels was important to the works' meaning. For White's failure to name his narrator in the trilogy seemed like a strategy for representing the ways gay life existed under erasure in the 1950s and 1960s. Consequently, his explicit identification of Austin and Julien from a more objective perspective suggested gay men's emergence into full social subjectivity – albeit circumstances dictated that White would remain ironically aware that a nurturing gay social subjectivity appeared in the West only at that moment when AIDS threatened to eradicate a generation of gay men.

But White's achievement in autobiographical fictions was not merely sociological. These works were also extraordinary examples of literary artistry, ones that experimented with formal conventions for representing clearly the struggle of middle-class white gay men to live openly and on their own terms. *A Boy's Own Story*, for instance, adapted to fiction a narrative from gay oral tradition, the "coming out" story. Before White, this narrative concerned the personal struggle to come to terms with one's homosexuality. But White complicated that triumphalist narrative of individual liberation by combining it with a vigorous anatomy of the deforming impact of American homophobia on his narrator's emergence into adult sexuality. Later autobiographical fictions forged different literary and rhetorical strategies for representing middle-class gay life. In *The Farewell Symphony*, White adapted conventions of memoir and reportage to fiction to emphasize the immense social creativity with which gay men in the 1970s and 1980s reinvented and reimagined possibilities for living outside the demeaning limits of American attitudes toward homosexuality to that point. The novel suggested that it was enough to represent life with journalistic accuracy when one was representing a completely new world of gay experience.

To be sure, White's trilogy and *The Married Man* do not represent the entirety of the author's achievement – either sociological or literary – in autobiographical forms. White's stories about AIDS in *The Darker Proof* (1987) – a collection co-authored with the English writer Adam Mars-Jones – and other stories collected in *Skinned Alive* (1995) as well as the stories from White's late collection, *Chaos* (2007), all clearly reflect aspects of White's own struggle to forge meaning out of his specifically gay experience. We may consider, too, what, in hindsight, looks like another thematic trilogy of works that reveal the complexities of White's response to the HIV epidemic. No single narrative or protagonist runs through the stories about AIDS, the last part of *The Farewell Symphony*, and *The Married Man*. But taken together, these works reflect White's developing literary response to the horror of the AIDS years.

In his stories, we see White once again experimenting with literary form to create fragmentary – and yet still traditionally epiphanic – narrative structures. He did so, he suggested, because he felt that mode was more appropriate for representing gay men at their individual moments of living with AIDS, rather than reproducing the seemingly inevitable trajectory toward death of the novel and then-fashionable AIDS memoirs. In *The Farewell Symphony*, when White's narrator comes to the moment when he has to describe the death from AIDS of his partner Brice, he simply breaks off the narrative with heartrending words echoing the absurdist vision of Samuel Beckett, "I can't go on. I can't tell this story, neither its happy beginning nor its tragic end" (White 1997, p. 411). And, finally, in *The Married Man*, White explored fully, and in brutal physical proximity, the suffering of Julien and the psychological devastation of those who survive their partners' and friends' deaths.

White is, too, the author of eight (so far) novels in non-autobiographical modes. Each is, in its own way, a highly individuated masterwork, and their ongoing, virtuosic experimentation with form and style suggests the degree to which the author is interested in the modes and limits of the novel itself. But they are also linked by a common thematic core: White's concern with the ways puritanical sexual hypocrisy intersects with and distorts American sexualities, intellection, and manners.

White's first two published novels, *Forgetting Elena* (1973) and *Nocturnes for the King of Naples* (1978), are highly accomplished experimental fictions, and they articulate themes that reflect on White's more contemporary work. *Forgetting Elena* is not a gay novel per se. Still, it concerns a young man's attempt to navigate a rarefied social world much like those in and around the gay communities on Fire Island in the 1960s. It is a satire of manners about a community in which aesthetic values have replaced moral and social ones. But one also discerns in it one of White's important themes: the need to refashion oneself in relation to the new modes of being emerging in the 1960s and 1970s. A similar idea lies behind *Nocturnes for the King of Naples*, White's first explicitly gay novel. *Nocturnes* concerns a young man who dwindles into emotional inconsequence when he leaves an older male lover whose importance to his psychological and cultural growth he recognizes only after that lover has died. The novel's highly saturated prose infuses a baroque spirit into its heady evocations of gay desire. So, *Nocturnes* reminds us that in White's work the spirit cannot be easily divorced from what its narrator calls the "hydraulics of passion" (1978, p. 74).

Such themes come to important fruition in *Caracole* (1985), a sprawling Baroque canvas of motifs from various literary and historical sources that may be White's most awkwardly constructed novel. *Caracole* is, on its most fundamental level, a satire of the New York intellectual scene in the 1970s, with characters who are, perhaps unfortunately, all-too-identifiable as real historical personages. Although it contains no gay characters, one critic argues that it was, nonetheless, written from its author's gay perspective (Bartlett 1996, p. 65). And, to the point, it constitutes a potent critique of the dominant intellectual disregard of sexual experience at the time of its writing – and the social knowledge that followed such experience. Certainly, the novel elaborates complexly White's conviction that experience, including sexual experience, is to be valorized over naiveté and innocence. Thus, it anticipates a polemical strain in White's later work, especially his memoirs, that advocates for the need to see sex as a significant epistemological category of inquiry.

Of White's later, twenty-first-century fictions, two are historical novels about nineteenth-century America, *Fanny: A Fiction* (2003) and *Hotel de Dream: A New York Story* (2007). Two others, *Jack Holmes and His Friend* (2012) and *Our Young Man* (2016), are stories about life in New York in the period from the 1960s to the 1980s (thus, in their own ways, they are "historical"). And White's recent novel, *A Saint from Texas* (2020), focuses uncharacteristically, like *Fanny*, on the lives of two women, in this case identical twins from Texas, in the 1950s. These works reflect a broadening of White's focus on forms of desire other than gay men's, and, in fact, seem to constitute an increasingly complex deconstruction of dominant American ideas about sex.

Among its many metatextual turns, *Fanny* satirizes the mode of biographical writing. In it, the fictionalized historical figure, the English writer Frances Trollope, purports to write the biography of another important figure in American life, the Scottish utopian and social reformer Frances Wright. But over the course of the novel, Trollope reveals her disdain for her biographical subject, in some measure on the grounds that Wright's reformist projects fail to account for the desires (sexual and otherwise) of the very people she would help. And in *Hotel de Dream* White pens a rather fierce response to American sexual hypocrisy. He imagines the last days of the great American realist author Stephen Crane, who died young of tuberculosis. The novel is written in a pastiche of Crane's style and American realism. And it imaginatively recreates a novel-within-a-novel about a young gay male prostitute the real-life Crane was rumored to have written before he died. A supposed companion to *Maggie: A Girl of the Streets* (1893), the manuscript was reportedly destroyed by Hamlin Garland to protect Crane's reputation. *Hotel de Dream*, however, attributes this mythical act of gay literary destruction to Henry James, portrayed in the novel as a closeted gay man who stands for a puritanical American hypocrisy that denies gay intellection and achievement its voice. White reveals in both novels, as he did in *Caracole* and perhaps *Forgetting Elena*, a skepticism about modes of thought that cannot accommodate or that attempt too rigidly to systematize sexual sensibility. And in both, he keeps his eye tuned to the ways history and literature – biography and novel – construct or inhibit social possibilities.

Jack Holmes and His Friend as well as *Our Young Man* concern life in New York in the 1970s and early 1980s in ways that stick close to White's lived experience of the period. At times tinged with the nostalgia of their aging author, they are, nevertheless, highly sophisticated literary works. *Jack Holmes* is particularly noteworthy because it is a rare exploration in American letters of a long-term and intimate friendship between a straight man, Will Wright, and a gay one, Holmes. Friendship had been a dominant theme in White's work from the beginning; it was the glue that cemented the kinds of community bonds White explored in gay men's forging a new life for themselves in his autobiographical novels. In *Jack Holmes*, however, White not only explores the differences between straight and gay men's conceptions of friendship, but by shifting the authorial perspective and the characters' point of view from Will to Jack in different parts of the novel, he reveals insightfully how at least one gay and one straight man might see and be seen by one another. The strategy allows White to produce a subtlety expansive, though not apologetic, view of gay life. *Our Young Man* revives White's satiric mode in its story about a young French fashion model, Guy, whose Dorian Gray-like beauty fails to fade after a number of years on the circuit, making him both rich and seemingly endlessly desirable. The novel's brilliance lies in the nuance with which White calls into question exactly what it is that is being satirized – the fashion industry or the world that pretends to a less shallow existence? The point is borne home by the novel's enigmatic closing sentence (Mukherjee 2016). When at the end Guy leaves his young lover, Kevin, to resume his relationship with Andrés, a previous lover who had gone to jail for Guy's sake, White writes that Kevin "felt older and wiser – but in what way wiser?" (2016, p. 282). Thus, he calls into question precisely where true knowledge lies and whether or not the novel, as a form, can answer the questions born of a desire for beauty.

Finally, in *A Saint from Texas*, White tells the story of twin sisters from Texas who lead very different lives – one is a brilliant social climber who grows up to become a sexually sentient French baroness and the other a devout nun who is on her way to sainthood by the novel's end. It is a premise that allows White to explore the ways self-righteous puritan self-denial overlaps the kinds of sexual desires it criticizes. The novel gestures toward the similarity of devotion that sustains both, and becomes a profound meditation on the bifurcated nature of American ideas about self- and sexual fulfillment.

White has also been a significant author of memoir and nonfictional autobiography. It is not clear what precisely counts in this category – works such as White's early and important gay ethnography, *States of Desire* (1980), for instance, combine elements of memoir with sociological analysis. However, *My Lives: An Autobiography* (2005), *City Boy: My Life in New York during the 1960s and '70s* (2009), and *Inside a Pearl: My Life in Paris* (2014) definitely do. Each is a unique literary achievement, and all provide valuable information useful to apprehending the author's autobiographical fiction. To this group we might add as well *The Unpunished Vice: A Life of Reading* (2018), in which White puts on display his considerable erudition about world literature and the ways it has affected his own thought and writing.

What is perhaps most telling about these memoirs as literary works is that they were nearly all written after the great vogue for gay life writing of the 1970s. That movement had something in common with White's autobiographical fictions in that it sought to discover and legitimize a voice or the voices of gay men that had been erased from history up to that time. But in his true autobiographies White does not struggle to find his voice. He writes, instead, as an authoritative guide. In this sense, the memoirs reflect the fruition of his longstanding concern with articulating gay perspectives as essential to American thought and writing. In his memoirs, White is keenly aware that his gay perspective provides a significant and legitimate position from which to anatomize not only gay life but Western culture at large.

Appropriate to this goal, we might also take brief note of White's superior achievement as an author of literary essays as well as his brilliant sociological essays on aspects of gay life and literature – many of them collected in *The Burning Library* (Bergman 1994). Not only has White become something of an arbiter of taste in the reading world, but he is also perhaps our most perspicuous chronicler of the changing discourses of gay life from the late 1960s onward. He is also the author of a magisterial biography of the great French writer Jean Genet (1993) as well as two shorter biographies of writers whose homosexuality he brings front and center in our understanding of their works, Marcel Proust (1999) and Arthur Rimbaud (2008).

The recipient of a number of important awards, White was named by the French government a *Chevalier de l'ordre des arts et lettres* in 1993 for his work on *Genet*, and he was awarded the *Premio Letterario Internazionale Mondello* by the Italian government in 2010 for his biography of Rimbaud. In his own country, he was honored with the PEN/Saul Bellow Award for Achievement in American Fiction in 2018 and once again with the National Book Award Medal for Distinguished Contribution to American Letters in 2019.

SEE ALSO: Mixed-Genre Fiction; Multiculturalism; Queer and LGBT Fiction; Realism after Poststructuralism

REFERENCES

Bartlett, Neil. (1996). Caracole. *Review of Contemporary Fiction* 16 (3): 61–68.

Bergman, David. (ed.) (1994). *The Burning Library: Essays*. New York: Knopf.

Mukherjee, Neel. (2016). *Our Young Man* by Edmund White review – sparkling and steamy tale of a male model. *The Guardian* (June 2, 2016). https://www.theguardian.com/books/2016/jun/02/our-young-man-edmund-white-review-male-model-fashion (accessed July 16, 2021).

White, Edmund. (1978). *Nocturnes for the King of Naples*. New York: St. Martin's Press.

White, Edmund. (1997). *The Farewell Symphony*. London: Chatto & Windus.

White, Edmund. (2016). *Our Young Man*. New York: Bloomsbury.

FURTHER READING

Basiuk, Tomasz. (2013). Theory in life writing, life writing in theory: Edmund White's *City Boy* and gay men's life writing. In *Theory That Matters: What Practice After Theory* (ed. Magorzata Myk and Kacper Bartczak), 125–141. Cambridge: Cambridge Scholars Press.

Bergman, David. (2004). *The Violet Hour: The Violet Quill and the Making of Gay Culture*. New York: Columbia University Press.

Brantley, Will and Roche, Nancy M. (eds.) (2017). *Conversations with Edmund White*. Jackson: University of Mississippi Press.

Purvis, Tony. (2008). America's "white" cultural and sexual dissensus: the fictions of Edmund White. *Journal of American Studies* 42 (2): 293–316.

Radel, Nicholas F. (2013). *Understanding Edmund White*. Columbia: University of South Carolina Press.

Whitehead, Colson

RALPH CLARE
Boise State University, USA

Colson Whitehead's substantial body of work has made him a pivotal twenty-first-century American author. Whitehead is part of a generation of post-postmodern authors, including those whose writing has been called "post racial." Whitehead's novels recall Thomas Pynchon's and Don DeLillo's critiques of power, media, and technology, as well as Toni Morrison's of race, memory, and American history. They resonate with Ishmael Reed's and Jonathan Lethem's riffs on pop culture and genre, and echo George Saunders and David Foster Wallace's eschewal of cynical and media-imposed forms of irony. Yet Whitehead's novels experiment with new literary forms and new understandings of race and racism in America, placing him alongside post-racial writers like Percival Everett, Danzy Senna, Salvador Plascencia, Junot Díaz, and others.

The term "post-racial," however, as Ramón Saldívar writes "does not mean we are *beyond* race" but that we must discover "what meaning the *idea* of race carries in our own time" (2011, p. 575). For Whitehead and other post-Civil Rights Black writers and artists, whose work may be described as "post-black" (Touré 2011, pp. 4–6) or "post-soul" (Neal 2002, pp. 2–3), the result is an explosion of possibilities for what Bertram D. Ashe calls "*blaxploration* or the propensity to trouble blackness" (2007, p. 614). Today's writers, Elda María Román puts it, have the "freedom to push against expectations of ethnic writing and racial-ethnic identities," particularly "through formal play, narrative hybridity, and unconventional character portrayals" (2018, p. 27).

Such a "post-racial" imaginary is evident in both the form and content of Whitehead's work. It explores contemporary American Black identity and historical and present-day forms of racism and exclusion, while self-consciously playing with genre, popular culture, and literary form.

Whitehead's African American protagonists frequently experience the complexities of racial identity and "blackness" in contemporary America. Nowhere is this more evident than in *Sag Harbor* (2009), Whitehead's semi-autobiographical novel about Benji, the 15-year-old son of middle-class Black professionals who spend their summers in Sag Harbor, Long Island, a kind of African American Hamptons. The adult Benji's semi-nostalgic story of these summers loosely follows his teenage fantasy of forging a "New Me" (2011a, pp. 23, 68).

Tellingly, racism isn't a main theme of this post-racial coming-of-age story. Whitehead's true focus is on the nuances of this particular seasonal Black community, its strengths and its contradictions. Racism here does not detract from what is a success story of Black self-determination, both individually and collectively. For example, Benji likens his grandparent's generation (who built Sag Harbor) to "pioneers" (2011a, pp. 51–52, 77), taking pride in their accomplishments.

Sag Harbor becomes a place that Benji and others can experiment with and create their own forms of Blackness. The project is difficult, since they are, paradoxically, "black boys with beach houses" (2011a, p. 57). A W.E.B Du Bois-like double-consciousness dilemma results: either "embrace the beach part" or "the black part – take some idea you had about what real blackness was, and make theater of it" (p. 58). Benji, for instance, normally listens to "white" music, though he learns to mix his tastes with rap and hip-hop in Sag Harbor (pp. 61–63, 143). Indeed, Benji learns to embrace these "contradictions" so that "what you call paradox, I call *myself*" (p. 58). Yet not everyone can. When Benji and his buddies buy BB guns, it allows one friend to "bury his prep school weakness [...] in the scowl of a thug [...]. A kind of blackface" (p. 126). This unfortunate conflation of "authentic" Blackness with being gangsta creates a false binary in which "[y]ou were hard or you were soft" (p. 146). And the "hard" performance can turn real, as "[l]ater some of us got real guns" (p. 147).

The previous generation has fueled this paradox in part by largely ceding the teaching of African American history to "white" prep schools. Moreover, popular culture, particularly *The Cosby Show*, offers a vision of professional Black life that Benji and his parents ambivalently accept as a model of successful "striving" (2011a, pp. 160, 188). However, a troubling race-tinged classism results. Benji's father, for instance, thinks his son's new haircut is too "street" (pp. 87–98), and while "the word *nigger*" is frowned upon by adults, they use it amongst themselves in a friendly way and also to denigrate lower class Blacks (p. 31). Such class divisions are also noticeable in *John Henry Days* (2001) "Strivers Row" (2002, pp. 279–280), in which Black characters appear to fear Blackness, and in *The Intuitionist* (1999), when protagonist Lila Mae Watson discovers that her intellectual hero, James Fulton, was a Black man who passed most of his life for white to avoid Jim Crow racism (2000, p. 151). Claiming

Blackness for these "striving" characters is a complicated and sometimes fraught practice. The post-Civil Rights generation is thus best encapsulated by Benji: "[w]e talked one way in school, one way in our homes, and another way to each other" (2011, p. 147). Inventing new ways to talk and new ways of being means finding new ways of connecting to Black history and creating Blackness in and for a post-racial era.

Whitehead's fiction doesn't just problematize the formation of individual and group racial identities in the post-racial era, it also underscores the structural and systemic forms of racism that have persisted since the founding of America. *The Intuitionist* is a noir-historical novel set around the Civil Rights era and follows Lila Mae Watson, the first African American woman elevator inspector, as she tries to solve the mystery of an elevator crash – which, in typical noir fashion, points to systemic corruption at higher levels of government and society. The novel imagines differing schools of elevator philosophy, the Empiricists and the Intuitionists, which become structural metaphors for a critique of entrenched, systemic forms of racism. While Empiricists fix elevators by attending to the visible, the Intuitionists "sense" the elevator's problems. Intuitionists also believe in its founder James Fulton's utopian ideas about building a "black box" that would initiate a "second elevation" to "*another world beyond this one*" (2000, p. 63).

Lila Mae, who battles prejudice throughout her life, is a follower of Fulton's Intuitionism and tacitly believes in "racial uplift." Yet this alienates her from other African Americans, and her worldview is upended when she learns that Fulton was a Black man passing for white. Suddenly, Fulton's writings seem to be a cruel joke. His notions that "*horizontal thinking in a vertical world is the race's curse*" (2000, p. 151) and that though the race "*dream[s] of uplift [. . .], and hope[s] to remember the terms on waking*," but it "*never does, and that is our curse*" (p. 186) become not mystical visions of a collective "colorblind" future but bitter laments about the possibility of ever achieving racial equality: "He knows the other world he describes does not exist" (p. 240).

Thus, *The Intuitionist*'s metaphorization of infrastructure underscores the structural and systemic aspects of racism. While moments of individual racism abound in the book, the increasingly disgruntled Black community (2000, pp. 12, 22, 27) and inflated nationalist rhetoric about America ending prejudice (p. 80) point to the fact that, despite the seeming progress, the underlying structures of "verticality" – meaning racial, class, social, and political hierarchies – persist. Such verticality undermines the promise of "horizontality" or true equality, evidenced in the segregated "colored city (yet another city in this city, always one more city)" (p. 166). The intuitionists' idealistic belief that society can build another world entails a belief in transcending race and class, but this turns out to be based upon Fulton's lie.

Individuals only have so much agency (like Lila Mae who makes many mistakes) within these already existing structures, institutions, and systems. To be sure, that Lila Mae finds no one reason for "the crash" means that this "crash" – which more broadly means American slavery and the resulting racist social structures – cannot be solved by simple individual means and/or euphemistic rhetoric – it's systemic, a structure that tends to reproduce itself in and through the people who inhabit it.

John Henry Days also explores material infrastructure as symbolic of racial inequality (the transcontinental railroad was built largely by African American and immigrant labor), yet it expands into the territory of "immaterial" infrastructures or America's racial and historical ideologies as perpetuated through popular culture and the media. The novel follows New York journalist J. Sutter who is covering "John Henry Days," a small Southern town's celebration of the man-myth who allegedly died there. Mainly set in the 1990s, the novel flashes back to various moments in history, including a retelling of the Henry myth. Whitehead therefore makes connections between myth, history, and the media.

J., for example, is a cynical, hack journalist, writing fluff that is little but corporate ads: "[n]ot stories, not articles, but content. Like it is a mineral" (2002, p. 21). J., who is increasingly compared to John Henry throughout the novel (pp. 388–389), is thus building media or immaterial infrastructure in a way analogous to how John Henry built railroads. Yet both become tools of capitalism, J.'s experience being likened to ducks being fattened before killing (p. 30).

Worse, J.'s coverage of John Henry Days will contribute to the emptying of history into a discourse of American "progress." The John Henry myth, long ago commodified, ought to be "secreted in altered lines like memory" (2002, p. 103), shared, and collectively changed (p. 159) but is instead profited upon by whites (pp. 255–256). In the novel's present, John Henry is used by the USPS on a new stamp and by the town to sanitize history (pp. 37, 49, 66). J. sees one poster of Henry as signifying "the forging of a nation [...] some real hokey shit" (p. 40). The hokiness, of course, comes from ignoring issues of slavery, capitalism, nationalism, and racism that John Henry's story – whether mythical or not – contains. This flattening of history is evident in a simplified mural of American history in *The Intuitionist* (2000, p. 47), the horrifying "museum" in *The Underground Railroad* (2016, pp. 109–110), and the corporate boosterism that replaces real history in *Apex Hides the Hurt* (2006, pp. 59, 127–129).

Another major theme related to "structures" in Whitehead's work is the question of who "built" America and what progress really means. For, "[p]rogress may be imagined as a railroad line, its right-of-way surveyed through rough plains of trial and error, deep gullies of botched innovation, until the terminus of perfection is reached" (2002, p. 341). *The Intuitionist* also questions the possibility of such perfection in Fulton's failed "other world." Nevertheless, *John Henry*'s ending, in which J. is a new John Henry and may or may not be killed by a mass shooter, suggests J. may have decided to write a real story after all. He finally comes to see the complexity in Henry's myth: "You could look at it and think the fight continued, that you could resist and fight the forces and you could win and it would not cost you your life because he had given his life for you" (p. 378). That the novels' final section is called "Adding Verses" (p. 341) metafictionally suggests that if J. does survive, then the novel we are reading may be the product of J. himself, and it is certainly an indication of the way in which literature can combat pop culture and capitalism's triumphalist rhetoric of America and its past.

Apex Hides the Hurt similarly punctures the notion of progress by exposing American history to be little more than a capitalist advertising scheme. The novel's unnamed protagonist is yet another professional African American, this time an adman with a talent for thinking up catchy names (2006, p. 35). When the small town of Winthrop – named after a white industrialist who "made" the town and whose descendent still holds great civic influence – hires the protagonist to rename/rebrand the fast-growing city, Whitehead explicitly ties advertising language and capital to the making of history and myth.

The protagonist finds himself amidst a political struggle to rename the town either the business inspired "New Prospera" or the historically accurate "Freedom," which the freed slaves who founded the town named it before whites forcibly took it. One character argues for "Freedom" because the name "didn't cover up history" (2006, p. 129) as the Winthrop family's self-serving corporate history has. The protagonist's greatest achievement, however, was imagining the slogan, "Apex Hides the Hurt," for a brand of variously colored bandages for multicultural consumers that promised "[t]he deep psychic wounds of history and the more recent gashes ripped by the present [...] could be covered by this wonderful, unnamed multicultural adhesive bandage. It erased. Huzzah" (p. 90). The ad itself suggested "the commonality of wound, they were all brothers now" (p. 109).

But when we learn that the protagonist once used Apex bandages to cover an injured toe that was eventually amputated, the implications of covering up problems become clear. Indeed, he comes to understand his job anew: "he just slapped a bandage on it to keep the pus in" (2006, p. 183), as Whitehead tightens the metaphorical knot between physical and psychic wounds. Yet the protagonist's epiphany and decision to name the town "Struggle" once again deflates a false vision of America and, like J. rewriting Henry's myth in *John Henry Days*, insists upon the positive power of language. For, the slaves knew that "[t]o give yourself a name is power" and that "to say, I Am This – that was freedom" (2006, p. 206). Whitehead thus lambastes a so-called post-racial America's ideal "apex" of "freedom" as forming a colorblind and history-blind society by pointing out that euphemism and capitalist ad-speak simply mask underlying structural problems that persist and are worsening.

Whitehead's post-postmodern slave narrative, *The Underground Railroad*, and its literalized metaphor of a subterranean transit system continues the thematic "line" of building and structuring of America of *John Henry Days* and *The Intuitionist*. As one refrain in the novel goes, "*[i]f you want to see what this nation is all about, you have to ride the rails*" (2016, p. 262). The novel's reimagining of the slave narrative explicitly connects antebellum, Jim Crow, and contemporary times through the material underground tunnels' surreal, time-travelling aspect. The underground railroad, then, is not simply a one-time (and highly mythologized) route of escape and resistance for slaves and abolitionists but becomes Whitehead's most powerful statement to date about the mutually informing legacies of racism and capitalism in America. Cora, the novel's protagonist and escaped slave, ties the two together with an apt train metaphor: "[s]tolen bodies working stolen land. It was an engine that did not stop, its hungry boiler fed with blood" (p. 117).

Whitehead also twists the slave narrative genre, in which an escaped slave gains physical and psychological freedom. First, Cora, like Lila Mae Watson, is a stoic character, one "who didn't know what *optimistic* meant" (2016, p. 108). Whitehead keeps the reader emotionally distanced from Cora, despite her trials, unlike Toni Morrison's *Beloved* (1987), which stresses community remembering and emotional healing. This resistance to emotional investment calls attention not just to the psychological effects of slavery, racism, and being forever on the run, as in *Beloved*, but also to its systemic or biopolitical (the political management of life and death) side, one that creates and controls subjectivities and bodies through soft and hard forms of power. Hence, the novel's look at "the ledger of slavery" with "[e]very name an asset, breathing capital, profit made flesh" (2016, p. 215). In the end, "'[t]he underground railroad is bigger than its operators" (p. 267).

Second, similar to *Apex*, in which Winthrop is renamed "Struggle," Whitehead emphasizes struggle over freedom, as Cora finds that "freedom" is never quite freedom no matter the place (the North) or the time (post-Emancipation). Indeed, Cora is still running at the novel's end, after learning that "[f]reedom was a thing that shifted as you looked at it" and that "[b]eing free had nothing to do with chains or how much space you had" (2016, p. 179). One must always face up to "[t]he manifold frustrations of liberty" (p. 253).

Yet even after the novel deflates myths of freedom and Manifest Destiny, one character claims that while America is "a delusion" it is a "useful" one (2016, p. 285). He also tells Cora that the Declaration of Independence (which earlier in the novel has been spoken by a parrot and parroted by a slave) "'is like a map. You trust that it's right, but you only know by going out and testing it yourself'" (p. 240). Freedom is an ongoing project. Thus, the novel offers no triumphant, feel-good ending, but a guarded endorsement of aspiring to, but never achieving and thus freezing, American ideals. In the metaphor of the railroad there exists the potential of a harmful system dominated by industry, ideology, and slavery to be transformed by those whom it has harmed and who, after all, built it.

Whitehead's work also responds to genre in a post-postmodern fashion, revisiting and revising it generally to non-ironic and reparative ends. *The Intuitionist*, *John Henry Days*, and *The Underground Railroad* can all be seen as "postsoul historical metafiction" (Maus 2014, pp. 6–11) that is interested not simply in tearing down harmful ideological structures but in laying groundwork for more historically grounded futures; *Sag Harbor* is a *Bildungsroman*; and there are magical, realist, speculative, or fantastical elements in *The Intuitionist* and *The Underground Railroad*.

Whitehead's strangest genre experiment is *Zone One* (2011), a post-apocalyptic zombie novel inspired by George Romero's films. While one might expect Whitehead to "color" this often "white-associated" genre, he largely decenters questions of race to intriguing ends. We only learn that the protagonist, Mark Spitz, is African American late in the novel, and he is presented as perfectly "*average*," as though race hardly matters (2011b, p. 9). Nevertheless, Whitehead's zombies constitute satirical pokes at daily American lives and concerns, from consumerism to exclusionary politics – with grim conclusions. In short, the before and after of this zombie dystopia isn't as distinct as it should be (Maus 2014, pp. 115–116). Curiously, then, Whitehead offers a colorblind or "race free" society that coincides with the very end or destruction of society.

Overall, *Zone One* demonstrates that race neither dominates nor is exclusively the focus of the post-racial writer as it may have been for earlier generations of writers. The novel, like all of Whitehead's works, nonetheless reveals that simply "e-racing" race from "future" genres of literature entails that post-postmodern literature itself might become zombified – "generic" in the pejorative sense – and that forms-of-life, which are like literary genres, are still as nuanced as ever, still full of potential, and still disrupting and reimagining expectations. Whitehead's post-racial fictions, by engaging critically with American history, pop culture, and literary forms, thus guardedly suggest that the genre of democracy that we call "America" and how we interpret its troubled legacy is forever open to contestation and transformation.

SEE ALSO: After Postmodernism; DeLillo, Don; Díaz; Junot; Mixed-Genre Fiction; Multiculturalism; Post-Soul and/or Post-Black Fiction; Pynchon, Thomas; Reed, Ishmael

REFERENCES

Ashe, Bertram D. (2007). Theorizing the post-soul aesthetic: an introduction. *African American Review* 41 (4): 609–623.

Maus, Derek C. (2014). *Understanding Colson Whitehead*. Columbia: University of South Carolina Press.

Neal, Mark Anthony. (2002). *Soul Babies: Black Popular Culture and the Post-Soul Aesthetic*. New York: Routledge.

Román, Elda María. (2018). "Post" ethnic form. In: *American Literature in Transition, 2000–2010* (ed. Rachel Greenwald Smith), 17–29. Cambridge: Cambridge University Press.

Saldívar, Ramón. (2011). Historical fantasy, speculative realism, and postrace aesthetics in contemporary American fiction. *American Literary History* 23 (3): 574–599.

Touré. (2011). *Who's Afraid of Post-Blackness: What it Means to be Black Now*. New York: Free Press.

Whitehead, Colson. (2000). *The Intuitionist*. New York: Anchor; 1st ed. 1999.

Whitehead, Colson. (2002). *John Henry Days*. New York: Anchor; 1st ed. 2001.

Whitehead, Colson. (2006). *Apex Hides the Hurt*. New York: Doubleday.

Whitehead, Colson. (2011a). *Sag Harbor*. London: Vintage; 1st ed. 2009.

Whitehead, Colson. (2011b). *Zone One*. London: Vintage.

Whitehead, Colson. (2016). *The Underground Railroad*. New York: Doubleday.

FURTHER READING

Dischinger, Matthew. (2017). States of possibility in Colson Whitehead's *The Underground Railroad*. *The Global South* 11 (1): 82–99.

Elam, Michelle. (2011). *The Souls of Mixed Folk: Race, Politics, and Aesthetics in the New Millennium*. Stanford: Stanford University Press.

Selzer, Linda. (2009). Instruments more perfect than bodies: romancing uplift in Colson Whitehead's *The Intuitionist*. *African American Review* 43 (4): 681–698.

Wideman, John Edgar

D. QUENTIN MILLER
Suffolk University, USA

John Edgar Wideman (b. 1941) grew up a first-hand witness to the conditions of the so-called urban ghettos of the 1950s and 1960s. His initial response to the blight, neglect, and decline he saw in Homewood – his Pittsburgh neighborhood – was not to immerse himself in it as his contemporaries in the Black Arts Movement did, but rather to remove himself physically, emotionally, and aesthetically. In his early work Wideman did not look directly to Homewood or to his family's stories for inspiration. Once he did, beginning in 1981, he became the leading literary voice regarding mass incarceration that has come to dominate discourse about race in America. Wideman might best be described as a post-Black Arts Movement writer who was aware of that movement's concerns, yet not a full participant in them. He forged a unique path that makes his work and career difficult to classify even as critics hail his undeniable importance. His long and varied career has blurred the lines between fiction and nonfiction, scrutinized the troubled ethics of writing about family, and merged esoteric ideas and popular cultural expressions to create a new literary aesthetic.

The eldest of five siblings, Wideman's initial journey was away from the neighborhood of his youth and into the notably white world of Ivy League education: he notes of his cohort, without exaggeration, "About ten of the seventeen hundred men and women who entered the University of Pennsylvania as freshmen in 1959 were black" (1984, p. 29). At Penn Wideman gained notoriety as a brilliant student and standout basketball player while he was taught a white, Eurocentric literary tradition that he emulated and adapted in his first three novels, published between 1967 and 1973. As the Black Arts Movement flourished by embracing Black vernacular speech and the chaos of the contemporary streets, Wideman employed challenging modernist models such as Joyce and Eliot as lenses to his world. Following this initial creative burst, Wideman took seven years off from writing to retrench, reemerging in the early 1980s to publish his acclaimed Homewood trilogy (1981–1983).

Part of Wideman's stated aim in publishing this trilogy consisting of a short story collection and two novels was to reach Black readers who might have found his early novels difficult to access. One of the reasons behind his seven-year hiatus was an incident at the University of Pennsylvania where he taught in the early 1970s: a group of Black students asked him to offer a course in African American literature and he declined, claiming he was not familiar enough with that tradition. This realization constituted a turning point: in exile from Homewood at Penn (both as a student and later as an instructor), at Oxford (where he studied on a Rhodes scholarship), and at the University of Wyoming (where he taught in the 1970s), he realized that he had cut himself off from his past and his community in the name of success and notoriety. The return to Homewood in these works was a return not only to his childhood home, but to the people, language, and traditions that comprised an essential but buried part of him.

The first two books of the trilogy – the story collection *Damballah* and the novel *Hiding Place*, both published in 1981 – connect mythology to personal experience. *Damballah* begins with a letter to his brother Robby (to whom the volume is dedicated), a family tree, and a "begat chart." Genealogy – a persistent concern in Wideman's writings – becomes a way to connect his personal past to the ancestral past. The title story is set in the era of slavery and focuses on a slave named Orion who refuses to obey the mandate that he speak English and convert to Christianity. Orion is murdered and decapitated for his rebellion, and a young boy impulsively throws his head into the water, unconsciously creating a ritual that becomes an essential if cryptic origin story for all of the modern inhabitants of Homewood. Orion identifies the boy as "the one" who "could learn the story and tell it again" (1981a, p. 18). In this way the boy is Wideman's direct literary ancestor charged with telling the Homewood stories that would otherwise be lost to history. *Damballah* represents Wideman's first attempts to retell the family stories heard throughout his youth, before he lost his "Homewood ear" (1984, p. 76). In doing so, and in repeating certain stories both within this collection and in later works, he adds mythological significance to stories that might be overlooked or considered unimportant and he also emphasizes the act of storytelling as a vital means to preserve culture.

One of the family stories he tells for the first time in *Damballah* is based on his brother Robby's experience, which would become the most significant recurrent story in his oeuvre. In 1975 Robby was involved in a botched armed robbery that resulted in murder. John became involved when Robby and his fugitive accomplices arrived at his door in Wyoming, catalyzing a complex response to his brother that involves a tug of war between his urge to succeed in academic and literary worlds and his responsibility to the family he left behind. Wideman's first engagement with this tale is a story called "Tommy" in which his brother's character is introduced against the backdrop of a decaying Homewood: the title character notes of his neighborhood, "All these old houses ain't nothing but rotten teeth" (1981a, p. 160). Robby perceives the decline of Homewood as one of the primary factors that leads him to a life of street crime. In "Solitary," the penultimate story in the collection, it is clear how Robby's incarceration affects John and his mother.

These two short works are just the outline of Robby's story which Wideman tells much more fully in *Hiding Place*, the next installment in the trilogy. This novel paints a much fuller portrait of Robby (still called Tommy) by showing not only his crime and his attempts to evade the law, but also by putting him into conversation with his great aunt Bess, who temporarily hides him while he is on the lam. She is also in exile from Homewood, fleeing from the psychological damage she suffered there through the losses of her husband, her son, and her great grandniece. Homewood residents regard her warily because she has willfully left her community, but she finds it too painful to stay. Looking at Homewood from her house positioned above it, Tommy concludes that his neighborhood is a trap and that even the living are "all dead and dying down there on the same jive-ass merry-go-round. All of them lost as him" (1981b, p. 37). Because its families have begun to disintegrate under the pressure of urban blight, Homewood seems to present two possibilities to its residents: leave (as John and Bess do) or stay and subject yourself to ruin (which is the fate of Robby and his friends).

Although Robby's story is revisited in the third of the Homewood novels, *Sent for You Yesterday* (1983), it receives its fullest treatment in *Brothers and Keepers* (1984), Wideman's acclaimed work of nonfiction published just a year later. Critics have wrestled with the classification of this work as it is at once John's autobiography and Robby's biography. Though it begins with John's voice, the author gradually acknowledges the importance of allowing Robby to tell his story in his own voice based on many interviews conducted in the prison's visiting room. Moreover, John says that he uses narrative techniques he has learned as a novelist to retell this story, but he does not label this rendition of Robby's story fiction and he reiterates that he is striving as much as possible for authenticity through the faithful reproduction of his brother's voice. It is a complex and moving work that chronicles John's anguish over leaving Homewood and abandoning his family, Robby's descent into a kind of nihilism that led to the outcome of life in prison without parole, and the relationship between these two brothers who ended up a long way down two starkly different paths. It initiates a pattern that dominates the rest of his career in which he connects personal anguish to broad social, cultural, and historical forces.

If Wideman's first three novels are marked by the challenging intellectual and aesthetic distance of modernism and the Homewood books return to the power of vernacular storytelling, *Brothers and Keepers* brings these two modes together. The book's overwhelmingly positive critical reception not only put Wideman decisively on the literary map, but it launched him into the role of spokesman for a growing movement to reform incarceration in the United States. Wideman partially embraced this role, writing (for example) the foreword to a popular memoir by the journalist and death row inmate Mumia Abu-Jamal and advocating for many years for his brother's sentence to be reduced (which finally happened in 2019 after nearly half a century in prison), but his primary interest in aesthetic innovation was somewhat at odds with his role as an activist. When it comes to mass incarceration (and many other subjects), Wideman's tendency toward complex thinking did not lend itself easily to his becoming a spokesperson or crusader for a cause. His engagement with the subject of incarceration is personal, cultural, intellectual, and emotional, not simply political. His work after *Brothers and Keepers* tends toward the academic as he connects the legacy of slavery in the United States and the extreme rise in incarceration in the late twentieth century. In many ways his work anticipates more recent work on race and incarceration such as Michelle Alexander's prominent work *The New Jim Crow* (2010).

During the 1980s and into the 1990s Wideman continued to publish prolifically, and his works of this era are daring, original, and experimental, though they have never matched the critical and popular success of the Homewood trilogy and

Brothers and Keepers. Another Homewood novel, *Reuben*, was published in 1987 followed by the story collection *Fever* in 1989. He published three additional novels in the 1990s – *Philadelphia Fire* (1990), *The Cattle Killing* (1996) and *Two Cities* (1998) – as well as the memoir *Fatheralong* (1994). His importance was recognized with a MacArthur "genius grant" in 1993, among a growing number of awards and honors including a Rea Award for significant contributions to the short story genre and the American Book Award for *Philadelphia Fire*. In these mid-career works, Wideman moves away from the pattern and types of narratives he established in the early 1980s. His primary subjects include some overlooked or marginal subjects of history, from the government destruction of the MOVE compound in Philadelphia in 1985 to the Xhosa tribe's slaughter of cattle in the nineteenth century to avoid European oppression. At the center of many of these historically-minded works is a tormented consciousness that represents a dimension of the author, specifically that dimension that manifested as guilt in *Brothers and Keepers*. Is it enough, these works collectively muse, to record incidents of traumatic oppression and to render them in experimental fiction? He becomes increasingly critical of writing as a profession, admonishing himself for stealing his brother's and father's stories for his own glory and referring to writers as "parasites" (2019, p. 81). The title character of *Reuben* is one manifestation of this tormented consciousness. A street lawyer who has suffered oppression in the form of a hate crime, he is on a quest to reunite a woman deemed an unfit mother with her lost son. He criticizes his own efforts to work to remedy society's ills, calling himself "Mountebank. Charlatan. Fool. Witch doctor" (1987, p. 71). Within outbursts such as these, Wideman indicates the crisis of his own calling: an alienated intellectual who on one hand feels compelled to speak for the oppressed and on the other feels powerless to really do anything about the patterns of oppression he observes, both in history and in the world he inhabits. It could be said that this self-doubt is the logical outcome of a lifetime of intense critical scrutiny of the African American self in the context of a hostile, racist society. There is also a latent violence in much of his work that represents Wideman's deep-seated anger at war with the realization that releasing that anger in a mindless, uncontrolled way carries potentially lethal consequences.

Wideman's recognition of the power of storytelling emboldens him to push outward on the boundaries between fiction and nonfiction. His three 1990s novels and his later novel *Fanon* (2008) as well as many of his late career short stories feature postmodern appearances of the author within the stories he is telling. As his career progresses and he frequently repeats the Igbo proverb "all stories are true," Wideman is both the creator of and subject of his writing, no matter the ostensible topic. Just as he was "on the outside, looking in" (1984, p. 87) at Robby's life in *Brothers and Keepers*, he steps outside his own fictional works, distancing himself through history, legend, geography, and imagination, then steps back in, rendering John Wideman as a real character within fictional settings.

Wideman's 1994 memoir *Fatheralong* similarly examines both his father's story and his own role as a father, both in the context of his family history and the broader context of race in America. His role as a spokesman against mass incarceration and his aspirations to be a more involved parent than his father was became more complicated in 1986 when his teenaged son Jacob, suffering a psychic break, committed murder at a summer camp and was, like Robby, sentenced to life in prison. Wideman's willingness to write about his brother's case in fiction and nonfiction and to pen open letters and essays about incarceration's devastating cultural and psychological effects is balanced by a reticence to discuss his son's situation. Jacob's story is broached indirectly for the first time at the end of *Fatheralong*, but the attendant pain associated with this dimension of Wideman's personal story has largely been absent from his oeuvre until a brief mention in his most recent collection *American Histories* (2018) and a fuller treatment in the uncollected story "Arizona" (2019) in which he confesses, "I have tried to write [Jacob's] story many, many times.... Each attempt failed" (2019, p. 80).

Although the subjects of *Fatheralong* are wide-ranging, the through line is the strained, awkward relationship Wideman had with his taciturn father, and the theme of clumsy attempts at male bonding against the background of a racially segregated society becomes another prominent, recurrent concern that reaches its fullest expression in *Hoop Roots* (2001). His father was consistently tough through John's childhood and into his adulthood; for instance, he refuses to visit Robby in prison. John attempts to get closer to his elderly father, but the final essay indicates that his loss of Jacob who now inhabits the penal system he has fought against for years constitutes a sense of grief so deep that any attempts to understand his own father cannot begin to heal it. *Hoop Roots* honors the father figures and lessons in masculinity he sought on playground basketball courts.

The overwhelming strains on the contemporary African American family may be at the heart of Wideman's writing, but many other topics radiate out from that central concern. He often turns attention to Black men who have been erased from the historical record: his novel *Fanon* about the Martiniquan intellectual and radical author Frantz Fanon, his multi-genre work *Hoop Roots* about the vital importance of playground basketball to African American culture and the forgotten men who excelled at it, and his investigative work *Writing to Save a Life* (2016) about the father of civil rights martyr Emmett Till all contribute to this dimension of Wideman's work. Along with *The Island: Martinique* (2003) and the stories in *American Histories*, they are all profoundly original and difficult to categorize in terms of genre. This resistance to literary convention can be seen as Wideman's way of asserting the principle he inherited from the Black Arts Movement and adapted to his own purposes: that Black experience cannot be rendered fully or authentically if one works strictly within accepted forms of white literature. These late works are demanding of the reader who must be willing to navigate, for instance, a single sentence that runs nearly thirty pages, or the switch from a lengthy travel memoir which interrogates a difficult moment in Wideman's relationship with his second wife to a fanciful time-traveling tale about the Martiniquan legendary figure Pere Labat. This impulse can perhaps be linked to improvisation, an aesthetic principle derived from jazz and blues music, which is another recurrent topic of inquiry within Wideman's work.

Yet Wideman has always been a writer eager to challenge his readers. Despite the variations in his subjects, styles, and themes over time, there is a marked consistency in the way his works are characterized by emotional and intellectual intensity. This intensity seems to have taken a toll on the author: Wideman's blistering productivity of the 1980s and 1990s diminished considerably after his most recent novel (*Fanon*) in 2008. In that novel, which contains a good deal of self-critique, he even predicts this trend: "I realize time's running out. I won't be writing many more books, if any" (2008, p. 5). In the 2010s he published a collection of flash fiction (*Briefs* [2010]), the long-anticipated project on Emmett Till's father, and a collection of longer short stories,

American Histories. These final two works indicate that he is still involved in his craft, even as he has retired from teaching and become an increasingly private figure. A recent story entitled "Writing Teacher" fittingly summarizes the anxiety of what it means to be John Edgar Wideman; the narrator, addressing a writing student in his mind, asks, "Isn't your story, like every story a masquerade ... Do you care if your mask slips and uncovers your face. I often worry mine's slipping" (2018, p. 85). This worry has catalyzed Wideman's entire career, characterized by fashioning protective masks in fiction and tearing them off to reveal the vulnerable, damaged self underneath.

SEE ALSO: Danticat, Edwidge; Everett, Percival; Gaines, Ernest; Mixed-Genre Fiction; Morrison, Toni; Post-Soul and/or Post-Black Fiction; Reed, Ishmael; Trauma and Fiction; Ward, Jesmyn; Whitehead, Colson

REFERENCES

Wideman, John Edgar. (1981a). *Damballah*. Boston: New York: Mariner.
Wideman, John Edgar. (1981b). *Hiding Place*. Boston: New York: Mariner.
Wideman, John Edgar. (1984). *Brothers and Keepers*. New York: Henry Holt.
Wideman, John Edgar. (1987). *Reuben*. New York: Viking Penguin.
Wideman, John Edgar. (2008). *Fanon*. Boston: Houghton Mifflin.
Wideman, John Edgar. (2018). *American Histories*. New York: Scribner.
Wideman, John Edgar. (2019). Arizona. *The New Yorker* (November 25, 2019). https://www.newyorker.com/magazine/2019/11/25/arizona (accessed August 2, 2021).

FURTHER READING

Byerman, Keith. (2013). *The Life and Work of John Edgar Wideman*. Santa Barbara, CA: Praeger.
Coleman, John W. (1989). *Blackness and Modernism: The Literary Career of John Edgar Wideman*. Jackson: University Press of Mississippi.
Guzzio, Tracie C. (2011). *All Stories Are True: History, Myth, and Trauma in the Works of John Edgar Wideman*. Jackson: University Press of Mississippi.
Miller, D. Quentin. (2018). *Understanding John Edgar Wideman*. Columbia: University of South Carolina Press.
TuSmith, Bonnie. (ed.) (1998). *Conversations with John Edgar Wideman*. Jackson: University Press of Mississippi.

Williams, Sherley Anne

GRETCHEN MICHLITSCH
Winona State University, USA

Black writer Sherley Anne Williams is best known for the liberation narrative *Dessa Rose*, which garnered critical and popular acclaim when it was published in 1986. In the novel, the eponymous heroine Dessa rises up against slaveholders, builds a life outside of slavery, and ultimately tells her own story. Prior to *Dessa Rose*, Williams's two books of poetry also received considerable attention; *The Peacock Poems* (1975) was named a National Book Award finalist and a television performance of poems from *Some One Sweet Angel Chile* (1982) was awarded an Emmy. Her book of literary criticism, *Give Birth to Brightness: A Thematic Study in Neo-Black Literature* (1972) helped shape literary movements of the 1970s and 1980s. Williams was sought after as a literary critic, and her introductions to Zora Neale Hurston's 1937 *Their Eyes Were Watching God* (1978) and Mark Twain's 1894 *The Tragedy of Pudd'nhead Wilson* (1996) reframed these canonical books for contemporary reading audiences seeking to understand how to think about the ways that Blackness meant in earlier fiction. In the 1990s, Williams drew on biographical material from her poetry to create two children's picture books, *Working Cotton* (1992) and *Girls Together* (1999), with *Working Cotton* being named a Caldecott Honor Book and a Coretta Scott King Honor Book. Williams was also highly successful as a scholar and teacher. Awarded her MA in American Literature from Brown University in 1972, Williams taught at California State University, Fresno for a year before joining the faculty at the University of California, San Diego, in 1973. At UCSD, she served as chair of the Literature Department from 1977 to 1980 and remained on the faculty until her early death from cancer on July 6, 1999. As a child, Williams grew up dirt poor among the fruit orchards and cotton fields of California's San Joaquin Valley, losing her father at age eight and her mother when she was sixteen. In her writing, Williams drew on the rhythms and cadences of the blues; she brought what she called "the way black people talk" into writing (Gable 1986, p. 27). Williams wrote to give voice to those whose voices she had not found in the books she loved to read as a child, to those whose perspectives were missing from the written historical record.

The daughter of migrant workers, Sherley Anne Williams was born in 1944 in Bakersfield, CA and grew up in Fresno, CA. Her mother, Lena-Lelia (Siler) Williams, was from rural Texas. Her father Jesse Winston Williams, who loved books, died of tuberculosis when Sherley was eight years old. Williams and her three sisters grew up poor and on welfare. She later explained that "Even in a poverty-stricken environment, we were enormously poor" (Gable 1986, p. 24). Each week the three older sisters checked out the maximum five books per person from the library and shared them among themselves (Phelgyal 2000). Embarrassed to ask a librarian in case there weren't any, Williams perused the shelves at the local library for books by Black writers and found Richard Wright's *Black Boy* (1945) and Eartha Kitt's *Thursday's Child* (1956). When their mother died, Sherley's older sister Ruby Louise, known as "Ruise," took in the 16-year-old Sherley. When they needed money, they worked in the cotton and fruit fields surrounding Fresno. An eighth-grade science teacher had encouraged Sherley to take college prep classes and she applied for college on the advice of a high school chemistry teacher. In her first year at Fresno State University, she took an Introduction to Literature class with poet Philip Levine. After Williams's death in 1999, Levine remembered the young Williams as "clearly a very bright, very talented student ... She was eager, eating everything up." He also described her as "highly opinionated about what she read" and willing to argue with her professor in class. By 1999, Levine no longer recalled the details of their argument about Ralph Ellison's *Invisible Man* (1952), but he did remember conceding the point to the young Williams (Phelgyal 2000).

Williams established her position as a critic with her 1972 *Give Birth to Brightness: A Thematic Study in Neo-Black Literature*. This focused yet wide-ranging book analyzes the oeuvre of Neo-Black writers of the twentieth century, tracing and contextualizing representations of Black heroes predominantly through the work of male writers, including Amiri Baraka, James Baldwin, and Ernest Gaines. Williams's interrogation of the definitions of "hero," "Black," "negro," and "rebel" foreshadow the construction of her later female protagonist in *Dessa Rose*. The success of *Give Birth to Brightness*, which she dedicated to her son Malcolm, led Williams to leave the PhD program at Brown University and begin the career she wanted as a teacher and a writer.

Part of Williams's own genius as a writer lay in her skill in representing in written form the sounds of the language she knew growing up in California's San Joaquin Valley. The characters in Williams's early short stories – "Tell Martha Not to Moan" (1968) and "The Lawd Don't Like Ugly" (1974) – speak this language. Her attention to language likewise centers her nuanced essays "The Blues Roots of Contemporary Afro-American Poetry" (1977) and "Returning to the Blues: Esther Phillips and Contemporary Blues Culture" (1991), which provide intellectual frameworks through which we can also read her own writings. In the 1977 essay, Williams highlights the significance of the blues as a verbal genre developed at the juncture of African oral and European written traditions, studying the songs of Billie Holiday and the poetry of Langston Hughes and Lucille Clifton. In the latter essay, she compares her own time as "a graduate student at an old New England university" in the 1970s to James Baldwin's time in Switzerland: "Anchored in those cold and alien surroundings by some old recordings of Bessie Smith and a typewriter [Baldwin] returned to his earliest cultural roots and in so doing uncovered his writing voice." Williams herself had been "in school looking for our history, to learn the skills by which I would ferret it out from wherever white folks had hidden it." However, "unlike Baldwin, . . . [she] was not ashamed of loving this living culture" (Williams 1991, p. 820). In addition, Williams identified the poets Langston Hughes and Sterling Brown (with whom Williams studied at Howard University) as early influences on her work: "I was just totally captivated by their language, their speech, and their character," she said, "because I've always liked the way black people talk. So I wanted to work with that in writing" (Gable 1986, pp. 24–25). Similarly, Williams tells in her 1978 Foreword to *Their Eyes Were Watching God* of her first encounter with Zora Neale Hurston's work. When it was finally Williams's turn to read a copy of *Their Eyes Were Watching God* in a graduate class at Howard University, she "became Zora Neale's for life." Hurston's "fidelity to diction, metaphor, and syntax ... rings ... with an aching familiarity that is a testament to Hurston's skill and to the durability of black speech," Williams wrote, adding that Hurston's "ear for speech rhythms must have been remarkable."

Williams's admiration for Hurston's "deftness with language" offers a window into her own authorial creation: "In the speech of [Hurston's] characters I heard my own country voice and saw in the heroine something of my own country self" (Williams 1978, pp. vii, xi).

Williams's own deftness with language was fully established with *The Peacock Poems*, published by Wesleyan University Press in 1975. This three-part collection introduces themes of a longing for home and of the importance of togetherness. The first section includes first-person poems about being pregnant, about giving birth, and about the longing that the one-sided bed blues convey. Her driving poems testify to a twentieth-century landscape traversed by cars. The speaker of the prose poem "The Valley" introduces the potential of *"going into labor in the Grapevine"*: *"The winds up there are treacherous, the curves and grades deceptive, and I'd almost hold my breath until that spot in the Grapevine, just before the highway makes its final curving descent into the Valley."* By "The Folding of the Feathers / the Counting of the Birds," readers hear the voice of "a deep sea diva with a steady stroke" who is

the singer /
the song   the road /
the power   the new world loa.

By the time " ... the lines converge here ..." in the third section, "Quartet" speaks to "what my mamma told / me. Her rhythm, her tone – now / mine" as the poet writes of "piec[ing] together my child / hood for my son." The speaking voices of "I Sing This Song for Our Mothers," Odessa and Odessa Son, prefigure the characters and framing of *Dessa Rose*. Ultimately, the wealth of material gathered into *The Peacock Poems* gave birth to several other projects.

The rich and varied poems in the collection *Some One Sweet Angel Chile* were dedicated to Williams's mother Lena-Lelia Marie and published by William Morrow in 1982. "Letters from a New England Negro" builds via a set of epistolary poems the voice of a young school teacher who goes South to teach the freed men and women and children after the Civil War. This opening project, which Williams also shaped into a one-woman play, invites comparison to the voice of the eponymous protagonist of *Dessa Rose* – a character reclaimed from history and given her own voice. "Regular Reefer" pays homage to Bessie Smith, Empress of the Blues, evoking Smith's voice and her influence in this blues-themed section, which includes a reprise of *The Peacock Poems*' "one-sided bed Blues." In "fragments:," the poet speaks of Smith: "What / happen is in the / record: She could walk / a man like water; / she touched me; and I / knowed her." Williams ends this second section with another of her driving poems that measure time and elevation by light and dark and in-between. "down torrey pines road:" slows down for the curves in the road: "The way the moonlight washes / out all colors and / the high beams bounce shadows off / the overhanging / trees, the way the cars come round the / curves gathering speed / for the climb up the road to / the canyon rim is / something like Mississippi . . ." The poet ponders her parents' lives in "The Iconography of Childhood" and "the wishon line" and "california light," and her second children's book draws from these texts. In this final section, with the drumming and strumming and singing of "The Janus Love" and a grounding in the rhythms of Ray Charles and Thelonious Monk and Johnny Watson & George Duke, this collection returns to gather the poet's family and friends.

Williams's 1986 novel *Dessa Rose* opens with Dessa pregnant and chained in a root cellar as the leader of a slave revolt, sentenced to death once she gives birth. Readers meet Dessa's family and friends only through her dreams. The pen is in the hand of the antagonist Adam Nehemiah, Williams's reincarnation of Nehemiah Adams, the historical author of *The South-Side View of Slavery, or, Three Months at the South, in 1854* whose controversial text was republished in 1969 by Negro Universities Press. A primary conflict in the novel represents the real-world conflict over who has the power to record history. In this opening section, titled "The Darky," the third-person narrator frames Nehemiah's own writing down of Odessa's story and subtly undermines his credibility as an expert on slaves.

This opening of *Dessa Rose* revises Williams's novella "Meditations on History," which was initially rejected by editors who liked the writing but found the white male character Adam Nehemiah problematic and unbelievable. In 1980, Mary Helen Washington included the novella in her collection *Midnight Birds: Stories of Contemporary Black Women Writers*. The expanded plot of *Dessa Rose* recalls the three-part arc of Hurston's *Their Eyes Were Watching God* and plays with William Faulkner's Sutpen's Hundred and Mark Twain's *Adventures of Huckleberry Finn* (1884). Against a backdrop of legal slavery and accepted, blatant racism, Dessa faces antagonists. She ultimately "friends" the white woman Ruth Elizabeth, called "Rufel," and, with her collaborators, bests the white man Adam Nehemiah. Williams explains her inspiration for the novel in the Author's Note: she followed Angela Davis's telling of a pregnant woman sentenced to die in Kentucky in 1829 as the leader of a slave revolt to Herbert Aptheker's record, and there found also the account of a white woman in North Carolina who provided sanctuary to people who had escaped slavery. Though there is very little trace of either woman in the historical record, in fiction, Williams could bring them together.

Dessa Rose means on multiple levels. The book is a fictional creation of a missing history, a counterpoint that provides missing voices – voices that Williams creates based on a combination of recorded history and lived experience. It is also a rejoinder, a winning counterargument presented to those who make certain claims about historical Black experiences. At the same time, it remains a story with a purpose to entertain, sharing human thoughts, feelings, struggles.

A plethora of critical works analyze Williams's material in "Meditations on History" and *Dessa Rose*. Several early essays provide a foundation for later critics. Mae G. Henderson, in one essay in 1989, addresses Williams's claim to discursive power in the relationship between Dessa and Nehemiah, attending to "Meditations on History" as Williams's incensed reply to William Styron's blasphemous reimagining of history in his 1967 *The Confessions of Nat Turner*. Ashraf Rushdy's 1993 essay attends extensively to Dessa and Rufel's relationship, including their struggles over the naming power of the word "Mammy." Deborah McDowell's 1989 essay similarly focuses on these relationships between Dessa and Nehemiah and between Dessa and Rufel, foregrounding the characters' struggles over who tells the story. When the novel was first published, it was compared to Alice Walker's *The Color Purple* (1982). Since then, it has frequently been analyzed together with Toni Morrison's *Beloved* (1987), which was published the year after *Dessa Rose* and similarly provides the perspective of a slave woman who escaped, claimed liberty, gave birth, and raised children outside of slavery. *Dessa Rose* has also been read in relation to a range of material from Harriet Jacobs's autobiography and Nella Larsen's *Passing* (1929) to Octavia Butler's *Kindred* (1979) and Kara Walker's "A Subtlety" (2014).

The last section of *Dessa Rose* recalls a Mark Twain ending, in both tone and direction. The final romp of the characters from Sutton's Glen is playful and picaresque, even as it underlines the seriousness of the freedom of the Black body. Ultimately, the fictional Dessa retroactively subverts the historic Nehemiah Adams, rewrites the ending of the *Adventures of Huckleberry Finn* from a Black woman's perspective, and lights out for the territory to claim life, freedom, and a place and a way to raise the son she birthed. *Dessa Rose* concludes with an Epilogue in which Dessa, who has claimed the narrative voice by the end of the book, assures that the children have heard these stories from "our own lips," with those who know the story best claiming the power to represent their experience to future generations.

Williams's two published children's books partner her poetry with the work of award-winning artists. The writer and the illustrators shared a passion for creating for younger generations the stories, the images that they knew were missing from published literature – the stories of people who looked like and sounded like them. Illustrator Carole Byard won her fourth Coretta Scott King Illustrator Award for the 1992 *Working Cotton,* and together Williams and Byard won the Coretta Scott King Award for the book, which was also a Caldecott Honor Book. Williams's text draws from an autobiographical poem in *The Peacock Poems* and names her sisters. Byard's wonderfully detailed cotton plants nestle the images of the young protagonist among her family – father, mother, and sisters eking out a living as migrant workers among the cotton. *Working Cotton* conveys feelings of togetherness among a migrant family laboring long hours to pick as many pounds of cotton as they can, keeping the youngest as safe and as warm as possible.

The 1999 *Girls Together*, with paintings by the iconoclastic illustrator Synthia Saint James, emerges from a poem in *Some One Sweet Angel Chile* to tell part of a day in the life of girls Hatti Jean, ViLee, and Lois together with "Ruise and me." Through the young narrative voice, full of similes, metaphors, and comparison, Williams conveys the cadences of the language and the life of these girls of "the Project" where they live. Set on a morning with "Sun just barely looking and everything quiet except for the birds. Air feel like if you fell into a trailer full of cotton; it's just that soft on your skin," *Girls Together* also contains echoes of Williams's own childhood. Saint James's illustrations depict girls in action – linking arms while they walk, hanging amongst the flowers in a magnolia tree. As she did frequently throughout her work, Williams again paid tribute to her sister Ruby Louise, known as Ruise. While one girl in the story, Lois, is "the tallest, so dark she look black, her face pretty as any doll's," Ruise, "the oldest, skinny as a snake, have a grin makes you grin with her." As a writer, Williams created the books that she herself could not find in the library when she was young.

Throughout her career, Williams was both writer and teacher. Notable among the scholars who brought Afro-American Literature classes into the mainstream at US universities, Williams taught classes from Origins of Afro-American Literature and Literature and the Blues to The Black Detective and The Pan-African Historical Novel. She taught The Craft of Fiction to undergraduates and Imaginative Writing to graduate students. In 1984, she was a Senior Fulbright Lecturer at the University of Ghana. In 1987, the UCSD Alumni Association named her distinguished Professor of the Year.

Williams was working on two books when she died, including a sequel to *Dessa Rose*. Her early death dealt a great loss to American literature.

SEE ALSO: Bambara, Toni Cade; Butler, Octavia; Gaines, Ernest; Johnson, Charles; Marshall, Paule; McMillan, Terry; Morrison, Toni; Multiculturalism; Reed, Ishmael; Walker, Alice

REFERENCES

Gable, Mona. (1986). Understanding the impossible: poet and professor Sherley Anne Williams, who once picked cotton in Fresno, has become a surprise best-selling novelist. *Los Angeles Times Magazine* (December 7, 1986): 22, 24, 27–28.

Henderson, Mae G. (1989). (W)riting the work and working the rites. *Black American Literature Forum* 23 (4): 631–660.

McDowell, Deborah E. (1989). Negotiating between tenses: witnessing slavery after freedom – Dessa Rose. In: *Slavery and the Literary Imagination* (ed. Deborah E. McDowell and Arnold Rampersad), 144–163. Baltimore, MD: Johns Hopkins University Press.

Phelgyal, Jangchup. (2000). Sherley Williams – from Fresno to La Jolla: raised not to hope too hard. *San Diego Reader* (April 13, 2000). https://www.sandiegoreader.com/news/2000/apr/13/cover-raised-not-hope-too-hard (accessed August 15, 2021).

Rushdy, Ashraf H.A. (1993). Reading Mammy: the subject of relation in Sherley Anne Williams's *Dessa Rose*. *African American Review* 27 (3): 365–389.

Williams, Sherley Anne. (1978). Foreword. In: *Their Eyes Were Watching God* (by Zora Neale Hurston), v–xv. Urbana: University of Illinois Press; 1st ed. 1937.

Williams, Sherley Anne. (1991). Returning to the blues: Esther Phillips and contemporary blues culture. *Callaloo* 14 (4): 816–828.

FURTHER READING

Harris, Trudier. (2011). History as fact and fiction. In: *Cambridge History of African American Literature* (ed. Maryemma Graham and Jerry W. Ward, Jr.), 451–496. Cambridge: Cambridge University Press.

Henderson, Mae G. (2014). *Speaking in Tongues and Dancing Diaspora: Black Women Writing and Performing*. Oxford: Oxford University Press.

Mitchell, Angelyn. (2002). *The Freedom to Remember: Narrative, Slavery, and Gender in Contemporary Black Women's Fiction*. New Brunswick, NJ: Rutgers University Press.

Tate, Claudia. (1986). Interview with Sherley Anne Williams. In: *Black Women Writers at Work* (ed. Claudia Tate), 205–213. New York: Continuum.

Williams, Sherley Anne. (1993). The lion's history: the ghetto writes b[l]ack. *Soundings* 76 (2–3): 245–259.

Wolfe, Tom

SETH STUDER
South Dakota State University, USA

By 1980, Tom Wolfe, who turned 50 that year, had already enjoyed a prodigious literary career. One of the nation's most prominent journalists, over the next decade Wolfe would remake himself as a novelist. Prior to 1980, Wolfe had advocated importing the tools and techniques of fiction into journalism. Now, he would advocate bringing the style and sensibilities of journalism to fiction. He enjoyed his greatest success in 1987 with *The Bonfire of the Vanities*, an energetically written tale of a beleaguered Wall Street bond trader who must navigate the byzantine society and explosive racial politics of 1980s New York City. Social status, racial tensions, and Wolfe's trademark style would recur in all his later novels. In 1989, Wolfe set forth his theory of fiction in "Stalking the Billion-Footed Beast," a manifesto that railed against the growing irrelevance of novels in American society, a trend he blamed on contemporary literature's obfuscated style and obsession with formal experimentation. *Bonfire* made Wolfe into a recognizable celebrity beyond the literary world. With his trademark white suits, dandy style, and conservative views, Wolfe became an avatar of the backlash against postmodernism and the leading proponent of a return to literary realism.

The son of a newspaper editor, Wolfe was born on March 2, 1930, in Richmond, Virginia. An avowed Southerner (the young Wolfe was accepted by Princeton but chose to attend Washington and Lee University in Lexington, Virginia), Wolfe pursued his literary ambitions in the North, first as a graduate student of literature at Yale (he wrote a PhD dissertation on Communist organization among American writers) and then as a reporter in New York City. In 1963, during a newspaper strike, Wolfe traveled for *Esquire* magazine to investigate the custom car scene that had blossomed in southern California. As the deadline for the article approached, Wolfe became severely inhibited by writer's block. Desperate, he wrote a rambling letter to his editor explaining the spirit of what he wanted to achieve in the piece. The letter made liberal use of Wolfe's own perspective, featuring colorful interjections, cascades of adjectives, dialogue, individual scenes, exclamation marks, and even sound effects. His editor published the letter under the title "There Goes (Varoom! Varoom!) That Kandy-Kolored (Thphhhhhh!) Tangerine-Flake Streamline Baby (Rahghhh!) Around the Bend (Brummmmmmmmmmmmmmmm). . .," and the piece became the first instance of Wolfe's signature style in journalism (Wolfe 1963).

Wolfe would make his name as a leading figure of the New Journalism, a confederation of writers – including Truman Capote, Norman Mailer, Hunter S. Thompson, and Joan Didion – who applied the techniques of fiction to journalism. These authors abandoned the disinterested narrative voice, lean prose, and assumed objectivity of midcentury journalistic convention. Instead, they wrote from their own self-consciously subjective perspectives and employed highly stylized prose unique to each author. In 1968, Wolfe published his first book-length work in this style: *The Electric Kool-Aid Acid Test* documented the psychedelic adventures of Ken Kesey and his Merry Pranksters and, more generally, reflected on the countercultural developments of the late 1960s. This turn toward cultural politics marked the beginning of a preoccupation that would last the rest of Wolfe's career. In 1970 his latent political conservatism became explicit in two longform pieces, "Radical Chic" and "Mau-Mauing the Flak Catchers," which attempted to portray the hypocrisies of racial politics in the United States: first at a fundraising party hosted by Leonard Bernstein for the Black Panther Party, and second among civil servants who must "catch flak" from minorities who know how to game the government dole. Wolfe lambasted modern art in 1975's The Painted Word and modern architecture in 1981's From Bauhaus to Our House. His 1976 essay for New York magazine, "The 'Me' Decade and the Third Great Awakening," was a widely cited think piece on the 1970s. Wolfe argued that the post-World War II expansion of the US middle class, which now included members of the former working class, had produced a deadly individualism, a phenomenon exacerbated by the excesses of the sexual revolution and hippie counterculture. He conflated the resurgence of revivalistic Evangelical Christianity, associated with then-presidential candidate Jimmy Carter, with the New Age movement, associated with California governor Jerry Brown, as two sides of the same coin: a "Third Great Awakening." But Wolfe's most successful work prior to 1980 was The Right Stuff (1979), a bombastic and often sentimental appraisal of the early days of the US. space program and of the Mercury Seven astronauts. The book's tone – robustly pro-Cold War and pro-American, with a nostalgic view back to the halcyon days of Dwight Eisenhower – anticipated the tone and tenor of Ronald Reagan's presidential campaign, which would succeed in making Reagan president the following year. Wolfe would hail Reagan as a champion of the new middle class he described in "The 'Me' Decade." Meanwhile, Wolfe's critiques of wealthy liberals and undeserving Black welfare recipients would be echoed by the Reagan campaign.

Throughout this period of rich journalistic output, Wolfe perceived an apparent and, for him, troubling lack of ambitious novels about American society. Wolfe felt that no American novel had sufficiently chronicled the hippie counterculture or the seismic racial divides of modern New York City. Wolfe's aesthetic sensibilities already ran toward the journalistic naturalism of Emile Zola and Upton Sinclair, as well as the sentimental realism of Charles Dickens (even as his political sensibilities ran counter to the social progressivism of those earlier writers). Novelists, Wolfe argued, had rejected realism at their peril and had, consequently, lost their audiences and cultural relevance. The death of the novel and the influence of French poststructuralism on the literary scene were perennial concerns for Wolfe; he stringently rejected postmodernism in literature just as he had in art and architecture. Prior to 1980, Wolfe seemed to celebrate the novel's demise. The New Journalists had, Wolfe wrote, "wipe[d] out the novel as literature's main event" (Wolfe 1973, p. 9). But he would grow increasingly maudlin about the fate of the novel, and at the beginning of the 1980s he embarked on a project that would become The Bonfire of the Vanities.

Wolfe began Bonfire with research. He studied the cases that came before the Manhattan Criminal Court, worked with homicide detectives in the Bronx, and covered bond traders on Wall Street. Over time, he developed the character of Sherman McCoy, a Manhattan writer who is thrust into New York racial politics after nearly killing a Black high school student with his car. Wolfe took his novel's title from the late medieval practice of destroying secular trifles by fire, particularly the 1497 bonfire in Florence, in which the radical Dominican friar Girolamo Savonarola led the burning of innumerable books, works of art, and other worldly "vanities." By 1984, Wolfe had enough material to pitch his novel to *Rolling Stone* magazine. He intended to publish the novel serially, in the manner of the nineteenth-century realists he so admired but also because the deadlines that helped him combat his recurrent struggles with writer's block. Wolfe described writing "a chapter every two weeks with a gun at my temple" (1989, p. 54). *Bonfire* was published by *Rolling Stone* in twenty-seven installments beginning in July 1984.

As the first installments appeared, Wolfe grew dissatisfied with his novel. He was, it seemed, hamstrung by his strict adherence to literary naturalism. Current events in the 1980s quickly rendered much of the original version of *Bonfire* outdated. First, there was the heavily publicized subway shooting by gunman Bernard Goetz of a group of young, would-be pickpockets. The case was heavily politicized: Goetz was white while his targets were Black. The incident mirrored a scene in Wolfe's first draft of *Bonfire*, in which a white character confronts a group of Black youths on the subway. Wolfe disdained even the appearance that his plot had been ripped from the headlines and cut the scene. As the 1980s progressed, Wolfe realized that the main story of contemporary New York City would be the roaring bond market, which made millionaires overnight and contributed to a Reagan economy that was simultaneously high-performing and bedeviled by inequality. As Wolfe began to contemplate the final version of his novel, under contract with Farrar, Straus and Giroux, he changed Sherman McCoy's occupation from writer to bond trader.

The final version of *Bonfire* appeared in November 1987, just weeks after Black Monday, when the Dow Jones Industrial Average plummeted 508 points, the largest one-day crash in history. This time, events conspired in Wolfe's favor. The public was hungry for a morality tale of Wall Street collapse, and *Bonfire* appeared as if on cue. In this version, Sherman McCoy is a married bond trader whose dalliances with his 26-year-old mistress lead him to take a wrong turn off the Triborough Bridge into the Bronx. He hits a young Black high school student, Henry Lamb, with his car and then flees the scene. When Lamb enters a coma as a result of his injuries, a prominent Black minister, Reginald Bacon, takes up the youth's cause. Bacon enlists a cynical, alcoholic British journalist, Peter Fallow, to investigate the hit-and-run. Fallow's investigation leads him to McCoy and the incident becomes a fulcrum for public outrage over racial injustice in the city. The Bronx district attorneys, under pressure to make a show of McCoy's trial, prosecute the case furiously. As a result of the publicity, McCoy loses his job, his wife, and his status in society.

The feature of *Bonfire* that most captured the public's imagination was its exhaustive portrayal of New York high society of the 1980s. Wolfe offers the reader a tour of glamorous parties, spacious Manhattan apartments, Hamptons summer retreats, and richly adorned Wall Street offices, all described with the careful eye for detail that he had mastered in his journalism. Also appealing to readers was the sense, provided by Wolfe, that all this wealth was built on nothing. McCoy famously describes himself and his fellow bond traders as "Masters of the Universe." But in one scene, when his daughter asks him how he makes his money, McCoy struggles to answer. His daughter has just learned that her friend's father "makes books, and he has eighty people working for him" (2004, p. 236). What does McCoy *do*, she insists? How many people work for him? He tries to answer in simple terms, embarrassingly: something about retrieving crumbs while other people are exchanging slices of cake. He also tries to tie his work to funds used for roads and hospitals. His daughter excitedly asks, "You build roads and hospitals, Daddy?" to which he must reply, "No, I don't actually build them. . ." (p. 235). Wolfe's critique of finance capitalism is not especially original, but by 1987, the public was ready for a broad-brushed caricature of the financiers who had lately caused the nation so much trouble. *Bonfire* was a runaway bestseller and Wolfe was now the public face of middle-class backlash against Wall Street. *Entertainment Weekly* noted that, despite its 659 pages and 2343 exclamation points (part of Wolfe's characteristic style), *Bonfire* sold 725,000 copies in hardcover. Rights to print the paperback were sold for $1.5 million; the subsequent edition spent forty-one weeks on the bestseller list.

Despite the novel's association with Wall Street excess, the politics of *Bonfire* is primarily racial, and here the novel remains controversial. The 1987 version of the novel opens with a vignette of an embattled New York City mayor (a thinly disguised Ed Koch) confronting an angry audience of minority voters in Harlem. He imagines the scene from the perspective of his affluent white supporters downtown: "Do you really think this is *your* city any longer?" he asks them and then exclaims, "It's the Third World down here!" (2004, p. 5). The character of Reverend Reginald Bacon is especially controversial, portrayed as an opportunistic leader of the Black community who manages to consolidate both power and wealth from the political crises he stokes, such as the Henry Lamb case (Wolfe portrays Lamb as a lackluster student, but in Bacon's hands he becomes a sympathetic star of his high school). Liberal critics accused Wolfe of racism for his portrayal of Bacon. But after the Tawana Brawley rape case caught national attention and catapulted Reverend Al Sharpton into a public figure, Wolfe merely demurred that his portrayal of Bacon had not been extreme enough.

Accusations of racism in his novels would persist. Part of Wolfe's stated goal for *Bonfire* was to portray the full social strata of 1980s New York City. But readers will find huge omissions and truncations in Wolfe's portrait. Homosexuals are discussed secondhand (AIDS is mentioned twice). Leftwing activists, including those who had recently staged the world's largest anti-nuclear demonstration in Central Park, do not appear. Non-Black minorities and immigrant communities are not seen or heard. Wolfe's Black characters, drawn from diverse communities across the Five Boroughs, are all taxonomized as either poor and dangerous or well-to-do and corrupt. In a period when diverse vocabularies of hip-hop exploded across the city, Wolfe's Black youth share essentially the same vocabulary and walk with the same (crudely termed) "pimp roll." Likewise, white youth culture in the 1980s – its niches and ecologies varying at times from street to street – is basically ignored. Reagan Democrats, ubiquitous among the city's white working class, appear mostly as cops. And the full scale of white flight (perhaps the truly big sociological story of 1980s New York) is never really conveyed.

In November 1989, two years after the publication of *Bonfire*, Wolfe published "Stalking the Billion-Footed Beast" in *Harper's* magazine. The essay amounted to a manifesto for a new social realism modeled on *Bonfire* itself. Wolfe was not modest about his achievements: he declared *Bonfire* a template for the future of American fiction. After World War II, he argued, the US intelligentsia sought to build a native American literature by looking to Europe. There, they discovered Absurdism, Magical Realism, Minimalism, and a variety of poststructuralist language games that captured the imagination of novelists but not novel readers. This preference for the abstract and difficult, argued Wolfe, was the result of a latent Marxist prejudice against nineteenth-century bourgeois taste. Middle-class readers preferred realistic fiction; therefore, serious fiction must not be realistic. This spelled doom for fiction in the United States.

By turning away from the powerful capacity of realism to evoke emotion and provoke sympathy, argued Wolfe, novelists were abandoning the most essential technology of fiction itself.

By the 1980s, of course, literary realism was resurgent, particularly among the Dirty Realists, a movement associated with Raymond Carver and others. But these works were, in Wolfe's estimation, too narrow in scope. Wolfe demanded that novelists conduct painstaking research and render broad, society-wide portraits. Wolfe was particularly attentive to the idea of status, which for him seemed to supersede the category of class (Wolfe arguably wanted literary naturalism without its traditional left politics and focusing too much on class would complicate that endeavor). In "Stalking the Billion-Footed Beast," Wolfe described his method of characterization as status modified by personality, paraphrasing Lionel Trilling ("class traits modified by personality" [2008, p. 262], without the class). He once commented that "every living moment of a human being's life. . .is controlled by a concern for status" (Wolfe 1989, p. 51).

More than a decade would pass before Wolfe's second novel, *A Man in Full* (1998). Its publication was a major event. Wolfe appeared on the cover of *Time* magazine in his trademark white suit; more than a million copies were sold to bookstores in advance. The novel was similar to *Bonfire* in themes and structure, moving from 1980s New York City to 1990s Atlanta and from the bond market to the real estate market. Again, Wolfe tackled racial themes, and his portrayal of Black characters again courted controversy. But *A Man in Full* marked the beginning of a major backlash against Wolfe's literary style. John Irving, Norman Mailer, and John Updike each criticized the novel's breathless, somewhat flabby prose, full of italicizations and exclamation points. This prompted a harsh retort from Wolfe, who accused the three luminaries of professional jealousy.

By the publication of his third novel, *I Am Charlotte Simmons* (2004), Wolfe had become a divisive cultural figure, openly endorsing George W. Bush (who, in return, was seen carrying a copy of *Charlotte Simmons*). The title essay of Wolfe's collection *Hooking Up* (2000) documented and railed against sexual promiscuity in US high schools and universities. Wolfe's research for the essay served as the basis for *Charlotte Simmons*, which portrayed the title character's sexual exploits at an elite US university with embarrassingly clinical detail. The novel's many sex scenes provoked widespread ridicule. Wolfe's final novel, *Back to Blood* (2012), returned to the themes that had made him famous: status and race. Set in Miami, the novel explored the tensions associated with immigration, foregrounding a subject that would prove critical to US political discourse in the 2016 presidential election and beyond. Nevertheless, the novel was Wolfe's first major commercial failure. His one defense against critics of his style – that his books sold well – now seemed defunct. He increasingly retreated to obscure preoccupations: bizarre critiques of Chomskyan linguistics and of the Darwinian theory of evolution. He published a nonfiction treatise on these subjects, *The Kingdom of Speech* (2016), two years before his death at age 88 on May 14, 2018.

Critics generally prefer Wolfe's journalism over his fiction. He remains, however, an essential practitioner and advocate of literary realism at the end of the twentieth century, and *Bonfire* remains an essential novel of the 1980s. Wolfe's literary project was part of a wider backlash against postmodernism in fiction, one that included such diverse movements as Dirty Realism in the 1980s and the New Sincerity in the 1990s and 2000s. Jonathan Franzen's own manifesto for social relevance, "Perchance to Dream" (published in 1996 in *Harper's*), is a descendant of "Stalking the Billion-Footed

Beast," to which it refers directly. Franzen would reach different conclusions from Wolfe, but he shared many of Wolfe's core assumptions about realism and the direction of American fiction – as well as his emphasis on white, middle-class readership and taste.

SEE ALSO: Carver, Raymond; The Culture Wars; Franzen, Jonathan; Irving, John; Mailer, Norman; Realism after Poststructuralism; Updike, John

REFERENCES

Trilling, Lionel. (2008). *The Liberal Imagination: Essays on Literature and Society*. New York: New York Review Books; 1st ed. 1950.
Wolfe, Tom. (1963). There goes (varoom! varoom!) that kandy-kolored (thphhhhhh!) tangerine-flake streamline baby (rahghhhh!) around the bend (brummmmmmmmmmmmmmmmm…). *Esquire* (November 1, 1963). https://classic.esquire.com/article/19631101121/print (accessed September 24, 2021).
Wolfe, Tom. (1989). Stalking the billion-footed beast. *Harper's Magazine* (November 1989): 45–56.
Wolfe, Tom. (2004). *Bonfire of the Vanities: A Novel*. New York: Picador.

FURTHER READING

Best, Joel. (2001). "Status! Yes!" Tom Wolfe as a sociological thinker. *The American Sociologist* 32 (4): 5–22.
Hitchens, Christopher. (2000). Running on empty. In: *Unacknowledged Legislation: Writers in the Public Sphere*, 379–388. New York: Verso.
Kennedy, Liam. (1997). "It's the third world down here!": urban decline and (post)national mythologies in *Bonfire of the Vanities*. *Modern Fiction Studies* 43 (1): 93–111.
Scura, Dorothy. (ed.) (1998). *Conversations with Tom Wolfe*. Jackson: University Press of Mississippi.
Weingarten, Marc. (2010). *The Gang That Wouldn't Write Straight: Wolfe, Thompson, Didion, Capote, and the New Journalism Revolution*. New York: Random House.

Wolitzer, Meg

BETH WIDMAIER CAPO
Illinois College, USA

A writer of adult literary fiction and books for younger readers, Meg Wolitzer is known for her sweeping novels of acute social observation. Her writing dissects romantic, familial, marital, and platonic relationships, gender, and issues both timeless (grief, aging, death) and contemporary (HIV, feminism, birth control and sexuality). Wolitzer's accessible novels have received minimal critical or scholarly attention as yet, but they have found popular success, particularly *The Female Persuasion* (2018) and *The Wife* (2003). Many of her adult novels have inhabited the *New York Times* Best Seller list and several have been adapted for film or television.

Wolitzer's focus on women's lives and relationships, lack of experimental narrative devices, wry and witty tone, and empathetic approach to serious topics code her work as populist, "droll and entertaining novels of ideas" (Corrigan 2018). In "The Second Shelf," a 2012 *New York Times Book Review* essay, Wolitzer comments on how "many first-rate books by women and about women's lives never find a way to escape 'Women's Fiction' and make the leap onto the upper shelf" of literary fiction deemed worthy of respect. "Women's Fiction," defined as "literature that happens to be written by women," is often ignored by reviewers and award committees, as well as by male readers, while fiction by male writers such as Jonathan Franzen and Jeffrey Eugenides, to whom Wolitzer has been compared, garners acclaim and scholarly attention (Wolitzer 2012). This "continuing critical bias against women" may contribute to Wolitzer's relative neglect (Wolitzer 2012). Meg Wolitzer's work, significant for its realistic depictions of contemporary issues, engages with debates about gendered reception and the value and definition of "popular," including Young Adult (YA), versus "literary" fiction.

Born on Long Island, New York, in 1959, daughter of author Hilma Wolitzer, Meg Wolitzer studied English at Brown University. She sold her first novel, *Sleepwalking* (1982), when still a college senior. Her work is usually set in or around New York City, where she currently lives with her husband, science writer Richard Panek. Wolitzer teaches in the MFA program at Stony Brook Southampton.

Wolitzer's fiction explores women's lives with great empathy for the mundane dramas of human experience. A self-identified feminist, her work depicts flawed, fully-human characters navigating relationships, career, and family. *Sleepwalking* describes the friendship of three Swarthmore students each obsessed with a different female poet who committed suicide – Anne Sexton, Sylvia Plath, and fictional Lucy Ascher. Wolitzer's interest in writers and her background as an English major are apparent in many of her novels, with literary references and frequent artist and writer characters. These poets capture the sense of isolation of young, sensitive, educated women, and validate their sense of sadness in a culture that demands they smile and look pretty. Protagonist Claire is still coming to terms with the death of her younger brother and her parents' bitter grief; her contact with Lucy's parents provides an uncomfortable catalyst for healing. This somber first novel captures with great pathos the love of parents for their children, the difficulties of communicating across generations, and the struggle of intelligent young women to come of age.

Wolitzer has stated "I feel I'm a feminist so I write like a feminist. But I am interested primarily in following and exploring the stories of people who feel like real people, as opposed to writing a polemic" (O'Kelly 2018). Since the 1980s her novels have implicitly considered the debates within contemporary feminism. In her second novel, *Hidden Pictures* (1986), Wolitzer offers an extended meditation on love and parenthood. The protagonist takes her young son and leaves her unhappy marriage. A successful artist and loving mother, she finds fulfillment in a lesbian relationship, although she and her partner face homophobia after leaving New York for its safer suburbs. This relationship is paralleled by the marriage of her ex-husband. The novel portrays marriage, parenting, divorce, and the families we create. The theme of individuals negotiating sexuality, including birth control and infertility, remain a constant thread in her work throughout the decades.

Humor marks the examination of mother/daughter and sororal relationships in *This Is Your Life* (1988). The memorable protagonist, Dottie, is an obese comedienne often on the road, a single mother supporting her daughters. Set in Manhattan in the 1970s and 1980s, the novel narrates the impact of their mother's fame and its eventual loss on Erica and Opal, and Dottie's struggle with money and her health. Each daughter chooses a divergent path into adulthood, and the novel insightfully depicts the challenges facing women as they create an identity, find a career, and build satisfying relationships. Nora Ephron adapted the novel for her first film, *This is My Life* (1992), and the novel was reprinted in 2014 under that title.

Wolitzer employs an expanded cast of characters and a witty, observant style in *Friends for Life* (1994), which focuses on female friendships. The opening line, "Three women in a restaurant: *what a cliché*," warns readers that the novel will play with and enlarge stereotypes of female friendships (1994, p. 3). The novel tracks three women who have been friends since suburban grade school as they work to maintain their friendship with each other as adults in New York City while pursuing careers and the tribulations of relationships and families. Through job changes, marriage, childbirth, jealousy and misunderstanding, female friendship offers a haven of security and understanding.

Wolitzer's next novel, *Surrender, Dorothy* (1999), further explores friendship, mother/daughter relationships, and sexual relationships. Friends since freshman year of college, Sara, Adam, and Maddy escape New York City each summer by renting a dilapidated beach house. A sudden tragedy ending the first chapter focuses the novel on grief and facing the truth of our imperfect understanding of others. The novel compassionately examines the death of a child, postpartum depression, marital dissatisfaction, homosexuality, career success and failure, and aging. As she had in *Sleepwalking*, Wolitzer probes the topic of grief and its survival and offers an uplifting but realistic message: "When a child dies there was only one truth: You could not get over it, ever, but still you had to live" (2014a, p. 214). Diane Keaton starred in a television-movie adaptation in 2006.

The Wife, perhaps Wolitzer's best-known novel thanks to the 2017 film adaptation starring Glenn Close, uses first-person voice to tell through flashbacks the story of the wife of a famous novelist. Across four decades, Joan Castleman details her transformation from a college freshman at 1950s Smith to the wife of an award-winning writer who encapsulates male privilege. In "a voice of controlled rage and pissed-off humor" (Wolitzer 2019), Joan details decades of cultural sexism and her decisions as a writer, wife, and mother. She enjoyed being "the wife," but at age sixty-four, at the moment of her husband's greatest triumph, she has decided to leave him. Through Joan, Wolitzer reveals sexism in the publishing industry and gender roles more broadly, but also how women, as agentic individuals, are complicit.

The Position (2005) offers insight into family dynamics as it examines social change in gender and sexual roles. A novel about "sex and the family" (Cox 2011), it recognizes how four children were affected by the sex manual their suburban Long Island parents published in the mid-1970s. As with *This Is Your Life*, the novel examines how parental fame can affect children. Twenty-eight years after they found the book, the children are drawn together when their long-divorced parents fight over reissuing *Pleasuring: One Couple's Journey to Fulfillment*. Depression, impotence, infidelity, drug use, and aimlessness are eventually salved through romantic relationships (both homosexual and heterosexual) and a reconnection with family. The novel answers the question "How did children raised in the same family end up so different from one another?" (2006, p. 281) with Wolitzer's signature respect for the complexity of human interaction. The parents are given voice, their decisions and choices narrated with wit and nonjudgmental ambivalence.

The Ten-Year Nap (2008) probes "the mommy wars" between women who opt out of work to stay at home and raise children and those who continue working. The tension between motherhood and ambition, or its lack, are apparent in Amy Lamb and her friends Jill, Roberta, and Karen in post 9/11 New York. The novel, set in Manhattan, captures the urban lifestyle of walk-ups, rent stabilization, nannies and coffeeshops of a privileged subset of women who recognize that their choice to opt out is "lucky" (2008, p. 60). Generational difference demonstrates the slow work of social change. Amy's mother, a second wave feminist, urges her to return to work, but Amy resents her mother's own absence from her childhood. Wolitzer lays bare the still unfulfilled promise of feminism, examining how and why women leave the workforce when they have children. Characters wrestle with what their own decisions mean, and the rhetoric of choice and its intersectionality with class are mirrored in an abortion subplot. It foregrounds the gendered division of labor still burdening women with emotional labor and primary caregiving responsibilities within institutional pay disparities and a lack of affordable day care. While the novel is grounded in feminist debates, it is not polemical. It is not, in itself, a feminist work, as "there is no call to action. Motherhood has defeated feminism. The personal is private, not political" (Michaels 2009, p. 320). As in her other work, Wolitzer plumbs the depths of women's ordinary experience and the dilemmas they face, creating an impression rather than an argument.

Female desire, a thread across Wolitzer's work, takes center stage in *The Uncoupling* (2011), a witty novel that strays from the realist mode to add an element of magic realism. The arrival of a high school drama teacher directing *Lysistrata* casts a spell over a suburban New Jersey town. Women in sexual relationships, no matter their age or marital status, are struck by a freezing of their libido. Passion suddenly turns to disgust and horror, and privately relationships stutter. While the spell removes women's agency, the concept and *Lysistrata* as its vehicle reflects on the power of "no" and the centrality of female desire in relationships and, for some women, in their sense of identity. The respite from sex forces a reexamination of their lives and relationships for both men and women. The spell finally breaks at the high school performance, and the drama teacher moves on to take the play and its magical effect elsewhere, to reset people's appreciation for sex and each other, to break them out of the rut of routine.

Based in part on her own experience at a summer performing arts camp as a teenager, *The Interestings* (2013) follows six teenagers who meet at a summer camp in the 1970s across four decades. The sweeping novel inspects ambition, success, aging, and how relationships evolve. With empathy and her signature flawed characters, the novel focuses on Jules Jacobson, a middle-class suburban girl who befriends five talented, wealthy New York teens at summer camp. What is success? While Jules gives up her dream of becoming a comedic actor, she creates a comfortable life filled with meaningful work, friendship, and a loving family. Two of her friends, a talented cartoonist and animator and a theater director, marry and grow to enormous wealth and fame but confront familial and personal challenges. The novel's vivid details create memorable and realistic characters enacting multiple subplots, touching on rape, drug use and cults, depression, autism, homosexuality, wealth disparity, and child labor. The novel offers nonjudgmental observation of individual moral choices. As with Wolitzer's other work, the novel was a bestseller, with some critics faulting the straightforward style. Goldfield, for example, wrote, "*The Interestings* is serious, and literary, and sweeping, but, in contrast to Franzen, for example, who, for his other flaws, writes with a virtuosic, poetic authority, Wolitzer's obvious, pedestrian style and tendency toward sentimentality severely limits her" (2013). A TV pilot was made in 2016.

While *The Interestings* aimed for an adult audience, Wolitzer's 2014 novel *Belzhar* was written for young adults (YA). Wolitzer has published several novels for younger readers. In "Look Homeward, Reader," a 2014 piece for the *New York Times,* she describes her experience in a "kid lit" book group and "what drew me to write Y.A. in the first place: the desire for a particular *feeling*." Rather than indulging nostalgia, Wolitzer describes reading and writing beyond the realm of adult literary fiction as "broadening" and points to the growing number of respected writers "crossing over" (Wolitzer 2014b). The slippery boundaries between YA and adult fiction often are more marketing than substance, as demonstrated by Wolitzer's first novel, *Sleepwalking,* which was originally marketed as an adult novel but was issued in paperback as YA. Set in a Vermont boarding school for "emotionally fragile, highly intelligent" teenagers (2014c, p. 1), *Belzhar*'s setting recalls the camp scenes of *The Interestings*. The novel's invocation of poet Sylvia Plath as a touchstone for troubled teenagers recalls *Sleepwalking*. The novel focuses on five students in Special Topics in English whose journaling assignments transport them to an alternate reality where they can briefly relive the period before their individual tragedies. This magical narrative device is reminiscent of the sex-strike spell in *The Uncoupling*. The novel also returns to the topic of grief and healing, as the protagonist and her fellow students in Special Topics confront the tragedies of their past in order to move beyond them. The novel demonstrates Wolitzer's abiding interest in and respect for the psychology of young people.

Female mentorship and feminism are central to *The Female Persuasion*. The novel is dedicated to eight women, including her mother, that mentored the author. In smart, perceptive writing, the novel follows Greer Kadetsky, her boyfriend, and her college roommate through their twenties. The conflicts between second- and third-wave feminism are evident in Greer and second wave feminist icon Faith Ford, her mentor. Her long-running feminist magazine having folded to competition from third-wave blogs, Faith leads a venture-capital funded feminist speakers bureau heavy on celebrity, media, and receptions with sparkling wine. Faith mentors by listening, encouraging, and giving women permission to pursue their ambitions. The idealism of youth – that of Faith, Greer, and other characters – is muted and transformed by personal tragedy, depression, economic hardship, and uncompromising reality even as individuals strive for effective activism. How is self-help "female empowerment" different from real power? This "novel of ideas" critiques overconfident ideological purity as insufficient in the face of personal and political challenges: "As Wolitzer dramatizes, life isn't that straightforward and art shouldn't be either" (Corrigan 2018).

How do people survive the challenges and dilemmas they confront, and what mundane and moral choices do they make? Throughout her fiction Meg Wolitzer realistically identifies the issues facing contemporary women and men. Her novels center sex and sexuality, and their accompanying complications, of contraception, pregnancy, abortion, childbirth, and parenting. These are, as Sarah Lyall describes them, "big, substantial, old-fashioned books that allow her characters room to breathe, change and grow into adulthood and beyond" (2018). Her characters are always flawed and often funny. Her work is deeply human. But it is also limited to a mostly white, urban, upper- and middle-class experience, and the topical nature of her themes can make them feel dated a decade later. Wolitzer's empathetic and ambitious novels blend humor and drama to detail a slice of American life.

SEE ALSO: Chick Lit and the New Domesticity; The Culture Wars; Third-Wave Feminism; Young Adult Boom

REFERENCES

Corrigan, Maureen. (2018). Meg Wolitzer traces the arc of the feminist movement in "The Female Persuasion." *NPR* (April 11, 2018). https://www.npr.org/2018/04/11/601370601/meg-wolitzer-traces-the-arc-of-the-feminist-movement-in-the-female-persuasion (accessed July 18, 2021).

Cox, Erin L. (2011). Meg Wolitzer talks about humor, film, and the end of sex. *Publishing Perspectives* (April 7, 2011). https://publishingperspectives.com/2011/04/meg-wolitzer-talks-about-humor-film-and-the-end-of-sex/ (accessed July 18, 2021).

Goldfield, Hannah. (2013). Camp people: Meg Wolitzer's *Interestings*. *VQR Online* (December

17, 2013). https://www.vqronline.org/camp-people-meg-wolitzers-interestings (accessed July 18, 2021).

Lyall, Sarah. (2018). Why now may (finally) be Meg Wolitzer's moment. *The New York Times* (March 23, 2018). https://www.nytimes.com/2018/03/23/books/meg-wolitzer-the-female-persuasion.html (accessed July 19, 2021).

Michaels, Meredith W. (2009). Mothers "opting out": facts and fiction. *WSQ: Women's Studies Quarterly* 37 (2): 317–322. doi:10.1353/wsq.0.0193

O'Kelly, Lisa. (2018). Meg Wolitzer: "I feel I'm a feminist, so I write like a feminist." *The Guardian* (November 25, 2018). https://www.theguardian.com/books/2018/nov/25/meg-wolitzer-interview-im-a-feminist-so-i-write-like-a-feminist-the-female-persuasion-the-wife (accessed July 18, 2021).

Wolitzer, Meg. (2006). *The Position*. New York: Scribner; 1st ed. 2005.

Wolitzer, Meg. (2008). *The Ten-Year Nap*. New York: Riverhead Books.

Wolitzer, Meg. (2012). The second shelf. *The New York Times* (March 30, 2012). https://www.nytimes.com/2012/04/01/books/review/on-the-rules-of-literary-fiction-for-men-and-women.html (accessed July 18, 2021).

Wolitzer, Meg. (2014a). *Surrender, Dorothy*. New York: Scribner; 1st ed. 1999.

Wolitzer, Meg. (2014b). Look homeward, reader. *The New York Times* (October 17, 2014). https://www.nytimes.com/2014/10/19/fashion/a-not-so-young-audience-for-young-adult-books.html (accessed July 18, 2021).

Wolitzer, Meg. (2014c). *Belzhar*. New York: Dutton Books for Young Readers.

FURTHER READING

Brockes, Emma. (2018). Meg Wolitzer: "You go for what feels human, and it transcends a political moment." *The Guardian* (June 1, 2018). https://www.theguardian.com/books/2018/jun/01/meg-wolitzer-interview

Schwartz, A. (2018). Meg Wolitzer rides the feminist waves. *The New Yorker* (April 2, 2018). https://www.newyorker.com/magazine/2018/04/09/meg-wolitzer-rides-the-feminist-waves

Teisch, Jessica. (2018). Meg Wolitzer. *Bookmarks* (July): 24.

Writers' Collectives

FLORIAN SEDLMEIER
Freie Universität Berlin, Germany

While writers' collectives have a long history even before the historical avant-garde, their contemporary iterations are inextricable from the shifting institutional conditions of literary production and reception. Assuming a dialectical understanding of individual possessive authorship and writers' collectives, we can identify different provisional formations taking shape under divergent conditions and with various motivations. Two such developments and their related constructions of collectivity in paratexts are at the center of this entry, which builds on the conceptual metaphors of Pierre Bourdieu. First, the reshuffling of the literary field and its history according to cultural difference creates demographic collectives that correlate to distinctive identity poetics understood as literary capital. In the specific context of African American literature, the imagined transhistorical writers' collective prompts reactive collectives from within. Ranging from postmodern playfulness to gestures of activism, these affiliations pursue alternative aesthetic programs. Second, against the backdrop of creative writing programs and the literary center New York City, contemporary magazines and publishing platforms create competing institutions. Negotiating the relation between digitization and print culture, the resulting writers' collectives explore the conditions for collaborative cultural criticism and social engagement. In effect, though, these collectives often depend upon the prominence of individual authors who move them from niche to mainstream. While literary blogs and social media interfaces afford new modes of connectivity, the collectives of the digital sphere are a symptom of the economic precariousness affecting literary culture. As such, they compensate for a lack of connections to the established institutions that continue to hold symbolic capital.

If the writers' collective has not yet entered our critical lexicon in a substantial way, then one reason for this may be the persistence of individual possessive authorship, which finds its institutional manifestation in practices of anthologizing national literary histories by authors' names and of archiving authors' papers (Chen 2020). However, the formation of writers' collectives equally structures both literary history and the literary field, at least in the twentieth century. We may consider the collaborative novel *The Family* (1907–1908), the twelve contributing writers of which were affiliated with literary realism and consolidated the status of *Harper's* as a major publishing venue (Howard 2001). We may look at the various, often short-lived little magazines, which became the platforms for the historical avant-garde in the early twentieth century and for later avant-gardes, as they renegotiated the relation between literature and lived experience (Bürger 1984), not only in literary practice but also in a sprawling paratext (Genette 1997) that featured the manifesto with its performative collective speech act as a crucial genre (Lyon 1999). Similarly, various countercultural movements of the 1950s, 1960s, and 1970s imagine notions of artistic collectivity against the backdrop of a perceived cultural consensus with its established literary and political institutions (Puchner 2006).

These instances suggest several criteria for a working definition of writers' collectives cast in the language of Pierre Bourdieu, who remains influential for the heterogeneous "*new* sociology of literature" (English 2010, p. v). First, individual possessive authorship and writers' collectives are best conceived dialectically, with the two poles constituting and challenging one another as writers compete for symbolic capital in the literary field, at times to the effect that some authors' names stand in synecdochic relation to larger movements. Second, for their formation and consolidation, writers' collectives rely on specific publication venues including anthologies, forums, magazines (print and digital), specific book series and imprints, social media interfaces and platforms, all of which can be ascribed varying degrees of symbolic capital. Third, writers' collectives need to produce a paratext, reflecting on and legitimizing their own raison d'être. Political declarations and poetological statements take the form of editorials, essays, interviews, manifestos, mission statements, prefaces, or reviews, and often include the choice of a label to coalesce around. These paratexts react to previous pronouncements of other groups, whether past or contemporaneous, in order to create distinct positions in the literary field. Fourth, writers' collectives chafe at established literary institutions. They constitute themselves vis-à-vis the symbolic capital these institutions hold. While invested in the building of "anti-institutional institutions" (Bourdieu 1996, p. 258), they are themselves an effect of the literary field, which always already accommodates alternative positions and dissenting voices. Fifth, contemporary writers' collectives differ from previous ones because of the proliferation of institutional frameworks, including creative writing programs at colleges and universities. There is an increasing reciprocity between academically constructed author collectives, their labeling in para-academic criticism and marketing, and writers' collectives.

COLLECTIVES OF CULTURAL DIFFERENCE

With respect to contemporary American literature, a first iteration of writers' collectives is inextricable from the emergence of "women's writing" and "minority writers," which serve as categories of classification and analysis, but also as markers of distinction and legitimation. The emergence of such categories and markers, in turn, cannot be separated from the formation of artistic and political groups in the literary field of the 1960s and 1970s, constituted by second-wave feminism, decolonization, and the Civil Rights movement. For instance, the Black Arts Movement and the Black Aesthetic, as proclaimed by Addison Gayle, Jr., Hoyt W. Fuller, Larry Neal, and others, are situated against the backdrop of the Black Power movement. Disillusioned by the failures of integration and fueled by an interventionist cultural separatism, they envision artistic collectives that claim to represent an imagined demographic community by means of a distinct aesthetic and the control of the means of production. Tenets of activist groupings like the Combahee River Collective (1974–1980) – situated at the intersection of feminism, lesbianism, Blackness, and socialism (Springer 2005) – influence group formation in the literary field and inform the ensuing academic rewriting of literary histories. From the late 1960s onward, the incentives of author collectives, which are legitimated by the shared biographical experience of structural discrimination and institutional exclusion, find their manifestation in anthologies. Most early collections, often edited by writers or writers who are also scholars, are organized by cultural identity as exemplified in *Black Fire: An Anthology of Afro-American Writing* (1968), *We Are Chicano: An Anthology of Mexican-American Literature* (1973), and *Aiiieeeee! An Anthology of Asian-American Writers* (1974). As instances of self-institutionalization to counter existing institutions while attempting to acquire the symbolic capital they hold, the writers' collectives imagined by these anthologies find their institutional manifestations in the restructuring of English and comparative literature departments. In particular, they influenced the widespread redefinition of American literary studies as studies of ethnic and racial difference, with the decades of the 1980s and 1990s witnessing the institutional rise of cultural studies, gender studies, multiculturalism, and postcolonial studies. While they prompted rhetorically hard-fought debates about core curricula, selective syllabi, and the revision of the canon, these studies redefined American literary production not least by viewing "writers primarily, if not exclusively, as members of various ethnic and gender groups" (Sollors 1986, p. 14).

The writers' collectives that scholars reconstruct under the conditions of the institutionalization of these new fields of study are transhistorical, redirecting and multiplying the question of "a usable past" for American literature, which Van Wyck Brooks had posed in 1918. These pasts equally rest on the formulation of a distinct poetics that combines the corrective rewriting of colonial master texts and stereotypical tropes with the retrieval of culturally specific modes of expression and narration. A pastiche of self-narration, historiographical essay, cultural manifesto, and poetry, Gloria Anzaldúa's bilingual *Borderlands/La Frontera: The New Mestiza* (1987) imagines a postcolonial collective based on an intersectional consciousness and the contradictions resulting from annexation and colonial contact in border regions. The complex textuality of her account performs the program of an identity poetics shifting between the personal pronouns "I," "we," and "she" that navigate the line between individual and collective authorship. Henry Louis Gates, Jr.'s *The Signifying Monkey* (1988) provides another case in point. By means of the concepts of "signifying" and "trickster," he reconstructs African American literary history and criticism as a collective endeavor structured by intra- and intertextual references. Resituating semiotic theory and deconstructionist reading practice in African and African American mythologies, Gates recreates a transhistorical genealogy where the texts of Black authors signify upon previous texts to affiliate themselves with a culturally distinct tradition.

With his focus on citational and significatory practices to reconstruct a literary history, Gates is skeptical of the more general bent of multiculturalism to "allow intellectual work to be the expression and medium of identity," as the Chicago Cultural Studies Group (1992, p. 541) puts it. In the collectively authored "Critical Multiculturalism," the group records their discussions, which reflect upon various benefits and shortcomings of an identity-based multiculturalism with respect to the alliances and separations its imagined collectives announce.

On the one hand, the underlying operation of mapping demographic collectives onto collectives of scholars, critics, and writers is an indispensable strategy to secure the social relevance and symbolic capital of literature as cultural studies. It spurs the ongoing revisions of both the canon and literary history as a crucial "corrective to the biases and blindness of nonacademic gatekeepers" (Bérubé 1992, p. 30). These gatekeepers may be the cultural custodians engaged in the "culture wars." They may also be publishers and marketeers in the field of cultural production, which often absorbs cultural difference in exoticist terms (Huggan 2001), but which, in any case, uses markers of ethnicity as marketing strategies for contemporary American literature (Ween 2003). On the other hand, the desideratum of authenticity, based on the anthropological figure of the native informant, generates what Deepika Bahri calls "the burden of representation" (2003, p. 4). The expectation and pressure for writers to function as representatives of demographic groups often glosses over the possibility that difference and culture may be syncretic categories (Sollors 1986), which make it difficult to hold on to the strategically proclaimed stability of scripts of identity.

Notably, writers who operate from within the marking and marketing of ethnic collectives carve out alternative positions, leading to different senses of collectivity. Drawing on the citational and stylistic eclecticism of postmodernism, writer and academic Trey Ellis proclaims a New Black Aesthetic to emphasize the hybrid heterogeneity of African American cultural production beyond the confines of an aesthetic anchored in the patterns of call and response, characteristic of spirituals and blues, as well as in the syncopated rhythms of jazz. Like the proponents of a Black Aesthetic, however, Ellis legitimizes his positioning as "a cultural mulatto" (1989, p. 235) with personal experience and maps it onto a generationally defined collective endowed with less restricted literary license. Building on Ellis, a text by novelist Denzy Senna accompanied the reprinting of Fran Ross's long forgotten novel *Oreo* (1974). In her introduction, part of which was also printed in *The New Yorker*, Senna mobilizes her biography to place her writing in transhistorical continuity with Ross's satirical picaresque novel, thus carving out a field position around a presumably underrepresented aesthetic genealogy from within African American literature (Senna 2015). Ellis's and Senna's moves reverberate in the scholarship of Ramón Saldívar and others, who explore the conditions of a post-soul or postracial aesthetic in terms of generation, genre, and range of references to construct different writers' collectives. Adapting Bourdieu's framework, sociologists Mustafa Emirbayer and Matthew Desmond (2015) accordingly account for the heterogeneity from within multicultural collectives when they chart a "Field of Literary Blackness." In this field, the differing degrees to which tropes of Blackness are cited index clusters of writers and serve as symbolic capital. Such capital correlates with commercial and avant-garde value, as well as with a dialectic of literary realism and experimental writing.

In notable distinction to culturalist playfulness, and against the backdrop of the renewed public attention to structural violence and police brutality, some African American writers collectivize as literary activists against racial oppression. Drawing on James Baldwin and prompted by the shooting of Black teenagers Michael Brown, Jr., Trayvon Martin, and Tamir Rice (among many others) at the hands of white police officers, the anthology *The Fire This Time: A New Generation Speaks about Race* (2016) assembles deeply personal texts written in different genres. In her introduction, editor and National Book Award-winning novelist Jesmyn Ward, after relating her individual attempt to find her words through rereading Baldwin's essays, explains her vision for the collection: "A book that would gather new voices in one place, in a lasting, physical form, and provide a forum for those writers to dissent, to call to account, to witness, to reckon" (2016, p. 8). The book, a *New York Times* bestseller, becomes the material manifestation of a generationally marked writers' collective, an attempt to cope with, speak out against, and compensate for communal loss. If its intent is "to provide a forum" for the critique of governmental institutions and structural racism, then the implication is also that other publication formats, whether prominent magazines or newspapers, rarely afford such collective formation. Ward ends her introduction with a reader address: "I hope this book makes each one of you, dear readers, feel as if we are sitting together, you and me and Baldwin and Tretheway and Wilkerson and Jeffers and Walters and Anderson and Smith and all the serious, clear-sighted writers here – and that we are composing our story together" (p. 11). Implicating the reader, whether Black or white, the conjunction of individual names, aligned by their demographic and professional identity, leads to a collective story composition to the effect that "we are writing an epic where black lives carry worth" (p. 11), a national epos of existential self-validation.

THE SCHOOL AND ITS COUNTER-INSTITUTIONS

Writers' collectives of cultural and racial difference, while anti-institutional and self-instituting in their gesture, are always already an effect of the literary field and its interplay with literary institutions. Suggesting such an institutional lens and adopting some tenets of systems theory, Mark McGurl's influential *The Program Era: Postwar Fiction and the Rise of Creative Writing* (2009) has changed the perception of scholars, para-academic critics, and many writers of contemporary American literature. He identifies a shared, institutionally induced investment in autopoiesis that characterizes what he labels high cultural pluralism, lower-middle-class modernism, and technomodernism (as well as their overlaps) as claims to aesthetic distinction. While McGurl's diagnosis of a "systematic creativity" (2009, p. 46) invites us to rethink the notion of the oeuvre of individual authors like Philip Roth as a feedback loop of sorts, where each novel incorporates the reception of the previous one and generates new provocations, it also makes it possible to think different options of grouping authors framed by "the school" and "the workshop." Writers may coalesce qua institutional affiliation, influenced by other writers who are their teachers and peers in the programs; they may be aligned by their investment in different genres including "the ethnic family saga" or "the meta-slave narrative"; and they may find their collective manifestation in formats such as "the workshop story collection" (p. 49).

Reacting to McGurl, the writer Chad Harbach, co-founder and editor of the journal *n+1*, identifies two competing, yet overlapping literary cultures organized by literary form. In the context of creative writing programs, he argues, authors are invested in the short story, which "has become a primary pedagogical genre form" (2014, p. 17). Its condensed brevity lends itself to detailed discussion with professors and workshop peers, and its subsequent publication in quarterly journals and story collections endows MFA writers with the credentials to apply for positions at colleges and universities, where they themselves teach the writing of stories. The writers' collective generated by "the program" and "the school," we could say, depends upon literary capital ascribed to the short story, which enables the accrual of institutional capital on a career path within the educational system. The complementary writers' collective identified by Harbach in his polemic is based in New York City, the central hub of the publishing world and home to many of the most credentialed writers from different generations including Philip Roth, Siri Hustvedt, Michael Chabon, Colson Whitehead, and Nicole Krauss. Lacking the institutional security of the MFA writers-as-teachers, NYC authors depend on their success as novelists, which is the form they tackle in a highly competitive market that awards most of its economic and symbolic capital to the few and already established. These writers are pressed to define their positions in both the field and the market, producing, as Harbach notes, "a combination of public and academic acclaim" (p. 23).

The macroscopic institutional perspective with its interrelated clusters, created by the institutions MFA and NYC, prompts questions about the status of alternative collective formations. Perhaps the most successful anti-institutional literary institution of the past two decades has been McSweeney's, an independent and multifaceted publishing conglomerate located in San Francisco. Founder Dave Eggers, who does not hold an MFA degree, who began his writing career in local journalism, and who worked as a graphic designer, started out with *Timothy McSweeney's Quarterly Concern* (1998–). Partly modeled on the publication format of the miscellany, which collects rather than selects, the magazine features an extensive paratext of ironic commentary on editorial conventions in many of its issues, performing its self-awareness and initial position on the margins of the contemporary literary field. The inaugural issue, with a run of just 2500 print copies, some of which Eggers distributed himself and placed in bookstores, announces a decisive break with gatekeeping mechanisms, explicitly inviting the submission of unsolicited manuscripts. It marks itself as a forum for the writing which has been rejected elsewhere, which has been leftover in a drawer or file, and which may engage genres and forms that do not meet the expectations of the market and the publishing industry. In retrospect, Eggers notes in the introduction to the collection *The Best of McSweeney's*: "I began wondering if it were possible to start a new journal, assembled from [. . .] articles not fit for other magazines," which could result in "a quarterly of orphaned stories" (2004, p. viii). The publication of several "Best-of" and "Better-of" volumes indicates something else as well. While the magazine constitutes itself as a miscellany harboring a heterogeneous writers' collective committed to quirky experimentalism, the anthologies in book format follow the logic of canonization and symbolic capital by selecting some of the most acclaimed and prolific contemporary novelists, including Jonathan Lethem, Zadie Smith, and David Foster Wallace, whose careers had launched before the magazine took off.

The name "Timothy McSweeney's" itself serves not only as a pen name for the individual author Eggers, but also "metonymically represents the various authorial and editorial voices for which McSweeney's provides a forum" (Bollen, Craps, and Vermeulen 2013). The writers' collective thus formed – "the McSweeney's coterie of writers" (Starre 2015, p. 69) – invests in a range of aesthetic effects taken from avant-garde magazines and do-it-yourself culture to foreground the conditions of production and reception. The humorous, arabesque, and meandering style of many contributions is paired with reflections on print culture, including the use of specific fonts with their histories. Developed against the backdrop of the digitization of the book market, the journal can be viewed, with Alexander Starre, as "an exemplary institution of print culture in the digital era." It ceaselessly addresses its own mediality, "monitor[ing] its own reception and comment[ing] on it in subsequent issues" (p. 68). The writers' collective held together by the periodical *McSweeney's* thus reinforces and adapts itself in a feedback loop. One may stress, though, that this also implies the permanent refinement of a literary field position, which changes from sophisticated bookishness to middlebrow mainstream, and an ambivalent attitude toward economic profit (Brouillette 2003; O'Dell 2017).

The underlying model may be Dave Eggers's authorial strategy of "courting publicity while also mocking it" (Hamilton 2010, p. 3). As such, it navigates and collapses the line between art, commodity, and social commitment. Paired with a gesture of humanitarian engagement, Eggers's savvy entrepreneurship shows itself in various other venues of the platform McSweeney's. These include the nonprofit project 826 Valencia, which tutors structurally disadvantaged children in reading and writing, and Voice of Witness, "an oral history book series," which the accompanying web page promotes as having "amplified hundreds of voices." Informed by a belief in the transformative power of storytelling, the documentary gesture of the project, which transcribes the testimonials of unprivileged individuals, casts the writers' collective as an editorial one. In his related collaborative texts *What is the What* (2006) and *Zeitoun* (2009), whose hardcover editions were published with McSweeney's, Eggers also negotiates the gesture of authorial self-effacement in editorial terms. Based on journalistic research and interviews with his subjects, Eggers writes here, respectively, the stories of Valentino Achak Deng, a Sudanese war refugee on his path to US citizenship and a college education, and of a US family of Muslim faith, focusing on the father Abulrahman Zeitoun, a Syrian American who is detained and tortured in the aftermath of Hurricane Katrina. Both texts feature extensive paratexts and draw on the conventions of auto/biography and literary nonfiction. In the convention of possessive authorship, Eggers holds the copyright, thus inevitably profiting for his own authorial brand and the McSweeney's collective. The proceeds, however, go to the individuals, whose experiences are narrated, or rather, they go to foundations in their name. These self-instituted organizations are committed to underlying social causes and formulate a critique of political institutions. This commitment and critique finds expression in a gesture of literary philanthropy, which constitutes itself, its complex collaborative authorship, and collective investment, by opening up in both texts the channels between paratexts and actual narration (Sedlmeier 2018).

While situated outside the Program, "McSweeney's as an institution exists within a literary field that has already *schooled* writers" (Hungerford 2016, p. 667). The visibility of this counter-school as writers' collective remains inextricable from Dave Eggers. He leads "the Eggersards," "a tight network of associates of the impresario Dave Eggers," as the editors of the inaugural issue of *n+1* frame it in "A Regressive Avant-Garde" (2004), one of several editorials commenting on "The Intellectual Situation." In rhetorically effective polemics, the text turns the defining criteria of McSweeney's against itself, listing its "identifiable style" and its strategy to publish "sub-literary work" to classify the magazine and the platform as "a regressive avant-garde" in a double sense. In terms of content, the diagnosis is an avoidance of substantive "ethical" concerns that would result in a retreat, both sentimental and ironic, into an "obsession with childhood" and an affective investment in "popular culture." In terms of form, style, and technique, the charge is the repetition of "old innovations" in "typography and tone," an excessive play of "paratextual games" that ceaselessly comments on its own modes of production and reception (The Editors 2004a).

Founded by Mark Greif, Chad Harbach, Benjamin Kunkel, and others, the New York-based *n+1* (2004–) operates in a para-academic setting of public intellectualism. Its paratext is no less extensive and serves to carve out a shared position by "Negation" (the title of the inaugural issue) of other imagined collectives associated with magazines. The other editorials of the first issue perform *n+1*'s own sense of authorial collectivity in contradistinction to the left-leaning *The New Republic* (1914–) and the neo-conservative *The Weekly Standard* (1995–2018), publications that in turn are ascribed a coherent sense of collectivity. The latter is an easy target. In "PoMo NeoCons," its contributors are defined by a brand of "conservative-themed cultural studies" that adopts strategies of "the language of the oppressed," the purview of "the academic left," to the effect of disguising their own elitist status (The Editors 2004d). In the editorial "Designated Haters," the former is credited with perfecting a type of literary criticism that generates attention by taking down prominent writers, both academic and literary. At the same time, the editors charge the longstanding institution with an investment in "fake refinement" and with letting "authority fill the place of thinking" (The Editors 2004b).

The emphasis on "thinking," with a Marxist bent, defines the self-positioning of the writers' collective of *n+1* in intellectual terms against what the "Editorial Statement" calls "demented self-censorship" (The Editors 2004c). The sense of collectivity is enhanced by the fact that Benjamin Kunkel dedicates his novel *Indecision* (2005) to the magazine: "for *n+1*" (Kunkel 2005). Given the proclaimed return to a political criticism of this collective against the backdrop of 9/11 and the Bush administration, we may even view Eggers's turn in the second half of the 2000s to collaborative creative nonfiction, which criticizes political institutions, as a correction of his own field position against the charges of *n+1*. Writers' collectives, that is, react to one another in a game of oneupmanship where the conditions of converting literary into political and social capital are permanently redrawn.

Recently, critical interest in contemporary literary magazines and publishing outlets has increased and provides further avenues for thinking about writers' collectives. Sophie Seita draws our attention to the literary communities and movements constituted by little magazines from the early twentieth century to the present. Suggesting a diachronic view, she understands these periodicals as "protoforms": the avant-gardes they constitute are "provisional networks of affiliation" and their hospitable heterogeneity is contingent upon "media, genres, and groups" (2019, p. 3). The emergence of publications such as *Triple Canopy* (2007–) or *ON: Contemporary Practice* (2008–), which negotiate the conditions of digitization and their medial status against the culture of print (see Seita 2019, pp. 160–189), suggests a notion of writers' collectives that depends on the rise of the Internet, digital publishing, and social media. The new sense of connectivity afforded by these technological developments transforms the cultural, economic, and social conditions of "the network society," as theorized by Manuel Castells (2010).

Against the backdrop of declining advertising revenue with subsequent budget cuts and layoffs, Evan Kindley traces the shifts of the literary culture in the 2000s from McSweeney's and *n+1* to the literary blogs and little magazines published exclusively online. With respect to the latter, he notes that "they presented themselves as collective enterprises rather than individual projects" (2017, p. 354). While McSweeney's and *n+1* (ironically) cater to professional academic discourse, the amateur gesture of these new outlets imagines writers' collectives outside of such discussions. And yet, as Kindley also shows, the "*semiprofessional*" part-time workers and freelancers behind these collectives are often "highly educated and credentialed people" (p. 357), who, in earlier decades, would have held secure employment in journalism, the book industry, or academia. Along these lines, we may say that the writers' collectives emerging in the digital sphere make virtue of necessity, since the dire job prospects in literary culture are partly an effect of digitization. Their emphasis on connectivity compensates for and is an effect of a lack of connections. In order to obtain both symbolic and economic capital, the fluctuating and jumbled digital sphere, which institutionalizes itself and competes for attention and resources, still relies on the acceptance of the literary field and its institutions.

SEE ALSO: Chabon, Michael; The Culture Wars; Eggers, Dave; Hustvedt, Siri; Krauss, Nicole; Lethem, Jonathan; Literary Magazines; Multiculturalism; Post-Soul and/or Post-Black Fiction; Program Culture; Roth, Philip; Senna, Danzy; Wallace, David Foster; Ward, Jesmyn; Whitehead, Colson

REFERENCES

Anzaldúa, Gloria. (1987). *Borderlands/La Frontera: The New Mestiza*. San Francisco: Aunt Lute Books.

Bahri, Deepika. (2003). *Native Intelligence: Aesthetics, Politics, and the Postcolonial*. Minneapolis: University of Minnesota Press.

Bérubé, Michael. (1992). *Marginal Forces/Cultural Centers: Tolson, Pynchon, and the Politics of the Canon*. Ithaca: Cornell University Press.

Bollen, Katrien, Craps, Stef, and Vermeulen, Pieter. (2013). *McSweeney's* and the challenges of the marketplace for independent publishing. CLCWeb: Comparative Literature and Culture 15 (4). https://docs.lib.purdue.edu/cgi/viewcontent.cgi?article=2092&context=clcweb (accessed September 21, 2021).

Bourdieu, Pierre. (1996). *The Rules of Art: Genesis and Structure of the Literary Field* (trans. Susan Emanuel). Cambridge: Polity Press; 1st ed. 1992 (in French).

Brooks, Van Wyck. (1918). On creating a usable past. *The Dial* (April 11, 1918): 337–341.

Brouillette, Sarah. (2003). Paratextuality and economic disavowal in Dave Eggers' *You Shall Know Our Velocity*. Reconstruction: Studies in Contemporary Culture 3 (2).

Bürger, Peter. (1984). *Theory of the Avant-Garde* (trans. Michael Shaw). Minneapolis: University of Minnesota Press.

Castells, Manuel. (2010). *The Rise of the Network Society*, 2nd ed. Chichester: Wiley-Blackwell; 1st ed. 1996.

Chen, Amy Hildreth. (2020). *Placing Papers: The Literary Archives Market*. Amherst: University of Massachusetts Press.

Chicago Cultural Studies Group. (1992). Critical multiculturalism. Critical Inquiry 18 (3): 530–555.

Eggers, Dave. (2004). Introduction. In: *The Best of McSweeney's* (ed. Dave Eggers and Jordan Bass), vii–xiii. London: Hamish Hamilton.

Ellis, Trey. (1989). The New Black Aesthetic. Callaloo 38: 233–243.

Emirbayer, Mustafa and Desmond, Matthew. (2015). *The Racial Order*. Chicago: University of Chicago Press.

English, James F. (2010). Everywhere and nowhere: the sociology of literature after "the Sociology of Literature." New Literary History 41 (2): v–xxiii.

Gates, Henry Louis, Jr. (1988). *The Signifying Monkey: A Theory of Afro-American Literary Criticism*. New York: Oxford University Press.

Genette, Gérard. (1997). *Paratexts: Thresholds of Interpretation* (trans. Jane E. Lewin). Cambridge: Cambridge University Press; 1st ed. 1987 (in French).

Hamilton, Caroline D. (2010). *One Man Zeitgeist: Dave Eggers, Publishing and Publicity*. London: Bloomsbury.

Harbach, Chad. (2014). MFA vs. NYC. In: *MFA vs. NYC: The Two Cultures of American Fiction* (ed. Chad Harbach), 9–28. New York: n+1/Faber.

Howard, June. (2001). *Publishing the Family*. Durham, NC: Duke University Press.

Huggan, Graham. (2001). *The Postcolonial Exotic: Marketing the Margins*. London: Routledge.

Hungerford, Amy. (2016). *Making Literature Now*. Stanford: Stanford University Press.

Kindley, Evan. (2017). Little magazines, blogs, and literary media. In: *American Literature in Transition, 2000–2010* (ed. Rachel Greenwald Smith), 345–359. Cambridge: Cambridge University Press.

Kunkel, Benjamin. (2005). *Indecision*. New York: Random House.

Lyon, Janet. (1999). *Manifestoes: Provocations of the Modern*. Ithaca: Cornell University Press.

McGurl, Mark. (2009). *The Program Era: Postwar Fiction and the Rise of Creative Writing*. Cambridge, MA: Harvard University Press.

O'Dell, Jacqueline. (2017). The gift network: Dave Eggers and the circulation of second editions. NANO: New American Notes Online 11.

Puchner, Martin. (2006). *Poetry of the Revolution: Marx, Manifestos, and the Avant-Gardes*. Princeton: Princeton University Press.

Saldívar, Ramón. (2011). Historical fantasy, speculative realism, and postrace aesthetics in contemporary American fiction. American Literary History 23 (3): 574–599.

Sedlmeier, Florian. (2018). The paratext and literary narration: authorship, institutions, historiographies. Narrative 26 (1): 63–80.

Seita, Sophie. (2019). *Provisional Avantgardes: Little Magazine Communities from Dada to Digital*. Stanford: Stanford University Press.

Senna, Denzy. (2015). An overlooked classic about the comedy of race. *New Yorker* (May 7, 2015). https://www.newyorker.com/books/page-turner/an-overlooked-classic-about-the-comedy-of-race (accessed July 22, 2021).

Sollors, Werner. (1986). *Beyond Ethnicity: Consent and Descent in American Culture*. Oxford: Oxford University Press.

Springer, Kimberley. (2005). *Living for the Revolution: Black Feminist Organizations, 1968–1980*. Durham, NC: Duke University Press.

Starre, Alexander. (2015). *Metamedia: American Book Fictions and Literary Print Culture after Digitization*. Iowa City: University of Iowa Press.

The Editors. (2004a). A regressive avant-garde. *n+1* (1). https://nplusonemag.com/issue-1/the-intellectual-situation/regressive-avant-garde/ (accessed July 22, 2021).

The Editors. (2004b). Designated haters. *n+1* (1). https://nplusonemag.com/issue-1/the-intellectual-situation/designated-haters/ (accessed July 22, 2021).

The Editors. (2004c). Editorial statement. *n+1* (1). https://nplusonemag.com/issue-1/letters/editorial-statement/ (accessed July 22, 2021).

The Editors. (2004d). PoMo NeoCons. *n+1* (1). https://nplusonemag.com/issue-1/the-intellectual-situation/pomo-neocons/ (accessed July 22, 2021).

Voice of Witness: Amplifying Unheard Voices. (n.d.). https://voiceofwitness.org/about/ (accessed July 22, 2021).

Ward, Jesmyn. (2016). Introduction. In: *The Fire This Time: A New Generation Speaks about Race* (ed. Jesmyn Ward), 3–11. New York: Scribner's.

Ween, Lori. (2003). This is your book: marketing America to itself. PMLA 118 (1): 90–102.

FURTHER READING

Foucault, Michel. (1998). What is an author? In: *The Foucault Reader* (ed. Paul Rabinow; trans. Josué V. Harari), 101–120. New York: Pantheon.

Glass, Loren. (ed.) (2007). *After the Program Era: The Past, Present, and Future of Creative Writing*. Iowa City: University of Iowa Press.

Morris, Ian and Diaz, Joanne. (eds.) (2015). *The Little Magazine in Contemporary America*. Chicago: University of Chicago Press.

Spahr, Clemens and Löffler, Philipp. (2012). Introduction: concepts of collectivity in contemporary American literature. Amerikastudien/American Studies 57 (2): 161–176.

Y

Yamanaka, Lois-Ann

LEANNE DAY
University of Hawaiʻi at Hilo, USA

As one of the most prominent and controversial contemporary Asian American writers, Lois-Ann Yamanaka's unapologetic work launched Hawaiʻi's unique literary scene into critical debates about the discipline and political stakes of Asian American Studies, Asian American Literature, and Ethnic Studies in the 1990s. With its incisive wit, evocative images, and explosive utilization of Hawaiʻi Creole English (HCE), known colloquially as pidgin, Yamanaka's work is renowned for its unflinching examination of working-class Japanese American adolescent girls that rejects stereotypical versions of a paradisiacal Hawaiʻi. Her work has simultaneously received high praise for its strong female protagonists and criticism for its negative representations of Filipino men as sexual predators. *Blu's Hanging* (1997) was selected for the annual Association of Asian American Studies (AAAS) Book Award in 1998 amidst intense protests. The award was subsequently rescinded and remains a watershed moment in Asian American Studies and Asian American literature. Still, Yamanaka received national recognition as one of the most polarizing and exciting contemporary literary voices. Her poetry received two Pushcart Prizes in 1993 and 1994 and the AAA National Book Award in 1994. Her fiction was recognized for a 1994 Rona Jaffe Award for Women Writers, a Lannan Literary award in 1996, the Elliot Cades Award for Literature, and Hawaiʻi Book Award for Literature. She is the author of six novels, one poetry collection, and a children's book. She lives on Oʻahu where she runs a writing, mentoring, and academic success program called Naʻau.

Born in 1961 in Hoʻolchua, Molokai and raised on the island of Hawaiʻi in Hilo, Kona, and Pahala, Yamanaka is a third-generation Japanese American and the oldest of four sisters. She is the daughter of school teachers whose father later became a taxidermist and makes a fictional appearance in *Heads by Harry* (1999). Attending the University of Hawaiʻi at Mānoa for both her bachelor's in 1983 and master's in Education in 1987, Yamanaka became a public-school teacher on Oʻahu in English, Drama, and Speech. At 27 years old, she began writing fiction and poetry inspired by her experiences on Molokaʻi, Hawaiʻi island, and Oʻahu. Yamanaka is the co-founder and head of Naʻau Place of Learning in Honolulu, which opened in 2003. Naʻau evolved out of a shared dream with her graduate school colleague and business partner Melvin E. Spencer III. Naʻau espouses

---

The Encyclopedia of Contemporary American Fiction 1980–2020, First Edition. Edited by Patrick O'Donnell, Stephen J. Burn, and Lesley Larkin.
© 2022 John Wiley & Sons Ltd. Published 2022 by John Wiley & Sons Ltd.

a holistic approach to teaching creative and academic writing and mentoring for students from pre-Kindergarten to Grade 12.

Published in 1993, Yamanaka's debut poetry collection *Saturday Night at the Pahala Theater* established her influence on contemporary American fiction through an expansive use of HCE, a focus on working-class families, and unflinching portrayals of Japanese American female adolescence. Her approach to teenage sexuality, violence, and local racial hierarchies in Hawai'i communities placed Yamanaka's work in the crosshairs of controversy and celebration. *Saturday Night at the Pahala Theater* highlights the overlapping influences of US popular culture and Hawai'i-based expectations of sociality, beauty, and status. Published by Bamboo Ridge Press, a literary press created by Darrell Lum and Eric Chock in 1979 to promote creative works with an "island sensibility," *Saturday Night at the Pahala Theater* asserts a distinct representation of multi-ethnic communities that contrasts with continental Asian American experiences. "Local," in Hawai'i, culturally functions as not simply a geographical identifier but as distinct from "haole," meaning foreigner of any ethnicity, and "native," Kanaka Maoli, the Indigenous peoples of Hawai'i. Derived from mid-twentieth century interracial labor movements among plantation workers, "local" differentiated a multi-ethnic working class from elite, often white, plantation owners and businessmen. "Local" became both a political framework for organizing and as a cultural marker of belonging to Hawai'i, often through the erasure of and substitution for Kanaka Maoli. Central to the concept of "local" is the use of HCE that emerged out of necessity on the plantations for communication between immigrants from China, Japan, Okinawa, Korea, and the Philippines. Viewed as inferior to Standard English, HCE was often associated with ignorance. Consequently, *Saturday Night at the Pahala Theater* valorizes pidgin through its colloquial use for local communities and as distinct from 'Ōlelo Hawai'i, Hawaiian.

Saturday Night at the Pahala Theater includes the voices of six main female protagonists around ages twelve to thirteen, including most notably, Kala, Tita, Lucy, and Girlie, in what might be classified as a poetic novella set on the island of Hawai'i. The narrative poems jointly reinforce how social acceptance operates and how girls should approach adolescence, sex, and relationships, even as their advice is often unreliable. The collection opens with "Kala Gave Me Anykine Advice Especially About Filipinos When I Moved to Pahala" and offers a range of survival tips, including how local Japanese girls should be fearful of sexual assault by Filipino men. This is the central contention for critics of Yamanaka who claim her work bolsters racism. Relying on well-documented negative historical stereotypes of Filipino men as sexual predators, the speaker recounts how Kala offers dubious warnings, such as which clothes to wear to avoid being raped, to not use another person's deodorant, and to avoid making certain faces. The poem begins, "No whistle in dark/or you call the Filipino man. . .he goin to drag you to his house,/ tie you to the vinyl chair,/ the one he sit outside all day, / and smile at you with his yellow teeth/ and cut off your bi-lot with the cane knife./ He going fry um in Crisco for dinner./ That's what Kala told me" (1993, p. 15). Kala situates the possibility of imminent assault by the unnamed "Filipino man" or by Felix, mentioned later and unidentified by ethnicity, but presumably Filipino, who is already accused of rape. Kala's reference to these rumors of previous assaults highlights the constant threat for local Japanese girls. Even further, the dramatic inclusion that the speaker's "bi-lot," or in Tagalog, "vagina," will be removed and eaten further amplifies the dangerous nature of the accused perpetrator

Felix as a stand-in for all Filipino men. Thus, the literal and metaphoric consumption of local Japanese girls circulates through Kala's gossip even as the speaker's first sexual experience occurs because of pressure from her own uncle and with a Japanese peer, Jimmy (Baiada 2016, p. 46) . This complicates the accusation that Filipino men are the sole source of sexual violence and instead calls into question how local Asian communities often reinforce silence around gendered violence and child molestation.

Saturday Night at the Pahala Theater won two Pushcart Prizes and the AAAS Annual Book Prize in 1994 (despite vigorous protests from the Filipino American Studies Caucus). Yamanaka's collection continues to incite controversial conversations around racial stereotypes, local racism, working-class plantation life, and the gendered struggles of growing up. In 2004, James Sereno adapted the sections by the character Kala into a short film, *Silent Year*, and received first runner up at the prestigious British Academy Awards in Los Angeles. In January 2012, local theater company Kumu Kahua Theater adapted Yamanaka's collection into a play, which was met with overwhelming praise.

Following *Saturday Night at the Pahala Theater*, Yamanaka began work on her first novel with support from a Carnegie Foundation Grant and a National Endowment for the Arts Creative Writing Fellowship. Published in 1996, *Wild Meat and the Bully Burgers* explores similar themes of growing up and feeling like an outsider in Hawai'i, a feeling that is reinforced by the desire to fit into both American and local community notions of belonging. Based in Hilo in the 1970s, the novel is narrated by an awkward and bullied adolescent Japanese American girl named Lovey Nariyoshi. Lovey's stories demonstrate her overwhelming dream to be what she perceives as a typical middle-class white American girl who is thin with blonde hair, eats "Minute rice with lots of butter," and is named "Lovey Beth Cole" (1996, p. 34). In worshipping *Charlie's Angels*, Farrah Fawcett, *Gone with the Wind* (1939), Barbie, and *The Brady Bunch,* but also the hallmarks of consumerism through brands like Dixie Cup, Kraft, and Pez, Lovey fixates on the external appearance of wealth and success. Yet, Lovey and her queer best friend, Jerome, manage to find solidarity in each other, as both are outsiders and subject to harassment from the popular local Japanese American girls.

Wild Meat and the Bully Burgers is the first book in Yamanaka's Hilo trilogy and explores the complexities of the Americanization of Hawai'i, the centrality of plantation immigration, and the idiosyncratic turmoil of growing up as a social outcast. The novel received critiques for its explicit use of sexuality, profanity, and pidgin, similar to the criticism about *Saturday Night at the Pahala Theater*. In Hawai'i, the novel was banned by some schools and Yamanaka was uninvited to talks. Nationally, criticism of Yamanaka's portrayal of racist stereotypes of Filipinos continued and incited protests again from the Filipino American Caucus at the AAAS in 1997. The Book Award committee first voted to award the annual honor to *Wild Meat and the Bully Burgers,* but then in an attempt to avoid controversy decided to not give any fiction award that year. Still, the novel did win the Rona Jaffe Award for Women Writers. In 2005, Kayo Hatta adapted stories from the novel into a film *Fishbowl* that aired nationally on PBS the following year.

In 1997, Yamanaka published *Blu's Hanging* as the second novel in her Hilo trilogy, which amplified critiques about her work as intensely racist and violent towards Filipino men. As her most well-known novel, *Blu's Hanging*'s notoriety embodies the larger crises in Asian

American Studies over the politics of literary form, representation, and inter-ethnic hierarchies within the concept of "Asian American." The AAAS chose *Blu's Hanging* as the recipient for the annual fiction prize in 1998, which was vehemently protested by members of the Filipino American Caucus in addition to earlier letters sent by faculty and students to the board. After the award vote, the committee voted to rescind the award, and most of the AAAS executive board resigned as a result of potential legal ramifications. This conflict over the validity of Yamanaka's fiction placed aesthetics and the perpetuation of historical opposition in radical opposition; critics later suggested that a book award may not have been the most productive site for this discussion. Still, the legacy of *Blu's Hanging* continues in its frequent appearance on college syllabi and ongoing analysis by critics.

Blu's Hanging focuses on the impoverished Japanese American Ogata family on Molokai in the aftermath of the mother's death. The narrator, 13-year-old Ivah, she attempts to care for her two younger siblings, Blu and Maisie, while their father turns to drugs. Ivah's development involves reckoning with the public shame of Hansen's Disease because both parents, Bertram and Eleanor, had previously been incarcerated at the Kalaupapa leprosy colony. The stigma around Leprosy and Eleanor's death haunt the characters as they struggle to reconcile their grief and survive in a community divided by class and ethnic lines. Ivah's difficulties in taking care of Blu, teased at school for his family's lack of money and perceived oddness, and Maisie, who stops talking after Eleanor's death, are amplified by their father's silence. The Ogatas are juxtaposed with their equally poor neighbors, the Reyes family. The community judges, but does not intervene in, the fact that Uncle Paulo Reyes repeatedly rapes his four nieces, who have an absentee mother and a Japanese father who abandoned them. Eventually, Uncle Paulo rapes Blu before Ivah leaves to go to boarding school on Oahu to pursue her intellectual ambitions. The villainous character of Uncle Paulo Reyes is at the heart of the controversy over the novel even amidst a milieu of homophobic, masculinist, and misogynistic characters where the impending threats of sexual violence and surveillance are pervasive. Blu's violent assault by Uncle Paolo makes visible the intersection of poverty, drugs, and alienation where sexual violence affects not only Blu and the Reyes girls, but also serves as a critique of the community's silence around these issues. Ivah declares at the end "us can all be mama now" (1997, p. 259), as if to gesture towards a communal sense of care that hinges on her departure and the uncertain future of the rest of the family. The novel's uneasiness with closure and the inability to resolve the continuation of trauma in the Ogata family is what remains unsettling about the narrative and is not isolated to Blu's rape.

The national media emphasized the controversy over the novel as an issue of freedom of speech and prominent Asian American writers like Amy Tan and Maxine Hong Kingston publicly supported Yamanaka's work. However, pitting creative license against historical systemic racism foreclosed any meaningful engagement beyond the rescinding of the award and resignation of the executive board. The novel as an aesthetic form seemed to be eclipsed in the conversation; the complexity of narrative style and a problematic multicultural local community became obscured by Blu's rape as a single incident. Ultimately, the novel refuses to pardon the majority of the community for the ongoing abuse of children and its silent complicity, even as Ivah has the privilege to leave. *Blu's Hanging*, as a novel, and its surrounding controversy elucidate how Asian American Studies has had to grapple with the pervasive desire for national inclusion, the enduring legacies of settler colonialism both in Hawai'i and on the continent, and the embedded inter-ethnic disparities in the field.

In 1999, Yamanaka ended her Hilo trilogy with *Heads by Harry*, which won the Hawai'i Book Award. Narrated by the Yaguu family's middle daughter, Toni, who is 18 years old, the story is about the family's taxidermy shop and Toni's desire to join the business instead of going to college. The Yagyuu family consists of Toni's mother who is a school teacher, her older queer brother, Sheldon, and her younger beloved sister, Bunny. Toni feels constantly overlooked and inferior to her successful and well-liked siblings. Similar to Yamanaka's previous works, *Heads by Harry* depicts the complexity of familial expectations of success through college education, internal struggles to find self-confidence, and the challenges of finding meaningful relationships. The Yagyuu family is the most emotionally and financially stable compared to the families in the previous novels in the trilogy. While the central conflict rests on Harry's refusal to let Toni join his taxidermy business as he believes it is not suitable for women, the overall plot explores Toni's navigation of wild college parties, drugs, and her own sexual and professional desires. Still, Toni's childhood friends and intermittent lovers, the Santos brothers, act as her support system and become co-baby daddies (as it is unclear which one is the father) to her daughter, Harper. After Toni flunks out of college, Harry acquiesces to her passion for taxidermy and hands over the family business to her and the Santos brothers. *Heads by Harry* wraps up the Hilo trilogy with the success of Toni gaining confidence in her passion to follow her dreams.

Yamanaka's subsequent novel, *Fathers of the Four Passages* (2001), begins her experimental phase with utilizing first- and third-person narration, nonlinear temporality, and not using pidgin. The protagonist, Sonia Kurisu, struggles as a single mother and Las Vegas lounge singer, who faces the emotional and traumatic consequences of her three abortions. The novel explores the unfulfilled possibility of these three lost sons through their ghostly presence and haunting. The living child, Sonny Boy, is autistic and becomes the embodiment of not only Sonia's guilt over her previous abortions, but also of the extended family's sins. Sonia repeatedly engages in surreal conversations and letters with her lost sons that extend in sometimes tortured sequences that attempt to absolve her. In *Father of the Four Passages*, Yamanaka's exploration of narration styles and temporality enhances the novel's themes of ghostliness, redemption, fantasies of infanticide, and dysfunctional families.

Utilizing a chorus of ghosts and hints of magical realism, Yamanaka goes on to play with narrative style in her only historical novel *Behold the Many* (2006). Yamanaka experiments aesthetically through abandoning a strong first-person narrator and gestures towards the interconnections of the spirit world, the land, and humans. Set in 1913 on O'ahu, the novel follows three young Japanese and Portuguese American sisters, Anah, Aki, and Leah who have contracted tuberculosis and are sent to an orphanage called St. Joseph's in Kalihi Valley. Based on Yamanaka's historical research, *Behold the Many*'s lyrical and nonlinear temporality centers the ghosts of Anah's deceased sisters, parents, and suggested ancestors. Yamanaka returns to using pidgin and most explicitly engages with an Indigenous-centered cosmology in exploring how haunting is not only about Anah's family, but also reveals the absence of Kanaka Maoli as animated presence in the valley. This explicit reckoning with Hawaiian notions of 'āina, land as a living genealogical relation, is significant, as the criticism of Yamanaka's work has not only been about her racism against Filipinx communities, but also her erasure of Kanaka Maoli and refusal to acknowledge settler colonialism. Readers may have been surprised by Yamanaka's turn to Indigeneity as grounded in place, though she ultimately returns to her central themes of the challenges of female adolescence, parental loss, and the local community's ideas of shame associated with disease.

Yamanaka is still an incredibly contentious author, and critics remain fixated on the crisis over *Blu's Hanging* and its unmasking of the inter-ethnic tensions present in the field and AAAS that persist today, even as both have turned towards centering settler colonialism and racial hierarchies within "Asian America." The question of the racist nature of Yamanaka's work continues to haunt not only her oeuvre, but can also be framed as a litmus test for contemporary ethnic literature that continues to struggle with the politics of aesthetic representation and the drive towards national assimilation. Unsurprisingly, Yamanaka's work continues to be taught throughout the United States. and consistently generates new scholarship and discussions of Asian American literary form and the stakes of engaging with gendered and intra-communal issues of violence and sexual abuse that often are erased. While Yamanaka may not be well-liked, her explosive use of pidgin, attentiveness to the complex social norms of minority communities, unapologetic female adolescent narrators, and distinct imagery of Hawai'i ensure that her work will continue to resonate, inspire, and incite discussions.

SEE ALSO: Fiction and Affect; Hagedorn, Jessica; Indigenous Narratives; Kingston, Maxine Hong; Lee, Chang-rae; Literature of the Americas; Multiculturalism; Nguyen, Viet Thanh; Tan, Amy; Trauma and Fiction

REFERENCES

Baiada, Christa. (2016). Loving the unlovable body in Yamanaka's *Saturday Night at the Pahala Theater*. *Asian American Literature: Discourses and Pedagogies* 7: 39–53.

Yamanaka, Lois-Ann. (1993). *Saturday Night at the Pahala Theater*. Honolulu: Bamboo Ridge Press.

Yamanaka, Lois-Ann. (1996). *Wild Meat and the Bully Burgers*. New York: Farrar, Straus and Giroux.

Yamanaka, Lois-Ann. (1997). *Blu's Hanging*. New York: Farrar, Straus and Giroux.

FURTHER READING

Chuh, Kandice. (2003). *Imagine Otherwise: On Asian Americanist Critique*. Durham, NC: Duke University Press.

Fujikane, Candace. (2000). Sweeping racism under the rug of "censorship." The controversy over Lois-Ann Yamanaka's *Blu's Hanging*. *Amerasia Journal* 26 (2): 158–194.

Ninh, erin Khuê. (2015). Teaching *Blu's Hanging*. *Pedagogy* 15 (2): 223–251.

Rodrigues, Darlene. (2000). Imagining ourselves: reflections on the controversy over Lois-Ann Yamanaka's *Blu's Hanging*. *Amerasia Journal* 26 (2): 195–207.

Nguyen, Viet Thanh. (2002). *Race and Resistance: Literature and Politics in Asian America*. New York: Oxford University Press.

Yamashita, Karen Tei

VINCE SCHLEITWILER
University of Washington, USA

One of the most inventive, versatile, and intellectually challenging authors of her time, Karen Tei Yamashita is the author of eight genre-bending books, ranging across fiction, essay, and performance, which incorporate extensive research and Yamashita's cosmopolitan life experiences in formally playful and innovative ways. A Sansei, or third-generation Japanese American, Yamashita has written extensively about the experiences of people of the Japanese diaspora, the Nikkei, in Latin America, the United States, and Japan. Her work is also often associated with the multiracial geography of greater Los Angeles. As part of a cohort of writers and artists emerging in the wake of the late 1960s-early 1970s Asian American movement, Yamashita carries forward the less-acknowledged legacy of radical experimentalism that marked the arrival of a self-consciously Asian Americanist tradition.

Despite numerous accolades, Yamashita's broader literary reputation may not reflect the great esteem in which she is held by specialists in Asian American literary studies – though it is likely to grow as the field's marginalization within US literary studies continues to diminish. The sophisticated and expansive intellect characterizing her writing has made it a touchstone for scholarly illuminations of various critical concepts that have been prominent over the course of her career, from postmodernism and magical realism to diaspora and globalization to ecocriticism and speculative fiction, and, most consistently, transnationalism. Ultimately, her formal versatility and wide-ranging curiosity have meant that disparate critical interests have centered around each of her novels: *Brazil-Maru* (1992), *Through the Arc of the Rainforest* (1990), *Tropic of Orange* (1997), and *I Hotel* (2010). Strong cases can be made for nominating each of these books as Yamashita's masterpiece, but it is arguably the latter, a *sui generis* panorama of the Asian American movement and the social and artistic revolutions it imagined, that can be read as grounding both Yamashita's own oeuvre and the larger literary/critical field it exemplifies.

Yamashita's grandparents, on both her father's (Yamashita) and her mother's (Sakai) side, were first-generation immigrants from Japan, or Issei, who established themselves as small-business owners in the San Francisco Bay Area, raising seven and nine children, respectively. Within their segregated, striving immigrant community, they seem to have achieved some modest status, despite fluctuating fortunes; both of Yamashita's parents, (Hiroshi) John Yamashita and Asako Sakai, graduated from the University of California, Berkeley, prior to World War II. In 1942, both families were forcibly removed from their homes and held in US concentration camps, first at the temporary facility at Tanforan racetrack and then at a permanent War Relocation Authority camp at Topaz, Utah, like approximately 126,000 other Japanese Americans incarcerated by the US government during World War II.

As the military and political tides of war shifted, many Nisei, or second-generation Japanese Americans, were encouraged by the WRA to leave the camps to resettle away from their prewar West Coast communities, particularly well-educated, Christian high achievers who were seen as evidence of the WRA's success at rehabilitating their community. A number of Yamashita's older relatives left camp, including her father, John, who moved to Evanston, Illinois to attend seminary at the Garrett Biblical Institute. An admirer and mentee of the influential African American theologian and civil rights leader Howard Thurman, John became a Methodist minister. Yamashita's parents met after the war, and were married in 1948. Further information and reflections on Yamashita's family history and wartime experience can be found in *Letters to Memory* (2017), as well as the *Yamashita Family Archives* website at the University of California, Santa Cruz.

Yamashita was born on January 8, 1951, in Oakland, California, and a year later, her family moved to Los Angeles, where John served as pastor at the Japanese American Centenary Methodist Church. Karen and her younger sister, Jane, grew up deeply embedded in a Nikkei community, or what, in her 2020 essay "Growing Up Sansei in LA," she describes "a series of Japanese American bubbles." The trajectory of the family's residential migration through segregated Los Angeles exemplifies a history of the shifting racial and social status of Japanese Americans in the postwar era, beginning from a parsonage in a predominantly working-class, Black and Japanese American neighborhood near Fifth Avenue and Jefferson Boulevard, and continuing to a new parsonage in Crenshaw, whose residents she describes as "slightly better off, perhaps white collar and professional, business owners, a mix of Asians, Blacks, Jews, and disappearing white folks." After John suffered a stroke and left the church, Yamashita's mother, Asako, became an elementary school teacher and the primary breadwinner, and the family moved to Gardena, a suburb dominated by Nisei who had fled central LA with their Sansei children, where Yamashita's high school social circle was virtually all "JA." For Yamashita, this JA "bubble was a kind of reorganized camp" (Yamashita 2020).

To escape this bubble, she attended Carleton College in Minnesota, where she studied English and Japanese literature, and did a junior year abroad at Waseda University in Tokyo. After graduation, she won a prestigious Thomas J. Watson fellowship, which she used to study Nikkei communities in Brazil, which developed after anti-Japanese exclusion movements ended mass migration to the United States. She ended up living there for nine years, marrying Brazilian architect Ronaldo Lopes de Oliveira in 1977, and giving birth to two children. In 1984, Yamashita and her family moved back to LA, where she found a job with the local public television station KCET, and continued working as a writer, translator, and experimental playwright. With the publication of her first three novels in 1990, 1992, and 1997, Yamashita's literary career was established.

Because most readers discovered Yamashita via her first two novels, *Through the Arc of the Rain Forest* and *Brazil-Maru*, her initial reception largely associated her work with US perceptions of Latin American writing. Though published second, *Brazil-Maru* was written first, a transformation of Yamashita's extensive ethnographic research on Japanese Brazilians for her Watson fellowship. A sprawling multigenerational epic that explores the rise and fall of the utopian settlements established by an idealistic band of immigrants, from their arrival in 1925 through to an epilogue set in 1992, the novel follows a more conventional, naturalistic format than Yamashita's other works, though its complex, intertextual engagements with philosophical ideas and its formally complex use of multiple narrative perspectives forecast characteristics of her later fiction. *Brazil-Maru* has been relatively neglected by scholars compared to Yamashita's other novels, but as US-based research in Japanese American and diasporic studies has begun to acknowledge the role of settler colonialism and Japanese imperialism in shaping Nikkei migration to the Americas – topics that were difficult to address as Asian American studies sought to establish itself – it is possible that more future readers will be better prepared to appreciate the complexities of this story.

With *Through the Arc of the Rain Forest*, Yamashita's earliest published novel, the satirical, dizzyingly inventive imagination characteristic of her writing was first unleashed for a broad audience. Narrated by a golf-ball-sized sphere that hoves six inches in front of the head of an immigrant Japanese engineer in Brazil – a quirk the author retained over the objections of her own editor – the book also features a three-armed US businessman and a mysterious, black, magnetic plastic discovered in the Amazon rainforest floor, and began as a collaboration with Yamashita's husband. Winner of an American Book Award and the Janet Heidinger Kafka Prize, the novel's reputation has outlived the heyday of US interest in Latin American magical realism, and continues to attract new analyses for its speculative imagination and its ability to stretch and recombine narrative forms, like the Brazilian TV *novela*, to encompass an environmentalist, post-Third-Worldist critique of global capitalism.

In *Tropic of Orange*, Yamashita brought that speculative imagination back to her hometown of Los Angeles, registering its transformations of its status as a multiracial metropolis and capital of globalization since her youth in a slowly homogenizing postwar "JA bubble." In seven sections of seven parts each, the novel follows seven characters over seven tumultuous days, narrating the confluence of neoliberal policies of free trade and militarized borders, liberal multiculturalism's mystification of complicity with violence through spectacles of difference, and the ecological devastations of global capitalism. Featuring another idea borrowed from her husband – a mystical orange that bears the Tropic of Cancer along with it, bending reality as it is carried northwards – as well as Manzanar Murakami, a homeless Sansei man born in camp who originally appeared in her 1989 play, *GiLArex* (included in her 2014 collection, *Anime Wong*), the novel gathers together previous currents in her work, along with themes drawn from the ongoing history of Black and Chicano LA.

Nineteen ninety-seven marked a turning point for Yamashita. In addition to publishing *Tropic of Orange*, she received a Japan Foundation Fellowship, spending six months living and researching in Japan. This provided the basis for her genre-hopping hybrid volume *Circle K Cycles* (2001), which explored the return migration of Japanese Brazilians to their ancestral homeland, and is therefore generally associated with her first two books, though a historicized understanding of Nikkei diasporic movements allows it to be integrated with other texts, as well. That same year, she began teaching at the University of California, Santa Cruz, continuing for over two decades before taking emerita status in 2019. Given the cleverness, erudition, and intellectual curiosity of her writing, Yamashita's move to academia seems to have been a good fit, though it may also have dampened the growth of her literary profile. In this sense, *Circle K Cycles* looks forward to her subsequent works, which are less approachable for new or more casual readers, because of their increasingly daunting complexity and/or more specialized interest.

In *I Hotel*, Yamashita's last novel published to date and a finalist for the National Book Award, the ability to obsessively pursue her interests that academia and her earlier successes provided is rewarded in a monumental, panoramic reimagination of the Asian American movement and the revolutionary imagination it unleashed, within which the history of something called "Asian American literature" is merely a subfield. The book comprises ten distinct novellas, each loosely organized around a single year (from 1968–1977), and a different combination of themes, settings, and characters (arranged within diagrams of unfolded cubes illustrating the extended table of contents) – though all of these elements, including the years, regularly overlap and interweave across the text's 600-plus pages. At its center is San Francisco's International Hotel, whose single-occupancy rooms for elderly, retired immigrant laborers and meeting spaces for artists and activists made it the movement's Northern California homebase. The long and bitterly fought campaign to save the hotel from the forces of urban renewal and gentrification defined an era.

Extensively researched, the book could variously be described as a *roman à clef* (though decoding all of the prominent and obscure real-life analogues of the characters, who are often hilariously clever mash-ups of several figures, would exhaust the capacity of a team of committed scholars) or as the most thorough historical reconstruction of the movement to date, notwithstanding the excellent emerging scholarship in this area by Karen Ishizuka (2016) and others. Within this history, the appearance of "Asian American literature" as it would be recognized by academic literary history to that point – a postmulticulturalist narrative of the field's consolidation in the mid-1970s by a narrow cultural nationalism that established a canon of "dead yellow men" – is both unfolded, revealing the complexity that narrative contained, and provincialized, revealed to be merely a subset of the broader cultural ferment of the movement. The multimedia, polygeneric experimentalism that the book thematizes draws on the radically innovative aesthetics of the movement's early days, when the effort to conjure a collective, revolutionary Asian American identity innovated new forms of expression and communication that did not respect boundaries between music and poetry, text and graphics, experimental film and documentary propaganda, performance and protest, or between making art and serving the people.

Perhaps the book might be most accurately characterized as a single-authored anthology, recognizing that the anthology is the literary genre that has proved most suited for and influential in establishing a specifically "Asian American" literature, as opposed to the ethnic designations ("Japanese American," "Chinese American," etc.) that better describe most novels in Asian American literary studies. Alternately, recognizing that "Asian American" is, historically speaking, fundamentally a political identification rather than a cultural identity, one might argue that *I Hotel* is the best, if not the only example of a truly Asian American novel.

From the vantage of *I Hotel*, another understanding of Yamashita's career emerges, which was obscured by the aesthetically conservative turn of late 1980s/early 1990s multiculturalism, which privileged realist narratives of cultural conflict, intergenerational family drama, and ethnic subject formation. Yet few writers' careers have been so thoroughly shaped by the networks and institutions of Asian American literary culture than Yamashita's. Her first short story, "The Bath," was published in *Amerasia Journal* in 1975, after editor Dick Osumi entered it in a short story contest without her knowledge; four years later, another story won the James Clavell American-Japanese contest for short fiction. Other early works appeared in community newspapers, including LA's *Rafu Shimpo* and Seattle's *International Examiner*; and several of her early plays were staged by the East West Players. She published pieces in anthologies edited by Janice Mirikitani, arguably the most significant figure in Asian American literature of the early 1970s, and Ishmael Reed, who may be the most influential non-Asian American writer in the emergence of the field. Her career was also shaped by other, less famous but deeply influential figures, like the journalist J.K. Yamamoto (nephew of the writer Hisaye Yamamoto), and the poet, painter, and editor Alan Chong Lau, who connected Yamashita to Coffee House Press, the publisher for all eight of her books.

This framing of Yamashita's career is supported by her three most recent books – the brilliant and demanding *Letters to Memory*, a meditation on the impact of World War II incarceration on her family's history, and especially the collections *Anime Wong: Fictions of Performance* (2014) and *Sansei and Sensibility* (2020). Edited by Stephen Hong Sohn with the participation of the author, *Anime Wong* collects Yamashita's often experimental theater and performance work, in a thematically unified collection that reflects on race, gender, and the dynamic historical manifestations of Orientalism. Though it includes some new work, and omits some older work that was important to her career at the time, *Anime Wong* is of interest in part because it illuminates Yamashita's career prior to her emergence as a novelist, when she was developing her craft and vision in collaboration with key institutions of the Asian American theater of the 1980s and 1990s. Relatedly, *Sansei and Sensibility* gathers Yamashita's short fiction, as far back as 1975's "The Bath," with newer work, pairing a deep dive into the "JA bubbles" of the author's upbringing (including a collection of "Sansei Recipes" and a timeline of Southern California Nikkei history) with stories inspired by Jane Austen – or more precisely, by her sister Jane's fandom for an author Yamashita had not previously gotten around to reading.

Looking back over the course of her career, Karen Tei Yamashita can be seen as a leading figure in a cohort of Asian American writers and artists, including Sesshu Foster and Jessica Hagedorn, who began their careers as the revolutionary social movements of the late 1960s and early 1970s were beginning to recede, and who carried forward movement traditions of politically committed, aesthetically innovative art – in the shadow of more prominent, naturalistic writers like Amy Tan and Jhumpa Lahiri, and as precursors to the more recent breakthroughs of writers like Viet Thanh Nguyen and Cathy Park Hong. Rather than seeing it as a repudiation of the limits of 1970s–1980s cultural nationalism or 1980s–1990s liberal multiculturalism, Yamashita's work – hilariously entertaining; formally sophisticated and inventive, in its rendering of global capitalism's racial violence and environmental devastation; worldly, in its cosmopolitan, erudite sensibility and its situated historical awareness, and yet otherworldly, following the speculative, visionary traditions of liberationist movements – demonstrates the unlimited potential of "Asian American literature," or of the radical imagination that could emerge from a "JA bubble." In September 2021, Yamashita was named the thirty-fourth recipient of the Medal for Distinguished Contribution to American Letters, the lifetime achievement award of the National Book Foundation, whose previous awardees include John Ashbery, Joan Didion, Maxine Hong Kingston, Toni Morrison, and Adrienne Rich.

SEE ALSO: Border Fictions; Ecocriticism and Environmental Fiction; Globalization; Literature of the Americas; Multiculturalism

REFERENCES

Ishizuka, Karen L. (2016). *Serve the People: Making Asian America in the Long Sixties*. New York: Verso.

Yamashita Family Archives. (n.d.). yamashitaarchives.ucsc.edu (accessed September 5, 2021).

Yamashita, Karen Tei. (2020). Growing up Sansei in LA. *Guernica* (June 23, 2020). https://www.guernicamag.com/growing-up-sansei-in-la (accessed August 9, 2021).

FURTHER READING

Eng, Chris A. (2017). Queer genealogies of (be)longing: on the thens and theres of Asian America in Karen Tei Yamashita's *I Hotel*. *Journal of Asian American Studies* 20 (3): 345–372.

Hsu, Ruth Y. and Thoma, Pamela. (eds). (2021). *Approaches to Teaching the Works of Karen Tei Yamashita*. New York: Modern Language Association of America.

Lee. A. Robert. (ed.) (2018). *Karen Tei Yamashita: Fictions of Magic and Memory*. Honolulu: University of Hawai'i Press.

Ling, Jinqi. (2012). *Across Meridians: History and Figuration in Karen Tei Yamashita's Transnational Novels*. Stanford: Stanford University Press.

Sheffer, Jolie A. (2020). *Understanding Karen Tei Yamashita*. Columbia: University of South Carolina Press.

Young Adult Boom

JACQUELINE BACH
Louisiana State University, USA

Young adult (YA) literature comprises texts written and marketed to 12- to 18-year-olds that feature young adult protagonists. It is a genre marked by its intention to capture the unique experiences of adolescence, their "coming of age" and "rites of passage." While books featuring young adults have a long history, YA established itself in the late 1960s, accompanied by the rise in adolescents' exploration of their cultural and social identities, increased leisure time, and the availability of spending money. The YA Boom began in the 1980s and can be organized into three movements with periods of decline between each: the rise of the books in a series and contemporary realistic fiction (1980s to mid-1990s), the rise of fantastical and speculative fiction (late 1990s to early 2000s), and the rise of the novel representing diverse experiences and social issues (2010 to today). One distinguishing aspect of YA's boom is the ongoing relationship among societal and cultural trends, and readers, educators, librarians, authors, and publishers. These forces often work together to find the next best-selling trend that teens will want to read.

The term young adult literature is often contested and has undergone a series of definitions and labels, including junior novels, adolescent fiction, teen fiction, juvenile fiction, and new adult. The term itself reflects the changing nature of what it means to be a "teenager" and what is considered "literature." Its definition often depends on how culture and society shape and identify those concepts (Cart 2016). While the field began with what authors felt adolescents needed to see in books about their own experiences in authentic language and settings, the field grew into one characterized by a strong community of authors, readers, teachers, librarians, and publishers who are mainly concerned with the quality, popularity, and longevity of the field.

CREATING THE REAL: 1960S TO EARLY 1980S

The first novel written and published for teenagers was likely *Seventeenth Summer* by Maureen Daly in 1942. However, 1967 marks the genre's first boom as it separated itself from adult fiction with the publications of S.E. Hinton's *The Outsiders* (1967), Robert Lipsyte's *The Contender* (1967), Chaim Potok's *The Chosen* (1967), and Ann Head's *Mr. and Mrs. Bo Jo Jones* (1967). Those titles were soon joined by Paul Zindel's *The Pigman* (1968) and John Donovan's *I'll Get There. It Better Be Worth the Trip* (1969). These novels were written explicitly for young adults and reflect a variety of adolescent experiences including social class, poverty, friendship, tragedy, sexual orientation, and the challenges of becoming an adult, with the language and characteristics aimed to relate to a young adult.

Considered the first golden age of YA (Cart 2016), the 1970s and early 1980s introduced a number of authors who would continue to define the field with realistic stories that reflected much of the adolescent experience: Judy Blume with sex (*Are You There God, It's Me, Margaret* [1970]); Robert Cormier with bullying and violence (*Chocolate War* [1974]); and Mildred Taylor with racism (*Roll of Thunder, Hear My Cry* [1976]). *Go Ask Alice* (1971), a best-selling diary written by an "anonymous author" who runs away and succumbs to drug abuse, has received both praise and critique. These novelists, among authors of these two decades, set what has come to define the young adult literary tradition of presenting stark, sometimes bleak, portrayals of sex, drugs, divorce, violence, incarceration, racism, and heartache.

REACTING TO THE REAL: 1980S TO MID-1990S

However, readers grew tired of the continuous bleak portrayals of their lives and longed for what their parents had read and were reading – stories of romance and adventure of a "less troubled" world in the romance novels of the 1940s and 1950s (Campbell 2010; Cart 2016). The lower sales of young adult literature were exacerbated as the realistic novel soon devolved into the "problem" novel being published with formulaic plotlines, characters, and melodramatic settings (Bucher and Hinton 2014; Cart 2016). A boom was on the horizon, however, fueled by two major movements: first, the publication of books in series; and second, the publication of high-quality young adult novels that continued in the tradition of the genre's founders of contemporary realism. However, by the end of the decade, sales of YA would drop as publishers began to focus on the growing middle school population and their library and school budgets (Nilsen, Blasingame, Jr., and Donelson 2005; Cart 2016).

In the early 1980s, fictional series found their way into the market as authors and publishers turned their focus from stand-alone books featuring protagonists dealing with realistic issues to novels with recurring characters in popular genres such as romance and horror. Readers could easily find their favorite series on the bookshelves as they searched for covers with spooky fonts (*Fear Street*, R.L. Stine [1989–2005]), a pink spine (*Sweet Valley High*, F. Pascal [1983–2012]), or an apple (*Baby-Sitters Club*, A.M. Martin [1986–2010]). This uniform look also made the books easier to organize on bookshelves and market for readers to find. While series like *Wildfire* and *Sweet Valley High* promised romance and drama, and R.L. Stine (*Goosebumps* [1992–1997]) and Christopher Pike promised gory suspense, these books overwhelmingly represented a particularly narrow adolescent experience, one filled with mainly white characters hanging out at teenage joints and parties, and featured slightly less serious problems such as not getting along with one's parents, first love, friends, and navigating clichés. The *Sweet Valley High* series alone sold over 60 million copies of its 156 books (Lodge 2008). The books were published frequently, sometimes once a month, and were better known by their series title than by the author's name (Cart 2016). Some series, including Pascal's, incorporated a team of writers to keep up with the demand. While never overly graphic or explicit, these books bridged children's literature and adult literature.

Almost since its inception young adult literature has struggled, at least among academics and critics, to demonstrate its quality, especially during the late 1980s and early 1990s in which the genre grew a reputation for producing commercialized quantities of formulaic plotlines and characters (Campbell 2010; Cart 2016). Another critique that emerged came from scholars, librarians, and educators who began calling for more diverse voices in the field. There was considerable agreement that young adults should have stories that feature windows for them into other worlds, mirrors that reflect their own experiences, and sliding glass doors that would allow them to step into other worlds (Bishop 1990). During the 1980s, several authors won substantial awards for their novels representing voices otherwise not found on bookshelves, including Walter Dean Myers, Laurence Yep, Virginia Hamilton, Gary Soto, and Sandra Cisneros. In addition, authors like Richard Peck (*A Long Way from Chicago* [1998]), short story anthology editor Don Gallo (*Sixteen* [1985]), and Chris Crutcher (*Staying Fat for Sarah Burns* [2003]) contributed well-crafted, realistic stories that focused on issues not often found in their contemporary counterparts including abuse, violence, and death. Finally, the Newbery award-winning and honored works in the early 1990s by Lois Lowry, Avi, Jerry Spinelli, Nancy Farmer, and Gary Paulsen helped bring literary recognition to young adult literature and were welcomed by teachers into their curriculums.

During this same period, there was a fear that young adult literature was dying as sales were down and fewer books were being published. Cart (2016) attributes this decline to editors publishing more books to attract the growing number of students found in middle schools, reduced budgets for libraries, the growing popularity of television, which featured many of the same plotlines found in the novels, and the reluctance of teenagers to spend money on hardcovers.

DISGUISING, FABULIZING, AND ACCEPTING THE REAL: MID-1990S TO EARLY 2000S

This trend was not to last and young adult literature was about to experience its second significant boom. During the late 1990s, the teenage population increased significantly (Cart 2016; Campbell 2010) as well as the amount of money they had to spend. By 2004, teenagers had an estimated $169 billion in disposable income (Rosen 2005). Young adult literature in this period owes its success to a number of issues: first, a larger teenage population; second, the publication of *Harry Potter* (J.K. Rowling, 1997–2019) and the multiple speculative fiction titles that followed. Next, several publishing and marketing practices designed to carve young adult literature its own spot gave the genre more attention. Finally, combined efforts by teen fans, librarians, award committees, bestseller lists, and educators brought attention the latest best books being published.

In 1997, British author J.K. Rowling published *The Sorcerer's Stone*, a book featuring an 11-year-old wizard, Harry Potter, and his two friends. For the next seven books, readers grew up as Harry Potter grew up and that time ushered in a slew of books featuring teenage issues in fantastical worlds that attracted children, young adults, and their parents. Harry Potter's was not the first wizarding school for young adults (that was in Ursula K. Le Guin's *Earthsea* trilogy, 1968–1972), but it set a standard by putting a magical world in the "real world" and showed publishers that young readers could handle books over 500 pages. *Harry Potter* was soon followed by a number of books set in magical worlds within the human world. Notable contributions would come from the former adult mystery author Rick Riordan who, in 2005, published the first installment in his bestselling *Percy Jackson* series (2005–2008), about a teenage boy who learns he is a Greek demi-god and works within a mythological world hidden from the real world to save the world from destruction. Also in 2005, Stephanie Myers published the first installment in her paranormal romance between a human and a vampire, *Twilight* (2005–2008). In 2008, Suzanne Collins published *The Hunger Games* (2008–2010), a world in which children engage in a battle to the death for the wealthy's enjoyment. After that dystopian fiction would become another avenue for authors. The work of Rowling, Riordan, Myers, and Collins led not only to spin-offs but also to blockbuster feature films. Other notable authors from these genres are Philip Pullman (*The Golden Compass* [1995]), Neal Shusterman (*Full Tilt* [2004]), and Scott Westerfeld (*Uglies* [2005]). One plot point that connected nearly all of these works would be the enormous pressure put on young heroes to save the world again and again from annihilation by evil forces.

The creation of several awards, bestseller lists, and marketing strategies helped establish young adult literature as its own genre and brought a new level of visibility and legitimization to its authors. While young adult authors had been recognized by awards such as the Coretta Scott King (for African American authors and illustrators) and the Newbery (for children's literature), one of the first awards dedicated strictly to honor a young adult author was the Margaret A. Edwards in

1998. That award has since been joined by the National Book Award, which added a category for Young People's Literature in 1996, the Alex Awards in 1998 for adult books that appeal to young adults, the Michael L. Printz Award in 2000 for excellence in young adult literature, and the William C. Morris Award for debut authors in 2009. Several states also began their own awards for young adult literature. In 2000 in response to Rowling's *Harry Potter* series dominating the bestseller list and in anticipation of the fourth installment (Smith 2000), the *New York Times* added a list for Children's Books. In 2012, the *New York Times* would separate their children's list into one for middle grades and one for young adult. Securing spots in book review journals and on awards and bestsellers lists meant that libraries would likely add these books to their collections and educators would read them and recommend them to students. Another notable factor adding to the visibility of the genre occurred in 1999 when publishers began to create imprints that specialized in young adult literature (Cart 2016). Book stores and libraries began creating new sections for YA – separate from children's and adult books (Campbell 2010). Finally, relationships between organizations dedicated to young adult literature such as Young Adult Library Association (YALSA) and the Assembly on Literature for Adolescents of the National Council of Teachers of English (ALAN), authors, publishers, and educators worked together to bring visibility and respectability for the field and its readers (Campbell 2010; Cart 2016).

The overwhelming popularity of fantastical and speculative fiction did not replace the desire for stand-alone realistic books that reflected a diverse set of experiences and cultures. Alongside the explosion in fantasy, paranormal, and speculative fiction were novels focused on bullying, sexual violence, racism, depression, and juvenile incarceration. Those include works by Sharon Flake (*The Skin I'm In* [1998]), Sharon Draper (*Forged by Fire* [1998]), Laurie Halse Anderson (*Speak* [1999]), and Walter Dean Myers (*Monster* [1999]). Another anomaly testifying to the autonomy of the adolescent reader of this time was the cult popularity of the novel *Perks of Being a Wallflower* (S. Chbosky, 1999), which was actually marketed to an older audience by MTV's publishing company, Pocket Books, but sold widely to readers under the age of 18. Well-known adult authors also began writing for young adults, like Carl Hiassen, Joyce Carol Oates, and Terry Pratchett. Finally, young adult literature such as Art Spiegelman's *Maus* (1980), Lois Lowry's *Number the Stars* (1990), and Markus Zusak's *The Book Thief* (2005), which capture the voices firsthand of characters traumatized by the Holocaust, became staples in the classroom canon of young adult literature. As the decade continued, standout authors such as Matt de la Peña (*Ball Don't Lie* [2008]), Sherman Alexie (*The Absolutely True Story of a Part-Time Indian* [2007]), and Gene Luen Yang (*American Born Chinese* [2008]) also earned awards for their stories of protagonists whose cultural identities clashed with mainstream white culture and norms.

As in the late 1980s, the field returned to the profitability of publishing books in a series, only this time the focus was on the upper-class lives of adolescents. This trend started with Cecily von Ziegersar's *Gossip Girls* (2002–2011), a series of fifteen books set in upper Manhattan that was based loosely on the author's own experiences and spawned its own television show. Readers devoured the stories of glamorous teenage girls who possessed lavish lifestyles, attended posh parties and prep schools, and embroiled themselves in elaborate romantic relationships. Several spin-offs emerged soon after, such as *The A-List* (Z. Dean, 2008–2010), *The Clique* (L. Harrison, 2004–2008), and *The Au Pairs* (M.

de la Cruz, 2004–2008) series. Marketing campaigns advertised that these books held the answers to becoming fashionable, popular, and savvy by featuring characters who have it all figured out. Most likely these titles became popular as a result of several popular television shows for adults in which the characters were obsessed with consumerism, such as *Sex in the City* (Bellafonte 2003). And the "morally bankrupt" characters reflected publishers' desires to sell novels rather than create complicated stories that would explore the intricacies of social class, family relationships, materialism, and consumerism (Glenn 2008).

Another factor that also contributed to the YA Boom at this time was the incorporation of experimental forms of storytelling, most notably the rise of the verse novel. While a few authors had been publishing verse novels for adolescents since the 1980s (Mel Glenn and Virginia Euwer Wolff), according to Friesner (2017), it was the award of the Newbery to Karen Hesse's *Out of the Dust* (1997) that opened the market for verse novels. Award-winning authors of verse novels include Nikki Grimes (Coretta Scott King and Laura Ingalls Wilder), Jacqueline Woodson (MacArthur Fellow, Margaret A. Edwards, National Book Award, the *New York Times* Best-Selling Author), Sonya Sones (Christopher Award), and Ellen Hopkins (American Library Association and Young Adult Libraries Association top 10 lists, the *New York Times* Best-Selling author), who set the standard of examining the topics of sex, sexual orientation, abuse, drugs, and racism. In the style of their predecessors, these characters told their stories in the first person, and their subtle, sparse, poetic form reflected the harsh realities of growing up.

An increase in technology (especially social media) in this decade revolutionized the ways texts were written as well as the way they were marketed. Authors began to look to new platforms for expanding their stories other than just in printed books, including social media, apps, video games, and interactive texts. As more adolescents gained access to the Internet and cell phones, their ways of communication and language changed. In M.T. Anderson's cyberpunk *Feed* (2002), characters have devices implanted in them which allow them to access a vast digital network and expose them to increased commercialization and corporate control. In 2004, Myracle's *ttyl* became the first book to be written entirely in text speak, and Cory Doctorow's *Little Brother* (2008) incorporated text speak and email messages while also being published for free online under the Creative Commons License to allow readers to remix it. These books, among others such as Patrick Carman's *Skeleton Creek* (2009), which combines text and video, and Michael Grant's *BZRK* (2012), which features an app, social media tie-ins, and video games, reflected the changing way young adults were communicating with each other in digital spaces and the increasing influence of social media on their lives.

Representing the Real: 2010–2020

In 2012, *Publishers Weekly* reported on a study showing that "55 percent of books intended for a YA audience (readers aged 12 to 17) were bought by adults, and 78 percent of those purchases were for the buyer's own reading" (*Publishers Weekly* 2012). YA continues to dominate markets as its audience extends to readers outside this age frame. The most recent boom in YA is the focus on social movements and diverse voices, including those involved with the field (editors, publishers, educators, critics), film and television adaptations, and the influence of social media on shaping the field. YA is finally reaching the notice of mainstream scholars and reviewers and receiving a hard-earned (and well-deserved) acknowledgment for its quality. Currently, the field is focusing on diversifying itself and its representations and bringing recognition to high-quality authors and titles.

In response to an all-white, all-male featured panel of children's and young adult authors at the 2014 BookCon, two young adult authors, Ellen Oh and Malinda Lo, took to Twitter and Facebook to call for more diverse representation in the field. That public interaction led to the founding of the movement #weneeddiversebooks, and readers, librarians, authors, and publishers are all focusing efforts on diversifying the field. We Need Diverse Books (WNDB) is now a volunteer-run nonprofit with "programs to celebrate diverse books, to mentor diverse writers and illustrators, to support diverse publishing professionals, and to provide books to classrooms nationwide" (WNDB 2021).

In 2015, with the rise of social movements across the United States, young adult authors sought to represent the effects these events have on young adults as well as to showcase ways in which young adults might become involved in society's social issues. Stories began to reflect headlines covering the shootings of Black men by police, social class, #blacklivesmatter, #metoo, gender identity, and sexual orientation. This new group of fictional teenagers are not dealing with just social concerns; they are engaging with social protests and movements. Jason Reynold's and Brenden Kiely's 2001 *All-American Boys*, Nic Stone's 2017 *Dear Martin*, and Angie Thomas's 2017 *The Hate U Give* are examples of narratives in which the protagonists confront police brutality through the violence and shooting of a Black teenage boy. Another issue that authors have taken up relates to the #MeToo movement, scandals regarding the sexual abuse of preteen girls, and the growing number of young girls who are victims of sexual harassment and abuse (de Leon 2020). A recent increase also includes a focus on mental health, again reflecting society's growing willingness to address mental health issues and the increasing number of young people diagnosed with mental illness. According to the World Health Organization (2020), "Half of all mental health conditions start by 14 years of age but most cases are undetected and untreated." Recent books focusing on mental health issues in young adult literature include titles by Laurie Halse Anderson, A.S. King, John Green, Francisco X. Stork, Emily X.R. Pan, and Neal Schusterman. The responsibility for the field to "get it right" is more important than ever as authors tackle issues for younger audiences.

In addition to the field seeking to diversify itself, authors are also seeking to diversify the representation of characters from historically underrepresented backgrounds who may traditionally have had only one narrative path, for example the story of an urban youth of color who faces racism, incarceration, or hardship, or the coming out story of an LGBTQ character. In an effort to provide windows, mirrors, and sliding glass doors (Bishop 1990), these singular representations are being challenged as authors include the multiple experiences of young adults. And experimental forms, such as verse novels, continue to impress award committees. One notable example is Elizabeth Acevedo's *The Poet X* (2018), which was awarded the National Book Award for Young People's Literature, the Michael L. Printz Award, and an Odyssey Award for the audio recording. Kwame Alexander's *The Crossover* (2014) was the 2015 winner of a Newbery Award and a Coretta Scott King Honor Book and has now become a series. Furthermore, genres that have been traditionally dominated by white, straight protagonists are also seeing new authors and characters. For example, Toliver (2019) asserts that 2018 caused an earthquake in the field of speculative fiction as the popular films *Black Panther* (dir. Ryan Coogler, 2018) and the reboot of *A Wrinkle in Time* (dir. Ava DuVernay, 2018) with a Black actress in the leading role contributed to the rise of Black speculative fiction (many of which have become series) written by Black women. L.L. McKinney (*A Blade So Black* [2018]), Justina Ireland (*Dread Nation* [2017]), and Tomi Adeyemi (*Children of Blood and Bone* [2018]) joined the few previous authors Virginia Hamilton (*The Magical Adventures of Pretty Pearl* [2018]), Malorie Blackman (*Noughts & Crosses* [2001–2019]), and Zetta Elliott (*A Wish after Midnight* [2010]).

Some topics in young adult literature started with its inception and are only just now reaching the visibility hoped for by readers, educators, and authors. In 1969, John Donovan published *I'll Get There. It Better Be Worth the Trip*, the first young adult novel featuring a gay character. *Ruby* by Rosa Guy in 1976 featured one of the first protagonists who was a queer adolescent of color. The number of books featuring LGBTQ+ issues and characters has been steadily increasing each decade from eight in the 1970s, forty in the 1980s, and seventy-five in the 1990s. In the 1980s, 73% of books featuring LGBTQ+ characters and themes included gay men and only 27% lesbian women (Cart 2016). Lo (2003) tracked books with main characters who were LGBTQ and published by major publishers, and found that there was an average of fifteen titles per year since 2011. However, with the increase of the number of books, the number of LGBTQ protagonists decreased as they became secondary characters (Cart 2016). While early narratives were critiqued for featuring mainly coming out stories with bleak endings and featuring mainly white gay males (Cart 2016), this genre continues to become more diverse. Standout authors include Jacqueline Woodson, David Leviathan, and Francesca Lia Block. As fiction and nonfiction for young adults featuring LGBTQ+ characters and themes have increased, so has the number of characters who are LGBTQ+ appearing in the works of best-selling authors who may not have included these characters or themes in their earlier works. One example is Rick Riordan, who won a Stonewall Award (an award established in 2010 with a category dedicated to children's and young adult literature) for including a transgender, gender-fluid character in his best-selling *Magnus Chase* (2015–2018) series.

The increasing number of novels adapted for film and television also accompanied the increasing popularity of YA. After the success of film versions of Harry Potter, Twilight, and the Hunger Games, directors looked to adapt successful young adult stand-alone and book series. Recent books are also appearing on streaming services such as an adaptation of Jay Asher's *13 Reasons Why* (2007) and Philip Pullman's *His Dark Materials* (1995–2000). Other notable film adaptations include Veronica Roth's *Divergent* (2014), John Green's *The Fault in Our Stars* (2012), and Angie Thomas's *The Hate U Give* (2017).

A final feature of the field that accounts for its current boom is the role of technology. Social media has extended the relationships between young adult authors and their readers through Instagram, Twitter, YouTube, Facebook, and TikTok. No matter what platform comes next, those interactions are not only visible, but to varying extents shape what gets published and how it is received. As much as the online community is able to enact change regarding who gets noticed, read, or praised, it has also caused several books not to be published, condemned authors for plotlines, and strongly influenced how books are reviewed and promoted.

CONCLUSION: TODAY, CONSTRUCTING THE REAL

Between 2018 and 2019, adult literature sales dropped 2.7% while children's and YA literature increased 6.8% (Association of American

Publishers 2020). That figure is just over 2 billion dollars a year (Milliot 2020). Clearly, from a profitability standpoint, young adult literature will endure and has learned its lesson that if there is a drop in population or funding, it must reach into other age groups, change its marketing, and return to what it does best: reflecting the unique experiences of adolescents in new ways. Young adult literature's booms have always been accompanied by its ability to transform and meet the changing experiences of its readers. But that change is shaped as readers, authors, librarians, educators, and publishers clamor to find the next great book, preferably the first in a series. Because of the dynamic changes in society, the move to online purchasing, and digital books and e-readers, the relationship among readers, publishers, authors, and educators will continue to be marketed and packaged differently – but all of this includes the search for what readers want to read, what educators want them to read, and how publishers and authors can market and sell those ideas to their audiences.

As Campbell (2010) notes, the field continues to be bifurcated into two distinct genres, contemporary realist fiction and speculative fiction, with a few standouts in nonfiction and historical fiction. And certain titles such as Hinton's *The Outsiders*, Lowry's *The Giver* (1993), Zusak's *The Book Thief*, and Thomas's *The Hate U Give* have made it into the canon of middle and high school classrooms. Outside of required reading, it is word of mouth among readers, educators, and librarians that continues to play a role in what gets read; today, that same social approach has moved into a virtual realm where those conversations have become very public through social media posts, online reviews, and networks. As Aronson (2002) points out, no matter what form the genre takes, it will always "remain the direct expression of teenage experience and the invention of new worlds as wild, dangerous and profound as this one feels to the teenagers who are first learning to master it."

SEE ALSO: Alexie, Sherman; Anders, Charlie Jane; Cyberpunk; Debut Novels; The Graphic Novel Le Guin, Ursula; Mixed-Genre Fiction; Oates, Joyce Carol; Queer and LGBT Fiction

REFERENCES

Aronson, Marc. (2002). Coming of age. *Publishers Weekly* (February 11, 2002). https://www.publishersweekly.com/pw/print/20020211/30452-coming-of-age.html (accessed July 22, 2021).

Association of American Publishers. (2020). AAP November 2019 statshot report: industry up 0.9% year-to-date for 2019. https://publishers.org/news/aap-november-2019-statshot-report-industry-up-0-9-year-to-date-for-2019/ (accessed July 22, 2021).

Bellafonte, Ginia. (2003). CULTURAL STUDIES: poor little rich girls, throbbing to shop. *The New York Times* (August 17, 2003). https://www.nytimes.com/2003/08/17/style/cultural-studies-poor-little-rich-girls-throbbing-to-shop.html (accessed July 22, 2021).

Bishop, Rudine S. (1990). Mirrors, windows, and sliding glass doors. Perspectives: Choosing and Using Books for the Classroom 6 (3): ix–xi.

Bucher, Katherine T. and Hinton, KaaVonia. (2014). *Young Adult Literature: Exploration, Evaluation, and Appreciation*, 3rd ed. Boston: Pearson; 1st ed. 2006.

Campbell, Patty. (2010). *Campbell's Scoop: Reflections on Young Adult Literature*, vol. 38. Lanham, MD: Scarecrow Press.

Cart, Michael. (2016). *Young Adult Literature: From Romance to Realism*, 3rd ed. Chicago: Neal Shuman; 1st ed. 1996.

De Leon, Concepción. (2020). Why more children's books are tackling sexual harassment and abuse. *The New York Times* (June 17, 2020). https://www.nytimes.com/2020/06/17/books/childrens-books-middle-grade-metoo-sexual-abuse.html (accessed July 22, 2021).

Friesner, Brenna. (2017). *The Verse Novel in Young Adult Literature*, vol. 53. Lanham, MD: Rowman & Littlefield.

Glenn, Wendy. (2008). Gossiping girls, insider boys, A-list achievement: examining and exposing young adult novels consumed by conspicuous consumption. Journal of Adolescent & Adult Literacy 52 (1): 34–42.

Lo, Malinda. (2003). LGBT young adult books 2003–13: a decade of slow but steady change. https://www.malindalo.com/blog/2013/10/lgbt-young-adult-books-2003-13-a-decade-of-slow-but-steady-change (accessed July 22, 2021).

Lodge, Sally. (2008). Sweet Valley High: back in session. *Publishers Weekly* (March 27, 2008). https://www.publishersweekly.com/pw/by-topic/childrens/childrens-book-news/article/1995-sweet-valley-high-back-in-session.html (accessed July 22, 2021).

Milliot, Jim. (2020). Industry sales posted small gain in 2019. *Publishers Weekly* (March 14, 2020). https://www.publishersweekly.com/pw/by-topic/industry-news/financial-reporting/article/82693-industry-sales-posted-small-gain-in-2019.html (accessed July 22, 2021).

Nilsen, Alleen P., Blasingame, James, Jr., and Donelson, Ken. (2005). 2004 honor list: an encouraging illustration of extended horizons. The English Journal 103.

Publishers Weekly. (2012). New study: 55% of YA books bought by adults. https://www.publishersweekly.com/pw/by-topic/childrens/childrens-industry-news/article/53937-new-study-55-of-ya-books-bought-by-adults.html (accessed July 22, 2021).

Rosen, Judith. (2005). As if! Marketing books to older teens. *Publishers Weekly* (July 15, 2005). https://www.publishersweekly.com/pw/print/20050718/23360-as-if-marketing-to-older-teens.html (accessed July 22, 2021).

Smith, Dinitia. (2000). *The Times* plans a children's best-sellers list. *The New York Times* (June 24, 2000). https://www.nytimes.com/2000/06/24/books/the-times-plans-a-children-s-best-seller-list.html (accessed July 22, 2021).

Toliver, Stephanie. (2019). On the history (and future) of YA and speculative fiction by Black women. *Lit Hub* (August 8, 2019). https://lithub.com/on-the-history-and-future-of-ya-and-speculative-fiction-by-black-women/ (accessed July 22, 2021).

WNDB. (2021). We need diverse books. https://diversebooks.org/ (accessed July 22, 2021).

World Health Organization. (2020). Adolescent mental health. https://www.who.int/news-room/fact-sheets/detail/adolescent-mental-health (accessed July 22, 2021).

FURTHER READING

Cart, Michael. (2008). The value of young adult literature. https://www.ala.org/yalsa/guidelines/whitepapers/yalit

Cart, Michael and Jenkins, Christine A. (2006). *The Heart has its Reasons: Young Adult Literature with Gay/Lesbian/Queer Content, 1969–2004*. Lanham, MD: Scarecrow Press.

Lenz, Millicent and Mahood, Ramona M. (1980). *Young Adult Literature: Background and Criticism*. Chicago: American Library Association.

Thomas, Ebony E. (2019). *The Dark Fantastic: Race and the Imagination from Harry Potter to The Hunger Games*. New York: NYU Press.

Zipes, Jack. (2001). *Sticks and Stones: The Troublesome Success of Children's Literature from Slovenly Peter to Harry Potter*. New York: Routledge.

Yu, Charles

THOMAS B. BYERS
University of Louisville, USA

As of this writing, Charles Yu has published two short story collections: *Third Class Superhero* (2006) and *Sorry Please Thank You* (2012); and two novels: *How to Live Safely in a Science Fictional Universe* (2010) and *Interior Chinatown* (2020). All have attracted acclaim; most notably, Richard Powers selected Yu for the National Book Foundation's 5 Under 35 prize for *Third Class Superhero*, and *Interior Chinatown* won the National Book Award for Fiction in 2020. Examples of Yu's fiction fit into many categories such as social satire, Asian American literature, science fiction, and metafiction. One of his prominent subjects is the hardships of contemporary working life; another is parent–child relations. He frequently explores characters' self-awareness outside, or on the edge of, an aspirational model or goal such as Americanness, or success, or loving connection, or simply having a decent life. Recently he has profoundly analyzed the difficulties of Asian American identity. At the same time, his work is noted for pleasurable imaginative conceits, metafictional virtuosity, and humor. As Leslie Bow notes, "Yu is a master at externalizing the arbitrary or inane simulacra that govern contemporary bourgeois existence … Yet at the heart of Yu's fiction lies an affective and relatable core" (Bow 2017, p. 2).

Born in Los Angeles in 1976, Yu is the son of Taiwanese immigrants. He graduated from UC Berkeley, where he majored in biology but "minored in creative writing (in poetry) … [taking] several poetry workshops with people like Thom Gunn and Ishmael Reed" (Birnbaum 2012). He aspired to become an MD, but by his own account "did not get into medical school" (Birnbaum 2012). He went to Columbia Law School, and then worked as a corporate lawyer, writing fiction after hours (Sternbergh 2020). Eventually, however, he "got a call from HBO" (Sternbergh 2020) and became a television writer, first on *Westworld* (for which he received two Writers Guild of America Award nominations in 2017) and then on a number of other shows.

Writers whom Yu claims as influences include Isaac Asimov (Harvilla 2020), Donald Barthelme (Birnbaum 2012), Don DeLillo (Clarke 2015a), and George Saunders (Yu 2021). He has expressed admiration for Philip Roth (Clarke 2015c), William Gibson (Birnbaum 2012), Jonathan Lethem (Birnbaum 2012; Clarke 2015b), Richard Powers (Bow 2017, p. 4), and Ben Lerner (Birnbaum 2012). He has been compared to Italo Calvino (Nance 2012, p. 35; Clute 2020), Kurt Vonnegut (Clute 2020), Junot Díaz (Bow 2017, p. 1), and Ted Chiang (Shiu 2014). Notably absent from these partial lists are women and (other than Chiang) Asian American writers. While scholars such as Brian McHale (2015, p. 185), Frances Tran (2016), and Anthony Sze-Fai Shiu (2014) discuss Yu in an Asian American context, journalistic writing and his own statements in interviews associate him primarily with white male authors. One comparison worth exploring would be to Karen Tei Yamashita, whose *The I-Hotel* (2010), like *Interior Chinatown*, combines formal and generic play, Asian American history, and moving stories of individual characters. The remainder of this entry samples each of Yu's books in hopes of whetting the reader's appetite for his fiction.

Though the narrator of the title story of *Third Class Superhero* has graduated from superhero school, his application for official superhero status keeps failing, year after year, as he sees his more talented classmates surpassing him. The humorous center of his problem is his quite limited superpower:

> My power, if you can call it that, and I don't think you can, is that I am able to take about two gallon of water from the moisture in the air and shoot it in a stream or a gentle mist. Or a ball. Which is useful for water-balloon fights, but not all that helpful when trying to stop Carnage and Mayhem from robbing a bank.
>
> (2006, loc. 59)

He reads self-help books and studies physics, history, and theory, but cannot "change the fact that I'm minor. Not even minor. A sideshow. A human water fountain" (loc. 63). Eventually, he wonders, "even if the rest of my life is one long lucky streak until the day I die, where does that get me? Middle management? A teaching post? Adjunct lecturer…?" (loc. 183). In desperation, by selling a group of colleagues into an ambush where one is killed, he obtains, on the black market, the ability to fly, but thus also betrays his status as a (literally) card-carrying "good guy." In the end, while flying for the first time, he assesses himself thus: "I'm not a superhero. I'm background. I'm a good person wrapped in a mediocre soul. I want to be better. I really do. But even now in my greatest moment I know this is as good as it will ever get for me and it's not that good" (loc. 290).

The superhero framework provides humor and entertainment, but the story addresses a serious situation: the condition of the white-collar working class (the narrator's "day job" is as "a records clerk for a big midtown law firm" [2006, loc. 47]). Our hero aspires to a position that only the most highly qualified and talented will ever get (indeed that's the allegorical meaning of "superhero" here). He has already lowered his expectations dramatically: "[I]t's not like I'm asking for a lot. I don't need to be an all-star. I just want a suit and a cape, steady work, a paycheck that covers groceries. Decent health insurance. But I'll have to wait another year" (loc. 39–43). But even this kind of basic success is beyond the reach even of many graduates. Those few with superhuman gifts flourish in the spotlight. For everyone else, even if they work hard and follow the rules, the economy of inequity offers only struggle for minor success.

The narrator lays his limitations to not having been "born gifted," a deficiency he can't overcome even through special effort. One wishes the story showed more awareness that in reality the "gifts" separating the elite from everyone else are often matters of privilege, not talent. What it *does* do, through a comedic situation but a convincing and poignant narrative voice, is convey how it feels to realize that one is doomed to a life of mediocrity.

"Standard Loneliness Package," the lead story of *Sorry Please Thank You*, is one of Yu's finest works. It concerns a horrible labor situation that its world accepts as normal. The story's narrator works in a call center in Bangalore where "I feel pain for money. Other people's pain. Physical, emotional, you name it" (2012, p. 3). People contract for his time in half-hour segments and their pain is shifted, via an implanted chip, to him. For "twelve dollars per hour, plus reimbursement for pain-killers" (p. 3), he endures their broken legs and broken hearts; hernias, root canals and migraines; incarcerations, unrequited loves, and bereavements. Periodically through the story he quotes prices, such as:

Death of an aunt is seven hundred. Death of an uncle is six.
Bad day in the market is a thousand. Kid's recital is one twenty-five an hour. Church is one fifty.

(2012, p. 19)

Thus are the worker's body, nervous system, and consciousness commodified and monetized.

In this world as in ours, productivity experts have constructed the employees' time for full efficiency. Waiting time at the doctor's office, for instance, which might provide a brief respite, has been eliminated (2012, p. 3). Indeed, "They have gotten it down to a science. How much a human being can take in a given twelve-hour shift ... and the end result is you leave work every day right about at your exact breaking point" (pp. 9–10).

Still, Yu's speaker has been successfully interpellated into his station: "It's ok for me," he tells us. "It's a good job. I didn't do that well in school, after all.... [M]aybe this is about where I belong in the grand scheme of things, in terms of high-end low-end for me as a person" (2012, p. 8). He does have an idea, however, of what both his high end and low end would be. The low would be to sell his whole life, rather than just each workday. This is what his father did: he mortgaged his life for forty years to provide for his family, "and if he made it full term [which, sadly, he did not] ... he could stop, he could come back to us" (p. 28). This low end literalizes the way many men sell themselves to their jobs and in doing so lose their families.

The narrator's high end would be to buy a prepackaged life, made from "the leftover slices of life," like the time in the doctor's waiting room, that were "smushed all together into a kind of reconstituted life slab, a lifeloaf" (2012, p. 13). He has his eye on one:

> Not a DreamLife®, not top of the line, but ... a good one. Standard possibility. Low volatility. A kind-hearted wife with nice hair, 0.35 kids, no actuals ... but some potential kids, a solid thirty-five percent chance of having one. Normal life-expectancy, average health, median aggregate amount of happiness. I test-drove it once, and it felt good, it felt right. It fit just fine.
>
> (2012, p. 15)

He does admit, however, that "I just thought there might be more to it all than this" (2012, p. 15).

This story's premise symbolizes the reality that the labor market is, for billions of workers, simply a place where they sell their toleration for misery – and that what wealth buys is, too often, the suffering of others. The narrator's may not be, as he claims, "a good job" (2012, p. 8); but it is, all too truly, a job like many others. Perhaps its saddest implication is that its holder thinks it is all he deserves.

Turning to the novels, the work of Yu's that most partakes of, or plays with, the science fiction genre is *How to Live Safely in a Science Fictional Universe*. Its protagonist/narrator (whose name is Charles Yu) "fix[es] time machines for a living" (2010, p. 5), and otherwise generally spends his time alone in his TM-31 time machine, a piece of "chronodiegetical technology: a six cylinder grammar drive built on a quad-core physics engine ... allowing for free-form navigation within a rendered environment, such as, for instance, a story space and, in particular, a science-fictional universe" (p. 4). The combination of physics and grammar here recalls the Nefastis machine in Thomas Pynchon's *Crying of Lot 49* (1967) with its blending of entropy in physics and in communication science. In Yu's text, "memory and regret are ... the set of necessary and sufficient elements required to produce a time machine" (Yu 2010, p. 34), and thus the machine may actually be consciousness, or writing itself.

Early in the book, the narrator keeps to himself. Having never recovered from his father's abandonment of the family, he has rejected chronological time, choosing to live in the "present-indefinite" tense (2010, p. 3), so as "to suppress memory, to ignore the future" (p. 56) in "a hidden cul-de-sac of space-time ... the most uneventful piece of time I could find.... That's why I chose it. I know for a fact that nothing bad can happen to me in here" (p. 15). He has chosen "A life without danger. A life without the risk of Now" (p. 22).

He suggests at least two reasons, beyond his own self-protective instincts, that one might choose not to live in chronological time: one concerns looking forward, the other looking back. His father lived toward the future, reading books about "actualization, realization, ... self as a DIY project. Self as a kind of problem to be solved" (2010, p. 38). He "spent all the time he had with us thinking about how he wished he had more time" (p. 18) rather than living in the time he had. Both the myth of progress and the hyperconsciousness of chronological limitation became ways of not living a present life. Moreover, once the myth failed, "His time machine broke down, and he got trapped in the past ... permanently stuck in his own history" (p. 232). These two traps of future and past are very common: "Most people I know live their lives moving in a constant forward direction, the whole time looking backward" (p. 22). In this, they repeat Walter Benjamin's Angel of History who "would like to stay, awaken the dead, and make whole what has been smashed," but who cannot do so both because he is borne forward by "progress" and because he can only focus on the past as "catastrophe" and "wreckage" (Benjamin 1969, pp. 257–258).

The narrator gets caught in a time-loop in which, over and over, his future self shoots his past self. Finally, however, he meets another version of himself, who gives him a comic but existential slap in the face, telling him,

> only you know what you need to do ... Now get back to your life and quit being such a whiny little wuss. Be a man. Find your father. Tell him you love him. Then let him go. Then go and marry that girl you never married.... Anything is possible in this kind of world. You idiot. Go marry Marie. And have a life. And grow a heart. And a pair.
>
> (2010, pp. 138–139)

At this point, the narrator begins to use his time machine to confront his past. He reviews in particular the painful day his father tried to demonstrate his time machine invention to his company's CEO, and it would not work. This was the day Charles learned the bitter lessons of classism and immigrant status and impostor syndrome, and learned too how he had let his father down by lacking confidence in him, and "realized ... how good a man my father was and is" (2010, p. 183). Ultimately, having faced all this, the narrator realizes he must step out of the box, leave the time machine caught in the loop, and enter "the world of time and risk and loss again. Move forward, into the empty plain ... Enjoy the elastic present" (p. 233). There is no living safely that is really living.

Yu's first three books have relatively little focus on Asian American identity or issues. Indeed, in a 2012 interview, he stated, "I have not identified myself as an Asian-American writer. I am aware that others have" (Birnbaum 2012). *Interior Chinatown*, however, presents a different case. Its title refers in part to the text's formal conceit, that the protagonist lives in a world that is also a television show in which he is a bit player and for which the book is a script. But it also refers to having Chinatown, with all its historical, cultural, and stereotypical meanings, in – or as – one's own interiority. A map of it might take the form of a Venn diagram, wherein a literal, historical place, in some iterations created as "a literal, legally defined ghetto" (Yu 2020, pp. 202, 232), intersects with an orientalist site (or TV set) created by white imagination for the playing out of stories in which the residents of the space are simply supporting characters, villains, or background. They are perpetually alien and peripheral and never individual, the men identified in the script only as versions of "Generic Asian Man." They're not even "Generic Asian American," because the American in Asian American is always under erasure. It is so not only because they are in a perpetual state of arrival (see p. 74), but also because the real subjects of American history are Black and White (which is also the name of the TV show about two detectives of those two "races" which the book scripts). Generic Asian Man has internalized the notion that, despite its long and outrageous history, the racial oppression of Asian Americans "is second-class" (p. 248) "because it does not include the original American sin – of slavery" (p. 247).

The use of the TV show in *Interior Chinatown* highlights the importance of the gaze and performance in the lives of Asian Americans. There is a cruel paradox in such lives: the dominant culture's measure of their success is the degree to which they remain unseen. If racial difference is signaled by one's appearance, to be a "model minority" is to model invisibility. Yet in mainstream life in general, and especially on television, success is linked to visibility: the more attention one attracts, the higher one is rated. The desire to be seen is the desire to be at center stage rather than in the background, to stand out rather than blend in, to be a star, not an extra. For Yu's protagonist, life and television are at once stages on which one seeks to appear and panopticons in which one constantly monitors and restricts oneself for fear of the regulatory gaze. Thus, as the heroic figure "Older Brother" says in the climactic court scene (where the protagonist finds himself "on trial for my own disappearance"),

> Chinatown and indeed being Chinese is and always has been, from the very beginning, a construction, a performance of features, gestures, culture, and exoticism. An invention, a reinvention, a stylization. Figuring out the show, finding our place in it, which was the background, as scenery, as non-speaking players. Figuring out what you're allowed to say.
>
> (2020, p. 252)

Interior Chinatown is Yu's most fully realized book to date. Its framing of life as both a reality and a TV show is pulled off brilliantly and, as in his other fictions, the formal and metafictional pyrotechnics and the humor maintain a fine balance with the serious and moving human stories. One can only look forward eagerly to his future fictions.

SEE ALSO: Chiang, Ted; DeLillo, Don; Diaz, Junot; Gibson, William; Globalization; Intermedial Fiction; Powers, Richard; Reed, Ishmael; Saunders, George; Vonnegut, Kurt

REFERENCES

Benjamin, Walter. (1969). Theses on the philosophy of history [1940]. In *Illuminations* (ed. Hannah Arendt; trans. Harry Zohn), 253–264. New York: Schocken Books.

Birnbaum, Robert. (2012). Charles Yu. *The Morning News* (November 1, 2012). https://themorningnews.org/article/charles-yu (accessed July 22, 2021).

Bow, Leslie. (2017). An interview with Charles Yu. *Contemporary Literature* 58 (1): 1–17.

Clarke, Jaime. (2015a). Influenced by D. *Believer Magazine* (January 22, 2015). https://believermag.com/logger/2015-01-22-influenced-by-17/ (accessed July 22, 2021).

Clarke, Jaime. (2015b). Influenced by L. *Believer Magazine* (February 3, 2015). https://believermag.com/logger/2015-02-03-influenced-by-9/ (accessed July 22, 2021).

Clarke, Jaime. (2015c). Influenced by. *Believer Magazine* (February 9, 2015). https://believermag.com/logger/2015-02-09-influenced-by-5/ (accessed July 22, 2021).

Clute, John. (2020). Yu, Charles. *SFE: The Science Fiction Encyclopedia* (March 5, 2020). http://sf-encyclopedia.com/entry/yu_charles (accessed July 22, 2021).

Elias, Amy J. (2013). Tense and sensibility. *American Book Review* 34 (4): 7–8.

Harvilla, Rob. (2020). The multiple dimensions of Charles Yu. *The Ringer* (January 29, 2020). https://www.theringer.com/2020/1/29/21113080/charles-yu-interior-chinatown-new-book-interview (accessed July 22, 2021).

McHale, Brian. (2015). *The Cambridge Introduction to Postmodernism*. Cambridge: Cambridge University Press.

Nance, Kevin. (2012). Me, you and Charles Yu. *Poets & Writers* 40 (4): 33–38.

Shiu, Anthony. (2014). The ethics of race, failure, and Asian American (ethno)futures. *Extrapolation* 55 (3): 299–321.

Sternbergh, Adam. (2020). With his fourth book, Charles Yu finally feels like a writer. *The New York Times* (January 22, 2020). https://www.nytimes.com/2020/01/22/books/charles-yu-interior-chinatown.html (accessed July 22, 2021).

Tran, Frances. (2016). How to live un safely: toward a better good life for Asian American studies. *Journal of Asian American Studies* 19 (2): 213–235.

Yu, Charles. (2006). *Third Class Superhero*. Harvest. Kindle e-book.

Yu, Charles. (2010). *How to Live Safely in a Science Fictional Universe*. New York: Vintage Books.

Yu, Charles. (2012). *Sorry Please Thank You*. New York: Vintage Books.

Yu, Charles. (2020). *Interior Chinatown*. New York: Europa.

Yu, Charles. (2021). Author Q&A: a conversation with Charles Yu. https://www.penguinrandomhouse.com/books/203055/how-to-live-safely-in-a-science-fictional-universe-by-charles-yu/ (accessed July 22, 2021).

FURTHER READING

Treisman, Deborah. (2016). This week in fiction: Charles Yu on therapy and storytelling. *The New Yorker* (May 23, 2016). https://www.newyorker.com/books/page-turner/fiction-this-week-charles-yu-2016-05-30

Yu, Charles. (2020). What it's like to never ever see yourself on TV. *Time* (January 21, 2020). https://time.com/5767738/what-its-like-to-never-see-yourself-on-tv/

Yu, Charles. (2020). The pre-pandemic universe was the fiction. *The Atlantic* (April 15, 2020). https://www.theatlantic.com/culture/archive/2020/04/charles-yu-science-fiction-reality-life-pandemic/609985/

Yu, Charles. (n.d.). www.charlesyuauthor.com

Index

Entries in **bold** indicate subjects covered by a main article; page locators in **bold** indicate main articles. This index uses letter-by-letter alphabetization.

10:04 (Lerner), 818–822, 940
13th Valley, The (Del Vecchio), 281
2008 global financial crisis, 169–170, 256, 488, 1286, 1325–1326
2666 (Bolaño), 167, 170–172, 174
Abraham Lincoln: Vampire Hunter (Grahame-Smith), 937, 940
Abu-Jaber, Diana, 1–6
  Arabian Jazz (Abu-Jaber), 2
  awards and acclaim, 1
  Birds of Paradise (Abu-Jaber), 3–4
  Crescent (Abu-Jaber), 2–3
  Language of Baklava, The (Abu-Jaber), 4–5
  life and works, 1
  Life without a Recipe (Abu-Jaber), 4–5
  Origin (Abu-Jaber), 3–4
  themes, 2–5
  writing devices and techniques, 5
Acker, Kathy, 6–11
  1990 onwards, 9–10
  Blood and Guts in High School (Acker), 686–687
  Empire of the Senseless (Acker), 7–8
  influence, themes, and writing style, 6–7
  In Memoriam to Identity (Acker), 8–9
  Kathy Goes to Haiti (Acker), 7
  legacy, 10
  life and early works, 6–7
  mid- to late 1980s, 7–9
  My Mother: A Demonology (Acker), 9
  Pussy, King of the Pirates (Acker), 9–10
Acts of Intervention (Román), 669
Adichie, Chimamanda Ngozi, 11–17
  Americanah (Adichie), 12, 14–16
  awards and acclaim, 12–14
  citizenship and identity, 11
  Half of a Yellow Sun (Adichie), 13–14
  Igbo culture, 13, 16
  influence and impact, 15–16
  life and early work, 11–13
  nonfiction, 15–16
  Purple Hibiscus (Adichie), 12
  Thing around Your Neck, The (Adichie), 12, 14
  We Should All Be Feminists (Adichie), 15–16
Adventures of Lucky Pierre, The (Coover), 28–30, 306
affect *see* Fiction and Affect
African Diaspora, The (Palmer), 158
Afrofuturism, 17–26
  Afrofuturism's fictive kin, 23–25
  apocalyptic and postapocalyptic, 19–21, 24
  Beloved (Morrison), 19
  Between the World and Me (Coates), 23
  Black Atlantic, 164
  Black Futures (Drew and Wortham), 22
  Black music, 20
  Black Panther (Coogler), 20–21
  Butler, Octavia, 17, 19–21
  Citizen: An American Lyric (Rankine), 23
  complex temporalities, 19–21
  decolonization, 21–24
  Delany, Samuel R., 357–362
  Dery, Mark, 17–18
  Díaz, Junot, 19, 24
  Gomez, Jewelle, 567, 569–571
  history and definitions, 17–19
  hypertext fiction and network narratives, 660
  Johnson, Mat, 729–730
  mixed-genre fiction, 939
  Nelson, Alondra, 18

The Encyclopedia of Contemporary American Fiction 1980–2020, First Edition. Edited by Patrick O'Donnell, Stephen J. Burn, and Lesley Larkin.
© 2022 John Wiley & Sons Ltd. Published 2022 by John Wiley & Sons Ltd.

Afrofuturism *(cont'd)*
  Octavia's Brood (Imarisha), 17, 21–22
  Okorafor, Nnedi, 17–20
  queer and LGBT fiction, 1140
  Underground Railway, The (Whitehead), 21
  usable past, 18–20
  visionary fiction and nonfiction, 21–23
  Water Dancer, The (Coates), 21, 23
  When They Call You a Terrorist (bandele and Cullors), 22–23
  Womack, Ytasha, 18–19
afternoon (Joyce), 661–662
After Postmodernism, 26–35
  Adventures of Lucky Pierre, The: Directors' Cut (Coover), 28–30
  Barth, John, 32
  Chabon, Michael, 240–246
  context, 26–27
  Eggers, Dave, 398–404
  fiction and affect, 472–475
  Foer, Jonathan Safran, 495–501
  Geek Love (Dunn), 29
  Gold Bug Variations, The (Powers), 29–30
  Internet, 32–33
  Jones, Stephen Graham, 744–749
  Lerner, Ben, 818–823
  Middlesex (Eugenides), 30
  Oates, Joyce Carol, 1017–1022
  politics and culture war, 33
  post-9/11 narratives, 31–32
  Pynchon, Thomas, 29–31, 1130–1136
  religion, 31–32
  Satanic Verses, The (Rushdie), 30–31
  Saunders, George, 31
  Sokal, Alan D., 28, 33
  Spiotta, Dana, 1256–1261
  Vollmann, William T., 1371–1376
  Wallace, David Foster, 26–27, 30–32, 1388–1393
  Whitehead, Colson, 1415–1421
After the Workshop (McNally), 1122
Against the American Grain (Kutzinski), 839
AIDS *see* HIV/AIDS
Alameddine, Rabih, 35–40
  Angel of History, The: A Novel (Alameddine), 39
  awards and acclaim, 39
  Hakawati, The (Alameddine), 37
  I, the Divine: A Novel in First Chapters (Alameddine), 37–38
  Koolaids: The Art of War (Alameddine), 36–37
  life and themes, 35–36
  multiculturalism, 981–982
  Perv, The (Alameddine), 37

  Unnecessary Woman, An (Alameddine), 38–39
  works and influence, 35–36
Alarcón, Daniel, 40–45
  At Night They Walk in Circles (Alarcón), 43–44
  awards and acclaim, 41
  impact and influence, 44–45
  King Is Always Above the People, The (Alarcón), 44
  life and context, 40–42
  Lost City Radio (Alarcón), 40, 42–43
  Radio Ambulante (podcast), 41, 44
  themes, 41–42
  translation work, 44
  War by Candlelight: Stories (Alarcón), 40, 42
Alexie, Sherman, 45–50
  awards and acclaim, 46
  Business of Fancydancing, The (Alexie), 46–47
  cultural hybridity, 47–48
  Indian Killer (Alexie), 47–48
  legacy, 49–50
  life, 46
  Reservation Blues (Alexie), 47
  Ten Little Indians (Alexie), 48–49
  Toughest Indian in the World, The (Alexie), 48
  War Dances (Alexie), 49
  young adult fiction, 49–50
Allende, Isabel, 50–56
  awards and acclaim, 50, 55
  Daughter of Fortune (Allende), 53–54
  Eva Luna (Allende), 52
  House of the Spirits, The (Allende), 51–55
  Inés of My Soul (Allende), 54
  Infinite Plan, The (Allende), 52–53
  In the Midst of Winter (Allende), 55
  Island Beneath the Sea (Allende), 54–55
  legacy, 55
  life, 51–52
  Long Petal in the Sea, A (Allende), 55
  Paula (Allende), 53
  Portrait in Sepia (Allende), 54
  style, influences, and themes, 50–51
  young adult fiction, 55
Allison, Dorothy, 56–60
  awards and acclaim, 56, 58, 60
  Bastard Out of Carolina (Allison), 58–59
  Cavedweller (Allison), 59–60
  legacy, 60
  life and early writings, 56–57
  sexual violence, controversy, and censorship, 59
  themes and style, 57
  Trash: Short Stories (Allison), 58
  women's movement and controversy, 56–58
Almanac of the Dead (Silko), 680–681, 843, 1232–1234

Álvarez, Julia, 60-65
  How the García Girls Lost Their Accents (Álvarez), 61, 63, 1275-1277
  In the Time of the Butterflies (Álvarez), 62
  life and key themes, 60-61
  Wedding in Haiti, the Story of a Friendship, A (Álvarez), 64-65
  ¡Yo! (Álvarez) and expectations of ethnic literature, 61-62
American Dirt (Cummins), 262, 555
American Marriage, An (Jones), 269
American Splendor (Pekar), 575
Anaya, Rudolfo, 65-70
  Alburquerque (Anaya), 69
  awards and acclaim, 68-69
  Bless Me, Última (Anaya), 66-67, 69
  Heart of Aztlán (Anaya), 67
  higher education and activism, 67-69
  legacy, 69-70
  life and writing themes, 65-67
  near-death experience and recovery, 67
  nonfiction, 68
  Tortuga (Anaya), 67
Anders, Charlie Jane, 70-75
  All the Birds in the Sky (Anders), 70, 72-74
  awards and acclaim, 70-71
  Butler, Octavia, 73-74
  Choir Boy (Anders), 70-72
  City in the Middle of the Night, The (Anders), 70-71, 74-75
  impact and future directions, 75
  Le Guin, Ursula K., 72, 74
  publications, collaborations, and themes, 70-71
Annihilation (VanderMeer), 1095
Antinomies of Realism (Jameson), 1149
Antrim, Donald, 76-82
  Afterlife, The (Antrim), 76, 78, 80-81
  criticism, 79
  Elect Mr. Robinson for a Better World (Antrim), 76-77, 79, 81
  Emerald Light in the Air (Antrim), 78-80
  Hundred Brothers, The (Antrim), 77, 79
  life and education, 76
  memoir, 80-81
  Verificationist, The (Antrim), 77-79
  writing style and themes, 76-77, 79-81
Apostol, Gina, 82-87
  awards and acclaim, 86-87
  Bibliolepsy (Apostol), 83-84
  context and themes, 82-83
  Gun Dealers' Daughter (Apostol), 85
  Hagedorn, Jessica, 82, 85-86

  Insurrecto (Apostol), 85-86
  Revolution According to Raymundo Mata, The (Apostol), 84-85
Argonauts, The (Nelson), 1141-1142
Art of Fielding, The (Harbach), 354
Atmospheric Disturbances (Galchen), 200, 203-204
Auster, Paul, 87-92
  4321 (Auster), 87, 91-92
  Book of Illusions, The (Auster), 90, 685-686
  Brooklyn Follies, The (Auster), 90-92
  impact, 92
  intermedial fiction, 685-686
  In the Country of Last Things (Auster), 88-89
  Invisible (Auster), 90-91
  Leviathan (Auster), 89
  Man in the Dark (Auster), 90-91, 1082-1083
  Moon Palace (Auster), 89
  Mr. Vertigo (Auster), 89-90
  Music of Chance, The (Auster), 89
  New York Trilogy, The (Auster), 87-88, 91
  Oracle Night (Auster), 90
  post-9/11 narratives, 1082-1083
  themes, writing style, and life, 87-88
  Timbuktu (Auster), 89-90
  Travels in the Scriptorium (Auster), 90-91
Authoring Autism (Yergeau), 672-673
Autonomía cultural americana (Ballón), 839
Autonomous (Newitz), 140
AVA (Maso), 867-868, 996

Bachman, Richard *see* King, Stephen
Baker, Nicholson, 93-98
  Human Smoke (Baker), 97
  impact and legacy, 97-98
  life, themes, and writing style, 93-94
  Mezzanine, The (Baker), 93-96
  nonfiction, 95-97
  Room Temperature (Baker), 95-96
  Traveling Sprinkler (Baker), 93, 96
  U and I (Baker), 94-96
  Vox (Baker), 96
Ball, Jesse, 98-102
  awards and acclaim, 98
  Census (Ball), 99-101
  Cure for Suicide, A (Ball), 99-101
  Divers' Game, The (Ball), 100-101
  How to Set Fire and Why (Ball), 99
  impact, 101-102
  influences and comparisons, 100-101
  life and education, 99
  Samedi the Deafness (Ball), 99-100
  themes and writing style, 98-99

Bambara, Toni Cade, 102–107
  activism, 102–107
  filmmaking, 103
  Gorilla, My Love (Bambara), 103–105
  impact and legacy, 102, 106–107
  influences and writing themes, 102–104
  intersectionality, 103–105
  life and education, 102–103
  Morrison, Toni, 103–104, 106–107
  publications and awards, 103
  Salt Eaters, The (Bambara), 103–106
  Seabirds Are Still Alive, The (Bambara), 103, 105
  Those Bones Are Not My Child (Bambara), 103, 105–107
Banks, Russell, 107–112
  Affliction (Banks), 108–111
  awards and acclaim, 107–108
  Bildungsroman, 111
  Cloudsplitter (Banks), 108–111
  Continental Drift (Banks), 108–110
  Darling, The (Banks), 108, 111–112, 481
  fiction and terrorism, 481
  Hamilton Stark (Banks), 108–110
  Kerouac, Jack, 108–109
  life, context, and writing themes, 107–109
  publications, 108
  Rule of the Bone (Banks), 108, 110–111
  Sweet Hereafter, The (Banks), 108–110
Barth, John, 112–117
  after postmodernism, 32
  Book of Ten Nights and a Night, The: Eleven Stories (Barth), 116
  Coming Soon!!! (Barth), 115
  context and early works, 112–113
  criticism, 112–115
  Development, The (Barth), 116
  Every Third Thought (Barth), 116
  Last Voyage of Somebody the Sailor, The (Barth), 114–115
  LETTERS (Barth), 112–113
  Once Upon a Time: A Floating Opera (Barth), 114–115
  recent works, 116
  Sabbatical (Barth), 113
  themes and writing style, 112–115
  Tidewater Tales, The (Barth), 113–114
Bascombe books (Ford), 1290
Beast, The (Martínez), 189
Beattie, Ann, 117–122
  criticism and reviews, 117–120
  life and context, 117–118
  literary magazines, 117–118
  Munro, Alice, 117, 119–120
  Picturing Will (Beattie), 119
  recent works, 120–122
  Rorty, Richard, 120–122
  State We're In, The (Beattie), 121–122
  Updike, John, 117–120
  writing style and themes, 118–122
  "Yancey" (Beattie), 121–122
Beatty, Paul, 122–128
  awards and acclaim, 122–123
  Hokum: An Anthology of African-American Humor (Beatty), 123–127
  Joker, Joker, Deuce (Beatty), 123
  key publications, 122–123
  post-soul and/or post-Black fiction, 1104
  Sellout, The (Beatty), 123–124, 126–127, 1292–1293
  Slumberland (Beatty), 125–126
  suburban narratives, 1292–1293
  Tuff (Beatty), 123–124
  White Boy Shuffle, The (Beatty), 122–124, 1104
  writing style and themes, 122
Beauty Myth, The (Wolf), 1309
Behold the Dreamers (Mbue), 1325–1326
Bellefleur (Oates), 931–932, 1017
Beloved (Morrison), 19, 157, 159, 227, 961, 963, 1321–1322
Bennett, Brit, 128–133
  awards and acclaim, 128–129
  Between the World and Me (Coates), 129
  Bluest Eye, The (Morrison), 129–130
  essays, 128–129
  life and context, 128
  Morrison, Toni, 128–132
  Mothers, The (Bennett), 128–130, 132
  Paradise (Morrison), 131
  Passing (Larsen), 130–131
  Sula (Morrison), 130
  Vanishing Half, The (Bennett), 128–132
  writing style and themes, 128–129
Bergdorf Blondes (Sykes), 254
Berger, Thomas Louis, 133–138
  Adventures of the Artificial Woman (Berger), 137–138
  awards and acclaim, 133–134
  Being Invisible (Berger), 137–138
  Best Friends (Berger), 136
  Changing the Past (Berger), 137
  Feud, The (Berger), 134–135
  Houseguest, The (Berger), 134–136
  Little Big Man (Berger), 133–135
  Meeting Evil (Berger), 136–137
  Neighbors (Berger), 134–135, 137–138
  Nowhere (Berger), 137

publications, writing style, and themes, 133–134
Return of Little Big Man, The (Berger), 134–135
Berlin trilogy (Lute), 576, 580
Be Safe I Love You (Hoffman), 286, 288
Between the World and Me (Coates), 23, 129
Beyond Cyberpunk (Murphy and Vint), 325
Beyond the Culture Wars (Graff), 311
Big Data, 138–147
   Autonomous (Newitz), 140
   Bleeding Edge (Pynchon), 144
   Circle, The (Eggers), 145–146
   concept and overview, 138–139
   conclusion, 146
   data fictions before big data, 139–141
   extractive economies, 144–145
   global village, 139
   He, She, and It (Piercy), 139–140
   inequalities, 139–140
   Infomocracy (Older), 146
   In Persuasion Nation (Saunders), 143–144
   knowledge economy, 141–142
   Known World, The (Jones), 144
   Lowland, The (Lahiri), 141–142
   Neuromancer (Gibson), 140
   Orfeo (Powers), 143
   Pale King, The (Wallace), 144–145
   Person of Interest, A (Choi), 141
   Purity (Franzen), 145
   Recursion (Crouch), 145
   Shteyngart, Gary, 1222–1223
   sociality, 145–146
   Tale for the Time Being, A (Ozeki), 141–142
Billy Lynn's Long Halftime Walk (Fountain), 285–286
Binky Brown Meets the Holy Virgin Mary (Green), 577
Biological Fictions, 147–156
   biological imagination and molecular language, 154–156
   Biopunk (Wohlsen), 151
   body and embodiment, 6–10, 129–132, 293–295, 581–586, 895–900, 997–998, 1306–1315
   Butler, Octavia, 227–228
   concept and context, 147–149
   Constructing Postmodernism (McHale), 151
   Dragon's Island (Williamson), 149
   End of Ordinary, The (Ashton), 148–149
   from scientific language of biofictions to biopunk, 149–152
   Gray, Amelia, 581–586
   impact of, 155–156
   legitimacy of knowledge and control of information in the Bacterial Age, 153–154
   Next (Crichton), 148–150, 155

   Orfeo (Powers), 148–149, 152–154
   Oryx and Crake (Atwood), 149
   Three Days in April (Ashton), 148
   Tomasula, Steve, 1315–1319
   Windup Girl, The (Bacigalupi), 148
Birdwell, Cleo *see* DeLillo, Don
Black Atlantic, 156–166
   African Diaspora, The (Palmer), 158
   Allen, Jafari S., 163–164
   Beloved (Morrison), 157, 159
   Black Atlantic expands
      Black Atlantic, Afrofuturist Atlantic, 164
      Black Atlantic beyond the Atlantic, 160–161
      Black Lives Matter in the wake, 164–165
      critical response, 160
      gender and sexuality in the Black Atlantic, 163–164
      the non-Anglophone Black Atlantic, 161–163
   Black Atlantic literatures, 158–160
   Black Atlantic, The: Modernity and Double Consciousness (Gilroy), 156–165
   Butler, Octavia, 159, 164, 226–229
   Catherine Carmier (Gaines), 158
   Chango, The Biggest Badass (Olivella), 162
   Cliff, Michelle, 271
   Corregidora (Jones), 162
   cyberpunk, 329
   Dark Princess, The (Du Bois), 161
   Dawn (Butler), 164
   Delany, Samuel R., 164
   Demonic Grounds (McKittrick), 163
   double consciousness, 156–157, 162
   Du Bois, W.E.B., 157–158, 161
   Evans, Lucy, 163
   Gaines, Ernest J., 522–527
   Guillén, Nicolás, 159–160
   Hate You Give, The (Thomas), 165
   historical context, 157–158
   Hughes, Langston, 159
   Icarus Girl, The (Oyeyemi), 163
   James, Marlon, 702–704
   Johnson, Charles, 716–721
   Johnson, Mat, 727–730
   Jones, Edward P., 732, 735–737
   Jones, Gayl, 739–743
   Looking for Transwonderland (Saro-Wiwa), 163
   Lose Your Mother: A Journey Along the Atlantic Slave Route (Hartman), 163
   Marshall, Paule, 860–865
   migrations, 158, 161, 163
   modernity, 156–157, 159, 161–164
   Morrison, Toni, 961–962
   Mumbo Jumbo (Reed), 162

Black Atlantic (*cont'd*)
  origins of the Black Atlantic, 156–157
  Perkins-Valdez, Dolen, 1063–1068
  Pinto, Samantha, 163–164
  Praisesong for the Widow (Marshall), 158–160
  program culture, 1122
  Reed, Ishmael, 1157, 1159–1160
  rememory, 159
  Robinson, Marilynne, 1179
  Saunders, George, 1195, 1197
  Sharpe, Christina, 165
  "thirsty" (Brand), 165
  Tinsley, Omise'eke Natasha, 164
  transnational relationships, 159–161
  Whitehead, Colson, 1417–1420
  Wideman, John Edgar, 1422
  Williams, Sherley Anne, 1426–1427, 1429–1430
  Zeleza, Paul T., 160–161
Black Futures (Drew and Wortham), 22
Black Hole (Burns), 580
Black Mirror: Bandersnatch (Slade), 662
Black Panther (Coogler), 20–21, 1469–1470
Black Regions of the Imagination (Dunbar), 294
Black, White and Jewish: Autobiography of a Shifting Self (Walker), 1307, 1311
Blankets (Thompson), 578
Bleeding Edge (Pynchon), 144, 1134–1135
Blindsight (Watts), 1095–1096
Blown Away (Sukenick), 689–690
Blow-Up (Antonioni), 210–211
Bluest Eye, The (Morrison), 129–130, 959, 962
Bodily Natures (Alaimo), 389–390
Body Artist, The (DeLillo), 362, 365–366, 1154–1155
Bolaño Effect, The, 166–175
  2008 global financial crisis, 169–170
  2666 (Bolaño), 167, 170–172, 174
  autoethnography, 168–171
  autofiction, 171–172
  autopoiesis, 172–174
  Bolaño and his aftermath, 166–168
  border fictions, 167, 174
  Brief Wondrous Life of Oscar Wao, The (Díaz), 169
  By Night in Chile (Bolaño), 166–167, 170
  City On Fire (Hallberg), 170
  Crack movement, 168
  Distant Star (Bolaño), 170–171
  fascism, 167–170
  Flamethrowers, The (Kushner), 170
  Fuguet, Alberto, 168–169
  Great Believers, The (Makkai), 170
  Hatred of Poetry, The (Lerner), 172–173
  Kirsch, Adam, 171–172
  Leaving the Atocha Station (Lerner), 172
  Lethem, Jonathan, 169
  Lost Children Archive (Luiselli), 173–174
  magic realism, 166, 168–169
  McOndo movement, 168
  Motherless Brooklyn (Lethem), 169
  Nazi Literatures in the Americas (Bolaño), 167, 170
  neoliberalism, 167, 169–170, 172–174
  poetry, 167, 172–173
  Savage Detectives, The (Bolaño), 167, 169–172
  Third Reich, The (Bolaño), 167
  Topeka School, The (Lerner), 172–173
  Tuesday Nights in 1980 (Prentiss), 170–171
  Volpi, Jorge, 168–169
Book Clubs, 175–184
  Best Seller lists, 175–176, 181–182
  Black Lives Matter, 175
  BookBrowse, 179–180
  book club phenomenon, the, 178–180
  Book Clubs: Women and the Uses of Reading in Everyday Life (Long), 179
  Book Group Book, The (Slezak), 179
  Book of the Month Club, 177–178, 181
  chick lit and the new domesticity, 253
  Faludi, Susan, 178
  Feeling for Books, A (Radway), 177–178
  Feminism and its Fictions (Hogeland), 178
  Forgotten Readers: Recovering the Lost History of African American Literary Societies (McHenry), 177, 183
  How to Read and Why (Bloom), 175
  Intimate Practices: Literacy and Cultural Work in U.S. Women's Clubs (Gere), 176–177, 180
  introduction, 175–176
  Making of Middlebrow Culture, The (Rubin), 177
  Morrison, Toni, 175, 181, 183
  Oprah's Book Club, 175–176, 180–183, 267, 507, 509
  Paris Was a Woman (Schiller), 178
  Reading Oprah (Konchar Farr), 181–183
  Reading Sites: Social Difference and Reader Response (Schweickart and Flynn), 175–176, 180
  Reese's Book Club, 176
  second-wave feminism, 178
  Shakespeare and Company (Beach), 178
  social and historical contexts, 176–178
  This Book is An Action (Harker and Konchar Farr), 178
  Uses of Literature (Felski), 178–179
  Well-Read Black Girl, 176
Border Fictions, 184–193
  Acosta, Abraham, 189–190
  Álvarez, Julia, 60, 63–65

Anaya, Rudolfo, 68
Anzaldúa, Gloria, 186–188, 193
as *reconquista* (reconquest) narrative, 188
Beast, The (Martínez), 189
Bolaño Effect, the, 167, 174
border fictions for children, 187–188
Borderlands/La Frontera (Anzaldúa), 186–187, 885–886, 977–978, 985, 987, 1444
Caballero: A Historical Novel (González), 186
Canícula: Snapshots of a Girlhood en la Frontera (Cantú), 192–193
Capirotada: A Nogales Memoir (Ríos), 192–193
Castillo, Ana, 237–239
"Child, The" (Ríos), 191
Cisneros, Sandra, 263
contemporary Chicanx border fictions, 192
context and overview, 184–185
corridos, 185–187, 191
Danticat, Edwidge, 338–342
Desert Blood: The Juárez Murders (Gaspar de Alba), 190
Devil's Highway, The (Urrea), 189–190
feminism, 186–187, 192
gender and sexuality, 186–187, 192
Huesos en el desierto (Bones in the Desert) (Rodríguez), 190–191
Jones, Gayl, 740–741
life on the border, 192–193
McCarthy, Cormac, 884–890
millennial fiction, 913–914
new border consciousness, 186–188
No Country for Old Men (McCarthy), 188
Pérez, Emma, 192–193
Power of the Dog (Winslow), 191
racism and sexism, 185–186, 192
Touch of Evil (Welles), 185–187
Urrea, Luis Alberto, 1348–1353
violence of the border
 border crossing and migrant narratives, 189–190
 border writing on feminicide, 190
 narco fictions, 190–191
 overview, 188–189
Vollmann, William T., 1374
"With His Pistol in His Hand" (Paredes), 186
writing against colonial histories, 185–186
Boyle, T.C., 194–199
Budding Prospects (Boyle), 195
criticism and scholarship, 195–196
Drop City (Boyle), 195, 197
Friend of the Earth, A (Boyle), 1291–1292
Harder They Come, The (Boyle), 195–198
life, influences, and comparisons, 194

suburban narratives, 1291–1292
Terranauts, The (Boyle), 196
Tortilla Curtain (Boyle), 194–195, 198
Water Music (Boyle), 195, 197
writing style and themes, 194–198
Boy Meets Boy (Levithan), 1140
Boy's Own Story, A (White), 1137, 1139–1140, 1411
Brain and American Fiction, The, 199–208
Alzheimer's, 203
amnesia, 203
Atmospheric Disturbances (Galchen), 200, 203–204
Burn, Stephen, 201–206
Capgras syndrome, 203, 205
Character of Consciousness, The (Chalmers), 200
Chiang, Ted, 248–249
concepts and the neuroscientific turn, 199–200
DeLillo, Don, 201
Dennett, Daniel, 199–200, 202
Echo Maker, The (Powers), 200, 203–206
Elusive Brain, The (Tougaw), 200–206
explanatory gap, the, 200
Franzen, Jonathan, 206
Gaedtke, Andrew, 199, 204
Galatea 2.2 (Powers), 202–203
historical context, 201–202
How the Mind Works (Pinker), 199–200
Hustvedt, Siri, 653–658
Lowboy (Wray), 200, 203–205
Man Walks into a Room (Krauss), 203
Motherless Brooklyn (Lethem), 200, 203–205
Powers, Richard, 1112–1117
Roth, Marco, 199–202, 205
schizophrenia, 203–205
self, the, and selfhood, 205–207
Tourette's syndrome, 203–205
Unnamed, The (Ferris), 206
Braschi, Giannina, 208–214
Blow-Up (Antonioni), 210–211
Calderón de la Barca, Pedro, 211, 213
Close-Up (Kiarostami), 210
criticism and comparison, 209–213
El imperio de los sueños (Empire of Dreams) (Braschi), 208–210, 212–213
Hamlet (Shakespeare), 209, 211
life and context, 208–210
Spanish Golden Age, 211–212
United States of Banana, The (Braschi), 208–213
writing style and themes, 208–213
Yo-Yo Boing! (Braschi), 208–212
Brideshead Revisited (Waugh), 273
Bridget Jones's Diary (Fielding), 252–255, 1310
Brief History of The Dead (Brockmeier), 1244

Brief Wondrous Life of Oscar Wao, The (Díaz), 169, 367–368, 370–371
Bright Lights, Big City (McInerney), 470–472
Brooks, Geraldine, 214–219
  Caleb's Crossing (Brooks), 215–219
  context and comparison, 215
  Little Women (Alcott), 217–218
  March (Brooks), 215–219
  memoir, 215
  People of the Book (Brooks), 216
  summary of contemporary positioning, 218–219
  writing style and themes, 214–216
Building Stories (Ware), 573–574
Buried in Shades of Night (Stratton), 1399
Burnt Shadows (Shamsie), 485
Burroughs, William S., 219–225
  1960s to 1990s, 220–222
  2000s and beyond, 223–224
  collaborations, 221–222
  cut-up method, 220–224
  death and legacy, 223–224
  Ginsberg, Allen, 220, 222, 224
  Grauerholz, James, 221–223
  Harris, Oliver, 223
  impact and influence, 219–221
  life and context, 219–222
  multimedia works, 222–223
  Naked Lunch (Burroughs), 220–221, 223
  previously unseen archival materials, 223–224
  prose trilogy, 221–222
  scholarship, 222–224
  Western Lands, The (Burroughs), 222, 224
  works of autobiography, 222
  Yage Letters, The (Burroughs and Ginsberg), 220
Bury, Stephen *see* Stephenson, Neal
Butler, Octavia, 225–230
  Anders, Charlie Jane, 73–74
  awards and acclaim, 225
  Beloved (Morrison), 227
  cover art and themes, 226
  Dawn (Butler), 164, 227–228
  ecocriticism and environmental fiction, 392
  Fledgling (Butler), 229–230, 939
  Kindred (Butler), 227, 1068
  life, influence, and legacy, 225–226, 229–230
  mixed-genre fiction, 939
  Parable series (Butler), 20–21, 229, 1166–1168, 1292
  Patternmaster (Butler), 226
  Perkins-Valdez, Dolen, 1068
  religion and contemporary fiction, 1166–1168
  suburban narratives, 1292
  Wild Seed (Butler), 226–227
  Xenogenesis series, 227–229
Butterfly Moon (Endrezze), 682–683
By Night in Chile (Bolaño), 166–167, 170

Caballero: A Historical Novel (González), 186
California (Lepucki), 1292
Canícula: Snapshots of a Girlhood en la Frontera (Cantú), 192–193
Capirotada: A Nogales Memoir (Ríos), 192–193
Capital City (Tyree), 1340–1341, 1346
Carver, Raymond, 231–235
  awards and acclaim, 232, 235
  Cathedral (Carver), 234
  death and legacy, 235
  life and context, 232–234
  Lish, Gordon, 233–234
  minimalism and maximalism, 926–927, 929
  posthumous collections, 235
  What We Talk About When We Talk About Love (Carver), 233–234
  Where I'm Calling From (Carver), 234–235
  Will You Please Be Quiet, Please? (Carver), 232–233
  writing style and themes, 231–232
Castillo, Ana, 235–240
  Black Dove: Mamá, Mi'jo, and Me (Castillo), 238–239
  Guardians, The (Castillo), 238–239
  Invitation, The (Castillo), 236
  life and context, 236
  Massacre of the Dreamers (Castillo), 235–236, 239
  Mixquiahuala Letters, The (Castillo), 236–237, 239
  My Father Was a Toltec (Castillo), 237
  So Far From God (Castillo), 237–240
  writing style and themes, 235–236
  Xicanisma, 235–236
Catherine Carmier (Gaines), 158
Caucasia (Senna), 1104–1105, 1210–1214
Centenal Cycle, The trilogy (Older), 560
Chabon, Michael, 240–246
  Amazing Adventures of Kavalier and Clay, The (Chabon), 242–244
  Final Solution, The: A Story of Detection (Chabon), 243
  future directions, 245
  Gentlemen of the Road (Chabon), 243
  Kingdom of Olives and Ash (Chabon and Waldman), 245
  life and context, 240–241
  Maps and Legends (Chabon), 243–244
  Model World, A (Chabon), 241
  Moonglow (Chabon), 245

Mysteries of Pittsburgh, The (Chabon), 241
Summerland (Chabon), 242–243
Telegraph Avenue (Chabon), 244–245
Werewolves in Their Youth (Chabon), 242–244
Wizard of Earthsea, A (Le Guin), 243
Wonder Boys (Chabon), 241–242
writing style and themes, 241
Yiddish Policemen's Union, The (Chabon), 243–245
Chango, The Biggest Badass (Olivella), 162
Character of Consciousness, The (Chalmers), 200
Cheat, The (DeMille), 1175–1176
Cherry (Walker), 287
Chiang, Ted, 246–251
 "Anxiety is the Dizziness of Freedom" (Chiang), 247, 251
 awards and acclaim, 246
 "Dacey's Patent Automatic Nanny" (Chiang), 248
 "Division by Zero" (Chiang), 249–251
 "Evolution of Human Science, The" (Chiang), 249
 "Exhalation" (Chiang), 249
 "Hell is the Absence of God" (Chiang), 250
 life, context, and writing themes, 246
 "Lifecycle of Software Objects, The" (Chiang), 248
 "Liking What You See: A Documentary" (Chiang), 247–248, 251
 "Merchant and the Alchemist's Gate, The" (Chiang), 247
 "Omphalos" (Chiang), 250–251
 "Seventy-Two Letters" (Chiang), 250
 "Story of Your Life" (Chiang), 246–247, 251
 "Tower of Babylon" (Chiang), 250
 "Truth of Fact, the Truth of Feeling, The" (Chiang), 248, 251
 "Understand" (Chiang), 246, 249, 251
 "What's Expected of Us" (Chiang), 247
Chick Lit and the New Domesticity, 251–260
 2008 global financial crisis, 256
 assimilation, 255
 Bergdorf Blondes (Sykes), 254
 book clubs, 253
 Bridget Jones's Diary (Fielding), 252–255
 chick culture, 253–254
 Chick-Lit: Postfeminist Fiction (Mazza and DeShell), 252
 context and emergence of, 251–252
 cover art, 252
 defining chick lit, 252–254
 ethnicity, 253, 255
 Fault in Our Stars, The (Green), 257
 future directions, 258–259
 genealogies and developments, 254–256
 Gill, Rosalind, 257
 heteronormativity, 257–259
 lad lit, 256–257
 Pride and Prejudice (Austen), 254–255
 racism, 255
 reception and criticism, 256–259
 Sex and the City (Bushnell), 252–254
 subgenres of, 253
 third-wave feminism, 1309–1310
 This Is Not Chick Lit (Merrick), 256
 Waiting to Exhale (McMillan), 253
China Tidal Wave (Lixiong), 557–558
Christmas Carol, A (Dickens), 1158
Circle, The (Eggers), 145–146, 402–403, 664–665
Cisneros, Sandra, 260–265
 American Dirt (Cummins), 262
 awards and acclaim, 262
 Bad Boys (Cisneros), 262
 Caramelo (Cisneros), 263–264
 children's fiction, 263–264
 contribution, impact, and life, 260–261, 264
 House of My Own, A: Stories from My Life (Cisneros), 264
 House on Mango Street, The (Cisneros), 260, 262–263, 928, 1274–1275
 Loose Woman (Cisneros), 263
 minimalism and maximalism, 928
 My Wicked, Wicked Ways (Cisneros), 263
 Puro Amor (Cisneros), 264
 story cycles, 1274–1276
 writing themes, 261–262
Citizen: An American Lyric (Rankine), 23, 475
City On Fire (Hallberg), 170
class and classism
 Allison, Dorothy, 56–58
 Álvarez, Julia, 61–65
 Banks, Russell, 107–112
 Beattie, Ann, 117–119
 Carver, Raymond, 231–235
 downwardly mobile middle class, 490–492
 Ferré, Rosario, 457–461
 Johnson, Denis, 722–725
 Johnson, Mat, 727–728
 Jones, Edward P., 732–733, 737
 Ng, Celeste, 1001–1005
 Revoyr, Nina, 1173–1174
 Schwartz, Lynne Sharon, 1198–1204
 suburban narratives, 1285–1286, 1290–1293
 third-wave feminism, 1307–1312
 trauma and fiction, 1325–1327
 Viramontes, Helena María, 1364–1365
 Whitehead, Colson, 1416
 Wolfe, Tom, 1432–1436
 Yu, Charles, 1473–1474

Cleage, Pearl, 265–270
  American Marriage, An (Jones), 269
  awards and acclaim, 269
  Baby Brother's Blues (Cleage), 267–268
  essays, 266–267
  Flyin' West (Cleage), 265–267
  free womanhood, 265, 267–268
  illness and disability narratives, 669
  influence and impact, 269
  life and influences, 265
  novels, 267
  plays, 266
  poetry, 268
  political work, 266, 268–269
  presence in Atlanta's cultural scene, 268–269
  Seen It All and Done the Rest (Cleage), 268
  Some Things I Never Thought I'd Do (Cleage), 267
  What Looks Like Crazy on an Ordinary Day (Cleage), 267–268, 669
Cliff, Michelle, 270–275
  Abeng (Cliff), 270–272
  Bodies of Water (Cliff), 271
  Brideshead Revisited (Waugh), 273
  Claiming an Identity They Taught Me to Despise (Cliff), 270
  Free Enterprise (Cliff), 271–273
  Into the Interior (Cliff), 271–273
  legacy, 273–274
  life and context, 270
  Multidirectional Memory (Rothberg), 273–274
  nonfiction, 270–271
  No Telephone to Heaven (Cliff), 271–274
  Store of a Million Items (Cliff), 271
  writing style and themes, 271–273
Climate Trauma (Kaplan), 1326–1327
Closer to Freedom (Camp), 1064
Close-Up (Kiarostami), 210
Closing of the American Mind (Bloom), 310, 314
Coldest Winter Ever, The (Souljah), 1342–1344
Cold Mountain (Frazier), 353, 511–512, 515
Cole, Teju, 275–280
  awards and acclaim, 275
  comparison, writing style, and themes, 276–277
  Every Day is for the Thief (Cole), 275–277
  globalization, 554–555
  Open City (Cole), 275–279, 554–555
  photography, 279
  publications, life, and context, 275–276
  use of social media, 275, 279
colonialism/postcolonialism/neocolonialism
  Abu-Jaber, Diana, 2
  Apostol, Gina, 82–87
  border fictions, 185–186
  Braschi, Giannina, 208–209, 212–213
  Brooks, Geraldine, 216–217
  Cole, Teju, 275–279
  contemporary regionalisms, 291–296
  cyberpunk, 327, 329
  decolonization, 21–24, 296, 739–741, 743
  ecocriticism and environmental fiction, 384, 387
  Hagedorn, Jessica, 593–598
  Hogan, Linda, 641–642
  imperialism, 208–209, 483, 485, 837–841
  Indigenous narratives, 675–684
  James, Marlon, 702–704
  Kincaid, Jamaica, 756–760
  Kingsolver, Barbara, 768–769
  Kushner, Rachel, 781–783
  literature of the Americas, 836–840
  Marshall, Paule, 860–865
  multiculturalism, 975–977
  Truong, Monique, 1329
  Vizenor, Gerald, 1366–1371
  Welch, James, 1404–1408
  writers' collectives, 1444
  Yamanaka, Lois-Ann, 1454–1458
Colorist, The (Daitch), 686
Color Purple, The (Walker), 1137, 1139–1140, 1161, 1383–1385
Comedy of Survival (Meeker), 385
Community (TV series), 673–674
Condition of Postmodernity, The (Harvey), 1122–1123
Constructing Postmodernism (McHale), 151
Contemporary American Short-Story Cycle, The (Nagel), 1276
Contemporary Fictions of War, 280–289
  13th Valley, the (Del Vecchio), 281
  Adichie, Chimamanda Ngozi, 13
  Afghanistan and Iraq
    combat zone and realism, 287
    context and overview, 284–285
    focus on the home front, 286–287
    globalization, 558
    Hosseini, Khaled, 648–652
    women protagonists and non-American points of view, 287–288
  Alameddine, Rabih, 36–39
  Alarcón, Daniel, 40–44
  Allende, Isabel, 51–55
  Álvarez, Julia, 62–65
  Apostol, Gina, 85–86
  Auster, Paul, 91
  Be Safe I Love You (Hoffman), 286, 288
  Billy Lynn's Long Halftime Walk (Fountain), 285–286

Cherry (Walker), 287
conclusion, 288
context, 280
Englander, Nathan, 422–424
Fobbit (Abrams), 285, 287
Foer, Jonathan Safran, 496–499
gender, sexism, assault, 287–288
globalization, 557–559
Good Lieutenant, The (Terrell), 287–288
Good Scent from a Strange Mountain, A (Butler), 283
Hannah, Barry, 600–601
Healer's War, The (Scarborough), 282–283
Heller, Joseph, 613–614, 616
Hinojosa, Rolando, 635
Hosseini, Khaled, 647–653
I'd Walk With My Friends If I Could Find Them (Goolsby), 286–287
In Country (Mason), 282
Irving, John, 697
Israeli occupation of Palestine, 422–424
Johnson, Denis, 723–724
Lee, Chang-rae, 803–804
Louts Eaters, The (Soli), 283–284
Mailer, Norman, 847–849
Nguyen, Viet Thanh, 1011–1016
O'Brien, Tim, 1022–1027
One Hundred and One Nights (Buchholz), 284–285, 288
Paco's Story (Heinemann), 281–282
queer and LGBT fiction, 1137
Remasculinization of America (Jeffords), 287–288
Sand Queen (Benedict), 284, 287–288
Sparta (Robinson), 286
Spoils (Van Reet), 287–288
Stone, Robert, 1267–1271
story cycles, 1278
Sympathizer, The (Nguyen), 284
Things They Carried, The (O'Brien), 283, 285
Tree of Smoke (Johnson), 283–284
Vidal, Gore, 1356–1360
Vietnam War, 280–284, 697, 723–724, 1011–1016, 1022–1027, 1137, 1269–1270
Vonnegut, Kurt, 1377–1381
Yellow Birds, The (Powers), 285–286
Contemporary Regionalisms, 289–298
assimilation, 292
Banks, Russell, 107–112
Black Regions of the Imagination (Dunbar), 294
Carver, Raymond, 231–235
colonialism, 291–296
concept and overview, 289
COVID-19 pandemic, 297

decolonialism, 296
diaspora, 291, 295–296
Erdrich, Louise, 292–293
Eyes Bottle Dark with a Mouthful of Flowers (Skeet), 293–294
Frazier, Charles, 511–516
Gaines, Ernest J., 522–527
Gilead (Robinson), 293
globalization, 289, 291, 297
Groff, Lauren, 586–591
Hillbilly Elegy (Vance), 290
Kennedy, William, 751–756
Kingsolver, Barbara, 765–770
language and linguistics, 294–295
Laymon, Kiese, 294
Mason, Bobbie Ann, 870–876
McCarthy, Cormac, 295, 884–890
Morrison, Toni, 293
Paradise (Morrison), 293
Phillips, Jayne Anne, 1068–1074
Proulx, Annie, 1125–1130
regional futures, 296–297
regionalism in critical discourse, 1980–2020
    critical regionalism, 291
    overview, 289
    recovery and legacies of nineteenth-century regionalism, 290
    regionalism and indigeneity, 291–292
    transnational turn in American studies, 291
Robinson, Marilynne, 1177–1182
Shark Dialogues (Davenport), 295
Simpson, Mona, 1235–1240
Sing, Unburied, Sing (Ward), 293
Smiley, Jane, 1240–1245
some works of literary regionalism, 1980–2020
    community within region, 292–293
    overview, 292
    regional histories, 295–296
    region and the body, 293–295
story cycles, 1275–1276
suburban narratives, 1287–1289
There There (Orange), 295–296
Train Dreams (Johnson), 295
Tripmaster Monkey (Kingston), 295–296
Truong, Monique, 1328–1334
Ward, Jesmyn, 293, 1393–1398
Washburn, Frances, 1398–1404
Whereas (Long Soldier), 294–295
Contract with God, A (Eisner), 575
Cooper, Dennis, 298–303
Closer (Cooper), 300–302
context and themes, 298
early prose and fiction, 299–300

Cooper, Dennis (*cont'd*)
  Frisk (Cooper), 300–301
  George Miles cycle, 300–301
  God Jr. (Cooper), 301–302
  influences, 298–299
  Little Ceasar (magazine), 299
  Marbled Swarm, The (Cooper), 302
  My Loose Thread (Cooper), 301
  post-cycle works, 301–302
  Safe (Cooper), 300
  Sluts, The (Cooper), 302
  Tenderness of the Wolves, The (Cooper), 299–300
  Terror of Earrings, The (Cooper), 299
  Wrong: A Critical Biography of Dennis Cooper (Hester), 301
  Zac'a Haunted House (Cooper), 298
Coover, Robert, 303–308
  Adventures of Lucky Pierre, The (Coover), 306
  Briar Rose (Coover), 304–306
  Brunist Day of Wrath, The (Coover), 307–308
  contribution and impact, 304, 308
  Enchanted Prince, The (Coover), 305
  Gerald's Party (Coover), 306
  Ghost Town (Coover), 306–307
  Huck Out West (Coover), 307
  hypertext fiction and network narratives, 663
  Origin of the Brunists, The (Coover), 307
  Pinocchio in Venice (Coover), 305
  Pricksongs and Descants (Coover), 663
  Public Burning, The (Coover), 304, 307
  Spanking the Maid (Coover), 304
  Stepmother (Coover), 305
  writing style and themes, 303–304
Corregidora (Jones), 162, 738–740, 742–743
Cosmopolis (DeLillo), 365, 559–560, 1061
COVID-19 pandemic, 297, 488, 560–561, 668, 670–671, 914
Cruel Optimism (Berlant), 1036
Cultural Capital (Guillory), 315
Cultures of United States Imperialism (Kaplan and Pease), 840, 976
Culture Wars, The, 308–316
  after postmodernism, 33
  Age of Reagan, 309
  Beyond the Culture Wars (Graff), 311
  Braschi, Giannina, 208–214
  Cheney, Lynne, 308, 310
  Closing of the American Mind (Bloom), 310, 314
  conservative attack, the, 308–311
  Cultural Capital (Guillory), 315
  feminism, 309, 311–314
  fiction and the culture wars
    culture wars novel, the, 313–314
    overview, 311
    revision of the canon and multiculturalism, 311–313
    rise of literary theory, 314–316
  Human Stain, The (Roth), 313–314
  language and linguistics, 315
  migration, 311, 313
  Myth of Political Correctness, The (Wilson), 311
  neoliberalism, 309–311, 314
  Oleanna (Mamet), 313–314
  post 9-11 narratives, 314
  writers' collectives, 1445
Cunningham, Michael, 316–321
  awards and acclaim, 316
  Flesh and Blood (Cunningham), 318–319
  Golden States (Cunningham), 316–317
  Home at the End of the World, A (Cunningham), 317–319, 1288
  Hours, The (Cunningham), 319–320
  life and early career, 316–317
  recent novels, 321
  Specimen Days (Cunningham), 320
  suburban narratives, 1288
  writing style and themes, 316–317
Cyberpunk, 321–331
  Beyond Cyberpunk (Murphy and Vint), 325
  colonialism and postcolonialism, 327, 329
  conclusion, 329–330
  feminism, 328–329
  Gibson, William, 322–330, 542–547
  hypertext fiction and network narratives, 659–660
  introduction: origins and critical history, 321–325
  Islands in the Net (Sterling), 326–328
  key texts
    Islands in the Net (Sterling), 326–328
    Neuromancer (Gibson), 324–326, 329
    "Pretty Boy Crossover" (Cadigan), 328–329
    Snow Crash (Stephenson), 328
    Synners (Candigan), 329
  Mirrorshades (Sterling), 322, 328
  neoliberalism, 323–328
  racism, 328–329
  sexualities, 329
  slavery, 329
  Stephenson, Neal, 1261–1266
  Sterling, Bruce, 322–324, 326–328
  young adult boom, 1468

Damascus Gate (Stone), 479–480, 1269–1270
Dance Boots, The (LeGarde Grover), 679

Danielewski, Mark Z., 333–338
  Familiar, The (Danielewski), 335–337
  Fifty Year Sword, The (Danielewski), 334–335
  House of Leaves (Danielewski), 333–337, 663–664, 685, 687, 1152–1153
  hypertext fiction and network narratives, 663–664
  impact and future directions, 337
  Little Blue Kite, The (Danielewski), 333, 337
  Only Revolutions (Danielewski), 335–336
  realism after poststructuralism, 1152–1153
  recent works, 335–337
  writing style and themes, 333–334
Danticat, Edwidge, 338–342
  awards and acclaim, 338, 341
  Breath, Eyes, Memory (Danticat), 339–340
  Claire of the Sea Light (Danticat), 341
  Dew Breaker, The (Danticat), 340–342, 911
  essays, 341
  Krik? Krak! (Danticat), 340
  life and context, 339–340
  Mengestu, Dinaw, 911
  writing style and themes, 338–339
  young adult fiction, 340–341
Dara, Evan, 342–347
  Easy Chain, The (Dara), 344–346
  Flee (Dara), 345–346
  Gaddis, William, 346–347
  Hugh Selwyn Mauberly (Pound), 344
  Joyce, James, 344
  Lost Scrapbook, The (Dara), 342–347
  Provisional Biography of Mose Eakins, A (Dara), 346
  pseudonym and anonymity, 342
  writing style and themes, 343–347
Darconville's Cat (Theroux), 931
Dark Knight Returns, The (Miller), 573
Dark Princess, The (Du Bois), 161
Davis, Lydia, 347–352
  awards and acclaim, 348
  End of the Story, The (Davis), 348–350
  "Foucault and Pencil" (Davis), 349
  "Grammar Questions" (Davis), 349–350
  "Letter, The" (Davis), 349
  "Marie Curie, So Honorable Woman" (Davis), 350
  pastiche and citational works, 350
  publications and influences, 348–349
  "Story" (Davis), 349
  translations, 350–351
  writing style and themes, 347–348
Dead Voices (Vizenor), 682
Debut Novels, 352–357
  Art of Fielding, The (Harbach), 354
  awards and prizes, 354–355
  book deals, advances, and the cascading effect, 353–354
  Cold Mountain (Frazier), 353
  concept and significant novels, 352
  controversy and debate, 355
  debut buzz and its impact, 355–356
  Everything is Illuminated (Foer), 356
  historical context, 352–353
  Homegoing (Gyasi), 354
  Künstlerroman, 354
  Lincoln in the Bardo (Saunders), 355
  New York Magazine (magazine), 353, 356
  New York Times, The (newspaper), 353
  Nielsen BookScan, 353
  Publishers Weekly (journal), 352, 354
  #PublishingPaidMe, 355
Delany, Samuel R., 357–362
  awards and acclaim, 357–358
  Babel-17 (Delany), 357
  Black Atlantic, 164
  Dhalgren (Delany), 357–359
  Hogg (Delany), 360–361
  hypertext fiction and network narratives, 659–660, 664
  illness and disability narratives, 669
  Jewel-Hinged Jaw, The (Delany), 358
  life, experiences, and worldview, 357–359
  Mad Man, The (Delany), 669, 1142–1144
  marginalization and discussions of transgressive erotica, 359–361
  Return to Nevèrÿon series, 359, 361
  Stars in My Pockets Like Grains of Sand (Delany), 659–660, 664
  Times Square Red, Times Square Blue (Delany), 358, 360–361
  writing style and themes, 357–359
DeLillo, Don, 362–367
  Body Artist, The (DeLillo), 362, 365–366, 1154–1155
  brain and American fiction, the, 201
  Cosmopolis (DeLillo), 365, 559–560, 1061
  ecocriticism and environmental fiction, 390
  Falling Man (DeLillo), 366, 477–478, 482, 1080–1081
  globalization, 559–560
  Libra (DeLillo), 363–364, 366
  life, career, and awards, 362–363
  Mao II (DeLillo), 364
  minimalism and maximalism, 932–933
  Names, The (DeLillo), 362–363, 366, 1059–1061
  periodization, 1055, 1059–1062
  Point Omega (DeLillo), 366
  post-9/11 narratives, 1080–1081

DeLillo, Don (cont'd)
  realism after poststructuralism, 1154–1155
  religion and contemporary fiction,
    1162–1166
  Silence, The (DeLillo), 367
  Spiotta, Dana, 1257–1259
  suburban narratives, 1287–1288, 1291
  Underworld (DeLillo), 362, 364–365
  White Noise (DeLillo), 363, 367, 390, 1164–1166,
    1287–1288, 1291
  writing style and themes, 362–363
  Zero K (DeLillo), 366–367
Democracy of Objects, The (Bryant), 1094
Demonic Grounds (McKittrick), 163
Desert Blood: The Juárez Murders (Gaspar de Alba),
  190
Devil's Highway, The (Urrea), 189–190, 1349–1352
Dew Breaker, The (Danticat), 340–342, 911
Dialectics of Our America, The (Saldívar), 975
diaspora *see* migrations and diaspora
Díaz, Junot, 367–372
  Afrofuturism, 19, 24
  awards and acclaim, 367–368
  Bolaño Effect, the, 169
  Brief Wondrous Life of Oscar Wao, The (Díaz), 169,
    367–368, 370–371
  Drown (Díaz), 367–371
  Islandborn (Díaz), 367, 372
  life and career, 367–368
  This Is How You Lose Her (Díaz), 367–368,
    371–372
  tíguere, 369–371
  writing style and themes, 367–368
DICTEE (Cha), 996–997
Digital Modernism (Pressman), 688
disability *see* Illness and Disability Narratives
Disorder Peculiar to the Country, A (Kalfus), 1079,
  1081–1083
Distant Star (Bolaño), 170–171
Divergent series (Roth), 913
Doctorow, E.L., 373–377
  Andrew's Brain (Doctorow), 376
  awards and acclaim, 373
  Book of Daniel, The (Doctorow), 373–374, 377
  City of God (Doctorow), 376
  early work, 373–374
  Homer and Langley (Doctorow), 373, 376
  legacy, 376–377
  life and career, 373
  March, The (Doctorow), 373, 375–377
  Ragtime (Doctorow), 373–377
  Waterworks (Doctorow), 375–376
  writing style and themes, 373–374

Dog Stars, The (Heller), 930
Doktor Faustus (Mann), 1245–1246
Don Quixote (Cervantes), 1149–1150
Do the Americas Have a Common Literature? (Pérez
  Firmat), 839
Dragon's Island (Williamson), 149
Dreaming in Cuban (García), 528–529, 1277–1278
Drowning in Fire (Womack), 1144
Ducks, Newburyport (Ellmann), 933
Ducornet, Rikki, 377–382
  Carroll, Lewis, 380–381
  collections, 380–381
  Complete Butcher's Tales, The (Ducornet), 380–381
  Entering Fire (Ducornet), 378–380
  Fountains of Neptune, The (Ducornet), 379–380
  Jade Cabinet, The (Ducornet), 380–381
  life, career, and comparisons, 378
  recent work and impact, 382
  Stain, The (Ducornet), 378–379
  Surrealism, 378–379
  writing style and themes, 377–379

Echo Maker, The (Powers), 200, 203–206, 1116
Ecocriticism and Environmental Fiction, 383–393
  Anaya, Rudolfo, 69
  Anders, Charlie Jane, 72–75
  Bodily Natures (Alaimo), 389–390
  Boyle, T.C., 194–196, 390
  Butler, Octavia, 392
  climate fiction and dystopian fiction, 391–392
  Comedy of Survival (Meeker), 385
  concepts and context, 383–384
  cosmopolitanism, 384, 387
  Danticat, Edwidge, 341
  Ecocriticism Reader, The (Glotfelty), 383, 385–386
  ecofeminism, 383–386
  End of Nature, The (McKibben), 386
  environmental fiction, 390–392
  environmental justice, 386–388
  environmental studies, 385
  globalization, 387, 560–561
  Groff, Lauren, 588, 590–591
  Hogan, Linda, 391, 638–643
  Indigenous narratives, 681
  inequalities, 386–387
  interspecies relationality, 388
  Kingsolver, Barbara, 391, 765–770
  Kushner, Rachel, 786
  Le Guin, Ursula K., 812–817
  materiality, affect, and scale, 388–390
  origins of ecocriticism, 384–386
  Ozeki, Ruth, 391, 1033–1037
  postcolonialism, 384, 387

Powers, Richard, 391
Proulx, Annie, 1129
racism, 386–387
Robinson, Kim Stanley, 392
Romanticism, 383–384
Russell, Karen, 1187–1191
Sense of Place, Sense of Planet (Heise), 387
sexualities, 389
Silko, Leslie Marmon, 1230–1235
slow violence, 389
Storyworld Accord, The (James), 390
suburban narratives, 1291–1292
Uncommon Ground (Cronon), 386
Viramontes, Helena María, 1363–1365
Vollmann, William T., 1375
Vonnegut, Kurt, 1378–1379
White Noise (DeLillo), 390
Effect of Living Backwards, The (Julavits), 483
Egan, Jennifer, 393–398
  awards and acclaim, 393
  "Black Box" (Egan), 396–397
  fiction and terrorism, 478–480
  hypertext fiction and network narratives, 664–665
  Invisible Circus, The (Egan), 394–395
  Joyce, James, 394
  Keep, The (Egan), 393–396
  legacy and future directions, 397–398
  Look at Me (Egan), 394–395, 478–480, 664
  Manhattan Beach (Egan), 397
  story cycles, 1278–1279
  Visit from the Goon Squad, A (Egan), 395–397, 664, 1278–1279
  writing style and themes, 393–394, 397–398
Eggers, Dave, 398–404
  big data, 145–146
  Circle, The (Eggers), 145–146, 402–403, 664–665
  fiction and affect, 474
  Heartbreaking Work of Staggering Genius, A (Eggers), 398–400, 474
  Heroes of the Frontier (Eggers), 403
  Hologram for the King, A (Eggers), 402, 556–557
  hypertext fiction and network narratives, 664–665
  life and authorial evolution, 398–399
  McSweeney's, 400–401, 403
  recent works and legacy, 403
  Timothy McSweeney's Quarterly Concern (magazine), 400–401, 403
  What Is the What (Eggers), 401
  writers' collectives, 1447–1449
  writing style and themes, 398–399
  Your Fathers, Where Are They? And the Prophets, Do They Live Forever? (Eggers), 402

You Shall Know Our Velocity (Eggers), 400, 403
Zeitoun (Eggers), 401–403
Elkin, Stanley, 404–410
  context and legacy, 404, 410
  George Mills (Elkin), 405–407
  Living End, The (Elkin), 404
  MacGuffin, The (Elkin), 407–409
  Magic Kingdom, The (Elgin), 406–407
  Mrs. Ted Bliss (Elkin), 409–410
  Rabbi of Lud, The (Elkin), 407
  Van Gogh's Room at Arles (Elkin), 408–409
  writing style and themes, 404–405
Ellis, Bret Easton, 410–415
  American Psycho (Ellis), 412–415
  controversy, 410–411, 415
  fiction and terrorism, 480
  film adaptations, 415
  Glamorama (Ellis), 480
  Imperial Bedrooms (Ellis), 414–415
  Informers, The (Ellis), 413, 415
  Less Than Zero (Ellis), 411–412, 414–415, 469–473
  life and career, 411–412
  Lunar Park (Ellis), 414
  nonfiction, 410–411, 415
  Rules of Attraction, The (Ellis), 412, 414
  Tartt, Donna, 1300–1301
  Wall Street (Stone), 412–413
  writing style and themes, 410–411
Ellroy, James, 416–420
  American Tabloid (Ellroy), 418–419
  Black Dahlia, The (Ellroy), 417, 420
  Blood's a Rover (Ellroy), 419–420
  breakthrough and the LA Quartet novels, 417–419
  Clandestine (Ellroy), 416
  L.A. Confidential (Ellroy), 417–418
  life and influences, 416
  Lloyd Hopkins trilogy, 416–417
  nonfiction, 419–420
  Perfidia (Ellroy), 420
  recent work and legacy, 420
  Underworld USA trilogy, 418–419
Elusive Brain, The (Tougaw), 200–206
Emperor's Children, The (Messud), 1085–1087
End of Nature, The (McKibben), 386
End of Ordinary, The (Ashton), 148–149
Englander, Nathan, 420–425
  Dinner at the Center of the Earth (Englander), 423–424
  For the Relief of Unbearable Urges (Englander), 421–422
  kaddish.com (Englander), 424
  Metaphysics (Aristotle), 422
  Ministry of Special Cases, The (Englander), 422

Englander, Nathan (cont'd)
  translation of the Haggadah, 423
  What We Talk About When We Talk About Anne Frank (Englander), 422–423
  writing style and themes, 420–421
environmental fiction *see* Ecocriticism and Environmental Fiction
Erasure (Everett), 443–444, 1104, 1342
Erdrich, Louise, 425–430
  autobiographical publications, 429
  awards and acclaim, 429
  Bingo Palace, The (Erdrich), 428
  contemporary regionalisms, 292–293
  Indigenous narratives, 676–678
  Last Report on the Miracles at Little No Horse, The (Erdrich), 426–427
  life and education, 425–426
  Love Medicine (Erdrich), 425–428
  Night Watchman, The (Erdrich), 677
  novels, 427
  poetry and short stories, 426
  writing style and themes, 425–428
  young adult fiction, 428–429
Erickson, Steve, 430–434
  Arc d'X (Erickson), 431–433
  context and influences, 430
  Days Between Stations (Erickson), 430–431
  impact and criticism, 434
  Our Ecstatic Days (Erickson), 430, 433
  Rubicon Beach (Erikson), 431–432
  Shadowbahn (Erickson), 433–434
  Tours of the Black Clock (Erickson), 432–433
  writing style and themes, 430–431
Eugenides, Jeffrey, 434–440
  Fresh Complaint (Eugenides), 434–435
  life and influences, 434–435
  Marriage Plot, The (Eugenides), 434–435, 438–439
  Middlesex (Eugenides), 434–438
  Virgin Suicides, The (Eugenides), 434–438
  writing style and themes, 434–435
Everett, Percival, 440–445
  award and acclaim, 440–441
  Erasure (Everett), 443–444, 1104, 1342
  fiction and terrorism, 483–484
  For Her Dark Skin (Everett), 443
  Glyph (Everett), 995
  life, context, and influences, 440–442
  new experimentalism/the contemporary avant-garde, 995
  Percival Everett by Virgil Russell (Everett), 442
  post-soul and/or post-Black fiction, 1104
  So Much Blue (Everett), 444
  urban fiction, 1342

  Water Cure, The (Everett), 442–443, 483–484
  Westerns, 443
  writing style and themes, 440–441
Everything is Illuminated (Foer), 356, 495–500
Evil Dead Center (LaFavor), 1144
Exit West (Hamid), 691–692
Extremely Loud & Incredibly Close (Foer), 482, 484, 495–500, 1081
Eye Killers (Carr), 683
Eyes Bottle Dark with a Mouthful of Flowers (Skeet), 293–294

Falling Man (DeLillo), 366, 477–478, 482, 1080–1081
Fault in Our Stars, The (Green), 257
Faust (Goethe), 517–518
Federman, Raymond, 447–451
  Aunt Rachel's Fur (Federman), 449–450
  autobiographical works, 449
  Beckett, Samuel, 447–448, 450
  Critifiction (Federman), 449
  Double or Nothing (Federman), 448, 450
  impact and legacy, 450–451
  life and context, 447–448
  My Body in Nine Parts (Federman), 449
  Return to Manure (Federman), 448–449
  Shhh: The Story of a Childhood (Federman), 448–449
  Smiles on Washington Square (Federman), 449–451
  translations, 450
  Twofold Vibration, The (Federman), 448
  Voice in the Closet, The/La voix dans le cabinet de débarras (Federman), 448, 450
Feeling for Books, A (Radway), 177–178
Feinberg, Leslie, 452–456
  Drag King Dreams (Feinberg), 454–455
  legacy, 456
  life and context, 452
  queer and LGBT fiction, 1141
  Rainbow Solidarity in Defense of CUBA (Feinberg), 455–456
  Stone Butch Blues (Feinberg), 452–456, 1141
  Transgender Liberation: A Movement Whose Time Has Come (Feinberg), 452, 454
  Transgender Warriors (Feinberg), 454
  Well of Loneliness, The (Feinberg), 453
  writing style and themes, 452–453
Feminism and its Fictions (Hogeland), 178
Ferré, Rosario, 457–461
  Eccentric Neighborhoods (Ferré), 458
  essays, 461
  House on the Lagoon, The (Ferré), 458–459, 461
  life and context, 457–458
  Maldito Amor (Ferré), 459–461

Memoria (Ferré), 458–459, 461
Papeles de Pandora (Ferré), 457, 459–460
translation works, 460–461
writing styles and themes, 457–458
Zona de carga y descarga (journal), 457
Ferris, Joshua, 462–467
brain and American fiction, the, 206
impact and future directions, 466
life, influences, and comparison, 462–464, 466
Roth Philip, 466
Then We Came to the End (Ferris), 462–464
To Rise Again at a Decent hour (Ferris), 462, 465–466
Unnamed, The (Ferris), 206, 462, 464–465
writing style and themes, 462–466
Yates, Richard, 463–464, 466
Fiction and Affect, 467–476
affect–emotion distinction, 468–469
Allison, Dorothy, 56–60
autofiction, 475
Bright Lights, Big City (McInerney), 470–472
Citizen: An American Lyric (Rankine), 475
commodification and consumerism, 468–469, 472, 474–475
concepts and historical context, 467–469
Cunningham, Michael, 316–321
ecocriticism and environmental fiction, 388–390
generation X and the affect of affectlessness, 469–472
Generation X: Tales for an Accelerated Culture (Coupland), 470–472
Heartbreaking Work of Staggering Genius, A (Eggers), 474
Infinite Jest (Wallace), 473–474
Jameson, Fredric, 471–472
Lerner, Ben, 818–823
Less Than Zero (Ellis), 469–473
Morrison, Toni, 958–963
neoliberalism, 469, 474
Ng, Celeste, 1001–1005
post-apocalypse, 474–475
post-postmodernism, sincerity, and empathy, 472–475
Proulx, Annie, 1125–1130
racism, 475
Simpson, Mona, 1235–1240
Sontag, Susan, 1245–1251
story cycles, 1272–1274
Strout, Elizabeth, 1280–1285
Tan, Amy, 1295–1300
Wallace, David Foster, 1388–1393
Williams, Raymond, 467–469, 472, 475
Zone One (Whitehead), 474–475

Fiction and Terrorism, 476–486
American writer's response to 9/11 attacks, 477–478
Auster, Paul, 89
Burnt Shadows (Shamsie), 485
Damascus Gate (Stone), 479–480
Darling, The (Banks), 481
DeLillo, Don, 363–367
Effect of Living Backwards, The (Julavits), 483
Erickson, Steve, 430–434
Extremely Loud & Incredibly Close (Foer), 482, 484
Falling Man (DeLillo), 477–478, 482
fiction dramatizing the 9/11 attacks, 481–482
gender, 481
Glamorama (Ellis), 480
humanizing the terrorist, 478–481
imperialism, 483, 485
Look at Me (Egan), 478–479
Mao II (DeLillo), 482
political satire, 483
religion, 478–481, 484–485
Reluctant Fundamentalist, The (Hamid), 479
Submission, The (Waldman), 484–485
terrorist incidents in the US, 477
Terrorist (Updike), 476–480
Updike, John, 1339
Water Cure, The (Everett), 483–484
Zero, The (Walters), 483–484
Fictions of Work and Labor, 486–495
Álvarez, Julia, 64
care work, 489, 493
changes in work and the composition of labor, 487–488
context and overview, 486–487
COVID-19 pandemic, 488
deindustrialization and residual blue-collar work, 489–490
Elkin, Stanley, 405–407
Feinberg, Leslie, 452–456
Ferris, Joshua, 462–467
finding work and labor in contemporary fiction, 488–489
future directions, 493–494
global financial crisis (2008), 488
interactive service work, 492–493
Kennedy, William, 751–756
Kushner, Rachel, 783–786
meditations on temporary work, 491
migration, 487, 493–494
millennial fiction, 914–918
minimalism and maximalism, 490
multiethnic fiction, globalization, and work, 493
Ng, Fae Myenne, 1007–1011

Fictions of Work and Labor (*cont'd*)
   office satire, 491
   office work and the downwardly mobile middle class, 490–492
   politics and policy, 487–488
   postapocalyptic fiction, 491–492
   Saunders, George, 1193–1198
   start-up novels, 494
   Truong, Monique, 1328–1334
   Viramontes, Helena María, 1363–1364
   Vonnegut, Kurt, 1377
   Wallace, David Foster, 1392
   Wall Street and financial thrillers, 490–491
   Yu, Charles, 1474–1475
Fire This Time, The (Ward), 1397, 1446
Fire with Fire (Wolf), 1309
Flamethrowers, The (Kushner), 170, 781, 783–786
Fledgling (Butler), 229–230, 939
Florida (Long), 1293
Flyy Girl (Tyree), 1341–1342
Fobbit (Abrams), 285, 287
Foer, Jonathan Safran, 495–501
   debut novels, 356
   Everything is Illuminated (Foer), 356, 495–500
   Extremely Loud & Incredibly Close (Foer), 482, 484, 495–500, 1081
   fiction and terrorism, 482, 484
   Here I Am (Foer), 495–499
   key works and life, 495–496
   nonfiction, 495
   One Hundred Years of Solitude (Márquez), 496
   Slaughterhouse-Five (Vonnegut), 497
   writing style and themes, 495–496
forced migration *see* migrations and diaspora
Ford, Richard, 501–506
   awards and acclaim, 502, 505
   Bascombe books (Ford), 1290
   Canada (Ford), 502–503
   Independence Day (Ford), 502–504
   Lay of the Land, The (Ford), 502, 504–505
   "Leaving for Kenosha" (Ford), 504
   Let Me Be Frank with You (Ford), 502–503
   life and early writing, 501–502
   Sportswriter, The (Ford), 502–503
   writing style and themes, 501–502
Forgotten Readers: Recovering the Lost History of African American Literary Societies (McHenry), 177, 183
Frank (Berry), 995
Frankenstein (Shelley), 761, 796, 995
Franzen, Jonathan, 506–511
   big data, 145
   brain and American fiction, the, 206
   context, controversy, and criticism, 506–507, 510
   Corrections, The (Franzen), 506–507, 510
   Discomfort Zone, The (Franzen), 508
   essays, 507–510
   Freedom (Franzen), 509–510
   How to Be Alone (Franzen), 507–508
   Marcus, Ben, 857–858
   Oprah's Book Club, 507, 509
   Purity (Franzen), 145, 510
   Strong Motion (Franzen), 508–509
   Twenty-Seventh, The (Franzen), 508–509
   Wallace, David Foster, 510
Frazier, Charles, 511–516
   Cold Mountain (Frazier), 353, 511–512, 515
   debut novels, 353
   Nightwoods (Frazier), 511–512, 514–515
   Thirteen Moons (Frazier), 511–513
   Varina (Frazier), 511–515
Free Life, A (Jin), 554–555
Freestyle (exhibition), 1100–1101
Fun Home (Bechdel), 578–579

Gaddis, William, 517–522
   Agapē Agape (Gaddis), 517, 521
   awards and acclaim, 517
   Carpenter's Gothic (Gaddis), 517, 519–520
   Dara, Evan, 346–347
   Faust (Goethe), 517–518
   Frolic of His Own, A (Gaddis), 517, 519–520
   influence and legacy, 521
   J R (Gaddis), 518–520
   life and death, 517
   Marcus, Ben, 857
   minimalism and maximalism, 931
   Recognitions, The (Gaddis), 517–518, 521, 931
   Rush for Second Place, The (Gaddis), 521
   writing style, themes, and influences, 517–521
Gaines, Ernest J., 522–527
   Autobiography of Miss Pittman, The (Gaines), 526
   Black Atlantic, 158
   Catherine Carmier (Gaines), 158
   Gathering of Old Men, A (Gaines), 522–523
   Lesson Before Dying, A (Gaines), 523–524, 526
   life and body of work, 522
   Mozart and Leadbelly (Gaines), 524–526
   Tragedy of Brady Sims, The (Gaines), 526–527
   writing style and themes, 522
Galatea 2.2 (Powers), 202–203, 1113, 1115–1116
García, Cristina, 527–532
   Dreaming in Cuban (García), 528–529, 1277–1278
   Handbook to Luck, A (García), 530–531
   Here in Berlin (García), 531–532

King of Cuba (García), 530
Lady Matador's Hotel, The (García), 531
life, awards, and acclaim, 527–528
Monkey Hunting (García), 530
story cycles, 1277–1278
writing style and themes, 528
Gardens in the Dunes (Silko), 680, 1233–1234
Gass, William H., 532–537
   awards and acclaim, 533
   Cartesian Sonata and Other Novellas (Gass), 535
   Eyes (Gass), 537
   Finding a Form (Gass), 534–535
   impact and legacy, 533, 537
   intermedial fiction, 686–687
   life, influence, and influences, 532–533
   Life Sentences (Gass), 536
   Middle C (Gass), 536–537
   Reading Rilke (Gass), 535–536
   realism after poststructuralism, 1152
   Temple of Texts, A (Gass), 536
   Tests of Time (Gass), 536
   Tunnel, The (Gass), 534–536
   Willie Masters' Lonesome Wife (Gass), 686–687
   writing style and themes, 533–534
Gay, Roxane, 538–542
   Ayiti (Gay), 538–541
   Bad Feminist (Gay), 538
   Difficult Women (Gay), 540–541
   Hunger (Gay), 540
   impact and legacy, 538, 541
   life and context, 538
   PANK (online magazine), 538
   Small Place, A (Kincaid), 539
   Untamed State, An (Gay), 539–540
   World of Wankanda series (Marvel comics), 541
   writing styles and themes, 538
Geek Love (Dunn), 29, 674–675
gender
   Acker, Kathy, 6–10
   Allende, Isabel, 53
   Álvarez, Julia, 62
   Black Atlantic, 163–164
   border fictions, 186–187
   Boyle, T.C., 194–198
   Butler, Octavia, 226–230
   contemporary fictions of war, 282, 287–288
   Eugenides, Jeffrey, 434–439
   Feinberg, Leslie, 452–456
   fiction and terrorism, 481
   intersex, 436–438
   Irving, John, 697–698
   Le Guin, Ursula K., 814–816
   Maupin, Armistead, 877–879

McMillan, Terry, 904
Middlesex (Eugenides), 434–438
millennial fiction, 916–917
Ng, Celeste, 1001–1005
program culture, 1121
Senna, Danzy, 1212–1213
suburban narratives, 1292
third-wave feminism, 1306–1315
transphobia, 71
Truong, Monique, 1328–1334
Viramontes, Helena María, 1360–1366
young adult boom, 1470
Generation X: Tales for an Accelerated Culture (Coupland), 470–472
Ghost Fleet (Singer and Cole), 558
Ghost Singer (Walters), 680
Ghost World (Clowes), 575
Gibson, William, 542–547
   Agency (Gibson), 546–547
   Archangel (Gibson), 546
   big data, 140
   Blue Ant trilogy (Gibson), 544–545
   Bridge trilogy (Gibson), 544
   context and impact, 542
   Difference Engine, The (Gibson and Sterling), 545–546
   globalization, 560
   hypertext fiction and network narratives, 659–660, 664
   Neuromancer (Gibson), 140, 324–326, 329, 542, 560, 659–660
   Pattern Recognition (Gibson), 664
   Peripheral, The (Gibson), 546
   Sprawl trilogy (Gibson), 542–544
   writing styles and themes, 542
Gilda Stories, The (Gomez), 567, 569–571, 1140–1141
Gilead (Robinson), 293, 1168–1169, 1179–1181
Gilroy, Paul *see* Black Atlantic
Glamorama (Ellis), 413–414, 480
Glancy, Diane, 547–552
   Claiming Breath (Glancy), 550
   Cold-and-Hunger Dance, The (Glancy), 549, 551
   Designs of the Night Sky (Glancy), 550
   impact, 551
   Island of the Innocent (Glancy), 550–551
   life and context, 547–548
   Mask Maker, The (Glancy), 549–550
   Native American Renaissance (Lincoln), 547–548
   Pushing the Bear (Glancy), 548–549
   Stone Heart (Glancy), 549–550
   writing style and themes, 548

Globalization, 552–562
　Afghanistan, invasion of, 558
　American Dirt (Cummins), 555
　capitalism, 553, 556–557, 559–561
　Centenal Cycle, The trilogy (Older), 560
　China Tidal Wave (Lixiong), 557–558
　comings and goings, 553–556
　contemporary regionalisms, 289, 291, 297
　context and overview, 552–553
　Cosmopolis (DeLillo), 559–560
　COVID-19 pandemic, 560–561
　cultural hybridity, 553, 555
　dystopia, 557, 560–561
　ecocriticism and environmental fiction, 387, 560–561
　fictions of work and labor, 493
　Free Life, A (Jin), 554–555
　future directions, 561
　García, Cristina, 527–532
　Ghost Fleet (Singer and Cole), 558
　Hologram for the King, A (Eggers), 556–557
　immigration literature, 553–554
　Iraq War (2003–2011), 558
　Kushner, Rachel, 781–785
　Lazarus Project, The (Hemon), 556
　Mandibles, The: A Family (Shriver), 556–557
　millennial fiction, 912, 914–916, 919
　Modernity At Large (Appadurai), 559
　Neuromancer (Gibson), 560
　New York 2140 (Robinson), 560–561
　Open City (Cole), 554–555
　post-9/11 narratives, 558–559
　Sand Queen (Benedict), 558
　Shteyngart, Gary, 1224–1225
　Snow Crash (Stephenson), 560
　speculative fiction, 560–561
　Stephenson, Neal, 560
　Tan, Amy, 1295–1300
　Thucydides Trap, 558
　Tomasula, Steve, 1315–1319
　towards a globalized unicity, 559–561
　United States in the world, 556–559
　Windup Girl, The (Bacigalupi), 560–561
　Yamashita, Karen Tei, 1459, 1461
Glossary of Literary Terms, A (Abrams), 1148
Glyph (Everett), 995
Gold Bug Variations, The (Powers), 29–30, 1113, 1115
Golden, Marita, 562–567
　After (Golden), 566
　And Do Remember Me (Golden), 564–565
　context and impact, 562–564
　criticism and scholarship, 562–563
　Edge of Heaven, The (Golden), 565–566

　Long Distance Life (Golden), 564
　Migrations of the Heart (Golden), 563–564
　Specifying (Willis), 562–563
　Wide Circumference of Love, The (Golden), 566
　Worrying the Line (Wall), 562
　writing style and themes, 562–566
Goldfinch, The (Tartt), 1288–1289, 1291, 1301–1305
Gomez, Jewelle, 567–572
　activism, 567–571
　awards and acclaim, 567, 571
　Flamingoes and Bears (Gomez), 568–569
　Gilda Stories, The (Gomez), 567, 569–571, 1140–1141
　legacy, 571
　life and context, 567–568
　Lipstick Papers, The (Gomez), 568
　other publications, 571
Good Faith (Smiley), 1289–1290
Good Kings, Bad Kings (Nussbaum), 672
Good Lieutenant, The (Terrell), 287–288
Good Life, The (McInerney), 1085–1087
Good Lord Bird, The (McBride), 882–883, 1170–1171
Gossip Girls series (Ziegesar), 1467–1468
Graphic Novel, The, 572–581
　American Splendor (Pekar), 575
　Berlin trilogy (Lute), 576, 580
　Binky Brown Meets the Holy Virgin Mary (Green), 577
　Black Hole (Burns), 580
　Blankets (Thompson), 578
　Building Stories (Ware), 573–574
　coming of a singularized cultural good, 572–574
　context, 572
　Contract with God, A (Eisner), 575
　Dark Knight Returns, The (Miller), 573
　Ducornet, Rikki, 380–381
　essential structural features, 574
　from alternative comics to graphic novels, 574–576
　Fun Home (Bechdel), 578–579
　Ghost World (Clowes), 575
　Gibson, William, 546
　Here (McGuire), 576
　In the Shadow of No Towers (Spiegelman), 578
　Jimmy Corrigan (Ware), 576–577
　Johnson, Mat, 726–732
　Maus: A Survivor's Tale (Spiegelman), 572–573
　My Friend Dahmer (Backderf), 579
　New Orleans After the Deluge (Neufeld), 580
　One Hundred Demons (Barry), 577–578
　On the Ropes (Vance and Burr), 580
　Palahniuk, Chuck, 1043, 1047
　Palestine (Sacco), 579, 581

Rusty Brown (Ware), 577
Sabrina (Drnaso), 580–581
second wave of the graphic novel
   context, 576–577
   graphic journalism, 579–580
   rise of the graphic memoir, 577–579
   works of other subgenres, 580–581
Stitches (Small), 578–579
System, The (Kuper), 576
third-wave feminism, 1313
War-Fix (Axe), 579–580
Watchmen (Moore and Gibbons), 573
young adult fiction, 580
Grass Dancer, The (Power), 683, 1107–1110
Gray, Amelia, 581–586
   AM/PM (Gray), 582
   comparisons, 583
   Gutshot (Gray), 583, 585
   Isadora (Gray), 585–586
   life and context, 581–582
   Museum of the Weird (Gray), 582–583
   THREATS (Gray), 583–586
   writing style and themes, 582
Great Believers, The (Makkai), 170
Great Republic, The (Bailyn et al.), 974
Groff, Lauren, 586–591
   Arcadia (Groff), 587–591
   Delicate Edible Birds (Groff), 587–589
   Fates and Furies (Groff), 588–590
   Florida (Groff), 586–591
   life, awards, and acclaim, 586–587
   Monsters of Templeton, The (Groff), 586–591
   writing style and themes, 586–587
Gulf War Did Not Take Place, The (Baudrillard), 662

Hacker Crackdown, The (Sterling), 660
Hagedorn, Jessica, 593–598
   Apostol, Gina, 82, 85–86
   Charlie Chan is Dead (Hagedorn), 595–596
   Dangerous Music (Hagedorn), 595
   Dogeaters (Hagedorn), 593–594
   Gangster of Love, The (Hagedorn), 594–595
   impact and legacy, 596–597
   life, works, and context, 593–594
   Manila Noir (Hagedorn), 596–597
   writing style and themes, 593–595
Hamlet (Shakespeare), 209, 211
Hannah, Barry, 598–603
   Bats Out of Hell (Hannah), 599–600
   Faulkner, William, 598–600
   Geronimo Rex (Hannah), 598
   life, awards, and key works, 598–599
   Ray (Hannah), 598–599, 601–602

Southern Writer in the Postmodern World, The (Hobson), 601–602
   "That Was Close Ma" (Hannah), 600–601
   writing style and themes, 598–599
   Yonder Stands Your Orphan (Hannah), 602
Harrison, Jim, 603–609
   acclaim, 603–604
   Brown Dog (Harrison), 607–608
   Dalva (Harrison), 605–607
   death and legacy, 608
   influences, 604–605
   Just Before Dark (Harrison), 608
   Legends of the Fall (Harrison), 603–604
   life and works, 603–604
   Off to the Side (Harrison), 605
   Road Home, The (Harrison), 605–606
   True North (Harrison), 605–607
   Woman Lit by Fireflies, A (Harrison), 607
   writing style and themes, 604–605
Harry Potter books (Rowling), 1466–1467
Hate You Give, The (Thomas), 165
Hatred of Poetry, The (Lerner), 172–173
Hawkes, John, 609–613
   Adventures in the Alaskan Skin Trade (Hawkes), 611
   Cannibal, The (Hawkes), 609–610
   Charivari (Hawkes), 609
   Frog, The (Hawkes), 612
   Irish Eye, An (Hawkes), 612
   legacy, 613
   life, influences, and early work, 609–610
   Lime Twig, The (Hawkes), 610, 612
   Passion Artist, The (Hawkes), 611
   Second Skin (Hawkes), 610–611
   Sweet William (Hawkes), 612
   Virginie (Hawkes), 611
   Whistlejacket (Hawkes), 611–612
   writing style and themes, 609, 612–613
Heads of the Colored People (Thompson-Spires), 1103–1104
Healer's War, The (Scarborough), 282–283
Heartbreaking Work of Staggering Genius, A (Eggers), 398–400, 474
Heller, Joseph, 613–618
   Catch-22 (Heller), 613–614, 616
   Closing Time (Heller), 616–617
   God Knows (Heller), 614–615
   Good as Gold (Heller), 614–616
   impact and context, 613–614
   Picture This (Heller), 615–616
   Portrait of an Artist, as an Old Man (Heller), 617
   Something Happened (Heller), 613–614
   writing style and themes, 613–614

Hemispheric American Studies (Levander and Levine), 840
Hemon, Aleksandar, 618–623
  collaborations, 622
  globalization, 556
  Lazarus Project, The (Hemon), 556, 620–621
  life and context, 618–619
  Love and Obstacles (Hemon), 621–622
  Making of Zombie Wars, The (Hemon), 621–622
  nonfiction essays, 622
  Nowhere Man (Hemon), 620–621
  Question of Bruno, The (Hemon), 620
  writing style and themes, 618–619
Hempel, Amy, 623–628
  At the Gates of the Animal Kingdom (Hempel), 625–626
  awards and acclaim, 623, 625
  Collected Stories of Amy Hempel, The (Hempel), 626–627
  Dog of the Marriage, The (Hempel), 626
  Hand That Feeds You, The (Ciment and Hempel), 626–627
  "In the Cemetery Where Al Jolson is Buried" (Hempel), 625
  life, context, and influences, 623–625
  Lish, Gordon, 624–625
  Tumble Home (Hempel), 626
  writing style and themes, 623–625
Here (McGuire), 576
Hijuelos, Oscar, 628–633
  awards and acclaim, 628
  Beautiful Maria of My Soul (Hijuelos), 630
  Dark Dude (Hijuelos), 632
  Empress of the Splendid Season, The (Hijuelos), 631
  Fourteen Sisters of Emilio Montez O'Brian (Hijuelos), 630–631
  life and career, 628
  Mambo Kings Play Songs of Love, The (Hijuelos), 629–630
  Mr. Ives' Christmas (Hijuelos), 631
  Our House in the Last World (Hijuelos), 629
  Simple Habana Melody (From When the World Was Good), A (Hijuelos), 631–632
  Twain & Stanley Enter Paradise (Hijuelos), 632
  writing style and themes, 628–629
Hillbilly Elegy (Vance), 290
Hinojosa, Rolando, 633–638
  awards and acclaim, 634
  Böll, Heinrich, 637
  Claros varones de Belken (Fair Gentlemen of Belken County) (Hinojosa), 635–636
  context and publications, 633

Dear Rafe (Hinojosa), 635–636
influence and legacy, 637–638
Klail City Death Trip, The series (Hinojosa), 634–637
Korean Love Songs (Hinojosa), 634–635
life and career, 633–634
Mi querido Rafa (Hinojosa), 635–636
Useless Servants, The (Hinojosa), 634–635
We Happy Few (Hinojosa), 637
Historia comparada de las literaturas americanas (Sánchez), 836–837
Historical Novel, The (Lukács), 1207–1209
History of the Americas: A Syllabus with Maps (Bolton), 841
HIV/AIDS
  Alameddine, Rabih, 36–37, 39
  Burroughs, William S., 221–222
  Cleage, Pearl, 267
  Cunningham, Michael, 317–319
  Delany, Samuel R., 359, 361
  illness and disability narratives, 668–669
  Irving, John, 694, 697
  Leavitt, David, 799
  Maso, Carole, 866–867
  Maupin, Armistead, 878, 880
  Nava, Michael, 983–984, 986
  queer and LGBT fiction, 1137, 1143–1144
  White, Edmund, 1410–1412
Hogan, Linda, 638–643
  awards and acclaim, 639
  Calling Myself Home (Hogan), 638–640
  Daughters, I Love You (Hogan), 640–641
  impact and legacy, 642
  life and career, 638–639
  Mean Spirit (Hogan), 640–641
  People of the Whale (Hogan), 641–642
  Power (Hogan), 641–642
  Solar Storms (Hogan), 640, 642
  writing style and themes, 638–639
Holocaust
  Federman, Raymond, 447, 450–451
  Foer, Jonathan Safran, 495–499
  Gass, William H., 534
  Krauss, Nicole, 775–779
  Maso, Carole, 867–868
  Ozick, Cynthia, 1037–1041
  trauma and fiction, 1321–1324
  young adult boom, 1467
Hologram for the King, A (Eggers), 402, 556–557
Home at the End of the World, A (Cunningham), 317–319, 1288
Homegoing (Gyasi), 354

Homes, A.M., 643–647
   Cheever, John, 645
   End of Alice, The (Homes), 644–645
   In a Country of Mothers (Homes), 643–644
   Jack (Homes), 643
   Lolita (Nabokov), 644–645
   May We Be Forgiven (Homes), 645–646
   Mistress's Daughter, The (Homes), 643
   This Book Will Save Your Life (Homes), 645
   writing style and themes, 643
Hosseini, Khaled, 647–653
   And the Mountains Echoed (Hosseini), 651–652
   awards and acclaim, 648
   Kite Runner, The (Hosseini), 648–652
   life, education, and humanitarian work, 647–648
   Sea Prayer (Hosseini), 652
   Thousand Splendid Suns, A (Hosseini), 650–652
House Made of Dawn (Momaday), 675, 943–945, 947
House of Leaves (Danielewski), 333–337, 663–664, 685, 687, 1152–1153
House of Sand and Fog (Dubus III), 1291
House on Mango Street, The (Cisneros), 260, 262–263, 928, 1274–1275
How the Mind Works (Pinker), 199–200
How to Read and Why (Bloom), 175
How We Became Posthuman (Hayles), 1089
Huesos en el desierto (Bones in the Desert) (Rodríguez), 190–191
Hugh Selwyn Mauberly (Pound), 344
Human Stain, The (Roth), 313–314, 1184–1185
Humument, A (Phillips), 687
Hunger Games, The (Collins), 1466
Hustvedt, Siri, 653–658
   awards and acclaim, 654
   Blazing World, The (Hustvedt), 653, 655–658
   Blindfold, The (Hustvedt), 656
   Delusions of Certainty, The (Hustvedt), 655
   Enchantment of Lily Dahl, The (Hustvedt), 656–657
   life, publications, and career, 653–654
   Sorrows of an American, The (Hustvedt), 656
   "Three Emotional Stories" (Hustvedt), 657
   What I Loved (Hustvedt), 655–656
   writing style and themes, 653–655
   "Yonder" (Hustvedt), 655
Hypertext Fiction and Network Narratives, 658–666
   Afrofuturism, 660
   afternoon (Joyce), 661–662
   Black Mirror: Bandersnatch (Slade), 662
   Choose Your Own Adventure books, 660–661
   Circle, The (Eggers), 664–665
   context and overview, 658–659

   cyberpunk, 659–660
   Ensslin, Astrid, 661
   Gulf War Did Not Take Place, The (Baudrillard), 662
   Hacker Crackdown, The (Sterling), 660
   House of Leaves (Danielewski), 663–664
   Infinite Jest (Wallace), 663
   Landow, George P., 661
   legacy, 665
   Look At Me (Egan), 664
   Neuromancer (Gibson), 659–660
   Pattern Recognition (Gibson), 664
   post-9/11 narratives, 664
   Pricksongs and Descants (Coover), 663
   realism after poststructuralism, 1152
   Stars in My Pockets Like Grains of Sand (Delany), 659–660, 664
   Storyspace (Eastgate Systems software), 661–662
   Timecode (Figgis), 661
   Victory Garden (Moulthrop), 662
   Visit from the Goon Squad, A (Egan), 664
   Watchmen (Moore), 661

Icarus Girl, The (Oyeyemi), 163
Ideology and Classic American Literature (Bercovitch et al. eds.), 975–976
I'd Walk With My Friends If I Could Find Them (Goolsby), 286–287
I Know Why the Caged Bird Sings (Angelou), 1341
I'll Get There. It Better Be Worth the Trip (Donovan), 1470
Illness and Disability Narratives, 667–675
   Acts of Intervention (Román), 669
   Antrim, Donald, 77–81
   Authoring Autism (Yergeau), 672–673
   Ball, Jesse, 99–102
   Community (TV series), 673–674
   COVID-19, 668, 670–671
   Cunningham, Michael, 317–319
   disability, 671–674
   Geek Love (Dunn), 674–675
   Good Kings, Bad Kings (Nussbaum), 672
   Heller, Joseph, 616–617
   HIV/AIDS, 668–669
   illness, 668–671
   Illness as Metaphor (Sontag), 668, 671–672, 1246
   introduction: understanding "and", 667–668
   Just Say No (Kramer), 668
   LaValle, Victor, 794–795
   Leavitt, David, 799
   Mad Man, The (Delany), 669
   Matrix, The (Wachowski and Wachowski), 670
   My Brother (Kincaid), 669

Illness and Disability Narratives (cont'd)
   Narrative Prosthesis: Disability and the Dependencies of Discourse (Mitchell and Snyder), 672
   Normal Heart, The (Kramer), 668–669
   Phillips, Jayne Anne, 1069–1072
   Severance (Ma), 670–671
   What Looks Like Crazy on an Ordinary Day (Cleage), 669
Illness as Metaphor (Sontag), 668, 671–672, 1246
I Love Dick (Kraus), 941
Inanimate Alice (Pullinger and Joseph), 687
In Country (Mason), 282, 872–873
Indigenous Narratives, 675–684
   Afrofuturism, 23–24
   Almanac of the Dead (Silko), 680–681
   animals and sentience, 682–683
   assimilation, 679–680
   biopolitics, 678–679
   Butterfly Moon (Endrezze), 682–683
   Castillo, Ana, 236–240
   context and overview, 675–676
   crime fiction, 677–678
   Dance Boots, The (LeGarde Grover), 679
   Dead Voices (Vizenor), 682
   ecocriticism and environmental fiction, 681
   Erdrich, Louise, 425–430
   Eye Killers (Carr), 683
   family, 677–680, 683
   fictionalization of historical events and alternative histories, 680–681
   fictions speaking of the difficulties of urban indigeneity, 677–678
   Gardens in the Dunes (Silko), 680
   General Allotment Act (1887), 676–677
   Ghost Singer (Walters), 680
   Glancy, Diane, 547–552
   Grass Dancer, The (Power), 683
   Hogan, Linda, 638–643
   horror, 682–683
   House Made of Dawn (Momaday), 675
   Igbo culture, 13, 16
   Indian Relocation Act (1956), 677
   Indian Removal Act (1830), 676
   Jones, Stephen Graham, 744–749
   kinship, 682–683
   looting of burial grounds and theft of cultural property, 680
   Mapping the Interior (Jones), 683
   millennial fiction, 916–917
   Momaday, N. Scott, 943–948
   Native American Graves Protection and Repatriation Act (1990), 1109
   Night Watchman, The (Erdrich), 677
   Ojibwe culture, 425–429
   Power, Susan, 1107–1112
   queer and LGBT fiction, 1144
   retelling and reimagining of traditional and culturally significant stories, 680–681
   Sacred Smokes (Van Alst), 677
   sexual abuse, 678–679
   sexualities, 679
   Silko, Leslie Marmon, 1230–1234
   Song of the Turtle (Allen), 675
   spirituality, 680–681
   Storyteller (Silko), 679–680, 683
   violence, 677–678, 681
   Vizenor, Gerald, 1366–1371
   Washburn, Frances, 1398–1404
   Way of Thorn and Thunder, The (Heath Justice), 676, 682
   Welch, James, 1404–1410
   Yamanaka, Lois-Ann, 1453–1458
Infinite Jest (Wallace), 30–32, 473–474, 663, 932, 1196, 1388–1392
Infomocracy (Older), 146
In Persuasion Nation (Saunders), 143–144, 1197
Interceptor Pilot, The (Gangemi), 686
Intermedial Fiction, 684–694
   Blood and Guts in High School (Acker), 686–687
   Blown Away (Sukenick), 689–690
   bookishness, 691–692
   Book of Illusions, The (Auster), 685–686
   Colorist, The (Daitch), 686
   context and overview, 684–685
   Coover, Robert, 305–306
   Danielewski, Mark Z., 333–338
   Digital Modernism (Pressman), 688
   Erickson, Steve, 430–434
   Exit West (Hamid), 691–692
   historicizing intermedial fiction, 688–692
   House of Leaves (Danielewski), 685, 687
   Humument, A (Phillips), 687
   Inanimate Alice (Pullinger and Joseph), 687
   Interceptor Pilot, The (Gangemi), 686
   Krazy Kat (Cantor), 685–686
   other perspectives on media and fiction, 692
   range of intermedial fiction, 685–688
   Three Farmers on Their Way to a Dance (Powers), 690
   Vidal, Gore, 1357–1358
   Vineland (Pynchon), 690
   Willie Masters' Lonesome Wife (Gass), 686–687
In The Dream House (Machado), 934–935
In the Shadow of No Towers (Spiegelman), 578

Intimate Practices: Literacy and Cultural Work in U.S. Women's Clubs (Gere), 176–177, 180
Irving, John, 694–699
  context, impact, and life, 694–696
  Hotel New Hampshire, The (Irving), 696–698
  Prayer for Owen Meany, A (Irving), 697
  World According to Bensenhaver, The (Irving), 695–696
  World According to Garp, The (Irving), 694–698
  writing style and themes, 694–698
I Sailed with Magellan (Dybek), 1274–1275
Islands in the Net (Sterling), 326–328

James, Marlon, 701–705
  Black Leopard, Red Wolf (James), 702–703, 705
  Book of Night Women, The (James), 702–704
  Brief History of Seven Killings, A (James), 701–703
  John Crow's Devil (James), 702–704
  life, awards, and acclaim, 701
  Shame (Rushdie), 701
  writing style and themes, 701–704
Jarrar, Randa, 706–711
  acclaim, 706
  Him, Me, Muhammad Ali (Jarrar), 706, 708–710
  life and context, 706
  Map of Home, A (Jarrar), 706–708
  writing style and themes, 706–707
Jen, Gish, 711–716
  Girl at the Baggage Claim, The: Explaining the East-West Cultural Gap (Jen), 715
  life, writing style, and themes, 711–712
  Love Wife, The (Jen), 713
  Mona in the Promised Land (Jen), 712
  nonfiction, 714–715
  Resisters, The (Jen), 714
  Typical American (Jen), 712
  Who's Irish? (Jen), 712–713
  World and Town (Jen), 713–714
Jimmy Corrigan (Ware), 576–577
Johnson, Charles, 716–721
  awards and acclaim, 720
  collaborations, 720
  Faith and the Good Thing (Johnson), 716
  life and career, 716
  Middle Passage (Johnson), 717–718
  Oxherding Tale (Johnson), 716–717
  Sorcerer's Apprentice, The (Johnson), 719
  Soulcatcher and Other Stories (Johnson), 719–720
  television scripts, 720
  writing style and themes, 716–717
Johnson, Denis, 721–726
  contemporary regionalisms, 295
  death and legacy, 725

Jesus' Son (Johnson), 721, 723, 725
Largesse of the Sea Maiden, The (Johnson), 722, 725
Laughing Monsters, The (Johnson), 724–725
life, awards, and acclaim, 721
Resuscitation of a Hanged Man (Johnson), 721–724
Train Dreams (Johnson), 295
Tree of Smoke (Johnson), 283–284, 721–724
writing style and themes, 721–723
Johnson, Mat, 726–732
  collaborations, 728–729
  Drop (Johnson), 727
  Great Negro Plot, The (Johnson), 727–728
  Hunting in Harlem (Johnson), 727–728
  Incognegro (Johnson), 727–729
  life and context, 726–727
  Loving Day (Johnson), 730–731, 1104–1105
  Pym (Johnson), 727, 729–730
  writing style and themes, 726–727, 731
Jones, Edward P., 732–738
  All Aunt Hagar's Children (Jones), 732–734
  awards and acclaim, 732
  big data, 144
  Dubliners (Joyce), 732
  "First Day, The" (Jones), 733–735
  Known World, The (Jones), 144, 732, 735–738
  life and education, 733–734
  Lost in the City (Jones), 732–734
  writing style and themes, 732–734
Jones, Gayl, 738–744
  Corregidora (Jones), 162, 738–740, 742–743
  Eva's Man (Jones), 739, 742–743
  Healing, The (Jones), 741–743
  impact and context, 739
  legacy, 743
  life and education, 738–739
  Mosquito (Jones), 740–741, 743
  nonfiction, 742
  Song for Anninho (Jones), 739–740, 743
  writing style and themes, 739–740
Jones, Stephen Graham, 744–749
  2000s, 746–747
  2010s to present, 747–748
  early writing, 745–746
  Fast Red Road, The (Jones), 745–747
  Growing up Dead in Texas (Jones), 747
  impact and future directions, 748
  Indigenous narratives, 683
  influences, 745–746
  Ledfeather (Jones), 747
  life, career, and context, 744–745
  Mapping the Interior (Jones), 683, 748
  writing style and themes, 744–748

Joy Luck Club, The (Tan), 1276, 1295–1296, 1298
Just Say No (Kramer), 668

Kennedy, William, 751–756
  awards and acclaim, 752–753
  Billy Phelan's Greatest Game (Kennedy), 752–753, 755
  Changó's Beads and Two-Tone Shoes (Kennedy), 755–756
  Flaming Corsage, The (Kennedy), 755
  Ink Truck, The (Kennedy), 751–752
  Ironweed (Kennedy), 753–754
  legacy, 756
  Legs (Kennedy), 752–753
  life and context, 751–752
  nonfiction, 756
  Quinn's Book (Kennedy), 754–756
  Roscoe (Kennedy), 755
  Very Old Bones (Kennedy), 755
Kincaid, Jamaica, 756–760
  Annie John (Kincaid), 758
  At the Bottom of the River (Kincaid), 758
  Autobiography of My Mother, The (Kincaid), 758–759
  Gay, Roxane, 539
  illness and disability narratives, 669
  life, writings, and context, 756–758
  Lucy (Kincaid), 758
  Mr. Potter (Kincaid), 759–760
  My Brother (Kincaid), 669, 759
  See Then Now (Kincaid), 760
  Small Place, A (Kincaid), 539
Kindred (Butler), 227, 1068
King, Stephen, 760–765
  Bachman, Richard, 765
  Bill Hodges Trilogy (King), 765
  Cell (King), 764
  context, awards, acclaim, and legacy, 760–761
  Dark Tower series (King), 763–764
  Doctor Sleep (King), 764–765
  Dolores Claiborne (King), 763
  Frankenstein (Shelley), 761
  IT (King), 761–765
  Misery (King), 763–764
  Pet Sematary (King), 761, 763
  Song of Susannah (King), 764
  Stand, The (King), 762, 764
Kingdom of Olives and Ash (Chabon and Waldman), 245
King Lear (Shakespeare), 1241–1242
Kingsolver, Barbara, 765–770
  Animal Dreams (Kingsolver), 767–768
  Bean Trees, The (Kingsolver), 766–767

  context and career, 765–766
  Flight Behavior (Kingsolver), 769–770
  Lacuna, The (Kingsolver), 769
  Pigs in Heaven (Kingsolver), 766–767
  Poisonwood Bible, The (Kingsolver), 768–769
  Prodigal Summer (Kingsolver), 769
  Unsheltered (Kingsolver), 770
Kingston, Maxine Hong, 770–775
  acclaim, impact, and future directions, 774
  activism, 771, 773–774
  China Men (Kingston), 771
  contemporary regionalisms, 295–296
  Fifth Book of Peace, The (Kingston), 773–774
  Hawai'i One Summer (Kingston), 771–772
  I Love a Broad Margin to My Life (Kingston), 773–774
  life, writing style, and themes, 770–771
  multiculturalism, 979–980
  To Be the Poet (Kingston), 772–773
  Tripmaster Monkey: His Fake Book (Kingston), 295–296, 772–773
  Woman Warrior, The (Kingston), 771, 774
Known World, The (Jones), 144, 732, 735–738
Krauss, Nicole, 775–780
  acclaim, writing style, and themes, 775–776
  brain and American fiction, the, 203
  Forest Dark (Krauss), 778–779
  Great House (Krauss), 778–779
  History of Love, The (Krauss), 776–779
  Holocaust, 775–779
  life and education, 776
  Man Walks into a Room (Krauss), 203, 776–777, 779
Krazy Kat (Cantor), 685–686
Kushner, Rachel, 780–786
  acclaim, 780
  Flamethrowers, The (Kushner), 170, 781, 783–786
  life and education, 781
  Mars Room, The (Kushner), 781, 784–786
  Telex from Cuba (Kushner), 781–785
  writing style and themes, 780–781

Lahiri, Jhumpa, 787–792
  big data, 141–142
  impact and future directions, 791–792
  In Altere Parole (In Another Language) (Lahiri), 791–792
  Interpreter of Maladies (Lahiri), 787–790
  life, awards, and acclaim, 787–789
  Lowland, The (Lahiri), 141–142, 787, 791
  Namesake, The (Lahiri), 787–791
  "Sexy" (Lahiri), 788
  Unaccustomed Earth (Lahiri), 787, 790–791
  writing style and themes, 787–788

language and linguistics
    bilingualism, 264, 447–451, 633–638, 791–792, 1027–1032
    biological fictions, 148–156
    Braschi, Giannina, 208–214
    contemporary regionalisms, 294–295
    culture wars, the, 315
    Davis, Lydia, 348–351
    Delany, Samuel R., 358
    Everett, Percival, 442–443
    Gass, William H., 532–537
    Hagedorn, Jessica, 596–597
    Marcus, Ben, 854–858
    Maso, Carole, 865–870
    Morrison, Toni, 958–963
    posthumanism, 1094–1095
    translation, 348–351, 423, 450, 460–461, 633–638, 815
    Washburn, Frances, 1400
    Williams, Sherley Anne, 1427–1428
    Yamanaka, Lois-Ann, 1453–1458
Last Street Novel, The (Tyree), 1345–1346
LaValle, Victor, 792–797
    Ballard of Black Tom, The (LaValle), 795–796
    Big Machine (LaValle), 793–794
    Changeling, The (LaValle), 796–797
    Destroyer comic series (LaValle), 796–797
    Devil in Silver, The (LaValle), 793–795, 797
    Ecstatic, The (LaValle), 793
    Frankenstein (Shelley), 796
    "Horror at Red Hook, The" (Lovecraft), 795–796
    influences and comparisons, 795
    life, awards, and acclaim, 793, 796
    Slapboxing with Jesus (LaValle), 793
    writing style and themes, 792–793
Lazarus Project, The (Hemon), 556, 620–621
Leaving the Atocha Station (Lerner), 172, 818–819, 821–822
Leavitt, David, 797–802
    Arkansas (Leavitt), 800–801
    context and influences, 797–798
    Equal Affections (Leavitt), 799–801
    Lost Language of Cranes, The (Leavitt), 798–799
    Martin Bauman (Leavitt), 799, 801
    "New Lost Generation, The" (Leavitt), 797–798
    Two Hotel Francforts, The (Leavitt), 800–801
    While England Sleeps (Leavitt), 800–801
    writing style and themes, 797–799
Lee, Chang-rae, 802–806
    Aloft (Lee), 804
    awards and acclaim, 802–803
    Gesture Life, A (Lee), 803
    life and context, 802–803
    Native Speaker (Lee), 802–805
    On Such A Full Sea (Lee), 805–806
    Surrendered, The (Lee), 803–804
Lee, Don, 806–812
    awards and acclaim, 806–807
    Collective, The (Lee), 807
    Country of Origin (Lee), 807
    life and context, 806–808
    Lonesome Lies Before Us (Lee), 807–808
    Wrack & Ruin (Lee), 807
    writing style and themes, 807–808
    Yellow (Lee), 807–812
Le Guin, Ursula K., 812–817
    activism and legacy, 817
    Anders, Charlie Jane, 72, 74
    Chabon, Michael, 243
    children's books, 816
    Dispossessed, The (Le Guin), 813–815
    Earthsea Cycle (Le Guin), 813–814
    essays, 815–816
    Left Hand of Darkness, The (Le Guin), 813–814
    life, awards, and acclaim, 812
    translations, 815
    Wizard of Earthsea, A (Le Guin), 243
    writing style and themes, 812–813
Lerner, Ben, 818–823
    10:04 (Lerner), 818–822, 940
    Bolaño Effect, the, 172–173
    Hatred of Poetry, The (Lerner), 172–173
    Leaving the Atocha Station (Lerner), 172, 818–819, 821–822
    mixed-genre fiction, 940
    poetry, 818
    Topeka School, The (Lerner), 172–173, 818–822
    writing style and themes, 818
Less (Greer), 1122
Less Than Zero (Ellis), 411–412, 414–415, 469–473
Lethem, Jonathan, 823–828
    Bolaño Effect, the, 169
    brain and American fiction, the, 200, 203–205
    Chronic City (Lethem), 826
    Dissident Gardens (Lethem), 827
    Feral Detective, The (Lethem), 827
    Fortress of Solitude, The (Lethem), 169, 825–826
    Girl in Landscape (Lethem), 824–825, 827
    Gun, with Occasional Music (Lethem), 824–825, 827
    life, context, and influences, 823–824
    Motherless Brooklyn (Lethem), 169, 200, 203–205, 825, 827
    other works and influences, 826–827
    Searchers, The (Ford), 825
    writing style and themes, 823–827

Let That Be the Reason (Stringer), 1343
Lincoln in the Bardo (Saunders), 355, 939–940, 1195, 1198
Linden Hills (Naylor), 988, 990, 1292–1293
Literary Magazines, 828–835
  Americas Review, The (magazine), 829
  anticommercialism and anti-institutionalism, 831
  archives and databases, 834
  Beattie, Ann, 117–118
  BOMB (magazine), 830
  Callaloo (magazine), 829–830, 834
  Community of Literary Magazines and Presses, 828, 830, 833
  context, 828
  Cooper, Dennis, 299
  defined by diversity, 828–830
  digittle magazines, 834
  Eggers, Dave, 400–401, 403
  Erickson, Steve, 434
  Ferré, Rosario, 457
  Floating Bear (magazine), 833
  Fuck You/a magazine of the arts (magazine), 833
  future directions, 833–834
  Gay, Roxane, 538
  Granta (magazine), 829, 831–832
  Little Caesar (magazine), 299, 829–830
  Little Magazine in Contemporary America, The (Morris and Diaz), 831
  McSweeney's (magazine), 831, 833
  n+1 (magazine), 831, 1446–1450
  Ng, Celeste, 1001
  nonverbal arts, 830–831
  PANK (online magazine), 538
  program culture, 832, 1120
  Scalawag (magazine), 834–835
  Semanteme (magazine), 1001
  technological change, 833–834
  the campus and the city, 832
  the "literary" and the "little", 830–832
  Timothy McSweeney's Quarterly Concern (magazine), 400–401, 403
  Umbra (magazine), 851
  underground literary and arts zines, 832
  web-based titles, 833
  Zona de carga y descarga (journal), 457
Literature of the Americas, 835–844
  Against the American Grain (Kutzinski), 839
  Almanac of the Dead (Silko), 843
  Autonomía cultural americana (Ballón), 839
  concept and definition, 835–836
  contemporary context and future directions, 841–844

  Cultures of United States Imperialism (Kaplan and Pease), 840
  Do the Americas Have a Common Literature? (Pérez Firmat), 839
  education and pedagogy, 840–841
  Hemispheric American Studies (Levander and Levine), 840
  Hemispheric Studies, 839–844
  Historia comparada de las literaturas americanas (Sánchez), 836–837
  historical context and development of, 836–840
  History of the Americas: A Syllabus with Maps (Bolton), 841
  how might literature of the Americas transform the study of contemporary American fiction?, 841–844
  nationalism, 838, 840–841, 844
  Nueva historia de la literatura americana (Sánchez), 836–837
  Panorama das literaturas das Américas (Carvalho), 837
  Readings from the Americas (Cardwell), 837–838
  slavery, 842–843
  "Spanish American Literature Compared with That of the United States" (Umphrey), 837
  Spanish Background of American Literature, The (Williams), 838, 840, 842–843
  Teaching and Studying the Americas (Pinn, Levander, and Emerson), 841
  US imperialism, 837–841
Little Women (Alcott), 217–218
Location of Culture, The (Bhabha), 977
Lolita (Nabokov), 644–645, 1227
Look at Me (Egan), 394–395, 478–480, 664–665
Looking for Transwonderland (Saro-Wiwa), 163
Lose Your Mother: A Journey Along the Atlantic Slave Route (Hartman), 163
Lost Children Archive (Luiselli), 173–174
Lotus Eaters, The (Soli), 283–284
Loving Day (Johnson), 730–731, 1104–1105
Lowboy (Wray), 200, 203–205
Lowland, The (Lahiri), 141–142, 787, 791

Mad Man, The (Delany), 669, 1142–1144
Magic Kingdom, The (Elgin), 406–407
Mailer, Norman, 845–850
  Ancient Evenings (Mailer), 847–849
  Castle in the Forest, The (Mailer), 849
  context and acclaim, 845
  Executioner's Song, The (Mailer), 845–846
  Gospel According to the Son, The (Mailer), 848–849
  Harlot's Ghost (Mailer), 848

Naked and the Dead, The (Mailer), 847
Of Women and Their Elegance (Mailer), 846
Tough Guys Don't Dance (Mailer), 847–848
Why Are We in Vietnam? (Mailer), 845
Major, Clarence, 850–854
   All-Night Visitors (Major), 850
   Dirty Bird Blues (Major), 853
   Emergency Exit (Major), 851–852
   life and context, 850
   My Amputations (Major), 852–853
   NO (Major), 850–851
   One Flesh (Major), 853–854
   Painted Turtle (Major), 853
   Reflex and Bone Structure (Major), 851
   short fiction, 854
   Such Was the Season (Major), 852–854
   Umbra (magazine), 851
   writing style and themes, 850–854
Making of Middlebrow Culture, The (Rubin), 177
Mandibles, The: A Family (Shriver), 556–557
Man Walks into a Room (Krauss), 203, 776–777, 779
Mao II (DeLillo), 364, 482
Mapping the Interior (Jones), 683, 748
Marcus, Ben, 854–860
   Age of Wire and String, The (Marcus), 855–856
   awards and acclaim, 855
   context, life, and career, 854–855
   Flame Alphabet, The (Marcus), 858
   Franzen, Jonathan, 857–858
   Gaddis, William, 857
   influences, 856
   Leaving the Sea (Marcus), 858–859
   Notable American Women (Marcus), 856–857
   Notes from the Fog (Marcus), 858–859
   writing style and themes, 854–856
Marshall, Paule, 860–865
   Brown Girl, Brownstones (Marshall), 861–862
   Chosen Place, The Timeless People, The (Marshall), 862
   Daughters (Marshall), 861, 863
   essays, 864
   Fisher King, The (Marshall), 863–864
   life, context, and acclaim, 860–862
   Praisesong for the Widow (Marshall), 158–160, 863
   short stories, 864
   Triangular Road: A Memoir (Marshall), 861, 864–865
   writing style and themes, 860–862
Mars Room, The (Kushner), 781, 784–786
Maso, Carole, 865–870
   American Woman in the Chinese Hat, The (Maso), 867
   Art Lover, The (Maso), 866–867, 869

Aureole, Defiance (Maso), 868
AVA (Maso), 867–868, 996
Break Every Rule (Maso), 866, 869
Ghost Dance (Maso), 865–866, 868
life, context, and acclaim, 865
Mother and Child (Maso), 868
new experimentalism/the contemporary avant-garde, 996
writing style and themes, 865–866
Mason, Bobbie Ann, 870–876
   Atomic Romance, An (Mason), 872–873
   Clear Springs (Mason), 870–871
   contemporary fictions of war, 282
   context and acclaim, 870–871, 873
   Feather Crowns (Mason), 871–872, 874–875
   Girl in the Blue Beret, The (Mason), 871, 874
   In Country (Mason), 282, 872–873
   Nancy Culpepper (Mason), 871–872
   Shiloh and Other Stories (Mason), 870–871, 873–874
   Spence + Lila (Mason), 873
Maupin, Armistead, 876–881
   Dickens, Charles, 877, 879
   Logical Family: A Memoir (Maupin), 876
   Michael Tolliver Lives (Maupin), 877–880
   Night Listener, The (Maupin), 876, 880
   Tales of the City series (Maupin), 876–878
   Wolfe, Thomas, 879–880
Maus: A Survivor's Tale (Spiegleman), 572–573, 1322–1324
McBride, James, 881–884
   Color of Water, The (McBride), 881–883
   context, awards, and acclaim, 881
   Good Lord Bird, The (McBride), 882–883, 1170–1171
   impact, 883
   Kill 'Em and Leave (McBride), 883
   religion and contemporary fiction, 1170–1171
   Song Yet Sung (McBride), 883
   writing style and themes, 881–882
McCarthy, Cormac, 884–890
   Blood Meridian (McCarthy), 884–886, 888–889
   Borderlands/La Frontera (Anzaldúa), 885–886
   Border trilogy (McCarthy), 884–887
   Joyce, James, 885–886
   minimalism and maximalism, 928–930
   No Country for Old Men (McCarthy), 188, 887
   Road, The (McCarthy), 884, 887, 1326–1327
   trauma and fiction, 1326–1327
   writing style and themes, 884–885
McElroy, Joseph, 890–895
   Actress in the House (McElroy), 890, 893–894
   Cannonball (McElroy), 890, 893–894

McElroy, Joseph (cont'd)
  context, comparisons, and publications, 890
  Letter Left to Me, The (McElroy), 890, 892–893
  Preparations for Search (McElroy), 892–893
  Women and Men (McElroy), 890–893, 895
  writing style and themes, 890–895
McKnight, Reginald, 895–900
  awards and acclaim, 896
  context and life, 895–896
  He Sleeps (McKnight), 895–898
  I Get on the Bus (McKnight), 895–897
  Kind of Light That Shines on Texas, The (McKnight), 899–900
  Moustapha's Eclipse (McKnight), 898–899
  White Boys (McKnight), 900
  writing style and themes, 895–899
McMillan, Terry, 900–907
  chick lit and the new domesticity, 253
  context and life, 900–901
  Day Late and A Dollar Short, A (McMillan), 903–904
  Disappearing Acts (McMillan), 902
  Getting to Happy (McMillan), 904–905
  How Stella Got Her Groove Back (McMillan), 903
  I Almost Forgot about You (McMillan), 905–906
  impact and legacy, 906
  Interruption of Everything, The (McMillan), 904
  Mama (McMillan), 900–901
  Waiting to Exhale (McMillan), 253, 902–904
  Who Asked You? (McMillan), 905
Meeting the Universe Halfway (Barad), 1095
Mengestu, Dinaw, 907–912
  All Our Names (Mengestu), 908, 910–911
  awards and acclaim, 908
  Beautiful Things that Heaven Bears, The (Mengestu), 908–909
  Dew Breaker, The (Danticat), 911
  How to Read the Air (Mengestu), 908–910
  life, context, and career, 907–908
  writing style and themes, 907–908
Metaphysics (Aristotle), 422
MFA vs. NYC: The Two Cultures of American Fiction (Harbach), 1118
Middlesex (Eugenides), 30, 434–438
migrations and diaspora
  Alameddine, Rabih, 35–40
  Alarcón, Daniel, 40, 42–45
  Allende, Isabel, 51–55
  Álvarez, Julia, 60–61, 64
  assimilation, 61, 255, 292, 593–594, 628, 679–680, 706–707, 787–792
  Black Atlantic, 156–166
  Braschi, Giannina, 209–211
  Cisneros, Sandra, 260–264
  Cliff, Michelle, 270–275
  contemporary regionalisms, 291, 295–296
  culture wars, the, 311, 313
  fictions of work and labor, 487, 493–494
  García, Cristina, 527–530
  Hemon, Aleksandar, 618–623
  Hijuelos, Oscar, 628–633
  Hosseini, Khaled, 648–649
  Jarrar, Randa, 706–711
  Kincaid, Jamaica, 756–760
  Kingston, Maxine Hong, 771–772
  Lahiri, Jhumpa, 787–792
  Lee, Chang-rae, 802–806
  Lee, Don, 806–812
  Marshall, Paule, 860–865
  Mengestu, Dinaw, 907–912
  Mukherjee, Bharati, 969–973
  Ng, Fae Myenne, 1006–1011
  Nguyen, Viet Thanh, 1011–1016
  Ortiz Cofer, Judith, 1027–1032
  Shteyngart, Gary, 1220–1225
  story cycles, 1276–1277
  suburban narratives, 1286–1287
  Syrian refugee crisis, 652
  trauma and fiction, 1325–1326
  Truong, Monique, 1328–1334
  Viramontes, Helena María, 1363–1364
  Yamashita, Karen Tei, 1458–1463
Millennial Fiction, 912–920
  apocalypse and post-apocalypse, 912–916, 919
  border fictions, 913–914
  capitalism, 914–916
  concept and overview, 912
  Divergent series (Roth), 913
  ethnic, cultural, and gender diversity of, 916–917
  fictions of work and labor, 914–918
  globalization, 912, 914–916, 919
  historiographic metafiction, 916–917
  hybridity, 916–917
  Indigenous narratives, 916–917
  millennial theme in millennial fiction, the, 912–914
  My Year of Rest and Relaxation: A Novel (Moshfegh), 917–919
  new work order in millennial fiction, 914–916
  pandemics, 914
  post-9/11 narratives, 918–919
  post-ethnicity and the end of history in millennial fiction, 917–919
  Pynchon, Thomas, 919
  Severance (Ma), 913–916, 919
  Silko, Leslie Marmon, 916–917

transnationalism, 913–914, 916
young adult fiction, 913
Millhauser, Steven, 920–925
   "August Eschenburg" (Millhauser), 922–923
   awards and acclaim, 920–921
   Edwin Mullhouse (Millhauser), 921
   "Eisenheim the Illusionist" (Millhauser), 924
   From the Realm of Morpheus (Millhauser), 921–922
   "Little Kingdom of J. Franklin Payne" (Millhauser), 922–923
   Martin Dressler: The Tale of an American Dreamer (Millhauser), 920, 923–924
   "New Automaton Theater, The" (Millhauser), 922
   Portrait of a Romantic (Millhauser), 921
   We Others (Millhauser), 921, 923–925
   writing style and themes, 920–921
Milou North *see* Erdrich, Louise
Mimesis (Auerbach), 1148
Minimalism and Maximalism, 925–934
   Bellefleur (Oates), 931–932
   Carver, Raymond, 926–927, 929
   concepts and context, 925–926
   Coover, Robert, 303–308
   Darconville's Cat (Theroux), 931
   DeLillo, Don, 932–933
   Dog Stars, The (Heller), 930
   Ducks, Newburyport (Ellmann), 933
   fictions of work and labor, 490
   Ford, Richard, 501–505
   geopolitics, 926
   Hempel, Amy, 625–626, 927
   House on Mango Street, The (Cisneros), 928
   Infinite Jest (Wallace), 932
   In The Dream House (Machado), 934–935
   Mason, Bobbie Ann, 870–876
   McCarthy, Cormac, 928–930
   Morrison, Toni, 932
   Palahniuk, Chuck, 1043–1048
   postmodernism, 926, 931
   Pynchon, Thomas, 932–933
   Recognitions, The (Gaddis), 931
   Saunders, George, 1193–1198
   Three Farmers on Their Way to a Dance (Powers), 932
   Towelhead (Erian), 929
   Wallace, David Foster, 1388–1393
   Weather (Offill), 930–931
Minor Feelings: An Asian American Reckoning (Hong), 981
Mirrorshades (Sterling), 322, 328
Mixed-Genre Fiction, 934–943
   10:04 (Lerner), 940
   Abraham Lincoln: Vampire Hunter (Grahame-Smith), 937, 940
   Bildungsroman, 935, 937–938
   blurring the boundaries between fiction and nonfiction, 940–941
   conclusion, 941–942
   Fledgling (Butler), 939
   Hannah, Barry, 598–603
   I Love Dick (Kraus), 941
   introduction, 934–936
   Kingston, Maxine Hong, 770–775
   LaValle, Victor, 792–797
   Lethem, Jonathan, 823–828
   Lincoln in the Bardo (Saunders), 939–940
   mashup fiction as a catalyst for generic hybridity, 936–937
   My Soul to Take (Due), 939
   Ortiz Cofer, Judith, 1027–1032
   politics of genre-mixing in the contemporary US novel, 937–940
   Pride and Prejudice and Zombies (Grahame-Smith), 936–938
   queer and LGBT fiction, 1145–1146
   Reality Hunger (Shields), 941–942
   Silko, Leslie Marmon, 1230–1234
   Specimen Days (Whitman), 941–942
   Zone One (Whitehead), 938–939
Moby-Dick (Melville), 1228
Model Home (Puchner), 1289–1290
Modernity At Large (Appadurai), 559
Momaday, N. Scott, 943–948
   Ancient Child, The (Momaday), 944–945
   awards and acclaim, 943–944
   children's stories, 948
   essays, 946–948
   House Made of Dawn (Momaday), 675, 943–945, 947
   In the Bear's House (Momaday), 947–948
   In the Presence of the Sun (Momaday), 945–946
   Man Made of Words, The (Momaday), 946–948
   poetry collections, 948
   Three Plays (Momaday), 947
   Way to Rainy Mountain, The (Momaday), 944
   writing style and themes, 943–944
Monkey Bridge (Cao), 1286–1287, 1293
Monkeys (Minot), 1275
Moody, Rick, 948–953
   awards and acclaim, 948–949, 953
   Black Veil, The (Moody), 949, 951
   Diviners, The (Moody), 952
   Garden State (Moody), 949
   Hotels of North America (Moody), 952–953
   Ice Storm, The (Moody), 949–950, 952
   life, context, and influences, 948–949, 952–953
   Purple America (Moody), 949–951
   short fiction collections, 951–952
   writing style and themes, 949–950

Moore, Lorrie, 953–958
  Anagrams (Moore), 955–956
  awards and acclaim, 953–954, 958
  Bark (Moore), 957–958
  Birds of America (Moore), 956–957
  Gate at the Stairs, A (Moore), 957
  impact and future directions, 958
  life, writing style, and themes, 954
  Like Life (Moore), 956
  Self-Help (Moore), 954–956
  Who Will Run the Frog Hospital (Moore), 956
Morrison, Toni, 958–963
  Afrofuturism, 19–20, 23
  awards and acclaim, 959
  Bambara, Toni Cade, 103–104, 106–107
  Beloved (Morrison), 19, 157, 159, 961, 963, 1321–1322
  Bennett, Brit, 128–132
  Bluest Eye, The (Morrison), 129–130, 959, 962
  book clubs, 175, 181, 183
  contemporary regionalisms, 293
  Jazz (Morrison), 960
  legacy, 962–963
  life and impact, 959
  Love (Morrison), 960
  Mercy, A (Morrison), 960
  minimalism and maximalism, 932
  Paradise (Morrison), 131, 293, 960–962
  Playing in the Dark (Morrison), 958–959, 961
  "Recitatif" (Morrison), 960–961
  Song of Solomon (Morrison), 959
  Sula (Morrison), 130
  Tar Baby (Morrison), 959–960
  writing style and themes, 958–959
Mosley, Walter, 963–969
  awards and acclaim, 963, 968
  Devil in a Blue Dress (Mosley), 965
  Easy Rawlins series (Mosley), 965–966
  Fearless Jones (Mosley), 966
  Killing Johnny Fry (Mosley), 968
  legacy, 968
  Leonid McGill (Mosley), 967
  life, context, and influences, 963–965
  Man in My Basement, A (Mosley), 967
  Parishioner (Mosley), 966
  Socrates Fortlow series (Mosley), 966
  writing style and themes, 963–965
Motherless Brooklyn (Lethem), 169, 200, 203–205, 825, 827
Mukherjee, Bharati, 969–973
  awards and acclaim, 970
  Darkness (Mukherjee), 970
  Holder of the World, The (Mukherjee), 971–973
  Jasmine (Mukherjee), 969–971
  legacy, 973
  life and influences, 969–970
  Middleman and Other Stories, The (Mukherjee), 970
  Miss New India (Mukherjee), 970, 972
  Scarlet Letter, The (Mukherjee), 971–973
  Tiger's Daughter, The (Mukherjee), 969–970
  Wife (Mukherjee), 970–971
  writing style and themes, 969–970
Multiculturalism, 973–982
  Adichie, Chimamanda Ngozi, 11–16
  Alameddine, Rabih, 35–40
  Apostol, Gina, 82–86
  Appiah, Kwame Anthony, 978, 980
  Bender, Thomas, 980
  Borderlands/La Frontera (Anzaldúa), 977–978
  Cole, Teju, 275–280
  context, 973–974
  cosmopolitanism, 973, 978, 980–981
  Cultures of United States Imperialism (Kaplan and Pease), 976
  Dialectics of Our America, The (Saldívar), 975
  Elkin, Stanley, 409–410
  emergent literatures, 973, 978–981
  Everett, Percival, 441–442
  Great Republic, The (Bailyn et al.), 974
  Hemon, Aleksandar, 618–623
  Hollinger, David, 975
  hybridity, 976–978
  Ideology and Classic American Literature (Bercovitch et al. eds.), 975–976
  Jen, Gish, 711–716
  Jones, Gayl, 738–744
  Kingston, Maxine Hong, 979–980
  Lee, Chang-rae, 803
  Lee, Don, 806–812
  Location of Culture, The (Bhabha), 977
  Mengestu, Dinaw, 907–912
  Minor Feelings: An Asian American Reckoning (Hong), 981
  nationalism, 973–975, 980
  Ortiz Cofer, Judith, 1027–1032
  particularistic multiculturalism, 978–979
  Patchett, Ann, 1048–1053
  pluralism, 974–975, 978
  Poetics of the Americas (Cowan and Humphries), 976–977
  postcolonialism, 975–977
  racism, 981
  Reed, Ishmael, 1156–1162
  Simpson, Mona, 1235–1240
  story cycles, 1275–1277

Truong, Monique, 1328–1334
universalism, 973–974, 978, 980–981
Urrea, Luis Alberto, 1348–1353
Virgin Land: The American West as Symbol and Myth (Nash Smith), 976
"What We Know That We Don't Know" (Porter), 975
Williams, Raymond, 973, 979–980
Multidirectional Memory (Rothberg), 273–274
Mumbo Jumbo (Reed), 162
My Brother (Kincaid), 669, 759
My Friend Dahmer (Backderf), 579
My Soul to Take (Due), 939
Mystery and Manners (O'Connor), 1301
Myth of Political Correctness, The (Wilson), 311
My Year of Rest and Relaxation: A Novel (Moshfegh), 917–919

Names, The (DeLillo), 362–363, 366, 1059–1061
Narrative Prosthesis: Disability and the Dependencies of Discourse (Mitchell and Snyder), 672
Native American Renaissance (Lincoln), 547–548
Naughty Bits series (Gregory), 1307, 1313
Nava, Michael, 983–987
  awards and acclaim, 986–987
  Borderlands/La Frontera (Anzaldúa), 985, 987
  City of Palaces, The (Nava), 984–986
  essays and nonfiction, 984
  Henry Rios series (Nava), 983–987
  Lay Your Sleeping Head (Nava), 983
  life, impact, and context, 983–984, 986–987
  nonfiction, 984
  Street People (Nava), 987
  writing style and themes, 983–984
Naylor, Gloria, 987–993
  1996 (Naylor), 988, 992
  awards and acclaim, 988
  Bailey's Café (Naylor), 991
  Children of the Night (Naylor), 987–989
  legacy, 992
  life, context, and impact, 987–988
  Linden Hills (Naylor), 988, 990, 1292–1293
  Mama Day (Naylor), 990–992
  Men of Brewster Place, The (Naylor), 989–990
  suburban narratives, 1292–1293
  Women of Brewster Place, The (Naylor), 988–992
  writing style and themes, 988–989
Nazi Literatures in the Americas (Bolaño), 167, 170
neocolonialism *see* colonialism/postcolonialism/neocolonialism
Neodomestic American Fiction (Jacobson), 1290
network narratives *see* Hypertext Fiction and Network Narratives

Neuromancer (Gibson), 140, 324–326, 329, 542, 560, 659–660, 1262
New Experimentalism/The Contemporary Avant-Garde, 993–1001
  AVA (Maso), 996
  Burroughs, William S., 219–224
  concept and examples, 993–994
  Danielewski, Mark Z., 333–338
  Davis, Lydia, 347–352
  DICTEE (Cha), 996–997
  digital literature, 994
  Ducornet, Rikki, 377–382
  embodiment, 997–998
  experiments with authorship, 998–999
  extreme experiments, 999–1000
  Federman, Raymond, 447–451
  fictional boundaries, 998–999
  Frank (Berry), 995
  Frankenstein (Shelley), 995
  Glyph (Everett), 995
  impact of, 1000
  impossibility of expression, 995–996
  Marcus, Ben, 854–860
  Martone, Michael, 998
  narrative stability, 995
  novel as physical object, 997–998
  "Orange World" (Russell), 995
  page's relationship to words, 996–997
  "Parcel Post" (Milletti), 995
  progressive political movements, 994–995
  queer and LGBT fiction, 1141–1143
  Ravickian trilogy (Gladman), 996
  S. (Abrams and Dorst), 997
  Schizophrene (Kapil), 999
  Skin (Jackson), 999
  SNOW (Jackson), 999
  story cycles, 1278–1279
  Tomasula, Steve, 1315–1319
  VAS (Tomasula), 997–998
  Wallace, David Foster, 1388–1393
  writing process, 998–999
  young adult boom, 1468
New Orleans After the Deluge (Neufeld), 580
New York 2140 (Robinson), 560–561
Next (Crichton), 148–150, 155
Ng, Celeste, 1001–1006
  awards and acclaim, 1001–1002
  Everything I Never Told You (Ng), 1001–1003
  life and context, 1001–1002
  Little Fires Everywhere (Ng), 1001–1005
  Semanteme (magazine), 1001
  writing style and themes, 1001–1002

Ng, Fae Myenne, 1006–1011
   awards and acclaim, 1006–1007
   "Backdaire" (Ng), 1007
   Bone (Ng), 1006–1010
   impact, 1010
   life, context, and influences, 1006–1007
   "Red Sweater, A" (Ng), 1007
   Steer Toward Rock (Ng), 1008–1010
   Strangers from a Different Shore (Takaki), 1007
   writing style and themes, 1006–1007
Nguyen, Viet Thanh, 1011–1016
   awards and acclaim, 1011
   Committed, The (Nguyen), 1015
   Displaced, The (Nguyen), 1015
   impact and legacy, 1015–1016
   life, career, and influences, 1011–1012
   Nothing Ever Dies (Nguyen), 1014
   Race and Resistance (Nguyen), 1011–1013
   Refugees, The (Nguyen), 1014–1015
   Sympathizer, The (Nguyen), 284, 1013–1014
Night Watchman, The (Erdrich), 677
No Country for Old Men (McCarthy), 188, 887
Normal Heart, The (Kramer), 668–669
Nox (Carson), 1153
Nueva historia de la literatura americana (Sánchez), 836–837

Oates, Joyce Carol, 1017–1022
   Accursed, The (Oates), 1018
   awards and acclaim, 1017, 1021
   Because It Is Bitter, and Because It Is My Heart (Oates), 1019
   Bellefleur (Oates), 931–932, 1017
   Black Water (Oates), 1019–1020
   Blonde (Oates), 1020
   Bloodsmoor Romance, A (Oates), 1018
   Gravedigger's Daughter, The (Oates), 1021
   legacy, 1021
   Lives of the Twins (Oates), 1019
   Marya: A Life (Oates), 1018–1019
   memoir, 1021
   minimalism and maximalism, 931–932
   Missing Mom (Oates), 1021
   My Heart Laid Bare (Oates), 1018
   Mysteries of Winterthurn (Oates), 1018
   nonfiction, 1020
   We Were The Mulvaneys (Oates), 1020
   What I Lived For (Oates), 1019
   Wild Nights! (Oates), 1020–1021
   You must Remember This (Oates), 1018–1019
O'Brien, Tim, 1022–1027
   context, awards, and acclaim, 1022–1023
   Going After Cacciato (O'Brien), 1024–1025
   In the Lake of the Woods (O'Brien), 1025–1026
   July, July (O'Brien), 1026
   Northern Lights (O'Brien), 1022
   Nuclear Age, The (O'Brien), 1022–1023
   story cycles, 1278
   Things They Carried, The (O'Brien), 283, 285, 1023–1026, 1278
   Tomcat in Love (O'Brien), 1026
   Traumatic Imagination, The (Arva), 1024
   writing style and themes, 1022–1023
Octavia's Brood (Imarisha), 17, 21–22
Oleanna (Mamet), 313–314
Olive, Again (Strout), 1272–1274, 1280, 1282–1284
Olive Kitteridge (Strout), 1272–1274, 1280–1282, 1284
Once in a Promised Land (Halaby), 1079, 1083–1084
One Hundred and One Nights (Buchholz), 284–285, 288
One Hundred Demons (Barry), 577–578
One Hundred Years of Solitude (Márquez), 496
On the Ropes (Vance and Burr), 580
Open City (Cole), 275–279, 554–555
Orange World and Other Stories (Russell), 995, 1190–1191
Oreo (Ross), 1103, 1105, 1213–1214
Orfeo (Powers), 143, 148–149, 152–154
Ortiz Cofer, Judith, 1027–1032
   awards and acclaim, 1031–1032
   contribution to the discussion of the art of writing, 1031
   Cruel Country, The (Ortiz), 1031
   impact and legacy, 1027–1028, 1031–1032
   life, career, and influences, 1028–1029
   Line of the Sun, The (Ortiz), 1030
   poetry collections, 1029–1030
   Silent Dancing (Ortiz), 1030
   young adult fiction, 1030
Oryx and Crake (Atwood), 149
Out of the Dust (Hesse), 1468
Overstory, The (Powers), 143, 1113, 1116–1117
Ozeki, Ruth, 1033–1037
   All Over Creation (Ozeki), 1033–1035
   big data, 141–142
   Cruel Optimism (Berlant), 1036
   Halving the Bones (Ozeki), 1033
   life, influences, and acclaim, 1033
   My Year of Meats (Ozeki), 1033–1034
   realism after poststructuralism, 1154
   Tale for the Time Being, A (Ozeki), 141–142, 1035–1037, 1154
   writing style and themes, 1033

Ozick, Cynthia, 1037–1042
  awards and acclaim, 1037–1038
  Cannibal Galaxy, The (Ozick), 1038–1039
  essays, 1042
  Heir to the Glimmering World (Ozick),
    1041–1042
  life, context, and influences, 1038–1039
  nonfiction, 1040–1041
  poetry, 1039–1040
  Puttermesser Papers, The (Ozick), 1038,
    1040–1042
  "Shawl, The" (Ozick), 1038
  Trust (Ozick), 1038–1039
  writing style and themes, 1038–1042

Paco's Story (Heinemann), 281–282
Palahniuk, Chuck, 1043–1048
  Choke (Palahniuk), 1045–1046
  context, works, and acclaim, 1043–1045
  current and future directions, 1047
  Fight Club (Fincher), 1043–1044
  Fugitives and Refugees (Palahniuk), 1046
  Haunted (Palahniuk), 1046–1047
  Invention of Sound and Consider This, The
    (Palahniuk), 1047
  Invisible Monsters (Palahniuk), 1045–1046
  Lullaby (Palahniuk), 1046–1047
  Survivor (Palahniuk), 1045–1046
  writing style and themes, 1044–1045
Pale King, The (Wallace), 144–145, 1151, 1154–1155,
  1391–1392
Palestine (Sacco), 579, 581
Panorama das literaturas das Américas
  (Carvalho), 837
Parable series (Butler), 20–21, 229, 1166–1168,
  1292
Paradise (Morrison), 131, 293, 960–962
Paris Was a Woman (Schiller), 178
Passing (Larsen), 130–131
Patchett, Ann, 1048–1053
  awards and acclaim, 1048
  Bel Canto (Patchett), 1051–1052
  Commonwealth (Patchett), 1050
  Dutch House, The (Patchett), 1050–1051
  life and context, 1048–1049
  Magician's Assistant, The (Patchett), 1049
  Patron Saint of Liars, The (Patchett), 1049–1050
  Run (Patchett), 1051
  State of Wonder (Patchett), 1051–1053
  Taft (Patchett), 1051
  writing style and themes, 1048–1049
Pattern Recognition (Gibson), 664, 1079
People of Paper, The (Plascencia), 1153

Percy Jackson series (Riordan), 1466
Periodization, 1053–1063
  anti-periodism and anti-postmodernism, 1058
  context and overview, 1053–1056
  Cosmopolis (DeLillo), 1061
  Hartog, François, 1057
  Hayot, Eric, 1057
  moving target: the contemporary, 1059–1062
  Names, The (DeLillo), 1059–1061
  paraperiod, 1055, 1059–1062
  post-Cold War, 1054–1056, 1059–1061
  Postmodernist Fiction (McHale), 1062
  post World War II, 1054, 1060
  trouble with period, the, 1056–1057
  Trumpener, Kate, 1058
Perkins-Valdez, Dolen, 1063–1068
  awards and acclaim, 1068
  Balm (Perkins-Valdez), 1063, 1066–1068
  Closer to Freedom (Camp), 1064
  Kindred (Butler), 1068
  life and context, 1064
  Remember Me to Miss Louisa (Green),
    1064–1065
  Roll, Jordan, Roll (Genovese), 1064
  Wench (Perkins-Valdez), 1063–1068
  writing style and themes, 1063–1064
Perks of Being a Wallflower (Chbosky), 1467
Person of Interest, A (Choi), 141
Phillips, Jayne Anne, 1068–1074
  Black Tickets (Phillips), 1069
  critical response, 1073
  Fast Lanes (Phillips), 1069
  Lark & Termite (Phillips), 1071–1072
  Machine Dreams (Phillips), 1069–1070, 1072
  Motherkind (Phillips), 1071, 1073
  Quiet Dell (Phillips), 1072–1073
  Shelter (Phillips), 1070–1071
  writing style and themes, 1068–1069
Piercy, Marge, 1074–1078
  big data, 139–140
  context and acclaim, 1074
  Cost of Lunch, Etc., The (Piercy), 1078
  Fly Away Home (Piercy), 1075
  Gone to Soldiers (Piercy), 1075–1076
  He, She, and It (Piercy), 139–140, 1076–1077
  Summer People (Piercy), 1076–1077
  Three Women (Piercy), 1077
  Vida (Piercy), 1075
  Woman on the Edge of Time (Piercy),
    1074–1075
  writing style and themes, 1074
Poetics of the Americas (Cowan and Humphries),
  976–977

Post-9/11 Narratives, 1079–1088
  after postmodernism, 31–32
  alternate worlds, 1082–1083
  Auster, Paul, 87–88, 91
  Barth, John, 115–116
  Braschi, Giannina, 208–213
  context and overview, 1079–1080
  culture wars, the, 314
  DeLillo, Don, 366
  Disorder Peculiar to the Country, A (Kalfus), 1079, 1081–1083
  Emperor's Children, The (Messud), 1085–1087
  Erickson, Steve, 433–434
  Extremely Loud & Incredibly Close (Foer), 1081
  Falling Man (DeLillo), 1080–1081
  falling (wo)men, 1080–1082
  Foer, Jonathan Safran, 495–500
  Gibson, William, 542, 544–547
  globalization, 558–559
  Good Life, The (McInerney), 1085–1087
  Hosseini, Khaled, 647–653
  hypertext fiction and network narratives, 664
  Islamophobia, 1079–1080, 1084–1085
  Johnson, Denis, 724–725
  King, Stephen, 764
  Man in the Dark (Auster), 1082–1083
  millennial fiction, 918–919
  Once in a Promised Land (Halaby), 1079, 1083–1084
  Ozeki, Ruth, 1035–1037
  Pattern Recognition (Gibson), 1079
  Pynchon, Thomas, 1133–1135
  social histories, 1085–1087
  Submission, The (Waldman), 1084–1085
  suburban narratives, 1286
  transnational politics, 1083–1085
  Zero, The (Walters), 1083
post-Black fiction *see* Post-Soul and/or Post-Black Fiction
postcolonialism *see* colonialism/postcolonialism/neocolonialism
Posthumanism, 1088–1097
  Althusser, Louis, 1091
  Annihilation (VanderMeer), 1095
  antihumanism, transhumanism, posthumanism, 1090–1095
  as literary theory, 1095–1096
  Blindsight (Watts), 1095–1096
  Braidotti, Rosi, 1092
  context and overview, 1088–1089
  "Cyborg Manifesto, A" (Haraway), 1088–1089, 1092–1093
  Democracy of Objects, The (Bryant), 1094
  Ferrando, Francesca, 1092
  Foucault, Michel, 1091–1092
  Freud, Sigmund, 1091
  How We Became Posthuman (Hayles), 1089
  humanism, 1089–1090
  materiality, 1094
  Meeting the Universe Halfway (Barad), 1095
  Nietzsche, Friedrich, 1090–1091
  "Reeling for the Empire" (Russell), 1093
  Said, Edward, 1096
  Tenth of December (Saunders), 1096
  Tomasula, Steve, 1315–1319
  Vibrant Matter (Bennett), 1094
  What is Posthumanism? (Wolfe), 1088–1090, 1093–1094
Postmodernist Fiction (McHale), 1062
Post-Soul and/or Post-Black Fiction, 1097–1107
  Bell, Bernard W., 1101
  Caucasia (Senna), 1104–1105
  Crawford, Natalie, 1101–1102
  Daniels-Rauterkus, Melissa, 1102
  early efforts at defining the new aesthetics, 1098–1100
  Ellis, Trey, 1098–1103
  Erasure (Everett), 1104
  Everett, Percival, 441–443
  evolution of post-soul and post-Black discourse, 1101–1103
  exemplars of post-soul and post-Black fiction, 1103–1106
  Freestyle (exhibition), 1100–1101
  future directions, 1105–1106
  George, Nelson, 1098–1101
  Golden, Thelma, 1100–1101
  Heads of the Colored People (Thompson-Spires), 1103–1104
  Hughes, Langston, 1098
  Johnson, Mat, 726–732
  Loving Day (Johnson), 1104–1105
  McBride, James, 881–884
  McKnight, Reginald, 895–900
  music, 1099
  Neal, Mark Anthony, 1101–1102
  new millennium and the arrival of post-Blackness, 1100–1101
  Oreo (Ross), 1103, 1105
  Sag Harbor (Whitehead), 1104–1105
  Sweet Sweetback's Baadasssss Song (Van Peebles), 1100
  Tate, Greg, 1098–1101, 1103
  Trouble with Post-Blackness, The (Baker and Simmons), 1102
  What Was African American Literature? (Warren), 1097–1098

White Boy Shuffle, The (Beatty), 1104
Whitehead, Colson, 1415–1421
Who's Afraid of Post-Blackness? (Touré), 1102–1103
Wideman, John Edgar, 1421–1426
Power of the Dog (Winslow), 191
Power, Susan, 1107–1112
  awards and acclaim, 1107
  critical debate, 1111
  Grass Dancer, The (Power), 683, 1107–1110
  "Museum Indians" (Power), 1108–1109
  Native American Graves Protection and Repatriation Act (1990), 1109
  Roofwalker (Power), 1108–1111
  Sacred Wilderness (Power), 1108–1111
  "Stone Women" (Power), 1111
  "Watermelon Seeds" (Power), 1111
  writing style and themes, 1107
Powers, Richard, 1112–1117
  awards and acclaim, 1113
  big data, 143
  biological fictions, 148–149, 152–154
  context, writing style, and themes, 1112–1113
  Echo Maker, The (Powers), 200, 203–206, 1116
  ecocriticism and environmental fiction, 391
  Gain (Powers), 1113
  Galatea 2.2 (Powers), 202–203, 1113, 1115–1116
  Gold Bug Variations, The (Powers), 1113, 1115
  intermedial fiction, 690
  life, 1113–1114
  minimalism and maximalism, 932
  Operation Wandering Soul (Powers), 1115
  Orfeo (Powers), 143, 148–149, 152–154
  Overstory, The (Powers), 143, 1113, 1116–1117
  Plowing the Dark (Powers), 1115
  Prisoner's Dilemma (Powers), 1114–1115
  Three Farmers on Their Way to a Dance (Powers), 690, 932
Praisesong for the Widow (Marshall), 158–160, 863
Pride and Prejudice and Zombies (Grahame-Smith), 936–938
Pride and Prejudice (Austen), 254–255
Program Culture, 1118–1125
  After the Workshop (McNally), 1122
  Condition of Postmodernity, The (Harvey), 1122–1123
  gender and sexism, 1121
  how, 1122
  introduction, 1118
  Iowa model, 1122
  Künstlerroman, 1118, 1125
  Less (Greer), 1122
  literary magazines, 832, 1120

MFA vs. NYC: The Two Cultures of American Fiction (Harbach), 1118
  O'Connor, Flannery, 1121
  postmodernism, 1118, 1122–1124
  Program Era, The (McGurl), 1118–1125
  queer and LGBT fiction, 1121
  racism, 1121–1122
  what, 1122–1125
  when, 1119
  where, 1119–1120
  who, 1120–1122
Program Era, The (McGurl), 1118–1125, 1446
Proulx, Annie, 1125–1130
  Accordion Crimes (Proulx), 1128
  awards and acclaim, 1125–1126
  Barskins (Proulx), 1129
  "Brokeback Mountain" (Proulx), 1126
  contribution and impact, 1125–1126
  Heart Songs and Other Stories (Proulx), 1127
  life, context, and influences, 1126–1127
  Postcards (Proulx), 1125, 1127–1129
  scholarly interest, 1129–1130
  Shipping News, The (Proulx), 1126, 1128
  That Old Ace in the Whole (Proulx), 1128–1129
  writing style and themes, 1125–1130
  Wyoming Stories books (Proulx), 1128–1129
Purity (Franzen), 145, 510
Push (Sapphire), 1307, 1312, 1342
Pynchon, Thomas, 1130–1136
  Against the Day (Pynchon), 1133–1135
  awards and acclaim, 1131
  big data, 144
  Bleeding Edge (Pynchon), 144, 1134–1135
  Crying of Lot 49, The (Pynchon), 1131–1132
  Gravity's Rainbow (Pynchon), 1133
  Inherent Vice (Pynchon), 1134
  intermedial fiction, 690
  legacy, 1135
  life and publications, 1131
  Mason & Dixon (Pynchon), 1133, 1135
  millennial fiction, 919
  minimalism and maximalism, 932–933
  Vineland (Pynchon), 690, 1132–1133, 1135
  writing style and themes, 1130–1132

Queer and LGBT Fiction, 1137–1145
  Afrofuturism, 1140
  Allison, Dorothy, 56–60
  Anders, Charlie Jane, 71–75
  Argonauts, The (Nelson), 1141–1142
  Bennett, Brit, 131–132
  Black Atlantic, 163–164
  border fictions, 186–187, 192

Queer and LGBT Fiction (cont'd)
  Boy Meets Boy (Levithan), 1140
  Boy's Own Story, A (White), 1137, 1139–1140
  Civil Rights movement, 1137
  Cliff, Michelle, 270–275
  Color Purple, The (Walker), 1137, 1139–1140
  Cooper, Dennis, 298–303
  Cunningham, Michael, 317–321
  cyberpunk, 329
  Delany, Samuel R., 357–362
  Drowning in Fire (Womack), 1144
  erotic and pornographic fiction, 1142–1143
  Evil Dead Center (LaFavor), 1144
  Feinberg, Leslie, 452–456
  Gilda Stories, The (Gomez), 1140–1141
  Gomez, Jewelle, 567–572
  HIV/AIDs, 1137, 1143–1144
  homophobia, 71, 74–75, 878–879, 983–986, 1411
  Indigenous narratives, 1144
  James, Marlon, 701–705
  Leavitt, David, 797–802
  Mad Man, The (Delany), 1142–1144
  Maso, Carole, 865–870
  Maupin, Armistead, 876–881
  mixed-genre fiction, 1145–1146
  Nava, Michael, 983–987
  new experimentalism/the contemporary avant-garde, 1141–1143
  New Narrative, 1142–1143
  post-punk queer aesthetics, 1312–1314
  program culture, 1121
  speculative fiction, 1140–1141
  Stone Butch Blues (Feinberg), 1141
  Stonewall, 1137, 1139–1141
  third-wave feminism, 1307, 1313–1314
  Vanishing Rooms (Dixon), 1144
  Vidal, Gore, 1355–1360
  Vietnam War, 1137
  White, Edmund, 1410–1415
  young adult boom, 1464, 1467–1470
  Zami: A Biomythography (Lorde), 1137–1141

Rabbit series (Updike), 1293, 1335–1337
Race, Space, and the Law (Razack), 1172
racism and impacts of
  Adichie, Chimamanda Ngozi, 11–15
  Allende, Isabel, 53–55
  Álvarez, Julia, 61–65
  Anaya, Rudolfo, 66–68
  Auster, Paul, 89–90
  Bambara, Toni Cade, 103–105
  Beatty, Paul, 122–127
  Bennett, Brit, 128–133
  border fictions, 185–186, 192
  Boyle, T.C., 196–198
  Butler, Octavia, 225–230
  Castillo, Ana, 236–239
  chick lit and the new domesticity, 255
  Cleage, Pearl, 265–269
  Cliff, Michelle, 270–275
  culture wars, the, 308–316
  cyberpunk, 328–329
  debut novels, 355
  ecocriticism and environmental fiction, 386–387
  Ferré, Rosario, 457–461
  fiction and affect, 475
  Ford, Richard, 503–504
  Gaines, Ernest J., 522–527
  Golden, Marita, 562–567
  Gomez, Jewelle, 567–572
  Hosseini, Khaled, 648
  James, Marlon, 701–705
  Jen, Gish, 711–716
  Johnson, Charles, 716–721
  Johnson, Mat, 726–732
  Kingston, Maxine Hong, 770–775
  LaValle, Victor, 794–797
  Lee, Chang-rae, 803–806
  Lee, Don, 806–812
  literature of the Americas, 838–842
  Marshall, Paule, 860–865
  McBride, James, 881–884
  McKnight, Reginald, 895–900
  McMillan, Terry, 905
  Mengestu, Dinaw, 911
  Morrison, Toni, 958–963
  Mosley, Walter, 963–969
  multiculturalism, 981
  Naylor, Gloria, 992
  Ng, Celeste, 1001–1005
  Ng, Fae Myenne, 1006–1011
  Nguyen, Viet Thanh, 1011–1016
  Ozeki, Ruth, 1033–1037
  passing, 270–272, 716–717, 727–729, 1210–1215
  Perkins-Valdez, Dolen, 1063–1068
  program culture, 1121–1122
  Reed, Ishmael, 1156–1162
  Revoyr, Nina, 1172–1177
  Roth, Philip, 1186
  Senna, Danzy, 1210–1215
  Sontag, Susan, 1247
  suburban narratives, 1292–1293
  third-wave feminism, 1307–1312
  Truong, Monique, 1328–1334
  Viramontes, Helena María, 1364–1365
  Ward, Jesmyn, 1393–1398

Whitehead, Colson, 1415–1421
Wideman, John Edgar, 1423–1425
Wolfe, Tom, 1432–1436
Yamanaka, Lois-Ann, 1454–1458
young adult boom, 1467–1470
Yu, Charles, 1476–1477
Radio Ambulante (podcast), 41, 44
Ravickian trilogy (Gladman), 996
Reading Oprah (Konchar Farr), 181–183
Readings from the Americas (Cardwell), 837–838
Reading Sites: Social Difference and Reader Response (Schweickart and Flynn), 175–176, 180
Realism after Poststructuralism, 1147–1155
  Apostol, Gina, 83–85
  Body Artist, The (DeLillo), 1154–1155
  Carver, Raymond, 231–235
  context and concepts, 1147–1149
  Doctorow, E.L., 373–377
  Don Quixote (Cervantes), 1149–1150
  Egan, Jennifer, 393–398
  Eugenides, Jeffrey, 434–439
  Frazier, Charles, 511–516
  future directions, 1155
  Gass, William H., 1152
  Glossary of Literary Terms, A (Abrams), 1148
  Hannah, Barry, 598–603
  Hijuelos, Oscar, 628–633
  House of Leaves (Danielewski), 1152–1153
  hypertext fiction and network narratives, 1152
  impact of quantum physics, 1152–1154
  intertextuality, 1154
  Lerner, Ben, 818–823
  Mimesis (Auerbach), 1148
  Novel, The: An Alternative History (Moore), 1148–1149
  Nox (Carson), 1153
  Pale King, The (Wallace), 1151, 1154–1155
  People of Paper, The (Plascencia), 1153
  Realism (Morris), 1148
  Reed, Ishmael, 1152
  S. (Abrams and Dorst), 1153–1154
  self-reflexivity, 1150
  Smiley, Jane, 1240–1245
  Tale for the Time Being, A (Ozeki), 1154
  Tomasula, Steve, 1153
  Wallace, David Foster, 1150–1151
  Waugh, Patricia, 1150, 1155
  young adult boom, 1467
Realism (Morris), 1148
Reality Hunger (Shields), 941–942
Reckless Eyeballing (Reed), 1160–1161
Recognitions, The (Gaddis), 517–518, 521, 931
Recursion (Crouch), 145

Redeployment (Klay), 1278
Reed, Ishmael, 1156–1162
  Black Atlantic, 162
  Christmas Carol, A (Dickens), 1158
  Color Purple, The (Walker), 1161
  Conjugating Hindi (Reed), 1157, 1159–1160
  context and acclaim, 1156
  Haunting of Lin-Manual Miranda, The (Reed), 1156–1158
  Japanese by Spring (Reed), 1160–1161
  Mumbo Jumbo (Reed), 162
  "Neo-Hoodoo Manifesto" (Reed), 1160–1161
  realism after poststructuralism, 1152
  Reckless Eyeballing (Reed), 1160–1161
  Terrible Threes, The (Reed), 1159
  Terrible Twos, The (Reed), 1156–1160
  writing style and themes, 1156
refugees *see* migrations and diaspora
Religion and Contemporary Fiction, 1162–1172
  Adichie, Chimamanda Ngozi, 12, 14
  after postmodernism, 31–32
  Anaya, Rudolfo, 66–67, 69
  beyond disenchantment, 1162–1164
  Brooks, Geraldine, 216–219
  Butler, Octavia, 228–229
  Castillo, Ana, 236–238
  Cisneros, Sandra, 263
  context and overview, 1162–1164
  Englander, Nathan, 420–425
  Ferris, Joshua, 465–466
  fiction and terrorism, 478–481, 484–485
  Foer, Jonathan Safran, 497, 499
  Franchot, Jenny, 1163
  Gaddis, William, 519
  Gaines, Ernest J., 524, 526
  Gilead (Robinson), 1168–1169
  Glancy, Diane, 548–551
  Good Lord Bird, The (McBride), 1170–1171
  Heller, Joseph, 614–615
  Homes, A.M., 645–646
  Irving, John, 697
  Islamophobia, 649, 957, 1079–1080, 1084–1085
  Jen, Gish, 713–714
  Johnson, Denis, 721–725
  Judaism, 420–425, 1184
  Kaufmann, Michael, 1163–1164
  LaValle, Victor, 794
  Le Guin, Ursula K., 813, 815
  Mailer, Norman, 849
  Momaday, N. Scott, 943–945, 947
  Naylor, Gloria, 991
  Ozeki, Ruth, 1036–1037
  Ozick, Cynthia, 1037–1042

Religion and Contemporary Fiction (cont'd)
  Parable series (Butler), 1166–1168
  Patchett, Ann, 1048–1049
  Piercy, Marge, 1076–1078
  Power, Susan, 1109–1110
  Puritanism, 216–219
  Robinson, Marilynne, 1177–1182
  spirituality and mysticism, 249–250, 680–681
  Stone, Robert, 1267–1271
  third-wave feminism, 1308
  Vidal, Gore, 1358–1359
  White Noise (DeLillo), 1164–1166
Reluctant Fundamentalist, The (Hamid), 479
Remasculinization of America (Jeffords), 287–288
Remember Me to Miss Louisa (Green), 1064–1065
Rent Girl (Tea and McCubbin), 1313
Representative Short Story Cycles of the Twentieth Century (Ingram), 1272
Revoyr, Nina, 1172–1177
  Age of Dreaming, The (Revoyr), 1175–1176
  awards and acclaim, 1172
  Cheat, The (DeMille), 1175–1176
  life and context, 1172–1173
  Lost Canyon (Revoyr), 1174–1175
  Necessary Hunger, The (Revoyr), 1176
  Race, Space, and the Law (Razack), 1172
  Southland (Revoyr), 1173
  Student of History, A (Revoyr), 1173–1176
  Wingshooters (Revoyr), 1172, 1176
  writing style and themes, 1172–1173
Road, The (McCarthy), 884, 887, 1326–1327
Robinson, Marilynne, 1177–1182
  awards and acclaim, 1181–1182
  Gilead (Robinson), 293, 1168–1169, 1179–1181
  Housekeeping (Robinson), 1178–1180
  impact, 1181–1182
  influences and comparisons, 1180–1181
  Jack (Robinson), 1179–1180
  life and context, 1177–1179
  nonfiction, 1181
  writing style and themes, 1177–1179
Roll, Jordan, Roll (Genovese), 1064
Roth, Philip, 1182–1187
  American Pastoral (Roth), 1184–1185
  awards and acclaim, 1182, 1186–1187
  Counterlife, The (Roth), 1183
  culture wars, the, 313–314
  Everyman (Roth), 1186
  Ferris, Joshua, 466
  Ghost Writer, The (Roth), 1183–1184
  Goodbye, Columbus and Other Stories (Roth), 1182
  Human Stain, The (Roth), 313–314, 1184–1185
  I Married a Communist (Roth), 1184–1185
  legacy, 1187
  memoir, 1183–1184
  Nemesis (Roth), 1186–1187
  Operation Shylock (Roth), 1184, 1186
  Patrimony (Roth), 1183–1184
  Plot Against America, The (Roth), 1186
  Portnoy's Complaint (Roth), 1182–1184
  Sabbath's Theater (Roth), 1184
Rubicon Beach (Erikson), 431–432
Russell, Karen, 1187–1191
  awards and acclaim, 1187–1188
  life and influences, 1187–1188
  new experimentalism/the contemporary avant-garde, 995
  Orange World and Other Stories (Russell), 995, 1190–1191
  posthumanism, 1093
  "Reeling for the Empire" (Russell), 1093
  St. Lucy's Home for Girls Raised by Wolves (Russell), 1188–1189
  Swamplandia! (Russell), 1189–1190
  Vampires in the Lemon Grove (Russell), 1190
  writing style and themes, 1187–1188
Rusty Brown (Ware), 577

S. (Abrams and Dorst), 997, 1153–1154
Sabrina (Drnaso), 580–581
Sacred Smokes (Van Alst), 677
Sag Harbor (Whitehead), 1104–1105, 1416, 1420
Sand Queen (Benedict), 284, 287–288, 558
Satanic Verses, The (Rushdie), 30–31, 1246
satire *see* comedy and satire
Saunders, George, 1193–1198
  after postmodernism, 31
  awards and acclaim, 1196–1198
  big data, 143–144
  CivilWarLand in Bad Decline (Saunders), 1195–1196
  debut novels, 355
  Infinite Jest (Wallace), 1196
  In Persuasion Nation (Saunders), 143–144, 1197
  life and influences, 1193–1195
  Lincoln in the Bardo (Saunders), 355, 939–940, 1195, 1198
  mixed-genre fiction, 939–940
  Pastoralia (Saunders), 1196–1197
  posthumanism, 1096
  Slaughterhouse-Five (Vonnegut), 1194
  Tenth of December (Saunders), 1096, 1197
  writing style and themes, 1193–1195
Savage Detectives, The (Bolaño), 167, 169–172
Schizophrene (Kapil), 999

Schwartz, Lynne Sharon, 1198–1204
Disturbances in the Field (Schwartz), 1202–1203
Face to Face (Schwartz), 1199, 1203
Fatigue Artist, The (Schwartz), 1202
In the Family Way (Schwartz), 1200–1202
Leaving Brooklyn (Schwartz), 1199, 1202–1203
Referred Pain (Schwartz), 1202
Rough Strife (Schwartz), 1199–1201
writing style and themes, 1198–1199
Scott, Joanna, 1204–1210
Arrogance (Scott), 1205–1206
awards and acclaim, 1204–1205
Careers for Women (Scott), 1207–1208
Closest Possible Union, The (Scott), 1204
De Potter's Grand Tour (Scott), 1206
Historical Novel, The (Lukács), 1207–1209
Manikin, The (Scott), 1204
Various Antidotes (Scott), 1205–1206
writing style and themes, 1204
Searchers, The (Ford), 825
Second Life (online platform), 1262–1264
Second Sex, The (Beauvoir), 1309
Senna, Danzy, 1210–1215
awards and acclaim, 1210–1211
Caucasia (Senna), 1103–1105, 1210–1214
Enigma (journal), 1211
impact and future directions, 1214
life and influences, 1210–1211
New People (Senna), 1211, 1213
Oreo (Ross), 1213–1214
post-soul and/or post-Black fiction, 1104–1105
Symptomatic (Senna), 1211–1213
Where Did You Sleep Last Night? (Senna), 1212
writers' collectives, 1445
You Are Free (Senna), 1212–1213
Sense of Place, Sense of Planet (Heise), 387
Serros, Michele, 1215–1220
Chicana Falsa and Other Stories of Death, Identity, and Oxnard (Serros), 1215–1218
Honey Blonde Chica (Serros), 1216, 1219
How to Be a Chicana Role Model (Serros), 1216, 1218–1219
impact and legacy, 1216, 1219
life, influences, and acclaim, 1215–1216
poetry, 1215–1216
Seventeenth Summer (Daly), 1464
Severance (Ma), 670–671, 913–916, 919
Sex and the City (Bushnell), 252–254
sexism
Bambara, Toni Cade, 105
border fictions, 186, 192
Castillo, Ana, 236–239
Cleage, Pearl, 265–269
contemporary fictions of war, 287–288
culture wars, the, 308–316
Ferré, Rosario, 457–461
Golden, Marita, 562–567
Hustvedt, Siri, 653, 655–658
Marshall, Paule, 860–865
McKnight, Reginald, 895–898
Ng, Celeste, 1001–1005
program culture, 1121
Wolitzer, Meg, 1439
sexualities
Acker, Kathy, 6–10
Alameddine, Rabih, 35–40
Allison, Dorothy, 56–60
Baker, Nicholson, 96
Black Atlantic, 163–164
Boyle, T.C., 195–198
Cooper, Dennis, 298–303
Delany, Samuel R., 357–362
Díaz, Junot, 370–371
Ducornet, Rikki, 377–382
ecocriticism and environmental fiction, 389
Ellis, Bret Easton, 411–412, 414–415
Eugenides, Jeffrey, 435–439
Gay, Roxane, 540
Gomez, Jewelle, 571
heteronormativity, 257–259
Indigenous narratives, 679
Irving, John, 697–698
Jones, Gayl, 742–743
Le Guin, Ursula K., 814
Mailer, Norman, 847
McKnight, Reginald, 895–898
McMillan, Terry, 905–906
Mosley, Walter, 968
Piercy, Marge, 1076–1078
suburban narratives, 1288
Viramontes, Helena María, 1362–1363
Walker, Alice, 1384–1387
Wolfe, Tom, 1436
Wolitzer, Meg, 1438–1441
young adult boom, 1464, 1467–1469
Shakespeare and Company (Beach), 178
Shame (Rushdie), 701
Shark Dialogues (Davenport), 295
Shteyngart, Gary, 1220–1225
Absurdistan (Shteyngart), 1222
Lake Success (Shteyngart), 1224–1225
life and context, 1220
Little Failure (Shteyngart), 1220, 1223–1224
memoir, 1220, 1223–1224
Russian Debutante's Handbook, The (Shteyngart), 1221–1222

Shteyngart, Gary (cont'd)
  Super Sad True Love Story (Shteyngart), 1222–1223
  writing style and themes, 1220–1221
Siegel, Lee, 1225–1230
  City of Dreadful Night, The (Siegel), 1227, 1229
  context, life, and influences, 1225–1227
  Lolita (Nabokov), 1227
  Love and Other Games of Chance (Siegel), 1226, 1228–1230
  Love and the Incredibly Old Man (Siegel), 1229–1230
  Love in a Dead Language (Siegel), 1226–1228, 1230
  Moby-Dick (Melville), 1228
  Net of Magic (Siegel), 1227
  Trance-Migrations (Siegel), 1227
  Who Wrote the Book of Love (Siegel), 1226, 1228–1230
Signifying Monkey, The (Gates), 1444–1445
Silko, Leslie Marmon, 1230–1235
  Almanac of the Dead (Silko), 680–681, 843, 1232–1234
  Ceremony (Silko), 1230–1232
  essays, 1233
  Gardens in the Dunes (Silko), 680, 1233–1234
  impact and legacy, 1234–1235
  life, context, and acclaim, 1230–1232
  literature of the Americas, 843
  millennial fiction, 916–917
  Oceanstory (Silko), 1234
  Sacred Water (Silko), 1232–1233
  Storyteller (Silko), 679–680, 683, 1231–1232
  Turquoise Ledge, The (Silko), 1234
  writing style and themes, 1230–1231
  Yellow Woman and a Beauty of the Spirit (Silko), 1233
Simpson, Mona, 1235–1240
  Anywhere But Here (Simpson), 1236–1237
  awards and acclaim, 1235–1236
  Casebook (Simpson), 1239–1240
  impact, 1240
  life and context, 1235–1236
  Lost Father, The (Simpson), 1237–1238
  My Hollywood (Simpson), 1239
  Off Keck Road (Simpson), 1239
  Regular Guy, A (Simpson), 1238–1239
  writing style and themes, 1235–1236
Sing, Unburied, Sing (Ward), 293, 1396–1397
Skin (Jackson), 999
Slaughterhouse-Five (Vonnegut), 497, 1194, 1376–1378
Small Place, A (Kincaid), 539

Smiley, Jane, 1240–1245
  awards and acclaim, 1241
  Brief History of The Dead (Brockmeier), 1244
  Good Faith (Smiley), 1289–1290
  Greenlanders, The (Smiley), 1242–1244
  Horse Heaven (Smiley), 1243–1244
  King Lear (Shakespeare), 1241–1242
  Last One Hundred Years Trilogy, The (Smiley), 1241–1245
  life, education, and publications, 1240–1241
  suburban narratives, 1289–1290
  Thousand Acres, A (Smiley), 1241–1242
  Understanding Jane Smiley (Nakadate), 1242
  writing style and themes, 1241–1242
Snow Crash (Stephenson), 328, 560, 1262, 1265–1266
SNOW (Jackson), 999
Song of the Turtle (Allen), 675
Sontag, Susan, 1245–1251
  Against Interpretation and Other Essays (Sontag), 1246
  Benefactor, The (Sontag), 1247–1248
  Death Kit (Sontag), 1248
  Doktor Faustus (Mann), 1245–1246
  illness and disability narratives, 668, 671–672
  Illness as Metaphor (Sontag), 668, 671–672, 1246
  impact and legacy, 1246, 1250
  In America (Sontag), 1249–1250
  life, context, and acclaim, 1245–1247
  On Photography (Sontag), 1246–1247
  Promised Lands (Sontag), 1247
  Regarding the Pain of Others (Sontag), 1246–1247
  Satanic Verses, The (Rushdie), 1246
  Under the Sign of Saturn (Sontag), 1249
  Volcano Lover, The (Sontag), 1248–1249
Sorrentino, Gilbert, 1251–1256
  Aberration of Starlight (Sorrentino), 1253, 1255
  Abyss of Human Illusion, The (Sorrentino), 1255–1256
  awards and acclaim, 1251
  Blue Pastoral (Sorrentino), 1253
  Crystal Vision (Sorrentino), 1253
  Gold Fools (Sorrentino), 1255
  Imaginative Qualities of Actual Things (Sorrentino), 1252–1255
  life and career, 1251
  Mulligan Stew (Sorrentino), 1251–1253
  Pack of Lies (Sorrentino), 1253–1254
  Red the Fiend (Sorrentino), 1255
  Sky Changes, The (Sorrentino), 1251, 1253, 1255
  Strange Commonplace, A (Sorrentino), 1255
  writing style and themes, 1251–1252
Southern Writer in the Postmodern World, The (Hobson), 601–602

Spanish Background of American Literature, The (Williams), 838, 840, 842–843
Sparta (Robinson), 286
Specifying (Willis), 562–563
Specimen Days (Whitman), 941–942
Spiotta, Dana, 1256–1261
    DeLillo, Don, 1257–1259
    Eat the Document (Spiotta), 1258–1259
    Innocents and Others (Spiotta), 1256, 1260–1261
    life, context, and influences, 1256–1257
    Lightning Field (Spiotta), 1257–1260
    Stone Arabia (Spiotta), 1259–1260
    writing style and themes, 1256–1257
Spoils (Van Reet), 287–288
Stars in My Pockets Like Grains of Sand (Delany), 659–660, 664
Stephenson, Neal, 1261–1266
    Cryptonomicon (Stephenson), 1263
    Diamond Age, The (Stephenson), 1263
    globalization, 560
    In the Beginning Was the Command Line (Stephenson), 1263–1264
    McGurl, Mark, 1265–1266
    Mongoliad, The (Stephenson), 1265
    Neuromancer (Gibson), 1262
    REAMDE (Stephenson), 1264–1265
    Second Life (online platform), 1262–1264
    Seveneves (Stephenson), 1265–1266
    Snow Crash (Stephenson), 328, 560, 1262, 1265–1266
    Subutai Corporation, 1265
    writing style and themes, 1261–1262
Stitches (Small), 578–579
Stone Butch Blues (Feinberg), 452–456, 1141
Stone, Robert, 1267–1271
    awards and acclaim, 1271
    Bay of Souls (Stone), 1270
    Children of Light (Stone), 1269
    "Coda" (Stone), 1271
    context, life, and influences, 1267–1269
    Damascus Gate (Stone), 479, 1269–1270
    death and legacy, 1271
    Death of a Black-Haired Girl (Stone), 1270–1271
    Dog Soldiers (Stone), 1269
    fiction and terrorism, 479
    Flag for Sunrise, A (Stone), 1269–1270
    Hall of Mirrors, A (Stone), 1269
    Outerbridge Reach (Stone), 1270
    Prime Green (Stone), 1268
    writing style and themes, 1267
Story Cycles, 1271–1280
    affect, 1272–1274
    concept and context, 1272–1273

Contemporary American Short-Story Cycle, The (Nagel), 1276
contemporary fictions of war, 1278
contemporary regionalisms, 1275–1276
Danticat, Edwidge, 340–342
Díaz, Junot, 367–372
Dreaming in Cuban (García), 1277–1278
experimentalism, 1278–1279
family and family history, 1275–1278
flash fiction, 1279
House on Mango Street, The (Cisneros), 1274–1275
How the García Girls Lost Their Accents (Álvarez), 1275–1277
I Sailed with Magellan (Dybek), 1274–1275
Joy Luck Club, The (Tan), 1276
Lister, Rachel, 1273
Lynch, Gerald, 1274
migrations, 1276–1277
Monkeys (Minot), 1275
multiculturalism, 1275–1277
Olive Again: A Novel (Strout), 1272–1274
Olive Kitteridge (Strout), 1272–1274
Proulx, Annie, 1128–1129
Redeployment (Klay), 1278
Representative Short Story Cycles of the Twentieth Century (Ingram), 1272
Strout, Elizabeth, 1280–1285
Things They Carried, The (O'Brien), 1278
Thrailkill, Jane, 1273–1274
Transcultural Reinventions (Davis), 1276
Visit from the Goon Squad, A (Egan), 1278–1279
Winesburg, Ohio (Anderson), 1275
Storyteller (Silko), 679–680, 683, 1231–1232
Storyworld Accord, The (James), 390
Strangers from a Different Shore (Takaki), 1007
Street Life (Jihad), 1344
Strout, Elizabeth, 1280–1285
    Abide With Me (Strout), 1280–1283
    Amy & Isabelle (Strout), 1280–1281, 1283–1284
    Anything is Possible (Strout), 1280, 1282, 1284
    awards and acclaim, 1281
    Burgess Boys, The (Strout), 1280–1281
    My Name is Lucy Barton (Strout), 1280–1284
    Olive, Again (Strout), 1280, 1282–1284
    Olive Kitteridge (Strout), 1272–1274, 1280–1282, 1284
    writing style and themes, 1280–1281
Submission, The (Waldman), 484–485, 1084–1085
Suburban Narratives, 1285–1294
    2008 global financial crisis, 1286
    alienation, 1286–1287, 1290, 1293
    American Dream, 1289–1293

Suburban Narratives (*cont'd*)
  Bascombe books (Ford), 1290
  California (Lepucki), 1292
  class and classism, 1285–1286, 1290–1293
  context, 1285
  ecocriticism and environmental fiction, 1291–1292
  Eugenides, Jeffrey, 434–439
  Florida (Long), 1293
  Ford, Richard, 501–505
  Friend of the Earth, A (Boyle), 1291–1292
  gender, 1292
  global influences, 1286–1287
  Goldfinch, The (Tartt), 1288–1289, 1291
  Good Faith (Smiley), 1289–1290
  Home at the End of the World, A (Cunningham), 1288
  House of Sand and Fog (Dubus III), 1291
  Jurca, Catherine, 1285–1286
  Knapp, Kathy, 1286, 1290
  Linden Hills (Naylor), 1292–1293
  migrations, 1286–1287
  Model Home (Puchner), 1289–1290
  Monkey Bridge (Cao), 1286–1287, 1293
  Neodomestic American Fiction (Jacobson), 1290
  Parable of the Sower (Butler), 1292
  post-9/11 narratives, 1286
  Rabbit series (Updike), 1293
  racism, 1292–1293
  regionalisms, 1287–1289
  Schwartz, Lynne Sharon, 1198–1204
  Sellout, The (Beatty), 1292–1293
  sexualities, 1288
  Simpson, Mona, 1235–1240
  Updike, John, 1335–1340
  White Noise (DeLillo), 1287–1288, 1291
  Wideman, John Edgar, 1422–1423
Sula (Morrison), 130
Sweet Sweetback's Baadasssss Song (Van Peebles), 1100
Sweet Valley High series (Pascal), 1465
Sympathizer, The (Nguyen), 284, 1013–1014
Synners (Candigan), 329
System, The (Kuper), 576

Tale for the Time Being, A (Ozeki), 141–142, 1035–1037, 1154
Tan, Amy, 1295–1300
  awards and acclaim, 1295
  Between Worlds: Women Writers of Chinese Ancestry (Tan), 1295
  Bonesetter's Daughter, The (Tan), 1297–1298
  children's books, 1296
  Hundred Secret Senses, The (Tan), 1296–1297
  Joy Luck Club, The (Tan), 1276, 1295–1296, 1298
  Kitchen God's Wife, The (Tan), 1296
  life and context, 1295–1296
  Opposite of Fate, The: A Book of Musings (Tan), 1295, 1298
  Saving Fish from Drowning (Tan), 1298
  story cycles, 1276
  Valley of Amazement, The (Tan), 1298–1299
  writing style and themes, 1295
Tartt, Donna, 1300–1306
  awards and acclaim, 1300, 1302, 1304
  Ellis, Bret Easton, 1300–1301
  Goldfinch, The (Tartt), 1288–1289, 1291, 1301–1305
  legacy, 1305
  life, context, and comparisons, 1300–1302
  Little Friend, The (Tartt), 1301–1304
  Mystery and Manners (O'Connor), 1301
  poetry, 1305
  Secret History, The (Tartt), 1300–1302
  suburban narratives, 1288–1289, 1291
  writing style and themes, 1301–1302
Teaching and Studying the Americas (Pinn, Levander, and Emerson), 841
Telex from Cuba (Kushner), 781–785
Tenth of December (Saunders), 1096, 1197
terrorism *see* Fiction and Terrorism
Terrorist (Updike), 476–480, 1339
There There (Orange), 295–296
Things They Carried, The (O'Brien), 283, 285, 1023–1026, 1278
Third Reich, The (Bolaño), 167
Third-Wave Feminism, 1306–1315
  Adichie, Chimamanda Ngozi, 14–16
  Allende, Isabel, 50–53
  Allison, Dorothy, 56–60
  anthologies and essays, 1308
  Bambara, Toni Cade, 103–107
  Beauty Myth, The (Wolf), 1309
  "Becoming the third wave" (Walker), 1310–1311
  Bennett, Brit, 129–132
  Black, White and Jewish: Autobiography of a Shifting Self (Walker), 1307, 1311
  border fictions, 186–187, 192
  Bridget Jones's Diary (Fielding), 1310
  Brooks, Geraldine, 214–219
  Butler, Octavia, 225–230
  Castillo, Ana, 235–240
  Cisneros, Sandra, 260–265
  Cleage, Pearl, 265–270
  Cliff, Michelle, 270–275
  context and overview, 1306–1307

culture wars, the, 309, 311–314
cyberpunk, 328–329
ecocriticism and environmental fiction, 383–386, 388–389
ecofeminism, 383–386
Feinberg, Leslie, 452–456
Fire with Fire (Wolf), 1309
Gomez, Jewelle, 567–572
Le Guin, Ursula K., 814
Maso, Carole, 865–870
Naomi Wolf and chick lit, 1309–1310
Naughty Bits series (Gregory), 1307, 1313
Ozeki, Ruth, 1033–1037
Piercy, Marge, 1074–1078
post-feminism, 251–260
"Post-Feminism and Popular Culture" (McRobbie), 1311
Push (Sapphire), 1307, 1312
Rebecca Walker and third-wave intersectionality, 1310–1312
religion, 1308
Rent Girl (Tea and McCubbin), 1313
Riot Grrrl and post-punk queer aesthetics, 1312–1314
Second Sex, The (Beauvoir), 1309
second-wave feminism, 178
sexual harassment, 1310–1312
third-wave politics of the personal, 1307–1309
Vagina Monologues, The (Ensler), 1307, 1312
violence against women, 1307, 1312
Walker, Alice, 1383–1388
Wolitzer, Meg, 1437–1442
This Book is An Action (Harker and Konchar Farr), 178
This is My Life (Ephron), 1438
This Is Not Chick Lit (Merrick), 256
Three Days in April (Ashton), 148
Three Farmers on Their Way to a Dance (Powers), 690, 932, 1113–1114
tíguere, 369–371
Timecode (Figgis), 661
Tomasula, Steve, 1315–1319
  Book of Portraiture, The: A Novel (Tomasula), 1316–1317
  IN&OZ (Tomasula), 1317
  realism after poststructuralism, 1153
  TOC: A New Media Novel (Tomasula), 1317–1318
  VAS: An Opera in Flatland (Tomasula), 997–998, 1315–1317
  "Visualization, Scale, and the Emergence of Posthuman Narrative" (Tomasula), 1318–1319
  writing style and themes, 1315

Topeka School, The (Lerner), 172–173, 818–822
Touch of Evil (Welles), 185–187
Towelhead (Erian), 929
Train Dreams (Johnson), 295
Transcultural Reinventions (Davis), 1276
Trauma and Fiction, 1319–1328
  Alameddine, Rabih, 35–40
  Allison, Dorothy, 56–60
  American Dream, 1325–1326
  animals, 1324–1325
  apocalypse, 1326–1327
  Apostol, Gina, 85–86
  Behold the Dreamers (Mbue), 1325–1326
  Beloved (Morrison), 1321–1322
  class, 1325–1327
  Cliff, Michelle, 270–274
  Climate Trauma (Kaplan), 1326–1327
  context, 1319–1320
  Danticat, Edwidge, 338–342
  Díaz, Junot, 367–372
  dystopia, 1326–1327
  Ellroy, James, 416–420
  family and childhood trauma, 1324–1325
  Federman, Raymond, 447–451
  Foer, Jonathan Safran, 495–500
  García, Cristina, 527–532
  Gay, Roxane, 538–542
  Harrison, Jim, 604–605
  Hemon, Aleksandar, 618–623
  Holocaust, 1321–1324
  Hosseini, Khaled, 647–653
  Journal of Literature and Trauma Studies (journal), 1327
  Krauss, Nicole, 775–780
  Maus (Spiegelman), 1322–1324
  McKnight, Reginald, 895–900
  McMillan, Terry, 900–907
  Mengestu, Dinaw, 907–912
  migrations, 1325–1326
  minimalism and maximalism, 927–934
  Morrison, Toni, 958–963
  Ng, Celeste, 1001–1005
  O'Brien, Tim, 1022–1027
  origins of, 1320
  Ozick, Cynthia, 1037–1042
  recent contemporary fiction, 1327
  Road, The (McCarthy), 1326–1327
  slavery, 1321–1322
  Tartt, Donna, 1300–1306
  Trauma Fiction (Whitehead), 1324
  Urrea, Luis Alberto, 1348–1353
  Vonnegut, Kurt, 1376–1382
  Ward, Jesmyn, 1393–1398

Trauma and Fiction (cont'd)
   We Are All Completely Beside Ourselves (Fowler), 1324–1325
   Wideman, John Edgar, 1421–1426
Traumatic Imagination, The (Arva), 1024
Tree of Smoke (Johnson), 283–284, 721–724
Tripmaster Monkey (Kingston), 295–296, 772–773
Trouble with Post-Blackness, The (Baker and Simmons), 1102
True to the Game (Woods), 1343
Truong, Monique, 1328–1334
   awards and acclaim, 1328
   Bitter in the Mouth (Truong), 1328–1330
   Book of Salt, The (Truong), 1328–1329
   nonfiction, 1333
   Sweetest Fruits, The (Truong), 1328, 1330–1332
   writing style and themes, 1328–1329
Tsoai-talee *see* Momaday, N. Scott
ttyl (Myracle), 1468
Tuesday Nights in 1980 (Prentiss), 170–171

Uncommon Ground (Cronon), 386
Underground Railroad, The (Whitehead), 21, 1418–1420
Unnamed, The (Ferris), 206, 462, 464–465
Updike, John, 1335–1340
   Afterlife, The (Updike), 1337–1338
   awards and acclaim, 1335–1336
   Beattie, Ann, 117–120
   Bech at Bay (Updike), 1338–1339
   Couples (Updike), 1335–1336
   critical writings, 1338
   fiction and terrorism, 476–480
   legacy, 1339
   life and context, 1335–1336
   My Father's Tears (Updike), 1339
   Rabbit series (Updike), 1293, 1335–1337
   Roger's Version (Updike), 1337
   Self-Consciousness (Updike), 1335–1336
   Terrorist (Updike), 476–480, 1339
   Toward the End of Time (Updike), 1338
   Witches of Eastwick, The (Updike), 1337, 1339
   writing style and themes, 1335–1336
Uptown Thief (de Leon), 1346
Urban Fiction, 1340–1348
   Capital City (Tyree), 1340–1341, 1346
   Coldest Winter Ever, The (Souljah), 1342–1344
   context and emergence of, 1340
   Erasure (Everett), 1342
   Flyy Girl (Tyree), 1341–1342
   Foye, K'wan, 1344
   Graaff, Kristina, 1343, 1346
   hip-hop, 1340–1342, 1344–1345, 1347

   I Know Why the Caged Bird Sings (Angelou), 1341
   impact and legacy, 1347
   impact on Black American writers and the publishing industry, 1344–1345
   incarceration, 1343–1347
   Last Street Novel, The (Tyree), 1345–1346
   Let That Be the Reason (Stringer), 1343
   Push (Sapphire), 1342
   scholarship on, 1346
   sex work, 1346–1347
   Street Life (Jihad), 1344
   Stringer, Vickie, 1343–1344
   True to the Game (Woods), 1343
   Uptown Thief (de Leon), 1346
   "Urban Street Literature Retirement, An" (Tyree), 1345
   Weber, Carl, 1344
Urrea, Luis Alberto, 1348–1353
   Across the Wire (Urrea), 1348–1349
   awards and acclaim, 1348
   By the Lake of the Sleeping Children (Urrea), 1348–1349
   Devil's Highway, The (Urrea), 189–190, 1349–1352
   House of Broken Angels, The (Urrea), 1351–1352
   Hummingbird's Daughter, The (Urrea), 1351
   Into the Beautiful North (Urrea), 1351
   Nobody's Son: Notes from an American Life (Urrea), 1348–1350, 1352
   nonfiction and memoir, 1348–1350, 1352
   Wandering Time (Urrea), 1352
   writing style and themes, 1348–1349
Uses of Literature (Felski), 178–179

Vagina Monologues, The (Ensler), 1307, 1312
Vanishing Rooms (Dixon), 1144
VAS: An Opera in Flatland (Tomasula), 997–998, 1315–1317
Victory Garden (Moulthrop), 662
Vidal, Gore, 1355–1360
   awards and acclaim, 1355
   City and the Pillar, The (Vidal), 1356
   Creation (Vidal), 1355, 1358–1359
   death and legacy, 1359–1360
   Golden Age, The (Vidal), 1356–1358
   Hollywood (Vidal), 1357
   life and context, 1355–1356
   Lincoln (Vidal), 1357
   Myra Breckinridge (Vidal), 1356
   Narratives of Empire (Vidal), 1355, 1357
   Palimpsest (Vidal), 1355–1357
   Smithsonian Institution, The (Vidal), 1356–1357
   writing style and themes, 1355–1356
Vineland (Pynchon), 690, 1132–1133, 1135

Viramontes, Helena María, 1360–1366
   awards and acclaim, 1361–1362
   Chicana Creativity and Criticism (Viramontes), 1361–1362
   Chicana (W)rites: On Word and Film (Viramontes), 1361–1362
   impact and future directions, 1361, 1365
   life, career, and influences, 1361–1362
   Moths and Other Stories, The (Viramontes), 1362–1363
   Their Dogs Came with Them (Viramontes), 1364–1365
   Under the Feet of Jesus (Viramontes), 1363–1364
   writing style and themes, 1360–1361
Virgin Land: The American West as Symbol and Myth (Nash Smith), 976
Visit from the Goon Squad, A (Egan), 395–397, 664, 1278–1279
Vizenor, Gerald, 1366–1371
   Bearheart (Vizenor), 1368
   context, awards, and acclaim, 1366–1367
   Dead Voices (Vizenor), 682
   Griever: An American Monkey King in China (Vizenor), 1368–1369
   Harold of Orange (Vizenor), 1370
   Heirs of Columbus, The (Vizenor), 1369
   Interior Landscapes: Autobiographical Myths and Metaphors (Vizenor), 1367–1368
   Ishi and the Wood Ducks (Vizenor), 1370
   nonfiction and collaborations, 1367, 1369–1371
   poetry collections and Ojibwe stories and songs, 1367
   "Sand Creek Survivors" (Vizenor), 1369
   Tribal Scenes and Ceremonies (Vizenor), 1369
   Trickster of Liberty, The (Vizenor), 1369
   writing style and themes, 1367–1368
Vollmann, William T., 1371–1376
   Afghanistan Picture Show, An (Vollmann), 1372–1373
   awards and acclaim, 1371
   Carbon Ideologies (Vollmann), 1375
   Europe Central (Vollmann), 1374
   Imperial (Vollman), 1374
   life and influences, 1372
   Rising Up and Rising Down (Vollmann), 1372–1373
   Seven Dreams volumes (Vollmann), 1373–1374
   writing style and themes, 1371–1372
   You Bright and Risen Angels (Vollmann), 1371–1372
Vonnegut, Kurt, 1376–1382
   artworks, 1378–1381
   Bluebeard (Vonnegut), 1379–1380

Breakfast of Champions (Vonnegut), 1378–1380
Cat's Cradle (Vonnegut), 1377
children's books, 1378
Deadeye Dick (Vonnegut), 1379
Foer, Jonathan Safran, 497
Galápagos (Vonnegut), 1379
God Bless You, Dr. Kevorkian (Vonnegut), 1381
God Bless You, Mr. Rosewater (Vonnegut), 1377–1378
Hocus Pocus (Vonnegut), 1380
impact and legacy, 1376, 1381
Jailbird (Vonnegut), 1378
life and context, 1376–1377
Man Without a Country, A (Vonnegut), 1381
Palm Sunday (Vonnegut), 1378–1379
Player Piano (Vonnegut), 1377
plays, 1378
Slapstick (Vonnegut), 1378
Slaughterhouse-Five (Vonnegut), 497, 1194, 1376–1378
Timequake (Vonnegut), 1380–1381
writing style and themes, 1376–1377

Waiting to Exhale (McMillan), 253, 902–904
Walker, Alice, 1383–1388
   awards and acclaim, 1383
   By the Light of My Father's Smile (Walker), 1383, 1386–1387
   Color Purple, The (Walker), 1137, 1139–1140, 1161, 1383–1385
   legacy, 1387
   life and context, 1383
   Now Is the Time to Open Your Heart (Walker), 1383, 1387
   Possessing the Secret of Joy (Walker), 1383, 1385–1386
   Reed, Ishmael, 1161
   Temple of My Familiar, The (Walker), 1383–1385
   writing style and themes, 1383–1384
Wallace, David Foster, 1388–1393
   big data, 144–145
   Brief Interviews with Hideous Men (Wallace), 1391
   Broom of the System, The (Wallace), 1388–1390
   Franzen, Jonathan, 510
   Girl with Curious Hair (Wallace), 1390
   hypertext fiction and network narratives, 663
   Infinite Jest (Wallace), 30–32, 473–474, 663, 932, 1196, 1388–1392
   life and publications, 1388
   Oblivion (Wallace), 1390–1391
   Pale King, The (Wallace), 144–145, 1151, 1154–1155, 1391–1392
   realism after poststructuralism, 1150–1151
   writing style and themes, 1388–1389

war *see* Contemporary Fictions of War
Ward, Jesmyn, 1393–1398
  awards and acclaim, 1393, 1395–1397
  Faulkner, William, 1395, 1397
  Fire This Time, The (Ward), 1397, 1446
  life and context, 1393–1394, 1397–1398
  Men We Reaped (Ward), 1394, 1396
  Salvage the Bones (Ward), 1394–1396
  Sing, Unburied, Sing (Ward), 293, 1396–1397
  Where the Line Bleeds (Ward), 1394–1395
  writers' collectives, 1446
  writing style and themes, 1393–1395
War-Fix (Axe), 579–580
Washburn, Frances, 1398–1404
  Buried in Shades of Night (Stratton), 1399
  Elsie's Business (Washburn), 1398, 1400–1401, 1403
  life and contribution, 1398–1399
  Peoplehood Matrix, 1400
  Red Bird All-Indian Traveling Band (Washburn), 1398, 1402–1403
  Sacred White Turkey, The (Washburn), 1398, 1401–1403
  writing style and themes, 1398–1400
Watchmen (Moore and Gibbons), 573, 661
Water Cure, The (Everett), 442–443, 483–484
Water Dancer, The (Coates), 21, 23
Way of Thorn and Thunder, The (Heath Justice), 676, 682
We Are All Completely Beside Ourselves (Fowler), 1324–1325
We Are All Multiculturalists Now (Glazer), 974–975
Weather (Offill), 930–931
Welch, James, 1404–1410
  awards and acclaim, 1404, 1408
  Death of Jim Loney (Welch), 1406
  Fools Crow (Welch), 1406
  Heartsong of Chargin Elk, The (Welch), 1407–1408
  Indian Lawyer, The (Welch), 1405–1407
  Killing Custer (Welch), 1407
  legacy, 1408–1409
  life, influences, and publications, 1404–1405
  poetry, 1404–1405
  Riding the Earthboy 40 (Welch), 1404–1405
  Winter in the Blood (Welch), 1405–1406, 1409
What is Posthumanism? (Wolfe), 1088–1090, 1093–1094
What Looks Like Crazy on an Ordinary Day (Cleage), 267–268, 669
What Was African American Literature? (Warren), 1097–1098

When They Call You a Terrorist (bandele and Cullors), 22–23
Whereas (Long Soldier), 294–295
White, Edmund, 1410–1415
  awards and acclaim, 1415
  Boy's Own Story, A (White), 1137, 1139–1140, 1411
  Burning Library, The (White), 1414–1415
  Caracole (White), 1412–1413
  essays, 1414
  Fanny: A Fiction (White), 1413
  Farewell Symphony, The (White), 1411–1412
  Forgetting Elena (White), 1412–1413
  Hotel de Dream (White), 1413
  impact and legacy, 1410, 1414
  Jack Holmes and His Friend (White), 1413–1414
  life, context, and influence, 1410–1411
  Married Man, The (White), 1411–1412
  memoir, 1414
  Nocturnes for the King of Naples (White), 1412
  Our Young Man (White), 1413–1414
  Saint from Texas, A (White), 1413–1414
  writing style and themes, 1410–1411
Whitehead, Colson, 1415–1421
  Afrofuturism, 18, 21
  Apex Hides the Hurt (Whitehead), 1418–1419
  context and comparisons, 1415–1416
  fiction and affect, 474–475
  Intuitionist, The (Whitehead), 1416–1420
  John Henry Days (Whitehead), 1416–1420
  mixed-genre fiction, 938–939
  Sag Harbor (Whitehead), 1104–1105, 1416, 1420
  Underground Railroad, The (Whitehead), 21, 1418–1420
  Zone One (Whitehead), 474–475, 938–939, 1420
White Noise (DeLillo), 363, 367, 390, 1164–1166, 1287–1288, 1291
Who's Afraid of Post-Blackness? (Touré), 1102–1103
Wideman, John Edgar, 1421–1426
  American Histories (Wideman), 1425–1426
  awards and acclaim, 1423–1424
  Brothers and Keepers (Wideman), 1423–1424
  Damballah (Wideman), 1422
  Fanon (Wideman), 1424–1425
  Fatheralong (Wideman), 1424–1425
  Hiding Place (Wideman), 1422–1423
  Hoop Roots (Wideman), 1425
  impact and legacy, 1424–1426
  life and context, 1421–1422
  Philadelphia Fire (Wideman), 1424
  Reuben (Wideman), 1424
  Sent for You Yesterday (Wideman), 1423
  writing style and themes, 1425

Williams, Sherley Anne, 1426–1432
  awards and acclaim, 1426–1427
  children's books, 1430–1431
  context, life, and publications, 1426–1427
  Dessa Rose (Williams), 1426–1427, 1429–1430
  Girls Together (Williams), 1430–1431
  Give Birth to Brightness (Williams), 1426–1427
  impact and legacy, 1431
  influence, 1427–1428
  nonfiction, 1427
  Peacock Poems, The (Williams), 1428–1430
  poetry collections, 1428–1430
  Some One Sweet Angel Chile (Williams), 1428–1430
  Working Cotton (Williams), 1430
  writing style and themes, 1427–1428
Willie Masters' Lonesome Wife (Gass), 686–687
Windup Girl, The (Bacigalupi), 148, 560–561
Winesburg, Ohio (Anderson), 1275
Wizard of Earthsea, A (Le Guin), 243
Wolfe, Tom, 1432–1437
  Back to Blood (Wolfe), 1436
  Bonfire of the Vanities, The (Wolfe), 1432–1436
  context, life, and comparisons, 1432–1433, 1436–1437
  Electric Kool-Aid Acid Test, The (Wolfe), 1432–1433
  I Am Charlotte Simmons (Wolfe), 1436
  Man in Full, A (Wolfe), 1436
  Maupin, Armistead, 879–880
  Right Stuff, The (Wolfe), 1433
Wolitzer, Meg, 1437–1442
  Belzhar (Wolitzer), 1440–1441
  context, comparisons, and life, 1437–1438
  Female Persuasion, The (Wolitzer), 1441
  Friends for Life (Wolitzer), 1438–1439
  Hidden Pictures (Wolitzer), 1438
  Interestings, The (Wolitzer), 1440–1441
  Position, The (Wolitzer), 1439
  Sleepwalking (Wolitzer), 1438–1441
  Surrender, Dorothy (Wolitzer), 1439
  Ten-Year Nap, The (Wolitzer), 1439–1440
  This is My Life (Ephron), 1438
  This Is Your Life (Wolitzer) 1438–1439
  Uncoupling, The (Wolitzer), 1440–1441
  Wife, The (Wolitzer), 1439
  writing style and themes, 1437–1438
work and labor *see* Fictions of Work and Labor
World of Wankanda series (Marvel comics), 541
Worrying the Line (Wall), 562
Writers' Collectives, 1442–1451
  Black Aesthetic, 1444–1445
  Borderlands/La Frontera (Anzaldúa), 1444

Bourdieu, Pierre, 1442–1443, 1445
Chicago Cultural Studies Group, 1445
collectives of cultural difference, 1443–1446
colonialism and postcolonialism, 1444
Combahee River Collective, 1444
culture wars, 1445
digital technologies and social media, 1449–1450
Eggers, Dave, 1447–1449
Ellis, Trey, 1445
Fire This Time, The: A New Generation Speaks about Race (Ward), 1446
Greif, Mark, 1449
Harbach, Chad, 1446–1447, 1449
introduction, 1442–1443
Kindley, Evan, 1450
Major, Clarence, 851–852
McSweeney's, 1447–1450
n+1 (journal), 1446–1450
New Black Aesthetic, 1445
Program Era, The (McGurl), 1446
Seita, Sophie, 1449
Senna, Danzy, 1445
Signifying Monkey, The (Gates), 1444–1445
the school and its counter-institutions, 1446–1450
Wrong: A Critical Biography of Dennis Cooper (Hester), 301

Yage Letters, The (Burroughs and Ginsberg), 220, 223
Yamanaka, Lois-Ann, 1453–1458
  awards and acclaim, 1453
  Behold the Many (Yamanaka), 1457–1458
  Blu's Hanging (Yamanaka), 1453, 1455–1458
  Fathers of the Four Passages (Yamanaka), 1457
  Heads by Harry (Yamanaka), 1453, 1457
  impact, 1458
  life and context, 1453–1454
  poetry, 1453–1455
  Saturday Night at the Pahala Theater (Yamanaka), 1454–1455
  Wild Meat and the Bully Burgers (Yamanaka), 1455
Yamashita, Karen Tei, 1458–1463
  Anime Wong (Yamashita), 1462–1463
  Brazil-Maru (Yamashita), 1459–1460
  Circle K Cycles (Yamashita), 1461
  context, life, and acclaim, 1458–1460
  I Hotel (Yamashita), 1459, 1461–1462
  Sansei and Sensibility (Yamashita), 1462–1463
  Through the Arc of the Rainforest (Yamashita), 1459–1461
  Tropic of Orange (Yamashita), 1459, 1461
  writing style and themes, 1458–1460
Yellow Birds, The (Powers), 285–286

Young Adult Boom, 1463–1472
- Alexie, Sherman, 49–50
- Allende, Isabel, 55
- Anders, Charlie Jane, 72–74
- *Black Panther* (Coogler), 1469–1470
- bullying, 1464, 1467
- conclusion: today, constructing the real, 1470–1471
- consumerism and glamour, 1467–1468
- context and overview, 1463–1464
- creating the real: 1960s to early 1980s, 1464
- cyberpunk, 1468
- Danticat, Edwidge, 340–341
- digital technology and social media, 1468–1471
- disguising, fabulizing, and accepting the real: mid-1990s to early 2000s, 1466–1468
- drug abuse, 1464, 1468
- Erdrich, Louise, 428–429
- fantasy and speculative fiction, 1466–1467, 1469–1470
- gender, 1470
- *Gossip Girls* series (Ziegersar), 1467–1468
- graphic novel, the, 580
- *Harry Potter* books (Rowling), 1466–1467
- Holocaust, 1467
- *Hunger Games, The* (Collins), 1466
- *I'll Get There. It Better Be Worth the Trip* (Donovan), 1470
- millennial fiction, 913
- Ortiz Cofer, Judith, 1030
- *Out of the Dust* (Hesse), 1468
- *Percy Jackson* series (Riordan), 1466
- *Perks of Being a Wallflower* (Chbosky), 1467
- queer and LGBT fiction, 1464, 1467–1470
- racism, 1467–1470
- reacting to the real: 1980s to mid-1990s, 1464–1466
- representing the real: 2010–2020, 1468–1470
- romance, 1464–1467
- Serros, Michele, 1216, 1219
- *Seventeenth Summer* (Daly), 1464
- sexual abuse and harassment, 1468–1469
- *Sweet Valley High* series (Pascal), 1465
- *ttyl* (Myracle), 1468
- verse novels, 1468
- violence, 1464–1465, 1467, 1469
- We Need Diverse Books, 1469
- Wolitzer, Meg, 1440–1441

Yu, Charles, 1472–1478
- *How to Live Safely in a Science Fictional Universe* (Yu), 1475–1476
- *Interior Chinatown* (Yu), 1473, 1476–1477
- life and influences, 1473
- publications and acclaim, 1472–1473
- *Sorry Please Thank You* (Yu), 1474–1475
- *Third Class Superhero* (Yu), 1473–1474
- writing style and themes, 1472–1473

Zami: A Biomythography (Lorde), 1137–1141
Zero, The (Walters), 483–484, 1083
Zone One (Whitehead), 474–475, 938–939, 1420